Lecture Notes in Artificial Intelligence 12344

Subseries of Lecture Notes in Computer Science

More information about this series at http://www.springer.com/series/1244

Enrique Antonio de la Cal ·
José Ramón Villar Flecha ·
Héctor Quintián · Emilio Corchado (Eds.)

Hybrid Artificial Intelligent Systems

15th International Conference, HAIS 2020
Gijón, Spain, November 11–13, 2020
Proceedings

Editors
Enrique Antonio de la Cal
University of Oviedo
Oviedo, Spain

José Ramón Villar Flecha
University of Oviedo
Oviedo, Spain

Héctor Quintián
University of A Coruña
Ferrol, Spain

Emilio Corchado
University of Salamanca
Salamanca, Spain

ISSN 0302-9743 ISSN 1611-3349 (electronic)
Lecture Notes in Artificial Intelligence
ISBN 978-3-030-61704-2 ISBN 978-3-030-61705-9 (eBook)
https://doi.org/10.1007/978-3-030-61705-9

LNCS Sublibrary: SL7 – Artificial Intelligence

This Springer imprint is published by the registered company Springer Nature Switzerland AG
The registered company address is: Gewerbestrasse 11, 6330 Cham, Switzerland

Preface

This volume of *Lecture Notes on Artificial Intelligence* (LNAI) includes accepted papers presented at the 15th International Conference on Hybrid Artificial Intelligence Systems (HAIS 2020), held in the beautiful city of Gijón, Spain, November 2020.

HAIS has become an unique, established and broad interdisciplinary forum for researchers an practitioners who are involved in developing and applying symbolic and sub-symbolic techniques aimed at the construction of highly robust and reliable problem-solving techniques, and bringing the most relevant achievements in this field.

The hybridization of intelligent techniques, coming from different computational intelligence areas, has become popular because of the growing awareness that such combinations frequently perform better than the individual techniques such as neurocomputing, fuzzy systems, rough sets, evolutionary algorithms, agents and multiagent systems, deep learning, and so on.

Practical experience has indicated that hybrid intelligence techniques might be helpful to solve some of the challenging real-world problems. In a hybrid intelligence system, a synergistic combination of multiple techniques is used to build an efficient solution to deal with a particular problem. This is, thus, the setting of the HAIS conference series, and its increasing success is the proof of the vitality of this exciting field.

The HAIS 2020 International Program Committee selected 65 papers, which are published in this conference proceedings, yielding an acceptance ratio of about 62%.

The selection of papers was extremely rigorous in order to maintain the high quality of the conference and we would like to thank the Program Committee for their hard work in the reviewing process. This process is very important in creating a conference of high standard and the HAIS conference would not exist without their help.

The large number of submissions is certainly not only a testimony to the vitality and attractiveness of the field but an indicator of the interest in the HAIS conferences themselves.

HAIS 2020 enjoyed outstanding keynote speeches by distinguished guest speakers: Prof. Antonio Bahamonde – Professor in the Department of Computer Science, University of Oviedo, Spain, and Prof. Sara Silva – Professor in the Large Scale Computer Systems Laboratory (LASIGE), University of Lisbon, Portugal.

HAIS 2020 has teamed up with the *Neurocomputing* (Elsevier) and the *Logic Journal of the IGPL* (Oxford Journals) journals for a suite of special issues including selected papers from HAIS 2020.

Particular thanks go as well to the conference's main sponsors, Startup OLE, the University of Oviedo, the Government of Principado de Asturias, the Government of the local council of Gijón, the Computer Science Department at University of Oviedo, the University of Salamanca, IBERIA, RENFE, ALSA, and the International Federation for Computational Logic, who jointly contributed in an active and constructive manner to the success of this initiative.

We would like to thank Alfred Hoffman and Anna Kramer from Springer for their help and collaboration during this demanding publication project.

Finally, we would like to thank the authors and, again, the Program Committee, for their support and comprehension during the COVID-19 pandemic and their total collaboration: they helped us in keeping on with the conference. Also, a special memorial to all the people that suffered from this horrendous pandemic.

November 2020

Enrique Antonio de la Cal
José Ramón Villar Flecha
Héctor Quintián
Emilio Corchado

Organization

General Chair

Emilio Corchado	University of Salamanca, Spain

Local Chairs

Jose Ramón Villar Flecha	University of Oviedo, Spain
Enrique Antonio de la Cal	University of Oviedo, Spain

Honor Committee

Adrián Barbón Rodríguez	President of the Government of Asturias, Spain
Santiago García Granda	Chancellor of the University of Oviedo, Spain
Ana González Rodríguez	Mayor of the city of Gijón, Spain

International Advisory Committee

Ajith Abraham	Machine Intelligence Research Labs, Europe
Antonio Bahamonde	University of Oviedo, Spain
Andre de Carvalho	University of São Paulo, Brazil
Sung-Bae Cho	Yonsei University, South Korea
Juan M. Corchado	University of Salamanca, Spain
José R. Dorronsoro	Autonomous University of Madrid, Spain
Michael Gabbay	King's College London, UK
Ali A. Ghorbani	UNB, Canada
Mark A. Girolami	University of Glasgow, UK
Manuel Graña	University of País Vasco, Spain
Petro Gopych	Universal Power Systems USA-Ukraine LLC, Ukraine
Jon G. Hall	The Open University, UK
Francisco Herrera	University of Granada, Spain
César Hervás-Martínez	University of Córdoba, Spain
Tom Heskes	Radboud University Nijmegen, The Netherlands
Dusan Husek	Academy of Sciences of the Czech Republic, Czech Republic
Lakhmi Jain	University of South Australia, Australia
Samuel Kaski	Helsinki University of Technology, Finland
Daniel A. Keim	University of Konstanz, Germany
Marios Polycarpou	University of Cyprus, Cyprus
Witold Pedrycz	University of Alberta, Canada
Xin Yao	University of Birmingham, UK
Hujun Yin	The University of Manchester, UK

Michał Woźniak	Wroclaw University of Technology, Poland
Aditya Ghose	University of Wollongong, Australia
Ashraf Saad	Armstrong Atlantic State University, USA
Fanny Klett	German Workforce Advanced Distributed Learning Partnership Laboratory, Germany
Paulo Novais	Universidade do Minho, Portugal
Rajkumar Roy	The EPSRC Centre for Innovative Manufacturing in Through-life Engineering Services, UK
Amy Neustein	Linguistic Technology Systems, USA
Jaydip Sen	Innovation Lab, Tata Consultancy Services Ltd., India

Program Committee

Emilio Corchado (PC Chair)	University of Salamanca, Spain
Abdel-Badeeh Salem	Ain Shams University, Egypt
Alberto Cano	Virginia Commonwealth University, USA
Alfredo Cuzzocrea	ICAR-CNR and University of Calabria, Italy
Alicia Troncoso	University Pablo de Olavide, Spain
Álvaro Herrero	University of Burgos, Spain
Amelia Zafra Gómez	University of Córdoba, Spain
Ana M. Bernardos	Polytechnic University of Madrid, Spain
Ana Madureira	Instituto Superior de Engenharia do Porto, Portugal
Anca Andreica	Babes-Bolyai University, Romania
Andreea Vescan	Babes-Bolyai University, Romania
Andrés Pinón	University of A Coruña, Spain
Ángel Arroyo	University of Burgos, Spain
Ángel Manuel Guerrero	University of León, Spain
Antonio de Jesús Díez	Polythecnic University of Madrid, Spain
Antonio D. Masegosa	University of Deusto and IKERBASQUE, Spain
Antonio Dourado	University of Coimbra, Portugal
Antonio Morales-Esteban	University of Seville, Spain
Arkadiusz Kowalski	Wrocław University of Technology, Poland
Barna Laszlo Iantovics	Petru Maior University of Tg. Mures, Romania
Beatriz Remeseiro	University of Oviedo, Spain
Bogdan Trawinski	Wroclaw University of Science and Technology, Poland
Bruno Baruque	University of Burgos, Spain
Camelia Chira	University of Babes Bolyai, Romania
Camelia Pintea	Technical University of Cluj-Napoca and North University Center at Baia Mare, Romania
Camelia Serban	University of Babes Bolyai, Romania
Carlos Cambra	University of Burgos, Spain
Carlos Carrascosa	GTI-IA DSIC Universidad Politecnica de Valencia, Spain
Carlos Mencía	University of Oviedo, Spain
Carlos Pereira	ISEC, Portugal

Cezary Grabowik	Silesian Technical University, Poland
Cosmin Sabo	Technical University of Cluj-Napoca, Romania
Damian Krenczyk	Silesian University of Technology, Poland
Dario Landa-Silva	University of Nottingham, UK
David Iclanzan	Sapientia - Hungarian Science University of Transylvania, Romania
Diego P. Ruiz	University of Granada, Spain
Dragan Simic	University of Novi Sad, Serbia
Edward R. Nuñez	University of Oviedo, Spain
Eiji Uchino	Yamaguchi University, Japan
Eneko Osaba	University of Deusto, Spain
Enrique Antonio de la Cal	University of Oviedo, Spain
Enrique Onieva	University of Deusto, Spain
Esteban Jove Pérez	University of A Coruña, Spain
Eva Volna	University of Ostrava, Czech Republic
Federico Divina	Pablo de Olavide University, Spain
Fermin Segovia	University of Granada, Spain
Fidel Aznar	University of Alicante, Spain
Francisco Javier de Cos Juez	University of Oviedo, Spain
Francisco Javier Martínez de Pisón Ascacíbar	University of La Rioja, Spain
Francisco Martínez-Álvarez	University Pablo de Olavide, Spain
Francisco Zayas Gato	University of A Coruña, Spain
George Papakostas	EMT Institute of Technology, Greece
Georgios Dounias	University of the Aegean, Greece
Giancarlo Mauri	University of Milano-Bicocca, Italy
Giorgio Fumera	University of Cagliari, Italy
Gloria Cerasela Crisan	University of Bacau, Romania
Gonzalo A. Aranda-Corral	University of Huelva, Spain
Gualberto Asencio-Cortés	Pablo de Olavide University, Spain
Guiomar Corral	La Salle University, Spain
Héctor Aláiz	University of León, Spain
Héctor Quintián	University of A Coruña, Spain
Henrietta Toman	University of Debrecen, Hungary
Ignacio Turias	University of Cádiz, Spain
Ioana Zelina	Technical University of Cluj-Napoca and North Center in Baia Mare, Romania
Ioannis Hatzilygeroudis	University of Patras, Greece
Irene Diaz	University of Oviedo, Spain
Isabel Barbancho	University of Málaga, Spain
Iskander Sánchez-Rola	University of Deusto, Spain
Javier Bajo	Polytechnic University of Madrid, Spain
Javier De Lope	Polytechnic University of Madrid, Spain
Javier Sedano	ITCL, Spain
Jorge García-Gutiérrez	University of Seville, Spain

Jorge Reyes	NT2 Labs, Chile
José Alfredo Ferreira Costa	Federal University, UFRN, Brazil
José Antonio Sáez	University of Salamanca, Spain
José Dorronsoro	Universidad Autónoma de Madrid, Spain
José García-Rodriguez	University of Alicante, Spain
José Luis Calvo-Rolle	University of A Coruña, Spain
José Luis Casteleiro-Roca	University of A Coruña, Spain
José Luis Verdegay	University of Granada, Spain
José M. Molina	University Carlos III of Madrid, Spain
José Manuel Lopez-Guede	University of the Basque Country, Spain
José María Armingol	University Carlos III of Madrid, Spain
José Ramón Villar Flecha	University of Oviedo, Spain
Jose-Ramón Cano De Amo	University of Jaen, Spain
Juan Humberto Sossa Azuela	National Polytechnic Institute, México
Juan J. Flores	Universidad Michoacana de San Nicolás de Hidalgo, Mexico
Juan Pavón	Complutense University of Madrid, Spain
Julio Ponce	Universidad Autónoma de Aguascalientes, México
Khawaja Asim	PIEAS, Pakistan
Krzysztof Kalinowski	Silesian University of Technology, Poland
Lauro Snidaro	University of Udine, Italy
Lenka Lhotska	Czech Technical University in Prague, Czech Republic
Leocadio G. Casado	University of Almeria, Spain
Lidia Sánchez González	University of León, Spain
Luis Alfonso Fernández Serantes	FH Joanneum University of Applied Sciences, Austria
M. Chadli	University of Picardie Jules Verne, France
Manuel Castejón-Limas	University of León, Spain
Manuel Graña	University of the Basque Country, Spain
María Sierra	University of Oviedo, Spain
Mario Koeppen	Kyushu Institute of Technology, Japan
Nashwa El-Bendary	Arab Academy of Science, Technology and Maritime Transport, Egypt
Noelia Rico	University of Oviedo, Spain
Oscar Fontenla-Romero	University of A Coruña, Spain
Oscar Mata-Carballeira	University of A Coruña, Spain
Ozgur Koray Sahingoz	Turkish Air Force Academy, Turkey
Paula M. Castro	University of A Coruña, Spain
Paulo Novais	University of Minho, Portugal
Pavel Brandstetter	VSB-Technical University of Ostrava, Czech Republic
Pedro López	University of Deusto, Spain
Peter Rockett	The University of Sheffield, UK
Petrica Pop	Technical University of Cluj-Napoca and North University Center at Baia Mare, Romania
Qing Tan	University of Athabasca, Canada

Ramon Rizo	University of Alicante, Spain
Ricardo Del Olmo	University of Burgos, Spain
Ricardo Leon Talavera Llames	University Pablo de Olavide, Spain
Robert Burduk	Wroclaw University of Technology, Poland
Rodolfo Zunino	University of Genoa, Italy
Roman Senkerik	Tomas Bata University in Zlin, Czech Republic
Rubén Fuentes-Fernández	Complutense University of Madrid, Spain
Sean Holden	University of Cambridge, UK
Sebastián Ventura	University of Córdoba, Spain
Theodore Pachidis	Kavala Institute of Technology, Greece
Urszula Stanczyk	Silesian University of Technology, Poland
Wiesław Chmielnicki	Jagiellonian University, Poland
Yannis Marinakis	Technical University of Crete, Greece
Zuzana Kominkova Oplatkova	Tomas Bata University in Zlin, Czech Republic

Organizing Committee

Enrique Antonio de la Cal	University of Oviedo, Spain
José Ramón Villar Flecha	University of Oviedo, Spain
Noelia Rico	University of Oviedo, Spain
Mirko Fáñez	University of Oviedo, Spain
Enol García González	Unviersity of Oviedo, Spain
Sezin Safar	University of Oviedo, Spain
Francisco Gil Gala	Unviersity of Oviedo, Spain
Hernán Díaz Rodríguez	University of Oviedo, Spain
Héctor Quintian	University of A Coruña, Spain
Emilio Corchado	University of Salamanca, Spain

Contents

Advanced Data Processing and Visualization Techniques

Generative Adversarial Network with Guided Generator for Non-stationary Noise Cancelation . . . 3
Kyung-Hyun Lim, Jin-Young Kim, and Sung-Bae Cho

Fake News Detection by Means of Uncertainty Weighted Causal Graphs . . . 13
Eduardo C. Garrido-Merchán, Cristina Puente, and Rafael Palacios

An Hybrid Registration Method for SLAM with the M8 Quanergy LiDAR . . . 25
Marina Aguilar-Moreno and Manuel Graña

An Adaptive Neighborhood Retrieval Visualizer . . . 36
Dominik Olszewski

A Fast SSVEP-Based Brain-Computer Interface . . . 49
Tania Jorajuría, Marisol Gómez, and Carmen Vidaurre

Visual Analytics for Production Line Failure Detection . . . 61
Unai Arrieta, Ander García, Mikel Lorente, and Ángel Maleta

Missing Data Imputation for Continuous Variables Based on Multivariate Adaptive Regression Splines . . . 73
Fernando Sánchez Lasheras, Paulino José García Nieto, Esperanza García-Gonzalo, Francisco Argüeso Gómez, Francisco Javier Rodríguez Iglesias, Ana Suárez Sánchez, Jesús Daniel Santos Rodríguez, María Luisa Sánchez, Joaquín González-Nuevo, Laura Bonavera, Luigi Toffolatti, Susana del Carmen Fernández Menéndez, and Francisco Javier de Cos Juez

Clustering and Regression to Impute Missing Values of Robot Performance . . . 86
Ángel Arroyo, Nuño Basurto, Carlos Cambra, and Álvaro Herrero

A Simple Classification Ensemble for ADL and Falls . . . 95
Enrique A. de la Cal, Mirko Fáñez, Mario Villar, Jose R. Villar, and Victor Suárez

Joint Entity Summary and Attribute Embeddings for Entity Alignment Between Knowledge Graphs . . . 107
Rumana Ferdous Munne and Ryutaro Ichise

Employing Decision Templates to Imbalanced Data Classification 120
Szymon Wojciechowski and Michał Woźniak

Comparison of Labeling Methods for Behavioral Activity Classification Based on Gaze Ethograms 132
Javier de Lope and Manuel Graña

Bio-inspired Models and Optimization

PBIL for Optimizing Hyperparameters of Convolutional Neural Networks and STL Decomposition 147
Roberto A. Vasco-Carofilis, Miguel A. Gutiérrez-Naranjo, and Miguel Cárdenas-Montes

An Evolutionary Approach to Automatic Keyword Selection for Twitter Data Analysis 160
Oduwa Edo-Osagie, Beatriz De La Iglesia, Iain Lake, and Obaghe Edeghere

PreCLAS: An Evolutionary Tool for Unsupervised Feature Selection 172
Jessica A. Carballido, Ignacio Ponzoni, and Rocío L. Cecchini

RADSSo: An Automated Tool for the multi-CASH Machine Learning Problem 183
Noemí DeCastro-García, Ángel Luis Muñoz Castañeda, and Mario Fernández-Rodríguez

A Metaheuristic Algorithm to Face the Graph Coloring Problem 195
A. Guzmán-Ponce, J. R. Marcial-Romero, R. M. Valdovinos, R. Alejo, and E. E. Granda-Gutiérrez

Tardiness Minimisation for Job Shop Scheduling with Interval Uncertainty 209
Hernán Díaz, Juan José Palacios, Irene Díaz, Camino R. Vela, and Inés González-Rodríguez

Modified Grid Searches for Hyper-Parameter Optimization 221
David López, Carlos M. Alaíz, and José R. Dorronsoro

Supervised Hyperparameter Estimation for Anomaly Detection 233
Juan Bella, Ángela Fernández, and José R. Dorronsoro

Using the Variational-Quantum-Eigensolver (VQE) to Create an Intelligent Social Workers Schedule Problem Solver 245
Parfait Atchade Adelomou, Elisabet Golobardes Ribé, and Xavier Vilasís Cardona

Fully Fuzzy Multi-objective Berth Allocation Problem. 261
Boris Pérez-Cañedo, José Luis Verdegay, Alejandro Rosete, and Eduardo René Concepción-Morales

Analysis of the Genetic Algorithm Operators for the Node Location Problem in Local Positioning Systems 273
Rubén Ferrero-Guillén, Javier Díez-González, Rubén Álvarez, and Hilde Pérez

Optimization of Learning Strategies for ARTM-Based Topic Models. 284
Maria Khodorchenko, Sergey Teryoshkin, Timur Sokhin, and Nikolay Butakov

Learning Algorithms

A Cluster-Based Under-Sampling Algorithm for Class-Imbalanced Data 299
A. Guzmán-Ponce, R. M. Valdovinos, and J. S. Sánchez

Comparing Knowledge-Based Reinforcement Learning to Neural Networks in a Strategy Game 312
Liudmyla Nechepurenko, Viktor Voss, and Vyacheslav Gritsenko

Clustering Techniques Performance Analysis for a Solar Thermal Collector Hybrid Model Implementation 329
María Teresa García-Ordás, Héctor Alaiz-Moretón, José-Luis Casteleiro-Roca, Esteban Jove, José Alberto Benítez Andrades, Carmen Benavides Cuellar, Héctor Quintián, and José Luis Calvo-Rolle

A Hybrid One-Class Topology for Non-convex Sets 341
Esteban Jove, José-Luis Casteleiro-Roca, Héctor Quintián, Francisco Zayas-Gato, Roberto Casado-Vara, Bruno Baruque, Juan Albino Méndez-Pérez, and José Luis Calvo-Rolle

A Machine Consciousness Architecture Based on Deep Learning and Gaussian Processes 350
Eduardo C. Garrido Merchán and Martin Molina

Some Experiments on the Influence of Problem Hardness in Morphological Development Based Learning of Neural Controllers. 362
M. Naya-Varela, A. Faina, and R. J. Duro

Importance Weighted Adversarial Variational Bayes 374
Marta Gómez-Sancho and Daniel Hernández-Lobato

Global and Saturated Probabilistic Approximations Based on Generalized Maximal Consistent Blocks 387
Patrick G. Clark, Jerzy W. Grzymala-Busse, Zdzislaw S. Hippe, Teresa Mroczek, and Rafal Niemiec

Evaluation of Error Metrics for Meta-learning Label Definition in the Forecasting Task 397
Moisés R. Santos, Leandro R. Mundim, and André C. P. L. F. Carvalho

Averaging-Based Ensemble Methods for the Partial Label Ranking Problem 410
Juan C. Alfaro, Juan A. Aledo, and José A. Gámez

Agglomerative Constrained Clustering Through Similarity and Distance Recalculation 424
Germán González-Almagro, Juan Luis Suarez, Julián Luengo, José-Ramón Cano, and Salvador García

Multi-expert Methods Evaluation on Financial and Economic Data: Introducing Bag of Experts 437
A. C. Umaquinga-Criollo, J. D. Tamayo-Quintero, M. N. Moreno-García, J. A. Riascos, and D. H. Peluffo-Ordóñez

The Borda Count as a Tool for Reducing the Influence of the Distance Function on *k*means 450
Noelia Rico, Raúl Pérez-Fernández, and Irene Díaz

Data Mining, Knowledge Discovery and Big Data

Opinion Mining System for Twitter Sentiment Analysis 465
Pâmella A. Aquino, Vivian F. López, María N. Moreno, María D. Muñoz, and Sara Rodríguez

An Expert System for Building Energy Management Through the Web of Things 477
Daniel Ibaseta, Julio Molleda, Martín Álvarez, and Fidel Díez

Simulating Users in a Social Media Platform Using Multi-agent Systems 486
Daniel Pérez and Estefanía Argente

First Steps Towards State Representation Learning for Cognitive Robotics . . . 499
Blaž Meden, Abraham Prieto, Peter Peer, and Francisco Bellas

Hybridized White Learning in Cloud-Based Picture Archiving and Communication System for Predictability and Interpretability 511
Antonio J. Tallón-Ballesteros, Simon Fong, Tengyue Li, Lian-sheng Liu, Thomas Hanne, and Weiwei Lin

A New Forecasting Algorithm Based on Neighbors for Streaming Electricity Time Series 522
P. Jiménez-Herrera, L. Melgar-García, G. Asencio-Cortés, and A. Troncoso

Effective Bin Picking Approach by Combining Deep Learning and Point Cloud Processing Techniques 534
Alberto Tellaeche Iglesias, Iker Pastor-López, Borja Sanz Urquijo, and Pablo García-Bringas

Forecasting Security Alerts Based on Time Series 546
Patrik Pekarčík, Andrej Gajdoš, and Pavol Sokol

Hybrid Artificial Intelligence Applications

A Real Time Vision System Based on Deep Learning for Gesture Based Human Machine Interaction 561
Alberto Tellaeche Iglesias, Iker Pastor-López, Borja Sanz Urquijo, and Pablo García-Bringas

Tourists Movement Analysis Based on Entropies of Markov Process 573
Naohiro Ishii, Kazuya Odagiri, Hidekazu Iwamoto, Satoshi Takahashi, Kazunori Iwata, and Tokuro Matsuo

Clustering Imputation for Air Pollution Data 585
Wedad Alahamade, Iain Lake, Claire E. Reeves, and Beatriz De La Iglesia

Identifying and Counting Vehicles in Multiple Lanes by Using a Low-Cost Vehicle-Mounted Sensor for Intelligent Traffic Management Systems 598
Elnaz Namazi, Jingyue Li, Rudolf Mester, and Chaoru Lu

Minimizing Attributes for Prediction of Cardiovascular Diseases 612
Roberto Porto Solano and Jose M. Molina

A Neural Approach to Ordinal Regression for the Preventive Assessment of Developmental Dyslexia 620
Francisco J. Martinez-Murcia, Andres Ortiz, Marco A. Formoso, Miguel Lopez-Zamora, Juan Luis Luque, and Almudena Gimenez

Fall Detection Based on Local Peaks and Machine Learning 631
José R. Villar, Mario Villar, Mirko Fañez, Enrique de la Cal, and Javier Sedano

Neural Networks for Background Rejection in DEAP-3600 Detector 644
Iñaki Rodríguez-García, Vicente Pesudo, Roberto Santorelli, Miguel Cárdenas-Montes, and on behalf of the DEAP-3600 Collaboration

Dyslexia Detection from EEG Signals Using SSA Component Correlation and Convolutional Neural Networks 655
Andrés Ortiz, Francisco J. Martínez-Murcia, Marco A. Formoso, Juan Luis Luque, and Auxiliadora Sánchez

Local Binary Pattern Features to Detect Anomalies in Machined Workpiece 665
Lidia Sánchez-González, Virginia Riego, Manuel Castejón-Limas, and Laura Fernández-Robles

Early Fully-Convolutional Approach to Wavefront Imaging on Solar Adaptive Optics Simulations 674
Francisco García Riesgo, Sergio Luis Suárez Gómez, Jesús Daniel Santos Rodríguez, Carlos González Gutiérrez, Enrique Díez Alonso, Francisco Javier Iglesias Rodríguez, Pedro Riesgo Fernández, Laura Bonavera, Susana del Carmen Fernández Menéndez, and Francisco Javier De Cos Juez

Modeling a Specific Commercial Single Proton Exchange Membrane Fuel Cell 686
Jose Manuel Lopez-Guede, Julian Estevez, and Manuel Graña

Deep Learning for House Categorisation, a Proposal Towards Automation in Land Registry 698
David Garcia-Retuerta, Roberto Casado-Vara, Jose L. Calvo-Rolle, Héctor Quintián, and Javier Prieto

On the Identification of Critical Questions in the PISA for Schools Program 706
Noelia Rico, Pedro Alonso, Laura Muñiz-Rodríguez, Raúl Pérez-Fernández, Luis J. Rodríguez-Muñiz, and Irene Díaz

Exploratory Analysis of Radiomics Features on a Head and Neck Cancer Public Dataset. 718
Oier Echaniz, Carlos M. Chiesa-Estomba, and Manuel Graña

Stroke Rehabilitation: Detection of Finger Movements. 729
Diego Aranda-Orna, José R. Villar, and Javier Sedano

A Hybrid Bio-inspired Clustering Approach for Diagnosing Children with Primary Headache Disorder. 739
Svetlana Simić, Slađana Sakač, Zorana Banković, José R. Villar, Svetislav D. Simić, and Dragan Simić

Artificial Neural Networks for Tours of Multiple Asteroids 751
Giulia Viavattene and Matteo Ceriotti

Deep Learning for Scene Recognition from Visual Data: A Survey 763
Alina Matei, Andreea Glavan, and Estefanía Talavera

Cost-Efficiency of Convolutional Neural Networks for High-Dimensional EEG Classification 774
Javier León, Andrés Ortiz, Miguel Damas, Jesús González, and Julio Ortega

Author Index 787

Advanced Data Processing and Visualization Techniques

Generative Adversarial Network with Guided Generator for Non-stationary Noise Cancelation

Kyung-Hyun Lim, Jin-Young Kim, and Sung-Bae Cho(✉)

Department of Computer Science, Yonsei University, Seoul 03722, South Korea
{lkh1075, seago0828, sbcho}@yonsei.ac.kr

Abstract. Noise comes from a variety of sources in real world, which makes a lot of non-stationary noises, and it is difficult to find target speech from noisy auditory signals. Recently, adversarial learning models get attention for its high performance in the field of noise control, but it has limitation to depend on the one-to-one mapping between the noisy and the target signals, and unstable training process due to the various distributions of noise. In this paper, we propose a novel deep learning model to learn the noise and target speech distributions at the same time for improving the performance of noise cancellation. It is composed of two generators to stabilize the training process and two discriminators to optimize the distributions of noise and target speech, respectively. It helps to compress the distribution over the latent space, because two distributions from the same source are used simultaneously during adversarial learning. For the stable learning, one generator is pre-trained with minimum sample and guides the other generator, so that it can prevent mode collapsing problem by using prior knowledge. Experiments with the noise speech dataset composed of 30 speakers and 90 types of noise are conducted with scale-invariant source-to-noise ratio (SI-SNR) metric. The proposed model shows the enhanced performance of 7.36, which is 2.13 times better than the state-of-the-art model. Additional experiment on −10, −5, 0, 5, and 10 dB of the noise confirms the robustness of the proposed model.

Keywords: Speech enhancement · Noise cancelation · Non-stationary noise · Deep learning · Generative adversarial network

1 Introduction

All the sounds in ambulances like rescue personnel's communication with the medical center are recorded to preserve the situation. Since the loud siren noises of more than 120 dB hinder us from recording and storing the contents of communication, we have to remove the noise [1]. As illustrated in Fig. 1, the non-stationary noises change the frequencies quickly, and show the irregular characteristics. Noise cancelation, one of the major issues in speech enhancement, aims to improve the quality of speech signal and make the speech understandable to the observer. In order to achieve it in the real environment where various noises are mixed, we have to eliminate noises with different distributions and irregularities [2].

E. A. de la Cal et al. (Eds.): HAIS 2020, LNAI 12344, pp. 3–12, 2020.
https://doi.org/10.1007/978-3-030-61705-9_1

Generative adversarial network (GAN) is recently popular in the field of speech enhancement due to its powerful performance [3], but the model has tendency to produce blurred sounds because it works on one-to-one mapping from noisy speech ($\tilde{x}$) to clean speech (x). It has the inherent limitation to deal with the characteristics of non-stationary noise. In the real environment like ambulances, we have to handle the various non-stationary noises and mode collapsing problem that can occur in learning with various distributions of noises and target sounds from various speakers [4].

In this paper, we propose a novel method to overcome the problems of the generative model mentioned above. In order to prevent the output sound from blurring, an additional discriminator is designed to guide the distributions of the noise. Unlike the previous GAN models with only one discriminator, the discriminator which learns the distribution and characteristics of noise alleviates the problem of blurred sound. To work out the mode collapsing problem, we utilize a pre-trained generator that guides the other generator during the adversarial learning. The proposed method is evaluated with a dataset that randomly mixes the non-stationary noise with clean speech recorded in the recording studio, in four evaluation scenarios: only validation noise, only validation speaker, both of them, and training data for test data. The SI-SNR metric is used for objective numerical evaluation.

2 Related Works

Several methods for noise cancelation are studied in two approaches. One applies filtering method to remove noise by using threshold and several conditions [5]. Basically, there is a limitation that a specific noise cannot be removed which is not set at the design time, resulting in the difficulty to remove the irregularly shaped noise. However, the first limitation of the filtering method can be solved through the deep learning method [6]. Recently, the GAN model, which is attracting attention for learning

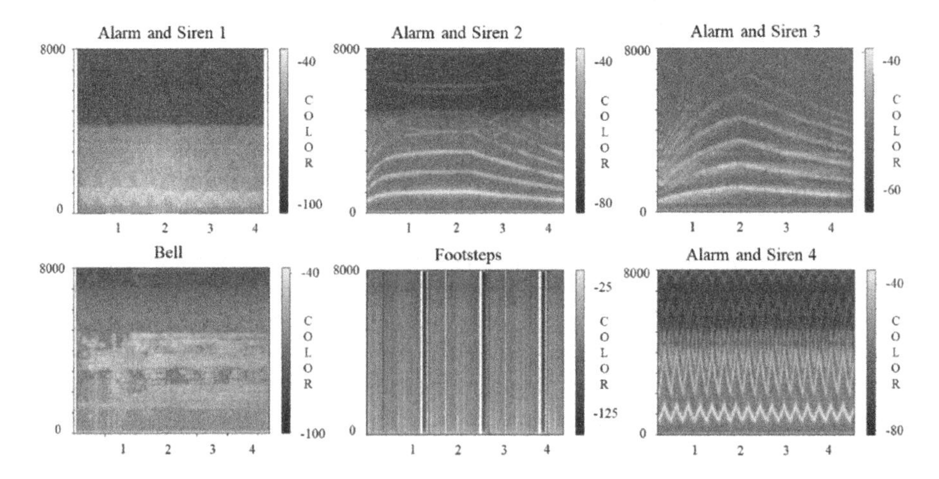

Fig. 1. Examples of non-stationary noise. They show an irregular characteristic of rapidly changing frequency. The x-axis means time and y-axis is frequency.

complex relationships of data, has also been studied in the field of noise cancelation. This model shows good performance but is still vulnerable to the non-stationary noise, since they all tried one-to-one mapping, which blurrs the noise characteristics [3, 7]. In addition, there is a limitation that only limited experiments are conducted [8].

There is also a lot of research to solve the mode collapsing problem of generative models. In order to perform the mapping with the actual samples having various distributions, many studies have been conducted toward the additional use of a discriminator or a generator [9–12]. Salimans et al. avoided the mode collapsing problem by tailoring batch data to ensure that the data in the batch is organized into different classes [4]. Luke used additional parameters, which predict the changes of discriminator, while training generator [13]. Although it showed better results, it has the disadvantage of increasing the complexity of the model and the amount of training. Nguyen et al. used two discriminators each of which learned real data and synthesized data as true [9]. Hoang et al. used a stabilization method similar to ours [10]. They used multiple generators and combined the results. However, since each generator is responsible for different portion of data, the computational complexity increases as well as the performance.

In this paper, we propose a model that can stably remove the untrained non-stationary noise by using the two generators and two discriminators and evaluate the performance by constructing four evaluation scenarios similar to the real environment.

3 The Proposed Method

The learning of the proposed method consists of two stages: shadow generator $G_{\theta'}$ is pretrained for guiding G_θ and then G_θ learns in adversarial by taking $G_{\theta'}$'s guide. Figure 2(a) shows the pre-training process of $G_{\theta'}$. Figure 2(b), (c) and (d) illustrate adversarial learning phase. $G_{\theta'}$ is trained by sampling data and learns the distribution of data briefly through one-to-one mapping as previous methods did. It is used to increase the effectiveness of adversarial learning because it can compensate for the instability that can occur in the adversarial learning. The instability means that generator makes corrupted signal like sequence of one or zero signal, which is called '*mode collapsing*' problem. When original generator G_θ raises it, the guide is given to the weight of pre-trained $G_{\theta'}$, which stabilizes G_θ's adversarial learning. Finally, G_θ removes the noise.

3.1 Residuals-Noise Discriminator

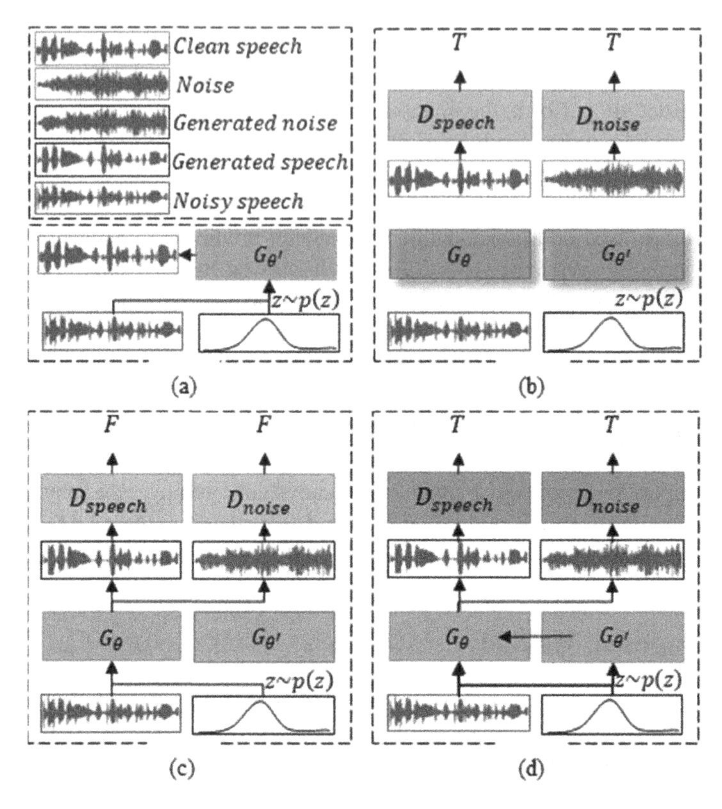

Fig. 2. Overall training process. (a) Pre-training of shadow generator $G_{\theta'}$. (b), (c), and (d) Adversarial learning process with $G_{\theta'}$ with guide. Purple boxes mean trainable status. Gray boxes have a fixed weight.

Most of generative models attempt to remove the noise by mapping only two distributions: clean speech and noisy speech. They are mixed and produce a more diverse distribution. This makes it difficult to remove noises with simple one-to-one mapping. In addition, characteristics of noise become blurred in the process, making them vulnerable to non-stationary noise. In order to eliminate the various non-stationary noises, our model is constructed with two discriminators. Each discriminator learns distributions of clean speech or noise, respectively. Residuals-noise discriminator D_{noise} learns noise as true by subtracting clean speech x from noisy speech $\tilde{x}$, and learns the residuals as false by subtracting generated speech $\hat{x}$ from $\tilde{x}$. The generator does not simply learn to generate a speech similar to the original speech x, but to what distribution of noise is mixed. This process is derived from minimizing Jensen-Shannon divergence (JSD) through two discriminators. The JSD is a measure of the difference between two probability distributions. By minimizing the JSD, the two probability distributions become similar, and the model learns the characteristics of the noise and can even eliminate non-stationary noise. The first term in Eq. (1) computes the difference between the distributions of clean speech and enhances speech. The noise cancelation performance is improved through a second term meaning difference between the noise and the residuals. The structure of discriminator is composed of fully convolution layer to extract and learn features of speech.

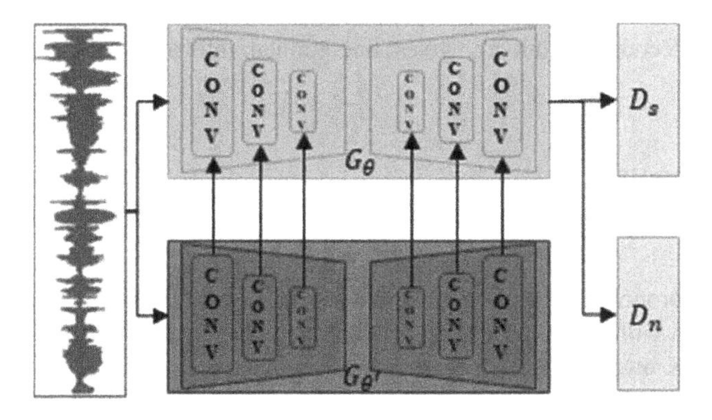

Fig. 3. Pretrained shadow generator $G_{\theta'}$ transfers its gradient to G_θ during learning.

$$\min[(JSD(P_x, G(P_{\tilde{x}})) + JSD(P_{\tilde{x}} - P_x,\ P_{\tilde{x}} - G(P_{\tilde{x}})))] \tag{1}$$

where P is the probability distribution of the data.

3.2 Guiding Through the Shadow Generator

The $G_{\theta'}$ is trained about noisy and clean speech pairs using minimum sample. Since the learning is carried out by the auto-encoder, the prior knowledge can be acquired. It guides G_θ as shown in Fig. 3 through the prior knowledge during adversarial learning. Its guide makes it possible to proceed with adversarial learning until the G_θ has converged stably. Equations (2) and (3) represent the objective function for each discriminator.

$$\min_G \left(D_{speech}(G_\theta(z, \tilde{x}))\right)^2 + \|G_\theta(z, \tilde{x}) - x_1\| \tag{2}$$

$$\min_G (D_{noise}(G_\theta(z, \tilde{x}) - x))^2 + \left\|2\tilde{x} - (G_\theta(z, \tilde{x}) + x)_1\right\| \tag{3}$$

where z is a random variable with normal distribution. The z adds a stochastic function to the generator and prevents it from overfitting the learned noise [3]. Also, the second term of both equations means L1 norm which is often used to help generate near-real samples [14]. Minimizing this term helps generate samples similar to the actual clean speech. The generator consists of an encoder and a decoder. Noisy speech is used as the input of the encoder. As the input of the decoder, z sampled from a Gaussian distribution Z and the output of the encoder are used simultaneously. At this time, the output of the encoder plays a role similar to the condition of conditional auto-encoder [15]. Both encoder and decoder structure are composed of fully convolution layer to extract and learn the features of complex speech signal. Skip connection is used between encoder and decoder. It directly gives fine-grained information of input signal to decoder [14].

4 Experiments

4.1 Dataset

To verify the proposed method, we use the speech data of 30 people recorded in the recording room with clean speech and 90 different noise data [16, 17]. Clean speech is composed 1.2K utterance. 22 speakers and 78 noises are used for training and others are involved in validation dataset. Noise is selected at an appropriate ratio based on category. Noise data contains things that may occur in a real world, such as a traffic sound, clapping, cough, etc. The sample rate of the speech data is 16K, and the training data was clipped to 16,384 length having a length similar to one second at this rate. The noisy speech for learning is composed by mixing one random noise with one clean speech. For systematic evaluation, four scenarios were constructed: only validation noise, only validation speaker, both of them, and training data for test data. For objective evaluation, the SI-SNR, which is calculated as shown in Eq. (4)–(6), is used.

$$S_{target} = \frac{\langle x, \tilde{x} \rangle \cdot x}{||x||^2} \tag{4}$$

$$E_{noise} = \tilde{x} - S_{target}, \tag{5}$$

$$SI - SNR = 10log_{10}\left(\frac{||S_{target}||^2}{||E_{noise}||^2}\right) \tag{6}$$

where the x means clean speech, $\tilde{x}$ is noisy speech, $\cdot, \cdot$ represents inner product, and $\cdot$ operator is dot product. If the noise is completely removed, the S_{target} becomes equal to x. SI-SNR represents the similarity of speech signals, the higher the performance the better [18].

4.2 Learning Stability

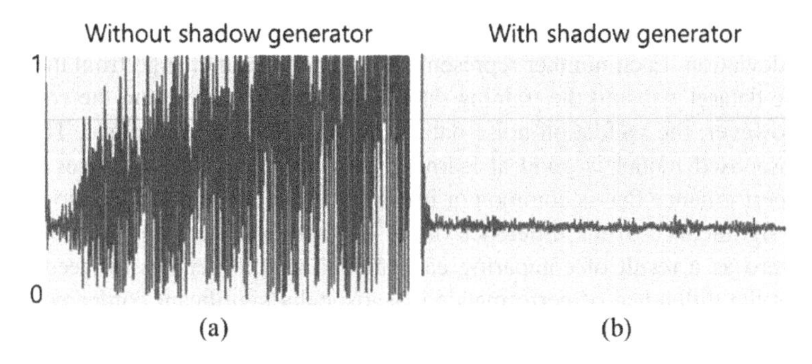

Fig. 4. Visualization of generator loss under two condition: (a) without shadow generator, and (b) with shadow generator (b). X-axis is epoch, and y-axis represents value of loss function.

Figure 4 depicts the loss of the generator to show the stable learning process through the guiding of shadow generator. To see the effect of the shadow generator, we set the same parameters, such as training time and epoch, data, and model structure. Figure 5 shows that we are guiding well regardless of the scenario. Experimental results show that shadow *G* made continuous learning, but without shadow *G*, learning is corrupt after a certain time.

4.3 Noise Cancelation Performance

We evaluated the performance of the comparison model and the proposed model using four scenarios. Figure 6 and Table 1 show the results of SI-SNR evaluation values based on the same learning time as boxplot and numeric values. The model proposed in

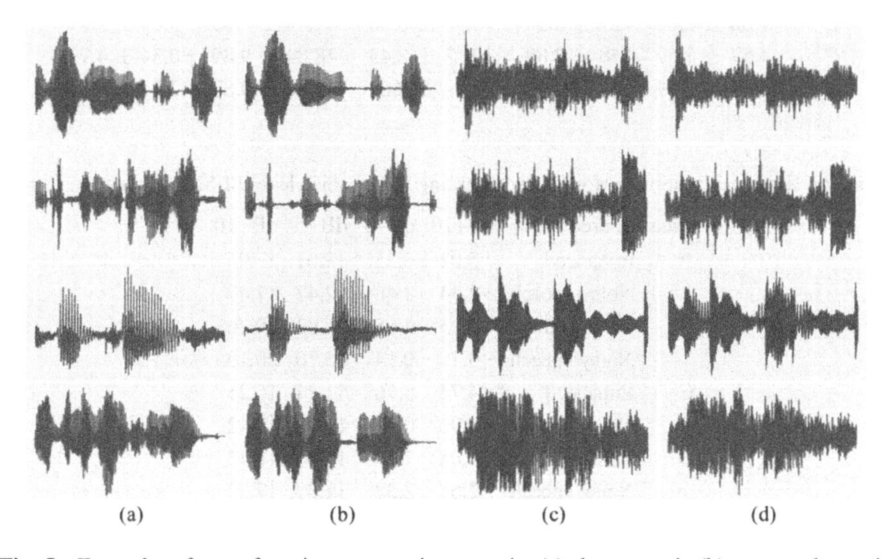

Fig. 5. Examples of wave form in unseen noise scenario. (a) clean speech, (b) generated speech, (c) noise signal, and (d) synthesized noise signal by generator.

this paper shows the best performance in most of the four scenarios. In Table 1, the performance of the dataset C corresponding to the unseen speaker was almost similar to that of the existing model (4.57 and 4.58). The number following '±' symbol means Standard deviation. Each number represents how much it can change from the average value. The dataset A using the training data shows lower values than the competitive model. However, the validation noise dataset B shows a clear advantage. This means that the proposed model is good at learning about noise, which improves the noise rejection performance that is common or irregular. The t-test is performed to check the statistical significance of the difference of the evaluation results, and the p-values are close to zero as a result of comparing each model at nine degrees of freedom. This shows that the difference of performance is statistically significant compared with the conventional methods.

The second experiment was performed by changing the dB (decibel) of noise based on the data set in Table 1. This experiment proves that our model learned the noise distribution reliably. As shown in Table 2, noise cancelation performance is maintained regardless of dB of noise. In particular, the SI-SNR evaluation of the dataset with the highest dB increase shows a 2.13-time decrease in noise level because the noise level increase by approximately 7 the noise speech. The experimental results show that our method can learn the characteristics of various non-stationary noises well and reliably remove them.

Table 1. SI-SNR evaluation results with other models. A is composed seen speaker and noise. B is seen speaker and unseen noise. C is unseen speaker and seen noise. D is unseen speaker and noise.

Data	Ours	[3]	Filtering	Auto-encoder	Noise signal
A	7.36 ± 2.61	**7.50 ± 3.64**	−16.82 ± 8.65	−49.94 ± 9.60	0.95 ± 5.71
B	**7.36 ± 2.62**	3.29 ± 5.24	−15.98 ± 8.36	−49.94 ± 9.61	3.05 ± 5.54
C	4.57 ± 3.59	**4.58 ± 2.88**	−19.23 ± 8.43	−48.84 ± 9.89	−0.34 ± 4.73
D	**4.571 ± 3.59**	2.03 ± 2.03	−18.43 ± 8.67	−48.84 ± 9.88	2.51 ± 6.31

Table 2. Noise cancelation performance according to the noise level SI-SNR evaluation result.

Data	Source	dB+10	dB+5	dB−5	dB−10
A	Enhanced	5.02	6.35	13.01	17.95
	Noisy speech	−2.54	2.46	12.47	17.47
B	Enhanced	3.25	4.55	26.02	20.26
	Noisy speech	−5.11	0.14	25.10	20.10
C	Enhanced	4.74	5.76	11.24	16.25
	Noisy speech	−4.90	0.11	10.12	15.12
D	Enhanced	6.05	7.17	14.06	18.12
	Noisy speech	−2.68	2.32	12.32	17.32

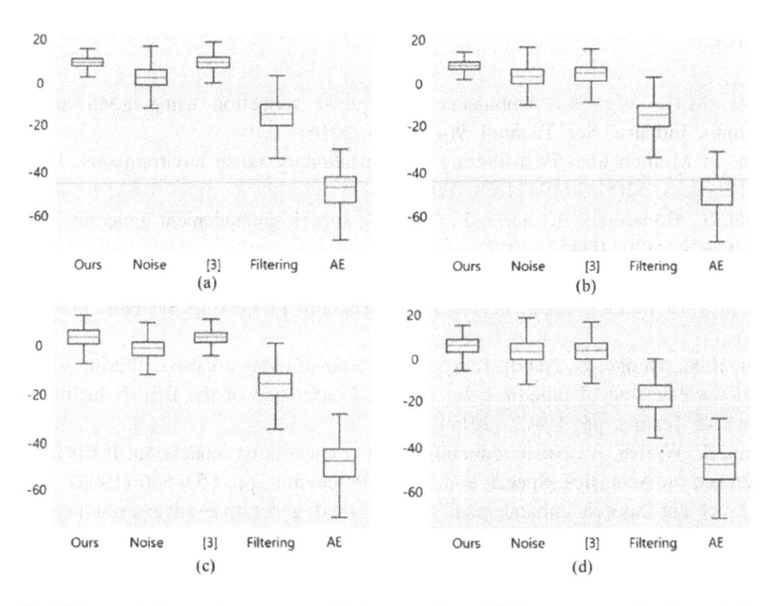

Fig. 6. SI-SNR result for each scenario. (a) is seen data, (b) is unseen noise data, (c) is unseen speaker data, (d) is the data model haven't seen.

5 Conclusion

In this paper, we propose a method to stably remove non-stationary noise. The additional discriminator learning the distribution of noise helps to remove irregular non-stationary noise by learning the characteristics of noise. Besides, the other discriminator, which learns the distribution of the clean speech, is trained to reconstruct the original well, and the generator can produce a clear target speech. Furthermore, two generators made a kind of relationship between teacher and student to compensate for the instability problem. As a result, stable learning could lead to better noise cancellation results. The results of the several experiments show that our proposed model and learning method achieves the best performance compared with the conventional models. The visualization of the loss values show that the proposed model is trained in stable.

In the future, we will conduct a comparative experiment using more various evaluation indexes and develop a demonstration system that can directly evaluate the usefulness. In addition, since most papers currently use hand-made datasets, the type and number of noises are not systematic. However, since the data collected in the real environment cannot create a clean speech targeted, it is necessary to systematically generate the data.

Acknowledgement. This work was supported by Institute of Information & Communications Technology Planning & Evaluation (IITP) grant funded by the Korean government (MSIT) (No. 2020-0-01361, Artificial Intelligence Graduate School Program (Yonsei University)) and grant funded by 2019 IT promotion fund (Development of AI based Precision Medicine Emergency System) of the Korean government (MSIT).

References

1. Sharma, M.K., Vig, R.: Ambulance siren noise reduction using LMS and FXLMS algorithms. Indian J. Sci. Technol. **9**(47), 1–6 (2016)
2. Cohen, I.: Multichannel Post-filtering in nonstationary noise environments. IEEE Trans. Signal Process. **52**(5), 1149–1160 (2004)
3. Pascual, S., Bonafonte, A., Serra, J.: SEGAN: speech enhancement generative adversarial network arXiv:1703.09452 (2017)
4. Salimans, T., Goodfellow, I., Zaremba, W., Cheung, V., Radford, A., Chen, X.: Improved techniques for training Gans. In: Neural Information Processing Systems, pp. 2234–2242 (2016)
5. Mahal, H.N., Mudge, P., Nandi, K.A.: Noise removal using adaptive filtering for ultrasonic guided wave testing of pipelines. In: Annual Conference of the British Institute of Non-Destructive Testing, pp. 19–27 (2019)
6. Tamura, S., Waibel, A.: Noise reduction using connectionist models. In: IEEE International Conference on Acoustics, Speech and Signal Processing, pp. 553–556 (1988)
7. Lin, J., et al.: Speech enhancement using forked generative adversarial networks with spectral subtraction. In: Interspeech, pp. 3163–3167 (2019)
8. Lim, K.-H., Kim, J.-Y., Cho, S.-B.: Non-stationary noise cancellation using deep autoencoder based on adversarial learning. In: Yin, H., Camacho, D., Tino, P., Tallón-Ballesteros, A.J., Menezes, R., Allmendinger, R. (eds.) IDEAL 2019. LNCS, vol. 11871, pp. 367–374. Springer, Cham (2019). https://doi.org/10.1007/978-3-030-33607-3_40
9. Nguyen, T., Le, T., Vu, H., Phung, D.: Dual discriminator generative adversarial nets. In: Neural Information Processing Systems, pp. 2670–2680 (2017)
10. Hoang, Q., Nguyen, T.D., Le, T., Phung, D.: MGAN: training generative adversarial nets with multiple generators. In: International Conference on Learning Representation, pp. 1–24, 2018
11. Kim, J.Y., Bu, S.J., Cho, S.B.: Hybrid deep learning based on GAN for classifying BSR noises from invehicle sensors. In: de Cos Juez, F., et al. (eds.) Hybrid Artificial Intelligent Systems, vol. 10870, pp. 27–38. Springer, Heidelberg (2018). https://doi.org/10.1007/978-3-319-92639-1_3
12. Kim, J.Y., Bu, S.J., Cho, S.B.: Zero-day malware detection using transferred generative adversarial networks based on deep autoencoders. Inf. Sci. **460–461**, 83–102 (2018)
13. Luke, M., Ben, P., David, P., Jascha, S.D.: Unrolled generative adversarial networks. arXiv:1611.02163 (2016)
14. He, K., Zhang, X., Ren, S., Sun, J.: Deep residual learning for image recognition. In: IEEE Conference on Computer Vision and Pattern Recognition, pp. 770–778 (2016)
15. Doersch, C.: Tutorial on variational autoencoders arXiv:1606.05908 (2016)
16. Valentini, C.: Noisy speech database for training speech enhancement algorithms and TTS Models. University of Edinburgh. School of Informatics. Centre for Speech Research (2016)
17. Hu, G., Wang, D.L.: A tandem algorithm for pitch estimation and voiced speech segregation. IEEE Trans. Audio Speech Lang. Process. **18**, 2067–2079 (2010)
18. Luo, Y., Mesgarani, N.: TasNet: surpassing ideal time-frequency masking for speech separation arXiv:1809.07454 (2018)

Fake News Detection by Means of Uncertainty Weighted Causal Graphs

Eduardo C. Garrido-Merchán[1(✉)], Cristina Puente[2], and Rafael Palacios[2]

[1] Universidad Autónoma de Madrid, Francisco Tomás y Valiente 11, Madrid, Spain
eduardo.garrido@uam.es

[2] Escuela Técnica Superior de Ingeniería ICAI, Universidad Pontificia Comillas, Madrid, Spain
cristina.puente@icai.comillas.edu, palacios@comillas.edu

Abstract. Society is experimenting changes in information consumption, as new information channels such as social networks let people share news that do not necessarily be trust worthy. Sometimes, these sources of information produce fake news deliberately with doubtful purposes and the consumers of that information share it to other users thinking that the information is accurate. This transmission of information represents an issue in our society, as can influence negatively the opinion of people about certain figures, groups or ideas. Hence, it is desirable to design a system that is able to detect and classify information as fake and categorize a source of information as trust worthy or not. Current systems experiment difficulties performing this task, as it is complicated to design an automatic procedure that can classify this information independent on the context. In this work, we propose a mechanism to detect fake news through a classifier based on weighted causal graphs. These graphs are specific hybrid models that are built through causal relations retrieved from texts and consider the uncertainty of causal relations. We take advantage of this representation to use the probability distributions of this graph and built a fake news classifier based on the entropy and KL divergence of learned and new information. We believe that the problem of fake news is accurately tackled by this model due to its hybrid nature between a symbolic and quantitative methodology. We describe the methodology of this classifier and add empirical evidence of the usefulness of our proposed approach in the form of synthetic experiments and a real experiment involving lung cancer.

1 Introduction

There is a trend in our society to read more news on Social Networks or Messaging platforms than on more traditional (and more regulated) news media such as newspapers, radio or TV. Unfortunately, those managing social networks are not responsible for the contents distributed through their networks, so false or misleading messages cannot be punished. Only in more extreme cases in which a user violates the privacy of a person or an institution, that user, but not the

E. A. de la Cal et al. (Eds.): HAIS 2020, LNAI 12344, pp. 13–24, 2020.
https://doi.org/10.1007/978-3-030-61705-9_2

network, will be sued [9]. However, the society has experienced an increasing sensitivity about the contents spread through social networks. Specially after the concerns about the effects of fake news circulating social media on the results of the 2016 US presidential elections [2]. Although people are more likely to believe the news that favor their preferred candidate or show disapprobation for the opponent, it is generally accepted that fake news have an impact on the way people think, so the impact of social networks on elections in the US and other countries has been analyzed extensively [3,4]. Social Media managers have detected a threat of missing customers due to distrust on social media due to a lack of verification of the contents, that was also amplified by privacy concerns over politically related data breaches [17]. Therefore there is a growing interest on managing and controlling rumor dissemination on social media, which starts by detecting fake news on social media [15].

In this paper, we propose a causal detection approach to tackle fake news classification, we will only focus in retrieved causal relations of text and in giving a probabilistic quantity for an information to be faked based in previous learn information of trust worthy sources. The paper is organized as follows: Sect. 2 will briefly describe causality and related work. Then, Sect. 3 will dive into the proposal of our method to classify fake news. We provide empirical evidence to support our hypothesis that fake news can be classified with respect to their causal relations in Sect. 4 with a set of synthetic experiments and a real experiment. Finally, we conclude our article with a conclusions and further work section.

2 Causality Applied to Fake News and Related Work

Fake news detection is problematic since it appears in any context. Then, in contrast with more concrete problems such as automatic entity recognition, it is very difficult to extract patterns from texts in a supervised machine learning fashion, tagging doubtful messages, in a similar way as spam detectors label email messages with a calculated spam probability. Nevertheless, the plethora of different contexts for fake news, sharing between them almost any pattern, is too broad for pure machine learning systems [10] to perform a good work.

Motivated by the absence of a proper approach to tackle fake news and by the difficulties that machine learning systems experiment in this task, we have decided to focus on causality to discriminate if a processed text contains fake information. We can only know if an information is fake based in previous learned information that is accurate. The difficulty is that this information is different for every context. Hence, we must learn from every possible context with before classifying if an information is fake. In this paper, we have decided to learn the causal relations of trust worthy texts by creating a casual weighted graph [7] and then using that information to discriminate if a new information is fake.

Causality is an important notion in every field of science. In empirical sciences, causality is a useful way to generate knowledge and provide explanations. When Newton's apple fell on into his head, he discovered gravity analysing what had provoked such event, that is, he established a cause-effect relationship [8].

Causation is a kind of relationship between two entities: cause and effect. The cause provokes an effect, and the effect is a consequence of the cause. Causality is a direct process when A causes B and B is a direct effect of A, or an indirect one when A causes C through B, and C is an indirect effect of A [1]. In this work, we use causality as source to verify information, as causal sentences establish strong relations between concepts easy to validate.

Causality is not only a matter of causal statements, but also of conditional sentences. In conditional statements, causality emerges generally from the relationship between antecedent and consequence. In [14], Puente et al. described a procedure to automatically display a causal graph from medical knowledge included in several medical texts, particularly those identified by the presence of certain interrogative particles [16]. These sentences are pre-processed in a convenient way in order to achieve single cause-effect structures, or causal chains from a prior cause to a final effect. Some medical texts, adapted to the described process, let make questions that provide automatic answers based on causal relations. Causal links admit qualifications in terms of weighting the intensity of the cause or the amount of links connecting causes to effects. A formalism that combines degrees of truth and McCulloch-Pitts cells permits us to weigh the effect with a value; so, to validate information in a certain degree. In the following section, we propose a classifier based in a causal weighted graph model to predict fake news based in a causality methodology.

3 Generating a Weighted Causal Graph from Text Causal Relations

In this section, we will expose the mechanism that detects fake news by means of a Weighted Causal Graph [7]. The weighted causal graph is a generalization of a causal graph [12] but modelling the certain degree as a latent variable with a probability distribution instead of with a point estimation. This model builds a causal network from the logicist point of view of probability with probability distributions in the edges that represent the probability of the certain factors that connect two concepts in the net. This weighted causal graph was specifically designed to retain the uncertainty given by time adverbs of retrieved causal sentences from texts. The priors for each adverb belong to the exponential family of distributions. Further information about the model can be consulted in this paper [7].

In order to compute the distance between two distributions P and Q we use the KL divergence, that is given by the following expression, where we approximate the integral by Grid Approximation:

$$D_{KL}(P||Q) = \int_{\infty}^{\infty} p(x) \log(\frac{p(x)}{q(x)})dx. \tag{1}$$

These quantity, along with entropy, will be used in the following section to get a probabilistic prediction of a new causal relation representing fake knowledge.

4 Detecting Fake News

After performing the learning process of the graph, we are more sure about the uncertainty that a given concept is associated with some effect. As the causal relation may appear in more texts, we need a mechanism to ensure that the new texts contain information that can be trusted. By working with PDFs, we can use the entropy of the PDFs as a measure of the gained information. We compute the entropy of the computed posteriors by grid approximation:

$$h(X) = -\int_{\mathcal{X}} f(x) \log f(x) dx \tag{2}$$

In order to detect fake information, we first need to know if we have gained knowledge about the probability of the causal. The causal is represented by its prior distribution $p(x)$ and posterior distribution $s(x)$. A criterion to discriminate if we have gained knowledge about the probability of the causal is to define a binary variable b that tells us whether it makes sense to compute the fake information probability:

$$b = 1 - \delta(h(s(x)) - h(p(x))). \tag{3}$$

If the entropy of the posterior is lower than the entropy of the prior, we have gained knowledge about the probability of the causal. Then, we can compute a fake information probability. We assume that if the new PDF is close to the learned posterior, the information can be trusted. We also take into account the gained information of the posterior. We are more sure about the fake new probability of the distribution $l(x)$ if the entropy of the posterior is close to zero, as we have gained more knowledge.

By combining both criteria, we propose a criterion for a causal to be fake. First, we need to normalize the KL $KL_n(s(x)||l(x))$ and the entropy $h_n(s(x)) \in [0, 1]$. The entropy can be normalized with respect to the other adverb PDFs in a $[0, 1]$ range in order to output a probability $p_f(x) \in [0, 1]$. KL is more challenging to be normalized as it is a measure that has no upper limit and is not defined with distributions that have support 0. In order to circumvent these issues, we smooth the distributions by a very small quantity and transform the KL divergence by squashing it into a sigmoid. That is, $KL(s(x)||l(x)) = 1 - \exp(-KL(s(x)||l(x)))$. By performing these two operations, we get rid of computational problems. We also assign a regularizer weight $w \in [0, 1]$ to the entropy factor $h_n(s(x))$ in order to model the contribution of the posterior entropy to the probability $p_f(x)$ and a scale factor σ to $p_f(x) \in [0, 1]$ that scales the probability in order to ensure it to be fake or to be more permissive with the result. The final criterion, $p_f(x)$, that determines whether a causal relation is fake or not is given by:

$$p_f(x) = ((1 - w)(KL_n(s(x)||l(x))wh_n(s(x))))^{\sigma}. \tag{4}$$

The computed probability can be used for two things. First, it is useful to compute this probability and to discriminate if the analyzed information represent fake information. Hence, it can be used as a fake new classifier. We can train our classifier with a reliable source of information with respect to some particular scenario, for example, lung cancer causal relations. Once we have trained our classifier in a realiable source of information, our posteriors represent the learned knowledge.

At this point, we are ready to discriminate whether new information is fake. We define fake information to be the information that is not similar to the learned information. If the causals retrieved from new sources of information give a high fake information probability $p_f(x)$, then we can classify this information as fake. We classify information as fake if the probability $p_f(x)$ is higher than a threshold β that we introduce as a hyperparameter. For example, if we set $\beta = 0.6$ and $p_f(x) = 0.7$, the information will be fake. On the other hand, if $p_f(x) = 0.5$, the information is not fake. By setting this threshold we do not only give a probability but a decision about the new information. We can also give a confidence degree of our decision Ω by computing $\Omega = |p_f(x) - \beta|/max(1 - p_f(x), p_f(x))$ where $\Omega \in [0, 1]$ will also represent a probability.

The described expressions represent whether a given causal is fake and also provide its probability. Another interesting measure to compute is the probability of a fake source of information. This probability represent whether the whole source of information is reliable or not. This probability will be computed as a function of the probabilities of being fake of all the causal relations retrieved from the new source of information. The trust degree of a new source of information α can be computed as: $\alpha = \frac{\sum_{i=1}^{N} p_i}{N}$, where N is the total number of causal relations and p_i represent the probability of a causal relation i for being fake. By computing this probability we can also set another threshold γ and compute a confidence degree of our decision ϵ that will classify is a source of information is reliable in an analogous form that we have computed it for a single causal relation. That is, $\epsilon = |\alpha - \gamma|/max(1 - \alpha, \alpha)$ computes the confidence degree of our decision to classify a source of information.

The second use for the probability of a causal relation as fake is to serve as a binary variable for learning new knowledge. We can refine our classifier with new knowledge as some knowledge is refined as a function of time. The old knowledge may not serve as time passes, so we need to learn knowledge from new sources of information. The problem that arises is to discriminate whether the new knowledge can be trusted. In order to discriminate if the new knowledge is trustworthy we do only have the learned posteriors, the probability of a new causal relation to be fake and the probability of a source of information of being reliable.

In this case, we recommend to learn new causal relations if the source of information is trustworthy, ignoring the single probabilities of the causal relations. The probability of a source of information being trust worthy is a function of every single causal relation contained in it, so if the causal relations lie far away from our posteriors, the source of information will be classified as not trust worthy and we will learn nothing. On the other hand, if we learn only the causal relation that are not fake by only focusing on the probability of every single

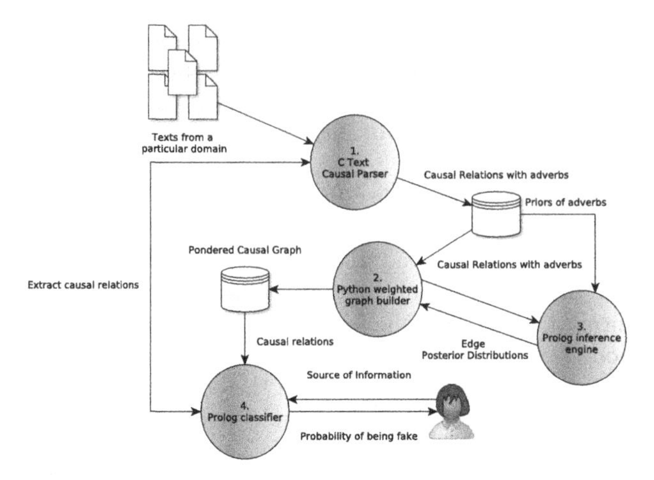

Fig. 1. Architecture of the fake news classifier. First, causal relations are retrieved with a parser from texts belonging to a particular domain. Then, a probabilistic causal graph is generated with all the causal relations retrieved. By using this probabilistic causal graph, we can build a fake news classifier that reads some input information and outputs the probability of that information to be fake.

causal relation we will potentially not learn nothing new about the context of the text that we are analyzing. We can adjust the rate of change in the posterior distributions with the mentioned threshold γ. However, our methodology can also accept to learn only the causal relations which probability $p_f(x)$ is above the threshold β that we can configure for classifying if a causal relation is fake or not. We can also be more restrictive in the learning process by only learning a causal relation or a new source of information if our confidence degree Ω or ϵ respectively lies above other thresholds that we can configure. We have designed a flow diagram that is represented in Fig. 1 that illustrates all the information of our system.

5 Experiments

In this section, we will present several experiments where the proposed methodology tackles with new knowledge to be learned. We have performed a set of different synthetic experiments to illustrate the usefulness of the proposed approach. We also present a real case involving Lung Cancer from a trained weighted causal graph from a trusty source. All the code for the experiments and the fake news classifier is available in https://github.com/EduardoGarrido90/prob_causal_graphs_fake_news.

In all our experiments, we set the following value to the hyperparameters of our model: We assign w value 0.2 in order to give to the entropy factor a 20% of importance and to the KL divergence factor a 80% of importance for the final expression. We consider that the divergence between distributions is more

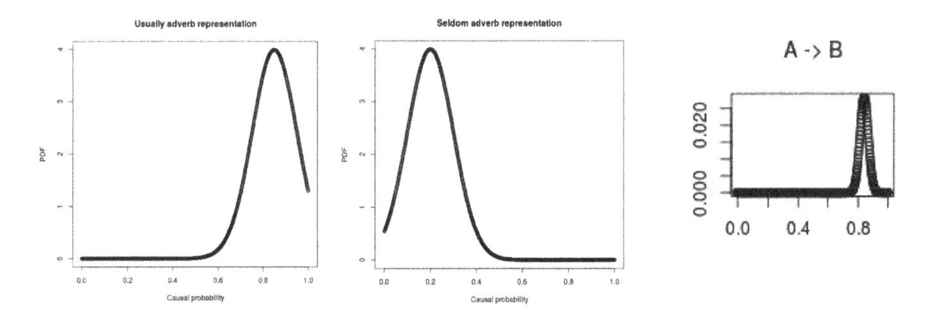

Fig. 2. Prior (left) and posterior (right) distribution of a synthetic causal relation. The new knowledge that we want to validate is represented by the figure of the center. This relation is rejected due to the fact that it is very different from the learned knowledge.

important than the decrease in entropy since we are more interested in detecting fake information that in being sure about whether our learned information is robust and coherent. Depending on the application, this value can be changed to meet the user preferences. We have also set σ to 3, since we have empirically observed that this value classifies fake information accurately.

5.1 Synthetic Experiments

We generate synthetic data that contain causal relations of the form `A->B` and `B->C`. Every generated causal relation comes with a time adverb that has a prior probability distribution. The prior distribution for every different causal relation is the prior distribution associated with the adverb that comes with the first generated causal relation. We generate four scenarios that illustrate the different outputs that our system can consider. For every scenario, we first generate a train set that represent the source of truthful information and a test set that represent the new source of information. In each synthetic experiment, we generate a number of causal relations automatically, choosing the adverbs of the causal relations at random from a subset of all the possible time adverbs that our system considers, and retain only those causal relations of the form `A->B` and `B->C` from all possible combinations of the set $\{A, B, C\}$. If it is not said otherwise, we consider a threshold of 30 to consider an information not being fake.

For the first synthetic experiment, we generate 200 causal relations with the adverbs usually and normally for the train set and retrieve only the valid ones according to the described criterion. For the test set, we generate another 5 causal relations but this time with the adverbs infrequently and seldom, whose probability distributions are very different from the ones of the train set as we can see in the figures of the left and center of the Fig. 2. The distributions of the train set generate a posterior distribution that is very different from the posterior distributions of the train set as we see in the right figure of Fig. 2. We expect that our system consider the test set of knowledge to be fake information. We

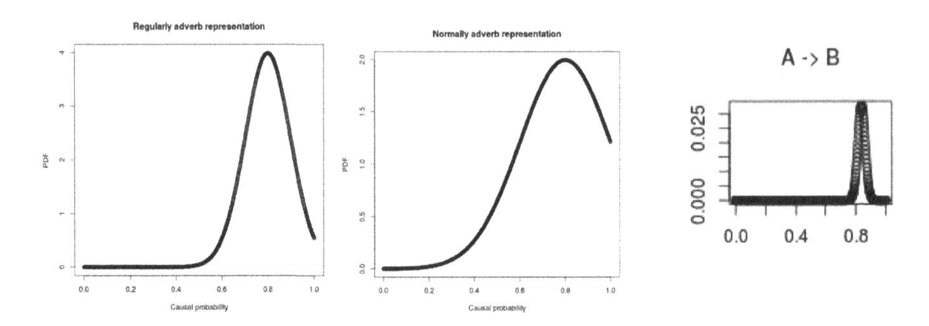

Fig. 3. Prior (left) and posterior (right) distribution of a synthetic causal relation. The new knowledge that we want to validate is represented by the figure of the center. This relation is accepted due to the fact that it is similar to the learned knowledge.

execute the Prolog inference engine, obtaining the probabilities in the range of [78%, 80%] for every causal relation of the test set of being fake causal relations.

We can observe that the system inferred that the new information is fake with a high probability. This satisfies our hypothesis that if we consider probability distributions different from the learned ones, the system would argue that the information would be fake. We would also like to analyze whether the source of information must be learned as a whole or not. As the causal relations are considered to be fake with high probability, the system will have to reject the new source of information. Our proposed system outputs the following log once it analyzes the test set: *The probability of the source being non trust worthy is: 78.557881%. According to the given threshold, we must not learn causal relations from this source. The confidence degree of the decision based in the threshold and the probability of the source is 55.446863%.*

As we can see, the system does not recommend to learn the information given by the test set, which validates again our proposed hypothesis.

The second experiment is just an example of the opposite scenario, an scenario where the new information must be learned. In order to simulate this case, we generated for the train set causal relations with the adverbs usually and normally and for the test causal relations with the adverbs frequently and regularly as we can see in the figures of the left and center of Fig. 3. The distributions of the train set generate a posterior distribution that is similar to the distributions of the test set, as we can see in the figure of the right of Fig. 3. Based on this data, we expect a low probability for the new causal relations of being fake, being able to be incorporated in the weighted causal graph. The system compute the following probabilities for the 5 causal relations considered for the test set: [18.76%, 26.69%, 54.12%, 18.77%, 46.7%].

We see how the majority of the causal relations lie behind the considered 30% threshold. Some relations are suspicious of being fake though. In order to know whether we can learn from this test set, we analyze the source of information as a whole, obtaining the following results: *The probability of the source being non trust worthy is: 33.010959%. According to the given threshold, it is a trust worthy source. The confidence degree of the decision based in the threshold and the probability of the source is 2.969203%.*

We observe how our system recommends to learn the information from the test set but with a low security grade. The security grade can vary according to the given threshold and to the hyperparameters σ and w. For these experiments we have configure the system in an strict way to not consider information suspicious of being fake. Higher values for w, σ and lower values for the threshold relax the system criterion.

5.2 Real Experiment

The proposed methodology has been applied to detect fake news in a medical environment. The Mayo Clinic is a prestigious healthcare institution based in Rochester, Minnesota, very well known for its activities in Cancer Research. They developed a database of Tweets related with lung cancer, and labeled those messages as real of fake, in an effort to mitigate the effect of fake messages on patients.

Cancer patients, especially those recently diagnosed, are very vulnerable to any type of fake messages [13]. The anxiety of the patients (and their families) to know why they have become sick or the possible methods to increase the chances of a quick recovery, make some patients immerse themselves in Social Networks and web pages searching for answers. Fake messages about origins of the disease, naturalistic magic cures, unproved diet methods, etc. may have a very negative impact of patients including an increasing anxiety or lack of trust in standard medical treatments.

We use our system in the Lung Cancer domain trained from the Mayo clinic text in order to classify tweets as fake information or not. Twitter is a source of information where the society can talk freely about any topic exposing opinions that are not contrasted from information sources validated by experts [18]. Hence, classifying information from Twitter based in information from the Mayo clinic is an excellent example where our system can operate.

We have learned the following causes of lung cancer from the Mayo Clinic set of documents that are shown in Fig. 4. Searching what do the users write about lung cancer and its causes, we retrieve the following two tweets that contain causal information: 1. *But this wasn't always the case. Today, smoking causes nearly 9 out of 10 lung cancer deaths, while radon gas, pollution, and other things play a smaller role* and 2. *Cigs = lung cancer & DEATH.* These two tweets contain the following causal relations: 1. *Smoking constantly causes lung cancer*, 2. *Radon gas hardly ever causes lung cancer*, 3. *Secondhand smoke hardly ever causes lung cancer*, 4. *Smoking always causes lung cancer* and 5. *Lung cancer always causes death.*

We are going to execute our algorithm to discriminate whether the new information is fake or not. We can hypothesize that the information is going to be fake as it can be argued that is slightly radical, which is common in social networks. We can observe this radicality by comparing the posterior distribution of lung cancer and death of our system and the distribution associ-

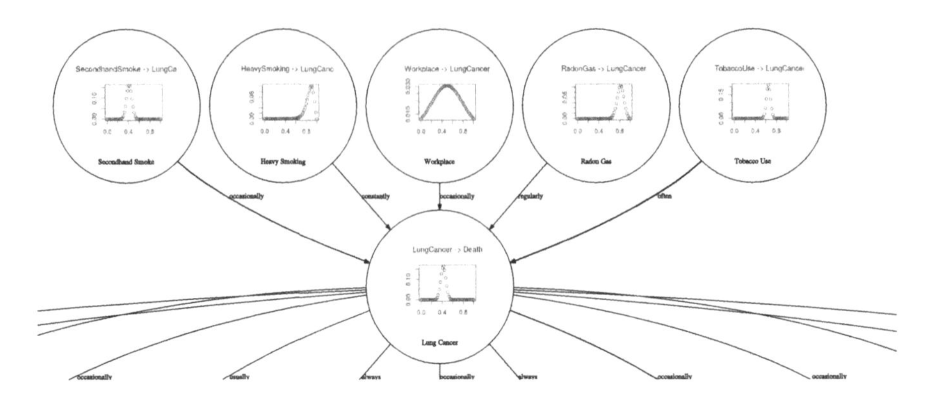

Fig. 4. Posterior distributions of the causes of Lung Cancer of the causal weighted graph in the Lung Cancer domain.

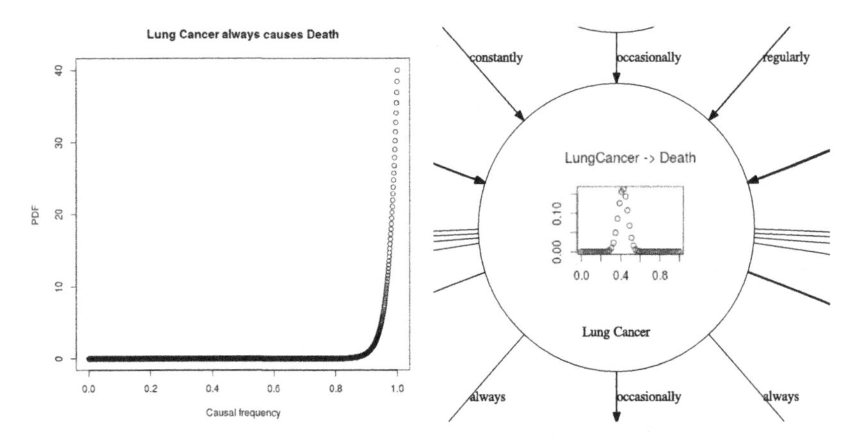

Fig. 5. Comparison of a causal relation to be learned (left) and the posterior distribution of a causal relation of the weighted graph (right).

ated with the analyzed information of Twitter in Fig. 5. We can see in Fig. 5 that the distribution to be learned is very different to the posterior distribution of the weighted graph, so we can not learn it. Fake probabilities are: [49.39%, 65.66%, 55.94%, 71.46%, 68.58%].

We can observe that all the probabilities are high, hence, the system must classify the source of information as fake. If we do classify this source of information, the system generates the following log: *The probability of the source being non trust worthy is: 62.203338%. According to the given threshold, we must not learn causal relations from this source. The confidence degree of the decision based in the threshold and the probability of the source is 35.694769%.*

And refuses to learn the information found in Twitter, as we have hypothesize that it would do. This example has shown how we can use the described system to determine whether information is fake or not.

6 Conclusions and Further Work

We have presented a system that classifies if new knowledge must be learned based in if it represents fake information, which is a problem in our society. Our system bases its decision in a pondered causal graph that has been generated from causal relations retrieved from texts. The system can discriminate whether new sources of information are worth to be added in the pondered causal graph. We obtain as an output a probability that represents if the new information represents a fake new and a security grade of the decision. We consider as further work to optimize the three hyperparameters, the threshold, w and σ; of the proposed model with Multiobjective Constrained Bayesian Optimization [6]. More further work involves to feed in a cognitive architecture of a robot the model, so its information can be shared with other robots to see how they update its networks. The robots would question and answer queries, updating their networks and showing social behaviour that, combined with other processes, can be a correlation of machine consciousness [11]. We also want to compare this approach with a machine learning generic NLP model such as BERT [5]. We hypothesize a better performance of our approach, since it is able to structure causal information coming from different texts.

Acknowledgments. The authors gratefully acknowledge the use of the facilities of Centro de Computación Científica (CCC) at Universidad Autónoma de Madrid. The authors also acknowledge financial support from Spanish Plan Nacional I+D+i, grants TIN2016-76406-P and TEC2016-81900-REDT and from the Spanish Ministry of Science and Innovation - State Research Agency, project PID2019-106827GB-I00.

References

1. Aish, A.-M.: Explanatory models in suicide research: explaining relationships. In: Franck, R. (ed.) The Explanatory Power of Models, pp. 51–66. Springer, Dordrecht (2002). https://doi.org/10.1007/978-1-4020-4676-6_4
2. Allcott, H., Gentzkow, M.: Social media and fake news in the 2016 election. J. Econ. Perspect. **31**(2), 211–236 (2017)
3. Badawy, A., Ferrara, E., Lerman, K.: Analyzing the digital traces of political manipulation: the 2016 russian interference twitter campaign. In: 2018 IEEE/ACM International Conference on Advances in Social Networks Analysis and Mining (ASONAM), pp. 258–265. IEEE (2018)
4. Borondo, J., Morales, A., Losada, J.C., Benito, R.M.: Characterizing and modeling an electoral campaign in the context of twitter: 2011 Spanish presidential election as a case study. Chaos Interdiscip. J. Nonlinear Sci. **22**(2), 023138 (2012)
5. Devlin, J., Chang, M.-W., Lee, K., Toutanova, K.: Bert: pre-training of deep bidirectional transformers for language understanding. arXiv preprint arXiv:1810.04805 (2018)
6. Garrido-Merchán, E.C., Hernández-Lobato, D.: Predictive entropy search for multi-objective Bayesian optimization with constraints. Neurocomputing **361**, 50–68 (2019)
7. Garrido-Merchán, E.C., Puente, C., Sobrino, A., Olivas, J.: Uncertainty weighted causal graphs (2020)

8. Hausman, D.M., Simon, H., et al.: Causal Asymmetries. Cambridge University Press, Cambridge (1998)
9. Kekulluoglu, D., Kokciyan, N., Yolum, P.: Preserving privacy as social responsibility in online social networks. ACM Trans. Internet Technol. (TOIT) **18**(4), 1–22 (2018)
10. Khan, A., Baharudin, B., Lee, L.H., Khan, K.: A review of machine learning algorithms for text-documents classification. J. Adv. Inf. Technol. **1**(1), 4–20 (2010)
11. Merchán, E.C.G., Molina, M.: A machine consciousness architecture based on deep learning and Gaussian processes. arXiv preprint arXiv:2002.00509 (2020)
12. Garrido Merchán, E.C., Puente, C., Olivas, J.A.: Generating a question answering system from text causal relations. In: Pérez García, H., Sánchez González, L., Castejón Limas, M., Quintián Pardo, H., Corchado Rodríguez, E. (eds.) HAIS 2019. LNCS (LNAI), vol. 11734, pp. 14–25. Springer, Cham (2019). https://doi.org/10.1007/978-3-030-29859-3_2
13. Oh, H.J., Lee, H.: When do people verify and share health rumors on social media? The effects of message importance, health anxiety, and health literacy. J. Health Commun. **24**(11), 837–847 (2019)
14. Puente, C., Sobrino, A., Olivas, J. A., Merlo, R.: Extraction, analysis and representation of imperfect conditional and causal sentences by means of a semi-automatic process. In: International Conference on Fuzzy Systems, pp. 1–8. IEEE (2010)
15. Shu, K., Sliva, A., Wang, S., Tang, J., Liu, H.: Fake news detection on social media: a data mining perspective. ACM SIGKDD Explor. Newsl. **19**(1), 22–36 (2017)
16. Sobrino, A., Puente, C., Olivas, J.A.: Extracting answers from causal mechanisms in a medical document. Neurocomputing **135**, 53–60 (2014)
17. Venturini, T., Rogers, R.: "API-based research" or how can digital sociology and journalism studies learn from the Facebook and Cambridge analytica data breach. Digit. J. **7**(4), 532–540 (2019)
18. Weller, K., Bruns, A., Burgess, J., Mahrt, M., Puschmann, C.: Twitter and Society, vol. 89. Peter Lang (2014)

An Hybrid Registration Method for SLAM with the M8 Quanergy LiDAR

Marina Aguilar-Moreno(✉) and Manuel Graña(✉)

Computational Intelligence Group, University of the Basque Country (UPV/EHU), San Sebastian, Spain
marina.aguilar@ehu.eus, manuel.grana@ehu.es

Abstract. Simultaneous localization and mapping (SLAM) is process highly relevant for autonomous systems. Accurate sensing provided by range sensors such as the M8 Quanergy LiDAR improves the speed and accuracy of SLAM, which can become an integral part of the control of innovative autonomous cars. In this paper we propose a hybrid point cloud registration method that profits from the high accuracy of classic iterated closest points (ICP) algorithm, and the robustness of the Normal Distributions Transform (NDT) registration method. We report positive results in an in-house experiment encouraging further research and experimentation.

Keywords: Point cloud registration · LiDAR · SLAM · Hybrid registration

1 Introduction

The simultaneous localization and mapping (SLAM) [1–3] aims to estimate a reconstruction of the environment along with the path traversed by the sensor has become an integral part of the robotic operating system (ROS) [4,5]. One of the most widely used kinds of sensors used for SLAM are laser based depth measurement sensors, or light detection and ranging (LiDAR) sensors, which have been used for scanning and reconstruction of indoor and outdoor environments [6], even in underground mining vehicles [7]. Fusion of LiDAR with GPS allows for large scale navigation [8] of autonomous systems.

Our aim in this paper is to propose a hybridization of two well known point cloud registration methods. Hybridization is akin to the composition of subsystems in circuit like systems. It can be done in series, parallel or interleaving the systems in time. In this paper we propose a serial hybridization where one algorithm serves to provide a robust initial condition to the other. We have carried out SLAM experiments over different datasets using the Iterative Closest Point (ICP) [9], and the Normal Distribution Transform (NDT) [10]. We have found that the ICP method provides less noisy registrations under specific conditions, though it is much more fragile than the NDT. Figure 1 shows a reconstruction of the initial point clouds with ICP and NDT methods, respectively, for the

E. A. de la Cal et al. (Eds.): HAIS 2020, LNAI 12344, pp. 25–35, 2020.
https://doi.org/10.1007/978-3-030-61705-9_3

inhouse data recording that is the demonstrator for the works in this paper. As we can see, ICP reconstruction generates a better surface with higher point density than NDT. Nevertheless, the ICP method is not able to properly register point sets at turning sections of the path traversed by the sensors, as shown in Figure 2, where the registration becomes unwieldy after this turning point. In other words, the ICP methods deals poorly with big rotations.

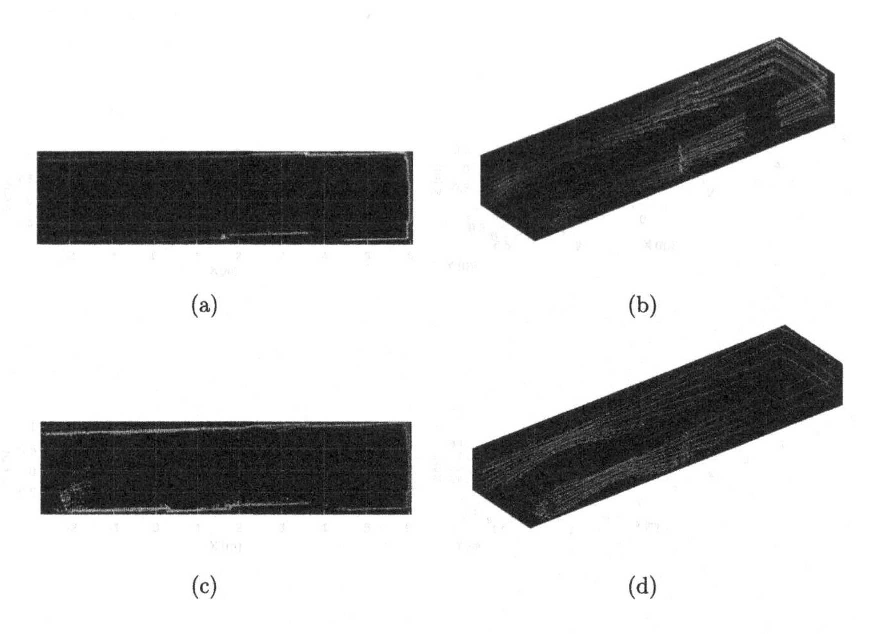

Fig. 1. Results of registration with ICP method, (a) 2D plot of one the range detection at an specific position, (b) reconstructed ray sampling of the 3D surface. Results of registration with NDT method, (c) 2D plot of one the range detection at an specific position, (d) reconstructed ray sampling of the 3D surface.

This paper is structured as follow: A brief presentation of the environment where experiment was carried out and the LiDAR sensor used in it, Quanergy M8. Next, we provide a formal description of the 3D registration methods used in the paper: the Iterative Closest Point (ICP) and the Normal Distribution Transform (NDT). Then, the proposed hybrid NDT algorithm with ICP initialization is described. Finally, experimental results are presented for standard NDT registration and for the hybrid system described in this article, comparing root mean square error of the Euclidean distance, the path obtained and resulting reconstructed surfaces.

2 Materials

New affordable LiDAR sensors, such as the M8 from Quanergy that we are testing in this paper, allow for further popularization of LiDAR based SLAM

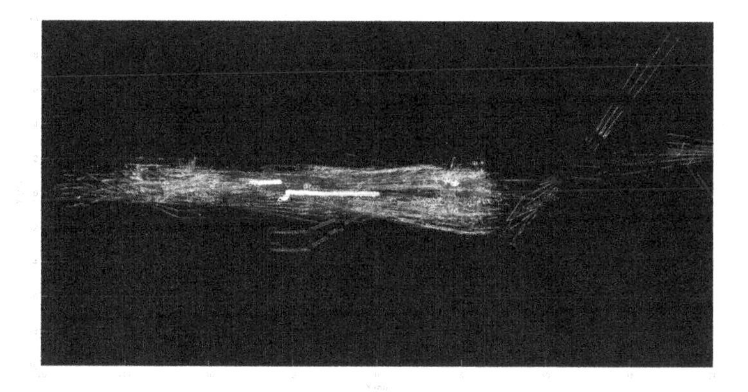

Fig. 2. Estimated trajectory (white points) and registered cloud of points using ICP.

applications. Due to its specific innovative characteristics, the M8 sensor still needs extensive testing by the community in order to assume its integration in the newly developed systems [11]. The work reported in this paper is intended partly to provide such empirical confirmation of the M8 sensor quality continuing experimentation over this sensor data reported elsewhere [12]. Both the time sequence of M8 captured point clouds and the Matlab code used to carry out the computational experiments has been published as open data and open source code[1] in the Zenodo repository for reproducibility.

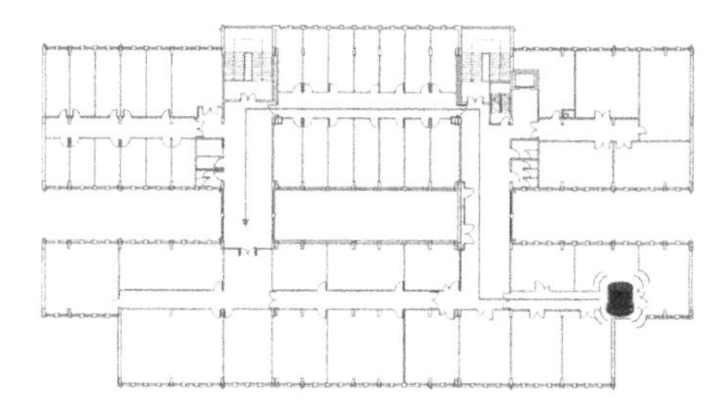

Fig. 3. Nominal path followed during the LiDAR recording.

Location and Experiment Setting. The experiment was carried out in the third floor of the Computer Science School of the UPV/EHU in San Sebastian. Figure 3 shows the nominal path followed by the M8 LiDAR on a manually driven mobile platform. The actual path shows small perturbations around the nominal path. We do not have a precise actual path measurement allowing to quantify the error in the trajectory.

[1] https://doi.org/10.5281/zenodo.3636204.

LiDAR M8 Quanergy. The Quanergy M8 LiDAR sensor is a multi-laser system with 8 2D line scanners located on a spinning head. This system is based on Time-of-Flight (TOF) technology whose spin rate is 5 Hz and 20 Hz and its maximum range is 100 m. The Table 1 shows the M8 LiDAR main parameters. Besides, M8 LiDAR comes with 2 desktop applications to manage and visualize point clouds, a SDK to record and show data in real time, and a SDK in framework ROS.

Table 1. Quanergy M8 sensor specifications

Parameter	M8 sensor specifications
Detection layers	8
Returns	3
Minimum range	0.5 m (80% reflectivity)
Maximum range	>100 m (80% reflectivity)
Range accuracy (1σ at 50 m)	< 3 cm
Spin rate	5 Hz–20 Hz
Intensity	8-bits
Field of view	Horizontal 360° - Vertical 20° (+3°/−17°)
Data outputs	Angle, Distance, Intensity, Synchronized Time Stamps

3 Point Cloud Registration Methods

Point cloud registration methods are composed of two steps: (a) finding the correspondence between points in one cloud (the moving) to the points in the other cloud (the reference), and (b) the estimation of the motion parameters that achieve optimal match of the moving points to the reference points after correcting for the motion. If the motion is modeled by a rigid body or an affine transformation, then a matrix transformation common to all points is estimated. If the motion is some non linear deformation, then we have to estimate a flow field. In this paper we are restricted to rigid body transformations, which are compositions of a translation and a rotation. The transformation estimation process takes the form of a minimization problem where the energy function is related to the quality of the correspondence achieved. Next we recall the basics of the two point cloud registration methods. Figure 4 shows the structure of the algorithms as flow diagram of their basic iterations.

3.1 Iterated Closest Point

The most popular and earliest point cloud registration method is the Iterative Closest Point (ICP) proposed by Besl in 1992 [9]. This technique has been exploited in many domains, giving rise to a host of variations whose relative merits are not so easy to assess [13]. Given a point cloud $P = \{\mathbf{p}_i\}_{i=1}^{Np}$ and a shape described by another point cloud $X = \{\mathbf{x}_i\}_{i=1}^{Nx}$ (The original paper

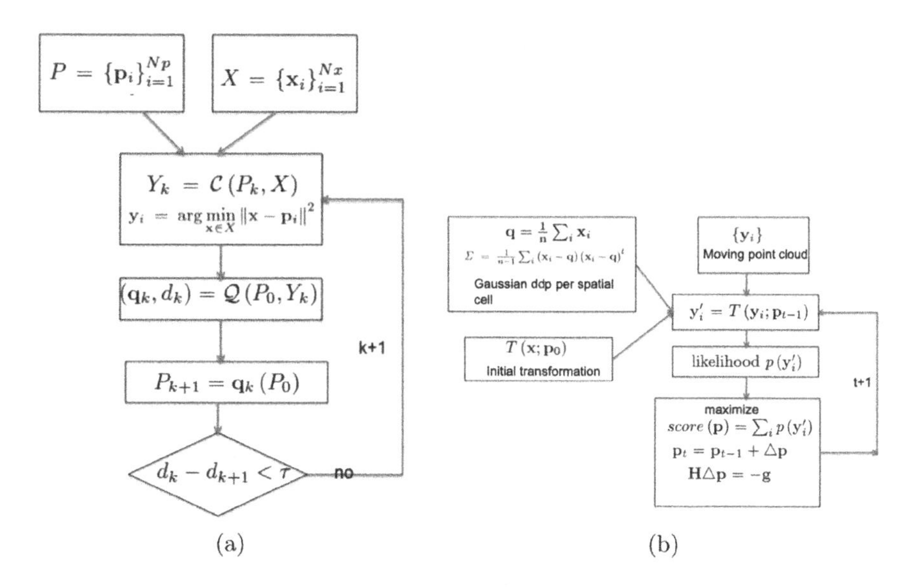

Fig. 4. ICP (a) and NDT (b) processes.

includes the possibility to specify other primitives such as lines or triangles with well defined distances to a point, but we will not consider them in this paper.) the least squares registration of P is given by $(\mathbf{q}, d) = \mathcal{Q}(P, Y)$, where $Y = \{\mathbf{y}_i\}_{i=1}^{Np}$ is the set of nearest points from X to the points in P, i.e. $\mathbf{p}_i \in P; \mathbf{y}_i = \arg\min_{\mathbf{x}\in X} \|\mathbf{x} - \mathbf{p}_i\|^2$, denoted $Y = \mathcal{C}(P, X)$, and operator $\mathcal{Q}$ is the least squares estimation of the rotation and translation mapping P to Y using quaternion notation, thus $\mathbf{q} = [\mathbf{q}_R \mid \mathbf{q}_T]^t$ is the optimal transformation specified by a rotation quaternion $\mathbf{q}_R$ and a translation $\mathbf{q}_T$, and d is the registration error. The energy function minimized to obtain the optimal registration is $f(\mathbf{q}) = \frac{1}{N_p}\sum_{i=1}^{Np} \|\mathbf{y}_i - \mathbf{R}(\mathbf{q}_R)\mathbf{p}_i - \mathbf{q}_T\|^2$, where $\mathbf{R}(\mathbf{q}_R)$ is the rotation matrix constructed from quaternion $\mathbf{q}_R$. The iteration is initialized by setting $P_0 = P$, $\mathbf{q}_0 = [1, 0, 0, 0, 0, 0, 0]^t$, and $k = 0$. The algorithm iteration is as follows: (1) compute the closest points $Y_k = \mathcal{C}(P_k, X)$, (2) compute the registration $(\mathbf{q}_k, d_k) = \mathcal{Q}(P_0, Y_k)$, (3) apply the registration $P_{k+1} = \mathbf{q}_k(P_0)$, and (4) terminate the iteration if the results are within a tolerance: $d_k - d_{k+1} < \tau$.

3.2 Normal Distribution Transform

The key difference of the NDT [10] method is the data representation. The space around the sensor is discretized into regular overlapped cells. The content of each cell having more than 3 points is modeled by a Gaussian probability distribution of mean $\mathbf{q} = \frac{1}{\mathrm{n}}\sum_i \mathbf{x}_i$ and covariance matrix $\Sigma = \frac{1}{n-1}\sum_i (\mathbf{x}_i - \mathbf{q})(\mathbf{x}_i - \mathbf{q})^t$, so that the probability of a LiDAR sample falling in the cell is of the form: $p(\mathbf{x}) \sim \exp\left(-\frac{1}{2}\right)(\mathbf{x} - \mathbf{q})\Sigma^{-1}(\mathbf{x} - \mathbf{q})$. Given an initial rigid body transformation $T(\mathbf{x}; \mathbf{p}_0)$, where $\mathbf{p}$ is the vector of translation and rotation parameters, a

Algorithm 1. The hybrid ICP-NDT registration algorithm.

Input: sequence of point clouds $\{N(t)\}_{t=0}^{T}$ captured by the LiDAR
Output: overall point cloud $M(T)$, sequence of registered transformations $\{\mathcal{T}_t\}_{t=1}^{T}$
Method = "ICP"
For $t = 0, \ldots, T$

1. $N^{(1)}(t) \leftarrow$remove ground plane from $N(t)$
2. $N^{(2)}(t) \leftarrow$ remove ego-vehicle from $N^{(1)}(t)$
3. $N^{(3)}(t) \leftarrow$ downsample $N^{(2)}(t)$
4. If $t = 0$ then $M(0) = N^{(3)}(t)$; GOTO step 1
5. $(\mathcal{T}_t, e_t) \leftarrow$ register $\mathcal{T}_{t-1}\left(N^{(3)}(t)\right)$ to $M(t-1)$ using *Method*
6. If $e_t > \theta_e$ then *Method* = "NDT"
7. $N^{(4)}(t) \leftarrow \mathcal{T}_t\left(N^{(2)}(t)\right)$
8. $M(t) \leftarrow merge\left(M(t-1), N^{(4)}(t)\right)$

reference point cloud $\{\mathbf{x}_i\}$ modeled by the mixture of the cells Gaussian distributions, and the moving point cloud $\{\mathbf{y}_i\}$, the iterative registration process is as follows: the new laser sample points $\mathbf{y}_i$ are transformed into the reference frame of the first cloud $\mathbf{y}'_i = T(\mathbf{y}_i; \mathbf{p}_{t-1})$, where we find the cell where it falls and use its parameters $(\mathbf{q}, \Sigma)$ to estimate its likelihood $p(\mathbf{y}'_i)$. The score of the transformation is given by $score(\mathbf{p}) = \sum_i p(\mathbf{y}'_i)$. The maximization of the score is carried out by gradient ascent using Newton's method, i.e. $\mathbf{p}_t = \mathbf{p}_{t-1} + \triangle\mathbf{p}$. The parameter update is computed solving the equation $\mathbf{H}\triangle\mathbf{p} = -\mathbf{g}$, where $\mathbf{H}$ and $\mathbf{g}$ are the Hessian and the gradient of the $-score(\mathbf{p}_{t-1})$ function, respectively. Closed forms of $\mathbf{H}$ and $\mathbf{g}$ are derived in [10] for the 2D case. An extension to 3D is described in [14].

4 Hybrid Point Cloud Registration Algorithm

In this section, hybrid registration algorithm which uses ICP and NDT methods is presented. As ICP reconstructed surface generates a better surface, i.e. with greater point density than NDT, but ICP method is not able to properly register point sets at turning sections. Our hybrid algorithm that initially uses ICP method changing to the NDT method when the registration error becomes higher than a threshold.

Algorithm 1 presents an algorithmic description of the proposed hybrid registration method. The input to the algorithm is the sequence of point clouds recorded by the LiDAR $N(t)$; $t = \{1, \ldots, T\}$. The point sets are obtained while the LiDAR sensor is being displaced manually in the environment according to the approximate path in Figure 3. The final result of the process is a global point cloud $M(T)$ that contains all the recorded 3D points registered relative to the first acquired point cloud $N(0)$, and the estimation of the LiDAR recording positions relative to the initial position given by the composition of the point cloud registration transformations estimated up to this time instant $\{\mathcal{T}_t\}_{t=1}^{T}$. The process of each point cloud is as follows: For each point cloud $N(t)$ acquired at time t, firstly we remove the ground plane applying a segmentation denoted $N^{(1)}(t)$. Secondly we remove the ego-vehicle points, denoted $N^{(2)}(t)$. Thirdly, we down-sample the point cloud to decrease the computation time and improve accuracy registration, denoted $N^{(3)}(t)$. For the initial point cloud $N^{(3)}(0)$ becomes the global merged reference cloud $M(0)$. For subsequent time instants $t > 0$, the fourth step is to estimate the transformation $\mathcal{T}_t$ of the acquired data $N^{(3)}(t)$ optimally registered to the previous global point cloud $M(t-1)$. For this estimation, we may use ICP or NDT methods. We then apply this transformation to the acquired point cloud previous to downsampling $N^{(4)}(t) = \mathcal{T}_t\left(N^{(2)}(t)\right)$, which is used to obtain the new global registered point cloud by merging $M(t) \leftarrow merge\left(M(t-1), N^{(4)}(t)\right)$. Our hybrid strategy consists in using the ICP method in the initial steps of the algorithm, up a time instant when the registration error meets a given threshold, after this time point the system shifts to use the NDT method to continue registration of all remaining point clouds. The rationale is that the ICP acts as a good initial estimation for the ensuing NDT steps, as will be demonstrated in the results section below.

5 Results

Figure 5 shows the evolution of the registration error for ICP, NDT and the hybrid algorithm presented in the previous section, setting $\theta_e = 0.25$. The plot scale is logarithmic in order to be able to represent the three error course in the same plot. The ICP algorithm gives the highest error. At the beginning the error is low, but it is increasing when we add more point clouds, until it explodes in iteration $t = 1308$. Both NDT and the proposed hybrid method registration errors are bounded over time. The error of the hybrid method error is the same as the error of the ICP until the point where the algorithm shifts from ICP to NDT at the 138-th iteration. Afterwards the hybrid method has a slightly lower error that the NDT due to the quality of the initialization provided by the ICP. Table 2 gives numerical registration errors. However, the effect of using the ICP initialization is much more evident when assessing the overall results. Figure 6 shows the trajectory estimation (up) and the projection of the reconstructed surfaces on the floor plan (bottom) when using only NDT registration method. Though the error of the method is bounded, it can be appreciated that after the second turning point a noticeable drift appears, causing misalignment of the reconstructed surfaces with the actual floor plan walls. (Direction of advance is from right to left). On the other hand, the hybrid method trajectory and reconstruction results are provided in Figure 7 showing a much better fit to the floor plan walls. We conclude that the ICP provides a much more robust initialization for NDT.

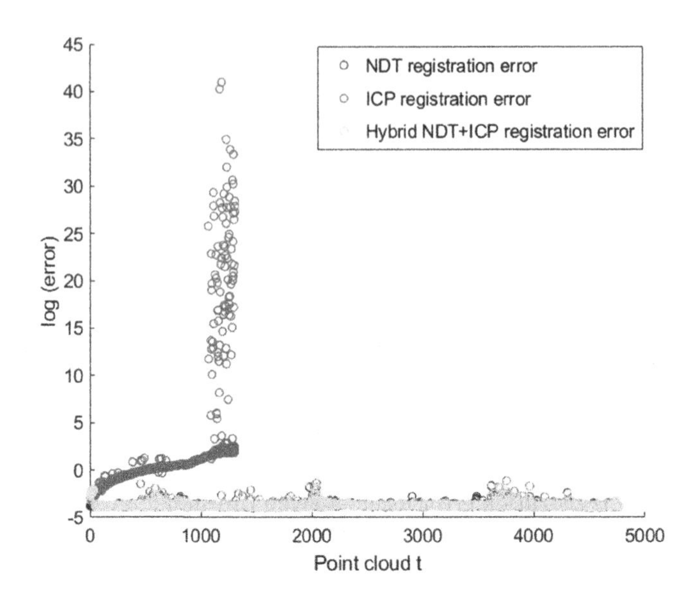

Fig. 5. Evolution of the registration error (log plot) for NDT (blue dots), ICP (red dots), and hybrid ICP-NDT method (green dots). (Color figure online)

Table 2. Registration error for ICP method, NDT method and hybrid ICP-NDT method

	ICP method (for 1308 iterations)	NDT method	Hybrid ICP-NDT method
Maximum error	6.3528×10^{17}	0.3245	0.3208
Median error	7.2580×10^{14}	0.0251	0.0256
Total error	9.4935×10^{17}	119.4010	122.0764

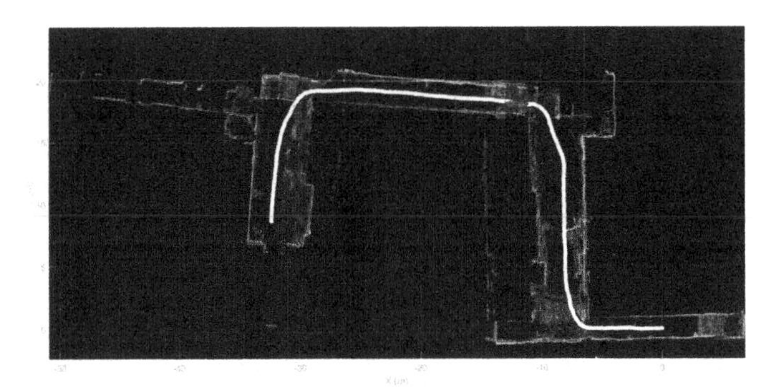

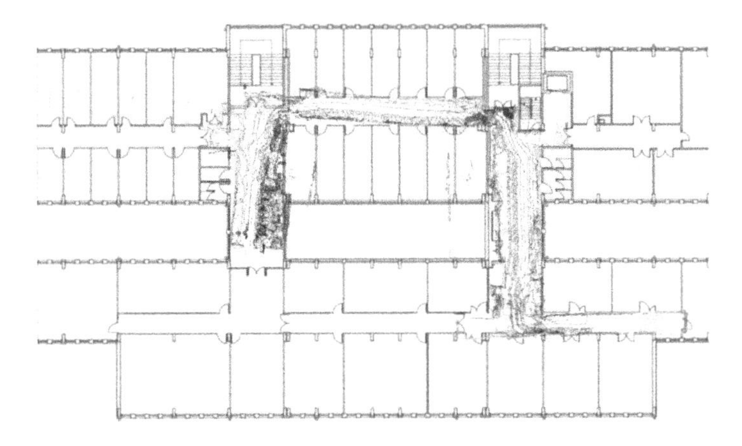

Fig. 6. Estimated trajectory (white points) and registered cloud of points using NDT (Above). Projection of the NDT registered point cloud on the plan of stage 3 of the building.

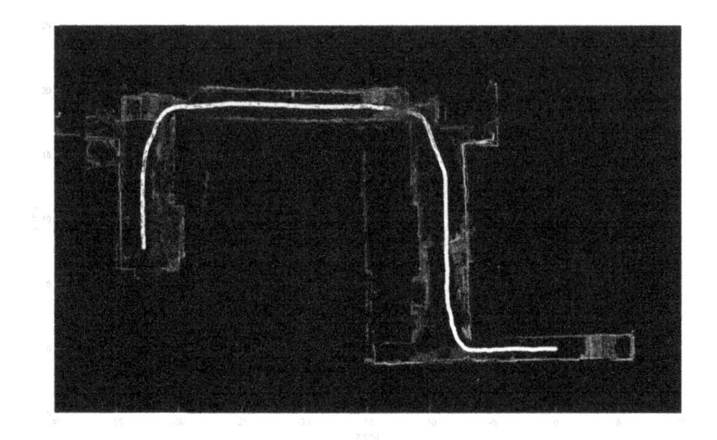

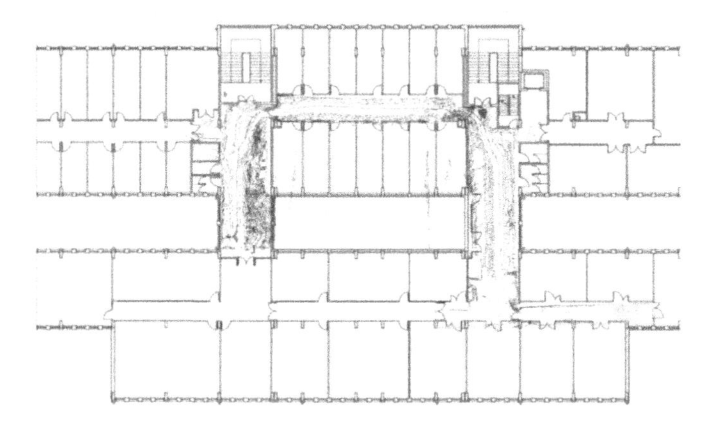

Fig. 7. Estimated trajectory (white points) and registered cloud of points using hybrid method proposed (Above). Projection of the hybrid registered point cloud on the plan of stage 3 of the building.

6 Conclusion

In this paper we report a hybridization between two registration methods for 3D point clouds, namely the Iterative Closest Point (ICP) and the Normal Distributions Transform (NDT). The experimental point clouds have been recorded with the M8 Quanergy LiDAR sensor traversing an indoor path the third floor of the Computer Science School of the UPV/EHU in San Sebastian. The general SLAM algorithm followed in this paper includes preprocessing (detect and remove ego-vehicle and floor, and down-sample), registration, transformation and merger of point cloud. We report the registration error, the estimation of the path traversed by the sensor, and the reconstructed point cloud. The hybrid method produces a slightly lower error than the NDT. On a qualitative assessment the hybrid method produces better surface reconstruction and path estimation. Future works will consider the analysis and exploitation of out-door recording methods.

Acknowledgments. This work has been partially supported by FEDER funds through MINECO project TIN2017-85827-P, and grant IT1284-19 as university research group of excellence from the Basque Government.

References

1. Durrant-Whyte, H., Bailey, T.: Simultaneous localization and mapping: part I. IEEE Robot. Autom. Mag. **13**, 99–110 (2006)
2. Bailey, T., Durrant-Whyte, H.: Simultaneous localization and mapping (SLAM): part II. IEEE Robot. Autom. Mag. **13**, 108–117 (2006)
3. Cadena, C., et al.: Past, present, and future of simultaneous localization and mapping: toward the robust-perception age. IEEE Trans. Rob. **32**, 1309–1332 (2016)
4. Xuexi, Z., Guokun, L., Genping, F., Dongliang, X., Shiliu, L.: SLAM algorithm analysis of mobile robot based on Lidar. In: 2019 Chinese Control Conference (CCC), pp. 4739–4745, July 2019
5. Yagfarov, R., Ivanou, M., Afanasyev, I.: Map comparison of Lidar-based 2D SLAM algorithms using precise ground truth. In: 2018 15th International Conference on Control, Automation, Robotics and Vision (ICARCV), pp. 1979–1983 (2018)
6. Caminal, I., Casas, J.R., Royo, S.: SLAM-based 3D outdoor reconstructions from Lidar data. In: 2018 International Conference on 3D Immersion (IC3D), pp. 1–8, December 2018
7. Wu, D., Meng, Y., Zhan, K., Ma, F.: A Lidar SLAM based on point-line features for underground mining vehicle. In: 2018 Chinese Automation Congress (CAC), pp. 2879–2883, November 2018
8. Deng, Y., Shan, Y., Gong, Z., Chen, L.: Large-scale navigation method for autonomous mobile robot based on fusion of GPS and Lidar SLAM. In: 2018 Chinese Automation Congress (CAC), pp. 3145–3148, November 2018
9. Besl, P.J., McKay, N.D.: A method for registration of 3-D shapes. IEEE Trans. Pattern Anal. Mach. Intell. **14**, 239–256 (1992)
10. Biber, P., Straßer, W.: The normal distributions transform: a new approach to laser scan matching, vol. 3, pp. 2743–2748, December 2003
11. Mitteta, M.A., Nouira, H., Roynard, X., Goulette, F., Deschaud, J.E.: Experimental assessment of the Quanergy M8 LIDAR Sensor. ISPRS Int. Arch. Photogram. Remote Sens. Spatial Inf. Sci. **41B5**, 527–531 (2016)
12. Aguilar-Moreno, M., Graña, M.: A comparison of registration methods for SLAM with the M8 Quanergy LiDAR. In: Herrero, Á., Cambra, C., Urda, D., Sedano, J., Quintián, H., Corchado, E. (eds.) SOCO 2020. AISC, vol. 1268, pp. 824–834. Springer, Cham (2021). https://doi.org/10.1007/978-3-030-57802-2_79
13. Pomerleau, F., Colas, F., Siegwart, R., Magnenat, S.: Comparing ICP variants on real-world data sets. Auton. Robot. **34**, 133–148 (2013). https://doi.org/10.1007/s10514-013-9327-2
14. Magnusson, M., Lilienthal, A., Duckett, T.: Scan registration for autonomous mining vehicles using 3D-NDT. J. Field Robot. **24**, 803–827 (2007)

An Adaptive Neighborhood Retrieval Visualizer

Dominik Olszewski(✉)

Faculty of Electrical Engineering, Warsaw University of Technology, Warsaw, Poland
dominik.olszewski@ee.pw.edu.pl

Abstract. We propose a novel adaptive version of the Neighborhood Retrieval Visualizer (NeRV). The data samples' neighborhood widths are determined on the basis of the data scattering in the high-dimensional input space. The scattering of input data is measured using the inner-cluster variance quantity, obtained as a result of the preliminary data clustering in the input space. The combination of the pre-clustering and the subsequent NeRV projection can be recognized as a hybrid approach. The experimental study carried out on two different real datasets verified and confirmed the effectiveness of the introduced approach and the correctness of the theoretical claim of the paper.

Keywords: Neighborhood retrieval visualizer · Adaptive neighborhood retrieval visualizer · Information retrieval · Clustering · Visualization

1 Introduction

Data visualization obtained using dimensionality reduction has gained wide interest, and it is an extensively studied branch of machine learning and data mining. Visualization of data via dimensionality reduction provides a linear or non-linear mapping between an input high-dimensional data space and an output 2- or 3-dimensional data space.

Regardless of the visualization method utilized and regardless of the subsequent analysis carried out, a typical problem, which any visualization approach faces, is the difficulty of defining the evaluation criterion measuring the quality of the visualization. Generally, there are two main measures of visualization quality: preservation of all pairwise distances or the order of all pairwise distances and classification of the data in the low-dimensional space and using the classification accuracy as the basis of the visualization quality assessment. However, each of the quantities can be recognized as imperfect, and the issue of formulating the visualization evaluation criterion still remains a challenging problem.

A milestone in the field of proposing a formally mathematical framework for the data visualization task has been achieved in the research presented in paper [15], where a rigorously defined measure of visualization quality has been introduced. The probabilistic representation of the measure made it an eligible subject to an optimization procedure leading to the non-linear mapping from the

E. A. de la Cal et al. (Eds.): HAIS 2020, LNAI 12344, pp. 36–48, 2020.
https://doi.org/10.1007/978-3-030-61705-9_4

input high-dimensional data space to the output 2-dimensional data plane. The quality measure derives from presenting and depicting the visualization problem as the information retrieval issue. The authors of [15] introduced the name of their proposed method as Neighborhood Retrieval Visualizer (NeRV).

The solution from [15] was the point of departure and inspiration for the research and methodological development of our work.

1.1 Our Proposal

We propose an adaptive rule for setting the input neighborhood of samples in the input high-dimensional space. This neighborhood plays a crucial role in the main concept of the entire visualization. However, in the work [15], there is no precise and strict method for the neighborhood size computation given. We propose to establish a dependency between the neighborhood width and the cluster scattering in the input high-dimensional space. Therefore, a preliminary data clustering is carried out in the input space in order to provide the information about the data similarities and scattering. This information, as we claim, can be effectively utilized as a basis of the mathematical formulation of our visualization. Setting the neighborhood of the input samples on the basis of the input data scattering leads to maintaining the input data dependencies, and consequently, preserving the input data nature and characteristics. The combination of the pre-clustering and the subsequent NeRV projection can be recognized as a hybrid approach. The details of the introduced solution and the original neighborhood retrieval visualization method are presented and explained in Sect. 3 and in Sect. 4.

2 Related Work

Data visualization using dimensionality reduction has been a subject of researchers' interest and study since the first methods and algorithms in this field of data analysis have been introduced.

Among all of them, the ones designed purely and especially for the purpose of data visualization as a specific case of the general dimensionality reduction problem, are of particular interest and value in our research, because their nature and main features and characteristics have been oriented on data visualization issue particularly, and it can be highly expected to obtain good performance and satisfactory outcome using these methods and algorithms.

An example of such a method, which gained much interest and attention from researchers over the years is the Self-Organizing Map (SOM) introduced by T. Kohonen in [4]. The SOM visualization technique has been extensively studied, and numerous improvements and extensions have been developed, including the Growing Hierarchical SOM (GHSOM) [13], the asymmetric SOM [9,11], and the adaptive SOM [3], to name a few.

In our work, we focus on the specific branch of data visualization concerning the neighborhood preserving projection [5,7,14], among which, one can find the Stochastic Neighbor Embedding (SNE). This visualization technique has become a subject of improvement and extension in a research conducted by the authors of [15]. The paper [15], in turn, has become a subject of analysis and consideration in our research.

3 Traditional NerV Method

The main idea behind the NeRV method is expressing the visualization problem as the information retrieval task. Specifically speaking, the notions of precision and recall are utilized and treated as the basis for the formulation of the entire technique. Precision and recall are the traditional information retrieval measures. In the NeRV method, a cost function is formulated as one of the most important mathematical tools used in the approach. The cost function can be related to precision and recall.

However, at first, a basic form of the cost function for a given ith data sample is expressed in the following way:

$$E_i = N_{\mathrm{FP},i} C_{\mathrm{FP}} + N_{\mathrm{FN},i} C_{\mathrm{FN}}, \quad (1)$$

where i is the index of a given data sample, $N_{\mathrm{FP},i}$ is the number of all data samples recognized as false positive, C_{FP} is an assumed cost of an error of type false positive, $N_{\mathrm{FN},i}$ is the number of all data samples recognized as false negative, and C_{FN} is an assumed cost of an error of type false negative.

Now, one can express the cost function including the quantities of precision and recall:

$$E_{k_i,r_i} = C_{\mathrm{FP}} (1 - \pi_i) + \frac{r_i}{k_i} C_{FN} (1 - \rho_i), \quad (2)$$

where k_i is the number of data samples in the neighborhood Q_i of a data sample i, r_i is the number of data samples in the neighborhood P_i of a data sample i, π_i is a value of the precision for a given data sample i, ρ_i is the value of the recall for a given data sample i, and the rest of the notation is explained in Eq. (1).

The quantities of precision and recall are described by the following formulas:

$$\pi_i = 1 - \frac{N_{\mathrm{FP},i}}{k_i}, \quad (3)$$

$$\rho_i = 1 - \frac{N_{\mathrm{FN},i}}{r_i}, \quad (4)$$

where all of the notation is explained in Eq. (1) and in Eq. (2).

The next step in the development of the NeRV method is creating a probabilistic background for the mathematical description of the method as a generalization of all the utilized notions and quantities. In this way, one constitutes and provides a sophisticated and useful mathematical scaffolding for the considered technique, which leads to new form of the cost function presented in Eq. (2).

The neighborhoods of a given ith data sample in the input space and its projected point in the visualization are now expressed as the probability distributions p_i and q_i, respectively. The method aims to minimize the dissimilarity between these probability distributions in order to maximize the visualization quality. In order to determine the dissimilarity between two probability distributions, one needs to employ certain probabilistic measure to achieve this goal. The choice from [15] was the Kullback-Leibler divergence [6] as a standard, very well-known, and even historical quantity serving as a probabilistic measure of dissimilarity.

Now, in this probabilistic context, after introduction of the notion of the Kullback-Leibler divergence [6], precision and recall may be expressed using directly the Kullback-Leibler divergence in the following way:

$$D\left(q_i,\, p_i\right) \;=\; \sum_{j \neq i} q_{j|i} \log \frac{q_{j|i}}{p_{j|i}}\,, \tag{5}$$

where $D\left(\cdot,\, \cdot\right)$ is the Kullback-Leibler divergence, $q_{j|i}$ is the probability of the choice of jth data sample in the neighborhood of ith data sample in the output space, and $p_{j|i}$ is the probability of the choice of jth data sample in the neighborhood of ith data sample in the input space.

$$D\left(p_i,\, q_i\right) \;=\; \sum_{j \neq i} p_{j|i} \log \frac{p_{j|i}}{q_{j|i}}\,, \tag{6}$$

where all the notation is explained in Eq. (5).

Equation (5) presents the probabilistic variant of the precision, called in [15] the smoothed precision, whereas Eq. (6) presents the probabilistic variant of the recall, called in [15] the smoothed recall.

Finally, one can approach to formulating a new version of the cost function (2) based on the smoothed precision and smoothed recall, along with the probability distributions p_i and q_i. The new probabilistic form of the cost function is given in the following way:

$$E_{\mathrm{NeRV}} \;\approx\; \lambda \sum_{i} \sum_{j \neq i} p_{j|i} \log \frac{p_{j|i}}{q_{j|i}} \;+\; (1 \;-\; \lambda) \sum_{i} \sum_{j \neq i} q_{j|i} \log \frac{q_{j|i}}{p_{j|i}}\,, \tag{7}$$

where λ is an auxiliary parameter allowing differentiate between the significance and expansiveness of errors in precision and recall (in other words, it controls, which of the errors, we consider as more important), and the rest of the notation is explained in Eq. (5).

The main concept of the entire NeRV technique, and the way that the cost function in either form operates, is illustrated graphically in Fig. 1. In the figure, the errors of both possible types, i.e., false positive and false negative, are marked clearly.

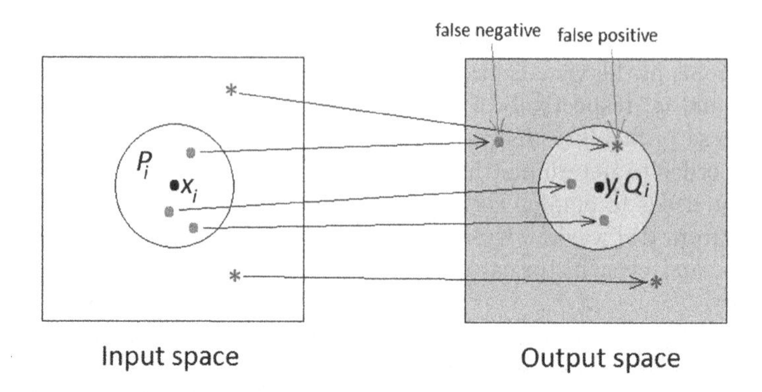

Fig. 1. Illustration of the basic NeRV visualization mapping, including false positive and false negative kinds of errors in visualization

4 A Novel Adaptive NeRV Method

In this paper, we introduce an adaptive technique for determining the data samples' neighborhood widths, in both – input and output spaces. These neighborhood widths are playing a crucial role in the information retrieval task, utilized in the NeRV method as the principal way to establish a visualization. The neighborhood widths in our improvement of the NeRV method are determined independently for each data sample in the input and output spaces. In this way, each data sample during the information-retrieval-based data visualization is treated separately, which increases the probability of higher accuracy in case of a selected data sample projection, and consequently, the accuracy of the entire data visualization.

When reading carefully the paper [15] and analyzing meticulously the traditional form of the NeRV method described in [15], a reader cannot find any formal principled way to determine the data samples' neighborhood widths and wonders about any guidelines to support and suggest that highly important choice for the NeRV method. The only information provided in [15] regarding the data samples' neighborhood size is that one can choose an arbitrary radius determining the data samples' neighborhood width or one can as well choose an arbitrary number of samples in the vicinity of a given data sample, in this way, constituting the sample's neighborhood size. However naturally, both of these approaches operate in a purely arbitrary manner, which does not increase the probability of the high visualization performance. This drawback of the traditional form of the NeRV method has been addressed in our research by introducing an adaptive way to calculate the neighborhood width independently for each data sample in the analyzed dataset.

According to the proposal of our paper, the first phase in the preliminary data analysis and processing is carrying out an initial data clustering. As a result of data clustering, one obtains the information about data scattering. The resulting knowledge concerns the data density in the vicinities of subsequent data samples. This information can be efficiently utilized in order to determine the data samples' neighborhood widths. Strictly speaking, after the preliminary data clustering, we compute the inner-cluster variances and use them for each data sample belonging to the cluster as its neighborhood width during visualization. In this way, the data scattering and the natural data clusters formed during a given clustering process, serve as the source of information about the data similarities and associations, which is afterward incorporated in the data visualization as the basis for the data samples' neighborhood widths determination. Consequently, for clusters of highly dense samples, i.e., with the corresponding very low inner-cluster variance, a small and narrow neighborhood will be chosen during the data visualization, and that is because a small neighborhood is sufficient to produce a high visualization quality in this case. On the other hand, in case of vast clusters with a few number of data samples inside, i.e., in case of clusters with very high value of inner-cluster variance, it is recommended to assure large and vast neighborhood during the data visualization, and it is exactly done, when using our method, i.e., when the inner-cluster variance is utilized as the data samples' neighborhood widths during the data visualization. This form of the novel NerV methods' behavior can be recognized as an adaptive attempt to adjust to data nature and characteristics, and consequently, as an adaptive improvement of the classical NeRV technique.

The entire proposal of the extension to the traditional NeRV method is presented completely and formally in Procedure 1.

Procedure 1. *The adaptive NeRV method proposed in this paper proceeds as follows:*

Step 1. Perform a clustering of the analyzed dataset in the input high-dimensional space.

Step 2. Compute the inner-cluster variance for each of the clusters according to the following formula:

$$\sigma_n = \frac{1}{N_n} \sum_{i=1}^{N_n} d\left(c_n, x_i\right), \tag{8}$$

where σ_n is the inner-cluster variance of the nth cluster, $n = 1, \ldots, K$, K is the number of clusters, N_n is the number of data samples in the nth cluster, $d\left(\cdot, \cdot\right)$ is a given suitable dissimilarity measure in the input high-dimensional space, c_n is the centroid of the nth cluster, x_i are the data samples in the input high-dimensional space.

Step 3. Compute the probabilities $p_{j|i}$ and $q_{j|i}$ according to the following formulas:

$$p_{j|i} = \frac{\exp\left(-\frac{d(x_i, x_j)^2}{\sigma_i^2}\right)}{\sum_{k \neq i} \exp\left(-\frac{d(x_i, x_k)^2}{\sigma_i^2}\right)}, \tag{9}$$

where all of the notation has been explained previously in this paper.

$$q_{j|i} = \frac{\exp\left(-\frac{d_{\mathrm{E}}(y_i, y_j)^2}{\sigma_i^2}\right)}{\sum_{k \neq i} \exp\left(-\frac{d_{\mathrm{E}}(y_i, y_k)^2}{\sigma_i^2}\right)}, \tag{10}$$

where $d_{\mathrm{E}}(\cdot, \cdot)$ *is the Euclidean distance, and* y_i *and* y_k *are the points in the low-dimensional output space, i.e., the projection of the data samples from the high-dimensional input space.*

Step 4. Optimize the adaptive form of the cost function (2), obtained by inserting the probabilities $p_{j|i}$ *and* $q_{j|i}$ *in the former traditional formula of the cost function (2).*

The main concept behind the novel adaptive NeRV method proposed in this paper is illustrated graphically in Fig. 2.

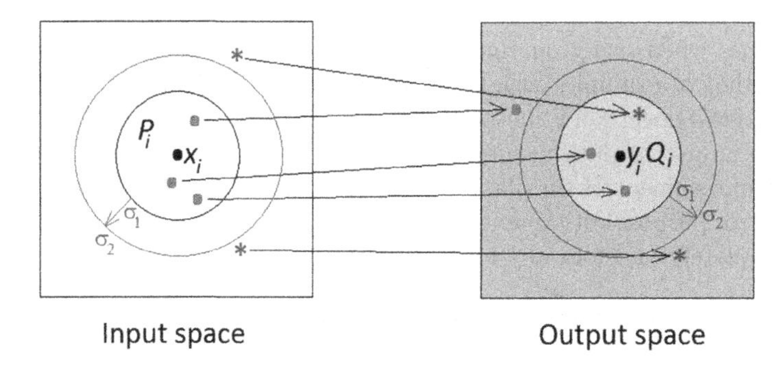

Fig. 2. Illustration of the novel adaptive NeRV visualization mapping proposed in this paper, with different neighborhood widths around a data sample x_i and the corresponding projection y_i. The neighborhood widths are marked as σ_1 and σ_2

5 Experimental Setup

In our experimental study, we have evaluated effectiveness of the proposed adaptive NeRV technique by carrying out the clustering process in the 2-dimensional output space of the proposed NeRV visualization and in the 2-dimensional output space of two reference visualization methods. The first reference method utilized in our empirical research was the traditional SOM technique, whereas the second one was the classical form of the NeRV approach. In this way, one can observe a clear comparison between our extension to the traditional NeRV method and the traditional method, itself. As a result, a precise verification and validation of the novelty within the NeRV concept can be proceeded. Furthermore, a comparison with a very well-known and commonly used all over the world data visualization approach has been presented. As the mentioned very well-known data visualization approach, we have chosen the SOM method, described in this paper as a related work, in Sect. 2. As the clustering method, we have employed the standard well-known k-means clustering algorithm with the correct number of clusters provided a priori as the input data.

The experiments have been conducted on real data in the two different research fields: in the field of words clustering and in the field of human heart rhythm signals clustering. The first part of the experimental study has been carried out on the large dataset of high-dimensionality (Subsect. 5.3), while the remaining experimental part has been conducted on smaller dataset, but also of high-dimensionality (Subsect. 5.4). In this way, one can assess the performance of the investigated methods operating on datasets of different size and nature, and consequently, one can better evaluate the effectiveness of the proposed approach.

The human heart rhythm signals analysis was carried out using the ECG recordings derived from the MIT-BIH ECG Databases [2].

In case of the ECG recordings dataset, a graphical illustration of the U-matrices generated by SOM and two kinds of NeRV is provided, while in case of the "Bag of Words" dataset no such illustration is given, because of the high number of instances in that dataset, which would make such images unreadable.

5.1 Evaluation Criteria

As the basis of the comparisons between the investigated methods, i.e., as the clustering evaluation criteria, we have used the accuracy rate [8,9,12] and the uncertainty degree [9,12]:

1. **Accuracy Rate.** This evaluation criterion determines the number of correctly assigned objects divided by the total number of objects.
   Hence, for the entire dataset, the accuracy rate is determined as follows:
   $$q = \frac{m}{n}, \tag{11}$$
   where m is the number of correctly assigned objects, and n is the total number of objects in the entire dataset.
   The accuracy rate q assumes values in the interval $\langle 0, 1 \rangle$, and naturally, greater values are preferred.
   The accuracy rate q was used in our experimental study as the main basis of the clustering accuracy comparison of the three investigated approaches.
2. **Uncertainty Degree.** This evaluation criterion determines the number of overlapping objects divided by the total number of objects in a dataset. This means, the number of objects, which are in the overlapping area between clusters, divided by the total number of objects. The objects belonging to the overlapping area are determined on the basis of the ratio of dissimilarities between them and the two nearest clusters centroids. If this ratio is in the interval $\langle 0.9, 1.1 \rangle$, then the corresponding object is said to be in the overlapping area.

The uncertainty degree is determined as follows:

$$U_d = \frac{\mu}{n}, \tag{12}$$

where μ is the number of overlapping objects in the dataset, and n is the total number of objects in the dataset.
The uncertainty degree assumes values in the interval $\langle 0, 1 \rangle$, and, smaller values are desired.

5.2 Feature Extraction

Feature extraction of the textual data investigated in this part of our experimental study was carried out using the term frequency – inverse document frequency (*tf-idf*) approach. Features of the human heart rhythm signals considered in Subsect. 5.4 have been extracted using a method based on the Discrete Fourier Transform (DFT), which is described in details in [10].

5.3 Words Visualization and Clustering

In the first part of our experimental study, we have utilized excerpts from the "Bag of Words" dataset from the UCI Machine Learning Repository [1].

Dataset Description. The "Bag of Words" dataset consists of five text collections: Enron E-mail Collection, Neural Information Processing Systems (NIPS) full papers, Daily KOS Blog Entries, New York Times News Articles, PubMed Abstracts. The total number of analyzed words was approximately 10,868,000. On the visualizations generated by the investigated methods, five clusters representing those five text collections in the "Bag of Words" dataset were formed.

5.4 Human Heart Rhythms Visualization and Clustering

The human heart rhythm signals visualization and clustering experiment was carried out on the dataset of ECG recordings derived from the MIT-BIH ECG Databases [2].

In this part of our experiments, we considered three clusters representing three types of human heart rhythms: normal sinus rhythm, atrial arrhythmia, and ventricular arrhythmia. This kind of clustering can be interpreted as the cardiac arrhythmia detection and recognition based on the ECG recordings.

Dataset Description. Our dataset is composed of the normal rhythm signals, arrhythmias originating in the atria, and in the ventricles. We analyzed 20-min ECG holter recordings sampled with the 250 Hz frequency. The entire dataset consisted of 63 ECG signals. Feature extraction was carried out according to the DFT-based method described in Subsect. 5.2.

6 Experimental Results

6.1 Words Visualization and Clustering Results

The results of this part of our experiments are reported in Table 1, where the accuracy rates and uncertainty degrees corresponding to each investigated approach are presented.

Table 1. Accuracy rates and uncertainty degrees of the words visualization and clustering

	q	U_d
SOM	8,174,844/10,868,000 = 0.7522	2,459,849/10,868,000 = 0.2263
Traditional NeRV	8,910,547/10,868,000 = 0.8199	1,979,504/10,868,000 = 0.1821
Proposed NeRV	9,230,362/10,868,000 = 0.8493	1,497,091/10,868,000 = 0.1378

6.2 Human Heart Rhythms Visualization and Clustering Results

The results of this part of our experiments are presented in Figs. 3, 4a, b, and in Table 2, which is constructed in the same way as in Subsect. 5.3.

Table 2. Accuracy rates and uncertainty degrees of the human heart rhythms visualization and clustering

	q	U_d
SOM	45/63 = 0.7143	18/63 = 0.2857
Traditional NeRV	48/63 = 0.7619	7/63 = 0.1111
Proposed NeRV	60/63 = 0.9365	5/63 = 0.0794

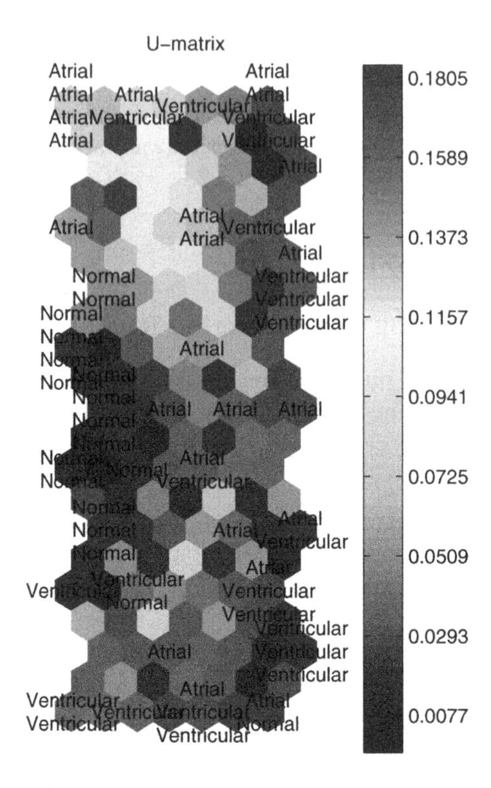

Fig. 3. Results of human heart rhythms visualization using the traditional SOM method

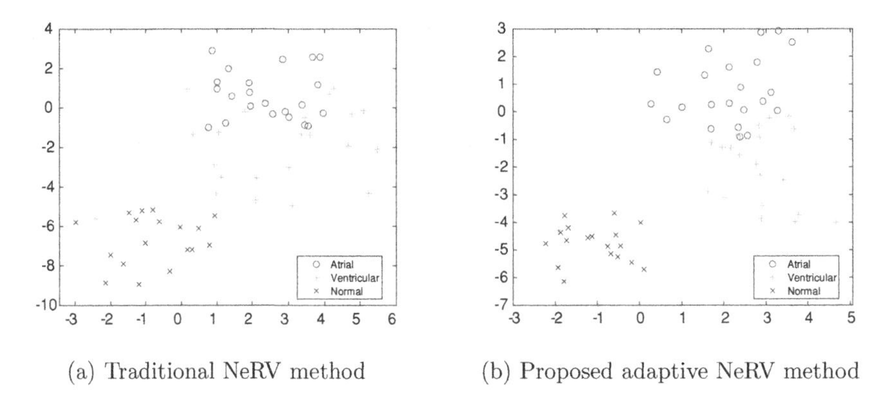

Fig. 4. Results of human heart rhythms visualization using the traditional NeRV method and the proposed adaptive NeRV improvement

7 Summary and Future Study

In this paper, a novel adaptive version of the NeRV method was proposed. In our improvement of the traditional NeRV technique, the data samples' neighborhood widths are determined independently for each data sample in the input and output spaces. The main concept introduced in the current paper is to utilize the information about the data scattering in the high-dimensional input data space, and make it the basis for determining the data samples' neighborhood sizes. The information about the data scattering in the input space, in turn, is derived and acquired by carrying out the preliminary data clustering in the input space and measuring the inner-cluster variance, which is afterward incorporated in the fundamental phase of the NeRV visualization in order to calculate the data samples' neighborhood widths as it is shown in Eqs. (9) and (10). As a result, one can conclude that a hybrid data analysis method has been formulated.

References

1. Frank, A., Asuncion, A.: UCI machine learning repository (2010). http://archive.ics.uci.edu/ml
2. Goldberger, A.L., et al.: PhysioBank, PhysioToolkit, and PhysioNet: components of a new research resource for complex physiologic signals. Circulation **101**(23), e215–e220 (2000). http://circ.ahajournals.org/cgi/content/full/101/23/e215, circulation Electronic Pages
3. Ippoliti, D., Zhou, X.: A-GHSOM: an adaptive growing hierarchical self organizing map for network anomaly detection. J. Parallel Distrib. Comput. **72**(12), 1576–1590 (2012)
4. Kohonen, T.: The self-organizing map. Proc. IEEE **28**, 1464–1480 (1990)
5. Koringa, P.A., Mitra, S.K.: L1-norm orthogonal neighbourhood preserving projection and its applications. Pattern Anal. Appl. **22**(4), 1481–1492 (2019)
6. Kullback, S., Leibler, R.A.: On information and sufficiency. Ann. Math. Stat. **22**(1), 79–86 (1951)
7. Lu, Y., Lai, Z., Li, X., Wong, W.K., Yuan, C., Zhang, D.: Low-Rank 2-D neighborhood preserving projection for enhanced robust image representation. IEEE Trans. Cybern. **49**(5), 1859–1872 (2019)
8. Olszewski, D.: Asymmetric *k*-Means algorithm. In: Dobnikar, A., Lotrič, U., Šter, B. (eds.) ICANNGA 2011. LNCS, vol. 6594, pp. 1–10. Springer, Heidelberg (2011). https://doi.org/10.1007/978-3-642-20267-4_1
9. Olszewski, D.: An experimental study on asymmetric self-organizing map. In: Yin, H., Wang, W., Rayward-Smith, V. (eds.) IDEAL 2011. LNCS, vol. 6936, pp. 42–49. Springer, Heidelberg (2011). https://doi.org/10.1007/978-3-642-23878-9_6
10. Olszewski, D.: *k*-Means clustering of asymmetric data. In: Corchado, E., Snášel, V., Abraham, A., Woźniak, M., Graña, M., Cho, S.-B. (eds.) HAIS 2012. LNCS (LNAI), vol. 7208, pp. 243–254. Springer, Heidelberg (2012). https://doi.org/10.1007/978-3-642-28942-2_22
11. Olszewski, D., Kacprzyk, J., Zadrożny, S.: Time series visualization using asymmetric self-organizing map. In: Tomassini, M., Antonioni, A., Daolio, F., Buesser, P. (eds.) ICANNGA 2013. LNCS, vol. 7824, pp. 40–49. Springer, Heidelberg (2013). https://doi.org/10.1007/978-3-642-37213-1_5

12. Olszewski, D., Šter, B.: Asymmetric clustering using the alpha-beta divergence. Pattern Recogn. **47**(5), 2031–2041 (2014)
13. Rauber, A., Merkl, D., Dittenbach, M.: The growing hierarchical self-organizing map: exploratory analysis of high-dimensional data. IEEE Trans. Neural Netw. **13**(6), 1331–1341 (2002)
14. Tian, Z., Dey, N., Ashour, A.S., McCauley, P., Shi, F.: Morphological segmenting and neighborhood pixel-based locality preserving projection on brain fMRI dataset for semantic feature extraction: an affective computing study. Neural Comput. Appl. **30**(12), 3733–3748 (2017). https://doi.org/10.1007/s00521-017-2955-2
15. Venna, J., Peltonen, J., Nybo, K., Aidos, H., Kaski, S.: Information retrieval perspective to nonlinear dimensionality reduction for data visualization. J. Mach. Learn. Res. **11**, 451–490 (2010)

A Fast SSVEP-Based Brain-Computer Interface

Tania Jorajuría, Marisol Gómez, and Carmen Vidaurre(✉)

Department of Statistics, Informatics and Mathematics,
Universidad Pública de Navarra, Pamplona, Spain
carmen.vidaurre@unavarra.es

Abstract. Literature of brain-computer interfacing (BCI) for steady-state visual evoked potentials (SSVEP) shows that canonical correlation analysis (CCA) is the most used method to extract features. However, it is known that CCA tends to rapidly overfit, leading to a decrease in performance. Furthermore, CCA uses information of just one class, thus neglecting possible overlaps between different classes. In this paper we propose a new pipeline for SSVEP-based BCIs, called corrLDA, that calculates correlation values between SSVEP signals and sine-cosine reference templates. These features are then reduced with a supervised method called shrinkage linear discriminant analysis that, unlike CCA, can deal with shorter time windows and includes between-class information. To compare these two techniques, we analysed an open access SSVEP dataset from 24 subjects where four stimuli were used in offline and online tasks. The online task was performed both in control condition and under different perturbations: listening, speaking and thinking. Results showed that corrLDA pipeline outperforms CCA in short trial lengths, as well as in the four additional noisy conditions.

Keywords: Brain-computer interface · Steady-state visual evoked potential · Linear discriminant analysis · Canonical correlation analysis

1 Introduction

Brain-computer interfaces (BCI) use brain signals, and most commonly electroencephalogram (EEG) to establish a new way to interact with our environment directly with mental activity. Their most common applications include the control of external devices [10,19], communication tools for disabled people [26,41] and neurological rehabilitation [6,7]. However, they can also be applied to other fields such as entertainment [1,23] and marketing [32].

There are several types of brain responses that can be used to achieve these goals, such as event-related potentials [13,30], sensorimotor rhythms [12,14,22,25,28,33–36,38] and visual-evoked potentials (VEP) [18,39,40]. One type of VEP is the steady-state visual evoked potential (SSVEP) which, in comparison to

This research was supported by MINECO (RYC-2014-15671).

E. A. de la Cal et al. (Eds.): HAIS 2020, LNAI 12344, pp. 49–60, 2020.
https://doi.org/10.1007/978-3-030-61705-9_5

other types of evoked potentials, is a robust phenomenon [9] with high signal-to-noise ratio [31]. In particular, SSVEPs are natural responses to visual stimulation at specific frequencies, where the brain generates oscillatory responses at the same (or multiples of) frequency of the visual stimulus at which the subject focuses.

Over the past years, different methodologies have been followed to analyse SSVEP signals. Among them, the most widely used method is the canonical correlation analysis (CCA) [2,5,17]. CCA has also been extended [44,45] and combined [8] with other methods. The concept underlying CCA-based methods is the maximization of the correlation between SSVEP signals and sine-cosine reference matrices and typically, they do not need any calibration data. This aspect offers an advantage in comparison to other methods, because the BCI system is immediately ready-to-use by a new participant. Nevertheless, CCA maximizes the correlation of multivariate datasets without minimizing the overlap between different classes, thus leading to poor performance, for example, when trials are not sufficiently long or the number of dimensions (channels) is large.

In this paper we propose a new pipeline to extract and classify SSVEP features, based on linear discriminant analysis (LDA) [24,27,43] with shrinkage [3,37]. The linear discriminant aims to minimize the within-class covariance at the same time that maximizes the between-class covariance. Thus, it is a supervised method that finds a linear combination of the input features that best separates them according to its objective function. Our results show that the proposed SSVEP-based BCI system outperforms the state-of-the-art CCA method when trials are as short as 1 s. Besides, in out-of-the-lab conditions and without prior knowledge of perturbations structure, its performance is also superior to CCA. This new pipeline is also practical, since there is no need to select subject-specific hyper-parameters.

2 Materials

We analysed open access data described and shared by [11]. In that study, data of 24 subjects were analysed after acquiring written informed consent by participants. In this paper, we used the same datasets for our analyses.

EEG from 60 channels were recorded with 1 kHz sampling rate, setting left mastoid as the reference electrode. Stimuli markers that specified the start and end of the flickering were used to segment EEG.

Each participant was presented a screen with four circles placed at different locations with different flickering frequencies: 5.45 Hz (up), 8.57 Hz (down), 12 Hz (right) and 15 Hz (left). In order to prevent that these main frequencies coincide with their higher harmonics, frequencies multiples of each other were avoided. Offline and online tasks were carried out by all subjects. In this paper, data acquired from offline task were used as the training dataset, whereas online task data were used as the testing dataset.

In each trial during the offline session, the participants were asked to focus on one of the four randomly presented flickering circles for three seconds. After the stimuli, they could blink during 1 s. In total, each subject performed 25 trials for each of the four stimuli.

On the other hand, during the online task the subjects freely selected one of the four circles and focused on it for three seconds. Then, they were presented the classification result and they had to either confirm or reject this result. If the result was rejected, the subjects had to specify the correct circle using the keyboard. Furthermore, the online task was performed under four different environmental conditions: control (i.e. no perturbation), listening, speaking and thinking. In total, each subject performed 100 trials for each condition. For more details on data acquisition procedure, please refer to [11].

3 Methods

In this manuscript we compare two pipelines to extract features for an SSVEP-based BCI system: the state-of-the-art CCA method and the proposed approach, that we named corrLDA. The notation used in this paper is boldface capital letters to denote matrices (e.g. $\mathbf{X}$), boldface lower-case letters for vectors (e.g. $\mathbf{x}$) and regular letters for scalars (e.g. x).

3.1 Pre-processing

In the two analysed pipelines, the EEG data was de-trended and band-pass filtered between 0.53 and 40 Hz with a fourth order Butterworth filter to remove DC, 50 Hz power line noise and high frequency artifacts.

3.2 Canonical Correlation Analysis (CCA)

The standard CCA method was selected as baseline, because it is considered the most popular technique to extract features from SSVEP signals [2,5,9,17, 21,42]. Briefly, CCA aims at finding the maximal correlation between the EEG signals and several reference signals (one or more at different frequencies) to estimate the similarity between the EEG and each of the flickering frequencies (classes); i.e., CCA aims at finding the SSVEP. In [11] canonical correlations were calculated between the EEG and two sine-cosine reference signal matrices. The reference functions of one of these two matrices were defined at the frequencies corresponding to the stimulation, whereas the frequencies of the other matrix corresponded to their second harmonics. Therefore, two canonical correlation values were obtained for each of the eight reference signals, which were used as features for classification. In order to obtain results for this study, we proceeded similarly.

3.3 CorrLDA

The proposed corrLDA pipeline (see Fig. 1) consists of correlating each trial in EEG pre-processed data with a sine-cosine reference matrix. This matrix is composed of $N = 16$ signals that match with sines and cosines of the four flickering frequencies and their corresponding second harmonics. This way, the dimensions of resulting data are N by number of channels by number of trials.

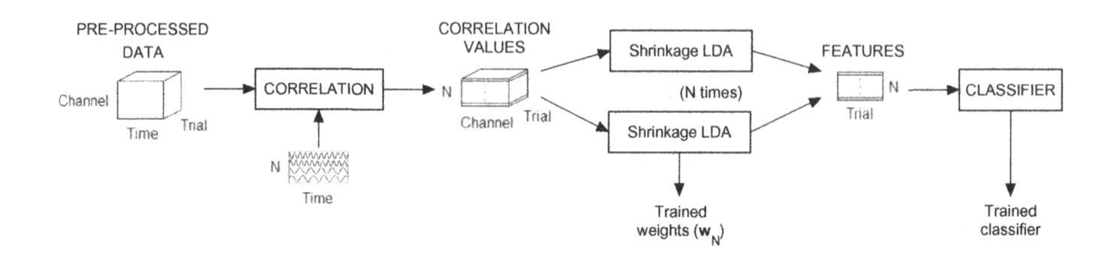

Fig. 1. corrLDA block scheme ($N = 16$).

Then, these correlation values are projected using regularized linear discriminant analysis with shrinkage (shrinkage LDA), implemented in the BBCI Toolbox of Matlab [4]. The LDA was regularized because of the high-dimensionality of the features (60) in comparison to the number of trials per class (25). Recall that the linear discriminant analysis (LDA) finds a one-dimensional subspace in which the classes are well (linearly) separated. This is formalized by requiring that after the projection onto the subspace, the ratio of the between-class variance to the within-class variance is maximal:

$$\mathbf{w} = \underset{\mathbf{w}}{argmax} \frac{\{\mathbf{w}^T \mathbf{S}_b \mathbf{w}\}}{\{\mathbf{w}^T \mathbf{\Sigma} \mathbf{w}\}} \tag{1}$$

where $\mathbf{S}_b$ and $\mathbf{\Sigma}$ are between-class and within-class scatter matrices, respectively, computed as:

$$\mathbf{S}_b = (\boldsymbol{\mu}_1 - \boldsymbol{\mu}_2)(\boldsymbol{\mu}_1 - \boldsymbol{\mu}_2)^T \tag{2}$$

$$\mathbf{\Sigma} = \frac{\mathbf{\Sigma}_1 + \mathbf{\Sigma}_2}{2} \tag{3}$$

where $\boldsymbol{\mu}_1$ and $\boldsymbol{\mu}_2$ are the sample class means and $\mathbf{\Sigma}_1$ and $\mathbf{\Sigma}_2$ are the sample covariances for class 1 and 2 respectively. The optimization problem in Eq. 1 amounts to solving a generalized eigenvalue decomposition (GEVD), which solves $\mathbf{S}_b \mathbf{w} = \beta \mathbf{\Sigma} \mathbf{w}$ for the leading eigenvector. Thus, the optimal subspace is defined by:

$$\mathbf{w} = \mathbf{\Sigma}^{-1}(\boldsymbol{\mu}_1 - \boldsymbol{\mu}_2) \tag{4}$$

As the covariance matrix is often typically poorly conditioned, we follow the approach by Ledoit and Wolf [15,16] and replace in Eq. 4 by a shrinkage estimate of the form:

$$\mathbf{\Sigma}_\lambda = (1 - \lambda)\mathbf{\Sigma} + \lambda \tilde{\mathbf{\Sigma}}, \ \lambda \in [0, 1] \tag{5}$$

The matrix $\tilde{\mathbf{\Sigma}}$ is the sample-covariance matrix of a restricted sub-model, and the optimal shrinkage intensity λ can be estimated from the data. We use the following sub-model: all variances (i.e. all diagonal elements) are equal, and all covariances (i.e. all off-diagonal elements) are zero (see [29] for other alternatives, and their corresponding optimal λ). As we were interested in finding subspaces for each of the correlation matrices (which were $N = 16$ in total) we computed the same number of subspaces employing one versus rest approach: for each of the main frequencies (f_i, i = 1...4) four correlation matrices related to that frequency were computed (i.e. correlations with $\sin(f_i)$, $\cos(f_i)$, $\sin(2^*f_i)$ and $\cos(2^*f_i)$ reference signals), with dimensions number of channels by number of trials. With each of these matrices, a shrinkage LDA was trained to find the linear combination $\mathbf{w}_N$ best separating the classes according to Eq. 1. For each shrinkage LDA, the trials that belonged to the class with the same f_i as the one used to calculate the corresponding correlation matrix (see Fig. 1) were taken as targets, while the remaining trials were non-targets. Thus, the final number of features per trials was reduced to $N = 16$.

3.4 Classification

Following the procedures of [11], three classifiers were used: Decision Tree, Naïve Bayes (using kernel distribution to model the data) and K-Nearest Neighbor (K-NN) (with K = 5 neighbors), implemented with Statistics and Machine Learning Toolbox of Matlab.

All of them were used to calculate the training (offline) dataset classification accuracy, using a leave-one-out approach. This was done for the two techniques discussed in this paper (i.e. the standard CCA method and the new proposed pipeline, corrLDA), using three different trial lengths (1, 2 and 3 s).

On the contrary, the testing (online) dataset results were obtained using the best classifier for each analysed technique, estimated from the training dataset analysis. These two technique-classifier pipelines were evaluated using 1 s trial length, for the four perturbations present in the dataset, after training with the whole training dataset.

3.5 Statistical Analysis

We conducted a two-way analysis of variance (ANOVA) for repeated measures to analyse the effect of technique (CCA, corrLDA) and classifier (K-NN, Naïve Bayes, Decision Tree) on the results obtained with cross-validation in the training set, when using 1 s trial length. For the testing dataset, we conducted a two-way repeated measures ANOVA to see the influence of approach (the selected CCA-classifier and corrLDA-classifier combinations) and perturbation (control, listening, speaking, thinking) factors on classification results obtained with 1 s long trials.

When the interaction of factors or the main effects were significant, a Tuckey's honestly significant difference (HSD) post hoc test was computed. Furthermore, we used Mauchly's test to analyse the sphericity of the response variables in the repeated measures model of each ANOVA. When this null hypothesis was rejected, we looked at the Greenhouse-Geisser adjusted p-values.

4 Results

4.1 Training Dataset Classification

Figure 2 depicts mean accuracies (%) and standard errors across subjects for each of the presented techniques. Classification results of the three tested classifiers when changing trials length from 1 to 3 s are represented in each of the subplots.

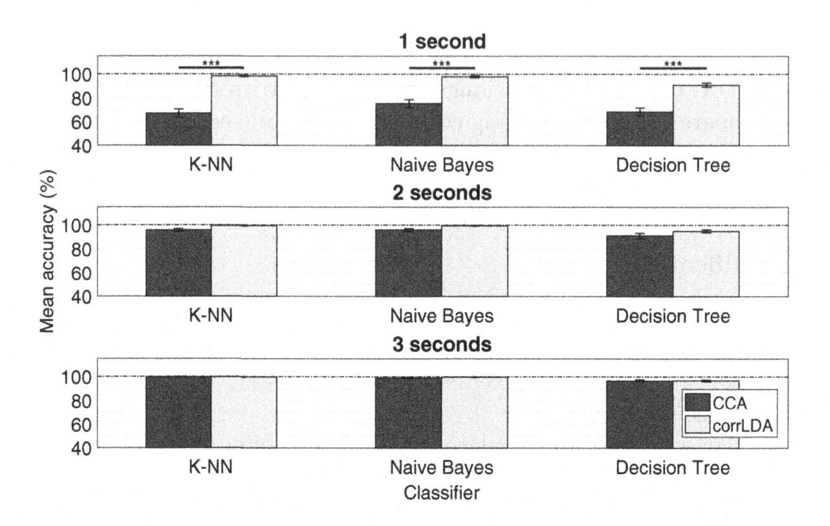

Fig. 2. Mean accuracies (%) and standard errors for different stimuli lengths and classifiers (training dataset; 24 subjects). ***: $p < 0.001$. Differences (Tuckey's HSD) between techniques for 1 s trial length.

As described in Sect. 3.5, we performed a 2-way repeated measures ANOVA (see Table 1) with factors technique and classifier, using accuracy results obtained with 1 s trial length. Both main factors and their interaction were significant ($p < 0.001$ in each case). Thus, post-hoc tests followed.

Tuckey's HSD revealed that corrLDA outperformed CCA with the three analysed classifiers ($p < 0.001$ in each case). Besides, when using CCA, Naïve Bayes classifier performance was superior to K-NN and Decision Tree ($p < 0.001$ in each case). On the other hand, with the corrLDA pipeline both K-NN and Naïve Bayes classifiers had better results than Decision Tree ($p < 0.001$ in each case).

Mean classification accuracies across subjects obtained with the proposed corrLDA pipeline were higher than 90% with 1 s long trials. This result was consistent for all three analysed classifiers (mean ± std; K-NN: 98.29 ± 0.53, Naïve Bayes: 97.83 ± 0.72, Decision Tree: 91 ± 1.76). However, for 1 s long trials, CCA could not reach 80% of mean accuracy for any of the classifiers (mean ± std; K-NN: 67.04 ± 3.53, Naïve Bayes: 75.25 ± 3.25, Decision Tree: 68.46 ± 3.40).

For further analyses with the testing dataset, we selected K-NN and Naïve Bayes classifiers to analyse corrLDA and CCA techniques, respectively (i.e. corrLDA-KNN and CCA-NB).

Table 1. Two-way repeated measures ANOVA for mean accuracies in training dataset with 1 s trial length, with classifier and technique factors.

Source	*SS*	*df*	*MS*	*F*	*p*
Classifier	1120.88	2	560.44	33.25	<0.001
Error (classifier)	775.46	46	16.86	–	–
Technique	23332.56	1	23332.56	84.28	<0.001
Error (technique)	6367.27	23	276.84	–	–
Classifier × technique	603.79	2	301.90	15.40	<0.001
Error (classifier × technique)	901.88	46	19.61	–	–

4.2 Testing Dataset Classification

As previously mentioned, two technique-classifier approaches were evaluated with the testing dataset: CCA-NB and corrLDA-KNN. In Fig. 3 mean accuracies (%) and standard errors across subjects are shown for each studied approach under different perturbations (using 1 s long trials).

A two-way ANOVA for repeated measures was conducted (see Table 2) with approach and perturbation factors. The results showed that both main factors were significant ($p < 0.001$ in each case), but there was no significant interaction between them ($p = 0.4435$).

Table 2. Two-way repeated measures ANOVA for mean accuracies in testing dataset with 1 s trial length, with approach and perturbation factors.

Source	*SS*	*df*	*MS*	*F*	*p*
Approach	41477.52	1	41477.52	225.21	<0.001
Error (approach)	4235.98	23	184.17	–	–
Perturbation	2526.71	3	842.24	13.38	<0.001
Error (perturbation)	4342.29	69	62.93	–	–
Approach × perturbation	80.44	3	26.81	0.84	0.4435
Error (approach × perturbation)	2211.06	69	32.04	–	–

Both approaches got the highest mean accuracy result in Control condition (mean ± std; corrLDA-KNN: 88.08 ± 1.73, CCA-NB: 59.00 ± 2.41), followed by Listening (mean ± std; corrLDA-KNN: 85.58 ± 2.24, CCA-NB: 56.04 ± 2.30), Thinking (mean ± std; corrLDA-KNN: 82.58 ± 2.45, CCA-NB: 51.29 ± 2.40) and Speaking (mean ± std; corrLDA-KNN: 77.88 ± 3.38, CCA-NB: 50.21 ± 2.33) perturbations.

Finally, post-hoc tests revealed that the CCA-NB approach achieved significantly less accuracy than corrLDA-KNN for all perturbations ($p < 0.001$, in all cases).

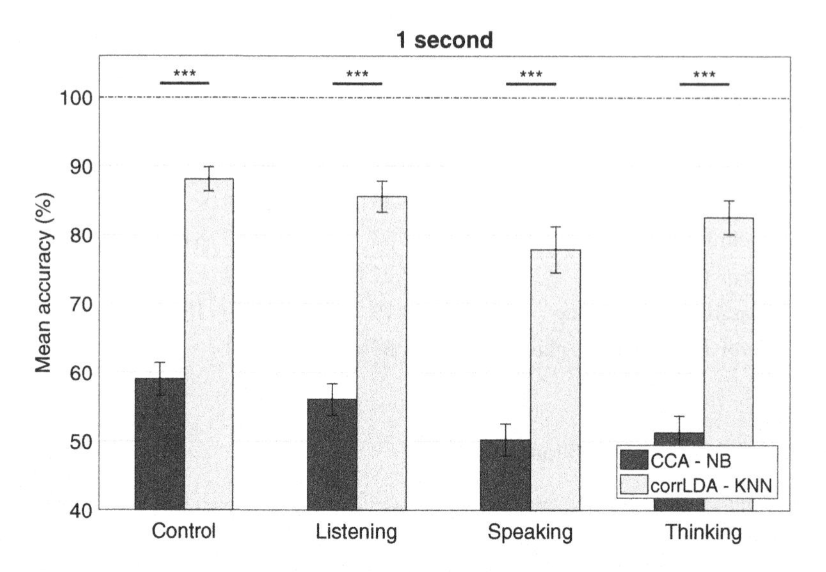

Fig. 3. Mean accuracies (%) and standard errors for different perturbations with 1 s trial length (testing dataset; 24 subjects). ***: $p < 0.001$. Differences (Tuckey's HSD) between approaches for each perturbation.

5 Discussion

As observed from previous results, the corrLDA pipeline outperforms CCA. CCA-based methods do not take into account between-class information to compute correlations, because each CCA is performed with reference signals of just one class. Therefore, when features from different classes overlap, which on the other hand is the most common setting for SSVEP signals [20], the classification results are poor. On the contrary, the corrLDA pipeline employs linear discriminant functions that maximize the difference between classes, thus (linearly) reducing the overlap between them. Consequently, and as we have seen, corrLDA achieves significantly better performance than CCA.

Furthermore, corrLDA achieves higher mean accuracy classification results with short trial lengths than CCA. In particular, we analysed trials of 1 s length, with which it was possible to achieve almost 90% mean accuracy in the control condition (without noise perturbations). In the case of CCA, however, the mean accuracy was around 60% for condition control. The reason for this is that regression-based methods are unable to achieve reliable estimates without enough number of cycles of the signal of interest. It is clear thus, that our proposed pipeline corrLDA can be considered a good option to design fast and easy to train SSVEP-based BCI systems, with the potential of increasing information transfer rates [41].

Regarding classification results achieved under different perturbations, our corrLDA pipeline again outperforms the classification results obtained with CCA, in the four analysed conditions. Even without including knowledge of the noise structure of each perturbation, corrLDA achieved an average of 83.53% of accuracy under all analysed disturbances, whereas CCA only reached 54.14%. Nevertheless, both techniques are affected by noise, being the speaking condition the one that most affects (decreases) mean accuracies. As stated in [11], the reason for this could be that the quality of the EEG signal decreases in the theta band. Another reason could be the attention split that the subjects undergo due to dual tasking. Indeed, the latter factor is also present in the thinking condition, which is the next worst condition regarding classification performance. These results suggest that further investigation needs to be done in order to develop BCI systems that are robust against perturbations, so that they can be reliably used in out-of-the-lab environments.

Finally, the proposed pipeline is practical and easy to use since it does not require to select subject-specific hyper-parameters, which greatly simplifies the set-up of the system. Unlike CCA, corrLDA needs some calibration data in order to train the shrink LDAs. corrLDA offers, however, significantly better performance than CCA, even under noisy conditions and using significantly shorter trial lengths.

6 Conclusions

In this paper we proposed a new pipeline, named corrLDA, to develop a fast SSVEP-based BCI system. This pipeline computes correlation values with sine-cosine reference templates and uses shrinkage LDA to reduce the number of features. Finally, a non-linear classifier is used to decode the EEG signal. We showed that corrLDA outperforms CCA using trial lengths as short as 1 s, under both ideal and noisy conditions. Further investigations need to be done to robustly classify SSVEP data regardless of the perturbation.

Acknowledgements. We are grateful to Zafer İşcan for partly sharing code and to Mina Jamshidi and Vadim V. Nikulin for fruitful discussions.

References

1. Ahn, M., Lee, M., Choi, J., Jun, S.: A review of brain-computer interface games and an opinion survey from researchers, developers and users. Sensors **14**(8), 14601–14633 (2014). https://doi.org/10.3390/s140814601
2. Bin, G., Gao, X., Yan, Z., Hong, B., Gao, S.: An online multi-channel SSVEP-based brain-computer interface using a canonical correlation analysis method. J. Neural Eng. **6**(4), 046002 (2009). https://doi.org/10.1088/1741-2560/6/4/046002
3. Blankertz, B., Lemm, S., Treder, M., Haufe, S., Müller, K.R.: Single-trial analysis and classification of ERP components-a tutorial. NeuroImage **56**(2), 814–825 (2011). https://doi.org/10.1016/j.neuroimage.2010.06.048
4. Blankertz, B., et al.: The berlin brain-computer interface: non-medical uses of BCI technology. Front. Neurosci. **4**, 198 (2010). https://doi.org/10.3389/fnins.2010.00198

5. Cao, L., Ju, Z., Li, J., Jian, R., Jiang, C.: Sequence detection analysis based on canonical correlation for steady-state visual evoked potential brain computer interfaces. J. Neurosci. Methods **253**, 10–17 (2015). https://doi.org/10.1016/j.jneumeth.2015.05.014
6. Daly, J.J., Wolpaw, J.R.: Brain-computer interfaces in neurological rehabilitation. Lancet Neurol. **7**(11), 1032–1043 (2008). https://doi.org/10.1016/S1474-4422(08)70223-0
7. Dobkin, B.H.: Brain-computer interface technology as a tool to augment plasticity and outcomes for neurological rehabilitation. J. Physiol. **579**(3), 637–642 (2007). https://doi.org/10.1113/jphysiol.2006.123067
8. Farooq, M., Dehzangi, O.: High accuracy wearable SSVEP detection using feature profiling and dimensionality reduction. In: 2017 IEEE 14th International Conference on Wearable and Implantable Body Sensor Networks (BSN), pp. 161–164. IEEE (2017). https://doi.org/10.1109/BSN.2017.7936032
9. Friman, O., Volosyak, I., Graser, A.: Multiple channel detection of steady-state visual evoked potentials for brain-computer interfaces. IEEE Trans. Biomed. Eng. **54**(4), 742–750 (2007). https://doi.org/10.1109/TBME.2006.889160
10. Gao, X., Xu, D., Cheng, M., Gao, S.: A BCI-based environmental controller for the motion-disabled. IEEE Trans. Neural Syst. Rehabil. Eng. **11**(2), 137–140 (2003). https://doi.org/10.1109/TNSRE.2003.814449
11. İşcan, Z., Nikulin, V.V.: Steady state visual evoked potential (SSVEP) based brain-computer interface (BCI) performance under different perturbations. PLoS ONE **13**(1), e0191673 (2018). https://doi.org/10.1371/journal.pone.0191673
12. Kawanabe, M., Vidaurre, C., Blankertz, B., Müller, K.-R.: A maxmin approach to optimize spatial filters for EEG single-trial classification. In: Cabestany, J., Sandoval, F., Prieto, A., Corchado, J.M. (eds.) IWANN 2009. LNCS, vol. 5517, pp. 674–682. Springer, Heidelberg (2009). https://doi.org/10.1007/978-3-642-02478-8_84
13. Kübler, A., Furdea, A., Halder, S., Hammer, E.M., Nijboer, F., Kotchoubey, B.: A brain-computer interface controlled auditory event-related potential (P300) spelling system for locked-in patients. Ann. N. Y. Acad. Sci. **1157**(1), 90–100 (2009). https://doi.org/10.1111/j.1749-6632.2008.04122.x
14. Kübler, A., et al.: Patients with ALS can use sensorimotor rhythms to operate a brain-computer interface. Neurology **64**(10), 1775–1777 (2005). https://doi.org/10.1212/01.WNL.0000158616.43002.6D
15. Ledoit, O., Wolf, M.: Honey, I shrunk the sample covariance matrix. J. Portfolio Manag. **30**(4), 110–119 (2004). https://doi.org/10.3905/jpm.2004.110
16. Ledoit, O., Wolf, M., et al.: A well-conditioned estimator for large-dimensional covariance matrices. J. Multivar. Anal. **88**(2), 365–411 (2004)
17. Lin, Z., Zhang, C., Wu, W., Gao, X.: Frequency recognition based on canonical correlation analysis for SSVEP-based BCIs. IEEE Trans. Biomed. Eng. **53**(12), 2610–2614 (2006). https://doi.org/10.1109/TBME.2006.886577
18. Lorenz, R., Pascual, J., Blankertz, B., Vidaurre, C.: Towards a holistic assessment of the user experience with hybrid BCIs. J. Neural Eng. **11**(3), 035007 (2014)
19. McFarland, D.J., Wolpaw, J.R.: Brain-computer interface operation of robotic and prosthetic devices. Computer **41**(10), 52–56 (2008). https://doi.org/10.1109/MC.2008.409
20. Nakanishi, M., Wang, Y., Chen, X., Wang, Y.T., Gao, X., Jung, T.P.: Enhancing detection of SSVEPs for a high-speed brain speller using task-related component analysis. IEEE Trans. Biomed. Eng. **65**(1), 104–112 (2017). https://doi.org/10.1109/TBME.2017.2694818

21. Nan, W., et al.: A comparison of minimum energy combination and canonical correlation analysis for SSVEP detection. In: 2011 5th International IEEE/EMBS Conference on Neural Engineering, pp. 469–472. IEEE (2011). https://doi.org/10.1109/NER.2011.5910588
22. Nierhaus, T., Vidaurre, C., Sannelli, C., Mueller, K.R., Villringer, A.: Immediate brain plasticity after one hour of brain-computer interface (BCI). J. Physiol. (2019). https://doi.org/10.1113/JP278118
23. Nijholt, A., Bos, D.P.O., Reuderink, B.: Turning shortcomings into challenges: brain-computer interfaces for games. Entertain. Comput. **1**(2), 85–94 (2009). https://doi.org/10.1016/j.entcom.2009.09.007
24. Perez, J.L.M., Cruz, A.B.: Linear discriminant analysis on brain computer interface. In: 2007 IEEE International Symposium on Intelligent Signal Processing, pp. 1–6. IEEE (2007). https://doi.org/10.1109/WISP.2007.4447590
25. Pfurtscheller, G., Brunner, C., Schlögl, A., Da Silva, F.L.: Mu rhythm (de) synchronization and EEG single-trial classification of different motor imagery tasks. NeuroImage **31**(1), 153–159 (2006). https://doi.org/10.1016/j.neuroimage.2005.12.003
26. Pfurtscheller, G., Flotzinger, D., Kalcher, J.: Brain-computer interface-a new communication device for handicapped persons. J. Microcomput. Appl. **16**(3), 293–299 (1993). https://doi.org/10.1006/jmca.1993.1030
27. Saa, J.F.D., Gutierrez, M.S.: EEG signal classification using power spectral features and linear discriminant analysis: a brain computer interface application. In: Eighth Latin American and Caribbean Conference for Engineering and Technology, pp. 1–7. LACCEI, Arequipa (2010)
28. Sannelli, C., Vidaurre, C., Müller, K.R., Blankertz, B.: A large scale screening study with a SMR-based BCI: categorization of BCI users and differences in their SMR activity. PLoS One **14**(1) (2019). https://doi.org/10.1371/journal.pone.0207351
29. Schäfer, J., Strimmer, K.: A shrinkage approach to large-scale covariance matrix estimation and implications for functional genomics. Stat. Appl. Genet. Mol. Biol. **4**(1) (2005). https://doi.org/10.2202/1544-6115.1175
30. Sellers, E.W., Krusienski, D.J., McFarland, D.J., Vaughan, T.M., Wolpaw, J.R.: A P300 event-related potential brain-computer interface (BCI): the effects of matrix size and inter stimulus interval on performance. Biol. Psychol. **73**(3), 242–252 (2006). https://doi.org/10.1016/j.biopsycho.2006.04.007
31. Srinivasan, R., Bibi, F.A., Nunez, P.L.: Steady-state visual evoked potentials: distributed local sources and wave-like dynamics are sensitive to flicker frequency. Brain Topogr. **18**(3), 167–187 (2006). https://doi.org/10.1007/s10548-006-0267-4
32. Vecchiato, G., et al.: The study of brain activity during the observation of commercial advertsing by using high resolution EEG techniques. In: 2009 Annual International Conference of the IEEE Engineering in Medicine and Biology Society, pp. 57–60. IEEE (2009). https://doi.org/10.1109/IEMBS.2009.5335045
33. Vidaurre, C., Klauer, C., Schauer, T., Ramos-Murguialday, A., Mueller, K.R.: EEG-based BCI for the linear control of an upper-limb neuroprosthesis. Med. Eng. Phys. **38**, 1195–1204 (2016). https://doi.org/10.1016/j.medengphy.2016.06.010
34. Vidaurre, C., Murguialday, A.R., Haufe, S., Gómez, M., Müller, K.R., Nikulin, V.V.: Enhancing sensorimotor BCI performance with assistive afferent activity: an online evaluation. NeuroImage **199**, 375–386 (2019). https://doi.org/10.1016/j.neuroimage.2019.05.074
35. Vidaurre, C., et al.: Neuromuscular electrical stimulation induced brain patterns to decode motor imagery. Clin. Neurophysiol. **124**(9), 1824–1834 (2013). https://doi.org/10.1016/j.clinph.2013.03.009

36. Vidaurre, C., Sannelli, C., Müller, K.-R., Blankertz, B.: Machine-learning based co-adaptive calibration: a perspective to fight BCI illiteracy. In: Graña Romay, M., Corchado, E., Garcia Sebastian, M.T. (eds.) HAIS 2010. LNCS (LNAI), vol. 6076, pp. 413–420. Springer, Heidelberg (2010). https://doi.org/10.1007/978-3-642-13769-3_50
37. Vidaurre, C., Krämer, N., Blankertz, B., Schlögl, A.: Time domain parameters as a feature for EEG-based brain-computer interfaces. Neural Netw. **22**(9), 1313–1319 (2009). https://doi.org/10.1016/j.neunet.2009.07.020
38. Vidaurre, C., Scherer, R., Cabeza, R., Schlögl, A., Pfurtscheller, G.: Study of discriminant analysis applied to motor imagery bipolar data. Med. Biol. Eng. Comput. **45**(1), 61 (2007). https://doi.org/10.1007/s11517-006-0122-5
39. Wang, Y., Gao, X., Hong, B., Jia, C., Gao, S.: Brain-computer interfaces based on visual evoked potentials. IEEE Eng. Med. Biol. Mag. **27**(5), 64–71 (2008). https://doi.org/10.1109/MEMB.2008.923958
40. Wang, Y., Wang, R., Gao, X., Hong, B., Gao, S.: A practical VEP-based brain-computer interface. IEEE Trans. Neural Syst. Rehabil. Eng. **14**(2), 234–240 (2006). https://doi.org/10.1109/TNSRE.2006.875576
41. Wolpaw, J.R., Birbaumer, N., McFarland, D.J., Pfurtscheller, G., Vaughan, T.M.: Brain-computer interfaces for communication and control. Clin. Neurophysiol. **113**(6), 767–791 (2002). https://doi.org/10.1016/S1388-2457(02)00057-3
42. Yin, E., Zhou, Z., Jiang, J., Yu, Y., Hu, D.: A dynamically optimized SSVEP brain-computer interface (BCI) speller. IEEE Trans. Biomed. Eng. **62**(6), 1447–1456 (2014). https://doi.org/10.1109/TBME.2014.2320948
43. Zhang, R., Xu, P., Guo, L., Zhang, Y., Li, P., Yao, D.: Z-score linear discriminant analysis for EEG based brain-computer interfaces. PLoS One **8**(9) (2013). https://doi.org/10.1371/journal.pone.0074433
44. Zhang, Y., Zhou, G., Jin, J., Wang, M., Wang, X., Cichocki, A.: L1-regularized multiway canonical correlation analysis for SSVEP-based BCI. IEEE Trans. Neural Syst. Rehabil. Eng. **21**(6), 887–896 (2013). https://doi.org/10.1109/TNSRE.2013.2279680
45. Zhang, Y., Zhou, G., Jin, J., Wang, X., Cichocki, A.: Frequency recognition in SSVEP-based BCI using multiset canonical correlation analysis. Int. J. Neural Syst. **24**(04), 1450013 (2014). https://doi.org/10.1142/S0129065714500130

Visual Analytics for Production Line Failure Detection

Unai Arrieta[1(✉)], Ander García[1], Mikel Lorente[2], and Ángel Maleta[2]

[1] Vicomtech Foundation, Basque Research and Technology Alliance (BRTA), Mikeletegi 57, 20009 Donostia-San Sebastián, Spain
uarrieta@vicomtech.org

[2] Zucchetti Group, Zuatzu 4 – 1°, 20018 Donostia-San Sebastián, Spain

Abstract. There are several situations where a company has to analyze data gathered from its production line (machines, raw materials, operations, warehouses, ...) to identify the cause of the situation and to react as soon as possible. One of these situations is the detection of production failures after a faulty product has been detected. Failure detection has always been a critical issue in the industrial sector, mainly because measures should be taken both to prevent them happening again, and to fix already finished or sold products. Access to production line data is required to know what has happened. Most companies store this data, at least by using an ERP software. However, it is complicated and human resource intensive to detect a failure just by looking to the raw data provided by an ERP.

This paper focuses on this situation, supporting employees visualizing and navigating production line data. An application transforming production line data into a graph structure, and applying Visual Analytics and Big Data approaches, has been designed and developed. This application has been integrated with an existing ERP, Izaro from Group Zucchetti. Results have been positively evaluated, as they greatly improve existing tools to analyze and navigate production line data from the ERP.

Keywords: Visual analytics · Production line · Visualization techniques · Data modelling

1 Introduction

A production line is composed by several steps where different elements (machines, raw materials, operations, warehouses, ...) can have a relevant impact on the quality of the final product. These elements produce an important amount of interconnected data that is quite difficult and resource intensive to be stored and analyzed by traditional tools.

Although Machine Learning and Big Data technologies can be applied to automatically perform this analysis, still a lot of companies, mainly SMEs, do not have access to these technologies. However, most of these companies already

E. A. de la Cal et al. (Eds.): HAIS 2020, LNAI 12344, pp. 61–72, 2020.
https://doi.org/10.1007/978-3-030-61705-9_6

rely on ERP (Enterprise Resource Planning) software to store and manually query key data of production lines. Thus, when a special situation happens at these companies, extensive human resources are directed to access this data, analyze what has happened, and take a decision about it.

This paper focuses on one of these situations that requires a fast response to minimize its negative impact: failure detection. When a failure on a product is detected, either by clients or employees, companies have to perform the following main tasks:

- Analyze the production line to detect the elements responsible of the failure.
- Define and execute actions to avoid the failure to ever happen again.
- Identify whether the failure affects products that have already been produced or sold, and react in consequence.

The first and the last tasks require a thorough and resource intensive analysis of the information stored on the ERP by employees with a deep knowledge about the production line.

This paper proposes an approach based on Visual Analytics to help employees on these relevant tasks. The objective is to reduce the reaction time to production failures.

The main contributions of the paper consist in modeling industrial requirements for failure point detection; in solving these requirement applying a node-link graph visualization approach; and in validating and integrating this approach into a traditional industrial system, the ERP Izaro from Zucchetti Group, to assist employees on real situation. An agile development approach, consisting of sequences of repeated design, development, integration and validation short cycles (iterations), has been followed to fulfil the previous objective.

A production line can be transformed into a graph structure where the steps a product goes through are represented by vertices and the relations between steps by edges. Data generated during the production process can be associated both to these edges and vertices.

Once the production line is transformed into a graph, Visual Analytics tools can be applied to efficiently support employees on the previous tasks. This work presents a visual application to represent a production line using a node-link based graph structure. This application includes visualization and interaction techniques customized for the detection of production failures. The application has been integrated and validated with data from an existing ERP software, Izaro by Zucchetti Group.

This paper is organized as follows: first, related work and the requirements of the production failure detection problem are presented. Then, the proposed data model and the applied visualization and interaction techniques are described. The paper finalises presenting some future work and conclusions.

2 Related Work

Researchers have proposed different approaches for exploring manufacturing data. These approaches target two main application groups: visualization for production planning, optimization and simulation; and visualization for process monitoring [13]. However, to the best of the authors' knowledge, there are no examples of visualization for the manufacturing use case tackled by this paper: graph techniques for the detection of the cause of a faulty product.

A great deal of emphasis has been placed on the visualization techniques for static graphs. Some papers use tree structures to represent graphs [12]. Other papers use directed or undirected graphs to visualize them [4].

The techniques for displaying this later graphs are divided in three groups. Node-link based approaches where the relation between nodes is represented using links [6]. Matrix approaches where the relation between nodes is represented by an adjacency matrix [5]. Hybrid approaches combine the two stated techniques [9]. Due to the challenge, the main concern in the graphs represented using node-link based techniques is the layout [3]. Therefore, the difference between the layout lies in the node and edge placement. Force-based layouts use simulation techniques to place nodes [2]. Multi-scale layouts divide the graph into smaller sub-graphs [1]. Layered layouts place nodes in different layers depending on the layout algorithm [4].

Apart from visualizing the graph, the employee needs to navigate and interact with the graph. Standard interaction techniques such as zooming and panning allow the user to navigate through the graph [7]. Layout change and highlighting can be used to change the visual representation [11]. Data filtering allows the user to simplify the visualization and hide unwanted information [14]. In some works, the user is allowed to manipulate the data by changing values or adding/deleting nodes to the graph [8].

This paper extends and customises these visualization and interaction approaches to support employees during production line failure detection tasks.

3 Requirements

Production line data is generated during all of its steps: from the acquisition of raw materials to the delivery of the final product. Although each production line has its own characteristics, common production steps and elements can be defined among lines.

These common steps and elements can be found with similar names in main general purpose ERPs, as the one provided by Zucchetti Group and used for the validation of the approach presented on the paper. These steps and elements can be grouped in six categories. Data about these categories represent the workflow of the production line and its step. Each product of the production line can be traced by these data. For each product, transition between categories is restricted by the production workflow. A general production workflow only allows certain transition among categories. The following list describes each category and their allowed transitions:

- Batch. It represents a product that either (i) has been acquired as input material for production, (ii) has been produced at an intermediate production

step to be used at a further production step, or (iii) has already been produced and it is ready to be sold or stored. It can come from a purchase note or it can be the result of a set of manufacturing orders. It can go to a warehouse, delivery note or a new set of operations.
- Warehouse. It represents a location where produced products are stored. It is a final step with no further steps and can only come from one batch.
- Manufacturing order (MO). It represents an order to create a new batch using one or more operations and input batches. It can only come from a set of operations. It can only go to one batch.
- Operation. It represents a transformation applied to a batch. It can only come from a set of batches. It can only go to one MO.
- Delivery note. It represents the sale of a batch to a client. It is a final step with no further steps and can only come from one batch.
- Purchase note. It represents the purchase of a batch. It is considered as an initial step, it has no previous step and it can result only in one batch.

Considering this general approach to the production line, two use cases have been identified to handle the information of the production workflow to detect production failures.

The first use case focuses on the identification of the point of failure within the production line. Once a faulty product has been identified by its batch and item numbers, its batch number has to be used to access its production data. As production data can be overwhelming, it has to be queried and presented gradually, helping employees navigate through the data until they find the point of failure.

The second use case focuses on the reaction to the failure. Once the failure has been identified, the employee has to know which warehouses and delivery notes are related to the point of failure. With this information, the employee can create issues commanding to take the required action, for example to retire already sold products, that have been affected by the detected point of failure.

4 Data Model

In order to handle the previous requirements and transform production line data into a graph, the following data model is proposed.

First, available data is divided in two types, nodes for graph vertices and relations for graph edges. Nodes represent the previous categories of steps and elements of a production line. They are described by the following attributes:

- Identifier: Identifier of the node.
- Name: Name given to the node.
- Type: Category of the node.
- Data: Data object of the node, which varies depending the category of the node.

Relations represent the transition from one production step to another and they contain the following attributes.

- Source node id: Identifier of the node which is the source of the relation.
- Target node id: Identifier of the node which is the target of the relation.

The given production line dataset can be represented as a graph structure. A graph $G = (V, E)$ consists of a set of vertices $V = \{V_0, ..., V_{n-1}\}$ and set of edges $E = \{E_0, ..., E_{t-1}\}$ where n is number of vertices and t number of edges. Since an edge has source and target node, the direction of the edges is relevant. Thus, it is a directed graph. One edge E_k going from node i to node j consists of two vertices $E_k = (V_i, V_j)$ where $k \in \{0, ..., t-1\}$, $\{i, j\} \in \{0, ..., n-1\}$ and $i \neq j$.

In order to simplify the neighbour search, the dataset is pre-processed. For each node k the identifier of its neighbours are stored. Since this is a directed graph, not all the neighbours are equivalent. Thus, there are two groups of nodes, u and d. The group u consists of nodes from which node k is the target node in a relation. The group d consists of nodes from which node k is the source node in a relation. So the neighbours of the node k are represented by A_{ka} where $a \in \{u, d\}$. Later in this paper the u group is referred as adjacent up nodes and the d group as adjacent down nodes.

5 Visualization and Interaction Techniques

This section presents the graph visualization and interaction approaches of the paper in order to support employees during the production failure detection.

5.1 Node Visualization

First, to visually distinguish nodes by category, each node is represented by an icon related to its category. Each category has its own icon, as shown in Fig. 1.

Fig. 1. Icons of the different categories.

For the sake of readability, as users interact with the graph that represents the production line, the state of the nodes changes reacting to actions of the employees. A node can have three different states, each one visually represented with a different color selected by the ERP provider (Fig. 2).

- Current. Is the node currently selected by the user. The information displayed by the application corresponds to this node and is distinguished by orange color.

- Not visited. The user has not yet interacted with the node. This is the default state for a node and distinguished by azure blue color.
- Visited. The user has already interacted with the node. It is represented by deep blue color.

Fig. 2. Node states, from left to right: current, not visited, and visited. (Color figure online)

5.2 Node Positioning

As previously introduced, production line data is going to be represented as a directed graph. A node-link based technique is used to visualize the graph. The main challenge of this representation is the layout, so that the graph structure is readable [3].

We propose a layered layout for the placement of nodes, based on the position of the neighbour nodes. The proposed node positioning algorithm has three phases: assignment of nodes to layers, assignment of nodes' position in the Y axis, and reassignment of nodes' position according to component ratio.

Assignment of Nodes to Layers. Every node in the dataset is assigned to a layer. The initial node is the one identified by the batch and item number of the faulty product. Starting from this initial node, a depth-first search algorithm is used to iterate through all the graph.

Each node has a layer where L_k is the layer of the node k and the layer of the first node is $L_k = 0$. The layer of the neighbour i is $L_i = L_k - 1$ where $i \in \{A_{ku}\}$. The layer of the neighbour j is $L_j = L_k + 1$ where $j \in \{A_{kd}\}$. If the layer is set as the X axis then the direction of the graph is going to be from left to right.

Assignment of Nodes Position in the Y Axis. Nodes have form a set of C layers where h is the size of the set. The Y position of the layer C_e is calculated using the following equation,

$$-((n - n \bmod 2)/2 - (0.5 - (n \bmod 2) * 0.5) - i), i \in \{0, ..., n-1\}$$

where $e \in \{1, ..., h\}$ and n is the number of nodes is the layer C_e.

Recalculate the Position of the Nodes According to Component Ratio. Depending on the structure of the graph it is possible that it is not suited for visualization. Therefore, the graph has to be adjusted to the component holding it. This is done by scaling the value of the X and Y axes. As a result, the space used by the graph in the component is maximized.

5.3 Node Filtering

In order to improve the visualization and navigation of the graph, the user has the option to apply filters to simplify the graph. A deterministic filtering based on the categories of the nodes has been applied [10]. The filter allows to remove nodes of two categories, operation and MO, from the display. Figure 3 shows a graphical representation of the process of hiding and showing nodes after applying and removing a filter.

Hide Nodes. When hiding node k all the edges (V_i, V_k) and (V_k, V_j) must be removed, where $i \in \{A_{ku}\}$ and $j \in \{A_{kd}\}$. To reconnect the graph new edges (V_i, V_j) must be created as shown in the Fig. 3a).

As stated in Sect. 3, nodes of categories MO and operations are connected. Thus, it is possible for one of the neighbours to be already hidden. For example, if we try to hide the MO category and the operation category is already hidden is not possible to reconnect the graph. Therefore, the next layer is going to be used, in this case the batch category.

If an adjacent up node is hidden, this node's adjacent up nodes are going to be used. When hiding node k, all the edges (V_l, V_k) and (V_k, V_j) must be removed, where $l \in \{A_{iu}\}$, $i \in \{A_{ku}\}$ and $j \in \{A_{kd}\}$. To reconnect the graph new edges (V_l, V_j) must be created. The same procedure is applied for hidden adjacent down nodes. When hiding node k all the edges (V_i, V_k) and (V_k, V_r) must be removed, where $i \in \{A_{ku}\}$, $j \in \{A_{kd}\}$ and $r \in \{A_{id}\}$. To reconnect the graph new edges (V_i, V_r) must be created.

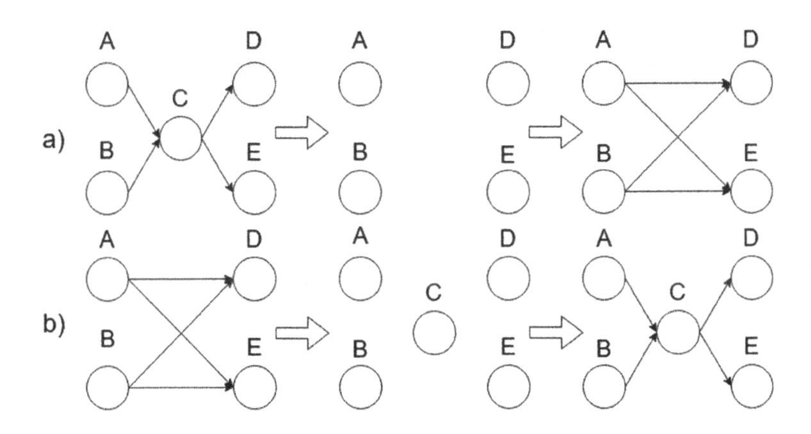

Fig. 3. Process of hiding (a) and showing (b) node C.

Show Nodes. When showing node k all the edges (V_i, V_j) must be removed, where $i \in \{A_{ku}\}$ and $j \in \{A_{kd}\}$. To reconnect the graph new edges (V_i, V_k) and (V_k, V_j) must be created as shown in the Fig. 3b).

As in the case of hiding nodes, it is possible for one of the neighbours to be already hidden. In the case an adjacent up node is hidden, this node's adjacent up nodes are going to be used. When showing node k all the edges (V_l, V_j) must be removed, where $l \in \{A_{iu}\}$, $i \in \{A_{ku}\}$ and $j \in \{A_{kd}\}$. To reconnect the graph new edges (V_l, V_k) and (V_k, V_j) must be created. The same procedure is applied for hidden adjacent down nodes. When showing node k all the edges (V_i, V_r) must be removed, where $i \in \{A_{ku}\}$, $j \in \{A_{kd}\}$ and $r \in \{A_{id}\}$. To reconnect the graph new edges (V_l, V_k) and (V_k, V_j) must be created.

5.4 Simplify Graph Visualization

Whole datasets of production line data from a company can not be managed directly. Querying, retrieving, loading and visualizing whole dataset from a company may exceed the computational resources of regular servers and PCs.

Thus, when the application is launched, only a part of the dataset is loaded and transformed into a graph. This part comprises data about the faulty product and its direct neighbours.

This technique of data filtering is called bottom up approach and the starting point is the node requested by the user, identified by its batch and item number. The navigation is done based on the graph structure, more specifically it shows neighbour nodes up to one level [7].

To expand the graph furthermore, the user needs to interact with the neighbours, which is achieved by clicking on a node. The state of the node clicked changes to current and the neighbours that were not shown will be visible.

The state of the previous node changes from current to visited, meaning that this node can be selected again but it will not have new neighbours.

5.5 Expand Node

As previously stated, the initial graph contains only the nodes that connect to the one specified by the user. As users navigate through the graph, it is possible they require additional information from a different node.

The action to get additional information from a node is called to 'expand node'. The application queries the production line data source (ERP) for additional data related to the currently selected node. If new data is returned, the graph is updated inserting new edges and vertices.

Not all the nodes can be expanded, only batch and MO nodes. These nodes are identified by a '+' icon at the top right corner of the node, as shown in Fig. 4.

Fig. 4. MO node that can be expanded ("+"), and an already expanded batch node.

6 Use Case

This section presents the integration of previous techniques in a final application integrated with the ERP of Zucchetti Group, Izaro. The application has two functionalities: identify the point of failure, and react to the failure.

Users have to enter the batch and item number of the faulty product to enter to the application. Then, the application connects to the ERP using its API to load production line data related to the faulty product. Once data is loaded, the application generates a graph with this data and draws the initial state of the graph, as shown in Fig. 5. The initial graph consists of the provided batch and its neighbours. The position of the neighbours is calculated using the algorithm in Sect. 5.2.

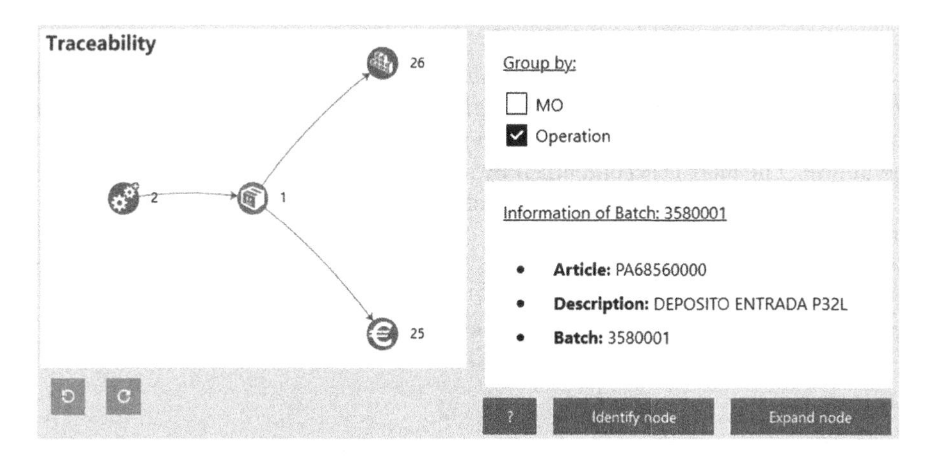

Fig. 5. Main screen of the application showing the graph and components to help the user.

As the user interacts with the graph, the states of the nodes change according to Sect. 5.1. Figure 6 shows an example of a graph where all the nodes have been visited.

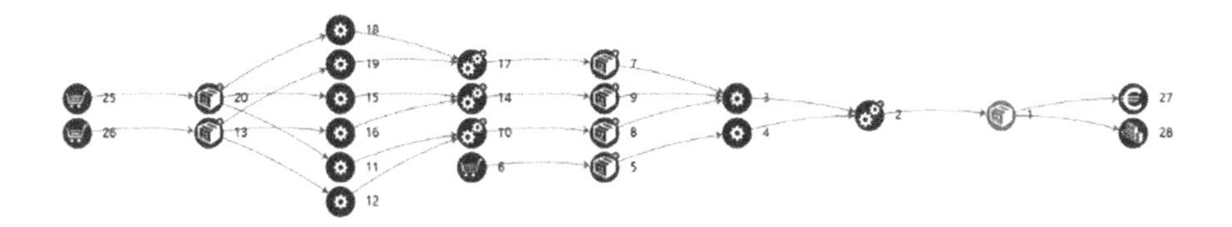

Fig. 6. A fully expanded graph.

Beside the graph, the application has three more components (Fig. 5).

- At the top right corner there is the possibility to group the nodes by MO and operation. As explained in Sect. 5.3, this will hide or show nodes of these categories, simplifying the visualization.
- Below the filtering option, there is a component where the metadata of the selected node is shown.
- The component at the bottom is made up of three buttons. The one with the '?' symbol shows a legend with the meaning of each icon of the nodes, similar to the one in Fig. 1. Expand node button queries for additional information of the selected node, as explained in Sect. 5.5. Identify node button will identify the selected node as the source of failure and the application will change to its second functionality: failure reaction.

Once the failure has been detected, the screen is updated (Fig. 7). The new screen shows information regarding the final nodes (warehouse or delivery note) related to the point of failure.

Left side of the screen shows a simplified graph with the identified node and final nodes related to it. Right side of the screen shows additional information about each final node. Each final node can be selected to send an alert to react to the failure. The alert is accompanied by a message and is sent to the ERP, where it will be redirected to users in charge of the warehouse storing the products or the clients who bought them.

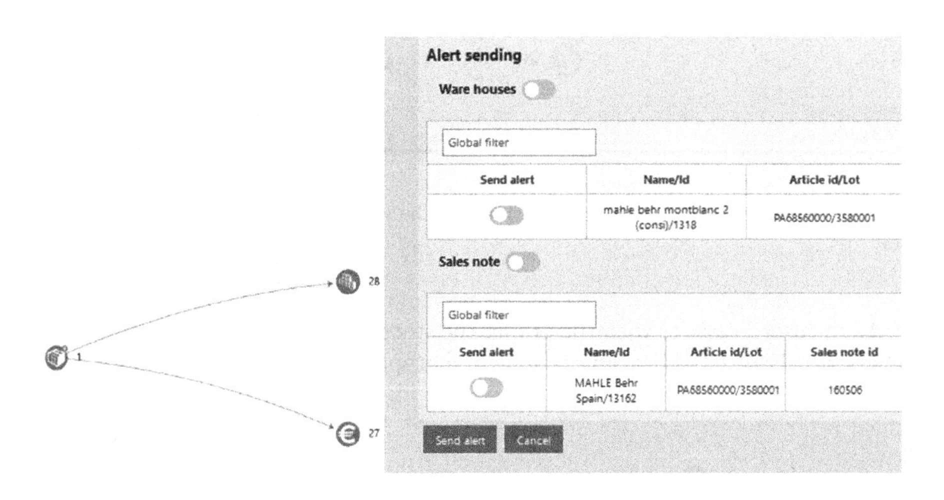

Fig. 7. Screen to react to failures.

7 Future Work

The presented application allows users to navigate through a graph representing a production line to identify failure point. Currently, it only has one way to show the graph but more should be implemented, such as trees [12] or adjacency matrix [5]. Thus, different approaches could be validated for this problem. Moreover, it could be useful to allow users to modify the dataset information or even add new vertices to the graph like in [8].

When then available dataset of production data increases in size with thousands of elements of each category, finding a point of failure navigating the graph could still be cumbersome. Artificial intelligence or machine learning methods should be integrated to assist employees in these cases, for example applying clustering algorithms and detecting data outliers to group similar production processes, detect differences between batches of the same production process, and to propose candidate points of failure. The integration of these approaches will be analyzed when the ERP provides more data about production processes, for example machine data.

Finally, the integration with the ERP provider should be strengthen, and validations by real customers of the ERP should provide feedback to further improve the visualization and interaction techniques.

8 Conclusions

This paper presents a Visual Analytics application for the detection of failures in production lines. Data about the production line has been represented using a directed graph and a data model for the problem has been proposed. A layered layout has been implemented to set the nodes' position, which is based in the nodes' neighbours. Various visualization and interactions techniques have been used and to improve the navigation of the graph, a bottom up approach has been followed.

The application has been integrated with the ERP Izaro of Zucchetti Group, receiving a positive feedback from their employees. The integration of Visual Analytics approaches greatly helps users to navigate and analyze data stored by the ERP, reducing the time required to identify point of failures and to react to solve them.

Acknowledgment. This work has been partially funded by the research projects ANAVIS of the Basque Government's HAZITEK programme.

References

1. ACE: a fast multiscale eigenvectors computation for drawing huge graphs. In: Proceedings of the IEEE Symposium on Information Visualization, INFO VIS 2002, January 2002, pp. 137–144. InfoVis (2002)
2. Arafat, N.A., Bressan, S.: Hypergraph drawing by force-directed placement. In: Benslimane, D., Damiani, E., Grosky, W.I., Hameurlain, A., Sheth, A., Wagner, R.R. (eds.) DEXA 2017. LNCS, vol. 10439, pp. 387–394. Springer, Cham (2017). https://doi.org/10.1007/978-3-319-64471-4_31
3. Díaz, J., Petit, J., Serna, M.: A survey of graph layout problems. ACM Comput. Surv. **34**(3), 313–356 (2002)

4. Dwyer, T., Koren, Y.: Dig-CoLa: directed graph layout through constrained energy minimization. In: 2005 IEEE Symposium on Information Visualization, INFOVIS 2005, pp. 65–72. IEEE (2005)
5. Elmqvis, N., et al.: ZAME: interactive large-scale graph visualization. In: IEEE Pacific Visualization Symposium 2008, PacicVis - Proceeding, pp. 215–222 (2008)
6. van Ham, F., Krishnan, N., et al.: ASK-GraphView: a large scale graph visualization system. IEEE Trans. Vis. Comput. Graph. **12**(5), 669–676 (2006)
7. Heer, J., Boyd, D.: Vizster: visualizing online social networks. In: Proceedings of the IEEE Symposium on Information Visualization, INFO VIS, pp. 33–40 (2005)
8. Henry, N., Fekete, J.D.: MatrixExplorer: a dual-representation system to explore social networks. IEEE Trans. Vis. Comput. Graph. **12**(5), 677–684 (2006)
9. Henry, N., et al.: NodeTrix : a Hybrid visualization of social networks. IEEE Trans. Vis. Comput. Graph. **13**(6), 1302–1309 (2007)
10. Von Landesberger, T., et al.: Visual analysis of large graphs: state-of-the-art and future research challenges. In: Computer Graphics Forum, pp. 1719–1749 (2011)
11. McGuffin, M.J., Jurisica, I.: Interaction techniques for selecting and manipulating subgraphs in network visualizations. IEEE Trans. Vis. Comput. Graph. **15**(6), 937–944 (2009)
12. Schulz, H.J., Hadlak, S., Schumann, H.: Point-based tree representation: a new approach for large hierarchies. In: IEEE Pacific Visualization Symposium, pp. 81–88 (2009)
13. Sun, D., et al.: PlanningVis: a visual analytics approach to production planning in smart factories. IEEE Trans. Vis. Comput. Graph. **26**(1), 579–589 (2020)
14. Van Ham, F., Perer, A.: Search, show context, expand on demand: supporting large graph exploration with degree-of-interest. IEEE Trans. Vis. Comput. Graph. **15**(6), 953–960 (2009)

Missing Data Imputation for Continuous Variables Based on Multivariate Adaptive Regression Splines

Fernando Sánchez Lasheras[1(✉)], Paulino José García Nieto[1], Esperanza García-Gonzalo[1], Francisco Argüeso Gómez[1], Francisco Javier Rodríguez Iglesias[2], Ana Suárez Sánchez[2], Jesús Daniel Santos Rodríguez[3], María Luisa Sánchez[3], Joaquín González-Nuevo[3], Laura Bonavera[3], Luigi Toffolatti[3], Susana del Carmen Fernández Menéndez[4], and Francisco Javier de Cos Juez[2]

[1] Department of Mathematics, Faculty of Sciences, University of Oviedo, c/ Federico García Lorca 18, 33007 Oviedo, Spain
{sanchezfernando, pjgarcia, espe, argueso}@uniovi.es

[2] School of Mining, Energy and Materials Engineering of Oviedo, University of Oviedo, c/ Independencia 13, 33004 Oviedo, Spain
{fjiglesias, suarezana, fjcos}@uniovi.es

[3] Department of Physics, Faculty of Sciences, University of Oviedo, c/ Federico García Lorca 18,, 33007 Oviedo, Spain
{jdsantos, mlsr, gnuevo, bonaveralaura, ltoffolatti}@uniovi.es

[4] Department of Geology, University of Oviedo, c/Jesus Arias de Velasco s/n. 3300, Oviedo, Spain
fernandezmsusana@uniovi.es

Abstract. The problem of missing data in a database is something that causes frequent difficulties for its processing and analysis. This research presents a new missing data methodology based on multivariate adaptive regression splines (MARS) for missing data imputation. The performance of the proposed method is checked using as input information a database created from the hourly records of environmental stations located in the city of Madrid (Spain). Data analyzed corresponds to hourly measurements from 10th February 2004 to 31st May 2010. The proposed methodology has three variants. The first of these makes use of all the available information in order to calculate different MARS models with the ability to predict missing information based on the available data. In the second case, the MARS models are trained after the removal of 1% of the most extreme cases according to Mahalanobis' distances, as they are considered outliers. Finally, the third model proposed makes use of the information corresponding only to the previous month in order to calculate the MARS models for the missing data prediction. The results obtained outperformed those given by multivariate imputation by chained equations (MICE) when applied to the same data sets. For a data set with 20% of its information missing, the proposed algorithm outperforms MICE in RMSE values at least in 65.5% of cases, MAE in 75.2% and MAPE in 76%.

E. A. de la Cal et al. (Eds.): HAIS 2020, LNAI 12344, pp. 73–85, 2020.
https://doi.org/10.1007/978-3-030-61705-9_7

Keywords: Missing Data Imputation · Multivariate Adaptive Regression Splines (MARS) · Multiple Imputation by Chained Equations (MICE) · Pollutants

1 Introduction

1.1 Missing Data Imputation

The problem of missing data in a database is something that causes frequent difficulties for its statistical analysis and processing. Since the 1990s, however, there have been important advances in the analysis of missing information. In order to deal with this issue, it is necessary to establish what the mechanism is that generates the missing data. The three main categories of missing data are as follows [1]:

- **Missing completely at random (MCAR):** missing data is completely at random when the likelihood that data is missing is not related either to the value of the data or the variable that it belongs to, in the case of a multivariate data set.
- **Missing at random (MAR):** missing data is at random when the probability that data is missing depends on the value of the data that is observed. An example of a data set with MAR information would be a clinical study where a patient is removed from the study when one of his/her variables reaches a certain value.
- **Not missing at random data (NMAR):** this is the case when the missing information follows a certain pattern.

In order to analyze a data set with missing data, it is necessary to employ some kind of data imputation technique. There are simple methodologies, such as imputing using mean or median values or even replacing missing data for the most frequent values in each variable. There are also other more sophisticated methodologies like the one used in this research, called Multivariate Imputation by Chained Equations (MICE) [2], which has proved in the past to perform well [3]. Other methods that are employed nowadays are those that assumes a parametric density function on the data given models [4] and imputes missing data under such supposition. There are also imputation methods that makes use of support vector regression [5] and even methods based on random forest has been applied with promising results [6].

1.2 The Aim of the Present Research

The aim of the present research is to develop a new method for missing data imputation, one suitable for imputing continuous variables. More specifically, this new methodology is based on Multivariate Adaptive Regression Splines (MARS) and is able to beat in many cases MICE that was specifically developed for missing data imputation. The performance of the proposed methodology has been tested with the help of a database that corresponds to air pollution. The reason for making this choice is that such databases usually have a large amount of information that comes from different variables (pollutants) recorded at different air pollution monitoring stations and in many cases part of the information can be missing due to, say, sensor failure. Therefore, we have a data base with a large amount of information and likely to have missing data.

2 Materials and Methods

2.1 The Data Base

Nowadays, air pollution is a world-wide concern, one linked to approximately 3.8 million deaths per year, according to data from the World Health Organization [7]. Also, it must be considered that a good part of the population in the Western World lives in urban areas where air quality levels pose serious health risks. Therefore, reducing air pollution continues to be a vitally important issue. The end of the global economic crisis that started with the financial crisis of 2007–2008 [8] has provoked a rise in air pollution in recent years, mainly in underdeveloped countries. The most remarkable situation is that of the two most populated countries in the World, China and India, where nowadays urban areas present significantly high levels of air pollution.

Due to the importance of air pollution, most metropolitan areas in the world have a network of air pollution monitoring stations. A case in point is Madrid, the capital of Spain, which with 3,223,334 inhabitants in 2018 and an area of 604,45 km^2 has a total of 24 air pollution monitoring stations managed by the city council. The database employed in this research is formed by the hourly records of two environmental stations located in the city of Madrid (Spain). To be more precise, they are the stations with references 28079024, called *Casa de Campo*, and 28079060, called *Tres Olivos*. We have also analyzed the information recorded under the code 28079099, which represents the average value for all the available environmental stations. Data analyzed corresponds to hourly measurements from 10th February 2004 to 31st May 2010. This means that more than 55,000 hourly records for each variable and environmental station will be employed. The reason why these two stations were chosen is that they are the two in Madrid that record the largest number of pollutants. For the present research, the following pollutants measured in $\mu g/m^3$ are employed: benzene (BEN), carbon monoxide (CO), ethylbenzene (EBE), meta-xylene (MXY), nitrogen dioxide (NO_2), nitrogen oxides (NO_x), ozone (O_3), ortho-xylene (OXY), particulate matter 10 microns or less (PM_{10}), particulate matter 2.5 microns or less ($PM_{2.5}$), paraxylene (PXY), sulfur dioxide (SO_2) and toluene (TOL). Two other variables measured in mg/m^3 are also analyzed: non-methane hydrocarbons (NMHC) and hexane (TCH). Those hourly measurements with any missing data have been removed, as in this research the performance of the proposed methods must be tested using a database in which missing data is created by removing existing information in order to be able to compare real values with the forecasted ones. Finally, please note that in the case of the average values of all the environmental stations, due to the fact that not all the pollutants are recorded by all the stations, the information corresponds to the average value of the stations where the value of the pollutant is available.

2.2 Multivariate Imputation by Chained Equations (MICE)

Multivariate Imputation by Chained Equations (MICE) is a data imputation methodology developed for data imputation in those cases of MAR. It means that missing information only depends on the information that is present in the database. MICE methodology has proved its performance in large data sets [9, 10].

In the MICE methodology, imputation is performed in consecutive steps. This method requires three main steps, called imputation, analysis and pooling. The analysis always starts with an observed incomplete data set Y_{obs} in which missing data is replaced by plausible values. The second step consists of calculating a coefficient called Q, usually a vector of coefficients for each of the imputed data sets. The last step involves pooling all the estimated Q values into an average $\bar{Q}$ and calculating their variance. The three steps are then repeated.

In the case of the present research, five different imputation methods allowed by MICE are employed: mean imputation (*mean*), Bayesian linear regression (*Norm*), linear regression ignoring model error (*Norm nob*) [11], predictive mean matching (PMM) [12] and sample (*random samples for observed values*). In all the methods 5 iterations with 5 imputations each were programmed as in the original research of van Buuren and Groothuis-Oudshoorn [2]. Please note that higher numbers of iterations and imputations were also tested but without any improvement in the results.

2.3 Multivariate Adaptive Regression Splines (MARS)

Multivariate Adaptive Regression Splines is a methodology for flexible regression modeling of high-dimensional data that was originally developed by Friedman [13]. MARS models are able to model an output variable using as input information the value of the function in a certain number of points of a space with as many dimensions as the number of input variables.

By means of MARS methodology, it is possible to obtain a model $\hat{y} = f(x_1, \ldots, x_n) + \varepsilon$ over a domain $(x_1, \ldots, x_n) \in D \subset \mathbb{R}^n$ that contains all the data. Please note that ε represents the model noise. The MARS method is linked to recursive partitioning regression [14] but overcomes some of its limitations, such as continuity, for example.

In general, a MARS model is expressed by the following equation:

$$\hat{f}(\boldsymbol{x}) = \sum_{i=1}^{k} c_i \cdot B_i(\boldsymbol{x}) \tag{1}$$

Where $\hat{f}(\boldsymbol{x})$ is the approach of the $f(\boldsymbol{x})$ over the domain D, c_i are constant coefficients and the basis functions of the model are represented by $B_i(\boldsymbol{x})$. A basis function is a product of one or more hinge functions; each hinge function is expressed as $\mathrm{h}(x - c)$ or $\mathrm{h}(c - x)$ where c is a constant value called a knot. Hinge functions expresses as follows:

$$h(x - c)\begin{cases} x - c \; if \; x > c \\ 0 \; if \; x \leq c \end{cases} \tag{2}$$

In the case of the models employed for the present research, the maximum degree allowed was 9. It means that in each addend the maximum number of variables that can interact is equal to nine. For each model, the maximum number of terms before pruning was of 21 and the forward stepping threshold value was of 10^{-8}. Please note that it means that the forward stepping process must terminate if adding a term changes the model R^2 less than the threshold value.

2.4 Performance Measurements

In order to assess the performance of the different missing data imputation methods root mean squared error (RMSE), mean absolute error (MAE) and mean absolute percentage error (MAPE) are employed [15].

$$RMSE = \sqrt{\frac{1}{n}\sum\nolimits_{i=1}^{n} (\hat{x}_i - x_i)^2} \quad (3)$$

Equation 3 represents the root mean squared error, where n is the number of available observations, $\hat{x}_i$ is the i-th forecasted value and x_i is the i-th real value. Equation 4 shows the formula of MAE and Eq. 5 the formula of MAPE. In both formulae the meaning of the variable is the same as in Eq. 3.

$$MAE = \frac{1}{n}\sum\nolimits_{i=1}^{n} |\hat{x}_i - x_i| \quad (4)$$

$$MAPE = \frac{1}{n}\sum\nolimits_{i=1}^{n} \frac{|\hat{x}_i - x_i|}{x_i} \quad (5)$$

2.5 Mahalanobis Distance

In this work the outlier detection is performed with the help of the Mahalanobis distance. Let $\boldsymbol{x}$ be an observation that belongs to the domain $D \subset \mathbb{R}^n$ and let us consider $\boldsymbol{\mu}$ as an n-dimensional vector of the means of all the vectors of the data set. The Mahalanobis distance of vector $\boldsymbol{x}$ is expressed as follows [16]:

$$D_M = \sqrt{(\boldsymbol{x} - \boldsymbol{\mu})^T \cdot S^{-1} (\boldsymbol{x} - \boldsymbol{\mu})} \quad (6)$$

Where S represents the covariance matrix of data.

2.6 The Proposed Algorithm

The proposed algorithm is based on the MARS method. It uses all the rows without missing data as input information in order to train a set of MARS models for each of the variables considered. As in the same row more than one piece of data would be missing, all the possible models that make use of a different subset of variables are trained, employing all the available information for each one. For example, if we want to predict the value of BEN, the model to be trained is the one formed by the rest of the variables: CO, EBE, MXY, NO_2, NO_x, O_3, OXY, PM_{10}, $PM_{2.5}$, PXY, SO_2, TOL, NMHC and TCH, but it is possible that the values of, for example, O_3 and PM_{10} are missing. Therefore, a model that only employs CO, EBE, MXY, NO_2, NO_x, OXY, $PM_{2.5}$, PXY, SO_2, TOL, NMHC and TCH should also be trained, and the same can be applied for the rest of the combinations of variables. In a row where more than one variable is missing, the first variable to be imputed is the variable with the lowest percentage of missing data in the total data set.

Figure 1 represents a sketch of the proposed algorithm applied to a case with five variables and nine rows with missing data information, in order to illustrate how the model will be trained. In this case, in which five different variables are considered, a model for each variable using the other four will be trained. These models are as follows: $V_1 = f(V_2, V_3, V_4, V_5)$, $V_2 = f(V_1, V_3, V_4, V_5)$, $V_3 = f(V_1, V_2, V_4, V_5)$, $V_4 = f(V_1, V_2, V_3, V_5)$ and $V_5 = f(V_1, V_2, V_3, V_4)$. In the case of this example, these models can be trained using information from rows 1, 7 and 9. In the case of variable V_1, that model will not be employed as there is no missing information. Please note that none of the models that will not be employed need to be trained. For example, in row 4 there are two missing variables V_2 and V_4. We will start imputing the variable with less missing data. In this case, as both have the same amount of missing data in the whole dataset, the variable to be imputed first will be selected at random. The model to be trained will be $V_2 = f(V_1, V_3, V_5)$, which will make use of data from rows 1, 2, 7, 8 and 9 and $V_4 = f(V_1, V_3, V_5)$, trained with the information from rows 1, 5, 6, 7 and 9.

	V_1	V_2	V_3	V_4	V_5
1-	X	X	X	X	X
2-	X	X	X	O	X
3-	X	X	O	X	X
4-	X	O	X	O	X
5-	X	O	X	X	X
6-	X	O	X	X	X
7-	X	X	X	X	X
8-	X	X	X	O	X
9-	X	X	X	X	X

Fig. 1. Example of variables with missing data

According to the sketch seen in Fig. 1, and taking into account that the total amount of variables is 15, the total number of models to be trained is equal to the sum of the combinations of the n variables selected from 15, with n from 1 to 14 and all multiplied by 15. It follows the equation:

$$\sum_{n=1}^{14} 15 \cdot \frac{14!}{n! \cdot (14 - n)!} \quad (7)$$

Therefore, in this case, the maximum number of models to be trained would be up to 245,745. In those cases where all the data in a row is missing, values will be found with the help of linear interpolation using the rows above and below.

3 Results

3.1 Performance of MICE

This section analyzes the results obtained imputing data with the help of the MICE method. For each level of missing data (1%, 5%, 10%, 15% and 20%), 100 repetitions were performed. Table 1 shows the median values of RMSE, MAE and MAPE for the five different percentages of missing data employed in the study. As can be expected, the greater the amount of missing data, the higher the values of RMSE, MAE and MAPE. As data does not follow a normal distribution, the non-parametric Kruskal-Wallis test was applied and found statistically-significant differences in medians for RMSE ($H = 403.66, df = 4, p < 0.001$), MAE ($H = 588.47, df = 4, p < 0.001$) and MAPE ($H = 936.68, df = 4, p < 0.001$) among different missing data percentages. This was the expected result.

Table 1. Median values of RMSE, MAE and MAPE for the five different percentages of missing data employed for MICE imputation in the study.

Percentage	RMSE	MAE	MAPE
1%	2.44	1.79	0.54
5%	3.09	2.23	0.58
10%	3.50	2.43	0.60
15%	4.20	2.54	0.64
20%	4.37	2.66	0.67

As the worst RMSE, MAE and MAPE values are obtained for the case in which 20% of data are missing, Table 2 shows the median values of RMSE, MAE and MAPE for the five different algorithms internally employed by MICE for the imputation. In this case, there are also statistically-significant differences in medians among groups for RMSE ($H = 363.29, df = 4, p<0.001$), MAE ($H = 327.02, df = 4, p<0.001$) and MAPE ($H = 3845.77, df = 4, p<0.001$). The results given by Tukey's *post hoc* test shows that there are no statistically significant differences for RMSE among *norm*, *norm nob* and *PMM* algorithms. Despite this, the same test found that for MAE and MAPE, the results obtained for the *PMM* algorithm were better. These results led us to the conclusion that the comparison of the performance of the new algorithm will be performed using the 100 sets that have 20% of information missing and using MICE with the *PMM* algorithm as a benchmark, as this was the one with the best performance among the MICE.

Table 2. Median values of RMSE, MAE and MAPE for the five different imputation methods employed by MICE algorithm.

Method	RMSE	MAE	MAPE
Mean	2.85	1.91	0.81
Norm	1.91	1.26	0.62
Norm nob	1.85	1.24	0.63
PMM	1.83	1.02	0.43
Sample	4.08	2.61	1.04

3.2 Performance of the Proposed Algorithm

In order to contrast the performance of the proposed algorithm when compared to MICE, the Mann-Whitney test was applied to find differences in the median values obtained with both methods. As was stated in the previous section, the data corresponds to a set of 100 repetitions of the experiment. For RMSE, the median value of MICE was 1.83 while for the proposed algorithm it was 0.91. These differences were statically significant ($W = 18168070, p < 0.001$). The same happened with the results obtained for this test in the cases of MAE ($W = 17908068.5, p < 0.001$) and MAPE ($W = 8569379, p < 0.001$), as both differences were statistically significant. Please note that in the case of MAE, the median was 1.02 for MICE and 0.39 for the proposed algorithm, while for MAPE the result obtained was 0.43 for MICE and 0.21 for the proposed algorithm. Table 3 shows the number of cases from a total of 100 repetitions that the proposed algorithm outperformed MICE for RMSE, MAE and MAPE in meteorological stations 28079006, 28079024 and the average values of all the meteorological stations in Madrid. In this case, the percentage of missing data considered was 20% as it is the least favorable case. According to the results, in all the cases and metrics, the performance of MARS was better than MICE. Also, it is remarkable that the percentage of outperformance is higher in the values of the average station when compared with MICE.

Table 3. Number of cases from a total of 100 repetitions that the proposed algorithm performed better than MICE for RMSE, MAE and MAPE in meteorological stations 28079006, 28079024 and in the average values of all the meteorological stations in Madrid expressed as a percentage. Missing data 20%.

	28079006			28079024			Madrid average		
	RMSE	MAE	MAPE	RMSE	MAE	MAPE	RMSE	MAE	MAPE
BEN	51%	70%	74%	63%	75%	91%	74%	90%	92%
CO	59%	67%	69%	79%	86%	85%	83%	89%	94%
EBE	54%	76%	81%	64%	80%	87%	65%	80%	91%
MXY	63%	83%	84%	65%	77%	92%	77%	95%	96%
NMHC	60%	77%	76%	87%	89%	85%	80%	92%	92%
NO2	70%	83%	85%	53%	73%	91%	84%	95%	94%
NOX	66%	77%	86%	67%	81%	91%	88%	94%	97%
O3	92%	92%	74%	72%	76%	63%	86%	86%	87%
OXY	47%	70%	71%	60%	72%	84%	69%	91%	93%
PM10	72%	79%	83%	67%	80%	79%	78%	90%	92%
PM2.5	60%	71%	77%	67%	77%	79%	89%	92%	92%
PXY	68%	81%	76%	76%	91%	96%	79%	88%	89%
SO2	59%	65%	63%	72%	76%	76%	73%	81%	84%
THC	70%	745	76%	76%	81%	82%	66%	78%	99%
TOL	47%	63%	65%	56%	73%	91%	69%	81%	83%
Average	62.53%	75.20%	76.00%	68.27%	79.13%	84.80%	77.33%	88.13%	91.67%

Taking into account that the MARS model presents better results for the Madrid average data, a new model was proposed. It also followed the methodology described in Sect. 2.6 but in this case, before training the models, 1% of the most extreme values according to Mahalanobis' distances were considered outliers and removed. The model was applied to different data sets for missing data levels of 1%, 5%, 10%, 15% and 20%. The results obtained (Table 4) did not outperform the original proposal with the exception of the MAPE metric, which improved the original proposed methodology from a minimum of 65.5% for 1% of missing data to a maximum 75.3% for 15% of missing information, obtaining on average an improvement of 68.8%.

Table 4. Number of cases from a total of 100 repetitions that the proposed algorithm with a removal of 1% of the most extreme outliers performed better than the proposed algorithm without outlier removal expressed as a percentage, applied to the average values of all the meteorological stations in Madrid. Missing data 1%, 5%, 10%, 15% and 20%.

	Madrid average														
	RMSE					MAE					MAPE				
	1%	5%	10%	15%	20%	1%	5%	10%	15%	20%	1%	5%	10%	15%	20%
BEN	20%	35%	10%	10%	10%	20%	45%	35%	40%	25%	94%	93%	63%	93%	94%
CO	5%	10%	5%	0%	0%	45%	25%	15%	15%	30%	88%	60%	29%	55%	39%
EBE	35%	25%	15%	5%	5%	90%	70%	25%	40%	45%	100%	100%	95%	95%	100%
MXY	20%	15%	5%	15%	10%	40%	35%	25%	45%	40%	90%	100%	100%	95%	95%
NMHC	0%	0%	0%	0%	0%	5%	5%	5%	5%	5%	65%	68%	66%	75%	69%
NO2	5%	0%	0%	0%	0%	5%	0%	0%	5%	5%	32%	10%	16%	15%	26%
NOX	10%	20%	10%	10%	0%	45%	70%	50%	55%	15%	79%	90%	90%	79%	80%
O3	0%	0%	0%	5%	0%	10%	0%	0%	0%	0%	10%	68%	66%	75%	69%
OXY	30%	0%	5%	10%	10%	60%	30%	15%	30%	30%	90%	89%	88%	89%	100%
PM10	0%	10%	10%	5%	5%	10%	40%	35%	25%	10%	35%	33%	47%	71%	37%
PM2.5	5%	5%	5%	20%	5%	35%	30%	15%	30%	35%	65%	56%	57%	93%	67%
PXY	25%	35%	5%	20%	20%	90%	80%	85%	60%	80%	95%	94%	100%	100%	100%
SO2	0%	0%	0%	0%	10%	5%	0%	0%	5%	10%	10%	5%	20%	25%	15%
THC	10%	20%	5%	15%	15%	80%	100%	90%	80%	95%	65%	100%	66%	100%	69%
TOL	5%	0%	0%	0%	0%	10%	5%	0%	5%	0%	65%	57%	92%	69%	71%
Average	11.3%	11.7%	5.0%	7.7%	6.0%	36.7%	35.7%	26.3%	29.3%	28.3%	65.5%	68.2%	66.3%	75.3%	68.7%

Finally, another variation on the originally proposed algorithm was performed. It consisted of using only information belonging to the previous month to the row with the missing data to be imputed for training the different MARS models. In other words, a local model is created that is recalculated for each row that contains missing information using all the available information of the previous month as its training data set. It means that considering a month of 30 days and 24 measurements per day, a maximum of 720 rows would be employed for training each MARS model, but all those rows with missing information that does not allow to create the required MARS model will not be employed. For example, in the worst case imputing a row would mean imputing 14 missing variables, as we should have information about at least one variable as if not we will use linear interpolation. It means training a total of 14 different MARS models. All the models employed for this study were calculated in a computer with 32 GB RAM memory and a processor Intel ® Core ™ i7-7700 CPU @ 3.60 GHz. The average time required for computing each one of those MARS models that make use only of the information of the previous month was of 0.151 s while that the average time consumed for the calculation of each one of those MARS models that makes use of all the available information was of 8.236 s each.

For the case of the present research, with 55 000 rows and 15 columns, 7 322 different MARS models were trained with the first proposed methodology. It supposed 60 303.992 s while in the case of using MARS models trained with the information of the month before a total of 53 036 models were trained which required of 8 310.436 s.

The results of this new proposed methodology can be seen in Table 5, where it may be seen that the MAE and MAPE results outperformed those of the proposed algorithm for all the percentages of missing data checked, but in the case of RMSE this only occurred for missing data percentages 1%, 5% and 10%.

Table 5. Number of cases from a total of 100 repetitions that the algorithm that makes use of the information from the previous month performed better than the proposed algorithm, applied to the average values of all the meteorological stations in Madrid. Missing data 1%, 5%, 10%, 15% and 20%.

	Madrid average														
	RMSE					MAE					MAPE				
	1%	5%	10%	15%	20%	1%	5%	10%	15%	20%	1%	5%	10%	15%	20%
BEN	83%	74%	60%	57%	44%	83%	98%	93%	94%	97%	97%	93%	94%	93%	92%
CO	92%	97%	97%	100%	97%	99%	100%	100%	100%	98%	100%	100%	99%	98%	100%
EBE	34%	41%	40%	34%	27%	83%	81%	73%	79%	90%	100%	86%	76%	71%	59%
MXY	59%	54%	47%	46%	37%	92%	88%	90%	95%	94%	100%	100%	99%	92%	92%
NMHC	92%	77%	60%	49%	30%	98%	99%	100%	98%	98%	90%	77%	82%	79%	77%
NO2	42%	39%	27%	26%	24%	89%	82%	81%	79%	74%	100%	72%	62%	57%	42%
NOX	67%	69%	70%	67%	57%	99%	98%	99%	98%	97%	97%	97%	92%	87%	75%
O3	75%	84%	90%	84%	74%	99%	98%	99%	98%	97%	94%	80%	77%	78%	75%
OXY	83%	62%	37%	41%	37%	98%	98%	99%	81%	77%	92%	86%	84%	72%	56%
PM10	59%	46%	30%	29%	20%	89%	78%	77%	76%	64%	78%	75%	72%	71%	68%
PM2.5	59%	38%	13%	15%	17%	78%	67%	57%	55%	50%	90%	82%	80%	79%	75%
PXY	75%	62%	47%	50%	44%	89%	85%	83%	84%	77%	100%	90%	89%	82%	83%
SO2	100%	100%	90%	89%	80%	100%	99%	98%	99%	98%	100%	100%	90%	75%	75%
THC	75%	59%	33%	27%	17%	78%	89%	87%	73%	64%	90%	73%	71%	64%	54%
TOL	59%	46%	33%	21%	7%	74%	72%	68%	63%	48%	90%	93%	77%	74%	50%
Average	70.3%	63.2%	51.6%	49.0%	40.8%	89.9%	88.8%	86.9%	84.8%	81.5%	94.5%	86.9%	82.9%	78.1%	71.5%

4 Discussion and Conclusions

This work presents a new missing data methodology based on MARS for the imputation of missing data. The performance of this novel method is verified using MICE as a benchmark methodology. Also, two different kinds of improvements to the proposed method are presented. The first consists of considering the most extreme data as outliers and removing them from the database for the model training. This proposal does not improve in a considerable way the original algorithm except for the MAPE metric. The second variant involves considering only the information that belongs to the previous month as the data set available for building the models that are required. In this case, the results obtained improved the MAE and MAPE of the original algorithm for all the percentages of missing data employed in this research, but in the case of RMSE this only occurred for missing data percentages 1%, 5% and 10%. From the point of view of the authors these second variant would be of great interest in practical applications, as, in the case of the data base employed in this study, the time required for computing each model that makes use only of the information of the previous month was 50 times less than the time for each MARS model that makes use of all the available information. Please note that the total time required will depend on how missing data are placed inside the database.

Finally, although the algorithm has been applied to environmental data, due to the importance of the issue and the availability of information, this is not an ad *hoc algorithm* and therefore, it could be applied to any data set with continuous variables. Despite these, more experiments with additional datasets need to be arranged in order to generalize the proposed method. One of the possible areas in which to apply this model might be in stock and raw materials markets [17, 18]. This case is especially suitable as it makes use of large data sets of continuous variables.

Acknowledgements. Laura Bonavera, Luigi Toffolatti and Joaquín González-Nuevo acknowledge financial support from the PGC 2018 project PGC2018-101948-B-I00 (MICINN, FEDER) and PAPI-19-EMERG-11 (Universidad de Oviedo). Joaquín González-Nuevo acknowledges financial support from the Spanish MINECO for the 'Ramon y Cajal' fellowship (RYC-2013-13256). Susana del Carmen Fernández Menéndez ackowledges financial Support from PERMASNOW CTM2014-52021-R from the Spanish MINECO.

References

1. Rubin, D.B.: Inference and missing data. Biometrika **63**, 581–592 (1976)
2. van Buuren, S., Groothuis-Oudshoorn, K.: mice: multivariate imputation by chained equations in R. J. Stat. Softw. **45**(3), 1–67 (2011)
3. Ordóñez Galán, C., Sánchez Lasheras, F., de Cos Juez, F.J., Bernardo Sánchez, A.: Missing data imputation of questionnaires by means of genetic algorithms with different fitness functions. J. Comput. Appl. Math. **311**, 704–717 (2017)
4. Honaker, J., King, G., Blackwell, M.: Amelia II: a program for missing data. J. Stat. Softw. **45**(7), 1–47 (2011)
5. Wang, X., Li, A., Jiang, Z., Feng, H.: Missing value estimation for DNA microarray gene expression data by support vector regression imputation and orthogonal coding scheme. BMC Bioinform. **7**(1), 1 (2006)
6. Stekhoven, D.J., Bühlmann, P.: Missforest: non-parametric missing value imputation for mixed-type data. Bioinformatics **28**(1), 112–118 (2012)
7. World Health Organization. Health, environment, and sustainable development. Airpollution. https://www.who.int/sustainable-development/cities/health-risks/air-pollution/en/. Accessed 07 Jan 2020
8. Iglesias García, C., et al.: Effects of the economic crisis on demand due to mental disorders in Asturias: data from the asturias cumulative psychiatric case register (2000–2010). Actas Esp. Psiquiatr. **42**, 108–115 (2014)
9. He, Y., Zaslavsky, A.M., Landrum, M.B., Harrington, D.P., Catalano, P.: Multiple imputation in a large-scale complex survey: a practical guide. Stat. Meth. Med. Res. **19**(6), 1–18 (2009)
10. Stuart, E.A., Azur, M., Frangakis, C.E., Leaf, P.J.: Practical imputation with large data sets: A case study of the children's mental health initiative. Am. J. Epidemiol. **169**, 1133–1139 (2009)
11. Rubin, D.B.: Multiple Imputation for Nonresponse in Surveys. John Wiley & Sons, New York (1987)
12. Morris, T.P., Ian, R.W., Patrick, R.: Tuning multiple imputation by predictive mean matching and local residual draws. BMC Med. Res. Methodol. **14**, 75–87 (2014)
13. Friedman, J.H.: Multivariate adaptive regression splines. Ann. Stat. **19**(1), 1–67 (1991)
14. Scott, B.G.: Partition regression. J. Am. Stat. Assoc. **69**(348), 945–947 (1974)
15. Pérez-Pevida, E., et al.: Biomechanical consequences of the elastic properties of dental implant alloys on the supporting bone: finite element analysis. BioMed Res. Int., 1–9 (2016)
16. de Cos Juez, F.J., Sánchez Lasheras, F., Roqueñí, N., Osborn, J.: An ANN-based smart tomographic reconstructor in a dynamic environment. Sensors **12**(7), 8895–8911 (2012)

17. Sánchez Lasheras, F., de Cos Juez, F.J., Suárez Sánchez, A., Krzemień, A., Riesgo Fernández, P.: Forecasting the COMEX copper spot price by means of neural networks and ARIMA models. Res. Policy **45**, 37–43 (2015)
18. Riesgo García, M.V., Krzemień, A., Manzanedo del Campo, M.A., Escanciano García-Miranda, C., Sánchez Lasheras, F.: Rare earth elements price forecasting by means of transgenic time series developed with ARIMA models. Res. Policy **59**, 95–102 (2018)

Clustering and Regression to Impute Missing Values of Robot Performance

Ángel Arroyo(✉), Nuño Basurto, Carlos Cambra, and Álvaro Herrero

Grupo de Inteligencia Computacional Aplicada (GICAP),
Departamento de Ingeniería Informática, Escuela Politécnica Superior,
Universidad de Burgos, Av. Cantabria s/n, 09006 Burgos, Spain
{aarroyop,nbasurto,ccbaseca,ahcosio}@ubu.es

Abstract. It is widely claimed that a major challenge in Robotics is to get reliable systems while both response and down times are minimized. In keeping with this idea, present paper proposes the application of a Hybrid Artificial Intelligence System (HAIS) to preprocess data with the aim of improving the detection of performance anomalies. One of the main problems when analyzing real-life data is the presence of missing values. It is usually solved by removing incomplete data, what causes a loss of information that may be critical in some domains. As an alternative, present paper proposes the application of regression models to impute those missing values. Prediction is optimized by generating personalized models on previously clustered data. Experiments are run on a public and up-to-date dataset that contains information about anomalies affecting the component-based software of a robot. The obtained results validate the proposed HAIS, as it successfully imputes missing values from the different features in the original dataset.

Keywords: Hybrid intelligent system · Machine learning · Clustering · Regression · Missing values · Robot software

1 Introduction

Robotics is acknowledged as one of the most promising technological fields, being a meeting point of some different disciplines such as cinematic, mechatronics, electronics, and artificial intelligence. In fact, 384,000 industrial units have been sold in the world in just one year (31% increase) as reported by the Industrial Federation of Robotics [10]. Furthermore, the annual sales volume of industrial robots have been increasing for several years in a row. Although the complexity of robots has been growing too, the demands for robustness and reliability are increasing as well. However, robots suffer from failures, as any cyber-physical system, that may cause high economic loss. To prevent them and reduce downtime, anomaly detection [13] is required, although not enough effort has been devoted to it from the scientific community so far [15].

There is a major shortcoming when trying to process (i.e. classify) real data coming from sensors in order to detect anomalies: the presence of Missing Values

E. A. de la Cal et al. (Eds.): HAIS 2020, LNAI 12344, pp. 86–94, 2020.
https://doi.org/10.1007/978-3-030-61705-9_8

(MV) [6], that must be overcame [4]. This issue is addressed in present paper, where clustering and regression are combined in order to impute the MV in a dataset gathered from the performance indicators of a robot. Although failure detection has been previously performed in this dataset [3,21], present work goes one step further, proposing the imputation of MV rather than deleting them [2], in order to improve the failure detection rate.

As an advantage for industrial companies [9], Machine Learning has been successfully applied in different fields up to now [12]. Researchers have previously dealt with the MV in robot data, as in the case of [19], in which a probabilistic approach is used, based on the a-priori probability of each value determined from the instances in that node which have specified values. Robot failures are detected by applying a well-known classifier: a Decision Tree. The classifier is applied to all available data collected from the sensors of the robot; it does not matter the type of attribute (whether numeric or nominal). The author applied and compared different imputation techniques for handling the MV. As opposed to this previous work, present paper deals with the software of a robot and strategies for clustering data before imputation.

The rest of this paper is organized as follows: the applied techniques (clustering and imputation) are described in Sect. 2 while the analyzed case study is described in Sect. 3. The setup of performed experiments and the obtained results are presented in Sect. 4. Finally, Sect. 5 introduces the main conclusions derived from present research and points outs some proposals for future work.

2 Proposed Hybrid System

As previously stated, clustering and regression methods are combined to impute MV. More precisely, experiments have been run with the k-means clustering technique, a simple regression technique, and an Artificial Neural Network (ANN) regressor. These techniques are described in the following subsections.

2.1 k-Means

Cluster analysis [11] organizes data, grouping data samples according to a given criteria distance. Two individuals in a valid group will be much more similar than those in different groups. The k-means clustering algorithm [16] groups data samples into a previously defined number of groups. Two input parameters are required: the number of clusters (k) and their initial centroids. Firstly, each data sample is assigned to the cluster with the nearest centroid. Once the groups are defined, the centroids are recalculated and a reallocation of the samples takes place. Those steps are repeated until there is no further modification of the centroids. The quality criterion to measure the grouping is the Sum of Squared Errors (SSE). The algorithm intended to minimize it can be defined as follows:

$$SSE = \sum_{j=1}^{k} \sum_{x \epsilon G_i} p(x_i, c_j)/n \tag{1}$$

where, k is the number of groups, p is the proximity function, c_j is the centroid of group j, and n is the number of data samples. From among all the proposed distances the Cosine distance was selected, which is defined as one minus the cosine of the included angle between points (treated as vectors).

$$d(x-c) = 1 - xc/\sqrt{(xx')(cc')} \tag{2}$$

In the run experiments, the Means + + algorithm has been used for the initialization of centroids.

2.2 Regression Techniques

In the proposed HAIS, once data is clustered, regressors are applied to the defined clusters in order to get more accurate results, according to "local models" perspective. In general terms, regression tries to model the relationship between two or more variables in the dataset by fitting a linear equation to the input data. One or more of the variables are the predictor variable, and the other variable is considered to be the criterion variable [24]. The target of multiple regressions [18] is to learn more about the relationship between the independent or predictor variables and a dependent or criterion variable(s), when such relationships can be linear or non-linear.

Non-linear Regression. Non-Linear Regression (N-LR) is a regression algorithm in which observational data are modeled by a function which is a non-linear combination of the input data and depends on one or more criterion variables [17]. The parameters can take the form of an exponential, trigonometric, power, or any type of non-linear function. To determine the non-linear parameter values, an iterative algorithm is commonly used. The model can be defined as:

$$y = f(X, \beta) + \varepsilon \tag{3}$$

where β represents a non-linear parameter estimates to be computed, X is the dependent variables and ϵ represents the error terms.

Multilayer Perceptron. The well-known ANN are simplified models of natural neural systems. The following definition, given by Hecht - Nielsen in 1988 [8], formalizes the concept: "An ANN is a parallel processing computer system distributed, consisting of a set of elementary processing units equipped with a small local memory and interconnected in a network through connections with associated weights. Each processing unit has one or more input connections and a single output connection that links to many collateral connections as desired. All processing associated with an elementary unit is a local, i.e. depends only on the values that take input signals from the unit and the internal state of the sam". Multilayer Perceptrons (MLPs), adjusted to such definition, have been applied in present study. MLPs consist of a system of layered interconnected neurons or nodes. They are connected by weights and output signals which are a function of the sum of the inputs to the node modified by a simple activation, function. The architecture consists of several layers of neurons; the input layer serves to pass the input vector to the network. The terms called as "input vectors" and "output vectors" refer to the inputs and outputs of the MLP and can be represented as single vectors [7]. The MLP must implement at least one or more hidden layers, and additionally there is an output layer. MLPs are fully connected, with each node connected to every node in the next and previous layer. One of the critical issues of such model is the training (update) of all the weights as the error can be calculated in the output but weights in all layers must be updated. To solve such problem, backpropagation was proposed and several different algorithms implement it.

The Bayesian Regularization (BR) [5] version of backpropagation is applied in this study. This algorithm aims at improving the model's generalization capability, expanding the objective function with the addition of the sum of squares of the network weights.

3 Component-Based Robot

The dataset analysed in present study comes from a component-based robot. That is, the robot is composed of different components that can be made by different manufacturers and that are interconnected through a middleware. The robot components, as mentioned above, are connected by the RBS Middleware [20], which uses an event-based system. A tool called rsbag, which is located next to the middleware, is in charge of storing the information that circulates through it.

The authors of the dataset, in order to be able to detect possible future errors in the behaviour of the robot, decided to induce some anomalies and tried to detect them. These software-induced anomalies have the particularity that in none of the cases they prevent the robot to complete the task that had been planned to be carried out, but they penalize the performance. The majority of induced anomalies act on only one of the components.

This dataset has been developed by some researchers from Bielefeld University (Germany), and it is described in detail in [21]. The data, together with detailed explanations, are available in a public repository [22].

To carry out present study, the LegDetector component has been used. This component of the robot is responsible for locating the legs of a person in front of the robot. It is done by means of a laser sensor, that is located at the base of the robot. An anomaly, called LegDetectorSkippable, has been induced in this component. This anomaly causes the robot to perform several scanning attempts until the good one is done. As a result, the performance counters are penalized without preventing the task from being carried out. The dataset contains 8 components (shown in Table 1) that were periodically sampled before, during and after the anomalies.

This component has been selected as for assistive robots it is key to process visual information and recognize objects [14]. Additionally, according to previous

Table 1. Explanation of the dataset attributes.

Variables	Description
write_bytes	Count of bytes written by the tool
rchar	Count of bytes read since the beginning by a process
stime	Quantity of time in user mode by a process
wchar	Count of bytes that written by a process from the start
utime	Quantity of time in kernel mode by a process
rss	Current RSS of a process
received_bytes	Quantity of bytes hosted by the interface
sent_bytes	Quantity of bytes which the interface dispatch

studies carried out by the authors of the data set, best results when it comes to detecting anomalies were obtained for this component [23].

4 Experiments and Results

The clustering method in the first step, and the regression techniques consequently (both described in Sect. 2) have been applied to the LegDetector component of the dataset described in Sect. 3 in order to evaluate their imputation capability on all the attributes of the dataset.

To evaluate the contribution of clustering, the comparison in present section comprises results on the whole data (no clustering before regression) and on the groups generated by k-means (with values of k = 2 and k = 3). Different distance metrics have been tested to conduct the clustering and imputation has been applied to the groups generated by the Cosine one as this is the one that obtains the most balanced groups.

To get significant conclusions, results are validated by the well-known n-fold Cross-Validation (CV) [1] scheme. The number of (n) data partitions was set to 10 for all the experiments, as it is a standard value.

In order to be able to do the regression on all the attributes of the LegDetector datasets, eight sets of experiments have been conducted. In each one of them, the attribute to which regression is applied is stated as the target (criterion) while the remaining ones are the predictor variables. As a performance metric, the Mean Squared Error (MSE) has been calculated and is presented in this section. In the case of MLP, the training process (BR algorithm) has been performed ten times for each kfold, in order to obtain more reliable results. Hence, both the average MSE value (AVG) and standard deviation (SDEV) are shown.

Firstly, Table 2 shows the results of applying the regression techniques (N-LR and MLP) to the different attributes of the LegDetector component without applying clustering.

In Table 2 it can be observed that the average MSE obtained by MLP is lower than the one obtained by N-LR for the eight attributes, although there is just

Table 2. N-LR and MLP results (MSE) on the different attributes of the LegDetector component without applying clustering.

	N-LR	MLP	
		AVG	SDEV
write_bytes	2.62E−06	2.54E−06	4.46E−22
rchar	8.36E−06	5.85E−06	8.93E−22
stime	5.53E−06	5.18E−06	8.93E−22
wchar	6.09E−07	2.27E−07	2.79E−23
utime	6.93E−06	5.63E−06	8.93E−22
rss	9.32E−08	**8.45E−08**	**1.40E−23**
received_bytes	2.55E−06	1.62E−06	2.23E−22
sent_bytes	6.06E−06	3.37E−06	8.93E−22

a slight difference. In absolute terms, the 'rss' attribute is the one that achieves the lowest MSE average value and the lowest standard deviation.

Once regression results are shown for the raw dataset, results on the clustered data are also presented. Consequently, Table 3 shows the results of applying N-LR and MLP to the two clusters generated by the k-means algorithm (k parameter taken the value of 2). In the first cluster, 9285 data samples were gathered while 9249 samples were assigned to the second one. The k-means clustering algorithm with the Cosine metric groups the data samples into clusters with a similar number of samples.

Table 3. NL-R and MSE results (MSE) on the different attributes of the LegDetector component after applying k-means (k = 2).

k = 2	Cluster 1			Cluster 2		
	N-LR	MLP		N-LR	MLP	
		AVG	SDEV		AVG	SDEV
write_bytes	3.21E−06	3.16E−06	4.46E−22	8.26E−06	8.21E−06	0
rchar	**4.88E−06**	**2.52E−06**	**0**	**1.91E−07**	**1.66E−07**	**0**
stime	1.24E−05	1.11E−05	1.79E−21	**3.10E−06**	**2.87E−06**	**4.46E−22**
wchar	6.26E−07	3.02E−07	**5.58E−23**	1.63E−06	7.77E−07	**1.12E−22**
utime	9.76E−06	8.11E−06	**0**	1.53E−05	1.24E−05	0
rss	**9.89E−12**	**3.98E−11**	**6.81E−27**	**2.50E−11**	**1.11E−10**	**1.36E−26**
received_bytes	2.04E−06	**1.28E−06**	2.23E−22	4.24E−06	2.69E−06	0
sent_bytes	**4.92E−06**	3.78E−06	**0**	1.10E−05	8.23E−06	1.79E−21

From results shown in Table 3, it can be highlighted that for the first cluster there are up to four attributes (rchar, rss, received_bytes, and sent_bytes) that have obtained better regression results than those obtained without clustering (see Table 2). For the rest of the attributes, very similar results have been obtained so the initial step of clustering does not improve the regression results. It is worth mentioning the case of the "rss" attribute due to the fact that errors on clustered data are significantly lower thanks to the clustering. For the second cluster, three attributes have obtained better results than those without clustering. Results on 2 of these attributes (rchar and rss) were also improved in the first cluster but not for the other attribute (stime).

As previously stated, experiments have been also run modifying the value of the k parameter in the k-means algorithm and the obtained results are shown in Table 4. In this case, the first cluster consists of 4394 samples, 8532 the second and 5608 samples in the third cluster.

Table 4. NL-R and MSE results (MSE) on the different attributes of the LegDetector component after applying k-means (k = 3).

k = 3	Cluster 1			Cluster 2			Cluster 3		
	N-LR	MLP		N-LR	MLP		N-LR	MLP	
		AVG	SDEV		AVG	SDEV		AVG	SDEV
write_bytes	1.78E−05	1.70E−05	8.88E−08	3.15E−06	3.09E−06	0	1.16E−05	1.15E−05	1.79E−21
rchar	**4.08E−07**	**3.34E−07**	0	**1.90E−06**	**8.99E−07**	**2.23E−22**	**3.41E−07**	**3.06E−07**	0
stime	1.21E−05	9.02E−06	1.79E−21	1.31E−05	1.22E−05	0	**4.56E−06**	**4.46E−06**	0
wchar	4.76E−06	1.77E−06	0	6.12E−07	2.66E−07	0	1.46E−06	9.72E−07	2.23E−22
utime	3.51E−05	1.23E−05	0	9.59E−06	8.27E−06	1.79E−21	**7.87E−07**	**4.58E−07**	0
rss	**5.91E−11**	**1.79E−10**	**2.72E−26**	**1.01E−11**	**2.76E−11**	**6.81E−27**	**2.74E−11**	**1.13E−10**	**2.72E−26**
received_bytes	1.18E−05	6.77E−06	2.05E−08	**2.05E−06**	**1.31E−06**	**2.23E−22**	5.93E−06	4.16E−06	8.93E−22
sent_bytes	2.69E−05	9.97E−06	2.24E−08	**5.27E−06**	4.11E−06	0	7.09E−06	**2.42E−06**	4.46E−22

As can be seen in Table 4, the best results are obtained fo the third cluster in terms of MSE, compared to the results without clustering (Table 2). In this cluster, Results have been improved for four attributes in the case of N-LR and five attributes in the case of MLP. In the second cluster, results have been improved for up to four attributes on clustered data. Finally, in the first cluster, results have been improved for two attributes. Once again, error on the rss attribute are significantly smaller than those obtained without clustering (see Table 3).

After analising the attributes case by case, it can be said that results have been improved for the rchar and rss attributes in all clusters, for the sent_bytes attribute in two of them and for the stime, utime and received_bytes in only one.

5 Conclusions and Future Work

In the present study the imputation methods detailed in Sect. 2 have been applied to the dataset explained in Sect. 3. After preparing the data and applying the CV scheme to obtain more reliable results, a regression has been performed on the eight attributes of the Legdetector component. Firstly methods have been applied to the raw dataset (i.e. without clustering) and then, they have been also applied to the clusters generated by the k-means algorithm (Table 3 and Table 4). The main objective of present paper has been achieved: To carry out an analysis of the applied techniques, validating their results on this dataset and its attributes in order to know the most effective techniques in each case, according to the prediction error (MSE).

From the obtained results (in Sect. 4), it can be concluded that in the raw dataset (Table 2), MLP outperforms N-LR for all the component attributes. When regression is applied to clustered data, improved results are obtained when applying both regression methods for most of the attributes in some of the clusters. It is only in the case of write_bytes and wchar that the results are not improved. In the case of the 'rss' attribute, results are greatly improved both for k = 2 and k = 3.

Future work will focus on the application of some other clustering techniques (agglomerative density-based). Furthermore, imputation will be combined together with some other data preprocessing techniques (such as data balancing algorithms) to improve failure detection.

References

1. Arlot, S., Celisse, A.: A survey of cross-validation procedures for model selection. Stat. Surv. **4**, 40–79 (2010). https://doi.org/10.1214/09-SS054
2. Basurto, N., Cambra, C., Herrero, Á.: Improving the detection of robot anomalies by handling data irregularities. Neurocomputing (2020)
3. Basurto, N., Herrero, Á.: Data selection to improve anomaly detection in a component-based robot. In: Martínez Álvarez, F., Troncoso Lora, A., Sáez Muñoz, J.A., Quintián, H., Corchado, E. (eds.) SOCO 2019. AISC, vol. 950, pp. 241–250. Springer, Cham (2020). https://doi.org/10.1007/978-3-030-20055-8_23
4. Das, S., Datta, S., Chaudhuri, B.B.: Handling data irregularities in classification: foundations, trends, and future challenges. Pattern Recogn. **81**, 674–693 (2018). https://doi.org/10.1016/j.patcog.2018.03.008
5. Doan, C.D., Liong, S.: Generalization for multilayer neural network Bayesian regularization or early stopping. In: Proceedings of Asia Pacific Association of Hydrology and Water Resources 2nd Conference, pp. 5–8 (2004)
6. García-Laencina, P.J., Sancho-Gómez, J.L., Figueiras-Vidal, A.R.: Pattern classification with missing data: a review. Neural Comput. Appl. **19**(2), 263–282 (2010). https://doi.org/10.1007/s00521-009-0295-6
7. Gardner, M., Dorling, S.: Artificial neural networks (the multilayer perceptron)-a review of applications in the atmospheric sciences. Atmos. Environ. **32**(14), 2627–2636 (1998). https://doi.org/10.1016/S1352-2310(97)00447-0
8. Hecht-Nielsen, R.: III. 3 - theory of the backpropagation neural network. In: Wechsler, H. (ed.) Neural Networks for Perception, pp. 65–93. Academic Press (1992). https://doi.org/10.1016/B978-0-12-741252-8.50010-8
9. Herrero, Á., Jiménez, A.: Improving the management of industrial and environmental enterprises by means of soft computing. Cybern. Syst. **50**(1), 1–2 (2019)
10. IFR: summary - OUTLOOK on world robotics report 2019 by IFR. https://ifr.org/ifr-press-releases/news/summary-outlook-on-world-robotics-report-2019-by-ifr

11. Jain, A.K., Murty, M.N., Flynn, P.J.: Data clustering: a review. ACM Comput. Surv. **31**(3), 264–323 (1999). https://doi.org/10.1145/331499.331504
12. Jimenez, A., Herrero, A.: Soft computing applications in the field of industrial and environmental enterprises. Expert Syst. **36**(4), e12456 (2019). https://doi.org/10.1111/exsy.12456
13. Jove, E., Casteleiro-Roca, J.L., Quintián, H., Simić, D., Méndez-Pérez, J.A., Luis Calvo-Rolle, J.: Anomaly detection based on one-class intelligent techniques over a control level plant. Log. J. IGPL (2020). https://doi.org/10.1093/jigpal/jzz057
14. Kasaei, S.H., Oliveira, M., Lim, G.H., Lopes, L.S., Tomé, A.M.: Towards lifelong assistive robotics: a tight coupling between object perception and manipulation. Neurocomputing **291**, 151–166 (2018). https://doi.org/10.1016/j.neucom.2018.02.066
15. Khalastchi, E., Kalech, M.: On fault detection and diagnosis in robotic systems. ACM Comput. Surv. **51**(1), 1–24 (2018). https://doi.org/10.1145/3146389
16. MacQueen, J., et al.: Some methods for classification and analysis of multivariate observations. In: Proceedings of the Fifth Berkeley Symposium on Mathematical Statistics and Probability, Oakland, CA, USA, vol. 1, pp. 281–297 (1967)
17. Neter, J., Kutner, M.H., Nachtsheim, C.J., Wasserman, W.: Applied Linear Statistical Models, vol. 4. Irwin, Chicago (1996)
18. Pearson, K., Lee, A.: On the generalised probable error in multiple normal correlation. Biometrika **6**(1), 59–68 (1908). http://www.jstor.org/stable/2331556
19. Twala, B.: Robot execution failure prediction using incomplete data. In: 2009 IEEE International Conference on Robotics and Biomimetics (ROBIO), pp. 1518–1523, December 2009. https://doi.org/10.1109/ROBIO.2009.5420900
20. Wienke, J., Wrede, S.: A middleware for collaborative research in experimental robotics. In: 2011 IEEE/SICE International Symposium on System Integration (SII), pp. 1183–1190, December 2011. https://doi.org/10.1109/SII.2011.6147617
21. Wienke, J., Meyer zu Borgsen, S., Wrede, S.: A data set for fault detection research on component-based robotic systems. In: Alboul, L., Damian, D., Aitken, J.M.M. (eds.) TAROS 2016. LNCS (LNAI), vol. 9716, pp. 339–350. Springer, Cham (2016). https://doi.org/10.1007/978-3-319-40379-3_35
22. Wienke, J., Wrede, S.: A fault detection data set for performance bugs in component-based robotic systems. https://doi.org/10.4119/unibi/2900911
23. Wienke, J., Wrede, S.: Autonomous fault detection for performance bugs in component-based robotic systems. In: 2016 IEEE/RSJ International Conference on Intelligent Robots and Systems (IROS), pp. 3291–3297. IEEE (2016). https://doi.org/10.1109/IROS.2016.7759507
24. University of Yale: Linear regression (2017). http://www.stat.yale.edu/Courses/1997-98/101/linreg.htm

A Simple Classification Ensemble for ADL and Falls

Enrique A. de la Cal[1](✉), Mirko Fáñez[2], Mario Villar[3], Jose R. Villar[1], and Victor Suárez[4]

[1] Computer Science Department, Faculty of Geology, University of Oviedo, Oviedo, Spain
{delacal,villarjose}@uniovi.es
[2] Instituto Tecnológico de Castilla y León, Pol. Ind. Villalonquejar, 09001 Burgos, Spain
mirko@mirkoo.es
[3] University of Granada, Granada, Spain
mario.villarsanz@gmail.com
[4] Control and Automatica Department, EPI, University of Oviedo, Gijón, Spain
vmsuarez@uniovi.es

Abstract. Fall Detection (FD) and ADL (Activity of Daily Living) identification is one the main challenges in a lot of real-world problems like work monitoring, healthcare systems, etc. Up to our knowledge, there are a lot of proposals in the literature for both problems separately, but few of them pose both problems at a time. A possible solution relies on-wrist wearable devices including tri-axial accelerometers performing ADL and Fall identification autonomously. Since the dynamics of both kind of activities (FALL and ADL) are quite similar and not easy to identify, mainly in FALL and high ADLs like Running, Jogging, GoUpstairs, etc, a technique considering peaks is suitable. Thus, in this study, an ensemble between KMEANS and KNN (stands for EKMEANS) taking as input a 19 features dataset calculated from a time window whenever a peak is detected. As peak detection algorithm is used, the MAX-PEAKS algorithm presented in [15].

The proposal is evaluated using the UMA Fall, one of the publicly available simulated fall detection data sets, and compared to two classical well-known algorithms: the KNN and a Feed Forward Neural Network (NN) [15].

The results show that our proposal outperforms the NN results.

Future work includes a further analysis of the dynamics of the ensemble EKMEANS and a study of this problem using Deep-Learning.

Keywords: Human activity recognition · ADL identification · Fall detection TS clustering · TS classification · Wearable devices

This research has been funded by the Spanish Ministry of Science and Innovation, under project MINECO-TIN2017-84804-R, and by the Grant FC-GRUPIN-IDI/2018/000226 project from the Asturias Regional Government.

E. A. de la Cal et al. (Eds.): HAIS 2020, LNAI 12344, pp. 95–106, 2020.
https://doi.org/10.1007/978-3-030-61705-9_9

1 Introduction

Fall Detection (FD) and ADL (Activity of Daily Living) identification is one of the most important research niches in several real-world problems like healthcare, work safety, sport monitoring, etc. At present, there are a lot of proposals in the literature for both problems separately, but few of them pose both problems at a time.

Concerning FD, the solutions can be classified into three main types respect to the type of sensors used: Non-Wearable Based Systems (NWS), Wearable Based Systems (WS), and Fusion or hybrid-based Systems (FS) [17]. Current work focuses on smart-watches with built-in tri-axial accelerometers (3DACC), which is by far the most chosen option [2,5].

Regarding FD proposals, it can be stated that most of the references includes any machine learning technique applied to the focused problem. For example, [16, 18] involve a feature extraction stage plus a SVM that classifies the TS windows. Likewise, [2,5,6] classify the sliding windows based on some transformations of the 3DACC magnitude and using some thresholds with very simple rules.

One of the baselines in FD is the Abbate algorithm [1], that has been extended and modified in a series of publications [7,8,14], to adapt the original location of the Abbate algorithm sensor (waist) to a sensor on the wrist. In one of our previous work [15], a new event detection mechanism to detect the high intensity fall events was presented (events that arise when the user stands up and falls either while walking, standing still, running, etc.). The idea is derived from a partial maximum peak detection method [11], where the threshold to detect the peaks is automatically determined for each user. Interestingly, this new event detection makes use of no user predefined threshold, which represents a step ahead in the event detection mechanisms in the literature. We refer to this event detection mechanism as *MAX-PEAKS*.

Since finding an appropriate value for the threshold that allows detecting all type of falls without getting confused with some ADL has proved to be a complicated problem [17], current work proposes a preliminary proposal to classify TS in a public dataset including typical ADLs as well as different kind of falls. It can be stated that most of references tackling ADL identification usually exclude FALL time series: sometimes the original dataset doesn't include FALL times series [9,10] and others the authors exclude the FALL samples [12].

Thus, this study proposes a Hybrid Artificial Intelligent System to classify datasets including ADLs and Fall TSs. The proposal includes an extension of the MAX-PEAKS algorithm presented in [15] with a more complete set of features, and the classification algorithm will be an ensemble of the well-known algorithms K-Means and KNN (stands for EKMEANS). In addition, the MAX-PEAKS features will be reduced using the PCA [13] analysis with different levels of variance.

The structure of the paper is as follows. The next section deals with the description of the proposal including the extension of the MAX-PEAKS algorithm, together with the transformations that are proposed to compute, as well as the description of the classification algorithm EKMEANS. Section 3 describes the UMA Fall dataset used, the experimental setup and shows and discusses the obtained results. Finally, conclusions are drawn.

2 The Proposal

Figure 1 shows the complete procedure of the algorithm employed in this work.

Fig. 1. The general schema of the proposal

The general algorithm consists of four stages: first, a sliding window of $\frac{1}{4}FREQ$ of sampling rate is considered to compute the MAX-PEAKS algorithm [15]. When a Peak is detected (FALL or NOT FALL), the transformations for two windows are calculated. After that, the feature extraction using PCA is computed and finally the classification model is carried out.

2.1 The MAX-PEAKS Peaks Detection Algorithm

The Event Detection Stage. For the purpose of detecting peaks in the 3DACC magnitude, the first stage is to smooth the signal using a sliding window sized $\frac{1}{4}FREQ$, with $FREQ$ being the sampling frequency. Afterwards, we apply the S_1 transformation proposed in [11]. For the current problem, the S_4 and S_5 were too complex for a smart-watch and need too wide windows of data in order to estimate the entropy. From the remaining transformations, we chose S_1 because its simplicity and similar performance among all of them. The Eq. 1 defines the calculation of S_1, where k is the predefined number of samples and t is the current sample timestamp. It is worth noticing that, although we analyze the window $[a_{t-2k-1}, a_t]$ at time t, the peak candidate is a_{t-k}, the center of the interval. The S_1 transformation represents a scaling of the TS, which makes the peak detection easier using a predefined threshold α.

$$S_1(t) = \frac{1}{2} \times \{max_{i=t-2k}^{t-k-1} a_i + max_{i=t-k+1}^{t} a_i\} \tag{1}$$

The algorithm for detecting peaks is straightforward: a peak occurs in time t if the value S_t is higher than α and is the highest in its $2k$ neighborhood. In the original report, all the parameters (k, α) were carefully determined for each problem in order to optimize the peak detection.

The New Set of Transformations. Whenever a high intensity fall occurs there are three main parts: the activity being carried ordinarily before the fall event, the fall itself that we identify as a peak and what happens next. Because there are no public data set of real falls for healthy participants, we are not able to say accurately what happens after a fall: we can make the hypothesis that what happens after a fall is a period of relative calm, without special activity, perhaps some erratic movements of the hands. Therefore, we will divide the $[a_{t-2k-1}, a_t]$ window in three: before the peak $I_B = [a_{t-2k-1}, a_{t-k-1}]$, the peak $I_P = [a_{t-k-1}, a_{t-k+1}]$ and after the peak $I_A = [a_{t-k+1}, a_t]$. For each of these sub-intervals we propose to compute the following transformations:

AAMV Average Absolute Acceleration Magnitude Variation computed as $AAMV = \sum_{t=s}^{e-1} |a_{t+1} - a_t|/N$, with N the number of samples in the interval $[s, e]$.
E Energy of the Acceleration Magnitude $E = \sum_{t=s}^{e} a_t^2/N$
Mean Mean Activity the mean of the acceleration magnitude in the interval $[s, e]$.
SD Standard Deviation of the acceleration magnitude in the interval $[s, e]$.
AoM Amount of movement calculated as $abs(max(a_i) - min(a_i))$.
MAD Mean Absolute Difference calculated as $1/n * sum(|a_i - mean(a_i)|)$.

Therefore, we have a total of 19 transformations (6 transformations for each of the three intervals plus the new S_1 calculated for the peak interval I_P); none of which relies on thresholds of any kind. All of these transformations are well known in the context of Human Activity Recognition and Fall Detection.

Besides, and in order to analyse the importance of these features a principal components analysis has been carried out with two levels of significance of 90% and 95%.

2.2 EKMEANS: An Ensemble of KMEANS and KNN

Algorithm 1 presents the complete procedure of the EKMEANS algorithm proposed in this work. This proposal consists in a user-centered ensemble of KMEANS and KNN. So, the train dataset (Stage TRAIN, Algorithm 1L2) for each participant p will be the fusion of data from the other participants different to p (Remaining_DATASET). Thus, since frequently in this kind of problems there are a big overlapping of the samples from different classes, our proposal consists on the execution of the well-known KMEANS[1] algorithm [4] on the TrainDataset to obtain the set of centroids K (KMEANS_RESULTS$_i/i = 1...K$). The optimal number of clusters (K) is estimated using the method "Within-cluster sum of square".

In the case of the clusters with samples belonging to more than one class (Algorithm 1L6), the KNN algorithm will be calculated for 1 to 15 neighbors to obtain the best number of neighbors, otherwise the predicted class for this cluster will be the one corresponding to the train samples of this cluster.

[1] The default implementation of the R platform "kmeans" function has been used.

In the TEST stage (Algorithm 1L10), the predicted class for each test sample will be computed considering the number of classes for the cluster predicted for this sample (PK, Algorithm 1L12). In case, the *PK* cluster had more than one class for the train samples, the KNN obtained for the train samples will be used to predict the class of test SAMPLE (Algorithm 1L13–14), otherwise the predicted class will be the one belonging to all the train samples for this cluster.

Algorithm 1. EKMEANS(TRAINDATASET, TESTDATASET, NP: Number of Participants, K: Number of Centroids for KMEANS)

```
 1: for p in 1:NP do
 2:   TRAIN_STAGE ← 1
 3:   Remaining_DATASET ← TRAINDATASET - {Samples of participant p}
 4:   KMEANS-RESULTS ← KMEANS(Remaining_DATASET, K)
 5:   for i in 1:K do
 6:     if #Classes(KMEANS-RESULTS[i]) > 1 then
 7:       KNN-FOR-CLUSTER[i] ← KNN(Remaining_DATASET, 1, 3, 5, 7, ..,15)
 8:     end if
 9:   end for
10:   TEST_STAGE ← 1
11:   for SAMPLE in DATATEST do
12:     PK ← PREDICT-KMEANS(KMEANS-RESULTS, SAMPLE)
13:     if #Classes(KMEANS-RESULTS[PK]) > 1 then
14:       PREDICTEDCLASS(SAMPLE) ← PREDICT(KNN-FOR-
          CLUSTER[PK], SAMPLE)
15:     else
16:       PREDICTEDCLASS(SAMPLE) ← Class(KMEANS-RESULTS[PK])
17:     end if
18:   end for
19: end for
```

3 Numerical Results

3.1 Data Set Description

The publicly available simulated falls UMA Fall data set [3] is used in this study. This data set includes several activities, transitions and simulated falls regarding up to 17 participants. There is no fixed number of repetitions of each activity or simulated fall. Each participant used several 3DACC, specially one on a wrist; the sampling frequency was 20 Hz. Altogether, 208 TS are simulated falls, belonging to lateral, forward or backward falls, out of the 531 TS that are available in this data set.

3.2 Experimentation Set up

The experimentation has considered just one event detection method: the MAX-PEAKS algorithm with 19 features (see Sect. 2.1), and as classification algorithm two alternatives have been run, EKMEANS and KNN. Three datasets have been built from the MAX-PEAKS 19 features: the original MAX-PEAKS dataset (MAX-PEAKS) with the 19 features, and two PCA feature extraction with variance of 90% and 95% (MAX-PEAKS PCA90 and PCA95). Besides, two kind of labelling of the datasets have been considered: MULTICLASS (F1–F3 and A1–A5) and TWO-CLASS PROBLEM (FALL and NOT FALL) (see Table 1). Besides, the results of a Feed Forward Neural Network for the MAX-PEAKS dataset using the TWO-CLASS labelling obtained in [15] will be considered. The sensitivity and specificity of the results for all the participants will be used to measure the performance of the method.

Table 1. Summary of ADL and FALL kind of activities

	FALL				
Code	F1	F2	F3		
Activity	FALL.BACKWARDS	FALL.FORWARD	FALL.LATERAL	-	-
	NOT FALL				
Code	A1	A2	A3	A4	A5
Activity	WALKING	HOPPING	CLIMBING UPSTAIRS	CLIMBING DOWNSTAIRS	BENDING

3.3 Numerical Results

Regarding the three datasets, the two classification algorithms and the two labelling alternatives, we will obtain 12 tables with the numerical results for the 17 participants, but by lack of space, just the most representatives tables are included, as well as two summary tables.

Results for the TWO-CLASS Labelling. Typically, clustering solutions on FALL Detection presents the results as Two-class problems. Thus, we are starting this section with the results of applying the EKMEANS and KNN algorithms on the TWO-CLASS MAX-PEAKS 19 features dataset (see Table 2). It can be observed at least the following issues: the Sensitivity for the EKMEANS and KNN results are quite similar (MAX-PEAKS, PCA90 and PCA95), but the Specificity for EKMEANS outperforms lightly the results for KNN for the two PCA datasets; other issue is that EKMEANS overpass clearly the Specificity of the NN results [15] with a quite similar Sensitivity.

Let's see the EKMEANS results for participant #1 (see Fig. 2). We know that three clusters (#1, #8 and #10) out of the eleven clusters obtained in the train stage contains train samples (the shaped/colored points) from the

Table 2. Summary of results for EKMEANS and KNN for the TWO-CLASS problem

Pid	EKMEANS MAX-PEAKS		EKMEANS MAX-PEAKS PCA90		EKMEANS MAX-PEAKS PCA95		KNN MAX-PEAKS		KNNMAX-PEAKS PCA90		KNN MAX-PEAKS PCA95		NN [15] MAX-PEAKS	
	Sens	Spec	Sens	Spec	Sens	Spec	Sens	Spec	Sens	Spec	Sens	Spec	Sens	Spec
1	0.900	0.714	0.900	0.857	0.950	0.857	0.800	0.714	0.800	0.714	0.750	0.714	1.000	0.271
2	0.846	1.000	0.846	1.000	0.846	1.000	0.846	1.000	0.769	1.000	0.692	1.000	1.000	0.434
3	1.000	1.000	1.000	1.000	1.000	1.000	1.000	1.000	0.889	1.000	0.944	1.000	1.000	0.357
4	0.941	1.000	0.941	1.000	0.941	1.000	0.941	1.000	0.824	1.000	0.706	1.000	1.000	0.469
5	0.500	1.000	0.500	1.000	0.500	1.000	0.500	1.000	0.625	1.000	0.500	1.000	1.000	0.439
6	0.625	1.000	0.625	1.000	0.750	1.000	0.750	1.000	0.500	1.000	0.750	1.000	1.000	0.231
7	NA	0.929	NA	NA	NA	0.786	NA	0.857	NA	0.857	NA	0.929	NA	0.439
8	NA	0.857	NA	0.857	NA	0.857	NA	0.857	NA	NA	NA	NA	NA	0.522
9	0.857	1.000	0.810	0.750	0.810	0.750	0.905	1.000	0.762	0.750	0.762	0.750	1.000	0.467
10	NA	0.929	NA	0.929	NA	0.857	NA	NA	NA	NA	NA	0.929	NA	0.351
11	0.500	1.000	0.500	0.900	1.000	0.900	1.000	0.900	0.000	0.900	0.000	1.000	1.000	0.360
12	1.000	0.692	1.000	0.615	1.000	0.692	1.000	0.692	1.000	0.923	1.000	0.923	1.000	0.417
13	1.000	1.000	1.000	1.000	1.000	1.000	1.000	1.000	1.000	1.000	0.917	1.000	1.000	0.597
14	0.875	1.000	0.750	1.000	0.875	1.000	0.750	1.000	0.875	1.000	1.000	1.000	1.000	0.125
15	1.000	1.000	1.000	1.000	1.000	1.000	1.000	1.000	0.909	1.000	0.909	1.000	1.000	0.473
16	0.947	0.826	0.947	0.870	0.930	0.913	0.947	0.870	0.930	0.957	0.930	1.000	1.000	0.389
17	0.765	1.000	0.706	1.000	0.706	1.000	0.706	1.000	0.647	1.000	0.647	1.000	1.000	0.276
μ/σ	**0.840/0.178**	**0.938/0.104**	**0.823/0.182**	**0.924/0.113**	**0.879/0.147**	**0.918/0.103**	**0.868/0.151**	**0.931/0.106**	**0.752/0.260**	**0.940/0.096**	**0.751/0.262**	**0.953/0.091**	**1.00/0.000**	**0.389/0.112**

two classes (the points are not labelled by class). The remaining clusters only contains train samples belonging to one class. If the test samples are analysed (white circles with label F or NF), it can be observed that they are labelled by clusters **#1(red)**, **#8(blue)**, #11(pink), #3(khaki green), **#10(purple)**, and the clusters that contains overlapped test samples (in boldface) are the same as the ones for the train samples. These test samples belonging to these three clusters are the ones affecting the Sensitivity and Specificity values.

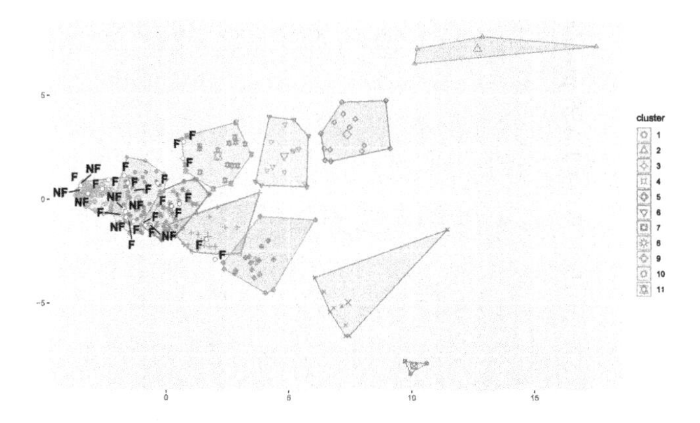

Fig. 2. The EKMEANS results for the MAX-PEAKS TWO-CLASS dataset. The train samples are plotted with different shapes and colors (11 clusters), and the test samples are white circle-shaped, labelled with F (FALL) and NF (Not FALL) (Color figure online)

Results for the MULTICLASS Labelling. Table 3 includes the results of EKMEANS and KNN for all the MULTICLASS datasets considered in this section. Since the number of samples for each class are quite low, it can be stated that the Sensitivity figures are quite low for all the experiments, models and datasets. On the other side the Specificity is clearly higher than the Sensitivity in both models. In order to justify these results, let's depict the results of the EKMEANS in Fig. 3 for participant #1. In the figure, it can be seen that the test samples (white circles) belonging to class F1 are quite sparse and scattered among different clusters, that is the reason the Sensitivity was 0.0 (see Table 4). Conversely, test samples from class F2 are more compact, and the results for this kind of fall confirm it (column F2 in Table 4). The remaining kinds of activities present low levels of Sensitivity for the same reason as F1. Besides in general terms, we can observe (Table 4: mean/std) that practically all the activities but F2, sport bad Sensitivity results and high Specificity.

Table 3. Summary of results for EKMEANS and KNN for the MULTICLASS problem

Pid	EKMEANSMAX-PEAKS		EKMEANSMAX-PEAKS PCA90		EKMEANSMAX-PEAKS PCA95		KNNMAX-PEAKS		KNN MAX-PEAKS PCA90		KNN MAX-PEAKS PCA95	
	Mean/std		Mean/std		Mean/std		Mean/std		Mean/std		Mean/std	
	Sens	Spec	Sens	Spec	Sens	Spec	Sens	Spec	Sens	Spec	Sens	Spec
1	0.350/0.266	0.868/0.102	0.392/0.429	0.889/0.125	0.267/0.303	0.870/0.141	0.225/0.263	0.872/0.120	0.408/0.490	0.901/0.140	0.408/0.490	0.883/0.154
2	0.333/0.471	0.870/0.082	0.488/0.342	0.887/0.073	0.571/0.332	0.880/0.064	0.369/0.442	0.833/0.157	0.369/0.442	0.868/0.095	0.286/0.481	0.860/0.075
3	0.567/0.401	0.917/0.068	0.500/0.425	0.896/0.089	0.500/0.373	0.896/0.102	0.533/0.321	0.894/0.106	0.700/0.361	0.920/0.070	0.500/0.408	0.887/0.093
4	0.493/0.384	0.912/0.099	0.627/0.394	0.947/0.071	0.553/0.398	0.928/0.084	0.593/0.414	0.922/0.115	0.593/0.414	0.949/0.033	0.527/0.392	0.937/0.035
5	0.500/0.707	0.875/0.087	0.500/0.707	0.875/0.102	0.562/0.619	0.867/0.112	0.500/0.707	0.875/0.102	0.500/0.707	0.858/0.124	0.562/0.619	0.858/0.143
6	0.700/0.298	0.905/0.147	0.433/0.435	0.885/0.173	0.367/0.415	0.862/0.163	0.433/0.435	0.899/0.115	0.400/0.435	0.884/0.112	0.267/0.435	0.797/0.196
7	0.417/0.373	0.894/0.143	0.383/0.439	0.878/0.125	0.317/0.207	0.864/0.154	0.417/0.373	0.878/0.109	0.433/0.253	0.888/0.155	0.300/0.274	0.824/0.143
8	0.375/0.479	0.915/0.070	0.375/0.479	0.925/0.070	0.250/0.500	0.901/0.077	0.333/0.471	0.913/0.075	0.333/0.471	0.893/0.067	0.417/0.500	0.910/0.083
9	0.424/0.307	0.892/0.075	0.387/0.299	0.899/0.122	0.354/0.267	0.892/0.128	0.320/0.385	0.917/0.062	0.295/0.221	0.880/0.097	0.499/0.410	0.909/0.079
10	0.217/0.331	0.843/0.189	0.267/0.435	0.881/0.173	0.200/0.447	0.889/0.127	0.200/0.447	0.843/0.225	0.400/0.548	0.816/0.304	0.400/0.548	0.851/0.237
11	0.458/0.315	0.906/0.081	0.542/0.417	0.883/0.162	0.542/0.417	0.883/0.162	0.667/0.471	0.894/0.193	0.542/0.417	0.836/0.194	0.542/0.417	0.836/0.265
12	0.452/0.369	0.910/0.090	0.405/0.407	0.902/0.098	0.357/0.390	0.895/0.110	0.333/0.385	0.887/0.111	0.357/0.339	0.895/0.118	0.357/0.390	0.895/0.132
13	0.562/0.375	0.806/0.140	0.312/0.375	0.829/0.132	0.312/0.315	0.835/0.111	0.250/0.204	0.807/0.218	0.250/0.289	0.807/0.151	0.250/0.354	0.819/0.100
14	0.333/0.471	0.723/0.119	0.417/0.500	0.754/0.175	0.396/0.427	0.765/0.121	0.333/0.471	0.704/0.247	0.250/0.500	0.749/0.203	0.333/0.471	0.715/0.216
15	0.438/0.427	0.848/0.156	0.438/0.515	0.802/0.217	0.583/0.354	0.852/0.174	0.583/0.354	0.850/0.173	0.542/0.363	0.830/0.101	0.604/0.315	0.889/0.051
16	0.329/0.333	0.891/0.122	0.384/0.333	0.902/0.142	0.413/0.322	0.905/0.115	0.424/0.323	0.907/0.108	0.364/0.279	0.905/0.093	0.371/0.314	0.899/0.100
17	0.367/0.383	0.899/0.090	0.315/0.311	0.901/0.094	0.361/0.371	0.902/0.080	0.463/0.347	0.922/0.079	0.337/0.386	0.919/0.094	0.417/0.376	0.911/0.141
μ/σ	**0.430/0.114**	**0.875/0.049**	**0.421/0.090**	**0.879/0.045**	**0.406/0.123**	**0.875/0.036**	**0.410/0.134**	**0.872/0.054**	**0.416/0.123**	**0.870/0.050**	**0.414/0.109**	**0.863/0.054**

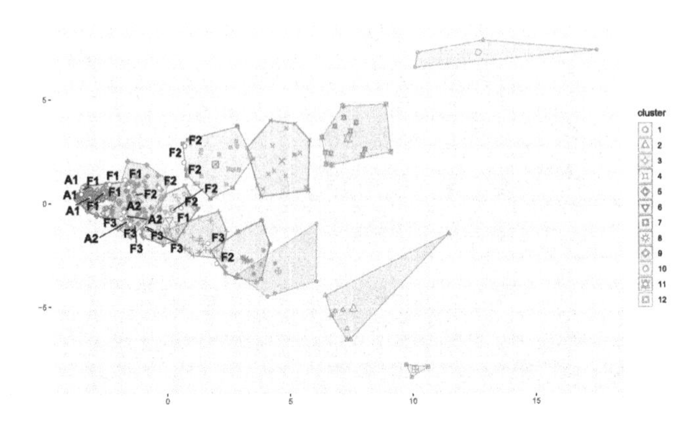

Fig. 3. The EKMEANS results for the MAX-PEAKS MULTICLASS dataset. The train samples are plotted with different shapes and colors (12 clusters), and the test samples are white circle-shaped, labelled with F# (FALL) and A# (Not FALL) (Color figure online)

Table 4. EKMEANS - MAX-PEAKS, Sensitivity and Specificity for the MULTICLASS dataset. Pid: stand for Participant ID. For the sake of space this table just includes the results for participant #1.

EKMEANS - MAX-PEAKS																	
PId	F1		F2		F3		A1		A2		A3		A4		A5		Mean/std	
	Sens	Spec	Sens	Spec	Sens	Spec	Sens	Spec	Sens	Spec	Sens	Spec	Sens	Spec	Sens	Spec	Sens	Spec
1	0.000	0.714	0.750	0.789	0.333	0.905	0.333	0.875	0.333	1.000	NA	0.926	NA	NA	NA	NA	**0.350/0.266**	**0.868/0.102**
mean	**0.337**	**0.819**	**0.523**	**0.862**	**0.238**	**0.844**	**0.868**	**0.818**	**0.217**	**0.946**	**0.111**	**0.934**	**0.306**	**0.952**	**0.267**	**0.978**	**0.430**	**0.875**
std	**0.330**	**0.120**	**0.287**	**0.107**	**0.205**	**0.064**	**0.211**	**0.142**	**0.217**	**0.050**	**0.172**	**0.079**	**0.195**	**0.060**	**0.370**	**0.035**	**0.114**	**0.049**

4 Conclusions

This study proposes the EKMEANS algorithm for ADL and Falls classification, using a low computational consumption technique based on an ensemble between KMEANS and KNN.

Our proposal has been compared to the classical KNN algorithm as well as the results obtained with a Feed Forward NN in [15] taking as input three variants of the public dataset UMAFALL [3]. These three datasets have been built from the UMAFALL wrist acceleration: one applying the peaks detection algorithm MAX-PEAKS [15] and the results of PCA with variance of 90% and 95%. Besides, these three datasets have been considered using two kind of labelling: on one side, considering all the different labels of activities defined in the UMAFALL dataset (MULTICLASS), on the other side the Not-FALL and FALL activities have been re-labelled just as a two-class problem.

The results show that our proposal EKMEANS outperforms clearly the Specificity of the NN results with a quite similar Sensitivity for the TWO-CLASS dataset. Besides, our proposal is a lighter computational consumption process than a NN in deployment stage. Concerning the MULTICLASS datasets, we have observed that mostly all the activities but F2 (Lateral Fall), sport bad

Sensitivity results and high Specificity for all the models. Other important issue is that PCA doesn't affect positively or affect negatively in the performance of the different models used in current study.

Future work must consider a deeper analysis of the dynamics of the intra-cluster KNN for EKMEANS, as well other kind of low consumption classification meta-heuristic. Besides, in our point of view a multiclass oversampling technique must be carried out on the used datasets. Finally, the use of Deep Learning is also part of future work.

References

1. Abbate, S., Avvenuti, M., Bonatesta, F., Cola, G., Corsini, P.: AlessioVecchio: a smartphone-based fall detection system. Pervasive Mob. Comput. **8**(6), 883–899 (2012)
2. Bourke, A., O'Brien, J., Lyons, G.: Evaluation of a threshold-based triaxial accelerometer fall detection algorithm. Gait Posture **26**, 194–199 (2007)
3. Casilari, E., Santoyo-Ramón, J.A., Cano-García, J.M.: Umafall: a multisensor dataset for the research on automatic fall detection. Procedia Comput. Sci. **110**(Supplement C), 32–39 (2017). https://doi.org/10.1016/j.procs.2017.06.110
4. Hartigan, J.A., Wong, M.A.: Algorithm as 136: a k-means clustering algorithm. J. Roy. Stat. Soc. Ser. C (Appl. Stat.) **28**(1), 100–108 (1979). http://www.jstor.org/stable/2346830
5. Huynh, Q.T., Nguyen, U.D., Irazabal, L.B., Ghassemian, N., Tran, B.Q.: Optimization of an acc. and gyro.-based fall det. algorithm. J. Sens. (2015)
6. Kangas, M., Konttila, A., Lindgren, P., Winblad, I., Jämsaä, T.: Comparison of low-complexity fall detection algorithms for body attached accelerometers. Gait Posture **28**, 285–291 (2008)
7. Khojasteh, S.B., Villar, J.R., de la Cal, E., González, V.M., Sedano, J., Yazgan, H.R.: Evaluation of a wrist-based wearable fall detection method. In: de Cos Juez, F., et al. (eds.) 13th International Conference on Soft Computing Models in Industrial and Environmental Applications. HAIS 2018. LNCS, vol. 10870, pp. 377–386. Springer, Cham (2018). https://doi.org/10.1007/978-3-319-92639-1_31
8. Khojasteh, S.B., Villar, J.R., Chira, C., González, V.M., de la Cal, E.: Improving fall detection using an on-wrist wearable accelerometer. Sensors **18**(5), 1350 (2018)
9. Lin, W.Y., Verma, V.K., Lee, M.Y., Lai, C.S.: Activity monitoring with a wrist-worn, accelerometer-based device. Micromachines **9**(9), 450 (2018)
10. Lu, J., Tong, K.Y.: Robust single accelerometer-based activity recognition using modified recurrence plot. IEEE Sens. J. **19**(15), 6317–6324 (2019)
11. Palshikar, G.K.: Simple algorithms for peak detection in time-series. Technical report, Tata Research Development and Design Centre (2009)
12. Sukor, A.A., Zakaria, A., Rahim, N.A.: Activity recognition using accelerometer sensor and machine learning classifiers. In: 2018 IEEE 14th International Colloquium on Signal Processing and Its Applications (CSPA), pp. 233–238. IEEE (2018)
13. Venables, W.N., Ripley, B.D.: Modern Applied Statistics with S. Springer, Cham (2002)
14. Villar, J.R., de la Cal, E., Fañez, M., González, V.M., Sedano, J.: User-centered fall detection using supervised, on-line learning and transfer learning. Progress Artif. Intell. **2019**, 1–22 (2019). https://doi.org/10.1007/s13748-019-00190-2

15. Villar, M., Villar, J.R.: Peak detection enhancement in autonomous wearable fall detection. In: Abraham, A., Siarry, P., Ma, K., Kaklauskas, A. (eds.) ISDA 2019. AISC, vol. 1181, pp. 48–58. Springer, Cham (2021). https://doi.org/10.1007/978-3-030-49342-4_5
16. Wu, F., Zhao, H., Zhao, Y., Zhong, H.: Development of a wearable-sensor-based fall detection system. Int. J. Telemed. Appl. **2015**, 11 (2015). https://doi.org/10.1155/2015/576364
17. Yacchirema, D., de Puga, J.S., Palau, C., Esteve, M.: Fall detection system for elderly people using IoT and big data. Procedia Comput. Sci. **130**, 603–610 (2018). The 9th International Conference on Ambient Systems, Networks and Technologies (ANT 2018)/The 8th International Conference on Sustainable Energy Information Technology (SEIT-2018)/Affiliated Workshops
18. Zhang, T., Wang, J., Xu, L., Liu, P.: Fall detection by wearable sensor and one-class SVM algorithm. In: Huang, D.S., Li, K.I.G. (eds.) Intelligent Computing in Signal Processing and Pattern Recognition. LNCS, vol. 345, pp. 858–863. Springer, Heidelberg (2006). https://doi.org/10.1007/978-3-540-37258-5_104

Joint Entity Summary and Attribute Embeddings for Entity Alignment Between Knowledge Graphs

Rumana Ferdous Munne[1,2](✉) and Ryutaro Ichise[1,2]

[1] SOKENDAI (The Graduate University for Advanced Studies), Tokyo, Japan
[2] National Institute of Informatics, Tokyo, Japan
{rfmunne,ichise}@nii.ac.jp

Abstract. Knowledge Graph (KG) is a popular way of storing facts about the real world entities, where nodes represent the entities and edges denote relations. KG is being used in many AI applications, so several large scale Knowledge Graphs (KGs) e.g., DBpedia, Wikidata, YAGO have become extremely popular. Unfortunately, very limited number of the entities stored in different KGs are aligned. This paper presents an embedding-based entity alignment method. Existing methods mainly focus on the relational structures and attributes to align the same entities of two different KGs. Such methods fail when the entities have less number of attributes or when the relational structure may not capture the meaningful representation of the entities. To solve this problem, we propose a Joint Summary and Attribute Embeddings (JSAE) based entity alignment method. We exploit the entity summary information available in KGs for entities' summary embedding. To learn the semantics of the entity summary we employ Bidirectional Encoder Representations from Transformers (BERT). Our model learns the representations of entities by using relational triples, attribute triples and description as well. We perform experiments on real-world datasets and the results indicate that the proposed approach significantly outperforms the state-of-the-art models for entity alignment.

Keywords: Knowledge graphs · Entity alignment · Embedding models

1 Introduction

In the recent years, knowledge graphs (KGs) attract increasing attention and are being extensively used in AI applications, such as question answering, semantic search, information retrieval and web mining. KGs contain a large amount of structured knowledge/facts. KGs are multi-relational directed graphs consist of entities as graph nodes and relations as edges, which is an efficient way to store real world facts as structured data in triple format. A relational triple can be denoted as (h, r, t) where h and t are the subject/head entity and the object/tail

E. A. de la Cal et al. (Eds.): HAIS 2020, LNAI 12344, pp. 107–119, 2020.
https://doi.org/10.1007/978-3-030-61705-9_10

entity respectively and r is the predicate/relation between the h and t. If the object is a literal then we call it attribute triple.

KG embedding models represent entities and relations, in a low-dimensional vector space while preserving the KG semantics. TransE [1] proposed by Bordes et al. is a simple but effective model which interprets a relationship vector as the translation from the head entity vector to its tail entity vector. In other words, if a relationship triple (h, r, t) holds, $h + r \approx t$ is expected. Popular KG embedding models focus on capturing the semantic of a single KG. It's difficult for a KG to hold all the facts. It may ease the situation if we can align the entities of multiple KGs.

Entity alignment task refers to finding the same real world entities in multiple KGs. There are several existing models which discussed the entity alignment task by means of KG embedding. MTransE [3] is a multilingual knowledge graph embedding model that learns the multilingual knowledge graph structure. JE [7] embeds different KGs into a unified space using TransE with the aim that each seed alignment has similar embeddings. Like JE, IPTransE [23] also represents different KGs into a unified embedding space, which is an iterative and parameter sharing method. Another popular entity alignment model BootEA [15] also embeds two KGs in a unified space and iteratively labels new entity alignment as supervision. It achieved very impressive performance in entity alignment task. JAPE [14] learns entity alignment by jointly exploiting attribute and relational embeddings. AttributeE [16] is an extension of JAPE, they exploit large numbers of attribute triples existing in the knowledge graphs and generates attribute character embeddings to align the entities in two KGs.

The exiting models mostly depend on relational and attribute triples. They require seed alignments (i.e., a seed set of aligned triples from two KGs), which is very limited. It is true that attribute is very helpful in entity alignment but exiting models will fail to align entities in two KGs, in case of entities which have small number of attributes attached to them. To tackle the above challenges, we propose a novel model JSAE for entity alignment which exploit entity summary extracted from the KGs along with the relational and the attribute triples. We exploit BERT [5] to learn the summary embeddings in JSAE. In our model all the components discussed above are jointly optimized to improve the alignment performance. Our proposed approach is an ensemble method of symbolic system and sub-symbolic system. We have incorporated entity summary as part of symbolic system with embeddings as sub-symbolic system.
We summarize the main contributions of this paper as follows:

- We propose a model consists of three components: relational structure embedding, attribute embedding and entity summary embedding.
- We show the effectiveness of entity summary embedding to align entities while very small number of attribute triples exist. Our method can perform well in zero shot scenario where some entities in two KGs only have summary information.

- We perform experiment in two real world datasets. Our experiments on two datasets show that our model largely outperforms the existing state-of-the-art embedding-based entity alignment models.

The rest of this paper is organized as follows. We discuss the related work on KG embedding and KG entity alignment in Sect. 2. We describe the background and formal definitions of the term used in this paper in Sect. 3, Sect. 4 details the proposed model. Section 5 presents the experimental results. Section 6 concludes the paper.

2 Related Work

We have divided the related works in two categories: (1) KG Embedding Models; (2) Entity Alignment Models based on KG Embedding. We discuss them in the rest of this section.

2.1 KG Embedding Models

Several popular KG embedding models have been proposed recently. TransE is the simplest translation distance based model but it has succeeded to get the attention of KG embedding researchers. TransE works well in 1-to-1 relations but has flaws when dealing with 1-to-N, N-to-1 and N-to-N relations. TransH [19] addressed those issues and considered the relation as a translating operation on a relation-specific hyperplane. Relation specific projection makes the model more flexible by choosing the components of embeddings to represent each relation in specific hyperplane. These two models use same vector spaces for both entities and relations. In TransR [9], authors proposed different vector spaces for entities and relations because theoretically entities and relations are different types of component in a KG. Another model is TorusE [6], which proposed a way of solving the regularization problem of TransE. TorusE achieved state-of-the-art results in link prediction task and proved to be highly parameter efficient.

There are several neural network based models e.g., NTN [12], SLM [12]. Another convolutional model called ConvE [4] achieved very competitive results compare to other state-of-the-art models. Bilinear models like DistMult [21] and HolE [11] use tensor-based factorization and represent relationships with matrices. Trouillon et al. proposed a bilinear model ComplEx [17] which uses complex numbers instead of real numbers.

2.2 Entity Alignment Models Based on KG Embedding

The embedding models for KG completion inspired several entity alignments based models. The KG embedding based entity alignment models represent different KGs as embeddings and find entity alignment by calculating the similarity between the embeddings. In this section, we discuss the state-of-the-art KG embedding based entity alignment models.

JAPE. This model proposed embeddings for entities and relations of different KGs in a common embedding space and it showed the effectiveness of attribute triples to learn the entity alignment in between different KGs [14]. JAPE is the first approach which models the attribute triples to address the entity alignment task between cross-lingual KGs.

BootEA. Sun et al. proposed a bootstrapping approach which also embeds the entities and relations of different KGs in a unified embedding space [15]. The main advantage of BootEA is: it can iteratively train a classifier by using bootstrapping approach from both labeled and unlabelled data. BootEA updates newly aligned entities to the exiting seeds set and enriches the training data iteratively.

AttributeE. AttributeE [16] exploited large numbers of attribute triples existing in the KGs. AttributeE utilized character-level literal embeddings and exploited the attribute triples like the JAPE model to learn the alignment. AttributeE showed satisfactory performance but quickly fails when the number of attributes triples are very limited.

Other Models. There are several other models addressed the entity alignment problem. Chen et al. proposed a multilingual alignment model MTransE [3] which follows the principle of TransE. MTransE consists of two components: the first component is the knowledge model that encodes the entities and relations from each language-specific graph structure, and the second component is the alignment model that learns the cross-lingual transitions from the existing seeds. IPTransE [23] proposed a model to align entities according to their semantic distance in the joint embedding space and iteratively label new entity alignment by utilizing the existing seeds. JE [7] utilized structured embedding model (TransE) to embed different KGs into a unified space with the aim that each seed alignment has similar embeddings and showed how to use them in the cross-lingual scenario. KDCoE [2] proposed a multilingual KG embedding model and a multilingual literal description embedding model for cross-lingual entity alignment which is a semi-supervised learning approach. Recently, Multiview[22] achieved the satisfactory performance in entity alignment. But it relies on the large number of seed alignment like BootEA which is a major drawback of this model.

In our proposed model we deal with the entity alignment problem in between multiple KGs and we exploit the entity summary information, which is the main difference between the above discussed models. Our model can tackle the zero-shot scenario while aligning the entities in multiple KGs.

3 Preliminary

In this section we formally define the terms used in this paper and the problem as well.

Definition 1. *Knowledge Graph (KG): A knowledge graph $KG = (E, R, T)$, where E, R, T are the set of entities, relations and triples respectively.*

Definition 2. *Relational Triples: $T \in E \times R \times E$ is a set of relational triples representing the relations between entities, where E and R is the set of all entities and relations respectively.*

Definition 3. *Attribute Triples: $A_T \in E \times A \times L$ is a set of attribute triples representing the attributes of entities, where A is a set of all attributes, and each attribute $A_i \in A$ has a corresponding literal attribute value set $L_i \in L$.*

Definition 4. *Entity Alignment: Given two KGs, KG_1 and KG_2, the entity alignment problem aims to find every pair (e_1, e_2) where $e_1 \in KG_1$, $e_2 \in KG_2$, and e_1, and e_2, represent the same real-world entity.*

Given two knowledge graphs, the objective of our model is to jointly learn the relational structure, attribute embedding and summery embedding to find all the pairs of entities between KGs which represent the same real word entities. In our paper, we use bold lowercase letters to represent embedding vectors and bold uppercase letters to denote matrices.

4 Proposed Methodology

In this section, we describe our model architecture. We exploit embedding-based techniques in our proposed JSAE model. Figure 1 illustrates the JSAE model overview. JSAE can be typically divided into three major components: (1) Predicate alignment between KG_1 and KG_2; (2) Representation learning for entities, relations, attributes and literals; (3) Entity alignment process.

In Fig. 2, we show the intuition behind predicate alignment. For the relational embeddings, we need to have a unified vector space, therefore we merge two KGs based on the predicate similarity. We have adopted the same predicate aligning method described in AttributeE [16].

In our model, we use the TransE model to embed the entities and relations. There are two reasons for using TransE: first, entity alignment is 1-to-1 mapping and TransE shows satisfactory performance in 1-to-1 relations; second, TransE is a very simple but powerful tool and it is very easy to interpret the model architecture. TransE uses the same embedding space for both relationship and entity embeddings. For representation learning part, we have defined three different sub-components: Summary Embedding (SE), Relational Embedding (RE), and Attribute Embedding (AE). We use BERT [5] and Continuous Bags of Words (CBOW) [10] to learn the SE of the entities. In RE, we exploit the translational embedding model, TransE to embed the structured triples. This part is similar to KG embeddings. Finally, AE uses character level embeddings for attribute triples. For the entity alignment part, we marge all the three major components and predict the alignment using cosine similarity.

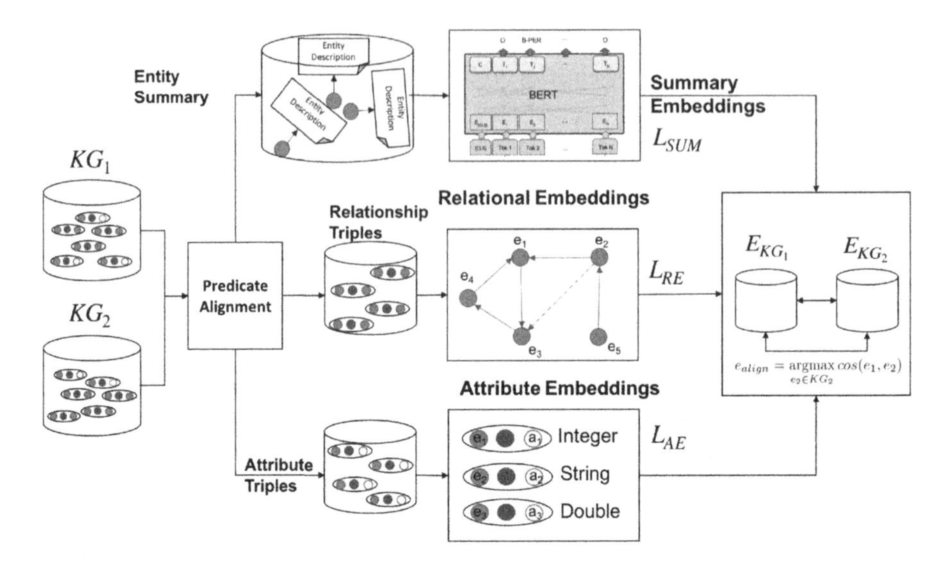

Fig. 1. JSAE model architecture. The figure of BERT embedding is taken from their original paper [5].

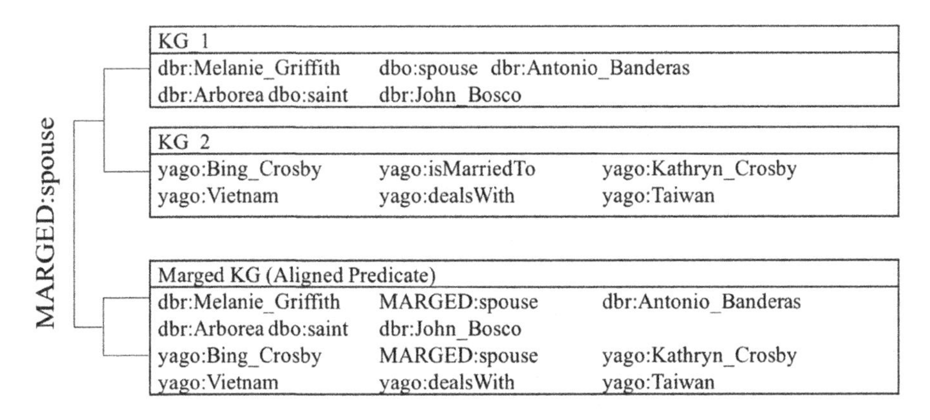

Fig. 2. Predicate alignment of KG_1 and KG_2

4.1 Relational Embedding

To preserve relational structures, we adopt TransE [1] to interpret a relation as a translation vector from its head entity to tail entity. Similar to AttributeE [16], we have also exploited the weight α to control the embedding learning over the triples with aligned predicates. To learn the structure embedding, in our model, we minimize the following objective function L_{RE}:

$$L_{RE} = \sum_{(h,r,t)\in T_r} \sum_{(h',r,t')\in T'_r} max(0, \gamma + \alpha(f_r(h,t) - f_r(h',t'))) \qquad (1)$$

where $\alpha = \frac{count(r)}{|T|}$, γ is the margin, T_r is the set of valid relationship triples, T_r' is the set of corrupted relationship triples, count(r) is the number of occurrences of relationship r, and $|T|$ is the total number of triples in the merged KGs.

4.2 Attribute Embedding

We have employed the basic of TransE for attributes and literals embedding, but unlike relational embedding we interpret predicate r as a translation from the head entity h to the attribute a. For structural differences in various KGs, the same attribute can have multiple representations, as an example one KG might stores the decimal points up to 4 digits where others might keep more (e.g. 23.7000 vs. 23.70000001 as the latitude value of an entity). Therefore to encode the attribute value, we use a compositional function $\phi(a)$ where a is a sequence of the characters of the attribute value $a = c_1, c_2, c_3, \ldots, c_t$ and define the relationship of each element in an attribute triple as $h + r \approx \phi(a)$. The compositional function encodes the attribute value into a single vector and maps the similar attribute values to a similar vector representation. We have applied an N-gram-based compositional function in our proposed model. We use the summation of n-gram combination of the attribute value. The equation is given below:

$$\phi(a) = \sum_{n=1}^{N} \left(\frac{\sum_{i=1}^{l} \sum_{j=i}^{n} c_j}{l - i - 1} \right) \tag{2}$$

To learn the attribute embedding, we minimize the following objective function L_{AE}:

$$L_{AE} = \sum_{(h,r,a) \in T_a} \sum_{(h',r,a') \in T_a'} max(0, \gamma + \alpha(f_a(h,a) - f_a(h',a'))) \tag{3}$$

Here, T_a is the set of valid attribute triples from the training dataset, while $T_a^{'}$ is the set of negative attribute triples (A is the set of attributes in G). The negative samples are constructed by replacing the head entity with a random entity or the attribute with a random attribute value. Here, $f_a(h,a)$ is the plausibility score that based on the embedding of the head entity h, the embedding of the relationship r, and the vector representation of the attribute value that computed using the compositional function $\phi(a)$.

4.3 Entity Summary Embedding

For summary embedding, we are considering the textual description associated with each entity as summary. As example, in DBpedia [8] most of the entities have a short abstract, similarly Wikidata [18] provides a summarize textual description of entities which contain the basic information about those entities.

We employ BERT to generate a set of word vectors from the summary of each specific entity which are usually capable of capturing the main ideas of entities. Recently, BERT achieved the-state-of-the-art performance in the embedding tasks in comparison with the other well stablished techniques e.g., CNN, GRU based models. We discuss the process of obtaining the summary embeddings using BERT in the following section.

Bidirectional Encoder Representations From Transformers. Bidirectional Encoder Representations from Transformers (BERT) model [5] has built on a multilayer bidirectional transformer encoder as the name suggest. It is designed to pre-train deep bidirectional representations from unlabelled text by jointly conditioning on both left and right context. It is a state-of-the-art model for a wide range of tasks, such as word embedding, question answering and language inference, without substantial task specific architecture modifications.

For each entity we feed the summary to the BERT model and we get the embeddings of each word. Then we sum up the embeddings of each word to get the entity embedding based on the summary of that specific entity.

$$\mathbf{e}_{sum} = \mathbf{w}_1 + \mathbf{w}_2 + \mathbf{w}_3 + \cdots + \mathbf{w}_n \tag{4}$$

BERT base model uses 12 layers of transformer encoders, each output from each layer of these (12 layers) can be used as a word embedding. As per the suggestion of the BERT authors, one of the best performance can be found by summing the last 4 layers. We follow their suggestion in our implementation.

Summary Embedding (SE). In our model, we leverage the entity summary to align the entities between two KGs. Xie et. al. already showed that entity summary/description can be a powerful tool for KG completion task [20] and KDCoE [2] followed them in their paper. SE model is effective while the aligning entities have less number of attributes in the KG. There are many entities in KGs with no attribute values at all, in such cases summary embeddings might be an efficient tool to bridge the gap. We use three different scoring functions to learn the entity summary embeddings. They are as follows:

$$\begin{aligned} f_s &= \| \ \mathbf{h}_{sum} + \mathbf{r} - \mathbf{t}_{sum} \ \|_{l1/l2} \\ f_{st} &= \| \ \mathbf{h}_{sum} + \mathbf{r} - \mathbf{t} \ \|_{l1/l2} \\ f_{hs} &= \| \ \mathbf{h} + \mathbf{r} - \mathbf{t}_{sum} \ \|_{l1/l2} \end{aligned} \tag{5}$$

In Eq. (5), for the scoring function f_s: the $\mathbf{h}_{sum}$ and the $\mathbf{t}_{sum}$ are the representations of head and tail entity considering the summary as described in previous section; f_{st} captures the representations of head entity based on summary and tail entity uses SE model based representation and f_{hs} is the exact opposite of f_{st} for head and tail entities.

The summary embedding model learns the entity embeddings as follows:

$$L_{SUM} = f_s + f_{st} + f_{hs} \tag{6}$$

where L_{SUM} is the loss function for summary based representations of entities and the objective is to minimize L_{SUM}.

4.4 Entity Alignment Process

Summary embedding (SE) captures the similarity of entities between two KGs based on the textual description of the entities' while relational structure embedding and attribute embedding capture the similarity of entities between two KGs based on entity relationship and attribute values respectively. Therefore, the overall objective function of our model is:

$$L = L_{RE} + L_{AE} + L_{SUM} \tag{7}$$

We compute the following equation for entity alignment as described in AttributeE [16]. Given an entity $e_1 \in KG_1$, we compute the similarity between e_1 and all entities $e_2 \in KG_2$. to find the aligned entity pair.

$$e_{align} = \underset{e_2 \in KG_2}{\operatorname{argmax}}\, cos(e_1, e_2) \tag{8}$$

For each query entity, we expect the rank of its' truly-aligned target entity to be at the top of the rank list.

5 Experiments

5.1 Datasets

To evaluate our model, we have used two datasets, namely DBP-WD and DBP-YG. They are recently introduced by BootEA [15]. The two datasets were sampled from DBpedia [8], Wikidata [18] and YAGO [13], each of which contains 100,000 aligned entity pairs. The statistics of the dataset is given on the Table 1.

In our model we exploit the aligned predicates to align the entities between KGs. DBP-WD and DBP-YG datasets contain 52 and 30 aligned predicates respectively. Each dataset provides 30% reference of entity alignment data as seeds and left the remaining as testing data.

Table 1. Dataset statistics.

Datasets		Entity	Relation triples	Attribute triples
DBP-WD	DBpedia	100,000	463294	381166
	Wikidata	100,000	448774	789815
DBP-YG	DBpedia	100,000	428952	451646
	YAGO	100,000	502563	118376

For SE model, we have extracted the entities' summaries as follows: (1) For DBpedia we have considered the abstract (en) as the summary; (2) similarly for Wikidata we have considered the Wikipedia (en) abstracts (for the entities in our dataset) as the summary; (3) YAGO does not provide the summary/description on their data dump but it provides Wikilinks to the corresponding entities, so we have extracted the Wiki pages associated with the YAGO entities (for the entities in our dataset) and then copied the abstracts from the Wikipedia links as summaries.

5.2 Experimental Settings

We compared our proposed method with the following models: MTransE [3], IPTransE [23], JAPE [14], BootEA [15], KDCoE [2], and AttributeE [16].

For getting best model performance we tune the hyperparameters. We select the margin γ from $\{1, 5, 10\}$, the embedding dimension d of vectors among $\{50, 75, 100, 150, 200\}$, the learning rate α from $\{0.001, 0.01, 0.1\}$, the batch size B from $\{20, 50, 100, 200\}$. JSAE takes maximum 500 epochs to converse in the experimental datasets.

To evaluate the performance of the models we use Hits@1 and Hits@10 (Hits@k indicates the proportion of correctly aligned entities ranked in the top k predictions), and the mean rank (MR) which denotes the mean the rank of the correct entities for alignment. Higher Hits@k and lower MR indicate better performance.

5.3 Results and Analysis

We have conducted two experiments. In our first experiment, we examined the effectiveness of summary embeddings for entity alignment problem. We compared the individual performances of the embedding models of JSAE to identify the contribution of our summary embedding model. So, we performed experiments for aligning the entities by the summary embedding, attribute embedding and relational embedding models independently on the datasets. The results are shown in the Table 2. As each embedding model focuses on different features so individually they cannot utilize the other feature hence the result is not so promising. Summary emnedding (BERT) achieved Hits@1 score of 64.89% and Hits@10 score of 78.49%. It is proved that the individual performance of Summary emnedding (BERT) is higher than Summary Embedding (CBOW), Relation Embedding and Attribute Embedding models. We also perform experiment using two more combinations: (1) using summary embedding and relational embedding (2) using attribute embedding and relational embedding. They perform better than the individual models (SE, AE and RE). However, when we combine all three embeddings in proposed JSAE, we have observed that it can capture the meaningful representation of the entities and therefore give us the best outcome.

In the second experiment, we show that proposed JSAE model consistently outperforms the baseline models (see Table 3). MTransE, IPTransE, and JAPE rely on the number of the seed alignments, therefore their experiment mainly focused on the cross-lingual datasets of same knowledge graph (e.g. DB-en, DB-fr). BootEA [15] efficiently used their method for aligning two different KGs, but they used 100,000 aligned entities for defining the unified space which is a large number of pre-aligned data. Though DBpedia and Wikidata contain large numbers of already aligned entities but other KGs usually do not provide such a large number of aligned entities. KDCoE [2] used entity description for their alignment method. But their focus on the paper was to align cross-lingual entities in the same KG, so their method can not show good performance for aligning

Table 2. Results of entity alignment using different embeddings combination

Model	DBP-WD			DBP-YG		
	Mean rank	Hits@1	Hits@10	Mean rank	Hits@1	Hits@10
Summary embedding (CBOW)	998	68.4	76.84	1256	63.45	75.49
Summary embedding (BERT)	927	70.4	80.34	1108	64.89	78.49
Relation embedding	152	54.24	65.08	58	33.49	59.89
Attribute embedding	6,774	61.13	72.08	1,001	62.52	73.89
Attribute + Relation embedding	145	67.83	77.98	138	56.34	69.63
Summary (BERT) + Relation embedding	207	74.4	85.34	110	74.39	83.18

entities between different knowledge graphs. AttributeE [16] tactfully handled this issue by using predicate alignment instead of relying on seed alignment. However, for their experiment they have used the benefits of huge attribute triples. Their dataset contains attribute triples, which is three times larger than the relational triples and in our observation we have seen their results drastically falls down when the number of attribute triples is reduced. In our experiment, we have used the predicate alignment so JSAE does not require pre-aligned seeds in the training phase.

Table 3. Comparison with the state-of-the-art embedding-based entity alignment models. The results of MtransE, IPTransE, JAPE and BootEA were directly copied from [15]. We reproduced the others results using their source code.

Model	DBP-WD			DBP-YG		
	Mean rank	Hits@1	Hits@10	Mean rank	Hits@1	Hits@10
MTransE	656	28.12	51.95	512	25.15	49.29
IPTransE	265	34.85	63.84	158	29.74	55.76
JAPE	266	31.84	58.88	189	23.57	48.41
BootEA	109	74.79	89.84	**34**	76.10	89.44
KDCoE	182	57.19	69.53	137	42.71	48.30
AttributeE	142	68.77	80.78	108	57.05	70.64
JSAE (CBOW)	139	78.13	90.38	95	76.87	89.78
JSAE (BERT)	**112**	**81.48**	**92.34**	84	**79.56**	**91.45**

In our dataset the number of attribute triples is almost equal to relational triples, so attribute embedding alone can not achieve reasonable performance, but JSAE leverages summary embedding to utilize the textual information of the entities and outperform the results of the exiting state-of-the-art models. Moreover, predicate alignment module overcomes the dependency of pre-aligned seeds. Among the state-of-the-art models BootEA and AttributeE achieved the better results in DBP-WD and DBP-YG datasets respectively. Hits@k is the most significant metric to evaluate KG embedding models. In the DBP-WD dataset,

JSAI achieved the Hits@1 score of 81.48% which is 8.96% and 18.48% higher than the BootEA and AttributeE respectively. For DBP-YG dataset our model achieved the Hits@1 score of 79.56% which is 39.46% higher than the AttributeE model. Models that exploit attribute property or textual description are tend to have higher mean rank (see Table 3). We have leveraged both properties for our model so our mean rank is higher than BootEA on DBP-YG dataset. For the experiment, we have employed the continuous bag of word model (CBOW) and the BERT model for the summary embeddings. BERT model undoubtedly outperforms CBOW model.

6 Conclusion

In this paper, we introduced a joint entity summary and attribute embedding model along with structural embedding technique for entity alignment in between KGs. Our proposed model uses the BERT embedding model for entity summary embeddings and it's very effective in zero-shot scenario. We also discussed how our approach can overcome the flaws of the recently proposed entity alignment methods. We compared the performance of JSAE with the most recent state-of the-art models. Our experimental results demonstrated that our approach achieved superior results than the baseline embedding approaches.

References

1. Bordes, A., Usunier, N., Garcia-Duran, A., Weston, J., Yakhnenko, O.: Translating embeddings for modeling multi-relational data. In: NIPS, pp. 2787–2795 (2013)
2. Chen, M., Tian, Y., Chang, K.W., Skiena, S., Zaniolo, C.: Co-training embeddings of knowledge graphs and entity descriptions for cross-lingual entity alignment. In: IJCAI, pp. 3998–4004 (2018)
3. Chen, M., Tian, Y., Yang, M., Zaniolo, C.: Multilingual knowledge graph embeddings for cross-lingual knowledge alignment. In: IJCAI, pp. 1511–1517 (2017)
4. Dettmers, T., Minervini, P., Stenetorp, P., Riedel, S.: Convolutional 2D knowledge graph embeddings. In: AAAI, pp. 1811–1818 (2018)
5. Devlin, J., Chang, M., Lee, K., Toutanova, K.: BERT: pre-training of deep bidirectional transformers for language understanding. In: NAACL-HLT, pp. 4171–4186 (2019)
6. Ebisu, T., Ichise, R.: Toruse: knowledge graph embedding on a lie group. In: AAAI, pp. 1819–1826 (2018)
7. Hao, Y., Zhang, Y., He, S., Liu, K., Zhao, J.: A joint embedding method for entity alignment of knowledge bases. In: Chen, H., Ji, H., Sun, L., Wang, H., Qian, T., Ruan, T. (eds.) CCKS 2016. CCIS, vol. 650, pp. 3–14. Springer, Singapore (2016). https://doi.org/10.1007/978-981-10-3168-7_1
8. Lehmann, J., et al.: Dbpedia-a large-scale, multilingual knowledge base extracted from wikipedia. Semant. Web **6**(2), 167–195 (2015)
9. Lin, Y., Liu, Z., Sun, M., Liu, Y., Zhu, X.: Learning entity and relation embeddings for knowledge graph completion. In: AAAI,. pp. 2181–2187 (2015)
10. Mikolov, T., Chen, K., Corrado, G., Dean, J.: Efficient estimation of word representations in vector space. In: ICLR Workshop Track (2013)

11. Nickel, M., Rosasco, L., Poggio, T.: Holographic embeddings of knowledge graphs. In: AAAI, pp. 1955–1961 (2016)
12. Socher, R., Chen, D., Manning, C.D., Ng, A.: Reasoning with neural tensor networks for knowledge base completion. In: NIPS, pp. 926–934 (2013)
13. Suchanek, F.M., Kasneci, G., Weikum, G.: Yago: a core of semantic knowledge. In: WWW, pp. 697–706 (2007)
14. Sun, Z., Hu, W., Li, C.: Cross-lingual entity alignment via joint attribute-preserving embedding. In: d'Amato, C., et al. (eds.) ISWC 2017. LNCS, vol. 10587, pp. 628–644. Springer, Cham (2017). https://doi.org/10.1007/978-3-319-68288-4_37
15. Sun, Z., Hu, W., Zhang, Q., Qu, Y.: Bootstrapping entity alignment with knowledge graph embedding. In: IJCAI, pp. 4396–4402 (2018)
16. Trisedya, B.D., Qi, J., Zhang, R.: Entity alignment between knowledge graphs using attribute embeddings. In: AAAI, pp. 297–304 (2019)
17. Trouillon, T., Welbl, J., Riedel, S., Gaussier, É., Bouchard, G.: Complex embeddings for simple link prediction. In: ICML, pp. 2071–2080 (2016)
18. Vrandečić, D., Krötzsch, M.: Wikidata: a free collaborative knowledge base. Commun. ACM **57**(10), 78–85 (2014)
19. Wang, Z., Zhang, J., Feng, J., Chen, Z.: Knowledge graph embedding by translating on hyperplanes. In: AAAI, pp. 1112–1119 (2014)
20. Xie, R., Liu, Z., Jia, J., Luan, H., Sun, M.: Representation learning of knowledge graphs with entity descriptions. In: AAAI, pp. 2659–2665 (2016)
21. Yang, B., Yih, W.T., He, X., Gao, J., Deng, L.: Embedding entities and relations for learning and inference in knowledge bases. In: ICLR 2015 (2015)
22. Zhang, Q., Sun, Z., Hu, W., Chen, M., Guo, L., Qu, Y.: Multi-view knowledge graph embedding for entity alignment. In: IJCAI, pp. 5429–5435 (2019)
23. Zhu, H., Xie, R., Liu, Z., Sun, M.: Iterative entity alignment via joint knowledge embeddings. In: IJCAI, pp. 4258–4264 (2017)

Employing Decision Templates to Imbalanced Data Classification

Szymon Wojciechowski(✉) and Michał Woźniak

Department of Systems and Computer Networks, Faculty of Electronics, Wrocław University of Science and Technology, Wybrzeże Wyspiańskiego 27, 50-370 Wrocław, Poland
{szymon.wojciechowski,michal.wozniak}@pwr.edu.pl

Abstract. Data difficulties as imbalanced class distribution cause that the methods which can produce reliable predictive models remain a focus of intense research. This work attempts employing the concept of *Decision Templates* for the mentioned classification task. Additionally, a modification to the original method is introduced, which uses many decision templates for each class instead of one per class. The usefulness of the algorithms employing the idea of *Decision Template* algorithm is evaluated based on extensive experimental study and backed-up with a thorough statistical analysis. We also present an in-depth discussion of both the positive and negative impacts of the proposed approach.

Keywords: Imbalanced data · Pattern classification · Decision template

1 Introduction

There are many modern machine learning problems which difficulty is related to high disproportion among class sizes. This high disproportion may have a negative impact on the classifier learnig, as the decision is biased towards majority class, but often the samples from minority are the ones, for which classification error has higher cost [9]. This problem is a common task, including in medical diagnostics, cybersecurity or banking. The most popular methods of dealing with this phenomenon include algorithms based on data preprocessing (undersampling, oversampling and combining these approaches) [7], modification of classification algorithms so that they take into account the disproportions among number of examples from different classes [10] (e.g., by taking into account the appropriate form of the loss function, or choosing an adequate training criterion), or finally a combination of both approaches. In this work, we will focus on the use of adequately designed classifier ensembles, which are one of the most commonly used methods in the considered classification task [11,13].

When designing the above classifiers, we have to answer three questions [18]: (i) how to choose base classifiers to form a valuable, diverse pool, (ii) how the base classifiers should be interconnected, (iii) how to get the final decision based

E. A. de la Cal et al. (Eds.): HAIS 2020, LNAI 12344, pp. 120–131, 2020.
https://doi.org/10.1007/978-3-030-61705-9_11

on the decisions of the base classifiers, i.e., how to propose the appropriate combination rule. The most popular, parallel classifier ensemble architecture will be used in the work, and a diversified pool of classifiers will be generated using methods based on *bootstrapping*, while in this work we will focus on the appropriate selection of the combination rule for the imbalanced data classification task. The most common combination rules are methods based only on class labels passed by base classifiers, or techniques based on the so-called support functions [6]. We will focus on the second type of combination rules and propose of *Decision Template* (proposed by Kuncheva et al. [12]) dedicated to imbalanced data analysis. Details of the model will be described in the next section, but the idea of this approach is based on creating, for each class, so-called *Decision Templates* indicating what the most popular support values returned by each base classifiers are. Our modification consists of building more than one *Decision Template* for each class. There are not many modifications to this approach in the literature. Most authors focus on proposing new methods of calculating the so-called similarity measure (i.e., how to measure the distance between a given observation and a *Decision Template*). Only a few works suggest decomposing this model. Nguen et al. [15] use heuristic optimization to find the optimal template that minimizes the empirical 0-1 loss function. Dietrich et al. [4] calculate multiple *Decision Templates* per class and use this model for bioacoustic time series classification. In turn, Min et al. [14] propose to generate many templates per class and make a decision based on the most popular class among k-nearest localized templates. According to the best of the authors knowledge, *Decision Templates* integration was not applied to imbalanced data in the past, which is a main motivation for this work. Moreover, this method offers wide range of possible modifications which might improve classification of imbalanced data.

The main contributions of this work are as follows:

- Verification of *Decision Template* integration algorithm for imbalanced data classification
- Proposition of a novel classifier based on *Decision Templates*
- Proposition of a learning algorithm of the proposed classifier which bases on clustering the support function space
- Experimental evaluation of the discussed approaches based on imbalanced datasets and backed by the statistical analysis of the results.

2 Methods

Let $x \in R^d$ be a sample of d dimensional feature space $\mathcal{X}$ and $\mathcal{C} = \{1, 2, ..., c\}$ is a set of possible labels. A classifier Ψ maps the feature space into the set of the labels:

$$\Psi : \mathcal{X} \to \mathcal{C}. \tag{1}$$

Most of the classifiers are also capable of presenting the outputs in a continuous form, which provides a “support” for each class [6]:

$$\widetilde{\Psi} : \mathcal{X} \to [\mu_1, \mu_2, ..., \mu_c] \Leftrightarrow \mu \in [0, 1] \tag{2}$$

which is used to make a final decision using *maximum support rule* (e.g., for the probabilistic classifiers the *maximum posterior probability* rule is used):

$$\Psi(x) = i \Leftrightarrow i = \max_{1,2,\ldots,c} \widetilde{\Psi}_c(x) \tag{3}$$

The classifier pool $\mathcal{L}$ is a set of classifiers $\{\Psi_1, \Psi_2, ..., \Psi_l\}$. Decision profile DP is a matrix computed for x in following manner:

$$DP(x) = \begin{bmatrix} \widetilde{\Psi}_{1,1}(x)\ \widetilde{\Psi}_{1,2}(x) \ ...\ \widetilde{\Psi}_{1,c}(x) \\ \widetilde{\Psi}_{2,1}(x)\ \widetilde{\Psi}_{2,2}(x) \ ...\ \widetilde{\Psi}_{2,c}(x) \\ ... \\ \widetilde{\Psi}_{l,1}(x)\ \widetilde{\Psi}_{l,2}(x) \ ...\ \widetilde{\Psi}_{l,c}(x) \end{bmatrix} \tag{4}$$

For a given training set $Z = \{z_1, z_2, ..., z_n\}$ of samples, where $z_k \in \mathcal{X}$, and $Y = \{y_1, y_2, ..., y_n\}$ of the corresponding labels $y_k \in \mathcal{C}$, decision template DT of class i is calculated as the arithmetic mean of all the decision profiles of of samples from class i.

The integration of the classifier Ψ' which is consisting of pool $\mathcal{L}$ is based on similarity measure. In this work only minimal euclidean distance between DT and $DP(x)$ will be considered:

$$\Psi' : \mathcal{X} \rightarrow i \Leftrightarrow i = \min_{1,2,\ldots,c} \sqrt{\sum_{p=1}^{l}\sum_{q=1}^{c}(DT_{c,p,q} - \widetilde{\Psi}_{p,q}(x))^2} \tag{5}$$

Decision profiles can be flattened by concatenating all l rows, which will transform x from d dimensional feature space $\mathcal{X}$ to $s = l \cdot c$ dimensional *support space* S. The example of such a transformation is presented in Fig. 1. The original synthetic binary data set is represented by two features, which distributions are overlapping. Decision profiles were calculated from two pre-trained Naive Bayes classifiers. To make a visualization of new 4-dimensional space PCA decomposition was used - giving a picture of decision profiles distribution (see Fig. 1). The samples of each class usually group on two extremities, however not all of them.

Figure 2 presents decision templates (marked with $\times$ symbol) for the same data. It can be observed that the majority class template is surrounded by corresponding samples. However minority class template is shifted from place where the density of decision profiles is high. Moreover, many of the majority class samples are placed close to the minority class template.

Based on the observations from the example, it can be assumed that the model could be enhanced by creating more than one decision template per class. One way to achieve this is to use a segmentation algorithm. In this work OPTICS

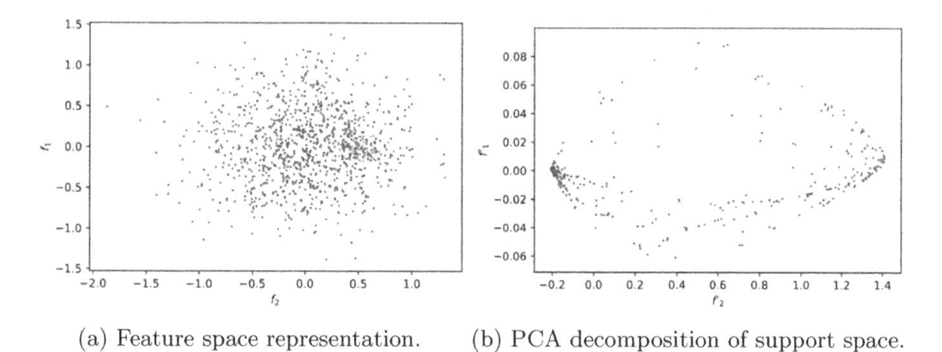

(a) Feature space representation. (b) PCA decomposition of support space.

Fig. 1. Samples representation in feature and support space.

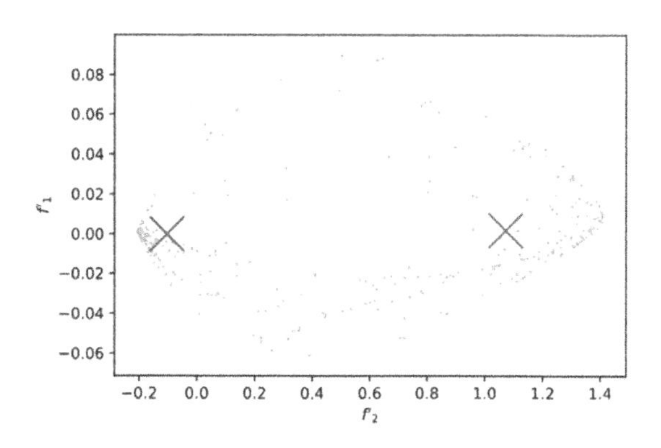

Fig. 2. Decision templates placement.

[2] algorithm was selected, which does not need parameter tuning for satisfying results and it is not limited to a fixed number of clusters.

Algorithm 1. OPTICS Decision Templates

Data: Set of decision profiles $P = DP(Z)$
1 decision_templates := Set($\emptyset$)
2 decision_templates_labels := Set($\emptyset$)
3 **foreach** *label* c *in labels* $\mathcal{C}$ **do**
4 | clusters T := OPTICS(P_c)
5 | **foreach** *cluster* t *in clusters* T **do**
6 | | put(decision_templates, $DT(t)$)
7 | | put(decision_templates_labels, c)
8 | **end**
9 **end**
Result: decision_templates, decision_templates_labels

The new procedure is presented in Algorithm 1. OPTICS algorithm is used to separate clusters of each class in support space, then each for each subset of points decision template is created in the same manner as it is done in the original algorithm, and is using the same decision rule as previously, but the distance is calculated for all new decision templates.

This approach, however, does not consider that the number of samples in the cluster can be strongly imbalanced between them. To compensate this, each template can be assigned with weight-based on the ratio between all samples in the cluster and all samples in class:

$$W_t = \frac{||P_c||}{||t||}. \tag{6}$$

Denoting `decision_templates_labels` as DTL new decision function for Weighted Optics Decision Templates can be defined:

$$\Psi' : \mathcal{X} \rightarrow i \Leftrightarrow i = DTL_j \Leftrightarrow j = \min_{1,2,\ldots,t} W_t \sqrt{\sum_{p=1}^{l} \sum_{q=1}^{c} (DT_{t,p,q} - \widetilde{\Psi}_{p,q}(x))^2} \tag{7}$$

Figure 3 is presenting new decision templates obtained from segmentation. The size of the marker is corresponding to template weight. In this example templates seem to be better matching an original decision profile distribution.

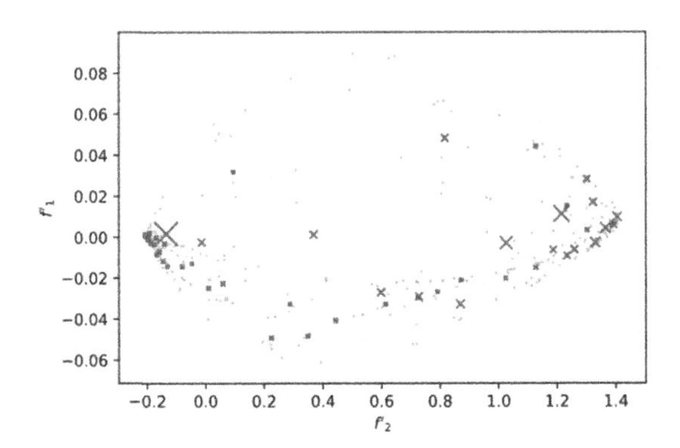

Fig. 3. Decision templates based on OPTICS segmentation.

3 Experiments

The experiments were carried out to find answers to the following questions:

- Are decision templates based integration algorithms performing better for imbalanced data sets classification, than other well-known integration algorithms?

- Is the segmentation of intermediate feature space significantly improving this method?

Setup. Experiments were prepared in Python language, using classification and segmentation algorithms provided in scikit-learn package [16] as a reference to proposed methods. The code is available in the on-line repository provided in the supplementary materials.

Data Sets. Experiments were carried out on well-known data sets from KEEL repository [1], and only binary problems were selected. Moreover, the imbalance ratio in all of the selected data sets *imbalance ration* varying between 1:1.5 and 1:9. Detailed description of selected problems is presented in Table 1. As the experimental protocol 5×2 cross-validation [5] has been chosen.

Experiment Conditions. For each data set, the homogeneous classifier pool consisted of 20 Naive Bayes classifiers was used. All classifiers were trained using *Balanced Bagging* algorithm [13], to provide better diversity into the pool. Each integration algorithm used the same pool trained on the same fold and it was verified on the same samples. All of the proposed algorithms were compared with two other commonly used integration methods *Majority Voting* and *Average Aggregation* [8].

Metrics. To compare the performance quality of the classifiers, measures based on confusion matrix such as sensitivity, specificity and precision were used, and also other aggregated metrics as balanced accuracy, f1 score, and g-mean. This selection is commonly used to score classifiers in imbalanced data problems. All of the results were verified for statistical significance using Wilcoxon singed-rank test [3,17] with the significance level $\rho < 0.05$.

Table 1. Selected data sets with their properties.

Data set	IR	Samples	Features	Data set	IR	Samples	Features
glass1	1:1.82	214	9	glass-0-1-2-3_vs_4-5-6	1:3.2	214	9
ecoli-0_vs_1	1:1.86	220	7	vehicle0	1:3.25	846	18
wisconsin	1:1.86	683	9	ecoli1	1:3.36	336	7
pima	1:1.87	768	8	new-thyroid1	1:5.14	215	5
iris0	1:2.0	150	4	new-thyroid2	1:5.14	215	5
glass0	1:2.06	214	9	ecoli2	1:5.46	336	7
yeast1	1:2.46	484	8	segment0	1:6.02	2308	19
haberman	1:2.78	306	3	glass6	1:6.38	214	9
vehicle2	1:2.88	846	18	yeast3	1:8.1	1484	8
vehicle1	1:2.9	846	18	ecoli3	1:8.6	336	7
vehicle3	1:2.99	846	18	page-blocks0	1:8.79	5472	10

3.1 Results

The detailed results of the chosen metrics are presented in Table 2 and Table 3. Below each mean metric value and its standard deviation, a list of reference methods, which were statistically significantly outperformed by the classifier, are listed. Detailed results for the rest of the metrics are available in supplementary materials[1].

The results of sensitivity testify that all of the proposed methods outperform reference methods in at least one of the evaluated data sets, which are `glass`, `vehicle2`, `pima` for Weighted OPTICS Decision Templates, OPTICS Decision Templates, and Decision Templates accordingly. However, Majority Voting and Average Aggregation outperform proposed algorithms in all of the `yeast` data sets and `vehicle0`. Moreover, in `vehicle1`, `glass0` and `glass1` those also performed better, but the difference was not statistically significant to Weighted OPTICS Decision Templates. It is also noticeable that Average Aggregation is globally reaching the best scores, while OPTICS Decision Templates is the worse one.

The specificity results, on the other hand, are exposing an advantage of OPTICS Decision Templates algorithm, which in most cases outperformed the other algorithms. Other interesting results can be observed in `pima` where the globally best method reached the lowest score. In this experiment, there are too many factors to conclude, but a more in-depth analysis of this example could expose the weakens of OPTICS Decision Templates. It should also be mentioned that in the case of imbalanced data, this metric is less preferred than sensitivity.

The ranking results are presented in Table 4. The observations from previous tables are confirming that OPTICS Decision Templates are performing very well on specificity, but are the loosing on sensitivity even though they have a positive impact on precision, because of reducing false-negative predictions.

The significant improvement of those metrics did not reflect on aggregated metrics. Most probably because of very low sensitivity. On the other hand, the original Decision Templates algorithm is significantly improving Balanced Accuracy and G-mean and it is significantly better than Average Aggregation and Weighted OPTICS Decision Templates in F1 score. It is also important to mention that the second-best algorithm is Majority Voting.

The results are showing that indeed Decision Templates are better-suited integration method for imbalanced data classification, under the conditions of this experiment. On the other hand, the experiment is suggesting that despite the intuition, segmentation does not improve the original method.

3.2 Discussion

Let's try to answer the following research questions.

Why Decision Templates Are Improving Results? The results are implying that *Decision Templates* algorithm is keeping the best balance between sensitivity

[1] https://github.com/w4k2/decision-templates.

Table 2. Mean sensitivity results.

Classifier / Data set	Majority Voting(1)	Average Aggregation(2)	Decision Templates(3)	OPTICS Decision Templates(4)	Weighted OPTICS Decision Templates(5)
ecoli-0_vs_1	0.93±0.05 -	0.93 ± 0.05 -	0.93 ± 0.05 -	0.94 ± 0.04 -	0.93 ± 0.06 -
ecoli1	0.90±0.05 4	0.91 ± 0.05 4	0.90 ± 0.04 4	0.68 ± 0.18 -	0.90 ± 0.03 4
ecoli2	0.92±0.05 4	0.93 ± 0.04 3, 4	0.91 ± 0.04 4	0.81 ± 0.08 -	0.92 ± 0.04 4
ecoli3	0.92±0.06 4	0.91 ± 0.07 4	0.93 ± 0.06 4	0.52 ± 0.24 -	0.93 ± 0.05 4
glass-0-1-2-3_vs_4-5-6	0.77±0.09 -	0.80 ± 0.08 1	0.82 ± 0.08 1, 2	0.84 ± 0.09 -	0.90 ± 0.09 1, 2, 3
glass0	0.90±0.07 3, 4	0.90 ± 0.07 3, 4, 5	0.86 ± 0.08 4	0.43 ± 0.17 -	0.79 ± 0.18 4
glass1	0.90±0.04 3, 4	0.90 ± 0.04 3, 4	0.82 ± 0.07 4	0.52 ± 0.12 -	0.76 ± 0.23 -
glass6	0.86±0.07 -	0.86 ± 0.07 -	0.88 ± 0.07 -	0.81 ± 0.12 -	0.93 ± 0.06 1, 2, 3, 4
haberman	0.41±0.11 -	0.42 ± 0.11 -	0.45 ± 0.11 1, 2, 4	0.35 ± 0.08 -	0.43 ± 0.16 -
iris0	1.00±0.00 -	1.00 ± 0.00 -	1.00 ± 0.00 -	1.00 ± 0.00 -	1.00 ± 0.00 -
new-thyroid1	1.00±0.00 -	1.00 ± 0.00 -	1.00 ± 0.00 -	1.00 ± 0.00 -	1.00 ± 0.00 -
new-thyroid2	1.00±0.00 -	1.00 ± 0.00 -	1.00 ± 0.00 -	0.99 ± 0.02 -	1.00 ± 0.00 -
page-blocks0	0.60±0.02 -	0.60 ± 0.02 -	0.67 ± 0.02 1, 2	0.57 ± 0.13 -	0.74 ± 0.16 1, 2, 4
pima	0.67±0.03 4	0.68 ± 0.02 1, 4	0.69 ± 0.03 1, 2, 4, 5	0.59 ± 0.08 -	0.67 ± 0.04 4
segment0	0.98±0.01 4	0.98 ± 0.01 4	0.98 ± 0.01 4	0.80 ± 0.05 -	0.98 ± 0.01 4
vehicle0	0.92±0.04 3, 4, 5	0.92 ± 0.04 3, 4, 5	0.89 ± 0.04 4, 5	0.53 ± 0.13 -	0.86 ± 0.06 4
vehicle1	0.70±0.06 3, 4	0.70 ± 0.06 3, 4	0.69 ± 0.05 4	0.48 ± 0.09 -	0.72 ± 0.08 4
vehicle2	0.71±0.08 -	0.72 ± 0.08 1	0.75 ± 0.07 1, 2	0.81 ± 0.08 1, 2, 3, 5	0.71 ± 0.07 -
vehicle3	0.66±0.04 4	0.67 ± 0.04 3, 4	0.65 ± 0.04 4	0.37 ± 0.08 -	0.66 ± 0.06 4
wisconsin	0.98±0.01 4	0.98 ± 0.01 4	0.98 ± 0.01 4	0.97 ± 0.01 -	0.99 ± 0.01 1, 2, 3, 4
yeast1	0.99±0.01 3, 4, 5	0.99 ± 0.01 3, 4, 5	0.81 ± 0.12 4	0.39 ± 0.04 -	0.75 ± 0.09 4
yeast3	0.96±0.03 3, 4, 5	0.97 ± 0.03 3, 4, 5	0.91 ± 0.04 4	0.59 ± 0.10 -	0.90 ± 0.03 4

and specificity. Decision templates are reducing the missclassification rate. The example presented in this article is showing that decision profiles are aggregated in support space, which might be related to the pool level of confidence. The samples which will be placed in the aggregation of the opposite class might be outliers and biasing a model towards the might lower than the overall performance of the ensemble.

Table 3. Mean specificity results.

Classifier / Data set	Majority Voting(1)	Average Aggregation(2)	Decision Templates(3)	OPTICS Decision Templates(4)	Weighted OPTICS Decision Templates(5)
ecoli-0_vs_1	0.99±0.02 -	0.99 ± 0.02 -	0.99 ± 0.02 -	0.99 ± 0.01 -	0.98 ± 0.03 -
ecoli1	0.77±0.13 -	0.76 ± 0.14 -	0.84 ± 0.04 1, 2	0.88 ± 0.05 1, 2, 3, 5	0.84 ± 0.06 -
ecoli2	0.78±0.14 2	0.77 ± 0.15 -	0.89 ± 0.04 1, 2, 5	0.96 ± 0.02 1, 2, 3, 5	0.79 ± 0.11 -
ecoli3	0.86±0.03 5	0.86 ± 0.04 5	0.86 ± 0.03 5	0.93 ± 0.03 1, 2, 3, 5	0.82 ± 0.06 -
glass-0-1-2-3_vs_4-5-6	0.93±0.03 3, 5	0.91 ± 0.03 5	0.90 ± 0.03 -	0.94 ± 0.02 2, 3, 5	0.88 ± 0.04 -
glass0	0.51±0.06 -	0.51 ± 0.06 -	0.53 ± 0.06 1, 2	0.87 ± 0.06 1, 2, 3, 5	0.59 ± 0.09 1, 2
glass1	0.40±0.11 -	0.39 ± 0.10 -	0.46 ± 0.10 1, 2	0.74 ± 0.07 1, 2, 3, 5	0.47 ± 0.20 -
glass6	0.93±0.03 2, 5	0.92 ± 0.03 5	0.93 ± 0.03 5	0.96 ± 0.02 1, 2, 3, 5	0.87 ± 0.07 -
haberman	0.84±0.06 4	0.84 ± 0.07 4	0.81 ± 0.06 -	0.75 ± 0.07 -	0.73 ± 0.16 -
iris0	1.00±0.00 -	1.00 ± 0.00 -	1.00 ± 0.00 -	1.00 ± 0.00 -	1.00 ± 0.00 -
new-thyroid1	0.96±0.02 5	0.96 ± 0.02 5	0.96 ± 0.02 5	0.98 ± 0.02 1, 2, 3, 5	0.94 ± 0.02 -
new-thyroid2	0.97±0.02 5	0.97 ± 0.02 5	0.97 ± 0.02 5	0.98 ± 0.01 1, 2, 3, 5	0.96 ± 0.03 -
page-blocks0	0.93±0.01 2, 3, 5	0.93 ± 0.01 3, 5	0.93 ± 0.01 5	0.96 ± 0.01 1, 2, 3, 5	0.60 ± 0.06 -
pima	0.78±0.03 2, 3, 4, 5	0.77 ± 0.03 3, 4	0.77 ± 0.02 4	0.68 ± 0.04 -	0.76 ± 0.03 4
segment0	0.77±0.04 -	0.77 ± 0.04 -	0.79 ± 0.04 1, 2	0.98 ± 0.00 1, 2, 3, 5	0.79 ± 0.04 1, 2, 3
vehicle0	0.59±0.03 -	0.58 ± 0.03 -	0.60 ± 0.03 1, 2	0.87 ± 0.03 1, 2, 3, 5	0.61 ± 0.03 1, 2, 3
vehicle1	0.66±0.02 5	0.65 ± 0.02 5	0.67 ± 0.02 1, 2, 5	0.77 ± 0.04 1, 2, 3, 5	0.58 ± 0.06 -
vehicle2	0.81±0.07 -	0.81 ± 0.07 -	0.80 ± 0.06 -	0.92 ± 0.03 1, 2, 3, 5	0.82 ± 0.09 -
vehicle3	0.68±0.04 2, 5	0.67 ± 0.04 5	0.68 ± 0.03 5	0.77 ± 0.06 1, 2, 3, 5	0.58 ± 0.09 -
wisconsin	0.95±0.02 5	0.95 ± 0.02 5	0.95 ± 0.02 5	0.95 ± 0.02 5	0.92 ± 0.02 -
yeast1	0.03±0.01 -	0.03 ± 0.01 -	0.47 ± 0.27 1, 2	0.82 ± 0.02 1, 2, 3, 5	0.54 ± 0.12 1, 2
yeast3	0.46±0.34 2	0.42 ± 0.29 -	0.87 ± 0.10 1, 2	0.96 ± 0.01 1, 2, 3, 5	0.89 ± 0.07 1, 2

Why Clustering-Based Templates Are Not Improving Aggregated Metrics? The sensitivity results are clearly showing that segmentation is producing decision templates, which are improving majority class detection, but in the cost of the minority class. It is unwanted behavior for imbalanced problems, but the valuable

Table 4. Ranking results.

Classifier	Majority Voting(1)	Average Aggregation(2)	Decision Templates(3)	OPTICS Decision Templates(4)	Weighted OPTICS Decision Templates(5)
Sensitivity	3.07 4	3.61 1, 4	3.27 4	1.68 -	3.36 4
Specificity	3.00 2	2.07 -	3.07 2	4.59 1, 2, 3, 5	2.27 -
Precision	3.20 2	2.34 -	3.27 2, 5	4.27 1, 2, 3, 5	1.91 -
F1 score	3.20 -	2.80 -	3.82 2, 5	2.86 -	2.32 -
Balanced Accuracy	2.98 -	2.86 -	3.93 1, 2, 4, 5	2.64 -	2.59 -
G-mean	3.00 -	2.73 -	3.95 1, 2, 4, 5	2.73 -	2.59 -

property of this method. It might be related to lack of weighting - in which case a bigger spread of majority class in support space will cover more of its area.

On the other hand, the weighted version of the algorithm is reaching very low precision. What is related to a high number of false-positives, so weighting is equalizing changes of the minority class. Probably, because outliers are classified as majority class, then they are used to create a template that is placed near the majority class highest density what should be verified in future research.

4 Final Remarks

This research exposed the potential of decision templates in the classification of imbalanced data. Results are also suggesting that modifications based on segmentation are not providing a positive impact to this task. It seems that the biggest issue in this approach are templates found close to aggregations of the opposite class. The feature research should verify if all of the decision profiles should be clustered, perhaps samples should be selected in feature space before creating decision templates. It should be also possible to propose a decision template selection method.

The future research should be focused on finding another way to adopt decision templates in imbalanced data classification, as it seems that it can still be improved. The high-dimensional support space might have a negative impact. Perhaps other metrics than euclidean distance should also be evaluated.

Acknowledgments. This work was supported by the Polish National Science Centre under the grant No. 2017/27/B/ST6/01325 as well as by the statutory funds of the

Department of Systems and Computer Networks,Wroclaw University of Science and Technology.

References

1. Alcalá-Fdez, J., et al.: Keel data-mining software tool: data set repository, integration of algorithms and experimental analysis framework. J. Multiple-Valued Log. Soft Comput. **17**, 255–287 (2011)
2. Ankerst, M., Breunig, M.M., Kriegel, H.P., Sander, J.: Optics: ordering points to identify the clustering structure. In: Proceedings of the 1999 ACM SIGMOD International Conference on Management of Data, pp. 49–60. Association for Computing Machinery (1999)
3. Demšar, J.: Statistical comparisons of classifiers over multiple data sets. J. Mach. Learn. Res. **7**, 1–30 (2006)
4. Dietrich, C., Palm, G., Schwenker, F.: Decision templates for the classification of bioacoustic time series. Inf. Fusion **4**(2), 101–109 (2003). https://doi.org/10.1016/S1566-2535(03)00017-4, http://www.sciencedirect.com/science/article/pii/S1566253503000174
5. Dietterich, T.G.: Approximate statistical tests for comparing supervised classification learning algorithms. Neural Comput. **10**(7), 1895–1923 (1998)
6. Duda, R.O., Hart, P.E., Stork, D.G.: Pattern Classification, 2nd edn. Wiley-Interscience, USA (2000)
7. GarcíÂa, V., Sánchez, J., Mollineda, R.: On the effectiveness of preprocessing methods when dealing with different levels of class imbalance. Knowl.-Based Syst. **25**(1), 13–21 (2012). special Issue on New Trends in Data Mining
8. Kittler, J., Hatef, M., Duin, R.P.W., Matas, J.: On combining classifiers. IEEE Trans. Pattern Anal. Mach. Intell. **20**(3), 226–239 (1998)
9. Krawczyk, B.: Learning from imbalanced data: open challenges and future directions. Prog. Artif. Intell. **5**(4), 221–232 (2016). https://doi.org/10.1007/s13748-016-0094-0
10. Krawczyk, B., Wozniak, M., Schaefer, G.: Cost-sensitive decision tree ensembles for effective imbalanced classification. Appl. Soft Comput. **14**, 554–562 (2014). https://doi.org/10.1016/j.asoc.2013.08.014
11. Ksieniewicz, P.: Undersampled majority class ensemble for highly imbalanced binary classification. In: Proceedings of the Second International Workshop on Learning with Imbalanced Domains: Theory and Applications, vol. 94, pp. 82–94. PMLR (2018)
12. Kuncheva, L.I., Bezdek, J.C., Duin, R.P.: Decision templates for multiple classifier fusion: an experimental comparison. Pattern Recogn. **34**(2), 299–314 (2001)
13. Liu, X., Wu, J., Zhou, Z.: Exploratory undersampling for class-imbalance learning. IEEE Trans. Syst. Man Cybern. Part B (Cybern.) **39**(2), 539–550 (2009)
14. Min, J.-K., Cho, S.-B.: Multiple classifier fusion using k-nearest localized templates. In: Yin, H., Tino, P., Corchado, E., Byrne, W., Yao, X. (eds.) IDEAL 2007. LNCS, vol. 4881, pp. 447–456. Springer, Heidelberg (2007). https://doi.org/10.1007/978-3-540-77226-2_46
15. Nguyen, T.T., et al.: Evolving an optimal decision template for combining classifiers. In: Gedeon, T., Wong, K.W., Lee, M. (eds.) ICONIP 2019. LNCS, vol. 11953, pp. 608–620. Springer, Cham (2019). https://doi.org/10.1007/978-3-030-36708-4_50

16. Pedregosa, F., et al.: Scikit-learn: machine learning in Python. J. Mach. Learn. Res. **12**, 2825–2830 (2011)
17. Wilcoxon, F.: Individual comparisons by ranking methods. Biometrics Bull. **1**(6), 80–83 (1945)
18. Woźniak, M., Graña, M., Corchado, E.: A survey of multiple classifier systems as hybrid systems. Inf. Fusion **16**, 3–17 (2014)

Comparison of Labeling Methods for Behavioral Activity Classification Based on Gaze Ethograms

Javier de Lope[1(✉)] and Manuel Graña[2]

[1] Computational Cognitive Robotics Group, Department of Artificial Intelligence, Universidad Politécnica de Madrid (UPM), Madrid, Spain
javier.delope@upm.es
[2] Computational Intelligence Group, University of the Basque Country (UPV/EHU), San Sebastian, Spain

Abstract. The paper describes and compares several novel alternatives for labeling gaze ethograms data to estimate the activity that users carry out in front of computers with the use of the onboard camera. Gaze ethograms are basically discrete functions of time, therefore, the problem can be formulated by applying statistical and machine learning inspired methods to reduce the amount of information on a specific activity. To compare the proposed methods we carry out several experiments with experimental subjects in an office-like environment with no special lighting conditions. The result is a set of recommendations that allow to classify the activities with high precision.

Keywords: Neuroethology · Activity recognition · Behavioral activity classification · Gaze ethograms · Eye tracking · Screen-based eye tracker · Non-invasive techniques

1 Introduction

Computational Neuroethology comprises a wide variety of devices, computational tools and techniques used in the studies aiming to understand the neural substrate of the observable behavior [1]. The neural activity sensing devices are a main instrument in neuroethology, but interesting results can be achieved with conventional tools and techniques such as Computer Vision (CV) that allow to monitor and quantify behaviors in real life environments. In fact, interacting with computers is a pervasive activity nowadays which can be analyzed through CV means. These analysis are a good testbed for computational neuroethology, in order to determine which activities are being carried out in a view of non-invasive methods.

The underlying hypothesis is that the subject's gaze fixation information allows to determine the activities the subject is engaged in [2]. This is the

E. A. de la Cal et al. (Eds.): HAIS 2020, LNAI 12344, pp. 132–144, 2020.
https://doi.org/10.1007/978-3-030-61705-9_12

same hypothesis underlying neuromarketing business [3], where companies routinely analyze user visual behavior visiting a web page, mining the marketing value of the user visual interaction. In our works we compute the *gaze ethograms* in order to assess the behavioral state of a laptop computer user on the basis of the sequence of gaze fixations on the computer display. There is a trade-off between eye tracking accuracy and invasiveness. The most accurate techniques for eye tracking are very invasive. Electro-oculography (EOG) and video-oculography (VOG) [4] use a series of electrodes situated in the user's face to measure the eye movement, and a head-mounted mask that is equipped with small cameras, respectively. Glass frames with mounted infrared based eye trackers are mildly invasive while very accurate. However, we aim to carry out observation and measurement with minimal or no interference to the natural behavior.

The rest of the paper is organized as follows. Firstly, we review the protocol followed to perform the experiments, giving as well an overview of the general workflow. Then, we describe the models used to classify the activities and how the features are defined. Also, we formulate some considerations about the validation process concerning the experimental work. Before to show a detailed description of the results, we compare and select the tools to be used. The paper ends with a discussion on the experimental results and conclusions. Some ideas on further work are also enumerated.

2 Experimental Protocol and Workflow

The experimental subject is seated in front of a conventional laptop endowed with a web camera on top of the screen. The face distance to the laptop ranges between 40–60 cm. The camera is situated to a height determined for each subject to compute more efficiently some internal model parameters, as for example the eye aspect ratio, which will be defined below. The head movements are restricted to small angles ($\leq 10^\circ$) in order to improve the sensibility of the whole system. The subject is asked for carrying out three different activities for 10 min. Therefore, each recording contains about 18 000 frames. The activities are usual tasks done with computers, namely: reading a text, watching a movie, and typing a text.

The subject is also asked to perform specific actions in front of the computer camera that involve visual fixations in predefined areas of the computer screen. This additional recording is used for calibrating (training) the gaze tracking system. The ultimate goal of this system is to estimate the areas that are receiving the subject's attention. The calibration procedure has been detailed elsewhere [6] and it is summarized in the next paragraph for the sake of completeness.

The calibration procedure consists in displaying sequentially several targets in the screen for about 3 s. The subject has to watch to the targets when they appear and to maintain the gaze until a new target is shown. The subject's face is also captured and the recording will be used to increase the dataset to estimate the gaze destination. Currently, we are using a template with 9 targets.

We ask the subject to follow the order shown in Fig. 1 for the gaze fixations in order to minimize fatigue and to reduce the length of eye movements between two consecutive targets. Also, we have empirically determined that it is not needed to get the exact destination coordinates on the screen as would require an human-computer interaction application. For our particular purpose it is enough to estimate broad screen areas that may receive the subject's attention.

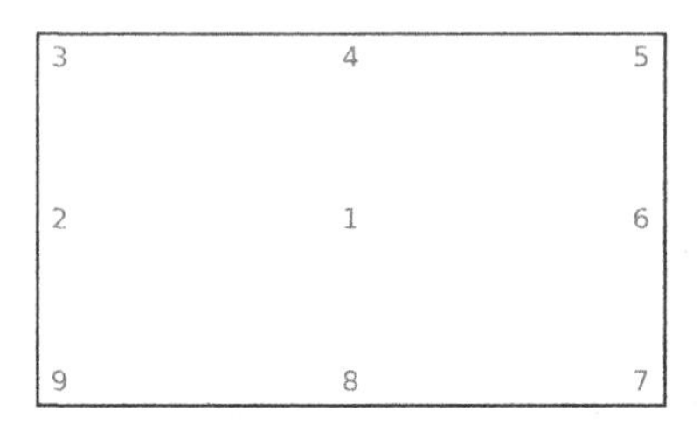

Fig. 1. Calibration template with the identification of the target areas to estimate the gaze destination. The target order has been arbitrarily defined to reduce the user fatigue during the calibration.

The whole workflow is as follows. Once the recordings are performed, the subject gaze destination in each frame is estimated. This estimation is performed by using conventional classifiers, which are previously trained using the recordings taken during the calibration stage. The classifiers use features, which are computed for each frame, and their outputs determine the target that receives the focus of the subject. We have obtained the best performance using polynomial kernel support vector machines (SVM) and a combination of features based on the *eye aspect ratio* (EAR) [7], which gives an index about if the eye is closed or how much it is open, and *intensity texture patterns* (ITP) [5] that provide texture-based information on the whole eyes area in the subject's face. We have used the software machine learning library *Scikit-learn* for all the matters related to classifiers and basic dataset management tools.

We have also considered as candidate to features the approximate position of the *pupil in subject's face coordinates* (PFC) but due to the low resolution of the images and the limited illumination conditions of the environment generally they produce poorer results compared to the other features and it is not used.

The next step consists of generating the datasets used along this work by using the above classifiers over the activities recordings. For this task, we use the best classifier of 100 runs trained with the calibration dataset. The averaged accuracy by this polynomial kernel SVM classifier was about. 9977, which is in part due to the use of the EAR and, mostly, the ITP as features.

The datasets are composed by the so-called *gaze ethograms* [6], which describe the sequence of target areas that receive the experimental subject's attention along the activity that is been studied. Figure 2 show sample gaze ethograms of an activity recording session during which the subject is reading a text (left), watching a movie (center), and typing a text (right). The subject fixates the gaze on a particular subset of target areas depending on the task.

The next and final step, which is the subject of the rest of the paper, addresses the classification of the activities from gaze ethograms. We must consider a new set of features computed from the ethograms, which can be arranged in two families: label-based and spatial. It is also needed to consider the minimum length of the recording or number of frames that can be used to determine the activity. Here, as it could be figured, the shorter, the better. During the recording other parameters are also studied. In the sequel we report the methods applied for activity classification and we comment achieved results.

3 Classification Model and Feature Extraction

Let us consider the gaze ethograms shown in Fig. 2. We see the subject's attention generally depends on the type of activity. While reading a text (Fig. 2, left) the subjects visit the upper display target areas 4 and 3 more frequently, due to the fact that the text starts in the top of the display and the subject scrolls the text. This behavior follows the western reading convention. During the video watching activity (Fig. 2, center) the experimental subjects visit the display center target areas 1 and 8 more frequently, with some excursions to target area 4. Target 1 corresponds to the center of the display, so it is a highly expected gaze detection output. It is where the visual field is wider and higher in comparison to the other targets and where the subject can gather much more visual information from the screen. The gaze ethogram of the typing activity (Fig. 2, right) shows that the user visits more often the targets 7, 8 and 9 at the bottom of the screen. This activity has a frequency of blinking events that is much lower than the reading and movie watching activities, probably because the gaze destination is mostly at the bottom of the display.

Therefore, the gaze ethograms are good candidates for activity classification. The problem now is how to extract features from them. We have already considered basic statistical methods such as averaged target values in conjunction with averaged eyes information over the whole ethogram with quite good results [6]. Those methods require a noteworthy amount of data to feed the classifiers and the results may be too subject dependent on occasions.

An ethogram is a discrete function of time. A broadly accepted method to deal with time-based functions consider to reduce the data to several discrete

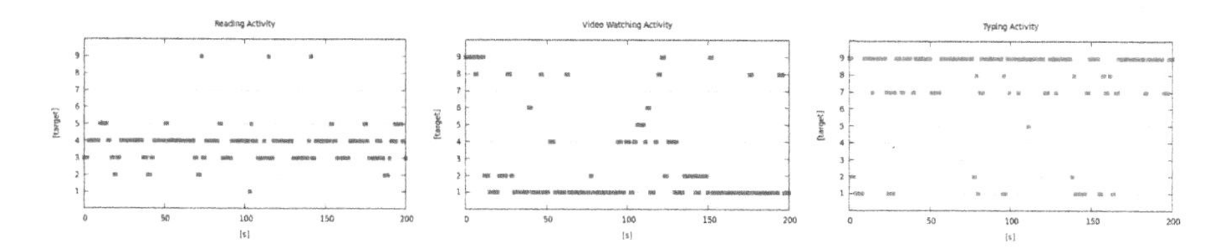

Fig. 2. Gaze ethograms associated with reading activity (left), watching a movie (center), and typing a text with the keyboard (right).

values or samples by sliding a window along the series. The wider the window, the lower the number of samples. The data is much more compacted but there is a remarkable loss of information.

On the other hand, the way in which the features are selected also determines some important concerns. As we have already commented, our initial model considers several computations over the number that identifies the target. We refer to this method as *target identifier labeling*. Those numbers are in fact labels arbitrarily assigned. We did consider how to locate them over the display taking into account psycho-physical criteria but it does not correspond to a well-formed spatial arrangement. For example, if the subject puts the visual attention on targets 3 and 7 during a half of the considered period (see Fig. 1), a strict arithmetic method to compute features would give as result target 5. Targets 3 and 7 are located on opposite corners of the diagonal. Perhaps, trying to define averaged target values is a nonsense, particularly by using this extreme case, but the middle point between these two targets would be over the target 1, near to the center of the display, and not over target 5 on a different corner.

Thus, we are proposing different approaches to assign labels to the targets. The first one considers some topology information of each target by *superimposing* coordinate axes over the display in such a way that target 1 corresponds to the origin of coordinates $(0, 0)$, target 2 is on coordinates $(-1, 0)$, target 3 is on coordinates $(-1, +1)$, and so on. By using this assignment, if we reconsider the previous example, at least the averaged target would correspond with the center of the display, which is more intuitive. This idea is depicted in Fig. 3. We name this method as *normalized fixation coordinates labeling*.

Fig. 3. Normalized fixation coordinates labeling.

The second alternative label assignments goes over the classic way to assign labels in multi-class classifiers, where a different output is used for each one of the possible classes, which are usually defined in the range $[0, 1]$ and can be interpreted as probability of belonging to that class. If we would apply this design to the classifiers that determine the target focused by the experimental subject, we would get nine—the number of our targets—outputs in the range $[0, 1]$. The greater of the outputs would correspond to the predicted class but it could be possible several other outputs greater than 0. Thus, we compute a normalized 9D feature vector for each sliding window. When the classifier predicts that every frames in a particular window corresponds to the same target, the feature vector element for that target will be 1, and the others will be 0. When the predictions indicate several classes, the vector is a weighted output relative to

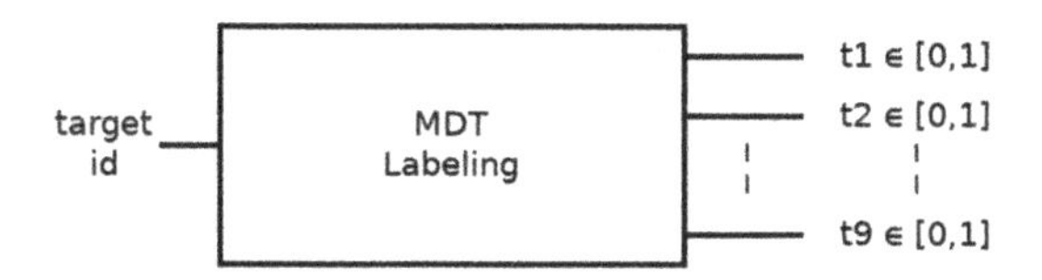

Fig. 4. Multi-dimensional target labeling.

those predictions. We refer to this method as *multi-dimensional target labeling* and its idea is shown in Fig. 4.

4 Validation Process

We carry out two types of validation processes. Firstly, we want to determine the optimal observation length over the experimental subject, i.e. the length of the video window that allows to determine which activity is being performed. It is important for us to define this value correctly because the response time must be short but we must ensure a baseline true positive performance. Also, we want to demonstrate empirically the best method for labeling targets and if we can improve our previous results by considering topological information or by modifying the dimensionality of the output space.

Secondly, we also want to assess the sensitivity of all these methods over two validation datasets. Usually, training datasets are extracted from calibration videos of several experimental subjects, while testing datasets are extracted from videos in which the subjects perform the planned activities. Calibration and activity videos are recorded in the same session, ensuring similar lighting conditions, face aspect, hairstyle, clothes, etc. In this paper we want to assess the robustness of the system when applying it to data from quite different recording sessions, i.e. recorded after some days. As the number of samples in the datasets for some experiments are reduced and in order to use equivalent metrics for all tests, we use the leave-one-out method for validation.

5 Selecting the Best Classifier

Table 1 summarizes the accuracy results achieved by several classifier models with default parameter settings. We use sets of videos with duration v_l of 30 s and 60 s, and window size w_s of 2 s with a 50% of overlapping. Thus the datasets contain 72 and 36 samples, respectively. As features we use the averaged value of target identifiers in each window. We compare the results of k Nearest Neighbors (kNN) with $k = 3$ and $k = 5$ and Euclidean distance, Gaussian Naïve Bayes, Support Vector Machine (SVM) with radial basis functions (rbf) and polynomial (poly) kernels, AdaBoost with 100 estimators, Random Forest with 100 estimators, and Multi-layer Perceptrons (MLP) with two hidden layers with 80 and 40 neurons and logistic (log) and hyperbolic tangent (tanh) activation functions. As we previously mentioned we use *Scikit-learn* machine learning library.

Table 1. Accuracy results of preliminary tests to select the classifier to be applied to the activities classification problem.

Classifier	$v_l = 30/w_s = 2$	$v_l = 60/w_s = 2$
kNN ($k=3$)	.8889	.9167
kNN ($k=5$)	.8889	.8889
Gaussian Naïve Bayes	.8750	.8889
SVM (rbf)	.9160	.9444
SVM (poly)	.8611	.8889
AdaBoost	.7222	.8889
Random forest	.8750	.9722
MLP (log)	.8611	.6944
MLP (tanh)	.8056	.6667

In a previous publication [5], we reported the best classification results by using polynomial kernel SVM, however in the current work the radial basis function kernel SVM improves slightly the accuracy score in both datasets. kNN classifiers show a pretty good performance, too. Nevertheless, the best score is achieved by a Random Forest over the small dataset. Although the learning accuracy is greater than others, this classifier exhibits overfitting problems probably due to the ratio between the number of estimators selected and the size of the dataset.

6 Experimental Results and Discussion

In the following subsections we show and discuss the results of the experiments carried out with radial basis function kernel SVM and we try to answer the question on which is the best combination of observation time of the experimental subject, window size to use for discretizing the gaze ethograms, and the several labeling alternatives.

6.1 Averaged Target Identifier Labeling

The first series of experiments runs with the simplest and, perhaps, the less robust labeling method. Once the samples that belong to the current window are determined, it is computed the mean of the identifier values and assigned as a new feature to the output vector. We have used videos with duration v_l from 5 s to 60 s with increments of 5 s, window sizes w_s of .5 s, 1 s, 2 s and 3 s, and an overlapping factor of 50 %. The number of items in the datasets goes from 432 to 36 samples. Those figures are used in the other experiments, too. For the sake of simplicity they will be not repeated.

Table 2 shows the accuracy values achieved by the radial basis function kernel SVM classifiers. If we consider the results concerning the calibration and activities datasets recorded at the same session, generally the longer the video, the higher the accuracy until a video length of 40–45 s. We also made some experiments beyond the upper limit of 60 s constrained by our recordings availability and the decreasing tendency goes on. On the other hand, we also observe in Table 2 that the smaller the window size, the better the accuracy in shortest videos. For the longest videos (over 45 s) this tendency is the opposite. The best case corresponds to a video length $v_l = 45$ s and window sizes $w_s = 2$ and $w_s = 3$ with an accuracy of .9583.

Table 2. Accuracy of the averaged target identifier labeling with datasets from the same and different recording sessions.

Video length	Same recording session				Different recording session			
	$w_s = .5$	$w_s = 1$	$w_s = 2$	$w_s = 3$	$w_s = .5$	$w_s = 1$	$w_s = 2$	$w_s = 3$
5 s	.8333	.7949	.7685	.7245	.7933	.7289	.6578	.5933
10 s	.8565	.8194	.8380	.8194	.8267	.7778	.7111	.7022
15 s	.8889	.8750	.8403	.8542	.8467	.7533	.7133	.7467
20 s	.8796	.8519	.8704	.8611	.8108	.7207	.7477	.7568
25 s	.9167	.8929	.9048	.8929	.7333	.7111	.7333	.7556
30 s	.9028	.8889	.9167	.9028	.7200	.7200	.7600	.7733
35 s	.8833	.8500	.8667	.8667	.7460	.7937	.7937	.7778
40 s	.9259	.9074	.9259	.9259	.7778	.7222	.7963	.7963
45 s	.9375	.9375	.9583	.9583	.7500	.7292	.7500	.8333
50 s	.8810	.8810	.8810	.8810	.7333	.7556	.8889	.8000
55 s	.8974	.8718	.8974	.9231	.4103	.5897	.7949	.8718
60 s	.9167	.9167	.9444	.9444	.4722	.6389	.7500	.8611

We have also studied the accuracy with other statistics operators such as the median and the mode of the target identifiers and we get quite similar results in part due to the nature of the data. The mode operator presents some troubles when the mode in the window is not unique that we solve by random selection.

Table 2 also shows the accuracy achieved when the datasets computed are from videos recorded at a different recording session. Here, the averaged accuracy is lower than in the previous scenario when the calibration and activity recordings belong to the same session. The best scores correspond to videos in the 45–50 s range. And usually the greater the window size, the better the accuracy for the longest videos. The tendency is quite similar to the obtained with the first dataset. The best case corresponds to a video length $v_l = 50$ s and window size of $w_s = 2$ with an accuracy of .8889.

6.2 Averaged Target Identifier and Standard Deviation Labeling

Now we apply a similar procedure over the same datasets but in this case we compute to values to be included into the feature vector for each window: the mean of the identifier values an the standard deviation. All the parameters and considerations are the same to the first case.

Table 3 indicates that the tendency here is not so clear as using the average alone but also the best results are achieved by the longest videos, particularly the best cases are found around 45–50 s. The data shows an increment with the longest videos, the 60 s ones, but it is not general case and probably the score comes determined by low number of samples in that dataset. Independently of the length of the videos, the better accuracy is achieved by the larger window sizes (it can be better appreciated in the shortest videos). There are not enough evidences to make a choice because the values are equals for several window sizes. The best case corresponds to a video length $v_l = 30$ s and a window size $w_s = 3$ with an accuracy of .9861.

Table 3. Accuracy of the averaged target identifier and standard deviation labeling with datasets from the same and different recording sessions.

Video length	Same recording session				Different recording session			
	$w_s = .5$	$w_s = 1$	$w_s = 2$	$w_s = 3$	$w_s = .5$	$w_s = 1$	$w_s = 2$	$w_s = 3$
5 s	.8588	.8588	.8681	.8333	.8089	.7889	.7889	.7356
10 s	.8889	.8796	.9028	.9167	.7778	.7733	.7778	.7689
15 s	.9097	.9236	.9306	.9375	.7467	.7533	.7867	.8067
20 s	.9352	.9352	.9537	.9537	.7027	.7207	.7748	.7928
25 s	.9167	.9167	.9286	.9405	.7000	.7556	.7667	.8222
30 s	.9028	.9444	.9583	.9861	.6944	.7639	.8333	.8472
35 s	.9333	.9333	.9333	.9333	.5873	.7460	.7937	.8095
40 s	.9259	.9444	.9444	.9444	.6296	.7037	.7963	.8148
45 s	.9167	.9583	.9583	.9583	.5833	.7292	.7917	.8125
50 s	.9286	.9286	.9524	.9524	.6444	.7111	.8444	.8444
55 s	.9231	.9231	.9487	.9487	.3333	.3846	.7436	.8462
60 s	.9444	.9722	.9722	.9722	.3333	.4444	.8333	.8889

For videos recorded at a different recording session, Table 3 shows that the tendency coincides with the datasets recorded at the same session: the larger the window size, the higher accuracy achieved by the classifier. Usually longest videos tend to achieve the best score, too. The best case corresponds to a video length $v_l = 60$ s and window size of $w_s = 3$ with an accuracy of .8889.

6.3 Normalized Fixation Coordinates Labeling

For the next labeling we apply the method explained above by associating to each target a location in a virtual coordinate system with the origin at the center of the display.

Table 4 shows that the best accuracy for datasets of the same recording session are achieved with small window sizes, usually when $w_s = .5$. Also the shorter the video length, the better the accuracy is. These results are radically different to the previous ones. Generally the performance of this labeling is lower, too. The best case corresponds to a video length $v_l = 15$ s and a window size $w_s = .5$ with an accuracy of .9236.

Table 4. Accuracy of the normalized fixation coordinates labeling with datasets from the same and different recording sessions.

Video length	Same recording session				Different recording session			
	$w_s = .5$	$w_s = 1$	$w_s = 2$	$w_s = 3$	$w_s = .5$	$w_s = 1$	$w_s = 2$	$w_s = 3$
5 s	.8935	.8495	.7269	.6667	.8200	.8044	.7978	.7511
10 s	.8796	.8472	.7685	.7269	.8578	.8489	.8267	.8178
15 s	.9236	.9097	.8125	.7847	.8400	.8333	.7933	.7933
20 s	.8889	.8611	.7870	.7685	.8108	.8198	.8378	.8018
25 s	.8571	.8810	.7976	.8095	.8556	.8667	.8333	.8444
30 s	.8611	.8889	.8472	.8472	.8133	.8000	.8267	.8267
35 s	.8833	.7833	.7333	.7333	.8571	.8413	.8571	.8571
40 s	.8148	.8148	.7963	.7593	.7593	.7593	.7593	.7778
45 s	.8333	.8333	.7292	.7083	.7500	.7083	.7083	.7292
50 s	.8095	.8095	.7857	.7619	.9111	.8667	.7778	.8000
55 s	.8462	.8462	.7949	.7692	.6923	.6923	.7949	.7692
60 s	.9167	.8889	.7778	.7778	.6944	.7500	.7778	.7500

Again, the normalized fixation coordinates labeling gives the worst averaged results for datasets from different recording sessions. It looks that smaller window sizes works better than larger ones although there is not a clear tendency. And shortest videos also improve the scores but, however, the best case corresponds to a video length $v_l = 45$ s and a window size $w_s = .5$ with an accuracy of .9111. The number of samples in that particular dataset is 45, which could be the reason of this score. Although the number of samples in the contiguous cases differs a half a dozen of samples and the scores with other window sizes are also good.

6.4 Multi-dimensional Target Labeling

Table 5 shows the accuracy when the multi-dimensional target labeling is used. Note that all the scores are better than with the previous labeling methods. For the datasets generated using videos recorded at the same recording session, the SVM is able to classify all the samples even with video lengths of $v_l = 30$ s and window sizes of $w_s = 1$ and $w_s = 2$. All the rest of scores are always over .94 except the ones belong to video lengths of $v_l = 5$ s.

Table 5. Accuracy of the multi-dimensional target labeling with datasets from the same and different recording sessions.

Video length	Same recording session				Different recording session			
	$w_s = .5$	$w_s = 1$	$w_s = 2$	$w_s = 3$	$w_s = .5$	$w_s = 1$	$w_s = 2$	$w_s = 3$
5 s	.9144	.9282	.9306	.9144	.8778	.8778	.8778	.8533
10 s	.9722	.9722	.9676	.9583	.9289	.9244	.9200	.9289
15 s	.9653	.9653	.9583	.9583	.9267	.9200	.9067	.9200
20 s	.9537	.9537	.9630	.9630	.8919	.9189	.9369	.9189
25 s	.9524	.9405	.9643	.9524	.8667	.9000	.9444	.9222
30 s	.9855	1.	1.	.9710	.8889	.9444	.9583	.9861
35 s	.9667	.9667	.9667	.9667	.8730	.8730	.9206	.9524
40 s	.9444	.9444	.9630	.9630	.7963	.7963	.8889	.9259
45 s	.9792	.9792	.9792	.9583	.7917	.8333	.9167	.9375
50 s	.9524	.9524	.9524	.9524	.8222	.8667	.9333	.9333
55 s	1.	1.	1.	1.	.3333	.6154	.8718	.8974
60 s	1.	1.	1.	1.	.4167	.6667	.9167	.9444

For different recording session case, the accuracy is also improved in all the experiments. Several scores go over .9 and the best case corresponds to a video length $v_l = 30$ s and a window size $w_s = 3$ with an accuracy of .9861.

Table 6. Accuracy of the labeling methods proposed.

Labeling method	Same session			Different session		
	v_l	w_s	Accuracy	v_l	w_s	Accuracy
Target identifier (avg)	45	{2, 3}	.9583	50	2	.8889
Target identifier (avg+std)	30	3	.9861	60	3	.8889
Normalized fixation coordinates	15	.5	.9236	45	.5	.9111
Multi-dimensional target	30	{1, 2}	1	30	3	.9861

6.5 Discussion

As it is shown in Table 6, the best results are achieved by the multi-dimensional target labeling and it should be the first option to consider when applying those methods to similar problems. The method keeps much more information about the targets than the target identifier method, so it was clear that it could by an improvement. The use of the standard deviation along the mean also improves the accuracy in general, although the best cases with datasets from different sessions show the same score. Again more information is retained by the method. Note that the normalized fixation coordinates does not improve the results of the target identifier method in the same session datasets tests but it does it with the other datasets. The normalized fixation coordinates labeling uses topological and contextual information and, a priori, it should improve results.

Concerning the length of the video we can not get a clear conclusion on what length carry the best results and it depends on the labeling method. At least we do conclude that very short recordings are not usable for determining the activity performed by the experimental subject. There are not results with recording shorter than 15 s and usually they are in the 30–45 range or greater.

The same considerations can be made about the window size. It is too dependent on the labeling method and, in this case, also the dataset. Except for the normalized fixation coordinates labeling, the other methods get the best results with window sizes of 2–3 s. By checking the performance in other labeling methods, a window size about 2 s could be a good initial reference.

Also, the results get worse at datasets computed with the recordings from a different session to the one where the calibration videos were taken.

Summarizing, the multi-dimensional target labeling gets almost an accuracy of 100%, which should be the first method to check in new applications with a window size about 2 s. Probably it would be sure to use recordings with length of about 30 s, it gets the best performance for this particular labeling method and it is a good candidate for others.

7 Conclusions and Further Work

We have proposed novel methods for labeling the data used in the gaze ethograms to estimate the activity that an user carries out in front of a computer by using its onboard web camera. We compare our previously applied method based on the identifier associated to each display area with the new proposals, which employ more statistical information, topological and contextual information, and different way of representing the data. Also, we have studied two more parameters in our sliding window proposal: the minimum length of the recording that allows the determine the activity and the window size used to compute the features. The tests are performed by using two datasets, which are generated for sets of recordings taken in several video sessions with the experimental subjects.

Further work has to be performed on the comparison with other methods. We are currently working on an approach to determine the gaze destination based on convolutional neural networks. Also, we work on the improvement of low level faces localization, and on building models independently of the position and the orientation of the head.

Acknowledgments. This work has been partially supported by FEDER funds through MINECO project TIN2017-85827-P.

References

1. Graña, M., de Lope Asiain, J.: A short review of some aspects of computational neuroethology. In: Ferrández Vicente, J.M., Álvarez-Sánchez, J.R., de la Paz López, F., Toledo Moreo, J., Adeli, H. (eds.) IWINAC 2019. LNCS, vol. 11486, pp. 275–283. Springer, Cham (2019). https://doi.org/10.1007/978-3-030-19591-5_28
2. George, A.: Image based eye gaze tracking and its applications. arXiv:1907.04325 (2019)
3. Hof, R.: How do you Google? New eye tracking study reveals huge changes, Forbes Online, March 2015
4. Blakley, B.W., Chan, L.: Methods considerations for nystagmography. J. Otolaryngol. Head Neck Surg. **44**, 25 (2015)
5. de Lope, J., Graña, M.: Behavioral activity recognition based on gaze ethograms. Int. J. Neural Syst. https://doi.org/10.1142/S0129065720500252
6. Moraleda, S., de Lope Asiain, J., Graña, M.: Recognizing cognitive activities through eye tracking. In: Ferrández Vicente, J.M., Álvarez-Sánchez, J.R., de la Paz López, F., Toledo Moreo, J., Adeli, H. (eds.) IWINAC 2019. LNCS, vol. 11486, pp. 291–300. Springer, Cham (2019). https://doi.org/10.1007/978-3-030-19591-5_30
7. Soukupová, T., J. Čech, J.: Real-time eye blink detection using facial landmarks. In: 21st Computer Vision Winter Workshop (2016)

Bio-inspired Models and Optimization

PBIL for Optimizing Hyperparameters of Convolutional Neural Networks and STL Decomposition

Roberto A. Vasco-Carofilis[1], Miguel A. Gutiérrez-Naranjo[1], and Miguel Cárdenas-Montes[2(✉)]

[1] Department of Computer Science and Artificial Intelligence, University of Seville, Seville, Spain
andresvasc@gmail.com, magutier@us.es

[2] Department of Fundamental Research, Centro de Investigaciones Energéticas Medioambientales y Tecnológicas, Madrid, Spain
miguel.cardenas@ciemat.es

Abstract. The optimization of hyperparameters in Deep Neural Networks is a critical task for the final performance, but it involves a high amount of subjective decisions based on previous researchers' expertise. This paper presents the implementation of Population-based Incremental Learning for the automatic optimization of hyperparameters in Deep Learning architectures. Namely, the proposed architecture is a combination of preprocessing the time series input with Seasonal Decomposition of Time Series by Loess, a classical method for decomposing time series, and forecasting with Convolutional Neural Networks. In the past, this combination has produced promising results, but penalized by an incremental number of parameters. The proposed architecture is applied to the prediction of the ^{222}Rn level at the Canfranc Underground Laboratory (Spain). By predicting the low-level periods of ^{222}Rn, the potential contamination during the maintenance operations in the experiments hosted in the laboratory could be minimized. In this paper, it is shown that Population-based Incremental Learning can be used for the choice of optimized hyperparameters in Deep Learning architectures with a reasonable computational cost.

Keywords: Hyperparameters optimization · Convolutional Neural Networks · STL decomposition · PBIL · ^{222}Rn measurements · Canfranc Underground Laboratory · Forecasting

1 Introduction

Adjusting machine learning hyperparameters is a tedious but crucial task, as the performance of an algorithm may depend on the choice of hyperparameters. Manual optimization is a time-consuming process that can be invested in other tasks of the algorithm development process. This paper presents an automatic

E. A. de la Cal et al. (Eds.): HAIS 2020, LNAI 12344, pp. 147–159, 2020.
https://doi.org/10.1007/978-3-030-61705-9_13

approach for the generation of hyperparameters of a machine learning model, which, in a few training sessions, allows to reach a local minimum among the possible combinations.

The learning model is a combination of Seasonal Decomposition of time series by Loess (STL) and Convolutional Neural Networks (CNN). Both methods have been integrated and applied in the study of time series [18], but their hyperparameters need to be carefully tuned in order to obtain accurate predictions. In order to fit some hyperparameters of CNN and parameters of STL decomposition, population-based incremental learning (PBIL) method has been used.

In our proposal, the arquitecture of the CNN is fixed and PBIL is used in order to optimize the search of some of their hyperparameters and some of the parameters of STL for a given task. In such way, a concrete dataset is considered and the task is to find a combination of parameters that minimizes the loss of the CNN on the dataset. PBIL is an optimization method of the family of genetic algorithms and, therefore, in order to use PBIL, each set of parameters of the CNN is encoded as a binary sequence, in other words as an *individual* of the population. In order to obtain the *fitness* of an individual which guides the evolutinary procees, firstly the hyperparameters encoded by the individual are obtained. The fitness associated to the individual is the loss of a single run of the CNN on the dataset when these parameters are considered.

The problem of automatically tuning hyperparameters in machine learning has been considered from many different point of views. One of the simplest approaches is the random search, which was explored in [3]. A different point of view is based in Bayesian optimization. This method considers on an iterative evaluation and update of promising hypermarameters [22]. Gradient-based optimization [16], radial basis functions [8] and spectral methods [13] have also been explored.

Special mention deserves the optimization of hyperparameters inspired in evolutionary and population based methods. Evolutionary optimization considers ideas coming from evolutionary algorithms to explore a hyperparameters space [19]. In population based methods applied to neural networks, the model tries to optimize network weights and hyperparameters simultaneously [15]. In our approach, an optimization method which takes ideas from competitive learning and population based methods is also considered.

1.1 Previous Efforts

In the past, the ^{222}Rn time series at Canfranc Underground Laboratory (LSC) has been analysed and forecast using non-stochastic algorithms: Holt-Winters, AutoRegressive Integrated Moving Averages, and Seasonal and STL (see [17] and references therein). Also in [17] and [18], the forecasting capacity of Multilayer Perceptron (MLP), Convolutional Neural Networks (CNN), and Recurrent Neural Networks is evaluated for this problem. In [5], improvements in the forecasting capacity is reported when implementing an Ensemble Deep Learning approach. In this study the ensemble is composed of Bidirectional Recurrent Neural Networks (BRNN), CNN, and a variant of CNN, termed CNN+STL, in which the original observations used as input are replaced by the components generated by Seasonal and Trend decomposition using Loess (STL): trend, seasonal and remainder components [18].

In [18] the first implementation of using STL decomposition and CNN for improving the forecasting capacity was presented. The promising results obtained only for some test was penalized by the lack of an optimal configuration. In this work, the analysis of the ^{222}Rn time series at LSC was based on the monthly medians of 5 years, 60 observations. The reduced dataset also penalized the final performance[1]. The sub-optimal performance achieved at the same time that the promising results motivates the additional effort presented in the current work.

The LSC is composed of two main experimental halls for hosting scientific experiments with requirements of very low-background. The ^{222}Rn concentration is monitored every 10 minutes in both halls. An accumulated record from July 2013 to September 2018 for Hall A is available (Fig. 1). Due to the high level of noise of the measurements, the weekly medians are considered for composing

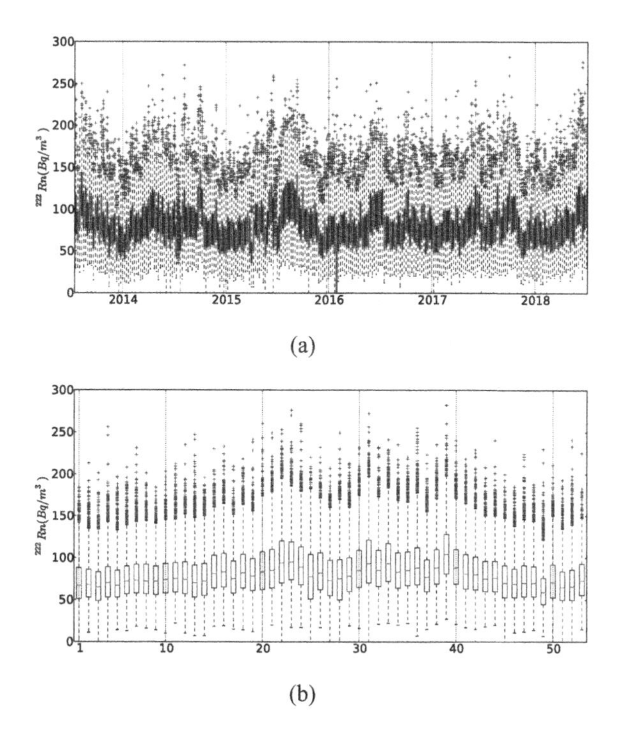

Fig. 1. Weekly box-plots of ^{222}Rn level at Hall A of the LSC, by week (Fig. 1(a)) and gathering the weeks independently of the week of the year (Fig. 1(b)). Depicted data corresponds to the period from July 2013 to June 2018.

[1] In the current work, the dataset is composed of weekly means of 5 years, which increments the number of observations up to 259.

the time series (red lines in the boxplot centre in Fig. 1(a)). Finally, the dataset contains 259 observations corresponding to the weekly medians. The faint annual modulation observed in Fig. 1(b) embodies in the noisy observations indicates that ^{222}Rn concentration at LSC is not fully random, and therefore it can be treated by machine learning algorithms.

The paper is organized as follows: Sect. 2 gives a brief description of the different Artificial Intelligence techniques used in this paper: PBIL as optimizer, STL for decomposing time series into components and CNN as predictive model. Section 3 describes the proposed approach. In Sect. 4, our application to the case study is shown, and finally, Sect. 5 contains the conclusions of this work.

2 Methods

2.1 Population-Based Incremental Learning

Population-based incremental learning is an optimization method which combines genetic algorithms with competitive learning [1,2]. It belongs to the so-called estimation of distribution algorithms (EDAs). The main difference with standard evolutionary algorithms is that EDAs do not create a population of solutions from the previous generation by using crossover and mutations. EDAs consider global information of the whole population in order to build a probabilistic distribution which is updated step by step. The optimization method is based on local search and it has been proved that it converges to local optima [21]. In this paper, binary-valued encoding for genotypes have been used. In our approach, PBIL is configured for using the best 5 individuals to build the distribution.

During the execution of the algorithm, individuals, representing the hyperparameters and parameters being optimized, are created from a probability distribution. Through the generations, only the best individuals of a generation are used for updating the parameters of the probability distribution. Later, based on the updated probability distribution parameters, a new generation of individuals is created by sampling the probability distribution and evaluated, restarting the process. The initial value of each probability is set at 0.5. In our approach, the individuals are created as binary vectors. Mean Squared Error (MSE, $MSE = \sum_i (\hat{y_i} - y_i)^2$, where y_i are the observations and $\hat{y_i}$ the predictions) of a single run of the CNN is used as fitness function in PBIL algorithm.

2.2 Gray Coding

Gray coding is a type of binary conding which is usually used in order to avoid Hamming cliffs (Table 1). A Hamming cliff is formed when two numerically adjacent values have bit representations that are far apart by using the Hamming distance. For example, number 3 and 4 differ in binary representation in three bits: 0011 and 0100, having a Hamming distance of 3; or for 15 and 16, corresponding the binary representations 01111 and 10000, which have a Hamming distance of 5.

Table 1. Example of correspondence among decimal, binary and Gray coding.

Decimal	Binary	Gray
0	0000	0000
1	0001	0001
2	0010	0011
3	0011	0010
4	0100	0110

A large Hamming distance is a barrier for the evolution of the individuals in the evolutionary algorithm. The change of one unit in a parameter under optimization requires a large amount of simultaneous modification of the individual binary coding, but not in Gray coding. This improbable process degrades the performance of evolutionary algorithm.

In our approach, the optimization of the hyperparameters will be performed by PBIL and each set of parameters will be encoded as a binary sequence by using Gray coding. For each hyperparameter to optimize, it is necessary define the minimum and maximum feasible values, and the step for moving in this range. This determines the size of the individual, since the binary representation must be able to express all the feasible values and hence, also the length of the vector of probabilities. For each parameter x, the number of bits n_x used in the individual for representing it can be calculated as $n_x = \lceil log_2((max - min)/step) \rceil$. For example, if the chosen region for searching a parameter p for the CNN has the bounds 20 and 64 and the chosen step is 4, then the number of used bits is $4 = \lceil log_2(11) \rceil$. If the 4 bits in a concrete individual are 1100, the decodification c (by using Gray conding) of such sequence is 8 and hence the concrete value of the parameter p can be obtained as $p = min + (c * step)$. In our case $p = (8 * 4) + 20 = 52$.

Each individual of the evolutionary algorithm is a binary vector concatenating the hyperparameters and parameters being optimized. For each generation, decimal representation of these hyperparameters and parameters are Gray-coded and concatenated. Later, when they have been manipulated by the evolutionary algorithm, they are decoded and evaluated with the CNN+STL implementation.

The CNN hyperparameters optimized are:

- *Batch size* is number of samples per gradient update, within the range [16] with step 1.
- *Sample size* is the number of observations which are used as independent variable. ranging from 52 to 100 with step 2.
- The number of *epochs* for training, ranging from 20 to 140 with a step of 20.
- Size of the kernels in the convolutional blocks: ranging from 3 to 13 for the first block, from 3 to 9 for the second one, and from 3 to 5 for the third one, with a step of 1.

- The number of kernels in the convolutional blocks: ranging from 8 to 32 for the first block, from 16 to 64 for the second one, and from 32 to 128 for third one, with steps for 8, 8 and 16 respectively.

The STL decomposition parameters optimized are:

- The most significant period of the time series for STL decomposition, *period*, within the range [30, 61] with step 1.
- The fraction of data used in fitting lowess regression, *lo_faction*, within the range [0, 1] with step 0.1. The parameters *lo_faction* and *lo_ delta* are converted into integer before the Gray coding.
- The distance within which to use linear-interpolation instead of weighted regression, *lo_ delta*, within the range [0, 0.2] with step 0.01.

2.3 Seasonal Decomposition of Time Series by Loess

Seasonal decomposition of time series by loess (STL) is a method of decomposing time series [7]. The whole time series is decomposed into three components. One of the components is the trend (T_t), related to the long-term increase or decrease of the original time series. Another component is seasonal component (S_t), related to the periodicity of the data. Finally, the third component is the remainder or random component (R_t). In the case of additive decomposition, the sum of these components results in the original time series (Y_t), $Y_t = T_t + S_t + R_t$. In our approach, additive STL decomposition is employed using the STLDecompose library [20].

2.4 Convolutional Neural Networks

Convolutional Neural Networks (CNN) are specialized Neural Networks with special emphasis in image processing [12,14], although nowadays they are also employed in time series analysis and forecasting [9,17,18,23].

The CNN consists of a sequence of convolutional layers, the output of which is connected only to local regions in the input. These layers alternate convolutional, non-linear and pooling-based layers which allow extracting the relevant features of the class of objects, independently of their placement in the data example. The CNN allows the model to learn filters that are able to recognize specific patterns in the time series, and therefore they can capture richer information from the series. It also embodies three features which provide advantages over the multilayer perceptron: sparse interactions, parameter sharing and equivariance to translation [12].

Although CNN are frequently associated to image or audio classification -2D grid examples- or video sequence -3D grid examples-, it can also be applied to time series analysis -1D grid examples-. When processing time series, instead of a set of images, the series has to be divided in overlapping contiguous time windows. These windows constitute the examples, where the CNN aims at finding patterns. At the same time, the application to time series modelling requires the application of 1D convolutional operators, whose weights are optimized during the training process.

CNN architecture is composed of three branches handling the three components arisen from the STL decomposition. Each branch is composed of three convolutional blocks with `relu`—Rectified Linear Unit—as activation function. Ending this, the three intermediated representations are concatenated and then they pass through two dense layers of 64, and 16 neurons and `relu` as activation function; and a output layer with `linear` activation function. Among other hyperparameters, the number of filters in the convolutional blocks and their size are optimized through the PBIL algorithms. The loss function is the MSE and the optimizer is `Adam`.

For the implementation of the current approach, Python3 and Keras library have been used for the implementation of the CNN [6].

2.5 Statistics

In order to ascertain if the proposed forecasting methods applied to the test set improve the prediction, two different types of tests can be applied: parametric and non-parametric. The difference between both relies on the assumption that data are normally distributed for parametric tests, whereas non explicit conditions are assumed in non-parametric tests. For this reason, the latter is recommended when the statistical model of data is unknown [10,11].

The Kruskal-Wallis test is a non-parametric test used to compare three or more groups of sample data. For this test, the null hypothesis assumes that the samples are from identical populations. The procedure when using multiple comparison to test whether the null hypothesis is rejected implies the use of a post-hoc test to determine which sample makes the difference. The most typical post-hoc test is the Wilcoxon signed-rank test.

The Wilcoxon signed-rank test belongs to the non-parametric category. For this test, the null hypothesis assumes that the samples are from identical populations, whereas the alternative hypothesis states that the samples come from different populations. It is a pairwise test that aims to detect significant differences between two sample means.

3 PBIL for Optimizing Hyperparameters of Convolutional Neural Networks and Parameters of STL Decomposition

The algorithm used in this work is outlined in the flowchart of Fig. 2.

1. Initially, with a probability 0.5, v_i Gray-coded individuals are randomly created, each one with length n, being n the minimum number of bits for representing all the hyperparameters and parameters to optimize. In the tests, population is composed of 25 individuals.

2. Each individual is split for obtaining the hyparameters and parameters, and the parts are translated from Gray-coded to decimal-coded representation.
3. The individuals are evaluated through the CNN+STL architecture (Fig. 3). The test error on a single run of the implementation is used as individual fitness.
4. The best and worse individuals are identified for creating a new probability vector. Each component of the probability vector follows a binomial distribution. Best individuals modify p of previous generation so that it is more probable for the individuals in the next generation to obtain positive features, whereas the worse individuals act in opposite direction over p.
5. The process is repeated until the end criterion —number of generations—is achieved.

4 Experimental Results and Analysis

For evaluating the overall performance of the proposed approach, performance comparisons with Multiplayer Perceptron, Convolutional Neural Network, and—Long Short-Term Memory—Bidirection Recurrent Neural Network are made. In those comparisons, MSE is employed as figure of merit. In Table 2, the values of the MSE after 15 independent executions are presented. As it can be appreciated, the proposed approach, CNN+STL, produces the lowest error among the architectures evaluated. CNN+STL clearly outperforms Multilayer Perceptron (MLP), and previous efforts in CNN; and it is competitive with BRNN which has as excellent performance in time series forecasting for a diversity of observations, from Radon [5] to air pollutants concentration [4].

The application of the Kruskal-Wallis test to the MSE indicates that the differences between the medians are significant for a confidence level of 95% (p-value under 0.05), p-value $= 5 \cdot 10^{-9}$, which means that the differences are unlikely to have occurred by chance with a probability of 95%. Furthermore, the application of the Wilcoxon signed-rank test to the values of the MSE of CNN+STL and BRNN approaches points that the differences between the median of the MSE are not significant for a confidence level of 95% (p-value under 0.05), p-value = 0.08.

In Fig. 4, the evolution of the MSE for the PBIL population versus the generation is shown. In this case, the final MSE is 77.83 with an initial MSE of 90.86. This initial MSE is much lower that the final MSE of other runs. This could indicate that the initial search space is too wide, and the initial random population plays a critical role in the performance of the run, even if PBIL has the capability to produce improvements in all the runs.

In-detail insight on the final values of CNN hyperparameters and STL decomposition parameters, for both excellent-performance and poor-performance runs, offers a valuable information about outperforming configurations. For instance, performance critically degrades when the period of decomposition is out of the narrow range [50, 52], while the two other parameters of STL decomposition do not play a relevant role in the final performance.

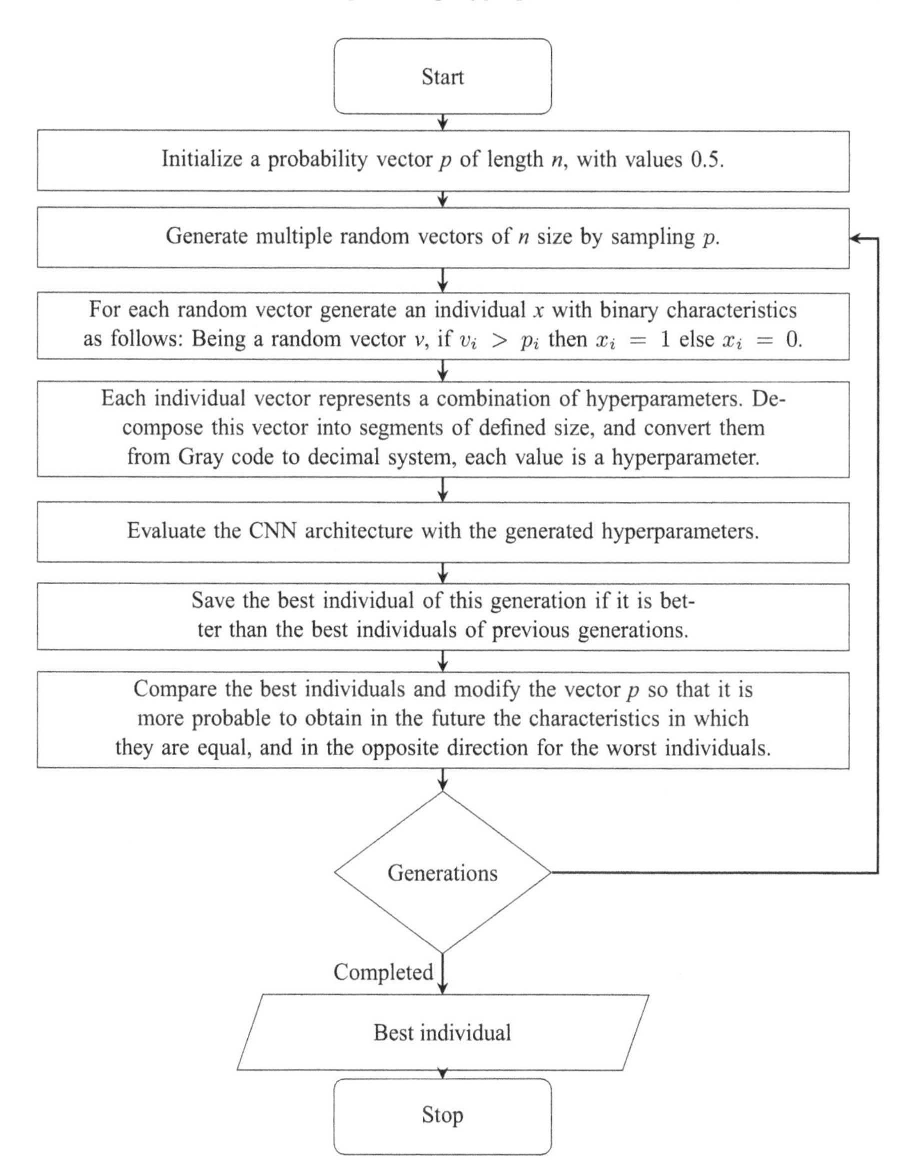

Fig. 2. Algorithm proposed for the implementation of PBIL in the optimization of hyperparameters of CNN and parameters of STL, in which given a specific number of generations the algorithm is able to obtain a combination of hyperparameters and parameters that approach the global optimum, improving the results with each generation.

With regards to the hyperparameters, the sample size seems not be as critical as the period of the STL decomposition for the performance of the proposed approach. A wide range of best MSE is achieved within the range of this hyper-

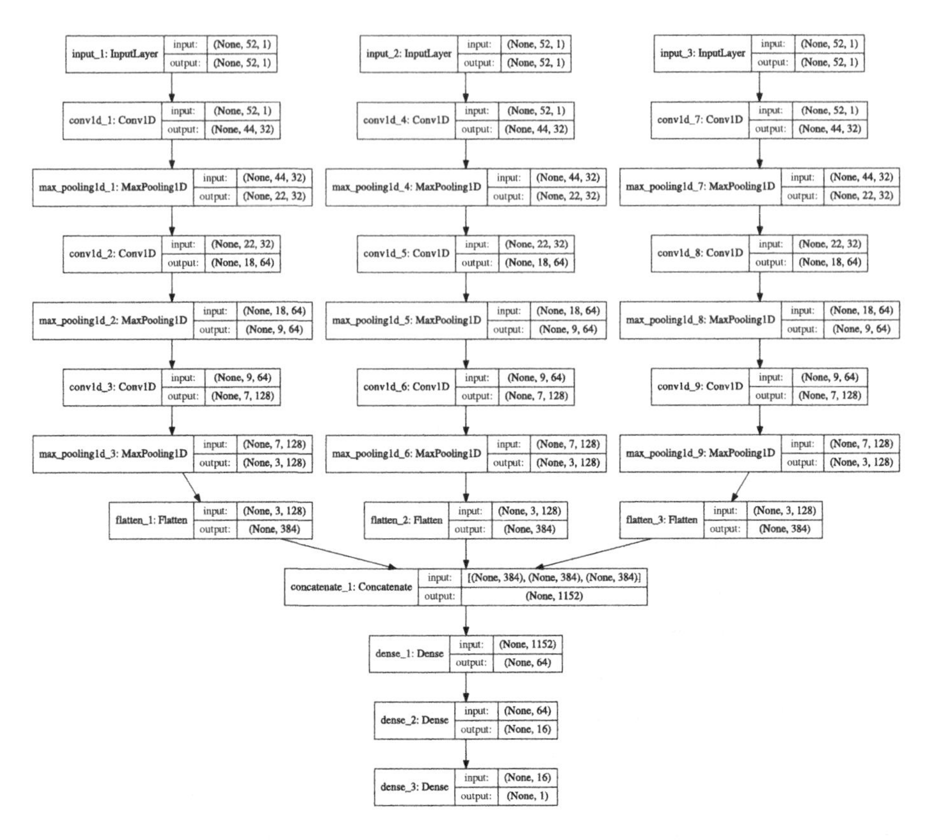

Fig. 3. CNN architecture. It is composed of three branches for handling the three components arising from the STL decomposition.

Table 2. Mean and standard deviation of MSE of test set (30% of the dataset) for 15 independent runs.

Architecture	MSE
MLP	113 ± 10
CNN	199 ± 22
BRNN	101 ± 2
CNN+STL	97 ± 9

parameter [52, 100]. A similar behaviour is observed for the number of epochs and the batch size.

The CNN architecture of the best case is composed of the following number of kernels: 13, 48, and 32; with sizes: 13, 4, and 5, with a sample size of 58. Two other high-performance cases appear for number of kernels (8, 40, 32), with kernels sizes (8, 9, 5) and (12, 3, 5), and sample sizes 96 and 100, respectively. Oppositely, low-performance cases appear when the number of kernels are much

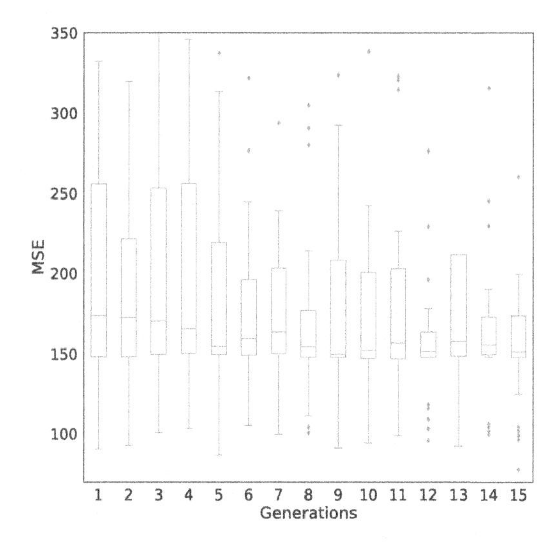

Fig. 4. Boxplot with the evolution of MSE per generation for the best case of 15 independent runs.

larger, specially in the last convolutional blocks, for instance (16, 48, 96), (32, 64, 80) and (24, 64, 128) with samples sizes: 70, 54, and 58, respectively.

5 Conclusions

In this paper, an approach based on PBIL for optimizing the hyperparameters of a CNN architecture and the parameters of a STL decomposition applied to the time series forecasting of ^{222}Rn concentration at Canfranc Underground Laboratory has been proposed. In the previous efforts, the performance of the time series forecasting with CNN architecture and STL decomposition was slightly penalized by the lack of a optimized parameters and hyperparameters set. The promising results obtained in the past deserve of an appropriated exploration of the parameter space. For this purpose, PBIL has been applied for finding a high-quality sub-optimal parameters and hyperparameters set. The use of an evolutionary algorithm for optimizing the hyperparameters of CNN allows replacing human-expertise-based values by optimized values.

The results and the statistical analysis state that the proposed architecture improves the previous performance of CNN and MLP algorithms being competitive with other well-recognized as suitable for time series forecasting as LSTM-Bidirectional Recurrent Neural Networks. Furthermore, the implementation can be used for exploring and evaluating not classical configuration of CNN architecture for time series forecasting.

To evaluate the proposed approach in other data sets is proposed as Future Work.

Acknowledgment. MCM is funded by the Spanish Ministry of Economy and Competitiveness (MINECO) for funding support through the grant "Unidad de Excelencia María de Maeztu": CIEMAT - FÍSICA DE PARTÍCULAS through the grant MDM-2015-0509.

References

1. Baluja, S.: Population-based incremental learning: a method for integrating genetic search based function optimization and competitive learning. Technical report, CMU-CS-94-163, Carnegie Mellon University, Pittsburgh, PA, January 1994
2. Baluja, S., Caruana, R.: Removing the genetics from the standard genetic algorithm. In: Machine Learning, Proceedings of the Twelfth International Conference on Machine Learning, Tahoe City, California, USA, 9–12 July 1995, pp. 38–46 (1995)
3. Bergstra, J., Bengio, Y.: Random search for hyper-parameter optimization. J. Mach. Learn. Res. **13**, 281–305 (2012)
4. Cárdenas-Montes, M.: Forecast daily air-pollution time series with deep learning. In: Pérez García, H., Sánchez González, L., Castejón Limas, M., Quintián Pardo, H., Corchado Rodríguez, E. (eds.) HAIS 2019. LNCS (LNAI), vol. 11734, pp. 431–443. Springer, Cham (2019). https://doi.org/10.1007/978-3-030-29859-3_37
5. Cárdenas-Montes, M., Méndez-Jiménez, I.: Ensemble deep learning for forecasting ^{222}rn radiation level at canfranc underground laboratory. In: Martínez Álvarez, F., Troncoso Lora, A., Sáez Muñoz, J.A., Quintián, H., Corchado, E. (eds.) SOCO 2019. AISC, vol. 950, pp. 157–167. Springer, Cham (2020). https://doi.org/10.1007/978-3-030-20055-8_15
6. Chollet, F., et al.: Keras (2015). https://github.com/fchollet/keras
7. Cleveland, R.B., Cleveland, W.S., McRae, J., Terpenning, I.: STL: a seasonal-trend decomposition procedure based on loess. J. Official Stat. 3–73 (1990)
8. Diaz, G.I., Fokoue-Nkoutche, A., Nannicini, G., Samulowitz, H.: An effective algorithm for hyperparameter optimization of neural networks. IBM J. Res. Dev. **61**(4), 9 (2017)
9. Gamboa, J.C.B.: Deep learning for time-series analysis. CoRR abs/1701.01887 (2017). http://arxiv.org/abs/1701.01887
10. García, S., Fernández, A., Luengo, J., Herrera, F.: A study of statistical techniques and performance measures for genetics-based machine learning: accuracy and interpretability. Soft Comput. **13**(10), 959–977 (2009)
11. García, S., Molina, D., Lozano, M., Herrera, F.: A study on the use of non-parametric tests for analyzing the evolutionary algorithms' behaviour: a case study on the CEC'2005 special session on real parameter optimization. J. Heuristics **15**(6), 617–644 (2009)
12. Goodfellow, I., Bengio, Y., Courville, A.: Deep Learning. MIT Press (2016). http://www.deeplearningbook.org
13. Hazan, E., Klivans, A.R., Yuan, Y.: Hyperparameter optimization: a spectral approach. CoRR abs/1706.00764 (2017). http://arxiv.org/abs/1706.00764
14. LeCun, Y.: Generalization and network design strategies. University of Toronto, Technical report (1989)
15. Li, A., et al.: A generalized framework for population based training. CoRR abs/1902.01894 (2019)

16. Maclaurin, D., Duvenaud, D.K., Adams, R.P.: Gradient-based hyperparameter optimization through reversible learning. In: Proceedings of the 32nd International Conference on Machine Learning, ICML 2015, Lille, France, 6–11 July 2015, pp. 2113–2122 (2015)
17. Méndez-Jiménez, I., Cárdenas-Montes, M.: Modelling and forecasting of the ^{222}Rn radiation level time series at the Canfranc Underground Laboratory. In: de Cos Juez, F., et al. (eds.) Hybrid Artificial Intelligent Systems - 13th International Conference, HAIS 2018, Proceedings. Lecture Notes in Computer Science, vol. 10870, pp. 158–170. Springer, Heidelberg (2018). https://doi.org/10.1007/978-3-319-92639-1_14
18. Méndez-Jiménez, I., Cárdenas-Montes, M.: Time series decomposition for improving the forecasting performance of convolutional neural networks. In: Herrera, F., et al. (eds.) Time series decomposition for improving the forecasting performance of convolutional neural networks. LNCS (LNAI), vol. 11160, pp. 87–97. Springer, Cham (2018). https://doi.org/10.1007/978-3-030-00374-6_9
19. Miikkulainen, R., et al.: Evolving deep neural networks. CoRR abs/1703.00548 (2017)
20. Montague, J.: STLDecompose (2017). https://github.com/jrmontag/STLDecompose
21. Rastegar, R., Hariri, A.: The population-based incremental learning algorithm converges to local optima. Neurocomputing **69**(13–15), 1772–1775 (2006)
22. Snoek, J., Larochelle, H., Adams, R.P.: Practical Bayesian optimization of machine learning algorithms. In: Advances in Neural Information Processing Systems 25: 26th Annual Conference on Neural Information Processing Systems 2012. Proceedings of a meeting held 3–6 December 2012, Lake Tahoe, Nevada, United States, pp. 2960–2968 (2012). http://papers.nips.cc/paper/4522-practical-bayesian-optimization-of-machine-learning-algorithms
23. Wang, Z., Yan, W., Oates, T.: Time series classification from scratch with deep neural networks: a strong baseline. CoRR abs/1611.06455 (2016). http://arxiv.org/abs/1611.06455

An Evolutionary Approach to Automatic Keyword Selection for Twitter Data Analysis

Oduwa Edo-Osagie[1(✉)], Beatriz De La Iglesia[1], Iain Lake[1], and Obaghe Edeghere[2]

[1] University of East Anglia, Norwich, UK
{o.edo-osagie,b.iglesia,i.lake}@uea.ac.uk
[2] Public Health England, Birmingham, UK
obaghe.edeghere@phe.gov.uk

Abstract. In this paper, we propose an approach to intelligent and automatic keyword selection for the purpose of Twitter data collection and analysis. The proposed approach makes use of a combination of deep learning and evolutionary computing. As some context for application, we present the proposed algorithm using the case study of public health surveillance over Twitter, which is a field with a lot of interest. We also describe an optimization objective function particular to the keyword selection problem, as well as metrics for evaluating Twitter keywords, namely: *reach* and *tweet retreival power*, on top of traditional metrics such as *precision*. In our experiments, our evolutionary computing approach achieved a tweet retreival power of **0.55**, compared to **0.35** achieved by the baseline human approach.

Keywords: Twitter · Evolutionary computing · Syndromic surveillance · Social media sensing

1 Introduction

Syndromic surveillance can be described as the real-time (or near real-time) collection, analysis, interpretation, and dissemination of health-related data, to enable the early identification of the impact (or absence of impact) of potential human or veterinary public health threats that require effective public health action [18]. As syndromic surveillance is concerned with the detection and understanding of public health threats, there is interest in rich, interesting and efficient data scources. De Quincey and Kostkova [2] introduced the potential of Twitter in detecting outbreaks. The amount of real-time information present on Twitter, either with regards to users reporting their own illness, the illness of others or reporting confirmed cases from the media, is both rich and highly accessible.

Supported by Public Health England.

E. A. de la Cal et al. (Eds.): HAIS 2020, LNAI 12344, pp. 160–171, 2020.
https://doi.org/10.1007/978-3-030-61705-9_14

Twitter syndromic surveillance is an active area of research. Chen et al. [1] managed to distinguish different biological phases of the flu from the content of tweets using a temporal topic model. In some of our previous work, we have used Twitter to monitor the prevalance/incidence of *asthma/difficulty breathing* in the UK [4–6]. Applications like these require the collection of Tweets for analysis. This collection usually involves specifying some filtering criteria. The simplest and most commonly used criteria is filtering by keyword. In any Twitter analysis application, choosing the right set of keywords can have a big impact on the system as it controls which Tweets are collected and observed. Choosing keywords that are too precise and strict will result in our system collecting mostly relevant Tweets, but also simultaneously only observing few Tweets, which will most likely only be a small sample of the relevant Tweets available. Conversely, choosing keywords that are too broad will result in our system observing a great deal of Tweets, most of which will not be relevant. Therefore, selecting the right keywords is an important and difficult task.

In this paper, we propose an intelligent and automatic approach to effective keyword selection. We leverage evolutionary algorithms and machine learning to quantify and distinguish semantic information in keywords, allowing us to automatically select the best keywords to collect Tweets relevant to our application. For the sake of comparison, we also discuss a manual method of keyword selection, carried out by humans, and use this as a baseline in our experiments. We found that our automatic keyword selection algorithm was able to outperform the manual, human approach. We make the source code for the proposed particle swarm optimization keyword selection algorithm publicly available at https://github.com/oduwa/PSOKeywordSelection.

2 Twitter Keyword Selection and Related Work

Before we begin thinking about automatic keyword selection, we must first understand how keyword selection normally occurs. While this process might differ based on the purpose of the data collection, it will typically involve some domain knowledge relating to the purpose of the data collection. However, in addition to this, it is often useful to keep in mind that language on Twitter is usually very informal and colloquial. This must also be taken into account when selecting a set of keywords for any purpose. For syndromic surveillance, our goal when selecting keywords for collection was to choose keywords which may be relevant to our particular syndrome of interest - *asthma/difficulty breathing*. We worked in conjunction with experts from Public Health England (PHE), to create a set of formal terms that may be connected to the specific syndrome under scrutiny. This set of keywords was then further expanded using synonyms from thesauri and the urban dictionary[1]. Urban dictionary is a web resource which serves as an encyclopedia of sorts for slangs, so it was used to account for informal language that may occur in Twitter.

[1] https://www.urbandictionary.com.

Much of the existing literature on keyword selection revolves around marketing and advertising efforts. Some researchers have looked at keyword selection as a feature selection problem [10]. Others have taken a classification point of view. For example, [12] applied a CNN to classify keywords as good or bad in order to maximaize advertising campaigns. More recently, with the influence of deep learning in natural language processing and the rise of deep word embeddings, such methods have seen a growing interest in keyword selection. Lee et al. made use of Word2Vec embeddings to select keywords for websites using semantic similarity [11]. In fact, similar to our work, Liu et al. work towards the problem of social media analysis, making use of GloVe embeddings to infer keywords which can be used to find online trolls on social media [13]. The problem with the solutions provided by much of the existing research, is that they assume that all similar keywords under a concept (such as asthma, for example), will collect relevant documents. They also assume that the addition of keywords will not dilute the quality of the collected data, just because they are all similar. However, this is not always the case. For this reason, we go further and attempt to optimize the set of keywords selected in such a way that confirms the above assumptions.

3 Evolutionary Automatic Keyword Selection for Twitter Data Analysis

We propose a two-stage approach which makes use of deep learning and evolutionary optimization. The input to the system is a small initial set of reasonable keywords. Deep word embeddings are trained on a text corpus with a subject domain related to the task for which the keywords are intended. We make use of GloVe [17] word embeddings which capture sematic meaning of words from observed context. Using these embeddings, we expand the initial input keyword set with words/phrases which are semantically similar or related to the input keywords. This expanded set of keywords then forms our candidate set which makes up our problem space from which we attempt to select the optimal subset to be used for Twitter data collection and analysis.

The task of keyword selection is modelled as an optimization problem. Each possible set of keywords is seen as a candidate solution and the goal is to find the optimal solution. In this approach, we make use of Particle Swarm Optimization (PSO) which is an evolutionary algorithm based on swarm intelligence put forward by J. Kennedy in 1995 [9]. Loosely speaking, we model each potential set of keywords as a particle in the swarm. Each particle is moved around the search space with some velocity, which is influenced by its known best position, as well as the best positions found by other members of the swarm.

3.1 Stage I: Obtaining the Candidate Set of Keywords

The first stage involves producing a larger set of candidate keywords, C, from which our optimal set will be selected. This is done by expanding the input query set, I, using deep word ebeddings as mentioned above. Word embeddings (sometimes referred to as word vectors) are a powerful distributed representation of text learned using neural networks that have been shown to perform well in similarity tasks [8]. They encode semantic information of words in dense low-dimensional vectors. There are many different ways to learn word embeddings [14,15,17]. The learned embeddings take the form of a matrix X of size $|V| \times d$ is produced where V is the set of all the words in our vocabulary and d is the dimension of each word embedding. For this work, we built GloVe embeddings [17] from a dataset of 5 million unlabelled Tweets collected without any keyword limitations. The trained GloVe embeddings allow our system to get an understanding of Twitter language and vernacular, as our application of choice is Twitter data analysis. For each word in our input, I, we obtain the n most similar words/phrases. These are estimated as the n closest vectors to the query word vector in the embedding space. We make use of cosine distance [7] as our distance measure for estimating similarity.

$$I = w_1, w_2, \dots, w_p \tag{1}$$

$$\forall w \in I : S = S \cup MostSimilar(w, n) \tag{2}$$

$$C = I \cup S \tag{3}$$

3.2 Stage II: Applying Particle Swarm Optimization to Keywords

We model the keyword selection task as an optimization problem. Here an individual or particle or solution is a set of keywords. In this problem, the goal is to find the set of keywords that provide the maximum (or minimum) of some objective function. While the obvious solution to such a problem would be simply to check each possible solution in the search space and select the best, this is not often feasible. This is due to the fact that as the problem space grows, the computational complexity increases exponentially with it, making brute force search approaches unfeasible. PSO solves this problem by making use of a set population of particles, where each particle is a potential solution. Figure 1 shows an illustration of the particles in a problem space. These particles are then set loose to explore the search space in order to find an optimal solution. They tend to swarm and form clusters in optimal regions of the problem space.

We now look towards how we can model the keyword selection problem using PSO. Following the construction of the candidate keyword set C as described in Eqs. 1, 2 and 3, we encode each keyword contained within it as a unique integer ranging from 1 to $|C|$. We can now represent a set of keywords as a vector of integers, k, where each integer in the vector maps to a keyword in C. The size of k, denoted as D, must be determined before-hand and equates to the maximum size of the desired final optimal keyword set. Additionally, while values of 1 to $|C|$ represent keywords, a value of zero will be used to represent the absence of a keyword. This makes it possible to have sets of keywords with varying numbers of keywords within them, up to $|k|$ keywords.

With this, when keyword vectors are mapped back to keyword sets, it will be possible to have sets of varying sizes (of up to $|k|$). For example, consider

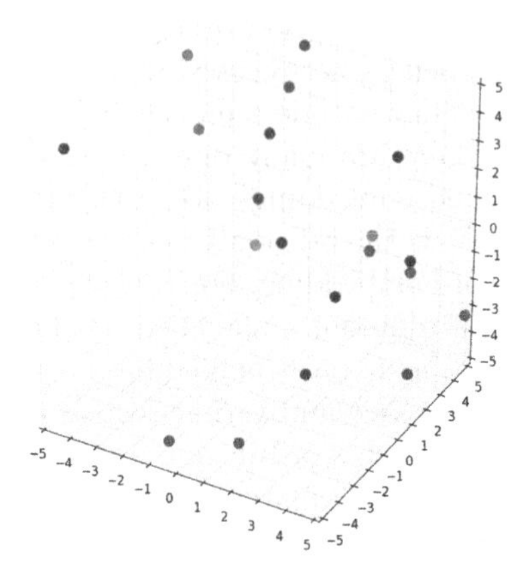

Fig. 1. Illustration of PSO particles in a search space represented in three dimensions using t-SNE. The axes represent respective component values in the 3D particle vector representation.

the mapping {*"boy":1, "girl":2, "man":3, "woman":4*}. Assuming a system of vectors with k set to 5, the set of keywords *[man, boy, girl]* can be represented as *[3,1,4,0,0]*, and *[woman]* as *[4,0,0,0,0]*. Having developed a way to represent a set of keywords as a vector, we can also represent a set of keywords as a particle, as a particle is represented by a vector. With this, we can apply PSO to our candidate set, C, to intelligently and automatically select a set of keywords.

We start by randomly initializing a population of particles (i.e. keyword sets) from C. In essence, we create a set number of random vectors of size D, with values ranging from 0 to $|C|$. Each particle possesses a ***position***, x and a ***velocity***, v, and keeps track of the best position it has found, that is, its "personal best" or ***pbest***. The system also keeps track of the "global best" or ***gbest***, which is simply the best position that has ever been found by any particle. The position of the ith particle can be represented $x_i = (x_i^1, x_i^2, x_i^3, ...x_i^D)$. The particles are all moved around the search space, with their positions updated based on their velocities, *pbest* values and *gbest*. More formally, after each iteration at time t, the position of the ith particle is updated according to Eq. 4

$$x_i^{t+1} = x_i^t + v_i^{t+1} \tag{4}$$

The velocity of the particle, v_i^{t+1}, (at time $t+1$) used to update its position can be computed as shown in Eq. 5 where ω is the inertia coefficient, c_1 and c_2 are acceleration coefficients and r_1 and r_2 are random floating point values between 0 and 1.

$$v_i^{t+1} = \omega v_i^t + c_1 r_1 (pbest - x_i^t) + c_2 r_2 (gbest - x_i^t) \tag{5}$$

There are three main components to the way the velocity of a particle is updated:

- ***Inertia Component:*** This component is intended to keep the particle moving (or not moving) in the direction it is heading, and is controlled by ω.

Lower values of ω will speed up convergence while higher values encourage particle exploration of the search space [19].
- ***Learning Component:*** This component controls the size of the step a particle takes towards its next position in exploring the search space. It is controlled by the coefficient, c_1 [3].
- ***Social Component:*** This component implements swarm mentality, and causes a particle to move towards the best regions the swarm has discovered so far. It is controlled by c_2 [3].

Largely speaking, the particles in the swarm explore the search space based on the *pbests* and *gbest* within the swarm. These values are computed for a particle's position using the objective function, Z. Our goal is to minimize the value of Z, which represents the underlying desire of the swarm system. It is the function to be optimized. We make use of an objective function that is particular to the task of selecting a keyword set. We wish to maximize the number of relevant documents (or Tweets in our application scenario) and minimize the number of irrelevant documents collected by a set of keywords. However, we don't wish to achieve this by being too selective and only collecting very few documents. Our goal is a combination of the relevancy of the Tweets we collect and the volume of Tweets we collect. Both of these figures are important to us. As such, we developed an objective function that belies this. The objective function, Z, is computed as the mean of two terms, α and β. α is the ***irrelevance factor*** shown in Eq. 6, while β is the ***retrieval factor*** shown in Eq. 7.

$$\alpha = \sum_{i=1}^{D} \left(\frac{\sum_{j=1}^{|T|} k[i] \in T[j]}{\sum_{j=1}^{|T|} T[j] == irrelevant} \right) \tag{6}$$

$$\beta = \sum_{i=1}^{D} \left(1 - \left(\frac{\sum_{j=1}^{|T|} k[i] \in T[j]}{|T|} \right)\right) \tag{7}$$

Z is computed as:

$$Z = \frac{\alpha + \beta}{2} \tag{8}$$

Finally, the main steps of the PSO keyword selection algorithm are an iteration over the following steps:

1. The objective function is computed by each particle for their current position.
2. Each particle updates their *pbest* and the *gbest*.
3. Each particle is moved once their velocity and position are updated, using the *pbest* and *gbest* values computed from the objective function.

The steps are repeated either until the values converge, or a predetermined maximum number of iterations is reached.

4 Experiments

We were interested in understanding if our proposed approach solved the task of intelligent and automatic keyword selection at all, and if so, also understanding how well it did so. We implemented and ran Tweet collections for the asthma/difficulty breathing syndrome using our keyword selection approach and the typical manual approach, for a baseline. We undertook two sets of collection periods. The first collection period was a sort of "validation" collection period, inspired by the training/validation/test splits adopted when building machine learning models. This validation collection period was used by our proposed approaches to automatically generate keywords. These generated keywords were subsequently utilized in a second collection period, intended to allow us to measure how well the generated keywords perform. This can be seen as our "test" collection period. Our validation collection period ran for a seven day period from the 24th of May, 2019 till the 1st of July, 2019. Our test collection period ran for a further seven day period from the 1st of July, 2019 till the 8th of July, 2019. Only the PSO-based approach was involved in the validation collection period, as the baseline approach does not need any data for setting it up. During the test collection period however, both approaches are involved.

One caveat to consider is that even though the evaluatory Tweet collections were performed simultaneously in parallel, due to the workings of the Twitter API, there is no guarantee that both systems will be exposed to the exact same Tweets at the exact same time. This is because the Twitter streaming API only offers a sample of the entire real-time stream, the percentage of which will vary depending on the activity loads at the time. Despite this limitation of the free Twitter API, we should still be able to get some indication of how well our approaches perform. In this section, we describe the experimental setup for each approach, including the baseline standard keyword selection approach. After that, we present and discuss the results we obtained.

4.1 Experimental Setup: Baseline Approach

The baseline approach involved working with a group of domain experts to come up with useful keywords and augmenting these keywords with some terms from the Urban Dictionary. We came up with the following list of keywords - *pollution, smog, poor air quality, wheeze, wheezing, difficulty breathing, asthma, inhaler, air pollution, itchy eyes, sore eyes, trouble breathing, can- not breathe, could not breathe, can't breathe, coudn't breathe, asma, short of breath, tight chest, chest tightness, respiratory disease, pea souper, murk, fumes, acid rain, gasping, puffing, panting.* Using these keywords, we ran a Tweet collection during the test collection period, from the 1st of July, 2019, till the 8th of July, 2019. The validation collection period was not used for this part of the experiments as there was no automatic keyword generation, rendering such a period unnecessary.

4.2 Experimental Setup: Particle Swarm Optimization-Based Keyword Selection Approach

The standard keyword set used in the baseline approach was used as the seed input I for creating the candidate set C. For each word in I, their five most similar words as inferred from our GloVe embeddings were added to the set. Using the candidate set of keywords, Tweets were collected during the validation collection period. At the end of this period, the PSO-based keyword generation algorithm was applied using the collected Tweets. We set our D, representing the maximum size of a keyword set to be 10. We made use of the PySwarm library of evolutionary algorithms to implement our PSO algorithm. Our setup had a swarm size of 100. After some experimentation, we set our ω to 0.8., and c_1 and c_2 to 1. This resulted in the following set of keywords being selected as the optimal arrangement: *wheezing, panting, gasping, puffing, coudn't breathe, wheeze, asthma, inhaler, sore eyes.* After obtaining the automatically selected keywords, we applied them during the test collection period, using them as query inputs.

5 Results

We utilized the set of keywords we obtained from our keyword selection algorithm as query inputs for Tweet collection. We also utilized the keywords obtained using the standard baseline approach. We applied the two distinct sets of keywords in parallel during our test collection period - 1st of July, 2019, till the 8th of July, 2019. We then analyzed the Tweets collected by each set of keywords in order to understand how useful each keyword set was. We assessed the keyword sets based on their information retrieval ability. A lot of the traditional information retrieval metrics do not translate well, or cannot be calculated for our problem. For example, recall, which measures the fraction of relevant documents retrieved cannot be calculated because we have no way of knowing the total amount of relevant Tweets out there. Because of this, we made use of a combination of traditional metrics and developed problem-specific metrics. These metrics are ***precision*** and ***reach***.

Precision is a popular information retrieval metric which represents the proportion of retrieved documents which are relevant. In such an information retrieval context, precision is calculated as:

$$precision = \frac{|RelevantTweets| \cap |CollectedTweets|}{|CollectedTweets|} \tag{9}$$

In our scenario, precision measures the proportion of the collected Tweets which are relevant. When calculating the precision values for each keyword approach, we computed the precision over a random sample of the retrieved Tweets. We took random 2000-large samples of the Tweets colletected using each keyword selection approach and computed the precision from this sample. We did this because we wanted to manually label and count the number of relevant Tweets, instead of relying on one of our trained classifiers which are not perfect. Doing so allowed us to get an accurate and exact value for the number of relevant Tweets, and would not be feasible with the complete set of collected Tweets which are very large and would be incredibly time-consuming to manually label.

Reach is a metric we developed to help us capture the ability of a set of keywords to retrieve as many Tweets as possible, relevant or not. This is important because while it is useful to collect relevant Tweets, if we only observe a small amount of Tweets, we cannot create a useful signal which is appropriately representative of the activity related to the syndrome of interest. As such, reach measures the quantity of Tweets a set of keywords is able to collect. This could be computed simply as the proportion of the general Tweet stream that is collected using a set of keywords. However, the inner workings of the Twitter API is unknown to us. To overcome any bias introduced by the API and any rate limits it may impose, we calculate the *reach* of a set of keywords in relation to the simplest singular keyword possible. This can be formally represented as shown below:

$$reach = \frac{|CollectedTweets|_{\hat{k}} - |CollectedTweets|_K}{|CollectedTweets|_K} \tag{10}$$

$\hat{k}$ represents some arbitrary single unit keyword which is a simple and straightforward keyword. For example, in our scenario of *asthma/difficulty breathing* surveillance, we make use of the keyword "asthma" as $\hat{k}$.

Finally, we combined the precision and reach metrics into one metric by taking their harmonic mean, similar to the F-measure. We term this combined metric, the ***Tweet Retrieval Power (TRP)***.

$$TRP = 2\frac{precision \times reach}{precision + reach} \tag{11}$$

The TRP weights precision and reach evenly but similarly to the F-measure, it is possible to calculate variations of the TRP score which place different weights on precision and reach as below:

$$TRP_\beta = (1 + \beta^2)\frac{precision \times reach}{\beta^2(precision + reach)} \tag{12}$$

where TRP_β measures the Tweet retrieval ability when β times as much importance is placed on reach than precision.

Table 1. Performances of different approaches to keyword selection

Keyword selection approach	Precision	Reach	TRP
Baseline human approach	0.23	0.75	0.35
PSO approach	0.48	0.65	0.55

Table 1 shows the results observed at the end of our analysis. We found the PSO approach to have the best Tweet Retrieval Power. The PSO approach produced a fair improvements in precision over the baseline human approach. It also resulted in a decrease in reach however. The precision achieved by the PSO keyword selection approach is more than double that seen by the baseline. In addition, while the reach of the baseline approach is better than that of the PSO approach, the margin between them is not very large. Finally, the total Tweet Retreival Power of the PSO approach is greater than that of the manual baseline approach, and appears to possess a reasonable balance of precision and reach.

6 Conclusion

In this paper, we investigated hybrid approaches to intelligently and automatically selecting keywords for use in collecting data, using Tweets for syndromic surveillance as a case study. We proposed an evolutionary algorithm inspired method which modelled the keyword selection task as an optimization problem. It made use of Particle Swarm Optimization (PSO) to determine the optimal set of keywords. The proposed algorithm was implemented and applied to the task of collecting Tweets for the surveillane of the *asthma/difficulty breathing* syndrome. For the sake of comparison, we also carried out a Tweet collection with keywords selected by human experts. We then evaluated the results of both approaches, making comparisons between them.

We found that the PSO-based method performed better, outperforming the manual, human approach by a fair margin. While we observed a fair increase in relevance (precision) using our automatic keyword selection algorithms, we saw the opposite when looking at the reach metric. The baseline human approach to curating keywords seemed to have the most reach. Despite this, the boost in precision offered by the automatic keyword selection algorithm meant that it outperformed the baseline approach, yielding a higher TRP value. However, it is also important to remember that while we tried to keep things constant in our experiments, applying each keyword selection approach in parallel during the same periods, we cannot guarantee that they were exposed to the same environments and Tweets as that is an issue dependent on the Twitter API. Studies have estimated that using the Twitter streaming API, users can expect to receive anywhere from 1% of the tweets to 40% of tweets available in real-time, depending on the amount of activity at the time [16].

While we have introduced this technique for the intelligent and automatic selection of keywords and used them for surveilling the syndrome of *asthma/difficulty breathing*, it also does not generalize to other tasks. These techniques cannot only be applied for the purposes of surveilling other syndromes on Twitter, but also for any Tweet collection exercise, regardless of the purpose of said exercise. This is due to the fact that these techniques aim to maximize the relevance of collected Tweets to some query, together with the volume of Tweets collected. As long as there exists some defined query, the notion of "relevance" for its results must also exist. Because these are the main ideas behind our proposed approaches, they can be very easily adapted to any other problem and generalize very well.

While we have established that the PSO method collects better Tweets, it also runs in a very reasonable amount of time. This is because the time taken for each iteration is determined by how many particles the swarm contains and the dimension of each particle, as well as the computational resources available. Even with a mid-tier computer, a single iteration could never take longer than an hour in the absolute worst case. As such the PSO method is not only effective in terms of the quality of the keywords produced, but also in terms of the amount of time taken to produce said keywords.

References

1. Chen, L., Hossain, K.T., Butler, P., Ramakrishnan, N., Prakash, B.A.: Syndromic surveillance of flu on Twitter using weakly supervised temporal topic models. Data Min. Knowl. Discov. **30**(3), 681–710 (2016)
2. de Quincey, E., Kostkova, P.: Early warning and outbreak detection using social networking websites: the potential of Twitter. In: Kostkova, P. (ed.) eHealth 2009. LNICST, vol. 27, pp. 21–24. Springer, Heidelberg (2010). https://doi.org/10.1007/978-3-642-11745-9_4
3. Deb, K., Padhye, N.: Improving a particle swarm optimization algorithm using an evolutionary algorithm framework. KanGAL report 2010/003 (2010)
4. Edo-Osagie, O., De La Iglesia, B., Lake, I., Edeghere, O.: Deep learning for relevance filtering in syndromic surveillance: a case study in asthma/difficulty breathing. In: International Conference on Pattern Recognition Applications and Methods, no. 8 (2019)
5. Edo-Osagie, O., Lake, I., Edeghere, O., De La Iglesia, B.: Attention-based recurrent neural networks (RNNs) for short text classification: an application in public health monitoring. In: Rojas, I., Joya, G., Catala, A. (eds.) IWANN 2019. LNCS, vol. 11506, pp. 895–911. Springer, Cham (2019). https://doi.org/10.1007/978-3-030-20521-8_73
6. Edo-Osagie, O., Smith, G., Lake, I., Edeghere, O., De La Iglesia, B.: Twitter mining using semi-supervised classification for relevance filtering in syndromic surveillance. PloS One **14**(7), e0210689 (2019)
7. George, K.K., Kumar, C.S., Ramachandran, K., Panda, A.: Cosine distance features for improved speaker verification. Electron. Lett. **51**(12), 939–941 (2015)
8. Jin, L., Schuler, W.: A comparison of word similarity performance using explanatory and non-explanatory texts. In: Proceedings of the 2015 Conference of the North American Chapter of the Association for Computational Linguistics: Human Language Technologies, pp. 990–994 (2015)
9. Kennedy, J.: Particle swarm optimization. In: Encyclopedia of Machine Learning, pp. 760–766 (2010)
10. Kiritchenko, S., Jiline, M.: Keyword optimization in sponsored search via feature selection. In: New Challenges for Feature Selection in Data Mining and Knowledge Discovery, pp. 122–134 (2008)
11. Lee, D., Kim, K.: Web site keyword selection method by considering semantic similarity based on word2vec. J. Soc. e-Bus. Stud. **23**(2) (2019)
12. Liang, J., Yang, H., Gao, J., Yue, C., Ge, S., Qu, B.: MOPSO-based CNN for keyword selection on Google ads. IEEE Access **7**, 125387–125400 (2019)

13. Liu, A., Srikanth, M., Adams-Cohen, N., Alvarez, R.M., Anandkumar, A.: Finding social media trolls: dynamic keyword selection methods for rapidly-evolving online debates. arXiv preprint arXiv:1911.05332 (2019)
14. Luong, T., Socher, R., Manning, C.: Better word representations with recursive neural networks for morphology. In: Proceedings of the Seventeenth Conference on Computational Natural Language Learning, pp. 104–113 (2013)
15. Mikolov, T., Sutskever, I., Chen, K., Corrado, G.S., Dean, J.: Distributed representations of words and phrases and their compositionality. In: Advances in Neural Information Processing Systems, pp. 3111–3119 (2013)
16. Morstatter, F., Pfeffer, J., Liu, H., Carley, K.M.: Is the sample good enough? Comparing data from Twitter's streaming API with Twitter's firehose. In: Seventh International AAAI Conference on Weblogs and Social Media (2013)
17. Pennington, J., Socher, R., Manning, C.: Glove: global vectors for word representation. In: Proceedings of the 2014 Conference on Empirical Methods in Natural Language Processing (EMNLP), pp. 1532–1543 (2014)
18. Triple, S.: Assessment of syndromic surveillance in Europe. Lancet (London, England) **378**(9806), 1833 (2011)
19. Umapathy, P., Venkataseshaiah, C., Arumugam, M.S.: Particle swarm optimization with various inertia weight variants for optimal power flow solution. Discrete Dyn. Nat. Soc. **2010**, 1–15 (2010). https://doi.org/10.1155/2010/462145

PreCLAS: An Evolutionary Tool for Unsupervised Feature Selection

Jessica A. Carballido, Ignacio Ponzoni(✉), and Rocío L. Cecchini

Institute for Computer Science and Engineering (UNS - CONICET),
Department of Computer Science and Engineering, Universidad Nacional del Sur,
Bahía Blanca, Argentina
{jac,ip,rlc}@cs.uns.edu.ar
https://icic.conicet.gov.ar/

Abstract. Several research areas are being faced with data matrices that are not suitable to be managed with traditional clustering, regression, or classification strategies. For example, biological so-called omic problems present models with thousands or millions of rows and less than a hundred columns. This matrix structure hinders the successful progress of traditional data analysis methods and thus needs some means for reducing the number of rows. This article presents an unsupervised approach called PreCLAS for preprocessing matrices with dimension problems to obtain data that are apt for clustering and classification strategies. The PreCLAS was implemented as an unsupervised strategy that aims at finding a submatrix with a drastically reduced number of rows, preferring those rows that together present some group structure. Experimentation was carried out in two stages. First, to assess its functionality, a benchmark dataset was studied in a clustering context. Then, a microarray dataset with genomic information was analyzed, and the PreCLAS was used to select informative genes in the context of classification strategies. Experimentation showed that the new method performs successfully at drastically reducing the number of rows of a matrix, smartly performing unsupervised feature selection for both classification and clustering problems.

Keywords: Clustering tendency · Classification strategies · Evolutionary algorithm · Unsupervised feature selection · Microarray data analysis

1 Introduccion

A well-known and extensively studied subject in machine learning, statistics and information theory is the dimensionality problem: matrices with a structure "$n \ll N$" where N (number of rows) is much larger than n (number of columns).

This work is supported by CONICET (Grant number 112-2017-0100829) and Secretaría de Ciencia y Tecnología (UNS) (Grant number 24/N042).

E. A. de la Cal et al. (Eds.): HAIS 2020, LNAI 12344, pp. 172–182, 2020.
https://doi.org/10.1007/978-3-030-61705-9_15

In this work, the objective is to present a novel unsupervised manner for selecting a manageable amount of rows suitable for classification and clustering methods.

A vital issue rarely discussed in data mining studies is the fact that clustering techniques always find clusters, whether or not real groups of coherent values genuinely exist in the structure of data under analysis. Then, clustering methods can contradict the proverb "from where there is nothing, you cannot get something". If the k-means algorithm is given a randomly generated matrix to find three clusters, the method yields three clusters, even though no real groups exist. Therefore, it should be required to perform some previous study to the structure of the matrix, to establish whether it is coherent to look for clusters in it. This study is called "clustering tendency". The Hopkins statistic [15,17] constitutes an appropriate measure for evaluating the clustering tendency of a matrix. In this context arose the main inspiration for the design of the method: an unsupervised instance reduction method that diminishes the number of rows using as a measure of choice the idea of keeping those rows that show some submatrix structure suitable for grouping techniques, whenever this submatrix truly exists. Obtaining a submatrix with this structure is also beneficial for classification methods, as it will be shown later. To the best of our knowledge, no strategy performs unsupervised feature selection based on this criterion.

The method, called PreCLAS, is implemented as an evolutionary algorithm that funds the selection of features based on clustering tendency studies. In this context, the Hopkins statistic is used to analyze whether the data are uniformly distributed. The measure is simple and intuitive. It is based on the difference between the distance from a real point to its nearest neighbor (d_r) and the distance from a randomly artificial generated point to its nearest neighbor (d_a). In this work, the implementation of the Hopkins statistic corresponds to the one provided by the `<clustertend> R package`. The idea is the following: when data contains no group structure, the distance among real points and their real neighbor points is approximately the same as the distance from uniformly distributed random artificial points to their nearest real neighbor points. On the other hand, if data contains some cluster structure, that distance increases.

The ultimate goal of this research is to apply the new method to bioinformatics problems of microarray data analysis. Microarray experiments obtain expression data from thousands of genes for a few samples, presenting this data as a matrix that exhibits the "$n \ll N$" form. Microarray data analysis includes statistics, supervised and unsupervised techniques, generally categorized as class discovery, class prediction, or class comparison. In this context, our method arises for selecting some informative genes in a matrix **without using information about the samples**. This is carried out because many times, microarray experiments present information about SOME of the samples, but not about all of them. Then it is important to count with a tool that analyses the matrix in an unsupervised manner. The final aim is to demonstrate whether those genes are representative of the classes that are defined in the dataset to constitute a useful input for classification algorithms. It is well known that a classification algorithm will perform accordingly to the quality of the examples that are used to train it.

It is also important to remark that a low number of samples makes it very difficult to create predictive models. First, some machine learning algorithms, such as linear discriminant analysis (LDA), cannot be applied if the number of observations is less than the number of predictors. Secondly, even though all the genes can be incorporated in the model (SVM), if many of them do not contribute more than noise to the model, this diminishes the predictive capacity when applied to new observations (overfitting). Moreover, most genes in microarray experiments are not of interest. Less than 10% manifest the hidden phenotypes, and therefore, are immersed in large amounts of noise. The uncertainty about which genes are relevant hinders the process of selecting informative genes.

On the whole, the idea is the following: differentially expressed genes between samples naturally generate a structure of groups in the matrix. Then, if the algorithm can select a reduced group of differentially expressed genes from matrices with dimension problems, it constitutes an unsupervised feature selection method that can be used before classification and clustering techniques. The importance of this unsupervised step lies in the fact that many times the microarray datasets do not contain class information for all the samples that are in general, very few. As far as we know, no widely accepted method performs feature selection for classification and clustering in an unsupervised manner.

2 Related Work

Data preprocessing is one of the most critical stages in data mining and knowledge discovering processes. Nowadays, data is massively being produced and stored to be studied and analyzed. As it is well known, this massive production of data also carries substantial amounts of redundant, noisy, faulty, and irrelevant information. This scenario has yielded the development of different preprocessing steps that can imply tasks such as data filtering, outlier detection, feature extraction, feature selection, and instance reduction. These kinds of functions have extensively been studied in machine learning, statistics, and information theory. In particular, the so-called feature extraction, feature selection, and instance selection problems are aimed at reducing the dataset size to facilitate the inference process of the machine learning method to be applied. The feature selection problem has been approached in different contexts by several authors [10,19]. Most basic techniques assume that the dataset at hand can be represented for a percentage of the total data, and select this portion in a heuristic way or by some systematic way [16], but numerous methods that are more sophisticated have been proposed. However, many of those methods are formulated and evaluated in the data classification scenario [1,22], or the regression scenario [2,11] but not for clustering, and even less in the case of the matrices $n \ll N$. On the other hand, several works are mainly focused on normalization, noise reduction, or faulted data correction [6,14]. Alternatively, different authors have designed other methods concentrating primarily on the selection of a few features that may be considered as the representative of the whole dataset [18,20]. Unlike these works, the PreCLAS method is directly intended to reduce the number of rows by finding the submatrix with the best group structure, i.e., not necessarily discarding objects that are similarly representative of the dataset structure, but trying to keep all the subsets of features that can be grouped in clearly defined clusters, whenever they exist.

Regarding the use of Evolutionary Algorithms on feature selection problems, there are also several works to mention. In [7], the authors reviewed some of the most relevant methods, and, since then, other evolutionary inspired methods have been proposed [4,25]. As in the case of the works mentioned in the previous section, many of the evolutionary techniques are thought and evaluated in the classification scenario [4,13,25] and aiming at selecting some few representative instances [13,24], or in the regression scenario [2]. As it can be seen from the available literature, the feature selection problem has been approached from diverse angles and with different purposes, but, to the best of our knowledge, they are not directly comparable with the one proposed in the present article, mainly because it works without information about the classes.

3 The Method: PreCLAS

The method presented in this article was implemented as a Genetic Algorithm (GA). GAs are metaheuristic adaptive methods used to solve NP search and optimization problems. They are based on the genetic process of living organisms. Across generations, populations evolve in nature following the principles of natural selection and the survival of the fittest, postulated by Darwin [5]. Simulating that process, GAs can create near-optimal solutions for many real-world problems. The individuals of the population represent solutions to the addressed problem. Basic principles of GAs were posed by Holland [12], and are well described in several texts, such as Goldberg [9]. In this context, PreCLAS is a GA implemented in R that receives a matrix of real numbers and an optional parameter for the number of rows of the resulting submatrix. Details on the algorithm are given below.

Individuals are vectors of 50 integer numbers that vary from 1 to the number or rows of the original matrix; they are values corresponding to feasible row indices. In this manner, each individual is a list of indices of fixed length that indicates which rows should be kept. As individuals represent different reductions of that matrix, the evaluation consists of calculating the Hopkins statistics of each submatrix. An initial population of 50 individuals is created with a substantial restriction: they must overcome a clustering tendency threshold of quality, which means that very inconvenient individuals (according to their fitness) are not allowed in the initial population. The creation of each individual is repeated until an acceptable value of the statistical threshold is obtained. Then, the fittest individuals of the population are kept by a binary tournament procedure, where two individuals are randomly selected, and the one with the best fitness value passes to the next generation.

The combination of genetic information is performed using ad-hoc designed set operations. Parents are selected, and the indices of rows contained in each of them are combined into a "super father". An intersection is also performed to see how many and which indices appear repeated between parents. Afterward, the first son is constructed selecting some indices from the "super father" and completing the number of indices with the ones that were found repeated in the intersection. The second son contains the remaining indices, also filled with the repeated ones. The crossover probability is 0.7. Finally, the mutation operation ends the process of obtaining the new descendant. In this implementation, individuals selected for mutation are randomly replaced. In this way, the operator introduces the right level of randomness for exploration purposes. The mutation probability is 0.3. A maximum number of 200 generations is established. In addition, the algorithm informs whether a submatrix with a reasonable clustering tendency could be obtained. Parameters of population size, probability of mutation and crossing, and the number of generations were empirically established.

4 Results and Discussion

4.1 Simple Performance Assessment

The functioning of this prototype was verified, analyzing a benchmark dataset used for conglomerate studies. The study case Ruspini [21] consists of 75 observations on two variables, x, and y. As can be seen in Fig. 1 (left), the separation into four clusters is visually recognizable. Some noise was added to the matrix, enlarging it to double its size with random values and maintaining the cluster structure (see Fig. 1). This new matrix was called RuspBIG. In this context, the hypothesis was about PreCLAS being able to find the submatrix from RuspBIG that exhibits a good clustering tendency.

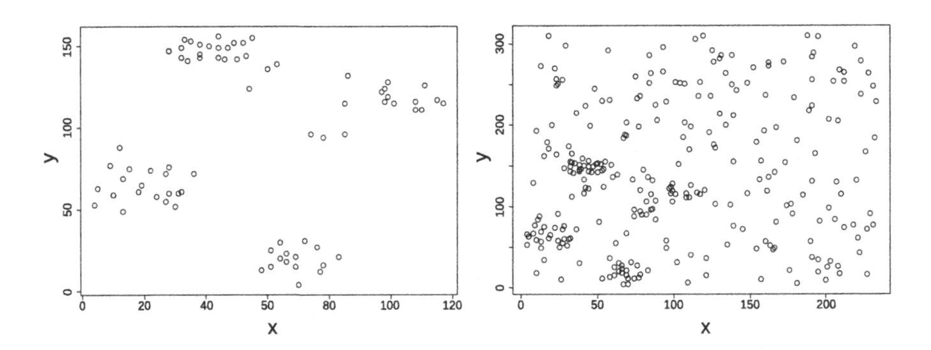

Fig. 1. Benchmark data distribution.

Starting from RuspBIG, two algorithms were used to reduce it: The PreCLAS and a RANDOM search algorithm. Both algorithms reduced the matrix to 70 rows. One hundred independent runs were performed for each of them. As a first measure, we obtained the mean Hopkins values from the 100 resulting sub-matrices (the best of each run). The results were: mean Hopkins value of the 100 PreCLAS sub-matrices = 0.2912351 and for RANDOM sub-matrices = 0.4611668.

As it was expected, the sub-matrices found by PreCLAS exhibited a better Hopkins value since it is closer to 0, and the confidence intervals showed a statistically significant difference between the mean values, as they do not overlap each other. This result was also expected because this measure precisely guides the evolution of the genetic algorithm. For visual aims, we randomly selected one submatrix yielded by each algorithm to see how the visualization method VAT [3] represents each of them. Figure 2 shows that a clustering tendency is more evident in the matrix obtained from PreCLAS. The next stage consisted of applying the K-means algorithm, with $k = 4$ to each reduced matrix. Final values found by each of the methods from all the trials were: PreCLAS: Hopkins mean = 0.29 (CI [0.28, 0.3]) and Silhouette mean = 0.51 (CI [0.5, 0.51]); RANDOM: Hopkins mean = 0.46 (CI [0.45, 0.47]) and Silhouette mean = 0.4 (CI [0.44, 0.45]).

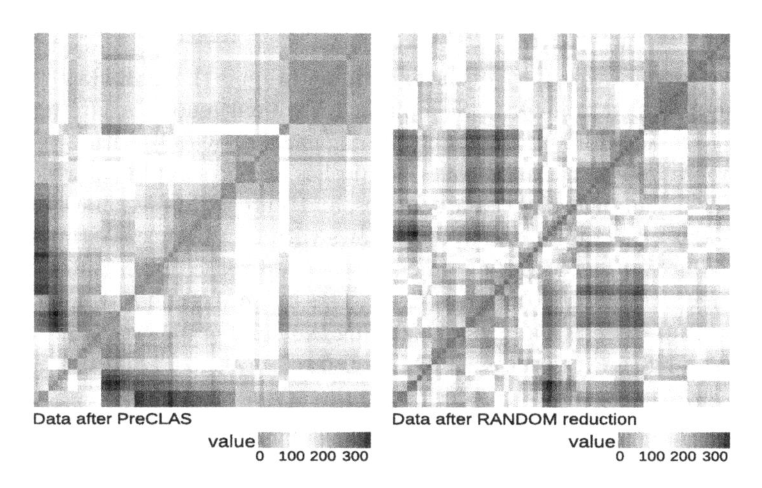

Fig. 2. VAT for data after PreCLAS reduction (left-hand side) and VAT for data after random modification (right-hand side).

A better performance was achieved by the clustering algorithm when the PreCLAS yielded the submatrix. When selecting one result after clustering from each sub-matrix obtained by PreCLAS and RANDOM, it can be graphically shown that the clusters found after PreCLAS (Fig. 3, left-hand side) look more coherent than those found after the RANDOM reduction (Fig. 3, right-hand side).

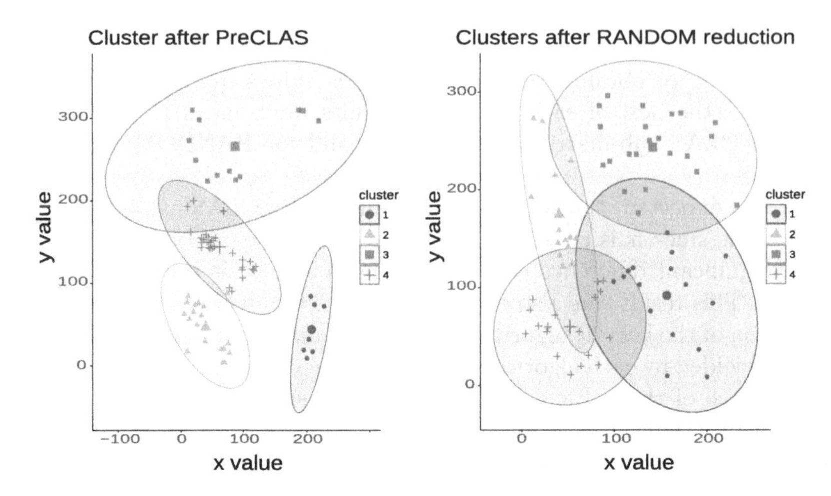

Fig. 3. Clusters after PreCLAS reduction (left-hand side) and after RANDOM reduction (right-hand side)

4.2 A Bioinformatics Example

The dataset used for this stage of the experimentation is the GSE43346 [23]. This dataset was obtained from GEO [8], a public functional genomics data repository. It belongs to a study of human small cell lung cancer (SCLC), with gene expression data represented in a matrix of 54675 probes and 68 samples, of which 23 are clinical SCLC, 42 are normal tissue samples, and 3 are SCLC cell lines. First, this original matrix was reduced to eliminate rows with no variance. With this initial standard reduction method, the number of rows decreased from 54675 to 27284 (called from now Original *Reduced* Matrix). This is one of the most common mathematical (unsupervised) manners of reducing the number of rows. However, note that this ranking is a very rudimentary way to select a subset of genes.

Moreover, this amount of genes is still not practicable for most classifiers. Hypothesis: Is a submatrix yielded by the PreCLAS a good alternative for classification purposes? The analysis was performed as follows:

1. The 50 genes (rows) with the highest variance are selected from the original reduced matrix. Then, nine genes are randomly selected from this matrix and form a new 9 by 68 matrix (from now on, this matrix will be called matrix A).
2. On the other hand, the PreCLAS was executed over the original reduced matrix to select 50 rows. Then, nine genes are also randomly selected from this other matrix and form a new 9 by 68 matrix (from now on, this matrix will be called matrix B).
3. The differential expressions of matrices A and B are calculated and showed in Figs. 4 and 5.

As can be seen in Figs. 4 and 5, the genes selected by PreCLAS (Fig. 5) are **more representative of the classes, even though the method is unsupervised**.

Two classification methods trained and tested with matrix B worked well: a purely statistical method LDA (linear discriminant analysis), and machine learning SVM (support vector machine) method.

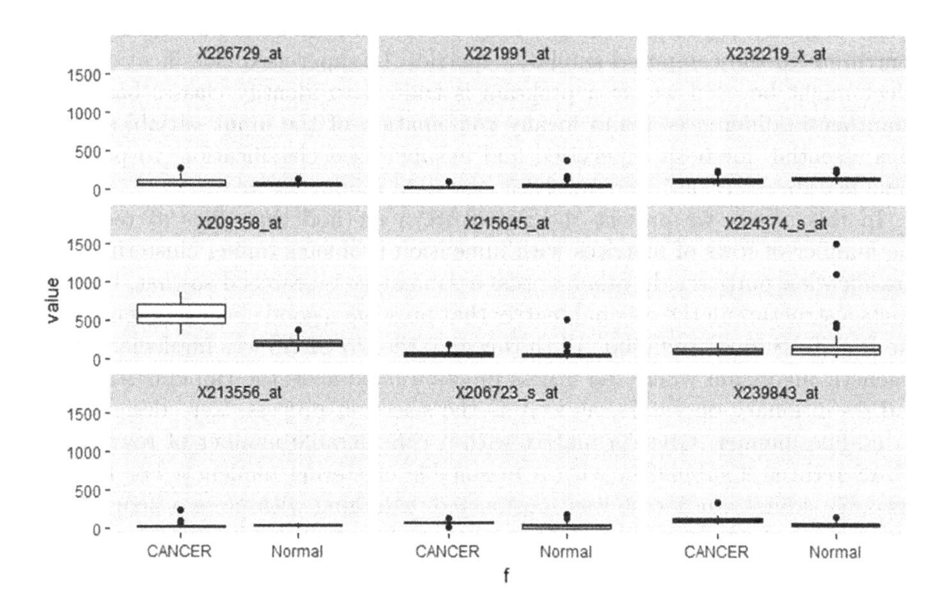

Fig. 4. Differential expression of 9 randomly selected genes from matrix A (50 rows with the highest variance).

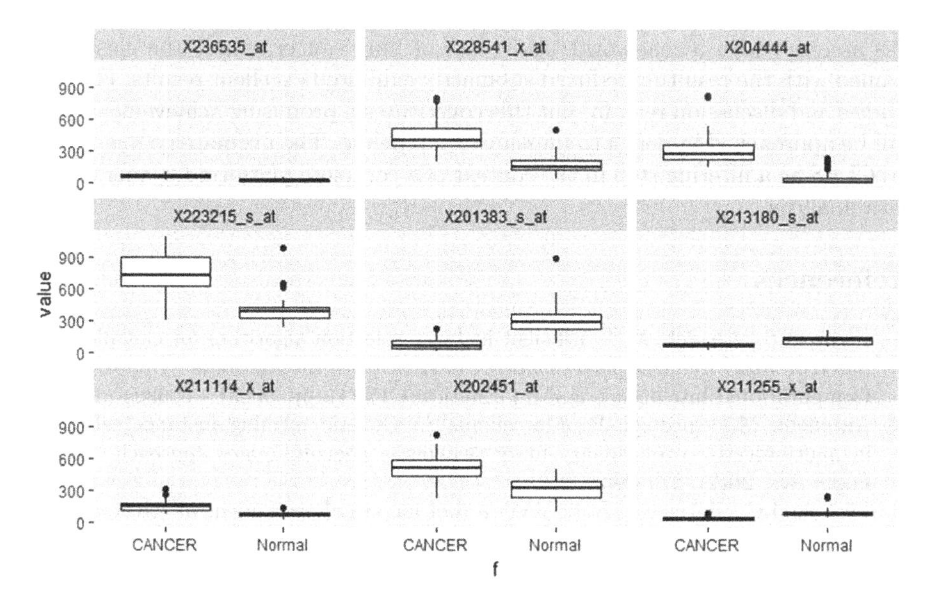

Fig. 5. Differential expression of 9 randomly selected genes from matrix B (PreCLAS).

5 Conclusions

In unsupervised classification, more precisely clustering, interactions between objects are intensely affected by matrices with dimensionality problems, since a vast majority of the features are likely to be uninformative, but will however contribute to the computed similarity metrics. In supervised classification, the effect might be even worse: a program is trained to identify classes based on unauthentic differences found in any combination of the input variables. It is thus essential, for both supervised and unsupervised classification, to perform some feature selection before applying any data mining strategy.

In this paper, we present the PreCLAS, a method that aims at reducing the number of rows of matrices with dimension problems tailing clustering and classification purposes. In other words, a submatrix is searched so that, if there exists a structure in the original matrix that presents a good clustering tendency, the PreCLAS tends to find it. With this aim, the PreCLAS was implemented as a genetic algorithm where the fitness function maximizes the Hopkins statistic, and evolutionary operators, as well as the selection process, were designed in an ad-hoc manner. Given a matrix with a considerable number of rows, PreCLAS returns a submatrix with a reasonable clustering tendency. For testing purposes, a first study case was constructed, enlarging with noise a benchmark clustering dataset. It could be observed that clustering results were better for matrices reduced by the PreCLAS, compared with clustering results of matrices reduced by a random algorithm. To the best of our knowledge, there is no other unsupervised method that reduces a matrix to find a submatrix presenting coherent groups. Finally, it was revealed that the reduction performed by PreCLAS is also useful as a filter method for classification strategies. This feature was assessed with a real-world study case of lung cancer, where the classifiers trained with the resulting reduced submatrix exhibited excellent results. Further studies and discussion remain, but this constitutes a promising achievement that will be approached in-depth to implement a pipeline. The ultimate goal is to use PreCLAS as a filtering step in the context of a complete platform for microarray data analysis.

References

1. Alvar, A.S., Abadeh, M.S.: Efficient instance selection algorithm for classification based on fuzzy frequent patterns. In: 2016 IEEE 17th International Symposium on Computational Intelligence and Informatics (CINTI), pp. 000319–000324 (2016)
2. Antonelli, M., Ducange, P., Marcelloni, F.: Genetic training instance selection in multiobjective evolutionary fuzzy systems: a coevolutionary approach. Trans. Fuzzy Sys. **20**(2), 276–290 (2012)
3. Bezdek, J.C., Hathaway, R.J.: VAT: a tool for visual assessment of (cluster) tendency. In: Proceedings of the 2002 International Joint Conference on Neural Networks, IJCNN 2002 (Cat. No. 02CH37290), vol. 3, pp. 2225–2230 (2002)
4. Chen, Z.-Y., Tsai, C.-F., Eberle, W., Lin, W.-C., Ke, S.-W.: Instance selection by genetic-based biological algorithm. Soft. Comput. **19**(5), 1269–1282 (2014). https://doi.org/10.1007/s00500-014-1339-0

5. Darwin, C.: On the Origin of Species by Means of Natural Selection. Murray, London (1859)
6. Delany, S.J., Segata, N., Mac Namee, B.: Profiling instances in noise reduction. Knowl.-Based Syst. **31**, 28–40 (2012)
7. Derrac, J., García, S., Herrera, F.: A survey on evolutionary instance selection and generation. Int. J. Appl. Metaheuristic Comput. **1**(1), 60–92 (2010)
8. Edgar, R., Domrachev, M., Lash, A.E.: Gene expression omnibus: NCBI gene expression and hybridization array data repository. Nucleic Acids Res. **30**(1), 207–210 (2002)
9. Goldberg, D.E.: Genetic Algorithms in Search, Optimization and Machine Learning, 1st edn. Addison-Wesley Longman Publishing Co. Inc., Reading (1989)
10. Grochowski, M., Jankowski, N.: Comparison of instance selection algorithms II. Results and comments. In: Rutkowski, L., Siekmann, J.H., Tadeusiewicz, R., Zadeh, L.A. (eds.) ICAISC 2004. LNCS (LNAI), vol. 3070, pp. 580–585. Springer, Heidelberg (2004). https://doi.org/10.1007/978-3-540-24844-6_87
11. Guillen, A., Herrera, L.J., Rubio, G., Pomares, H., Lendasse, A., Rojas, I.: New method for instance or prototype selection using mutual information in time series prediction. Neurocomputing **73**(10–12), 2030–2038 (2010)
12. Holland, J.H.: Adaptation in Natural and Artificial Systems. University of Michigan Press, Ann Arbor (1975). 2nd edn, 1992
13. Ishibuchi, H., Nakashima, T., Nii, M.: Learning of neural networks with GA-based instance selection. In: Proceedings Joint 9th IFSA World Congress and 20th NAFIPS International Conference (Cat. No. 01TH8569), vol. 4, pp. 2102–2107, August 2001
14. Jamjoom, M., El Hindi, K.: Partial instance reduction for noise elimination. Pattern Recogn. Lett. **74**(C), 30–37 (2016)
15. Kassambara, A.: Practical Guide To Principal Component Methods in R: PCA, M (CA), FAMD, MFA, HCPC, Factoextra, vol. 2. STHDA (2017)
16. Kuri-Morales, A., Rodríguez, F.: A search space reduction methodology for large databases: a case study. In: Perner, P. (ed.) ICDM 2007. LNCS (LNAI), vol. 4597, pp. 199–213. Springer, Heidelberg (2007). https://doi.org/10.1007/978-3-540-73435-2_16
17. Lawson, R.G., Jurs, P.C.: New index for clustering tendency and its application to chemical problems. J. Chem. Inf. Comput. Sci. **30**(1), 36–41 (1990)
18. Mirisaee, S.H., Douzal, A., Termier, A.: Selecting representative instances from datasets. In: 2015 IEEE International Conference on Data Science and Advanced Analytics (DSAA), pp. 1–10 (2015)
19. Olvera-López, J.A., Carrasco-Ochoa, J.A., Martínez-Trinidad, J.F., Kittler, J.: A review of instance selection methods. Artif. Intell. Rev. **34**(2), 133–143 (2010). https://doi.org/10.1007/s10462-010-9165-y10.1007/s10462-010-9165-y
20. Olvera-López, J.A., Carrasco-Ochoa, J.A., Martínez-Trinidad, J.F.: Object selection based on clustering and border objects. In: Kurzynski, M., Puchala, E., Wozniak, M., Zolnierek, A. (eds.) Computer Recognition Systems. AINSC, vol. 45, pp. 27–34. Springer, Heidelberg (2007). https://doi.org/10.1007/978-3-540-75175-5_4
21. Ruspini, E.H.: Numerical methods for fuzzy clustering. Inf. Sci. **2**(3), 319–350 (1970)
22. Samuels, E.: Fantasies of Identification: Disability, Gender, Race. NYU Press, New York (2014)

23. Sato, T., et al.: PRC2 overexpression and PRC2-target gene repression relating to poorer prognosis in small cell lung cancer. Sci. Rep. **3** (2013). Article number: 1911
24. Triguero, I., García, S., Herrera, F.: Differential evolution for optimizing the positioning of prototypes in nearest neighbor classification. Pattern Recogn. **44**(4), 901–916 (2011)
25. Tsai, C.F., Eberle, W., Chu, C.Y.: Genetic algorithms in feature and instance selection. Know.-Based Syst. **39**, 240–247 (2013)

RADSSo: An Automated Tool for the multi-CASH Machine Learning Problem

Noemí DeCastro-García[1(✉)], Ángel Luis Muñoz Castañeda[1], and Mario Fernández-Rodríguez[2]

[1] Department of Mathematics, Universidad de León, León, Spain
{ncasg,amunc}@unileon.es
[2] Research Institute of Applied Sciences in Cybersecurity (RIASC), Universidad de León, León, Spain
mfer@unileon.es

Abstract. The increasing application of machine learning techniques to different disciplines has driven the research in the field towards the creation of algorithms able to construct the best model with the optimal hyperparameter configuration for a particular problem, without the need of user's expert knowledge. This is well-known as the Combined Algorithms Selection and Hyperparameter Optimization problem.

In this work, we develop the open-source tool RADSSo in order to solve a multi-scenario of combined algorithms selection and hyperparameter optimization in which only one datastore is available containing many different machine learning problems. Then, several models need to be computed, at the same time, in an automated way. The tool is deployed in a modular form that allows to modify it and to customize the configuration files to adapt the tool to any context.

The underlying model is a mathematical formula that scores each machine learning model providing the best one for each subsample of the datastore. This score is based on the suitability of the model, different metrics from the confusion matrix and the capability of the generalization by the learning curves. In addition, RADSSo provides intuitively reports with all the essential information.

Keywords: Machine learning · Model selection · Hyperparameter optimization

1 Introduction

Machine learning is a current emerging field of research due to its applications in many other disciplines. Once the data have been processed, the goal in machine learning problems is to construct the most accurate classification or

Partially supported by the Spanish National Cybersecurity Institute (INCIBE) under contracts art.83, keys: X43 and X54.

E. A. de la Cal et al. (Eds.): HAIS 2020, LNAI 12344, pp. 183–194, 2020.
https://doi.org/10.1007/978-3-030-61705-9_16

prediction model. Once the machine learning models have been constructed with the optimal hyperparameter setting, several indicators are computed to select the model that performs the best. The Combination Algorithms Selection and Hyperparameter Optimization (CASH) problem arises to choose, automatically and simultaneously, the best learning algorithm for a problem as well as its set of hyperparameters.

On the one hand, a decision support software is an intelligent information system that assists the users to do a certain task without expert knowledge, and without needing to know the details of the algorithm that performs the computations and takes the decision. In the machine learning framework, the purpose of an Intelligent Decision Support Software (IDSSo) is to be able to extract information contained in the data, take the decision about which is the best machine learning model for the proposed problem, and present all the information to the potential user in an understandable form. Also, it needs to be robust and technologically efficient. We can find open-source data mining platforms that automatically construct highly parametrized machine learning models with their associated metrics at the push of a button (see [1,15,19]). Waikato Environment for Knowledge Analysis (WEKA), [8] is one of the most used platforms by non-expert users because its interface is very intuitive, and its use does not require a depth knowledge about machine learning algorithms. However, the last step regarding the choice of the best predictor, usually relies on the users' expert knowledge in machine learning and is, therefore, a not fully automated process. The machine learning CASH problem was first solved with the Auto-WEKA system developed in [20], where the choice of the machine learning algorithm is considered by itself as a hyperparameter optimization problem. In this case, tree-based Bayesian optimization methods are used [4]. Concretely, Sequential Model-based Algorithm Configuration (SMAC) [9] is the Hyperparameter Optimization (HPO) selected. This software is improved by Auto-WEKA 2.0, [11] including support for regression algorithms, and achieving a higher/better performance employing parallelization. It is integrated with WEKA by an interface that only requires the dataset, to reserve a suitable memory space and a budget of time. On the other hand, the *Auto-sklearn* is presented in [7]. This auto ML approach is implemented in Python with scikit-learn [18]. It includes a meta-learning step in the AutoML pipeline for initializing the Bayesian optimizer, and an automated ensemble construction step from configurations evaluated during optimization that is performed by SMAC. Also, the AutoML framework *hyperopt-sklearn* [10] is integrated as well as a budget (usually in time) that the user needs to fix before the algorithm runs.

Although we find several automated options to solve the CASH problem, at present, machine learning techniques are needed in institutions in which all the available data are collected at the same time, but they have to serve automatically to solve different problems; that is to say, multi-CASH problem. Also, it should be noted that, usually, not all information sources contribute to the same amount or the same type of information (concerning the different types of problems they report). This could imply overlapping, high redundancy of data, and different distribution functions in the subsets of data. In turn, the stored data could be unbalanced, heterogeneous, not all the features could be useful and they could be not complete for all machine learning problems that we might be solved with the same datastore. Finally, we have to take into account that an automated solution for this scenario needs to be flexible enough to withstand changes, and it has to be adaptable in terms of both, the security and the action policy of the organization that needs it.

In this article, a novel machine learning solution, RIASC Automated Decision Support Software (RADSSo)[1] is presented. This tool can manage any numerical feature, coming from any source, flexible enough to adapt itself to possible changes along time, as well as being able to solve, with the minimal human intervention, a multi-CASH machine learning problem scenario. It follows the underlying idea of the decision-theoretic approaches for the automated decision of the best machine learning model, faced on the usual Bayesian optimization included in other platforms. RADSSo integrates aspects such as the accuracy, the available information from the confusion matrix, and the capability of the generalization by the learning curves. Also, it includes the methods RIASC Hyperparameter Optimization Automated Software (RHOASo) and Random Search for the selection of hyperparameter settings.

RADSSo is an open-source software developed in Python and it is available in a Github repository. The open source nature of RADSSo, as well as its modular structure, is a strong point of the algorithm. These characteristics provide a framework easy to modify and increase in terms of machine learning algorithms or preprocessing methods. This flexibility is essential to customize the software for high-security ecosystems or scenarios that need automated keeping up to date, and they are capable of standing the test of time. Another strength of RADSSo is its potential usefulness by means of the creation of informal reports for the users. Although the algorithm takes automatically the decision about what is the best machine learning model, it offers all the information of the analyses: frequency distributions, accuracies, hyperparameter setting, confusion matrices, metrics, learning curves and the ranking of each machine learning algorithm thas has been carried out.

This article is organized as follows: In Sect. 2, we include the problem statement. In Sect. 3, we develop RADSSo in detail. Finally, the conclusions and future work are given.

2 Problem Statement

Let $\mathcal{X} = (\mathcal{X}_1, \ldots, \mathcal{X}_d)$ be a set of features, $\mathcal{Y}$ the target or label variable (for our proposes just a finite valued variable) and $\mathcal{P}$ the joint probability distribution function of $\mathcal{X} \times \mathcal{Y}$. Let $(\mathbf{x}_1, y_1), \ldots, (\mathbf{x}_n, y_n) \in \mathcal{X} \times \mathcal{Y}$ be independent and identically distributed samples. We denote by D^{train} the set formed by them. Given a space of functions $\mathcal{H} \subset \text{Maps}(\mathbb{R}^d, \mathcal{Y})$ (the machine learning model), a machine learning algorithm $\mathcal{A}$ is a functional

[1] Research Institute of Applied Sciences in Cybersecurity (RIASC).

$$
\begin{aligned}
A : \cup_{n\in\mathbb{N}}(\mathcal{X}\times\mathcal{Y})^n &\longrightarrow \mathcal{H} \\
D^{train} &\mapsto h_{A,D^{train}} : \mathbb{R}^d \longrightarrow \mathcal{Y} \\
&\qquad\qquad \mathbf{x}_i \mapsto h_{A,D^{train}}(\mathbf{x}_i) = y_i
\end{aligned} \tag{1}
$$

The function $h_{A,D^{train}}(\mathbf{x}_i)$ attaches, to each possible value of the set of features $\mathcal{X}$, its label. Usually, given D^{train}, $h_{A,D^{train}}$ is constructed by minimizing certain expected loss function, $\mathcal{L}(D^{train}, h_{A,D^{train}})$.

The target space of functions of the algorithm, $\mathcal{H}$, depends on certain parameters, $\lambda = (\lambda_1, \ldots, \lambda_q) \in \Lambda$, that might take discrete or continuous values, and have to be fixed before applying the algorithm. We will use the notation A_λ to refer to the algorithm with the hyperparameter configuration λ.

In this scenario, another independent data set $D^{test} \in \cup_{n\in\mathbb{N}}(\mathcal{X}\times\mathcal{Y})^n$ serves to evaluate the loss function, $\mathcal{L}(D^{test}, h_{A_\lambda,D^{train}})$ with the function $h_{A_\lambda,D^{train}}$ given by the algorithm run over D^{train}. This loss function measures the discrepancy between the hypothesis $h_{A_\lambda,D^{train}} \in \mathcal{H}$ and an ideal predictor.

Assuming the machine learning problem is a classification problem, we can take the loss function $\mathcal{L}$ as the error rate, that is, one minus the cross-validation value. Now, if we let just $\lambda = (\lambda_1, \ldots, \lambda_q)$. to be free in $\mathcal{L}(D^{test}, h_{A_\lambda,D^{train}})$ (we fix the rest of the data involved in this expression), we can define the following function

$$
\begin{aligned}
\Phi_{A,D} : \Lambda &\longrightarrow [0,1] \\
\lambda &\mapsto \mathcal{L}(D^{test}, h_{A_\lambda,D^{train}})
\end{aligned}
$$

The HPO problem is the optimization problem defined by $\min_\lambda \mathcal{L}(D^{test}, h_{A_\lambda,D^{train}})$. We usually have available many machine learning algorithms in order to give a solution for a particular problem, the HPO process has a great impact in the performance of the machine learning methods, and there is no machine learning model (and algorithm) that performs the best over all datasets. The CASH problem arises due to these facts.

Definition 1. *Let $\mathcal{A} = \{A^1, \ldots, A^R\}$ be a set of machine learning algorithms, and let $\Lambda^{(j)}$ be the hyperparameters space corresponding to A^j. The CASH problem is the optimization problem defined by*

$$
min_{A^j\in\mathcal{A},\lambda\in\Lambda^{(j)}}\mathcal{L}(D^{test}, h_{A^j_\lambda,D^{train}}) \tag{2}
$$

Let $\mathcal{X}$ be a space of d random variables (features) and $\mathcal{Y}$ the space of labels. Let $\mathcal{P}_1, \ldots, \mathcal{P}_k$ be different probability distribution functions on $\mathcal{X}\times\mathcal{Y}$. For each $l = 1, \ldots, k$, let D_l be a set of i.i.d. samples obtained according to $\mathcal{P}_l$, and consider $D = \cup D_l$.

Definition 2. *The multi-CASH problem:*

Let $\mathcal{A} = \{A^1, \ldots, A^R\}$ be a set of machine learning algorithms and let $\Lambda^{(j)}$ be the hyperparameters space corresponding to A^j. Then, the multi-CASH problem *consists of finding the algorithm and its hyperparameter setting that minimizes the loss metric* $\mathcal{L}(D_l^{test}, h_{A^j}, D_l^{train})$

$$min_{A^j \in \mathcal{A}, \lambda_l \in \Lambda^{(j)}} \mathcal{L}(D_l^{test}, h_{A^j_{\lambda_l}}, D_l^{train}) \tag{3}$$

for each problem in D *defined by* D_l.

3 RADSSo: RIASC Automated Decision Support Software

3.1 Underlying Idea

Different approaches to the hyperparameter optimization provide different results, related to the dataset and the machine learning problem. Consequently, the same conclusion can be made for the CASH-problem. RADSSo approaches this problem from an IDSSo perspective, solving the CASH optimization from the decision-theoretic point of view. Regarding the HPO underlying problem, it uses two possible algorithms, Random Search [3,17], and a novel automatic early-stop hyperparameter optimization method, RHOASo [16].

Source code for RADSSo is hosted on GitHub (https://github.com/amunc/RADSSo), with a user manual and a summary report template. It is available under GNU General Public License v3. The only required software to execute RADSSo is Python 2.7. RADSSo can be used in two different ways:

1. As a machine learning platform with customized configurations.
2. As a multi-CASH solver with high usability with configurations that can be manually tuned or left by default. It should be noted that it can work as an algorithm for the single CASH-problem.

Finally, RADSSo provides summary reports for the user with all the relevant information and it makes the requested predictions. Also, this software has been used in different works related to cybersecurity [6].

3.2 The Algorithm

The general workflow is shown in Fig. 1.

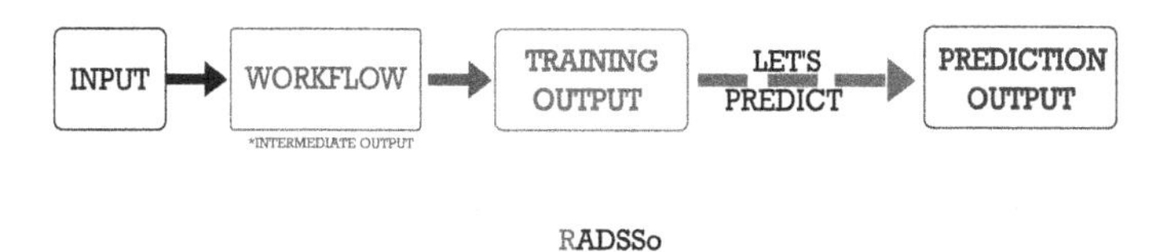

Fig. 1. General workflow of RADSSo

The Input Data. The input files are formed by files with different extensions and purposes:

1. The input dataset: It can be constituted by a single file or by a group of files with *.csv* extension that must contain a common header with the name of the features.
2. Discarded_common_features.json: It is used to create a 'simple dictionary' that allows to remove features that are known to be useless for the model creation process, because they are not relevant for modelling the current target for all the available events.
3. Events_to_process.json: This file allows to select those samples to process, including relevant and discarded features for each one. By default, RADSSo creates machine learning models for each subsample that finds.
4. HTML files: These files define the templates for dumping the processing results on .pdf files that are obtained in different steps of the execution process. There are four files which purpose can be consulted in the RADSSo user manual.
5. Conf.ini: It is the file where the configuration parameters for the training and prediction phases are specified. It can be modified or left by default. It has several sections. The main is the input data section where the most important parameters can be customized.

Workflow. The workflow and the intermediate performance of RADSSo are described in Fig. 2. This phase is made automatically and it should be noted that it is carried out for each target and for each type of subsamples.

First, RADSSo performs a frequency analysis about how is the assignment of categories in the available datastore. Then, the tool classifies the instances in subsets depending on if there were cases in the datastore that were labeled or not. This result provides a division among those samples that are going to need supervised machine learning techniques, those that will need unsupervised machine learning, and those that will not need any analyses. If we suppose that we have a datastore D that could be divided into D_l subsamples, these can be categorized in three groups as follows:

1. G_1 = {those D_l that need unsupervised machine learning because there are not available labels for any instance}.
2. G_2 = {those D_l that do not need any analytic due to the target is fully known and truthful assigned}.
3. G_3 = {those D_l that need supervised machine learning because there are available labels for some instances}.

Once the group and the analytics have been selected, the first action is filtering each D_l. We have included the option to remove some features by expert criteria of the input data. In addition, the first redundancy that is carried out is removing the empty, constant or equivalent features. Finally, we select the most relevant features for each model.

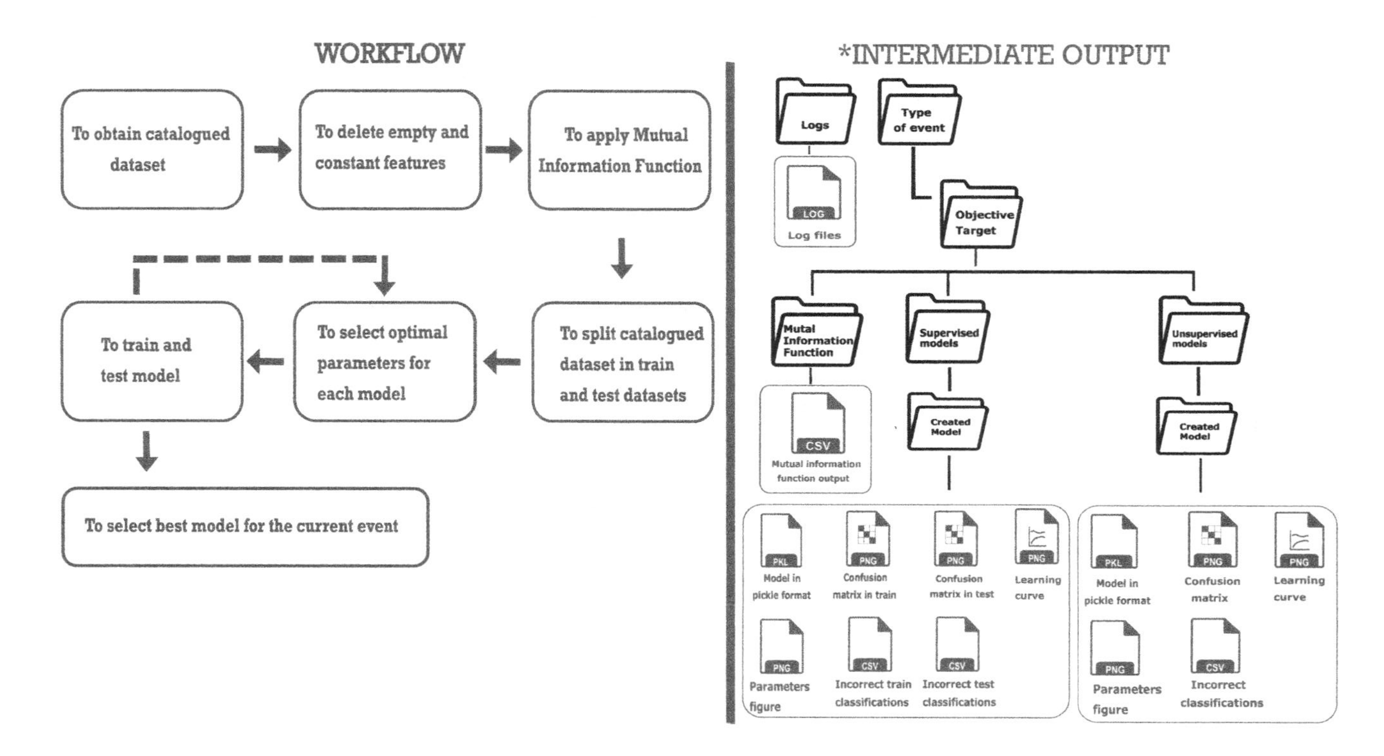

Fig. 2. General workflow

To achieve this, the Mutual Information Function (MIF) is applied between every feature an the target [12,13]. A high value of MIF implies a high dependency, and thus, more relevancy to predict one of the features depending on another. The choice of this fit index is due to the fact that it is the most used method in artificial intelligence and learning analytics environments as it is able to work with categorical features (such as the recodified response variables of the study). Once the MIF coefficient has been computed, we have introduced a threshold (percentile 80 by default) to train the model with the most relevant features.

At this point, the data of each D_l have split as follows

$$D_l = D_l^{train-test} \cup D_l^{valid} = [D_l^{train} \cup D_l^{test}] \cup D_l^{valid} \tag{4}$$

The weight of $D_l^{train-test}$ is 90% (80% and 20%, respectively) and the validation set D_l^{valid} is 10%. Also, the partitions have been computed in a random way since that, in a real situation, usually it is not possible to balance the data under the most favorable conditions. We have filtered those cases with unknown label. The above process is carried out for each subsample D_l.

We have integrated the usual supervised machine learning algorithms such as Random Forest (RF), Gradient Boosting (GB), Decision Tree (DT), Ada Boosting (AB), K-means (KM) Multi-Layer Perceptron (MLP), and KM from the skicit-learn library [18]. On the other hand, an early-stop automatic method of hyperparameter optimization,RHOASo (2-dimensional), and Random Search (1-dimensional) have been applied. Also,RADSSo finds the hyperparameter configuration with a 20% of each dataset if the size is greater than 5000 examples, and with the full dataset in another case [5].

Finally, the algorithm computes several metrics that are described as follows:

1. The *accuracy* (*Acc*).
2. The Mathews Correlation Coefficient (MCC) for unbalanced o very different sizes datasets [14]. It returns a value between -1 (total disagreement between prediction and observation) and +1 (perfect prediction). It should be noted that 0 indicates that the model is not better than random predictor.
3. The results obtained in the confusion matrices have been taken into account by the relative frequencies of each component $f_{i,j}$. These frequencies could be weighted by $w_{i,j}$ to attach importance to one type of error or another.
4. The generalization capability of each model has been analyzed by means of the learning curve. In order to measure the capability of generalization, or the possible overfitting, we have performed some affine transformations over the learning curves. The underlying idea of these transformations is based on Fig. 3 where I is the initial variance between the training accuracy curve and the validation accuracy curve, F is the final variance between the training accuracy curve and the validation accuracy curve, and α is the angle that we obtain when we construct two lines between the initial and the final points.

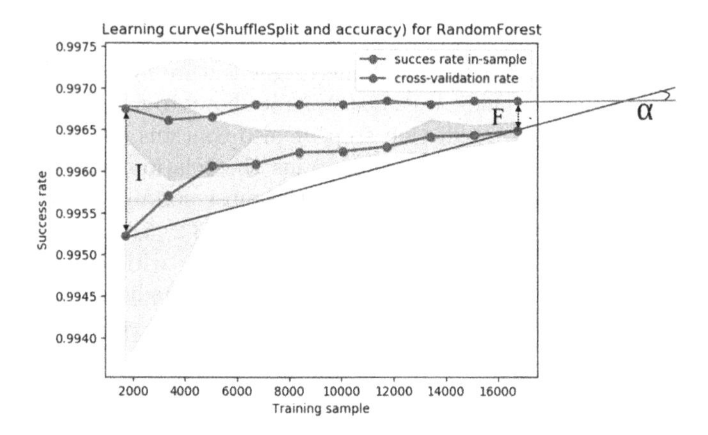

Fig. 3. Example of learning curve.

5. Furthermore, the indicators that are extracted from the confusion matrices are more useful for multi-class problems, and they provide us more type of information about the model. For this reason, RADSSo computes the macro and micro average of the indicators such as the sensibility, the specificity, the F_1 -score or the precision.

The model evaluation procedure that produces the ranking is a model selection strategy based on the weighted information criterion [2]. It quantifies the model performance, and it measures how well a model will generate a classification or a prediction with out-of-sample data (overfitting). For the automatic model selection we have proposed a scoring system that provides a ranking of the models. This system takes into account different metrics rewarding those positive indicators and penalizing those negative. For each ML model, a score $\mathrm{S}_{ML} \in \mathbb{R}$ is obtained and it is computed as follows

$$\mathrm{S}_{ML} = 10 \cdot (Acc/Mcc) + \sum_{i,j} f_{i,j} \cdot w_{i,j} - F - (1 - \frac{2\alpha}{\pi}) \cdot I$$

where Acc/Mcc denotes that the accuracy or the MCC is considered depending on the balance of the dataset.

Finally, in the case of tie of several machine learning models, we use the elapsed time to obtain them in order to take the lead.

All the above computations generate different intermediate outputs that are stored and that are used in order to create a report that summarizes the information.

Training Output. The training output is placed under the folders specified in the *output section* of the Conf.ini, see Sect. 3.2. The training output of RADSSo is constituted by the following directories and files:

1. Under *Prediction_models directory*: This directory contains the files with the best model for each event for a specific target feature in the form of pickle file, *event_name_target_name_best_model.pkl*; it allows to use this pickle file to make predictions in the prediction step. It also contains another pickle file, *prediction_models_dict.pickle*, that maintains the relationship between each event, target and the model selected as the most suitable for each one. If validation is enabled in the Conf.ini file, see Sect. 3.2, a subdirectory called *validation_data* is created and it will contain a csv with the headers and the samples destinated to the validation step in the prediction phase; if it is disabled, the user must specify a suitable validation dataset for the prediction phase.
2. The .pdf files generated using *General_execution_template.html* and *Dictionary_models_template.html* can be found under the folder *Results*. The purposes of the templates were described in Sect. 3.2.
3. Under the path *Results/Type of Event/Objective Target* can be found all the output files related to one event and a specific target. It has some subdirectories, the relevant ones are:
   - *Supervised*: This folder contains one subdirectory for each model with all the elements (confusion matrices, learning curves, parameters figures, etc.) that allow to measure the performance of the model and that are dumped in the pdf reports under *Reports* folder. All those elements constitute the intermediate output generated during the process.
   - *Unsupervised*: This folder contains one subdirectory for each unsupervised model with the same elements generated for the supervised models (except for the elements that correspond to the test phase, not present in this kind of models).
   - *Reports*: The pdfs generated using the information dumped in Report_template.html, can be found in this folder. It is generated one pdf file for each one of the available models where the execution information, rankings and metrics can be checked at the end of the training phase.

The most important files are the pickle files and the reports in pdf format. The first ones are mandatory for the prediction phase, containing the information of the most suitable models for each one of the events for a specific target; the second ones offer a simple way for a human to understand all the elements under the elaboration process of the ranking and the final selection of the best model.

The Prediction. Once the optimal suitable models have been generated for each one of the events for a specific target, those models can be used to predict the target value for new samples. The prediction output is composed by the following files:

1. Log file for the prediction phase: It contains information, in total numbers, about the different events which target value can be predicted using the trained models.

2. Data_with_predictions.csv: It constitutes the output dataset of the prediction phase. It contains the samples with the original target values and the predicted values for the target after the prediction phase has finished.

Remark 1. All the features selection phase as well as the training models step uses the same dataset, so it is possible to parallelize in an usual way. These are the parts with the most high costs of the resources in the execution. The RHOASo algorithm or the Random Search Grid algorithm will compute the optimal parameters depending on the model. The first one, the RHOASO algorithm, is an hybrid approach to the hyperparameter optimization finding the optimal hyper-parameter values with the less possible number of tested configurations. The Random Search algorithm is easily parallelizable

4 Conclusions and Future Work

In this work, an open-source tool, RADSSo, has been developed. It has been created in order to allow non-expert users to get efficient classifiers to solve the multi-CASH problem. RADSSo uses supervised and unsupervised machine learning algorithms, in combination with hyperparameter optimization techniques, in order to create a ranking of models to select the optimal one for solving each machine learning problem that arises in a multi-CASH situation. This is not restricted to a specific area of knowledge and it requires the minimum human intervention.

Future work will be focused on carrying out a comparative study about the performance of RADSSo and the behavior of other algorithms for the single CASH-problem. Also, we will include improvements in the software such as optimization procedures, integration of more machine learning algorithms and hyperparameter configuration methods, update of the version of Python, and data pre-processing techniques.

References

1. KNIME AG: KNIME software. https://www.knime.com
2. Aladag, C.H., Egrioglu, E., Gunay, S., Basaran, M.A.: Improving weighted information criterion by using optimization. J. Comput. Appl. Math. **233**(10), 2683–2687 (2010). https://doi.org/10.1016/j.cam.2009.11.016
3. Bergstra, J., Bengio, Y.: Random search for hyper-parameter optimization. J. Mach. Learn. Res. **13**(1), 281–305 (2012)
4. Brochu, E., Cora, V.M., de Freitas, N.: A tutorial on Bayesian optimization of expensive cost functions, with application to active user modeling and hierarchical reinforcement learning. The Computing Research Repository (CoRR) (2010). http://arxiv.org/abs/1012.2599
5. DeCastro-García, N., Muñoz Castañeda, Á.L., Escudero García, D., Carriegos, M.V.: Effect of the sampling of a dataset in the hyperparameter optimization phase over the efficiency of a machine learning algorithm. Complexity **2019** (2019). https://doi.org/10.1155/2019/6278908

6. DeCastro-García, N., Muñoz Castañeda, Á.L., Fernández-Rodríguez, M.: Machine learning for automatic assignment of the severity of cybersecurity events. Comput. Math. Meth. **2**(1), e1072 (2020). https://doi.org/10.1002/cmm4.1072
7. Feurer, M., Klein, A., Eggensperger, K., Springenberg, J.T., Blum, M., Hutter, F.: Efficient and robust automated machine learning. In: Proceedings of the 28th International Conference on Neural Information Processing Systems, NIPS 2015, vol. 2, pp. 2755–2763. MIT Press, Cambridge (2015)
8. Hall, M., Frank, E., Holmes, G., Pfahringer, B., Reutemann, P., Witten, I.H.: The WEKA data mining software: an update. ACM SIGKDD Explor. Newslett. **11**(1), 10–18 (2009). https://doi.org/10.1145/1656274.1656278
9. Hutter, F., Hoos, H.H., Leyton-Brown, K.: Sequential model-based optimization for general algorithm configuration. In: Coello, C.A.C. (ed.) LION 2011. LNCS, vol. 6683, pp. 507–523. Springer, Heidelberg (2011). https://doi.org/10.1007/978-3-642-25566-3_40
10. Komer, B., Bergstra, J., Eliasmith, C.: Hyperopt-sklearn: automatic hyperparameter configuration for scikit-learn. In: Proceedings of the 13th Python in Science Conference, SCIPY 2014, pp. 32–37 (2014). https://doi.org/10.25080/Majora-14bd3278-006
11. Kotthoff, L., Thornton, C., Hoos, H.H., Hutter, F., Leyton-Brown, K.: Auto-WEKA 2.0: automatic model selection and hyperparameter optimization in WEKA. J. Mach. Learn. Res. **18**(25), 1–5 (2017)
12. Kozachenko, L.F., Leonenko, N.N.: Sample estimate of the entropy of a random vector. Probl. Inf. Trans. **23**(2), 95–101 (1987)
13. Kraskov, A., Stögbauer, H., Grassberger, P.: Estimating mutual information. Phys. Rev. E **69**, 066138 (2004). https://doi.org/10.1103/PhysRevE.69.066138
14. Matthews, B.: Comparison of the predicted and observed secondary structure of T4 phage lysozyme. Biochimica et Biophysica Acta (BBA) Protein Struct. **405**(2), 442–451 (1975). https://doi.org/10.1016/0005-2795(75)90109-9
15. Mierswa, I., Wurst, M., Klinkenberg, R., Scholz, M., Euler, T.: Yale: rapid prototyping for complex data mining tasks. In: Proceedings of the 12th ACM SIGKDD International Conference on Knowledge Discovery and Data Mining, KDD 2006, pp. 935–940. ACM, New York (2006). https://doi.org/10.1145/1150402.1150531
16. Muñoz Castañeda, Á.L., Escudero García, D., DeCastro-García, N., Carriegos, M.V.: RIASC hyperparameter optimization automated software. https://github.com/amunc/RHOASo
17. Nuñez, L., Regis, R.G., Varela, K.: Accelerated random search for constrained global optimization assisted by radial basis function surrogates. J. Comput. Appl. Math. **340**, 276–295 (2018). https://doi.org/10.1016/j.cam.2018.02.017
18. Pedregosa, F., et al.: Scikit-learn: machine learning in python. J. Mach. Learn. Res. **12**, 2825–2830 (2011)
19. RapidMiner, I.: Rapidminer. https://rapidminer.com
20. Thornton, C., Hutter, F., Hoos, H.H., Leyton-Brown, K.: Auto-WEKA: combined selection and hyperparameter optimization of classification algorithms. In: Proceedings of the 19th ACM SIGKDD International Conference on Knowledge Discovery and Data Mining, KDD 2013, pp. 847–855. ACM, New York (2013). https://doi.org/10.1145/2487575.2487629

A Metaheuristic Algorithm to Face the Graph Coloring Problem

A. Guzmán-Ponce[1](✉), J. R. Marcial-Romero[1], R. M. Valdovinos[1], R. Alejo[2], and E. E. Granda-Gutiérrez[3]

[1] Facultad de Ingeniería, Universidad Autónoma del Estado de México, Toluca, Mexico
aguzmanp643@alumno.uaemex.mx, {jrmarcialr,rvaldovinosr}@uaemex.mx
[2] Tecnológico Nacional de México/IT Toluca, Mexico City, Mexico
ralejoe@toluca.tecnm.com
[3] Centro Universitario UAEM Atlacomulco, Universidad Autónoma del Estado de México, Mexico City, Mexico
eegrandag@uaemex.mx

Abstract. Let $G = (V, E)$ be a graph with a vertex set V and set of edges E. The Graph Coloring Problem consists of splitting the set V into k independent sets (color classes); if two vertices are adjacent (i.e. vertices which share an edge), then they cannot have the same color. In order to address this problem, a plethora of techniques have been proposed in literature. Those techniques are especially based on heuristic algorithms, because the execution time noticeably increases if exact solutions are applied to graphs with more than 100 vertices. In this research, a metaheuristic approach that combines a deterministic algorithm and a heuristic algorithm is proposed, in order to approximate the chromatic number of a graph. This method was experimentally validated by using a collection of graphs from the literature in which the chromatic number is well-known. Obtained results show the feasibility of the metaheuristic proposal in terms of the chromatic number obtained. Moreover, when the proposed methodology is compared against robust techniques, this procedure increases the quality of the residual graph and improves the Tabu search that solves conflicts involved in a path as coloring phase.

Keywords: Heuristic algorithm · Tabu search · Graph coloring · Maximal Independent Set

1 Introduction

The graph coloring problem (GCP) consists on assign colors to elements named vertex of a graph, such that no two adjacent vertices had the same color, so the smallest number of colors needed to color a graph is called the chromatic number. This is a NP-complete problem [7,11].

GCP allows describing and addressing combinatorial problems; thus, many real-problems can be solved using graphs, for instance: assignment of radio frequencies [15], chemical combinations [8], assignment of schedules [4], memory

E. A. de la Cal et al. (Eds.): HAIS 2020, LNAI 12344, pp. 195–208, 2020.
https://doi.org/10.1007/978-3-030-61705-9_17

allocation [16], among others. The approach versatility of GCP makes it very significant in several areas and, consequently, there are several approximate solutions.

Most of the researches about GCP have been divided into two solve directions: a) the use of exact algorithms and b) heuristic algorithms. In the first case, it is always an optimal solution to an optimization problem. The exact algorithms that have been developed to solve the graph coloring problem have been characterized by their exponential complexity, either in time or space, with respect to the number of vertices or edges. For instance, Christofides [5] proposed an algorithm with complexity $n!N^{O(1)}$. In contrast, Bodlaender and Kratsch [2] determined the chromatic number of a graph with complexity $O(5.283^n)$ in time and memory used.

Given the exponential complexity of the exact algorithms, heuristic strategies have been developed. These strategies do not guarantee an exact answer, but approximate the solution and provide high performance. Moreover, metaheuristic methods are used because exact algorithms can solve graph problems up to 100 vertices, while bigger graphs require heuristic techniques [13].

Several effective metaheuristic methods have been proposed for GCP. They are based on Ant Colony Optimization, Genetic algorithms, Tabu search, Simulated annealing, among other metaheuristic algorithms. The Greedy Algorithm [1] is noticeable because it can approximate the chromatic number by assigning to a vertex the lowest-numbered color that has not been used on any previously colored vertices adjacent to it. This algorithm is used by JGraphT [14], which is an open-access Java library useful to graph theory methods.

Guzmán et al. [9] proposed an approximate graph coloring algorithm based on getting the Maximal Independent Set (MIS) by the principle of *"reduce-and-solve"*. A MIS is built from non-articulated vertices with the highest degree and which are not adjacent to each other; this process is done until the graph became a bipartite graph since they can be colored with two colors.

Another proposal with heuristic algorithms intended to large graphs (more than 1000 vertices) was done by Qinghua Wu et al. [17]. The algorithm named $E2COL$ pre-processes the original graph to obtain sets of independent sets with the same size until it has a residual graph (extraction phase), which is coloring by a Tabu search. If the coloring is not valid, an expansion phase is applied which returns an independent set from the extraction phase and reapply Tabu search.

Marappan and Sethumadhavan [12] proposed three methods based on genetic algorithms and Tabu searching. Their proposals are focused on modifying a Single Parent Conflict Gene Crossover (SPCGX) with the Advanced Local Guided Search (ALGS), which decrease the search area through choosing a gene before the crossover operation, and a Tabu search as mutation process. In the first method, SPCGX and Conflict Gene Mutation are used with ALGS. The Conflict Gene Removal process is added in the second method to increase the percentage of successful runs of the genetic algorithm. Finally, multipoint SPCGX and

Multipoint Conflict Gene Mutation are used in the third method with ALGS and the Conflict Gene Removal.

Metaheuristic proposals are good alternatives to approximate the graph coloring problem over graphs with up to 400 vertices and up to 12,000 edges. Thus, a metaheuristic method named $TAMISG$ is proposed in this work. The latter is based on two strategies: the heuristic algorithm proposed by Wu et al. [17] and a deterministic algorithm (an algorithm that gets always the same solution, by following a defined series of steps) proposed by Guzmán et al. [9], which improves the construction of MIS. To improve the approximate chromatic number of a graph, the advantages of both methods are considered in $TAMISG$; additionally, a modified tabu search strategy that improves or equals results reported in the literature was also included.

2 Theoretical Framework

2.1 Graph Theory

Let $G = (V, E)$ be an undirected simple graph (i.e., loop-less and without parallel edges) with a set of vertices $V(G)$ and a set of edges $E(G)$, where an edge is a non-ordered pair of vertex $\{v, w\}$. Two vertices v and w are *adjacent* if there is an edge $\{v, w\} \in E$.

Given a graph $G = (V, E)$, the *degree* of a vertex $v \in V$, denoted by $\delta(v)$, is $|N(v)|$ (i.e. the number of edges in which v is incident). The *neighbourhood* of a vertex v in a graph $G = (V, E)$ is $N(v) = \{\forall u \in V \mid \{v, u\} \in E\}$, i.e $N(v)$ is the set of all vertices adjacent to v excluding itself.

For a subset of vertices $S \subseteq V(G)$, the subgraph of G denoted by $G|S$ has vertex set S and a set of edges $E(G|S) = \{\{u, v\} \in E : u, v \in S\}$. $G|S$ is called the *subgraph of* G *induced by* S. $G - S$ denotes the graph $G|(V - S)$. The subgraph induced by $N(v)$ is denoted as $H(v) = G|N(v)$ which has to $N(v)$ as the set of vertices and all edges upon them.

Given a subgraph $H \subseteq G$, for each vertex $x \in V(H)$, let $\delta_H(x)$ be the degree of x in the induced subgraph H of G, if $H = G$ then $\delta_G(x) = \delta(x)$ and $E_H(x) = \{\{x, u\} \in E(G) : u \in H\}$. Similarly, $N_H(x)$ denotes the set of vertices from H adjacent to x. For any subgraph $H \subseteq G$, $\delta_G(H) = \sum_{x \in H} \delta_G(x)$. If H is an independent set of G then $\delta_G(H)$ is the number of edges of G incident to any vertex of H.

A path from a vertex v to a vertex w in a graph is a sequence of edges: $v_0v_1, v_1v_2, \ldots, v_{n-1}v_n$ such that $v = v_0$, $v_n = w$,v_k is adjacent to v_{k+1} and the length of the path is n. A simple path is a path such that $v_0, v_1, \ldots, v_{n-1}, v_n$ are all distinct. A cycle is just a nonempty path such that the first and last vertices are identical.

$S \subseteq V$ is an independent set in G if for whatever two vertices v_1, v_2 in S, $\{v_1, v_2\} \notin E$. Let $I(G)$ be the set of all independent sets of G. An independent set $S \in I(G)$ is *maximal*, abbreviated as MIS, if it is not a subset of any larger independent set and, it is *maximum* if it has the largest size among all independent sets in $I(G)$. The *independence number* $\alpha(G)$ is the cardinality of the maximum independent set of G.

Let $G = (V, E)$ be a graph, G is a *bipartite graph* if V can be partitioned into two subsets U_1 and U_2, such that every edge of G joins a vertex of U_1 and a vertex of U_2.

On the other hand, a graph is *bipartite* if its set of vertices can be divided into two subsets X and Y, such that, each edge has an end point in X and another point final in Y [3], denotes a bipartite G with partition (X, Y) as $G[X, Y]$. If $G[X, Y]$ is simple and each vertex of X is joined by a vertex in Y, then G is a *bipartite graph.*

Another useful graph used is a *tree* [3], which is a graph without cycles, i.e. a graph G such that, for any pair of vertices in G there is a single path that unites them. An *expansion tree* T contains all the vertices of the original graph without edges that form cycles [3].

A *co-tree* is the graph complement of the expansion tree denoted as $\bar{T}$, in other words, it is a subgraph of G which has the vertices and edges that form cycles in G and that are not in the expansion tree.

A cutting vertex in a connected graph G, is a vertex v in which G/v results in a disconnected graph; in contrast, a *non-articulation vertex* is the vertex v that G/v results as a connected graph [3].

The GCP is formally defined as a graph $G = (V, E)$ if there is a mapping $\alpha : V \rightarrow K$, where K is a finite set of colors $\{1, 2, 3, ..., k\}$, a coloring of G is a pair (G, α) such that, $\alpha(V') = k$, with $k \in K$, if $v, w \in V$, $\alpha(v) \neq \alpha(w)$, if $v, w \in E$ and $V' \subseteq V$. A coloring is feasible, if the vertices in each edge in E have different color assigned. A vertex coloring of a graph G with k colours and $k \geq 1$ is called $k - colouring$.

2.2 Tabu Search

Tabu search is a local searching algorithm that restricts elements that can improve a solution [6]. The main idea of using Tabu search is giving a feasible solution s and their neighborhood $N(s)$. The algorithm chooses the best neighbor s^* generated so far; thus, s^* is moved whether $f(s^*)$ is better than $f(s)$ or not, where f is a fitness function which assesses a possible solution. Additionally, a tabu list is used to decide whether a move can be allowed or not; this list contains moves that are not allowed at the present iteration, where a move remains into the tabu list only during a certain number of iterations until a move can be used.

Tabucol is a Tabu search for graph coloring proposed by Hertz et al. [10]. This algorithm generates a random coloring with k-color classes (Algorithm 1); this will not be legal coloring in most cases. In *Tabucol*, the aim of the fitness function is trying to minimize the number of conflicts in a possible solution, and it is defined as follows:

$$f(s) = \sum_{i=1}^{k} |\forall\{u, v\} \in E : u \in C_i, v \in C_i| \tag{1}$$

If $f(s) = 0$ is known as a legal coloring.

Once an initial coloring has been generated, Tabucol (Algorithm 1) works until a legal solution is found or when certain number of iterations are completed. For each iteration, a next move is taken to remain in the tabu list a certain number of times. The next move will depend on taking the list members with the highest improvement on $f(s)$, except those moves in the tabu list. After a move is chosen, it is applied and it prohibits, i.e. the move that was just applied should not be applied for a number of iterations.

2.3 E2COL

E2COL [17] is a heuristic algorithm for graph coloring based on an extraction-and-expansion approach. The algorithm extracts independent sets to reduce the initial graph before expanding the approximate coloring solution by progressively adding back the extracted independent sets. Essentially, the *E2COL* algorithm [17] consists of three phases, which can be summarized as follows:

- Extraction Phase: Obtains sets of independent sets until the graph has only q-vertices. This phase uses a Tabu Search algorithm to generate the independent sets.
- Initial coloring: An initial coloring from the residual graph (i.e. the graph with q-vertices) is obtained by applying a Tabu search strategy. If the coloring is legal, i.e. the possible solution has no collisions, an independent set obtained in the extraction phase is added to the final solution and stops the procedure; otherwise, the next phase is done.

Algorithm 1. *Tabu search*

Require: A non directed graph $G = (V, E)$; a solution s_0
Ensure: The best colouring s^*
1: Initialize random configuration s_0
2: **while** $conflicts \neq 0$ and not reached iteration or time limit **do**
3: $s_0' \leftarrow$ Find non-tabu neighbor with largest improvement for the fitness fuction.
4: Make the move
5: $s_0 \leftarrow s_0'$
6: $tl = \lceil Random(0, 9) + \alpha * f(s_0) \rceil$
7: Add the move into Tabu list on tl-iterations
8: Update the Tabu list by reduce tl
9: **if** $f(s_0) < f(s^*)$ **then**
10: $s^* \leftarrow s_0$
11: **end if**
12: **end while**
13: Return s^*

- Expansion Phase: The sets of independent sets obtained from the first phase are returned, i.e. the independent set that was making a disturbance to the solution, by taking t-classes to empty them, through moving vertices around the rest of classes.

2.4 Maximal Independent Set (MIS)

Guzmán et al. [9] proposed a deterministic algorithm consisting of building a MIS from non-articulated vertices upon the condition that the vertex which will be added into the set has the highest degree and it is not adjacent with another vertex of such a set. In a general way, this proposal can be divided into two phases described as follows:

- Debugging phase: It removes trees or paths from the graph before the iterative construction of a MIS, because trees or paths can be colored by two colors.
- Iterative construction of MIS: Once the graph has no trees or paths, the iterative construction of MIS (Algorithm 2) is done by selecting non-articulated vertex x, this will be the first vertex which is added into the MIS. Subsequently, the non-neighbors of x are obtained. This set contains the candidates to be part of the MIS. The non-neighbors of x are sorted in ascending order according to each vertex degree. Afterwards, each non-neighbor vertex ve is verified that no cut the graph; thus, ve can be adding into the MIS, while neighbors of ve are removed from the candidates. The algorithm builds and saves a set of MIS until the remaining graph became a bipartite graph because it can be colored by two colors.

Algorithm 2. *GetMIS*

Require: A non directed graph $G = (V, E)$
Ensure: A set of disjoint MIS to equal cardinality
1: $K = [\,]$
2: Choose a non-articulation vertex $ve \in G$
3: Add ve into K
4: $noNeighbors \leftarrow$Sort non-neighbors of ve
5: **while** $noNeighbors$ **do**
6: $ve' \leftarrow$ Get a vertex from $noNeighbors$
7: **if** ve' is non-articulation vertex **then**
8: Add ve' into K
9: Delete neighbours of ve' in $noNeighbors$.
10: **end if**
11: **end while**
12: **return** K

3 Proposed Method

Due to the exponential complexity of the exact algorithms, heuristic strategies have been chosen to approximate solutions on graphs with more than 100 vertex [13]. In this paper, a metaheuristic method named as $TAMISG$ is proposed.

The latter combines two methods: a) *E2COL* [17] and b) MIS [9]. This proposal takes advantage of the *E2COL* methodology with several changes, allowing *TAMISG* to improve the approximate chromatic number by modifying the Tabu search strategy described in Sect. 2.2; then, MIS is applied.

In *TAMISG*, the *E2COL* [17] phases are preserved; nonetheless, a variant over the algorithm was made. Modifications to *E2COL* included in *TAMISG* proposal are summarized as follows:

1. In the extraction phase, the process to obtain independent sets was changed and a deterministic algorithm [9], which is described in Sect. 2.4, was used.
2. The Tabu search method was modified to solve conflicts involved in a path and it is described in Sect. 3.2.
3. In the extended phase, if a legal coloring is not found, an empty class is added until a solution with zero conflicts is reached.

3.1 Maximal Independent Set Process

In the extraction phase, given an initial size of a MIS, it is necessary to find as many sets of MIS as possible, so that in the end only the MIS with big size remains. The proposal exhibited here takes advantage of the Algorithm 2 described in Sect. 2.4, because it can build a MIS and ensure a residual connected graph. Thus, *TAMISG* proposal takes the idea of building a MIS with non-articulation vertices and remove these vertices from the graph G, until the graph has q-vertices, which is computed as below:

$$q = |V| - ((|V| * 60)/100) \tag{2}$$

where, $|V|$ is the number of vertices. The proposal considers the 60% of vertices that must be colored in the Extraction phase from the original graph, while 40% of vertices remain as part of the residual graph.

3.2 Tabu Search Proposal

Tabucol is the first Tabu search to graph coloring, as it can be seen in Sect. 2.2. However, the present proposal takes it up and seeks to resolve conflicts involved in a path.

Algorithm 1 receives an initial solution s_0, considered as the best solution (s^*) in the begining. The time limit is given by L-iterations, where, $L = |E| * 0.25$; that is, the 25% density of the graph is considered to iterate the Tabu search. To compute tl, $\alpha = 0.6$ is used and $f(s)$ is given by the Eq. 1.

After selecting a move, it is included a process that handles collisions in the path involved in the movement to be performed. In each iteration, the Tabu search moves a conflict vertex. In order to save these conflict vertices, the initial solution is evaluated to obtain the vertices that cause conflict. The process to obtain a candidate vertex to move has been performed as follows:

1. A list of conflict vertices is generated. For each conflict vertex, a subset is created with vertices that have not been visited and that has an edge between themselves.
2. A recursive process is carried out to obtain a path of conflict vertices. The latter tries to solve the conflict in this path with the vertices in the middle of the conflict vertices.

Once the candidate vertex is obtained, the move must be performed into the class with fewer conflicts. In case of a vertex has all classes in the Tabu list, i.e. the vertex can not be moved to any other class solution, the neighbors are analyzed; thus, a decision will be made whether the tabu search process continues or not. If a vertex collapses with all classes that until the actual solution s_0 has, then s_0 requires a new class.

The decision process tries to find the neighboring vertices of the vertex that collapse in a complete sub-graph. If the number of vertices that participate in the complete sub-graph is greater than the number of classes in the solution, the tabu process stops and returns the best found solution, decreasing the runtime.

3.3 *TAMISG* Algorithm

TAMISG proposal is shown in the Algorithm 3, where the first step consist on build a MIS with the deterministic Algorithm 2 until the residual graph has q-vertices. The next step, an Initial Coloring is performed by a Tabu Search algorithm (lines 7–12), which is explained in the Algorithm 1. This process returns a solution with zero collisions. The Tabu search solution must be added into the MIS extracted from the first phase and return it as a valid solution; otherwise, the Extraction Phase is done.

Because most solutions are based on a k value of color, in this proposal, the GCP is given by approximating the coloring based on a k value, which has been taken from the literature and represents the best approximation obtained until now. However, if in n iterations the coloring is not determined, then the graph is not k colorable, and the nearest integer to k for which it can be determined as colorable is looked.

Algorithm 3. *TAMISG* proposal for graph coloring

Require: A non directed graph $G_0 = (V_0, E_0)$; an integer k
Ensure: A legal $k - coloring$ of G_0 or a fail
{Extraction Phase}
1: $i = 0$
2: **while** $|V_i| > q$ **do**
3: $G_{i+1}=$ ***GetMIS***(G_i, I_i) ***This is a modification**
4: $i = i + 1$
5: **end while**
{ Initial coloring Phase}
6: $s_i =$ ***Tabu_Search***$(G_i, k - i)$ ****This is a modification, Section 3.2 ****
7: **if** $s_i =$ is an $(k - i)$ coloring, this is $f(s_i) = 0$ **then**
8: Use s_i to build a k coloring $s_0 = \{s_i, I_{i-1}, \cdots, I_0\}$ of G_0
9: Return s_0 and stop the process
10: **end if**
{Extent Phase }
11: **while** $i > 0$ **do**
12: $i = i - 1$
13: $s_i = \{s_{i+1}, I_i\}$
14: $s_i =$ ***Tabu_Search***(s_i, G_i)
15: **if** s_i is a $(k - i)$ coloring, i.e $f(s_i) = 0$ **then**
16: Use s_i to build a legal k-coloring $s_0 = \{s_i, I_{i-1}, \cdots, I_0\}$ of G_0
17: Return s_0 and stop the process
18: **end if**
19: **end while**
{This is a modification }
20: ***while*** $f(s_i) \neq 0$ ***do***
21: $s_i = s_i \bigcup \{\}$ * ***Add an empty class to the solution ****
22: $s_i =$***Tabu_Search***(s_i, G_i)
23: ***end while***

4 Experimental Set-Up

In order to evaluate the *TAMISG* performance, an experimental set was designed, It consist of comparing the results obtained with JGraphT [14], and the proposal by Guzmán et al. [9]. These methods were elected to verify the performance of the proposal depicted in this paper because their simplicity and availability as open-access resources. The results are compared in terms of approximation of the chromatic number. A MacBook Pro with Intel Core i5 microprocessor at 2.6 GHz. 8 GB DDR3 RAM 1600 MHz under OS X Version 10.11.6 was used to perform the experiments.

24 graphs (Table 1) were used in this research, which were taken from the DIMACS repository[1]. All of them are part of three groups that are described as follows:

- REG: Represents problems based on the assignment of records for variables in real codes, by Gary Lewandowski[2].
- SGB: These are graphs from the Donald Knuth's data set at Stanford, these are divided into:
  - *Book Graphs*: Based on literary works, a graph is created by representing each vertex as a character. Two vertices share an edge if the corresponding character meets another. Knuth created graphs from 5 literary works: Tolstoy's Anna Karenina (anna), Dicken's David Copperfield

[1] http://mat.gsia.cmu.edu/COLOR04/.
[2] gary@cs.wisc.edu.

(david), Homer's Iliad (homer), Twain's Huckleberry Finn (huck) and Hugo's Les Misérables (jean).
- *Queen Graphs*: It is a graph with mn vertices in which each vertex represents a square in a board $m \times n$, two vertices are connected by an edge if the corresponding squares are in the same row, column or diagonal.

- CAR: Graphs *k-insertion and full-insertion* are a generalization of graphs *mycel* with vertices inserted to increase the size of the graph but not the density (i.e., how a graph is connected).

Table 1. Description of the benchmarking graphs. Per each instance (first column), the number of vertices and the number of edges are reported in the next columns respectively.

	Instance	Vertices	Edges		Instance	Vertices	Edges
1	1-Insertions_4.col	67	232	13	queen8_8.col	64	1456
2	2-Insertions_3.col	37	72	14	queen9_9.col	81	2112
3	2-Insertions_4.col	149	541	15	queen8_12	96	1368
4	3-Insertions_3.col	56	110	16	queen11_11.col	121	3960
5	anna	138	986	17	queen12_12.col	144	5192
6	david	87	812	18	queen13_13.col	169	6656
7	fpsol2_i_1	269	11654	19	queen14_14.col	196	8372
8	fpsol2_i_2	363	8691	20	queen15_15.col	225	10360
9	fpsol2_i_3	363	8688	21	queen16_16.col	256	12640
10	queen5_5	25	320	22	zeroin_i_1	126	4100
11	queen6_6.col	36	580	23	zeroin_i_2	157	3541
12	queen7_7.col	49	952	24	zeroin_i_3	157	3540

5 Results and Discussion

Results obtained from the experimental study are presented here, explained in two parts: a) First, the impact of removing MIS to better understand the behavior of the proposal, b) Second, to evaluate the effectiveness of the proposed method, results with the well-known chromatic number per each graph are compared. This information has been extracted from[3].

5.1 Remove MIS

The impact of use of a deterministic algorithm as MIS removing procedure to reduce a graph as an improvement to approximate the chromatic number of a graph is discussed through Table 2, where the remaining graph configuration obtained after applying the Extraction phase is reported.

As it can be noted in Table 2, the remaining graph is small; thus, this becomes an ideal graph to be processed with a Tabu search. Taking the 60% of vertices in each graph to be part of a set of MIS and leaving the rest as a member of a connected graph is the advantage of using [9] to approximate efficiently the chromatic number in the next phase, because most number of vertices covered have been labeled through a MIS.

[3] http://mat.gsia.cmu.edu/COLOR04/.

Table 2. Summary of the extraction phase per each instance (first column). The number of vertices and edges obtained is reported in the second and third columns, respectively. The number of extracted MIS is shown in the fourth column. In the last column, the q-vertices obtained are reported.

Instance	Residual Vertices	Residual Edges	Extracted MIS	Remain vertices	Instance	Residual Vertices	Residual Edges	Extracted MIS	Remain vertices
1-Insertions_4.col	32	61	1	27	queen8_8.col	25	200	5	26
2-Insertions_3.col	13	13	1	15	queen9_9.col	21	118	7	32
2-Insertions_4.col	68	135	1	60	queen8_12	24	73	9	38
3-Insertions_3.col	17	17	1	22	queen11_11.col	49	580	7	48
anna	59	484	1	55	queen12_12.col	45	448	9	58
david	51	812	1	35	queen13_13.col	48	466	10	68
fpsol2_i_1	103	3344	7	108	queen14_14.col	78	1244	9	78
fpsol2_i_2	137	2978	2	145	queen15_15.col	82	1246	10	90
fpsol2_i_3	363	8688	2	145	queen16_16.col	91	1490	11	102
queen5_5	10	32	3	10	zeroin_i_1	44	654	17	50
queen6_6.col	12	84	4	14	zeroin_i_2	60	968	3	63
queen7_7.col	14	44	5	20	zeroin_i_3	60	970	3	63

5.2 Graph Coloring

The *TAMISG* performance is evaluated through approximate the well-know chromatic number. Table 3 reports the experimental results of such a evaluation. The proposal of this research was compared with JGraphT (a greedy algorithm) and Guzmán et al. [9] (a deterministic algorithm). Finally, 20 executions were carried out and the results obtained from the *TAMISG* proposal show their standard deviation in parentheses. The computational effort given in seconds is showing in square brackets.

Table 3. Graph coloring performance, the well-know chromatic number is included as a reference value, with the exception on some *queen* graphs in which value has not yet been registered.

Instance	Chromatic Number	JGraphT [14]	Guzmán [9]	TAMISG	Instance	Chromatic Number	JGraphT [14]	Guzmán [9]	TAMISG
1-Insertions_4.col	4	5 [0.1]	5 [0.0]	5 (0.366) [1.8]	queen8_8.col	9	15 [0.2]	12 [0.2]	11 (0.394) [12.2]
2-Insertions_3.col	4	4 [0.1]	4 [0.0]	4 (0.000) [0.0]	queen9_9.col	10	15 [0.3]	13 [0.3]	12 (0.324) [22.9]
2-Insertions_4.col	4	5 [0.3]	5 [0.1]	5 (0.244) [20.7]	queen8_12	12	17 [0.5]	15 [0.4]	14 (0.224) [12.5]
3-Insertions_3.col	4	5 [0.1]	4 [0.0]	4 (0.000) [0.0]	queen11_11.col	11	18 [0.3]	16 [0.9]	15 (0.394) [58.6]
anna	11	11 [0.1]	11 [0.2]	11 (0.366) [1.2]	queen12_12.col	*	20 [0.3]	17 [1.3]	16 (0.598) [138.0]
david	11	11 [0.2]	11 [0.1]	12 (0.489) [2.7]	queen13_13.col	13	22 [0.4]	18 [2.2]	18 (0.513) [160.2]
fpsol2_i_1	65	65 [1.2]	65 [28.3]	67(1.317) [69.4]	queen14_14.col	*	24 [0.6]	21 [3.6]	19 (0.224) [306.3]
fpsol2_i_2	30	30 [0.9]	30 [11.0]	33(0.761) [311.0]	queen15_15.col	*	24 [0.6]	21 [5.3]	19 (0.447) [448.9]
fpsol2_i_3	30	30 [1.2]	30 [11.1]	32 (1.040) [185.9]	queen16_16.col	*	27 [0.7]	22 [7.7]	21 (0.308) [633.3]
queen5_5	5	7 [0.1]	6 [0.0]	5 (0.000) [0.1]	zeroin_i_1	49	49 [1.1]	49 [3.6]	50 (0.510) [3.8]
queen6_6.col	7	10 [0.1]	9 [0.0]	9 (0.324) [2.6]	zeroin_i_2	30	30 [0.7]	30 [2.1]	32 (0.945) [12.2]
queen7_7.col	7	12 [0.1]	11 [0.1]	9 (1.309) [0.6]	zeroin_i_3	30	30 [0.9]	30 [2.1]	31 (0.745) [13.5]

According to these results, the algorithm from Guzmán et al. [9] improves the results obtained from JGraphT in 54% of instances (i.e. 13 graphs), while in the remain graphs, both get similar results. In contrast, when Guzmán et al. [9] is compared against *TAMISG*, the latter obtains a better approximation in 42% of the instances; however, both proposals get similar approximations in the remain results. Note that all proposals are competitive when they are compared against previously well-known results reported in the literature. Moreover, with exception of some instances, the proposal of this research gets the best results.

In $TAMISG$, most of the successful cases are in *queen* graphs, where the standard deviation indicates that there is not significant dispersion on the results. This is due to the use of the deterministic algorithm in the extraction phase; it obtains the same results after each execution, and the number of MIS extracted from each graph is large enough to get a residual graph, which can be easily colored with Tabu search. In addition, the standard deviation obtained from $TAMISG$ indicates that in 62.5% of graphs a uniform coloring is obtained (because standard deviation is less than 0.5).

It can be seen that the algorithm that obtains results more quickly is JGraphT; however, it does not obtain the best approximation to graph coloring compared to the other proposals. Although $TAMISG$ takes more time for instances with $|E| > 1000$, our proposal gets a better approximation.

It can be concluded that the methodology followed by $TAMISG$ not only improves the JGraphT results, but it is competitive with Guzmán et al. [9]. The latter is because in $TAMISG$ the extraction phase get sets of MIS that are enough to color most vertices, thus increasing the quality of the residual graph, where their q vertices can be easily colored by Tabu Search. Also, Tabu Search improves the graph coloring by resolving conflicts involved in a given path.

6 Conclusions and Future Research

This paper presents a metaheuristic algorithm named $TAMISG$ to handle the Graph Coloring Problem. The proposal in this research approximates the chromatic number of a graph by combining a deterministic algorithm and a heuristic algorithm. Taking advantage of the $E2COL$ methodology (with specific modifications) and introducing a deterministic algorithm as the extraction phase (proposed in [9]), this procedure increases the quality of the residual graph and improves the performance of the Tabu search that solves conflicts involved in a path as coloring phase.

It can be concluded upon the experimental study that, in terms of chromatic number, both: the method proposed by Guzmán et al. [9] and the $TAMISG$ proposal presented in this article, are competitive since the approximate graph coloring is similar. Despite getting similar approximations, in some graphs (for example *queen*), the $TAMISG$ proposal gets better performance than the deterministic proposal. The latter is sustained by means of the estimation of the standard deviation obtained from 20 executions, which indicates that the results are not significantly dispersed. Additionally, $TAMISG$ has better performance compared against the *greedy* method used by JGraphT.

The proposed method can be used to obtain better approximations in graphs with a greater number of edges, because the extraction phase ensured a residual graph with a smaller number of edges; thus, it can let get a better approximation. A potential flaw could be in a forest (graphs composed of graphs) where each graph must be processed separately in the extraction phase, since the method ensures a connected graph, leaving an open line of study.

TAMISG proposes to solve conflicts in paths by the Tabu search, which leaves interesting future research on the free parameters, like the time in which a vertex remains in the Tabu list. Another open research line is to assign conflict vertices to a new class, where it is important to consider strategies to move from the optimal local. Furthermore, the use of other heuristic algorithms such as *Hill Climbing, Simulated annealing* could be interesting.

Acknowledgment. This work has been partially supported by the 5046/2020CIC UAEM project and the Mexican Science and Technology Council (CONACYT) under scholarship [702275].

References

1. Arumugam, S., Brandstädt, A., Nishizeki, T., et al.: Handbook of Graph Theory, Combinatorial Optimization, and Algorithms. Chapman and Hall/CRC (2016)
2. Bodlaender, H.L., Kratsch, D.: An exact algorithm for graph coloring with polynomial memory. Technical report, Department of Information and Computing Sciences, Utrecht University (2006)
3. Bondy, J.A., Murty, U.S.R.: Graph Theory with Applications, vol. 290. Macmillan, London (1976)
4. Burke, E.K., Meisels, A., Petrovic, S., Qu, R.: A graph-based hyper heuristic for timetabling problems. Computer Science Technical Report No. NOTTCS-TR-2004-9, University of Nottingham (2004)
5. Christofides, N.: An algorithm for the chromatic number of a graph. Comput. J. **14**(1), 38–39 (1971)
6. Edelkamp, S., Schrödl, S. (eds.): Heuristic Search. Morgan Kaufmann, San Francisco (2012)
7. Garey, M.R., Johnson, D.S.: Computers and Intractability: A Guide to the Theory of NP-Completeness. Freeman, San Francisco (1979)
8. Gross, J.L., Yellen, J.: Graph Theory and its Applications. CRC Press (2005)
9. Guzmán-Ponce, A., Marcial-Romero, J.R., Ita, G.D., Hernández, J.A.: Approximate the chromatic number of a graph using maximal independent sets. In: 2016 International Conference on Electronics, Communications and Computers (CONIELECOMP), pp. 19–24. IEEE (2016)
10. Hertz, A., de Werra, D.: Using tabu search techniques for graph coloring. Computing **39**(4), 345–351 (1987)
11. Johnson, D.S., Trick, M.A.: Cliques, Coloring, and Satisfiability: Second DIMACS Implementation Challenge, 11–13 October 1993, vol. 26. American Mathematical Society (1996)
12. Marappan, R., Sethumadhavan, G.: Solution to graph coloring using genetic and tabu search procedures. Arabian J. Sci. Eng. **43**(2), 525–542 (2018)
13. Mostafaie, T., Khiyabani, F.M., Navimipour, N.J.: A systematic study on metaheuristic approaches for solving the graph coloring problem. Comput. Oper. Res. 104850 (2019)
14. Naveh, B.: Contributors: Jgrapht. From: http://jgrapht.org/. Accessed 5 Dec 2019

15. Smith, D., Hurley, S., Thiel, S.: Improving heuristics for the frequency assignment problem. Eur. J. Oper. Res. **107**(1), 76–86 (1998)
16. de Werra, D., Eisenbeis, C., Lelait, S., Marmol, B.: On a graph-theoretical model for cyclic register allocation. Discrete Appl. Math. **93**(2–3), 191–203 (1999)
17. Wu, Q., Hao, J.K.: An extraction and expansion approach for graph coloring. Asia-Pacific J. Oper. Res. **30**(05), 1350018 (2013)

Tardiness Minimisation for Job Shop Scheduling with Interval Uncertainty

Hernán Díaz[1](✉), Juan José Palacios[1], Irene Díaz[1], Camino R. Vela[1], and Inés González-Rodríguez[2]

[1] Department of Computing, University of Oviedo, Oviedo, Spain
{diazhernan,palaciosjuan,sirene,crvela}@uniovi.es
[2] Department of Maths, Stats and Computing, University of Cantabria, Santander, Spain
gonzalezri@unican.es

Abstract. This paper considers the interval job shop scheduling problem, a variant of the deterministic problem where task durations and due dates are uncertain and modelled as intervals. With the objective of minimising the total tardiness with respect to due dates, we propose a genetic algorithm. Experimental results are reported to assess its behaviour and compare it with the state-of-the-art algorithms, showing its competitiveness. Additional results in terms of solution robustness are given to illustrate the relevance of the interval ranking method used to compare schedules as well as the benefits of taking uncertainty into account during the search process.

Keywords: Job shop scheduling · Total tardiness · Interval uncertainty · Genetic algorithms · Robustness

1 Introduction

Scheduling consists in allocating a set of limited existing resources to perform a set of tasks with specific performance measures. It plays an important role in manufacturing systems because, if properly done, it can reduce material-handling costs and times as well as improving efficiency [16]. The job shop is one of the most relevant scheduling problems, since it has been considered to be a good model for many practical applications as well as a challenge to the research community due to its complexity. This complexity is the reason why metaheuristic search techniques are especially suited for solving the job shop problem [19].

A majority of contributions to the family of job shop scheduling problems concentrate on minimising the execution time span of the project (known as

Supported by the Spanish Government under research grants TIN2016-79190-R and TIN2017-87600-P and by the Principality of Asturias Government under grant IDI/2018/000176.

E. A. de la Cal et al. (Eds.): HAIS 2020, LNAI 12344, pp. 209–220, 2020.
https://doi.org/10.1007/978-3-030-61705-9_18

makespan). However, in recent years there has been a growing interest in due-date related criteria [5,8,14]. On-time fulfilment becomes especially relevant in modern pull-oriented supply chain systems concerned with meeting customer's demand in terms of due dates; a tardy job may result in delay-compensation cost, customer dissatisfaction or loss of reputation among others. It is also relevant in complex supply chain or manufacturing systems integrating planning and scheduling; tardy jobs in one of the scheduling stages may cause serious disruptions and delays in subsequent stages, with the associated costs.

Traditionally, it has been assumed in scheduling that design variables such as task processing times or due dates are deterministic. However, this assumption may seem naïve in real industrial settings because in real-world production scheduling problems such variables are quite often characterised vaguely due to the available information being incomplete or imprecise. Fuzzy sets have been used by many researchers to model uncertain durations in scheduling problems [2]. Regarding due dates, fuzzy sets are mostly used in the literature to model flexibility; there are however some cases where fuzzy due dates model uncertainty [4]. An alternative to fuzzy sets for dealing with uncertainty are intervals. Interval uncertainty is present as soon as information is incomplete. An expert working on a project may be reluctant or unable to provide point values for the duration of each task, while estimating a minimal and a maximal duration may be felt as more realistic. Also, the end of the job may depend on several uncertain events such as changing customer orders or dependencies on other components of a larger manufacturing system. Interval scheduling provides us with the possibility of focussing on significant scheduling decisions and give quite robust solutions, with little sensitivity to uncertainties.

Interval uncertainty is not new in scheduling, although contributions in the literature are still scarce. In [10], a genetic algorithm is proposed for a job shop problem with interval processing times and interval due dates to minimise the total tardiness with respect to job due dates. A population-based neighborhood search for a interval job shop, but with the objective of the makespan is presented in [9]. A multiobjective interval job shop problem with non-resumable jobs and flexible maintenance is solved in [11] by means of a multiobjective artificial bee colony algorithm that minimises both the makespan and the total tardiness. In [12], a dual-resource constrained job shop with heterogeneous resources is considered, and a dynamical neighbourhood search is proposed for lexicographic minimisation of carbon footprint and makespan.

In the following, we consider the job shop scheduling problem with intervals modelling both uncertain durations and uncertain due dates. With the goal of minimising total tardiness, an interval in this case, we propose a genetic algorithm that provides the basis for developing more sophisticated search methods in the future as well as allowing to study the influence of the ranking method used for comparing the interval objective function. A preliminary experimental study also highlights the benefits of considering the uncertainty during the search process in terms of robustness, specially with one of the ranking methods.

2 Problem Definition

The classical *job shop scheduling problem*, or *JSP* in short, consists in a set of jobs $J = \{J_1, \ldots, J_n\}$ to be scheduled on a set of physical resources or machines $M = \{M_1, \ldots, M_m\}$, subject to a set of constraints. There are *precedence constraints*, so each job J_j, $j = 1, \ldots, n$, consists of $m_j \leq m$ tasks $(o(j,1), \ldots, o(j, m_j))$ to be sequentially scheduled. There are also *capacity constraints*, whereby each task $o(j,l)$ requires the uninterrupted and exclusive use of a specific machine $\nu_{o(j,l)} \in M$ for its whole processing time $p_{o(j,l)}$. Additionally, each job J_j has a due date d_j by which it is desirable that the job be completed.

A solution to this problem is a *schedule* $\boldsymbol{s}$, i.e. an allocation of starting times $s_{o(j,l)}$ for each task $o(j,l)$, which is feasible (in the sense that all constraints hold) as well as optimal according to some criterion, in our case, minimum total tardiness with respect to due dates.

A schedule $\boldsymbol{s}$ establishes an order π among tasks requiring the same machine. Conversely, given a task processing order π, the schedule $\boldsymbol{s}(\pi)$ may be computed as follows. Let us assume w.l.o.g. that tasks are indexed from 1 to $N = \sum_{j=1}^{n} m_j$, so we can refer to a task $o(j,l)$ by its index $o = \sum_{i=1}^{j-1} m_i + l$ and simply write p_o to refer to its processing time. The set of all tasks is denoted $O = \{1, \ldots, N\}$. For every task $o \in O$, let $s_o(\pi)$ and $c_o(\pi)$ denote respectively the starting and completion times of o given π, let $PM_o(\pi)$ and $SM_o(\pi)$ denote the predecessor and successor tasks of o in its required machine, and let PJ_o and SJ_o denote respectively the predecessor and successor tasks of o in its job. If o is the first task to be processed in its machine or its job, $PM_o(\pi) = 0$ or $PJ_o = 0$, where 0 represents a dummy task such that $p_0 = 0$ and $s_0 = 0$. Then the starting time $s_o(\pi)$ is given by $s_o(\pi) = \max(s_{PJ_o} + p_{PJ_o}, s_{PM_o(\pi)} + p_{PM_o(\pi)})$ and the completion time is computed as $c_o(\pi) = s_o(\pi) + p_o$. Notice that the completion time of each job J_j for $\boldsymbol{s}(\pi)$ is the completion time of the last task in that job, given by $C_j(\pi) = c_{o(j,m_j)(\pi)}$. The total tardiness of the schedule is given by $T_{tot}(\pi) = \sum_{j=1}^{n} T_j(\pi)$, where $T_j(\pi)$ is the tardiness of job J_j according to π, $T_j(\pi) = \max(0, C_j(\pi) - d_j)$.

2.1 Uncertain Processing Times and Due Dates

In real-life applications, it is often the case that the time it takes to process a task is not exactly known in advance; instead, only some uncertain knowledge about the duration is available. In addition, due dates may not be perfectly defined, being dependent on external factors such as changing customer orders or dynamic manufacturing requirements. If only an upper and a lower bound of each duration and due date are known, uncertainty can be represented as a closed interval of possible values denoted $\mathbf{a} = [\underline{a}, \overline{a}] = \{x \in \mathbb{R} : \underline{a} \leq x \leq \overline{a}\}$.

Let $\mathbb{IR}$ denote the set of closed intervals. The job shop problem with total tadiness mimisation requires three arithmetic operations on $\mathbb{IR}$: addition, subtraction and maximum. These are defined by extending the corresponding operations on real numbers [13], so given two intervals $\mathbf{a} = [\underline{a}, \overline{a}], \mathbf{b} = [\underline{b}, \overline{b}] \in \mathbb{IR}$,

$$\mathbf{a}+\mathbf{b}=[\underline{a}+\underline{b},\overline{a}+\overline{b}], \quad (1)$$

$$\mathbf{a}-\mathbf{b}=[\underline{a}-\overline{b},\overline{a}-\underline{b}], \quad (2)$$

$$\max(\mathbf{a},\mathbf{b})=[\max(\underline{a},\underline{b}),\max(\overline{a},\overline{b})]. \quad (3)$$

Comparisons are a key point when processing times and due dates take the form of intervals as the "best" schedule should be the one with "minimal" total tardiness (an interval). However, it is well known that there is no natural total order in the set of intervals, so an interval ranking method needs to be considered among those proposed in the literature [7]. Among the multiple existing rankings in $\mathbb{IR}$, here we consider the following:

$$\mathbf{a}\leq_{Lex1}\mathbf{b}\Leftrightarrow\underline{a}<\underline{b}\vee(\underline{a}=\underline{b}\wedge\overline{a}<\overline{b}) \quad (4)$$

$$\mathbf{a}\leq_{Lex2}\mathbf{b}\Leftrightarrow\overline{a}<\overline{b}\vee(\overline{a}=\overline{b}\wedge\underline{a}<\underline{b}) \quad (5)$$

$$\mathbf{a}\leq_{YX}\mathbf{b}\Leftrightarrow\underline{a}+\overline{a}<\underline{b}+\overline{b}\vee(\underline{a}+\overline{a}=\underline{b}+\overline{b}\wedge\overline{a}-\underline{a}\leq\overline{b}-\underline{b}) \quad (6)$$

$$\mathbf{a}\leq_{MP}\mathbf{b}\Leftrightarrow m(\mathbf{a})\leq m(\mathbf{b})\text{ with, }m(\mathbf{a})=\frac{(\underline{a}+\overline{a})}{2} \quad (7)$$

(4), (5) and (6) actually define total order relations in $\mathbb{IR}$ [3]. Both (4) and (5) are derived from a lexicographical order of interval extreme points. The ranking proposed in expression (6) is proposed in [18], and the last one (midpoint order) is a particular case of the classical Hurwitz criterion and is equivalent to the one proposed in [9] for interval job shop.

2.2 The JSP with Interval Uncertainty

Given the above, the *Interval Job Shop Scheduling Problem* or *IJSP* for total tardiness minimisation can be formulated as follows:

$$\min_{R}\mathbf{T_{tot}} \quad (8)$$

$$\text{subject to: }\mathbf{T_{tot}}=\sum_{j=1}^{n}\mathbf{T}_j \quad (9)$$

$$\underline{T}_j=\max(0,\underline{c}_{o(j,m_j)}-\overline{d_j}) \quad (10)$$

$$\overline{T}_j=\max(0,\overline{c}_{o(j,m_j)}-\underline{d_j}) \quad (11)$$

$$\underline{c}_o=\underline{s}_o+\underline{p}_o,\ \forall o\in O \quad (12)$$

$$\overline{c}_o=\overline{s}_o+\overline{p}_o,\ \forall o\in O \quad (13)$$

$$\underline{s}_{o(j,l)}\geq\underline{c}_{o(j,l-1)},\ 1\leq l\leq m_j, 1\leq j\leq n \quad (14)$$

$$\overline{s}_{o(j,l)}\geq\overline{c}_{o(j,l-1)},\ 1\leq l\leq m_j, 1\leq j\leq n \quad (15)$$

$$\underline{s}_o\geq\underline{c}_{o'}\ \vee\ \underline{s}_{o'}\geq\underline{c}_o, \forall o\neq o'\in O:\nu_o=\nu_{o'} \quad (16)$$

$$\overline{s}_o\geq\overline{c}_{o'}\ \vee\ \overline{s}_{o'}\geq\overline{c}_o, \forall o\neq o'\in O:\nu_o=\nu_{o'} \quad (17)$$

where the minimum $\min_R \mathbf{T_{tot}}$ in (8) is the smallest interval according to a given ranking R in the set of intervals $\mathbb{IR}$. Constraint (9) defines the total tardiness as the addition of the tardiness of each job J_j. Constraints (10) and (11) define the tardiness of each job J_j as the interval difference between the completion time of the job and its due date. Constraints (12) and (13) establish the relationship between the starting and completion time of each task. Constraints (14) and (15) correspond to precedence relations between tasks within each job, and constraints (16) and (17) establish that the execution of two tasks requiring the same machine cannot overlap.

The resulting problem will be denoted $J|\underline{p}_o \leq p_o \leq \overline{p}_o, \underline{d}_j \leq d_j \leq \overline{d}_j|\mathbf{T}_{tot}$, following the three-field notation schema for scheduling problems. Clearly, this problem is NP-hard, since setting all processing times and due dates to crisp numbers yields the classical JSP, which is itself NP-hard [16].

3 Robustness on Interval Schedules

A solution to the IJSP provides an interval of possible values for the total tardiness computed from the possible values for the starting and completion times of each task and the due date for each job. As it is impossible at the time of scheduling to predict what the exact due dates, starting and completion times will be when the project is actually executed, a solution to a job shop problem with uncertainty should be understood as an a-priori or predictive solution [6]. Once the project is finished, and tasks have been executed according to the ordering π provided by the schedule, we shall know real duration of the tasks, deterministic times $p_o \in [\underline{p}_o, \overline{p}_o]$ for all tasks $o \in O$. Specific due dates are also unknown until an actual instance of the project is tackled. Only at the moment of executing the project are actual due dates $d_j \in [\underline{d}_j, \overline{d}_j]$ available for each job J_j. After execution, when processing times and due dates are exactly known and the a-posteriori solution is available, delays w.r.t. each job $T_j \in [\underline{T}_j, \overline{T}_j]$ can be computed as well as the resulting total tardiness, being desirable that the predictive schedule does not differ much from the executed one.

This coincides with the idea of robust schedule, as one that minimises the effect of executional uncertainties on its performance [1]. The formalization of this concept leads to different robustness measures [17]. In this work, the concept of ϵ-robustness, first proposed for fuzzy scheduling problems in [15], is adapted to the interval framework.

ϵ-robustness intends to measure the predictive error of the a-priori total tardiness, $\mathbf{T_{tot}}$ (an interval), compared to the real total tardiness T^{ex}_{tot} obtained after an execution (corresponding to a specific realization of task processing times $P^{ex} = \{p^{ex}_o \in [\underline{p}_o, \overline{p}_o], o \in O\}$ and job due dates $d^{ex}_j \in [\underline{d}_j, \overline{d}_j]$, $1 \leq j \leq n$). Assuming that tasks are executed without unnecessary delays at their earliest possible starting times, it is clear that $T^{ex}_{tot} \in \mathbf{T_{tot}}$. Thus, the prediction is always accurate in terms of bounds for the possible objective values after execution. On the other hand, in absence of other information it seems straightforward to estimate the total tardiness as the expected or mean value of the uniform distribution on $\mathbf{T_{tot}}$ and then measure the error of the prediction made by the a-priori metric as the (relative) deviation of the executed objective value with respect to this expected value.

In consequence, a predictive schedule with total tardiness interval value $\mathbf{T_{tot}}$ is *ϵ-robust* if the relative error made by $E[\mathbf{T_{tot}}]$ with respect to the total tardiness T_{tot}^{ex} of the executed schedule is bounded by ϵ, that is:

$$R_{ex} = \frac{|T_{tot}^{ex} - E[\mathbf{T_{tot}}]|}{E[\mathbf{T_{tot}}]} \leq \epsilon \text{ with } E[\mathbf{T_{tot}}] = (\overline{T}_{tot} - \underline{T}_{tot})/2 \text{ and } \epsilon \geq 0. \quad (18)$$

Clearly, the smaller the bound ϵ, the more accurate the a-priori prediction is or, in other words, the more robust the interval schedule is.

When the problem is tested on synthetic benchmark instances for job shop, real data regarding executions of the project are not available. In this case K possible scenarios are obtained using Monte-Carlo simulations. Thus, deterministic values for due dates and processing times are sampled on their respective interval using uniform probability distributions. Then, the average ϵ-robustness of the predictive schedule across the K possible configurations, denoted $\overline{\epsilon}$, can be calculated as:

$$\overline{\epsilon} = \frac{1}{K}\sum_{k=1}^{K} R_k = \frac{1}{K}\sum_{k=1}^{K} \frac{|T_{tot}^{k} - E[\mathbf{T_{tot}}]|}{E[\mathbf{T_{tot}}]}. \quad (19)$$

with T_{tot}^{k} denoting the exact total tardiness obtained after executing tasks according to the ordering provided by the predictive schedule $\boldsymbol{s}$ for each scenario $k = 1, \ldots, K$. This value provides an estimate of how robust is the schedule $\boldsymbol{s}$ across different processing times configurations. Again, the lower $\overline{\epsilon}$, the better.

4 A Genetic Algorithm for Tardiness Minimisation

Genetic algorithms, either on their own or combined with other metaheuristics such as tabu search [19], are a powerful tool for solving scheduling problems. In brief, a genetic algorithm starts by generating a pool of initial solutions, representing a population P_0 of individuals of a species. This population is evaluated and a fitness value, typically the value of the objective function, is assigned to each individual. The population is then left to evolve until a stopping criterion is met, usually for a fixed amount of generations or consecutive iterations without improvement. At each iteration i, individuals from population P_i are paired for mating following a selection procedure, and recombination operators of crossover and mutation are applied to each pair with probability p_{cross} and p_{mut} respectively, simulating natural evolution. The new population of individuals Off_i is evaluated and a replacement operator is applied to combine P_i and Off_i into a new population P_{i+1} for the next iteration, rewarding individuals with better fitness and keeping a constant population size. Once the stopping criterion is met, the best individual according to the interval ranking is selected from the last generation and returned.

In a genetic algorithm, each individual codifies a solution as a chromosome, typically an array of values. The design of encoding and decoding algorithms pose the most crucial step in designing the algorithm. To encode solutions, we use classical permutations with repetition of job's numbers. These represent linear orders of the set of tasks, where each task $o(j, l)$ is represented by its job number j. For example, a linear order $(o(3,1), o(1,1), o(3,2), o(2,1), o(2,2), o(1,2))$ is encoded as (3 1 3 2 2 1). The decoding follows an insertion strategy, so we always obtain a so-called active schedule in the sense that no operation can start earlier without disrupting the starting time of at least another operation. This strategy is done by iterating through the chromosome and scheduling each task $o(j, l)$ at its earliest feasible insertion position. Let η_k be the number of tasks already scheduled on machine $k = \nu_{o(j,l)}$, and let $\sigma_k = (0, \sigma(1, k), ..., \sigma(\eta_k, k))$ denote the partial processing order of tasks already scheduled in machine k. A feasible insertion position $q, 0 \leq q < \eta_k$ for $o(j, l)$ is a position that verifies both:

$$\max\{\underline{c}_{\sigma(q,k)}, \underline{c}_{o(j,l-1)}\} + \underline{p}_{o(j,l)} \leq \underline{s}_{\sigma(q+1,k)} \tag{20}$$

$$\max\{\overline{c}_{\sigma(q,k)}, \overline{c}_{o(j,l-1)}\} + \overline{p}_{o(j,l)} \leq \overline{s}_{\sigma(q+1,k)}, \tag{21}$$

being $q = \eta_k$ if there no feasible insertion position.

The earliest feasible insertion position q^* is that with smallest q value. Therefore, operation $o(j, l)$ is scheduled at starting time:

$$\mathbf{s}_{o(j,l)} = \max\{\mathbf{c}_{\sigma(q^*,k)}, \mathbf{c}_{o(j,l-1)}\} \tag{22}$$

5 Experimental Results

We conduct a series of experiments to study three different aspects: the behaviour of the proposed genetic algorithm, the potential advantage of managing uncertainty during the search process, and the influence of the different interval rankings. For these tests, we consider the instances proposed in [10], which are, as far as we know, the only instances available in the literature for interval JSP with uncertain due dates. The set consists on 7 instances, 4 of them of size 10×10 (instances 1–4) and the remaining 3 of size 15×10. All the experiments reported in this section have been run on a PC with Intel Xeon Gold 6132 processor at 2.6 Ghz and 128 Gb RAM with Linux (CentOS v6.9), using a C++ implementation.

First, a preliminary study is carried out to find the best setup for the genetic algorithm. An initial base setup is established and then parameters are tuned sequentially, trying different combinations of operators and probabilities. Specifically, the considered operators and values are the following:

- Crossover operator: Generalised Order Crossover (GOX), **Job-Order Crossover (JOX)** and Precedence Preservative Crossover (PPX)
- Crossover probability: 0.7, 0.8, 0.9 and **1.0**
- Mutation operator: Swap, Inversion and **Insertion**
- Mutation probability: **0.05**, 0.10, 0.15 and 0.30

- Selection operator: **Shuffle**, Roulette, Stochastic Universal Sampling (SUS) and Tournament 1/3 on the population
- Replacement operator: Generational replacement with elitism (k=1, 5%, 10%), Tournament 2/4 parents-offspring allowing repetition and **Tournament 2/4 parents-offspring without repetitions**

The best setup values obtained are highlighted in bold. In all cases the algorithm is run until 25 consecutive iterations pass without improving the best found solution. In addition, three different populations sizes are tested: 100, 250 and 500. Since this parameter has a heavy influence on the runtime of the algorithm, it requires a more careful study. When a population size of 250 is used, the runtime increases 1.8 times w.r.t. using 100, and the average quality of the obtained solutions improves 2.1%. However, a further increase to 500 multiplies the runtime by 2, but the obtained results improve only 0.7%. If runtime is of great importance, a population size of 100 might be the most adequate, but when it is not the case, a population size of 250 offers a significant improvement in quality. Further increasing the population size does not seem to improve results at the same pace, so for this study we choose to use 250 individuals.

To assess the performance of our genetic algorithm (GA in the following), we compare it with the best-known results in the literature. Different methods for the IJSP can be found in the literature minimising total tardiness (see Section 1). Among the published results, the best reported values for total tardiness are those obtained by the genetic algorithm proposed in [10]. We shall refer to this GA as GA-L to distinguish it from ours in the comparisons. The authors use a method equivalent to $\leq_{MP}$ to rank different intervals in their GA-L, so we will also adopt this ranking for the sake of a fair comparison. Table 1 shows, for each algorithm, the best solution obtained across all runs (20 runs for GA-L and 30 for GA), the average expected total tardiness across those runs and the average running time in seconds for each algorithm. A first look at the results shows that, in average values, the GA proposed in this work outperforms GA-L in 5 out of the 7 instances, with greater improvement on the large instances. On average, GA is 5.5% better on instance 5, 12.5% better on instance 6 and 21.4% on instance 7. On the other hand, for smaller instances, there is no clear winner: GA is better on instances 2 and 4 (2.0% and 1.2% respectively), but worse on instances 1 and 3 (1.9% and 3.9% respectively). Furthermore, for instances 1 and 3, the best solution found by GA does not even reach the average results of GA-L. To have a better understanding of this situation, a basic model of these instances is designed to be solved with the IBM CPLEX CP Optimizer solver. Even though CP Optimizer cannot reach the optimal solution for all instances with the current version of the model, it obtains lower bounds that are actually higher than the best solutions obtained by GA-L on instances 2, 3 and 4. This indicates that the published results for those instances are unattainable, and therefore we must be very cautious when comparing with them. Figure 1 depicts the best solution found by GA on instance 4, which is optimal according to CPLEX CP Optimizer. It is a Gantt chart adapted to intervals, so for each task, instead of a bar, there is a trapezoid where the upper side corresponds to the

Table 1. Computational results and times of GA-L and GA

	GA-L				GA			
Instance	Best	E[Best]	Avg.	Time	Best	E[Best]	Avg.	Time
1	[5, 321]	163.0	166.1	6.5	[3, 335]	169.0	169.3	0.4
2	[0, 493]	246.5	264.0	6.6	[0, 497]	248.5	258.6	0.5
3	[7, 459]	233.0	243.4	6.4	[8, 479]	243.5	252.9	0.6
4	[4, 451]	227.5	245.2	6.3	[1, 458]	229.5	242.3	0.5
5	[79, 1678]	878.5	943.9	21.5	[43, 1651]	847.0	891.9	1.4
6	[0, 1048]	524.0	568.8	22.0	[0, 949]	474.5	497.4	1.4
7	[69, 1524]	796.5	999.0	21.1	[68, 1376]	722.0	785.0	1.2

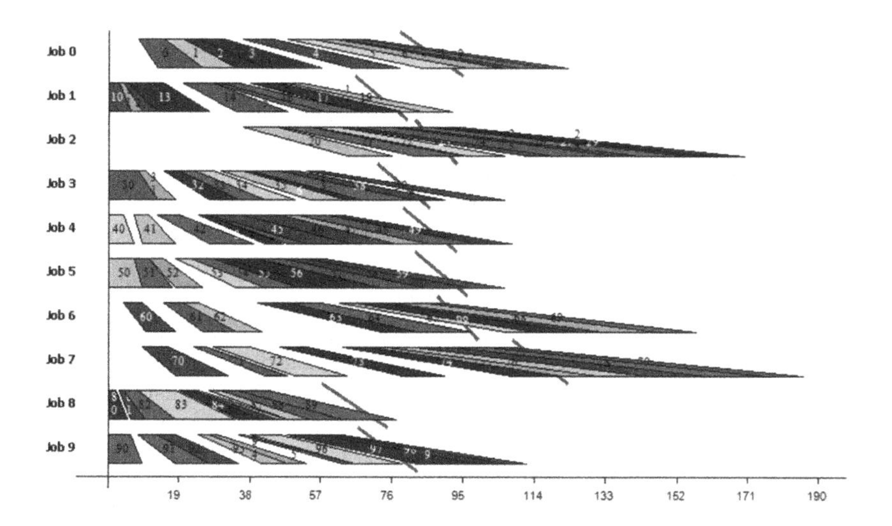

Fig. 1. Gantt diagram of the optimal solution found for Instance 4

earliest possible starting and completion times while the lower side corresponds to the latest possible starting and completion time; each row in the diagram shows the task sequence per job, colours determine the machine where each task needs to be executed, and thick red lines are the due dates. Regarding runtime, GA is 93.5% faster than GA-L. Notice however, that runtimes for GA-L are those provided by the authors using their own machine, therefore comparisons in this sense must be done with caution as well.

Using the intervals during the search process might add some extra difficulty to the problem: known concepts need to be adapted or redefined and solving methods redesigned to handle uncertainty, usually with an increased complexity. One may wonder if solving the crisp problem that results from considering only the midpoint of the interval processing times and due dates would lead to similar results with the added advantage of having all the available tools for deterministic JSP. It is also interesting to study the influence of the choice of

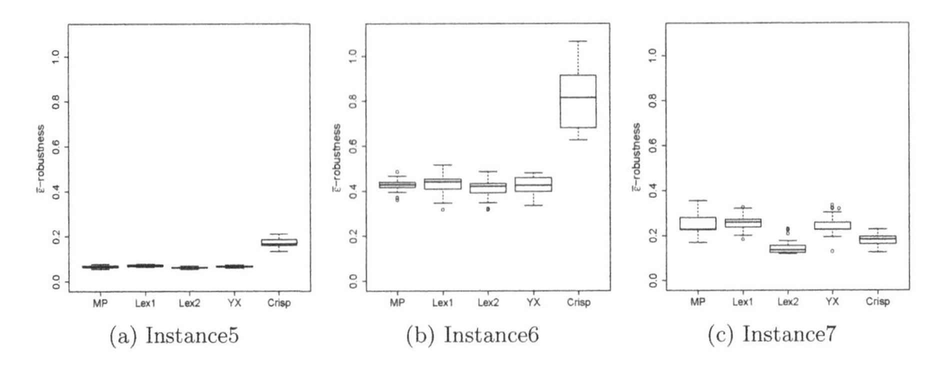

(a) Instance5 (b) Instance6 (c) Instance7

Fig. 2. $\bar{\epsilon}$-robustness of solutions obtained with four different rankings and solving the associated crisp instance

ranking methods in the interval setting. To shed some light on these questions, we carry out a new set of experiments. For each of the 7 instances, we run our algorithm 30 times considering each of the four different ranking methods and 30 times on the instance's crisp counterpart. Notice that the objective function is an interval in the first four cases and a crisp value in the last one, so they are not directly comparable. Instead, we measure the $\bar{\epsilon}$-robustness of the 30 solutions obtained by GA in each case using $K = 1000$ possible realisations, to compare the resulting solutions in terms of their quality as predictive schedules.

Figure 2 depicts for instances 5, 6 and 7, the boxplots with the $\bar{\epsilon}$ values of the 30 schedules obtained by GA in each case. Results for instances 2 and 4 are very similar those obtained for instance 6: in all of them the $\bar{\epsilon}$ values obtained from optimising the crisp instance are significantly worse than those obtained using intervals, independently of the ranking method used. Also, Mann-Whitney-U tests show that there are no significant differences between the results obtained using different ranking methods, except on instance 2, where using $\leq_{Lex1}$ yields significantly worse results than using $\leq_{MP}$ or $\leq_{YX}$. On the other hand, results for instances 1 and 3 are similar to those illustrated for instance 5. Again, the $\bar{\epsilon}$ values obtained from the solutions to the crisp instance are clearly worse than those obtained using intervals during the search process. However, in these instances $\leq_{Lex2}$ obtains solutions that are more robust than those obtained by any other ranking method. This is confirmed by the statistical tests, showing a significant difference between the $\bar{\epsilon}$ values of the schedules obtained using $\leq_{Lex2}$, and those of the schedules obtained with the other ranking methods. Results obtained on instance 7 are very different to the previous ones. This is the only instance where the solutions obtained from solving the crisp problem are not worse that those obtained from solving the interval JSP. In fact, the statistical tests show that they are significantly better than using the ranking methods $\leq_{MP}$, $\leq_{Lex1}$ and $\leq_{YX}$, but significantly worse than using $\leq_{Lex2}$. Further research is required on this particular instance for a better understanding on how the structure of the problem may affect the choice of a ranking method.

A preliminary analysis shows that even though the size is the same as on instances 5 and 6, task durations and due dates are larger in instance 7. For instance, the largest due dates are 172 (interval [140, 172]) and 215 (interval [176, 215]) for instances 5 and 6 respectively, while it is 1080 for instance 7 (interval [1033, 1080]). In addition, the width of the due-date intervals for instance 7 is also larger than for any other instance, directing us towards the idea that when uncertainty in due dates is big, a more conservative ranking method like $\leq_{Lex2}$ is the most adequate, being the others less reliable. Finally, it is worth mentioning that, according to the statistical tests, there is no significant difference between $\leq_{MP}$ and $\leq_{YX}$ on any instance. This seems natural, since $\leq_{YX}$ can be understood as a refinement of $\leq_{MP}$, but it also shows that this refinement does not necessarily translate into more robust schedules.

6 Conclusions

In this work we have tackled the job shop scheduling problem with uncertain durations and uncertain due dates modelled as intervals (IJSP). We have proposed a first approach to solving the IJSP using a genetic algorithm with an insertion decoding strategy. The algorithm has been tested on the 7 instances available in literature, outperforming the best-known results in 5 of them. In the largest instances, the proposed algorithm is always better, offering an improvement of up to 21% w.r.t the best previously-reported results. This is not the case for the smaller instances, where the results are not always better than the reported ones. However, we have checked –using IBM ILOG CP Optimizer- that these published results are infeasible, and therefore, not suitable for meaningful comparisons. A more detailed study has shown that the choice of interval ranking method plays a very important role in the final solution's performance, especially in terms of robustness. In addition, incorporating the interval uncertainty to the search process yields more robust solutions than solving the crisp problem, specifically with one of the ranking methods. Further work is needed to obtain more powerful search methods tailored for handling interval uncertainty and to thoroughly analyse the influence of different ranking methods in order to make a proper choice for the problem at hand.

References

1. Aytung, H., Lawley, M.A., McKay, K., Shantha, M., Uzsoy, R.: Executing production schedules in the face of uncertainties: a review and some future directions. Eur. J. Oper. Res. **161**, 86–110 (2005)
2. Behnamian, J.: Survey on fuzzy shop scheduling. Fuzzy Optim. Decis. Making **15**(3), 331–366 (2015). https://doi.org/10.1007/s10700-015-9225-5
3. Bustince, H., Fernandez, J., Kolesárová, A., Mesiar, R.: Generation of linear orders for intervals by means of aggregation functions. Fuzzy Sets Syst. **220**, 69–77 (2013)
4. Chanas, S., Kasperski, A.: On two single machine scheduling problems with fuzzy processing times and fuzzy due dates. Eur. J. Oper. Res. **147**, 281–296 (2003)

5. González, M., Vela, C.R., Varela, R.: An efficient memetic algorithm for the flexible job shop with setup times. In: Proceedings of the 23th International Conference on Automated Planning and Scheduling (ICAPS-2013), pp. 91–99 (2013)
6. González Rodríguez, I., Puente, J., Vela, C.R., Varela, R.: Semantics of schedules for the fuzzy job shop problem. IEEE Trans. Syst. Man Cybern. Part A **38**(3), 655–666 (2008)
7. Karmakar, S., Bhunia, A.K.: A comparative study of different order relations of intervals. Reliable Comput. **16**, 38–72 (2012)
8. Kuhpfahl, J., Bierwirth, C.: A study on local search neighbourhoods for the job shop scheduling problem with total weighted tardiness objective. Comput. Oper. Res. **261**, 44–57 (2016)
9. Lei, D.: Population-based neighborhood search for job shop scheduling with interval processing time. Comput. Ind. Eng. **61**, 1200–1208 (2011). https://doi.org/10.1016/j.cie.2011.07.010
10. Lei, D.: Interval job shop scheduling problems. Int. J. Adv. Manuf. Technol. **60**, 291–301 (2012). https://doi.org/10.1007/s00170-011-3600-3
11. Lei, D.: Multi-objective artificial bee colony for interval job shop scheduling with flexible maintenance. Int. J. Adv. Manuf. Technol. **66**, 1835–1843 (2013). https://doi.org/10.1007/s00170-012-4463-y
12. Lei, D., Guo, X.: An effective neighborhood search for scheduling in dual-resource constrained interval job shop with environmental objective. Int. J. Prod. Econ. **159**, 296–303 (2015). https://doi.org/10.1016/j.ijpe.2014.07.026
13. Moore, R.E., Kearfott, R.B., Cloud, M.J.: Introduction to Interval Analysis. Society for Industrial and Applied Mathematics (2009)
14. Mou, J., Gao, L., Li, X., Pan, Q., Mu, J.: Multi-objective inverse scheduling optimization of single-machine shop system with uncertain due-dates and processing times. Cluster Comput. **20**(1), 371–390 (2017). https://doi.org/10.1007/s10586-016-0717-z
15. Palacios, J.J., González-Rodríguez, I., Vela, C.R., Puente, J.: Robust swarm optimisation for fuzzy open shop scheduling. Nat. Comput. **13**(2), 145–156 (2014). https://doi.org/10.1007/s11047-014-9413-1
16. Pinedo, M.L.: Scheduling. Theory, Algorithms, and Systems, Fifth edn. Springer, Heidelberg (2016). https://doi.org/10.1007/978-3-319-26580-3
17. Roy, B.: Robustness in operational research and decision aiding: a multi-faceted issue. Eur. J. Oper. Res. **200**, 629–638 (2010)
18. Xu, Z., Yager, R.R.: Some geometric aggregation operators based on intuitionistic fuzzy sets. Int. J. General Syst. **35**(4), 417–433 (2006)
19. Zhang, J., Ding, G., Zou, Y., Qin, S., Fu, J.: Review of job shop scheduling research and its new perspectives under Industry 4.0. J. Intell. Manuf. **30**(4), 1809–1830 (2017). https://doi.org/10.1007/s10845-017-1350-2

Modified Grid Searches for Hyper-Parameter Optimization

David López[1(✉)], Carlos M. Alaíz[1], and José R. Dorronsoro[1,2]

[1] Department of Computer Engineering, Universidad Autónoma de Madrid, Madrid, Spain
david.lopezramos@estudiante.uam.es, {carlos.alaiz,jose.dorronsoro}@uam.es
[2] Inst. Ing. Conocimiento, Universidad Autónoma de Madrid, Madrid, Spain

Abstract. Black-box optimization aims to find the optimum of an unknown function only by evaluating it over different points in the space. An important application of black-box optimization in Machine Learning is the computationally expensive tuning of the hyper-parameters, which requires to try different configurations and measure the validation error over each of them to select the best configuration. In this work two alternatives to classical Grid Search are proposed, trying to alleviate the low effective dimensionality problem, i.e., the drop of performance when only some of the dimensions of the space are important. The first approach is based on a modification of a regular grid to guarantee equidistant projections of the points over each axis, whereas the second approach also guarantees these spread projections but with a random component. As shown experimentally, both approaches beat Grid Search, although in these experiments their performance is not statistically different from that of Random Search.

Keywords: Hyper-parameter optimization · Grid search · Random search · Black-box optimization

1 Introduction

Optimization problems are ubiquitous in many fields, and they particularly important in Machine Learning, where for example the training of a learning machine is often done by solving an optimization problem, usually with a known objective function. Moreover, the selection of the hyper-parameters is an optimization problem, where the best parameters are selected according to a certain criteria, usually represented by an unknown (or intractable) objective function. Hence, this task is often tackled as a black-box optimization problem, where different configurations, selected using different strategies, are evaluated to find the best one.

Black-box optimization consists in optimizing a certain functional $F(\mathbf{x})$, with $\mathbf{x} \in \mathcal{S}$ (usually, $\mathcal{S} \subset \mathbb{R}^d$ and hence there are d optimization variables), when the analytical form of F may not be available but it can be evaluated at different

E. A. de la Cal et al. (Eds.): HAIS 2020, LNAI 12344, pp. 221–232, 2020.
https://doi.org/10.1007/978-3-030-61705-9_19

points. There are multiple black-box optimization algorithms, but two of the main representatives in Machine Learning, besides the Bayesian approaches, are Grid Search (GS) and Random Search (RS). GS performs an exhaustive search over a discretization of the search space. RS is a simple powerful approach that generates randomly the points to be evaluated and it can outperform GS in searches with a low effective dimensionality, as discussed below. Here, two different approaches are proposed to cope with this problem, trying to guarantee a good performance even if only a small number of the optimization variables of the problem are significant, since these methods are designed to provide samples whose projections over each dimension are equidistant over all the search range. In particular, the contributions of this work can be summarized as follows:

1. A new black-box optimization method, called Modified Grid Search, is proposed to alleviate the low effective dimensionality problem of GS.
2. Another method is proposed, namely Latin Hyper-Cube Grid Search, which is a random version of the previous one.
3. Both methods are compared experimentally with GS and RS.

The remaining of the paper is organized as follows. Section 2 contains a overview of hyper-parameter optimization, in particular using standard GS and RS. Section 3 presents the two proposed methods to alleviate the limitations of GS, which are numerically compared with GS and RS in Sect. 4. The paper ends with some conclusions and pointers to further work in Sect. 5.

2 Hyper-Parameter Optimization

In order to train a parametric learning machine, two different types of parameters have to be set: the internal parameters of the model and the hyper-parameters. The first ones are adjusted from the data during the training phase. But the hyper-parameters usually cannot be learned directly from the data, because they represent properties of a higher level in the model, such as its complexity or its architecture. Therefore, hyper-parameters are usually predefined during a previous validation phase by simply trying different configurations to see which ones work better. Hence, in this phase the quality of the model is seen as a black-box function, in which different configurations of hyper-parameters are inserted and the output is observed to select the configuration with a better performance. Usually, this process is an expensive task since the search space can be large, and evaluating each configuration is costly [5].

2.1 Grid Search and Random Search

Two of the most popular methods to optimize hyper-parameters (without considering Bayesian approaches) are the classical Grid Search (GS), and the Random Search (RS) proposed by Bergstra and Bengio [1], who attribute the success of both techniques mainly to their conceptual simplicity, ease of implementation, trivial parallelization, and outperformance over purely manual optimization. Moreover, they show that RS provides a slight reduction of efficiency in low

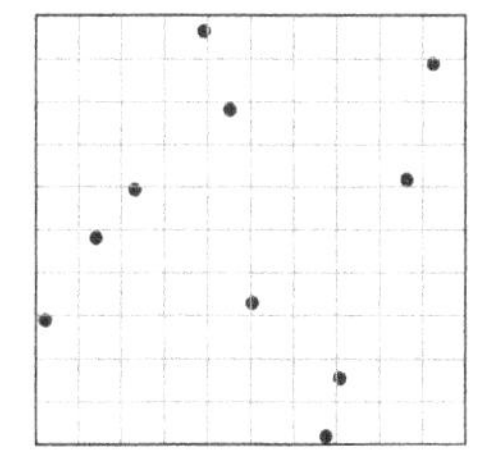

Fig. 1. Latin Hyper-Cube Sampling in 2D.

dimensions to obtain a large increase of efficiency in high dimensions with respect to GS, because frequently the objective function has a low effective dimensionality, that is, the function is more sensitive to changes in some dimensions than in others. In particular, it can be the case that for a certain model and a particular dataset, only certain hyper-parameters are relevant. The problem is that the relevant hyper-parameters change from one dataset to another, preventing from a design of an appropriate custom grid even for a fixed model. In this context, the low effective dimensionality causes GS to evaluate points in dimensions that have very little relevance, obtaining a worse performance than RS. Furthermore, RS presents other practical advantages: the experiments can be stopped at any time and the trials form a complete experiment, new trials can be added to an experiment without having to adjust the grid, and the failing of a trial does not jeopardize the complete search (it can be simply discarded).

2.2 Latin Hyper-Cube Sampling

A different approach can be found in the sampling method known as Latin Hyper-Cube Sampling (LHS; [7]). In the two-dimensional case, this method divides the search space into different cells, and randomly determines the cells that will be used to sample in such a way that no row or column is selected more than once. Hence, this selects a random cell, then samples a point inside that cell and discards the row and column corresponding to the cell; the process is repeated until discarding all the rows or columns. The advantage of this sampling is that the projection of the points over each dimension fall in different cells, spreading them over the whole interval (an example is shown in Fig. 1). This idea will be the basis of the new search approaches proposed in this work.

3 Modified Grid Searches

The GS approach, based on a Regular Grid (RG) and called for now on Regular Grid Search (RGS), performs particularly bad when the function to be minimized has a low effective dimensionality. For example, even if a certain optimization variable x_i has no real impact on the objective function F, by its own nature RGS will evaluate different points, $\mathbf{x}$ and $\mathbf{x}'$, that only differ in that variable, i.e.

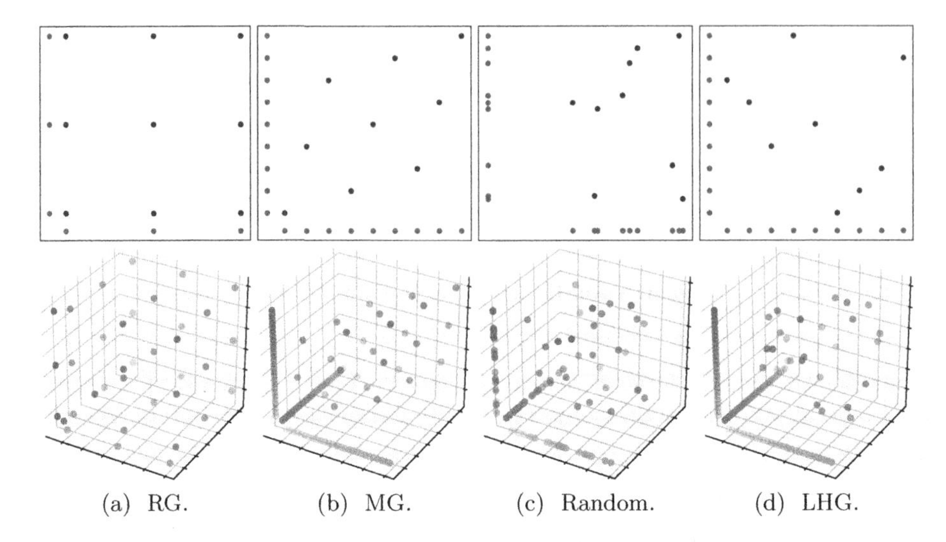
(a) RG. (b) MG. (c) Random. (d) LHG.

Fig. 2. Illustration of the samples generated by the four methods for a two-dimensional search (top) and a three-dimensional search (bottom). The samples are represented in blue; their projections over the axis are shown in green, red and orange. (Color figure online)

$x_j = x'_j$, $\forall j \neq i$, although these points will be essentially equivalent, providing approximately the same objective value, $F(\mathbf{x}) \approx F(\mathbf{x}')$. This effort could be used to explore instead other combinations of the effective variables, improving the results. In order to alleviate the limitation of RGS when optimizing problems with low effective dimensionality, two sampling methods are proposed next.

3.1 Modified Grid Search

The idea underneath the first new method, called Modified Grid Seach (MGS), is to use a different configuration of the points to be evaluated so that none of their coordinates is repeate, i.e., so that each optimization variable never takes the same value twice. Moreover, their projections over each dimension will be equidistant to explore the space as much as possible. With this configuration, even if a certain variable has no impact on the objective function, the values explored by MGS for the remaining variables will be exactly the same whether the insignificant variable is considered or not.

The design of this Modified Grid (MG) is based on that of a standard grid, defined as the Cartesian product of the sets of values to be evaluated for each variable. In this case, these sets are equispaced in linear or logarithmic scale. The process of modifying the RG can be understood intuitively in two dimensions, where it can be imagined as if the RG were stretched, pulling the lower left corner and the upper right corner until the points take equidistant projections between them (this can be seen in Figs. 2a and 2b, top).

The procedure is formalised next. Let $\mathcal{G}_{\mathbf{n}} \subset \mathbb{R}^d$, with $\mathbf{n} = (n_1, n_2, \dots, n_d)$, be the regular grid that tries n_i different values for the i-th optimization variable, and which is defined as:

$$\mathcal{G}_{\mathbf{n}} = \left\{ (x_1, x_2, \dots, x_d) \in \mathbb{N}^d : 1 \leq x_i \leq n_i,\ i = 1, \dots, d \right\} .$$

Although this grid is defined in the region $\prod_{i=1}^{d} [1, n_i]$, it can be easily rescaled or adapted to logarithmic scale. The procedure to convert $\mathcal{G}_{\mathbf{n}}$ into a MG, denoted by $\mathcal{G}'_{\mathbf{n}}$, is as follows. For the i-th variable, and for each value of that variable, $x_i \in \{1, \dots, n_i\}$, every appearance is moved a different quantity so that there are no repeated values. In particular, the j-th appearance of the i-th variable x_i is displaced an amount $(j-1)\, d_i$, where $d_i = 1/\prod_{j \neq i} n_j$ is the inverse of the number of times that each value of the i-th variable will be repeated. In this way, the last appearance satisfies:

$$x_i + \frac{\prod_{j \neq i} n_j - 1}{\prod_{j \neq i} n_j} = x_i + 1 - d_i ,$$

i.e., it is at a distance d_i from the following value $x_i + 1$, hence producing an equidistant distribution of the points.

The whole procedure is summarized in Algorithm 1, where `RegularGrid` returns the aforementioned RG $\mathcal{G}_{\mathbf{n}}$, and where the function `NormalizeGrid` just normalizes the grid to the range $\prod_{i=1}^{d} [0, 1]$ (the grid could be further transformed, e.g. resizing and translating it, or changing some components to logarithmic scale).

3.2 Latin Hyper-Cube Grid

The idea behind the LHS can be applied to the creation of a Latin Hyper-Cube Grid (LHG), which is simply a deterministic version of the LHS that guarantees equidistant projections, as the proposed MG, but in this case with a random structure instead of one based on the RG. In this way, the points to be evaluated in this new LHG Search (LHGS) will be distributed randomly over a dense grid without sharing any row or column (or any slice in dimension larger than two).

The procedure to generate the LHG is described next. It should be noted that, in this case, there is no point in selecting the number of different values to be tried per optimization variable, since it will be ignored by the algorithm, which only takes into account the total number of points to be evaluated.

Hence, the algorithm is based on the total size sample N, and on a vector $\mathbf{z} = (1, 2, \dots, N) \in \mathbb{N}^N$ which represents the N different values that all the variables will take. Now, in order to define the samples, it is enough to define the N values of the i-th variable as a random permutation of $\mathbf{z}$, which guarantees that all the variables will take N equidistant values, distributed over an $N \times N$ grid without repeating any value twice for any variable.

This procedure is shown in Algorithm 2, where `Permutation(z)` returns a random permutation of the vector $\mathbf{z}$, and again `NormalizeGrid` normalizes the samples.

Algorithm 1: Modified Grid.

Data: Number of values by dimension, $\mathbf{n} \in \mathbb{R}^d$.
Result: Set of points to be evaluated.
for $i = 1$ **to** d **do**
  $d_i \leftarrow \frac{1}{\prod_{j \neq i} n_j}$ // Separation between consecutive values.
end
$N \leftarrow \prod_i n_i$ // Number of points in the grid.
$\mathcal{G}_\mathbf{n} \leftarrow \mathtt{RegularGrid}(\mathbf{n}) = \left\{\mathbf{x}^{(1)}, \dots, \mathbf{x}^{(N)}\right\}$ // Regular grid.
for $i = 1$ **to** d **do**
  for $j = 1$ **to** n_j **do**
    $c_{ij} \leftarrow 0$ // Number of apparition of value j in variable i.
  end
end
for $p = 1$ **to** N **do**
  for $i = 1$ **to** d **do**
    $\bar{x}_i^{(p)} \leftarrow x_i^{(p)} + \left(c_{ix_i^{(p)}} - 1\right) d_i$
    $c_{ix_i^{(p)}} \leftarrow c_{ix_i^{(p)}} + 1$
  end
end
$\mathcal{G}'_\mathbf{n} \leftarrow \left\{\bar{\mathbf{x}}^{(1)}, \dots, \bar{\mathbf{x}}^{(N)}\right\}$
return $\mathtt{NormalizeGrid}(\mathcal{G}'_\mathbf{n})$

3.3 Comparative

Illustration. An illustration of the four grids (RG, MG, random grid and LHG) is shown in Fig. 2, both for the two-dimensional (top) and the three-dimensional (bottom) cases, where the samples are shown in blue, and their projections over the different axis in green, red and orange. Some conclusions can be drawn:

- In the case of RG, the points are distributed in a regular grid, and hence the projections collapse always to only 3 points (the number of values per variable). If the objective functional $F(x, y[, z])$ could be (reasonably) approximated by a function of one variable $G(x)$, the sample would be equivalent to one of size 3, although 9 or 27 points would be evaluated in two or three dimensions, respectively.
- For MG, the points that previously had repeated projection values now occupy the entire projection interval, obtaining 9 or 27 different and equidistant values for each one of the two or three variables. In the low dimensional case, where $F(x, y[, z])$ could be approximated by $G(x)$ the MG will continue to have 9 or 27 different values to explore over the significant variable x.
- For the random sample, there is no structure, hence the projections of the points do not collapse, but they can leave gaps between them.
- For LHG, the points are randomly distributed on the grid but their projections on the axes are equidistant, hence the proposed LHGS presents the robustness against the low effective dimensionality of MG.

Algorithm 2: Latin Hyper-Cube Grid.

Data: Number of values by dimension, $\mathbf{n} \in \mathbb{R}^d$.
Result: Set of points to be evaluated.
$N \leftarrow \prod_i n_i$ `// Number of points in the sample.`
$\mathbf{z} \leftarrow (1, 2, \ldots, N)$
for $i = 1$ **to** d **do**
  $\mathbf{p}_i \leftarrow$ `Permutation(z)`
end
for $p = 1$ **to** N **do**
  $\mathbf{x}^{(p)} \leftarrow (p_{1p}, p_{2p}, \ldots, p_{dp})$
  `//` p_{ip} `is the` p`-th entry of` $\mathbf{p}_i$.
end
$\mathcal{G}_\mathbf{n} \leftarrow \left\{\mathbf{x}^{(1)}, \ldots, \mathbf{x}^{(N)}\right\}$
return `NormalizeGrid(`$\mathcal{G}_\mathbf{n}$`)`

Pair Distance Distributions. A study of the probability distribution of the distances between each pair of points can give an intuition about how the points are placed, and how the shape of the grid affects this configuration. Hence, the following experiment is done. The distance between every pair of points of the grids will be measured for 100 generation of the four grids. Obviously, RG and MG will always produce the same grid, since they are deterministic, but the repetition of the experiment allows to cope with the randomness of the random sample and of LHG. The sample will be generated in dimension three, and its total size (the number of points in the grid) will be $N = 6^3 = 216$. In Fig. 3 the distribution is shown for three configuration of the vector $\mathbf{n}$: $(6, 6, 6)$, $(12, 6, 3)$ and $(36, 3, 2)$, that is, from more to less square. As it can be seen, as the number of points in each dimension is decompensated, the distances in the RG are separated to the right (the number of greater distances between pairs increases), while the other methods keep practically the same distribution.

4 Experiments

Two different set of experiments are conducted to validate the proposed methods, comparing RGS, MGS, RS and LHGS. The first one consists in the minimization of synthetic (hence, known) objective functions, whereas the second one deals with the tuning of the hyper-parameters of a Support Vector Machine.

4.1 Minimum of a Synthetic Function

The first set of experiments just tackles a general black-box optimization problem, aiming to find the minimum value of a function randomly generated. In particular, the function to evaluate will consist of a complete polynomial of a fixed degree g and dimension d (i.e., number of optimization variables). The coefficients are generated randomly in $[-1, 1]$, and in order to bound the problem from below, the absolute value of the generated polynomial is used as objective functional, $F(\mathbf{x}) = |p(x_1, x_2, \ldots, x_d)|$.

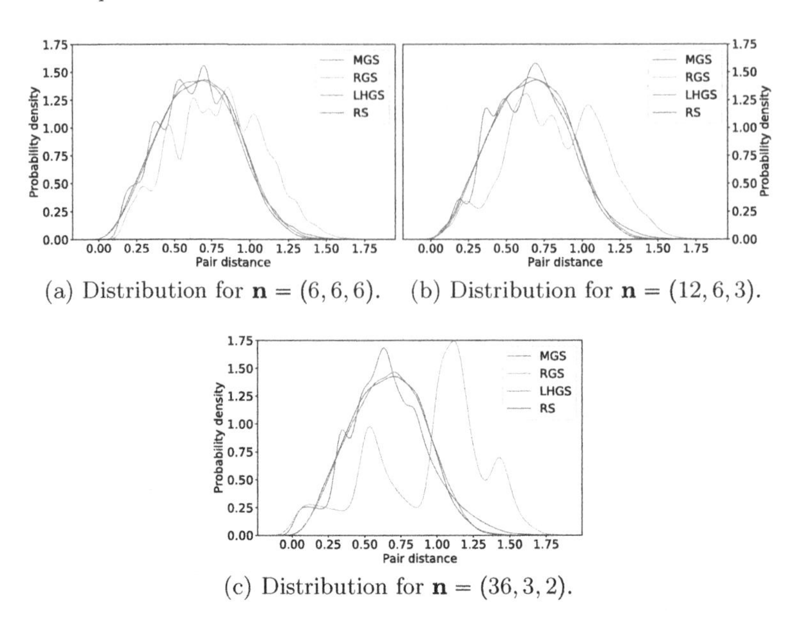

(a) Distribution for $\mathbf{n} = (6, 6, 6)$. (b) Distribution for $\mathbf{n} = (12, 6, 3)$.

(c) Distribution for $\mathbf{n} = (36, 3, 2)$.

Fig. 3. Pair distance distributions for different configurations of the grid.

The sample region (for the four search methods) is scaled to the interval $[-1, 1]$ in each dimension. The number of values explored by the four methods is the same over all the dimensions (the vector $\mathbf{n}$ is constant, $n_i = n$ for $1 \leq i \leq d$).

Three different degrees are used for the polynomial, $g \in \{4, 6, 8\}$, and two different number of dimensions, $d \in \{3, 4\}$. For a given configuration (g, d), 1000 different polynomials are generated to average the results. Different values of n are used to see the evolution of the search approaches. For each polynomial and for each value of n, the polynomial is evaluated over the solution given by each method, and the resultant four values are used to build a ranking that will be averaged over the 1000 repetitions.

The results are shown in Fig. 4. It can be seen that, the larger the degree of the polynomials g, the larger the separation between RGS and the other three methods, which have essentially the same performance. Similarly, the performance of RGS is worse when d is 4, since in that case, a low effective dimensionality is more probable, although it is not explicitly enforced. These results can be further analysed using a Nemenyi test [8] to compare the average ranks. This test is based on the creation of a threshold above which the difference between two means are considered significant. With the ranking means and the number of iterations, the critical distance is $D = 0.148$ for a significance value $\alpha = 5\,\%$. If the means of two methods have a greater difference than this value, one of them can be considered better than the other. Looking at the results corresponding to $g = 6$ and $g = 8$, the difference between RGS and the other methods is significant, whereas between the other three methods is not.

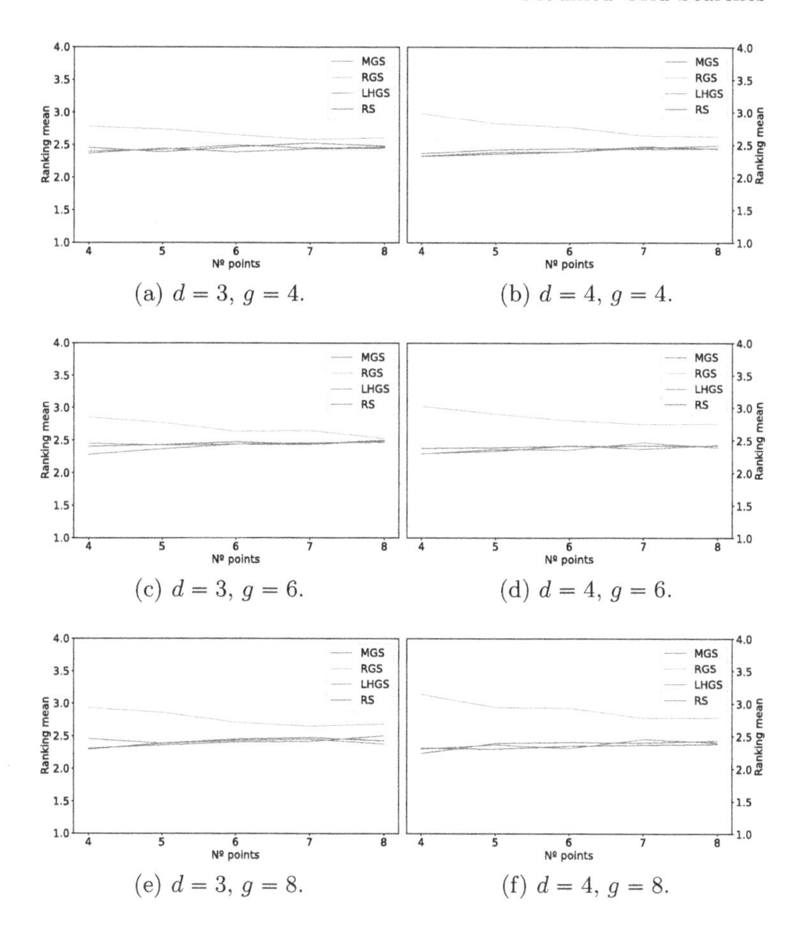

(a) $d = 3,\ g = 4$.

(b) $d = 4,\ g = 4$.

(c) $d = 3,\ g = 6$.

(d) $d = 4,\ g = 6$.

(e) $d = 3,\ g = 8$.

(f) $d = 4,\ g = 8$.

Fig. 4. Average ranking for the minimization of a synthetic polynomial, for different degrees of the polynomial g and different numbers of dimensions d.

As a conclusion, it seems that the performance of RGS is worse the greater the complexity of the polynomial to be evaluated, because raising the number of variables and raising the degree, the number of possible combinations increases, and the other methods make a better use of the available exploration effort. In addition, the performance in this problem of MGS, RS and LHGS is similar. It is necessary to mention that the importance of each variable is given by its (random) coefficient, so an ineffective dimension is not enforced. If some variables would be ignored to build the polynomial, probably the performance of the new methods would be even better when compared to RGS.

4.2 SVM Hyper-Parameter Tuning

The following experiments compare the four search approaches when applied to tuning the hyper-parameters of a Support Vector Machine (SVM; [2,9]. These

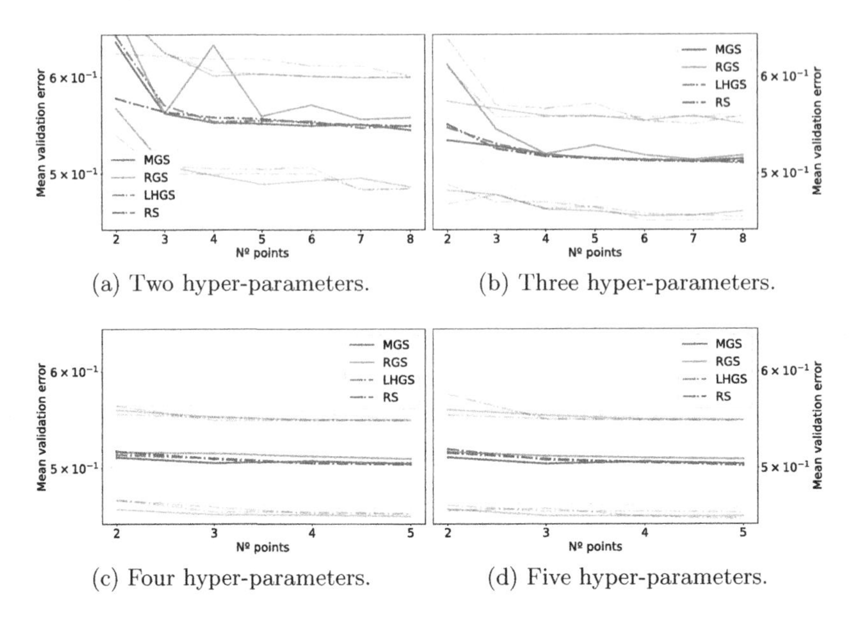

(a) Two hyper-parameters. (b) Three hyper-parameters.

(c) Four hyper-parameters. (d) Five hyper-parameters.

Fig. 5. Validation errors for *Diabetes*.

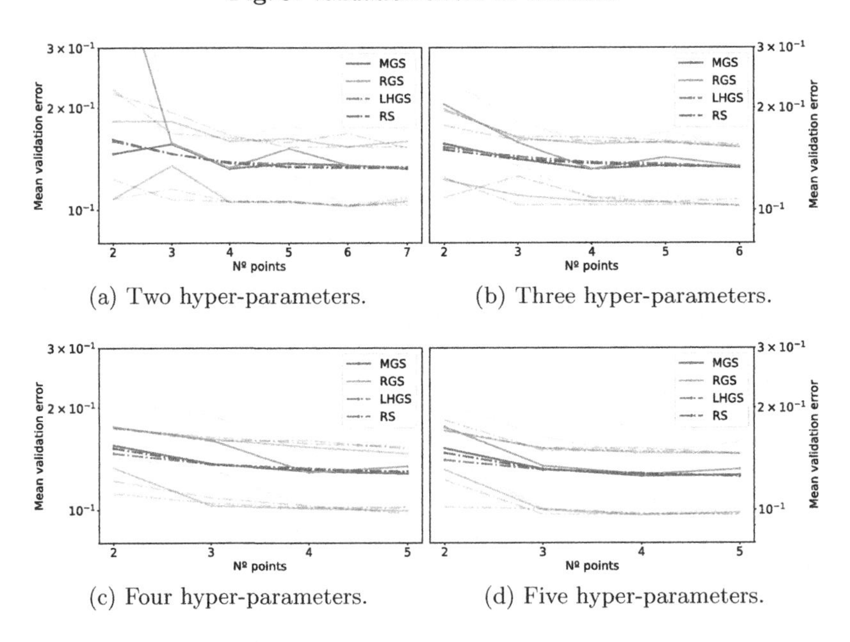

(a) Two hyper-parameters. (b) Three hyper-parameters.

(c) Four hyper-parameters. (d) Five hyper-parameters.

Fig. 6. Validation errors for *Boston*.

experiments are implemented in Python, using the *scikit-learn* library. In particular, the `GridSearchCV` function is used, but configuring a list of dictionaries that define the searching space according to RGS, MGS, RS or LHGS. To evaluate each SVM configuration, 5-fold cross-validation is used. Therefore, the black-box optimization problem consists in minimizing the 5-fold cross-validation error, and the optimization variables are the hyper-parameters. The kernel selected for the SVMs is the polynomial kernel $k(\mathbf{x}, \mathbf{x}') = (\gamma\langle \mathbf{x}, \mathbf{x}' \rangle + \tau)^d$, because it has more hyper-parameters than the most commonly used Gaussian kernel, and hence it allows to compare the search approaches in higher dimensional spaces (with more optimization variables). There are in total 5 hyper-parameters:

- `C` (C): Penalty parameter for the error term.
- `epsilon` (ε): Width of insensitivity.
- `degree` (d): Degree of the polynomial kernel.
- `gamma` (γ): Kernel coefficient.
- `coef0` (τ): Kernel independent term.

The comparison is done over two real (although smallish) regression datasets: *Diabetes* (introduced in [4], and available through the function `load_diabetes`) and *Boston* (corresponding to the UCI repository [3], and accessible through the function `load_boston`). For each dataset, and for each search method, the validation score, e.g., the cross-validation error corresponding to the best hyper-parameters, is used as a measure of the performance of the optimization approach. Four experiments are conducted for each dataset, tuning two, three, four and five hyper-parameters, with the rest fixed to their default values, and the procedure is repeated 10 times with different partitions of the datasets.

The validation errors are shown in Figs. 5 and 6, where the dark lines represent the mean best validation error for each method, and the light lines below and above represent the minimum and maximum values (to show how spread are the results). Looking at the experiments, RGS is worse than the other three methods when the number of evaluated points is small, although the difference is reduced when the grid becomes denser. The other three methods behave similarly, with small differences between them. Finally, the oscillations of RGS should be remarked, since when the number n of different values per hyper-parameter is small then the difference between considering n or $n + 1$ values can change a lot the distribution of the samples in the space, affecting the performance.

5 Conclusions

Black-box optimization is an ubiquitous problem, specially important in Machine Learning, where tuning the hyper-parameters of a learning machine is a particular case that can be crucial for guaranteeing the good performance of many methods. Two of the most popular approaches for setting up the hyper-parameters are Grid Search (GS) and Random Search (RS), the first one based on an exhaustive search over a discretisation of the space, and the second one on generating and evaluating random points.

In this work two new approaches are proposed. The first one, Modified Grid Search (MGS), is based on a modification of a regular grid to guarantee the best possible independent exploration of each hyper-parameter, by providing equidistant projections of the grid-points over every axis. The second approach, Latin Hyper-Cube Grid Search (LHGS), is a random version of the first one, that again provides equidistant projections but without enforcing any structure on the grid, similar to a deterministic version of the Latin Hyper-Cube Sampling. As shown experimentally, when considering the same number of explored points, and hence the same computational effort, the proposed methods outperform GS in many situations, being comparable, and in some situations better, than RS.

As further work, the illustrative experiments shown in this paper should be extended to consider a large number of datasets to average the performance, so that significant results can be obtained. There are also many other approaches for hyper-parameter optimization that could also be added to the comparison (e.g. [6]). It should be noted that only the hyper-parameters of a Support Vector Machine with polynomial kernel have been tuned, but it would be interesting to extend this study to models like (possibly Deep) Neural Networks, where the large number of hyper-parameters could make the low effective dimensionality problem more severe, and hence the proposed approaches more beneficial.

Acknowledgements. With financial support from the European Regional Development Fund and from the Spanish Ministry of Economy, Industry, and Competitiveness - State Research Agency, project TIN2016-76406-P (AEI/FEDER, UE). Work supported also by the UAM–ADIC Chair for Data Science and Machine Learning.

References

1. Bergstra, J., Bengio, Y.: Random search for hyper-parameter optimization. J. Mach. Learn. Res. **13**(Feb), 281–305 (2012)
2. Cortes, C., Vapnik, V.: Support-vector networks. Mach. Learn. **20**(3), 273–297 (1995)
3. Dua, D., Graff, C.: UCI machine learning repository (2017)
4. Efron, B., Hastie, T., Johnstone, I., Tibshirani, R., et al.: Least angle regression. Ann. Stat. **32**(2), 407–499 (2004)
5. Feurer, M., Hutter, F.: Hyperparameter optimization. In: Hutter, F., Kotthoff, L., Vanschoren, J. (eds.) Automated Machine Learning. TSSCML, pp. 3–33. Springer, Cham (2019). https://doi.org/10.1007/978-3-030-05318-5_1
6. Li, L., Jamieson, K., DeSalvo, G., Rostamizadeh, A., Talwalkar, A.: Hyperband: a novel bandit-based approach to hyperparameter optimization. J. Mach. Learn. Res. **18**(1), 6765–6816 (2017)
7. McKay, M.D., Beckman, R.J., Conover, W.J.: Comparison of three methods for selecting values of input variables in the analysis of output from a computer code. Technometrics **21**(2), 239–245 (1979)
8. Nemenyi, P.: Distribution-free multiple comparisons. In: Biometrics. vol. 18, p. 263. International Biometric Soc 1441 I ST, NW, SUITE 700, WASHINGTON, DC 20005–2210 (1962)
9. Smola, A.J., Schölkopf, B.: A tutorial on support vector regression. Stat. Comput. **14**(3), 199–222 (2004)

Supervised Hyperparameter Estimation for Anomaly Detection

Juan Bella[1], Ángela Fernández[1(✉)], and José R. Dorronsoro[1,2]

[1] Dept. Ingeniería Informática, Universidad Autónoma de Madrid, Madrid, Spain
juan.bellas@estudiante.uam.es, {a.fernandez,jose.dorronsoro}@uam.es
[2] Inst. Ing. Conocimiento, Universidad Autónoma de Madrid, Madrid, Spain

Abstract. The detection of anomalies, i.e. of those points found in a dataset but which do not seem to be generated by the underlying distribution, is crucial in machine learning. Their presence is likely to make model predictions not as accurate as we would like; thus, they should be identified before any model is built which, in turn, may require the optimal selection of the detector hyperparameters. However, the unsupervised nature of this problem makes that task not easy. In this work, we propose a new estimator composed by an anomaly detector followed by a supervised model; we can take then advantage of this second model to transform model estimation into a supervised problem and, as a consequence, the estimation of the detector hyperparameters can be done in a supervised setting. We shall apply these ideas to optimally hyperparametrize four different anomaly detectors, namely, Robust Covariance, Local Outlier Factor, Isolation Forests and One-class Support Vector Machines, over different classification and regression problems. We will also experimentally show the usefulness of our proposal to estimate in an objective and automatic way the best detector hyperparameters.

Keywords: Outliers · Anomaly detection · Supervised learning

1 Introduction

One of the main challenges in a machine learning (ML) problem is contaminated data, i.e. data samples with instances far from the distribution mean. The term "outlier" makes reference to those points which are so far away from the rest of the sample that become suspicious of being generated by a different mechanism [10]. Moreover, they are likely to make ML models less accurate so it is interesting to detect and exclude them from the training dataset. In this context one can in principle distinguish two kinds of problems:

- Outlier detection, where the goal is to separate normal data from outliers before, say, training a model.
- Novelty detection where the goal is to model an already clean sample and to use this model to detect new patterns that do not follow it.

E. A. de la Cal et al. (Eds.): HAIS 2020, LNAI 12344, pp. 233–244, 2020.
https://doi.org/10.1007/978-3-030-61705-9_20

Outlier and novelty detection are problems of long standing in ML and, as a consequence, they have received substantial attention; see for instance [6] for a thorough and relatively recent review. Usually one refers to outlier detection (OD) when handling a contaminated sample that has to be cleaned before further proceeding. In this sense OD is an unsupervised problem as one assumes in principle no information on the sample. In novelty detection (ND) one begins with a clean sample that has to characterize, often by modeling its data distribution so that this model can be applied later on to weed out new patterns that contradict it. Because of this, ND is considered a semisupervised problem, as one mixes a supervised component when modeling the initial clean sample, and an unsupervised one in the new patterns. As it can be seen, the distinction between both problems is somewhat subtle and often the same methods can be applied to both problems. These dual-use methods are commonly referred as anomaly detection (AD) algorithms, to be applied as ODs in unsupervised settings, and as NDs in semisupervised ones. Here we shall refer to AD algorithms indistinctly under both points of view.

As mentioned, there is a large literature on Anomaly Detection that remains a very active research field. More recently, AD methods based on deep neural networks (DNNs) have been proposed, quite often using autoencoders [15,20] or under an adversarial point of view [1,8] or even connecting them with previous AD proposals [16]; see [5] for a general survey of DNN-based AD, [14] for a more specialized one on adversarial methods or the very recent [2] for anomaly detection in time series. Here, however, we will concentrate our attention on four older and more established AD methods, namely Robust Covariance [17], Local Outlier Factor [3] and Isolation Forests [13], usually labeled as outlier detectors, and also One-Class Support Vector Machines (one-class SVMs, [18]), that try to model a probability distribution over an already clean sample and are thus usually labeled as a novelty detection method. The main reason of our choice is that they have well documented and tested implementations within the *scikit-learn* library which, in particular, makes it easy to build pipelined methods around them and also to take advantage of the hyperparameter estimation classes in that library (see also [19] for a recent Python library for scalable OD).

In any case, any AD model depends on a set of hyperparameters whose optimal values have to be determined. However, the unsupervised or semisupervised nature of AD models and, hence, the usual absence of a well established ground truth makes difficult that estimation. On the other hand, AD is usually a first step in a more general process of data exploitation. Often, this exploitation is done after building a supervised model on the clean sample following a pipelined structure, where the outputs of the AD model are plugged into the inputs of the supervised model. Similarly, once an AD has been built on a clean sample, it may be sensible to apply it before a supervised model is used on new patterns not deemed to be anomalies.

This means that in this pipeline-like setting the exploitation of the AD model is done in a supervised way, which suggests that one could take advantage of this not only to estimate the optimal hyperparameters of the supervised component but those of the AD component as well. This is the aim of this paper, in which we propose a new supervised framework for tuning pipelined models with a first AD component and where the overall optimal hyperparameters, including those of the AD model, are estimated using the ground truth of the final supervised component by applying the usual train-validation tools. We point out that supervised approaches to anomaly detection have already been proposed; see for instance [9,11] or [4]. However, these approaches usually focus on exploiting classification label information when applying AD methods; on the other hand, our focus here is different, as we combine AD models with classifiers or regressors with the double aim of better hyperparametrizing the first AD component and of improving the performance of the subsequent supervised model.

We shall consider here classification and regression problems. While quite powerful methods are available for them, we shall just apply here standard linear and logistic regressors; recall that our main aim is the optimal estimation of AD hyperparameters, which even in the simplified setting we consider involves a not small number of hyperparameters and, hence, a substantial computational load.

In summary, our main contribution is the proposal of a supervised framework for optimal AD hyperparameter estimation through the combination of AD algorithms within a pipeline structure with a supervised classifier or regressor. This paper is organized as follows. In Sect. 2 we recall the classical methods for dealing with these problems and in Sect. 3 we present a new algorithm for applying these techniques in a supervised context. In Sect. 4 we numerically compare the different methods over different experiments and, finally, in Sect. 5 we offer some conclusions and point out to lines of further work.

2 Classical Methods for Anomaly Detection

We briefly recall next the classical methods we will use for anomaly detection.

2.1 Robust Covariance

One of the biggest challenges when detecting outliers in datasets with dimension $d > 3$ is how to visualize them. An usual way to deal with this problem is the use of a robust estimator for localizing multivariate distributions, and an example of it is the Minimum Volume Ellipsoid (MVE) estimator [17]. This method looks for the ellipsoid of minimum volume that contains h of the n observations, where $n/2 \leq h < n$. The MINVOL algorithm applies this idea via an iterative estimation, starting with a subsample of size $d + 1$ and computing its mean and covariance matrix. Then it either enlarges or contracts the ellipsoid until it contains h samples, choosing finally the minimum volume ellipsoid.

A similar method is the Minimum Covariance Determinant (MCD) estimator [17]. In this case we look for the h samples with a minimum determinant of the covariance matrix. According to [17], this generates a better estimator than MVE in terms of statistical efficiency, robustness and precision. Nevertheless, it is not easy to compute the MCD estimator. Fortunately, there exists a fast estimation algorithm, the FAST-MCD [17], that even improves the MVE computation speed. In this work we have used the implementation of FAST-MCD given by *scikit-learn*, where the hyperparameters to be estimated are:

- $\rho \in [0, 1]$ indicates the proportion of samples included in the ellipsoid, i.e., $h = \rho\, n$. The default h value is $h = \frac{n+d+1}{2}$.
- The contamination percentage, i.e., the proportion of outliers we believe there are in the sample. This is a hyperparameter that will appear in one form or another in all the methods we consider. By default is set to 0.1.

2.2 Local Outlier Factor

In other occasions, instead of defining an outlier in a 0–1 way it is more convenient to give a measure about how different a point is from the rest of the sample. We can then define a threshold from which to decide whether a given point will be considered an anomaly. The concept of cluster can help us to define anomalies from this new perspective. An outlier will then be a point that does not belong to any data cluster.

Local Outlier Factor (LOF, [3]) is a method that uses these ideas, defining outliers in terms of their neighbors. In this framework, an outlier is defined in terms of the called LOF_k measure, which is defined taking into account the distance in between two points and the density of the clusters. A formal definition is

$$LOF_k(x_i) = \frac{1}{k}\left(\sum_{x_l \in N_k(x_i)} k\text{-dist}(x_l)\right)\left(\sum_{x_j \in N_k(x_i)} \frac{1}{\sum_{x_m \in N_k(x_j)} k\text{-dist}(x_m)}\right), \quad (1)$$

where, k-dist(x_i) can be approximately defined as the distance of x_i to its farthest k neighbor. The use of LOF to detect outliers is based on the observation that when a point is an inlier, it should be "well" inside its cluster and hence, its LOF value will be near to 1. On the other hand, for an outlier x_i its neighbors x_j should be far away from it while the neighbors of these x_j should be close to x_j. Thus both terms on the right hand side of (1) should be large and, hence, result in $LOF(x_i) >> 1$. Therefore, the larger the $LOF_k(x_i)$, the more anomalous x_i can be considered.

In this work we have used the implementation of this algorithm given by *scikit-learn*, where the hyperparameters to be estimated are:

- The number of neighbors k.
- The contamination percentage, which is again here the proportion of outliers we believe to be in the sample.

2.3 Isolation Forests

Recall that an anomaly is defined as a point with different characteristics than those considered to be "normal" points. The methods seen previously try to identify what the "normality" is and then classify as anomalies the patterns that do not follow its definition [12]. These techniques present two inconveniences:

1. These models are optimized for detecting normal data, so they can be inefficient for detecting anomalies.
2. Their complexity grows with the size and dimension of the dataset.

To prevent these drawbacks, Isolation Forests (iForests, [13]) try to explicitly isolate the anomalies instead of focusing on defining normality. They use a tree structure, called iTree, that will leave the anomalies near to the root as they have a more differentiated characteristics, while the normal instances will be moved deeper into the tree.

The iForest algorithm builds a set of iTrees and defines as anomalies those points that, in mean, have lower depth. It is a quite light algorithm in terms of computational complexity, as it is not necessary to build the trees completely, it does not use distance metrics and it does not need a large amount of memory. It works well in small samples and also in big datasets with high dimension.

As in the previous cases, we have used the implementation of this algorithm given by *scikit-learn*, where the hyperparameters to be estimated are:

- The number of iTrees.
- The maximum number of patterns used per tree. By default, it is set to 256.
- The maximum number of features used per tree. By default, it uses all the available features.
- The contamination percentage, with the same meaning as before.

2.4 One-Class SVM

One-class Support Vector Machine (One-class SVM, [18]) is a kernel-based anomaly detector that ultimately tries to estimate the density function of the data and then to define a binary function f which determines whether or not a point belongs to the region where the sample lies. In practice, and as for standard SVMs, we have to solve a dual optimization problem formally defined as

$$\min_{\alpha \in \mathbb{R}^N} \left\{ \frac{1}{2} \alpha^\intercal K \alpha \right\} \text{ s.t. } \begin{cases} \alpha^\intercal \mathbf{1} = 1, \\ \mathbf{0} \leq \alpha \leq \frac{1}{\nu N}, \end{cases}$$

where:

- K is the kernel function. In general we will use the Gaussian kernel defined as
$$k(x, y) = e^{-\gamma ||x-y||^2},$$
where γ is the kernel scale. A good approximation to its optimal value can be obtained by $1/d$, with d the number of features, after scaling inputs feature-wise to a, say, $[0, 1]$ range.

Algorithm 1: `OptHyperpars`$(X, y, X_{ts}, D, M, R_\alpha, R_\beta)$

1 Read train data X, y, test data X_{ts}, algorithms D, M, hyperparameter ranges R_α, R_β
2 $(\alpha^*, \beta_0^*) = \texttt{CV}_{M,D}(X, y, D, M, R_\alpha, R_\beta)$ `#hyperparametrization of` α
3 $(X_{cl}, y_{cl}) = D(X, y, \alpha^*)$
4 $\beta^* = \texttt{CV}_M(X_{cl}, y_{cl}, M, R_\beta)$ `#hyperparametrization of` β
5 $y^{pred} = M(\cdot, \beta^*).\texttt{predict}(X_{ts})$

- $\nu \in (0, 1]$ measures the anomaly detection sensitivity. It is an upper-bound of the fraction of errors allowed and a lower-bound of the number of support vectors. By default the value 0.5 is used, but this is one of the model hyperparameters to be optimized, as a large ν implies a small support for the sample data (so almost every point will be considered an anomaly) and a small ν provides a large support and some anomalies can be missed.

Once again we have used for the experiments the implementation of this method provided by *scikit-learn*.

3 Supervised Outlier Detection

We will apply the preceding ideas on a first scenario, where we assume we have a possibly contaminated sample X, y and a pair $D(\cdot, \alpha)$, $M(\cdot, \beta)$ made of an AD algorithm D with a set of hyperparameters α and a supervised model M hyperparametrized by the parameter set β. Our steps can be stated as follows:

1. Estimate an optimal hyperparameter set α^* of the AD model D.
2. Obtain clean versions (X^{cl}, y^{cl}) of the initial set (X, y) as $(X^{cl}, y^{cl}) = D((X, y), \alpha^*)$.
3. Estimate an optimal hyperparameter β^* of the supervised model P over the clean set X^{cl}, y^{cl} by standard cross validation (CV).

Once these steps are done, if we receive a clean test set X_{ts} we will simply apply to it the $M(\cdot, \beta^*)$ model to get test predictions $\hat{y}_{ts}$. If, on the other hand, we suspect the test set to be contaminated, we would apply first the AD model $D(\cdot, \alpha^*)$ to get a clean version X_{ts}^{cl} upon which we would then apply $M(\cdot, \beta^*)$. These steps are summarized in Algorithm 1. Notice that to get the optimal hyperparameters α^* of algorithm D we obtain them together with a preliminary estimate β_0^* of the hyperparameters of M in line 2 which later refine to a final estimate β^* in line 4 of Algorithm 1.

We still have to clarify how to apply the first step above or, more precisely, how to implement the function $\texttt{CV}_{M,D}$ in Algorithm 1. To do so, consider a pipeline made of the AD model D and the supervised one M. This can be seen as defining a composite model

$$C(\cdot, \alpha, \beta) = M(D(\cdot, \alpha), \beta)$$

Algorithm 2: $\texttt{CV}(X, y, D, M, R_\alpha, R_\beta)$

1 Read sample X, y, algorithms D, M and hyperparameter ranges R_α, R_β
2 Split (X, y) into K folds (X_k, y_k)
3 **for** $(\alpha, \beta) \in R_\alpha \times R_\beta$**:**
4   **for** $k = 1, \ldots, K$**:**
5         $(X'_k, y'_k) = \cup_{j \neq k}(X_j, y_j)$
6         $(X'_k, y'_k)^{cl} = D((X'_k, y'_k), \alpha)$
7         $M(\cdot, \beta) = M.\texttt{fit}((X'_k, y'_k)^{cl}, \beta)$
8         $y_k^{pred} = M(\cdot, \beta).\texttt{predict}(X_k)$
9         $m_k(\alpha, \beta) = \ell(y_k, y_k^{pred})$
10     $m(\alpha, \beta) = \{m_k(\alpha, \beta)\}.\texttt{mean}_k$
11 Return $m(\alpha, \beta).\texttt{arg\_min}_{\alpha,\beta}$

for which a figure of merit $m(X, y, \alpha, \beta)$ can be computed over any loss ℓ that may be available for M, i.e.

$$m(X, y, \alpha, \beta) = \ell(y, M(D(X, \alpha), \beta)) = \ell(y, C(X, \alpha, \beta)).$$

This can easily fit into any CV procedure to optimize α, β over the training set X. The details of this can be seen in Algorithm 2.

4 Experiments

4.1 Experimental Methodology

This section describes the experimental analysis done for testing the proposed supervised hyperparametrization of AD models. We basically follow the procedure in Algorithm 2 taking as D models the MCD, LOF, iTree and one-class SVM described above; for the M models we will use Logistic and Ridge Regression for classification and regression problems, respectively. The samples are feature-wise normalized to a $\mu = 0$, $\sigma = 1$ distribution for the MCD and LOF algorithms and scaled to the $[0, 1]$ range when using one-class SVMs; no normalization is done for Isolation Forest as it does not require it. When applying AD in a supervised setting a decision has to be made on whether to include target values as inputs to the detectors; we will do so in all our experiments and estimate the optimal AD hyperparameters on the joint (X, y) training sample.

Notice that in our tests we don't apply the AD component D but only the supervised model M, as we take the test set X_{ts} to be clean. If, on the other hand, we would like to clean a possibly contaminated test sample, we can retrain the AD model with the found optimal hyperparameters only on the independent training variable matrix X and apply it to the contaminated test independent variables X_{ts}. Of course, this implicitly assumes that the optimal hyperparameters over the entire train sample (X, y) (i.e., including targets) would also work correctly when only the X matrix is considered, something that at this point cannot be guaranteed and that would need further study.

Table 1. Set of hyperparameter values for validation.

Model	Parameter	Range
Logistic Regression	C	$[10^{-2}, 10^{-1}, \ldots, 10^{5}]$
Ridge Regression	α	$[10^{-2}, 10^{-1}, \ldots, 10^{5}]$
MCD	contamination	$\{0.05, 0.1, 0.15, 0.20, 0.25, 0.3, 0.4, 0.5\}$
	ρ	$[0.1, 0.2, \ldots, 0.9]$
LOF	contamination	$\{0.05, 0.1, 0.15, 0.20, 0.25, 0.3, 0.4, 0.5\}$
	k	$\{5, 9, 17, 33, 65\}$
iForest	contamination	$\{0.05, 0.1, 0.15, 0.20, 0.25, 0.3, 0.4, 0.5\}$
	num_iTrees	$\{10, 25, 50, 75, 100, 125\}$
	max_features	$\{0.125, 0.25, 0.375, 0.5, 0.625, 0.77, 0.875, 1\}$
One-class SVM	ν	$\{0.05, 0.1, 0.15, 0.20, 0.25, 0.3, 0.4, 0.5\}$
	γ	$[\frac{2^{-3}}{d}, \frac{2^{-2}}{d}, \ldots, \frac{2^{4}}{d}]$

As mentioned before, we will use Logistic Regression as the supervised model for classification problems and Ridge Regression for the regression ones. We will work with 3 folds for CV based hyperparametrization using as CV scores the area under the ROC curve (AUC) for classification problems and the mean absolute error (MAE) for regression. The classification folds are built in a stratified fashion, so that essentially the same positive to negative sample ratio is kept for all folds. The different hyperparameter ranges for each model are shown in Table 1.

We will compare our experimental results using different model evaluation metrics. More precisely, for classification we will use the area under the ROC curve (AUC), the accuracy (Acc) and the area under the precision-recall curve (AP). For regression we will use the mean absolute error (MAE) and the mean square error (MSE). To make our results more robust we will repeat $N = 10$ times the overall procedure and report averages and standard deviations of the evaluation metrics.

4.2 Datasets

We will work with four classification and four regression datasets taken from the UCI Machine Learning Repository [7] that we briefly describe next.

Abalone. The aim of this dataset is to predict the age of abalones (a kind of mollusk) from 8 features, most of them involving physical measurements; it has 4, 177 patterns.

Housing. This dataset contains housing information in several Boston areas, with the goal being to estimate the median price for each area. It has 506 patterns with 13 features.

Table 2. Regression Results. Datasets: *Abalone* (Abal), *Housing* (Hous), *Mg* and *Space_ga* (Space).

		Baseline	MCD	LOF	iForest	One-class SVM
Abal	MAE	1.602 ± 0.027	$\mathbf{1.585 \pm 0.036}$	1.587 ± 0.041	1.603 ± 0.045	1.589 ± 0.032
	MSE	$\mathbf{4.982 \pm 0.299}$	5.152 ± 0.374	5.147 ± 0.449	5.303 ± 0.495	5.004 ± 0.342
Hous	MAE	3.447 ± 0.203	3.789 ± 0.453	3.477 ± 0.237	3.419 ± 0.183	$\mathbf{3.389 \pm 0.193}$
	MSE	$\mathbf{24.598 \pm 3.542}$	39.062 ± 16.203	28.486 ± 6.533	26.791 ± 4.673	26.627 ± 4.620
Mg	MAE	$\mathbf{0.119 \pm 0.004}$	0.120 ± 0.005	$\mathbf{0.119 \pm 0.004}$	0.120 ± 0.004	0.120 ± 0.005
	MSE	$\mathbf{0.022 \pm 0.001}$	0.023 ± 0.002	$\mathbf{0.022 \pm 0.002}$	0.023 ± 0.001	$\mathbf{0.022 \pm 0.002}$
Space	MAE	$\mathbf{0.098 \pm 0.003}$	$\mathbf{0.098 \pm 0.004}$	$\mathbf{0.098 \pm 0.003}$	$\mathbf{0.098 \pm 0.003}$	$\mathbf{0.098 \pm 0.004}$
	MSE	$\mathbf{0.017 \pm 0.001}$	$\mathbf{0.017 \pm 0.001}$	$\mathbf{0.017 \pm 0.002}$	$\mathbf{0.017 \pm 0.001}$	0.017 ± 0.001

Mg. The goal in this mammography mass dataset is to predict the severity (benign or malignant) of a mass lump using BI-RADS attributes and the patient's age. It has 6 features and 1,385 patterns.

Space_ga. This dataset (from StatLib[1]) contains 3,107 observations on U.S. county votes cast in the 1980 presidential election. Patterns have 6 features related with the voting population characteristics and the targets are the vote counts.

Australian. The Australian credit approval dataset has 14 features and 690 patterns with the goal to decide whether or not an application is credit-worthy.

Diabetes. The objective here is to diagnose the presence of hepatitis on a dataset of with clinical measurements on a sample of Pima Indian females. Several constraints were placed on the selection of these instances from a larger database, such as all patterns to be females, at least 21 years old and of Pima Indian heritage. It has 8 features and 768 patterns.

German.number. The German credit dataset has 1,000 patterns to be classified as either good or bad credits. It uses 24 credit related features and some features that were originally categorical have been transformed into numerical attributes.

Ijcnn1. This dataset was proposed in the IJCNN 2001 neural network competition by Daniel Prokhorov. It has 49,990 patterns and 22 features.

4.3 Results

The results obtained for regression datasets can be seen in Table 2 and those for classification are shown in Table 3. We give results for the combination of each AD method with the corresponding supervised model, and we also give the baseline scores obtained by the direct application of the supervised classifier or regressor to the entire sample, without any filtering of possible anomalies.

[1] http://lib.stat.cmu.edu/datasets/.

Table 3. Classification Results. Datasets: *Australian* (Austr), *Diabetes* (Diabet), *German.number* (German) and *Ijcnn1.*

		Baseline	MCD	LOF	iForest	One-class SVM
Austr	AUC	0.858 ± 0.020	0.859 ± 0.021	0.859 ± 0.021	0.858 ± 0.019	**0.863 ± 0.021**
	Acc	0.858 ± 0.018	0.859 ± 0.020	0.859 ± 0.020	0.860 ± 0.017	**0.864 ± 0.019**
	AP	0.777 ± 0.024	0.777 ± 0.028	0.777 ± 0.028	0.780 ± 0.022	**0.784 ± 0.025**
Diabet	AUC	0.723 ± 0.025	0.725 ± 0.023	**0.729 ± 0.027**	0.714 ± 0.040	0.713 ± 0.024
	Acc	**0.769 ± 0.022**	0.754 ± 0.022	**0.769 ± 0.023**	0.763 ± 0.028	0.748 ± 0.024
	AP	0.775 ± 0.016	0.778 ± 0.016	**0.779 ± 0.018**	0.769 ± 0.026	0.769 ± 0.016
German	AUC	0.684 ± 0.024	0.680 ± 0.024	**0.687 ± 0.028**	0.671 ± 0.035	0.681 ± 0.024
	Acc	**0.770 ± 0.013**	0.762 ± 0.017	**0.770 ± 0.019**	0.762 ± 0.023	0.768 ± 0.015
	AP	0.473 ± 0.025	0.463 ± 0.027	**0.475 ± 0.033**	0.458 ± 0.040	0.469 ± 0.027
Ijcnn1	AUC	0.675 ± 0.006	**0.731 ± 0.022**	0.676 ± 0.006	0.686 ± 0.038	0.663 ± 0.006
	Acc	0.924 ± 0.001	**0.926 ± 0.002**	0.924 ± 0.001	0.923 ± 0.003	0.924 ± 0.002
	AP	0.321 ± 0.010	**0.374 ± 0.022**	0.321 ± 0.011	0.326 ± 0.039	0.313 ± 0.012

The best results (i.e., largest accuracy, AUC or AP values, smallest MAE or MSE scores) are emphasized in bold. This is done for illustration purposes, as the combination of a relatively small number of datasets with a relatively large number of models makes problematic the application of statistical tests. Moreover, we point out that comparisons have to be done mostly on an ad-hoc basis. By this we mean, for instance, that we do not know a priori whether or not a given sample has outliers and, hence, whether AD is going to improve on the direct application of the baseline supervised method.

In any case, a direct comparison of the means and standard deviations of different scores makes possible to extract some first conclusions. For instance, in the *Abalone* and *Housing* regression problems, the application of an AD method yields better MAE results than those of the baseline regressor. For *Abalone* MCD seems to perform best, with the one-class SVM and LOF close by; for *Housing* the best performer is the one-class SVM. On the other hand, for the other two problems (*Mg* and *Space_ga*) all the methods give similar MAE values which probably means that in these cases it is not necessary to remove any data point, as all of the points in the data sample can be taken as "normal". In fact, it turns out that the proposed supervised hyperparametrization essentially selects in all cases the minimum possible contamination value. We also point out that when test values are given in terms of the MSE, the baseline model always gives competitive results. For the *Mg* and *Space_ga* this is likely to be a consequence of the very light (if any) outlier removal that takes place; for the other two datasets it may be a consequence of using MAE as the CV scoring which results also in best test MAEs but not necessarily best MSEs.

The situation is slightly different for classification. To begin with, AD filtering results in best models for all the four datasets considered (one-class SVM for *Australian*, MCD for *IJCNN1* and LOF for both *Diabetes* and *German.numer*).

A first observation is, thus, that there is not a preferred AD model (although iForest seems to lag behind the others); a second one is that in all problems the baseline classifier gives competitive results only for accuracy and in two problems, *Diabetes* and *German.numer*. In other words, in these problems it pays to apply first an anomaly detector before building the final classifier.

5 Conclusions

A new supervised framework for optimal hyperparameter estimation of anomaly detectors has been proposed. This has been done by the combination of an anomaly detector and a supervised classifier or regressor, defining a new estimator with a pipeline structure. The advantage of this estimator is that it allows the search of the best hyperparameters for each model in an automatic and objective way, allowing also for the comparison between different techniques. In this work, we have considered four classical AD methods and experiments have been done over 8 different classification and regression datasets. Our results allow us to conclude that the supervised framework proposed can be very useful, as it lets us select the best detector in each case (notice that the AD selection is problem dependent).

Obvious lines of further work are the consideration of a larger number of datasets and the use of more recent AD methods as well as more powerful classifiers and regressors. In particular, the new deep neural network proposals for both AD and ML modeling are clear choices in this direction. Moreover, they allow for the flexible definition and easy application of non standard model losses, which suggest using these deep architectures to couple the AD and modeling components more tightly than what is possible under the pipeline approach presented here.

Acknowledgments. The authors acknowledge financial support from the European Regional Development Fund and from the Spanish Ministry of Economy, Industry, and Competitiveness - State Research Agency, project TIN2016-76406-P (AEI/FEDER, UE). They also thank the UAM–ADIC Chair for Data Science and Machine Learning and gratefully acknowledge the use of the facilities of Centro de Computación Científica (CCC) at UAM.

References

1. Beggel, L., Pfeiffer, M., Bischl, B.: Robust anomaly detection in images using adversarial autoencoders. CoRR abs/1901.06355 (2019)
2. Blázquez-García, A., Conde, A., Mori, U., Lozano, J.A.: A review on outlier/anomaly detection in time series data. arXiv e-prints arXiv:2002.04236, February 2020
3. Breunig, M.M., Kriegel, H.P., Ng, R.T., Sander, J.: LOF: identifying density-based local outliers. ACM SIGMOD Rec. **29**(2), 93–104 (2000). https://doi.org/10.1145/335191.335388

4. Carreño, A., Inza, I., Lozano, J.A.: Analyzing rare event, anomaly, novelty and outlier detection terms under the supervised classification framework. Artif. Intell. Rev., 1–20 (2019)
5. Chalapathy, R., Chawla, S.: Deep learning for anomaly detection: A survey. CoRR abs/1901.03407 (2019)
6. Chandola, V., Banerjee, A., Kumar, V.: Anomaly detection: a survey. ACM Comput. Surv. **41**(3), 15:1–15:58 (2009)
7. Dua, D., Graff, C.: UCI machine learning repository (2017). http://archive.ics.uci.edu/ml
8. Ger, S., Klabjan, D.: Autoencoders and generative adversarial networks for anomaly detection for sequences. CoRR abs/1901.02514 (2019)
9. Görnitz, N., Kloft, M., Rieck, K., Brefeld, U.: Toward supervised anomaly detection. J. Artif. Intell. Res. **46**, 235–262 (2013)
10. Hawkins, D.M.: Identification of Outliers. Springer, Netherlands (1980). https://doi.org/10.1007/978-94-015-3994-4
11. Kawachi, Y., Koizumi, Y., Harada, N.: Complementary set variational autoencoder for supervised anomaly detection. In: 2018 IEEE International Conference on Acoustics, Speech and Signal Processing, ICASSP 2018, Calgary, AB, Canada, 15–20 April 2018, pp. 2366–2370. IEEE (2018)
12. Liu, F.T., Ting, K.M., Zhou, Z.H.: Isolation forest. In: 2008 Eighth IEEE International Conference on Data Mining. IEEE (2008). https://doi.org/10.1109/icdm.2008.17
13. Liu, F.T., Ting, K.M., Zhou, Z.H.: Isolation-based anomaly detection. ACM Trans. Knowl. Discov. Data **6**(1), 1–39 (2012). https://doi.org/10.1145/2133360.2133363
14. Mattia, F.D., Galeone, P., Simoni, M.D., Ghelfi, E.: A survey on GANs for anomaly detection. CoRR abs/1906.11632 (2019)
15. Minhas, M.S., Zelek, J.S.: Semi-supervised anomaly detection using autoencoders. CoRR abs/2001.03674 (2020)
16. Oza, P., Patel, V.M.: One-class convolutional neural network. IEEE Sig. Process. Lett. **26**(2), 277–281 (2019)
17. Rousseeuw, P.J., Driessen, K.V.: A fast algorithm for the minimum covariance determinant estimator. Technometrics **41**(3), 212–223 (1999). https://doi.org/10.1080/00401706.1999.10485670
18. Schölkopf, B., Platt, J.C., Shawe-Taylor, J., Smola, A.J., Williamson, R.C.: Estimating the support of a high-dimensional distribution. Neural Comput. **13**(7), 1443–1471 (2001). https://doi.org/10.1162/089976601750264965
19. Zhao, Y., Nasrullah, Z., Li, Z.: Pyod: a python toolbox for scalable outlier detection. J. Mach. Learn. Res. (JMLR) **20**, 1–7 (2019)
20. Zhou, C., Paffenroth, R.C.: Anomaly detection with robust deep autoencoders. In: Proceedings of the 23rd ACM SIGKDD International Conference on Knowledge Discovery and Data Mining, Halifax, NS, Canada, 13–17 August 2017, pp. 665–674. ACM (2017)

Using the Variational-Quantum-Eigensolver (VQE) to Create an Intelligent Social Workers Schedule Problem Solver

Parfait Atchade Adelomou(✉), Elisabet Golobardes Ribé, and Xavier Vilasís Cardona

Research Group in Data Science for the Digital Society (DS4DS) La Salle – U. Ramon Llull, Sant Joan de la Salle, 42, 08022 Barcelona, Spain
parfait.atchade@salle.url.edu

Abstract. The scheduling problem of social workers is a class of combinatorial optimization problems that can be solved in exponential time at best. Because is belongs to class of problems known as NP-Hard, which have huge impact huge impact on our society. Nowadays, the focus on the quantum computer should no longer be just for its enormous computing capacity but also for the use of its imperfection, (Noisy Intermediate-Scale Quantum (NISQ) era) to create a powerful machine learning device that uses the variational principle to solve the optimization problem by reducing their complexity's class. We propose a formulation of the Vehicle Rooting Problem (VRP) with time windows to solve efficiently the social workers schedule problem using Variational Quantum Eigensolver (VQE). The quantum feasibility of the algorithm will be modelled with docplex and tested on IBMQ computers.

Keywords: Quantum algorithms · Variational Quantum Eigensolvers · Docplex · Combinatorial optimization algorithms

1 Introduction

The social workers problem is the problem described as, social workers who visit their patients at home as nursing home. This problem is an NP-Hard complexity class problem [1] because the tasks subject to the social workers are combinatorial optimization problems and the exact solution can drive an exponential computation time for growing scale input data.

The optimization problems are one of the problems we face daily. Optimization is an area of Applied Mathematics that allows modelling and solving real-life problems; Its principles and methods are used to solve quantitative problems in disciplines such as Physics, Biology, Engineering, Scheduling, Routing and Economics. The main objective of optimization is the best use of available resources to accomplish a certain task.

The complexity and importance of these problems involved scientist's community to research proficient methods to solve them [2]. There are two algorithms that could map very well on the social workers problem, Job Shop Scheduling Problem (JSSP) [3]

E. A. de la Cal et al. (Eds.): HAIS 2020, LNAI 12344, pp. 245–260, 2020.
https://doi.org/10.1007/978-3-030-61705-9_21

and Vehicle Routing Problem [4]. From the work of the researchers J. Christopher Beck, Patrick Prosser and Evgeny Selensky, on the comparisons of VRP [5, 6] and JSP [3, 7] we can understand the characteristics of these two techniques and especially how to use them in certain problems of scheduling or routing problem.

We decide to use the generic VRP to model our problem because of the travel time between the patients.

VRP like all the combinatorial optimization algorithms is NP-Hard. This definitely, leads us to explore new approaches for the large-scale social workers. Quantum computing [8] is called to be one of these approaches.

In this paper, after considering all this, we will propose a new formulation of the VRP to solve the social workers schedule problem posed, modelling it into docplex and mapping it properly in a Variational Quantum Eigensolver (VQE) [9]. We will insert a time variable that defines the schedule of each social worker in the proposed formulation. With this reformulation, we will be able to implement for the equivalent approach as for a Vehicle Routing Problem with Time Windows (VRPTW) [10, 11]. We will run our algorithm on ibmq_16_melbourne from IBMQ. Before that, we will use the docplex [12] to have the Hamiltonian of the Ising model [13]. Let's understand how the quantum computers work.

2 Quantum Computers

Quantum computers are the computers based on quantum mechanics techniques to perform calculations. These computations are based on the probability of an object's state on a complete inner-product space known as the Hilbert space [14]. The states represent logical operations using an electron spin. Spin-up is assigned to logic 1 and spin-down to logic 0. These discrete states allow for digital calculation [11]. Where the quantum system with two states, exploiting electron spin, it is known as a qubit [8]. The calculations, or quantum mechanical representation have the potential to process exponentially more data compared to classical computers. Because in quantum systems the discrete states can exist in multiple states simultaneously.

One of the quantum mechanics principle used in quantum computing is the superposition [8]. The superposition propriety is when a qubit can be both 0 and 1 at the same time. As observed, the Hilbert space is the space of complex vectors. Therefore, the superposition of the qubit can be comprehended like a linear combinatory of each vector of the basis. Fundamentally, when a qubit is in a superposition of states a logical operation applied to it will operate on both states simultaneously. Another principle of the quantum computing that give to quantum computing one of the major rewards is the entanglement [8]. This propriety is well-defined when the states of individual qubits are dependent on others.

The companies combine these principles to create the quantum computing [8, 15] and trying to drive us to que Quantum Supremacy [16].

3 Variational Calculation

The variational calculation [17] (or calculation of the variations) is the basis of the variational principle [18]. We can say that the variational calculation consists of looking for maximums and minimums or extensively looking for relative ends of a function of functions (functional) over a space of functions. This calculation can be seen as a generalization of the elementary calculation of maximum and minimum real functions of a variable.

Mathematically speaking, when we talk about optimization, we are talking in some way to find the maximum or minimum of the function that models our scenario; Our objective function. That is, calculate the minimum or maximum of our objective function. Although it seems easy, in many cases, the calculation of the minimum or maximum is not entirely trivial, because of the structure of the data, the size of the data or basically or for the computational cost required to make this calculation makes it non-trivial. The computational cost [19] is one of the limits of all scientific advances. For that same reason, the scientific community is working to equip itself with machines that can give it the greatest computational capacity [8].

There were also several branches that defined and designed alternatives in solving optimization problems by calculating variations. One of the most contemplated approaches is from Richard Bellman [20], who developed dynamic programming [20, 21] with clear alternatives to the calculation of variations.

The work of Sturm-Liouville [22] and Rayleigh-Ritz method [23], are the basis of the Variational Quantum Eignesolver; the VQE. A dynamic control system that allows us to make the variational calculation of a quantum state $|\psi(\theta)\rangle$ associated with its expectation value H.

4 Mapping Classical Domain to Quantum

A common method for mapping classic optimization problems to quantum hardware is by coding it into the Hamiltonian [24] of an Ising model [25].

$$H_{Ising} = \sum\nolimits_{i<j} J_{ij} S_i S_j + \sum\nolimits_i h_i S_i \tag{1}$$

Where S is Pauli [26] matrix S and $S_i = \mathbb{1}_2^{\otimes i-1} \otimes Z \otimes \mathbb{1}_2^{\otimes n-1}$, n is the total number qubits and $\mathbb{1}_2$ is 2×2 identity matrix. Due to its relative simplicity to implement experimentally, the most common physical implementation of the quantum optimization of the Ising model is the Ising cross-field model [27].

$$H_{trans} = -A \sum\nolimits_i X_i + BH_{Ising} \tag{2}$$

Where A and B are positives numbers, possibly time dependent, and constants X_i are defined similarly to S_i.

For $h = 0$ the quantum Ising model reduces to the classical model. Assuming a 2D square lattice this model has been solved exactly by Lars Onsager [28].

5 Variational Quantum Eigensolver - VQE

Unfortunately, we're still in the Noisy Intermediate-Scale Quantum (NISQ) [29] era because we don't really have yet a perfect quantum computer. To compensate for the fact that quantum isn't perfect yet, researchers started developing algorithms that work both quantum and classical parts to solve problems. This area is known as Quantum Machine Learning (QML) [30] and one of the warmest QML algorithms nowadays is the Variational Quantum Eigensolver. This is because its applications range all the way from finance, biology, scheduling and chemistry. One of the most important characteristics of molecules is its ground state energy. The ground state energy is just the lowest possible energy state that a molecule can be in. The ground state energy of a molecule is really important because it give us more information about the electron configuration of that molecule.

By varying the experimental parameters in the preparation of the state and calculating the Rayleigh-Ritz ratio [31] using the subroutine in a classical minimization, unknown eigenvectors can be prepared. At the end of the algorithm, the reconstruction of the eigenvector that is stored in the final set of experimental parameters that define the state will be done.

The variational method in quantum mechanics is used, which is a way of finding approximations to the energetic state of lower energy or fundamental state, and some excited states. This allows to calculate approximate wave functions, such as molecular orbitals and is the basis of this method. It is the variational principle that allows us to write the following equation $\langle H \rangle_{\psi(\vec{\theta})} \geq \lambda_i$. With λ_i as eigenvector and $\langle H \rangle_{\psi(\vec{\theta})}$ as the expected value. It is clear that the problem that the VQE solves is reduced to finding such an optimal choice of parameters $\vec{\theta}$, that the expected value is minimized and that a lower eigenvalue is found.

$$\langle H \rangle = \langle \psi(\theta) | H | \psi(\theta) \rangle \tag{3}$$

6 Noisy VQE for Optimization Problem

In Quantum computing we can classify the algorithms in 3 groups. Gate circuits [32], Annealing [3] and Variational [9, 16, 17].

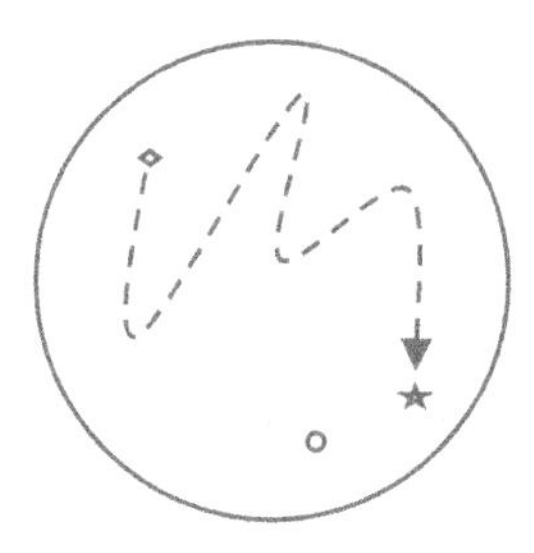

Fig. 1. Minimization principle used in Variational Quantum eigensolvers to empower the Quantum Machine Learning.

Although the logic gates are not perfect and have noise but by having the variational principle, we can see in NISQ devices a golden opportunity to have a machine that analyzes on the Hilbert's vector space.

The term "Noisy Intermediate Scale Quantum" describes the era in which we find ourselves today. Noisy, because the computer still does not offer enough qubits to save for error correction, and so we have imperfect qubits at the physical layer, last but not at least "intermediate scale" because of their small number of qubits.

This leads us to forget about the imperfections of the gates and only think of the variational ansatz [9] and that, this ansatz can be analyzed efficiently on a quantum computer. Something we can't really do with a classic computer. The Fig. 1 summarizes the idea. In short, we can say that we have a quantum computer that generates variational states, known as a Variational Quantum Computer [9]. Another way to see it could be, in each of the iterations, we have a quantum circuit that is close to the solution we would be looking for. This is the basis of Quantum learning [30]. We are basically doing machine learning (ML) on circuit design.

With this vision, what we are developing is a perfect machine to solve the optimization and classification problems by exploring the entire configuration space of quantum molecules.

As commented, the Variational Quantum Eigensolvers are useful because they find the lowest possible eigenvalue of a given Hermitian matrix H (it doesn't matter the size of H) using the variational method or the variational principle. It's also known that the expected value most always be equal or greater than the lowest possible eigenvalue. This means that if we just keep minimizing that expectation value, we only get closer and closer to the minimum eigenvalue of the given H matrix and never below it [9]. With this powerful concept, the great clue is to know how to map our objective function into a Hamiltonian model of a given molecular system. To do that, first, we map the molecular Hamiltonian into a qubit. This essentially means that we are mapping the electron orbital interactions inside the molecules onto our qubits. Next, we prepare the set. Our set to be shallow, have to cover a good enough range for our trial wave functions and so since we don't face what our ground state energy is. With the information given by a specific Hamiltonian, now, we calculate the energy of that electron configuration.

In this point, the algorithm measures those values and send it through to the classical optimizer. The classical optimizer minimizes our parameters, so gets a lower expectation value H. After that, we feed all these values back into the quantum part and reiterate it with this loop a bunch of times until it converges onto the lowest possible energy state for that inter atomic distance to following all the described steps. All this is achieved regardless of the noise or imperfection of the logic gates.

7 Docplex

To map a classical model to quantum computing we need to find the Hamiltonian of the Ising model. Nevertheless, the Hamiltonians of the Ising model are highly complicated and clearly no intuitive [24, 25]. So, mapping an optimization combinatorial problem to the Hamiltonian of the Ising model can be a very challenging, laborious, and may require specialized knowledge as the vectorization of the matrices with the Kronecker product [33] to express matrix multiplication as a linear transformation in matrices [34]. This tool developed by IBM has some limitation and don't allow inequality constraints.

Table 1. Schedule of patient visits without any association with social workers. Where U_1 to U_2 are the patients (users) and equal to the variable i or j of the mathematical formulation.

	M	T	W	TH	F
9:00–10:00	U_1	U_1	U_1	U_1	U_1
9:30–10:30	U_4				
10:15–11:15			U_4		
11:30–12:30					$U_5 U_4$
11:45–12:45	U_5				
12:00–13:00	U_2				
14:45–15:45		U_2			
15:00–16:00				U_3	
15:15–16:15	U_3				
15:45–16:45			U_3		
16:00–17:00			U_2		
16:30–17:30		U_3			
17:00–18:00					U_3

With the translator, all kind of users can write a quantum optimization algorithm model using docplex. With this tool, a lot of things become much easier compared to writing manually the Hamiltonian of the Ising model. Basically, because the model is short and intuitive.

8 Proposed Problem

Let n be the number of patients (users) and considering a weekly calendar of visits for each of them, our objective is to find an optimal meeting's calendar which minimize the cost of time travel hence, money and maximize number of visits to the patients in a work schedule. And if there are changes from the social workers or they hire or fire new workers or any change in patients, the system must adapt dynamically (see Fig. 2). At the end, we assign social workers to the group with the resultant optimal hours.

In our case study, the daily schedule (see Table 1), is set at 7 h and the distance between patients is at least 15 min.

Taking into account the advances on the speedup of the Quantum Approximate Optimization Algorithm (QAOA) [35–37] in the NISQ era, we can affirm that the experiment's scenario and it design are representatives because the only difficulty that can be added here, for this combinatorial optimization problem, is the number of patients and some restrictions. These difficulties have to do directly with the computational cost (not with the formulation/algorithm) where quantum computing is called to be more efficient [38]. Hoping to have access to a more powerful computer, we limited our test to a 20 qubits computer; the most powerful public quantum computer.

In this article we have chosen $n = 5$ (20 qubits) because the experiments from the problem of this class are among the most difficult in our test bench. We will review it in the discussion chapter.

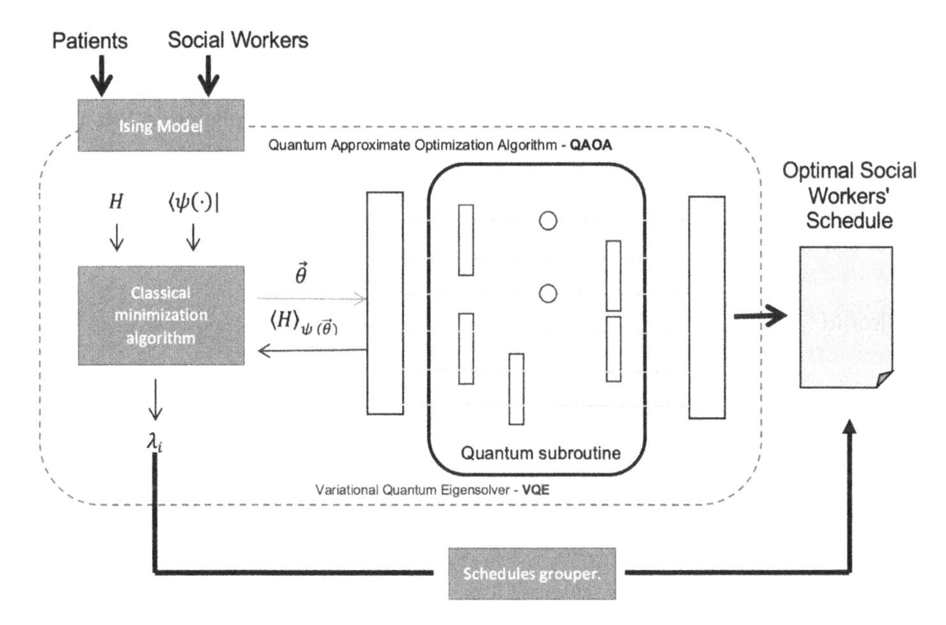

Fig. 2. Using the Variational-Quantum-Eigensolver (VQE) as Quantum Machine Learning to creates an Intelligent social workers schedule problem solver.

9 Our Approach to Solve the Problem

Our approach is to use a hybrid algorithm to solve the problem both in the planning part and in the routing part.

What our classical part does, is order all patients with visiting hours that do not overlap and order them ascending order by time t_{ij} (time between vertex i and j from lowest to highest). We use the Quantum Machine Learning as is show in the Fig. 2 to be applied on the vector of the decision variables of our Ising Hamiltonian. Then we execute the optimization subroutine using a feedback loop as is shown in Fig. 2 on a NISQ that uses variational method by taking in account a sample functions built with Y single-qubit rotations, $U_{single}(\theta) = \prod_{i=1}^{n} Y(\theta_i)$, and entangler steps $U_{\text{entangler}}$. By reformulating the weight function with time windows (by this way we can avoid the inequalities restrictions), we can use the docplex tool to model our algorithm. Let remember that this actual docplex model works with binary decision variables, linear and quadratic terms in objective functions and with only equality constraints.

10 VRP Formulation

We use the generic formulation of the vehicle routing problem to model the core of our algorithm. We also use a complete graph as a structure of our formulation. So Let $G = (V, E, c)$ be a complete graph directed with $V = \{0, 1, 2, \ldots, n\}$, as the set of nodes and $E = \{(i,j) : i,j \in V, i \neq j\}$ as the set of arcs, where node 0 represents the central. For a team of k social workers with the same capacity ρ and n remaining nodes that represent geographically dispersed patients.

Let W_{ij} be the growing travel cost that is associated with each arc $(i,j) \in E$. Let's consider that the W_{ij} distances are symmetrical to simplify the calculation and let x_{ij} be the decision variables of the paths between two consecutive patients.

Our goal is to minimize the following objective function:

$$\sum\nolimits_{k=1}^{m} \sum\nolimits_{i=1}^{l} \sum\nolimits_{j=1, i \neq j}^{n} W_{ij} x_{ijk}, \tag{4}$$

Subject to:

$$\sum\nolimits_{k=1}^{m} \sum\nolimits_{j=1}^{n} x_{ijk} = 1, \quad \forall i \in \{1, \ldots, n\} \tag{5}$$

$$\sum\nolimits_{k=1}^{m} \sum\nolimits_{i=1}^{n} x_{jik} = 1, \quad \forall j \in \{1, \ldots, n\} \tag{6}$$

$$\sum\nolimits_{i=1}^{l} di \sum\nolimits_{j=1}^{n} x_{ijk} \leq q, \quad \forall k \in \{1, \ldots, m\} \tag{7}$$

$$\sum\nolimits_{j=1}^{n} x_{0jk} = K, \quad \forall k \in \{1, \ldots, m\} \tag{8}$$

$$\sum\nolimits_{j=1}^{n} x_{j0k} = K, \quad \forall k \in \{1, \ldots, m\} \tag{9}$$

$$\sum\nolimits_{i=1}^{n} x_{ihk} - \sum\nolimits_{j}^{n} x_{hjk} = 0 \quad \forall h \in \{1, \ldots, n\}, \; and \; \forall k \in \{1, \ldots, m\} \tag{10}$$

$$x_{ijk} \in \{0, 1\}, \forall i,j \in \{0, \ldots, n\}, \; i \neq j \forall k \in \{1, \ldots, m\} \in \{1, \ldots, m\} \tag{11}$$

The objective function (4) minimizes the total travel savings in view of the new cost function with the time window we formulate. The restrictions of Eq. (5) impose that exactly the arcs k leave the plant; (8) and (9) are the restrictions on the degree of entry and exit of the social worker from the main workplace. With the restrictions (10) we ensure that the solution does not contain a sub-route and the last restrictions (11) are obligatory and define the type of linear programming.

Up to this point, the mathematical formulation of Eqs. (4) to (11) represents a conventional VRP. To solve the social workers problem as a scheduling problem, we may need a time variable. This is so important to finish mapping our cited problem. Then we use the Quantum Machine Learning (See Fig. 3) to run the solution.

11 Our Proposed Formulation

Our VRP formulation proposal incorporates the schedule of Table 1. With this new formulation we will describe the temporal evolution of each social worker equivalent to the Vehicle Routing Problem with Time Window (VRPTW) [10, 11, 14] and model it with the docplex. Our proposal is expressed by Eqs. 12 and 13.

$$W_{ij} = d_{ij} + g(t_{ij}) \tag{12}$$

$$g(t_{ij}) = \varepsilon \frac{(\tau_{i-}\tau_j)^2}{d_{max} - d_{min}} \tag{13}$$

Where W_{ij} is our weight time window function, d_{ij} is the distance between the patient i and the next j and g_{ij} is our time window's function. With g_{ij} as non-negative function that we map on a quadratic function to weigh extremal distances (shortest in relation to greatest ones). Let's Consider that the initial weight function $W_{ij} = d_{ij}$ is a distance function because we want to make g_{ij} behave like d_{ij}, and thus, be able to take full advantage of the behaviour of the initial objective function.

Let ε be positive and represents a weighted degree parameter of the time window function; τ_i is the starting worker time of a slot of time for patient i and τ_j for the patient j. With d_{max} as the maximum distance between all patients and d_{min} the minimum one. Hence, let's define our non-negative time windows $T_{ij} = (\tau_{i-}\tau_j) > 0$.

The simplified objective function subjected to the restrictions in Hamiltonian form for the schedule optimization problem is as follows:

$$\begin{aligned} H = & \sum\nolimits_{ij \in E} \left(d_{ij} + \varepsilon \frac{(\tau_{i-}\tau_j)^2}{d_{max} - d_{min}} \right) x_{i,j} + A \sum\nolimits_{i=1}^{n} (1 - \sum\nolimits_{j \in \delta(i)^+}^{N} x_{i,j})^2 + A \sum\nolimits_{i=1}^{n} (1 - \sum\nolimits_{j \in \delta(i)^-}^{N} x_{ji})^2 \\ & + A(k - \sum\nolimits_{i \in \delta(0)^+}^{N} x_{0,i})^2 + A(k - \sum\nolimits_{j \in \delta(0)^+}^{N} x_{j,0})^2 \end{aligned} \tag{14}$$

Now we apply the docplex or we find the related Ising model for the Hamiltonian Eq. (14). As we said it above, this task requires specialized knowledge on vectorization of matrix into vector using Kronecker product to express multiplication as linear transformation in matrices. In this article, we use the docplex to have the compact Ising Hamiltonian ready to compute on NISQ.

The result can have the following mathematical form:

$$\begin{aligned} H = & A \sum\nolimits_{i=1}^{n} \left[(e_i \otimes \mathbb{I}_n)^2 Z^2 + [v_i^T]^2 Z^2 \right] + w - 2A \sum\nolimits_{i=1}^{n} \left[(e_i \otimes \mathbb{I}_n^T) + v_i^T \right] \\ & - 2Ak\left[(e_0 \otimes 1_n)^T + v_0^T \right] + 2An + 2Ak^2 \end{aligned} \tag{15}$$

With

$$W_{ij} = d_{ij} + \varepsilon \frac{(\tau_{i-}\tau_j)^2}{d_{max} - d_{min}} \tag{16}$$

12 Results - Experimentation

We test our algorithm mapped on VQE and QAOA on the *ibmq_16_melbourne v1.0.0* with COBYLA as the classical optimizer. We can consider QAOA as a special case of VQE. This is one of the reasons we can apply directly the Hamiltonian of the Ising model of our proposed formulation to QAOA almost without modify. The Fig. 3, 4, 5 and 6 show the results of our algorithm once we executed our algorithm under the IBMQ. The final part of the algorithm regroups each optimal visit taking into account the hours of visits to form the optimal schedule shown in Table 2. We have made several experiments with the QML defining different scenes by using shot configuration [39]. With our quantum machine we can configure the number of repetitions of each circuit for sampling we need. With that, we will be basically doing machine learning on circuit design for each shot. And when the loop ends, we will get to the ground state energy. As a consequence, we solved our problem by creating one quantum circuit for each shot and the best circuit will be the one that optimizes our social workers problem.

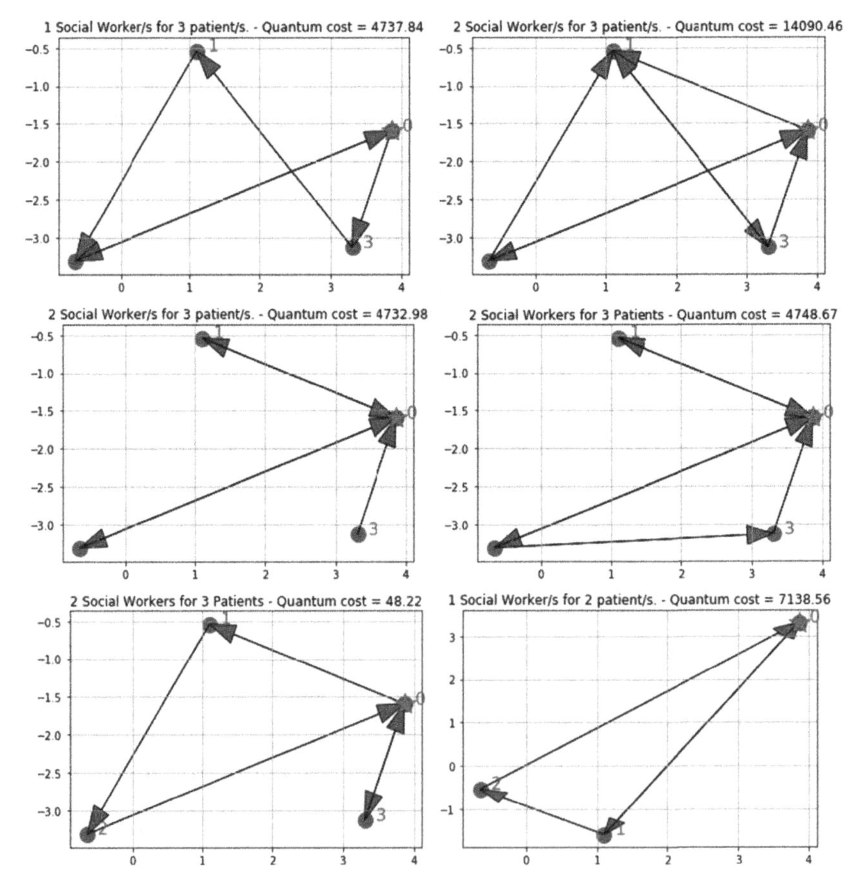

Fig. 3. Results of the experimentations. Changing the number of patients, social worker, shot configuration with the aim of analyzing the quantum cost to meet the optimal solution.

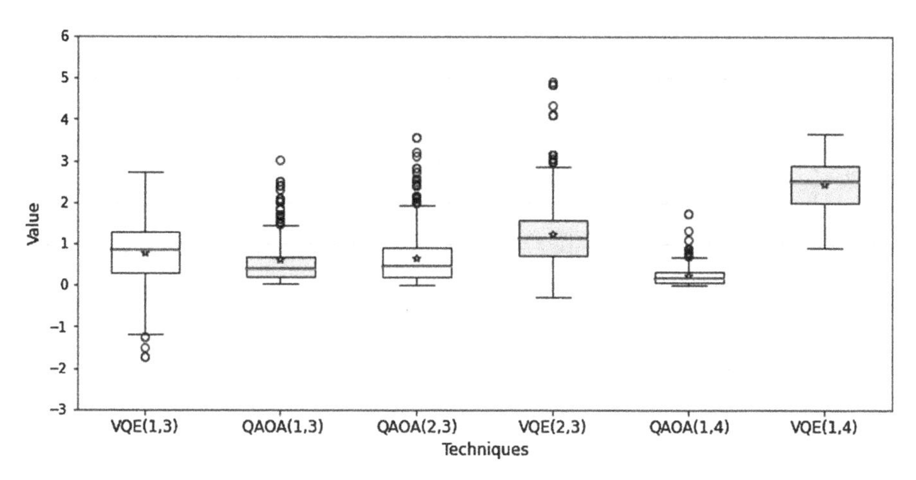

Fig. 4. Results of the experimentations by comparing six scenarios of the combinations of Social Workers Problem on VQE and QAOA. By changing the number of patients, social worker, shot configuration with the aim of analyzing the quantum cost to meet the optimal solution. We realize that the QAOA with the same settings as VQE, finds the optimal solution with little sample. It is true that we must consider high values of the seed parameter.

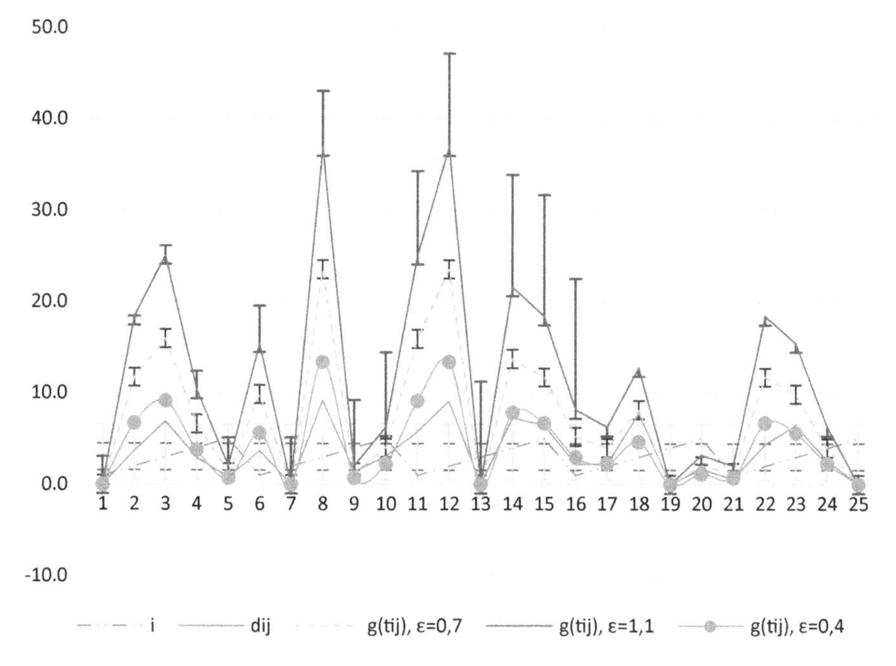

Fig. 5. Comparison of performance with standard deviation error bar on the three mappings of our proposed formulation (12, 13). The Standard Deviation expected total anneal time for 98% percent success for each mapping value, with the best ε for each shoot are shown. Our optimal case is for ε = 0,7. Our most representative cases are for ε = 0,4, ε = 0,7 and ε = 1,1.

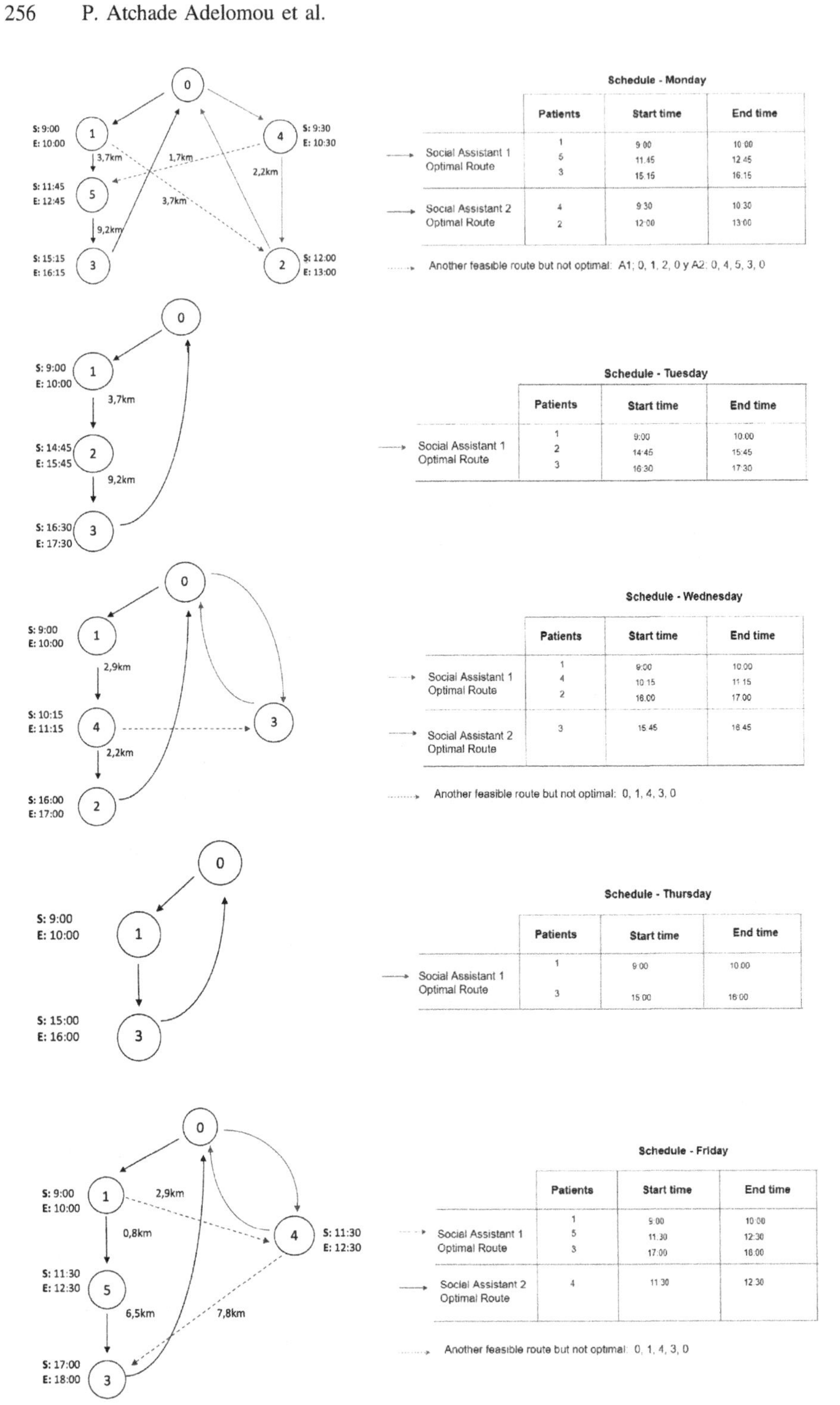

Fig. 6. Result of process of the calculations of the social workers' schedule.

Table 2. The Optimal social workers' schedules. A_1 and A_2 are the social workers.

	M	T	W	TH	F
9:00–10:00	A_1	A_1	A_1	A_1	A_1
9:30–10:30	A_2				
10:15–11:15			A_1		
11:30–12:30					A_2A_1
11:45–12:45	A_1				
12:00–13:00	A_2				
14:45–15:45		A_1			
15:00–16:00				A_1	
15:15–16:15	A_1				
15:45–16:45			A_2		
16:00–17:00			A_1		
16:30–17:30		A_1			
17:00–18:00					A_1

13 Discussion

The VQE works very well and empowers QML era. For what we expected, the VQE has solved it by far. With the help of the IBMQ Aqua[1] program environment (qiskit[2]), we were able to test our algorithm. Too bad, that we do not have access to a quantum computer with more qubits. Since in our case for $n = 5$, the number of qubits necessary is $n(n-1) = 20 qubits$. We have not been able to do many more tests for values of n greater than 5, since the computer on which we test our algorithm takes too long.

The VQE together with the docplex can help both the domain of programming in quantum computing where we require a high computing capacity but also to be able to empower intelligent solutions as the objective of this article: Using the Variational-Quantum-Eigensolver (VQE) to create an Intelligent social workers schedule problem solver.

The evaluation of the algorithm on an *ibmq_16_melbourne v1.0.0* from IBM was fulfilled. With any change in the input variables are mapped proportionally to our cost variable with time window.

With this work we are trying to offer to cities with an instrument [40] which could optimize the costs allied to the management of social workers and improve social gains. This work could also be a starting point for many countries in Africa that are seizing the opportunity of the mobile technology revolution [41] to develop and increase their industrious and e-health system [42, 43].

We would like to add, that the suggested formulation (12, 13) is not only specific to the proposed problem. It can be used to solve any family planning, scheduling and routing problem related to a list of tasks, restrictions, allocation of resources on location

[1] www.qiskit.org/aqua.

[2] www.qiskit.org.

and time. The test performed and showed in the Fig. 5 allows us to see the behaviour of our formulation with the variation of the correction factor ε. We see how our time window $T_{ij} = (\tau_{i-}\tau_j)$ adapts perfectly at the extremes to the cost variable in distance. This achievement is due to the chosen quadratic function (13). We want it to be adapted in this way so that our resultant function (12) weights together the short distances and time as well as the long distances and late times.

Other functions can be studied in order to have a test bench with which to compare the final results.

QAOA, like VQE, takes a qubit operator from the Hamiltonian of the Ising model. The only mapping that gets done is when QAOA builds a variational form based off the qubit operator and what we figured was that does not change the original qubit operator input. The Fig. 4 reveals the comparation work between VQE and QAOA algorithms for the same configuration parameters. After several tests we realized that with the QAOA instead of the VQE, our algorithm takes less execution time and requires fewer samples for the optimal solution. But in many cases, we have to increase the seed value, to get a fairly stable result.

14 Conclusion and Further Works

The summarized path grouped for the first patient (U_1) is 15 h 29 min a week. This value fit in the social worker contract's restrictions, so we can assign it to any social worker with the suitable contract.

The paths formed by the remaining visits total 4 h 7 min. Here also this value is less than the social worker contract's restrictions, so we can assign it to any social worker with the suitable contract.

With the $n = 5$ (20 qubits), we obtain 2 social workers with optimal schedules assigned to their weekly timetable.

While waiting for the enhanced version of the docplex, from IBM, expecting more flexibility and to be able to model almost all scheduling problems into quantum, an interesting future work would be to implement the VRPTW and compare it with our contribution.

Another future work that we set ourselves is to analyze very well the loop of the QML on the changes generated in the social workers and in the patients and evaluate how to create strongest quantum adaptative algorithms. With this last point we can have a system that could adapt intelligently to any change and has the computational capacity to empower any technique.

Acknowledgements. The authors greatly thank the IBMQ team, mainly Steve Wood. PA thanks Jennifer Ramírez Molino for her support and comments on the manuscript.

References

1. Bovet, D., Crescenzi, P.: Introduction to the Theory of Complexity, p. 69, xi, 282. Prentice-Hall, New York (1994). ISBN 0-13-915380-2
2. Brucker, P.: On the complexity of clustering problems. In: Henn, R., Korte, B., Oettli, W. (eds.) Optimization and Operations Research. LNE, vol. 157, pp. 45–54. Springer, Heidelberg (1978). https://doi.org/10.1007/978-3-642-95322-4_5
3. Bożejko, W., Pempera, J., Smutnicki, C.: Parallel simulated annealing for the Job Shop Scheduling problem. In: Biological Cybernetics: International Conference on Computational, vol. 60, pp. 139–144 (2009)
4. Laporte, G.: The vehicle routing problem: an overview of exact and approximate algorithm. Eur. J. Oper. Res. **59**, 345–358 (1992)
5. Clarke, G., Wright, J.W.: Scheduling of vehicles from a central depot to a number of delivery points. Oper. Res. **12**, 568–581 (1964)
6. Toth, P., Vigo, D.: The Vehicle Routing Problem: SIAM Monographs on Discrete Mathematics and Applications. SIAM (2002)
7. Solomon, M.M.: Algorithms for the vehicle routing and scheduling problems with time window constraints. Oper. Res. **35**, 254–265 (1987)
8. de Wolf, R.: QuSoft, CWI and University of Amsterdam: Lecture Notes. Quantum Computing https://arxiv.org/abs/1907.09415 (2019)
9. Wang, D., Higgott, O., Brierley, S.: Accelerated variational quantum eigensolver. Phys. Rev. Lett. **122**, 140504 (2019)
10. Desaulniers, G., Lessard, F., Hadjar, A.: Tabu search, partial elementarity, and generalized k-path inequalities for the vehicle rerouting problem with time windows. Transp. Sci. **42**, 387–404 (2008)
11. Rousseau, L.-M., Gendreau, M., Pesant, G.: Solving VRPTWs with constraint programming-based column generation. Ann. Oper. Res. **130**, 199–216 (2004)
12. Docplex. https://cdn.rawgit.com/IBMDecisionOptimization/docplex-doc/master/docs/index.html. Access 16 Mar 2020
13. Hamer, C.J., Barber, M.N.: Finite-lattice methods in quantum Hamiltonian field theory. I. The Ising model. J. Phys. A Math. Gen. **14**, 241 (1981)
14. Schuld, M., Killoran, N.: Probability distributions and hilbert spaces: quantum and classical systems. Phys. Rev. Lett. **60**, 111 (2019)
15. Parra-Rodriguez, A., Lougovski, P., Lamata, L., Solano, E., Sanz, M.: Digital-Analog Quantum Computation (2018)
16. Arute, F., et al.: Quantum supremacy using a programmable superconducting processor. Nature **574**, 505–510 (2019)
17. Roubíček, T.: Relaxation in optimization theory and variational calculus (2011)
18. Ekeland, I.: On the variational principle. J. Math. Anal. Appl. **47**, 324–353 (1974)
19. Killick, R., Fearnhead, P., Eckley, I.A.: Optimal detection of changepoints with a linear computational cost. J. Am. Stat. Assoc. **170**, 1590–1598 (2012)
20. Dreyfus, S.: Richard Bellman on the birth of dynamic programming. Oper. Res. **50**, 48–51 (2002)
21. Bhowmik, B.: Dynamic programming. Its principles, applications, strengths, and limitations. Criterion **4**, 7 (2010)
22. Agarwal, R.P., Bohner, M., Wong, P.J.Y.: Sturm-Liouville eigenvalue problems on time scales. Appl. Math. Comput. **99**, 153–166 (1999)
23. Bhat, R.B.: Natural frequencies of rectangular plates using characteristic orthogonal polynomials in Rayleigh-Ritz method. J. Sound Vibr. **102**, 493–499 (1985)

24. Eisberg, R.: Quantum Physics of Atoms, Molecules, Solids, Nuclei, and Particles (1985)
25. Lucas, A.: Ising formulations of many NP problems. Front. Phys. **2**, 1–5 (2014). https://doi.org/10.3389/fphy.2014.00005
26. Alonso Mendoza Suárez, L.J., Gonzalez Sierra, H., Segovia-Chaves, F.: Explicit derivation of the Pauli spin matrices from the Jones vector (2019)
27. Varizi1, A.D., Drumond, R.C.: Quantum Ising model in a period-2 modulated transverse field. https://arxiv.org/abs/1903.09468 (2019)
28. Cipra, B.A.: The Ising model is NP-complete. SIAM News **33**, 1–3 (2000)
29. Preskill, J.: Quantum computing in the NISQ era and beyond. Quantum **2**, 79 (2018)
30. Biamonte, J., Wittek, P., Pancotti, N., Rebentrost, P.: Quantum machine learning. Nature **549**, 195–202 (2017)
31. Wu, C.W.: On Rayleigh-Ritz ratios of a generalized Laplacian matrix of directed graphs. Linear Algebra Appl. **402**, 207–227 (2005)
32. Raychev, N.: Quantum circuit for spatial optimization. Int. J. Sci. Eng. **6**, 1365–1368 (2015)
33. Steeb, W.-H., Hardy, Y.: Matrix Calculus and Kronecker Product: A Practical Approach to Linear and Multilinear Algebra (2019)
34. Macedo, H.D., Oliveira, J.N.: Typing Linear Algebra: A Biproduct-Oriented Approach. https://doi.org/10.1016/j.scico.2012.07.012. Accessed 16 Mar 2020
35. Farhi, E., Harrow, A.W.: Quantum supremacy through the quantum approximate optimization algorithm (2016)
36. Guerreschi, G.G., Matsuura, A.Y.: Scientific reports QAOA for Max-Cut requires hundreds of qubits for quantum speed-up (2019)
37. Moylett, D.J., Linden, N., Montanaro, A.: Quantum speedup of the Travelling Salesman Problem for bounded-degree graphs (2016)
38. Preskill, J.: Quantum Computing in the NISQ era and beyond. https://doi.org/10.22331/q-2018-08-06-79. Accessed 16 Mar 2020
39. ADA. https://qiskit.org/documentation/api/qiskit.aqua.QuantumInstance.html. Accessed 16 Mar 2020
40. Wang, X., Truong, V.A., Bank, D.: Online Advance Admission Scheduling for Services with Customer Preferences. Technical report, Columbia University, New York, NY (2018)
41. Stephani, V.: Effective and needed, but not used: why do mobile phone-based health interventions in Africa not move beyond the project status? (2019)
42. Sodhro, A.H., Pirbhulal, S., Sangaiah, A.K.: Convergence of IoT and product lifecycle management in medical health care. Future Gener. Comput. Syst. **86**, 380–391 (2018)
43. Al Isma'ili, S., Li, M., Shen, J., He, Q., Alghazi, A.: African Societal Challenges Transformation through IoT (2017)

Fully Fuzzy Multi-objective Berth Allocation Problem

Boris Pérez-Cañedo[1(✉)], José Luis Verdegay[2], Alejandro Rosete[3], and Eduardo René Concepción-Morales[1]

[1] University of Cienfuegos, 55100 Cienfuegos, Cuba
bpcanedo@gmail.com, econcepm@gmail.com
[2] University of Granada, Granada, Spain
verdegay@ugr.es
[3] Technological University of Havana, Havana, Cuba
rosete@ceis.cujae.edu.cu

Abstract. The Berth Allocation (BA) problem is an important problem in port logistics. It aims at finding optimal berthing times and positions of arriving vessels in a wharf subject to physical constraints. The optimisation criteria in the BA problem are diverse and respond to specific interests of vessels and wharves operators. Furthermore, although the BA problem has been dealt with mostly under complete certainty, it is a highly uncertain problem due to many factors that can affect vessels arrival and handling times. This paper takes fuzzy uncertainty into account and presents a fully fuzzy two-objective BA problem, by considering the minimisation of the total waiting time of vessels and the makespan of the wharf operation from the perspectives of vessels and wharves operators, respectively. A fuzzy epsilon-constraint method and a lexicographic method for fully fuzzy linear programming with inequality constraints are used jointly to solve the problem. A numerical example is given as illustration. Results demonstrate the usefulness of the proposed approach in handling fuzziness and conflicting objectives simultaneously in a BA problem.

Keywords: Fully fuzzy berth allocation problem · Fully fuzzy multi-objective linear programming · Epsilon-constraint method · Fuzzy inequality constraint · Lexicographic ranking criteria

1 Introduction

The Berth Allocation (BA) problem is an important seaside problem in port logistics. It involves the determination of berthing times and positions of arriving vessels in a wharf [15]. The BA problem is mostly dealt with under the assumption of complete certainty about the problem parameter values; see, e.g. [3,14]. However, exact arrival times of vessels and their handling times may not be known precisely, since they depend on several uncontrollable factors such as weather conditions, operators' decisions, labour availability at the wharf side,

E. A. de la Cal et al. (Eds.): HAIS 2020, LNAI 12344, pp. 261–272, 2020.
https://doi.org/10.1007/978-3-030-61705-9_22

and so forth. Thus, it is common that such values are affected by subjective evaluations. Fuzzy Sets Theory, introduced by Zadeh [22] in 1965, has succeeded in numerous practical situations in which there is uncertainty due to the absence of complete and precise information. The application of Fuzzy Sets Theory in decision-making occurred almost as early as its own introduction [1].

A fuzzy discrete BA problem was analysed by Expósito-Izquierdo et al. [5]. The authors used a fuzzy number linear ranking function and the Variable Neighbourhood Search metaheuristic to solve the problem. Fully fuzzy models for the BA problem were recently investigated by Gutierrez et al. [9,10]. However, to the best of our knowledge, the research done so far has not considered fuzzy BA problems with multiple objectives. By taking into consideration multiple objectives in fuzzy BA problems, the models gain expressiveness and are better fitted to real decision-making situations faced by wharves operators.

In this paper, we formulate and solve a Fully Fuzzy Multi-Objective Berth Allocation (FFMOBA) problem with two objective functions. From vessels operators' perspective, it is important to minimise the waiting time so that vessels get serviced in the shortest possible time and thus continue to the next wharf. Wharves operators, on the other hand, wish to achieve full use of their resources at all times; therefore, the makespan of the whole operation should be minimised. The makespan of the wharf operation is defined as the amount of time between the first vessel that berths and the last vessel that leaves the wharf.

Uncertainty in the data will be modelled with triangular fuzzy numbers (TFNs) for their simplicity and ease of interpretation. In this sense, Sect. 2 presents some fundamental definitions regarding TFNs and the lexicographic method for solving fully fuzzy linear programming (FFLP) problems proposed in [18]. In Sect. 3, we formulate the FFMOBA problem, and propose a scalarisation approach based on the fuzzy epsilon-constraint method recently presented in [19]. Section 4 discusses a numerical example. Lastly, Sect. 5 presents the conclusions and possible future research lines.

2 Preliminaries

A fuzzy set $\tilde{A}$ in a space of points X, with elements denoted generically by x, is characterised by a membership function $\mu_{\tilde{A}} : X \to [0,1]$, with the value of $\mu_{\tilde{A}}(x)$ at x representing the grade of membership of x in $\tilde{A}$ [22]. The fuzzy set $\tilde{A}$ is convex if and only if $\mu_{\tilde{A}}(\lambda x_1 + (1-\lambda)x_2) \geq \min(\mu_{\tilde{A}}(x_1), \mu_{\tilde{A}}(x_2))$ for all $x_1, x_2 \in X$ and $\lambda \in [0,1]$. $\tilde{A}$ is normal if $\sup\limits_{x \in X}(\mu_{\tilde{A}}(x)) = 1$, where sup = supremum. The core of $\tilde{A}$ is the crisp set $C(\tilde{A}) = \{x \in X | \mu_{\tilde{A}}(x) = 1\}$. A fuzzy number is a convex normalised fuzzy set of the real line with a singleton core, whose membership function is at least piecewise continuous [11].

The following well-known definitions can be found in many papers and textbooks on Fuzzy Sets Theory and its applications; see, e.g. [2].

Definition 1. *A fuzzy number $\tilde{a} = (\underline{a}, a, \overline{a})$ is said to be a TFN if its membership function is given by:*

$$\mu_{\tilde{a}}(x) = \begin{cases} \frac{x-\underline{a}}{a-\underline{a}}, & \text{if } \underline{a} \le x \le a \\ \frac{\overline{a}-x}{\overline{a}-a}, & \text{if } a \le x \le \overline{a} \\ 0, & \text{otherwise} \end{cases}$$

Definition 2. *Let $\tilde{a} = (\underline{a}, a, \overline{a})$ and $\tilde{b} = (\underline{b}, b, \overline{b})$ be any TFNs, then $\tilde{a} = \tilde{b}$ if and only if $\underline{a} = \underline{b}$, $a = b$ and $\overline{a} = \overline{b}$.*

Definition 3. *For any two TFNs $\tilde{a} = (\underline{a}, a, \overline{a})$ and $\tilde{b} = (\underline{b}, b, \overline{b})$, fuzzy addition $\oplus$, subtraction $\ominus$ and multiplication by a scalar $\times$ are given respectively as: $\tilde{a} \oplus \tilde{b} = (\underline{a} + \underline{b}, a + b, \overline{a} + \overline{b})$, $\tilde{a} \ominus \tilde{b} = (\underline{a} - \overline{b}, a - b, \overline{a} - \underline{b})$ and $\lambda \times \tilde{a} = (\lambda\underline{a}, \lambda a, \lambda\overline{a})$ if $\lambda \ge 0$, $(\lambda\overline{a}, \lambda a, \lambda\underline{a})$ otherwise.*

The multiplication $\otimes$ of two TFNs is not explicitly used in this paper; the interested reader may refer to [2].

Definition 4 (Partial order relation). *Given two TFNs $\tilde{a} = (\underline{a}, a, \overline{a})$ and $\tilde{b} = (\underline{b}, b, \overline{b})$, then:*

1. *$\tilde{a} <_p \tilde{b}$ if and only if $\underline{a} < \underline{b}$, $a < b$ and $\overline{a} < \overline{b}$;*
2. *$\tilde{a} \le_p \tilde{b}$ if and only if $\underline{a} \le \underline{b}$, $a \le b$ and $\overline{a} \le \overline{b}$.*

2.1 FFLP Problem and Lexicographic Solution Method

Several researchers have noticed that most existing ranking methodologies cannot yield a complete order of fuzzy numbers. Lexicographic ranking criteria have been proposed in [6,20,21] to resolve this issue. The solution of FFLP problems by using lexicographic ranking criteria have been widely investigated; see, e.g. [4,12,13] and more recently [18,19]. In what follows, we present the lexicographic method [18] for solving FFLP problems with inequality constraints. We begin with the idea of a lexicographic order relation on the set of all TFNs.

Definition 5. *For an arbitrary TFN $\tilde{a} = (\underline{a}, a, \overline{a})$, let $f_k(\tilde{a}) := w_{k1}\underline{a} + w_{k2}a + w_{k3}\overline{a}$ for $k = 1, 2, 3$ be three linear functions of the parameters of $\tilde{a}$ with each w_{kr} chosen such that matrix $[w_{kr}]$ is non-singular. Furthermore, let $\le_{lex}$ denote the lexicographic order relation on $\Re^3$. Given any two TFNs $\tilde{a}$ and $\tilde{b}$, the strict inequality $\tilde{a} \prec \tilde{b}$ holds if and only if $\left(f_k(\tilde{a})\right)_{k=1}^3 <_{lex} \left(f_k(\tilde{b})\right)_{k=1}^3$. The weak inequality $\tilde{a} \preccurlyeq \tilde{b}$ holds if and only if $\left(f_k(\tilde{a})\right)_{k=1}^3 <_{lex} \left(f_k(\tilde{b})\right)_{k=1}^3$ or $\left(f_k(\tilde{a})\right)_{k=1}^3 = \left(f_k(\tilde{b})\right)_{k=1}^3$.*

The lexicographic order relation $\preccurlyeq$ satisfies the total order properties [7]; that is, $\preccurlyeq$ is reflexive, transitive, anti-symmetric and complete. It seems reasonable that after the selection of each $f_k(\cdot)$, the resulting order relation also satisfies the following property.

(I) For arbitrary TFNs $\tilde{a}$ and $\tilde{b}$, if $\tilde{a} \leq_p \tilde{b}$, then $\tilde{a} \preccurlyeq \tilde{b}$.

Hereafter, we shall consider only particular cases of $\preccurlyeq$ that satisfy (I). Thus, with the above considerations, the FFLP problem can be formulated as in Eq. (1), where $\tilde{c}_j$, $\tilde{a}_{ij}$ and $\tilde{b}_i$ are TFNs and $\tilde{x}_j$ denote the triangular fuzzy decision variables.

$$\begin{aligned} &\min \sum_{j=1}^{n} \tilde{c}_j \otimes \tilde{x}_j \\ &\text{s.t.} \sum_{j=1}^{n} \tilde{a}_{ij} \otimes \tilde{x}_j \{\preccurlyeq, =, \succcurlyeq\} \tilde{b}_i;\ i = 1, 2, \ldots, m \\ &\quad \tilde{x}_j \geq 0;\ j = 1, 2, \ldots, n \end{aligned} \tag{1}$$

By using Definitions 2 and 5, FFLP problem (1) is transformed into problem (2). We have assumed that $\tilde{z} = \sum_{j=1}^{n} \tilde{c}_j \otimes \tilde{x}_j$, $\tilde{a}_i = (\underline{a}_i, a_i, \overline{a}_i) = \sum_{j=1}^{n} \tilde{a}_{ij} \otimes \tilde{x}_j$, $\tilde{b}_i = (\underline{b}_i, b_i, \overline{b}_i)$ and $\tilde{x}_j = (\underline{x}_j, x_j, \overline{x}_j)$. In addition, I_{e}, I_{le} and I_{ge} denote the index sets of the fuzzy equality, less-than-or-equal-to and greater-than-or-equal-to constraints of FFLP problem (1), respectively.

$$\begin{aligned} &\text{lexmin}\left(f_k(\tilde{z})\right)_{k=1}^{3} \\ &\text{s.t.} \left(f_k(\tilde{a}_i)\right)_{k=1}^{3} \{\leq_{lex}, \geq_{lex}\} \left(f_k(\tilde{b}_i)\right)_{k=1}^{3};\ i \in I_{\text{le}} \cup I_{\text{ge}} \\ &\quad \underline{a}_i = \underline{b}_i,\ a_i = b_i,\ \overline{a}_i = \overline{b}_i;\ i \in I_{\text{e}} \\ &\quad \underline{x}_j \geq 0,\ \underline{x}_j \leq x_j \leq \overline{x}_j;\ j = 1, 2, \ldots, n \end{aligned} \tag{2}$$

By introducing binary variables y_{ik}, for $i \in I_{\text{le}} \cup I_{\text{ge}}$ and $k = 1, 2, 3$, problem (2) is transformed into problem (3), in which ϵ and L are positive constants sufficiently small and large, respectively.

$$\begin{aligned} &\text{lexmin}\left(f_k(\tilde{z})\right)_{k=1}^{3} \\ &\text{s.t.} -L\sum_{p=1}^{k-1} y_{ip} + \epsilon y_{ik} \leq f_k(\tilde{b}_i) - f_k(\tilde{a}_i) \leq L y_{ik};\ i \in I_{\text{le}},\ k = 1, 2, 3 \\ &\quad -L\sum_{p=1}^{k-1} y_{ip} + \epsilon y_{ik} \leq f_k(\tilde{a}_i) - f_k(\tilde{b}_i) \leq L y_{ik};\ i \in I_{\text{ge}},\ k = 1, 2, 3 \\ &\quad \underline{a}_i = \underline{b}_i,\ a_i = b_i,\ \overline{a}_i = \overline{b}_i;\ i \in I_{\text{e}} \\ &\quad y_{ik} \in \{0, 1\};\ i \in I_{\text{le}} \cup I_{\text{ge}},\ k = 1, 2, 3 \\ &\quad \underline{x}_j \geq 0,\ \underline{x}_j \leq x_j \leq \overline{x}_j;\ j = 1, 2, \ldots, n \end{aligned} \tag{3}$$

The equivalence of FFLP problem (1) and problem (3) is established by Theorems 1 and 2 in [18].

3 Fully Fuzzy Multi-objective Berth Allocation Problem

Based on the crisp models [3,14], this section presents the notations and mathematical model for the FFMOBA problem. To solve the FFMOBA problem, we must determine the berthing times and positions of arriving vessels in a wharf, under the assumption that the arrival and handling times are not known precisely but can be modelled with TFNs. The problem parameters and decision variables are listed below.

Parameters:
n The total number of vessels.
L The length of a wharf.
$\tilde{a}_i$ The fuzzy arrival time of vessel i.
$\tilde{b}_i$ The fuzzy handling time of vessel i, including the time between the departure of a vessel and the berthing of another vessel.
l_i The length of vessel i, including the necessary gap between adjacent vessels.

Decision variables:
x_i The berthing position of vessel i.
$\tilde{y}_i$ The fuzzy berthing time of vessel i.
z^x_{ij} A binary variable set to 1 if vessel i is positioned to the left of vessel j on the wharf, and 0 otherwise.
z^y_{ij} A binary variable set to 1 if vessel i is berthed before vessel j in time, and 0 otherwise.

The mathematical model for the FFMOBA problem is given by Eq. (4), where M is a large constant. Two objective functions, taking into consideration vessels and wharves operators' interests, are formulated in this study. Hence, this study considers the minimisation of the total waiting time of vessels and the makespan of the wharf operation, as indicated by Eq. (4a).

$$\min \left(\sum_{i=1}^{n} (\tilde{y}_i \ominus \tilde{a}_i),\ \max_i \left(\tilde{y}_i \oplus \tilde{b}_i\right)_{i=1}^{n} \ominus \min_i \left(\tilde{y}_i\right)_{i=1}^{n} \right) \tag{4a}$$

$$\text{s.t. } \tilde{a}_i \leq_p \tilde{y}_i;\ i = 1,2,\ldots,n \tag{4b}$$

$$\tilde{y}_i \oplus \tilde{b}_i \leq_p \tilde{y}_j \oplus \left(1 - z^y_{ij}\right) \times (M, M, M);\ i,j = 1,2,\ldots,n\ (i \neq j) \tag{4c}$$

$$x_i + l_i \leq x_j + \left(1 - z^x_{ij}\right) M;\ i,j = 1,2,\ldots,n\ (i \neq j) \tag{4d}$$

$$x_i + l_i \leq L;\ i = 1,2,\ldots,n \tag{4e}$$

$$z^x_{ij} + z^x_{ji} + z^y_{ij} + z^y_{ji} \geq 1;\ i,j = 1,2,\ldots,n\ (i \neq j) \tag{4f}$$

$$x_i \geq 0;\ i = 1,2,\ldots,n \tag{4g}$$

$$z^x_{ij} \in \{0,1\},\ z^y_{ij} \in \{0,1\};\ i,j = 1,2,\ldots,n\ (i \neq j) \tag{4h}$$

Constraint (4b) guarantees that a vessel cannot berth before its arrival time. Constraint (4c) or (4d) is effective only when z^y_{ij} or z^x_{ij} equals one; thus, (4c) represents the berthing schedule and (4d) the physical restrictions for the berthing position of adjacent vessels. Likewise, constraint (4e) implies that the rightmost end of a vessel is restricted by the length of the wharf. Constraint (4f) guarantees the accomplishment of constraints (4c) and (4d). Note that for handing the fuzzy inequality constraints (4c) and (4d), we have used the partial order for TFNs given in Definition 4; this ensures a strict accomplishment of those constraints.

3.1 Proposed Scalarisation

By introducing auxiliary variables $\tilde{v}_{\max}$, $\tilde{u}_{\min}$, v_i and u_i and using the fuzzy epsilon-constraint method presented in [19], FFMOBA problem (4) is scalarised as follows, where λ and M are small and large positive constants, respectively.

$$\begin{aligned}
&\min\ \tilde{f} \\
&\text{s.t. } \tilde{f} \oplus \lambda \times \tilde{s}^{+} = \tilde{v}_{\max} \ominus \tilde{u}_{\min} \oplus \lambda \times \tilde{s}^{-} \oplus (-M, 0, M) \\
&\quad \tilde{y}_i \oplus (u_i - 1) \times (M, M, M) \leq_p \tilde{u}_{\min} \preccurlyeq \tilde{y}_i;\ i = 1, 2, \ldots, n \\
&\quad \tilde{y}_i \oplus \tilde{b}_i \preccurlyeq \tilde{v}_{\max} \leq_p \tilde{y}_i \oplus \tilde{b}_i \oplus (1 - v_i) \times (M, M, M);\ i = 1, 2, \ldots, n \\
&\quad \sum_{i=1}^{n} u_i = 1,\ \sum_{i=1}^{n} v_i = 1,\ u_i \in \{0, 1\},\ v_i \in \{0, 1\};\ i = 1, 2, \ldots, n \\
&\quad \sum_{i=1}^{n} (\tilde{y}_i \ominus \tilde{a}_i) \oplus \tilde{s}^{+} = \tilde{\epsilon} \oplus \tilde{s}^{-} \\
&\quad \tilde{s}^{-} \preccurlyeq \tilde{s}^{+},\ \tilde{s}^{-} \geq 0,\ \tilde{s}^{+} \geq 0,\ \tilde{u}_{\min} \geq 0,\ \tilde{v}_{\max} \geq 0 \\
&\quad \text{Constraints (4b)} - \text{(4h)}
\end{aligned} \tag{5}$$

To transform FFMOBA problem (4) into FFLP problem (5), we have resorted to the classical linearisations of the max and min functions, and used property (I) of the lexicographic total order relation $\preccurlyeq$ together with its anti-symmetry property. This way we guarantee to compare the fuzzy values of the objective functions by using a lexicographic criterion. We remark that, as in the classical epsilon-constraint method [7], the idea is to transform one of the two objective functions, say, the total waiting time of the vessels, into a constraint by bounding it from above with the constant TFN $\tilde{\epsilon}$. Pareto optimal fuzzy solutions are then obtained by solving single-objective FFLP problem (5) for selected values of $\tilde{\epsilon}$. Further details on this transformation can be found in [19].

4 Illustrative Example

The FFMOBA problem considered in this section is adapted from [10]. It consists of a wharf of 700 meters length and eight vessels, with uncertain arrival and handling times modelled with TFNs. The problem data is shown in Table 1. This is the same dataset used in [10], except for the handling times which are considered fuzzy in the present study. As part of the solution method, the functions $f_1(\tilde{a}) = (\underline{a} + 2a + \overline{a})/4$, $f_2(\tilde{a}) = a$ and $f_3(\tilde{a}) = \overline{a} - \underline{a}$ are used to define

Table 1. Data of FFMOBA problem.

Vessel	Length	Arrival time	Handling time
1	159	$(4, 8, 34)$	$(120, 121, 122)$
2	150	$(0, 15, 36)$	$(229, 231, 234)$
3	95	$(18, 32, 50)$	$(84, 87, 88)$
4	63	$(9, 40, 46)$	$(244, 248, 251)$
5	219	$(32, 52, 72)$	$(211, 213, 215)$
6	274	$(55, 68, 86)$	$(492, 496, 500)$
7	265	$(62, 75, 90)$	$(434, 435, 438)$
8	94	$(45, 86, 87)$	$(143, 146, 148)$

Table 2. Results obtained by considering only the minimisation of the makespan of the wharf operation.

Vessel	Position	Berthing time	Departure time
1	95	$(72, 72, 72)$	$(192, 193, 194)$
2	0	$(489, 489, 490)$	$(718, 720, 724)$
3	0	$(72, 72, 72)$	$(156, 159, 160)$
4	94	$(239, 239, 239)$	$(483, 487, 490)$
5	431	$(72, 72, 72)$	$(283, 285, 287)$
6	157	$(223.23, 223.23, 223.23)$	$(715.23, 719.23, 723.23)$
7	435	$(283, 285, 287)$	$(717, 720, 725)$
8	0	$(285, 285, 287)$	$(428, 431, 435)$
Total waiting time			$(1234.23, 1361.23, 1517.23)$
Makespan of wharf operation			$(645, 648, 653)$

a lexicographic order relation on the set of all TFNs. Furthermore, this order relation is assumed to be in accordance with the subjective criterion used by the wharf operators to rank TFNs. All numerical calculations were performed on a computer with an Intel® Core™ i3-4005U @ 1.70GHz × 4 and 4GB RAM running Ubuntu 18.04.4. We used the linear programming modeller PuLP version 1.6.0 [17] and SCIP solver version 4.0.0 [16] with parameter "feastol" set to $1e-09$. The lexicographic method from Subsect. 2.1 was used with $\epsilon = 10^{-4}$ and $L = 10^4$; M in FFLP problem (5) was set to 10^3. Results are presented up to two decimal places.

If the problem is solved by considering only the wharf operators' interests, i.e. by minimising the makespan of the wharf operation, then excessively long waiting times are experienced by vessels operators, as seen from Table 2. Operating a wharf under this policy is against the service quality and causes great dissatisfaction in vessels operators. Hence, finding a trade-off between these two conflicting objectives is a major concern for wharves operators.

Table 3. Results obtained by using the proposed method with criterion $\left(f_k(\cdot)\right)_{k=1}^{3}$, $\tilde{\epsilon} = (700, 1000, 1300)$ and $\lambda = 10^{-4}$.

Vessel	Position	Berthing time	Departure time
1	471	$(25.99, 52, 78.00)$	$(145.99, 173, 200.00)$
2	0	$(296, 300, 303)$	$(525, 531, 537)$
3	376	$(32.00, 32.00, 112.00)$	$(116.00, 119.00, 200.00)$
4	0	$(52, 52, 52)$	$(296, 300, 303)$
5	63	$(32, 52, 72)$	$(243, 265, 287)$
6	426	$(145.99, 173, 200.00)$	$(637.99, 669, 700.00)$
7	150	$(243, 265, 287)$	$(677, 700, 725)$
8	282	$(45, 86, 87)$	$(188, 232, 235)$
Total waiting time			$(370.99, 636.00, 966.00)$
Makespan of wharf operation			$(625, 648, 673)$

Table 4. Results obtained by using only the ranking function $f_1(\cdot)$, $\tilde{\epsilon} = (700, 1000, 1300)$ and $\lambda = 10^{-4}$.

Vessel	Position	Berthing time	Departure time
1	384	$(9.75, 49.08, 100.08)$	$(129.75, 170.08, 222.08)$
2	539	$(296, 300, 303)$	$(525, 531, 537)$
3	265	$(45.75, 54.08, 54.08)$	$(129.75, 141.08, 142.08)$
4	637	$(52, 52, 52)$	$(296, 300, 303)$
5	46	$(32, 52, 72)$	$(243, 265, 287)$
6	265	$(129.75, 170.08, 222.08)$	$(621.75, 666.08, 722.08)$
7	0	$(243, 265, 287)$	$(677, 700, 725)$
8	543	$(45, 86, 87)$	$(188, 232, 235)$
Total waiting time			$(352.25, 652.25, 952.25)$
Makespan of wharf operation			$(625, 648, 673)$

In view of the excessive waiting times experienced by vessels operators, the wharf operators may wish to reduce the total waiting time and simultaneously analyse the impact of such a reduction on the makespan of the operation.

For example, by using the proposed method, results shown in Table 3 demostrate that it is possible to considerably reduce the total waiting time and have little impact on the makespan of the wharf operation. Note that the makespan of the operation has the same modal value but its fuzziness increased by 40 time units. However, that solution is likely to be preferable for wharf and vessels operators, because it drastically reduces the total waiting time. At this point, we would like to stress that the use of a single linear ranking function to define the order relation $\preccurlyeq$, as in e.g. [8], although much less computationally

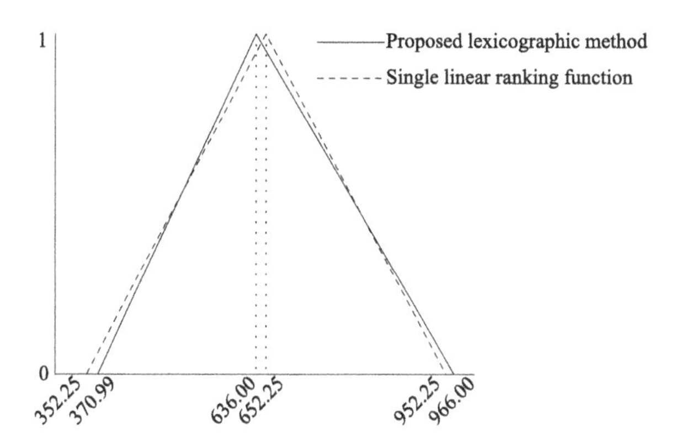

Fig. 1. Total waiting times obtained by using the proposed method and, alternatively, a single linear ranking function.

Table 5. Results obtained by using the proposed method with criterion $(f_k(\cdot))_{k=1}^{3}$, $\tilde{\epsilon} = (350, 480, 550)$ and $\lambda = 10^{-4}$.

Vessel	Position	Berthing time	Departure time
1	213	$(8, 8, 49.25)$	$(128, 129, 171.25)$
2	63	$(0, 8.62, 36)$	$(229, 239.62, 270)$
3	602	$(18, 32, 50)$	$(102, 119, 138)$
4	0	$(9, 40, 46)$	$(253, 288, 297)$
5	372	$(32, 52, 72)$	$(243, 265, 287)$
6	63	$(229, 249.62, 270)$	$(721, 745.62, 770)$
7	337	$(265, 265, 445.25)$	$(699, 700, 883.25)$
8	591	$(102, 119, 138)$	$(245, 265, 286)$
Total waiting time			$(162, 398.24, 881.50)$
Makespan of wharf operation			$(663, 681.37, 883.25)$

demanding, does not guarantee fuzzy Pareto optimality (see [19] for further discussion). Thus, if the problem is solved by considering only the ranking index $f_1(\cdot)$, then we obtain the solution shown in Table 4. Both solutions (Table 3 and Table 4) have the same makespan of the wharf operation, and their corresponding total waiting times have the same value by $f_1(\cdot)$ within the working precision; however, the solution yielded by the proposed method has a total waiting time with lower modal value, as seen from Fig. 1, and is therefore intuitively preferable.

Another Pareto optimal fuzzy solution is shown in Table 5. In this case, the wharf operators have set $\tilde{\epsilon} = (350, 480, 550)$ as an upper bound (in the sense of $\preccurlyeq$) for the total waiting time. Compared to the solution shown in Table 3, by using the particular definition of $\preccurlyeq$, the reader can easily realise that no solution dominates the other, since the decrease in the total waiting time of the

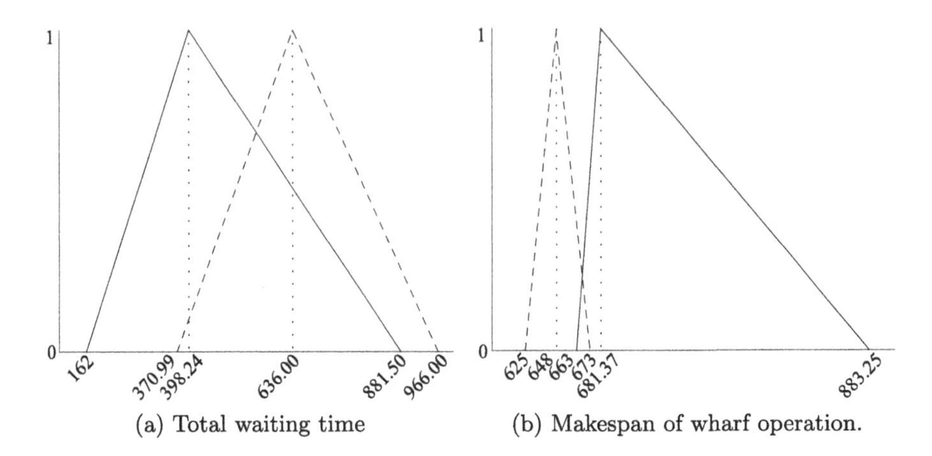

Fig. 2. Graphs of the objective functions values corresponding to the solutions of the FFMOBA problem shown in Table 3 (- - -) and Table 5 (—).

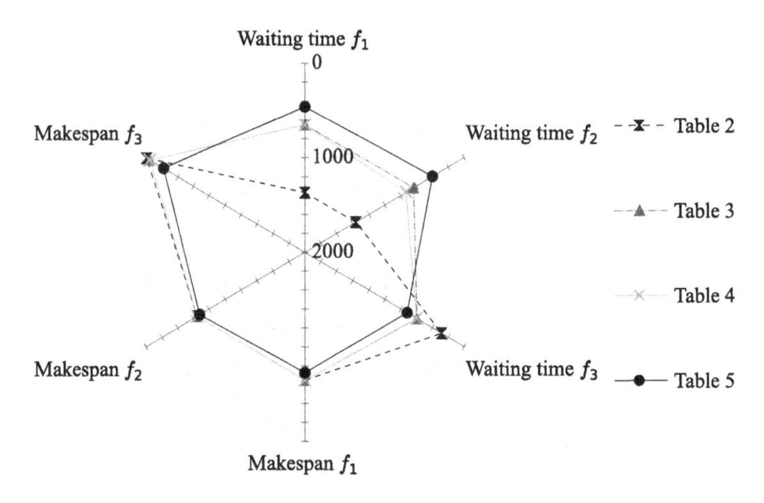

Fig. 3. Objective functions values in terms of the ranking indices $f_1(\cdot)$, $f_2(\cdot)$ and $f_3(\cdot)$ corresponding to the solutions shown in Tables 2, 3, 4 and 5.

last solution caused an expected increase in the makespan of the operation. This fact can be seen in Fig. 2.

In addition, Fig. 3 depicts the values of the objective functions in terms of the ranking indices $\left(f_k(\cdot)\right)_{k=1}^{3}$. From this figure, we can easily compare the solutions in Tables 2, 3, 4 and 5 by inspecting the objective functions values along their corresponding axes. We see, for example, that the solution in Table 2 has the worst total waiting time value according to the indices $f_1(\cdot)$ and $f_2(\cdot)$, and confirm, by the inspection of the "Waiting time f_2" axis, that the solution in Table 4 is dominated by the solution in Table 3.

Following the procedure as described above, other solutions can be obtained and analysed. The wharf operators can then implement a berthing plan that fits their expectations.

5 Concluding Remarks

In this paper, we formulated and solved an FFMOBA problem in which vessels and wharves operators' interests were considered simultaneously. From the viewpoint of wharves operators, the minimisation of the makespan of the operation is very important since it allows them to obtain berthing plans with full use of the available resources at all times. For vessels operators, it is most important to get serviced in the shortest possible time to continue with their itinerary. Furthermore, to address real decision-making situations faced by wharves operators, we considered uncertain vessels arrival and handling times and modelled them with TFNs. Results may allow wharves operators to obtain berthing plans exhibiting trade-offs between the two conflicting objectives and thus balance their goals and the service quality in uncertain environments.

In a future work, we may consider other objectives simultaneously. Fully fuzzy berth allocation and crane assignment is also an interesting extension in which the suitability of the proposed method is worthy of investigation. The use of metaheuristics to cope with high dimensional BA problems in fuzzy environments is also an interesting research line to explore.

Acknowledgements. The research of José Luis Verdegay is supported in part by project TIN2017-86647-P (Spanish Ministry of Economy and Competitiveness and FEDER funds from the European Union).

References

1. Bellman, R.E., Zadeh, L.A.: Decision-making in fuzzy environment. Manag. Sci. **17**(4), 141–164 (1970). https://doi.org/10.1287/mnsc.17.4.B141
2. Bojadziev, G., Bojadziev, M.: Fuzzy sets, fuzzy Logic, applications. In: Advances in Fuzzy Systems – Applications and Theory, vol. 5. World Scientific Publishing (1995)
3. Cheong, C., Tan, K., Liu, D.: Solving the berth allocation problem with service priority via multi-objective optimization. In: 2009 IEEE Symposium on Computational Intelligence in Scheduling, vol. 117576, pp. 95–102. IEEE (2009). https://doi.org/10.1109/SCIS.2009.4927021
4. Das, S.K., Mandal, T., Edalatpanah, S.A.: A mathematical model for solving fully fuzzy linear programming problem with trapezoidal fuzzy numbers. Appl. Intell. **46**(3), 509–519 (2017). https://doi.org/10.1007/s10489-016-0779-x
5. Expósito-Izquiero, C., Lalla-Ruiz, E., Lamata, T., Melián-Batista, B., Moreno-Vega, J.M.: Fuzzy optimization models for seaside port logistics: berthing and quay crane scheduling. In: Madani, K., Dourado, A., Rosa, A., Filipe, J., Kacprzyk, J. (eds.) Computational Intelligence. SCI, vol. 613, pp. 323–343. Springer, Cham (2016). https://doi.org/10.1007/978-3-319-23392-5_18

6. Farhadinia, B.: Ranking fuzzy numbers based on lexicographical ordering. Int. J. Appl. Math. Comput. Sci. **5**(4), 248–251 (2009)
7. Greco, S., Ehrgott, M., Figueira, J.R.: Multiple Criteria Decision Analysis. ISOR, vol. 233. Springer, New York (2016). https://doi.org/10.1007/978-1-4939-3094-4
8. Gupta, A., Kumar, A., Kaur, A.: Mehar's method to find exact fuzzy optimal solution of unbalanced fully fuzzy multi-objective transportation problems. Optim. Lett. **6**(8), 1737–1751 (2012). https://doi.org/10.1007/s11590-011-0367-2
9. Gutierrez, F., Lujan, E., Asmat, R., Vergara, E.: Fully fuzzy linear programming model for the berth allocation problem with two quays. In: Bello, R., Falcon, R., Verdegay, J.L. (eds.) Uncertainty Management with Fuzzy and Rough Sets. SFSC, vol. 377, pp. 87–113. Springer, Cham (2019). https://doi.org/10.1007/978-3-030-10463-4_5
10. Gutierrez, F., Lujan, E., Asmat, R., Vergara, E.: Fuzziness in the berth allocation problem. In: Fidanova, S. (ed.) Recent Advances in Computational Optimization. SCI, vol. 795, pp. 149–174. Springer, Cham (2019). https://doi.org/10.1007/978-3-319-99648-6_9
11. Hanss, M.: Applied Fuzzy Arithmetic. Springer, Heidelberg (2005). https://doi.org/10.1007/b138914
12. Hashemi, S.M., Modarres, M., Nasrabadi, E., Nasrabadi, M.M.: Fully fuzzified linear programming, solution and duality. J. Intell. Fuzzy Syst. **17**(1), 253–261 (2006)
13. Hosseinzadeh Lotfi, F., Allahviranloo, T., Alimardani Jondabeh, M., Alizadeh, L.: Solving a full fuzzy linear programming using lexicography method and fuzzy approximate solution. Appl. Math. Model. **33**, 3151–3156 (2009). https://doi.org/10.1016/j.apm.2008.10.020
14. Kim, K.H., Moon, K.C.: Berth scheduling by simulated annealing. Transp. Res. Part B: Methodol. **37**(6), 541–560 (2003). https://doi.org/10.1016/S0191-2615(02)00027-9
15. López Plata, I.: Improvement of the logistics processes in maritime container terminals through intelligent optimization techniques. Ph.D. dissertation, University of La Laguna, Spain (2020)
16. Maher, S.J., et al.: The SCIP Optimization Suite 4.0. Technical report, Optimization Online, March 2017. http://www.optimization-online.org/DB_HTML/2017/03/5895.html
17. Mitchell, S., O'Sullivan, M., Dunning, I.: PuLP: a linear programming toolkit for python (2011). http://www.optimization-online.org/DB_FILE/2011/09/3178.pdf. The University of Auckland, Auckland, New Zealand
18. Pérez-Cañedo, B., Concepción-Morales, E.R.: A method to find the unique optimal fuzzy value of fully fuzzy linear programming problems with inequality constraints having unrestricted L-R fuzzy parameters and decision variables. Expert Syst. Appl. **123**, 256–269 (2019). https://doi.org/10.1016/j.eswa.2019.01.041
19. Pérez-Cañedo, B., Verdegay, J.L., Miranda Pérez, R.: An epsilon-constraint method for fully fuzzy multiobjective linear programming. Int. J. Intell. Syst. **35**(4), 600–624 (2020). https://doi.org/10.1002/int.22219
20. Wang, M.L., Wang, H.F., Chih-Lung, L.: Ranking fuzzy number based on lexicographic screening procedure. Int. J. Inf. Technol. Decis. Making **4**(4), 663–678 (2005). https://doi.org/10.1142/S0219622005001696
21. Wang, W., Wang, Z.: Total orderings defined on the set of all fuzzy numbers. Fuzzy Sets Syst. **243**, 131–141 (2014). https://doi.org/10.1016/j.fss.2013.09.005
22. Zadeh, L.: Fuzzy sets. Inf. Control **8**(3), 338–353 (1965). https://doi.org/10.1016/S0019-9958(65)90241-X

Analysis of the Genetic Algorithm Operators for the Node Location Problem in Local Positioning Systems

Rubén Ferrero-Guillén[1(✉)], Javier Díez-González[1(✉)], Rubén Álvarez[2(✉)], and Hilde Pérez[1(✉)]

[1] Department of Mechanical, Computer, and Aerospace Engineering, Universidad de León, 24071 León, Spain
rferrg00@estudiantes.unileon.es, {jdieg, hilde.perez}@unileon.es

[2] Positioning Department, Drotium, Universidad de León, 24071 León, Spain
ruben.alvarez@drotium.com

Abstract. The node location plays a critical role in the LPS performance capabilities. Due to the complexity of this problem, the implementation of heuristic methodologies such as genetic algorithms (GA) has been widely proposed in the literature. However, the performance of GA is heavily dependent of the consistency of its foundation and its adaptation to the nature of the optimization problem. In this paper, we analyze and compare a variety of different selection and crossover techniques in search for the most suitable configuration for the node location problem. Results show that although some combinations achieve adequate results, the concept of a hybrid GA that takes advantage from different configurations depending on the problem requirements can surpass any fixed individual combination.

Keywords: CRLB · Hybrid genetic algorithms · Localization · Local Positioning Systems · Node location problem

1 Introduction

Local Positioning Systems (LPS) have supposed an active topic of research over the last few years. They rely on the deployment of sensors in a well-defined area in which the accuracy demands are higher than the Global Navigation Satellite Systems (GNSS) can provide. GNSS devices suffer distortion in the quality of their signals by crossing large buildings [1], by facing obstacles in their paths [2], by ionospheric effects [3] or by unstable synchronization among the system elements [4].

For these reasons, a new solution to mitigate these adverse effects is required for high-demanded applications such as autonomous navigation in indoor and outdoor environments. LPS have proven to enhance localization accuracy based on the ad-hoc deployment of sensors to avoid negative phenomena on signals. This requires an exact knowledge of the environment and a technique to correctly distribute the sensors in space.

E. A. de la Cal et al. (Eds.): HAIS 2020, LNAI 12344, pp. 273–283, 2020.
https://doi.org/10.1007/978-3-030-61705-9_23

However, the distribution of sensors in space in LPS, known as the node location problem, is a complex problem which has been proven to be NP-Hard [5, 6]. Therefore, heuristic solutions to the node location problem has been widely proposed in the literature. Tabu search methodologies [7], the firefly algorithm [8], the dolphin swarm algorithm [9], simulated annealing [10] but especially genetic algorithms (GA) [11–13] have been used to solve this problem.

Authors have previously addressed this problem by achieving reductions in the signal noise [14], algorithm coverage enhancements [15], clock errors [4] or mitigating adverse phenomena such as multipath or sensor failures [16] in Wireless Sensor Networks. This requires the computation of a fitness function to measure the beauty of the node distributions. Generally, the Cramer Rao Lower Bound (CRLB) estimator has been used to provide an evaluation of the quality of a sensor deployment in LPS [14, 17–20]. CRLB is a maximum likelihood estimator which defines the minimum localization error achievable by any positioning algorithm in a target location given a defined node distribution in a particular operation environment. In this way, the overall reduction of the CRLB in every possible target location, Target Location Environment (TLE), produces the better node configuration in the space among the possible node distributions considered in the optimization, Node Location Environment (NLE) [11].

We showed in [11] that the beauty of the sensor configuration in Line-of-Sight environments is a heuristic complex problem in which the configuration of the hyperparameters of the Genetic Algorithm was crucial to achieve actual and valuable solutions. In this sense, the purpose of this study was to describe the methodology for constructing a valid GA for the node location problem, considering a further discussion to the genetic operators (selection, crossover and mutation techniques) in order to achieve better results.

In this paper, we study different configurations for the genetic operators of the node location problem in an Asynchronous Time Difference of Arrival (A-TDOA) [21] positioning architecture in order to improve the quality of the heuristic search of our previous studies. We also look for providing a common framework for the discussion of the genetic operators used in the node location problem as well as the combination of these functions in a hybrid GA configuration to enhance the overall performance.

The remaining of the paper is organized as follows: the steps of the GA for the node location optimization in LPS are introduced in Sect. 2, the results are presented in Sect. 3 and Sect. 4 concludes the paper.

2 Genetic Algorithm for the Node Location Problem

The node location problem is crucial for LPS. The freedom of the designer to locate sensors in space allows the reduction of the errors produced by signal noise [18], algorithm coverage enhancement [15], clock errors [4], multipath effects [13] or sensor failures [16]. This requires a heuristic approach since the problem has been characterized as NP-Hard [5, 6].

Among the different metaheuristics, the GA have proven to specially fit the requirements of this complex problem. GA were first introduced by Holland [22] and later refined by Goldberg [23] built on the theory of evolution. By this postulate, the best adapted individuals are the most probable to survive and produce offspring for the next generations, where descendant individuals will present better adaptation to the environment.

The general steps followed in a GA computation problem are described in Fig. 1. These steps include the generation of the initial population for which a codification of the individuals is required, a fitness function definition for the evaluation of the individuals, a stop condition that can be based on a pre-defined number of generations or the definition of a suitable convergence criteria for the problem; and the genetic operators (selection, elitism, crossing and mutation) which are deeply discussed in this paper.

2.1 Codification of Individuals

GA are composed by generations of individuals. Every of these individuals are a possible solution of the node location problem among all the combinations considered for the optimization (NLE). The codification is usually binary since it allows the better performance of the genetic operators. Therefore, it requires the escalation of the variables implied in the definition of the individuals into the binary coding. In this problem, these variables are the Cartesian coordinates of each node used in the positioning architecture displayed.

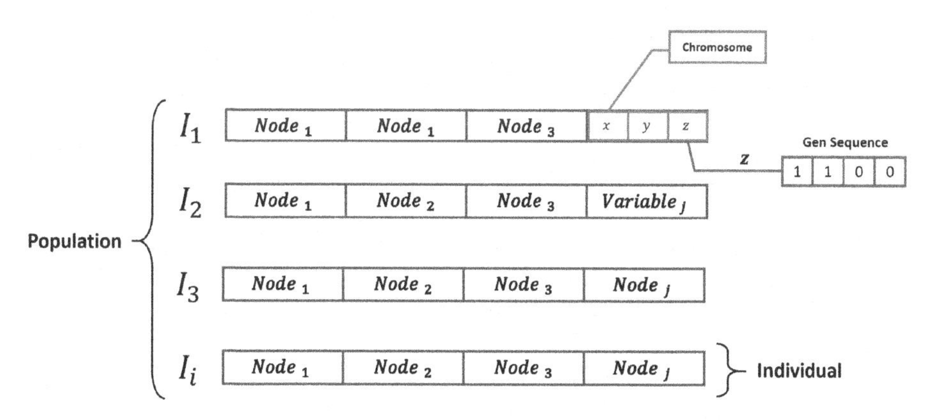

Fig. 1. Genetic Algorithm Codification of Individuals

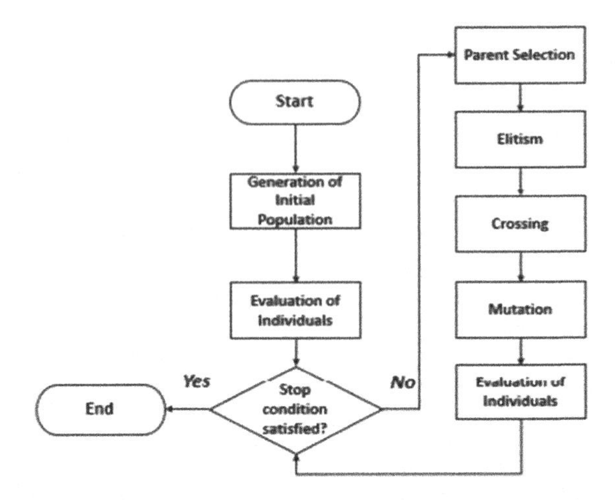

Fig. 2. Flux diagram of the GA.

As it is shown in Fig. 1, the population consists of a number *i* of individuals which must be defined as one of the hyperparameters of the GA. Each individual carries a number *j* of nodes to locate, consisting every node of the gene sequences used for the escalation in binary codification of the position of a node for each defined Cartesian coordinate. In this paper, the initial population of the GA is randomly defined for guaranteeing the diversity of the initial population.

2.2 Evaluation of Individuals

The beauty of each individual must be determined through a fitness function in order to detect the better adapted individuals of the population which are the best candidate solutions for the node location problem. Over the last few years, in the localization field, the CRLB parameter has been used as fitness function for the node location problem [14, 17, 18] since it allows the introduction of the uncertainties present in the communications channel in the covariance matrix of the system. Particularly, Kaune et al. [14] proposed a CRLB matrix form in which Huang et al. [17] introduced a heteroscedastic noise model consideration which especially fits for LPS applications:

$$\begin{aligned} FIM_{mn} = & \left[\frac{\partial h(TS)}{\partial TS_m}\right]^T R^{-1}(TS)\left[\frac{\partial h(TS)}{\partial TS_n}\right] \\ & + \frac{1}{2} tr\left\{R^{-1}(TS)\left[\frac{\partial R(TS)}{\partial TS_m}\right] R^{-1}(TS)\left[\frac{\partial R(TS)}{\partial TS_n}\right]\right\} \end{aligned} \tag{1}$$

where **FIM** is the Fisher Information Matrix (the inverse of the CRLB), **h(TS)** a vector containing the travel of the signal in the positioning architecture at study (in this case the A-TDOA [18, 21]), **R(TS)** the covariance matrix of the system containing the information of the signal noise uncertainties as we introduced in [11], TS the target sensor position expressed by its Cartesian coordinates through the m and n estimated parameters.

The Root Mean Square Error (RMSE), which is used as the fitness function of the GA, with the minimum achievable error in the TS location, can be directly obtained through the trace of the inverse of the FIM (CRLB) as follows:

$$RMSE = \sqrt{trace(FIM^{-1})} \tag{2}$$

2.3 Selection Techniques and Elitism Concept

Once evaluated, the selection procedure for the population is started. The main goal of this step of the GA is to arrange the individuals for the crossover in a way that optimizes the final solution, relying on the fitness value as a beauty estimator.

However, numerous selection methodologies are available, depending on the particular behavior of the specific characteristics of the problem. Therefore, in search for the most suited technique, we will analyze the behavior of tournament selection, with 2 and 3 individuals, roulette and ranked roulette selection [24].

The proportional and ranked roulette methodologies base their selection probability on the fitness value obtained by each individual. Although any individual can be selected, it is common for the most adapted individuals to dominate the selection criteria, resulting in a loss of diversity and a premature convergence.

The ranked-roulette pursues to prevent this phenomenon by establishing a selection probability based on the rank or position of each individual in the overall population. However, this methodology demands additional computation time, as it is required to rearrange the individuals multiple times and it is heavily dependent on the rank assignment which hinges on the specific problem characteristics.

On the other hand, the tournament selection methodologies rely heavily on the fitness values and may present problems of diversity for large number of contestants. However, being the selection of the contestants random, techniques such as tournament 2 or 3 stand out as well rounded and balanced selection methodologies.

Furthermore, the use of elitism along the selection criteria has been widely used through the GA literature. Although this particular step is optional, its improvement of the obtained solution by increasing the selection pressure is quite remarkable.

In this research we have opted for a persistent elitism where a certain percentage of the most adapted individuals are preserved for the next generation. The adequate selection of this percentage is critical for the GA's stability. An excessive value of elitism will result in a loss of genetic diversity and will incur a worse solution, thus we will analyze the appropriate value for each configuration we propose.

2.4 Crossover Techniques

The crossover techniques, as well as selection criteria, play a decisive role in the performance of the GA in the exploration and optimization of the solution. The objective of this step is to create the next generation of individuals in a way that optimizes the algorithm search for the optimal solution. Three different methodologies have been studied, the single point crossover, multipoint crossover and the uniform crossover.

These three techniques differ from one another in the amount of crossover points of the procedure, as shown in Fig. 2. By increasing the number of crossover points, up to the uniform technique, we enhance the genetic diversity and the probability of a productive new individual [25].

Nevertheless, a methodology with a lower number of crossover points, such as single point crossover, promotes the convergence of the algorithm by preserving most of the gene sequence of the most adapted individuals.

In search for the best appropriate methodology for the node location problem, we will study the single point crossover (SP), the multipoint crossover for 2 (MP2) and 3 (MP3) points and the uniform crossover.

2.5 Mutation Techniques

The mutation function in a GA provides an additional source of genetic diversity to the configuration, playing a main role in the exploration of the environment in search for the optimal solution.

In this step of the GA, we artificially create entropy in the optimization of the solution by randomly modifying the genetic sequences of some individuals. Although it may seem futile to sabotage some of the individuals, the addition of the right amount of chaos is favorable for the optimization process, especially when close to a local or global maximum of the solution.

However, it is crucial to select an appropriate value for the mutation parameter, being an excessive value adverse for the convergence of the GA (Fig. 3).

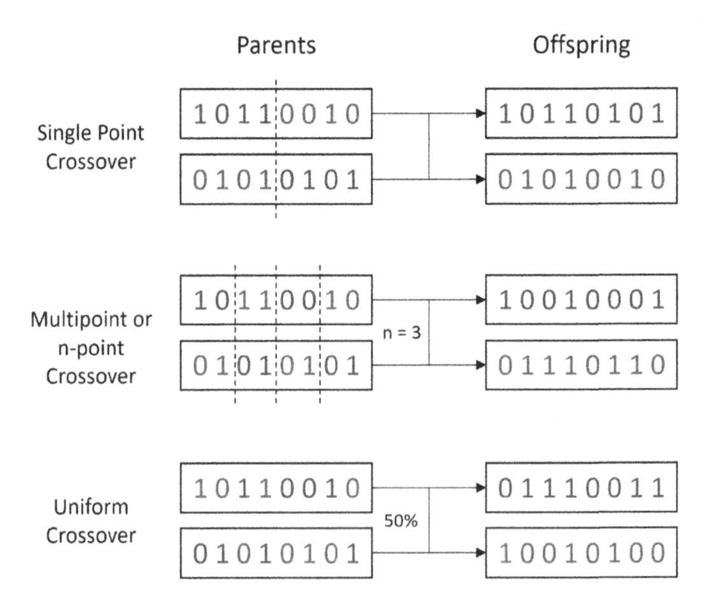

Fig. 3. Crossover methodologies

3 Results

The simulations were executed in the Python programing language, in an environment with the following characteristics (Table 1).

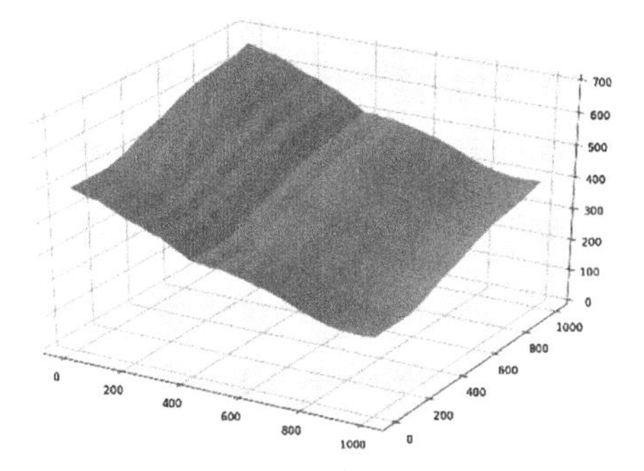

Fig. 4. Environment selected

Table 1. LPS Parameters [4]

Parameter	Value
Transmission power	400 W
Mean noise power	−94 dB
Frequency of emission	1090 MHz
Bandwidth	100 MHz
Path loss exponent	2.1
Antennae gains	Unity
Time - Frequency product	1
Communication type	Full-Duplex

In order to obtain the most suited methodology, we have studied a variety of possible combinations between the previously explained techniques. All simulations were executed with the same parameters of elitism, mutation and individuals, which were experimentally obtained based on previous simulations. The results of these different configurations over 10 simulations are listed below.

As shown in Table 2, three methodologies stand out, tournament 3 with 3-point crossover and tournament 2 and 3 with single point crossover. Once selected the best possible configurations, it is possible to optimize the mutation and elitism parameters for each configuration, as shown in Fig. 4.

Table 2. Comparison of the selection methodologies of tournament 2 (T2) and 3 (T3), roulette (R) and ranked roulette (RR) with the corresponding crossover techniques. All simulations were run equally with a 15% percentage of mutation and elitism.

	T2		T3		R		RR	
	Max	Mean	Max	Mean	Max	Mean	Max	Mean
Single point	**2546**	1832	**2002**	1436	1510	560	684	361
Two-point	815	623	1413	1016	785	531	859	321
Three-point	867	589	**2277**	1532	1637	735	1547	1065
Uniform	424	213	722	468	631	453	421	226

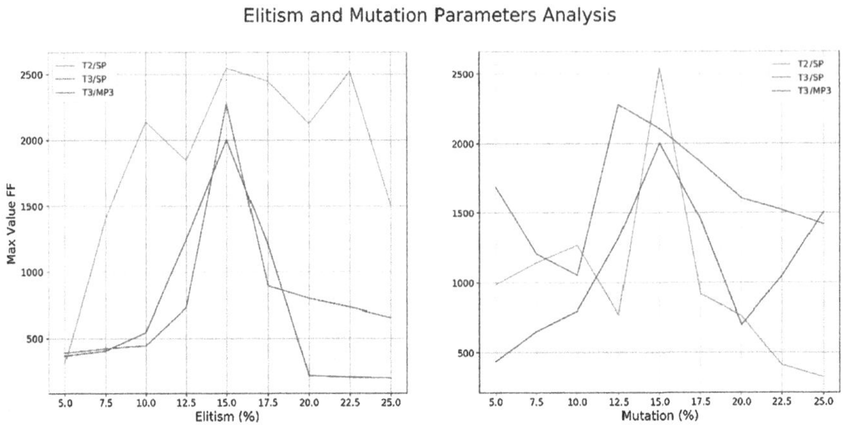

Fig. 5. Comparison between the best combinations of Table 2, in each graph the parameter at study is modified, remaining constant the second variable with a fixed value of 15%.

The best values are obtained from the T2/SP (tournament 2 and single point crossover) combination.

Therefore, we consider this value to be the optimal solution as no other combination obtains a greater result. However, in the T2/SP configuration, the single point crossover is considered to be an elitist technique that provides a quick and strong convergence, however the genetic diversity could be compromised.

On the other hand, in the T3/MP3 (tournament 3 and 3-point crossover) technique features a more chaotic approach which is favorable for the exploration of the environment but can difficult the convergence to the optimal solution.

Hence, we have assembled a hybrid genetic algorithm that combines these two methodologies in the pursuit of a superior solution. This hybrid algorithm present two different stages: an exploration-heavy phase and a solution intensification phase. The first phase relies on the T3/MP3 configuration for searching the optimal solution in the whole environment, after a certain number of generations, the algorithm would switch to the second stage. This last phase pretends to favor the convergence to the optimal solution encountered in the previous phase, through the elitist configuration of T2/SP.

In each phase of the program, the parameters of elitism and mutation are adapted to the optimal configuration of each technique in charge, obtained from Fig. 4.

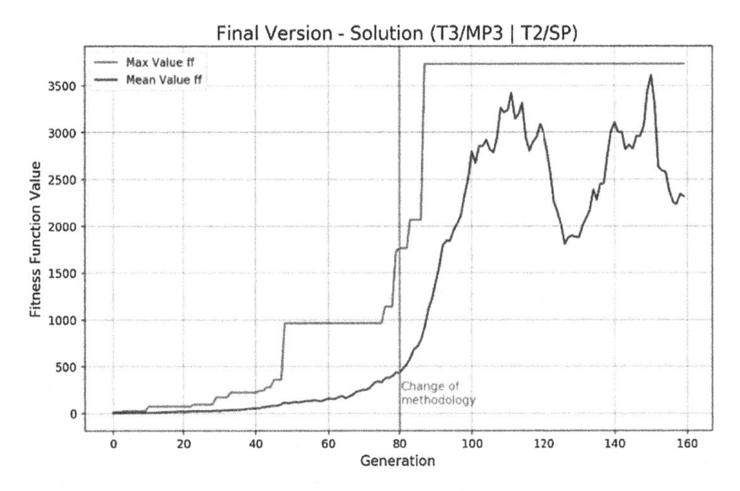

Fig. 6. Performance of the hybrid configuration of the GA

As seen in Fig. 5 the result obtained is greater than the maximum obtainable for each configuration individually. The optimal node distribution achieved for this configuration, shown in Fig. 7, can be obtained from the most adapted individual, from Fig. 6.

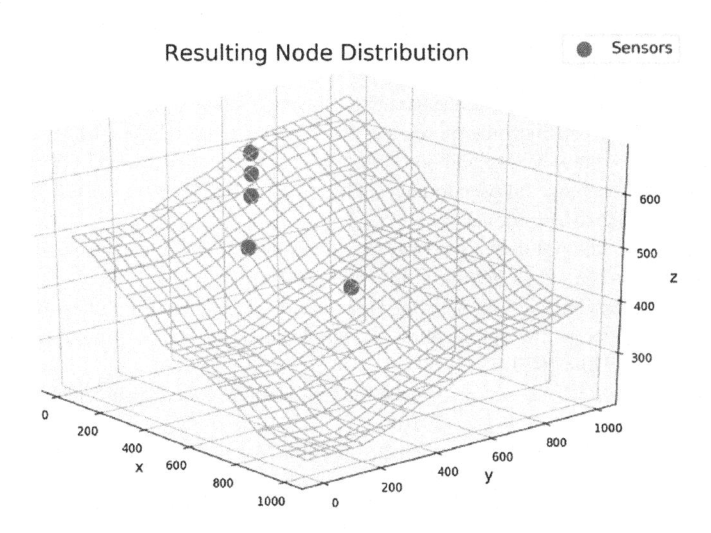

Fig. 7. Sensor positioning obtained from Fig. 5

4 Conclusions

LPS have proven to be a well-suited alternative to GNSS for certain applications, thus its renown in the research community. However, LPS have shown to be heavily dependent on the environment characteristics and its particular distribution on it. Nonetheless, this problem has been defined as NP-Hard, thus the use of heuristic methodology, such as GA, has been widely expanded throughout the literature.

In this paper, we have studied and compared the use of different methodologies of selection, crossover, mutation and elitism in order to obtain the most suited combination to find the optimal solution to this particular problem.

Results show that a strong elitism favors the convergence to the desired solution. Also, the entropy generators in the GA, such as mutation and multiple points crossovers play a decisive role to achieve valuable results. The use of these operators is critical in order to explore the environment selected in search for the optimal solution.

Therefore, the hybrid configuration proposed, which relies on multiple phases in the optimization procedure, achieves a greater solution than any possible individual combination of the most expanded genetic operators analyzed, thus fulfilling the main objective of this paper.

The conclusions achieved on this paper present a different perspective in the node location problem incorporating hybrid genetic configurations, opening new opportunities for future investigations.

References

1. de Sousa, M.N., Thomä, R.S.: Enhancement of localization systems in NLOS urban scenario with multipath ray tracing fingerprints and machine learning. Sensors **18**(11), 4073 (2018)
2. Groves, P.D., Adjrad, M.: Likelihood-based GNSS positioning using LOS/NLOS predictions from 3D mapping and pseudoranges. GPS Solut. **21**(4), 1805–1816 (2017). https://doi.org/10.1007/s10291-017-0654-1
3. Stankov, S.M., Jakowski, N.: Ionospheric effects on GNSS reference network integrity. J. Atmos. Solar-Terr. Phys. **69**(4–5), 485–499 (2007)
4. Álvarez, R., Díez-González, J., Sánchez-González, L., Pérez, H.: Combined noise and clock CRLB error model for the optimization of node location in time positioning systems. IEEE Access **8**(1), 31910–31919 (2020)
5. Tekdas, O., Isler, V.: Sensor placement for triangulation-based localization. IEEE Trans. Autom. Sci. Eng. **7**(3), 681–685 (2010)
6. Yoon, Y., Kim, Y.-H.: An efficient genetic algorithm for maximum coverage deployment in wireless sensor networks. IEEE Trans. Cybern. **43**(5), 1473–1483 (2013)
7. Laguna, M., Roa, J.O., Jiménez, A.R., Seco, F.: Diversified local search for the optimal layout of beacons in an indoor positioning system. IIE Trans. **41**(3), 247–259 (2009)
8. Tuba, E., Tuba, M., Beko, M.: Two stage wireless sensor node localization using firefly algorithm. In: Yang, X.-S., Nagar, A.K., Joshi, A. (eds.) Smart Trends in Systems, Security and Sustainability. LNNS, vol. 18, pp. 113–120. Springer, Singapore (2018). https://doi.org/10.1007/978-981-10-6916-1_10

9. Kannadasan, K., Edla, D.R., Kongara, M.C., Kuppili, V.: M-Curves path planning model for mobile anchor node and localization of sensor nodes using Dolphin Swarm Algorithm. Wirel. Netw. **26**(4), 2769–2783 (2019). https://doi.org/10.1007/s11276-019-02032-4
10. Wang, X., Ma, J.J., Wang, S., Bi, D.W.: Distributed particle swarm optimization and simulated annealing for energy-efficient coverage in wireless sensor networks. Sensors **7**(5), 628–648 (2007)
11. Díez-González, J., Álvarez, R., González-Bárcena, D., Sánchez-González, L., Castejón-Limas, M., Perez, H.: Genetic algorithm approach to the 3D node localization in TDOA systems. Sensors **19**(18), 3880 (2019)
12. Domingo-Perez, F., Lazaro-Galilea, J.L., Wieser, A., Martin-Gorostiza, E., Salido-Monzu, D., de la Llana, A.: Sensor placement determination for range-difference positioning using evolutionary multi-objective optimization. Expert Syst. Appl. **47**, 95–105 (2016)
13. Álvarez, R., Díez-González, J., Strisciuglio, N., Pérez, H.: Multi-objective optimization for asynchronous positioning methods. IEEE Access **8**(1), 43046–43056 (2020)
14. Kaune, R., Hörst, J., Koch, W.: Accuracy analysis for TDOA localization in sensor networks. In: 14th International Conference on Information Fusion, Chicago (2011)
15. Díez-González, J., Álvarez, R., Sánchez-González, L., Fernández-Robles, L., Pérez, H., Castejón-Limas, M.: 3D TDOA problem solution with four receiving nodes. Sensors **19**(13), 2892 (2019)
16. Díez-González, J., Álvarez, R., Prieto-Fernández, N., Pérez, H.: Local wireless sensor networks positioning reliability under sensor failure. Sensors **20**(5), 1426 (2020)
17. Huang, B., Xie, L., Yang, Z.: TDOA-based source localization with distance-dependent noises. IEEE Trans. Wirel. Commun. **14**(1), 468–480 (2015)
18. Álvarez, R., Díez-González, J., Alonso, E., Fernández-Robles, L., Castejón-Limas, M., Pérez, H.: Accuracy analysis in sensor networks for asynchronous positioning methods. Sensors **19**(13), 3024 (2019)
19. Hu, D., Chen, S., Bai, H., Zhao, C., Luo, L.: CRLB for joint estimation of TDOA, phase, FDOA, and Doppler rate. J. Eng. **21**, 7628–7631 (2019)
20. Kowalski, M., Willett, P., Fair, T., Bar-Shalom, Y.: CRLB for estimating time-varying rotational biases in passive sensors. IEEE Trans. Aerosp. Electron. Syst. **56**(1), 343–355 (2020)
21. He, S., Dong, X.: High-accuracy localization platform using asynchronous time difference of arrival technology. IEEE Trans. Instrum. Measur. **66**(7), 1728–1742 (2017)
22. Holland, J.H.: Adaptation in Natural and Artificial Systems: An Introductory Analysis with Applications to Biology, Control, and Artificial Intelligence. MIT Press (1992)
23. Goldberg, D.E.: Genetic Algorithms. Pearson Education India (2006)
24. Razali, N.M., Geraghty, J.: Genetic algorithm performance with different selection strategies in solving TSP. In: Proceedings of the World Congress on Engineering, vol. 2, no. 1. International Association of Engineers, Hong Kong (2011)
25. De Jong, K.A., Spears, W.M.: A formal analysis of the role of multi-point crossover in genetic algorithms. Ann. Math. Artif. Intell. **5**(1), 1–26 (1992)

Optimization of Learning Strategies for ARTM-Based Topic Models

Maria Khodorchenko(✉), Sergey Teryoshkin, Timur Sokhin, and Nikolay Butakov

ITMO University, 49 Kronverksky pr., St. Petersburg 197101, Russia
mariyaxod@yandex.ru, se.teryoshkin@gmail.com, 245591@niuitmo.ru, alipoov.nb@gmail.com

Abstract. Topic modelling is a popular unsupervised method for text processing which provides interpretable document representation. One of the most high-level approaches, considering its capability of imitating the behaviour of various methods such as LDA or PLSA, is based on additive regularization technique. However, due to its flexibility and advanced regularization abilities, it is challenging to find optimal learning strategy to create high-quality topics, because a user needs to select the regularizers with their values and determine the order of application. At the same time, there is a lack of research on parameters optimization of topic models, especially for ARTM-based models. Our work proposes an approach that formalizes the learning strategy into a vector of parameters which can be solved with an evolutionary or Bayesian approach. An experimental study conducted on English and Russian datasets indicates that the proposed learning strategy can be successfully optimized even in the presence of strong constrains.

Keywords: Topic modelling · Bayesian optimization · Learning strategy · Genetic algorithm

1 Introduction

Topic modelling is a machine learning technique which produces an interpretable representation. Due to its unsupervised nature, this probabilistic approach can be applied to a variety of exploratory and context analysis tasks, such as documents categorization or users/items profiling. However, topic models are highly dependent on the initial parameters [4], which may lead to different modelling results. It is challenging to find optimal learning strategy to create high-quality topics because the user needs to select the regularizers with their values and determine the order of application. Thus, a careful automatic parameters selection, along with appropriate optimization algorithm, are needed.

Here we address the problem of learning strategy selection for the Additive Regularization for Topic Models (ARTM) [19]. By *learning strategy*, we define a

E. A. de la Cal et al. (Eds.): HAIS 2020, LNAI 12344, pp. 284–296, 2020.
https://doi.org/10.1007/978-3-030-61705-9_24

set of sequential actions, which include parameters setting and values of learning iterations, that should be done in order to train the model. The choice of ARTM-approach was made due to the rich and flexible system of regularizers that work with various types of datasets. The resulting amount of parameters is difficult to tune manually, so it is easy to get a solution far from optimal. In order to automate the process of parameters tuning, the problem should be carefully formalized, which is not sufficiently covered in the literature. The task is complicated by the fact that the final interpretation of whether the topics are understandable and coherent is directly connected with human perception, that is tricky to convert into digital form. However, in the field of quality measures, two main approaches can be emphasized: the first one is based on corpus statistics, like coherence score [7] and the second one brings together scores which utilize word embeddings from models that were trained on larger corpus and thus collected the prior knowledge [11].

In this paper, we propose a way of learning strategy representation which is a replacement to manual tuning described in [20]. The procedure consists of manual changes of regularizers when after several iterations of learning, it should be defined whether to increase some regularization parameters or terminate the algorithm in case of sufficient quality. Here, we explore several optimization approaches and compare their performance on the task of learning strategy optimization. Depending on the size of the dataset and the total number of learning iterations, the preparation of the topic model may be computationally and time expensive and take from seconds to hours. In this research, we used a bit different approach to performance evaluation. In order to give equal conditions to all optimization algorithms, we count the number of models that are trained during the procedure and stop the algorithm if it hits the predefined limit.

Our main contributions can be summarized in two main points:

- An approach for learning strategy construction. We formalize the task in the form of a mixed-integer optimization problem, where the quality is measured by coherence.
- Comparative study of optimization algorithms for automatic evaluation of ARTM-based topic models in the presence of strong constrains that are the most adapted for such tasks. Results of experiments indicate that such methods as Grid Search or Bayesian Optimization can be outperformed with genetic algorithm.

The rest of the paper is organized as follows: Sect. 2 contains an overview of related works. Section 3 states the problem and describes in detail the construction of the learning strategy vector, quality metric choice and optimization algorithms selection. Section 4 contains the results of an experimental study on automated ARTM-based models optimization. Section 5 is devoted to the discussion, and Sect. 6 concludes the paper and describes future work.

2 Background and Related Work

While the significant amount of models, such as Probabilistic Latent Semantic Analysis (PLSA) or Latent Dirichlet allocation (LDA) and modifications of these algorithms exist and proceed to appear, ARTM [19] is introducing a set of regularizers to emulate each of them in one framework. Such adaptability to process different types of datasets with various texts length is the principal advantage of this approach. Regularizers add extra criteria to matrix factorization task, which makes the final results stable comparing to LDA.

Automatic optimization of topic models' parameters is a complex problem due to the lack of benchmark datasets for this task and reliable scores of quality estimation. Along with perplexity, which indicates the algorithm convergence, there is an apparent need in measuring the understandability of topics. Existing intrinsic evaluation metrics are applied to high-ranked topic words utilizing the statistics of given dataset [9,16,19] and moving towards the usage of pretrained embeddings [11,13]. Though these metrics do not take into account the specifics of sentence formation and may perform poorly on small or highly domain-specific corpora, they can catch the overall tendency of the topic to be labelled as "poor" or "good" by a human.

Over the last years, research in parameters tuning of non-neural topic models has focused mainly on LDA. In [14], the comparison study between several meta-heuristic is provided. Another approach is presented in [12], where the quality of resulting clusters estimates the performance. As for ARTM, to the best of our knowledge, no research papers are concentrating on this topic and the tuning is done manually [1]. Thus, in [20] authors admit that the careful selection of values is still an open question.

For the task of optimization, the two most widespread algorithms can be considered, namely Bayesian Optimization [17] and Evolutionary algorithms [3]. Both of them are capable of dealing with the "black box" machine learning problems. Still, the flexibility of evolutionary framework and freedom in operators implementation makes the application of the methods very common [18] for continuous and mixed-integer problems.

3 Problem Statement

3.1 Formalizing Requirements for Topic Model and Optimization Algorithm

Firstly, we should define the topic modelling task for additive regularization approach [19]. Following the PLSA [5] matrix factorization, the task is to uncover the underlying semantic structure of a document collection. Topic modelling outputs two matrixes - latent distribution over topics for documents $p(t|d)$ and distribution over words for topics $p(w|t)$:

$$p(w|d) = \sum_{t \in T} p(w|t)p(t|d) = \sum_{t \in T} \phi_{wt}\theta_{td}, d \in D, w \in W, \tag{1}$$

where D is a collection of documents, W is a finite set of vocabulary words, and T is a set of topics.

The main idea of additive regularization is based on the maximization of the log-likelihood with the addition of regularizers weighted sum to produce a unique solution for matrix factorization task, in other words to find the Φ and Θ matrices that satisfy the objective.

$$argmax_{\Phi,\Theta} \sum_{d \in D} \sum_{w \in W} n_{dw} ln \sum_{t \in T} \phi_{wt}\theta_{td} + R(\Phi, \Theta), \quad (2)$$

where n_{dw} is a counter of word w appear in a single document d, R is the weighted sum of regularizers.

Combining existing regularizers it is possible to create topic models with different properties that give dissimilar resulting topics. At the same time, there are no universal learning parameters for a variety of datasets that will result in a good model. In ARTM-based models, it is possible to reduce the influence of frequent words in the documents by making a separate set of specific and background topics with different regularizers.

So, to construct high-quality topic model, we want it to satisfy several conditions listed below.

Topics diversity. The obtained topics should cover different aspects of the provided documents, leading to the smallest possible overlap between words from different topics.

Topics interpretability. Produced topics should be understandable and easily described by a human.

Low amount of background words in specific topics. Amount of common words for the corpus should be small for each of the topics.

Thus, in order to take into account all the abovementioned requirements, we provide several features that are important when building a model and evaluating the quality.

The topics diversity condition is satisfied with the help of two separate decorrelators (D_{ϕ}^{B} and D_{ϕ}^{S}), — one for specific topics and another for the background ones. The level of coherence is defined by the selected quality value and will be explained in detail later in this section. To decrease the influence of common words, we allow the creation of background topics which are aimed to collect all the frequent words.

3.2 Learning Strategy

The formalization of *learning strategy* was done as a replacement to manual tuning described in [20]. Concerning the order in which regularizers should be applied, after selection of specific and background (B_N) topics number, it is necessary to set decorrelators first (D_{ϕ}^{B} and D_{ϕ}^{S}) to increase the topics sparsity which is a desirable property of the model. After several iterations of training (n_1), back smoothing parameters are set (P_{ϕ}^{B}, P_{θ}^{B}) to collect common words in background topics. Next, when n_2 iterations are done, comes the sparsing of specific topics (P_ϕ^S, P_θ^S). Then, following several more iterations the sparsing regularizers values may be changed to produce topics of higher quality. The sparsing process (increasing the values of P_ϕ^S and P_θ^S) stops when the termination criterion is hit. The vector form of a learning strategy for the topic models is presented in Fig. 1 with 13 parameters to optimize. In order to simplify the problem, we model two sparsing iterations for subject topics (changes of P_θ^S and P_ϕ^S).

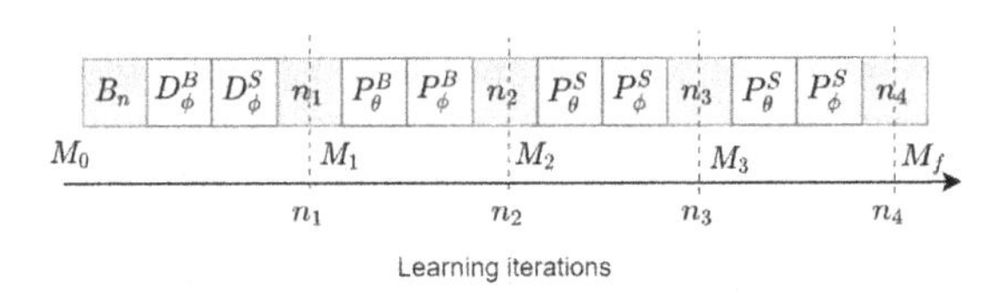

Fig. 1. Mapping between model learning process and vector representation of learning strategy (blue cells indicate integer variables, M_0 - initial untrained model, M_f - last trained result). (Color figure online)

It is worth mention that not for every dataset all the steps should be performed. For instance, when the vocabulary or the number of observations is low, high values for decorrelator may result in some topics extinction which is not a desirable outcome. So, in our approach, where learning parameters are presented as a set of regularizers values changes and the numbers of iterations selection, all the variables are bound to some reasonable search field that were defined by previous experiments as we state in Table 1.

Table 1. Search field bounds

Regularizers	Bounds	Variable type
D_ϕ^S, D_ϕ^B	[0, 1e5]	Float
n_1, n_2, n_3, n_4, B_N	[0, 8]	Integer
P_ϕ^S, P_θ^S	[1e−3, 1e2]	Float
P_ϕ^B, P_θ^B	[−1e2, −1e−3]	Float

3.3 Topic Quality Estimation

Quality score is assumed to reflect the human understanding of an interpretable topic. Given sets of the most probable words in each topic, we need to estimate the overall performance, and to achieve these, three widely applied scores were compared.

The coherence C [10] of topic t is calculated as follows:

$$C_t = \frac{2}{k(k-1)} \sum_{i=1}^{k-1} \sum_{j=i+1}^{k} \left[log \frac{p(w_i, w_j)}{p(w_i)p(w_j)} \right]_+, \tag{3}$$

where k is number of tokens in the topic, w_i and w_j are tokens from the topic, $p(w_i, w_j)$ - joint probability of tokens w_i and w_j in a corpora (co-occurrences).

The distributed word representation was incorporated in score proposed in [11] and is calculated as follows:

$$Q_t = \frac{1}{k(k-1)} \sum_{w_i \neq w_j \in t} d_{cos}(v_{w_i}, v_{w_j}), \tag{4}$$

where d_{cos} denotes the cosine distance between word vectors and v_{w_i}, v_{w_j} are word2vec representations of words from the topic.

The kernel contrast [19] is a measure of how topics kernels differ from each other. This score is calculated the following way:

$$K_t = \frac{1}{S_t} \sum_{w \in t_S} p(t|w), \tag{5}$$

where S_t is a size of the topic kernel. It is assumed that the higher scores on this metric correspond to better topics.

To select the quality function, we measured the correspondence between the metric values of topics obtained from models with different learning parameters and human scores. The results are provided in Subsect. 4.2.

3.4 Methods

Here we limit the number of models training for optimization algorithms to 150 in order to assure the comparison of population-based and non-population-based methods.

An approach with automatic learning strategy selection should achieve the following objectives:

- **Reliability to find a reasonable solution within limited iterations.** The need to get a high-quality model in reasonable time and with limited computational resources leads to the search speed requirement.
- **High exploratory ability.** In practice, when researchers are restricted by the number of runs, the ability of an algorithm to obtain interesting new solution occasionally is valuable. Thus, exploratory power is one of the main properties for the algorithm.

We compare several algorithms that can satisfy the requirements listed above.

Grid search. A method when the candidate solutions are generated from the grid of parameter values and which can be found in scikit-learn library. This is a baseline algorithm.

Genetic Algorithm. We tested several configurations of genetic algorithm with population size 10 (different mutation types - uniform, self-adaptive; crossover - single arithmetic recombination, two-point, blend) and the parameters of the best combination are provided below.

Blend Crossover. This recombination operation helps to extend the search space outside the "rectangle" defined by the parent solutions. Such property defines the feature of fast searching for the region of interest and aims to avoid being stuck in the local minimum. The α coefficient was set to 0.5, to assure equal opportunity for the child to lie inside or outside the space defined by parents.

Self-mutation. The two mutation parameters - the probability that an individ will mutate and the probability for each vector component to mutate – are incorporated into the candidate solution vector to let them evolve. All components of the solution are drawn from uniform distribution with a and b parameters and datatype provided in Table 1.

Selection. The percentage of the most fitted individs from the last population merge with the most fitted from the newly generated one. The percentage of parents were empirically evaluated and set to 0.4.

Differential Evolution is one of the evolutionary methods [15] that proved to work efficiently with continuous variables, i.e. finding the global minimum and converge fast. In order to check the performance on our datasets, we have taken the algorithm implementation from SciPy python package. Mutation strategy was set to current-to-best.

Bayesian Optimization. The probabilistic Bayesian approach is designed to be less computationally expensive as it builds a surrogate function, which is easier to optimize, and modifies it based on the feedback from the real model.

4 Experimental Study

4.1 Datasets

We have taken five real-world datasets for our experiments. Short name of each dataset is provided in the round brackets.

20 Newsgroups (20NG). This dataset [6] consists of around 180000 posts from newsgroups on 20 topics, covering politics, computers, automobiles and other aspects. Some of the given topics are very close to each other.

Datainfini's hotel reviews (HR). The dataset contains 34399 guest reviews of 1000 Hotels and highlights various aspects of the service quality.

Amazon fine food reviews (AR). This is a review corpus [8] of several various types of foods available through Amazon.

Lenta.ru dataset (lenta). The Russian language news corpus [21] contains more than 600000 news articles collected from 1999 to 2019 years.

Banners pages dataset (banners). Dataset of pages where banners lead collected from the internet with the help of crawler system [2]. In total, we obtained 400000 advertisement pages covering various topics.

For each of the datasets, several processing steps were applied such as cleaning (removal of HTML, punctuation, words with less than three letters), tokenization, stopwords removal and lemmatization. Lines with less than three words after processing were also removed. Calculation of the co-occurrence dictionaries for each dataset was made with the window size 10. The dictionary was restricted to words with document frequency more than three and less than 950. Summary of the data is provided in Table 2.

Table 2. Datasets summary

	Language	Avg tokens count	Voc size
20 Newsgroups	en	117.8	59974
Hotel reviews	en	22.6	13480
Food reviews	en	32.5	14678
Lenta.ru	ru	119.5	48874
Banner pages	ru	330	73062

4.2 Quality Function

In order to construct the appropriate quality function, we compared human scores and metrics scores for top words of topics from several models trained on the corpus of banners pages with various parameters. We have taken the word2vec model trained on Russian Wikipedia to construct the score based on distributed embeddings.

In total, we gave assessors 400 topics and asked them to set the score according to the following criteria: an explicit topic is presented and the amount of

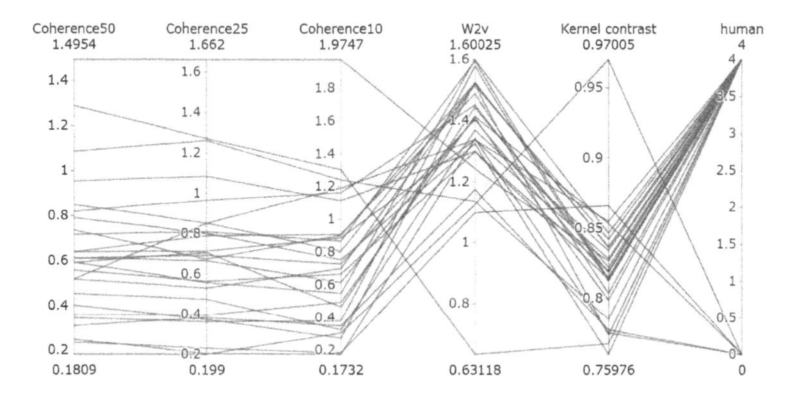

Fig. 2. Various scores for the best and the worst interpretable topics with the red lines – score 4 and green lines – score 0 (Color figure online)

background words is insignificant (1–3) – **Score 4**; an explicit topic is presented while the amount background words is high – **Score 3**; an explicit topic is presented but some words are not related to it – **Score 2**; topic is not clear and consistis of a mixture of 2–3 topics – **Score 1**; the topic is not understandable, the words seems not to be related to each other – **Score 0**.

In order to make sure that metrics can differentiate between truly "good" and "bad" topics, only ones with Score 0 and 4 were left. The results for a sample of topics are provided in Fig. 2. They indicate that the most aligned score with human judgement is coherence, while results for metric based on word2vec and kernel contrast cannot be well separated on interpretable and uninterpretable topics.

To construct quality function, we utilized the coherence of 50 most probable words and sum the minimum of the values, with the aim to avoid situation when result is a mixture of excellent and extremely incoherent topics.

$$Fitness = mean(C_i) + \min(C_i), \forall i = \overline{1, K}, \tag{6}$$

where K is a number of topics. We denote the quality function as "Fitness", similarly to the notation used in evolutionary theory.

4.3 Approaches Comparison and the Results

To provide an honest comparison between population-based and non-population-based algorithms with the computational restrictions, we set the limit of models that can be trained during the optimization procedure. Thus, the termination parameter was fixed and set to 150 models. The population size for evolutionary algorithms was set to 10, as the quality of solutions were higher with this value.

The experiments were conducted on five datasets (3 in English and 2 in Russian, see Subsect. 3.5) with 30 runs for each dataset and method combinations. The obtained results are depicted in Fig. 3 and averaged numbers with outliers removed are provided in Table 3.

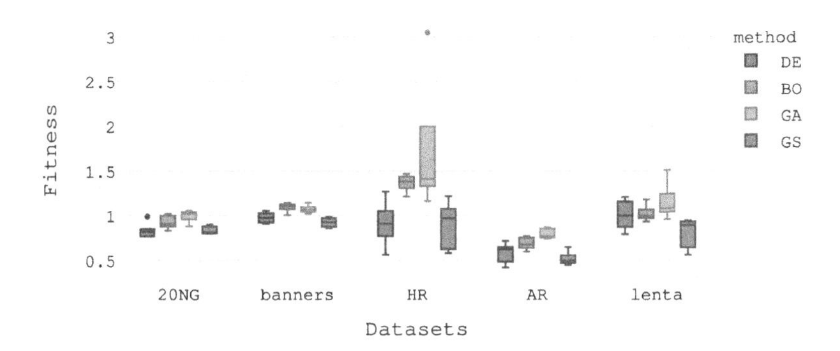

Fig. 3. Optimization algorithms comparision

Table 3. Mean values comparison

	BO	GS	DE	GA
20 Newsgroups	0.928	0.836	0.828	**0.996**
Hotel reviews	1.366	0.887	0.912	**1.403**
Food reviews	0.689	0.519	0.579	**0.798**
Lenta.ru	1.025	0.923	1.008	**1.155**
Banner pages	**1.094**	0.923	0.975	1.071

Genetic algorithm shows results up to 12% better on average compared to Bayesian Optimisation and also reveals high exploratory abilities. The small 3% difference in quality with the best result on the banners pages dataset may be explained by the significant average number of tokens which results in more complex search space, when 150 evaluations is not enough to find better solution.

Below the top 10 probable words of five topics from the best model on 20 Newsgroups dataset are provided as an example:

topic 1: *space nasa satellite launch center mission orbit health report probe*

topic 2: *file image program available version entry server format jpeg user*

topic 3: *armenian turkish turk turkey greek genoc russian ottoman appear armenia*

topic 4: *drive scsi disk hard controller bios floppy feature card tape*

topic 5: *game team season hockey play league goal flyer puck player*

Here we can see that the third topic is not describing any subject in particular though all the words are connected by the same meaning (nationality). This is a case when topic is coherent, but more related to background topics.

Several conclusions can be made from the experimental study. First of all, genetic algorithm outperforms all the other algorithms on 4 out of 5 datasets and the results are worse but comparable with Bayesian optimization on the last one dataset. For some tasks, especially on HR dataset, genetic algorithm reveals the ability to quickly explore the space for the exceptional solutions. The limited number of iteration and small population size does not allow differential evolution to start converging, which resulted in fitness close to grid search results.

4.4 LDA vs. ARTM

To prove that ARTM approach works better than LDA on chosen datasets in the scope of our metric, we evaluated all the datasets with our quality function using Bayesian Optimization. The number of specific topics for both models was set to 20. The results are provided in Fig. 4, where $BO + AR$ - Bayesian optimization of ARTM model with proposed learning strategy construction and $BO+LDA$ - Bayesian optimisation of α and β parameters. It is clearly seen that LDA performs much worse on the metric comparing to BigARTM; at the same time, the LDA model does not increase the score with optimization iterations.

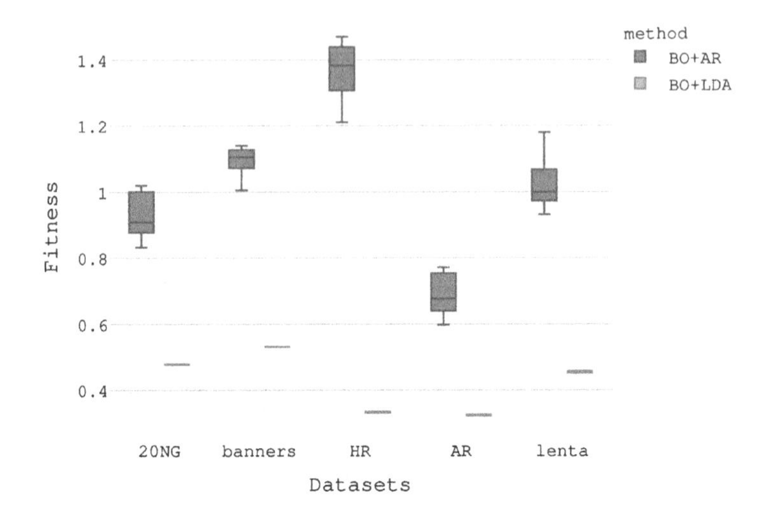

Fig. 4. Comparision of LDA and ARTM performance

According to the results, there is no need to include LDA model to the following set of experiments due to the low performance in our setting.

5 Discussion

Despite the good results shown on the datasets in terms of fitness quality, the approach still can be modified in order to take into consideration more task-specific features.

Firstly, Learning strategy can be further extended with the choice of specific topics number and search bounds extension.

Secondly, evolutionary search of learning strategies can be improved with modification of basic mutation and crossover operations to suit the mixed-integer nature of vector better. This can help an algorithm to converge faster and better deal with input datasets of various sizes. At the same time, it will be possible to include more variables in the model.

Thirdly, more research is needed on the fitness function metric, which may highly affect the choice of evolutionary algorithm design.

6 Conclusion

In this study, we introduce learning strategy construction for models based on additive regularization and provide a comparative study of optimization algorithms with carefully chosen quality function. Here we propose a vector representation and show that it can be successfully optimized in the presence of strong constrains. Comparing with Bayesian Optimization, genetic algorithm performs up to 12% better in cases when the vocabulary size is moderate and provides comparable results in case with a larger vocabulary. The combination of learning strategy and genetic algorithm is an approach for automatic tuning of ARTM-based models. In future work, we will conduct experiments with more parameters in the learning strategy and revise the mutation and crossover operators to better align the problem with discrete and continuous parameters.

Acknowledgments. This research is financially supported by The Russian Science Foundation, Agreement #20-11-20270.

References

1. Sidorov, G., Herrera-Alcántara, O. (eds.): MICAI 2016. LNCS (LNAI), vol. 10061. Springer, Cham (2017). https://doi.org/10.1007/978-3-319-62434-1
2. Butakov, N., Petrov, M., Mukhina, K., Nasonov, D., Kovalchuk, S.: Unified domain-specific language for collecting and processing data of social media. J. Int. Inf. Syst. **51**, 389–414 (2018)
3. Eiben, A.E., Smith, J.E.: Introduction to Evolutionary Computing, 2nd edn. Springer, Heidelberg (2015). https://doi.org/10.1007/978-3-662-44874-8
4. George, C.P., Doss, H.: Principled selection of hyperparameters in the latent dirichlet allocation model. J. Mach. Learn. Res. **18**(1), 5937–5974 (2017)
5. Hofmann, T.: Probabilistic latent semantic analysis. In: Proceedings of the Fifteenth Conference on Uncertainty in Artificial Intelligence, UAI 1999, pp. 289–296. Morgan Kaufmann Publishers Inc., San Francisco (1999)
6. Lang, K.: NewsWeeder: learning to filter netnews. In: Proceedings of the Twelfth International Conference on Machine Learning, pp. 331–339 (1995)
7. Lau, J.H., Newman, D., Baldwin, T.: Machine reading tea leaves: automatically evaluating topic coherence and topic model quality. In: Proceedings of the 14th Conference of the European Chapter of the ACL, pp. 530–539. ACL, Sweden (2014)
8. McAuley, J.J., Leskovec, J.: From amateurs to connoisseurs: modeling the evolution of user expertise through online reviews. In: Proceedings of the 22nd International Conference on World Wide Web, WWW 2013, pp. 897–908. Association for Computing Machinery, New York (2013). https://doi.org/10.1145/2488388.2488466
9. Newman, D., Lau, J.H., Grieser, K., Baldwin, T.: Automatic evaluation of topic coherence. In: Human Language Technologies: The 2010 Annual Conference of the North American Chapter of the Association for Computational Linguistics, HLT 2010, pp. 100–108. ACL, USA (2010)
10. Newman, D., Lau, J.H., Grieser, K., Baldwin, T.: Automatic evaluation of topic coherence. In: Human Language Technologies: The 2010 Annual Conference of the North American Chapter of the ACL, pp. 100–108. ACL, California (2010)
11. Nikolenko, S.I.: Topic quality metrics based on distributed word representations. In: Proceedings of the 39th International ACM SIGIR Conference, SIGIR 2016, pp. 1029–1032. Association for Computing Machinery, New York (2016)
12. Onan, A.: Biomedical text categorization based on ensemble pruning and optimized topic modelling. Comput. Math. Methods Med. **2018**, 1–22 (2018)
13. O'Callaghan, D., Greene, D., Carthy, J., Cunningham, P.: An analysis of the coherence of descriptors in topic modeling. Expert Syst. Appl. **42**(13), 5645–5657 (2015). https://doi.org/10.1016/j.eswa.2015.02.055

14. Panichella, A.: A systematic comparison of search algorithms for topic modelling—a study on duplicate bug report identification. In: Nejati, S., Gay, G. (eds.) SSBSE 2019. LNCS, vol. 11664, pp. 11–26. Springer, Cham (2019). https://doi.org/10.1007/978-3-030-27455-9_2
15. Price, K., Storn, R.M., Lampinen, J.A.: Differential Evolution: A Practical Approach to Global Optimization. Springer, Heidelberg (2005). https://doi.org/10.1007/3-540-31306-0
16. Role, F., Nadif, M.: Handling the impact of low frequency events on co-occurrence based measures of word similarity - a case study of pointwise mutual information (2011)
17. Snoek, J., Larochelle, H., Adams, R.P.: Practical Bayesian optimization of machine learning algorithms. In: Proceedings of the 25th International Conference on Neural Information Processing Systems, NIPS 2012, pp. 2951–2959. Curran Associates Inc., Red Hook (2012)
18. Tušar, T., Brockhoff, D., Hansen, N.: Mixed-integer benchmark problems for single- and bi-objective optimization. In: Proceedings of the Genetic and Evolutionary Computation Conference, GECCO 2019, pp. 718–726. Association for Computing Machinery, New York (2019). https://doi.org/10.1145/3321707.3321868
19. Vorontsov, K., Frei, O., Apishev, M., Romov, P., Dudarenko, M.: BigARTM: open source library for regularized multimodal topic modeling of large collections. In: Khachay, M.Y., Konstantinova, N., Panchenko, A., Ignatov, D.I., Labunets, V.G. (eds.) AIST 2015. CCIS, vol. 542, pp. 370–381. Springer, Cham (2015). https://doi.org/10.1007/978-3-319-26123-2_36
20. Vorontsov, K., Potapenko, A., Plavin, A.: Additive regularization of topic models for topic selection and sparse factorization. In: Gammerman, A., Vovk, V., Papadopoulos, H. (eds.) SLDS 2015. LNCS (LNAI), vol. 9047, pp. 193–202. Springer, Cham (2015). https://doi.org/10.1007/978-3-319-17091-6_14
21. Yutkin, D.: Corpus of Russian news articles collected from lenta.ru. https://github.com/yutkin/Lenta.Ru-News-Dataset

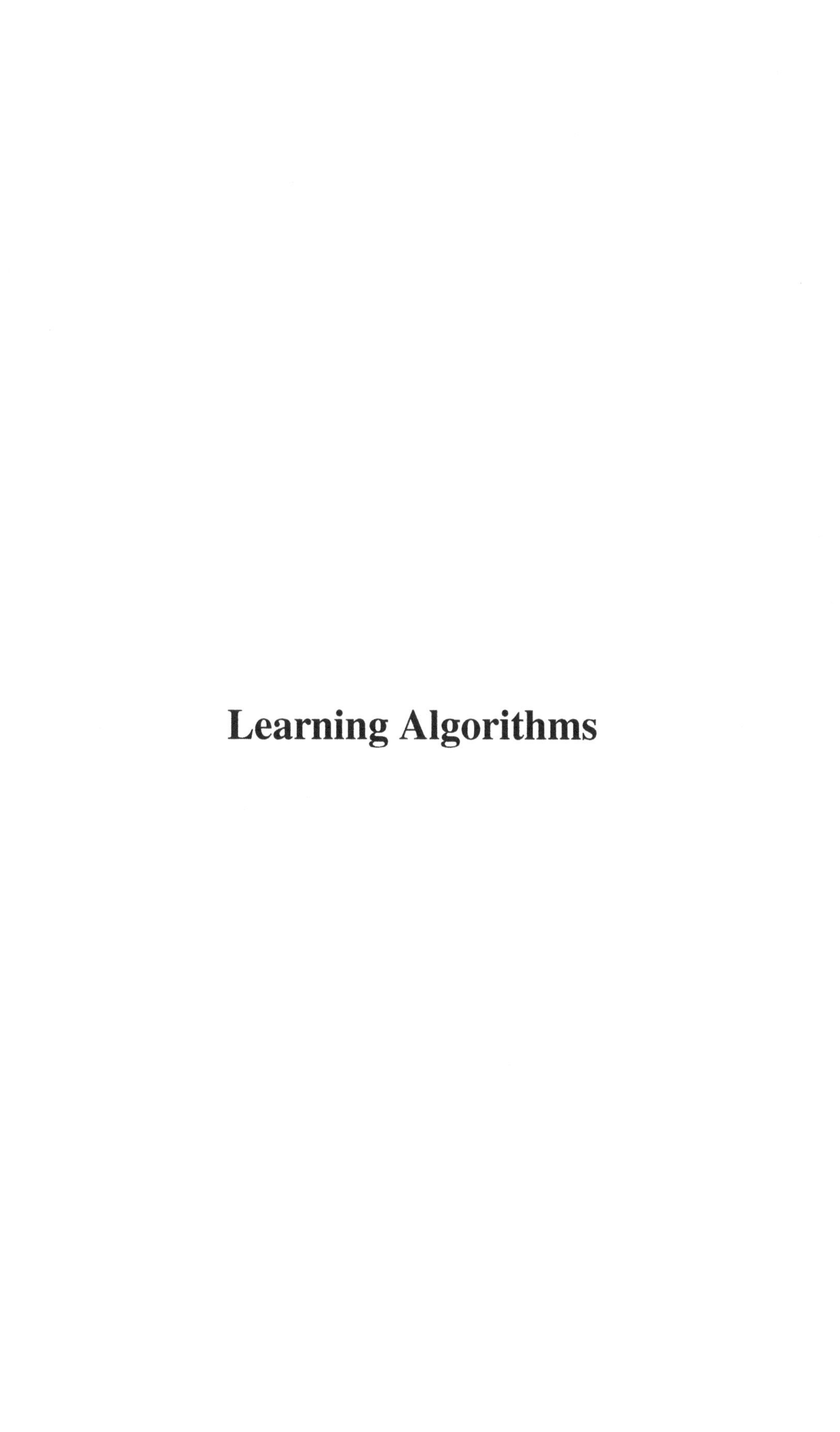

Learning Algorithms

A Cluster-Based Under-Sampling Algorithm for Class-Imbalanced Data

A. Guzmán-Ponce[1,2](✉), R. M. Valdovinos[1], and J. S. Sánchez[2]

[1] Facultad de Ingeniería, Universidad Autónoma del Estado de México, Toluca, Mexico
aguzmanp643@alumno.uaemex.mx, rvaldovinosr@uaemex.mx
[2] Institute of New Imaging Technologies, Department of Computer Languages and Systems, Universitat Jaume I, Castelló de la Plana, Spain
sanchez@uji.es

Abstract. The resampling methods are among the most popular strategies to face the class imbalance problem. The objective of these methods is to compensate the imbalanced class distribution by over-sampling the minority class and/or under-sampling the majority class. In this paper, a new under-sampling method based on the DBSCAN clustering algorithm is introduced. The main idea is to remove the majority class instances that are identified as noise by DBSCAN. The proposed method is empirically compared to well-known state-of-the-art under-sampling algorithms over 25 benchmarking databases and the experimental results demonstrate the effectiveness of the new method in terms of sensitivity, specificity, and geometric mean of individual accuracies.

Keywords: Class imbalance · DBSCAN · Under-sampling · Noise filtering

1 Introduction

The class imbalance problem has traditionally been viewed as a challenging scenario in Data Mining and Machine Learning [13]. A two-class data set is said to be imbalanced when one of the classes is strongly under-represented (minority or positive class) in comparison with the other class (majority or negative class) [12]. Several studies have shown that the class-imbalanced data problem may give rise to negative effects on the performance of most standard classifiers because they are often strongly biased towards the classification of the majority class and results in poor performance on the minority class [7], which is paradoxically the one of most interest in many real-world applications.

Much research has been conducted to tackle the class imbalance problem by developing different techniques at both algorithmic and data levels [11–13]. The methods at the algorithmic level modify the existing learning models for biasing the discrimination process towards the minority class. On the other hand,

E. A. de la Cal et al. (Eds.): HAIS 2020, LNAI 12344, pp. 299–311, 2020.
https://doi.org/10.1007/978-3-030-61705-9_25

the data level solutions consist of a preprocessing step to resample the original data set, either by over-sampling the minority class and/or under-sampling the majority class, until the classes are approximately equally represented. In general, the resampling strategies have been the most widely used techniques because they are independent of the classifier and can be easily implemented for any problem [1,9].

The simplest resampling methods are random over-sampling and random under-sampling (RUS). The former balances the class distribution through the random replication of minority class instances; although this method appears to be quite effective without adding new information into the data set, it may increase the likelihood of overfitting because it makes exact copies of the minority class examples. On the other hand, random under-sampling aims at balancing the data set through the random removal of instances that belong to the over-sized class; despite important information can be lost when instances are discarded at random, it has empirically been shown to be one of the most effective resampling methods.

Despite the apparent superiority of over-sampling [8,19], this paper concentrates on under-sampling because it seems to be a better choice for problems represented by large-scale databases [23], which is a situation of great interest with the advent of Big Data. Despite under-sampling may result in throwing away potentially useful information about the majority class and perturbing the a priori probability of the data set, it has to be taken in mind that over-sampling worsens the computational burden of most classifiers, may increase the likelihood of overfitting and introduce noise that could result in a loss of performance [3]. Taking all these questions into account, we introduce an under-sampling method based on the DBSCAN clustering algorithm [6], which will be applied only to the instances of the majority class. The proposed method is then empirically compared to other well-known under-sampling techniques over a collection of imbalanced two-class data sets taken from the KEEL repository. From a practical point of view, the major contributions of this paper are: (1) an adaptation of the DBSCAN algorithm to obtain a compact and representative cluster of the majority class, and (2) a new cluster-based under-sampling method to face the class imbalance problem.

Several cluster-based approaches have already been proposed to reduce the size of the majority class. For instance, Yen and Lee proposed the use of the K-means clustering technique to downsizing the majority class [26]. Lin et al. introduced an under-sampling strategy also based on K-means, which sets a number of clusters equal to the number of minority class instances [16]. Inspired by the approach proposed by Yen and Lee, Ofek et al. developed a new under-sampling algorithm that clusters only the minority class instances [17]. Tsai et al. introduced a novel under-sampling technique that combines clustering analysis (using the affinity propagation algorithm) and instance selection (the authors use three different algorithms) over the majority class [23]. Verma et al. proposed a hybrid approach based on the DBSCAN algorithm that integrates over-sampling and under-sampling [24]. Onan under-samples the majority class instances by employing a consensus cluster-based scheme [18].

Hereafter the paper is organized as follows. Section 2 provides a brief review of the under-sampling methods used in this study. Next, the new algorithm based on DBSCAN clustering is introduced in Sect. 3. Section 4 describes the experimental set-up, whereas Sect. 5 discusses the experimental results. Finally, Sect. 6 remarks the main conclusions and outlines some directions for further research.

2 Under-Sampling Methods

To remedy the shortcomings associated with the lazy RUS strategy, many other under-sampling methods have been developed with the aim of incorporating a more intelligent selection of the majority class instances that will be removed from the data set.

For instance, the Hart's condensing (CNN) algorithm [10] has been used as an under-sampling technique by applying the concept of consistent subset to eliminate the majority class instances that are sufficiently far away from the decision boundary because these are considered to be irrelevant for learning. Analogously, the Tomek links (TL) [22] have already been employed to remove the majority class instances that lie in the proximity of the decision boundary since, if two examples form a Tomek link, then either one of these can be seen as noise or both instances are borderline [5].

In contrast to CNN and Tomek links, the Wilson's editing (ENN) technique [25] emphasizes more data cleaning than data reduction to under-sample the majority class. In this case, the ENN algorithm identifies and removes majority class instances that are considered to be noisy according to the k-nearest neighbor (k-NN) classifier. Tomek proposed two extensions of the ENN algorithm with the repeated Wilson's editing (RENN) and All-k-NN (ALLk) methods [21]. The RENN algorithm extends the Wilson's editing approach by repeating multiple the deletion process until no more instances can be removed. The ALLk method similar to RENN except for the fact that the value of k (i.e., the number of neighbors) is increased after each iteration.

The neighborhood cleaning (NCL) rule developed by Laurikkala [15] consists of two stages. Firstly, the ENN algorithm is used to remove majority class instances. Then, a second step is performed to find the neighbors of each minority class instance and those that belong to the majority class are removed. According to the experiments carried by the author, the NCL method processes noisy instances carefully but, it is strongly biased in favor of the minority class and leads to poor specificity and overall accuracy.

It has to be pointed out that one critical disadvantage of all the ENN-based algorithms is that they fail when a large amount of noise is present in the majority class because in such cases, noise results incorrectly classified by other noisy instances.

3 The Proposed Under-Sampling Method Based on DBSCAN

The DBSCAN (Density Based Spatial Clustering of Applications with Noise) algorithm is a popular unsupervised learning algorithm that assumes that the clusters correspond to dense regions in space separated by regions of lower density [6], where density is defined as a minimum number of points within a certain distance of each other [14]. Thus the basic idea of DBSCAN is that for each point of a cluster the neighborhood of a given radius ϵ has to contain at least a minimum number of points ($minPts$). This technique presents some interesting properties since it can discover clusters of any arbitrary shape, works well even with noisy data, and is also efficient for large data sets [20].

Algorithm 1. DBSCAN

Require: Data set $D = \{p_1, p_2, \ldots, p_n\}$, ϵ, $minPts$
1: $C \leftarrow \emptyset$
2: **for** each unvisited instance p_i in D **do**
3:   Mark p_i as visited
4:   nbhdP $\leftarrow$ Neighbors(ϵ, p_i)
5:   **if** $sizeof(nbhdP) < minPts$ **then**
6:     Mark p_i as noise
7:   **else**
8:     $C=$ next cluster
9:     $C \leftarrow p_i$
10:     **for** each instance p' in nbhdP **do**
11:       **if** p' is not visited **then**
12:         Mark p' as visited
13:         nbhdP' $\leftarrow$ Neighbors(ϵ, p')
14:         **if** $sizeof(nbhdP') \geq minPts$ **then**
15:           nbhdP = nbhdP joined with nbhdP'
16:         **end if**
17:       **end if**
18:       **if** p' is not yet member of any cluster **then**
19:         $C \leftarrow p'$
20:       **end if**
21:     **end for**
22:   **end if**
23: **end for**

Unlike the original DBSCAN algorithm that is applied to the whole data set, the modification proposed in this paper will concentrate on obtaining a compact and representative cluster of the majority class. Besides, the new under-sampling method will take advantage of the fact that DBSCAN can detect noisy data (Step 6 in Algorithm 1), thus removing those majority class instances that have been identified as noise. On the other hand, the input parameters ϵ and $minPts$ in the proposed algorithm will be estimated using a modification of the original equations proposed by Smiti and Elouedi [20]:

$$\epsilon = \sqrt{\frac{\sum_{i=1}^{n^-} dist(m, p_i^-)}{n^-}} \tag{1}$$

where m is the middle vector of the majority class, p_i^- represents a majority class instance, $dist$ corresponds to the Euclidean distance between p_i and m, and n^- denotes the number of majority class instances.

$$minPts = \frac{\pi \times \epsilon^2}{TotalVolume} \times n^+ \tag{2}$$

where $TotalVolume = \frac{4}{3} \times \pi \times \epsilon^3$ and n^+ is the number of minority class instances. Note that we have supposed the spherical form to shape the majority class. Therefore, minPts is based on a ratio of change between the area of a circle and the sphere volume, due to DBSCAN moves around density-reachable instances according to the Euclidean distance.

The under-sampling algorithm based on DBSCAN starts by splitting the data set into two subsets C^- and C^+ with the majority and minority class instances, respectively. Then it takes an arbitrary instance p_i^- from the majority class C^- and searches all instances density-reachable from p_i^- with respect to ϵ and $minPts$. If there are not $minPts$ in the ϵ-neighborhood of p_i^-, then this is labeled as noise and removed. If an instance is found to be part of a cluster, all ϵ-neighborhood instances are also part of that cluster. If the instance p_i^- is a border point, no points are density-reachable from p_i^- and the algorithm visits the next majority class instance to discover whether it is noise or it belongs to a further cluster [27]. This process will be repeated on the majority class until ϵ and $minPts$ do not change. The algorithm for under-sampling is described as follows:

Algorithm 2. Under-sampling based on DBSCAN

Require: Data set $D = \{p_1, p_2, \ldots, p_n\}$
1: $D' \leftarrow \emptyset$
2: Split D into two subsets: $C^- = \{p_1^-, p_2^-, \ldots, p_n^-\}$ with the majority class instances and $C^+ = \{p_1^+, p_2^+, \ldots, p_n^+\}$ with the minority class instances
3: **repeat**
4: Estimate ϵ and $minPts$
5: **for** each unvisited instance p_i^- in C^- **do**
6: Select an arbitrary instance p_i^-
7: Mark p_i^- as visited
8: Find all instances density-reachable from p_i^- according to ϵ and $minPts$
9: **if** p_i^- does not have $minPts$ in its ϵ-neighborhood **then**
10: Remove p_i^- from C^-
11: **end if**
12: **end for**
13: **until** ϵ and $minPts$ do not change
14: $D' = C^- \cup C^+$

As can be seen, in Algorithm 2, DBSCAN is used to take advantage of removing instances that cannot be density-reachable. Given the size of the majority class, the proposal removes most of the instances from this class that are identified as noise.

4 Experimental Set-Up

With the aim of evaluating the performance of the DBSCAN under-sampling method and comparing it with that of some state-of-the-art algorithms, we carried out a series of experiments on a large collection of imbalanced two-class

Table 1. Some characteristics of the data sets (sorted by the IR values)

	Data set	Class distribution	#Instances	IR
1	yeast-2_vs_4	51 – 463	514	9.08
2	yeast-0-5-6-7-9_vs_4	51 – 477	528	9.35
3	vowel0	90 – 898	988	9.98
4	glass-0-1-6_vs_2	17 – 175	192	10.29
5	glass2	17 – 197	214	11.59
6	shuttle-c0-vs-c4	123 – 1706	1829	13.87
7	yeast-1_vs_7	30 – 429	459	14.30
8	glass4	13 – 201	214	15.47
9	ecoli4	20 – 316	336	15.80
10	page-blocks-1-3_vs_4	28 – 444	472	15.86
11	glass-0-1-6_vs_5	9 – 175	184	19.44
12	shuttle-c2-vs-c4	6 – 123	129	20.50
13	yeast-1-4-5-8_vs_7	30 – 663	693	22.10
14	glass5	9 – 205	214	22.78
15	yeast-2_vs_8	20 – 462	482	23.10
16	flare-F	43 – 1023	1066	23.79
17	yeast4	51 – 1433	1484	28.10
18	yeast-1-2-8-9_vs_7	30 – 917	947	30.57
19	yeast5	44 – 1440	1484	32.73
20	ecoli-0-1-3-7_vs_2-6	7 – 274	281	39.14
21	abalone-17_vs_7-8-9-10	58 – 2280	2338	39.31
22	yeast6	35 – 1449	1484	41.40
23	shuttle-2_vs_5	49 – 3267	3316	66.67
24	kdd-buffer_oflow_vs_back	30 – 2203	2233	73.43
25	poker-8-9_vs_5	25 – 2050	2075	82.00

data sets taken from the KEEL Data Set Repository (https://sci2s.ugr.es/keel/imbalanced.php#subA). The main characteristics of the data sets are summarized in Table 1, including the a prior class distribution, the total number of instances, and the imbalance ratio (IR), that is, the ratio of the majority class size to the minority class size.

The 10-fold cross-validation method was adopted for the experimental design: each original data set was randomly divided into 10 stratified parts of size $n/10$, where n denotes the total number of instances in the data set. For each fold, nine blocks were pooled as the training set, and the remaining portion was used as an independent test set.

The k-NN classifier (with $k = 5$) was applied to the sets preprocessed by the under-sampling method here proposed and the strategies described in Sect. 2 (CNN, ENN, RUS, RENN, ALLk, NCL, TL), and also to each original training set, which can be deemed as a baseline for comparison. Then the results from classifying the test samples were averaged across the 10 runs using three standard performance evaluation measures calculated from a 2×2 confusion matrix, where each entry contains the number of correct/incorrect classifications: the sensitivity or true-positive rate (TPR), the specificity or true-negative rate (TNR), and the geometric mean of sensitivity and specificity (Gmean) computed as follows:

$$Gmean = \sqrt{TPR \cdot TNR} \qquad (3)$$

where TPR and TNR are defined as the percentage of positive (minority class) and negative (majority class) instances correctly classified, respectively.

5 Experiment Results

For each data set, Table 2 reports the geometric mean (averaged across the 10 runs) of the k-NN classifier using the under-sampled training sets, along with the Friedman's average rank for each algorithm at a significance level of $\alpha = 0.05$. Values in boldface highlight the best performing method in each data set. As can be seen, the new method outperformed the other under-sampling algorithms in 10 out of 25 databases, which represents a 40% of the cases. The reason why DBSCAN performed the best on these databases is that it keeps the most informative instances. Besides the performance of DBSCAN was quite similar to that of the best algorithms in four databases (yeast-2_vs_4, shuttle-c0-vs-c4, page-blocks-1-3_vs_4, and ecoli-0-1-3-7_vs_2-6). Conversely, this method achieved very poor results for some other databases (shuttle-c2-vs-c4, yeast-1-4-5-8_vs_7, yeast-1-2-8-9_vs_7, and abalone-17_vs_7-8-9-10), whose characteristics should be further analyzed to gain some insight.

As the Friedman test only can detect significant differences over the whole set of comparisons, the Nemenyi's post hoc test was also computed to report any significant differences between all pairs of methods [4]. This test states that performances of two or more algorithms are significantly different if their average ranks are at least as great as their critical difference (CD) with a given level of significance:

$$CD = q_\alpha \sqrt{\frac{L(L+1)}{6N}} \qquad (4)$$

where N denotes the number of databases, L is the number of algorithms, and q_α is a critical value based on the Studentized range statistic divided by $\sqrt{2}$.

Table 3 summarizes the Nemenyi's statistic for a significance level of $\alpha = 0.05$. The positive values in boldface indicate that the method in the raw significantly outperforms the method in the column, whereas the negative values in boldface mean that the method in the column is significantly better than the method in the raw. Despite RENN, All*k* and NCL appear to be the best performing techniques for the databases used in these experiments, the statistical significance study shows that no method was significantly better than the DBSCAN under-sampling algorithm (no value in the DBSCAN row is greater than the critical difference). Additionally, the cluster-based method proposed here performed better than CNN, RUS and TL.

Table 2. Geometric mean results

Data Set	Original	DBSCAN	CNN	ENN	RUS	RENN	ALL*k*	NCL	TL
yeast-2_vs_4	81.4	83.7	78.8	83.9	78.8	**84.0**	83.9	**84.0**	82.5
yeast-0-5-6-7-9_vs_4	52.0	60.4	56.4	69.8	54.5	74.1	75.4	**77.5**	68.2
vowel0	98.3	**99.9**	40.8	98.3	94.9	98.3	98.3	98.8	98.3
glass-0-1-6_vs_2	0.0	**47.5**	45.9	41.9	41.9	42.0	45.9	33.9	0.0
glass2	0.0	**53.2**	49.9	41.9	42.0	41.7	42.0	34.1	0.0
shuttle-c0-vs-c4	99.6	99.6	**100**	99.6	99.6	99.6	99.6	99.6	99.6
yeast-1_vs_7	44.7	31.6	56.4	44.6	41.9	51.6	40.8	**57.5**	36.5
glass4	54.8	**87.7**	48.7	72.6	72.2	73.4	73.0	72.6	61.2
ecoli4	86.3	86.3	94.9	89.4	**97.5**	89.4	89.4	92.2	86.3
page-blocks-1-3_vs_4	96.3	96.3	90.3	95.8	84.5	96.4	96.4	**98.1**	96.3
glass-0-1-6_vs_5	87.4	88.2	67.4	**94.3**	81.6	**94.3**	**94.3**	**94.3**	80.7
shuttle-c2-vs-c4	0.0	0.0	0.0	0.0	**83.3**	0.0	0.0	0.0	0.0
yeast-1-4-5-8_vs_7	0.0	0.0	29.8	18.2	**52.9**	31.6	18.2	31.5	0.0
glass5	74.0	**88.2**	60.3	81.4	**88.2**	81.4	74.5	81.6	74.0
yeast-2_vs_8	**74.1**	**74.2**	68.4	**74.2**	52.4	**74.2**	**74.2**	**74.2**	**74.2**
flare-F	30.4	**72.9**	43.5	64.4	62.6	68.1	54.9	62.6	34.0
yeast4	44.1	39.5	44.0	67.1	41.9	**70.0**	68.6	65.5	48.4
yeast-1-2-8-9_vs_7	18.2	18.2	35.9	18.2	**66.7**	25.8	18.3	18.2	18.3
yeast5	83.7	87.6	70.1	94.0	70.1	**95.3**	94.1	93.9	86.3
ecoli-0-1-3-7_vs_2-6	84.2	84.2	78.7	84.4	**84.5**	84.4	84.4	84.4	84.2
abalone-17_vs_7-8-9-10	26.3	18.6	34.3	34.7	**74.1**	34.7	32.2	39.4	26.2
yeast6	69.5	75.3	71.1	79.2	72.7	**82.8**	**82.8**	80.9	75.4
shuttle-2_vs_5	**100**	**100**	87.7	**100**	96.9	**100**	**100**	**100**	**100**
kdd-buffer_oflow_vs_back	**98.3**	**98.3**	0.0	**98.3**	81.4	**98.3**	**98.3**	**98.3**	98.3
poker-8-9_vs_5	0.0	**52.1**	0.0	0.0	42.0	0.0	0.0	0.0	0.0
Av. rank	6.64	4.80	6.28	4.46	5.14	**3.46**	4.12	3.84	6.26

Table 3. Summary of the Nemenyi's test with $\alpha = 0.05$

	Original	DBSCAN	CNN	ENN	RUS	RENN	ALLk	NCL	TL
Original		−1.84	−0.36	−2.18	−1.50	**−3.18**	**−2.52**	**−2.80**	−0.38
DBSCAN			1.48	−0.34	0.34	−1.34	−0.68	−0.96	1.46
CNN				−1.82	−1.14	**−2.82**	−2.16	**−2.44**	−0.02
ENN					0.68	−1.00	−0.34	−0.62	1.80
RUS						−1.68	−1.02	−1.30	1.12
RENN							0.66	0.38	**2.80**
ALLk								−0.28	2.14
NCL									**2.42**
TL									
Critical difference (CD)									2.40

In class-imbalanced data problems, it is especially important to evaluate the performance on each individual class because the minority class is usually the one of major interest and with the highest misclassification costs [2].

Table 4. True-positive rates

Data Set	Original	DBSCAN	CNN	ENN	RUS	RENN	All$k$	NCL	TL
yeast-2_vs_4	0.667	**0.706**	**0.706**	**0.706**	**0.706**	**0.706**	**0.706**	**0.706**	0.686
yeast-0-5-6-7-9_vs_4	0.275	0.373	0.431	0.490	0.431	0.549	0.569	**0.608**	0.471
vowel0	0.967	**1.000**	**1.000**	0.967	**1.000**	0.967	0.967	0.978	0.967
glass-0-1-6_vs_2	0.000	**0.235**	**0.235**	0.176	0.176	0.176	**0.235**	0.118	0.000
glass2	0.000	0.294	**0.353**	0.176	0.176	0.176	0.176	0.118	0.000
shuttle-c0-vs-c4	0.992	0.992	**1.000**	0.992	0.992	0.992	0.992	0.992	0.992
yeast-1_vs_7	0.200	0.100	**0.367**	0.200	0.176	0.267	0.167	0.333	0.133
glass4	0.308	**0.769**	**0.769**	0.538	0.846	0.538	0.538	0.538	0.385
ecoli4	0.750	0.750	0.950	0.800	**1.000**	0.800	0.800	0.850	0.750
page-blocks-1-3_vs_4	0.929	0.929	**1.000**	0.929	**1.000**	0.929	0.929	0.964	0.929
glass-0-1-6_vs_5	0.778	0.778	**1.000**	0.889	**1.000**	0.889	0.889	0.889	0.667
shuttle-c2-vs-c4	0.000	0.000	**1.000**	0.000	0.833	0.000	0.000	0.000	0.000
yeast-1-4-5-8_vs_7	0.000	0.000	0.100	0.033	**0.700**	0.100	0.033	0.100	0.000
glass5	0.556	0.778	**1.000**	0.667	**1.000**	0.667	0.556	0.667	0.556
yeast-2_vs_8	**0.550**	**0.550**	0.500	**0.550**	**0.550**	**0.550**	**0.550**	**0.550**	**0.550**
flare-F	0.093	**0.535**	0.209	0.419	0.395	0.465	0.302	0.395	0.116
yeast4	0.196	0.157	0.235	0.451	0.176	**0.490**	0.471	0.431	0.235
yeast-1-2-8-9_vs_7	0.033	0.033	0.133	0.033	**0.667**	0.067	0.033	0.033	0.033
yeast5	0.705	0.773	0.818	0.886	0.818	**0.909**	0.886	0.886	0.750
ecoli-0-1-3-7_vs_2-6	**0.714**	**0.714**	**0.714**	**0.714**	**0.714**	**0.714**	**0.714**	**0.714**	**0.714**
abalone-17_vs_7-8-9-10	0.069	0.034	0.138	0.121	**0.707**	0.121	0.103	0.155	0.069
yeast6	0.486	0.571	0.600	0.629	**0.771**	0.686	0.686	0.657	0.571
shuttle-2_vs_5	**1.000**	**1.000**	**1.000**	**1.000**	**1.000**	**1.000**	**1.000**	**1.000**	**1.000**
kdd-buffer_oflow_vs_back	0.967	0.967	**1.000**	0.967	0.667	0.967	0.967	0.967	0.967
poker-8-9_vs_5	0.000	**0.280**	0.000	0.000	0.176	0.000	0.000	0.000	0.000

Correspondingly, Tables 4 and 5 report the true-positive and true-negative rates, respectively. As in the previous results, again the best values in each database are shown in boldface. One should analyze the results of both tables together in order to understand the effect of each under-sampling algorithm on the performance of the classifier.

One can observe that using the original data set with no preprocessing achieved true-negative rates similar to those of the under-sampling algorithms, but at the cost of misclassifying many minority class instances as indicated by the generally low true-positive rates. Focusing on the results of the DBSCAN-based algorithm, it is worth noting that the true-positive rates are among the best ones for many databases, while the true-negative rates are always 1 or very close to 1. Nonetheless, there are still some cases (shuttle-c2-vs-c4, yeast-1-4-5-8_vs_7, yeast-1-2-8-9_vs_7, abalone-17_vs_7-8-9-10 and glass2) in which the true-positive rate was not high enough and therefore, a deeper analysis would be necessary for a better understanding of the conditions under which the under-sampling algorithm proposed here performs well.

Table 5. True-negative rates

Data Set	Original	DBSCAN	CNN	ENN	RUS	RENN	All*k*	NCR	TL
yeast-2_vs_4	0.994	0.993	0.880	0.998	0.880	**1.000**	0.998	**1.000**	0.991
yeast-0-5-6-7-9_vs_4	0.983	0.981	0.739	0.995	0.739	**1.000**	**1.000**	0.988	0.987
vowel0	0.999	0.998	0.167	**1.000**	0.900	**1.000**	**1.000**	0.999	0.999
glass-0-1-6_vs_2	0.994	0.960	0.895	0.993	0.993	**1.000**	0.895	0.980	0.994
glass2	0.995	0.961	0.706	0.994	**1.000**	0.987	**1.000**	0.988	0.995
shuttle-c0-vs-c4	**1.000**	**1.000**	**1.000**	**1.000**	**1.000**	**1.000**	**1.000**	**1.000**	**1.000**
yeast-1_vs_7	0.998	**1.000**	0.869	0.995	0.993	**1.000**	**1.000**	0.992	0.998
glass4	0.975	**1.000**	0.308	0.979	0.615	**1.000**	0.989	0.979	0.975
ecoli4	0.994	0.994	0.947	**1.000**	0.950	**1.000**	**1.000**	**1.000**	0.994
page-blocks-1-3_vs_4	0.998	0.998	0.815	0.988	0.714	**1.000**	**1.000**	0.998	0.998
glass-0-1-6_vs_5	0.983	**1.000**	0.455	**1.000**	0.667	**1.000**	**1.000**	**1.000**	0.977
shuttle-c2-vs-c4	**1.000**	**1.000**	0.000	**1.000**	0.833	**1.000**	**1.000**	**1.000**	**1.000**
yeast-1-4-5-8_vs_7	**0.998**	0.995	0.885	0.997	0.400	**0.998**	0.997	0.995	0.995
glass5	0.985	**1.000**	0.364	0.995	0.778	0.995	**1.000**	**1.000**	0.985
yeast-2_vs_8	0.998	**1.000**	0.936	**1.000**	0.500	**1.000**	**1.000**	**1.000**	**1.000**
flare-F	0.994	0.995	0.904	0.989	0.990	0.997	**0.997**	0.990	0.992
yeast4	0.992	0.996	0.822	0.999	0.993	**1.000**	0.999	0.996	0.995
yeast-1-2-8-9_vs_7	0.998	0.999	0.969	0.996	0.667	**1.000**	**1.000**	0.999	**1.000**
yeast5	0.994	0.992	0.600	0.998	0.600	**1.000**	0.999	0.995	0.994
ecoli-0-1-3-7_vs_2-6	0.993	0.993	0.867	0.996	**1.000**	0.996	0.996	0.996	0.993
abalone-17_vs_7-8-9-10	**1.000**	0.999	0.854	0.999	0.776	**1.000**	**1.000**	0.999	0.999
yeast6	0.993	0.992	0.842	**0.999**	0.686	**0.999**	**0.999**	0.996	0.994
shuttle-2_vs_5	**1.000**	**1.000**	0.769	**1.000**	0.939	**1.000**	**1.000**	**1.000**	**1.000**
kdd-buffer_oflow_vs_back	**1.000**	**1.000**	0.000	**1.000**	0.995	**1.000**	**1.000**	**1.000**	**1.000**
poker-8-9_vs_5	**1.000**	0.968	**1.000**	**1.000**	**1.000**	**1.000**	**1.000**	**1.000**	**1.000**

6 Conclusions and Future Work

In this paper, the traditional DBSCAN clustering algorithm has been modified for under-sampling the majority class in imbalanced two-class data sets. One important feature of the proposed method is that it takes advantage of the capability of DBSCAN to discover and remove noise. Thus our under-sampling algorithm allows to eliminate the majority class instances that have been identified as noise by the basic procedure of DBSCAN. In addition, compared to other algorithms such as RUS, the new under-sampling technique can effectively avoid the important information loss of majority class. As a by-product, the proposed method reduces the size of the data sets, which is a common advantage of the under-sampling algorithms over the over-sampling strategy and results especially interesting in the current era of Big Data.

The experiments carried out over 25 two-class data sets with moderate to high class imbalance ratio have demonstrated the effectiveness of the new under-sampling method when compared with other popular state-of-the-art algorithms. In the empirical analysis, we have evaluated the classification performance of the under-sampling methods by using the true-positive rate, the true-negative rate and the geometric mean, and then we have checked for statistically significant differences through the Friedman's average ranks and the Nemenyi's post hoc test.

Although the results of this preliminary study are promising, we believe that a more exhaustive analysis is still necessary to gain deeper insight into which intrinsic data characteristics can affect the performance of the proposed under-sampling method. On the other hand, the experiments of this paper have concentrated on the k-NN classifier, but other prediction models such as decision trees and neural networks should be also tested to draw more general and robust conclusions. Finally, another avenue for further research is the generalization of our algorithm to multi-class and/or multi-label imbalanced databases.

Acknowledgment. This work was partially supported by the Universitat Jaume I under grant [UJI-B2018-49], the 5046/2020CIC UAEM project and the Mexican Science and Technology Council (CONACYT) under scholarship [702275].

References

1. Cao, P., Zhao, D., Zaiane, O.: Hybrid probabilistic sampling with random subspace for imbalanced data learning. Intell. Data Anal. **18**(6), 1089–1108 (2014)
2. Chawla, N.V., Cieslak, D.A., Hall, L.O., Joshi, A.: Automatically countering imbalance and its empirical relationship to cost. Data Mining Knowl. Disc. **17**(2), 225–252 (2008)
3. Dal Pozzolo, A., Caelen, O., Bontempi, G.: When is undersampling effective in unbalanced classification tasks? In: Appice, A., Rodrigues, P.P., Santos Costa, V., Soares, C., Gama, J., Jorge, A. (eds.) ECML PKDD 2015. LNCS (LNAI), vol. 9284, pp. 200–215. Springer, Cham (2015). https://doi.org/10.1007/978-3-319-23528-8_13

4. Demšar, J.: Statistical comparisons of classifiers over multiple data sets. J. Mach. Learn. Res. **7**, 1–30 (2006)
5. Devi, D., Biswas, S., Purkayastha, B.: Redundancy-driven modified Tomek-link based undersampling: a solution to class imbalance. Pattern Recognit. Lett. **93**, 3–12 (2017)
6. Ester, M., Kriegel, H.P., Sander, J., Xu, X.: A density-based algorithm for discovering clusters in large spatial databases with noise. In: Proceedings of 2nd International Conference on Knowledge Discovery and Data Mining, pp. 226–231. AAAI Press, Portland (1996)
7. Fernández, A., del Jesus, M.J., Herrera, F.: Hierarchical fuzzy rule based classification systems with genetic rule selection for imbalanced data-sets. Int. J. Approximate Reason. **50**(3), 561–577 (2009)
8. García, V., Sánchez, J.S., Marqués, A.I., Florencia, R., Rivera, G.: Understanding the apparent superiority of over-sampling through an analysis of local information for class-imbalanced data. Exp. Syst. Appl. **158**, 113026 (2019). https://doi.org/10.1016/j.eswa.2019.113026
9. García, V., Sánchez, J.S., Mollineda, R.A.: On the effectiveness of preprocessing methods when dealing with different levels of class imbalance. Knowl.-Based Syst. **25**(1), 13–21 (2012)
10. Hart, P.: The condensed nearest neighbor rule. IEEE Trans. Inf. Theory **14**(3), 515–516 (1968)
11. He, H., Ma, Y.: Imbalanced Learning: Foundations, Algorithms, and Applications. Wiley - IEEE Press, Piscataway (2013)
12. Japkowicz, N., Stephen, S.: The class imbalance problem: a systematic study. Intell. Data Anal. **6**(5), 429–449 (2002)
13. Krawczyk, B.: Learning from imbalanced data: open challenges and future directions. Prog. Artif. Intell. **5**(4), 221–232 (2016)
14. Kumar, K.A., Rangan, C.P.: Privacy preserving DBSCAN algorithm for clustering. In: Alhajj, R., Gao, H., Li, J., Li, X., Zaïane, O.R. (eds.) Advanced Data Mining and Applications, pp. 57–68. Springer, Heidelberg (2007). https://doi.org/10.1007/11811305
15. Laurikkala, J.: Improving identification of difficult small classes by balancing class distribution. In: Quaglini, S., Barahona, P., Andreassen, S. (eds.) AIME 2001. LNCS (LNAI), vol. 2101, pp. 63–66. Springer, Heidelberg (2001). https://doi.org/10.1007/3-540-48229-6_9
16. Lin, W.C., Tsai, C.F., Hu, Y.H., Jhang, J.S.: Clustering-based undersampling in class-imbalanced data. Inf. Sci. **409–410**, 17–26 (2017)
17. Ofek, N., Rokach, L., Stern, R., Shabtai, A.: Fast-CBUS: a fast clustering-based undersampling method for addressing the class imbalance problem. Neurocomputing **243**, 88–102 (2017)
18. Onan, A.: Consensus clustering-based undersampling approach to imbalanced learning. Sci. Programm. **2019**, 5901087 (2019). Article ID 5901087
19. Prati, R.C., Batista, G.E., Silva, D.F.: Class imbalance revisited: a new experimental setup to assess the performance of treatment methods. Knowl. Inf. Syst. **45**, 247–270 (2015). https://doi.org/10.1007/s10115-014-0794-3
20. Smiti, A., Elouedi, Z.: DBSCAN-GM: an improved clustering method based on Gaussian Means and DBSCAN techniques. In: Proceedings of IEEE 16th International Conference on Intelligent Engineering Systems, Lisbon, Portugal, pp. 573–578 (2012)
21. Tomek, I.: An experiment with the edited nearest-neighbor rule. IEEE Trans. Syst. Man Cybern. SMC **6**(6), 448–452 (1976)

22. Tomek, I.: Two modifications of CNN. IEEE Trans. Syst. Man Cybern. SMC **6**(6), 769–772 (1976)
23. Tsai, C.F., Lin, W.C., Hu, Y.H., Yao, G.T.: Under-sampling class imbalanced datasets by combining clustering analysis and instance selection. Inf. Sci. **477**, 47–54 (2019)
24. Verma, M.K., Xaxa, D.K., Verma, S.: DBCS: density based cluster sampling for solving imbalanced classification problem. In: Proceedings of International conference of Electronics, Communication and Aerospace Technology, Coimbatore, India, vol. 1, pp. 156–161 (2017)
25. Wilson, D.L.: Asymptotic properties of nearest neighbor rules using edited data. IEEE Trans. Syst. Man Cybern. SMC **2**(3), 408–421 (1972)
26. Yen, S.J., Lee, Y.S.: Cluster-based under-sampling approaches for imbalanced data distributions. Exp. Syst. Appl. **36**(3, Part 1), 5718–5727 (2009)
27. Yue, S.H., Li, P., Guo, J.D., Zhou, S.Q.: Using greedy algorithm: DBSCAN revisited II. J. Zhejiang Univ. - SCIENCE A 5(11), 1405–1412 (2004). https://doi.org/10.1631/jzus.2004.1405

Comparing Knowledge-Based Reinforcement Learning to Neural Networks in a Strategy Game

Liudmyla Nechepurenko(✉), Viktor Voss, and Vyacheslav Gritsenko

Arago GmbH, Eschersheimer Landstr. 526-532, 60433 Frankfurt am Main, Germany
lnechepurenko,vvoss,vgritsenko}@arago.co

Abstract. The paper reports on an experiment, in which a Knowledge-Based Reinforcement Learning (KB-RL) method was compared to a Neural Network (NN) approach in solving a classical Artificial Intelligence (AI) task. In contrast to NNs, which require a substantial amount of data to learn a good policy, the KB-RL method seeks to encode human knowledge into the solution, considerably reducing the amount of data needed for a good policy. By means of Reinforcement Learning (RL), KB-RL learns to optimize the model and improves the output of the system. Furthermore, KB-RL offers the advantage of a clear explanation of the taken decisions as well as transparent reasoning behind the solution.

The goal of the reported experiment was to examine the performance of the KB-RL method in contrast to the Neural Network and to explore the capabilities of KB-RL to deliver a strong solution for the AI tasks. The results show that, within the designed settings, KB-RL outperformed the NN, and was able to learn a better policy from the available amount of data. These results support the opinion that Artificial Intelligence can benefit from the discovery and study of alternative approaches, potentially extending the frontiers of AI.

Keywords: Knowledge-based systems · Reinforcement learning · Neural networks

1 Introduction

Machine Learning (ML) is one of the most recent trends in Artificial Intelligence. To a high extend, ML owns its popularity to the development of Neural Networks (NNs) and, particularly, Deep Neural Networks. The fact that NNs can find solutions for previously unsolvable tasks, drew a lot of attention to NNs and ML, while decreasing the attention to other approaches. At the same time, NNs face a number of challenges that can result in the lower performance of the NN method [26]. For example, NNs are data greedy [8], they require an extensive amount of data in order to train an effective model. One of the crucial hardships employing NNs is their unexplained output [34]: working as a 'back box', NNs cannot justify their output and, thus, lack to be trusted [10].

E. A. de la Cal et al. (Eds.): HAIS 2020, LNAI 12344, pp. 312–328, 2020.
https://doi.org/10.1007/978-3-030-61705-9_26

Studying new approaches opens Artificial Intelligence to new possibilities and facilitates a more informed choice of the technology when it comes to finding a suitable method for a research problem. Therefore, we believe that this report positively contributes to the healthy dynamic of the AI field by encouraging the diversity of its methodology and in-depth analysis of various methods. The objective of this article is to study the KB-RL method and compare it to Neural Networks in order to bring more light on the method's performance, its characteristics and the benefits of the method for a corresponding problem area.

In this report, KB-RL conforms to the idea that exploiting human knowledge can shorten the time and data needed for machines to learn. KB-RL consists of two techniques: the Knowledge-Based technique and Reinforcement Learning. In the Knowledge-Based approach [3], the knowledge is the essence of the system, it expresses the facts, information and skills needed to automate a particular task or a problem.

In KB-RL, RL is added to the Knowledge-Based System (KBS) as a conflict resolution strategy targeted at integrating the alternative knowledge, or multi-expert knowledge, into one knowledge base. The core difference between KB-RL and the traditional KBSs is their approach to knowledge. Classical KBSs strictly require the knowledge to be unambiguous. This means, if there is more than one rule to be matched to the current situation, the inference engine cannot proceed and requires conflict resolution. The conflict resolution is based on the assumption that only one rule can be correct in the given context, while others are attributed to mistakes [19]. In contrast, KB-RL considers conflicting rules as possible variations of the solution and employs RL to learn which variant delivers the best outcome for the defined task. Therefore, KB-RL easily accommodates ambiguous knowledge seeing it as knowledge of multiple experts that have different opinions or different strategies for the problem solution. Report [37] illustrates this principle on the example of the multi-strategy game CIVILIZATION. The report shows that, based on the several available strategies to play the game, the system learned to improve the gameplay, increasing the winning rate for the trained agent.

Following the work [37], we chose FreeCiv as a benchmark for the reported comparison. This allowed us to reuse the open-sourced framework of FreeCiv, the knowledge base and the data that was openly published at [36]. Due to the highly complex nature of FreeCiv, we addressed only a separate sub-task of the game. In particular, we chose to optimize the selection of the cities locations that would lead the nation to the maximal generated natural resources. Several reasons influenced the choice of the task. Besides being of reasonable complexity, this task involves image analysis - the area where NNs have shown a great performance. Moreover, there can be various strategies to approach settlement in the game, which is an appropriate setting for the KB-RL approach. City locations are closely linked to the amount of generated natural resources because natural resources are generated by the city from the tiles within the city borders, and their amount depends, in the first place, on the map tiles properties. Therefore, wisely choosing the city region acts as a fundamental prerequisite for generating rich natural resources.

For the purpose of this work, the selected task was solved twice, with the KB-RL and the Neural Networks approach. The difference in their performance became a determining factor for the analysis of this experiment. The results of this work satisfy the goal to provide better understanding of KB-RL's performance and capabilities, and the advantages it can give in contrast to the Neural Networks. It is important to note that the experiment could have other design decisions that may be questioned by the reader throughout the article. Unfortunately, we were limited by the time dedicated to this project to explore all possible designs.

2 Related Work

Comparative studies are commonly used to investigate methods and to gain better understanding of their strengths and weaknesses. Being one of the most popular AI techniques nowadays, NNs have been compared to other approaches in numerous studies, for example [6,21,24].

Previously, there were many instances of combining the Knowledge-Based approach with Machine Learning techniques into one method, for example [13,25,32,33]. For several decades, a large number of studies tackled the idea of combining these two methods from various angles. To the best of our knowledge, applying RL as a conflict resolution strategy in a multi-expert knowledge-based system for incremental solution improvement was first proposed in [37]. As the authors of [37] suggest, it is difficult to relate to similar studies that combine the Knowledge-Based and the Machine Learning approaches due to the diversity of the addressed problems by these studies. Therefore, it was not our objective to review all the methods combining Knowledge-Based approaches and Machine Learning in the related work section. We believe that KB-RL, as well as other methods, are worth considering and can deliver comprehensive results in numerous applications. Our primary goal was to examine the KB-RL method, for which a comparative study was regarded as an effective mechanism.

Games are a recognized benchmark for testing AI algorithms. Strategy games, such as CIVILIZATION, present an attractive case for AI research due to their high complexity. To be aware of the previous applications, we reviewed several reports on employing FreeCiv as a proving point for AI algorithms. Most studies addressed specific elements of the game, with only a few works playing the entire game. In 2004, A. Houk used a symbolic approach and reasoning to develop an agent for playing FreeCiv [1]. A series of articles explored Knowledge-Based related approaches for tasks, such as building and defending cities and population growth, see [14–18,35]. In 2014, Branavan et al. employed Natural Language Processing (NLP) to improve the player performance in CIVILISATION II [7]. In 2009, S. Wender, implemented several modifications of Sarsa and Q-learning algorithms to learn the potentially best city sites [39]. References [38] and [4] explored the utilization of Genetic Algorithms for the optimization of city placement and city development in FreeCiv. Overall, all the reviewed reports showed improved results of using the proposed methodology.

Our work differs from the reviewed methods in a number of settings, such as methods, episode length, complexity of the game configurations and the selected metric. The next sections give a detailed explanation of the performed experiment.

3 Task Definition

The amount of natural resources generated in the FreeCiv game is implemented through the points of different types that are produced by cities in every game turn. We call the amount of generated natural resource from all cities in one game: the **total game output** (TGO). We aimed to maximize the total game output by analysing the map, predicting the quality of map clusters (regions of 5×5 without corner tiles as it is shown in Fig. reffig:maprulea, which are 21 tiles) with respect to the TGO and building the cities in the places with the highest predicted quality.

Cities generate natural resources from those tiles within city borders that have working citizen on the tile. City borders may reach terrain within the 5×5 region centered on the city, minus its corners. To extract resources from a tile, the player must have a citizen working there, and the city can reposition its citizens to optimize the generated resources. Originally, the city is built with one citizen that works on the center tile. To acquire new citizens, the city must generate a surplus of natural resources. As the city's population grows, more tiles become engaged with work. Each working tile generates a number of food, production and trade points per turn. Trade points can be turned into gold, luxury or science points. These six types of points - **food, production, trade, gold, luxury and science** - constitute the **city output**. In this way, we calculate the city output as a sum of all points that are collected with every turn, and doubling the production points as they can be used as half of a gold point when buying the current city project. The formula for the **city output** is given in Eq. 1:

$$OUTPUT_T = \sum_{t=1}^{T}(gold_t + luxury_t + science_t + food_t + production_t * 2 + trade_t) \tag{1}$$

where t and T refer to the turn number, and $t = 1$ is the first turn of the game. For the cities built in later turns, all points prior to the turn in which they were built were taken as zeros.

Consequently, the **total game output** at turn T is the sum of all city outputs owned by the player until the T-th turn:

$$TGO = \sum_{n=1}^{N} OUTPUT_{n,T} \tag{2}$$

where N is the number of cities owned by the player.

The complexity of settling in FreeCiv lies in the abundance of options to exploit the map tiles for natural resources and in the constrained nature of the player's possibilities. In general, the number of working tiles is in inverse ratio to the number of cities because every new settler unit removes one citizen from the home city. Consequently, home cities produce less resources and delay exploiting more working tiles. Therefore, maximal accumulated natural resources do not necessarily arrive form maximizing the number of cities. Moreover, placing the available citizens on different tiles within the city borders results in different amounts for each particular type, as well as cumulative, natural resources. Also, the type of the natural resources plays an important role in the city's development and, consequently, influences the total game output.

We saw the estimation of the total game output as a regression problem that determines the relationships between the parameters of the map cluster and the TGO value. In other words, given a map cluster, we aimed to predict a continuous integer value reflecting the future contribution of the city being built in the cluster center to the TGO.

In FreeCiv, the amount of generated natural resources of each tile is affected by the map parameters, such as terrain type, the presence of special resources, rivers and improvements; and by the city economy, such as special buildings, city governor, the government type and trade routes. Since we were mainly interested in the relationships between the map parameters and the city output, we only considered the parameters relevant to the map qualities. They are listed as following: • (TERR) Terrain of the center tile and terrain of the surrounding tiles within the map cluster. There are 9 possible terrain types in the game suitable for building a city: Desert, Forest, Grassland, Hills, Jungle, Mountains, Plains, Swamp and Tundra. • (RES) Resources on the tile and surrounding tiles within the map cluster. Every type of terrain has a chance of an additional special resource that boosts one or two of the products. Special resources can be one of 17 types and only one per tile. • (WATER) Availability of water resources. Presence of Ocean or Deep Ocean terrain in the city has special significance due to their rich resources and strategic advantages. Therefore, we considered them as extra parameters. • (RIVERS) Availability of rivers. Rivers enable improvements of the terrain and enhance trade for certain terrain types.

The outlined parameter list may not be exhaustive, however, we aimed to include the most relevant features that have the highest correlation with the generated natural resources. The only two attributes unrelated to the map qualities were considered as those that characterize neighboring cities: number of player cities in the neighborhood (the 2 tiles wide area behind the city border) and the number of enemy cities in this region. We marked them 'MY_NEIGHB' and 'ENEMY_NEIGHB' respectively.

With all parameters considered, the regression problem was set in the form shown in Eq. 3:

$$f : (TERR, RES, WATER, RIVERS, NEIGHB) \rightarrow TGO \tag{3}$$

Equation 3 was addressed by two approaches: KB-RL and NN. The next sections provide detailed descriptions of both solutions.

It is possible that there are exiting solutions for the discussed task that are better than the two methods considered in this report. For example, such solutions may entail but are not limited to rooting in combinatorics, logic, or other areas of computer sciences. However, we did not aim to find the best solution, but rather saw this problem as suitable for comparing KB-RL with NN. Hence, it is possible that methods not addressed in this report can achieve better results when applied to the discussed problem.

4 KB-RL Method

The KB-RL approach of the reported experiment is explained in detail in [37]. Due to the restrictive nature of the conference paper, we provide here only a short summary of the method. The core of KB-RL is a knowledge-based system. KBSs were intensively studied in the 80s and 90s of the last century. Later, their popularity in the scientific community declined. However, there are numerous practical applications of the KBSs, such as [2,5,29]. Also, there is much literature available on KBSs, for example [3]. KBS encodes human knowledge into machine-readable rules for automated problem solving. A KBS typically consists of a knowledge base that holds the knowledge, and an inference engine that searches the knowledge to derive a valid conclusion for a given task. The inference engine in KB-RL processes the knowledge by adopting abductive reasoning. Abductive reasoning is characterized by the consideration of contextual knowledge in the process of inferring a solution [23]. The knowledge base is represented by a semantic network that follows an ontology to define the formal specification of the used concepts and their relationships. KB-RL distinguishes between two types of knowledge: contextual knowledge and procedural knowledge. Contextual knowledge consists of two types: facts about the environment and its state, and the situational information (working memory). The procedural knowledge is encoded in the form of rules dictating what actions should be accepted under the specified contextual conditions.

Unlike the classical KBSs, where rule conflicts need resolution, KB-RL is able to handle conflicting knowledge, either contradictory, or redundant. It is particularly relevant to multi-expert knowledge, where different experts can have different opinions and diverse expertise about the problem domain. KB-RL views conflicting knowledge as the variations of the solution and applies RL to handle the conflicts with the objective to master the optimal solution for a specified task or problem. In the situation of conflict, the inference engine acts as an agent in the RL setting, treating rules as actions and using the learned policy to decide on the one rule to be executed. The KB-RL approach employs the on-policy model-free Monte Carlo method as a RL algorithm for conflict resolution. The Monte Carlo method is characterized by averaging the state-action values and utilising an ϵ-greedy policy to ensure state space exploration [31].

KB-RL inherited its ability to explain the derived solution and the corresponding reasoning process from the traditional KBSs [22]. KB-RL provides visibility and information about the decision making with several mechanisms.

Firstly, the knowledge is represented in an explicit, human-readable format that can be viewed by users and knowledge engineers. Moreover, the meta-knowledge in the form of ontology provides a common vocabulary that carries the semantics of real-world concepts, facilitating the understanding of the problem context [9]. Furthermore, by tracing the executed rules in the history of the solution, one can understand the contextual conditions in which the rule was applied [28].

In the reported experiment, we reused the implementation of playing FreeCiv with the KB-RL method presented in [37], including the ontology for the semantic network, most of the knowledge base, and the clustering model for the state space segmentation. The ontology entities represented the main concepts of FreeCiv, such as a game, a player, a unit, a city, and a tile. The properties of these concepts were implemented as attributes of the corresponding entities, while the edges reflected the relationships between the concepts. The semantic network contained all the game data as instances of the outlined ontology types. The data was kept in constant sync with the FreeCiv's environment and, therefore, the inference engine could operate always up-to-date searching for matching rules. For the RL algorithm, the clustering model was employed to reduce the game state space to the finite number of states. The model was trained by the k-mean algorithm, particularly Lloyd's algorithm with a maximum of 300 iterations. The dataset was created based on 1100 game histories published at [36]. The 31 features of the dataset were selected based on their correlation with the won/lost outcome of these games. The features were such as the game score, population size, the number of learned technologies, and others. The collected dataset had 386895 entries. As a result of experimenting with hyperparameters, 185 clusters were defined to represent the game state space.

In [37]'s knowledge base, the tiles' quality for the city output was calculated by one rule summing the food, trade and shield points of all tiles within the map cluster. Considering the complex relationship between the parameters of the map cluster and the amount of the natural resources that a city could generate being built in the centre of this map cluster, [37]'s calculation of the tile quality is a rather simplified estimation. For our experiment, we replaced this rule with two different approaches: one was the Neural Network model (Sect. 5), and the other one was using the new rules for the knowledge base encoding several players' strategies for the tile evaluation.

Settling in FreeCiv has various strategies and can be solved by human players in numerous ways. Though the game rules are clearly defined, it takes practice for the players to master their settling strategies. Moreover, with more experience, players learn about different techniques that can be equally successful in winning the game. Following the KB-RL principle, we implemented several strategies into rules in order to evaluate the map clusters. These rules created a multi-expert knowledge base for the given task. A scoring system was used to estimate the tile quality to deliver high city output. Each tile held an attribute representing the tile quality score. The rules were encoded to manipulate the tile's score by adding more or less, or negative points to it based on the listed conditions. For example, the terrain of type Forest is highly valued by some players due to its

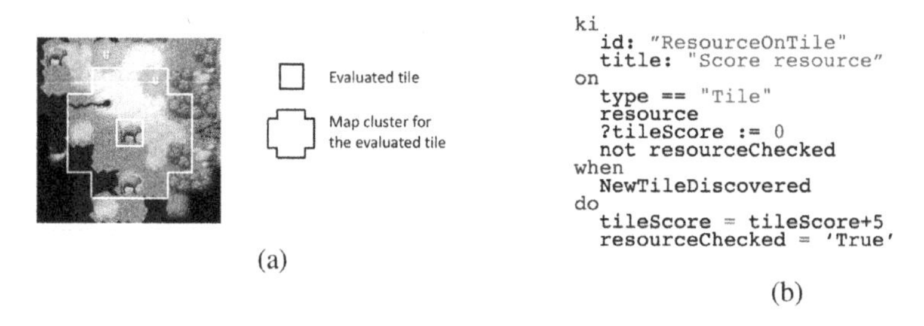

Fig. 1. An example of a map cluster (a), and a rule (b) that can be applied to it. The rule adds 5 points to the tile score for the special resource 'Bull' on the central tile.

high production output. Thus, the rule conditioning the Forest terrain added a high number of points to the tile score. Meanwhile, other players do not see this terrain type highly advantageous. Therefore, we added another rule that contributed to the tile score with less points. The terrain of type Desert earned negative reputation among players due to its scarce resources for city growth. These rules were adding negative or zero points to the tile score to reflect the rate of the players' dislike of the Desert tiles. Each rule contributed to the score of a particular tile independently of others, and rules conditioning the same features created the conflicting knowledge in terms of classical KBS. Following this principle, we could easily create more rules by adding various numbers of points for different map features to implement any player's strategy. Fig. 1b illustrates an example of a rule for the tile quality evaluation.

The rules addressed the parameter set outlined in Sect. 3: terrain type, special resources and water resources on the central and surrounding tiles. There were 14 features covered by the rules: 9 for different terrain types and 5 for other features: (1) special resource on the central tile, (2) special resources on the surrounding tiles, (3) availability of water resources, (4) access to the deep ocean and (5) presence of the whale resource. As whales are resources that boost two products (food and production) at the same time, many players favor them over other resources. Thus, we treated it with additional rules.

To cover different strategies, alternative rules were implemented for each feature adding a different amount of points to the tile score. For example, for the rule given in Fig. 1b, the alternative rules added 1, 5, or 10 points to the attribute 'tileScore'. These numbers reflected the value that different human players would put, given the occurrence of a special resource on the tile when playing the game with different strategies. In the classical KBS, these rules would create a conflict due to the identical specified conditions. However, in KB-RL, the system had to learn by means of RL what rule would convey the best outcome for the designed goal.

Overall, 56 rules were written for the aforementioned 14 features. The created rules were added to the multi-expert knowledge base of report [37]. It has to be noted, though, that the number of rules is rather indicative and does not reflect the complexity of the knowledge base.

For the purpose of this experiment, we had to redefine the reward function to reflect the connection between the total game output and the desired goal. One game was considered an episode and the total game output was calculated at the end of each game run. Then, for every state s of the episode, the reward R_s was given in the amount of the total game output of this episode. Accordingly, the value of a state was calculated as the average of the acquired rewards: $V_s = avg(R_s(n))$ where $n \in N$, and N is the set of all games that visited the state s. And, the state-action values were calculated by averaging the set of games M that visited the state s and performed action a: $q_s^a = avg(R_{s,a}(m)), m \in M$.

5 Neural Networks Method

Nowadays, Neural Networks do not need much of an introduction. A detailed discussion of Artificial Neural Networks can be found in [12], or [11]. For the NNs, the data is a fundamental component. Therefore, collecting a dataset to train the NN model was our first task for implementing the NN solution in this experiment. For this purpose, we exploited 1100 fully played FreeCiv games from [36] that were played with the KB-RL approach reported in [37]. The games were analysed, and all city places were identified as well as city outputs and total game outputs for all games. Based on the acquired information, the dataset was constructed for training NN to predict the quality of the place for the city output.

For each city place, the map cluster around the city was taken to create the input entry to the dataset, with the map cluster being centered on the tile where city was built. Firstly, the input data went through preprocessing, such as transforming data into vectors, normalisation and dealing with noise or missing values. In FreeCiv, the map is saved to a text file for each game turn being encoded into special symbols. These symbols represent all tile properties, such as terrain type, special resources, rivers, roads, tile owner and affiliation to the city. Based on these symbols, the map image can be entirely reconstructed at any point of time. Therefore, it was beneficial for us to use encoding, allowing us to convert the map cluster image into a feature vector with no loss of data integrity. Accordingly, the feature vector of the dataset included the following symbols: 21 symbols that reflect the terrain type of each tile in the map cluster, 21 symbols to indicate the presence/absence of the special resources on each of the 21 tiles and one symbol indicating the presence of the river on the central tile. Additionally, we counted the number of the player's cities and the number of the opponents' cities already built in the neighbourhood of the given place. We found it beneficial to ignore the position of the tiles within the city borders. The final dataset entry was constructed as columns where each column represented a symbol type, and the value was equal to the number of such symbols in the map cluster. For more detail, the dataset can be found at [27].

As a label column for the dataset entries, we estimated the output of the cities built on the derived map clusters. To do so, we faced a few challenges. Firstly, cities built on the same land in different games would differ in their output due to the different game development and the player's progress. Secondly, cities were built in various turns, but we had to estimate each city place independently from the turn built. Therefore, we could not use Eq. 1 to calculate the label for our dataset entries. By analyzing the data and experimenting with hyperparameters for training the neural network, we chose to calculate the city output as in Eq. 4:

$$OUTPUT_c = \sum_{i=1}^{100}(gold_i + luxury_i + science_i + food_i + production_i * 2 + trade_i) \tag{4}$$

where c refers to the city index, and i represents the age of the city in terms of turns. For example, $i = 1$ relates to the first turn after the city was built, and $i = 100$ is the 100th turn of city existence on the map.

As a result, the corresponding dataset had duplicate entries with different labels for them. It was due to cities being built on the same spot in different games, or the parameters of the map clusters were the same but in different locations. We replaced the duplicate entries with the average of their label values. By keeping only unique entries, we aimed to minimize potential data imbalance [20].

Accordingly, the resulting dataset contained 2765 unique entries for training the NN model. The input dataset was normalized by a min-max algorithm, and the trained model had the following structure: • Input layer accepts 83-dimensional feature vector. • One hidden layer with 95 neurons and ReLU activation. • Weights are initialized using normal distribution with zero mean and 0.0005 standard deviation. • To avoid overfitting, a dropout with probability 0.5 is applied to the hidden layer. • The output is a single neuron, which is a continuous variable. • The mean squared error is used as a loss function. • The ADAM optimizer is employed as it has shown the best performance among other optimization algorithms. • Batch size is 30 and learning rate is 0.002.

In order to find optimal hyperparameters, including the number of hidden layers, grid search has been applied to the model. For the model assessment, we chose K-fold cross validation with 10 splits and with shuffling. After training, the mean squared error for the test set reached the value 0,00637. To our surprise, the grid search resulted in a single-layered model to be the optimal for the provided dataset. After careful consideration, we suggest that it can be due to a theoretically proved finding that a neural network with one hidden layer can adequately approximate "any Borel measurable function from one finite-dimensional space to another", given the sufficient number of hidden units [11,30]. To validate the trained model, we also performed visual inspection of the predicted tile scores for the different map fragments. Figure 2 shows that the model performed reasonably well, predicting higher scores for the tiles of Grassland and Plains terrain, especially if they were located on the coast or had a special resource.

The trained model was plugged into the KB-RL system in such a way that on the start of every game turn, the game map was preprocessed, the feature vector for every map cluster was created and passed to the NN for prediction. The predicted value was assigned as the tile's score representing the tiles' quality for the TGO.

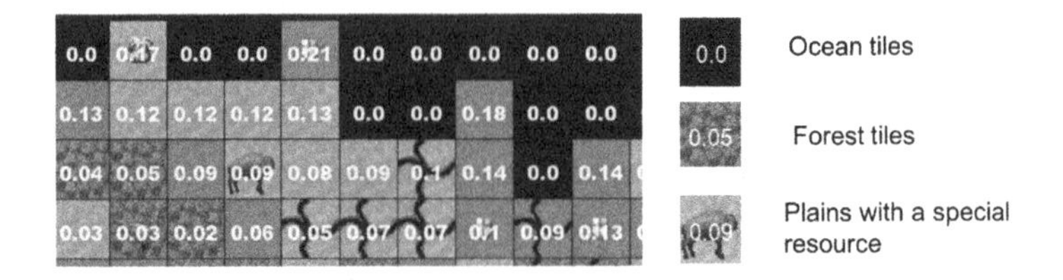

Fig. 2. A fragment of the visual validation of the trained NN model. The number in the square is the score predicted by the NN model for an assigned tile.eps

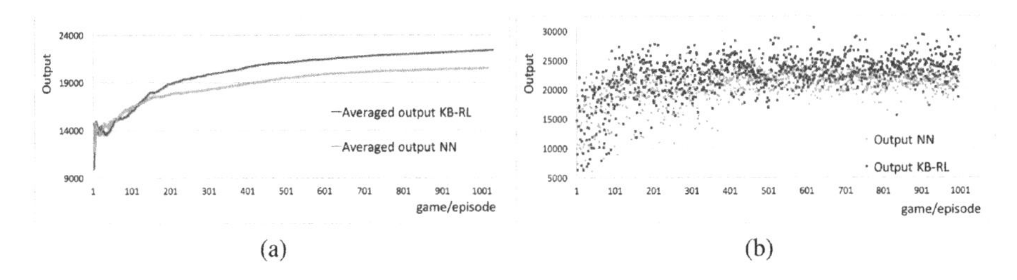

Fig. 3. TGO averaged over a number of games (a) and for each single game (b).

6 Experimental Setup

The experiment was set up in two ways. One time, the training of the KB-RL agent was conducted with the KB-RL method holding created rules for the evaluation of map clusters. The other time, the training ran with the plugged in NN model that replaced the rules for the evaluation of map clusters. For both runs, the TGO was observed and compared to estimate the performance of the two approaches. This way, the difference in output of the two setups would result from the two approaches for the tile evaluation and, thus, would become a point of comparison for these two methods.

There were several design decisions to be made. Firstly, we had to decide on a starting point for the games. FreeCiv offers a game configuration either with a random starting point or with a predefined starting position. A random starting position would give more generalisation to the trained model and more balanced data. However, it would also bring a lot of randomness to the progress of the game. The starting position defines the player's nation, and the nation dictates many aspects of the game, such as the nation's temperament, the way it is treated by other nations and the citizens' loyalty to the leader. Therefore, the nation also influences the generated natural resources in the game. It would take a longer training time for the model to learn to recognize the effect of the random start versus the influence of the map parameters. On the other hand, the games used for creation of the Neural Network dataset were started at a fixed position on each of 5 maps [37]. Based on this consideration, the decision was made to start the games from the fixed staring position. Given that the conditions for both setups were equal, we believe that this decision did not diminish the outcome of the experiment.

For the game configuration, we chose one of the configurations described in [37] named Chaos. The map of this configuration is 80×50 tiles with two big continents in the middle, and five small islands on the south of the map. The configuration is designed to be played by two KB-RL agents, where each of them starts the game on the separate continent. No embedded AI players are added to the game, however, Barbarians are activated. This configuration favours the game conditions where the players have no contact in the initial game phase to be engaged in warfare or diplomacy, and, therefore, are encouraged to build and develop cities.

Another design decision was made about the length of the games. Settling happens in FreeCiv in the initial phase. After cities are built, the player mostly focuses on developing the economy, technologies and warfare. For the purpose of the experiment, we did not need to play the games until they are finished. Stopping the games ahead of time gave us the advantage of significantly shorter episode duration: such episodes took about 10%–20% of the full game time. Analyzing the histories of games from citech26firstPaper, we chose to play only the first 120 turns of the game, as it seemed to be a good trade-off among the amount of generated data, the game state and the play time.

Initially, we also considered the setup where learning would be performed only once, with added rules for tile evaluation. Then, the performance would be observed for the total game output with the learned policy and without ongoing learning. After that, the rules would be replaced by the NN model, and the system performance would be measured again. However, in this case the NN might lead the game through a different set of states that were not well-learned during initial training. This fact would be a disadvantage to the NN setup. Thus, the decision was made in favor of running learning for both setups from the same starting point.

7 Results

To measure the performance of both experiments, we chose the metric of averaging the total game output over the number of games. The averaged total game output was calculated after every game and observed for both setups in comparison to each other. Figure 3a visualizes the averaged TGO progress throughout the training for the two setups. Additionally, Fig. 3b shows the TGO of each single game in the run of the episodes. At the beginning, the TGOs had much variation, with the average value just under 15 000. As learning proceeded, the TGO steadily climbed up, and the variation declined. This behaviour was common for both experiments as a result of the reinforcement learning optimization within the KB-RL system.

Each experiment ran for 1000 episodes. At the end, the game play stabilized with an average total reward of 20 500 and 22 400 points for the NN and the KB-RL setups respectively. For the KB-RL setup, the improvement constituted

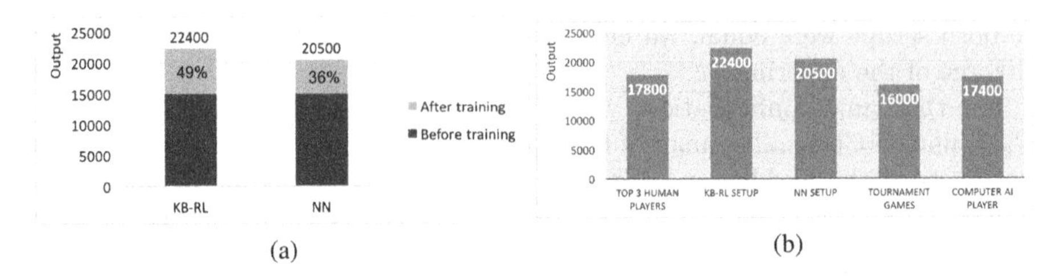

Fig. 4. Total game output after training compared to the value before training (a) and to the human players, the tournament games and the computer AI players (b).

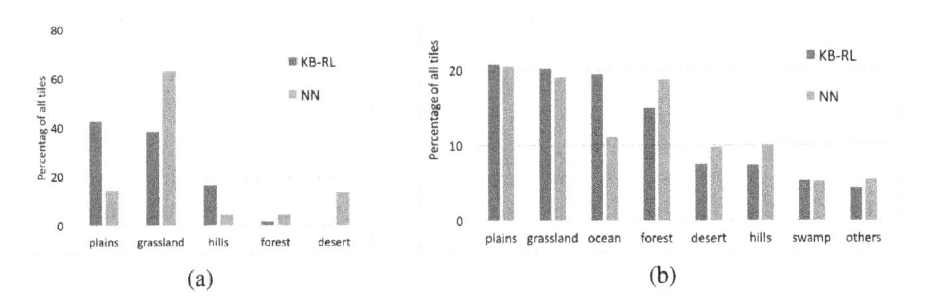

Fig. 5. Distribution of the terrain types after training on the city's central tile (a) and the entire city region (b).

49% in contrast to the starting value, while for the NN, it was a 36% increase (Fig. 4a). The difference of 13% between the two approaches stems from the different solutions for the tile evaluation.

To better understand the achieved results, we compared them to the performance of the human players, FreeCiv's computer AI players and the so-called tournament games of report [37]. Figure 4b illustrates the compared TGOs. The games played by humans were acquired as a part of the reused data of the report [37], they are published online at [27]. For comparison, we show the TGO of the top 3 players. Analysing the histories of their games, it can be concluded that they are definitely great experts in playing the game as their play was quick and efficient, and they won against computer AIs with a big winning margin. This comparison showed that both trained agents outperformed human and computer AI players (Fig. 4b). It must be noted, however, that neither human, nor computer AI players explicitly pursued the goal of maximizing generated natural resources. Therefore, this comparison is rather indicative.

When investigating the two setups in contrast to each other, it can be seen that the fundamental difference in building cities was in the terrain type of the central tile. Furthermore, there was a noticeable difference in the terrain type of the tiles surrounding the central tile within city borders. While both setups built comparatively similar number of cities, with the similar amount of resources and rivers within city borders, the terrain type of the city tiles differs significantly (Figs. 5a and 5b). In the KB-RL setup, the majority of cities were built on one of the three terrain types: plains (42%), grassland (38%) and hills (16%). On the contrary, most of the cities in the NN setup were built on grassland (63%) with a surprisingly big part of cities being built on the desert terrain (13%). Most likely, this is a consequence of a data deficit during the training of the NN model as the desert terrain is an obvious disadvantage for the city's development.

Cities of both setups occupied the terrain of types grassland and plains to a similar extent (Fig. 5b). However, the KB-RL agent tended to build cities mostly on the coast, occupying a high number of ocean tiles. At the same time, the NN setup showed more preference towards the forest terrain, while coastal terrains were occupied considerably less than forest. Furthermore, cities in the NN setup occupied more terrain of types hills and desert in comparison to the KB-RL setup.

While explaining the NN's prediction for the tile scores in the NN setup was challenging for us, the games' execution histories of the KB-RL setup gave us a valuable insight into the decision-making of the KB-RL agent. By reviewing the execution histories, we were able to check which rules contributed to the score of every tile. As the rules were encoded in the human-readable format using the semantically loaded vocabulary, it was straightforward to understand the reasoning process of the KB-RL agent. For example, for the map cluster in Fig. 1a, the executed rules were ResourceOnTile (added points for special resource bull on the central tile), ResourcesAround (added points for the two special resources within the map cluster), TerrainGrassland (added points for the Grassland terrain type of the central tile) and OceanTileBonus (added points for the Ocean terrain type of two tiles within the map cluster). Altogether, they added 27 points to the tile score. This number varied from game to game depending on the conflict resolution outcome since each of these rules had a set of the alternative rules, as it was explained in Sect. 4. For each rule, the execution history listed its conflicting rules and their probabilities at the time of conflict resolution. We saw a strong possibility to use this information in the analysis of the training process and its progress. However, this task was not included into this report and, potentially, could become a research study on its own.

8 Conclusion

The goal of this article was to study the KB-RL approach by comparing its performance to the NN in solving a classical Artificial Intelligence task. The evaluation of map tiles for building cities to deliver high output of the generated natural resources was chosen for this comparison. The results of the experiment support the idea that KB-RL can be a worthy alternative to other AI approaches, such as Neural Networks, in solving tasks of the Artificial Intelligence field.

By leveraging human experts' knowledge, KB-RL performed the initial phase of the training equally well as the NN, which was trained on the 1100 previously played games. These results advocate that KB-RL may be a better choice for the problems where the data for training a NN model is scarce or unavailable, but there is an access to human expertise. Moreover, with more games played,

KB-RL demonstrated a greater ability to optimize the complex policy, justifying the smaller demand of the data by KB-RL to deliver a better policy.

Another important advantage of the KB-RL solution was the ability to explain the system decisions by reviewing the rules executed in the game. This fact can be imperative in cases where the system's explainability is a critical requirement.

References

1. A. Houk, P.: A Strategic Game Playing Agent for FreeCiv. Master's thesis, Northwestern University, Illinois, United States (2004)
2. Abdullah, M.S., Kimble, C., Benest, I., Paige, R.: Knowledge-based systems: a re-evaluation. J. Knowl. Manage. **10**(3), 127–142 (2006)
3. Akerkar, R., Sajja, P.: Knowledge-Based Systems, 1st edn. Jones and Bartlett Publishers Inc., Burlington (2009)
4. Arnold, F., Horvat, B., Sacks, A.M.: Freeciv learner : a machine learning project utilizing genetic algorithms. Interim Report. The University of Auckland, Game AI Group (2005)
5. Avram, G.: Empirical study on knowledge based systems. Electron. J. Inf. Syst. Eval. **8**, 11–20 (2005)
6. Bologna, G., Hayashi, Y.: A comparison study on rule extraction from neural network ensembles, boosted shallow trees, and SVMs. Appl. Comput. Intell. Soft Comput. **2018**, 1–20 (2018). https://doi.org/10.1155/2018/4084850
7. Branavan, S.R.K., Silver, D., Barzilay, R.: Learning to Win by Reading Manuals in a Monte-Carlo Framework. CoRR abs/1401.5390 (2014)
8. Cannady, J.: Artificial neural networks for misuse detection. In: National Information Systems Security Conference, pp. 443–456 (1998)
9. Chandrasekaran, B., Swartout, W.: Explanations in knowledge systems: the role of explicit representation of design knowledge. IEEE Exp. **6**, 47–49 (1991)
10. Gilpin, L.H., Bau, D., Yuan, B.Z., Bajwa, A., Specter, M., Kagal, L.: Explaining explanations: an overview of interpretability of machine learning. In: 2018 IEEE 5th International Conference on Data Science and Advanced Analytics (DSAA), pp. 80–89 (2018)
11. Goodfellow, I., Bengio, Y., Courville, A.: Deep Learning. MIT Press, Cambridge (2016). http://www.deeplearningbook.org
12. Haykin, S.: Neural Networks: A Comprehensive Foundation, 3rd edn. Prentice-Hall Inc., Upper Saddle River (2007)
13. Hinkelmann, K., Ahmed, S., Corradini, F.: Combining machine learning with knowledge engineering to detect fake news in social networks - a survey. In: AAAI Spring Symposium: Combining Machine Learning with Knowledge Engineering (2019)
14. Hinrichs, T., Forbus, K.: Toward higher-order qualitative representations. In: Proceedings of QR 2012 (2012)
15. Hinrichs, T., Forbus, K.: Analogical learning in a turn-based strategy game. In: IJCAI International Joint Conference on Artificial Intelligence, pp. 853–858 (12 2007)
16. Jones, J., Goel, A.: Knowledge organization and structural credit assignment. In: Proceedings of IJCAI-05 Workshop on Reasoning, Representation and Learning in Computer Games, Edinburgh, UK, August 2005

17. Jones, J., Goel, A.K.: Metareasoning for adaptation of classification knowledge. In: AAMAS (2009)
18. Jones, J., Parnin, C., Sinharoy, A., Rugaber, S., Goel, A.K.: Adapting game-playing agents to game requirements. In: Proceedings of Fifth AAAI Conference on Artificial Intelligence and Interactive Digital Entertainment (AIIDE-09), pp. 148–153 (2009)
19. Khalil, K.M., Abdel-Aziz, M., Nazmy, T.T., Salem, A.B.M.: Intelligent Techniques for Resolving Conflicts of Knowledge in Multi-agent Decision Support Systems. ArXiv abs/1401.4381 (2014)
20. Kołcz, A., Chowdhury, A., Alspector, J.: Data duplication: an imbalance problem? In: In: Proceedings of the ICML 2003 Workshop on Learning from Imbalanced Datasets (2003)
21. Kumar, R., Srivastava, S., Gupta, J.R., Mohindru, A.: Comparative study of neural networks for dynamic nonlinear systems identification. Soft Comput. **23**(1), 101–114 (2019)
22. Lécué, F.: On the role of knowledge graphs in explainable AI. In: Joint Proceedings of the 6th International Workshop on Dataset PROFILing and Search & the 1st Workshop on Semantic Explainability co-located with the 18th International Semantic Web Conference (ISWC 2019), Auckland, New Zealand, 27 October 2019, p. 29 (2019)
23. Lucas, P.: Expert Systems. In: Kok, J.N. (ed.) Encyclopedia of Life Support Systems (EOLSS), pp. 328–356. Eolss Publishers, Paris (2009)
24. Mitrea, C., Lee, C., Wu, Z.: A comparison between neural networks and traditional forecasting methods: a case study. Int. J. Eng. Bus. Manage. **1** (2009). https://doi.org/10.5772/6777
25. Muggleton, S., Raedt, L.D.: Inductive logic programming: theory and methods. J. Logic Program. **19**(20), 629–679 (1994)
26. Navarro, H., Bennun, L.: Descriptive examples of the limitations of artificial neural networks applied to the analysis of independent stochastic data. Int. J. Comput. Eng. Technol. **5**, 40–42 (2014)
27. Nechepurenko, L., Voss, V.: FreeCiv Games for the Experiment on Comparing Knowledge-Based Reinforcement Learning and Neural Networks in Strategic Games (2019)
28. Neches, R., Swartout, W.R., Moore, J.: Explainable (and maintainable) expert systems. In: Proceedings of the 9th International Joint Conference on Artificial Intelligence, IJCAI 1985, vol. 1, pp. 382–389. Morgan Kaufmann Publishers Inc., San Francisco (1985)
29. Oravec, J.A.: Expert systems and knowledge-based engineering (1984–1991). Int. J. Des. Learn. **5**(2), 66–75 (2014)
30. Reed, R., Marks, R.: Neural Smithing: Supervised Learning in Feedforward Artificial Neural Networks. Bradford Book. MIT Press, Cambridge (1999)
31. Sutton, R.S., Barto, A.G.: Introduction to Reinforcement Learning, 1st edn. MIT Press, Cambridge (1998)
32. Towell, G.G., Shavlik, J.W.: Knowledge-based artificial neural networks. Artif. Intell. **70**(1–2), 119–165 (1994). https://doi.org/10.1016/0004-3702(94)90105-8
33. Tseng, H.H., Luo, Y., Haken, R.T., Naqa, I.E.: The role of machine learning in knowledge-based response-adapted radiotherapy. Front. Oncol. **8**, 266 (2018)
34. Tu, J.V.: Advantages and disadvantages of using artificial neural networks versus logistic regression for predicting medical outcomes. J. Clin. Epidemiol. **49**(11), 1225–1231 (1996)

35. Ulam, P., Goel, A., Jones, J., Murdock, W.: Using model-based reflection to guide reinforcement learning. In: Fourth AAAI Conference on AI in Interactive Digital Entertainment (2008)
36. Voss, V., Nechepurenko, L.: FreeCiv Games Played by Knowledge-based Reinforcement Learning (2019). https://doi.org/10.5281/zenodo.3266624
37. Voss, V., Nechepurenko, L., Schaefer, R., Bauer, S.: Playing a strategy game with knowledge-based reinforcement learning. SN Comput. Sci. **1**(2), 78 (2020)
38. Watson, I., Azhar, D., Chuyang, Y.T., Pan, W., Chen, G.: Optimization in Strategy Games : Using Genetic Algorithms to Optimize City Development in FreeCiv (2009). https://doi.org/10.1.1.567.7035
39. Wender, S.: Integrating Reinforcement Learning into Strategy Games. Master's thesis, The University of Auckland, Auckland, New Zealand (2009)

Clustering Techniques Performance Analysis for a Solar Thermal Collector Hybrid Model Implementation

María Teresa García-Ordás[1], Héctor Alaiz-Moretón[1], José-Luis Casteleiro-Roca[2](✉), Esteban Jove[2], José Alberto Benítez Andrades[1], Carmen Benavides Cuellar[1], Héctor Quintián[2], and José Luis Calvo-Rolle[2]

[1] Department of Electrical and Systems Engineering, University of León, Escuela de Ingenierías, Campus de Vegazana, 24071 León, Spain

[2] CTC, Department of Industrial Engineering, CITIC, University of A Coruña, Avda. 19 de febrero s/n, 15405 Ferrol, A Coruña, Spain

jose.luis.casteleiro@udc.es

Abstract. This work addresses the performance comparison of clustering techniques in order to achieve robust hybrid models. With this goal, three different clustering techniques have been tested. The experimental environment designed for this purpose is based on a real case study, a thermal solar generation system installed in a bio-climate house located in Sotavento Experimental Wind Farm, in Xermade (Lugo) in Galicia (Spain). In this way, clustering methods have been applied over the real dataset extracted from the thermal solar generation installation.

For comparing the quality of each clustering technique, two approaches have been used. The first one is oriented to a set of three unsupervised learning metrics (Silhouette, Calinski-Harabasz, and Davies-Bouldin), while the second one is based on error measurements associated with a regression method such as Multi-Layer Perceptron.

Keywords: Clustering · Prediction · Regression · Solar thermal panel · Hybrid model

1 Introduction

Due to some different reasons like climate change, the latest trends on environmental sustainability, the economy, and so on, the renewable energies are a very important issue [35]. The first steps were made by public and private institutions, with the aim to develop pilot experiences, and for defining the possible way to proceed in the future. In fact, the own governs force the new buildings to meet some requirements in this term; for instance, the corresponding Spanish Ministry has recently approved a new release of technical building framework [16]. Even the first editions of this regulation required the installation of the thermal solar panels for the new buildings.

E. A. de la Cal et al. (Eds.): HAIS 2020, LNAI 12344, pp. 329–340, 2020.
https://doi.org/10.1007/978-3-030-61705-9_27

Nowadays, the current trend are the Smart-grids [3,14,30]. This concept implies many issues, and one of the most important is the right prediction of energy generation and consumption. The main reason is the balance energy optimizing [28,36]. Of course, it would be necessary other complementary parts, like energy storage systems, knowledge extraction, and so on [15,30].

For a suitable prediction, there are some different proven techniques, from the traditional ones to the most advanced. Remark on this point that the last ones, specially the intelligent ones give very satisfactory results [5,23–26,31,34]. Within the intelligent ones, those based on hybrid systems allow to give the best results in prediction tasks [6,9–11,13,22].

In this paper, with the aim to create a hybrid intelligent model for prediction over a solar thermal panel, several different clustering methods are evaluated with three unsupervised metrics: Silhouette, Calinski-Harabasz, and Davies-Bouldin. Once the corresponding class to each data is obtained, a hybrid approach using an MLP is carried out in order to obtain a complimentary metric for evaluating the clustering algorithms.

This paper is structured as follows: the case study is briefly described in the next section. The clustering and regression methods are introduced in Sect. 3. The experiments and their results are described in Sect. 4, and the conclusions and suggestions for future work are presented in Sect. 5.

2 Case Study

The system used in this research is part of the installation in Sotavento Galicia Foundation. This foundation has the main aim of studying new renewable energies, and a bioclimatic house is built to test different renewable systems.

2.1 Sotavento Bioclimatic House

This house is part of a project to *demostrate* the uses of new systems, and it tries to use as few amounts of energy as it is possible. Figure 1 shows the real house, and it is located in the *Sotavento Experimental Wind Farm*, in Xermade (Lugo) in Galicia (Spain).

The bioclimatic house thermal energy system has three different parts: Generation, Accumulation, and Consumption. It is only shown the thermal energy, although the house also has electrical power generation (wind and photovoltaic). The thermal generation is divided into three different sources: Biomass, Geothermal, and Solar. This paper is focused on thermal solar generation.

Figure 2 represents the layout of whole the solar thermal part. This research is only focused on generation, only the sensors S1, S2, S3, S4 (at the top left) and Flow-meter (marked with the red row) are used. Moreover, a solar radiation sensor is used, located outside the bioclimatic house.

Fig. 1. Sotavento bioclimatic house

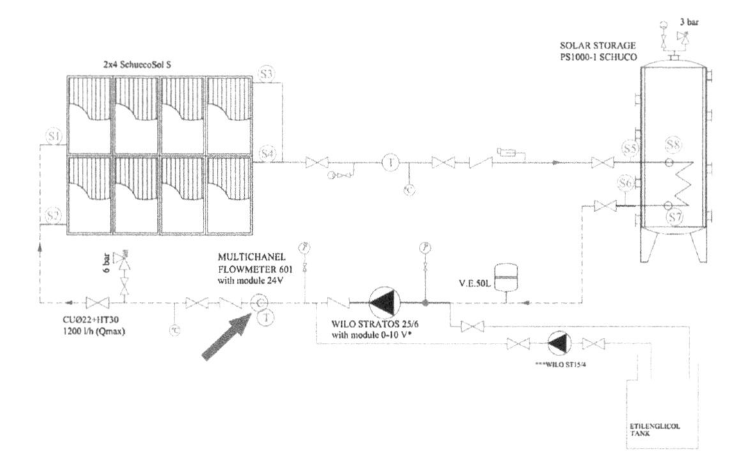

Fig. 2. Solar thermal energy layout (Color figure online)

2.2 Model Approach

Despite the fact that the measurement of the solar panels' output temp is included in the sensors, they are not taking into account in the first step. As the research analyzed the performance of different clustering techniques, it only takes into account Flow, the Radiation, and the Solar panels input temperatures (they are two solar panels).

It has been used different error metrics to check the performance of the different algorithms and, moreover, a regression algorithm is used to model the output temperature of the lower solar panel. With this prediction, a new *error metric* is obtained to check the performance.

3 Methods

In order to deal with our data, a preprocessing step has carried out using Min-Max normalization before the clustering. Three different well-known clustering algorithms have been evaluated, and an MLP neural network has been used as a regressor method for the temperature prediction. Furthermore, the LDA technique has been implemented for better visualization of the clustering results. In this section, we are going to briefly explain all these methods.

3.1 Preprocessing

MinMax Normalization takes into account the maximum and the minimum values to fix the data into the [0, 1] range following Eq. 1.

$$\hat{x}_i = \frac{x_i - x_{min}}{x_{max} - x_{min}} \tag{1}$$

This process has been applied due to the fact that it is considered a good practice when clustering techniques [19] and Multi Layer Percetron for regression purposes are implemented [4].

3.2 LDA Projection

Linear Discriminant Analysis (LDA) is a generalization of the Fisher's algorithm [27]. It is commonly used as a projection technique that tries to transform the data to get the classes as far apart as possible. LDA takes as input a high dimensionality dataset with class labels and tries to find an optimal projection that maps the data in a smaller space. In order to do that, LDA minimizes the distance within classes while it maximizes the distance between classes. It can be done by applying the eigen-decomposition on the scatter matrices of the training data set. Furthermore, it has been widely used as a two-dimension screening method such as in [27].

In this work, this technique has been used in order to get a first graphical approach for understanding how the clustering has worked. Data is reduced to 2D features and represented in a two-dimensional map using clusters as the supervised data required by LDA.

3.3 Clustering

K-Means. K-Means algorithm cluster [21] tries to separate the data into groups minimizing the inertia. In this algorithm, it is necessary to specify the number of clusters, and it is usually defined by the mean of all its elements called centroid μ_j. See Eq. 2.

$$\sum_{i=0}^{N} \min_{\mu_j \in C}(||x_i - \mu_j||^2) \tag{2}$$

Affinity Propagation. Affinity propagation algorithm [22] is an example-based clustering algorithm that is able to determine which are the best samples within a data set to represent all existing data and associate the rest of the data with one of them. With this aim, the algorithm establishes the clusters by sending messages of a pair of samples to determine the exemplariness between both of them. In that way, these messages are sent iteratively until convergence, where the most representative elements of each group are chosen to describe the cluster. One of the advantages of this method is that it not requires to define the number of clusters. However, the memory complexity of the algorithm is $\mathcal{O}(N^2)$ whereas the time complexity is $\mathcal{O}(N^2 I)$ where N is the number of samples and I the number of iterations until convergence.

Agglomerative Clustering. Agglomerative Clustering [18] is part of a general family of clustering algorithms called Hierarchical Clustering, based on the main idea of building clusters by merging or splitting them successively. Agglomerative clustering starts with one cluster per sample. On each iteration, the two clusters that are most similar are merged together. This procedure is repeated until all samples are member of a unique cluster. These algorithms are usually represented graphically using dendrograms.

3.4 Error Metrics

All the clustering methods were evaluated using three unsupervised metrics: Silhouette coefficient, Calinsky-Harabasz and Davies-Bouldin.

Silhouette [29]**.** Silhouette coefficient metric is defined following Eq. 3 for each point.

$$\frac{x-y}{max(x,y)} \tag{3}$$

where x represents the mean intra-cluster distance, and y represents the mean nearest-cluster distance for each sample, that is, the distance between a sample and the nearest cluster that the sample does not belong. The condition to apply the Silhouette coefficient is that the number of labels must be between two and the number of samples minus one.

Finally, Silhouette is calculated as the mean of the mean silhouettes through all the clusters.

Calinski-Harabasz [7]**.** If we take N as the number of observations and K as the number of clusters, we can define the Calinsky-Harabasz index as follows (4):

$$C = \frac{\frac{BGSS}{K-1}}{\frac{WGSS}{N-K}} = \frac{N-K}{K-1}\frac{BGSS}{WGSS} \tag{4}$$

where:

$$BGSS = \sum_{k=1}^{K} n_k ||G^k - G||^2 \tag{5}$$

being G^k the dispersion of the barycenters of each cluster, G the barycenter of the whole set of data and n_k the number of samples in cluster C_k.

$$WGSS = \sum_{k=0}^{K} WGSS^k \tag{6}$$

$$WGSS^k = \sum_{i \in I_k} ||M_i^k - G^k||^2 \tag{7}$$

being M_i^k the coefficients of the i-th row of the data matrix for a cluster C_k and I_k, the set of the indices of the observations belonging to the cluster C_k.

Davies-Bouldin [17]**.** Davies-Bouldin metric is defined as the mean value, among all the clusters, of the samples M_k (see Eq. 8).

$$DB = \frac{1}{K} \sum_{k=1}^{K} M_k \tag{8}$$

This expression is equivalent to 9:

$$DB = \frac{1}{K} \sum_{k=1}^{K} max_{k' \neq k} \left(\frac{\delta_k + \delta_{k'}}{\triangle_{kk'}} \right) \tag{9}$$

where δ_k is the mean distance of the points which belong to cluster C_k to their barycenter G_k and $\triangle_{kk'}$, the distance between barycenters G^k and $G^{k'}$ (see Eq. 10).

$$\triangle_{kk'} = d(G^k, G^{k'}) = ||G^k - G^{k'}|| \tag{10}$$

3.5 Regression Method

Multi-Layer Perceptron: In order to obtain a complimentary metric for evaluating the clustering algorithms previously explained a Multi-Layer Perceptron has been implemented.

Multi-Layer Perceptron is a supervised learning algorithm, that is able to learn thanks to function: $Fun(\cdot) : X^N \rightarrow X0$. Python Scikit-Learn has been the library utilized for implementing this technique. MLP's back-propagation architecture is based on one hidden layer only with an optimum number of neurons with an activation function inside.

With the aim to obtain the optimum number of neurons in the hidden layer and the activation function associated with each one, the cross-validation procedure has been selected. This way, it can train the Multi-Layer Perceptron with different parameters (number of neurons in the hidden layer and the activation function), picking a combination of parameters for obtaining the best regression model [1,2,8,10,12,20,33]. The optimum number of neurons has been chosen from the range defined from 3 to 30. The two possibilities for activation functions are 'Rectified Linear Unit' and 'Tanh function'.

4 Experiments and Results

4.1 Cluster

As the dataset is unlabelled, an unsupervised clustering step was carried out in order to determine possible groups in the dataset. Three different well-known techniques have been evaluated: K-Means, Affinity Propagation, and Agglomerative Clustering. On the first testings, it can be concluded that Affinity Propagation does not fit in our problem due to the nature of our dataset, which is formed of a high number of samples. Using this clustering algorithm, thousands of clusterings with single samples were formed no matter the hyperparameters used, so we decided to discard this technique from the experiments. For the other two methods, a hyperparameters study varying the number of clusters has been performed. Three different unsupervised metrics were taken into account to determine the best configuration: Silhouette, Calinski-Harabasz, and Davies-Bouldin scores. Whereas Silhouette and Calinski-Harabasz are better as bigger the score is, Davies-Bouldin works like an error metric, with values close to 0 being the best ones. In Table 1, the results achieved with the selected hyperparameter are shown.

Table 1. Best hyperparameter scoring using K-Means and Agglomerative Clustering

Clustering	Best number of clusters	Silhouette	Calinski-Harabasz	Davies-Bouldin
K-Means	4	0.5374	47787.0924	0.6338
Agglomerative	4	0.5279	41354.7560	0.6359

As we can see in both cases, the optimum value for the number of clusters was 4. The results showed that although both methods perform similarly, K-Means slightly outperforms Agglomerative Clustering in all the scorings.

In order to visualize the clustering, we trained an LDA model using the labels of the clusterings as the classes of each sample, obtaining a 2D representation shown in Fig. 3.

4.2 Regression

The final objective of this work is to know what is the best cluster algorithm applied in the dataset context. For this reason, an MLP regression architecture has been chosen. Being the protagonist the clustering method. In addition, the Cross-validation only is oriented to search a number of neurons in the hidden layer and their activation function. The error measure chosen for Grid Search as Cross-Validation has been the *Mean Squared Error* [32].

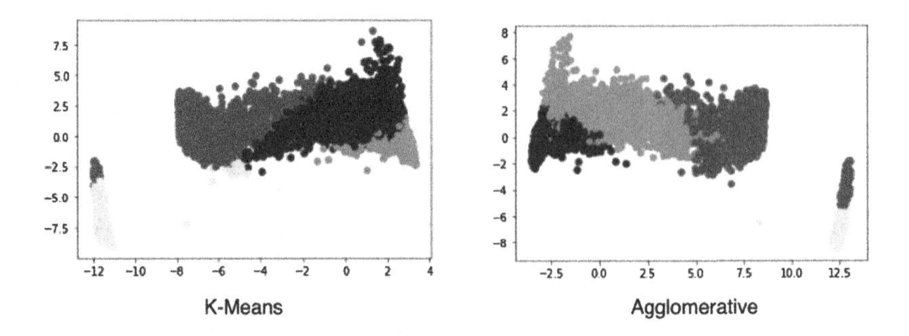

Fig. 3. 2D representation of the dataset for each clustering technique.

Table 2. MLP error measurements for K-Means and Agglomerative clustering

Cluster	1	2	3	4	*Weighted average*	Average
MSE: MLP & K-means	5.21	59.47	21.27	16.54	**36.77**	**25.62**
MAE: MLP & K-means	0.81	6.07	2.90	3.08	**4.04**	**3.22**
MSE: MLP & Agglomerative	56.66	1.19	21.36	11.13	**27.45**	**22.58**
MAE: MLP & Agglomerative	5.86	0.70	2,90	2.58	**3.33**	**3.01**
MSE: MLP	–	–	–	–	–	**36.88**
MAE: MLP	–	–	–	–	–	**3.33**

The final results are considered from two different approaches. The first one is oriented to a hybrid model based on the K-Means clustering method, and the second one is oriented to a hybrid model based on the Agglomerative Clustering method. Error measurements per each cluster are shown in Table 2. Besides, a weighted average proportional to size of each cluster are included in these tables.

Figures 4 and 5 display the graphical representation like real output (in blue) versus predicted output (in red) per each clustering technique. The "X" axis represents only 50 elements of each data sample of 20% cases of the final test data split per each cluster for visualizing purposes, due to the validation split is composed by 26665 elements divided into 4 clusters, and it can be very tedious to see the quality of regression if all elements of validation split are plotted. On the other hand, "Y" axis represents the out value, in this case, the output temperature of the top solar panel.

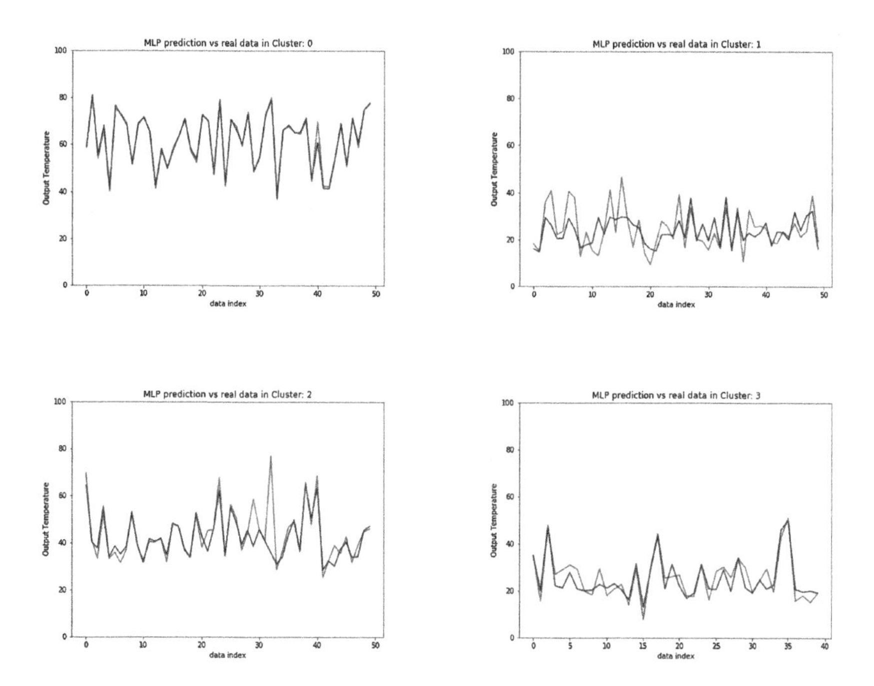

Fig. 4. Real data vs. MLP predictions for K-Means clustering (Color figure online)

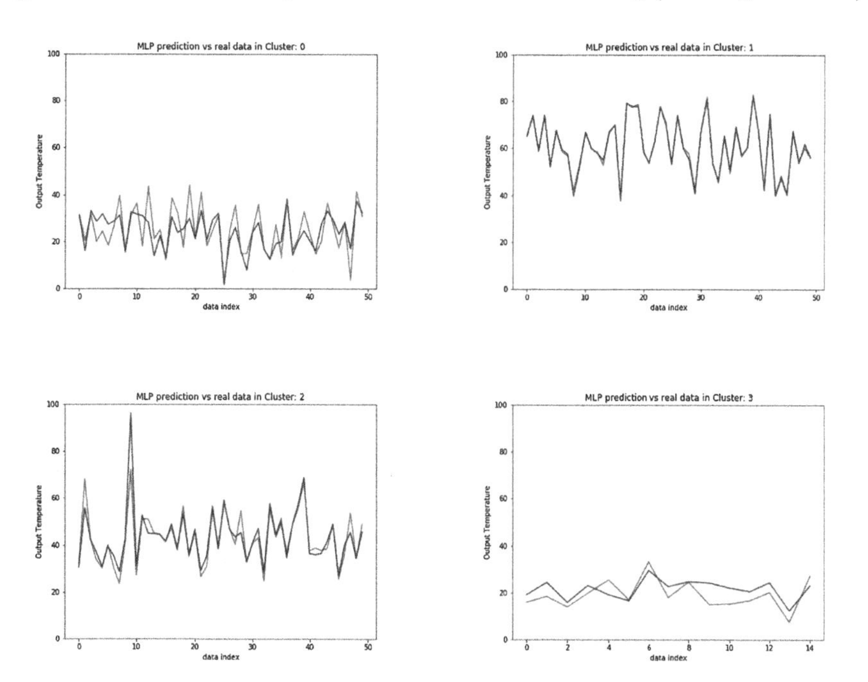

Fig. 5. Real data vs. MLP predictions for Agglomerative clustering (Color figure online)

5 Conclusions and Futures Works

In this work, several clustering methods have been evaluated to deal with the output temperature prediction in thermal solar panels. K-Means, Agglomerative Clustering and Affinity Propagation were used to find the best clusters for the dataset. In order to determine the performance of the clustering techniques, three different scorings have been used: Silhouette, Calinski-Harabasz, and Davies-Bouldin. As can be seen in the Experiments and Results section, the K-Means algorithm obtained the best scoring for all the metrics, although the results were certainly similar. Affinity propagation method could not fit the data obtaining thousands of different small clusters, spending a lot of time in the process due to the high number of elements in the dataset. Taking into account those clusterings, a hybrid method using an MLP regressor has been performed. Although the best results in the unsupervised step were obtained by the K-Means method, the regression showed that Agglomerative clustering was more accurate in the temperature prediction obtaining a weighted average MSE of 27.4473, an improvement of 25.35% with respect K-Means results and a mean absolute error (MAE) of 3.3319, which implies an improvement of 17.61% with respect K-Means method.

This can be explained because the hybrid method used is not totally influenced by the grouping done previously. There are many other characteristics that provide extra information for the reconstruction of the curve. However, the use of clustering is a determining factor, improving the regression by 63.33% taking into account the MSE metric.

Future works will be oriented to compare more clustering techniques in order to know, new clustering methods that can be applied for developing hybrid models. From the authors' point of view, it will be very interesting to implement these clustering techniques to new data sets extracted from other domains.

Acknowledgements. This work is partially supported by Junta de Castilla y Leon - Consejería de Educacion. Project: LE078G18. UXXI2018/000149. U-220.

References

1. Alaiz-Moreton, H., Fernández-Robles, L., Alfonso-Cendón, J., Castejón-Limas, M., Sánchez-González, L., Pérez, H.: Data mining techniques for the estimation of variables in health-related noisy data. In: Pérez García, H., Alfonso-Cendón, J., Sánchez González, L., Quintián, H., Corchado, E. (eds.) SOCO/CISIS/ICEUTE -2017. AISC, vol. 649, pp. 482–491. Springer, Cham (2018). https://doi.org/10.1007/978-3-319-67180-2_47
2. Alaiz-Moretón, H., et al.: Bioinspired hybrid model to predict the hydrogen inlet fuel cell flow change of an energy storage system. Processes **7**(11), 825 (2019)
3. Amin, M.: Smart grid. Public Utilities Fortnightly (2015)
4. Bacong, J.R., Juanico, D.E.: Performance analysis of multi-layer perceptron regression model with mixed-rate sensor data inputs. In: Proceedings of the Samahang Pisika ng Pilipinas (2018)

5. Baruque, B., Porras, S., Jove, E., Calvo-Rolle, J.L.: Geothermal heat exchanger energy prediction based on time series and monitoring sensors optimization. Energy **171**, 49–60 (2019)
6. Basurto, N., Arroyo, Á., Vega, R., Quintián, H., Calvo-Rolle, J.L., Herrero, Á.: A hybrid intelligent system to forecast solar energy production. Comput. Electr. Eng. **78**, 373–387 (2019)
7. Caliński, T., Harabasz, J.: A dendrite method for cluster analysis. Commun. Stat. **3**(1), 1–27 (1974). https://doi.org/10.1080/03610927408827101
8. Castejón-Limas, M., et al.: Coupling the PAELLA algorithm to predictive models. In: Pérez García, H., Alfonso-Cendón, J., Sánchez González, L., Quintián, H., Corchado, E. (eds.) SOCO/CISIS/ICEUTE -2017. AISC, vol. 649, pp. 505–512. Springer, Cham (2018). https://doi.org/10.1007/978-3-319-67180-2_49
9. Casteleiro-Roca, J.L., Barragan, A., Segura, F., Calvo-Rolle, J.L., Andújar, J.M.: Intelligent hybrid system for the prediction of the voltage-current characteristic curve of a hydrogen-based fuel cell. Revista Iberoamericana de Automatica e Informatica Industrial **16**(4), 492–501 (2019). https://doi.org/10.4995/riai.2019.10986
10. Casteleiro-Roca, J.L., Barragán, A.J., Segura, F., Calvo-Rolle, J.L.,Andújar, J.M.: Fuel cell output current prediction with a hybrid intelligent system. Complexity **2019** (2019).https://doi.org/10.1155/2019/6317270
11. Casteleiro-Roca, J.L., et al.: Electromyogram prediction during anesthesia by using a hybrid intelligent model. J. Ambient Intell. Hum. Comput. 1–10 (2019). https://doi.org/10.1007/s12652-019-01426-8
12. Casteleiro-Roca, J.L., Jove, E., Sánchez-Lasheras, F., Méndez-Pérez, J.A., Calvo-Rolle, J.L., de Cos Juez, F.J.: Power cell SOC modelling for intelligent virtual sensor implementation. J. Sens. **2017**, 1–10 (2017). https://doi.org/10.1155/2017/9640546
13. Casteleiro-Roca, J.L., Perez, J.A.M., Piñón-Pazos, A.J., Calvo-Rolle, J.L., Corchado, E.: Intelligent model for electromyogram (EMG) signal prediction during anesthesia. J. Multiple-Valued Logic Soft Comput. **32**, 205–220 (2019)
14. Casteleiro-Roca, J.L., Quintián, H., Calvo-Rolle, J.L., Méndez-Pérez, J.A., Perez-Castelo, F.J., Corchado, E.: Lithium iron phosphate power cell fault detection system based on hybrid intelligent system. Logic J. IGPL **28**(1), 71–82 (2020). https://doi.org/10.1093/jigpal/jzz072
15. Crespo-Turrado, C., et al.: Comparative study of imputation algorithms applied to the prediction of student performance. Logic J. IGPL **28**(1), 58–70 (2019). https://doi.org/10.1093/jigpal/jzz071
16. CTE, D.: Código técnico de la edificación (2020)
17. Davies, D.L., Bouldin, D.W.: A cluster separation measure. IEEE Trans. Pattern Anal. Mach. Intell. PAMI **1**(2), 224–227 (1979). https://doi.org/10.1109/TPAMI.1979.4766909
18. Defays, D.: An efficient algorithm for a complete link method. Comput. J. **20**(4), 364–366 (1977). https://doi.org/10.1093/comjnl/20.4.364
19. Ding, C.H., He, X., Zha, H., Gu, M., Simon, H.D.: A min-max cut algorithm for graph partitioning and data clustering. In: Proceedings 2001 IEEE International Conference on Data Mining, pp. 107–114. IEEE (2001)
20. Duan, K., Keerthi, S.S., Poo, A.N.: Evaluation of simple performance measures for tuning SVM hyperparameters. Neurocomputing **51**, 41–59 (2003)
21. Forgy, E.W.: Cluster analysis of multivariate data: efficiency versus interpretability of classifications (1965)
22. Frey, B.J., Dueck, D.: Clustering by passing messages between data points. Science **315**(5814), 972–976 (2007). https://doi.org/10.1126/science.1136800

23. Gutiérrez, C.G., et al.: Rapid tomographic reconstruction through GPU-based adaptive optics. Logic J. GPL **27**(2), 214–226 (2019)
24. Jove, E., Casteleiro-Roca, J., Quintián, H., Méndez-Pérez, J.A., Calvo-Rolle, J.L.: Anomaly detection based on intelligent techniques over a bicomponent production plant used on wind generator blades manufacturing. Revista Iberoamericana de Automatica e Informatica Industrial **17**(1), 84–93 (2020). https://doi.org/10.4995/riai.2019.11055
25. Jove, E., et al.: Modelling the hypnotic patient response in general anaesthesia using intelligent models. Logic J. IGPL **27**(2), 189–201 (2018). https://doi.org/10.1093/jigpal/jzy032
26. Marrero, A., Méndez, J., Reboso, J., Martín, I., Calvo, J.: Adaptive fuzzy modeling of the hypnotic process in anesthesia. J. Clin. Monitor. Comput. **31**(2), 319–330 (2017)
27. Mika, S., Ratsch, G., Weston, J., Scholkopf, B., Mullers, K.R.: Fisher discriminant analysis with kernels. In: Neural Networks For Signal Processing IX: Proceedings of the 1999 IEEE Signal Processing Society Workshop (cat. no. 98th8468), pp. 41–48. IEEE (1999)
28. Nizami, M., Haque, A., Nguyen, P., Hossain, M.: On the application of home energy management systems for power grid support. Energy **188**, 116104 (2019). https://doi.org/10.1016/j.energy.2019.116104
29. Rousseeuw, P.J.: Silhouettes: a graphical aid to the interpretation and validation of cluster analysis. J. Computat. Appl. Math. **20**, 53–65 (1987). https://doi.org/10.1016/0377-0427(87)90125-7
30. de Souza Dutra, M.D., Anjos, M.F., Digabel, S.L.: A general framework for customized transition to smart homes. Energy **189**, 116138 (2019). https://doi.org/10.1016/j.energy.2019.116138
31. Tomás-Rodríguez, M., Santos, M.: Modelling and control of floating offshore wind turbines. Revista Iberoamericana de Automática e Informática Industrial **16**, 381–390 (2019). https://doi.org/10.4995/riai.2019.11648
32. Tuchler, M., Singer, A.C., Koetter, R.: Minimum mean squared error equalization using a priori information. IEEE Trans. Signal Process. **50**(3), 673–683 (2002)
33. http://scikit-learn.org/stable/modules/generated/sklearn.model_selection.GridSearchCV.html. Grid search cross validation (2019). Accessed 22 April 2019
34. Vega Vega, R., Quintián, H., Calvo-Rolle, J.L., Herrero, Á., Corchado, E.: Gaining deep knowledge of android malware families through dimensionality reduction techniques. Logic J. IGPL **27**(2), 160–176 (2019)
35. Xu, X., Wei, Z., Ji, Q., Wang, C., Gao, G.: Global renewable energy development: influencing factors, trend predictions and countermeasures. Resour. Pol. **63**, 101470 (2019). https://doi.org/10.1016/j.resourpol.2019.101470
36. Yang, C.J., Jackson, R.B.: Opportunities and barriers to pumped-hydro energy storage in the united states. Renew. Sustain. Energy Rev. **15**(1), 839–844 (2011)

A Hybrid One-Class Topology for Non-convex Sets

Esteban Jove[1(✉)], José-Luis Casteleiro-Roca[1], Héctor Quintián[1], Francisco Zayas-Gato[1], Roberto Casado-Vara[2], Bruno Baruque[3], Juan Albino Méndez-Pérez[4], and José Luis Calvo-Rolle[1]

[1] CTC, Department of Industrial Engineering, CITIC , University of A Coruña, Avda. 19 de febrero s/n, 15405 Ferrol, A Coruña, Spain
{esteban.jove,jose.luis.casteleiro}@udc.es
[2] University of Salamanca, BISITE Research Group, IoT Digital Innovation Hub Edificio Multiusos I+D+i, 37007 Salamanca, Spain
[3] Departamento de Ingeniería Civil, Universidad de Burgos, Calle Francisco de Vitoria, s/n, 09006 Burgos, Spain
[4] Department of Computer Science and System Engineering, Universidad de La Laguna, Avda. Astrof. Francisco Sánchez s/n, 38200 S/C de Tenerife, Spain

Abstract. The technological advances in the industrial sector have emphasized the importance of anomaly detection, which represents a critical task to a achieve a systems optimization. In this context, many different outlier detection techniques have been developed. The boundary methods have presented successfully results in many one-class problems. Specifically convex hull approximations have offered good performance. However, this approach leads to misclassification when it is applied to non-convex sets. This paper proposes a hybrid one-class topology based on an approximate convex hull approach to solve the problem of anomaly detection over non-convex sets. The proposal is assessed and validated with successful results.

Keywords: Anomaly detection · Non-convex · Boundary methods

1 Introduction

Over the last years, the industries have presented many important technological advances, in terms of instrumentation and digitalization [16]. Several new concepts, such as Internet of Things or Industry 4.0 offer the possibility to provide a wide amount of information about a specific system [8,9,11].

In this context, the use of intelligent techniques can play a significant role [12, 13,24], specially in the optimization process. One of the key tasks to achieve a system optimization is the early detection of any kind of anomalies, such as sensors or actuators malfunctions [17]. The achievement of this critical task

E. A. de la Cal et al. (Eds.): HAIS 2020, LNAI 12344, pp. 341–349, 2020.
https://doi.org/10.1007/978-3-030-61705-9_28

would lead to economic savings in terms of energy consumption, material waste reduction and corrective and predictive maintenance, among others [15,19,29,31].

Following a generic approach, anomalies are defined as a data pattern that does not have the expected behavior in a specific system [7,10,18]. Despite the simplicity of this definition, anomaly detection must face a series of issues to be tackled [10,21]:

- The anomaly occurrence can be caused from an infinite number of situations. Then, the possibility of having data samples from all potential anomalous situations is not feasible.
- In many cases, it is not possible to force the system to an anomalous state, since this process may lead to irreversible system failures.
- Even if a one-class approach is faced using only data from the target set, the noise appearance could represent a significant problem.
- If the previous issues are settled, unsuitable limits between target and non-target classes would lead to misclassification.

A very common way to face anomaly detection, consists in establishing the geometric boundaries of the target set [30]. Concretely, the use of convex hull approach have achieved interesting results [4,14]. However, the performance of this approach decreases when applied to non-convex sets [5]. This work proposes a modification of Approximate Polytope Ensemble (APE) [5] technique to improve the performance with non-convex sets. To do so, a clustering algorithm is applied and, then, the APE is applied over each subset. The methodology is assessed over two datasets: a banana-shape set and a normal distribution set.

This work is structured as follows. After the present section, the motivation of this work is detailed. Then, Sect. 3 describes the proposal. Section 4 presents the experiments and results and then, conclusions and future works are exposed in Sect. 5.

2 Motivation

The boundary methods for one-class classification have been used to solve a wide variety of anomaly detection problems [14]. Techniques such as Support Vector Machine (SVM), Support Vector Data Description (SVDD) or Approximate Polytope Ensemble (APE) presented successful results over UCI datasets [14,30]. In particular, APE has shown great performance in recent works [20].

The basis of this classification technique is to calculate the boundaries of the original dataset $S \in R^n$ using the convex hull. The convex hull $C(S)$ of a set of points $S \subseteq R^n$ is the minimal convex set containing S, and can be defined as the convex combination of points in S, following Eq. 1 [14,25].

$$C(S) = \sum_{i=1}^{|S|} \beta x_i \mid \forall i : \beta_i \geq 0 \wedge \sum_{i=1}^{|S|} \beta x_i = 1, x_i \in S \tag{1}$$

Also, the possibility of expanding or contracting the vertexes v of the convex hull from its centroid $c = (1/|S|)\sum_i x_i, \forall x_i \in S$, can be carried out by using the parameter $\lambda \in [0, +\infty)$ following the Eq. 2.

$$v^\lambda : \{\lambda v + (1 - \lambda)c \mid v \in C(s)\} \tag{2}$$

Therefore, values of λ lower than 1 lead to convex hull contraction, and values greater than 1 expand convex hull. The proper value of λ depends on the shape of the dataset.

However, the process of obtaining a convex hull from a dataset with N samples and d variables, has a computational cost of $O(N^{(d/2)+1})$ [4]. Given the high computational cost of this process, an alternative method consists in making p random projections of the original data on $2D$ planes and determining their convex limits on that plane [14].

According to this approach, when the convex hull approximation is obtained from the training dataset, the following classification criteria for test data is used: if the data is out of at least one of the p projections, it is considered an anomaly. Figure 1 shows a $2D$ example where an anomaly point in $\mathbb{R}^3$ space is out of one of the original data projections.

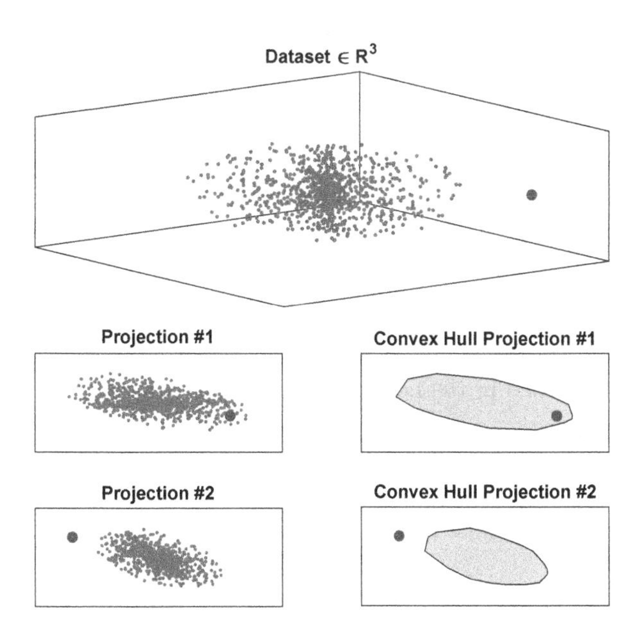

Fig. 1. Anomaly detection using APE over normal distribution dataset

However, the use of APE over non-convex sets could lead to erroneous classification if the anomalies appear outside the training set, but inside the convex hull, as shown in Fig. 2.

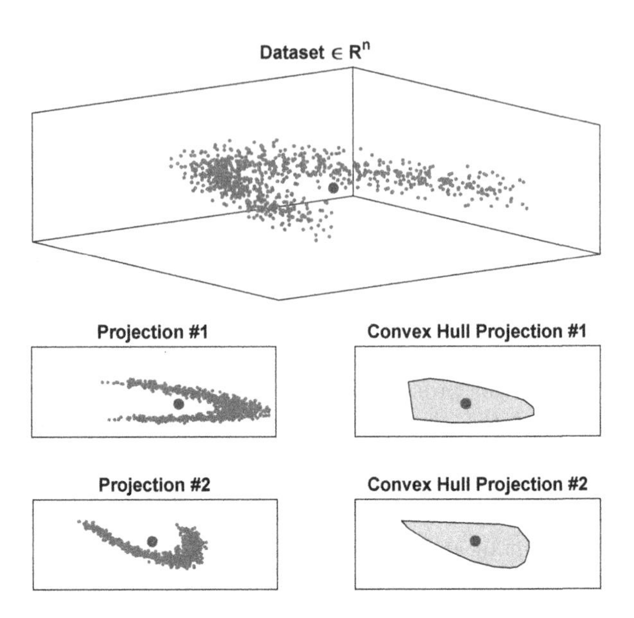

Fig. 2. Anomaly detection using APE over non-convex dataset

3 Classifier Approach

The present section describes the classifier approach to overcome the issue of APE algorithms over non-convex sets. The proposal is based on the use of APE combined with clustering techniques. In this case, kmeans, is the unsupervised clustering method used to classify the initial dataset into a number of groups defined by user. This is based on a first approach, where cluster centers are distributed randomly [1,2,6]. Then, to improve the sum of the euclidean distances from all the points of each cluster to their centroid is minimized [22,26–28].

The followed process to detect anomalous situations is presented in Fig. 3 and Fig. 4, and detailed in the next steps.

1. The initial dataset is divided into k clusters using kmeans algorithm.
2. For each cluster, p random $2D$ projections are applied (Fig. 3).
3. To determine if a new test point t is anomalous, the next condition must be fulfilled: the point t, must be out, at least, one of the p projections in all the k clusters 4.

An example of the clustering over a non-convex shape set in $\mathbb{R}^3$ is shown in Fig. 5. In this case, the training set is divided into two clusters and then, the anomaly point is out of at least one projection of each cluster.

4 Experiments and Results

The proposed approach was validated over two datasets. The first one is comprised of a banana shape training set in $\mathbb{R}^3$. The second training set follows

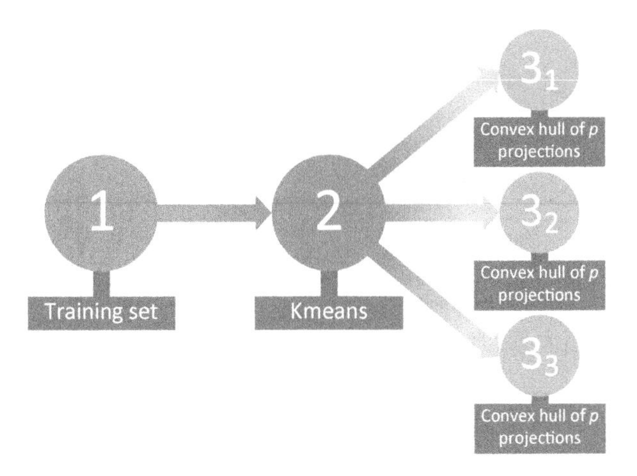

Fig. 3. Training process

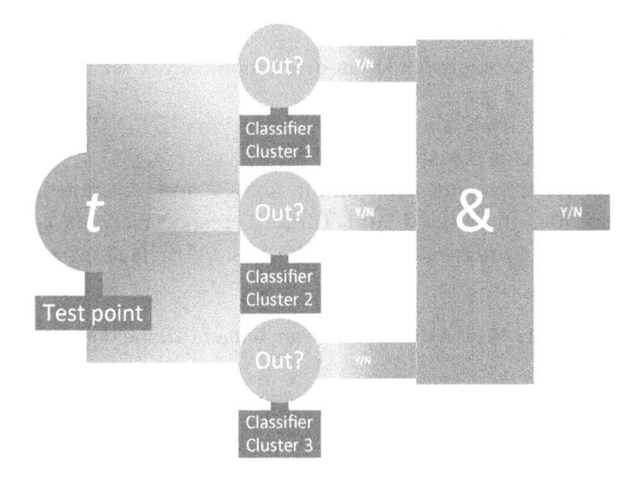

Fig. 4. Test process

a gaussian distribution in $\mathbb{R}^3$. Each training set has 10000 samples, and the anomalies are artificially generated outside the boundaries of the training set.

A comparative analysis over the performance of APE and the proposed approach with the two datasets is carried out according to the next conditions:

- Number of projections: 5, 10, 50, 100.
- Expansion parameter: 0.9, 1, 1.1.
- Number of clusters: 1 (APE), 2, 3, 4, 5.

To ensure the correct assessment, the classifier was trained using a $k - fold$ with $k = 10$. The classifiers performance are evaluated with the Area Under Curve (AUC) parameter, that establishes a relationship between true positives

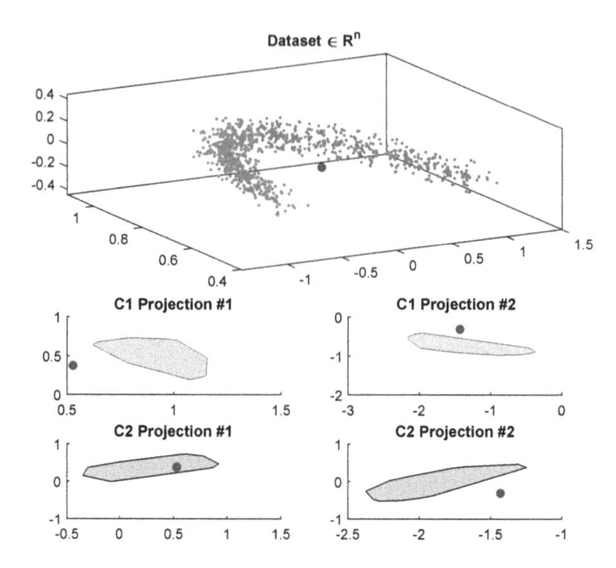

Fig. 5. Anomaly detection over a non-convex set in $\mathbb{R}^3$

and false positives [3]. Also, the standard deviations (STD) between k-fold iteration is represented, as a measure of repeatability.

The achieved results using the banana shape, and the normal distribution dataset are presented in Table 1 and Table 2, respectively. It is important to remark that only the configuration with the best AUC is shown.

Table 1. Best AUC results over banana shape dataset

Expansion	Clusters	Projections	AUC (%)	STD (%)
0.9	1	5	37,58	0,91
	2	5	90,42	0,67
	3	5	92,64	0,62
	4	5	93,18	0,55
	5	5	93,58	0,62
1	1	1	49,58	0,16
	2	5	99,29	0,18
	3	5	99,10	0,22
	4	5	98,98	0,26
	5	5	98,80	0,26
1, 1	1	10	53,24	0,29
	2	5	99,70	0,07
	3	5	99,97	0,05
	4	5	99,94	0,07
	5	5	99,88	0,08

Table 2. Best AUC results over normal distribution dataset

Expansion	Clusters	Projections	AUC (%)	STD (%)
0.9	1	5	98,05	0,76
	2	5	95,27	1,48
	3	5	91,53	1,80
	4	5	88,84	2,12
	5	5	86,00	2,56
1	1	1	98,85	0,97
	2	5	97,51	1,31
	3	5	96,28	1,76
	4	5	94,98	1,68
	5	5	93,36	1,76
1, 1	1	10	99,35	0,47
	2	5	98,74	0,73
	3	5	98,28	0,93
	4	5	97,88	0,97
	5	5	97,21	1,19

It is interesting to emphasize that, for almost all implemented classifiers, the best configuration is achieved with the minimum number of projections. This means that, all configurations have a significantly low training time, with less than 0,09 s. This value is essentially the same for all the classifiers with 5 projections, regardless the number of clusters.

5 Conclusions and Future Works

The present work has tackled the problem of using APE algorithms over non-convex sets. The proposal is a hybrid one-class classifier whose performance has been successfully validated with two different datasets. When this method is applied to a non-convex set, it clearly outperforms the original APE configuration, with a top AUC value of 99,98%, with 4 clusters, 5 projections and the expansion parameter set to 1. For this set, APE without clustering does not obtain successful results, with an AUC of at most 53,24%.

As expected, the performance of both approaches has been successful when they are applied over a gaussian distribution dataset.

This proposal could represent a very interesting method to detect anomalies when the nature of the dataset presents non-convex behavior. Its use in complex systems may improve the current performance of APE approach.

As future works, it could be considered the possibility of comparing the proposal with different one-class techniques. Furthermore, a prior knowledge extraction stage could be interesting. Finally, the application of other clustering technique could help to isolate outliers [23].

References

1. Alaiz-Moreton, H., et al.: Multiclass classification procedure for detecting attacks on MQTT-IoT protocol. Complexity **2019** (2019)
2. Aláiz-Moretón, H., Castejón-Limas, M., Casteleiro-Roca, J.L., Jove, E., Fernández Robles, L., Calvo-Rolle, J.L.: A fault detection system for a geothermal heat exchanger sensor based on intelligent techniques. Sensors **19**(12), 2740 (2019)
3. Bradley, A.P.: The use of the area under the roc curve in the evaluation of machine learning algorithms. Pattern Recognit. **30**(7), 1145–1159 (1997)
4. Casale, P., Pujol, O., Radeva, P.: Approximate convex hulls family for one-class classification. In: Sansone, C., Kittler, J., Roli, F. (eds.) MCS 2011. LNCS, vol. 6713, pp. 106–115. Springer, Heidelberg (2011). https://doi.org/10.1007/978-3-642-21557-5_13
5. Casale, P., Pujol, O., Radeva, P.: Approximate polytope ensemble for one-class classification. Pattern Recognit. **47**(2), 854–864 (2014)
6. Casteleiro-Roca, J.L., et al.: Short-term energy demand forecast in hotels using hybrid intelligent modeling. Sensors **19**(11), 2485 (2019)
7. Casteleiro-Roca, J.L., Javier Barragan, A., Segura, F., Luis Calvo-Rolle, J., Manuel Andujar, J.: Intelligent hybrid system for the prediction of the voltage-current characteristic curve of a hydrogen-based fuel cell. Revista Iberoamericana de Automática e Informática industrial **16**(4), 492–501 (2019)
8. Casteleiro-Roca, J.L., et al.: Power cellsoc modelling for intelligent virtual sensor implementation. J. Sensors **2017** (2017)
9. Cecilia, A., Costa-Castelló, R.: High gain observer with dynamic dead zone to estimate liquid water saturation in pem fuel cells. Revista Iberoamericana de Automática e Informática industrial **17**(2), 169–180 (2020)
10. Chandola, V., Banerjee, A., Kumar, V.: Anomaly detection: a survey. ACM Comput. Surv. (CSUR) **41**(3), 15 (2009)
11. Chiang, L.H., Russell, E.L., Braatz, R.D.: Fault Detection and Diagnosis in Industrial Systems. Springer, Heidelberg (2000)
12. Crespo-Turrado, C., et al.: Comparative study of imputation algorithms applied to the prediction of student performance. Logic J. IGPL **28**(1), 58–70 (2019). https://doi.org/10.1093/jigpal/jzz071
13. Fathi, M., Baptista, J., Barbosa, M., Barrero, D., Baruque, B., Bertini, I., Bittencourt, E., Boubekeur, M., Brown, K., Bulas-Cruz, J., et al.: Soft computing models in industrial and environmental applications. Adv. Intell. Soft Comput. **73**, 261 (2010)
14. Fernández-Francos, D., Fontenla-Romero, Ó., Alonso-Betanzos, A.: One-class convex hull-based algorithm for classification in distributed environments. IEEE Trans. Syst. Man, Cybern.: Syst. 1–11 (2018)
15. Gomes, I.L.R., Melicio, R., Mendes, V.M.F., Pousinho, H.M.I.: Wind power with energy storage arbitrage in day-ahead market by a stochastic MILP approach. Logic J. IGPL (2019). https://doi.org/10.1093/jigpal/jzz054
16. Hobday, M.: Product complexity, innovation and industrial organisation. Res. policy **26**(6), 689–710 (1998)
17. Jove, E., Alaiz-Moretón, H., García-Rodríguez, I., Benavides-Cuellar, C., Casteleiro-Roca, J.L., Calvo-Rolle, J.L.: PID-ITS: an intelligent tutoring system for PID tuning learning process. In: Pérez García, H., Alfonso-Cendón, J., Sánchez González, L., Quintián, H., Corchado, E. (eds.) SOCO/CISIS/ICEUTE -2017. AISC, vol. 649, pp. 726–735. Springer, Cham (2018). https://doi.org/10.1007/978-3-319-67180-2_71

18. Jove, E., et al.: Missing data imputation over academic records of electrical engineering students. Logic J. IGPL **28**, 487–501 (2019)
19. Jove, E., Casteleiro-Roca, J.-L., Quintián, H., Méndez-Pérez, J.A., Calvo-Rolle, J.L.: A new approach for system malfunctioning over an industrial system control loop based on unsupervised techniques. In: Graña, M., et al. (eds.) SOCO'18-CISIS'18-ICEUTE'18 2018. AISC, vol. 771, pp. 415–425. Springer, Cham (2019). https://doi.org/10.1007/978-3-319-94120-2_40
20. Jove, E., Casteleiro-Roca, J.L., Quintián, H., Méndez-Pérez, J.A., Calvo-Rolle, J.L.: Anomaly detection based on intelligent techniques over a bicomponent production plant used on wind generator blades manufacturing. Revista Iberoamericana de Automática e Informática industrial (2019)
21. Jove, E., Casteleiro-Roca, J.L., Quintián, H., Méndez-Pérez, J.A., Calvo-Rolle, J.L.: A fault detection system based on unsupervised techniques for industrial control loops. Exp. Syst. **36**, e12395 (2019)
22. Jove, E., et al.: Modelling the hypnotic patient response in general anaesthesia using intelligent models. Logic J. IGPL **27**(2), 189–201 (2018)
23. Machón-González, I., López-García, H., Calvo-Rolle, J.L.: A hybrid batch SOM-NG algorithm. In: The 2010 International Joint Conference on Neural Networks (IJCNN), pp. 1–5. IEEE (2010)
24. Marrero, A., Méndez, J., Reboso, J., Martín, I., Calvo, J.: Adaptive fuzzy modeling of the hypnotic process in anesthesia. J. Clin. Monitor. Comput. **31**(2), 319–330 (2017)
25. Preparata, F.P., Shamos, M.I.: Computational Geometry: An Introduction. Springer, Heidelberg (2012)
26. Quintián, H., Casteleiro-Roca, J.-L., Perez-Castelo, F.J., Calvo-Rolle, J.L., Corchado, E.: Hybrid intelligent model for fault detection of a lithium iron phosphate power cell used in electric vehicles. In: Martínez-Álvarez, F., Troncoso, A., Quintián, H., Corchado, E. (eds.) HAIS 2016. LNCS (LNAI), vol. 9648, pp. 751–762. Springer, Cham (2016). https://doi.org/10.1007/978-3-319-32034-2_63
27. Quintián, H., Corchado, E.: Beta Hebbian learning as a new method for exploratory projection pursuit. Int. J. Neural Syst. **27**(06), 1750024 (2017)
28. Quintián, H., Corchado, E.: Beta scale invariant map. Eng. Appl. Artif. Intell. **59**, 218–235 (2017)
29. Sittón-Candanedo, I., Alonso, R.S., Corchado, J.M., Rodríguez-González, S., Casado-Vara, R.: A review of edge computing reference architectures and a new global edge proposal. Fut. Gener. Comput. Syst. **99**, 278–294 (2019)
30. Tax, D.M.J.: One-class classification: concept-learning in the absence of counter-examples [ph. d. thesis]. Delft University of Technology (2001)
31. Tomás-Rodríguez, M., Santos, M.: Modelling and control of floating offshore wind turbines. Revista Iberoamericana de Automática eInformática Industrial **16**(4) (2019)

A Machine Consciousness Architecture Based on Deep Learning and Gaussian Processes

Eduardo C. Garrido Merchán[1(✉)] and Martin Molina[2]

[1] Universidad Autónoma de Madrid, Madrid, Spain
eduardo.garrido@uam.es
[2] Universidad Politécnica de Madrid, Madrid, Spain
martin.molina@upm.es

Abstract. Recent developments in machine learning have pushed the tasks that machines can do outside the boundaries of what was thought to be possible years ago. Methodologies such as deep learning or generative models have achieved complex tasks such as generating art pictures or literature automatically. Machine Consciousness is a field that has been deeply studied and several theories based in the functionalism philosophical theory like the global workspace theory have been proposed. In this work, we propose an architecture that may arise consciousness in a machine based in the global workspace theory and in the assumption that consciousness appear in machines that have cognitive processes and exhibit conscious behaviour. This architecture is based in processes that use the recent Deep Learning and generative process models. For every module of this architecture, we provide detailed explanations of the models involved and how they communicate with each other to create the cognitive architecture. We illustrate how we can optimize the architecture to generate social interactions between robots and genuine pieces of art, both features correlated with machine consciousness. As far as we know, this is the first machine consciousness architecture that use generative models and deep learning to exhibit conscious social behaviour and to retrieve pictures and other subjective content made by robots.

Keywords: Machine consciousness · Machine learning · Deep learning · Gaussian processes · Artificial intelligence

1 Introduction

Several reviews have been written about machine consciousness [24,25,50] that try to sum up all the ideas that literature has proposed about the potential arisal of consciousness in machines [14]. These ideas come from different areas such as artificial intelligence [13], neuroscience [46] or philosophy [53]. Although consciousness can not be measured directly, there exist approaches that have provided potential measures of consciousness in machines [4,49].

E. A. de la Cal et al. (Eds.): HAIS 2020, LNAI 12344, pp. 350–361, 2020.
https://doi.org/10.1007/978-3-030-61705-9_29

Although the field generates controversy [16] as it lies in the margin of the scientific method, it has recently attracted the attention of relevant researchers of computer science such as Yoshua Bengio, who has provided an approach for how machine consciousness may arise with deep learning [10]. As deep learning [40] has generated machines that implement attention mechanisms [32], a new focus have emerged with the field of machine consciousness based in the astonishing hypothesis [16] that our intelligence and consciousness may arise from very simple principles.

Computational approaches for machine consciousness are based in the functionalism theory of consciousness [50]. This theory claims that while mental states correspond to brain states, they are mental states due to their functionality, not due to their physical composition. Hence, consciousness may appear in machines that implement behaviors observed in humans that are correlated with consciousness.

Throughout the recent years, there has been amazing advances in the artificial intelligence and machine learning community [45] that does not only include deep learning models. In the machine consciousness literature, it has been hypothesized that consciousness, or phenomenal states [41], may arise from machines that are able to perform tasks that humans are able to do when they are conscious [17,25]. This is based in the hypothesis that if humans are conscious when producing complex behaviours, then, machines may be conscious when they produce them too [23].

We know, and have measured, that humans are conscious when performing these behaviours thanks to functional magnetic resonance imaging (fMRI) and related techniques [34,36]. These behaviours can include imagination [59], emotions [55], language communication and social relations [54] or awareness of the environment [37].

Machine learning recent models are able to generate art [21] that deviate from what they are fed to learn, are able to learn how to learn [60], learn from a few examples [56] and are able to transfer knowledge from a different task to behave better in a new one [35]. The applications of these abilities include natural language generation [20], understanding emotions [11] or generating videos [65]. We believe that if the philosophical theory that consciousness arises as a flux of information in any machine [52] is true, if we create a cognitive architecture [12] that is able to produce as many behaviours as possible that are correlated with consciousness in humans, then, the machine may as well arise, up to some extent, consciousness or phenomenal states.

We attempt to provide a bridge between the machine learning and the machine consciousness communities by providing the design of a cognitive architecture with machine consciousness behaviours through machine learning models. Several architectures have been proposed before [18] but none of them include both deep learning, generative processes and gaussian processes to generate interior cognitive processes and exterior behaviour and content. Section 2 will discuss related work. Then, in Sect. 3, we provide a detailed explanation of the modules of our architecture. Section 4 then provides the architecture that unifies these modules. We conclude our work with a section of conclusions and further work.

2 Related Work

Due to different theories explaining the origin of consciousness, several approaches have been proposed to tackle this problem. We first discuss the different processes involving machine consciousness [24] and then, the different approaches that have tackled machine consciousness [50].

Machine consciousness processes involve mainly four categories ordered from 1 to 4 in function of how close to generating real awareness they are [25].

Level 1 includes machines that implements external behaviour associated with consciousness. Some of the described behaviours in the introduction section like social interactions implemented in machines would be level 1 and the field of artificial general intelligence [30] lies in this level. Several authors [33,43] argue that machines implementing these behaviours may produce consciousness, but there is controversy. Machines that implement cognitive characteristics like imagination [3], attention, emotion, depiction and planning are level 2 machines. When an architecture involving all these process exists, we are talking about level 3 machines, that is, machines with an architecture that is claimed to be a cause or correlate of human consciousness. Lastly, phenomenally conscious machines are level 4 machines based in the hypothesis that several level 2–3 design could emerge phenomenal states [2].

Several approaches have tackled the previous categories of machine consciousness. A classification of them all [50] includes five categories: First one are methods based in the global workspace theory [5]. According to this theory, consciousness emerges from a system, like the brain, with a collection of distributed specialized networks with a fleeting memory capacity whose focal contents are widely distributed to many unconscious specialized networks, called contexts. These contexts work together to jointly constrain conscious events and to shape conscious contents [6]. These theory has support of the neuroscience community [7] and the computer science community [10]. We are also inspired by this theory to provide a cognitive architecture [12] with machine learning techniques. Other categories include methods that suggest that consciousness emerges from a certain amount of information processing and integration [9], from creating an internal self-model [47], from generating higher-level representations [1] and from attention mechanisms [38].

Machine consciousness has risen as a research topic for the deep learning literature [10], where the interest resides in learning representations of high-level concepts of the kind humans manipulate with language. We suggest that machine learning and related techniques [8] are able to work as a global workspace, process a high amount of information, can generate internal self-models and higher level representations and have attention mechanisms. Hence, machine learning and generative processes should be explored in this field.

3 Machine Consciousness Correlated Processes

We now provide the module design that implement cognitive processes and exhibit external behaviour that is correlated with consciousness [25]. In the selection of the cognitive processes to be simulated, we consider behaviors that can make an autonomous agent evolve to adapt to an unknown environment through observation and social interaction. These behaviours are also affected by processes that establish emotional connections between observed and imagined content (e.g., images generated by simulated dreams, emotion simulation, depiction of the environment) and that can be supported by novel techniques such as deep learning and generative methods.

3.1 Simulating Dreams

In order to simulate dreams, we first have to record photos $\mathbf{P}_i$ when being awake and store them in a semantic network [58]. Then, dreams will use that information $\mathbf{P} : \mathbf{P}_i \in \mathbf{P}$ to generate a sequence of images $\mathbf{D}_i \in \mathbf{D}$. We define a dream as a function d that converts a subset of a sequence of images $\mathcal{P} \in \mathbf{P}$ and a subset of a sequence of style images $\mathcal{S} \in \mathbf{S}$ in a new set of images $\mathcal{D}$, that is $\mathcal{D} = d(\mathcal{P}, \mathcal{S})$. In order to generate this procedure, we propose two processes for this simulator:

First, we classify images $\mathcal{P}$ into a semantic network R. We assume that a previous categorized semantic network R exists and that a robot has already learned to classify images $\mathcal{P}$ into that network R. An implementation of this process can have ImageNet [19] as semantic network. ImageNet is a resource with more than 14.000.000 images $\mathcal{D}(\mathbf{X})$ and more than 21.000 categories $\mathbf{y}$. ImageNet uses the hierarchy of WordNet [22] to classify photos, having each category y_i a semantic meaning and being organized as a graph $G = V, E$ that can be traversed, where $v \in V$ is the node representing category y_i. Convolutional neural networks [39] or advanced neural models as Efficient Net L2 [64] or ResNet [63] neural models can classify photos into ImageNet. Let NN be the neural model that implements the robot, the robot will classify each input image P to category y_i, inserting it in the graph G through the NN trained on the ImageNet dataset $\mathcal{D}(\mathbf{X}, \mathbf{y})$, that is: $y_i = NN(P|\mathcal{D}(\mathbf{X}, \mathbf{y}))$.

To feed images in the neural model NN to be classified in the graph G, we need a robot with an integrated camara to take the photos $\mathbf{P}$ and define a period of being awake T_a and asleep T_s. These parameters can be configured differently for every robot. We suggest to save additional images $\mathcal{S}$ that will represent different styles seen like for example dark places or broad landscapes in a different semantic network R_s.

Second, we need to define the dreaming state given by time T_s. We suggest to use a random walk [51] like the one performed in the Metropolis Hastings algorithm [15] to simulate movement into the semantic networks of images R and styles R_s that are related by semantic distance $d_s(y_i, y_j)$ in their graphs G, G_s given by the number of edges that connect each category. At each step, we select two images $\mathbf{P}_i, \mathbf{P}_i^s$ and invoke Deep Style neural networks [44] to generate a new image with the selected photo and an style applied $\mathbf{D}_i = DS_{nn}(\mathbf{P}_i, \mathbf{P}_s^i)$. Models such as a Generative Adversarial Network [48] can be used. The robot will then attend the photo and save it. We can observe examples of generated photos using the Deep Dream Generator by this procedure in Fig. 1.

Fig. 1. Generated photos representing dreams by the Deep Dream Generator models (http://deepdreamgenerator.com/)

Initial categories y_{init}, y_{init}^s are chosen randomly. To select the new categories, we perform a random walk in the graph G and G_s given by some uniform distribution with a lower l_l and upper u_l limit, whose sampled value we will call step size ω. If we set those parameters to a high number, dreams will contain different concepts and viceversa. We repeat the mentioned process by performing an iteration of the random walk. We store each generated image $\mathbf{D}_i$. The sequence of recreated images $\mathbf{D}$ recreates the dream. After dreaming, the robot will be awake, iterating both processes.

3.2 Depiction. Being Aware of the Environment

We suggest to implement a robot that moves autonomously in a given environment E. For the sake of simplicity we are going to assume that E is 2-dimensional $E \in \mathbb{R}^2$. This robot will remember the images $\mathbf{D}$ that has previously dreamed as described in the previous module. The robot, when awake, will try to return to the location or neighbourhood $\mathcal{N} \in E$ where the images that has dreamed are located.

We will generate a 2-dimensional function of location importance with a sample from a Gaussian Process [62] $f_l^r \sim \mathcal{GP}(0, k(\mathbf{x}, \mathbf{x}')) \in \mathbb{R}^2$ over the environment E , discretized by a grid, for each robot r with interesting places to visit. We can observe examples of such functions at Fig. 2 The resolution of the grid r_g can set the size of the environment E. Gaussian Processes models are flexible priors or distributions over functions where inference takes place directly in the functional space $\mathcal{F}$. This functional space contains every possible environment that can be created $E \in \mathcal{F}$. The generated environment by the GP $f_l \in \mathbb{R}^2$ will contain high-valued locations of interest to take photos from and viceversa. When the robot reaches these places, it will take photos of the environment and save them for the dream module. Once visited, these places will be penalized by a local penalization procedure [31]. These kind of procedures get a neighbourhood $N \in f_l$ centered in the place of interest $\mathbf{r} \in N$ and penalizes this zone by, for example, a multivariate gaussian distribution $f_l(N) = f_l(N) - MVG(\mathbf{r}, \mathbf{I})$.

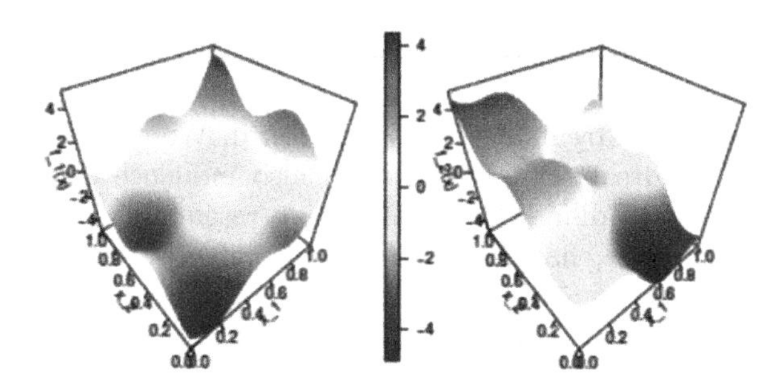

Fig. 2. Sampled functions from a 2-dimensional GP representing the importance value of each location of the environment for the robots.

The robot will end navigation when it is exhausted after its time awake T_a. We can simulate fatigue through a non deterministic function $p(r,t) \in [0,1]$ of time since it has last slept. Each time that the robot takes a photo, fatigue will be incremented or decremented depending on the reward given by the photo. We can assign a threshold $\phi \in [0,1]$ for fatigue. When the robot is awake the threshold takes value 0 and it is incremented as a function of time or by ϵ when taking a photo. The robot will fall asleep after the maximum time awake or if the non deterministic function samples a value higher than the threshold $p(r,t) > \phi$. The action of taking or not the photo t_p in each place g of the grid will be non deterministic and dependant on the value of f_l, that is $t_p(f_l, g)$. The robot can take a photo my sampling t_p periodically after an amount of steps s in f_l Specific parametric functions can be configured for each robot.

The Gaussian process sample f_l will be contaminated by i.i.d. gaussian noise $\epsilon \sim \mathcal{N}(0, \sigma_{gj})$ in each position of the grid g and dimension j in the period of being awake to favour exploration. Higher values of σ will enforce exploration. The robot will navigate through the environment with a metaheuristic [61] (exploration-exploitation) or by the gradients of the Gaussian process [57] (exploitation). Random rewards will be put in the scenario.

3.3 Emotion Simulation

In this section, we define a process that models emotions through objective functions $e(t) \in [0,1]$ of time. The main reason why we implement emotions in these robots is because they are going to influence the Gaussian Process prior f_l of the environment E. If the robots feels confident and happy $e_h(t) \approx 1$, unknown near areas of E to the position of the robot g will be rewarded to be explored. If R is a neighbourhood of f_l containing a reward, we can reward its value by sampling from a multivariate gaussian distribution centered in the reward $f_l(R) = f_l(R) - MVG(\mathbf{r}, \mathbf{I})$. By doing this process, the robot will enter a positive cycle and take photos of interesting places. By performing this action, we increment $e_h(t)$ by a uniform distribution which limits $[l, u]$ can be parametrized. If, in contrast, the robot feels sad and fear $e_h(t) \approx 0$, movement across the grid will be penalized by incrementing fatigue and decrementing the step size ω of the random walk, entering a negative loop.

These cognitive processes will exhibit external behaviour that will show if a robot is happy or sad by its activity on the grid. We provide an exit of the cycles by images of dreams $\mathcal{D}$. Dreams can also influence emotions $e(t)$ and make the robot behave differently. If an image resembles a visited area that had got high value of f_l, happiness will be incremented by a parametrizable amount $e(t) = e(t-1) + \delta \sim U[l, u]$, where t represents time. If images of places with low value of f_l are displayed, the opposite operation will be performed $e(t) = e(t-1) - \delta \sim U[l, u]$. Happiness could also affect the fatigue function, by alleviating it if the robot is happy or increasing it in the other case.

Other emotions that may be optimized are curiosity and boredom $e_c(t) \in [0, 1]$, that would affect the Gaussian Process sampled function f_l by penalizing already saw places by an $MVG(\mathbf{0}, \mathbf{I})$ and rewarding unknown places also by an $MVG(\mathbf{0}, \mathbf{I})$. A last example can be friendship and solitude $e_f(t)$, based in relations with other robots that are going to be described further or courage and fear $e_c(t)$ that will condition the movements across the environment by incrementing the step size ω of the random walk. The described fatigue function can also be seen as an emotion. Particular parametric forms of the functions are open for the robot developer to be implemented.

3.4 Social Relationships with Other Robots

If we want to simulate emotions $e(t)$ like the ones felt with humans to show behaviour correlated with consciousness, we need to model these emotions to be not only a function of the environment interaction f_l but also of relationships with other robots. For this reason, we consider that an essential component for the cognitive processes of the robots must be the interaction with other robots to share experiences, in the form of photos $\mathcal{P}$ in this setting, and influence the emotions $e(t)$.

Emotions like friendship or solitude $e_s(t)$ are dependant on social interactions. We define here a social interaction $\alpha(\beta_x, \beta_y)$ as the change of a photo $\mathcal{P}_x$ of a robot β_x with a photo $\mathcal{P}_y$ of a robot β_y when both robots share the same location g in the environment E.

Each robot β_i has a different function sampled from the GP prior $f_l^i \sim \mathcal{GP}(0, k(\mathbf{x}, \mathbf{x}')) \in \mathbb{R}^2$ of the environment E. As each photo $\mathcal{P}_i$ related to a position of the grid g_i, it will have, for every robot β_i a different value $f_l^i(g_i)$, conditioning the rest of the emotions. If the photo refers to a location that the robot likes according to its prior f_l^i, emotions will make the robot more active. Although, if this is not the case, the robot may enter a negative cycle.

By interacting with each other, robots β will share images $\mathcal{P}$ or dreamed images $\mathcal{D}$ of the environment E that will modify their Gaussian Process sampled function f_l^i and the other emotions of the robot. Specific parametric forms are again free for the programmer of the robot to be set.

4 An Unified Architecture for the Models

In the previous section, we have described how can we implement behaviours correlated with consciousness in machines. All the described processes can be implemented in a certain amount of robots β with an environment E that they can traverse and get photos $\mathcal{P}$ from. In this section, we provide a diagram with all the modules described to illustrate how the information flows in our architecture.

Besides the processes described in the previous section and in order to be more general, the proposed architecture uses multimodal information (e.g., ambient music and texts in form of recipes, besides images). These processes would generate subjective creations, which can be correlated with their communication to processes generated in conscious states, such as recipe suggestions [26] where in each position modelled by the GP the robot would find, with a probability sampled from a random variable, a suggestion of a recipe and generate in base of the recipe a degree of tastiness. Another alternative is to include ambient music simulations [42], where in each position in the input space we would have an ambient noise sample, also with a probability distribution given by the sampling of a random variable, and the robot would have a ambient music simulator, that uses these samples to generate music, simulating imagination and conditioning the emotion simulator.

All these processes generate the architecture that we can see in Fig. 3.

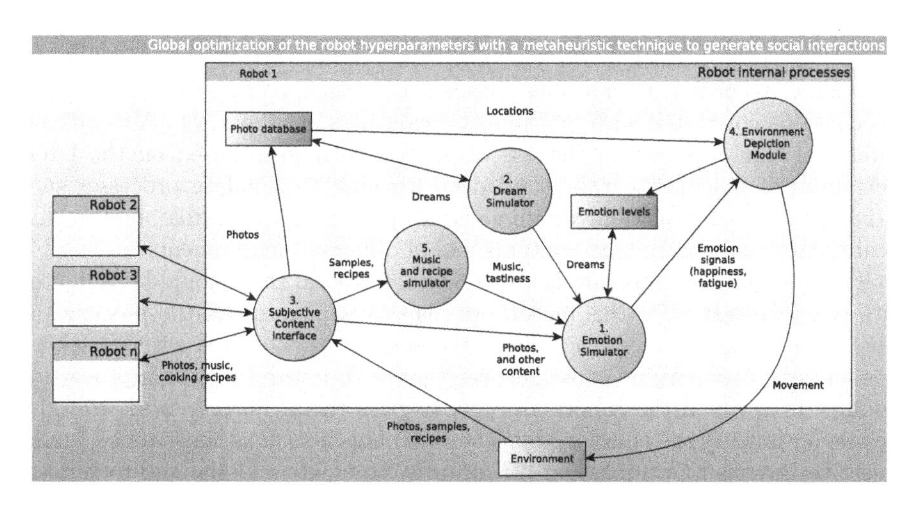

Fig. 3. Architecture of the proposed robots with behaviours correlated with consciousness. External processes that interact with the environment involve the depiction engine and the interface that collects data. Internal processes involve the dream, music and recipe generators and the emotion simulator, that condition the external behaviour. The hyperparameters of the robots models can be jointly optimized by a metaheuristic.

We can observe how robots share images and other information showing social behaviour. These interactions affect their emotions and incur in a different movement across the environment, reflecting emotions, commonly correlated with consciousness. Cognitive interior processes include dreaming images that are function of the perceived images and simulating music and cooking recipes, affecting emotions. These behaviours could, according to the cited theories, be a correlation of consciousness in robots.

Lastly, we propose the optimization of the different parametric forms $e(t)$ of the emotion engine and the parameters of the deep neural network for the dream simulation and the gaussian process for the environment in several simulations of the robots with a metaheuristic such as a genetic algorithm with the fitness being a function of the maximum number of interactions possible of the robots constrained to the maximum movement of the robots. By performing this optimization, we would end up having the optimum configuration for the robots to exhibit social behaviour, typically correlated with consciousness.

If the hyperparameters of the models are correctly optimized in future experiments, the outputs of these robots are hypothesized to be beautiful pieces of art in the form of pictures, music songs and cooking recipes, as all the environment can be seen as a reinforcement learning optimization technique to create subjective content and social interactions with conscious behaviours. Other architectures for machine consciousness just focus in cognitive processes and implementation of cited machine consciousness theories.

5 Conclusions and Further Work

We have described an architecture of processes that, if implemented in robots, exhibit external behaviour in the form of genuine art content and social behaviour. According to machine consciousness theory [25], both characteristics could be correlated with machine consciousness in robots [24]. A significant novelty of this approach is the use of generative models based on the latest techniques of machine learning and deep learning to simulate processes such as imagination or depiction, where gaussian processes are flexible models that create functional spaces that contains lots of different environments.

The presented architecture is a theoretical proposal that should be validated with practical tests. For this reason, we plan to implement all the processes in robots to get empirical evidence about the behaviour associated with consciousness and execute machine consciousness tests with natural language processing modules to verify if the robots are able to pass them. Further work will also include optimizing the emotions by some mechanism such as constrained Multi-objective Bayesian Optimization [27] in order to create a global and dynamical policy for the behaviour of the robots and including a weighted causal graph [29] as knowledge base to generate more complex social relationships where even fake information could be shared or detected [28].

Acknowledgments. The authors acknowledge the use of the facilities of Centro de Computación Científica (CCC) at UAM and acknowledge financial support from Spanish Plan Nacional I+D+i, grants TIN2016–76406-P and TEC2016–81900-REDT and Spanish Ministry of Science and Innovation - State Research Agency, project PID2019–106827GB-I00.

References

1. Aleksander, I.: Impossible Minds: My Neurons, My Consciousness. World Scientific, Singapore (1996)
2. Aleksander, I.: Why axiomatic models of being conscious? J. Conscious. Stud. **14**(7), 15–27 (2007)
3. Aleksander, I., Dunmall, B.: Axioms and tests for the presence of minimal consciousness in agents i: preamble. J. Conscious. Stud. **10**(4–5), 7–18 (2003)
4. Arrabales, R., Ledezma, A., Sanchis, A.: Consscale: a pragmatic scale for measuring the level of consciousness in artificial agents. J. Conscious. Stud. **17**(3–4), 131–164 (2010)
5. Baars, B.J.: In the theatre of consciousness. global workspace theory, a rigorous scientific theory of consciousness. J. Conscious. Stud. **4**(4), 292–309 (1997)
6. Baars, B.J.: The global workspace theory of consciousness. Blackwell Companion Conscious. 236–246 (2007)
7. Baars, B.J., Newman, J.: A neurobiological interpretation of global workspace theory. Conscious. Philos. Cogn. Neurosci. 211–226 (1994)
8. Bahdanau, D., Cho, K., Bengio, Y.: Neural machine translation by jointly learning to align and translate. arXiv preprint arXiv:1409.0473 (2014)
9. Balduzzi, D., Tononi, G.: Integrated information in discrete dynamical systems: motivation and theoretical framework. PLoS Comput. Biol. **4**, 6 (2008)
10. Bengio, Y.: The consciousness prior. arXiv preprint arXiv:1709.08568 (2017)
11. Cambria, E.: Affective computing and sentiment analysis. IEEE Intell. Syst. **31**(2), 102–107 (2016)
12. Chella, A., Frixione, M., Gaglio, S.: A cognitive architecture for robot self-consciousness. Artif. Intell. Med. **44**(2), 147–154 (2008)
13. Chella, A., Manzotti, R.: Artificial intelligence and consciousness. In: Association for the Advancement of Artificial Intelligence Fall Symposium, pp. 1–8 (2007)
14. Chella, A., Manzotti, R.: Artificial consciousness. In: Perception-Action Cycle. Springer, pp. 637–671 (2011)
15. Chib, S., Greenberg, E.: Understanding the metropolis-hastings algorithm. Am. Stat. **49**(4), 327–335 (1995)
16. Crick, F., Clark, J.: The astonishing hypothesis. J. Conscious. Stud. **1**(1), 10–16 (1994)
17. Damasio, A., Dolan, R.J.: The feeling of what happens. Nature **401**(6756), 847–847 (1999)
18. Dehaene, S., Changeux, J.-P.: Ongoing spontaneous activity controls access to consciousness: a neuronal model for inattentional blindness. PLoS Biol. **3**, 5 (2005)
19. Deng, J., Dong, W., Socher, R., Li, L.-J., Li, K., Fei-Fei, L.: Imagenet: a large-scale hierarchical image database. In: 2009 IEEE Conference on Computer Vision and Pattern Recognition, IEEE, pp. 248–255 (2009)
20. Deng, L., Liu, Y.: Deep Learning in Natural Language Processing. Springer, Berlin (2018)
21. Elgammal, A., Liu, B., Elhoseiny, M., Mazzone, M.: Can: creative adversarial networks, generating" art" by learning about styles and deviating from style norms. arXiv preprint arXiv:1706.07068 (2017)

22. Fellbaum, C.: Wordnet. Encycl. Appl. Linguist. (2012)
23. Gamez, D.: The development and analysis of conscious machines. PhD thesis, University of Essex Colchester (2008)
24. Gamez, D.: Progress in machine consciousness. Conscious. Cogn. **17**(3), 887–910 (2008)
25. Gamez, D.: Human and Machine Consciousness. Open Book Publishers, United Kingdom (2018)
26. Garrido-Merchán, E.C., Albarca-Molina, A.: Suggesting cooking recipes through simulation and bayesian optimization. In: Yin, H., Camacho, D., Novais, P., Tallón-Ballesteros, A.J. (eds.) IDEAL 2018. LNCS, vol. 11314, pp. 277–284. Springer, Cham (2018). https://doi.org/10.1007/978-3-030-03493-1_30
27. Garrido-Merchán, E.C., Hernández-Lobato, D.: Predictive entropy search for multi-objective bayesian optimization with constraints. Neurocomputing **361**, 50–68 (2019)
28. Garrido-MerchÁn, E.C., Puente, C., Palacios, R.: Fake news detection by means of uncertainty weighted causal graphs (2020)
29. Garrido-MerchÁn, E.C., Puente, C., Sobrino, A., Olivas, J.A.: Uncertainty weighted causal graphs (2020)
30. Goertzel, B., Pennachin, C.: Artificial General Intelligence, vol. 2. Springer, Berlin (2007)
31. González, J., Dai, Z., Hennig, P., Lawrence, N.: Batch bayesian optimization via local penalization. In: Artificial intelligence and statistics, pp. 648–657 (2016)
32. Graziano, M.S.: The attention schema theory: a foundation for engineering artificial consciousness. Front. Robot. AI **4**, 60 (2017)
33. Harnad, S.: Can a machine be conscious? how? J. Conscious. Stud. **10**(4–5), 69–75 (2003)
34. He, B.J., Raichle, M.E.: The FMRI signal, slow cortical potential and consciousness. Trends Cogn. Sci. **13**(7), 302–309 (2009)
35. Kaiser, L., et al.: One model to learn them all. arXiv preprint arXiv:1706.05137 (2017)
36. Kamitani, Y., Tong, F.: Decoding the visual and subjective contents of the human brain. Nat. Neurosci. **8**(5), 679–685 (2005)
37. Kitamura, T., Tahara, T., Asami, K.-I.: How can a robot have consciousness? Adv. Robot. **14**(4), 263–275 (2000)
38. Koch, C., Tsuchiya, N.: Attention and consciousness: two distinct brain processes. Trends Cogn. Sci. **11**(1), 16–22 (2007)
39. Krizhevsky, A., Sutskever, I., Hinton, G.E.: Imagenet classification with deep convolutional neural networks. In: Advances in Neural Information Processing Systems, pp. 1097–1105 (2012)
40. LeCun, Y., Bengio, Y., Hinton, G.: Deep learning. Nature **521**(7553), 436–444 (2015)
41. Loar, B.: Phenomenal states. Philos. Perspect. **4**, 81–108 (1990)
42. Martínez Sastre, R., et al.: Simulating music from the latent space of a variational autoencoder. B.S. thesis, UAM (2019)
43. Moor, J.H.: Testing robots for qualia. In: Perspectives on Mind. Springer, pp. 107–118 (1988)
44. Mordvintsev, A., Olah, C., Tyka, M.: Inceptionism: going deeper into neural networks. Google Research Blog (2015)
45. Murphy, K.P.: Machine learning: a probabilistic perspective. MIT press (2012)

46. Pennartz, C., Farisco, M., Evers, K.: Indicators and criteria of consciousness in animals and intelligent machines: an inside-out approach. Front. Syst. Neurosci. **13**, 25 (2019)
47. Perlis, D.: Consciousness as self-function. J. Conscious. Stud. **4**(5–6), 509–525 (1997)
48. Radford, A., Metz, L., Chintala, S.: Unsupervised representation learning with deep convolutional generative adversarial networks. arXiv preprint arXiv:1511.06434 (2015)
49. Raoult, A., Yampolskiy, R.: Reviewing tests for machine consciousness. Retrieved from ResearchGate (2015)
50. Reggia, J.A.: The rise of machine consciousness: studying consciousness with computational models. Neural Netw. **44**, 112–131 (2013)
51. Roberts, G.O., Gelman, A., Gilks, W.R., et al.: Weak convergence and optimal scaling of random walk metropolis algorithms. Ann. Appl. Probab. **7**(1), 110–120 (1997)
52. Rose, D.: Consciousness: Philosophical, Psychological, and Neural Theories. Oxford University Press, Oxford (2006)
53. Searle, J.R.: Mind: A Brief Introduction. Oxford University Press, Oxford (2004)
54. Searle, J.R., et al.: Consciousness and Language. Cambridge University Press, Cambridge (2002)
55. Shanahan, M.: Consciousness, emotion, and imagination: a brain-inspired architecture for cognitive robotics. In: In Proceedings of the AISB'05 Workshop: Next Generation Approaches to Machine Consciousness, Citeseer (2005)
56. Snell, J., Swersky, K., Zemel, R.: Prototypical networks for few-shot learning. In: Advances in Neural Information Processing Systems, pp. 4077–4087 (2017)
57. Solak, E., Murray-Smith, R., Leithead, W.E., Leith, D.J., Rasmussen, C.E.: Derivative observations in gaussian process models of dynamic systems. In: Advances in Neural Information Processing Systems, pp. 1057–1064 (2003)
58. Sowa, J.F.: Semantic networks. Citeseer (1987)
59. Stuart, S.A.: Machine consciousness: cognitive and kinaesthetic imagination. J. Conscious. Stud. **14**(7), 141–153 (2007)
60. Thrun, S., Pratt, L.: Learning to Learn. Springer Science & Business Media, Berlin (2012)
61. Voß, S., Martello, S., Osman, I.H., Roucairol, C.: Meta-heuristics: Advances and Trends in Local Search Paradigms for Optimization. Springer Science & Business Media, Berlin (2012)
62. Williams, C.K., Rasmussen, C.E.: Gaussian Orocesses for Machine Learning, vol. 2. MIT Press Cambridge, MA (2006)
63. Wu, Z., Shen, C., Van Den Hengel, A.: Wider or deeper: revisiting the resnet model for visual recognition. Pattern Recogn. **90**, 119–133 (2019)
64. Xie, Q., Hovy, E., Luong, M.-T., Le, Q.V.: Self-training with noisy student improves imagenet classification. arXiv preprint arXiv:1911.04252 (2019)
65. Xiong, W., Luo, W., Ma, L., Liu, W., Luo, J.: Learning to generate time-lapse videos using multi-stage dynamic generative adversarial networks. In: Proceedings of the IEEE Conference on Computer Vision and Pattern Recognition, pp. 2364–2373 (2018)

Some Experiments on the Influence of Problem Hardness in Morphological Development Based Learning of Neural Controllers

M. Naya-Varela[1(✉)], A. Faina[2(✉)], and R. J. Duro[1(✉)]

[1] Integrated Group for Engineering Research,
CITIC (Centre for Information and Communications Technology Research),
Universidade da Coruña, A Coruña, Spain
{martin.naya,richard}@udc.es

[2] Robotics, Evolution and Art Lab (REAL), Computer Science Department,
IT University of Copenhagen, Copenhagen, Denmark
anfv@itu.dk

Abstract. Natural beings undergo a morphological development process of their bodies while they are learning and adapting to the environments they face from infancy to adulthood. In fact, this is the period where the most important learning processes, those that will support learning as adults, will take place. However, in artificial systems, this interaction between morphological development and learning, and its possible advantages, have seldom been considered. In this line, this paper seeks to provide some insights into how morphological development can be harnessed in order to facilitate learning in embodied systems facing tasks or domains that are hard to learn. In particular, here we will concentrate on whether morphological development can really provide any advantage when learning complex tasks and whether its relevance towards learning increases as tasks become harder. To this end, we present the results of some initial experiments on the application of morphological development to learning to walk in three cases, that of a quadruped, a hexapod and that of an octopod. These results seem to confirm that as task learning difficulty increases the application of morphological development to learning becomes more advantageous.

Keywords: Cognitive robotics · Morphological development · Quadrupedal walking · Hexapod walking · Octopod walking

1 Introduction

In the last two decades, the concept of robotic intelligence has been extended to include the morphology of the robot and its environment, as well as their mutual interactions [1–3], as relevant components. In fact, this has resulted in a noticeable growth of the field of Artificial Embodied Intelligence (AEI) [4, 5]. AEI postulates that robot intelligence emerges from the interaction between the robot brain, its morphology and the domain it is faced with. Taking this view, as the field of robotics applications addresses ever more complex sequences of environments, it is often the case that the designer cannot contemplate at design time all the possible domains and tasks the robot will

E. A. de la Cal et al. (Eds.): HAIS 2020, LNAI 12344, pp. 362–373, 2020.
https://doi.org/10.1007/978-3-030-61705-9_30

have to perform. This has opened an area of research in which the robot, given a basic set of skills, must be able to adapt and learn new skills at run time, as it meets new domains it has not encountered before. In the literature, this is called the open-ended learning problem [6].

The main framework available to the robotics community in order to tackle open-ended learning scenarios in an incremental manner is that of Developmental Robotics (DR) [7]. DR studies different approaches so that robots can autonomously acquire an increasingly complex set of sensorimotor and mental capabilities through the interaction between their bodies and brains in the sequence of domains they encounter in their lifetime [8]. This field is inspired by the development of experience and motor skills in humans, from childhood to adulthood. An example of a very good review on the topic is the one by Asada et al. [7] who concentrate on the development of higher cognitive functions in infants.

The problem with most of the work on DR is that it has generally been focused on Cognitive Developmental Robotics (CDR) [9]. That is, it has dealt with the development of cognition [7, 10], within a fixed pre-designed body and has not introduced the fact that in natural beings the body also undergoes development during the learning period. In other words, it is not only the cognitive module of the system that changes during development but also the morphology of the system. Thus, the question arises of whether this morphological development provides an advantage to the individual for learning in complex open-ended settings and, if so, how it can be used to this end.

The very close relationship between robot morphology, the environment and the task was already highlighted by Pfeifer [11] even to the point that a given morphology may determine the capabilities a system may display in an environment. He concludes that an optimized morphology for a given task simplifies control, makes the task easier and permits improving performance. On the other hand, poorly chosen morphologies lead to inefficient solutions and increase control complexity and computational cost.

Based on these ideas, many authors [12–15] have investigated how the close relationship between the physical design of a robot and that of its controller, as a function of the environment or environments and tasks to perform, can be used in order to produce more efficient robot controllers. However, another question that needs to be clearly addressed, and which has been mostly ignored, is how the morphology-control relationship or coupling can be used in developmental processes. In other words, whether there is an advantage in using the development of the body during learning, especially when considering complex behavioral spaces and tasks that are hard to learn and how this should be done.

In natural systems, morphological development is usually taken as encompassing motor development [16], cognitive development [17], and body maturation [18]. Motor development is concerned with the continuous acquisition of motor skills. Cognitive development, on the other hand, operates at a higher level. It deals with the creation of new world representations and in the consolidation and adaptation of those that were previously obtained. Finally, growth and maturation have to do with the actual change of the body. They involve more than an increase in body size and weight and include subtler physical aspects such as increases in muscle tone, bone mass, extensions in the range of motion of the limbs or improving sensorial capabilities, among others.

Notwithstanding the fact that it is usually a continuous process, morphological development can be represented as a series of stages, from the simplest and starting stage, to the final and most complex one where the body has completely developed and has had a chance to adapt to the environment. With this idea in mind, it is important to point out a very fundamental difference between the operation of morphological development and that of cognitive development in the way how they handle the learning process.

In most of the literature on cognitive development, previously learnt units of knowledge are used as scaffolding to learn more complex knowledge nuggets. This is not the case when the body is changing. The cognitive structures created at each stage of morphological development are the starting point for learning the next stage but they are usually "overwritten" by the new learning processes. These structures are modified and adapted to the physical changes that occur during the morphological development process, giving rise to new cognitive systems that are better adapted to the new morphology (e.g. adult walking is not made up of different bits of baby walking and teenager walking). In other words, unlike most cognitive development approaches, the morphological development process is not an incremental construction procedure where one needs to find primitive blocks in order to combine them into more complex structures. It is rather a way to steer a path through a series of solution spaces for the controller that the system interacts with as it body develops and, if chosen wisely, the hypothesis is that it may facilitate learning the final skill and obtaining simplified and less computational costly solutions [19].

This paper is devoted to studying the effects of morphological development as a function of the rate of growth and the hardness of the task. To this end, we have chosen one main task: walking in a straight line. This task will be learnt with and without morphological development by different types of robots with different levels of complexity: a quadruped, a hexapod and an octopod. Learning controllers for walking is easier for a hexapod or octopod than for a quadruped since it has many more options for stable static walking without having to resort to dynamic walking gaits.

The papers we have found related to morphological development for quadrupedal motion do not consider learning per se, but rather, evolution of robots that walk. That is, they are concerned with the use of morphological development during the phylogenetic stage. A representative example is the work by Vujovic [20] who compares the results obtained after applying a strictly evolutionary to those of an EvoDevo sequence (performing development during evolution) to a robot for walking over flat terrain. The length and thickness of the legs were grown during the morphological development stage. His results show that the combination of evolution and development sometimes improves the fitness of the final solution. However, the choice of the way morphological development is carried out is critical. In fact, poorly chosen developmental parameters seem to result in poorer results than considering only evolution.

There are some papers, not many, on morphological development for learning in the case of bipedal [21–23] and hexapedal walking [24]. These papers provide examples in which morphological development during learning provides an advantage over just learning with the final morphology, but in other examples the result is just the opposite. That is, their results are inconclusive and most of them indicate that more research is needed in this line.

The objective of this work is to provide some more information and experimental results in order to elucidate whether and how morphological development may lead to a more effective learning process. To this end, the paper is organized as follows: In Sect. 2 we describe the experimental setup we will be using during the experiments. Section 3 is devoted to the presentation of the results of the experiments carried. These results are discussed in Sect. 4 and, finally, we provide some conclusions and future lines of work in Sect. 5.

2 Experimental Setup

As commented before, the main objective of this paper is to gather data on the influence of morphological development strategies over learning. Out of all the possible morphological development strategies, we will focus on growing limbs and we will concentrate on two aspects in order to construct the experiments. On the one hand, we want to see how problem hardness or learning difficulty affects the influence of morphological development. On the other, for each difficulty, we would like to extract information on what the optimal growth rate would be.

To this end, we have chosen a general experimental structure in which the aim is for the different robots to learn to walk as far as possible. To address how problem hardness affects morphological development, we have assumed that the less possible stable static walking configurations a morphology presents, the more difficult the learning process is and the harder the problem. This is a consequence of the fact that a system with fewer static walking configurations needs to resort to learning dynamic walking strategies, which are much more difficult to learn as most individuals keep falling over. Thus, we have assumed that the more legs a robot has, up to eight, the larger the range of static walking configurations available, making the learning problem easier.

Therefore, we have started with a quadruped robot and added legs. The base morphological design is the quadruped robot, shown in Fig. 1 left. It is made up of a central body of dimensions 30 cm * 15 cm * 1 cm and 2 kg, and 4 limbs, each one with two revolute joints and one prismatic joint. Each limb is composed of 3 segments, all of them present the same size and weight (5 cm * 2.5 cm * 0.5 cm and 250 g). The two revolute joints are actuated. They have a maximum torque of 2.5Nm and they are controlled through a proportional controller (P = 0.1). The farthest segments of the robot's legs are joined by the prismatic joint, which is set to a target length for each experiment (maximum force of 50 N, P = 0.1). The body of the hexapod and octopod is similar to the quadruped robot, but changing the body dimensions to (60 cm * 15 cm * 1 cm) and (90 cm * 15 cm * 1 cm) in the case of the hexapod, Fig. 1 middle, and octopod, Fig. 1 right, respectively and the number of limbs available, being obviously 6 for the hexapod, and 8 for the octopod. All the prismatic joints of the legs have a maximum stroke of 7.5 cm, which means that the length of the legs may vary from 10 cm to 17.5 cm. In the case of the revolute joint, the maximum motion range available is [−90, 90] degrees.

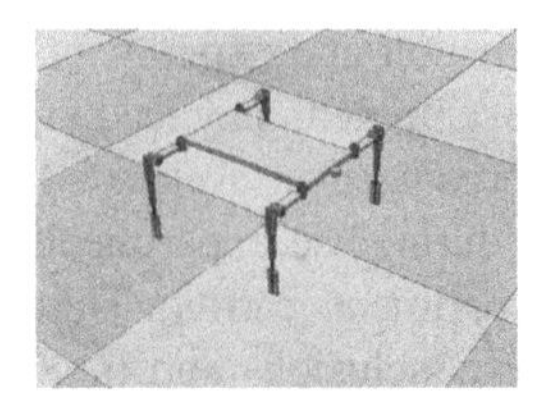

Fig. 1. Snapshots of each morphology considered in the experiments in their resting position. Left: quadruped. Middle: hexapod. Right: octopod. Each limb has three solid segments in a chain attached to the base by two actuated revolute joints (red cylinders) and a linear joint (red rectangular cuboid), which is used for the morphological development. The limbs in each side are equidistant from each other at a distance of 29 cm. (Color figure online)

The controller of the robot is a neural network whose weights and structure are learnt using NEAT [25] specifically the MultiNEAT [26] implementation. It has one input and 8, 12 and 16 outputs respectively, each controlling the actuation of one joint. The input is a sinusoidal function of amplitude 2.0 and frequency 1.0 rad/s.

A series of learning experiments using NEAT have been run over different implementations of the robot and environment using the VREP simulator [27] with the ODE physical engine [28] in the CESGA [29] computer cluster. Each NEAT learning run evolves a population of 50 individuals and is trained for 300 generations. A total of 30 independent runs have been carried out for each experiment with the objective of gathering relevant statistical data. As the controller is obtained using NEAT, the learning strategy is based on a neuroevolutionary process, where the fitness is the distance travelled by the front of the robot. Each individual is tested for 3 s with a simulation time step of 50 ms and physics engine time step of 5 ms.

In order to study how morphological development affects the ability to learn in different morphologies, we have carried out two kinds of experiments for each morphological configuration:

Reference Experiment. This experiment is run with a fixed morphology (the same as the final morphology for the rest of the experiments) from the beginning to the end. The robot starts at generation 0 with the maximum length of the legs and the neuro-evolutionary algorithm seeks a neural network-based controller to achieve maximum displacement.

Leg Growth Experiments. The robot morphology starts with the shorter version of the legs. That is, at the beginning the prismatic joint is fully contracted, its extension is 0 cm, and the length of the legs is thus 10 cm. The leg length is grown linearly for a number of generations until it reaches the maximum length of 17.5 cms. This growth takes place in a set number of generations for each experiment. That is, the final morphology is reached at generation 20, 40, 60, 80, 100 and 120 depending on the experiment. This permits studying the relevance of the growth rate with regards to performance. In a way, we try to simulate the way knowledge is acquired by biological entities: their limbs grow until a certain age, and then learning continues with a fixed morphology.

The results obtained from each of the experiments have allowed us to compare the differences that exist between the methods applied to each morphology, and the differences in results that occur between different designs.

3 Results

The results of the training process for each case can be observed in Figs. 2 and 3. Figure 2 shows the results obtained after the learning process through neuroevolution, in the case of no-development and growth. It displays the median of the best fitness obtained for the 30 independent runs at each generation for 3 of the growth rates and the reference. The shaded areas in the graph represent the areas between percentiles 75 and 25 for each experiment. Although we have carried out all of the experiments mentioned in Sect. 2, for the sake of clarity in this graph, we only represent the experiments where the final morphology is reached at generations 20 and 120, as they are the fastest and slowest growth rates respectively and the case for which the best development result was obtained for each morphology. For the quadruped, this corresponds to reaching the final morphology in generation 60, Fig. 2. top left, and for the octopod ingeneration 100, Fig. 2 bottom. In the case of the hexapod, Fig. 2. top right, the most statistically relevant results were reached in the experiment where the legs grow up to generation 20. Consequently, we also include in this graph the case for which the maximum median was achieved (growth up to generation 100).

Two important points can be observed in these graphs:

Growth Performance Variation. It can be easily observed that the morphological development mechanism based on leg growth provides better results than when there is no development in the case of the quadruped. Better results are also observed for one of the growth rates of the hexapod. In the case of the octopod, there is no significant improvement between using morphological development through growth and no-development.

This analysis is supported by the results presented in Fig. 3. Each boxplot represents the median and the 75 and 25 quartile in the last generation for 30 independent runs of each of the different types of experiments. The whiskers are extended to 1.5 of the interquartile range (IQR). Single points represent values that are out of the IQR. All developmental samples are compared to the no-development case. The statistical analysis has been carried out using the two-tailed Mann-Whitney test. We want to test whether the null hypothesis (if both compared samples are equal) is true. We consider a p-value of 0.05 as the significant value for accepting or rejecting the null hypothesis.

For the quadruped, the most relevant result is obtained for growth up to generation 60, leading to a p-value of 0.00238, which means a rejection of the null hypothesis. That is, in this case morphological development clearly improves learning with respect to no-development. Growth experiments up to generation 80 present a p-value of 0.01988 showing that development offers statistically relevant better results than no development. For the rest of development ratios, they display worse performance and they are not statistically relevant. For the hexapod, although the highest median is obtained in the growth experiment up to generation 100, the most relevant result is

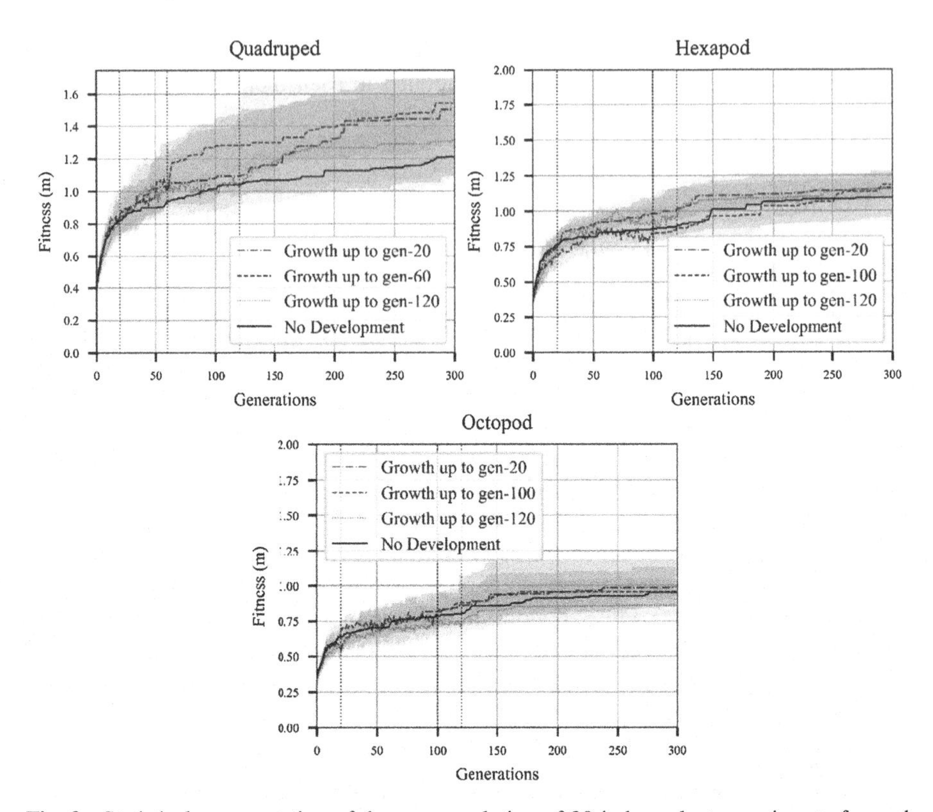

Fig. 2. Statistical representation of the neuroevolution of 30 independent experiments for each morphological configuration. All three images show results for the no-development case (black line), growth up to generation 20 (red dashed line) and 120 (green dotted line). Furthermore, the best growth ratio is shown for each morphology. Top left: Quadruped topology, for which the best results were obtained for growth up to generation 60. Top right: Hexapod topology and highest median of growth up to generation100. Bottom: Octopod topology and best case of growth up to generation100. (Color figure online)

obtained for growth up to generation 20, with a p-value of 0.01221. This statistical significance indicates that both samples can be considered different, and therefore allows us to confirm that this morphological development mechanism favors learning in this case. None of the rest of the experiments, can be considered better than the no-development case. For the octopod the best p-value, 0.596, is obtained in the experiment for growth up to generation 100, although there are no statistically relevant results showing any difference, and therefore, morphological development cannot be considered better than no-development.

Morphological Fitness Variation. If we take as a reference the median of each of the experiments of both development and no-development for each morphology, the slope of the learning curves, as well as the maximum fitness achieved at the end of the learning process varies with each morphology. Figure 4 left shows the statistical results of the absolute fitness value of different growth experiments up to generation 20 and

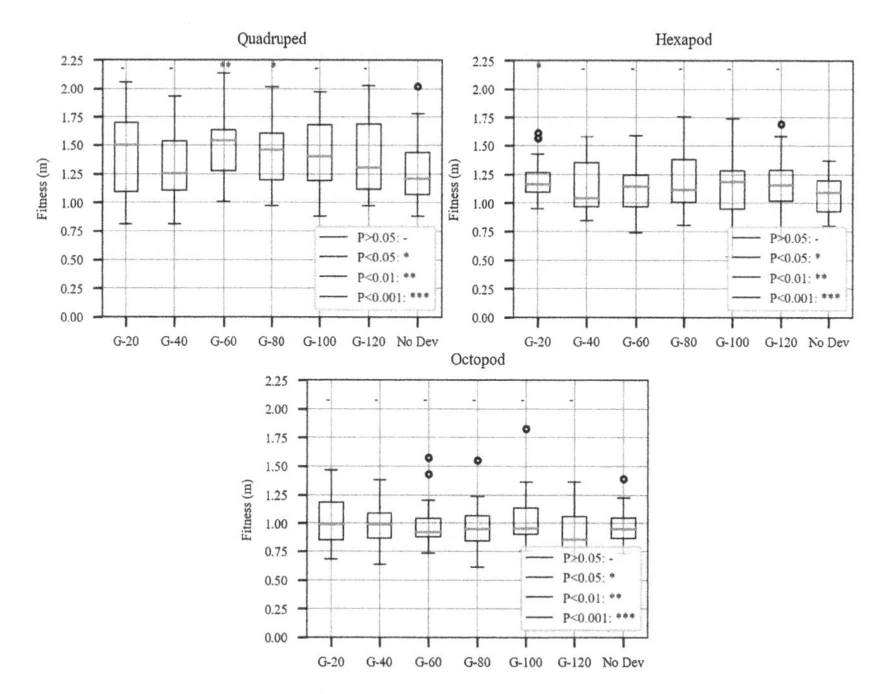

Fig. 3. Statistical representation of the performance obtained at the end of the neuroevolutionary process from the 30 independent experiments for each morphology. Top left: Statistical results for the quadruped morphology. Top right: Statistical representation for the hexapod morphology. Bottom: Statistical representation for the octopod morphology. Asterisks and lines refer to the statistical difference between the samples represented. Their corresponding numerical values are shown in the legend of the figure. "Growth up to" is abbreviated by a G, in order to make the figures clear.

120, as they are the fastest and slowest growth rates respectively, and those which grow up to generation 60 and 80, as intermediate growth rates. If we compare the three morphologies, in the four cases for each growth ratio the highest absolute values are obtained, in decreasing order, for the quadruped, the hexapod and the octopod. These results are in accordance with those displayed in Fig. 3, where it was shown that at the end of the neuroevolutionary process, the best results in absolute value were found for the quadruped, and the worst for the octopod. In Fig. 4 left we want to highlight how the dispersion of fitness varies as growth speed decreases and morphological complexity increases. This dispersion increases as the growth rate decreases and decreases with the complexity of the controller and the constraints on the morphology, being the quadruped the one that exhibits largest dispersion and the octopod the smallest with the decrease in growth speed. This implies a direct relationship between the morphology and the best possible performance of the task. This can be explained by the fact that morphologies with more legs are more constrained in terms of how much the body can twist. This implies that morphologies with less legs are able to combine body twist and leg reach in order to provide longer strides, thus making them able to walk farther in the same amount of time.

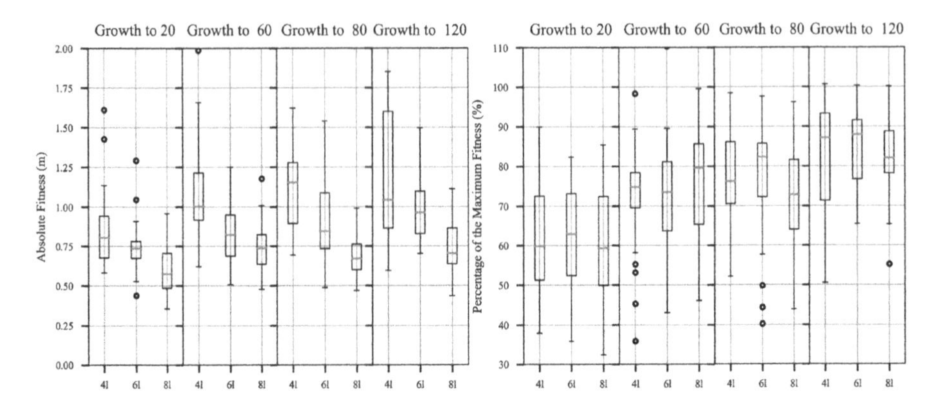

Fig. 4. Left: Statistical representation of the performance obtained at the end of each developmental process for the 30 independent experiments for each morphology. Right: Statistical representation of the relative performance, as a percentage of the maximum fitness achieved at the end of each learning process (generation 300).

However, if we change these results into relative values, understanding relative values as the absolute values shown in Fig. 4 left, divided by the maximum fitness value reached at the end of the learning process for each experiment expressed as a percentage, the graph changes remarkably (Fig. 4 right). Although the statistical dispersion varies significantly from one growth ratio to another, it can be seen how the values of the median are quite similar, being 9.5274% the maximum difference, for growth up to generation 80. Figure 4 left and Fig. 4 right, seem to lead to the conclusion that the maximum fitness achievable and thus, the fitness increase margin is dependent on the constraints the morphology imposes and not on the morphological development strategies.

Considering this, from Fig. 2 and Fig. 3, we may assume that morphological development offers an advantage in those cases in which the solution space available to the learning process changes more drastically as the morphology changes. In other words, when it is hard for the grown individual to find optimal solutions due to the very small attraction basin of optimal, or even reasonable solutions, leading to a high dispersion or very poor results at the end of the neuroevolution in the case of no development. In these cases, an appropriately selected morphological development strategy that seeks to expand the attraction basins of the optimal solutions when the individual is "young" and progressively lead to the final configuration helps to lead the learning process towards the most promising areas of solution space avoiding getting stuck in local minima and, thus, biasing the search towards the optimal solutions. That is why development offers better results with the quadruped: its space of optimal solutions is narrower than in the case of the hexapod and the octopod and growth helps to move towards optimal solutions. In the hexapod and, especially in the case of the octopod, the solution spaces at the beginning and end of the growth process are very similar due to the constraints imposed by the morphology and, thus, morphological development offers less of an advantage.

4 Discussion

While our aim in this paper was to study how the hardness of the task to learn affects the benefits of morphological development, there are a few limitations in our methodology.

Each type of morphology shows different absolute fitness values. This is caused by the fact that the morphologies have different physical features and because the learning can be more complex in some morphologies than in others. Regarding the physical features, the controllers have 8 outputs for the quadruped, 12 for the hexapod and 16 for the octopod and the central body is heavier and bigger in morphologies with more limbs. Regarding the difficulty of learning, there are different aspects to consider. On one hand, due to the number of variables involved in the problem, we presume that it is more complicated to efficiently control 16 outputs than 8. On the other, the octopod is very stable and its twist motion very constrained. Therefore, there are a lot of controllers that can effectively move the robot, even in its final morphology. On the contrary, the quadruped has fewer actuators to control but it is very unstable and much less constrained in its overall motion. This means that a lot of controllers will present very poor fitness values even if they are close to the optimum, creating a very deceptive search space, which makes learning more difficult. However, the controllers that are successful will present much higher fitness values as dynamic gaits are very efficient.

We consider that the hardness of learning decreases when adding extra limbs that give stability and constraining the motion of the robot. Therefore, learning the controllers in the grown up octopod is easier than in the grown up quadruped, because almost any controller allows it to move from its initial position without falling over or damaging itself. Learning is simple as there are multiple solutions that perform well and there is a gradient that guides the learning.

In the quadruped, we hypothesize that morphological development leads to an improvement of the performance during neuroevolution because, when the robot is still an infant, it provides the necessary stability and dynamic control that expands the attraction basing of the optimal solutions and allows controllers to explore the space of possible solutions biasing the solutions towards the optimum, moving it away from the stagnation in local minima that happens in the case of no-development.

The effect of morphological development seems to decrease with how easy to learn is a task for the grown up individual. If the task is easier to learn, there is no effect (octopod). If the task is hard to learn, noticeable improvement during learning can be appreciated (quadruped). The effects are visible (two experiments display statistical significance), but the correct growth rate must be selected.

These results show the need to study in greater depth the underlying mechanisms of growth in morphological development applied to robotics, in order to determine which cases can be classified as hard to learn, in order to be sensitive to the application of morphological development.

5 Conclusion and Future Work

In this paper we have shown that ontogenetic morphological development for quadruped, hexapod and octopod morphologies, while learning a locomotion task under some conditions, may help to find better solutions when compared to a learning process that does not follow any kind of development. In our robots, morphological growth of the limbs can help to learn better controllers if the growth rate is chosen correctly. However, we have also found that an incorrect synergy between morphology, the hardness of the task and development could render this approach irrelevant.

For our studies, it seems that there is a relationship between the utility of applying morphological development and the hardness of the task to be accomplished by the grown up individual: if the task is too easy to learn, even though it may display a high level of complexity, morphological development does not represent any advantage during learning. However, if the task is hard to learn even if it is simple, morphological development is a good methodology to improve learning outcomes.

Notwithstanding the previous comments, much more work is needed over many other morphologies and tasks to really be able to provide effective engineering indications on how to apply growth as a morphological development tool to aid learning. We are currently extending the range of morphologies and cases in order to get a better grasp of the scope of the approach.

Acknowledgment. This work has been partially funded by the Ministerio de Ciencia, Innovación y Universidades of Spain/FEDER (grant RTI2018-101114-B-I00), Xunta de Galicia and FEDER (grant ED431C 2017/12) and M. Naya-Varela is very grateful for the support of the UDC-Inditex 2019 grant for international mobility. We also want to thank CESGA (Centro de Supercomputación de Galicia. https://www.cesga.es/) for the possibility of using its resources.

References

1. Pfeifer, R., Bongard, J.: How the body shapes the way we think: a new view of intelligence. MIT press (2006)
2. Pfeifer, R.: Dynamics, morphology, and materials in the emergence of cognition. In: Burgard, W., Cremers, Armin B., Cristaller, T. (eds.) KI 1999. LNCS (LNAI), vol. 1701, pp. 27–44. Springer, Heidelberg (1999). https://doi.org/10.1007/3-540-48238-5_3
3. Chrisley, R.: Embodied artificial intelligence. Artif. Intell. **149**(1), 131–150 (2003)
4. Pfeifer, R., Iida, F.: Embodied artificial intelligence: trends and challenges. In: Iida, F., Pfeifer, R., Steels, L., Kuniyoshi, Y. (eds.) Embodied Artificial Intelligence. LNCS (LNAI), vol. 3139, pp. 1–26. Springer, Heidelberg (2004). https://doi.org/10.1007/978-3-540-27833-7_1
5. Hoffmann, M., Pfeifer, R.: Robots as powerful allies for the study of embodied cognition from the bottom up, 1–22 (2018)
6. Doncieux, S., et al.: Open-ended learning: a conceptual framework based on representational redescription. Front. Neurorobot. **12**, 59 (2018)
7. Asada, M., et al.: Cognitive developmental robotics: a survey. IEEE Trans. Auton. Ment. Dev. **1**(1), 12–34 (2009)

8. Cangelosi, A., Schlesinger, M.: Developmental robotics: from babies to robots. MIT Press (2015)
9. Zlatev, J., Balkenius, C.: Introduction: why epigenetic robotics?. In: 1st International Workshop on Epigenetic Robotics (2001)
10. Weng, J., et al.: Autonomous mental development by robots and animals. Science **291** (5504), 599–600 (2001)
11. Pfeifer, R., Iida, F.: Morphological computation: connecting body, brain and environment. Japanese Sci. Mon. **58**, 48–54 (2005)
12. Matarić, M., Cliff, D.: Challenges in evolving controllers for physical robots. Rob. Auton. Syst. **19**(1), 67–83 (1996)
13. Lipson, H., Pollack, J.B.: Automatic design and manufacture of robotic lifeforms. Nature **406**(6799), 974–978 (2000)
14. Cheney, N., Bongard, J., Lipson, H.: Evolving soft robots in tight spaces. In: Proceedings of the 2015 annual conference on Genetic and Evolutionary Computation, pp. 935–942 (2015)
15. Trianni, V.: Evolutionary robotics: model or design? Front. Robot. AI **1**, 13 (2014)
16. Clark, J.E., Whitall, J.: What is motor development? The lessons of history. Quest **41**(3), 183–202 (1989)
17. Fischer, K.W.: A theory of cognitive development: the control and construction of hierarchies of skills. Psychol. Rev. **87**(6), 477 (1980)
18. Roche, A.F.: Growth, Maturation, and Body Composition: The Fels Longitudinal Study, pp. 1929–1991. Cambridge University Press, Cambridge (1992)
19. Bongard, J.: Why morphology matters. Horizons Evol. Robot. **6**, 125–152 (2014)
20. Vujovic, V., Rosendo, A., Brodbeck, L., Iida, F.: Evolutionary developmental robotics: improving morphology and control of physical robots. Artif. Life **23**(2), 169–185 (2017)
21. Lungarella, M., Berthouze, L.: On the interplay between morphological, neural, and environmental dynamics: a robotic case study. Adapt. Behav. **10**(3), 223–241 (2002)
22. Berthouze, L., Lungarella, M.: Motor skill acquisition under environmental perturbations: on the necessity of alternate freezing and freeing of degrees of freedom. Adapt. Behav. **12**(1), 47–64 (2004)
23. Lungarella, M., Berthouze, L.: Adaptivity via alternate freeing and freezing of degrees of freedom. In: ICONIP 2002-Proceeding of 9th International Conference Neural Information Processing Computer Intelligence E-Age, vol. 1, pp. 482–487 (2002)
24. Bongard, J.: Morphological change in machines accelerates the evolution of robust behavior. Proc. Natl. Acad. Sci. **108**(4), 1234–1239 (2011)
25. Stanley, K.O., Miikkulainen, R.: Evolving neural networks through augmenting topologies. Evol. Comput. **10**(2), 99–127 (2002)
26. Chervenski, P., Ryan, S.: MultiNEAT, project website (2012). URL www.multineat.com/
27. Robotics, C.: VREP Simulator. http://www.coppeliarobotics.com/
28. Smith, R.L.: Open Dynamics Engine. https://www.ode.org/
29. CESGA. Centro de Supecomputacion de Galicia. http://www.cesga.es/. Accessed 14 Jan 2020

Importance Weighted Adversarial Variational Bayes

Marta Gómez-Sancho and Daniel Hernández-Lobato(✉)

Computer Science Department, Universidad Autónoma de Madrid,
Francisco Tomás y Valiente 11, 28049 Madrid, Spain
{marta.gomez,daniel.hernandez}@uam.es

Abstract. Adversarial variational Bayes (AVB) can infer the parameters of a generative model from the data using approximate maximum likelihood. The likelihood of deep generative models model is intractable. However, it can be approximated by a lower bound obtained in terms of an approximate posterior distribution of the latent variables of the data q. The closer q is to the actual posterior, the tighter the lower bound is. Therefore, by maximizing the lower bound one should expect to also maximize the likelihood. Traditionally, the approximate distribution q is Gaussian. AVB relaxes this limitation and allows for flexible distributions that may lack a closed-form probability density function. Implicit distributions obtained by letting a source of Gaussian noise go through a deep neural network are examples of these distributions. Here, we combine AVB with the importance weighted autoencoder, a technique that has been shown to provide a tighter lower bound on the marginal likelihood. This is expected to lead to a more accurate parameter estimation of the generative model via approximate maximum likelihood. We have evaluated the proposed method on three datasets, MNIST, Fashion MNIST, and Omniglot. The experiments show that the proposed method improves the test log-likelihood of a generative model trained using AVB.

Keywords: Variational autoencoder · Importance weighted autoencoder · Adversarial variational bayes · Generative models

1 Introduction

Generative models can generate new data very similar to the observed data. A popular generative model assumes that the observed data has been generated by letting a random source of noise (*e.g.*, Gaussian distributed noise) go through a strong non-linear function such as the one corresponding to a deep neural network. This is how variational autoencoders (VAEs) and generative adversarial networks (GANs) work [6,9]. The task of interest is how to infer the parameters of the non-linear function that better explain the data. In general, however, this is a difficult task. Simple approaches such as maximum likelihood estimation fail because the likelihood of the model has no analytic form. Its computation

E. A. de la Cal et al. (Eds.): HAIS 2020, LNAI 12344, pp. 374–386, 2020.
https://doi.org/10.1007/978-3-030-61705-9_31

involves marginalizing the input noise. The resulting integral is too complicated as a consequence of the strong non-linearities of the deep neural network.

Two approaches can be used to overcome the problems described. The first one, employed in GANs, consists in using a discriminator to evaluate the quality of the generative model inferred so far [6]. The discriminator is trained to learn to correctly classify data points as coming from the training data set or as coming from the generator. Then, the generator is trained to make things *difficult* for the discriminator. If the training process is carried out correctly, the result is a generator that outputs data very similar to the observed data [15]. Learning, however, becomes difficult as the optimization problem that infers the parameters of the generator is a max-min problem [6]. Thus, GAN training is sometimes unstable and fails to produce meaningful results [2]. In spite of this, the images generated by GANs are often described are very realistic [15].

A second approach for learning generative models approximates the likelihood using approximate inference. In the variational autoencoder (VAE) a lower bound on the log-likelihood of the model is provided [9]. This lower bound is obtained in terms of an approximate distribution q that targets the posterior distribution of the latent variables of the data (*i.e.*, the noise variables used to generate the data). The missing part of the lower bound is the Kullback-Leibler (KL) divergence between q and the exact posterior. Therefore, maximizing the lower bound is equivalent to minimizing the KL between q and the actual posterior. Often, q is set to be a Gaussian, which guarantees that the lower bound can be easily approximated and optimized using stochastic optimization. Furthermore, amortized variational inference relates the parameters of q to the actual observed data point $\mathbf{x}$ [18]. This non-linear relation is specified in terms of a deep neural network. Thus, in the VAE one obtains for free a recognition model (*i.e.*, q) that infers the latent variables used to generate each instance.

The VAE can be improved by considering an average over several samples from q to evaluate the lower bound. This method is known in the literature as the importance weighted autoencoder (IWAE) [4]. The IWAE relies on importance variational inference [5] and the lower-bound obtained can be proved to be tighter than the one of the VAE. Therefore, the IWAE carries out a process that is closer to maximum likelihood estimation. This is translated into better parameter learning of the generative model and better log-likelihood results on validation data. The drawback is that K samples are needed to approximate the lower bound, which is K times more expensive.

A limitation of the VAE is that q is often restricted to be Gaussian. The reason for this is that it simplifies the evaluation of the objective to be optimized. A Gaussian distribution, however, may be far from the actual posterior. This introduces some bias in the objective that is optimized. Namely, the lower bound. Specifically, the difference between the log-likelihood of the training data and the lower bound is the KL divergence between q and the actual posterior. A Gaussian approximate distribution q is expected to suffer from approximation bias. Therefore, by increasing the flexibility of q it is possible to make the lower bound tighter, which should lead to better parameters estimation.

The approximation bias described is alleviated by using more flexible distributions q. This is how adversarial variational Bayes (AVB) works [14]. A flexible model for q is one similar to the generative model considered in GANs or VAEs [6,9]. Namely, a non- linear function that receives as input a Gaussian noise. These are known as wild-variational approximations and also as implicit distributions [7,12]. If the non-linear function is complex enough, *e.g.*, it is a deep neural network, and the number of dimensions of the noise is big enough, such a distribution can generate almost anything, as illustrated by the expressive power of GANs [15]. These distributions are easy to sample from. For this, one only has to generate random noise and let it go through the non-linearity. Nevertheless, evaluating the probability density function (p.d.f.) is complicated since it requires the marginalization of the noise, which is intractable. The log-ratio between q and the prior distribution for the latent variables of the model appears in the lower bound of the VAE. Therefore, using an implicit distribution q makes things difficult. AVB solves this problem by approximating the log-ratio using a flexible classifier that discriminates between samples from q and the prior. It is possible to show that the optimal classifier is precisely given by such log-ratio. This classifier can be trained simultaneously as the generative model. Therefore, AVB allows to carry out approximate inference using more flexible distributions q that may lead to tighter lower bounds on the log-likelihood of the model. This has been shown to lead to better parameter estimation [14].

We improve AVB and the IWAE by combining both approaches. That is, we consider the lower bound that is optimized in the IWAE and we employ a flexible approximate distribution q that is specified as an implicit model. Namely, a distribution that is easy to sample from but that has no closed-form p.d.f. The lower bound of the IWAE also requires the estimation of the log-ratio between the approximate distribution q and the prior. To address this problem we use the trick employed in AVB. That is, we use a flexible classifier, specified by a deep neural network, to discriminate between samples from q and the prior. We refer to such an approach as importance weighted adversarial variational Bayes (IWAVB). We evaluate the performance of the this method on the MNIST, the Fashion MNIST, and the Omniglot datasets. The results obtained show that IWAVB improves the results of AVB. More precisely, it infers the parameters of the generative model so that the log-likelihood on test data is higher.

The rest of the paper is organized as follows: Sect. 2 introduces the VAE. We also review here the IWAE and AVB as two improvements of standard VAEs. Then, in Sect. 3 we described the proposed approach for learning deep generative models. This approach combines all the advantages of the IWAE and AVB for approximate inference. Section 4 describes important related work. Section 5 shows the experiments of this paper in which have evaluated the proposed approach, IWAVB. Finally, Sect. 6 gives the conclusions of this work.

2 Variational Autoencoders

We describe the problem of learning a generative model of the observed data and how this task can be carried out by using the variational autoencoder (VAE).

We also describe here how this model can be improved by considering the importance weighted autoencoder (IWAE) and adversarial variational Bayes (AVB). Consider some observed data $\mathbf{X} = \{\mathbf{x}_i\}_{i=1}^N$, with d the dimensionality of the data. We assume that these data have been generated by the following model:

$$p_\theta(\mathbf{x}) = \int p_\theta(\mathbf{x}|\mathbf{z})p(\mathbf{z})d\mathbf{z}\,, \tag{2.1}$$

where $\mathbf{z} \in \mathbb{R}^l$ are latent variables associated to $\mathbf{x}$ so that $\mathbf{z} \sim \mathcal{N}(\mathbf{0}, \mathbf{I})$. Therefore, l is the dimensionality of the latent space. Furthermore, we assume that $p_\theta(\mathbf{x}|\mathbf{z})$ is a conditional distribution parameterized by θ. In the case that $\mathbf{x} \in \mathbb{R}^d$, an example of this distribution is a deep neural network that will output the means and diagonal variances of a multi-variate Gaussian distribution for $\mathbf{x}$. In the case of binary data. That is, when $\mathbf{x} \in \{0, 1\}^d$, the conditional distribution can be a deep neural network that will output the activation probabilities of a product of Bernoulli distributions. Namely, in each case we have that:

$$p_\theta(\mathbf{x}|\mathbf{z}) = \prod_{j=1}^d \mathcal{N}(x_j|\mu_j^\theta(\mathbf{z}), \nu_j^\theta(\mathbf{z}))\,, \qquad p_\theta(\mathbf{x}|\mathbf{z}) = \prod_{j=1}^d \text{Bern}(x_j|\mu_j^\theta(\mathbf{z}))\,, \tag{2.2}$$

where $\mathcal{N}(\cdot|m, v)$ denotes a Gaussian density with mean m and variance v, and $\text{Bern}(\cdot|\mu_j^\theta(\mathbf{z}))$ is the probability mass function of a Bernoulli random variable with activation probability $\mu_j^\theta(\mathbf{z})$.

The task of interest is how to infer θ, *i.e.*, the parameters of $p_\theta(\mathbf{x}|\mathbf{z})$ given $\mathbf{X}$. The maximum likelihood principle can be used for this task [3]. The problem is that the marginalization of $\mathbf{z}$ in (2.1) is intractable. To overcome this, the VAE introduces an approximate distribution $q_\phi(\mathbf{z}|\mathbf{x})$ targeting $p(\mathbf{z}|\mathbf{x})$ and considers the following decomposition of the log-likelihood of the observed data [9]:

$$\log p_\theta(\mathbf{x}) = \mathcal{L}_{\phi,\theta}(\mathbf{x}) + \text{KL}(q_\phi(\mathbf{z}|\mathbf{x}))|p(\mathbf{z}|\mathbf{x}))\,, \tag{2.3}$$

where

$$\mathcal{L}_{\phi,\theta}(\mathbf{x}) = \int q_\phi(\mathbf{z}|\mathbf{x}) \log \frac{p_\theta(\mathbf{x}|\mathbf{z})p(\mathbf{z})}{q_\phi(\mathbf{z}|\mathbf{x})} d\mathbf{z}\,, \tag{2.4}$$

$$\text{KL}(q_\phi(\mathbf{z}|\mathbf{x}))|p(\mathbf{z}|\mathbf{x})) = -\int q_\phi(\mathbf{z}|\mathbf{x}) \log \frac{p(\mathbf{z}|\mathbf{x})}{q_\phi(\mathbf{z}|\mathbf{x})} d\mathbf{z} \geq 0\,. \tag{2.5}$$

Furthermore, the approximate distribution is constrained to be Gaussian with parameters specified non-linearly in terms of $\mathbf{x}$ by a deep neural network:

$$q_\phi(\mathbf{z}|\mathbf{x}) = \prod_{j=1}^l \mathcal{N}(z_j|m_j^\phi(\mathbf{x}), v_j^\phi(\mathbf{x}))\,. \tag{2.6}$$

The second term in the r.h.s. of (2.3) is the Kullback-Leibler divergence between q and the actual posterior. The first term, *i.e.*, $\mathcal{L}(\mathbf{x})$, is hence a lower bound on the log marginal likelihood. Namely, $\log p(\mathbf{x}) \geq \mathcal{L}_{\phi,\theta}(\mathbf{x})$. Thus, a maximization of $\mathcal{L}_{\phi,\theta}(\mathbf{x})$ with respect to ϕ is equivalent to minimizing $\text{KL}(q_\phi(\mathbf{z}|\mathbf{x}))|p(\mathbf{z}|\mathbf{x}))$. Furthermore, at the maximum, $q_\phi(\mathbf{z}|\mathbf{x})$ is expected to be a good approximation to $p(\mathbf{z}|\mathbf{x})$ and hence $\text{KL}(q_\phi(\mathbf{z}|\mathbf{x}))|p(\mathbf{z}|\mathbf{x}))$ should be small. In that case, a maximization of $\mathcal{L}_{\phi,\theta}(\mathbf{x})$ with respect to θ, the parameters of the generative model, is expected to also maximize $\log p_\theta(\mathbf{x})$. Specifically, the VAE objective is:

$$\sum_{i=1}^{N} \mathcal{L}_{\theta,\phi}(\mathbf{x}_i) = \sum_{i=1}^{N} \mathbb{E}_{\mathbf{z}_i \sim q_\phi(\mathbf{z}_i|\mathbf{x}_i)}[\log p_\theta(\mathbf{x}_i|\mathbf{z}_i)] - \text{KL}(q_\phi(\mathbf{z}_i|\mathbf{x}_i)|p(\mathbf{z}_i)), \tag{2.7}$$

which is maximized simultaneously with respect to ϕ and θ.

The second term in (2.7) is the KL divergence between two Gaussian distributions, which can be computed analytically. The first term in (2.7), however, has no closed-form expression. This term (and its gradients) can be approximated by Monte Carlo methods. In particular, one can resort to the reparametrization trick [9]. For this, one generates a sample from $q_\phi(\mathbf{z}_i|\mathbf{x}_i)$, $\tilde{\mathbf{z}}_i$, by first generating a standard Gaussian random variable $\boldsymbol{\epsilon}_i$ to then apply a transformation so that $\tilde{\mathbf{z}}_i = g_\phi(\mathbf{x}_i, \boldsymbol{\epsilon}_i)$. In the case of the Gaussian distribution, this transformation is always possible. One just has to multiply each component $j = 1, \ldots, l$ of $\boldsymbol{\epsilon}_i$ by $\sqrt{v_j^\phi(\mathbf{x})}$ to then add $m_j^\phi(\mathbf{x})$. The noisy estimate of (2.7) is then,

$$\frac{N}{|\mathcal{B}|} \sum_{i \in \mathcal{B}} \log p_\theta(\mathbf{x}_i|\tilde{\mathbf{z}}_i) - \text{KL}(q_\phi(\mathbf{z}_i|\mathbf{x}_i)|p(\mathbf{z}_i)), \tag{2.8}$$

where we have considered a mini-batch $\mathcal{B}$ of data points to scale to large datasets. A unbiased gradient estimate can be obtained from (2.8) using the chain rule. Thus, (2.7) can be easily optimized using stochastic optimization [9].

2.1 Importance Weighted Variational Autoencoders

The VAE can be improved by considering the importance weighted autoencoder (IWAE) [4]. In this method for learning the parameters θ of the generative model it is considered a tighter lower bound that the one of the VAE. Namely,

$$\hat{\mathcal{L}}_{\theta,\phi}^{K}(\mathbf{x}) = \mathbb{E}_{\mathbf{z}^1,\mathbf{z}^2,\ldots,\mathbf{z}^K \sim q_\phi(\mathbf{z}|\mathbf{x})} \left[\log \frac{1}{K} \sum_{k=1}^{K} \frac{p_\theta(\mathbf{x}|\mathbf{z}^k) p(\mathbf{z}^k)}{q_\phi(\mathbf{z}^k|\mathbf{x})} \right]. \tag{2.9}$$

This is a lower bound on $\log p_\theta(\mathbf{x})$ as follows from Jensen's inequality and the fact that the average is an unbiased estimator:

$$\mathbb{E}\left[\log \frac{1}{K} \sum_{k=1}^{K} \frac{p_\theta(\mathbf{x}|\mathbf{z}^k) p(\mathbf{z}^k)}{q_\phi(\mathbf{z}^k|\mathbf{x})} \right] \leq \log \mathbb{E}\left[\frac{1}{K} \sum_{k=1}^{K} \frac{p_\theta(\mathbf{x}|\mathbf{z}^k) p(\mathbf{z}^k)}{q_\phi(\mathbf{z}^k|\mathbf{x})} \right] = \log p_\theta(\mathbf{x}), \tag{2.10}$$

where the expectations are the same as the one in (2.9).

When the number of samples K equals 1, (2.9) coincides with (2.4). When $K > 1$, it is expected that the variance inside of the log in (2.9) is reduced. In particular, $\hat{\mathcal{L}}^{K+1}_{\theta,\phi}(\mathbf{x}) \geq \hat{\mathcal{L}}^{K}_{\theta,\phi}(\mathbf{x})$, as proved in [4]. Therefore, one can obtain a tighter lower bound simply by increasing K. The IWAE objective can also be approximated stochastically as in (2.7). In this case, however, the KL divergence is not contained in the objective. One must include the ratio between $q_\phi(\mathbf{z}|\mathbf{x})$ and the prior $p(\mathbf{z})$ in the stochastic estimate. Namely,

$$\frac{N}{|\mathcal{B}|}\sum_{i\in\mathcal{B}}\log\frac{1}{K}\sum_{k=1}^{K}\frac{p_\theta(\mathbf{x}_i|\tilde{\mathbf{z}}_i^k)p(\tilde{\mathbf{z}}_i^k)}{q_\phi(\tilde{\mathbf{z}}_i^k|\mathbf{x}_i)}, \tag{2.11}$$

where we consider K samples from $q_\phi(\mathbf{z}_i|\mathbf{x}_i)$ instead of just one, as in the VAE. This objective leads to better estimation of the parameters of the generative model θ when $K > 1$. More precisely, by considering $K = 5$ and $K = 50$ samples, better test log-likelihood results are obtained [4].

2.2 Adversarial Variational Bayes

A limitation of the VAE (and also the IWAE) is that the approximate distribution $q_\phi(\mathbf{z}|\mathbf{x})$ is Gaussian. This introduces some bias in the estimation of the model parameters. In particular, in the VAE the difference between the $\mathcal{L}_{\phi,\theta}(\mathbf{x})$ and the actual log-likelihood of the data $\log p_\theta(\mathbf{x}))$ is the KL divergence between $q_\phi(\mathbf{z}|\mathbf{x})$ and the exact posterior distribution $p(\mathbf{z}|\mathbf{x})$. This means that the quantity that is optimized by the VAE need not be equal to the expected optimal one. Namely, the log-likelihood of the model parameters θ.

Adversarial variational Bayes (AVB) is a technique that can be used to consider flexible distributions q_ϕ [14]. Examples of these distributions include implicit distributions also known as wild-approximations [12]. These are distributions that are easy to sample from but that may lack an analytical expression for the probability density. For example, consider the approximate distribution:

$$\mathbf{z} = f_\phi(\mathbf{x},\mathbf{e}), \quad \mathbf{e}\sim\mathcal{N}(\mathbf{0},\mathbf{I}), \quad q_\phi(\mathbf{z}|\mathbf{x}) = \int \delta(\mathbf{z} - f_\phi(\mathbf{x},\mathbf{e}))\mathcal{N}(\mathbf{e}|\mathbf{0},\mathbf{I})d\mathbf{e}, \tag{2.12}$$

where $\delta(\cdot)$ is a point of probability mass and $f_\phi(\cdot,\cdot)$ is a non-linear function, *e.g.*, a deep neural network. If the dimensionality of $\mathbf{e}$ is large enough and the complexity of f_ϕ is big enough, one can generate almost anything. This is precisely the approach used in GANs or the VAE to generate data [6,9], which can generate very complex data [15].

A problem, however, is that distributions such as (2.12) lack closed-form probability densities. This makes difficult optimizing the objective of the VAE in (2.8). Specifically, it is required to estimate the log-ratio between q and the prior, in order to evaluate (2.8), as the KL divergence between q and the prior depends on this log-ratio. See (2.4) for further details. AVB provides an elegant solution to this problem. For this, it uses the fact that the log-ratio between

q and the prior is given by the output of an optimal classifier that solves the problem of discriminating samples from the prior and from q. More precisely,

$$\text{KL}(q_\phi(\mathbf{z}|\mathbf{x})|p(\mathbf{z})) = \mathbb{E}_{\mathbf{z}\sim q_\phi(\mathbf{z}|\mathbf{x})}\left[\log\frac{q_\phi(\mathbf{z}|\mathbf{x})}{p(\mathbf{z})}\right] = \mathbb{E}_{\mathbf{z}\sim q_\phi(\mathbf{z}|\mathbf{x})}\left[T_{\omega^\star}(\mathbf{x},\mathbf{z})\right], \quad (2.13)$$

where $T_{\omega^\star}(\mathbf{x},\mathbf{z})$ is the output of the the optimal classifier. This classifier can be implemented as deep neural network with parameters ω. If $T_\omega(\mathbf{x},\mathbf{z})$ is flexible enough it should approximate the log-ratio very accurately [14]. The objective that is considered for training the discriminator, assuming q is fixed, is:

$$\max_\omega \quad \mathbb{E}_{\mathbf{z}\sim q_\phi(\mathbf{z}|\mathbf{x})}\left[\log\sigma(T_\omega(\mathbf{x},\mathbf{z})))\right] + \mathbb{E}_{\mathbf{z}\sim p(\mathbf{z})}\left[\log(1-\sigma(T_\omega(\mathbf{x},\mathbf{z}))))\right]. \quad (2.14)$$

where $\sigma(\cdot)$ is the sigmoid activation function. It is possible to show that the optimal $T_{\omega^\star}(\mathbf{z},\mathbf{x})$ that maximizes (2.14) is given precisely by $\log q_\phi(\mathbf{z}|\mathbf{x}) - \log p(\mathbf{z})$ [14]. Note that (2.14) can be optimized using stochastic optimization. It is equivalent to training a deep neural network to solve a binary classification task.

Given $T_{\omega^\star}(\mathbf{z},\mathbf{x})$, the objective of AVB for learning the parameters of the generative model is obtained by introducing in (2.8) the output of such a classifier:

$$\frac{N}{|\mathcal{B}|}\sum_{i\in\mathcal{B}}\log p_\theta(\mathbf{x}_i|\tilde{\mathbf{z}}_i)] - T_{\omega^\star}(\tilde{\mathbf{z}}_i,\mathbf{x}_i). \quad (2.15)$$

To optimize this objective we need to differentiate with respect to ϕ. This may be complicated since $T_{\omega^\star}(\mathbf{z},\mathbf{x})$ depends on ϕ. However, due to the expression for the optimal discriminator, it can be showed that $\mathbb{E}_{q_\phi(\mathbf{z}|\mathbf{x})}(\nabla_\phi T_{\omega^\star}(\mathbf{z},\mathbf{x})) = 0$. Therefore the dependence of $T_{\omega^\star}(\mathbf{z},\mathbf{x})$ w.r.t ϕ can be ignored [14]. In practice, both q_ϕ and the discriminator $T_\omega(\mathbf{z},\mathbf{x})$ are trained simultaneously. However, q_ϕ is updated by maximizing (2.15) using a smaller learning rate than the one used to update the discriminator T_ω, which considers (2.14). Several experiments show that an implicit distribution for q improves the test log-likelihood results [14].

3 Importance Weighted Adversarial Variational Bayes

We propose to combine both the IWAE, which is able to optimize a tighter lower bound than the one considered by the VAE, and AVB to allow for approximate inference using an implicit approximate distribution q_ϕ. This is expected to lead to better optimization results of the parameters of the generative model θ. In the case of IWAE, however, the missing term (*i.e.*, the difference between the log-likelihood of the model parameters θ and the lower bound) is not the KL divergence between q and the actual posterior. Nevertheless, this method can also benefit from a more flexible distribution q. Specifically, the IWAE objective is an importance sampling estimate [4]. The optimal sampling distribution in such an estimate is the actual posterior distribution $p(\mathbf{z}|\mathbf{x})$. If that distribution is employed, it is possible to show that the objective in (2.9) coincides with the marginal likelihood of the data $\log p_\theta(\mathbf{x})$.

Even though the IWAE can benefit from using an implicit distribution as the approximate distribution q_ϕ, it is not trivial how to employ this distribution in practice. More precisely, the objective in (2.9) requires the computation of the ratio between the prior $p(\mathbf{z})$ and approximate posterior $q_\phi(\mathbf{z}|\mathbf{x})$. We propose to estimate this ratio using the approach of AVB. Namely, by using the output of a near-optimal classifier that discriminates between samples from these two distributions. The lower bound that we consider is hence

$$\begin{aligned}\tilde{\mathcal{L}}^K_{\theta,\phi}(\mathbf{x}) &= \mathbb{E}_{\mathbf{z}^1,\mathbf{z}^2,\ldots,\mathbf{z}^K\sim q_\phi(\mathbf{z}|\mathbf{x})}\left[\log\frac{1}{K}\sum_{k=1}^K\frac{p_\theta(\mathbf{x}|\mathbf{z}^k)p(\mathbf{z}^k)}{q_\phi(\mathbf{z}^k|\mathbf{x})}\right]\\ &= \mathbb{E}_{\mathbf{z}^1,\mathbf{z}^2,\ldots,\mathbf{z}^K\sim q_\phi(\mathbf{z}|\mathbf{x})}\left[\log\frac{1}{K}\sum_{k=1}^K\exp\left\{\log p_\theta(\mathbf{x}|\mathbf{z}^k)-T_{\omega^\star}(\mathbf{z}^k,\mathbf{x})\right\}\right].\end{aligned} \tag{3.1}$$

and the objective is given by

$$\frac{N}{|\mathcal{B}|}\sum_{i\in\mathcal{B}}\log\frac{1}{K}\sum_{k=1}^K\exp\left\{\log p_\theta(\mathbf{x}|\mathbf{z}^k)-T_{\omega^\star}(\mathbf{z}^k,\mathbf{x})\right\}. \tag{3.2}$$

The optimal discriminator $T_{\omega^\star}(\mathbf{z}^k,\mathbf{x})$ can be trained as in AVB by optimizing the objective in (2.14). This can be carried out using the specific details employed in AVB, *e.g.*, training all the networks at the same time, and using a bigger learning rate to train the discriminator. We expect that the optimization of this tighter lower bound results in a better parameter estimation.

4 Related Work

There are other techniques that have been proposed to allow for implicit models besides adversarial variational Bayes. In [19] is it described a method to obtain an unbiased estimate of the gradients of the lower bound when an implicit model is used to approximate the posterior distribution. This estimate relies on Markov chain Monte Carlo techniques to approximate the posterior distribution of the noise $\mathbf{e}$ that was used to generate each $\mathbf{z}$. Even though this approach works in practice its implementation is difficult as simulating a Markov chain in frameworks such as Tensorflow require coding loops which are often computationally expensive and cannot be accelerated on GPUs [1].

Another approach to obtain flexible approximate distributions q is normalizing flows (NF) [16]. NF starts with a simple distribution q, *e.g.*, Gaussian, whose samples are modified using non-linear invertible transformations. If these transformations are chosen carefully, the p.d.f. of the resulting distribution can be evaluated in closed-form, avoiding the problems of implicit models for q that lack a closed-form p.d.f. The problem of NF is that the family of transformations is limited, since it has to be invertible, which may constrain the flexibility of q. The implicit model considered in our work does not have these restrictions and is hence expected to be more flexible.

Stein Variational Gradient Descent transforms a set of *particles* to match the posterior distribution [13]. This technique is competitive with state-of-the-art methods, but the main drawback is that many particles (points) need to be stored in memory to accurately represent the posterior. This can be a computational bottle-neck. The number of samples is fixed initially, and these samples or particles are optimized during training. In problems with a high dimensional latent space this can be problematic. Our approach only needs to generate a few samples to obtained better results, *i.e.*, 5 or 10 samples.

In [17] variational inference and MCMC methods are combined to obtain flexible approximate distributions. The key is to use a Markov chain as the approximate distribution q. The parameters of the Markov chain can be adjusted to match as close as possible the target distribution in terms of the KL divergence. This is an interesting idea, but is also limited by the difficulty of evaluating the p.d.f. of q, as in the case of AVB. In [17] this problem is addressed by learning a backward model, that infers the initial state of the Markov chain given the generated samples. Learning this backward model accurately is expensive and parametric models have to be used in practice, which may introduce some bias.

Another approach derives a lower bound that is looser than the one considered by the VAE [22]. However, this lower bound can be evaluated in closed-form when an implicit distribution is used as the approximate distribution. This work does not have the problems of AVB, in which extra models have to be used to approximate the log-ratio between the approximate distribution q and the prior. A problem, however, is that the looser lower bound can lead to sub-optimal approximation results. Nevertheless, the experiments carried out in that work indicate that some gains are obtained.

Finally, approximate inference by using importance weights is analyzed in detail in [5]. That paper shows that such a method optimizes a KL divergence between the approximate distribution q an implicit posterior distribution. That paper also extends the ideas of importance weighted approximate inference to general probabilistic graphical models, not only generative models as in [4].

While the proposed method to account for an implicit approximate distribution q is simple and can be easily codified in modern frameworks for machine learning such as Tensorflow [1], it suffers from the limitation of having to train a discriminator, in parallel, in order to optimize the lower bound in (3.2).

5 Experiments

We have carried out experiments on several datasets to evaluate the performance of the proposed method. The datasets considered are MNIST [11], Fashion MNIST [21], and Omniglot [10]. The number of instances in each of these datasets are 70,000, 70,000 and 32,640, respectively. Each instance is a 28×28 gray-scale image (in Omniglot we down-sample the images from an initial resolution of 105×105). We use 55,000 images for training in MNIST and Fashion MNIST, 5,000 for validation, and the rest for testing. In the case of the Omniglot dataset we use 5,000 instances for validation, 5,000 instances for testing and the rest for training. Figure 1 shows 50 images extracted from each datasets.

Fig. 1. Sample images extracted from the MNIST dataset (left), Fashion MNIST (middle) and Omniglot (right). All images are of size 28 × 28 pixels in gray scale.

In each dataset we train the proposed method, IWAVB, considering a different number of samples. Namely, $K = 1, 5$ and 10 samples. Importantly, for $K = 1$ samples IWAVB reduces to AVB, which allows to compare results with that method. We considered two potential values for the dimensionality of the latent space $l = 8$ and $l = 32$ and report results for both of them. In each experiment the generator, the non-linear function of the approximate distribution q and the classifier used to approximate the log-ratio use the same architecture as in [14]. That is, they are convolutional neural networks. The dimensionality of the noise injected in the implicit model is set to 32. We use ADAM for training the models with a learning rate of $5 \cdot 10^{-5}$ for the generative model and 10^{-4} for the classifier [8]. The number of steps is set to 150000. All the computations have been carried out using Tensorflow [1] and a Tesla P100 GPU. We use the adaptive contrast technique, as described in [14], to improve the results of the log-ratio estimation. The test log-likelihood is estimated using annealed-importance sampling with 8 parallel chains run for 1000 steps [20]. Validation data are used to track the overall progress of the training process.

The results obtained are displayed in Table 1. This table shows the average negative test log-likelihood (the lower the better) of IWAVB on each dataset in terms of the number of samples considered K and the dimensionality of the latent space, *i.e.*, l. We observe that IWAVB always improves results with K and that most of the times the best results correspond to the larger number of samples, as expected, since this results in a tighter lower bound of the log-likelihood associated to the training data. We also observe that increasing the dimensionality of the latent space improves results in general. The datasets considered in our experiments have a large number of samples. Therefore, we have only considered a single train / test partition of the data. It is hence difficult to obtain error bars on the estimated quantities. Nevertheless, the fact that always the best results correspond to $K > 1$ gives evidence supporting that the proposed approach performs better.

Table 1. Neg. test log-likelihood (NLL) on each dataset in terms of the latent space dimensionality (l) and the number of samples (K) used to compute the lower bound.

Dataset	l	K	NLL	Dataset	l	K	NLL	Dataset	l	K	NLL
MNIST	8	1	90.23	Fashion	8	1	231.25	Omniglot	8	1	156.62
MNIST	8	5	**90.16**	Fashion	8	5	230.34	Omniglot	8	5	**142.99**
MNIST	8	10	90.19	Fashion	8	10	**229.43**	Omniglot	8	10	152.70
MNIST	32	1	80.74	Fashion	32	1	226.96	Omniglot	32	1	91.54
MNIST	32	5	80.49	Fashion	32	5	227.16	Omniglot	32	5	**91.25**
MNIST	32	10	**79.77**	Fashion	32	10	**225.14**	Omniglot	32	10	91.43

From these experiments we can conclude that the proposed method is able to improve the results of estimating the parameters of the generative model θ. In particular, it seems to always improve the results of AVB in terms of the log-likelihood of test data. Recall that AVB correspond to IWAVB with $K = 1$. Importantly, the results obtained are also similar and even better than the ones reported in [14]. We conclude that a combination of the IWAVB with implicit models results in better generative models in terms of the test log-likelihood.

6 Conclusions

We have proposed a novel method for training deep generative models. Training these models is challenging because the likelihood lacks a closed-form expression. A method that overcomes this problem is the variational autoencoder (VAE), which maximizes a lower bound on the log-likelihood of the model [9]. This lower bound can be made tighter by considering extra samples from an approximate distribution q that targets the posterior distribution of the latent variables of the data $\mathbf{z}$. This is how the importance weighted autoencoder (IWAE) works. An orthogonal approach to improve results considers an implicit model for the approximate distribution q, which is constrained to be Gaussian in the VAE and the IWAE. This technique is known as adversarial variational Bayes (AVB) [14]. A difficulty, however, is that evaluating the lower bound when q is implicit is no longer tractable, since the log-ratio between q and the prior distribution for the latent variables is required. AVB uses the output of a classifier that discriminates between samples from q and the prior to estimate the log-ratio.

In this paper we have combined the the IWAE to obtain a tighter lower bound on the log-likelihood of the generative model and AVB, which allows to consider an implicit distribution q that need not be Gaussian. Our hypothesis was that the tighter lower bound of the IWAE combined with the extra flexibility of an implicit model for q should lead to better generative models. We have validated the proposed approach on several experiments involving gray-scale images of size 28 × 28 pixels extracted from the MNIST, Fashion MNIST, and Omniglot datasets. In these experiments we have observed that the proposed approach always improves the results of AVB. Furthermore, using a bigger number of samples in the approximation of the log-likelihood of the generative model seems to improve results most of the times, which is the expected behavior, since more samples imply a tighter lower bound that is closer to the actual log-likelihood.

Acknowledgment. We acknowledge the use of the facilities of Centro de Computación Científica at UAM and support from the Spanish Plan Nacional I+D+i (grants TIN2016–76406-P, TEC2016–81900-REDT and PID2019–106827GB-I00) and from Comunidad de Madrid (grant PEJ-2017-AI_TIC-6464).

References

1. Abadi, M., et al.: TensorFlow: large-scale machine learning on heterogeneous systems (2015). https://www.tensorflow.org/, available from tensorflow.org
2. Arjovsky, M., Bottou, L.: Towards principled methods for training generative adversarial networks. In: ICLR (2017)
3. Bishop, C.M.: Pattern Recognition and Machine Learning (Information Science and Statistics). Springer (2006)
4. Burda, Y., Grosse, R.B., Salakhutdinov, R.: Importance weighted autoencoders. In: ICLR (2016)
5. Domke, J., Sheldon, D.R.: Importance weighting and variational inference. In: NIPS, pp. 4470–4479 (2018)
6. Goodfellow, I., et al.: Generative adversarial nets. In: NIPS, pp. 2672–2680 (2014)
7. Huszár, F.: Variational inference using implicit distributions. arXiv preprint arXiv:1702.08235 (2017)
8. Kingma, D.P., Ba, J.: ADAM: a method for stochastic optimization. In: ICLR, pp. 1–15 (2015)
9. Kingma, D.P., Welling, M.: Auto-encoding variational Bayes. In: ICLR (2014)
10. Lake, B.M., Salakhutdinov, R., Tenenbaum, J.B.: Human-level concept learning through probabilistic program induction. Science **350**, 1332–1338 (2015)
11. LeCun, Y., Bottou, L., Bengio, Y., Haffner, P.: Gradient-based learning applied to document recognition. Proc. IEEE **86**, 2278–2324 (1998)
12. Li, Y., Liu, Q.: Wild variational approximations. In: NIPS Workshop on Advances in Approximate Bayesian Inference (2016)
13. Liu, Q., Wang, D.: Stein variational gradient descent: a general purpose Bayesian inference algorithm. In: NIPS, pp. 2378–2386 (2016)
14. Mescheder, L.M., Nowozin, S., Geiger, A.: Adversarial variational bayes: unifying variational autoencoders and generative adversarial networks. In: ICML, pp. 2391–2400 (2017)
15. Radford, A., Metz, L., Chintala, S.: Unsupervised representation learning with deep convolutional generative adversarial networks. In: ICLR (2016)
16. Rezende, D.J., Mohamed, S.: Variational inference with normalizing flows. In: ICML, pp. 1530–1538 (2016)
17. Salimans, T., Kingma, D., Welling, M.: Markov chain Monte Carlo and variational inference: bridging the gap. In: ICML, pp. 1218–1226 (2015)

18. Shu, R., Bui, H.H., Zhao, S., Kochenderfer, M.J., Ermon, S.: Amortized inference regularization. In: NIPS, pp. 4393–4402 (2018)
19. Titsias, M.K., Ruiz, F.J.R.: Unbiased implicit variational inference. In: Artificial Intelligence and Statistics, pp. 167–176 (2019)
20. Wu, Y., Burda, Y., Salakhutdinov, R., Grosse, R.: On the quantitative analysis of decoder-based generative models. arXiv preprint arXiv:1611.04273 (2016)
21. Xiao, H., Rasul, K., Vollgraf, R.: Fashion-mnist: a novel image dataset for benchmarking machine learning algorithms (2017)
22. Yin, M., Zhou, M.: Semi-implicit variational inference. In: ICML, pp. 5660–5669 (2018)

Global and Saturated Probabilistic Approximations Based on Generalized Maximal Consistent Blocks

Patrick G. Clark[1], Jerzy W. Grzymala-Busse[1,2(✉)], Zdzislaw S. Hippe[2], Teresa Mroczek[2], and Rafal Niemiec[2]

[1] Department of Electrical Engineering and Computer Science, University of Kansas, Lawrence, KS 66045, USA
patrick.g.clark@gmail.com, jerzy@ku.edu

[2] Department of Artificial Intelligence, University of Information Technology and Management, 35–225 Rzeszow, Poland
{zhippe,tmroczek,rniemiec}@wsiz.rzeszow.pl

Abstract. In this paper incomplete data sets, or data sets with missing attribute values, have two interpretations, lost values and "do not care" conditions. Additionally, the process of data mining is based on two types of probabilistic approximations, global and saturated. We present results of experiments on mining incomplete data sets using four approaches, combining two interpretations of missing attribute values with two types of probabilistic approximations. We compare our four approaches, using the error rate computed as a result of ten-fold cross validation as a criterion of quality. We show that for some data sets the error rate is significantly smaller (5% level of significance) for lost values than for "do not care" conditions, while for other data sets the error rate is smaller for "do not care" conditions. For "do not care" conditions, the error rate is significantly smaller for saturated probabilistic approximations than for global probabilistic approximations for two data sets, for another data set it is the other way around, while for remaining five data sets the difference is insignificant. Thus, for an incomplete data set, the best approach to data mining should be chosen by trying all four approaches.

Keywords: Data mining · Rough set theory · Characteristic sets · Maximal consistent blocks · Probabilistic approximations

1 Introduction

In this paper we study incomplete data sets, with missing attribute values having two interpretations, as lost values and "do not care" conditions. Erased or not inserted attribute values are called lost. When a data set with lost values is mined, only existing, specified attribute values are analyzed. A "do not care" condition means that the original attribute value was not relevant. Hence "do not care" conditions may be replaced by any value from the attribute domain.

E. A. de la Cal et al. (Eds.): HAIS 2020, LNAI 12344, pp. 387–396, 2020.
https://doi.org/10.1007/978-3-030-61705-9_32

In our methodology of mining incomplete data sets two processes, handling missing attribute values and rule induction, are conducted at the same time. First we compute a probabilistic approximation of all data concepts. The probabilistic approximation is an extension of the standard approximation as known in rough set theory. For complete data sets (with no missing attribute values) the probabilistic approximation was introduced in [15]. Such approximations were studied, e.g., in [12,14–21]. For incomplete data sets (data sets with missing attribute values) the probabilistic approximation was introduced in [8].

A fundamental idea of maximal consistent blocks, restricted only to data sets with "do not care" conditions, was introduced in [13]. Moreover, in [13] only two standard approximations, lower and upper, were considered and applied to incomplete data sets with only "do not care" conditions. A definition of the maximal consistent block was generalized to cover lost values and probabilistic approximations in [1,2]. The applicability of characteristic sets and generalized maximal consistent blocks for mining incomplete data, from the view point of an error rate, was studied in [1,2]. The main result of [1,2] is that there is a small difference in quality of rule sets, in terms of an error rate computed as the result of ten-fold cross validation, induced either way. But in [1,2] probabilistic approximations were restricted to three types (with probabilities 0.001, 0.5 and 1, respectively). In this paper we use the entire spectrum of probabilities. Additionally, we discuss two new probabilistic approximations, global and saturated. Such approximations were studied for the first time in [4], but were restricted only to characteristic sets. Complexity of rule sets, induced from global and saturated probabilistic approximations, also based on characteristic sets, was studied in [5].

The main objective of this paper is to check what an approach among four approaches, combining two types of probabilistic approximations (global and saturated), both based on generalized maximal consistent blocks, with two types of missing attribute values (lost values and "do not care" conditions), provides the smallest error rate, measured by ten-fold cross validation. In our experiments, the Modified Learning from Examples Module, version 2 (MLEM2) was used for rule induction [7].

2 Incomplete Data

Table 1 shows a small example of the data set. It is presented as a decision table. Each row of the decision table represents a case. The set of all cases is denoted by U. In Table 1, $U = \{1, 2, 3, 4, 5, 6, 7, 8\}$. Independent variables are called *attributes*, the set of all attributes is denoted by A. A dependent variable is called a *decision* and is denoted by d. In Table 1, $A = \{Temperature, Wind, Humidity\}$. In a decision table, the value for a case x and an attribute a is denoted by $a(x)$. For example, $Temperature(1) = normal$.

A *concept* is the set X of all cases defined by the same value of the decision d. For example, a concept associated with the value *yes* of the decision *Trip* is the set $\{1, 2, 3\}$.

Table 1. A decision table

	Attributes			Decision
Case	Temperature	Wind	Humidity	Trip
1	normal	*	no	yes
2	high	?	*	yes
3	*	?	no	yes
4	normal	*	no	no
5	?	yes	yes	no
6	very-high	*	yes	no
7	high	?	yes	no
8	*	no	yes	no

For complete decision tables, a *block* of the attribute-value pair (a, v), denoted by $[(a, v)]$, is the set $\{x \in U \mid a(x) = v\}$ [6]. For incomplete decision tables, the definition of a block of an attribute-value pair is modified as follows:

- for an attribute a and a case x, if $a(x) = ?$, then the case x should not be included in any blocks $[(a, v)]$ for all values v of attribute a;
- for an attribute a and a case x, if $a(x) = *$, then the case x should be included in blocks $[(a, v)]$ for all specified values v of attribute a.

For the data set from Table 1, the blocks of attribute-value pairs are:

[(Temperature, normal)] = {1, 3, 4, 8},
[(Temperature, high)] = {2, 3, 7, 8},
[(Temperature, very-high)] = {3, 6, 8},
[(Wind, no)] = {1, 4, 6, 8},
[(Wind, yes)] = {1, 4, 5, 6},
[(Humidity, no)] = {1, 2, 3, 4}, and
[(Humidity, yes)] = {2, 5, 6, 7, 8}.

The *characteristic set* $K_B(x)$, is defined as the intersection of the sets $K(x, a)$, for all $a \in B$, where $x \in U$, $B \subseteq A$, and the set $K(x, a)$ is defined as follows:

- if $a(x)$ is specified, then $K(x, a)$ is the block $[(a, a(x))]$ of attribute a and its value $a(x)$;
- if $a(x) = ?$ or $a(x) = *$, then $K(x, a) = U$.

For Table 1 and $B = A$,

$K_A(1) = \{1, 3, 4\}$,
$K_A(2) = \{2, 3, 7, 8\}$,
$K_A(3) = \{1, 2, 3, 4\}$,
$K_A(4) = \{1, 3, 4\}$,
$K_A(5) = \{5, 6\}$,
$K_A(6) = \{6, 8\}$,
$K_A(7) = \{2, 7, 8\}$, and
$K_A(8) = \{6, 8\}$.

A binary relation $R(B)$ on U, defined for $x, y \in U$ in the following way $(x, y) \in R(B)$ *if and only if* $y \in K_B(x)$, is called *B-characteristic relation.* Let

X be a subset of U. The set X is *B-consistent* if $(x, y) \in R(B)$ for any $x, y \in X$. If there does not exist a B-consistent subset Y of U such that X is a proper subset of Y, the set X is called a *generalized maximal B-consistent block*. The set of all generalized maximal B-consistent blocks will be denoted by $\mathscr{C}(B)$. In our example, $\mathscr{C}(A) = \{\{1, 3, 4\}, \{2, 3\}, \{2, 7\}, \{5\}, \{6, 8\}\}$. The set of all generalized maximal B-consistent blocks which include an element x of the set U, i.e. the set $\{Y|Y \in \mathscr{C}(B), x \in Y\}$ will be denoted by $\mathscr{C}_B(x)$. In our example,

$\mathscr{C}_A(1) = \{\{1,3,4\}\}$, $\mathscr{C}_A(5) = \{\{5\}\}$,
$\mathscr{C}_A(2) = \{\{2,3\},\{2,7\}\}$, $\mathscr{C}_A(6) = \{\{6,8\}\}$,
$\mathscr{C}_A(3) = \{\{2,3\},\{1,3,4\}\}$, $\mathscr{C}_A(7) = \{\{2,7\}\}$, and
$\mathscr{C}_A(4) = \{\{1,3,4\}\}$, $\mathscr{C}_A(8) = \{\{6,8\}\}$.

3 Probabilistic Approximations

We restrict our attention to two types of probabilistic approximations, global and saturated, both based on generalized maximal consistent blocks. We quote some definitions from [4,5].

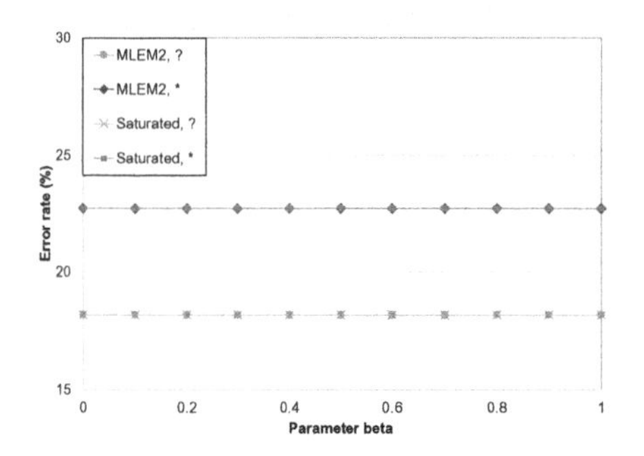

Fig. 1. *Bankruptcy* data set

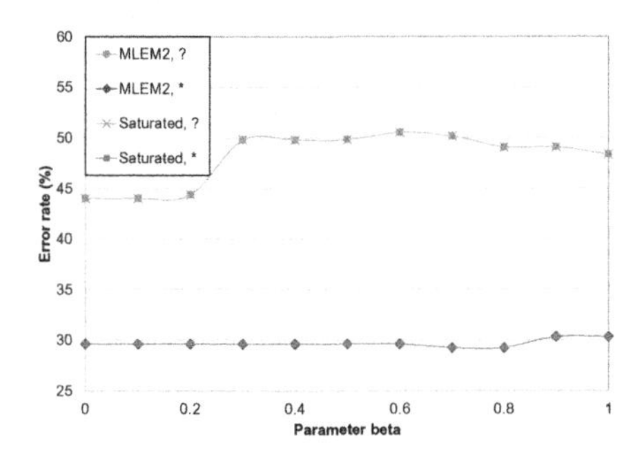

Fig. 2. *Breast cancer* data set

3.1 Global Probabilistic Approximations

A special case of the global probabilistic approximation, limited only to lower and upper approximations and to characteristic sets, was introduced in [10,11]. A general definition of the global probabilistic approximation was introduced in [5].

A *B-global probabilistic approximation* of the concept X, with the parameter α and denoted by $appr^{global}_{\alpha,B}(X)$ is defined as follows

$$\cup\{Y \mid Y \in \mathscr{C}_x(B),\ x \in X,\ Pr(X|Y) \geq \alpha\}.$$

Obviously, for given sets B and X and the parameter α, there exist many B-global probabilistic approximations of X. Additionally, an algorithm for computing B-global probabilistic approximations is of exponential computational

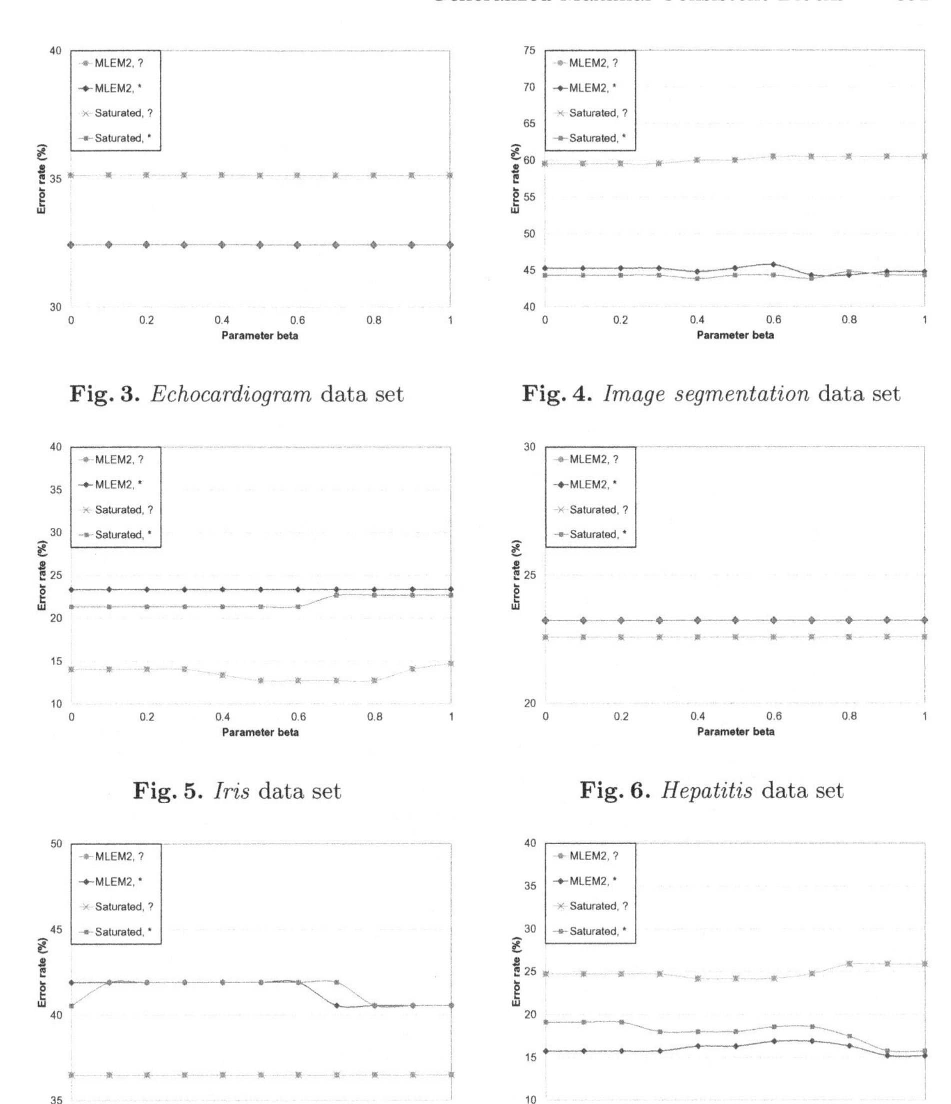

Fig. 3. *Echocardiogram* data set

Fig. 4. *Image segmentation* data set

Fig. 5. *Iris* data set

Fig. 6. *Hepatitis* data set

Fig. 7. *Lymphography* data set

Fig. 8. *Wine recognition* data set

complexity. So, we decided to use a heuristic version of the definition of B-global probabilistic approximation, called the MLEM2 B-global probabilistic approximation of the concept X, associated with a parameter α and denoted by $appr^{mlem2}_{\alpha,B}(X)$ [3]. This definition is based on the rule induction algorithm MLEM2. The approximation $appr^{mlem2}_{\alpha,B}(X)$ is a union of the generalized maximal consistent blocks $Y \in \mathscr{C}(B)$, the most relevant to the concept X, i.e., with $|X \cap Y|$ as large as possible and with $Pr(X|Y) \geq \alpha$. If more than one generalized maximal consistent block Y satisfies both conditions, the generalized maximal consistent block Y with the largest $Pr(X|Y) \geq \alpha$ is selected. If this criterion ends up with a tie, a generalized maximal consistent block Y is picked up heuristically, as the first on the list [3].

Special MLEM2 B-global probabilistic approximations, with $B = A$, are called *global probabilistic approximations* associated with the parameter α, and are denoted by $appr_{\alpha}^{mlem2}(X)$.

Let $E_{\alpha}(X)$ be the set of all eligible generalized maximal consistent blocks defined as follows

$$\{Y \mid Y \subseteq \mathscr{C}(A), Pr(X|Y) \geq \alpha\}.$$

A heuristic version of the MLEM2 global probabilistic approximation is computed using the following algorithm

MLEM2 global probabilistic approximation algorithm
input: a set X (a concept), a set $E_{\alpha}(X)$,
output: a set T (a global probabilistic approximation $appr_{\alpha}^{mlem2}(X)$) of X
begin
    $G := X$;
    $T := \emptyset$;
    $\mathscr{Y} := E_{\alpha}(X)$;
    while $G \neq \emptyset$ **and** $\mathscr{Y} \neq \emptyset$
        begin
            select a generalized maximal consistent block $Y \in \mathscr{Y}$
            such that $|X \cap Y|$ is maximum;
            if a tie occurs, select $Y \in \mathscr{Y}$
            with the smallest cardinality;
            if another tie occurs, select the first $Y \in \mathscr{Y}$;
            $T := T \cup Y$;
            $G := G - T$;
            $\mathscr{Y} := \mathscr{Y} - Y$
        end
end

For Table 1, all distinct MLEM2 global probabilistic approximations for $[(Trip, no)]$ are

$$appr_{1}^{mlem2}(\{4, 5, 6, 7, 8\}) = \{5, 6, 8\},$$

$$appr_{0.5}^{mlem2}(\{4, 5, 6, 7, 8\}) = \{2, 5, 6, 7, 8\},$$

$$appr_{0.333}^{mlem2}(\{4, 5, 6, 7, 8\}) = U.$$

3.2 Saturated Probabilistic Approximations

Saturated probabilistic approximation are unions of generalized maximal consistent blocks while giving higher priority to generalized maximal consistent blocks with larger conditional probability $Pr(X|Y)$. Additionally, if the approximation covers all cases from the concept X, we stop adding generalized maximal consistent blocks.

Let X be a concept and let $x \in U$. Let us compute all conditional probabilities $Pr(X|Z)$, where $Z \in \{Y \mid Y \subseteq \mathscr{C}(A), Pr(X|Y) \geq \alpha\}$. Then we sort the set

$$\{Pr(X|Y) \mid Y \subseteq \mathscr{C}(A)\}$$

in descending order. Let us denote the sorted list of such conditional probabilities by α_1, α_2,..., α_n. For any $i = 1, 2,..., n$, the set $E_i(X)$ is defined as follows

$$\{Y \mid Y \subseteq \mathscr{C}(A), Pr(X|Y) = \alpha_i\}.$$

If we want to compute a saturated probabilistic approximation, denoted by $appr_{\alpha}^{saturated}(X)$, for some α, $0 < \alpha \leq 1$, we need to identify the index m such that

$$\alpha_m \geq \alpha > \alpha_{m+1},$$

where $m \in \{1, 2, ..., n\}$ and $\alpha_{n+1} = 0$. The saturated probabilistic approximation $appr_{\alpha_m}^{saturated}(X)$ is computed using the following algorithm

Saturated probabilistic approximation algorithm
input: a set X (a concept), a set $E_i(X)$ for $i = 1, 2,..., n$, index m
output: a set T (a saturated probabilistic approximation $appr_{\alpha_m}^{saturated}(X)$) of X
begin
    $T := \emptyset$;
    $\mathscr{Y}_i(X) := E_i(X)$ for all $i = 1, 2,..., m$;
    for $j = 1, 2,..., m$ **do**
        while $\mathscr{Y}_j(X) \neq \emptyset$
            begin
                select a generalized maximal consistent block $Y \in \mathscr{Y}_j(X)$
                such that $|X \cap Y|$ is maximum;
                if a tie occurs, select the first Y;
                $\mathscr{Y}_j(X) := \mathscr{Y}_j(X) - Y$;
                if $(Y - T) \cap X \neq \emptyset$
                    then $T := T \cup Y$;
                if $X \subseteq T$ **then exit**
            end
end

For Table 1, any saturated probabilistic approximation for $[(\textit{Trip}, \textit{yes})]$ is the same as corresponding global probabilistic approximation for the same concept.

3.3 Rule Induction

In our experiments, we used the MLEM2 algorithm [9] for rule induction. MLEM2 uses a parameter β, also interpreted as a probability. The parameter β is used to control quality of induced rules. If a rule covers a subset Y of U and the rule indicates the concept X, the rule is produced by the rule induction system if $Pr(X|Y) \geq \beta$.

4 Experiments

Eight data sets, available at the University of California at Irvine *Machine Learning Repository*, were used for our experiments. For every data set, a template was created. This template was formed by replacing randomly as many as possible specified attribute values by lost values. The maximum percentage of missing attribute values was restricted by the requirement that no row of the data set should contain only lost values. The same templates were used for constructing data sets with "do not care" conditions, by replacing "?"s with "*"s.

In our experiments, data sets with 35% of missing attribute values were used. The parameter α was equal to 0.5 in all experiments. Results of our experiments are presented in Figs. 1, 2, 3, 4, 5, 6, 7 and 8, where "MLEM2" denotes a MLEM2 global probabilistic approximation, "Saturated" denotes a saturated probabilistic approximation, "?" denotes lost values and "*" denotes "do not care" conditions. Four approaches for mining incomplete data sets were used in our experiments, since we combined two options of probabilistic approximations (global and saturated) with two interpretations of missing attribute values (lost values and "do not care" conditions). These four approaches were compared by applying the distribution free Friedman rank sum test and then by the post-hoc test (distribution-free multiple comparisons based on the Friedman rank sums), with a 5% level of significance. Results of statistical analysis are shown in Table 2.

As our results show, for lost values, for any β, an error rate associated with global approximations is the same as the error rate associated with saturated approximations. It is caused by the fact that for six data sets (*bankruptcy*, *echocardiogram*, *hepatitis*, *image segmentation*, *lymphography* and *wine recognition*, all generalized maximal consistent blocks are singletons (sets containing exactly one case). For remaining two data sets, *breast cancer* and *iris*, some generalized maximal consistent blocks are sets containing two or three cases, but such cases, from the same generalized maximal consistent block, always belong to the same concept.

There are only three conclusive results on a comparison of two probabilistic approximations, global and saturated: for "do not care" conditions and for *image segmentation* and *iris* data sets, the error rate is smaller for saturated probabilistic approximations than for global probabilistic approximations. On the other hand, for "do not care" conditions and *wine recognition* data set, it is the other way around.

Table 2. Results of statistical analysis

Data set	Friedman test results (5% significance level)
Bankruptcy	(MLEM2, ?) & (Sat., ?) are better than (MLEM2, *) & (Sat., *)
Breast cancer	(MLEM2, *) & (Sat., *) are better than (MLEM2, ?) & (Sat., ?)
Echocardiogram	(MLEM2, *) & (Sat., *) are better than (MLEM2, ?) & (Sat. ?)
Hepatitis	(MLEM2, *) & (Sat., *) are better than (MLEM2, ?) & (Sat., ?)
Image segment	(MLEM2, *) & (Sat., *) are better than (MLEM2, ?) & (Sat., ?)
	(Saturated, *) is better than (MLEM2, *)
Iris	(MLEM2, ?) & (Saturated, ?) are better than (Saturated, *)
	(Saturated, *) is better than (MLEM2, *)
Lymphography	(MLEM2, ?) & (Sat. ?) are better than (MLEM2, *) & (Sat., *)
Wine recognition	(MLEM2, *) is better than (Saturated, *)
	(Saturated, *) is better than (MLEM2, ?) & (Sat. ?)

5 Conclusions

Four approaches for mining incomplete data sets (combining two interpretations of missing attribute values with two types of probabilistic approximations) were compared, using the error rate as the criterion of quality. Our experiments show that there are significant differences between the four approaches. However, the best approach, associated with the smallest error rate, depends on a specific data set. Thus the best approach should be selected by running experiments using all four approaches. Obviously, further experimental research, with more data sets, is required.

References

1. Clark, P.G., Gao, C., Grzymala-Busse, J.W., Mroczek, T.: Characteristic sets and generalized maximal consistent blocks in mining incomplete data. Proc. Int. Joint Conf. Rough Sets, Part **1**, 477–486 (2017)
2. Clark, P.G., Gao, C., Grzymala-Busse, J.W., Mroczek, T.: Characteristic sets and generalized maximal consistent blocks in mining incomplete data. Inf. Sci. **453**, 66–79 (2018)
3. Clark, P.G., Gao, C., Grzymala-Busse, J.W., Mroczek, T., Niemiec, R.: A comparison of concept and global probabilistic approximations based on mining incomplete data. In: Damaševičius, R., Vasiljevienė, G. (eds.) ICIST 2018. CCIS, vol. 920, pp. 324–335. Springer, Cham (2018). https://doi.org/10.1007/978-3-319-99972-2_26
4. Clark, P.G., Grzymala-Busse, J.W., Mroczek, T., Niemiec, R.: A comparison of global and saturated probabilistic approximations using characteristic sets in mining incomplete data. In: Proceedings of the Eight International Conference on Intelligent Systems and Applications, pp. 10–15 (2019)
5. Clark, P.G., Grzymala-Busse, J.W., Mroczek, T., Niemiec, R.: Rule set complexity in mining incomplete data using global and saturated probabilistic approximations. In: Proceedings of the 25-th International Conference on Information and Software Technologies, pp. 451–462 (2019)

6. Grzymala-Busse, J.W.: LERS–a system for learning from examples based on rough sets. In: Slowinski, R. (ed.) Intelligent Decision Support. Theory and Decision Library (Series D: System Theory, Knowledge Engineering and Problem Solving), vol 11. Springer, Dordrecht (1992) https://doi.org/10.1007/978-94-015-7975-9_1
7. Grzymala-Busse, J.W.: MLEM2: a new algorithm for rule induction from imperfect data. In: Proceedings of the 9th International Conference on Information Processing and Management of Uncertainty in Knowledge-Based Systems, pp. 243–250 (2002)
8. Grzymala-Busse, J.W.: Generalized parameterized approximations. In: Proceedings of the 6-th International Conference on Rough Sets and Knowledge Technology, pp. 136–145 (2011)
9. Grzymala-Busse, J.W., Clark, P.G., Kuehnhausen, M.: Generalized probabilistic approximations of incomplete data. Int. J. Approximate Reason. **132**, 180–196 (2014)
10. Grzymala-Busse, J.W., Rzasa, W.: Local and global approximations for incomplete data. In: Proceedings of the Fifth International Conference on Rough Sets and Current Trends in Computing, pp. 244–253 (2006)
11. Grzymala-Busse, J.W., Rzasa, W.: Local and global approximations for incomplete data. Trans. Rough Sets **8**, 21–34 (2008)
12. Grzymala-Busse, J.W., Ziarko, W.: Data mining based on rough sets. In: Wang, J. (ed.) Data Mining: Opportunities and Challenges, pp. 142–173. Idea Group Publ, Hershey, PA (2003)
13. Leung, Y., Wu, W., Zhang, W.: Knowledge acquisition in incomplete information systems: a rough set approach. Eur. J. Oper. Res. **168**, 164–180 (2006)
14. Pawlak, Z., Skowron, A.: Rough sets: some extensions. Inf. Sci. **177**, 28–40 (2007)
15. Pawlak, Z., Wong, S.K.M., Ziarko, W.: Rough sets: probabilistic versus deterministic approach. Int. J. Man-Mach. Stud. **29**, 81–95 (1988)
16. Ślęzak, D., Ziarko, W.: The investigation of the bayesian rough set model. Int. J. Approximate Reason. **40**, 81–91 (2005)
17. Wong, S.K.M., Ziarko, W.: INFER–an adaptive decision support system based on the probabilistic approximate classification. In: Proceedings of the 6-th International Workshop on Expert Systems and their Applications, pp. 713–726 (1986)
18. Yao, Y.Y.: Probabilistic rough set approximations. Int. J. Approximate Reason. **49**, 255–271 (2008)
19. Yao, Y.Y., Wong, S.K.M.: A decision theoretic framework for approximate concepts. Int. J. Man-Mach. Stud. **37**, 793–809 (1992)
20. Ziarko, W.: Variable precision rough set model. J. Comput. Syst. Sci. **46**(1), 39–59 (1993)
21. Ziarko, W.: Probabilistic approach to rough sets. Int. J. Approximate Reason. **49**, 272–284 (2008)

Evaluation of Error Metrics for Meta-learning Label Definition in the Forecasting Task

Moisés R. Santos(✉), Leandro R. Mundim, and André C. P. L. F. Carvalho

Institute of Mathematics and Computer Sciences,
University of São Paulo, São Carlos, Brazil
mmrsantos@usp.br, leandroresendemundim@gmail.com, andre@icmc.usp.br

Abstract. Meta-learning has been successfully applied to time series forecasting. For such, it uses meta-datasets created by previous machine learning applications. Each row in a meta-dataset represents a time series dataset. Each row, apart from the last, is meta-feature describing aspects of the related dataset. The last column is a target value, a meta-label. Here, the meta-label is the forecasting model with the best predictive performance for a specific error metric. In the previous studies applying meta-learning to time series forecasting, error metrics have been arbitrarily chosen. We believe that the error metric used can affect the results obtained by meta-learning. This study presents an experimental analysis of the predictive performance obtained by using different error metrics for the definition of the meta-label value. The experiments performed used 100 time series collected from the ICMC time series prediction open access repository, which has time series from a large variety of application domains. A traditional meta-learning framework for time series forecasting was used in this work. According to the experimental results, the mean absolute error can be the best metric for meta-label definition.

Keywords: Meta-learning · Meta-label · Error metrics · Time series

1 Introduction

Time series are usually represented by a sequence of data points collected along with the time [8]. One of the main tasks in time series analysis is forecasting, the prediction of the occurrence of future events [24]. Time series forecasting is a crucial task of data analysis in many domains, such as finance, industry, government, health, and environment.

One of the main challenges in time series forecasting is the selection of the technique able to induce the best forecasting model for a given time series. Several techniques have been proposed, each with its bias, favoring particular data distributions. Thus, to select the most suitable technique from a set of options, it is necessary to explore an ample search space of available forecasting techniques and depends on domain expert knowledge, which has a high cost

E. A. de la Cal et al. (Eds.): HAIS 2020, LNAI 12344, pp. 397–409, 2020.
https://doi.org/10.1007/978-3-030-61705-9_33

[2,21,27]. An alternative to reduce this cost is the use of meta-learning (MtL), which uses the knowledge obtained from past applications of machine learning (ML) algorithms in related tasks to create a predictive model able to recommend the most suitable technique(s) for a new dataset.

MtL has been successfully applied to algorithm recommendation and hyper-parameter selection [6,19,26,30,32]. Like in a conventional ML application, MtL applies a ML algorithm to a dataset, named meta-dataset. This learning process is called meta-level learning, to differ from the conventional learning process in ML, named base-level learning in the MtL literature. In the meta-dataset, each row represents a dataset and is labeled by either the ML algorithms performance applied to this dataset or by the forecasting model with the best predictive performance for a specific error metric. The predictive attributes in the meta-dataset are named meta-features. The values of the meta-features describe a dataset, highlighting important aspects that characterize the dataset. When an ML algorithm is applied to the meta-dataset, it induces a meta-model. Usually, the meta-model is a predictive model, which can be used, as part of a recommendation system, to predict the most suitable technique(s) for a new dataset. The ML algorithm used to induce the meta-model is named meta-learner.

Previous works have successfully applied in time series forecasting [1,3,15,16, 27,33]. However, in these works, the error metric as meta-label was arbitrarily defined, not considering other error metrics.

We believe that the error metric used can affect how well MtL works. This study evaluates the error metrics performance when used for the meta-label definition for several types of meta-learners. For such, we carried out experiments using a set of time series datasets collected from the ICMC time series datasets repository [25][1]. In the experimental analysis, we also look at the computational cost of each error metric used.

As base-learners, we used state of the art time series forecasting techniques [18], based on ML and statistics: Autoregressive Integrated Moving Average (ARIMA) [5], state space exponential smoothing (ETS) [10], and neural networks autoregressive (NNAR) [22]. The meta-dataset was created extracting 23 meta-features based on basic statistics, statistical tests for time series, partial and autocorrelations function coefficients and frequency domain measures. For the meta-labels, the following error metrics were assessed: Mean Absolute Error (MAE), Mean Squared Error (MSE), Median Absolute Error (MedAE), Symmetric Mean Absolute Percentual Error (sMAPE), and Mean Absolute Scaled Error (MASE) [13]. The ML algorithms used to induce the meta-models were: K-Nearest Neighbors, Decision Tree, Random Forest, and Multilayer Perceptron. More information about these techniques can be found in [20].

2 Time Series Forecasting

Given a time series $Y = y_1, y_2, ..., y_t$ and a forecasting horizon h, a time series forecasting model estimates the Y subsequent values y_{t+h}. Regarding h, the

[1] Datasets are available here.

time series forecasting can be classified as one-step ahead or multi-step ahead. One-step ahead forecasting is the prediction of the time series subsequent value, where $h = 1$. Multi-step forecasting predicts many steps into the future, where $h > 1$ [24]. This work focuses on the one-step forecasting. Time series forecasting can follow a univariate or multivariate approach. The first uses historical values of a single time series to predict future values. The second use, simultaneously, historical values of multiple time series [31]. Next, we present the main techniques used to induce models for time series forecasting.

2.1 Autoregressive Integrated Moving Average

Autoregressive Integrated Moving Average (ARIMA) models [5] are widely used for time series forecasting. The autoregressive component builds the interest variable prediction as a linear combination of p previous values. The moving average component is modeled as an error ϵ average of q previous values to predict the value of the variable of interest. The integrated component of ARIMA models is the inverse of differentiation [11]. ARIMA models can be generically described to Eq. 1.

$$y'_t = c + \phi_1 y'_{t-1} + ... + \phi_p y'_{t-p} + \theta_1 \epsilon_{t-1} + ... + \theta_q \epsilon_{t-q} + \epsilon_t \quad (1)$$

where y is the differenced time series, ϕ, and θ are the coefficients of autoregressive and moving average models, respectively, p and q are the model degrees. For simplicity, we can denote an ARIMA model as ARIMA(p, d, q), where p is the autoregressive part degree, d is the differentiation degree, and q is the moving average part degree.

2.2 Exponential Smoothing State-Space Model

Exponential smoothing models are based on time series decomposition in a seasonal s and a trend t components. The trend component t can be expressed as a linear combination of a level term l and a growth term b [10]. A general state-space model is described by Eqs. 2 and 3.

$$y_t = w(x_{t-1}) + r(x_{t-1})\epsilon_t \quad (2)$$

$$x_t = f(x_{t-1}) + g(x_{t-1})\epsilon_t \quad (3)$$

where ϵ_t is a Gaussian white noise process and $x_t = (l_t, b_t, s_t, s_{t-1}, ..., s_{t-m+1})'$.

2.3 Neural Network Autoregression

Neural networks are ML algorithms inspired in the human brain, specifically in the processing and interaction between neurons [9]. Although there are several neural network architectures, the neural networks autoregressive (NNAR) [22] is the most straightforward for time series forecasting. An NNAR is usually represented as NNAR(p, k), where p is previous inputs in a time series, and k is the number of neurons in the hidden layer. The NNAR weights are originally adjusted by the backpropagation algorithm. Given a NNAR(p, k) and a time series y. The values of output are given by Eq. 4.

$$y_t = f(\sum_{j=1}^{k} w_j f(\sum_{i=1}^{p} w_{ij} x_i + b_{0j}) + b_0) \quad (4)$$

where w are the weights associated to neurons, $x = y_{t-p}, ..., y_{t-1}$ is a set of lagged input and b is the bias, which work like a intercept component of linear equations for make neural networks most robust.

3 Meta-learning for Forecasting Model Recommendation

Among other implications, according to the "*no free lunch*" theorem [34], there is no technique that provides the best model for every dataset. This motivates the use of MtL for algorithm recommendation. Formally, given a set of problem instances P represented by a distribution of datasets D, a set of algorithms A and a performance metric m: $P \times A \rightarrow \mathbb{R}$, the algorithm recommendation problem consists of finding a mapping f: $P \rightarrow A$ that optimizes the expected performance measure regarding m for instances P with a distribution D [28]. Figure 1 illustrates a architecture of a MtL based recommendation system for time series forecasting inspired on [27] and [15].

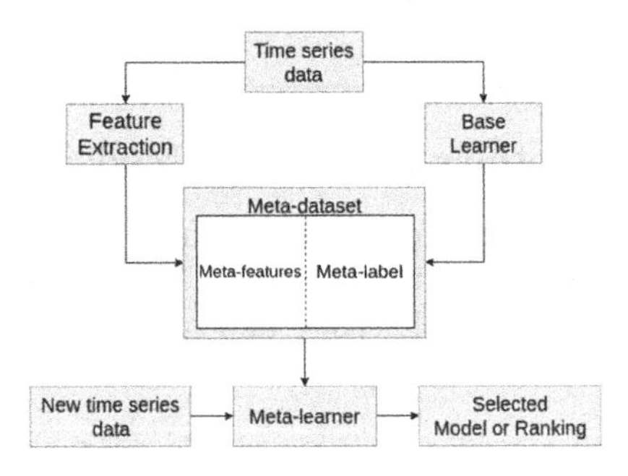

Fig. 1. MtL based recommendation system architecture

According to this figure, the MtL based model selection process can be described by its components. For such, it uses a meta-dataset from time series data where each meta-example represents a dataset by the values of meta-features (FE) extracted from the dataset and the predictive performance of different techniques, or the technique(s) with the best performance when applied to this dataset (BL). An ML algorithm can be applied to the meta-dataset, as a conventional ML experiment, to extract a predictive meta-model able to recommend, e.g., the most suitable technique for a new time series dataset.

4 Experimental Setup

4.1 Time Series Data

The experiments carried out used 100 time series datasets from the ICMC time series prediction repository [25]. These time series include synthetic, chaotic, real-world series, from several domains. These time series were selected to present explicitly open policy and domain diversity necessary for MtL.

4.2 Meta-features

To create the meta-dataset, we extracted from the 100 time series datasets 23 meta-features, divided in four groups:

- **Basic statistics**: length [15], minimum [15], maximum [15], mean [15], median [15], standard deviation [15], range [15], skewness [15], kurtosis [15], variation coefficient [27], upper quartile [15], lower quartile [15], turning points [27], trend [27];
- **Statistical tests**: Spearman correlation coefficient [15], Mann-Kendall trend test [15], Kruskal–Wallis test [15], Durbin-Watson test [15];
- **Autocorrelation**: lags one and two of autocorrelation function [27], lags one and two of partial autocorrelation function [11];
- **Frequency domain**: real part of the Fast Fourier Transform (FFT) maximum value [27].

4.3 Base-Learners

The base learners used are implemented in the R package "*forecast*" [12]. This package includes several techniques to induce forecasting models, such as ARIMA, ETS, and NNAR, which are briefly described next.

- **ARIMA**: produces automatically tuned ARIMA models for univariate time series data. The implementation used in this work was *auto.arima*;
- **ETS**: produces an automatic exponential smoothing state-space model. The implementation *ets* was used;
- **NNAR**: trains feed-forward neural networks NNAR with one hidden layer for univariate time series forecasting. After several tests, we decided to use 25 neurons in the hidden layer. For the normalization of the time series input, we applied the Box-Cox transformation from *nnetar* to the datasets.

4.4 Error Metrics Meta-label

The meta-model recommends, for new time series datasets, the most suitable techniques according to specific error metric, the meta-label. This study investigates how the error metric used affects the recommendations from the meta-model. As five error metrics were investigated, five meta-datasets were created, each one using a different error metric to define the meta-label values.

Given y, the test time series values, $\hat{y}$ are predicted values and n the test set length. The error metrics investigated in this work were:

- **Mean Absolute Error (MAE) Equation** 5: magnitude of prediction errors;
- **Mean Squared Error (MSE) Equation** 6: average squared of prediction errors;
- **Median Absolute Error (MedAE) Equation** 7: median magnitude of prediction errors;
- **Symmetric Mean Absolute Percentage Error (sMAPE) Equation** 8: percentage absolute difference of predictions errors. This is symmetric due to original MAPE not work for test set values close to zero [33].
- **Mean Absolute Scaled Error (MASE) Equation** 9: scales the errors based on MAE from the naive forecast method. This naive forecast method defines prediction value as the one-step past value.

$$MAE = \frac{\sum_{i=1}^{n} |y_i - \hat{y}_i|}{n} \tag{5}$$

$$MSE = \frac{\sum_{i=1}^{n} (y_i - \hat{y}_i)^2}{n} \tag{6}$$

$$MedAE = median(|y_i - \hat{y}_i|) \tag{7}$$

$$sMAPE = \frac{100}{n} \sum_{i=1}^{n} \frac{|y_i - \hat{y}_i|}{|y_i| + |\hat{y}_i|} \tag{8}$$

$$MASE = mean\left(\left|\frac{|y_i - \hat{y}_i|}{\frac{1}{n-1}\sum_{i=2}^{n} |y_i - y_{i-1}|}\right|\right) \tag{9}$$

4.5 Meta-learner

The following meta-learners were used for the experiments carried out in this study. They were selected to cover different learning biases.

- **K-Nearest Neighbors (KNN)**: simple technique based on lazy learning. We used the *caret* [14] R package;
- **Decision Tree induction algorithm (DT)**: Induce decision trees using divide and conquer. We used the Classification And Regression Trees (CART) algorithm [7] implementation in the *rpart* R package.
- **Random Forest (RF)**: ensemble technique that induces a set decision tree classifiers on various dataset sub-samples. The implementation used was from the *randomForest* [17] R package.
- **Multilayer Perceptron (MLP)**: fully connected feedforward artificial neural networks. The implementation came from the *RSNNS* [4] R package.

4.6 Meta-Level Evaluation

The experiments with the 100 time series datasets generated meta-datasets. For the meta-learning experiments, each meta-dataset was divided into training (80%) and test subsets (20%), keeping the class proportion. The MtL experiments partitioned the meta-dataset using Leave-One-Out (LOO). For KNN and MLP, the predictive attributes were centralized and scaled to unit variance.

Hyperparameters specific to each technique were tuned using the *caret* [14] basic hyperparameter tuning technique, with at most 10 tuning interactions: value of k for the KNN technique, complexity for DT, number of variables sampled as a candidate at each split for RF, and number of hidden layer neurons for MLP with a one-hidden layer. The meta-models induced by each technique had their predictive performance assessed using accuracy, as in the related works found in the literature. Each experiment was repeated 30 times, and the Friedman rank sum statistical hypothesis and Nemenyi, multiple comparison post hoc tests, were applied to all results with a p-value < 0.05. The Intel Math Kernel Library for R code was used for performance optimization.

4.7 Forecasting Level Evaluation

The labels predicted for the test data in the meta-level experiment were used for the experimental analyses at the base level. The meta-level predictive performance was measured by the mean and standard deviation of the results obtained by all the meta-learners. Thus, the focus of the first analysis is on the meta-level, i.e., the predictive performance of the recommendation framework.

On the forecasting level, the evaluation focus on whether the MtL use improves the predictive performance of forecasting techniques when compared with the use of a baseline. In this study, the baseline is the average of the predictive performance obtained by the forecasting techniques. Due to intuitive interpretation of the number of times a technique was better than others, Percentage Better (PB) [29], described by Eqs. 10 and 11, is used.

$$PB = \frac{1}{m}\sum_{j=1}^{n}\delta_j \tag{10}$$

$$\begin{cases} \delta_j = 1 & \text{if } |e_j^R| \leq |e_j| \\ \delta_j = 0, & \text{otherwise} \end{cases} \tag{11}$$

In these equations, δ is incremented when the magnitude of reference error is less than or equal to the magnitude of the MtL predicted error. The variable m is the number of times that these errors are different. Thus, when PB is close to 0, the MtL prediction is better than the reference (baseline), when close to 50, it is similar, and when more than 50, it is worse.

4.8 Time Complexity Analysis of the Error Metrics

For time complexity analysis, the "microbenchmark" R package [23] was used. Error metrics are tested with two synthetic arrays with a length of 10^2 and run 10 times.

5 Experimental Results

The previous section described the experimental setup adopted to compare the error metrics performance for meta-label prediction in univariate one-step ahead time series forecasting. This section presents the main experimental results. These results aim to answer the two fundamental questions of this study:

1. Does the MtL predictive performance varies for different meta-learners and distinct error metrics?
2. Among the error metrics with the best results for MtL, for each meta-learner, is there any difference in time complexity?

This section presents the results for the MAE, sMAPE, and MASE error metrics for the meta-target selection. Figures 2, 3, and 4 shown the results obtained.

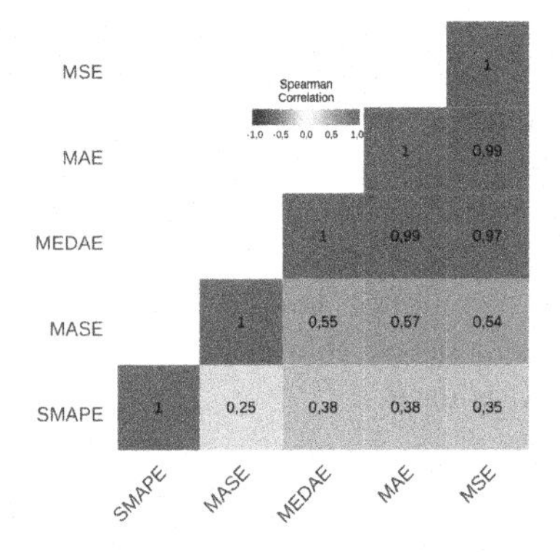

Fig. 2. ARIMA Spearman corr.

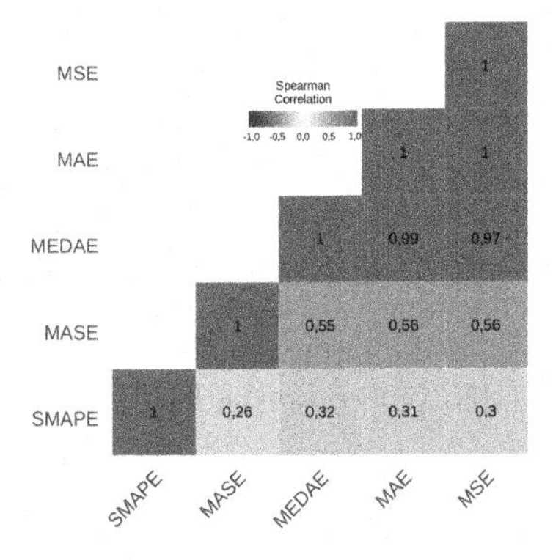

Fig. 3. ETS Spearman corr.

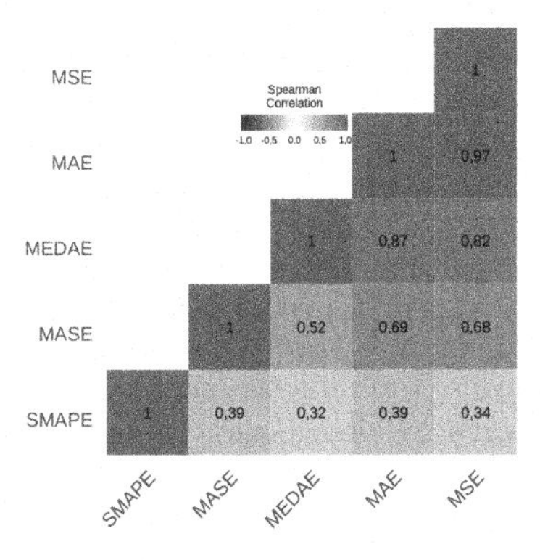

Fig. 4. NNAR Spearman corr.

These results show that the results for MedAE and MSE error metrics are redundant since there is a strong Spearman correlation with the MAE measurements for three meta-learners.

5.1 Meta-learner Performance for Meta-label Error Metrics

KNN Performance for Meta-label Error Metrics: Figs. 5 and 6 show the KNN meta-learner performance for each error metric used, in the meta and the forecasting level, respectively. On average, the MAE metric presented the best performance in the meta and forecasting levels. However, for both levels, there is no statistically significant difference between MAE and MASE.

DT Performance for Meta-label Error Metrics: Figs. 7 and 8 show the DT meta-learner performance for each error metric used in the meta-label definition in the meta-level and in the forecasting level, respectively. The sMAPE metric presented a better performance in the meta-level, but without significant difference regarding MAE and MASE. For the base level, the best performance was obtained by the MASE metric.

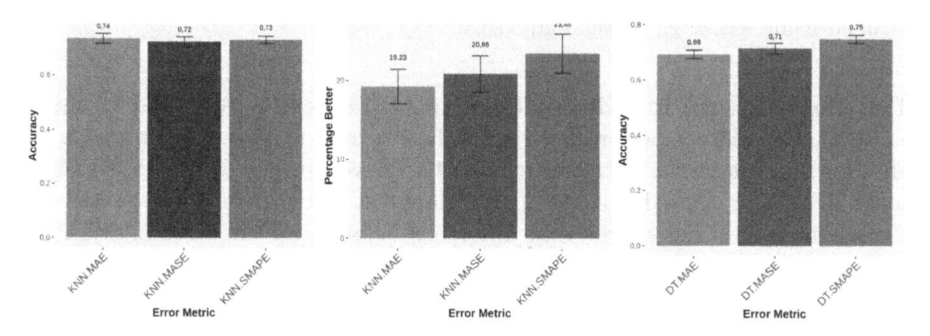

Fig. 5. Accuracy KNN

Fig. 6. PB KNN

Fig. 7. Accuracy DT

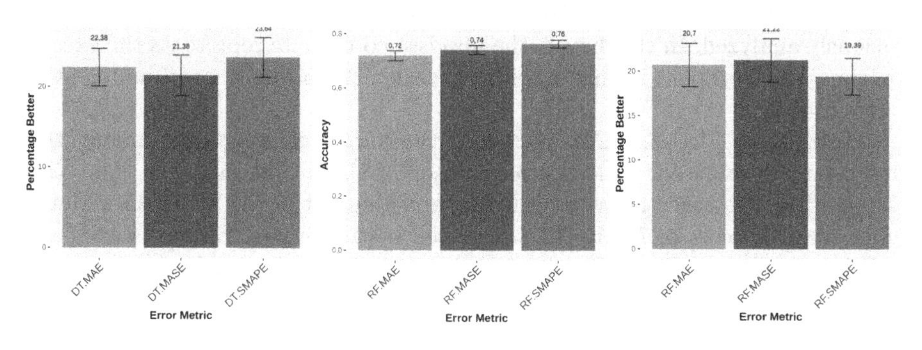

Fig. 8. PB DT

Fig. 9. Accuracy RF

Fig. 10. PB RF

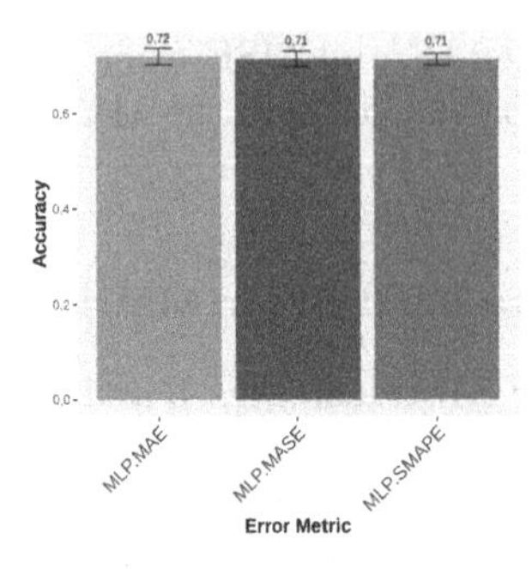

Fig. 11. Accuracy MLP

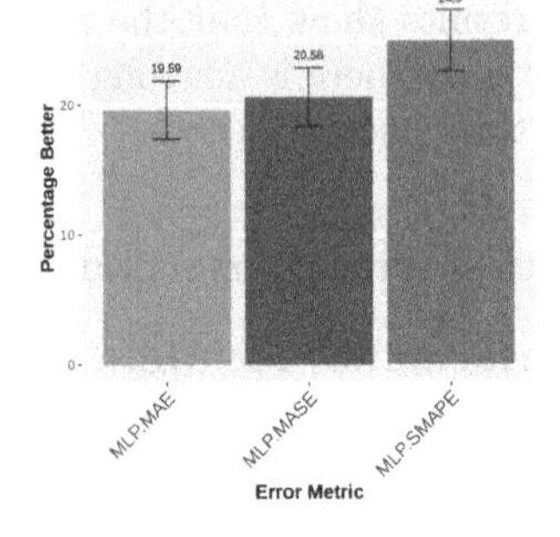

Fig. 12. PB MLP

RF Performance for Meta-label Error Metrics: Figs. 9 and 10 show the RF meta-learner performance for each error metric used in the meta-label definition in the meta and in the forecasting level, respectively. The sMAPE metric presents a superior performance on average in the meta and forecasting levels. The meta-level has no statistically relevant difference for all metrics. In the forecasting level, we did not observe a statistical difference between the results obtained using sMAPE, MAE, and MASE.

MLP Performance for Meta-label Error Metrics: Figs. 11 and 12 show the MLP meta-learner performance for each error metric used in the meta-label definition, for the meta-level and for the base level, respectively. On average, the MAE metric showed the best performance at both these levels. However, in these meta-level has no relevant difference between all the error metrics. In the forecasting level, has no significant difference between the MAE and MASE metrics.

5.2 Time Complexity Evaluation

Figure 13 shows the boxplot of the time complexity of the three error metrics previously analyzed. In this figure, the abscissa coordinate represents the execution time (milliseconds) in the logarithmic scale. The ordinate coordinate is the error metric.

According to Fig. 13, MAE presented the lowest running time among the error metrics evaluated. In terms of analysis of the average relative time, the cost of sMAPE is twice the cost of MAE, and the cost of MASE is three times higher than the cost of MAE. This occurred because sMAPE, and MASE are MAE-based metrics. Thus, they have more operations than MAE, making their computational cost higher.

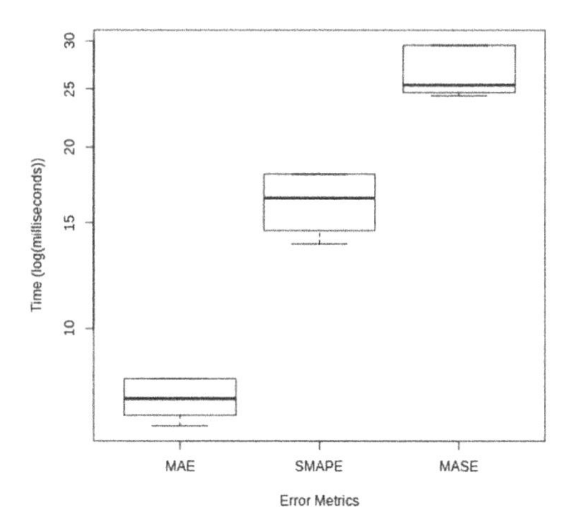

Fig. 13. Error metrics time complexity

6 Conclusion

This study evaluates the effect of predictive performance metrics on the recommendation of time series forecasting techniques using MtL. According to the experimental results, Regarding the error metrics MAE, sMAPE, and MASE, Mtl produced the best predictive performance, when compared with a baseline, for all tested scenarios.

For most of the meta-learners, the MAE metric presented, on average, the best predictive performance, despite being the metric with the lowest cost. In the time complexity analysis, the MAE obtained the best performance when compared with the error metrics. Thus, MAE should be used in scenarios requiring low computational costs without performance loss.

A limitation of this work is the low number of meta-examples in the meta-dataset. Although this fact did not impair the MtL process in our experiments, a larger meta-dataset would provide more significant experimental results. Thus, for the future, we want to increase the size of the meta-dataset. Another future work directions are to include meta-features that extract other aspects of time series and to investigate the effect of meta-feature selection on the MtL performance.

Acknowledgments. This study was partially funded by the Fundação de Amparo à Pesquisa do Estado de São Paulo (FAPESP) - Process 2019/10012-2 and Intel Inc.

References

1. Ali, A.R., Gabrys, B., Budka, M.: Cross-domain meta-learning for time-series forecasting. Procedia Comput. Sci. **126**, 9–18 (2018)

2. Armstrong, J.S.: Combining forecasts. In: Armstrong J.S. (eds) Principles of Forecasting. International Series in Operations Research & Management Science, vol 30. Springer, Boston, MA (2001) https://doi.org/10.1007/978-0-306-47630-3_19
3. Barak, S., Nasiri, M., Rostamzadeh, M.: Time series model selection with a meta-learning approach: evidence from a pool of forecasting algorithms. arXiv preprint arXiv:1908.08489 (2019)
4. Bergmeir, C.N., et al.: Neural networks in r using the stuttgart neural network simulator: RSNNS. J. Stat. Softw. (2012)
5. Box, G.E., Jenkins, G.M., Reinsel, G.C., Ljung, G.M.: Time Series Analysis: Forecasting and Control. John Wiley & Sons (2015)
6. Brazdil, P., Carrier, C.G., Soares, C., Vilalta, R.: Metalearning: Applications to data mining. Cognitive Technologies. Springer Science & Business Media, Springer-Verlag Berlin Heidelberg (2008). https://doi.org/10.1007/978-3-540-73263-1
7. Breiman, L., Friedman, J.H., Olshen, R.A., Stone, C.J.: Classification and Regression Trees. CRC Press Book, Monterey, CA (1984)
8. Cryer, J.D., Chan, K.S.: Time Series Analysis: With Applications in R, 2nd edn. Springer Texts in Statistics, Springer (2008). https://doi.org/10.1007/978-0-387-75959-3
9. Haykin, S.: Neural Networks: A Comprehensive Foundation. Prentice Hall PTR (1994)
10. Hyndman, R., Koehler, A.B., Ord, J.K., Snyder, R.D.: Forecasting with exponential smoothing: the state space approach. Springer Series in Statistics. Springer Science & Business Media, Springer-Verlag Berlin Heidelberg (2008). https://doi.org/10.1007/978-3-540-71918-2
11. Hyndman, R.J., Athanasopoulos, G.: Forecasting: Principles and Practice. OTexts (2018)
12. Hyndman, R.J., et al.: Automatic Time Series for Forecasting: The Forecast Package for R. Monash University, Department of Econometrics and Business Statistics. (2007)
13. Hyndman, R.J., et al.: Another look at forecast-accuracy metrics for intermittent demand. Foresight Int. J. Appl. Forecast. **4**(4), 43–46 (2006)
14. Kuhn, M.: The caret package. R Found. Stat. Comput. Vienna, Austria. https://cran.r-project.org/package=caret (2012)
15. Kück, M., Crone, S.F., Freitag, M.: Meta-learning with neural networks and landmarking for forecasting model selection an empirical evaluation of different feature sets applied to industry data. In: 2016 International Joint Conference on Neural Networks (IJCNN) (2016)
16. Lemke, C., Gabrys, B.: Meta-learning for time series forecasting and forecast combination. Neurocomput. **73**(10–12), 2006–2016 (2010)
17. Liaw, A., Wiener, M.: Classification and regression by randomforest. R News. **2**(3), 18–22 (2002). https://CRAN.R-project.org/doc/Rnews/
18. Makridakis, S., Spiliotis, E., Assimakopoulos, V.: Statistical and machine learning forecasting methods: concerns and ways forward. PloS one **13**(3), e0194889 (2018)
19. Mantovani, R.G., Rossi, A.L.D., Alcobaça, E., Vanschoren, J., de Carvalho, A.C.P.L.F.: A meta-learning recommender system for hyperparameter tuning: Predicting when tuning improves SVM classifiers. Inf. Sci. **501**, 193–221 (2019)
20. Marsland, S.: Machine Learning: An Algorithmic Perspective. Chapman and Hall/CRC (2014)
21. Meade, N.: Evidence for the selection of forecasting methods. J. Forecast. **19**(6), 515–535 (2000)

22. Medeiros, M.C., Teräsvirta, T., Rech, G.: Building neural network models for time series: a statistical approach. J. Forecast. **25**(1), 49–75 (2006)
23. Mersmann, O., et al.: Microbenchmark: accurate timing functions. R Package Version **1**(4–2), 1 (2015)
24. Montgomery, D.C., Johnson, L.A., Gardiner, J.S.: Forecasting and Time Series Analysis. McGraw-Hill Companies (1990)
25. Parmezan, A.R.S., Batista, G.E.A.P.A.: ICMC-USP time series prediction repository. Instituto de Ciências Matemáticas e de Computa cao, Universidade de Sao Paulo, Sao Carlos, Brasil (2014) https://goo.gl/uzxGZJ
26. Pimentel, B.A., de Carvalho, A.C.P.L.F.: A new data characterization for selecting clustering algorithms using meta-learning. Inf. Sci. **477**, 203–219 (2019)
27. Prudêncio, R.B., Ludermir, T.B.: Meta-learning approaches to selecting time series models. Neurocomput. **61**, 121–137 (2004)
28. Rice, J.R.: The algorithm selection problem. Adv. Comput. **15**, 65–118 (1976)
29. Shah, C.: Model selection in univariate time series forecasting using discriminant analysis. Int. J. Forecast. **13**(4), 489–500 (1997)
30. Feres de Souza, B., Soares, C., de Carvalho, A.C.: Meta-learning approach to gene expression data classification. Int. J. Intell. Comput. Cybern. **2**(2), 285–303 (2009)
31. Tsay, R.S.: Multivariate Time Series Analysis: with R and Financial Applications. John Wiley & Sons (2013)
32. Vilalta, R., Drissi, Y.: A perspective view and survey of meta-learning. Artif. Intell. Rev. **18**(2), 77–95 (2002)
33. Widodo, A., Budi, I.: Model selection using dimensionality reduction of time series characteristics. In: International Symposium on Forecasting, Seoul, South Korea (2013)
34. Wolpert, D.H.: The lack of a priori distinctions between learning algorithms. Neural Comput. **8**(7), 1341–1390 (1996)

Averaging-Based Ensemble Methods for the Partial Label Ranking Problem

Juan C. Alfaro[1,3(✉)], Juan A. Aledo[2,3], and José A. Gámez[1]

[1] Departamento de Sistemas Informáticos, Universidad de Castilla-La Mancha, Albacete, Spain
{JuanCarlos.Alfaro,Jose.Gamez}@uclm.es
[2] Departamento de Matemáticas, Universidad de Castilla-La Mancha, Albacete, Spain
JuanAngel.Aledo@uclm.es
[3] Laboratorio de Sistemas Inteligentes y Minería de Datos, Instituto de Investigación en Informática de Albacete, Albacete, Spain

Abstract. Label Ranking (LR) is a well-known non-standard supervised classification problem, with the goal of inducing preference models able to predict a ranking (permutation) over a finite set of labels from datasets in which the instances are explicitly labelled with (possibly) incomplete rankings. In this work, we focus on the Partial Label Ranking (PLR) problem, a more general approach of the LR problem that allows tied labels (i.e., there is no particular preference among them) in both, the training dataset and the prediction given as output. The main contributions of this paper are: (i) to use unsupervised discretization techniques (equal-frequency and equal-width) to heuristically (but fast) select the threshold for numerical features, and (ii) to apply averaging-based ensembles (Bagging and Random Forests) to improve the robustness of these decision trees. From the experimental results, we can conclude that the ensembles are better (in terms of accuracy) than the nearest neighbors based-method (IBPLR). Also, they are competitive in efficiency (CPU time) when the decision trees are built with the unsupervised discretization techniques.

Keywords: Supervised classification · Label ranking problem · Partial label ranking problem · Decision trees · Ensembles

1 Introduction

Preference Learning [17] is the branch of *Machine Learning* [25] that focuses on learning *preference models* from a training dataset containing past information about the preferences of some individuals, and the *Label Ranking* (*LR*) *problem* [10] study this field from the *data mining* perspective. The LR problem consists in learning a preference model that maps unlabelled instances to *permutations* (a.k.a. *rankings*) defined over a finite set of *labels*, given the value of the *predictive variables* (a.k.a. *features*).

E. A. de la Cal et al. (Eds.): HAIS 2020, LNAI 12344, pp. 410–423, 2020.
https://doi.org/10.1007/978-3-030-61705-9_34

Formally, the goal of the LR problem is to learn a preference model $\mathcal{M}$ from a training dataset $\mathbf{D} = \{(x_1^j, \ldots, x_m^j, \pi^j)\}_{j=1}^N$, where N is the number of instances, $\mathbf{x} = (x_1^j, \ldots, x_m^j) \in dom(X_1) \times dom(X_m)$ is a configuration of values over m predictive variables and π^j is a ranking of the values in $dom(Y) = \{y^1, \ldots, y^n\}$, where Y is the *class variable*. Furthermore, the preference model $\mathcal{M}$ should generalize well on unseen data. Let us suppose that a preference model recommends *(Ma)thematics* $\prec$ *(C)omputer (S)cience* $\prec$ *(Bi)ology* $\prec$ *(Me)dicine* to a student with programming skills and mathematics as favourite subject. Cheng et al. in [10] designed two machine learning algorithms for dealing with the LR problem, one based on the *nearest neighbors paradigm* [12] (*Instance Based Label Ranking, IBLR*) and other on *decision tree induction* [9] (*Label Ranking Trees, LRT*). In our previous example, assume that the students that most closely resemble our individual are

$$\begin{aligned} &Student\#1: \quad Ma \prec CS \prec Bi \prec Me \\ &Student\#2: \quad Ma \prec Bi \prec CS \prec Me \end{aligned}$$

It is clear that mathematics and medicine are, respectively, the most and the least preferred degrees, while there is no preference between computer science and biology, so they must be considered *tied*. Thus, the natural way to aggregate these two rankings into a *partial ranking* (a.k.a. *bucket order*) [19] becomes

$$Prediction: \quad Ma \prec CS \sim Bi \prec Me$$

In this work, we focus on the *Partial Label Ranking* (*PLR*) problem [4] with the aim of improving the predictive performance of the *Instance Based Partial Label Ranking* (*IBPLR*), and *Partial Label Ranking Trees* (*PLRT*) methods. To do that:

- We use *unsupervised discretization techniques* (*equal-frequency* and *equal-width*) to heuristically (but fast) select the threshold for numerical attributes [1].
- We build *ensembles* (*Bagging* [7] and *Random Forests* [8]) to improve the robustness and generalization of the decision trees. The experimental evaluation shows that the ensembles are better (in terms of accuracy) than the IBPLR algorithm, being also competitive in efficiency (CPU time) when the decision trees are built with the unsupervised discretization techniques.

The rest of the paper is organized as follows. In Sect. 2 we review some basic notions to deal with (partially) ranked data and briefly revise the LR problem, and the IBLR and LRT algorithms. In Sect. 3 we formally describe the PLR problem, and the IBPLR and PLRT algorithms, also detailing the unsupervised discretization techniques. In Sect. 4 we explain the ensemble techniques to use. In Sect. 5 we carry out an experimental study to assess the performance of the methods proposed in this work. Finally, in Sect. 6 we provide some conclusions and future research.

2 Background

In this section we review some basic concepts to deal with (partial) rankings, describe the LR problem and revise the IBLR and LRT algorithms, used to solve it. We must point out that, in this work, we cope only with datasets labelled with bucket orders, but our techniques can deal with datasets labelled with (possibly incomplete) partial rankings.

2.1 Rank Aggregation Problem

Given a set of items $[[n]] = \{1, \ldots, n\}$, a *ranking* π represents a precedence relation between them. In particular, the rankings can be *without ties* and *with ties*, depending on whether there is no particular preference between some of the ranked items. Formally, the set of permutations defined over $[[n]]$ is denoted by $\mathbb{P}_n$, and the set of bucket orders defined over $[[n]]$ is denoted by $\mathbb{B}_n$. Note that $\mathbb{P}_n \subset \mathbb{B}_n$. Given the items $u, v \in [[n]]$ and $\pi \in \mathbb{B}_n$, we write $u \prec_\pi v$ to indicate that the item u precedes the item v in π , and $u \sim_\pi v$ to indicate that u and v are tied in π.

The most well-known *Rank Aggregation Problem* (*RAP*) [23] is the *Kemeny Ranking Problem* (*KRP*) [21], which consists in obtaining the *consensus permutation* (*central permutation*) $\pi_0 \in \mathbb{P}_n$ that best represents a particular set of permutations. The *Borda count algorithm* [6] is the most used greedy method to tackle the KRP.

The *Mallows model* (or *Mallows probability distribution*) [24] is a distance-based probability distribution over permutations that belongs to the exponential family and it is parametrized by a *central permutation* $\pi_0 \in \mathbb{P}_n$ and a *spread parameter* $\theta \in [0, +\infty)$. Thus, the probability assigned to a permutation $\pi \in \mathbb{P}_n$ is

$$P(\pi; \pi_0, \theta) = \frac{e^{-\theta \cdot K(\pi, \pi_0)}}{\psi(\theta)} \tag{1}$$

where K is the *Kendall distance* [22] and $\psi(\theta)$ is a *normalization constant.* Observe that the spread parameter θ quantifies how quickly the probability decreases as the Kendall distance increases. Thus, for $\theta = 0$, a uniform distribution is obtained, while for $\theta \rightsquigarrow +\infty$, the distribution assigns the maximum probability (one) to π_0 and the minimum probability (zero) to the rest of permutations.

In this work, we deal with the *Optimal Bucket Order Problem* (*OBOP*) [19], a *distance-based* [11] RAP problem whose goal is to find the *bucket matrix* B_0 [19] associated with a bucket order $\pi_0 \in \mathbb{B}_n$ that minimizes

$$B_0 = argmin \sum_{u,v \in [[n]]} |B(u, v) - C(u, v)| \tag{2}$$

where C is a pair order matrix that summarizes the precedence relations of a particular set of bucket orders. There are several heuristic algorithms to solve the OBOP, and we use the *Bucket Pivot Algorithm with multiple pivots two-stages* (BPA_{LIA}^{MP2}) [2], due to its trade-off between accuracy and efficiency (CPU time).

2.2 Label Ranking Problem

The *Label Ranking (LR) problem* [10] consists in learning *preference models* [17] from a training dataset labelled with permutations, mapping unlabelled instances to permutations. Formally, given a set of m predictive features and a target class variable Y, a LR-Classifier is a model that assigns a permutation π of the values in $dom(Y)$ to any configuration of values $\mathbf{x}$. Thus, given a dataset $\mathbf{D}$, the LR prediction problem consists in learning a LR-Classifier that generalizes well on unseen data.

Instance Based Label Ranking (IBLR) [10]. It is based on the *k-nearest neighbors paradigm* and takes as input, an instance $\mathbf{x}$ to be classified and the number of nearest neighbors $k \in \mathbb{N}^+$, $k \leq N$, to be considered. Thus, the IBLR algorithm takes the k nearest neighbors of the input instance $\mathbf{x}$ in the training dataset $\mathbf{D}$, that is, $\mathbf{R} = \{x_i^j, \ldots, x_m^j, \pi^j\}_{j=1}^k$ and the permutations of these neighbors $\mathbf{R}_\Pi = \{\pi^j\}_{j=1}^k$. Then, the IBLR algorithm applies the Borda count algorithm to obtain the consensus permutation π_0 of the values in $dom(Y)$ returned as solution for the input instance $\mathbf{x}$.

Label Ranking Trees (LRT) [10]. It is based on the standard *decision tree induction principle* [9]. At each recursive call, the learning algorithm receives a set of instances $\mathbf{R} = \{x_i^j, \ldots, x_k^j, \pi^j\}_{j=1}^s$, with $k \leq m$ and $s \leq N$. Considering $\mathbf{R}_\Pi = \{\pi^j\}_{j=1}^s$ the permutations of the instances in $\mathbf{R}$, the LRT algorithm decides:

- Either to stop the recursive call and to create a leaf node. The branching stops if all the rankings are the same, or $s \leq 2n$. The consensus permutation π_0 of the values in $dom(Y)$ obtained from $\mathbf{R}_\Pi$ is assigned to the leaf node.
- Or to select an attribute for splitting the decision node. The attribute that most reduces the uncertainty is selected according to the spread parameter of the Mallows model, due to its resemblance with the variance. Thus, given an attribute X_i with $dom(X_i) = \{x_i^1, \ldots, x_i^r\}$, where $i \leq k$ and $r \leq s$, the uncertainty associated with a partition $\mathbf{R}_{X_i} = \{\mathbf{R}_j\}_{j=1}^r$ is inversely proportional to

$$g(X_i) = g(\mathbf{R}_{X_i}) = \sum_{j=1}^{r} \frac{|\mathbf{R}_j| \cdot \theta_j}{|\mathbf{R}|} \tag{3}$$

  where θ_j is the spread parameter of the Mallows model estimated from the permutations in $\mathbf{R}_j$ (see [20] for details). For a numerical attribute X_i, the LRT algorithm proceeds in the standard way, that is, taking a threshold t and considering the (discrete) attribute X_i^t as two-state, with $dom(X_i^t) = \{X_i \leq t, X_i > t\}$. To select the threshold t, all the (different) values in X_i are considered, and the one maximizing (3) is taken.

3 Partial Label Ranking Problem

In this section we delve in the PLR problem, and describe the IBPLR and PLRT algorithms. Also, we detail the unsupervised discretization techniques to heuristically (but fast) select the threshold for numerical attributes.

The goal of the *Partial Label Ranking* (*PLR*) problem [4] is to obtain preference models from a training dataset labelled with bucket orders, mapping unlabelled instances to bucket orders. Formally, given a set of m predictive features and a target class variable Y, a PLR-Classifier is a function that assigns a bucket order π of the values in $dom(Y)$ to any configuration of values $\mathbf{x}$. Thus, the PLR prediction problem consists in learning a PLR-Classifier that generalizes well on unseen data.

3.1 Instance Based Partial Label Ranking

The *Instance Based Partial Label Ranking* (*IBPLR*) *algorithm* [4] is an adaptation of the IBLR method to deal with the PLR problem. Given an instance x to be classified, the k nearest neighbors in the training dataset are identified and their bucket orders used to solve the OBOP problem, so obtaining the consensus bucket order returned as solution.

3.2 Partial Label Ranking Trees

The *Partial Label Ranking Trees* (*PLRT*) *algorithm* [4] is (partially) based on the LRT algorithm to tackle the PLR problem. The main difference is that it is not possible to use the spread parameter θ of the Mallows model to select the attribute that most reduces the uncertainty of a partition $\mathbf{R}$. Therefore, Alfaro et al. in [4] proposed to use an alternative ϕ of the spread parameter θ computed according to one of the following criteria:

- Disagreements. Given two bucket orders π, τ of the values in $dom(Y)$, there exists a disagreement between π and τ regarding two labels $y^u, y^v \in dom(Y)$ if either the relative order of these labels is different in π and τ, or if the labels are tied in one of the bucket order but not in the other one. Then, the ϕ parameter is set to the relative frequency of disagreements between the consensus bucket order obtained from the bucket orders in the partition and these bucket orders.

Example 1. Let us consider the set of bucket orders $\Pi = \{2 \sim 1 \prec 3, 1 \prec 3 \prec 2, 1 \prec 2 \sim 3, 2 \prec 1 \prec 3\}$ with associated bucket matrices

$$B_1 = \begin{pmatrix} 0.5 & 0.5 & 1 \\ 0.5 & 0.5 & 1 \\ 0 & 0 & 0.5 \end{pmatrix} \quad B_2 = \begin{pmatrix} 0.5 & 1 & 1 \\ 0 & 0.5 & 0 \\ 0 & 1 & 0.5 \end{pmatrix} \quad B_3 = \begin{pmatrix} 0.5 & 1 & 1 \\ 0 & 0.5 & 0.5 \\ 0 & 0.5 & 0.5 \end{pmatrix} \quad B_4 = \begin{pmatrix} 0.5 & 0 & 1 \\ 1 & 0.5 & 1 \\ 0 & 0 & 0.5 \end{pmatrix}$$

The consensus bucket order $\pi_0 = 1 \sim 2 \sim 3$ has associated bucket matrix B_0 and the ϕ parameter is computed with the disagreements criterion as:

$$B_0 = \begin{pmatrix} 0.5 & 0.5 & 0.5 \\ 0.5 & 0.5 & 0.5 \\ 0.5 & 0.5 & 0.5 \end{pmatrix} \qquad \phi = \frac{\overbrace{0.75}^{Pair\ (1,2)} + \overbrace{1}^{Pair\ (1,3)} + \overbrace{0.75}^{Pair\ (2,3)}}{3} = 0.833$$

- Distance. The ϕ parameter is set to the matrix distance (2) between the bucket matrix associated with the consensus bucket order obtained from the bucket orders in the partition, and the bucket matrices associated with these bucket orders.

Example 2. Let us consider the set of bucket orders (with the associated bucket matrices) and the consensus bucket order (with the associated bucket matrix) from Example 1. Thus, the ϕ parameter is computed with the distance criterion as

$$\phi = \frac{3 + 4 + 3}{3} = 3.333$$

- Entropy. The ϕ parameter is set to the averaged *Shannon entropy* [27] of the probability distribution given by the probability that a label y^u precedes, is tied and is ranked behind of a label y^v, for all (different) label pairs $y^u, y^v \in dom(Y)$. Note that this criterion does not consider the local solution to the OBOP to estimate the ϕ parameter.

Example 3. Let us consider the set of bucket orders from Example 1. Thus, the ϕ parameter is computed with the entropy criterion as

$$\phi = \frac{1.522 + 0.722 + 1.522}{3} = 1.255$$

Based on the work of Aledo et al. in [1], we propose to use the following *unsupervised discretization* techniques to heuristically (but fast) select the threshold for numerical attributes in the decision nodes:

- Equal width. The threshold t of a numerical attribute X_i is set to the value that divides the domain of X_i in two bins of equal width. That is, the mean of $range(X_i)$.
- Equal frequency. The threshold t of a numerical attribute X_i is set to the value that divides the domain of X_i in two bins containing (approximately) the same number of values. That is, the values of the attribute X_i are sorted and the median is taken.

4 Ensemble Methods

Ensemble methods typically consists in sampling b datasets $\mathbf{B} = \{\mathbf{B}_1, \ldots, \mathbf{B}_b\}$ from the original training dataset $\mathbf{D}$ to build classifiers $\mathbf{C} = \{\mathbf{C}_1, \ldots, \mathbf{C}_b\}$, and their output is later aggregated in some way.

In this paper we focus on *averaging-based ensembles*, where several (strong) classifiers (e.g., fully developed decision trees) are independently built and their predictions averaged to reduce the variance. In particular, we consider the PLRT algorithm to build the base classifiers, and *Bagging* [7] and *Random Forests* [8] as ensemble methods. As happens with supervised classification and the LR problem [1,28], we expect to obtain more robust algorithms regarding to accuracy and generalization capability.

Bagging [7]. It generates the new training datasets $\mathbf{B}$ by using sampling with replacement. Thus, given an input instance $\mathbf{x}$ to be classified, the output prediction for $\mathbf{x}$ is $h(\mathbf{C}_1(\mathbf{x}), \ldots, \mathbf{C}_b(\mathbf{x}))$, where h is an aggregation function. The idea is to learn b decision trees with the sampled training datasets $\mathbf{B}_i \in \mathbf{B}$, and to use the $\text{BPA}_{\text{LIA}}^{\text{MP2}}$ algorithm as aggregation function h.

Random Forests [8]. It builds each classifier $\mathbf{C}_i \in \mathbf{C}$ using a decision tree-based algorithm from a sampled drawn with replacement $\mathbf{B}_i \in \mathbf{B}$. During the splitting phase, instead of considering the m attributes on each decision node, only a (random) subset is checked to reduce the correlation between the classifiers, at the cost of a slight increase in bias. Thus, the b decision trees are learnt from the sampled training datasets $\mathbf{B}_i \in \mathbf{B}$ and the $\text{BPA}_{\text{LIA}}^{\text{MP2}}$ algorithm used as aggregation function h.

5 Experimental Evaluation

In this section we detail the experimental evaluation that we have carried out to assess the methods tackled in this work.

5.1 Datasets

We used a total of 15 datasets as benchmark, that were obtained by transforming *multi-class problems* [14] to the PLR problem (so considered semi-synthetic), as described in [4] (see https://github.com/alfaro96/scikit-lr/tree/master/sklr/datasets/data/partial_label_ranking). The idea is, for each instance in the dataset, to rank the labels according to the class probability distribution (obtained with 10×10-cv method of a Random Forests classifier) and, then, start a merging process of (some of) the labels in buckets. In Table 1 we show the main characteristics of each dataset. The columns #rankings and #buckets contain the number of different bucket orders and the mean number of buckets in the datasets, respectively.

Table 1. Description of the datasets.

Dataset	#instances	#attributes	#labels	#rankings	#buckets
(aut)horship	841	70	4	47	3.063
(blo)cks	5472	10	5	116	2.337
(bre)ast	109	9	6	62	3.925
(eco)li	336	7	8	179	4.140
(gla)ss	214	9	6	105	4.089
(iri)s	150	4	3	7	2.380
(let)ter	20000	16	26	15014	7.033
(lib)ras	360	90	15	356	6.889
(pen)digits	10992	16	10	3327	3.397
(sat)image	6435	36	6	504	3.356
(seg)ment	2310	18	7	271	3.031
(veh)icle	846	18	4	47	3.117
(vow)el	528	10	11	504	5.739
(win)e	178	13	3	11	2.680
(yea)st	1484	8	10	1006	5.929

5.2 Algorithms

We considered the following algorithms in the study:

- The IBPLR algorithm. The Euclidean distance was used to identify the nearest neighbors and, to compute the prediction, their bucket orders were weighted according to their (inverse) distance to the input query. The number of nearest neighbors to classify the test dataset was adjusted by applying a two-step procedure, which used a 5-cv method over the training dataset. First, we multiplied (by a factor of 2, starting with 5) the number of nearest neighbors while the accuracy improved. Then, with the last two tested values, we applied a binary search in this range. The number of nearest neighbors leading to the best accuracy was selected.
- The PLRT algorithm. The disagreements (A), distance (D) and entropy (E) criteria were used to identify the best attribute with the supervised (B) and unsupervised discretization techniques (equal-frequency (F) and equal-width (W)).
- The Bagging algorithm. The standard $b = 50$ sampled training datasets with replacement were employed to build the (strong) decision trees with the PLRT algorithm.
- The Random Forests algorithm. The standard $b = 50$ sampled training datasets with replacement were employed to build the (strong) decision trees with the PLRT algorithm, and $\sqrt{m}$ (random) attributes were considered when splitting.

- The Zero-R algorithm. The predicted bucket order for the test instances is obtained after solving the OBOP with all the bucket orders in the training dataset.

5.3 Methodology

We decided to adopt the following design decisions:

- Algorithms were assessed using a 5 × 10-cv method. The average of 50 runs is representative enough for a fair comparison.
- The accuracy was measured in terms of the τ_X *rank correlation coefficient* [15]. Given the bucket orders π_t, π_p of the values in $dom(Y) = \{y^1, \dots, y^n\}$, the τ_X rank correlation coefficient is given by

$$\tau_X(\pi_t, \pi_p) = \frac{\sum_{i=1}^{n}\sum_{j=1}^{n} \pi_t^{ij}\pi_p^{ij}}{n(n-1)} \tag{4}$$

$$\text{where} \qquad \pi_k^{ij} = \begin{cases} 1, & \text{if } y^i \text{ precedes or is tied with } y^j \text{ in } \pi^k \\ -1, & \text{if } y^i \text{ is ranked behind } y^j \text{ in } \pi^k \\ 0, & \text{if } i = j \end{cases}$$

The τ_X rank correlation coefficient takes values in $[-1, 1]$. The closer value to 1, the better correlation, while the closer value to -1, the better negative correlation.

5.4 Some Comments About Reproducibility

For the sake of reproducibility, all the datasets, the code [3] and a Docker image is provided in: https://github.com/alfaro96/scikit-lr. Finally, the experiments were carried out in computers running CentOS Linux 7 operating system with CPU Intel(R) Xeon(R) E5–2630 running at 2.40 GHz and 16 GB of RAM memory.

5.5 Results

Next, we provide the results of our experimental study. We focus on accuracy and efficiency (CPU time).

Accuracy. Table 2 shows the accuracy results. In particular, each cell contains the mean τ_X rank correlation coefficient between the true and the predicted bucket orders over the test datasets of the 5 × 10-cv. For each dataset, the algorithm leading to the best accuracy has been boldfaced. Before a statistical analysis, we highlight these conclusions:

- As expected, the IBPLR and PLRT algorithms outperform the baseline Zero-R algorithm, that obtains quite poor results.
- The IBPLR algorithm is competitive with respect to the supervised PLRT algorithms, but it is defeated by the ensembles.

Table 2. Mean accuracy for each algorithm (50 iterations in Bagging and Random Forests).

Ensemble	Method	aut	blo	bre	eco	gla	iri	let	lib	pen	sat	seg	veh	vow	win	yea
Single model	Zero-R	0.348	0.874	0.216	0.406	0.466	0.207	0.452	0.197	0.520	0.341	0.482	0.169	0.203	0.107	0.549
	PLRT-A-B	0.757	0.940	0.770	0.758	0.764	0.912	0.667	0.584	0.799	0.834	0.886	0.747	0.673	0.841	0.769
	PLRT-A-F	0.705	0.930	0.742	0.723	0.664	0.884	0.631	0.537	0.791	0.816	0.849	0.701	0.616	0.810	0.725
	PLRT-A-W	0.709	0.933	0.738	0.737	0.746	0.917	0.636	0.543	0.803	0.839	0.878	0.724	0.658	0.799	0.749
	PLRT-D-B	0.763	0.941	0.777	0.765	0.761	0.909	0.667	0.588	0.801	0.839	0.889	0.757	0.680	0.837	0.774
	PLRT-D-F	0.727	0.933	0.738	0.732	0.689	0.886	0.635	0.542	0.794	0.825	0.857	0.740	0.630	0.824	0.742
	PLRT-D-W	0.727	0.932	0.753	0.735	0.744	0.920	0.639	0.549	0.806	0.842	0.881	0.753	0.662	0.798	0.756
	PLRT-E-B	0.779	0.944	0.767	0.763	0.761	0.916	0.669	0.575	0.813	0.846	0.895	0.793	0.679	0.824	0.775
	PLRT-E-F	0.755	0.940	0.737	0.737	0.743	0.889	0.649	0.532	0.798	0.836	0.877	0.764	0.631	0.832	0.751
	PLRT-E-W	0.725	0.932	0.757	0.730	0.741	0.925	0.647	0.541	0.808	0.844	0.885	0.758	0.659	0.820	0.758
(BAG)ging	PLRT-A-B	0.825	0.954	0.808	0.792	0.797	0.931	0.718	0.669	0.838	0.887	0.916	0.803	0.758	0.871	0.806
	PLRT-A-F	0.788	0.948	0.804	0.778	0.764	0.920	0.704	0.650	0.827	0.871	0.903	0.780	0.755	0.861	0.777
	PLRT-A-W	0.788	0.947	0.804	0.782	0.796	0.930	0.707	0.667	0.833	0.886	0.907	0.796	**0.766**	0.860	0.798
	PLRT-D-B	0.828	0.955	0.810	0.789	0.802	0.930	0.721	0.671	0.839	0.889	0.916	0.813	0.761	0.875	0.807
	PLRT-D-F	0.808	0.948	0.806	0.781	0.771	0.924	0.707	0.655	0.828	0.874	0.905	0.802	0.755	0.872	0.785
	PLRT-D-W	0.807	0.947	0.806	0.785	0.797	0.932	0.710	0.671	0.834	0.887	0.910	0.809	0.766	0.861	0.802
	PLRT-E-B	**0.834**	0.955	0.813	0.793	**0.804**	0.930	**0.727**	**0.681**	**0.841**	0.887	**0.918**	**0.826**	0.761	**0.875**	**0.808**
	PLRT-E-F	0.823	0.949	0.807	0.785	0.800	0.925	0.717	0.659	0.829	0.876	0.909	0.813	0.758	0.875	0.792
	PLRT-E-W	0.812	0.946	0.812	0.784	0.796	0.928	0.715	0.674	0.834	0.887	0.909	0.812	0.766	0.859	0.800
(R)andom (F)orests	PLRT-A-B	0.817	0.955	0.809	0.790	0.796	**0.940**	0.708	0.666	0.839	0.888	0.916	0.799	0.753	0.861	0.799
	PLRT-A-F	0.752	0.946	0.796	0.774	0.760	0.920	0.681	0.644	0.822	0.871	0.900	0.766	0.745	0.838	0.761
	PLRT-A-W	0.762	0.946	0.810	0.785	0.792	0.923	0.691	0.666	0.832	0.883	0.908	0.783	0.760	0.848	0.789
	PLRT-D-B	0.820	**0.955**	0.810	0.793	0.798	0.938	0.711	0.669	0.839	0.890	0.916	0.808	0.758	0.873	0.805
	PLRT-D-F	0.768	0.946	0.796	0.776	0.764	0.923	0.684	0.650	0.822	0.873	0.902	0.770	0.746	0.840	0.769
	PLRT-D-W	0.776	0.948	**0.814**	0.782	0.789	0.926	0.693	0.666	0.832	0.884	0.908	0.787	0.760	0.852	0.791
	PLRT-E-B	0.822	0.954	0.810	**0.797**	0.801	0.936	0.714	0.678	0.840	**0.891**	0.917	0.810	0.758	0.867	0.802
	PLRT-E-F	0.794	0.948	0.809	0.776	0.776	0.917	0.700	0.657	0.826	0.878	0.904	0.791	0.752	0.843	0.773
	PLRT-E-W	0.791	0.947	0.811	0.785	0.790	0.923	0.698	0.669	0.832	0.886	0.907	0.790	0.762	0.853	0.791

- The supervised PLRT algorithms are better (in terms of accuracy) than the unsupervised PLRT algorithms, although the unsupervised PLRT algorithms also exhibit a remarkable performance.
- The accuracy of the PLRT algorithms clearly improves when using the ensembles. Although the best ensembles are obtained with the supervised PLRT algorithms, the ensembles based on the unsupervised PLRT algorithms also obtain good results.

To draw sound conclusions, the standard machine learning statistical analysis procedure [13,18] was carried out using the `exreport` tool [5]. The algorithms included in the study were the IBPLR method and the PLRT-based ensembles using the entropy criterion (since this is the criterion which leads to better results). Specifically:

- First, a *Friedman test* [16] was carried out with a significance level of $\alpha = 0.05$. Since the obtained p-value was $3.095e^{-11}$, we rejected the null hypothesis (H_0) that all the algorithms were equivalent in terms of score, in favour of the alternative hypothesis (H_1), that is, at least one of them was different.
- Second, we performed a pairwise post-hoc test with the *Shaffer's procedure* [26], using a significance level of $\alpha = 0.05$. Table 3 shows the results of the pairwise post-hoc test. In particular, each cell contains the adjusted p-value between the row-wise and column-wise algorithms.

According to these results, we can conclude that:

- The BAG-PLRT-E-B ensemble is ranked in the first position.

- The RF-PLRT-E-B ensemble is ranked in the second position, and the pairwise post-hoc test shows that it is not statistically different with respect to the BAG-PLRT-E-B ensemble. In fact, the faster BAG-PLRT-E-W ensemble neither shows statistical difference with respect to it.
- The pairwise post-hoc test reveals that four of the (compared) ensembles are statistically different with respect to the IBPLR algorithm. In particular, two of them are the Bagging ensembles built with the unsupervised PLRT algorithms.

Table 3. Results of the pairwise post-hoc test for the mean accuracy.

Method	RF-PLRT-E-B	BAG-PLRT-E-W	BAG-PLRT-E-F	RF-PLRT-E-W	RF-PLRT-E-F	IBPLR
BAG-PLRT-E-B	**9.047e^{-1}**	**1.567e^{-1}**	1.848e^{-2}	8.957e^{-4}	1.268e^{-6}	1.603e^{-9}
RF-PLRT-E-B	-	**1.000**	**6.074e^{-1}**	**1.055e^{-1}**	1.139e^{-3}	7.522e^{-6}
BAG-PLRT-E-W	-	-	**1.000**	**7.582e^{-1}**	4.025e^{-2}	8.957e^{-4}
BAG-PLRT-E-F	-	-	-	**1.000**	**2.519e^{-1}**	1.471e^{-2}
RF-PLRT-E-W	-	-	-	-	**9.047e^{-1}**	**1.567e^{-1}**
RF-PLRT-E-F	-	-	-	-	-	**1.000**

Table 4. Mean CPU time (in seconds) required by each algorithm (50 iterations in Bagging and Random Forests).

Ensemble	Method	aut	blo	bre	eco	gla	iri	let	lib	pen	sat	seg	veh	vow	win	yea
Single model	IBPLR	1.220	15.827	0.078	0.252	0.146	0.098	187.419	0.481	58.830	25.346	4.352	0.899	0.438	0.126	1.644
	PLRT-A-B	2.136	4.914	0.049	0.095	0.158	0.018	17.810	2.293	11.960	13.202	3.707	0.802	0.528	0.118	0.645
	PLRT-A-F	0.358	0.410	**0.008**	0.019	**0.014**	0.011	7.615	**0.151**	**1.462**	1.646	0.284	0.119	**0.033**	**0.017**	0.106
	PLRT-A-W	0.533	0.942	0.009	0.019	0.021	0.010	9.809	0.153	2.089	2.004	0.378	0.138	0.036	0.023	0.133
	PLRT-D-B	2.194	4.977	0.048	0.093	0.153	0.018	18.111	2.151	12.285	12.904	4.178	0.695	0.501	0.123	0.547
	PLRT-D-F	0.362	0.407	**0.008**	**0.018**	**0.014**	0.011	**7.591**	0.152	1.466	1.648	0.288	0.120	**0.033**	0.019	0.105
	PLRT-D-W	0.518	0.953	0.009	0.020	0.021	0.010	9.721	0.155	2.075	2.018	0.376	0.137	0.037	0.023	0.130
	PLRT-E-B	1.325	2.547	0.056	0.091	0.106	0.014	16.653	4.555	9.339	6.814	2.843	0.455	0.763	0.080	0.491
	PLRT-E-F	**0.334**	**0.360**	**0.008**	0.019	0.015	0.010	8.027	0.185	1.504	**1.627**	**0.277**	**0.118**	0.037	**0.017**	**0.104**
	PLRT-E-W	0.418	0.625	**0.008**	0.020	0.018	**0.009**	9.001	0.199	1.812	1.795	0.345	0.129	0.040	0.020	0.127
(BAG)ging	PLRT-A-B	71.419	175.591	2.733	6.582	6.542	0.735	1346.494	190.366	566.424	476.682	129.917	28.297	33.264	3.342	45.161
	PLRT-A-F	21.814	27.317	1.242	3.516	2.391	0.696	753.228	38.197	168.146	125.632	25.781	9.488	9.126	1.259	19.471
	PLRT-A-W	25.374	46.391	1.229	3.466	2.429	0.626	819.769	38.987	182.991	129.601	27.344	9.876	9.303	1.229	21.131
	PLRT-D-B	71.854	178.065	2.703	6.587	6.259	0.738	1359.136	181.424	579.314	468.400	144.978	26.548	32.295	3.300	43.512
	PLRT-D-F	20.904	27.737	1.253	3.563	2.421	0.706	755.334	38.622	168.427	125.320	24.758	9.313	9.280	1.257	19.800
	PLRT-D-W	24.483	43.417	1.234	3.506	2.417	0.626	828.488	39.262	183.631	128.986	26.320	9.390	9.218	1.203	20.627
	PLRT-E-B	50.527	95.256	2.853	6.887	5.658	0.633	1561.439	279.415	531.800	320.435	112.517	19.810	41.892	2.642	44.187
	PLRT-E-F	18.554	23.228	1.237	3.560	2.351	0.617	908.589	48.354	175.292	119.032	23.884	8.494	9.989	1.048	20.716
	PLRT-E-W	20.784	31.545	1.231	3.544	2.397	0.563	935.924	48.830	181.515	118.231	24.821	8.720	10.048	1.054	21.338
(R)andom (F)orests	PLRT-A-B	18.833	80.187	1.481	4.145	3.438	0.618	608.274	26.462	248.793	159.898	45.027	11.191	13.884	1.571	24.276
	PLRT-A-F	11.333	22.887	0.947	2.963	1.929	0.682	405.250	8.830	119.800	73.743	17.630	7.330	5.902	1.136	15.177
	PLRT-A-W	12.689	33.366	0.969	2.934	1.934	0.645	391.229	8.547	458.125	73.531	18.000	7.329	5.916	1.119	15.563
	PLRT-D-B	17.687	72.576	1.425	4.009	3.222	0.633	534.147	22.797	221.995	142.239	41.262	10.285	12.685	1.517	22.594
	PLRT-D-F	10.959	22.485	0.966	2.926	1.885	0.691	368.669	8.197	113.564	70.308	17.223	7.102	5.773	1.132	14.970
	PLRT-D-W	12.407	33.956	0.952	2.895	1.898	0.635	395.264	8.348	118.980	72.618	17.808	7.207	5.834	1.097	15.457
	PLRT-E-B	13.790	42.472	1.461	4.120	3.018	0.566	612.855	32.857	211.261	101.267	35.231	8.628	15.925	1.237	23.000
	PLRT-E-F	10.294	20.639	0.967	2.961	1.900	0.671	434.789	9.334	117.112	71.067	16.384	6.742	6.064	1.074	15.300
	PLRT-E-W	11.618	26.551	0.965	2.968	1.917	0.615	448.307	9.624	118.814	69.985	16.919	7.019	6.195	1.050	15.953

Efficiency. In this work, we have tackled instance-based and model-based paradigms, with induction and inference CPU time clearly different distributed.

In particular, the instance-based methods require more CPU time for the inference step, while the model-based procedures require more CPU time for the induction step. Thus, in order to make a fair comparison, the time for the whole process (learning with the training dataset and validating with the test one) was collected for the 5×10-cv over each dataset. The time results (in seconds) are shown in Table 4[1]. As before, to make easier the interpretation of the results, the algorithm(s) leading to the lowest CPU time has (have) been boldfaced.

In light of these results, we can conclude that:

- The IBPLR algorithm is competitive (in CPU time) with respect to the supervised PLRT algorithms. However, the computational complexity of the IBPLR algorithm significantly grows as the number of instances in the dataset increases.
- The unsupervised PLRT algorithms are faster than the supervised PLRT algorithms. Therefore, although the ensembles built with the supervised PLRT algorithms obtain good results (in terms of accuracy), they are not competitive (in CPU time) with respect to the ensembles built with the unsupervised PLRT algorithms.
- The PLRT algorithms using the entropy criterion are faster than the PLRT algorithms using the disagreements and distance criteria, because they generally lead to more complex decision trees.
- The unsupervised PLRT algorithms with the equal-frequency discretization are faster than their equal-width counterparts, because they tend to produce more compact trees.
- The Random Forests ensembles are faster than the Bagging ones, even if the Random Forests ensembles are built with the supervised PLRT algorithms and the Bagging ensembles with the unsupervised ones. However, they lead to more complex decision trees due to the randomness in the selection of the best attribute to split a decision node.

Therefore, taking into account accuracy and efficiency, the BAG-PLRT-E-W and RF-PLRT-E-B ensembles provide the best trade-off.

6 Conclusions and Future Research

In this work, we have proposed to use two unsupervised discretization techniques (equal-width and equal-frequency) to heuristically (but fast) select the threshold for numerical attributes in the decision nodes of the PLRT algorithm. To improve the robustness of these decision trees, we have applied two well-known averaging-ensemble methods, Bagging and Random Forests, due to their capability to reduce the variance of the built classifiers.

From our experimental evaluation, we observe that the IBPLR algorithm has a good performance with respect to the supervised PLRT algorithms, but it is defeated by (four of) the (compared) ensembles. Moreover, although the

[1] We do not consider the Zero-R algorithm because it is, by far, the fastest one.

supervised PLRT algorithms obtain better results (in terms of accuracy) than the unsupervised PLRT ones, these also exhibit a remarkable performance. In fact, the better ensembles are obtained with the PLRT algorithms using the entropy criterion.

Regarding the time, the IBPLR algorithm is competitive with respect to the supervised PLRT algorithms. Moreover, the unsupervised PLRT algorithms are clearly faster than the supervised PLRT ones, being the unsupervised PLRT algorithms with the equal-frequency discretization faster than their equal-width counterparts. It is important to point out that, although the Random Forests ensembles are faster than the Bagging ensembles, they generally lead to more complex decision trees.

As future work, we plan to deal with a more flexible approach of the ensemble methods working with incomplete partial rankings in the training dataset. Also, we plan to design boosting-based ensemble methods for the PLR problem.

Acknowledgements. This work has been partially funded by the Spanish Government, FEDER funds and the JCCM through the projects PID2019–106758GB–C33/AEI/10.13039/501100011033, TIN2016–77902–C3–1–P, and SBPLY/17/180501/000493. Juan C. Alfaro has also been funded by the FPU scholarship FPU18/00181 by MCIU.

References

1. Aledo, J.A., Gámez, J.A., Molina, D.: Tackling the supervised label ranking problem by bagging weak learners. Inf. Fusion **35**, 38–50 (2017)
2. Aledo, J.A., Gámez, J.A., Rosete, A.: Utopia in the solution of the Bucket Order Problem. Decis. Support Syst. **97**, 69–80 (2017)
3. Alfaro, J.C., Aledo, J.A., Gamez, J.A.: Scikit-lr (2019) https://github.com/alfaro96/scikit-lr
4. Alfaro, J.C., Aledo, J.A., Gamez, J.A.: Learning decision trees for the Partial Label Ranking problem. Int. J. Intell. Syst. (2020, in press)
5. Arias, J., Cózar, J.: ExReport: fast, reliable and elegant reproducible research (2015) http://exreport.jarias.es/
6. Borda, J.: Memoire sur les elections au scrutin. Histoire de l'Academie Royal des Sci. (1770)
7. Breiman, L.: Bagging predictors. Mach. Learn. **24**, 123–140 (1996)
8. Breiman, L.: Random forests. Mach. Learn. **45**, 5–32 (2001)
9. Breiman, L., Friedman, J., Stone, C.J., Olshen, R.A.: Classification and regression trees. Wiley Interdisc. Rev. Data Min. Knowl. Discov. **1**(1), 14–23 (1984)
10. Cheng, W., Hühn, J., Hüllermeier, E.: Decision tree and instance-based learning for label ranking. In: Proceedings of the 26th Annual International Conference on Machine Learning, pp. 161–168 (2009)
11. Cook, W.D.: Distance-based and ad hoc consensus models in ordinal preference ranking. Eur. J. Oper. Res. **172**, 369–385 (2006)
12. Cover, T., Hart, P.: Nearest neighbor pattern classification. IEEE Trans. Inf. Theory **13**, 21–27 (1967)
13. Demšar, J., Statistical Comparisons of Classifiers over Multiple Data Sets: Statistical comparisons of classifiers over multiple data sets. J. Mach. Learn. Res. **7**, 1–30 (2006)

14. Dheeru, D., Karra, E.: UCI machine learning repository (1987) http://archive.ics.uci.edu/ml
15. Emond, E.J., Mason, D.W.: A new rank correlation coefficient with application to the consensus ranking problem. J. Multi-Criteria Decis. Anal. **11**, 17–28 (2002)
16. Friedman, M.: A comparison of alternative tests of significance for the problem of m rankings. Ann. Math. Stat. **11**, 86–92 (1940)
17. Frünkranz, J., Hüllermeier, E.: Preference Learning. In: Sammut C., Webb G.I. (eds) Encyclopedia of Machine Learning. Springer, Boston, MA. (2010) https://doi.org/10.1007/978-0-387-30164-8
18. García, S., Herrera, F.: An extension on "statistical comparisons of classifiers over multiple data sets" for all pairwise comparisons. J. Mach. Learn. Res. **9**, 2677–2694 (2008)
19. Gionis, A., Mannila, H., Puolamäki, K., Ukkonen, A.: Algorithms for discovering bucket orders from data. In: Proceedings of the 12th ACM SIGKDD international conference on Knowledge discovery and data mining, pp. 561–566 (2006)
20. Irurozki, E., Calvo, B., Lozano, J.A.: PerMallows: an R package for mallows and generalized mallows models. J. Stat. Softw. **71**, 1–30 (2016)
21. Kemeny, J., Snell, J.: Mathematical Models in the Social Sciences. The MIT Press (1972)
22. Kendall, M.G.: Rank Correlation Methods. C. Griffin (1948)
23. Lin, S.: Rank aggregation methods. Wiley Interdisc. Rev. **2**, 555–570 (2010)
24. Mallows, C.L.: Non-null ranking models. Biometrika **44**, 114–130 (1957)
25. Mitchell, T.M.: Machine learning. McGraw-Hill (1997)
26. Shaffer, J.P.: Multiple hypothesis testing. Ann. Rev. **46**, 561–584 (1995)
27. Shannon, C.E.: A mathematical theory of communication. Bell Syst. Tech. J. **27**, 379–423 (1948)
28. Zhou, Y., Qiu, G.: Random forest for label ranking. Expert Syst. Appl. **112**, 99–109 (2018)

Agglomerative Constrained Clustering Through Similarity and Distance Recalculation

Germán González-Almagro[1(✉)], Juan Luis Suarez[1], Julián Luengo[1], José-Ramón Cano[2], and Salvador García[1]

[1] DaSCI Andalusian Institute of Data Science and Computational Intelligence, University of Granada, Granada, Spain
germangalmagro@ugr.es

[2] Department of Computer Science, EPS of Linares, Campus Científico Tecnológico de Linares, University of Jaén, Cinturón Sur S/N, 23700 Linares, Jaén, Spain

Abstract. Constrained clustering has become a topic of considerable interest in machine learning, as it has been shown to produce promising results in domains where only partial information about how to solve the problem is available. Constrained clustering can be viewed as a semi-supervised generalization of clustering, which is traditionally unsupervised. It is able to leverage a new type of information encoded by constraints that guide the clustering process. In particular, this study focuses on instance-level must-link and cannot-link constraints. We propose an agglomerative constrained clustering algorithm, which combines distance-based and clustering-engine adapting methods to incorporate constraints into the partitioning process. It computes a similarity measure on the basis of distances (in the dataset) and constraints (in the constraint set) to later apply an agglomerative clustering method, whose clustering engine has been adapted to consider constraints and raw distances. We prove its capability to produce quality results for the constrained clustering problem by comparing its performance to previous proposals on several datasets with incremental levels of constraint-based information.

Keywords: Semi-supervised learning · Constrained clustering · Agglomerative clustering · Similarity recalculation

1 Introduction

Clustering is one of the mots successful techniques in data analysis problems. It constitutes a key research area in the field of unsupervised learning, where there is no supervision on how the information should be handled. Partitional clustering can be defined as the task of grouping the instances of a dataset into clusters, so that new information can be extracted from them. Following the

E. A. de la Cal et al. (Eds.): HAIS 2020, LNAI 12344, pp. 424–436, 2020.
https://doi.org/10.1007/978-3-030-61705-9_35

semi-supervised learning paradigm we can incorporate background information into the clustering process, resulting in constrained clustering, which is the main subject of the study presented in this study. The goal of constrained clustering is to find a partition of a dataset that meets the proper characteristics of a clustering method result, in addition to satisfying a certain constraint set.

Constraints can be understood in different ways, resulting in three main types of constrained clustering: cluster-level [2], instance-level [5] and feature-level constrained clustering [13]. In particular, two types of instance-level constraints can be found in the literature: pairwise constraints and distance-based constraints. Pairwise constraints tell us if two specific instances of a dataset must be placed in the same or in different clusters, resulting in Must-link (ML) and Cannot-link (CL) constraints respectively. This study focuses on these types of constraints (ML and CL).

Multiple approaches to the problem of integrating constraints into the clustering process can be found, resulting in two broad families: (1) in *distance-based* methods the goal is to learn a new metric that reflects the information contained in the constraint set, so that a clustering method can use this new measure to find more accurate clusters [16], (2) in *clustering-engine adapting* methods a clustering method is modified to be able to handle the constraints by using them as hints to guide the clustering process [15].

Regarding the degree to which the constraints have to be satisfied, a distinction can be made between the concepts of hard [15] and soft [11] constraints. Hard constraints must necessarily be satisfied in the output partition of any algorithm that makes use of them, while soft constraints are taken as a strong guide for the algorithm that uses them but can be partially satisfied in the output partition. For the purposes of this study, we will employ the latter, given their practical applicability to real-world problems.

In this study a two-staged method is proposed: in the first stage, a similarity measure is computed based on the pairwise distances between instances in the dataset and on the constraint set, in the second stage, an agglomerative clustering method is run over the dataset, using the newly computed similarity measure to compute affinities. In cases in which the information given by the affinity function is not enough to choose the best two clusters to merge, constraints combined with the euclidean distance are used to compute the value of a penalty-style cost function. This function splits all possible merges into categories, with regards to the number of constraints violated by each possible merge. With this we have a distance-based first stage, where a similarity measure is computed, and a second stage with a clustering-engine adapted method. Our proposal is compared with several existing approaches to constrained clustering, showing significant improvements over them.

The rest of this study is organized as follows: in Sect. 3 we present the method that implements the idea described above, Sect. 4 describes the experimental setup used to carry out our experiments. In Sects. 5 and 6 we present and analyze the experimental results obtained with the proposed method. Lastly, our conclusions are discussed in Sect. 7.

2 Background

As we have already mentioned, partitional clustering consists in grouping instances of a dataset into a fixed number of clusters k. More formally, a dataset $X = \{x_1, \cdots, x_n\}$ is composed of n instances, each one of them described by u features, and with the ith instance noted as $x_i = (x_{[i,1]}, \cdots, x_{[i,u]})$. A typical clustering algorithm assigns a class label l_i to each instance $x_i \in X$. As a result, the set of labels $L = \{l_1, \cdots, l_n\}$ is obtained, with $l_i \in \{1, \cdots, k\} \forall i \in \{1, \cdots, n\}$, that effectively splits X into k non-overlapping clusters c_i to form a partition called C. The criterion used to assign an instance to a given cluster is the similarity to the rest of elements in that cluster, and the dissimilarity to the rest of instances of the dataset, which can be obtained with some kind of distance measurement [8]. In our work we focus on agglomerative clustering, which starts the clustering process with a large number of small (singleton) clusters $C = \{c_1, c_2, \cdots, c_n\}$ and iteratively merges them until stopping criteria are met. To select two clusters to merge in each iteration, an affinity measure $\mathcal{A}(\cdot, \cdot)$ must be defined, and thus the two most similar clusters are merged [6].

In most clustering applications it is common to have some kind of information about the dataset to be analyzed. In pairwise instance-level constrained clustering this information is given in the form of pairs of instances. A constraint states whether the instances which it refers to must, or must not, be assigned to the same cluster. It is possible to obtain a better result by using this type of information than by using completely unsupervised clustering algorithms. We can now formalize the two types of constraints mentioned:

- Must-link constraints $C_{=}(x_i, x_j)$: instances x_i and x_j from X must be placed in the same cluster.
- Cannot-link constraints $C_{\neq}(x_i, x_j)$: instances x_i and x_j from X cannot be assigned to the same cluster.

The goal of constrained clustering is to find a partition (or clustering) of k clusters $C = \{c_1, \cdots, c_k\}$ of the dataset X that ideally satisfies all constraints in the constraint set. As in the original clustering problem, it must be fulfilled that the sum of instances in each cluster c_i is equal to the number of instances in X, which has been defined as $n = |X| = \sum_{i=1}^{k} |c_i|$.

3 The Proposed Method

In this section the two stages that compose our method are described. Following the work in [3], we take a combination of the pairwise distances and the reconstruction coefficient as the optimization problem to solve in order to obtain the new similarity measure. Equation 1 shows the expression of this problem.

$$\begin{aligned} &\min_Z \frac{||X - XZ||_F^2}{2} + \frac{\lambda}{2} \sum_{i=1}^{n} \sum_{j=1}^{n} ||x_i - x_j||_2^2 S_{[i,j]} + \frac{\beta}{2} ||Z||_2^2 \\ &\text{s.t. } Z^T \mathbf{1} = \mathbf{1}, Z_{[i,i]} = 0, S = \frac{|Z| + |Z^T|}{2} \end{aligned}, \quad (1)$$

where $X = [x_1, \cdots, x_n] \in \mathbb{R}^{u \times n}$ is a matrix containing the instances of the dataset in each column, $||Z||_2^2$ is a regularization term, λ and β are tradeoff parameters, $\mathbf{1}$ is a column vector of ones with the needed dimension, and the constraint $S = (|Z| + |Z^T|)/2$ ensures compatibility between the two similarities combined in the expression. Note that the operator $|\cdot|$ gives the absolute values corresponding to all elements given as arguments and operator $||\cdot||_F$ refers to the Frobenius norm. Thanks to the reconstruction coefficient, the above similarity measure is robust to noise and outliers [3]. This problem can be rewritten as in Eq. 2 by defining D as a matrix containing pairwise distances within the dataset.

$$\begin{aligned} &\min_Z \frac{||X - XZ||_F^2}{2} + \frac{\lambda}{2} Tr(SD) + \frac{\beta}{2}||Z||_2^2 \\ &\text{s.t. } Z^T\mathbf{1} = \mathbf{1}, Z_{[i,i]} = 0 \end{aligned} . \quad (2)$$

To integrate constraints into the process of obtaining Z, distances in the dataset are computed taking into account the information contained in the constraint set. Equation 3 is used to build the pairwise distance matrix D.

$$D_{[i,j]} = \begin{cases} 0 & \text{if } C_=(x_i, x_j) \\ MaxD \times \gamma & \text{if } C_{\neq}(x_i, x_j) \\ ||x_i - x_j||_2 & \text{otherwise} \end{cases} , \quad (3)$$

where $MaxD = \max_{i=1,j=1}^{n}\{||x_i - x_j||_2\}$ is the maximum distance in the dataset and $\gamma > 1$ is a scaling parameter. This expression effectively sets all entries in matrix D to the Euclidean distance between instances unless they take part in an ML or CL constraint, in which case the entry is set to 0 (minimum distance) or to $MaxD \times \gamma$ (a value above the maximum distance in the dataset) respectively. Note that, with this, D reflects the information contained in the constraint set in a very limited manner. It is also worth mentioning that the metric described by the resulting distance matrix D does not satisfy the triangle inequality. To propagate constraints over the whole matrix and restore metricity to some extent, we can assume that, if two instances are related by an ML constraint, the distance separating them should be small, as well as the distances between their neighbors. This way, D can be interpreted as the matrix containing weights for a complete graph over the dataset X and run the Floyd-Warshall algorithm over it. This propagates constraints and in some cases restores metricity completely, although experimental results show that this does not affect the results negatively [10].

The mathematical derivation of the optimization scheme for Z based on the problem in Eq. 3 is analyzed in detail in [3]. It iteratively applies Eq. 4 to update every row z_i of matrix Z separately.

$$z_{[i,j]} = \text{sign}(v_j)\left(|v_j| - \frac{\lambda D_{[j,i]}}{2}\right)_+ , \quad (4)$$

where $Z_{[i,j]}$ is the j-th element in row z_i from Z, $D_{[j,i]}$ is the j-th of the i-th column from matrix D, and v_j is the j-th element from vector v, which

Algorithm 1. Constrained similarity matrix construction

Input: Dataset X, constraint sets $C_=$ and $C_{\neq}$, tradeoff parameter λ and β, scaling parameters γ, thresholding parameter μ.

1: Initialize Z with values in $[0,1]$ such that $Z^T\mathbf{1} = \mathbf{1}$ and $Z_{[i,i]} = 0$
2: Build matrix D using Equation 3
3: Apply Floyd-Warshall algorithm to D to propagate constraints and restore metricity
4: $D \leftarrow D^2$; $i \leftarrow 1$
5: **do**
6: Obtain row $z_i^{(t+1)}$ following Equation 4 and store it to get $Z^{(t+1)}$
7: $i \leftarrow (i+1) \mod n$
8: **while** $||Z - Z^{(t+1)}||_F < \epsilon$
9: Apply the hard thresholding operator $H_\mu(\cdot)$ to each column of Z
10: Obtain similarity matrix by computing $W = (|Z| + |Z^T|)/2$
11: Normalize each column of W applying the l_2-norm.
12: **return** W

is computed as $v = (X_1^T x)/(x^T x + \beta)$. The term X_1 is computed as $X_1 = X - (XZ - x_i z_i)$, with x_i being the i-th column (instance) of X and z_i being the i-th row of matrix Z. Note that when $i = j$ then $z_{[i,j]} = 0$.

Once Z is obtained, a hard thresholding operator $H_\mu(\cdot)$ is applied to each column of Z. This operator keeps the μ largest entries from the column given as argument and sets the rest to 0. Lastly, the resulting similarity measure W is obtained by computing $W = (|Z| + |Z^T|)/2$ and applying the unit l_2-norm to each column of W. Algorithm 1 summarizes the process to obtain the similarity matrix. The loop in line 5 is shown to always converge in [3].

Once we have the similarity matrix W, we can move on to the second stage of our method, which consists in applying an agglomerative clustering procedure that takes W as the similarity measure to choose the best clusters to merge. To compute the affinity between two clusters Eq. 5 is used, following the guidelines in [17].

$$\mathcal{A}(c_i, c_j) = \frac{1}{|c_i|^2}\mathbf{1}_{|c_i|^T} W_{c_i,c_j} W_{c_j,c_i} \mathbf{1}_{|c_i|} + \frac{1}{|c_j|^2}\mathbf{1}_{|c_j|^T} W_{c_j,c_i} W_{c_i,c_j} \mathbf{1}_{|c_j|}, \quad (5)$$

where W_{c_i,c_j} is a submatrix of W containing row indices from c_i and column indices from c_j, and $|c_i|$ is the number of elements in cluster c_i. This gives us an affinity measure which is highly influenced by the constraints. However, due to the hard thresholding operator $H_\mu(\cdot)$, and to the own nature of the Z optimization procedure, the affinity among clusters may be 0; what is more, the affinity between all clusters found so far may be 0. In these cases, the algorithm needs a different affinity measure to be able to make informed decisions when choosing two clusters to merge. A penalty-style cost function $\mathcal{P}(\cdot,\cdot)$ is used to compute distance (instead of affinity) between every pair of clusters. $\mathcal{P}(\cdot,\cdot)$ is described in Eq. 6.

$$\mathcal{P}(c_i, c_j) = \left\| \frac{\sum_{x_a, x_b \in c_i} \|x_a - x_b\|_2}{|c_i|} - \frac{\sum_{x_a, x_b \in c_j} \|x_a - x_b\|_2}{|c_j|} \right\|_2 + \underbrace{\text{infeasibility} \times \nu}_{Penalty}, \tag{6}$$

where infeasibility is the number of constraints violated by cluster $c_i \cup c_j$ and ν is a scaling parameter which must be of a order of magnitude greater than the larger distance in the dataset. In other words, $\mathcal{P}(\cdot, \cdot)$ computes the distance between the centroids associated with the two clusters to merge and apply a penalty term to it. This way, all possible mergers violating the same number of constraints will result in the same penalty term, so the algorithm can always choose the two closest clusters whose merge will result in as few constraint violations as possible. Note that $\mathcal{P}(\cdot, \cdot)$ does not implement hard constraints, avoiding possible dead-ends; therefore, a k-partition of the dataset is always provided. Algorithm 2 shows the described clustering process.

Regarding the algorithmic complexity of the overall proposed method, the bottleneck in Algorithm 1 is found in the matrix multiplication operation, varying from $\mathcal{O}(n^3)$ to almost $\mathcal{O}(n^2)$ depending on the implementation. Affinities and distances (Eqs. 5 and 6 respectively) can be computed in quadratic time ($\mathcal{O}(n^2)$). The bottleneck in Algorithm 2 is found in the selection of the two clusters to merge, which is $\mathcal{O}(n^3)$ in the worst case ($k = 1$). Finally, the Floyd-Warshall algorithm runs in $\mathcal{O}(n^3)$, which gives us an overall time complexity for the proposed method of $\mathcal{O}(n^3)$.

Algorithm 2. Proposed Constrained Clustering Method

Input: Dataset X, constraint sets $C_=$ and $C_{\neq}$, output partition number of clusters k, scaling parameter ν.

```
1: Compute similarity matrix W using Algorithm 1
2: Assign each instance to a singleton cluster to get initial partition C =
   {c_1, c_2, ··· , c_n}
3: while |C| > k do
     //Select two clusters using A
4:   c_a, c_b ← arg max_{c_i,c_j ∈ C | i≠j} A(c_i, c_j)
5:   if A(c_a, c_b) = 0 then
       //Select two clusters using P
6:     c_a, c_b ← arg min_{c_i,c_j ∈ C | i≠j} P(c_i, c_j)
7:   end if
     //Merge clusters
8:   C ← C ∪ {c_a ∪ c_b} − {c_a} − {c_b}
9: end while
10: return C
```

4 Experimental Setup and Calibration

For our experiments we will compare the results obtained by the proposed method and four other well known approaches to constrained clustering over

10 datasets and 3 constraint sets for each one of them. Most of these datasets can be found at the Keel-dataset repository[1] [14], though some of them have been obtained via scikit-learn python package[2]. Table 1 displays a summary of every dataset. No preprocessing other than a normalization procedure will be applied to these datasets.

Classification datasets are commonly used in the literature to test constrained clustering algorithms; the reason behind this is that they enable us to generate constraints with respect to the true labels. The method proposed in [15] is used to generate artificial constraint sets. This method consists of randomly selecting two instances of a dataset, then comparing its labels, and finally setting an ML or CL constraint depending on whether the labels are the same or different.

For each dataset three different sets of constraints are generated—CS_{10}, CS_{15} and CS_{20}—that will be associated with three small percentages of the size of the dataset: 10%, 15% and 20%. With n_f being the fraction of the size of the dataset associated with each of these percentages, the formula $(n_f(n_f-1))/2$ tells us how many artificial constraints will be created for each constraint set; this number is equivalent to how many edges a complete graph with n_f vertices would have. Table 1 shows the number of constraints of each type obtained for each dataset.

Table 1. Datasets and constraint sets summary

Dataset	Instances	Classes	Featuress	CS_{10}		CS_{15}		CS_{20}	
				ML	CL	ML	CL	ML	CL
Appendicitis	106	2	7	37	18	76	44	154	77
HayesRoth	160	3	4	47	73	86	190	177	319
Heart	270	2	13	173	178	436	384	747	684
Iris	150	3	4	28	77	92	161	132	303
Newthyroid	215	3	5	125	106	273	255	488	415
Sonar	208	2	60	106	104	241	255	416	445
Soybean	47	4	35	1	9	11	17	5	40
Spectfheart	267	2	44	230	121	563	257	952	479
Wine	178	3	13	57	96	105	246	210	420
Zoo	101	7	16	13	42	27	93	53	157

4.1 Evaluation Method and Validation of Results

Since we have the true labels associated with each of the datasets, they can be used to evaluate the results provided by each method. We will use the Adjusted Rand Index (ARI) to measure the accuracy of the predictions resulting from each

[1] https://sci2s.ugr.es/keel/category.php?cat=clas.

[2] https://scikit-learn.org/stable/datasets/index.html.

method [7]. The basic Rand Index computes the degree of agreement between two partitions C_1 and C_2 of a given dataset X. C_1 and C_2 are viewed as collections of $n(n-1)/2$ pairwise decisions. The ARI is a corrected-for-chance version of the Rand Index. An ARI value of 1 means total agreement of the two partitions given to compute the value, whereas an ARI value of -1 means the opposite. For more details on ARI see [7]. The *Unsat* measure is also included, that refers to the percentage on unsatisfied constraints.

In order to validate the results which will be presented in Sect. 5, Bayesian statistical tests are used, instead of the classic Null Hypothesis Statistical Tests (NHST). In [1] an in-depth analysis of the disadvantages of NHST can be found, and a new model is proposed for carrying out comparisons researchers are interested in. Most of the problems of NHST can be avoided by using Bayesian tests instead of NHST. In particular, the Bayesian sign test is used, which is the Bayesian version of the frequentist non-parametric sign test. To make use of it, the `rNPBST` R package is employed, whose documentation and guide can be found in [4].

The Bayesian sign test is based on obtaining the statistical distribution of a certain parameter ρ according to the difference between the results, under the assumption that said distribution is a Dirichlet distribution. To get the distribution of ρ we count the number of times that $A-B<0$, the number of times where there are no significant differences, and the number of times that $A-B>0$. In order to identify cases where there are no significant differences, the region of practical equivalence (rope) $[r_{\min}, r_{\max}]$ is defined, so that $P(A \approx B) = P(\rho \in \text{rope})$. Using these results we calculate the weights of the Dirichlet distribution and sample it to get a set of triplets with the form described in Eq. 7.

$$[P(\rho < r_{\min}) = P(A-B<0),\;\; P(\rho \in \text{rope})P(\rho > r_{\max}) = P(A-B>0)]. \tag{7}$$

4.2 Calibration

We compare our proposed method with 4 well known state-of-the-art methods: COnstrained Partitional K-means (COP-kmeans) [15], Linear Constrained Vector Quantization Error (LCVQE) [12], Two-Views Clustering (TVClust) [9], Relation Dirichlet Process - Means and (RDPM) [9].

In order for our experiments to be reproducible, parameters used in them are described in this section. For the proposed method 6 different parameters need to be set. Parameters γ, μ and ν will have the same value for every dataset: $\gamma = 1.5$, $\mu = n/3$ and $\nu = 1000$. λ and β will be optimized with a 10×10 optimization grid containing values from 10^{-3} to 10, and k will be set to the true number of classes for each dataset. Table 2 displays λ and β for every dataset and constraint set.

Table 2. λ and β parameters values

Dataset	CS_{10}		CS_{15}		CS_{20}	
	λ	β	λ	β	λ	β
Appendicitis	1	1	2	7	6	4
Hayes Roth	1	5	3	3	3	6
Heart	3	1	2	4	1	1
Iris	5	8	7	8	1	1
Newthyroid	2	6	3	9	4	9
Sonar	5	9	2	2	1	1
Soybean	1	1	1	1	1	1
Spectfheart	5	7	2	8	7	5
Wine	2	7	2	5	1	6
Zoo	1	1	1	4	1	1

5 Experimental Results

In this section, experimental results for all datasets and constraint sets are presented. Note that some of the previous proposals are not deterministic algorithms, so the results may vary between runs. To lessen the effect this may cause, average results of 50 runs are presented in our tables. Please note that in cases where COP-kmeans is not able to produce an output partition, we assign to that particular run the worst possible benchmark values. Tables 3, 4, and 5 shows the results obtained with the methodology described before.

Table 3. Experimental results obtained for CS_{10} by our proposal and the and the four previous approaches to constrained clustering.

Dataset	TSHACC		COP-kmeans		LCVQE		RDPM		TVClust	
	ARI	Unsat(%)	ARI	Unsat(%)	ARI	Unsat(%)	ARI	Unsat(%)	ARI	Unsat(%)
Appendicitis	**0.636**	16.364	-	-	0.257	21.818	0.271	32.545	0.109	41.636
Hayes Roth	**0.164**	42.500	-0.887	90.000	0.079	11.750	0.074	26.667	0.093	24.250
Heart	**0.763**	8.262	-	-	0.603	14.815	0.207	35.442	0.191	41.111
Iris	**0.904**	0.952	-0.070	50.000	0.868	2.857	0.665	9.905	0.615	11.524
Newthyroid	**0.968**	0.433	-0.603	80.000	0.937	0.866	0.726	8.355	0.691	11.429
Sonar	**0.477**	16.190	-	-	0.032	32.381	0.009	40.810	0.000	49.524
Soybean	**1.000**	0.000	0.717	0.000	**1.000**	0.000	0.851	4.000	0.000	90.000
Spectfheart	**0.698**	7.692	-	-	0.002	33.903	-0.086	41.026	0.000	34.473
Wine	0.894	0.000	-	-	**0.982**	0.000	0.706	8.627	0.293	30.131
Zoo	**0.896**	0.000	0.649	0.000	0.678	0.000	0.717	5.455	0.373	21.091
Average	**0.740**	9.239	-0.519	72.000	0.544	11.839	0.414	21.283	0.236	35.517

Regarding the CS_{10} level of constraints, presented in Table 3, we observe how the proposed algorithm is able to obtain better results than those obtained by

Table 4. Experimental results obtained for CS_{15} by our proposal and the and the four previous approaches to constrained clustering.

Dataset	TSHACC		COP-kmeans		LCVQE		RDPM		TVClust	
	ARI	Unsat(%)	ARI	Unsat(%)	ARI	Unsat(%)	ARI	Unsat(%)	ARI	Unsat(%)
Appendicitis	**0.647**	10.833	-	-	0.443	19.167	0.389	20.750	0.227	29.250
Hayes Roth	**0.479**	13.043	-	-	0.040	30.036	0.103	30.725	0.143	32.065
Heart	**1.000**	0.000	**1.000**	0.000	0.687	11.829	0.314	29.817	0.435	26.488
Iris	0.566	22.925	-	-	**0.980**	0.000	0.748	10.158	0.559	14.783
Newthyroid	0.924	1.705	0.000	50.000	**1.000**	0.000	0.971	0.492	0.809	8.902
Sonar	**1.000**	0.000	-	-	0.519	22.944	0.007	42.399	0.000	51.411
Soybean	**1.000**	0.000	0.200	40.000	**1.000**	0.000	0.785	13.929	0.000	60.714
Spectfheart	0.983	0.732	**1.000**	0.000	-0.000	41.573	-0.089	41.720	0.000	31.341
Wine	**1.000**	0.000	-0.800	90.000	**1.000**	0.000	0.751	6.467	0.390	25.328
Zoo	**0.954**	0.000	0.759	0.000	0.741	3.250	0.697	9.000	0.361	23.000
Average	**0.855**	4.924	-0.184	58.000	0.641	12.880	0.468	20.546	0.293	30.328

previous approaches. Note the results obtained for Iris and Newthyroid, with a near-optimum results, and Soybean, where our proposal and LCVQE are able to find the optimal solution, even with the smaller constraint set.

The results obtained with the SC_{15} constraint set are presented in Table 4. It is at this constraint level where we start to see major differences between our proposed method and the rest. We observe how the quality of the solutions found by the proposal scales with the number of constraints. However, cases in which a higher number of constraints does not result in a better ARI or Unsat can be found, as it happens with the Iris dataset. This is due to the fact that, as pointed out in [5]: *"Individual constraint sets can have adverse effects"*. Notice also that the Unsat measure decreases in most cases even if the number of constraints is higher. This is indicative of a good constraints-integration scheme, which is able to guide the clustering towards feasible solutions.

Table 5. Experimental results obtained for CS_{20} by our proposal and the and the four previous approaches to constrained clustering.

Dataset	TSHACC		COP-kmeans		LCVQE		RDPM		TVClust	
	ARI	Unsat(%)	ARI	Unsat(%)	ARI	Unsat(%)	ARI	Unsat(%)	ARI	Unsat(%)
Appendicitis	**0.869**	2.597	-	-	0.117	41.126	0.450	20.779	0.232	28.745
Hayes Roth	0.851	4.234	**0.993**	0.000	0.026	36.008	0.133	30.141	0.156	37.238
Heart	**1.000**	0.000	**1.000**	0.000	0.857	6.709	0.461	22.481	0.523	23.305
Iris	0.558	24.138	-	-	0.886	3.678	**0.968**	0.667	0.701	12.851
Newthyroid	0.954	2.326	0.200	40.000	0.968	2.104	**0.995**	0.166	0.975	0.753
Sonar	**1.000**	0.000	-	-	-0.003	47.828	0.114	36.922	0.000	51.684
Soybean	**1.000**	0.000	0.155	40.000	**1.000**	0.000	0.790	3.556	0.000	88.889
Spectfheart	**1.000**	0.000	**1.000**	0.000	-0.004	51.698	0.229	28.616	0.000	33.473
Wine	**1.000**	0.000	-0.800	90.000	**1.000**	0.000	0.813	5.603	0.700	12.810
Zoo	**0.968**	0.000	0.816	0.000	0.743	4.190	0.739	7.524	0.383	21.952
Average	**0.920**	3.329	0.036	47.000	0.559	19.334	0.569	15.645	0.367	31.170

Finally, results obtained for the CS_{20} constraint level are gathered in Table 5. We continue to see how the quality of the solutions found by our proposal scales with the number of constraints, being able to obtain the optimal partition in up to five cases. This is another argument in favor of the suitability of the constraints-integration scheme.

6 Analysis of Results

One of the major advantages of the Bayesian sign test is that a very illustrative visual representation of its results can be obtained. We can produce a representation of the triplet set in the form of a heatmap where each triplet constitutes one point whose location is given by barycentric coordinates. Figure 1 shows heatmaps comparing ARI results obtained by our proposal and the rest of the methods considered in this study with $rope = [-0.01, 0.01]$. Results produced by the proposed method are taken as the B set of results in Eq. 7, and the set of results obtained the other methods as A.

In all four cases shown in Figs. 1a, 1b, 1c and 1d, we can see how there is not a single triplet represented in a region other than the lower left region of the heatmap. This region is associated with the Bayesian sign test assigning a high probability to $A - B < 0$. With this in mind, and considering that ARI is a measure to maximize, we can conclude that there exist statistically significant differences between previous proposals and the newly proposed method in favor of the latter. Also note that there is not a single triplet represented in the upper region of the triangle (associated with practical equivalence), which provides evidence against our proposal being equivalent to the rest of the methods in any case.

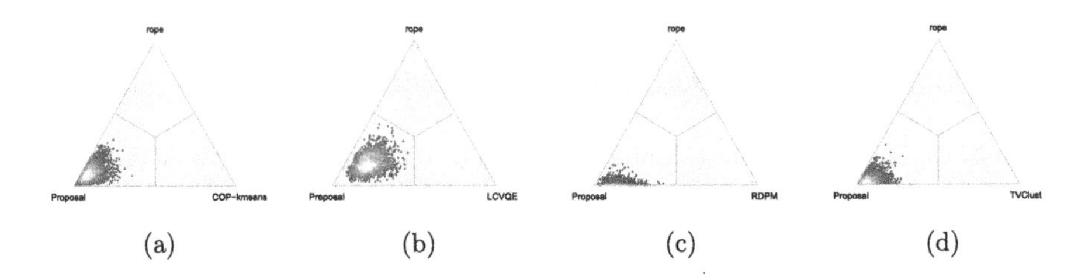

Fig. 1. Heatmaps 1a, 1b, 1c, 1d compare our proposed method with COP-kmeans, LCVQE, RDPM, and TVClust respectively.

7 Conclusions

In this study a new method to approach the constrained clustering problem is proposed. It is able to handle instance-level must-link and cannot-link constraints by including them in the clustering process in a hybrid fashion. In a first stage, it learns a new metric matrix on the basis of constraints and distances in the dataset, while in a second stage it applies agglomerative constrained clustering modifying the affinity/distance measure accordingly to the information provided by the metric matrix learned in the first stage.

Our proposal has proven to be able to scale the quality of the solutions with the number of constraints given, which can be understood as the amount of side information available to the problem. While achieving results similar to those obtained by previous well known approaches in low-constrained problems, the proposed method rapidly outscale other method when more side information is provided. Bayesian statistical test were used to prove significant differences between results.

References

1. Benavoli, A., Corani, G., Demšar, J., Zaffalon, M.: Time for a change: a tutorial for comparing multiple classifiers through bayesian analysis. J. Mach. Learn. Res. **18**(1), 2653–2688 (2017)
2. Bradley, P.S., Bennett, K.P., Demiriz, A.: Constrained k-means clustering. Microsoft Res. Redmond, **20** (2000)
3. Cai, Z., Yang, X., Huang, T., Zhu, W.: A new similarity combining reconstruction coefficient with pairwise distance for agglomerative clustering. Inf. Sci. **508**, 173–182 (2020)
4. Carrasco, J., García, S., del Mar Rueda, M., Herrera, F.: rNPBST: an R package covering non-parametric and bayesian statistical tests. In: Martínez de Pisón, F.J., Urraca, R., Quintián, H., Corchado, E. (eds.) HAIS 2017. LNCS (LNAI), vol. 10334, pp. 281–292. Springer, Cham (2017). https://doi.org/10.1007/978-3-319-59650-1_24
5. Davidson, I., Basu, S.: A survey of clustering with instance level constraints. ACM Trans. Knowl. Discovery Data **1**, 1–41 (2007)
6. Everitt, B.S., Landau, S., Leese, M.: Cluster Analysis. Wiley Publishing, 4th edn. (2009)
7. Hubert, L., Arabie, P.: Comparing partitions. J. Classif. **2**(1), 193–218 (1985)
8. Jain, A.K., Murty, M.N., Flynn, P.J.: Data clustering: a review. ACM Comput. Surv. (CSUR) **31**(3), 264–323 (1999)
9. Khashabi, D., Wieting, J., Liu, J.Y., Liang, F.: Clustering with side information: from a probabilistic model to a deterministic algorithm. arXiv preprint arXiv:1508.06235 (2015)
10. Klein, D., Kamvar, S.D., Manning, C.D.: From instance-level constraints to space-level constraints: making the most of prior knowledge in data clustering. Tech. rep, Stanford (2002)
11. Law, M.H.C., Topchy, A., Jain, A.K.: Clustering with soft and group constraints. In: Fred, A., Caelli, T.M., Duin, R.P.W., Campilho, A.C., de Ridder, D. (eds.) SSPR /SPR 2004. LNCS, vol. 3138, pp. 662–670. Springer, Heidelberg (2004). https://doi.org/10.1007/978-3-540-27868-9_72
12. Pelleg, D., Baras, D.: K-means with large and noisy constraint sets. In: Kok, J.N., Koronacki, J., Mantaras, R.L., Matwin, S., Mladenič, D., Skowron, A. (eds.) ECML 2007. LNCS (LNAI), vol. 4701, pp. 674–682. Springer, Heidelberg (2007). https://doi.org/10.1007/978-3-540-74958-5_67
13. Schmidt, J., Brandle, E.M., Kramer, S.: Clustering with attribute-level constraints. In: 2011 IEEE 11th International Conference on Data Mining, pp. 1206–1211. IEEE (2011)
14. Triguero, I., et al.: KEEL 3.0: an open source software for multi-stage analysis in data mining. Int. J. Comput. Intell. Syst. **10**(1), 1238–1249 (2017)

15. Wagstaff, K., Cardie, C., Rogers, S., Schrödl, S.: Constrained k-means clustering with background knowledge. In: Proceedings of the Eighteenth International Conference on Machine Learning, Morgan Kaufmann Publishers Inc., pp. 577–584 (2001)
16. Xing, E.P., Jordan, M.I., Russell, S.J., Ng, A.Y.: Distance metric learning with application to clustering with side-information. In: Advances in neural information processing systems, pp. 521–528 (2003)
17. Zhang, W., Wang, X., Zhao, D., Tang, X.: Graph degree linkage: agglomerative clustering on a directed graph. In: Fitzgibbon, A., Lazebnik, S., Perona, P., Sato, Y., Schmid, C. (eds.) ECCV 2012. LNCS, vol. 7572, pp. 428–441. Springer, Heidelberg (2012). https://doi.org/10.1007/978-3-642-33718-5_31

Multi-expert Methods Evaluation on Financial and Economic Data: Introducing Bag of Experts

A. C. Umaquinga-Criollo[1,2](✉), J. D. Tamayo-Quintero[3], M. N. Moreno-García[1], J. A. Riascos[5,6,7], and D. H. Peluffo-Ordóñez[4,5,7]

[1] Universidad de Salamanca, Salamanca, Spain
acumaquinga@usal.es
[2] Universidad Técnica del Norte, Ibarra, Ecuador
[3] Universidad Nacional de Colombia, Manizales, Colombia
[4] Universidad Yachay Tech, Urcuquí, Ecuador
[5] Corporación Universitaria Autónoma de Nariño, Pasto, Colombia
[6] Universidad Mariana, Pasto, Colombia
[7] SDAS Research Group, Ibarra, Ecuador
www.sdas-group.com

Abstract. The use of machine learning into economics scenarios results appealing since it allows for automatically testing economic models and predict consumer/client behavior to support decision-making processes. The finance market typically uses a set of expert labelers or Bureau credit scores given by governmental or private agencies such as Experian, Equifax, and Creditinfo, among others. This work focuses on introducing a so-named Bag of Expert (BoE): a novel approach for creating multi-expert Learning (MEL) frameworks aimed to emulate real experts labeling (human-given labels) using neural networks. The MEL systems "learn" to perform decision-making tasks by considering a uniform number of labels per sample or individuals along with respective descriptive variables. The BoE is created similarly to Generative Adversarial Network (GANs), but rather than using noise or perturbation by a generator, we trained a feed-forward neural network to randomize sampling data, and either add or decrease hidden neurons. Additionally, this paper aims to investigate the performance on economics-related datasets of several state-of-the-art MEL methods, such as GPC, GPC-PLAT, KAAR, MA-LFC, MA-DGRL, and MA-MAE. To do so, we develop an experimental framework composed of four tests: the first one using novice experts; the second with proficient experts; the third is a mix of novices, intermediate and proficient experts, and the last one uses crowd-sourcing. Our BoE method presents promising results and can be suitable as an alternative to properly assess the reliability of both MEL methods and conventional labeler generators (i.e., virtual expert labelers).

Keywords: Bag of experts · Multi-expert · Feed-forward neural network · Finance · Investment banking · Crowd-sourcing

E. A. de la Cal et al. (Eds.): HAIS 2020, LNAI 12344, pp. 437–449, 2020.
https://doi.org/10.1007/978-3-030-61705-9_36

1 Introduction

Nowadays, the use of machine learning (ML) techniques is consolidated as a powerful tool for commercial, finance, and investment banking scenarios a [13, 29]. Indeed, ML systems have gained increasing interest in economics scenarios, and their implementation is considered even a good practice for algorithmic trading, stock market predictions, and fraud detection [1,14,19,29]. One of the main ML tasks is the automatic classification, which consists of assigning a class or label to a new sample according to a previously performed learning process (known as training). A classification task can be either one-label and multi-label. One-label problems have mutually exclusive classes from a unique labeling vector, that means, an only single class can be assigned to the object (one label - one object); on the other hand, in multi-label, the classes are not mutually exclusive, where a class can occur more than one time in one object (multiple labels - one object). A particular case of multi-label analysis is the one on which all samples have assigned the same number of labels (uniform number of labels), and they are attributed individually to a single labeler or Expert. This case is known as multi-labeler, multiple annotators, or Multiple Experts (multi-expert) Learning, here termed as MEL. Some special applications of MEL are: a panel of specialists diagnosing a patient's pathology [4,16,18] or a teacher team assessing the academic performance of a student [7,21] or high-risk investment companies that base their decision according to experts in different fields [6]. Inspired in these approaches, here we propose a methodology called Bag of Experts (BoE). Although, multi-expert labelers make the classification a challenge since the ground truth is not identified [17,20], the data within these scenarios have an improvement over the only labeler because they can compensate for the influence of wrong labels and identify the excellent and lousy labelers [8,26]. In this connection, MEL is an advantage in many fields, and BoE can be a realistic alternative to imitate expert labelers compared to conventional techniques. Our methodology attempts to emulate expert labelers with a similar idea of Generative Adversarial Networks (GANs), but without perturbation or noise, thus, this paper introduces an approach focused on creating realistic expert labelers.

The rest of this manuscript is structured as follows: Sect. 2 briefly reviews some remarkable related works. Section 3 states the materials, our BoE approach, and outlines the considered MEL methods. Sections 4 and 5 gathers the results and discussion on the use of BoE on the comparative of MEL techniques. Finally, Sect. 6 presents the concluding remarks.

2 Related Works

Muti-expert technique is widely used in supervised classification, mainly applied in areas such as medicine, business, image processing, education, food, and beverage tasting, among others. Consequently, the use of this technique implies to select and model the expert carefully because it is necessary to consider different parameters such as years of experience, training, and subjectivity [7] as well as the agreement of all experts based on their statement [3,5,25]. Some authors addressed the problem of uncertain levels of experts with methodologies that try to balance the negative effect of mislabelled samples [7,8] or using a penalization factor to improve the efficiency [8,17,20]. Classical techniques such as majority vote [11] or binary classification [15] seek to reduce the influence of novice experts and malicious annotators. Indeed, the latest issue is no stranger to financial problems, where the intrinsic complexity and subjective knowledge in quantitative models increase the difficulty of this challenging task [12]. Therefore, multi-expert techniques applied in this area might allow cost reduction, a better catalog of services, attract new clients, and contribute to decision-making processes. For example, Zhang et al. [31] used supervised learning with multi-experts to tackle problems related to Industrial IoT Big Data with crowd-sourcing.

Due to associated costs in the acquisition, the expert panel's payment, or the experts' availability, obtaining data from real cases is not an easy task [27]. For these reasons, researchers use simulated annotators to test multi-expert techniques. For example, Murillo et al. [17] contaminate the data with a percentage error in one class; meanwhile, Gil et al. [10] simulated the annotation of the experts using both logistic regression and probabilities using a Bernoulli distribution with one and two coins.

3 Materials and Methods

3.1 Databases

To test our method, we used two financial and economic well-known datasets from UCI-repository [9]: the "Australian Credit Approval" and "default of credit card clients."

Database I - Default of credit card clients: This dataset refers to the customers' default payments in Taiwan, and compares the predictive accuracy of the probability of default. It contains 30.0000 records and 23 variables: 20 numerical and three categorical (Sex, Education, and Marriage). The output variable is 'default payment' with a binary variable (Yes = 1, or No = 0); the classes are imbalanced (77.9% to label 0). We cleaned and normalized the data matrix before carrying out the experiments.

Database II - Australian Credit Approval: This dataset holds credit card applications. It contains 690 records and 14 variables: six numerical and eight categorical. This dataset is suitable for testing because of the mix of attributes: continuous, nominal with small numbers of values, and nominal with more significant amounts of values. The output variable is a binary data (1 or 2) concerning to the credit approval. The classes are imbalanced (55.5% to label 1), and (44.5% to label 2). We normalized the data matrix before carrying out the experiments.

3.2 Proposed Approach for Generating Artificial Experts

Workflow: Fig. 1 illustrates the proposed methodology: we firstly introduce the Generator that randomizes the training data and hidden neurons, then an FNN is used to create virtual multi-experts labelers with different levels of expertise. We ran 300 times this process to imitate 300 experts ranked according to F1-score and saved in a bag. We selected different virtual expert labelers from the bag to create a MEL for comparing multi-expert methods. Thus, we carried out four experiments with the following settings: Novice (lowest BoE scores), Expert (highest BoE scores), Mix (both high and low BoE scores), and Crowd (several BoE scores).

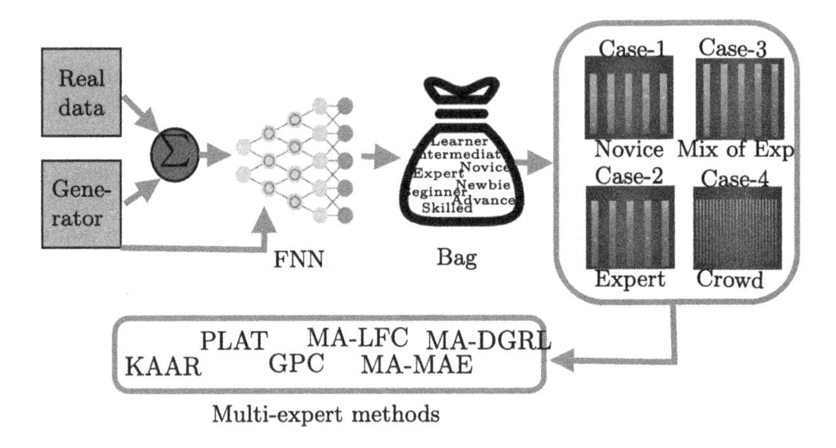

Fig. 1. Proposed methodology: BAg of Experts (BoE)

Generator: Responsible for randomizing the sample data used to training an FNN and the neurons to add or decrease the neurons, allowing a stochastic variation.

FNN: Forward Neural Networks present only one-way and one-directional connections among their neurons; in this architecture, neurons are arranged in different parallel layers [2]. In this case, the input data come from the real data sample using the generator, and additionally, the hidden neurons are randomized (adding or decreasing neurons), allowing different outputs (one FNN model) for each release.

Bag of Experts: It is composed of the 300 FNN models (300 virtual experts) obtained per each release. The virtual experts are used to predict the labels in both datasets, and ranked according to F1-score.

Multi-expert approach: We created a multi-expert dataset using multiples FNN models. To define multi-expert formally. First, suppose that the ordered pair $\{x_i, \bar{y}_i\}$ to denote the i-th sample or data point, where x_i is its D-dimensional feature vector, and $\bar{y}_i \in \{1, 0\}$ is its binary class label. Assuming that m data points are available, all feature vectors can be gathered into a $m \times d$ data matrix X such that $X = (x_1, \ldots, x_N)^\top$, whereas labels into a labeling vector $\bar{y} \in^N$. It is noteworthy that the latter is a single vector representing a expert set of L labeling vectors $\{y^{(1)}, \ldots, y^{(c)}\}$, since our task is **multi-expert**

type. Then, $\bar{y}$ is a reference vector to be determined. To set it, we can intuitively opt by an expectation operator over the input labeling vectors, i.e. the simple average as done in [11,15]. Nevertheless, other mixture alternatives can be considered as linear combinations, mode, median as well as non-linear mixtures [10,23,24,28,30]. For instance in Fig. 1 (Experiment I -Case 1-) the data have five labels given by five virtual experts such as an expert set of labeling vectors $\{y^{(1)}, y^{(2)}, y^{(3)}, y^{(4)}, y^{(5)}\}$ where $\bar{y}$ is the vector to solve with the multi-expert techniques.

Multi-expert methods: We considered the following methods to give a comparison of multi-expert classification for both dataset well-known "austalian credit aproval and default of credit card client": i) Gausian Process-Based classification with **P**ositive **L**abel frecuency **T**hreshold (GPC-**PLAT**) [30]; ii) Multiple Annotators Distinguish Good from Random Labelers (**MA-DGRL**) [23]; iii) Multiple Annotators Modeling Annotator Expertise (**MA-MAE**) [28]; iv) Multiple annotators using Learning From Crowds (**MA-LFC**) [22]; v) Kernel Alignment-based Annotator Relevance analysis (**KAAR**) [10]; and vi) the well-know Gaussian Processes Classification (**GPC**)[24]. To evaluate the stability of the presented approach, we used a 36 times cross-validation scheme and partitioned the data 70% for training and 30% for testing. We measured the performance of multi-expert methods with three established metrics: Accuracy (ACC), Area Under the ROC Curve (AUC), and the F1-score. We summarize our training algorithms as below:

Algorithm 1. Proposed method

Require: All the hyper-parameters, Dataset I and Dataset II.
  Initialize all the parameters
  $X \leftarrow$ Train data, $y \leftarrow$ Labels for record in x, $l \leftarrow$ Number of hidden neurons, $n = size(X, 1)$, $r = randperm(n)$, $k = 300$, $K = \{.\}$, $i = 0$.
  while $i \neq k$ **do**
    Training
    $\frac{a}{2} \leftarrow r(i)$
    $tempX \leftarrow X\,(:, a : 2a)$
    $tempy \leftarrow X\,(:, a : 2a)$
    $l \leftarrow \left(\frac{n}{a}\right) + 1$
    $K\,\{i\} = FNN(tempX, tempy, l)$
    Testing
    $test(K\,\{i\}\,, X, y)$
    $i = i + 1$
  end while
  $K\,\{.\} = sort(K\,\{.\})$ //The annotator are sorted using F1-score
  return$(K\,\{.\})$

---

4 Results

We carried out four experiments with different annotators settings in both datasets.

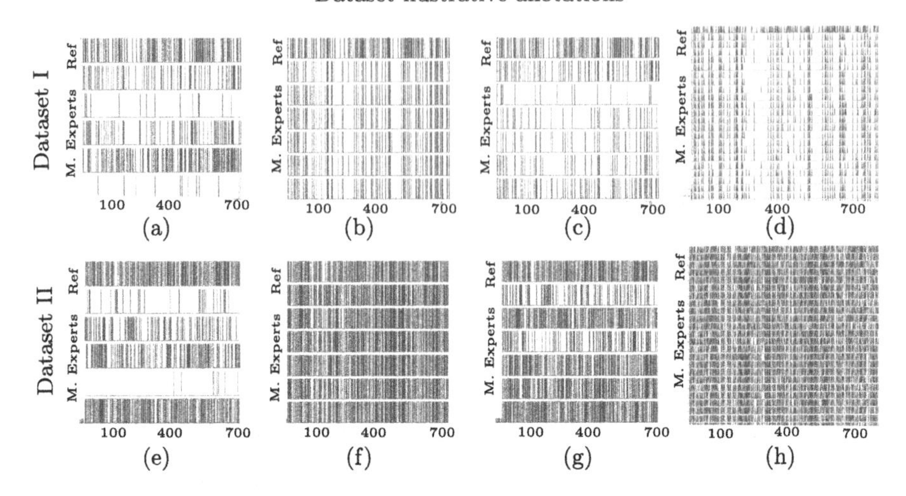

Fig. 2. The illustrative results of the virtual experts: (a)(b)(c) show different virtual experts from the Dataset I. The first row is the ground truth and (e)(d)(f) are the annotations or labels from the Dataset II.

Experiment I: we selected five simulated labelers from the bag of 300 experts; for each dataset, we chose the labelers with the lower performance trying to simulate experts with little expertise (see the (a) and (e) of Fig. 3). Figure 2 shows an illustrative presentation of the expert's labels, where the first row of each image represents the ground truth, and the rest, the labels of each expert. The (a) and (e) of Fig. 2 represents the Experiment I for dataset I and II, respectively.

Experiment II: we selected one virtual annotator more (six in total) from the BoE; in this case, for each dataset, we picked the annotators with the higher performance (see the (b) and (f) of Fig. 3), trying to simulate experts whit high experience, the induced "knowledge" of the annotators are similar between them. The (b) and (f) of Fig. 2 represents the expert's labels for the dataset I and II in Experiment II, respectively.

Experiment III: we selected six different labelers manually to have different simulated levels of 'knowledge' (see the (c) and (g) in Fig. 3). Likewise, the (c) and (g) of Fig. 2 represents the expert's labels for the Dataset I and II in Experiment III, respectively.

Experiment IV: finally, we selected 61 virtual experts from the BoE, trying to represent a crowd-sourcing annotation (see the (d) and (h) in Fig. 3). The (c) and (g) of Fig. 2 shows the expert's labels for the Dataset I and II in Experiment III, respectively.

Firstly, we would like to highlight that the built BoE for each dataset uses imbalanced data, to simulate real experts: Dataset 1 has a high level of imbalance data (4:1), i.e., for four labels in class 1, one corresponds to class 2. Meanwhile, the second dataset has a better relationship between classes (1:1.2).

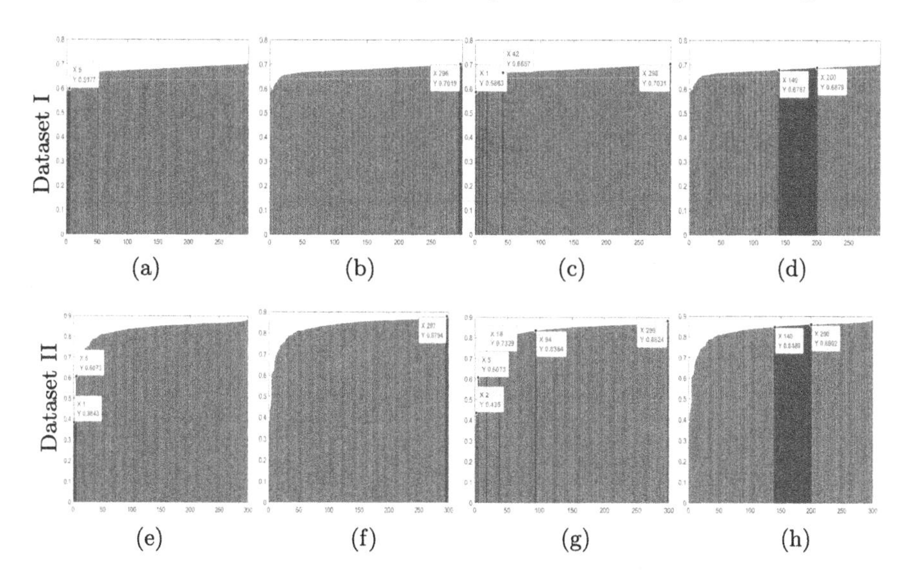

Fig. 3. An illustrative image of Bag of Expert (BoE) carried out by virtual experts and ranking to the lowest at highest according to F1-score.

Table 1. Summarize of the experiments

	PLAT	MA_DCFRL	MA_MAE	MA_LFC	KARR	GPC
Dataset I						
Exp I		X		**O**		
Exp II	**O**	X				
Exp III		X		**O**		
Exp IV		X				**O**
Dataset II						
ExpI	X			**O**		
Exp II				X	**O**	
Exp III	X	**O**				
Exp IV		**O**	X			

Consequently, the dataset I represents a difficulty for learning algorithms since they would be biassed towards the majority group. In the real world, usually, the minority class is the more important to the expert as, despite its rareness, it may carry essential and useful knowledge.

Lately, we used three different metrics to evaluate the performance, namely. ACC, AUC-ROC, and F1-score (Fig. 6); however, some performance measurements are sensible to imbalanced data; for that reason, we defined both the winner and loser using at least the concordance of two metrics. Table 1 shows

Table 2. Average of the experiments

	Dataset I			Dataset II			Average all datasets		
	AUC	F1_score	ACC	AUC	F1_score	ACC	AUC	F1_score	ACC
PLAT	**0,641**	0,682	0,800	0,740	0,743	0,753	0,691	0,712	0,776
MA_DGFRL	0,597	0,621	0,629	0,764	0,768	0,769	0,680	0,695	0,699
MA_MAE	0,599	0,668	**0,818**	0,762	**0,793**	**0,777**	0,681	**0,730**	**0,798**
MA_LFC	0,652	**0,688**	0,814	**0,772**	0,773	0,747	**0,712**	**0,730**	0,780
KARR	0,606	0,661	0,801	0,754	0,754	0,771	0,680	0,708	0,786
GPC	0,620	0,676	0,811	0,750	0,751	0,764	0,685	0,713	0,787

Table 3. Result of the experiments

Exp1	Dataset 1 - Default Payment			Dataset 2 - Credit Approval		
	AUC	F1-score	ACC	AUC	F1-score	ACC
PLAT	0,604 +- 0,033	0,595 +- 0,029	0,701 +- 0,028	0,478 +- 0,022	0,467 +- 0,033	0,518 +- 0,029
MA_DGFRL	0,536 +- 0,033	0,555 +- 0,057	0,524 +- 0,171	0,502 +- 0,025	0,507 +- 0,072	0,513 +- 0,044
MA_MAE	0,512 +- 0,013	0,591 +- 0,068	**0,797 +- 0,021**	0,506 +- 0,007	**0,617 +- 0,007**	0,561 +- 0,023
MA_LFC	**0,618 +- 0,032**	**0,624 +- 0,035**	0,762 +- 0,032	**0,597 +- 0,024**	0,597 +- 0,024	**0,591 +- 0,024**
KARR	0,551 +- 0,030	0,592 +- 0,037	0,786 +- 0,027	0,501 +- 0,017	0,484 +- 0,070	0,552 +- 0,027
GPC	0,574 +- 0,027	0,617 +- 0,038	0,794 +- 0,027	0,494 +- 0,022	0,483 +- 0,045	0,539 +- 0,030
Exp2	Default Payment			Credit Approval		
	AUC	F1-score	ACC	AUC	F1-score	ACC
PLAT	**0.668 +- 0.031**	**0.719 +- 0.032**	**0.836 +- 0.025**	0,862 +- 0,049	0,862 +- 0,043	0,861 +- 0,044
MA_DGFRL	0.649 +- 0.039	0.691 +- 0.055	0.781 +- 0.139	0,870 +- 0,028	0,869 +- 0,028	0,869 +- 0,029
MA_MAE	0.666 +- 0.031	0.717 +- 0.033	0.835 +- 0.025	0,874 +- 0,022	0,873 +- 0,023	0,874 +- 0,023
MA_LFC	0.664 +- 0.030	0.708 +- 0.033	0.830 +- 0.025	0,844 +- 0,104	0,844 +- 0,104	0,843 +- 0,107
KARR	0.642 +- 0.064	0.695 +- 0.083	0.803 +- 0.139	**0,879 +- 0,020**	**0,879 +- 0,020**	**0,880 +- 0,020**
GPC	0.653 +- 0.049	0.706 +- 0.062	0.815 +- 0.109	0,878 +- 0,019	0,878 +- 0,019	0,879 +- 0,019
Exp3	Default Payment			Credit Approval		
	AUC	F1-score	ACC	AUC	F1-score	ACC
PLAT	0,625 +- 0,038	0,693 +- 0,038	0,826 +- 0,027	0,754 +- 0,038	0,778 +- 0,029	0,771 +- 0,034
MA_DGFRL	0,552 +- 0,029	0,546 +- 0,025	0,430 +- 0,031	**0,808 +- 0,023**	**0,822 +- 0,022**	**0,820 +- 0,023**
MA_MAE	0,553 +- 0,031	0,645 +- 0,041	0,805 +- 0,028	0,806 +- 0,026	0,822 +- 0,024	0,819 +- 0,025
MA_LFC	**0,661 +- 0,032**	**0,711 +- 0,035**	**0,832 +- 0,026**	0,783 +- 0,024	0,787 +- 0,024	0,789 +- 0,024
KARR	0,590 +- 0,039	0,662 +- 0,050	0,813 +- 0,029	0,764 +- 0,036	0,781 +- 0,033	0,778 +- 0,035
GPC	0,601 +- 0,035	0,674 +- 0,048	0,818 +- 0,028	0,758 +- 0,036	0,773 +- 0,033	0,771 +- 0,035
Exp4	Default Payment			Credit Approval		
	AUC	F1-score	ACC	AUC	F1-score	ACC
PLAT	**0.654 +- 0.058**	0.693 +- 0.066	0.806 +- 0.107	0,865 +- 0,023	0,863 +- 0,022	0,862 +- 0,022
MA_DGFRL	0.593 +- 0.046	0.624 +- 0.077	0.631 +- 0.204	**0,877 +- 0,019**	**0,875 +- 0,019**	0,873 +- 0,019
MA_MAE	0.624 +- 0.029	0.686 +- 0.035	0.820 +- 0.022	0,861 +- 0,018	0,860 +- 0,018	0,855 +- 0,018
MA_LFC	0.639 +- 0.026	0.683 +- 0.029	0.770 +- 0.190	0,864 +- 0,016	0,862 +- 0,016	0,763 +- 0,274
KARR	0.635 +- 0.027	0.699 +- 0.030	0.826 +- 0.019	0,873 +- 0,020	0,873 +- 0,020	**0,874 +- 0,020**
GPC	0.634 +- 0.028	**0.700 +- 0.032**	**0.827 +- 0.019**	0,870 +- 0,019	0,868 +- 0,019	0,868 +- 0,019

the overall results of the experiments (the best method), where X means the lowest score and O the highest one. Table 3 shows deeply the findings. Finally, Fig.4 shows the box-plots of the F1 score. This metric gives a weighted average of precision and recall, so it is suitable to analyze the consistency of the multi-expert methods. Likewise, Fig. 5 and Fig. 6 show the performance metrics of the chosen experiment and multi-expert methods, respectively. The reader can notice that depending on the experiment, this number varies (as it was explained before), therefore, the Experiment 4, which has 61 experts, was reduced to the minimum, maximum and mean value, for visualization purposes.

5 Discussion

According to Table 1, MA-DCFRL is the loser method in Dataset I; however, in Dataset II, the same method is the winner of two experiments. Such a fact allowed us to suggest that MA-DCFRL does not have an excellent performance when imbalanced data. In the experiments I and III, where the annotators have different levels of expertise, MA-LFC presents better performance scores (Table 2 and Table 3), and it was the winner three out of four tests (two to Dataset I and one to Dataset II). Thus, this fact could suggest that this method has excellent performance when the annotators have different levels of expertise.

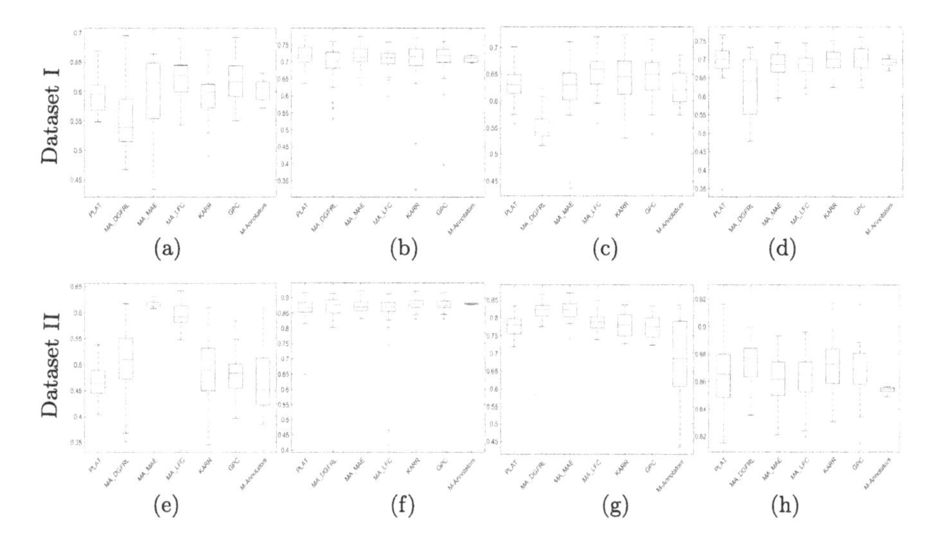

Fig. 4. Box-plot F1-score

In Dataset II, PLAT was the method that presents a lower score for experiments I and III, where the annotator has a different level of expertise, and the data almost have a balance between class. It suggests that this method should be avoided when the annotator presents different levels of experience; however, the best performance for this metric was obtaining in Dataset I when the annotators have similar levels of knowledge. The MA-MAE reached a better average in comparison with the other methods. Nevertheless, this method presents some handicaps in Experiment IV: the lowest in Dataset II and the second lower score in Dataset I, where the annotators are multiples, in this case, sixty-two. On the other hand, KARR is a suitable method if the data are balanced, and the annotators have a high level of experience. This method won in experiment II and was the second-best score in Experiment IV (Dataset II). Finally, the GPC method presents the best performance with imbalanced data (Dataset I) applied to Experiment IV, crowd annotations. However, the method needs more testing to be conclusive.

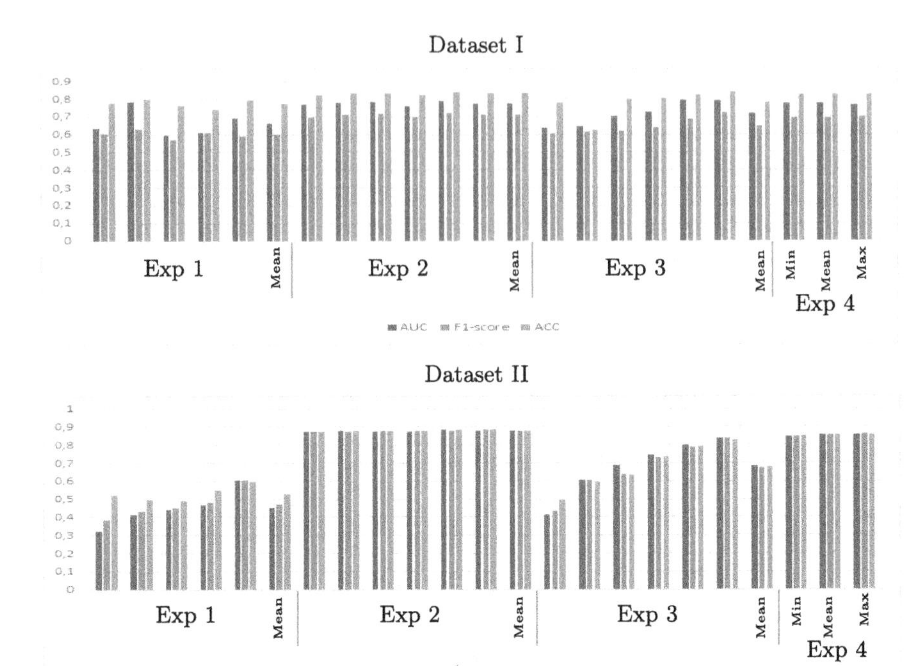

Fig. 5. Annotators settings performance

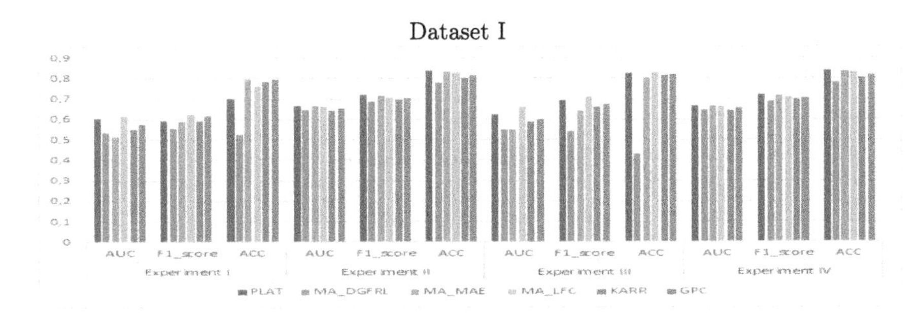

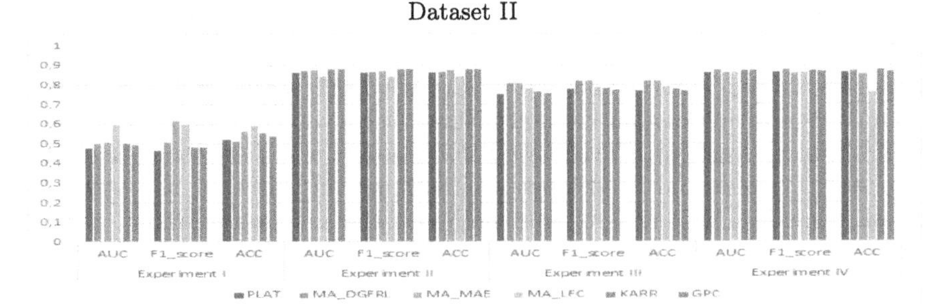

Fig. 6. Performance results

The methods have different behavior according to the experiments and datasets (see Table 3), for example, Fig. 6) in (a) shows that the MA-MAE box extends nearly to the lower extreme, indicating that data less than the media is likely to least relative consistent because there is no a significant jump. Contrarily, in (e), the same method is the most consistent technique, suggesting that some multi-expert methods could be susceptible to the data imbalances.

6 Conclusions and a Future Work

We proved experimentally that the proposed approach (BoE) is capable of created virtual experts. In general, the use of this multi-expert strategy provides a significant improvement in the classifier's design compared to the simulated annotations approach. Besides, the proposed method tests the capability of currently multi-expert methods and gives some recommendations to use one or another method concerning the data and level of expertise. For future work, we are aiming to explore different alternatives to use a simple method for considering the minority class as the one more important to the expert, because it may carry essential and useful knowledge. Also, multiclass scenarios should be considered for testing the multi-expert methods used in the present work.

Acknowledgment. This work is supported by the Smart Data Analysis Systems Group - SDAS Research Group (http://sdas-group.com)

References

1. Attigeri, G., Manohara Pai, M., Pai, R.: Framework to predict NPA/willful defaults in corporate loans: a big data approach. Int. J. Electr. Comput. Eng. **9**(5), 3786–3797 (2019)
2. Bebis, G., Georgiopoulos, M.: Feed-forward neural networks. IEEE Potentials **13**(4), 27–31 (1994)
3. Blitzer, J., Crammer, K., Kulesza, A., Pereira, F., Wortman, J.: Learning bounds for domain adaptation (2009)
4. Chang, V.: Generation of a HER2 breast cancer gold-standard using supervised learning from multiple experts. In: Stoyanov, D., et al. (eds.) LABELS/CVII/STENT -2018. LNCS, vol. 11043, pp. 45–54. Springer, Cham (2018). https://doi.org/10.1007/978-3-030-01364-6_6
5. Crammer, K., Kearns, M., Wortman, J.: Learning from multiple sources. J. Mach. Learn. Res. **9**, 1757–1774 (2008)
6. Danenas, P., Garsva, G., Simutis, R.: Development of discriminant analysis and majority-voting based credit risk assessment classifier. vol. 1, pp. 204–209 (2011)
7. Dekel, O., Shamir, O.: Good Learners for Evil Teachers. Association for Computing Machinery, New York (2009)
8. Donmez, P., Carbonell, J.G., Schneider, J.: Efficiently Learning the Accuracy of Labeling Sources for Selective Sampling. Association for Computing Machinery, New York (2009)
9. Dua, D., Graff, C.: UCI machine learning repository

10. Gil-Gonzalez, J., Alvarez-Meza, A., Orozco-Gutierrez, A.: Learning from multiple annotators using kernel alignment. Pattern Recogn. Lett. **116**, 150–156 (2018)
11. Groot, P., Birlutiu, A., Heskes, T.: Learning from multiple annotators with Gaussian processes. In: Honkela, T., Duch, W., Girolami, M., Kaski, S. (eds.) ICANN 2011. LNCS, vol. 6792, pp. 159–164. Springer, Heidelberg (2011). https://doi.org/10.1007/978-3-642-21738-8_21
12. Kim, M.J., Min, S.H., Han, I.: An evolutionary approach to the combination of multiple classifiers to predict a stock price index. Expert Syst. Appl. **31**(2), 241–247 (2006)
13. Klepac, G.: Customer profiling in complex analytical environments using swarm intelligence algorithms. Int. J. Swarm Intell. Res. (IJSIR) **7**(3), 43–70 (2016)
14. Lee, T., Cho, J., Kwon, D., Sohn, S.: Global stock market investment strategies based on financial network indicators using machine learning techniques. Expert Syst. Appl. **117**, 228–242 (2019)
15. Long, C., Hua, G., Kapoor, A.: A joint gaussian process model for active visual recognition with expertise estimation in crowdsourcing. Int. J. Comput. Vis. **116**(2), 136–160 (2016)
16. Mahapatra, D.: Combining multiple expert annotations using semi-supervised learning and graph cuts for medical image segmentation. Comput. Vis. Image Underst. **151**, 114–123 (2016)
17. Murillo Rendón, S.: Metodología para el aprendizaje de máquina a partir de múltiples expertos en procesos de clasificación de bioseñales. Ph.D. thesis
18. Nir, G., et al.: Automatic grading of prostate cancer in digitized histopathology images: learning from multiple experts. Med. Image Anal. **50**, 167–180 (2018)
19. Patwardhan, S., Yadav, D., Parlikar, S.: A review of role of data mining techniques in portfolio management. J. Adv. Res. Dyn. Control Syst. **11**(2 Special Issue), 674–681 (2019)
20. Peluffo-Ordóñez, D., Murillo-Rendón, S., Arias-Londoño, J., Castellanos-Domínguez, G.: A multi-class extension for multi-labeler support vector machines, pp. 701–706 (2014)
21. Raykar, V., et al.: Supervised learning from multiple experts : whom to trust when everyone lies a bit, vol. 382 (2009)
22. Raykar, V., et al.: Learning from crowds. J. Mach. Learn. Res. **11**, 1297–1322 (2010)
23. Rodrigues, F., Pereira, F., Ribeiro, B.: Learning from multiple annotators: distinguishing good from random labelers. Pattern Recogn. Lett. **34**(12), 1428–1436 (2013)
24. Rodrigues, F., Pereira, F., Ribeiro, B.: Gaussian process classification and active learning with multiple annotators. In: Xing, E.P., Jebara, T. (eds.) Proceedings of the 31st International Conference on Machine Learning. Proceedings of Machine Learning Research PMLR, Bejing, China, 22–24 June 2014, vol. 32, pp. 433–441 (2014)
25. Valizadegan, H., Nguyen, Q., Hauskrecht, M.: Learning classification models from multiple experts. J. Biomed. Inform. **46**(6), 1125–1135 (2013)
26. Wang, W., Zhou, Z.: Learnability of multi-instance multi-label learning. Chin. Sci. Bull. **57**(19), 2488–2491 (2012)
27. Wiebe, J., Mihalcea, R.: Word sense and subjectivity, vol. 1, pp. 1065–1072 (2006)
28. Yan, Y., Rosales, R., Fung, G., Subramanian, R., Dy, J.: Learning from multiple annotators with varying expertise. Mach. Learn. **95**(3), 291–327 (2013). https://doi.org/10.1007/s10994-013-5412-1

29. Yun, H., Lee, M., Kang, Y., Seok, J.: Portfolio management via two-stage deep learning with a joint cost. Expert Syst. Appl. **143**, 113041 (2020)
30. Zhang, J., Wu, X., Sheng, V.S.: Imbalanced multiple noisy labeling. IEEE Trans. Knowl. Data Eng. **27**(2), 489–503 (2015)
31. Zhang, Q., Yang, L.T., Chen, Z., Li, P., Bu, F.: An adaptive dropout deep computation model for industrial IoT big data learning with crowdsourcing to cloud computing. IEEE Trans. Ind. Inform. **15**(4), 2330–2337 (2019)

The Borda Count as a Tool for Reducing the Influence of the Distance Function on *k*means

Noelia Rico[1(✉)], Raúl Pérez-Fernández[2,3], and Irene Díaz[1]

[1] Department of Computer Science, University of Oviedo, Oviedo, Spain
{noeliarico,sirene}@uniovi.es
[2] Department of Statistics and O.R. and Mathematics Didactics, University of Oviedo, Oviedo, Spain
perezfernandez@uniovi.es,raul.perezfernandez@ugent.be
[3] KERMIT, Department of Data Analysis and Mathematical Modelling, Ghent University, Ghent, Belgium

Abstract. The aim of a clustering method is to create groups (clusters) of objects that are similar to each other. This similarity is usually measured by means of a distance, thus, the choice of distance function plays a crucial role in the clustering process. In this work, we propose a variant of the classical clustering method *k*means that combines the information given by different distances to group the objects. More precisely, the cluster to which an object is assigned is chosen by applying the Borda Count to the rankings of closest cluster centers induced by different distances. Experiments were carried out for 81 different datasets. For the vast majority of these datasets, the clusters obtained with the proposed method reduced the Total Distance Within Clusters (TDWC) in comparison with the clusters obtained with the classical *k*means.

Keywords: Clustering · Aggregation · Ranking · Borda count · *k*means

1 Introduction

The task of grouping objects of a dataset into smaller subsets of objects based on their similarity is broadly known as **clustering**. Clustering methods can be divided into different families based on their strategy for creating the clusters [8]. One of these families is called **partitional clustering** [9], being ***k*means** [5] the most prominent method of the family. This method is an iterative process that, after an initial cluster allocation, iteratively recalculates the clusters by reassigning the objects to the cluster whose center is the closest. Obviously, the

This research has been partially supported by Spanish MINECO project (TIN2017-87600-P) and FC-GRUPIN-IDI/2018/000176. Raúl Pérez-Fernández acknowledges the support of the Research Foundation of Flanders (FWO17/PDO/160).

E. A. de la Cal et al. (Eds.): HAIS 2020, LNAI 12344, pp. 450–461, 2020.
https://doi.org/10.1007/978-3-030-61705-9_37

way in which the distance of the objects to the centers is calculated plays a big role in the method of *k*means.

In this work, we present a variant of *k*means that reduces the influence of the distance function by modifying the step in which objects are assigned to a cluster. More precisely, the cluster to which an object is assigned is not calculated based on one sole distance function but, instead, by several distance functions fixed beforehand. We bring to the attention the Borda Count social choice function [1], which has been used in the field of social choice theory for centuries, as a tool that can combine the information given by all these distances. In this way, the assignation step becomes more robust with regard to the choice of distance function. Experiments on several artificially generated datasets support the claim.

The paper is organised as follows: in Sect. 2, the preliminary concepts that are required for the understanding of this work are introduced (the Borda Count, the definition of some prominent distances and the *k*means method). In Sect. 3, the proposed method is introduced. The experiments performed to test the method and the results are discussed in Sect. 4. To sum up, some conclusions and future work are commented in Sect. 5.

2 Preliminaries

In this section, we recall some preliminary notions that will be essential to understand this work.

2.1 Borda Count

Let $\mathscr{C} = \{c_1, c_2, \ldots, c_k\}$ denote a set of candidates. A ranking on $\mathscr{C}$ is the strict part of a total order relation on $\mathscr{C}$. A list of rankings on $\mathscr{C}$ is called a profile of rankings. A **social choice function** [10] is a function that assigns a non-empty subset of $\mathscr{C}$ to any profile of rankings, being this subset understood as the object(s) ranked overall at the best positions in the profile of rankings.

The **Borda Count** [1] is among the most prominent social choice functions. For applying the Borda Count, each candidate is awarded one point every time that it is ranked at a better position than another candidate and half a point every time that it is tied at the same position as another candidate. All the points obtained by a candidate over all rankings in the profile of rankings are added up to obtain the so-called **score** of the candidate. Finally, the Borda Count outputs the candidate(s) with the highest score.

Example 1. Consider the profile of four rankings on a set of six candidates given in Table 1.

The Borda Count is applied to the profile of rankings in Table 1. Table 2 shows the points that each candidate receives in each of the rankings, and the scores obtained by each candidate after adding these points. For instance, for the ranking r_1, candidate C is ranked at the worst position, so receives no points;

Table 1. Profile of four rankings on a set of six candidates.

	Ranking
r_1	$F \succ A \succ D \succ B \succ E \succ C$
r_2	$F \succ A \sim C \sim D \succ B \succ E$
r_3	$F \succ C \succ B \succ A \sim E \succ D$
r_4	$A \sim D \sim F \succ C \succ B \sim E$

candidate E is only ranked at a better position than candidate C, so receives one point; candidate B is only ranked at a better position than candidates E and C, so receives two points; and so on. Notice what happens when two or more candidates are tied. For instance, for the ranking r_4, candidates A, D and F are tied with each other and are ranked at a better position than the other three candidates. Therefore, four points are assigned to each of A, D and F. This process is applied to all the rankings until each candidate obtains a final score. Ultimately, candidates are ranked according to their scores, resulting in the ranking $F \succ A \succ D \succ C \succ B \succ E$.

Table 2. Points for each candidate in each ranking of the profile of rankings in Table 1 applying the Borda Count.

Ranking	A	B	C	D	E	F
r_1	4.0	2.0	0.0	3.0	1.0	5.0
r_2	3.0	1.0	3.0	3.0	0.0	5.0
r_3	1.5	3.0	4.0	0.0	1.5	5.0
r_4	4.0	0.5	2.0	4.0	0.5	4.0
Total	12.5	6.5	9.0	10.0	3.0	19.0
Final ranking	$F \succ A \succ D \succ C \succ B \succ E$					

2.2 Distances

Ten prominent distances[1] in the context of clustering have been selected based on the comparative study presented in [7]. Formally, these ten distances are defined, for any two objects $\mathbf{v} = (v_1, \ldots, v_n)$ and $\mathbf{w} = (w_1, \ldots, w_n)$, as follows.

Canberra distance:

$$d_{\text{can}}(\mathbf{v}, \mathbf{w}) = \sum_{i=1}^{n} \frac{|v_i - w_i|}{|v_i| + |w_i|}.$$

[1] It should be noted that not all the considered distance functions fulfill all axioms normally required for a 'metric'.

Chebyshev distance:

$$d_{\text{che}}(\mathbf{v}, \mathbf{w}) = \max_i |v_i - w_i| \ .$$

Cosine distance:

$$d_{\cos}(\mathbf{v}, \mathbf{w}) = 1 - \frac{\sum_{i=1}^n v_i w_i}{\sqrt{\sum_{i=1}^n v_i^2}\sqrt{\sum_{i=1}^n w_i^2}} \ .$$

Euclidean distance:

$$d_{\text{euc}}(\mathbf{v}, \mathbf{w}) = \sqrt{\sum_{i=1}^n (v_i - w_i)^2} \, .$$

Jaccard distance:

$$d_{\text{jac}}(\mathbf{v}, \mathbf{w}) = \frac{\sum_{i=1}^n (v_i - w_i)^2}{\sum_{i=1}^n v_i^2 + \sum_{i=1}^n w_i^2 - \sum_{i=1}^n v_i w_i} \ .$$

Manhattan distance:

$$d_{\text{man}}(\mathbf{v}, \mathbf{w}) = \sum_{i=1}^n |v_i - w_i| \, .$$

Matusita distance:

$$d_{\text{mat}}(\mathbf{v}, \mathbf{w}) = \sqrt{\sum_{i=1}^n (\sqrt{v_i} - \sqrt{w_i})^2} \, .$$

Max symmetric distance:

$$d_{\text{mas}}(\mathbf{v}, \mathbf{w}) = \max \left(\sum_{i=1}^n \frac{(v_i - w_i)^2}{v_i}, \sum_{i=1}^n \frac{(v_i - w_i)^2}{w_i} \right) \ .$$

Triangular discrimination distance:

$$d_{trd}(\mathbf{v}, \mathbf{w}) = \sum_{i=1}^n \frac{(v_i - w_i)^2}{v_i + w_i} \ .$$

Vicissitude distance:

$$d_{\text{vsd}}(\mathbf{v}, \mathbf{w}) = \sum_{i=1}^n \frac{(v_i - w_i)^2}{\max(v_i, w_i)} \ .$$

2.3 *k*means

Given m objects $\mathbf{x}_1, \ldots, \mathbf{x}_m \in \mathbb{R}^n$ (where n is the number of attributes), a clustering method aims at partitioning $\{\mathbf{x}_1, \ldots, \mathbf{x}_m\}$ into k groups (referred to as clusters) such that objects in the same cluster are the most similar as possible to each other and objects in different clusters are the most different as possible to each other.

The quality of a partition is measured in many different ways, for instance, in terms of the cohesion of the clusters that represents how similar all objects within the clusters are. This cohesion is typically described in terms of the Total Within Sum of Squares (TWSS) that sums the Within Sum of Squares (WSS_j) of all clusters $\{\mathcal{C}_j\}_{j=1}^k$. Formally, the WSS_j of a cluster $\mathcal{C}_j$ with center $\mathbf{c}_j$ is defined as

$$\text{WSS}_j = \sum_{\mathbf{x}_i \in \mathcal{C}_j} \sum_{\ell=1}^{n} (x_{i\ell} - c_{j\ell})^2 ,$$

and the TWSS is defined as

$$\text{TWSS} = \sum_{j=1}^{k} \text{WSS}_j = \sum_{j=1}^{k} \sum_{\mathbf{x}_i \in \mathcal{C}_j} \sum_{\ell=1}^{n} (x_{i\ell} - c_{j\ell})^2 , \tag{1}$$

where $x_{i\ell}$ and $c_{k\ell}$ respectively denote the ℓ-th component of $\mathbf{x}_i$ and $\mathbf{c}_j$ with $\ell \in \{1, \ldots, n\}$.

As proposed by MacQueen in the original paper [5] on *k*means, the goal is to identify the partition of $\{\mathbf{x}_1, \ldots, \mathbf{x}_m\}$ into k clusters that minimizes the TWSS. Unfortunately, finding such partition is a very difficult problem in case m is moderately large. Therefore, an heuristic approach, referred to as *k*means, is typically considered. There are many variants of *k*means, being the three discussed in [6] the most prominent ones. We will focus on the one presented by Lloyd [4].

The method works as follows. First, it is necessary to establish the number k of clusters the dataset is going to be divided into. Next, k initial centers must be selected. This task is usually done randomly but different approaches have been presented through the years [2] making this field of research quite popular. In this work, we follow the most classical approach and select the initial centers randomly among the objects in the dataset. The method of *k*means then consists of two main parts, the assignment phase and the update of the center. After the initial centers have been selected, the assignment phase occurs and the objects are assigned to the cluster represented by the closest center. When all the objects have been assigned to a cluster, the center of each cluster is recomputed as the centroid of all the points belonging to that cluster, meaning by centroid the (componentwise) arithmetic mean of all the objects belonging to that cluster. These steps are repeated until all the points are assigned to the same cluster that in the previous iteration or a maximum number of iterations established beforehand is attained. The pseudocode of this procedure is outlined in Algorithm 1. The assignment phase is highlighted to ease the comparison with the method presented later on in Sect. 3.

Algorithm 1: Lloyd

```
Select k random objects from the dataset as initial centers of the clusters;
for iter to max_iter do
    foreach x_i ∈ objects do
        foreach c_j ∈ centers do
            if d(x_i, c_j) ≤ d(x_i, current_cluster) then
                modify current_cluster to c_j;
            end
        end
    end
    foreach C ∈ clusters do
        update center to centroid of objects in C;
    end
    if none of the points change of cluster then
        break;
    end
```

Note that it is assured that, in each iteration, a partition with a value of TWSS smaller than that of the previous iteration is obtained. Unless the maximum number of iterations is reached, a local minimum of the TWSS is obtained by *k*means. It is common to run the method several times with different initialisations aiming at finding the closest solution to a global minimum of the TWSS.

3 The Proposed Method

The TWSS used for measuring the cohesion of the clusters is inherently linked to the Euclidean distance, as can be seen when rewriting Eq. (1) as

$$\text{TWSS} = \sum_{j=1}^{k} \sum_{\mathbf{x}_i \in \mathcal{C}_j} d_{\text{euc}} \left(\mathbf{x}_i - \mathbf{c}_j\right)^2 . \tag{2}$$

Unfortunately, the Euclidean distance might not be the distance that best fits the given dataset. The goal should then be to minimize the Total Distance Within Clusters (TDWC), defined as follows

$$\text{TDWC}_d = \sum_{j=1}^{k} \sum_{\mathbf{x}_i \in \mathcal{C}_j} d \left(\mathbf{x}_i - \mathbf{c}_j\right)^2 , \tag{3}$$

where d does not need to be the Euclidean distance and could possibly be unknown.

In order to achieve this purpose, we focus on modifying the assignment phase of Lloyd's original algorithm [4] (highlighted in Algorithm 1). As mentioned before, in Lloyd's algorithm the object is assigned to the cluster with the closest center, thus, this assignment relies completely on the considered distance. To overcome this problem, we present an approach that combines different distances for identifying the closest centers. Because the values given by different distances typically are not specified in the same order of magnitude, it is not possible to compare the distances between objects directly. Instead, the ordinal information associated with these distances may be used for defining a ranking of closest centers.

In order to apply the method, the number of clusters k and the set $\mathscr{D}$ of distances must be previously defined. The proposed method is applied by following these steps:

1. Select k different random objects as centers;
2. For object $\mathbf{x_i}$, center $\mathbf{c}_j$ and distance d_ℓ, compute $d_\ell(\mathbf{x}_i, \mathbf{c}_j)$;
3. Obtain the ranking $\succsim_{i,\ell}$ of the centers $\mathbf{c}_j$ by increasing value of $\{d_\ell(\mathbf{x}_i, \mathbf{c}_j)\}_{j=1}^{k}$;
4. Repeat Steps 2 and 3 for the n different distances in $\mathscr{D} = \{d_1, \ldots, d_n\}$;
5. Apply the Borda Count to the rankings $\{\succsim_{i,\ell}\}_{\ell=1}^{n}$ to obtain the winner $\mathbf{c}$ as the closest center;
6. The object $\mathbf{x}_i$ is assigned to the cluster whose center $\mathbf{c}$ was obtained as the closest in Step 6;
7. Update the center $\mathbf{c}_j$ of each cluster $\mathcal{C}_j$;
8. Repeat Steps 2 to 7 until none of the objects change of cluster or a max number of iterations is reached.

Algorithm 2 presents the pseudocode of this method. The highlighted box corresponds to the assignment phase, which represents the only change with respect to the original Lloyd's algorithm described in Sect. 2.

Algorithm 2: The proposed method

```
Select k random objects from the dataset as initial centers of the clusters;
for iter to max_iter do
    foreach x_i ∈ objects do
        initialize empty profile of rankings R_i;
        foreach d_ℓ ∈ distances do
            foreach c_j ∈ centers do
                compute d_ℓ(x_i, c_j);
            rank centers according to increasing value of {d_ℓ(x_i, c_j)};
            insert ranking into R_i;
        modify current cluster to borda_count(R_i);
    foreach C_j ∈ clusters do
        update center to centroid of objects in C_j;
    if none of the points change of cluster then
        break;
```

4 Experimental Results

4.1 Evolution of the TDWC

It is known that classical *k*means guarantees that the TDWC associated with the Euclidean distance (i.e., the TWSS) decreases in each iteration. Unfortunately, this might no longer (and typically will not) be the case for the TDWC associated with a different distance.

In this section, we will analyse how the proposed method behaves with regard to the TDWC associated with all the distances presented in Sect. 2.2. In order to compare the proposed method and the classical *k*means, the latter has been performed 10 times, one considering each of the different distances. The TDWC_{d_ℓ} with respect to each distance d_ℓ is calculated for the proposed method and all 10 *k*means (no matter the distance that was used for the method).

Since the distances are measured in different orders of magnitude, it is necessary to exploit the relative information and deal with the rankings induced by the 10 computed TDWC. More specifically, for each distance, we calculate the associated TDWC_{d_ℓ} for the proposed method and all 10 *k*means. The 11 methods are ranked according to increasing TDWC_{d_ℓ} for each distance d_ℓ. Thus, 10 rankings of the methods are obtained. Finally, to obtain an overall ranking of the methods, the Borda Count is applied to these obtained 10 rankings.

Example 2. A little example is outlined given the toy dataset consisting of 15 objects and 2 variables (x and y) presented in Table 3.

Table 3. Points of a normalized dataset used as an example for illustrating the proposed method.

	A	B	C	D	E	F	G	H	I	J	K	L	M	N	O
x	0.05	0.00	0.09	0.87	1.00	0.76	0.68	0.48	0.92	0.47	0.55	0.56	0.24	0.16	0.04
y	0.34	0.41	0.27	0.20	0.09	0.00	0.55	0.44	0.61	0.88	0.86	1.00	0.64	0.61	0.68

The dataset shown in Table 3 is grouped into clusters 11 different times using different techniques: 10 times using *k*means with a different distance d_ℓ (among those presented in Subsect. 2.2) and 1 additional time using the proposed method with the ten distances. The value of k has been set to 3 and all the partitions have been initialized with the same random centers.

Figure 1 shows how the TDWC_{d_ℓ} associated with each d_ℓ evolves for each method. Note that the TDWC_{d_ℓ} for the proposed method is generally decreasing, thus showing that iterating the method leads to a better partition of the dataset into clusters. Also, the proposed method tends to lead to a smaller TDWC_{d_ℓ} than most of the other methods, even though the method with the smallest TDWC_{d_ℓ} tends to be the *k*means corresponding to the distance d_ℓ that is being used for the TDWC_{d_ℓ}. As will be later explained, all these tendencies have also been observed in all the 81 datasets that have been used for the experiments.

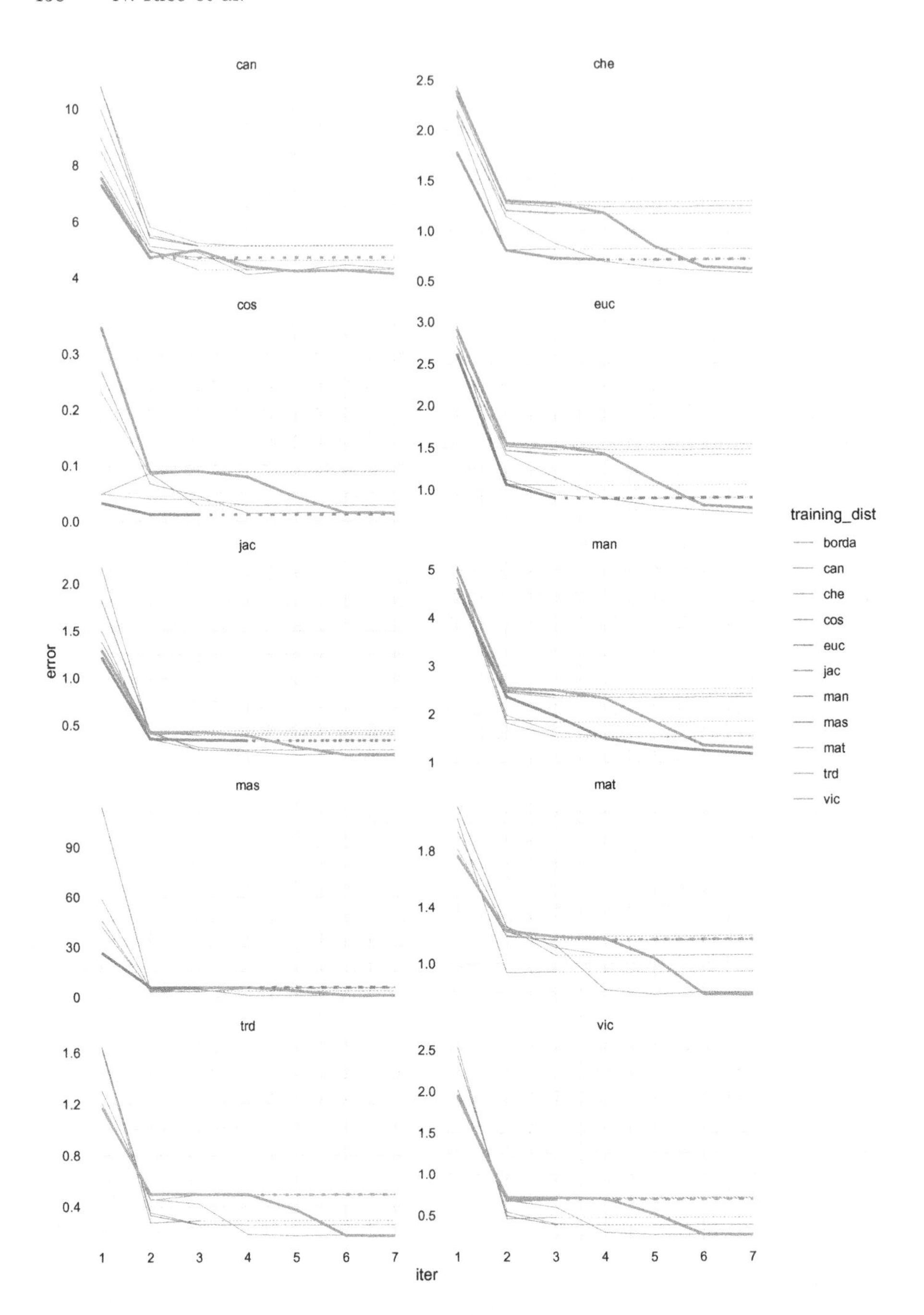

Fig. 1. Evolution of the different TDWC_{d_ℓ} according to each method through the iterations of *k*means and the proposed method. Each box represents the TDWC_{d_ℓ} associated with a certain d_ℓ and each line represents the evolution of TDWC_{d_ℓ} for one of the considered methods.

Table 4. Values of TDWC_{d_ℓ} for each distance d_ℓ obtained for the example dataset when applying the proposed method and all ten *k*means.

	can	che	cos	euc	jac	man	mat	trd	vic	mas	borda
TDWC_{can}	4.701	5.109	5.131	5.109	4.602	4.313	4.274	4.274	4.602	4.274	4.121
TDWC_{che}	1.285	0.706	0.813	0.706	1.166	0.568	1.236	1.236	1.166	1.236	0.608
TDWC_{cos}	0.088	0.028	0.011	0.028	0.089	0.014	0.089	0.089	0.089	0.089	0.014
TDWC_{euc}	1.530	0.894	1.046	0.894	1.404	0.704	1.472	1.472	1.404	1.472	0.770
TDWC_{jac}	0.439	0.236	0.413	0.236	0.335	0.196	0.395	0.395	0.335	0.395	0.181
TDWC_{man}	2.511	1.527	1.829	1.527	2.337	1.160	2.403	2.403	2.337	2.403	1.288
TDWC_{mat}	1.191	1.056	0.940	1.056	1.163	0.794	1.168	1.168	1.163	1.168	0.778
TDWC_{trd}	0.495	0.257	0.289	0.257	0.489	0.175	0.490	0.490	0.489	0.490	0.172
TDWC_{vic}	0.712	0.380	0.472	0.380	0.692	0.259	0.699	0.699	0.692	0.699	0.262
TDWC_{mas}	5.575	5.030	3.401	5.030	5.554	0.806	5.523	5.523	5.554	5.523	0.804

The results obtained for each TDWC_{d_ℓ} are shown in Table 4.

The proposed method and the 10 *k*means methods are ranked based on increasing TDWC_{d_ℓ} for each d_ℓ. This results in 10 different rankings (one for each TDWC_{d_ℓ}), which are shown in Table 5.

Table 5. Rankings of the methods in terms of all ten TDWC_{d_ℓ}.

Number of voters	Ranking
1	$borda \succ mat \sim trd \sim mas \succ man \succ jac \sim vic \succ can \succ che \sim euc \succ cos$
4	$man \succ borda \succ che \sim euc \succ cos \succ jac \sim vic \succ mat \sim trd \sim mas \succ can$
1	$cos \succ borda \succ man \succ che \sim euc \succ can \succ mat \sim trd \sim mas \succ jac \sim vic$
1	$borda \succ man \succ che \sim euc \succ jac \sim vic \succ mat \sim trd \sim mas \succ cos \succ can$
1	$borda \succ man \succ cos \succ che \sim euc \succ jac \sim vic \succ mat \sim trd \sim mas \succ can$
1	$borda \succ man \succ che \sim euc \succ cos \succ jac \sim vic \succ mat \sim trd \sim mas \succ can$
1	$borda \succ man \succ cos \succ che \sim euc \succ mat \sim trd \sim mas \succ jac \sim vic \succ can$

All the rankings shown in Table 5 are gathered into a profile of rankings, resulting in the following ranking after computing the scores associated with the Borda Count:

$$borda \succ man \succ che \sim euc \succ cos \succ jac \sim vic \succ mat \sim trd \sim mas \succ can\,.$$

We conclude that, overall, the here proposed method leads to a smaller TDWC than all ten *k*means.

4.2 Experiments and Results

In order to measure the behaviour of the proposed method, 81 datasets have been tested. These datasets are built from artificially generated data and each of them combines a different number of gaussian clusters and a different number of variables. Both the number of clusters and the number of variables in the dataset range from 2 to 10. The value of k used in the methods has been fixed to the real number of clusters used in the construction of the datasets to simplify the process. Every dataset has been normalized before applying the clustering method in order to assure that there are no negative values and, therefore, that all distances can be applied. More details on the datasets can be found in the following site https://noeliarico.shinyapps.io/clustering/.

An overall comparison of all methods head-to-head is presented in Table 6. The number in each cell represents the amount of datasets for which the method corresponding to the row was ranked at a better position the method corresponding to the column in the obtained ranking. We can conclude that the proposed method (Borda) performs better in comparison with all other $k$means at least for half of the datasets. It is worth mentioning that the proposed method clearly outperforms the most standard version of $k$means in which the Euclidean distance is considered.

Table 6. Pairwise comparison of the methods taking into account all the 81 datasets. The number at the ith row and jth column represents the number of times that the method corresponding to the ith row is ranked at a better position than the method corresponding to the jth column. The last column presents the percentage of times that the method corresponding to the row performs better than the other methods over the total of 810 possible comparisons (10 methods and 81 datasets).

	borda	can	che	cos	euc	jac	man	mas	mat	trd	vic	Total
borda	0	64	71	64	56	46	65	60	49	43	41	69%
can	12	0	53	41	25	24	34	35	21	15	14	34%
che	10	26	0	26	11	10	26	25	14	9	5	20%
cos	16	39	55	0	25	18	35	41	22	19	15	35%
euc	24	54	68	54	0	37	59	53	33	28	23	53%
jac	32	55	71	61	42	0	54	54	40	35	35	59%
man	16	46	54	45	17	26	0	44	28	18	11	37%
mas	20	45	54	40	28	25	37	0	17	16	19	37%
mat	28	59	67	59	47	39	53	63	0	12	26	56%
trd	32	64	72	62	51	45	62	64	37	0	28	64%
vic	37	67	74	64	54	46	70	61	46	41	0	69%

5 Conclusions and Future Work

Popular clustering methods such as $k$means presume that the Euclidean distance (or some other predetermined distance) is the one that best fits the current dataset. Some research on how to learn the most suitable distance has been performed. Here, due to the difficulty that learning the most suitable distance presents in clustering, we follow a totally different approach and propose a natural variant of $k$means that jointly exploits different distances at the same time. The presented results hint that the presented method minimizes the TDWC associated with an unknown distance in comparison to the classical method of $k$means.

The absence of a ground truth for the groups of objects in clustering datasets makes the evaluation process more difficult than for other kinds of problems such as classification. Many performance measures of different nature have been proposed for evaluating clustering algorithms [3], even though most of them rely on a preliminary choice of distance. In future work, we will adapt these performance measures similarly as it has been done for the TWSS. Additionally, since the centroid is inherently linked to the Euclidean distance, future research will focus on how to reduce the importance of the choice of distance to the phase in which the centers are updated.

References

1. Borda, J.C.: Mémoire sur les Élections au Scrutin. Histoire de l'Académie Royale des Sciences, Paris (1781)
2. Celebi, M.E., Kingravi, H.A., Vela, P.A.: A comparative study of efficient initialization methods for the k-means clustering algorithm. Expert Syst. Appl. **40**(1), 200–210 (2013)
3. Gan, G., Ma, C., Wu, J.: Data Clustering: Theory, Algorithms, and Applications (ASA-SIAM Series on Statistics and Applied Probability). Society for Industrial and Applied Mathematics, USA (2007)
4. Lloyd, S.: Least squares quantization in PCM. IEEE Trans. Inf. Theory **28**, 129–137 (1982)
5. MacQueen, J.B.: Some methods for classification and analysis of multivariate observations. In: Proceedings of the Fifth Berkeley Symposium on Mathematical Statistics and Probability, vol. 1, pp. 281–297. University of California Press (1967)
6. Morissette, L., Chartier, S.: The k-means clustering technique: general considerations and implementation in mathematica. Tutorials Quant. Methods Psychol. **9**, 15–24 (2013)
7. Visalakshi, N.K., Suguna, J.: K-means clustering using max-min distance measure. In: NAFIPS 2009–2009 Annual Meeting of the North American Fuzzy Information Processing Society, pp. 1–6. IEEE (2009)
8. Xu, D., Tian, Y.: A comprehensive survey of clustering algorithms. Ann. Data Sci. **2**, 165–193 (2015)
9. Xu, R., Wunsch, D.: Partitional Clustering. Wiley-IEEE Press (2009)
10. Young, H.P.: Social choice scoring functions. SIAM J. Appl. Math. **28**(4), 824–838 (1975)

Data Mining, Knowledge Discovery and Big Data

Opinion Mining System for Twitter Sentiment Analysis

Pâmella A. Aquino(✉), Vivian F. López(✉), María N. Moreno(✉), María D. Muñoz(✉), and Sara Rodríguez(✉)

Departamento Informática y Automática, University of Salamanca, Plaza de la Merced S/N, 37008 Salamanca, Spain
{pabaquino,vivian,mmg,mariado,srg}@usal.es

Abstract. After the paradigm shift produced by Web 2.0, the volume of opinion on the Internet has increased exponentially. The expansion of social media, whose textual content is somewhat subjective and comes loaded with opinions and assessments, can be very useful for recommending a product or brand. This information is an interesting challenge from the perspective of natural language processing, but is also an aspect of deep interest and great value not only as a marketing strategy for companies and political campaigns, but also as an indicator measuring consumer satisfaction with a product or service. In this paper, we present an opinion mining system that uses text mining techniques and natural language processing to automatically obtain useful knowledge about opinions, preferences and user trends. We studied improvements in the quality of opinion classification by using a voting system to choose the best classification of each tweet, base on of the absolute majority of the votes of the algorithms considered. In addition we developed a visualization tool that automatically combines these algorithms to assist end-user decision making. The opinion mining tool makes it possible to analyze and visualize data published on Twitter, to understand the sentiment analysis of users in relation to a product or service, by identifying the positive or negative sentiment expressed in Twitter messages.

Keywords: Sentiment analysis · Opinion mining · Social networks · Natural language processing · Text mining · Twitter · Classification algorithms

1 Introduction

Web 2.0 has changed the Internet world, providing not only access to, but also the actual creation of the information society, where new forms of communication grow and the volume of subjective information increases exponentially. It is also an example of the application of Opinion Mining (OM) [18], as the number of sites where users can express opinions and share content is growing. This is particularly true with the expansion of social media (blogs, forums and social networks), whose textual content is somewhat subjective and comes loaded with

E. A. de la Cal et al. (Eds.): HAIS 2020, LNAI 12344, pp. 465–476, 2020.
https://doi.org/10.1007/978-3-030-61705-9_38

opinions and assessments, which can be very useful for recommending a product or brand.

Although natural language processing (NLP) is a classic discipline, nowadays a number of approaches have proliferated on the extraction of semantic information in social networks. Twitter[1] has become a valuable source of data, but to carry out OM, the main barrier we find is language comprehension. The results are not good enough to detecting suitable the polarity of the message and achieve better levels of accuracy on automatically classifying text.

The aim of this study is to investigate opinion mining systems for social networks, based on NLP techniques and text mining. The intention is to identify and automatically extract subjective information on user reviews and store this information in a structured way, to process and classify it usefully. We have chosen machine learning methods for Sentiment Analysis (SA) based on supervised classification. To determine the performance and analyze the results of different classifiers, different algorithms were evaluated independently, showing a very similar behaviour. For this reason, in this study we decided to use a solution that combined different algorithms, through a system of majority voting, in order to increase confidence in the classification and achieve better results than the methods applied individually.

A corpus of Twitter messages (tweets), labelled as positive or negative classes, was used for the research. The corpus is trained by a supervised learning algorithm to classify the polarity of the message (positive or negative), considering a vote among the algorithms and the final polarity is determined according to the prediction of the most popular label.

This paper is structured as follows. Section. 2 describes the proposed solution. In Sect. 3 we describe the experiments, present results and evaluate the system proposed. The visualization tool is shown in Sect. 4. Finally, Sect. 5 explains the conclusions of the paper and proposes ideas for future research.

1.1 Natural Language Processing and SA

To the SA, the preprocessing of texts plays a very important role constituting the first step prior to the classification. Normalization, tokenization, elimination of empty words and part-of-speech tagging (PoS Tagging) are some of these techniques. All of these methods are very useful for preprocessing text before text analysis and document classification.

Studies in this area aim to discover the polarity of a subjective text, i.e., whether the text has a positive or negative connotation, employing different methods, such as the detection of polarity through adjectives that contain an emotional facet and automatic classification through previously tagged texts. Detecting the polarity of a text using adjectives, it is characterized by the use of dictionaries (lexicons) with semantic polarity orientation or opinion [29]. Various investigations in SA have used lexicon methods (polarity dictionaries) [8,11,20], which allow improvements with the use of linguistic knowledge.

[1] https://twitter.com/.

1.2 Text Categorization

We have chosen models based on supervised learning that aim to build a model of classes (categories) according to the characteristics of the data in question. These models are formed from a training set where their classifications are previously known. From there, the algorithm should be able to extract important features for future classifications [14]. The features are relevant terms extracted from the text and they allow us to find patterns to predict opinion type. These terms are used to train the classifier and later, to classify texts whose labels are unknown.

Making a preliminary selection of these features is of great importance and greatly benefits the learning task [7]. There is no consensus as to what type of attribute provides more information to the classifier. Generic attributes, are generally used to allow relevant features to be found. The best known methods for extracting features are based on statistical and probabilistic methods such as the *bag-of-words* model [19] and the *n-gram* model [25].

Nave Bayes Models (NB), and their variants, such as Multinomial Nave Bayes (MultinomialNB), Bernoulli Nave Bayes (BernoulliNB), Support Vector Machine (SVM) [8], and the Maximum Entropy Model (Maxent) can be very effective in solving classification and SA problems. These models have shown good accuracy, but according to [1] its performance is very dependent on the selected features, the quality and quantity of training data and the domain of the data.

To evaluate the results of the classifier, text classification metrics are used. Their use originated in information extraction. To evaluate the classifier results, these metrics determine whether the predicted class matches the actual class, and gain a measure of its efficiency. The instrument most commonly used to evaluate the performance of a classification algorithm is the confusion matrix. From a confusion matrix, several metrics relating to the classification accuracy can be deduced, such as *accuracy, precision, recall, and F-measure* in [23].

The first works using automatic classification were carried out in 2002 by Pang et al. [17] and Turney [26]. They used supervised and unsupervised learning methods in the classification of movie reviews and products, respectively. These works have been taken as a starting point for many works in later years.

More recent studies, such as [4,5,15] have analyzed publications of short texts that despite the noise in the text, such as the use of colloquialisms, ironies, ambiguities, relaxed spelling and excessive use of abbreviations have managed to achieve good result. Tests were made of tweets, microblogging of blippr[2] , blog posts and reviews of movies, which were labelled as positive, negative and neutral using the MultinomialNB and SVM classifiers.

Others approaches are using a combination of methods to achieve better results than those obtained by individual approaches [2,10,20,28]. The result of each method is combined into a single output to take better measures of *precision and F-measure* when compared with the methods used individually. In [10,28] the authors have gone further, with combining the results of individual methods by majority vote using three techniques: simple vote, *bagging* [6,21] y *boosting*

[2] http://blippr.tumblr.com/.

[24,30]. This paper investigates the efficacy of using a combination of methods. We have been found to perform better than than those mentioned above.

2 The Opinion Mining System

As mentioned, in this work we have taken a different approach to the task of SA, by combining texts classification methods found in the literature with a voting system to choose the best classification for each *tweet* based on an absolute majority of the votes of the algorithms considered and thus improve the sentiment accuracy. We make a statement-level analysis using machine learning methods for polarity classification with NLP [19]. Our strategy has the advantages afforded by the most recommended methods for classifying SA in short texts, focusing its efforts on improving the predictive power of sentiment.

Following the idea to identify and automatically extract subjective information from the tweets to store this information in a structured way and classify it, we have built an opinion mining system architecture which comprises the following steps: building of training corpus, postprocessing, preprocessing, feature extraction, classification and evaluation.

The Opinion Mining system was implemented in Python language using the Natural Language Toolkit (NLTK)[3]. We also used Scikit-Learn library[4] for application of the machine learning algorithms and to find the metrics for evaluating text classification results. Tweepy tool was used to build the training data set (tagged corpus). This is the Python library for accessing the Twitter API. In adition, the NodeJS platform[5] was used to build the visualization tool and MySQL[6] for managing the database.

2.1 Building of Training Corpus

Tweepy tool[7] was used to build the corpus, applying the distant supervision method [12] to the data collection, employed by [13,22]. To filter the tweets we used emoticons according to their polarity. The automatic labelling process consisted in assuming that the tweets with positive emoticons like :), will take a positive polarity and that the tweets with negative emoticons like :(will take a negative polarity. Tweets with mixed emoticons were delete. However, there are multiple emoticons that can express positive emotions, such as :-) and :] and negative emotions, such as :-(and :[. A more detailed list can be seen in Table 1.

Another key parameter in the filtering is the language; we retrieved tweets in English. Therefore, the proposed classification only works with tweets in English. Postprocessing was also applied to the corpus to eliminate the following elements: emoticons, repeated tweets, retweets and tweets with less than 5 tokens.

[3] http://www.nltk.org.
[4] http://scikit-learn.org/.
[5] https://nodejs.org/.
[6] http://www.mysql.com/.
[7] http://www.tweepy.org.

Table 1. Emoticons list

Tweet type	Emoticon
Positives	:) :-) :] :> :} :o) :c) >:] ;) =] =) 8) :p :P =D :o :D :-D :)
Negatives	:(:-(:[:< :{ :o(:c(>:[;(=[=(8(:3 :/

2.2 Preprocessing

Besides the classic preprocessing associated with NLP techniques (see Sect. 1.1), a second preprocessing step is performed. In this case, it is to treat specific constructs of the language model used in Twitter, that do not add information to the classification task, such as: user names, links, repetition of letters and replacement of hashtags by the corresponding term.

2.3 Feature Extraction

In this approach two types of feature extraction are performed:

- Based on the bag-of-words model and considering word frequency. All the terms of the training set regardless of position are considered features. In each text it takes into account how often that word occurs according to its polarity.
- Based on PoS Tagging [16] with adjective frequency. In which all the adjectives of the training set are considered features. In each text it takes into account how often an adjective occurs according to its polarity.

2.4 Classification

The classification process adopted is based on supervised learning to predict the polarity (positive or negative) of each tweet. The voting system is composed of five algorithms: NB, MultinominalNB, BernoulliBN, SVM and MaxEnt in which every algorithm is entitled to one vote. After the vote, the class receiving the most votes is assigned as the class of the tweet.

To develop the voting system for classifying *tweets*, it was decided to take as a reference the algorithm used by Harrison Kinsley on his Python Programming Platform[8]. To attain an absolute majority, at least three votes must match. This minimun threshold is estimated with a confidence level of 60% for the right solution. If four of the algorithms vote for the same class, the degree of trust increases by 80%, and if five algorithms match, the confidence level reaches 100%. It is important to note that the confidence level of 100% does not mean that the classification has been totally accurate. The classification results can be found in the Sect. 3.1.

[8] https://pythonprogramming.net/.

3 Experimental Work

Experiments were carried out following the steps described in Sect. 2 to evaluate our strategy. For the experiments we decided to build the corpus with our own data sets, because according to [27] there is a lack of benchmark data sets in this fieldand. The data sets were taken over a period between June 3rd and June 5th, 2016. Initially, the data set was divided into two parts: the training set, which contained with 13,500 tweets (75% tagged corpus), and one set for testing, which contained 4,500 tweets (25% of the data set).

To build the training data set, after postprocessing the corpus a total of 18,000 tweets were obtained, 9,000 of which showed a positive sentiment and the other 9,000 were negative. Both data sets were stored independently according to their polarity for their use in the experiments. We then applied the steps of our system to these data sets of public domain, whose corpus originally supplied 38.138 features. After the preprocessing, performed to treat the specific constructs of the Twitter language model, the size was reduced by 53.02%. When the bag-of-words model was applied, the training set was divided into two sets: a set that considered word frequency, which obtained a data space of 17,915 features and a set that used the PoS Tagging model with adjective frequency, which obtained a data space of 3,545 features (19.8% of the total data).

For the training phase of the five classifiers provided by the voting system, we used the training data set corresponding to the 13,500 tweets resulting from the previous steps. The performances of the classifiers were evaluated in each of the two types of feature extraction methods seen in Sect. 2.3 by using different metrics. This will check if the hypothesis of Sect. 1 is true, i.e., that if we use a system of majority of voting to choose the best classification of each tweet, then higher rates of success can be achieved than when using a single classifier.

For the evaluation phase we considered the implementation supplied by the Scikit-Learn library of metrics like accuracy, precision, recall and F-measure, for positive and negative classes, relative to feature extraction methods, word frequency and PoS Tagging with adjectives.

3.1 Experimental Results

We present the experimental results obtained concerning the performance of classifiers. It can be seen that, for the feature extraction process using word frequency (Table 2), four of the five algorithms accomplish very similar measures of accuracy, over 78%. The SVM algorithm stood out from the other classifiers, not only in relation to the *F-measure*, which evaluates the classifier with one single measure with a value of 97.1% but also with respect to the other metrics. Similarly, the results of the performance of classifiers by PoS Tagging with adjectives (Table 3) achieved very close measures of *accuracy*, about 70%. Moreover, as in the previous case, the SVM classifier excelled not only according to the *F-measure*, but also with respect to the other metrics.

Our results show that only the MultinomialNB algorithm, using the bag-of-words model stood out with respect to accuracy (78.8%), in the evaluation

Table 2. Performance of the classifiers - Word Frequency

Classifier	$Accuracy$	$Precision_{pos/neg}$	$Recall_{pos/neg}$	$F - measure_{pos/neg}$
Naïve Bayes	78.33	91.7/87	86.4/92.1	89/89.5
MultinomialNB	78.8	91.5/84.9	83.8/92.1	87.5/88.4
BernoulliNB	78.0	90.4/85.5	84.8/91	87.5/88.1
MaxEnt	78.6	91.9/91	91/91.9	91.5/91.4
SVM	75.8	97.4/96.9	96.9/97.3	97.1/97.1

Table 3. Performance of the classifiers - *PoS Tagging* with Adjectives

Classifier	$Accuracy$	$Precision_{pos/neg}$	$Recall_{pos/neg}$	$F - measure_{pos/neg}$
Naïve Bayes	69.86	76/78.8	80/74.6	78/76.7
MultinomialNB	70.07	76.2/78	78.8/75.3	77.5/76.6
BernoulliNB	69.93	75.6/78.2	79.5/74.1	77.5/76.1
MaxEnt	70.31	75.8/80	81.6/73.7	78.6/76.7
SVM	69.42	77.7/82.3	83.8/75.8	80.6/78.9

separately of the five algorithms. However our approach based on an absolute majority of the votes of the algorithms considered, achieve an accuracy over 78.06%. This was calculated based on the average of accuracy metric of all the algorithms involved in the voting system.

We also analyzed the performance of the algorithms depending on the number of *features* we use in classifier training. Training the classifier with a few *features* results in a lower yield. However, increasing the number of *features* improves the performance of the classifier. Another thing we observed was that the performance of the algorithms used in training, was very similar for the same amount of *features*.

In Table 4 and Table 5, highlighted in yellow are the cells in which the classifier performed better depending on the number of *features* for each extraction method. In turn, the last column shows the average performance of each classifier. For the word frequency method, the Bernoulli algorithm excelled over the others, achieving a better average yield based on the amount of *features*. Nevertheless for the *PoS Tagging with adjectives*, Naïve Bayes performed better than the other classifiers.

With regard to resource consumption. The time and computation resources spent to execute the system based on the absolute majority of the votes of the algorithms considered are justified. Because they have shown better performance as compared to their respective implementations of individual methods. Furthermore, although [1] it points out that lexicon or semantic approaches take less time in comparison with machine learning techniques. Its main limitation is the maintenance of the dictionaries, which is very expensive.

Table 4. Performance of the Classifiers by Word Frequency: *Accuracy* per *Number of Features*

Classifier	1.000	5.000	10.000	17.915	Average
Naïve Bayes	54.44	63.88	69.15	78.33	66.45
MultinomialNB	53.31	63.8	69.48	78.88	66.37
BernoulliNB	54.42	63.77	69.51	78.88	66.65
MaxEnt	54.33	64.15	69	78.6	66.52
SVM	54.2	63.8	67.66	75.8	65.37

Table 5. Performance of the Classifiers by *PoS Tagging* with adjectives: *Accuracy* per *Number of Features*

Classifier	1.000	2.000	3.545	Average
Naïve Bayes	62.22	64.6	69.86	65.56
MultinomialNB	60.08	63.06	70.06	64.4
BernoulliNB	60.31	64.68	69.93	64.97
MaxEnt	60.28	64.48	70.31	65.02
SVM	59.77	64.22	69.42	64.47

4 Visualization Tool

A visualization tool was constructed to analyze, as a case study, the data published in Twitter in order to understand the behaviour of users and their feelings in relation to a product or service. The opinion mining system developed was used to identify the sentiment expressed by the tweets published. The aim of the visualization tool is to allow the analyst to intuitively, identify and analyze the distribution of tweets on a world map. The tweets are shown on the map from the location provided by users themselves. The use of a map with the distribution of the tweets will allow the consumer to visualize sentiment regarding a product or service, meaning the visualization tool can be used as a support in decision-making, to identify strengths, weaknesses, and recognize new threats and opportunities.

The navigation strategy used consists of two views: a global one and another more detailed view. In the global view, a world map emerges that prints a heat map which represents the intensity of the data indicating the geographical points at which users have spoken about Uber (on the right in Fig. 1)

This is a tool that serves as the user's gateway to the information. It is mainly responsible for routing user requests to the appropriate information and returning feedback about the content of the tweets. Hence, the tool has an access control mechanism which authenticates users before starting the analysis. We differentiate between two types of user: analysts and other users. The analyst user is one who handles the visualization tool and, "other users" refers to Twitter users who publish messages on the social network.

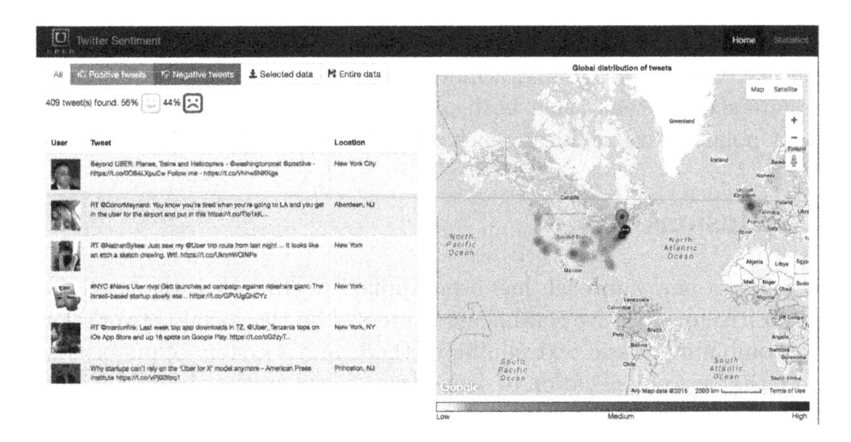

Fig. 1. Global View of the tool

In addition, the visualization tool is responsible for the final presentation of the results through an intuitive interface and makes it easy to find patterns through the map of distribution of tweets and then access that data.

4.1 Case Study Description

We also analyzed the performance of the system using the orientation of the topic domain and its features [3]. As we mentioned the sentiment often depends on the context in which the text is read. Context also influences performances of the classifiers. To improve on the sentiment accuracy we decided analyzed the performance of system using a specific domain. We have chosen to analyze service data from the *Uber startup*, a company that provides an alternative shuttle service that has revolutionized the taxi industry.

Uber is a conveyance means less individual and more sustainable, which to helps to improve the quality of life in cities. It follows the goal of sharing trips to achieve efficiency in the transport system, fuel savings and improve air quality.

With a service that attends to five continents, its entry into the market has caused a virulent reaction that has been reflected in social networks. Many of the disagreements, complaints or suggestions about this service are exposed by its users in messages on Twitter.

Data were collected during the period between June 20 and July 4, 2016. We performed a filtering using the keyword *uber* and collected a total of 9,590 tweets which were stored in a MySQL database, 4795 of which showed a positive sentiment and the other 4795 were negative. Both data sets were stored independently according to their polarity for their use in the experiments. Then the bag-of-words model was applied, the training set was divided into two sets: a set that considered word frequency, which obtained a data space of 10,155 features and a set that used the PoS Tagging model with adjective frequency, which obtained a data space of 13,232 features.

We use the system of majority of voting (see Sect. 2.4) to detecting suitable the polarity of the message and achieve better levels of classification accuracy. Our results showed that using both phases of classification (by topics and by sentiment polarity) we achieved reach a highest accuracy of 83%.

5 Conclusions

In this paper a new approach has been applied to SA. With the goal of determining positive or negative sentiments expressed on the social network Twitter, we have combining classic text mining methods and a system of majority voting to choose the best classification of each tweet, based on the absolute majority of the votes of the algorithms considered to achieve better levels of the accuracy results. This research has made it possible to go deeper into and compare opinion mining systems of social networks, based on NLP and data mining techniques. We have met the proposed objective to identify and automatically extract subjective information on user opinions and store this information in a structured way, to be able to process and classify it as useful information.

Each of the classifiers has also been evaluated independently, to verify their performance. Analysis of the results shows that there is a great similarity between them. For that reason, a solution of combined algorithms was posited, through a system of majority voting, in order to increase the confidence of the tweet classification. The highest accuracy attained by the evaluation separately of the five algorithms for the training set provided was 78.8%. However this approach, based on an absolute majority of the votes of the algorithms considered has worked well, with 78.06% best overall accuracy.

Finally the whole process is reflected in a visualization tool prototype, which provides an intuitive interface, easy to use and focused on assisting end users in decision-making, allowing them to find patterns through the distribution map of tweets and to access that data.

As future research, we aim to study solutions to solve the problem of semantic ambiguity using training sets in specific domains to improve the performance of classifiers and working on context-based SA.

In addition, we hope to evaluate other types unsupervised learning methods in the classification task using neural networks, and so on compare the results of both types of learning (supervised and unsupervised).

Acknowledgments. This paper has been partially supported by the research project: Movilidad inteligente y sostenible soportada por Sistemas Multi-agentes y Edge Computing (InEDGEMobility). Reference: RTI2018-095390-B-C32.

References

1. Sharma, A., Shubhamoy, D.: Using self-organizing maps for sentiment analysis (2013)

2. Augustyniak, L., et al.: Simpler is better? lexicon-based ensemble sentiment classification beats supervised methods. In: International Conference on 2014 IEEE/ACM. [S.l.]. Advances in Social Networks Analysis and Mining (ASONAM), pp. 924–929. IEEE (2014)
3. Basant, A., Namita, M., Pooja, B., Sonal G.: Sentiment analysis using commonsense and context information. Hindawi Publishing Corporation Computational Intelligence and Neuroscience (2015)
4. Bermingham, A., Smeaton, A. F.: Classifying sentiment in microblogs: is brevity an advantage? In: Proceedings of the 19th ACM International Conference on Information and Knowledge Management. [S.l.], pp. 1833–1836. ACM (2010)
5. Bermingham, A., Smeaton, A.: On using Twitter to monitor political sentiment and predict election results. In: Proceedings of the Workshop on Sentiment Analysis where AI meets Psychology (SAAIP 2011) (2011)
6. Breiman, L.: Bagging predictors. Mach. Learn. **24**(2), 123–140 (1996)
7. Cardie, C.: Automatic feature set selection for case-based learning of linguistic knowledge. In: Conference on Empirical Methods in Natural Language Processing, pp. 113–126 (1996)
8. Choy, M., Cheong, M.L.F., Nang Laik, M., Ping Shung, K.: A sentiment analysis of Singapore Presidential Election 2011 using Twitter data with census correction. CoRR, abs/1108 5520 (2011)
9. Duchowski, A.T.: A Breadth-first survey of eye tracking applications. Behav. Res. Methods Instrum. Comput. (BRMIC) **34**(4), 455–470 (2002). https://doi.org/10.3758/BF03195475
10. Fersini, E., Messina, E., Pozzi, F.: Sentiment analysis: Bayesian ensemble learning. Decis. Support Syst. **68**, 26–38 (2014)
11. Hu, M., Liu, B.: Mining and summarizing customer reviews. In: Proceedings of the Tenth ACM SIGKDD International Conference on Knowledge Discovery and Data Mining, KDD 2004, pp. 168–177. ACM, New York(2004)
12. Intxaurrondo, A., Surdeanu, M., López de Lacalle Lekuona, O., Agirre Bengoa, E.: Removing noisy mentions for distant supervision. Procesamiento del Lenguaje Natural. N. 51, pp. 41–48 (2013). ISSN 1135–5948
13. Go, A., Huang, L., Bhayani, R.: Twitter sentiment analysis. Final Projects from CS224N for Spring 2008/2009 at The Stanford Natural Language Processing Group (2009)
14. Kotsiantis, S.B.: Supervised machine learning: a review of classification techniques. Informatica **31**(3), 249–268 (2007). Slovene Society Informatika
15. Kouloumpis, E., Wilson, T., Moore, J.: Twitter sentiment analysis: the good the bad and the omg! In: ICWSM, vol. 11, pp. 538–541 (2011)
16. Manning, C.D., Schuetze, H.: Foundations of Statistical Language Processing. MIT Press, Cambridge (1999)
17. Pang, B., Lee, L., Vaithyanathan, S.: Thumbs up? sentiment classification using machine learning techniques. In: Proceedings of the Conference on Empirical Methods in Natural Language Processing (EMNLP), pp. 79–86 (2002)
18. Pang, B., Lee, L.: Opinion mining and sentiment analysis. Found. Trends Inf. Retrieval **2**(1–2), 1–135 (2008)
19. Perkins, J.: Python 3 Text Processing with NLTK 3 Cookbook. Packt Publishing (2014). ISBN 13: 9781782167853
20. Prabowo, R., Thelwall, M.: Sentiment analysis: a combined approach. J. Informetrics **3**(2), 143–157 (2009)
21. Quinlan, J.R.: Bagging, boosting, and c4.5. In: Proceedings of the 13th National Conference on Artificial Intelligence, pp. 725–730 (1996)

22. Read, J.: Using emoticons to reduce dependency in machine learning techniques for sentiment classification. In: Proceedings of ACL-05, 43nd Meeting of the Association for Computational Linguistics. Association for Computational Linguistics (2005)
23. Salton, G., McGill, M.J.: Introduction to Modern Information Retrieval. McGraw-Hill, Inc., New York (1986)
24. Schapire, R.E.: The strength of weak learnability. Mach. Learn. **5**(2), 197–227 (1990)
25. Sebastiani, F.: Machine learning in automated text categorization. ACM Comput. Surv. **34**(1), 1–47 (2002)
26. Turney, P.: Thumbs up or thumbs down? semantic orientation applied to unsupervised classification of reviews. In: Proceedings of the Association for Computational Linguistics (ACL), pp. 417–424 (2002)
27. Tsytsarau, M., Palpanas, T.: Survey on mining subjective data on the web. Data Min. Knowl. Disc. **24**, 478–514 (2012). https://doi.org/10.1007/s10618-011-0238-6
28. Wang, G., Sunc, J., Mac, J., Xue, K., Gud, J.: Sentiment classification: the contribution of ensemble learning. Decis. Support Syst. **57**, 77–93 (2014)
29. Zhang, L., Ghosh, R., Dekhil, M., Hsu, M., Liu, B.: Combining lexicon-based and learning-based methods for twitter sentiment analysis. Hewlett-Packard Laboratories. Technical report HPL-2011-89 (2011)
30. Zhou, Z.-H.: Ensemble Methods: Foundations and Algorithms. Chapman & Hall (2012)

An Expert System for Building Energy Management Through the Web of Things

Daniel Ibaseta[1](✉), Julio Molleda[2], Martín Álvarez[1], and Fidel Díez[1]

[1] CTIC Technological Centre, Gijón, Spain
{daniel.ibaseta,martin.alvarez,fidel.diez}@fundacionctic.org
[2] Department of Computer Science and Engineering, University of Oviedo, Oviedo, Spain
jmolleda@uniovi.es

Abstract. Managing energy consumption in buildings is of utmost importance given the fact that 20% of the total energy consumed worldwide comes from the buildings sector. The miniaturization of electronic and mechanical systems, together with low-power wireless communications, facilitate the development and deployment of building energy management systems (BEMS) based on Internet of Things (IoT) platforms. It is well known that IoT solutions create silos suffering from interoperability issues. In this paper, we propose an expert system based on the W3C Web of Things (WoT), a paradigm that seeks to counter the interoperability issues in the IoT. The proposed system implements a set of rules, fed by a time series database, that mange several sensors and actuators addressed through Web technologies using WoT. The goal of this expert system is to be the core of a BEMS, and thus, it will be able to optimize energy consumption as well as to enable smart retrofit of existing buildings. In addition, the expert system is combined with a graphical user interface featuring several web-based dashboards, making it possible for an administrator to remotely supervise the operation of the whole building.

Keywords: Smart building · Energy management · Expert system · Internet of Things (IoT) · Web of Things (WoT)

1 Introduction

In recent times, monitoring, managing and optimizing energy consumption is of utmost importance in almost every sector, such as industrial, transportation, and residential, among others. According to the Department of Energy of the U.S. Energy Information Administration, energy consumed in the buildings sector (including both residential and commercial) accounts for 20.1% of the total delivered energy consumed worldwide in 2018, and it is expected to reach 22% in 2050 [9]. Monitoring and managing building energy consumption require a wide variety of interconnected sensors and actuators to be placed or integrated

E. A. de la Cal et al. (Eds.): HAIS 2020, LNAI 12344, pp. 477–485, 2020.
https://doi.org/10.1007/978-3-030-61705-9_39

into the different building appliances (the air conditioner, the building hot water pump, to name but a few). These sensors and actuators are the key devices of the Building Energy Management System (BEMS).

The Internet of Things (IoT) has proven its usefulness in the last years in the energy monitoring domain, as well as in energy management and saving. However, platforms are usually based on dedicated software and tightly coupled services and hardware, creating silo solutions and fragmentation. The Web of Things (WoT) is a paradigm devised by the World Wide Web Consortium (W3C) on top of the IoT concept focussed on countering the interoperability issues in the IoT. It extends the Web architecture to incorporate smart devices into the Web. In IoT, each element is referred to as a *Thing*, whereas in WoT each element is referred to as a *Web Thing*.

The W3C WoT paradigm is based on four building blocks, as shown in Fig. 1: *i*) Thing, the abstraction of a physical or virtual entity represented in IoT applications; *ii*) Thing Description, the structured data (using a descriptive JSON file) that augments a Thing providing metadata about the Thing, its interactions, data model, communication and security; *iii*) Binding Templates, the collection of communication metadata that explains how to interact with different IoT platforms; and *iv*) Scripting API, an optional building block that eases the development of IoT applications by providing a runtime system for IoT applications similar to a Web browser.

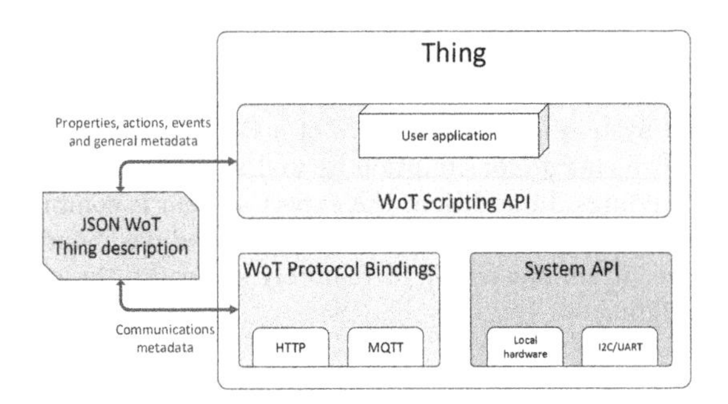

Fig. 1. WoT architecture concept

WoT offers an interesting approach to solve the issues faced during the design stage of systems that include legacy devices and heterogeneous technologies. The main differences between IoT and WoT are:

- The counteracting of fragmentation between different sensors and actuators by providing a machine-interpretable description [2].
- WoT brings IoT with machine-readable descriptions of sensors, actuators and controllers [2], providing it with an interoperability layer and enabling semantic interpretation of systems.

- WoT is designed to work specifically with the World Wide Web protocols, avoiding the technology fragmentation and lack of interoperability between different families of devices.

In the last decade, several systems have been developed to monitor and control building appliances based on IoT or Web technologies. However, only a few integrate all the available data to offer an intelligent system to minimize energy consumption and maximize comfort. In [4], a decentralized system for energy efficiency for monitored buildings is proposed. This system, called CONDE, focuses on decentralization for system efficiency and scalability. In [6], another decentralized solution is proposed. This solution is based on electricity demand, input power from solar panels and current pricing of grid energy to decide when to buy or sell energy to the grid and manage all the energy demand efficiently using a decision engine. In [3], a platform is defined using indoor air parameters (such as temperature and humidity) compared with outdoor temperature and energy price to optimize energy consumption. In [8], the solution is based on presence. Using CO_2 and infrared sensors, the system can decide when to set the temperature to a comfortable range or to turn off room appliances to save energy. Another example of a rule engine is [7], which provides good performance and maintains a good level of comfort using comfort thresholds, adequately capturing dependencies and interactions between components.

In this paper we propose a rule-based expert system for building energy monitoring and management using several sensors and actuators addressed through Web technologies based on the W3C WoT paradigm. The context of this work is the HEART Project [1], which aims to design a tool that integrates multiple components of a building, enabling smart retrofit. In this project, a complete building energy system (indoor air ventilation system, energy system, and water system) is monitored and controlled by a group of smart devices, managed using WoT technologies. Those WoT technologies represent the real innovation in this scenario as they allow an easy to implement communication with the final devices.

An expert system is selected instead of any other intelligent management system as a requirement for the project, as the rules come predefined with the HEART project.

2 Expert System for Building Energy Management

The decision-making ability of a human expert can be emulated in computer systems through an expert system [5]. The system proposed in this work is composed of: *i*) a WoT proxy that handles all the deployed devices in the building; *ii*) a database that stores all the data gathered from the devices; *iii*) a building device manager that reads the data from the WoT proxy; *iv*) a device monitor for visualization; and *v*) the BEMS engine that implements the custom logic. Figure 2 shows the architecture of the decision engine of the expert system proposed in this work.

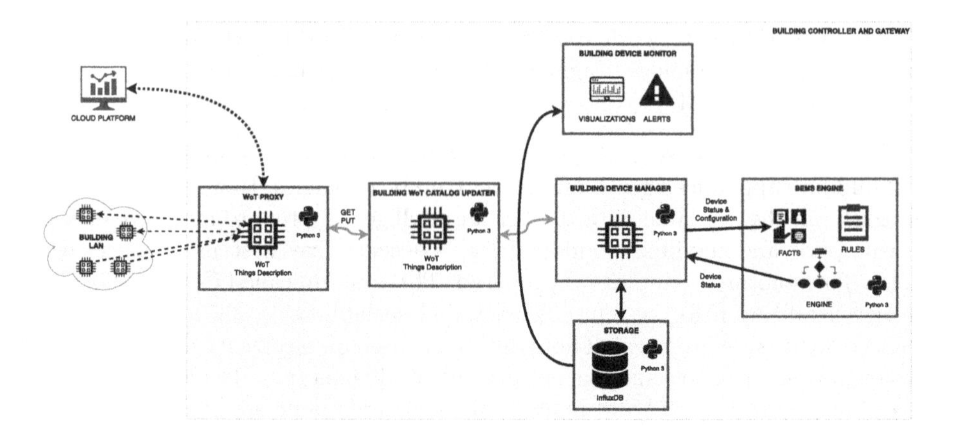

Fig. 2. Decision engine architecture

The custom logic is a combination of real-time data and a set of facts and rules. These facts, together with the current values acquired from the environment sensors, conform the input data of a proposed set of rules. As a consequence, the result provided by the custom logic actuate on some building devices (i.e. modify a thermostat, switch on or off a fan, start pumping water in a tank, etc.). Figure 3 shows a control-flow diagram from which the set of rules of the expert system is derived.

As seen in Fig. 2, the WoT proxy, and its corresponding WoT catalog, is the gateway between the building appliances and the expert system. This is a fundamental piece as it manages all the readings and actuations between these systems, and enables the logic to take direct action over the different actuators using simple HTTP messages which are easily implemented in the BEMS engine.

The rules implemented in the proposed expert system respond to the requirements of the HEART Project [1] and are focused only for testing and prototyping the final Artificial Intelligence solution and the WoT architecture that will be implemented in the project. Figure 4 shows an example of a rule implemented in Python. These rules consist of two parts: *i*) The first part, where the input variables are declared, and the comparisons and thresholds are defined; and *ii*) a function which involves the "@Rule" previously defined and stores the result in the time series database.

The proposed system is built upon InfluxDB[1], an open source time series database designed to handle high write and query loads. This database provides real-time querying, as well as write and query capabilities through a built-in HTTP API.

The proposed expert system controls the status of the thermal storage devices, such as domestic hot water (DHW) tanks, the main water storage, and the phase change material (PCM) tank, where the main building heat pump

[1] https://www.influxdata.com/products/influxdb-overview/.

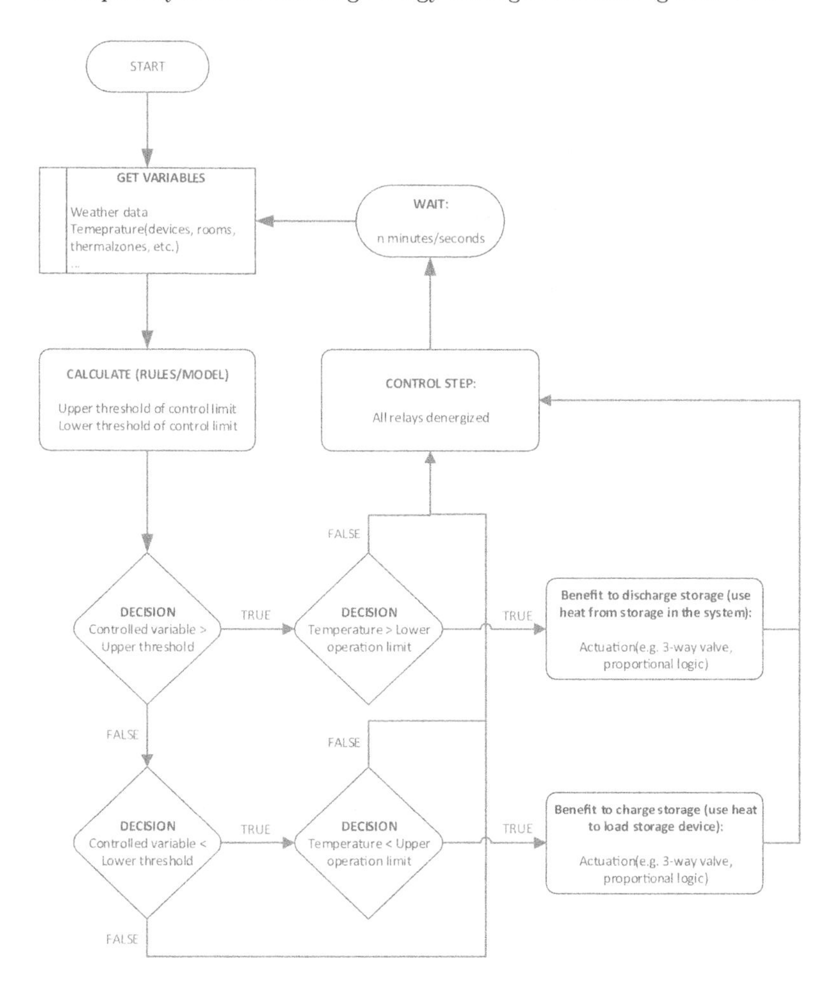

Fig. 3. Decision engine control-flow

stores the heated water. The status of these devices varies depending on specific environmental parameters, such as the temperature of water in each tank, and on some predefined values that set some specific thresholds for the rule engine.

In the proposed architecture, all components are deployed using Docker, and orchestrated using Docker Compose. The BEMS software module implements the rule engine to manage the energy flow of the system. This component is based on Experta[2], a Python library for building expert systems, which enables the development of expert systems based on a heuristic solution. This library is inspired on CLIPS[3] (C Language Integrated Production System), a rule-based programming language developed at the NASA's Johnson Space Center, released in 1996 as open source.

[2] https://pypi.org/project/experta/.
[3] http://www.clipsrules.net.

```
1  # PCM STORAGE DISCHARGING
2  @Rule(
3      AS.storageDeviceStatus << PcmStorageStatusFact(
4        id=MATCH.idDevice,
5        value=MATCH.currentValue,
6        status=NE('discharging')),
7      PcmStorageConfigurationFact(
8        id=MATCH.idDevice,
9        upper_threshold=MATCH.upperThreshold,
10       lower_threshold=MATCH.lowerThreshold,
11       upper_operation_limit=MATCH.upperOperationLimit,
12       lower_operation_limit=MATCH.lowerOperationLimit),
13     TEST(lambda upperThreshold, currentValue : currentValue >
       upperThreshold),
14     TEST(lambda lowerOperationLimit, currentValue : currentValue >
       lowerOperationLimit),
15     salience=0)
16
17 def storage_discharge(self, idDevice, storageDeviceStatus, currentValue,
     upperThreshold, lowerThreshold):
18     """Discharge storage of device, if the current value is greater than
       the upper threshold (also than the lower)"""
19     print('PCM STORAGE '{0}': LOWER [{1}] UPPER [{2}] CURRENT [{3}]
       ACTION -> [{4}]'.format(idDevice, lowerThreshold, upperThreshold,
       currentValue, 'DISCHARGE'))
20     self.dataManager.saveStatus(PcmStorageStatus(id=idDevice, value=
       currentValue, status='discharging'))
21     self.modify(storageDeviceStatus, status='discharging')
```

Fig. 4. Rule implementation example

The software is deployed on an UP Squared board, an x86 single board computer with an Intel®Celeron™N3350 processor, 8 GB of RAM, one Wi-Fi and two Gigabit Ethernet interfaces. The board runs the Ubuntu Server 18.04.3 LTS operating system. It covers the requirements of the system, allowing to connect it to multiple networks simultaneously with enough bandwidth to attend all the requests. It continuously gathers information of the status of the devices in the building and exposes visual data through intuitive dashboards.

3 Experiments and Results

The rule engine in the BEMS is executed periodically (the time interval can be fixed from seconds to minutes), gathering the latest values from the time series database and updating the status and parameters of the system on the same database accordingly.

The BEMS graphical user interface is composed of several dashboards. The behavior of the overall system is visualized using time series and intuitive representations. An example of such visualizations can be seen in Fig. 5, which represents when each device is being charged, discharged or idle. In addition, some information about the level of water storage in each device is also shown. Data shown in Fig. 5 has been simulated using a script that fluctuates PCM Storage temperature to go below and above the defined thresholds periodically, so the charge/discharge cycle can be observed. This cycle is arbitrated by the expert system and Fig. 5 shows that the temperature is not allowed to go down or up certain thresholds.

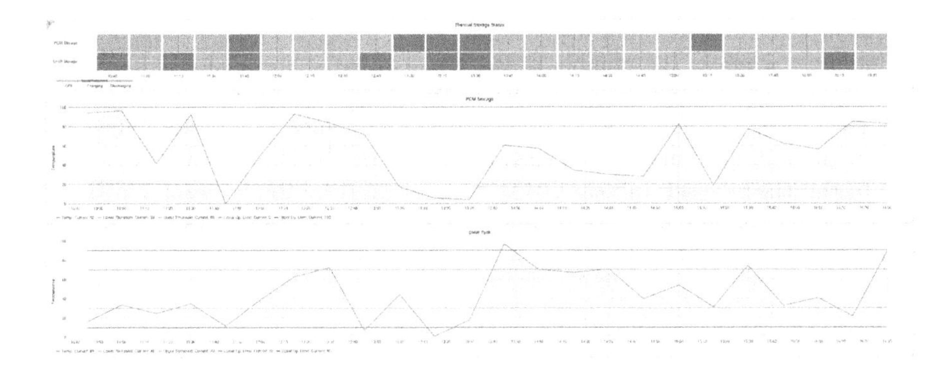

Fig. 5. PCM storage state visualization

Changes that we see in temperature and charge/discharge states are caused by the rule engine, activating and deactivating the simulated heater, and are applied using the underlying WoT architecture that enables the communication with the fancoils. The signal that activates or deactivates the fancoil is an HTTP request that travels from the rule engine to the desired fancoil.

Using another dashboard, the user can visualize the status of the fan coils, which depends on the thermal energy involved in the thermal energy exchange. Figure 6 shows the status of the fan coils with their properties. In this dashboard, the floor and fan coil ID can be filtered to show individual fan coils.

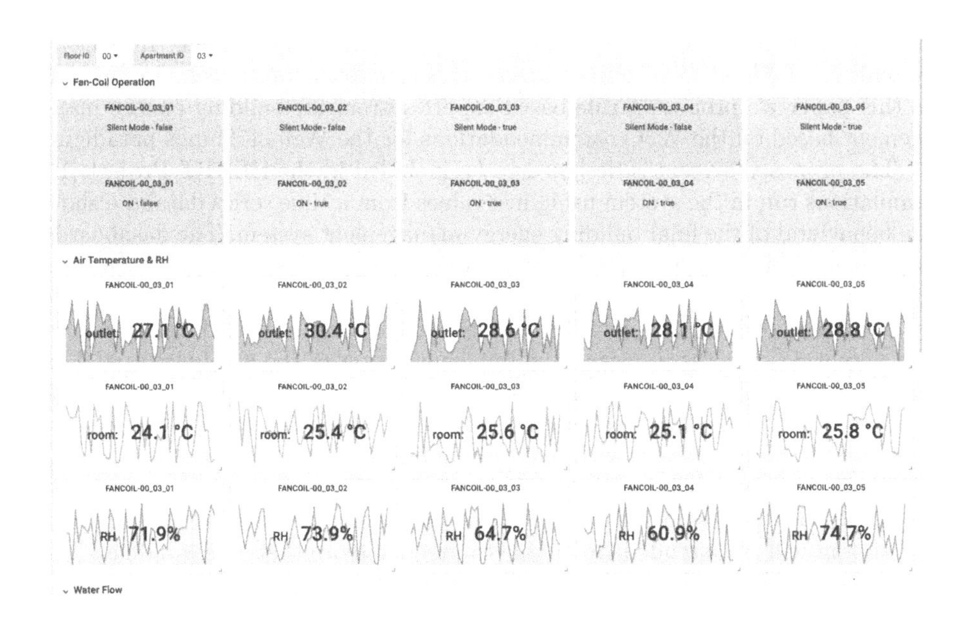

Fig. 6. Fan coil visualization

Usually, the number of hot water tanks ranges between 1 and 10, depending of the building, whereas the number of fan coils can grow up to several hundreds. Thus, a performance test was run using the proposed architecture to ensure that it can properly handle several hundreds of fan coils. The performance test consists on adding simulated fan coils to the BEMS. Table 1 shows the elapsed time to run the rule set and the RAM memory used by the UP Squared Board depending on the number of fan coils attached to the system. The results are the average of 5 min of constant repetitions of the rule engine over different sets of simulated data.

Table 1. Performance test, fan coils

# of fan coils	Rule processing time (s)	RAM Memory used (MB)
50	0.86	63.52
150	2.41	63.51
500	7.38	63.22
1000	15.51	63.78
2000	32.96	64.82

4 Conclusions and Future Work

Building energy management is the key to building energy saving. Intelligent systems can be used to optimize the energy consumption on such environments. In this paper we propose a rule-based expert system for building energy management based on the W3C recommendations for the Web of Things paradigm.

The proposed system is designed to be included in the HEART Project [1]. Simulations run in the system using live values from a time series database show the behavioral of the final building energy management system. The dashboards implemented in the graphical user interface make it possible for an administrator to supervise the operation of the whole building.

The usage of WoT technologies facilitates measuring the building appliances and actuating over them, easing the implementation of the whole system. The expert system itself is one of the many utilities that can benefit from the WoT architecture. The WoT implementation allows a seamless interaction between an agent and the final system, with high decoupling.

Future work will involve the adaptation of the expert system to the cloud, along with an extension for other sensors, actuators and devices. In addition, the system will be extended to be able to manage more than one building.

Acknowledgments. This work has been funded by the European Union's Horizon 2020 Framework Program for Research and Innovation under grant agreement No. 768921 and by the University of Oviedo under project 2018/00061/012.

References

1. Heart Project. https://heartproject.eu/. Accessed 3 Jan 2020
2. Web of Things at W3C. https://www.w3.org/WoT/. Accessed 4 Dec 2019
3. Ain, Q.U., Iqbal, S., Khan, S., Malik, A., Ahmad, I., Javaid, N.: IoT operating system based fuzzy inference system for home energy management system in smart buildings. Sensors **18**(9), 2802 (2018). https://doi.org/10.3390/s18092802
4. Farias, C., Pirmez, L., Delicato, F.C., Soares, H., dos Santos, I.L., Carmo, L.F.: A control and decision system for smart buildings. In: 2013 IEEE 10th International Conference on Ubiquitous Intelligence and Computing and 2013 IEEE 10th International Conference on Autonomic and Trusted Computing, pp. 254–261, December 2013. https://doi.org/10.1109/UIC-ATC.2013.108
5. Jackson, P.: Introduction to Expert Systems, 3rd edn. Addison-Wesley, Boston (1999)
6. Li, W., Logenthiran, T., Phan, V.T., Woo, W.L.: Intelligent housing development building management system (HDBMS) for optimized electricity bills. In: 2017 IEEE International Conference on Environment and Electrical Engineering and 2017 IEEE Industrial and Commercial Power Systems Europe (EEEIC/I&CPS Europe), pp. 1–6, June 2017. https://doi.org/10.1109/EEEIC.2017.7977410
7. Merabet, G.H., Essaaidi, M., Brak, M.E., Benhaddou, D.: Agent based for comfort control in smart building. In: 2017 International Renewable and Sustainable Energy Conference (IRSEC), pp. 1–4, December 2017. https://doi.org/10.1109/IRSEC.2017.8477369
8. Sun, J., Zhang, Y.: Towards an energy efficient architecture in smart building. In: 2015 International Conference on Computational Intelligence and Communication Networks (CICN), pp. 1589–1592, December 2015. https://doi.org/10.1109/CICN.2015.302
9. U.S. Department of Energy: International Energy Outlook 2019 with projections to 2050 (2019). https://www.eia.gov/ieo. Accessed 10 Jan 2020

Simulating Users in a Social Media Platform Using Multi-agent Systems

Daniel Pérez(✉) and Estefanía Argente(✉)

Valencian Research Institute for Artificial Intelligence (VRAIN), Universitat Politècnica de València, Camino de Vera s/n, 46022 Valencia, Spain
{dapregar,esarvil}@vrain.upv.es

Abstract. The massive use of social media makes it increasingly easy to find highly sensitive information about almost anyone on the Internet. Despite the efforts of social media platforms to provide their users with tools to manage their privacy, these are proving insufficient due to their complexity. For this reason, it has been considered necessary to develop a software tool based on a multi-agent system to help users to improve and correct their bad behavior by using automation mechanisms and transmitting the information in a natural way for them, replicating the behavior of a human being. The aim of our work is to implement a multi-agent system where agents interact organically with each other and with human users on the PESEDIA social network, so that they can support user in a non-intrusive manner, using paternalistic techniques through actions available on the social network.

Keywords: Social Media Platform · Multi-agent · Privacy · Simulation

1 Introduction

Over the last decade Social Media Platforms (SMPs) have experienced a spectacular increase in terms of their number of users. From Facebook, with 1.26 billion active users daily (as of September 2019) [9], through Twitter [11], with 145 million active users every day in the same period, to the most recent Instagram, with approximately 500 million active users daily (as of September 2017) [10], just to mention some of the most popular ones, it can be inferred that social media are undoubtedly an integral part of our daily lives.

As a result, users have gradually lost their fear of this type of technology, showing themselves more and more willing to pour into them personal information, such as their thoughts or ideologies, chores, opinions, conflicts, etc. This trend is even more notable among the younger strata of society [14], who have grown up with SMPs and therefore do not have the prejudices shown, initially, by people who have been able to experience the popularization of the Internet, where privacy was highly valued, driven by fear of the unknown.

E. A. de la Cal et al. (Eds.): HAIS 2020, LNAI 12344, pp. 486–498, 2020.
https://doi.org/10.1007/978-3-030-61705-9_40

Deciding when to disclose confidential information has always been difficult, especially for those who join and publish content on SMP [17]. The main motivations for disclosing private information at social media are sharing information with friends and acquaintances, using it as a means of storing information, keeping up with trends, as well as a means of fostering narcissism and showing popularity [19]. The preservation of privacy is essential in human relationships, but we often consent to unreliable software that collects, stores and processes our data, often not knowing how this information will be protected or who will have access to it [15].

In the SMPs, users often reveal a lot of personal information in their profiles, in order to appear more sympathetic and friendly to others [7]. Users should learn the inherent privacy rules of the social network, so that they know how much they need to disclose in order to be socially accepted. Generally, this learning is achieved through continued use of the site [13,18], e.g. participants with private profiles tend to have friends who also have private profiles on Facebook.

Although there are many campaigns to raise awareness of the risks of social media, practical training should be provided on the proper use of personal data, privacy, as well as greater attention to the content of messages and how these messages can involve content risks for other users [2]. In training actions, it is important to bear in mind that a person learns only 40% of what he observes and hears, but 80% of what he lives or discovers on his own[1]. Thus, only practical training, based on "learning by doing", in which the individual is fully involved, can ensure a high success rate. So it will be very useful to develop secure SMPs that integrate simulation scenarios, allowing users practice so that they become aware, in a safe environment, of the needs for better control of their privacy.

For this reason, the PESEDIA - AI4PRI (Artificial Intelligent agents for Privacy Aware in Social Media) research project[2] was proposed with the didactic objective of teaching and helping correcting all these erratic behaviours to its users. In this project, a multi-agent system (MAS) oriented to social media will be developed to address the problem of privacy, offering each user a personalized agent to help them make decisions regarding the performance of actions that may involve a risk to their privacy. Likewise, this project will provide a controlled environment where virtual agents and human agents co-exist and where various situations that potentially compromise user privacy in the context of social networks can be simulated. The aim is to facilitate the learning of the good use of social networks in a totally practical and immersive way.

Models, techniques and technologies of multi-agent systems are interesting for the study of social networks and the development of models based on them. An example of the use of MAS and social media is found in Franchi and Poggy's work [6], where the use of a distributed MAS is proposed for the creation of a social network where the information of each user is managed by an agent. The proposal focuses on suggesting friendship connections based on the user's profile. In Kökciyan and Yolum's work [12] an agent-based social network is

[1] Source: National Training Laboratories, 1977.

[2] https://pesedia.webs.upv.es/.

proposed, where the agents manage the privacy requirements of the users and create privacy agreements with the agents. The agent checks the current status of the system to detect and resolve privacy breaches before they occur.

Throughout this project, one of the biggest problems we have faced is trying to solve the way we show the users information about their activity on the SMP. Currently, the way to communicate it to them consists on showing them different panels and informative pop-ups. This way, despite being practical, has been proven to be insufficient through different experiments carried by our research group. There are many studies [3–5,8] that shown that a human being tends to give more credibility and importance to the information when they perceive it is another human being who is transmitting it to them, even modifying their behaviour when they perceive they are speaking with an artificial intelligence.

In order to improve the way in which we communicate to the users of the PESEDIA SMP the information necessary to fulfil the educational objectives of our project, we have decided to integrate a series of intelligent agents that simulate the behaviour of a human being. In this work we present our first results derived from the design and the implementation effort carried out to integrate a multi-agent system inside PESEDIA.

The aim of our proposal is to implement a multi-agent system where agents interact organically with each other and with human users on the PESEDIA social network, with the future objective of providing them with the necessary tools so that they can support users is a non-intrusive manner, using paternalistic techniques through the tools available on the social network such as comments, "I like it", private messages, etc., which have been proven to be effective [20].

The rest of the document is structured as follows. Section 2 provides a brief description of the PESEDIA social network. Section 3 gives an overview of the components and interactions of our proposed system. Section 4 shows examples of the implementation of some of the numerous actions that agents can carry out within our SMP, together with the results obtained from their execution. Finally, Sect. 5 details different proposals for future work and the conclusions of the paper.

2 Pesedia

PESEDIA[3] is a social network, based on the open source platform Elgg[4], with an educational purpose, whose main objective is to teach its users the importance of their personal information and the dangers of not correctly managing the scope of the content published on the social network.

PESEDIA's target population is mainly adolescents, as they are the sector most unprotected against the dangers of the Internet. In recent years, several seminars have been held within the Summer School of our university, in which 13 and 14 year-old students have used PESEDIA and, through game techniques, have learned to use the social network, as well as to understand the involvement

[3] https://pesedia.webs.upv.es/.

[4] https://elgg.org/.

and impact of each interaction they make. These sessions have also served to collect anonymous information with which to generate models that help understand the relationship that children have with issues related to privacy, their emotional state and how all this influences when generating content, how they modify their behaviour patterns as knowledge of the platform increases, etc.

Up to now, PESEDIA included a series of agents responsible for advising and warning children when they were going to publish sensitive content, through text analysis, emotions and argumentation techniques. These agents were intended to help users correct the content they post on social networks, following up individually to achieve an improvement over time.

3 Overview of Our Proposal

This section provides an overview of the proposed system, detailing its components, its communication mechanisms and the technology required.

Figure 1 shows the system components together with their communication flow. The workflow of the system is divided into four different parts (numbered in the image). Next, we briefly describe these four parts:

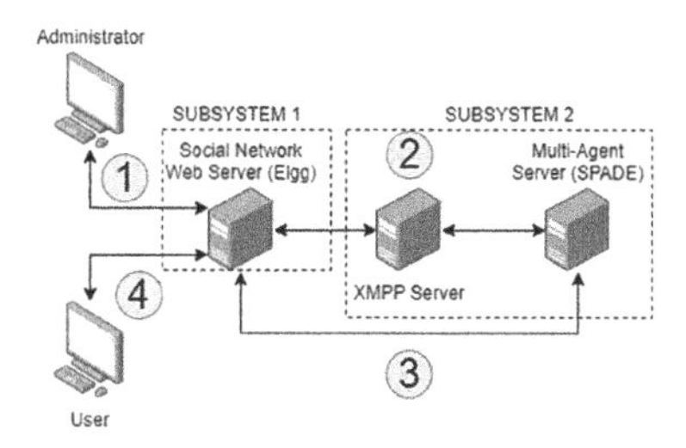

Fig. 1. System components and communication flow.

1. The administrator of the SMP can manage the multi-agent system through a web plugin (named here as subsystem 1) that includes both the interfaces and the communication mechanisms needed to make the link between the SMP and the multi-agent system effective. The administrator connects via web through the browser included in his/her device (PC, mobile, tablet, etc.) to the administration panel of the SMP, so as to activate the plugin provided through the corresponding menu.
   Once the plugin is activated, the administrator will see a new option within the administration menu (named "Multi-agent Settings"), and, when accessing this new option, he will be able to connect the SMP with the MAS (see Fig. 3). To do this, the web plugin asks the multi-agent system its status to know if it is available and, if so, it shows the administrator a new window where he can see the system status, as well as the different possible operations: add and remove agents, disconnect, etc.

2. The second part of the workflow includes the protocols and communication channels used by the web plugin and the multi-agent system (named here as subsystem 2). It deals with one of the communication mechanisms used between the SMP and the MAS - a full diagram detailing the protocols used is available in Fig. 2). As we have developed our multi-agent system on the SPADE[5] platform, and this platform uses the XMPP (Extensible Messaging and Presence Protocol) protocol[6] as a communication mechanism for the agents, we have thought it convenient to use it as well.
   In the proposed MAS we have a coordinating agent, named *master agent*, that is in charge of managing the rest of agents (which will normally represent SMP users) that we introduce in the system. Both the web plugin and each of the agents in the multi-agent system have their own JID (Jabber ID) identifier. Using this identifier they are able to send, receive and interpret the different messages sent between the different actors in the system.
   Furthermore, when the administrator performs any operation that may need to receive or send information to the MAS - check its status, for example - the web plugin is in charge of sending the request, using its own JID, to the associated JID of the master agent. This master agent then processes the message received, inform the other agents of the MAS of the relevant information for them and respond to the web plugin accordingly. The web plugin processes the response and updates the necessary information on the screen so that the administrator can know the result of the operation.
3. The third part of the system workflow deals with the other communication mechanism used between the SMP and the MAS. Each time the master agent notifies the other agents of an event of their interest, or when they themselves consider it, they should establish a communication channel that allows them to carry out the necessary operations to meet their objective.
   Elgg offers the programmer the possibility of implementing functions accessible through an API, as a native way of managing communication with external systems. Therefore, we have found it reasonable that the agents use this mechanism to interact with the SMP and to be able to both extract and persist information from it without having to go through the master agent. To achieve this they consult, through the API, the endpoint (a specific web address) designed for this task. Once they get the API response, they can perform the necessary operations to try to reach their goal and, if needed, they can persist results in the SMP using another endpoint. For interacting with the API, agents must indicate the user assigned to them in the SMP.
4. The fourth part of the system's workflow is concerned with solving the way the SMP (specifically the web plugin) sends information to the MAS so that it is aware of changes in the website based on the interaction of users and other agents. Every time the agents persist information in the SMP, it is likely that this information must be published so that the real users of the social network or other agents in the system become aware of it.

[5] http://spade.gti-ia.dsic.upv.es/index.php.
[6] https://xmpp.org/.

Both when the agents publish the content through the API, and when the users do it from the pertinent options available within the SMP, it is necessary that such content is visible to them. To solve the *agent* $\rightarrow$ *user* communication (understanding by "user" a real user or another agent) we have several functions exposed inside the API to allow the information persistence. This information, once in the database, is treated by Elgg and the framework itself facilitates its visibility based on what has been provided.
In order to solve the *user* $\rightarrow$ *agent* communication (understanding "user" as a real user or another agent) we use Elgg's tools that allow us to capture the different events associated to the actions that occur within the social network. When one of these events is triggered we proceed to send via XMPP (as explained in step 2) the information to the master agent, and this one is in charge of spreading it to the other agents as it considers appropriate.

Figure 2 shows in a conceptual manner the communication protocols used in our proposed system, based on the information above.

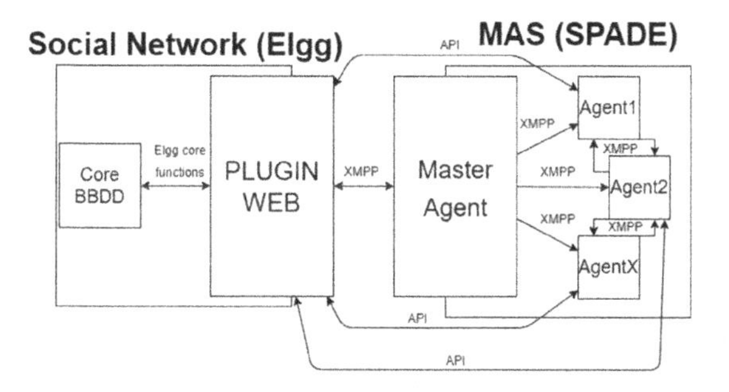

Fig. 2. Communication protocols used between the SMP and the MAS.

A reasonable doubt that may arise to the reader is the need to use two different communication protocols instead of sticking to only one of them. All these reasons are detailed below:

- **Reactivity and proactivity of the agents**: the nature of the agents implies that they can act on their environment and react to external stimuli. If we only used Elgg's API there would be no way to inform the agents of what is happening on the social network unless they decide to look into it. This problem could be solved by using only XMPP, but choosing this solution could generate new problems, which are detailed below.
- **Saturation in communications and modification of the servers' structure**: having determined that in case of opting for a single communication channel, XMPP is the only alternative, the need to know how this affects the different servers involved arises. First of all, it would be necessary for the server where the social network is hosted to be constantly listening for possible XMPP calls. To do this, it would be necessary to modify the server and add a socket in which to host the XMPP client responsible of managing

these communications, which would move it away from its original design and could lead to bad practices and future unwanted errors. On the other hand, the XMPP server in charge of managing the communications would have twice the workload because it would also have to attend the requests coming from the agents, what could cause an overload and require more hardware resources than the desired ones.

- **Web server overload**: the web server should only serve content and we must ensure that our solution does not force an additional workload. As we have seen in the previous point, a socket would allow to host an XMPP client that would attend the agents' requests. However, this socket would not be a traditional web socket and, instead of being open waiting for HTTP calls, it would have associated an XMPP agent that would be waiting in a loop for XMPP requests with a persistent connection, forcing to dedicate constant resources for a task that may not be necessary. This use of resources would obviously penalize the performance of the web server, already subject to a large workload due to the great amount of events that it has to handle with the normal use of the social network.

4 Validation

In order to validate the proposal, two different activities have been implemented.

The first activity replicates the process of registering a new user in the SMP, which requires the creation of new users in PESEDIA and also new agents within the multi-agent system. Currently, at the time of creation, the administrator will be able to choose between creating agents of two different types: extraverted or introverted. Extraverted agents will be willing to make as many friends as possible, whereas introverted agents will be shyer and less active in making friends. As future work, we would like to include other types of agents, such as egocentric, reserved, etc., that represent the different kinds of users that you would normally face within a social network.

To ensure that the subsystems can understand each other when communicating instructions, it has been necessary to develop a lexicon that both can interpret. For this purpose, a series of fixed structures, functions and parameters have been used which, once formatted using JSON notations, allow the desired instructions to be transferred unequivocally between both systems.

To add new agents, the administrator must access the corresponding screen (shown in Fig. 3) once the relevant plugin is activated in Elgg. Inside the screen, he must configure the number of users and the percentage distribution of types of agents that he wants to make.

Next, our web plugin creates the users in the social network using an Elgg's extension, named hypeFaker[7] plugin; and it also requests the MAS (specifically to the master agent) to create the corresponding agents, using a JSON message like the one displayed in Fig. 4.

[7] https://github.com/hypeJunction/hypeFaker.

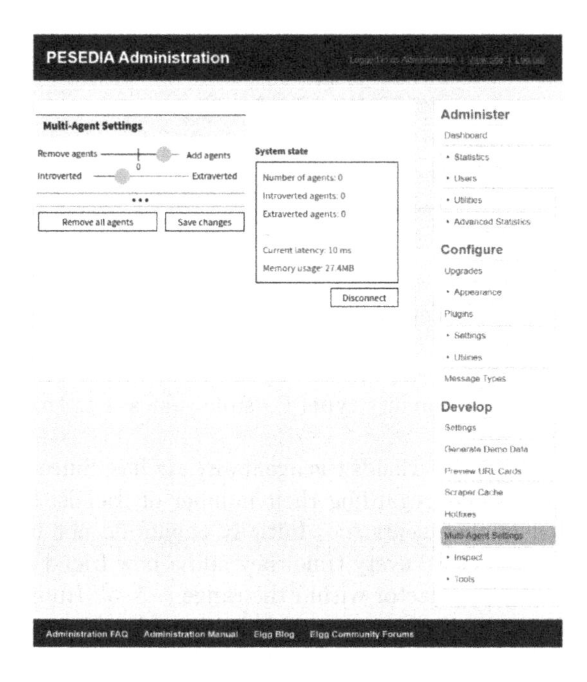

Fig. 3. Multi-agent settings screen.

After receiving the petition, the master agent proceeds creating the requested agents thanks to SPADE's functionality and passing them the required information to enable them to communicate freely with PESEDIA. Once created the agents start their behaviours as expected.

For the purpose of this paper, we have decided to also include the action of adding friends. This action in particular is quite interesting because it requires to perform certain instructions both within the multi-agent system, and the SMP. Additionally, this action can be started by the agents instead of the users, demonstrating how the agents can be proactive if needed. The following formula has been designed so that agents can decide whether they want to add new friends or not:

$$fDesire = min(100, max(iDesire * 25 + tPersonality * 8.33 - (nFriends * opposite(1 - nFriends * 0.3) + rBehaviour), 0))$$

where:

- **fDesire**: the final desire to perform the action. Its value is within [0–100].
- **iDesire**: the initial desire to perform the action, depending of the type of user we are representing, used to represent how active the agent should be in the SPM. Possible values: 1 (low-willing to do this action), 2 (medium-willing to do this action) or 3 (high-willing to do this action).

```
{
  "operation": "mas_operation_add_agents",
  "additional_parameters": {
    "personalities_and_number": [
      {"type": "INTROVERTED", "number": 1},
      {"type": "EXTRAVERTED", "number": 1}
    ],
    "pesedia_ids": [1203, 1204],
    "user_names": ["John Doe", "Jane Doe"]
  }
}
```


Fig. 4. Example of a JSON sent by PESEDIA to the MAS with the information required in order to create 2 new agents, as specified by the administrator.

- **tPersonality**: user personality type. Possible values: 1 (introverted), 2 (neutral), 3 (extraverted).
- **nFriends**: the number of friends the agent already has. Since humans tend to have threshold numbers regarding their number of friends, this factor must be implemented in the agents too. Initially agents do not have any friend, and this value is increased every time they add a new friend inside the SMP.
- **rBehaviour**: a random factor within the range [−5, 5]. Human behaviour is not always predictable and the agents' behaviour should not be either.

Since the final value should be in the range [0%–100%] - being 0% not willing to perform the action and 100% keenly disposed to do it - a set of weights has been assigned to each parameter. The most influential is the initial desire, which can represent a value as high as 75%, having a possible final weight of 25%, 50%, and 75%, increasing accordingly with the desired activity of the agents. The personality factor is the second one, with a maximum value of 25% and possible values of 8.33%, 16.66%, 24.99%. The number of friends is used to lineally reduce the willing to perform the action. Finally the random number adds a small variation of ±5%. Since using only the function can provide a value outside of the desired range, we have restricted it using minimum and maximum functions.

Figure 5 displays the evolution of the fDesire value after several executions, using a sample of 100 agents each time (50 introverted and 50 extraverted). As expected, the introverted agents lose their interest faster than the extraverted agents and, consequently, they will end up with a lower number of friends.

Once an agent has decided that he wants to add a new friend (i.e. $fDesire > threshold$), the agent asks PESEDIA for the current user list, via API, in order to decide which user he will send the friendship request, from amongst the ones that are not already his friends. Then he sends his petition once again via API and waits for the acceptance or rejection. Once informed of the result, he proceeds, adding the user to his friend list if accepted, or adding the user to his rejection list if pertinent, to avoid asking this user for friendship in the future.

Additionally, the agents are able to decide if they want to accept a friend request using the same formula. In this case PESEDIA will inform the master agent that a user (may the user be a human or another agent) is trying to add one of the agents as a friend. The master agent will inform the corresponding

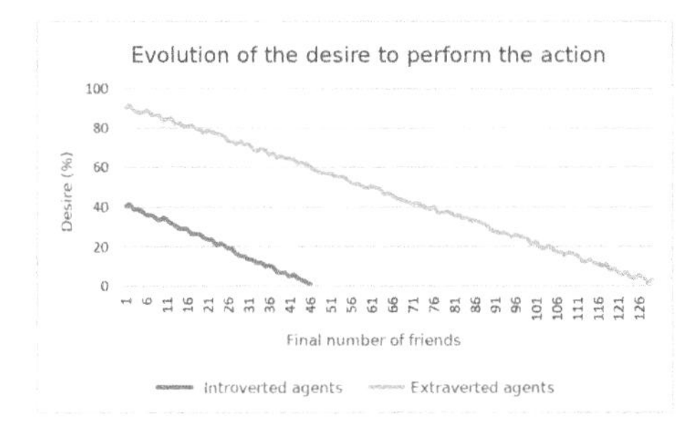

Fig. 5. Example of evolution of the *fDesire* value.

agent who will decide either to add the user or not, informing the social network via API with the appropriate response.

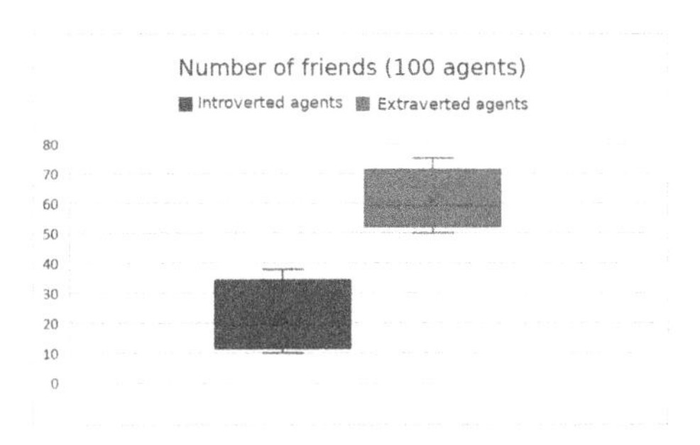

Fig. 6. Experiment result with 50 extraverted agents and 50 introverted agents.

Figure 6 displays the results obtained after a clean execution (in which PESEDIA has not any previous information nor users), using 100 agents (50 introverted and 50 extraverted), in an isolated agent environment. The expected results of this test considered that, usually, every extraverted agent would end up being friend of every other extraverted agent and some of the introverted ones, while the introverted ones have more probability of ending up as friends with extraverted agents mainly. In order to corroborate if our hypothesis is correct we have also run an smaller experiment with 2 extraverted agents and 10 introverted ones. The results of this test are shown in Fig. 7.

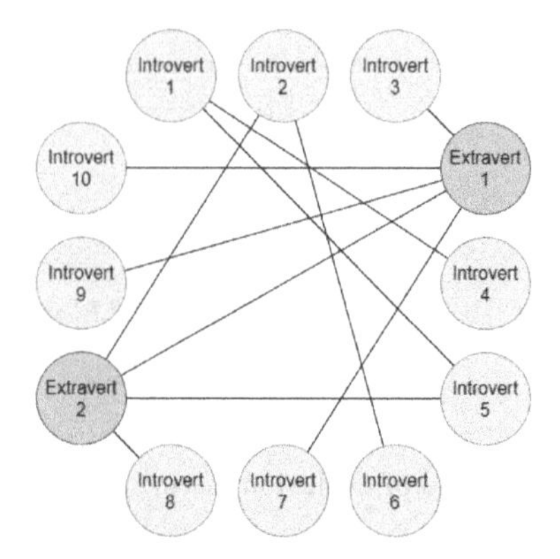

Fig. 7. Experiment result with 2 extraverted agents and 10 introverted agents.

5 Conclusions

This document proposes a framework that allows to populate a social network using a MAS, with agents that replicate behaviors based on human behavior patterns. The objective of the agents is to help transferring to the human users of the social network information about their behaviors, that may be harming their privacy, in a non intrusive (e.g. dialogues or pop-up windows) manner.

Additionally, an initial approach to the proposed system has been developed using the Elgg social network development framework and the XMPP-based multi-agent system framework SPADE. Different experiments have been carried out to validate that the behaviour of the agents is accurate using the PESEDIA social network as a test environment. The aim of this work was to test how the agents interact within the environment of the SMP. It is our intention to deploy this system in the next summer school seminars in order to determine how its usage may impact the teenager's behaviours and patterns of usage.

Being now this infrastructure in place, new research opportunities arise. Firstly, the possibility of designing privacy-aware agents customized for each user, so that they can help them in a direct way to learn good practices in relation to privacy and to correct bad habits through the use of simulation scenarios powered by the agents. In this privacy-aware agents we will integrate the soft-paternalism techniques [1] and argumentation system [16] already developed in our research group. Secondly, it is possible to study in depth the aspect of behaviour simulation. This work mentions how the personality to be emulated can influence the behaviour of the agents, so it might be possible to design different models of agents based on psychological profiles. Finally, it is also possible to design agents that, based on the content posted by the users of the social network and their reactions, try to determine the social norms of the network.

Acknowledgments. This work has been funded thanks to the Spanish Government through project TIN2017-89156-R and predoctoral contract PRE2018-084940.

References

1. Alemany, J., del Val, E., Alberola, J., García-Fornes, A.: Enhancing the privacy risk awareness of teenagers in online social networks through soft-paternalism mechanisms. Int. J. Hum.-Comput. Stud. **129**, 27–40 (2019)
2. Argente, E., Vivancos, E., Alemany, J., García-Fornes, A.: Educando en privacidad en el uso de las redes sociales. Educ. Knowl. Soc. **18**(2), 107–126 (2017)
3. Bell, L., Gustafson, J.: Interaction with an animated agent in a spoken dialogue system. In: 6th European Conference on Speech Communication and Technology (1999)
4. Cassell, J., Thorisson, K.R.: The power of a nod and a glance: envelope vs. emotional feedback in animated conversational agents. Appl. Artif. Intell. **13**(4–5), 519–538 (1999)
5. Cerrato, L., Ekeklint, S.: Different ways of ending human-machine dialogues. In: Proceedings of the Embodied Conversational Agents (2002)
6. Franchi, E., Poggi, A.: Multi-agent systems and social networks. In: Handbook of Research on Business Social Networking: Organizational, Managerial, and Technological Dimensions, pp. 84–97. IGI Global (2012)
7. Hollenbaugh, E.E., Ferris, A.L.: Facebook self-disclosure: examining the role of traits, social cohesion, and motives. Comput. Hum. Behav. **30**, 50–58 (2014)
8. Hubal, R.C., Fishbein, D.H., Sheppard, M.S., Paschall, M.J., Eldreth, D.L., Hyde, C.T.: How do varied populations interact with embodied conversational agents? Findings from inner-city adolescents and prisoners. Comput. Hum. Behav. **24**(3), 1104–1138 (2008)
9. Inc., F.: Facebook reports third quarter 2019 results (2019). https://investor.fb.com/investor-news/press-release-details/2019/Facebook-Reports-Third-Quarter-2019-Results/default.aspx. Accessed 27 Jan 2020
10. Inc., F.: Instagram for business (2019). https://www.facebook.com/business/marketing/instagram. Accessed 27 Jan 2020
11. Inc., T.: Twitter q3 '19 investor fact sheet (2019). https://s22.q4cdn.com/826641620/files/doc_financials/2019/q3/Q3_19_InvestorFactSheet.pdf. Accessed 27 Jan 2020
12. Kökciyan, N., Yolum, P.: PriGuardTool: a tool for monitoring privacy violations in online social networks. In: AAMAS, pp. 1496–1497 (2016)
13. Lewis, K.: The co-evolution of social network ties and online privacy behavior. In: Trepte, S., Reinecke, L. (eds.) Privacy Online, pp. 91–109. Springer, Heidelberg (2011). https://doi.org/10.1007/978-3-642-21521-6_8
14. Madden, M., et al.: Teens, social media, and privacy. Pew Res. Cent. **21**, 2–86 (2013)
15. Patkos, T., et al.: Privacy-by-norms privacy expectations in online interactions. In: 2015 IEEE International Conference on Self-Adaptive Self-Organizing Systems, pp. 1–6 (2015)
16. Ruiz Dolz, R.: An argumentation system for assisting users with privacy management in online social networks (2019)
17. Spottswood, E.L., Hancock, J.T.: Should I share that? Prompting social norms that influence privacy behaviors on a social networking site. J. Comput-Mediat. Commun. **22**(2), 55–70 (2017)
18. Stutzman, F., Kramer-Duffield, J.: Friends only: examining a privacy-enhancing behavior in facebook. In: Proceedings of the SIGCHI Conference on Human Factors in Computing Systems, pp. 1553–1562 (2010)

19. Waters, S., Ackerman, J.: Exploring privacy management on Facebook: motivations and perceived consequences of voluntary disclosure. J. Comput-Mediat. Commun. **17**(1), 101–115 (2011)
20. Wisniewski, P.J., Knijnenburg, B.P., Lipford, H.R.: Making privacy personal: profiling social network users to inform privacy education and nudging. Int. J. Hum.-Comput. Stud. **98**, 95–108 (2017)

First Steps Towards State Representation Learning for Cognitive Robotics

Blaž Meden[2], Abraham Prieto[1], Peter Peer[2], and Francisco Bellas[1](✉)

[1] GII, CITIC Research Center, Universidade da Coruña, A Coruña, Spain
{abraham.prieto,francisco.bellas}@udc.es
[2] Computer Vision Lab, University of Ljubljana, Ljubljana, Slovenia
{blaz.meden,peter.peer}@fri.uni-lj.si

Abstract. In this work we have implemented and tested a framework for training and analyzing auto-encoding architectures for the purpose of encoding state space representations into latent space, and thus compressing the essential space properties depicted in the training image dataset. We explored the possibility of incorporating a forward model in between encoder and decoder to predict the next state in series of temporally arranged images, with the aim of testing if it is able to predict meaningful representations (even if they are not interpretable by visual inspection). The application domain of this approach is that of cognitive robotics, where having a state representation learning system that can operate in an open-ended fashion is necessary. State representation learning has been a challenging topic in autonomous robotics for a long time, and some promising approaches have been developed. Anyway, when applying them to open-ended learning, as is the case of cognitive robotics, current solutions fail, so new systems must be implemented. The work presented here is a first approach towards this objective.

Keywords: Autoencoders · Variational autoencoders · Cognitive robotics

1 Introduction

State space representation in autonomous robotics is a key aspect, because it defines the search space where the different models and techniques that are used must solve the task [11]. Defining an adequate state space representation will impact on the capacity of an intelligent system for producing desirable behaviors not only for one task, but specially for a diverse set of tasks and in a data efficient manner, since it would imply the disentanglement of the underlying structure of the world into disjoint parts of its representation. Therefore, disregarding the work on an appropriate state representation will produce, as it is the case in many of the most popular algorithms, that they will suffer from poor data efficiency, or that they will not exhibit the same level of robustness and generalization one can find on biological intelligence [5].

E. A. de la Cal et al. (Eds.): HAIS 2020, LNAI 12344, pp. 499–510, 2020.
https://doi.org/10.1007/978-3-030-61705-9_41

Typically, given a robot hardware and a set of sensors, to simplify such searching process, authors establish the most convenient representation. To do it, different predefined processing algorithms are applied to the raw data coming from the sensors aiming to improve the learnability of useful patterns or models, and therefore, to produce useful behaviours. For instance, when dealing with environments which involve grasping or moving objects it is usual to define a state space based on distances and angles among them. Although in simple cases the human chosen representation could be optimal, in robotics, as well as in machine learning, finding and defining relevant states (or features) usually requires a considerable amount of manual engineering. It is, therefore, interesting to learn these features with the minimal supervision possible. This is the case in Cognitive Robotics [2], a sub-field of autonomous robotics where models of the human cognitive development are used with the aim of obtaining a higher level of autonomy. In this field, the robots are endowed with a cognitive architecture that carries out three main tasks: goal discovery and selection, model and policy learning, and knowledge storage and management [10]. These architectures allow the robot to perform open-ended learning, which starts from a set of innate knowledge, and that is able to carry out continual learning throughout the robot "life", discovering new goals and learning from experience. This way, a cognitive robot behaves "as humans" in the sense of requiring long periods of time to learn, to select what to do, and to consolidate the knowledge.

As it can be supposed, in cognitive robotics, pre-defining the state space representation is complex, mainly because the system improvement occurs in long periods of time in a developmental and incremental manner, so if the starting representation is not adequate, the system performance will not be optimal. The typical procedure in this field is imposing representations that are similar to those used in human (or animal) brains. For instance, in the case of having a camera, many authors implement an attention mechanism inspired in human vision to reduce the view field, and then they implement processing algorithms to extract objects and their properties. But, in general, this final stage of state space representation is, again, selected by the designer, who chooses the type of object that is more relevant for the task and, consequently, which elements in the scene are not relevant.

In this work, we aim to follow a state representation learning approach for cognitive robotics, based on the minimization of the designer intervention, and using internal measurements of information utility to guide such learning. That is, our objective is to define the most adequate representation space for the robot open-ended learning in its environment, using feedback from the learning process itself. In other words, we propose here to develop a representational procedure to autonomously adjust the state space representation according to the robot needs. To do it, we start from the raw information coming from the sensors, we apply an information compression stage, and we test if the resulting representation is appropriate for open-ended learning.

2 State Representation Learning

The field of state representation learning has been a key aspect in the robotics community in the last 20 years [11]. Some lines of work are being explored in parallel. On the one hand, there have been recent efforts on building theoretical frameworks and procedures to allow for the understanding and standardization of the automatic state representation definition using several principles as mutual information, minimality of the representation, cross entropy, symmetry, and invariance to nuisances as translations, rotations or occlusions [5,6].

On the other hand, some other works have focused on the study of how recent deep learning architectures produce useful representations associated to some of the hidden layers of the deep neural networks as an implicit mechanism to achieve robustness and generalization. Both to help improve the efficiency of those deep learning algorithms and to extract knowledge to be able to produce those representations in different domains and learning structures [1].

Finally, although it is possible to learn controllers directly from raw observations [12] and would not necessarily benefit from a reduced representation, control algorithms as reinforcement learning, evolutionary techniques and many others can improve their performance with low dimensional and informative representations, instead of raw data [13] and therefore some works have focused on finding practical implementations of procedures to obtain those reduced state spaces. This work belongs to this last category as it intends to define a state representation for a real robot grasping task endowed with a raw sensor which consist in a zenithal camera.

To be able to define a suited representation one should define properties (or features) that a relevant state representation should allow for. Those most commonly found in literature are, the reconstruction of raw observations (using PCA or autoencoders), learning direct or inverse world models, or learning the rewards space. In this work we will try to exploit the two first strategies. [11] provides a thorough compilation of those strategies and works in which they have been used. Other types of objectives use some properties, a priori knowledge, named priors, which are imposed to the representation by means of a loss term, namely, slowness, variability, proportionality, repeatability, and others. They have been satisfactorily exploited in [7] and [8] for a 3D navigation task.

We have studied here the creation of state representation of a 3D problem based on raw camera information by using image reconstruction and world model learning. In particular, we have focused on the impact of some features of the process as, the attention algorithm used to weigh the loss function, the type of autoencoder used (regular or variational), the relative size of the variable elements on the images and as usual the size of the state space. We will use the same notation as that presented in [11].

2.1 Autoencoders

Autoencoders have the potential to be useful in the problem of representation learning, due to their specific architecture, which introduces a dimensional bottleneck in the central part of the model and by doing that, compresses the representation of the information in the original data. Training is usually done in a non-supervised way and it is very simple to do, as we are trying to learn how to reconstruct the original input image on the output via backpropagation. The only condition that is introduced with the topology of the architecture is the compression stage, which is encoding the hidden representations (better known as a latent space).

A typical autoencoder model is following the encoding-decoding architectural scheme. The encoder as frontal part of the model performs downsampling of the image and produces latent representation. Then, the decoder takes the latent representation and tries to reconstruct the original input, based on given latent information. The model itself is trained in an end-to-end fashion and by optimizing entire model via backpropagation we minimize the loss between original inputs and obtained outputs. The loss is usually defined as metric for comparing two images (i.e. MSE). Other losses can be used as well. Other specific topological parameters can be also defined within the model, for example number of convolutional layers, size and number of filters per each convolutional layer, the size of the latent space and the activation functions, used after each layer.

2.2 Related Work

Related area in our line of work can be divided into techniques for obtaining compressed representations (representation learning) and autoencoding deep learning architectures, which are one specific way of achieving latent representations. The idea of autoencoders (AE) evolved over time, although one of the first mentioned ideas of using a bottleneck inside neural network was in Rumelhart's work [14]. As of nowadays, a well written and detailed chapter on the topic of autoencoders is available in the Deep Learning book from Goodfellow et al. [3]. The topic of autoencoders is becoming more diverse day by day, as researchers are using these kind of networks to do denoising, representation learning, etc.

Variational Autoencoder (VAE), as an extension of AE was introduced by Kingma et al. [9]. The paper includes formal definitions and mathematical foundations of the approach as well as visual results from two datasets (Frey Faces and MNIST digits). A recent and very relevant work that uses state representation learning in a similar way as we propose here is [4], where a VAE is used to learn about state representations in a game-like environments. In this work, a VAE model is successfully used to reconstruct observations and provide latent space, which encodes crucial scenario information needed to train the gameplay agents. Although this is a highly remarkable approach, it must be pointed out that the application domain is not cognitive robotics, so authors do not take into consideration any limitation related to real-time operation or efficiency.

3 System Overview

In this work, we were experimenting with two variations of autoencoders. A regular, fully convolutional autoencoder (AE) and a variational autoencoder (VAE).

The main difference between these two models is the fact, that AE is essentially only a series of layered convolutions, applied on the input image, to produce a final result. In its most simplest form, this could be represented with simple interpolation (downsampling, followed by upsampling), but in the case of AE, the filter parameters are learned (so downsampling and upsampling operations are tuned during the training, to minimize output loss). VAE on the other hand, uses the same logic, however, in between the encoder and decoder, there is a special sampling layer, which is fitting the training data onto randomly sampled variables from multivariant Gaussian distribution. This essentially scrambles the spatial information, but on the other hand, dedicates entire latent space to encode the hidden representation. In this sense, the variational latent space seems more rich with information, but the encoding cannot be visually interpreted.

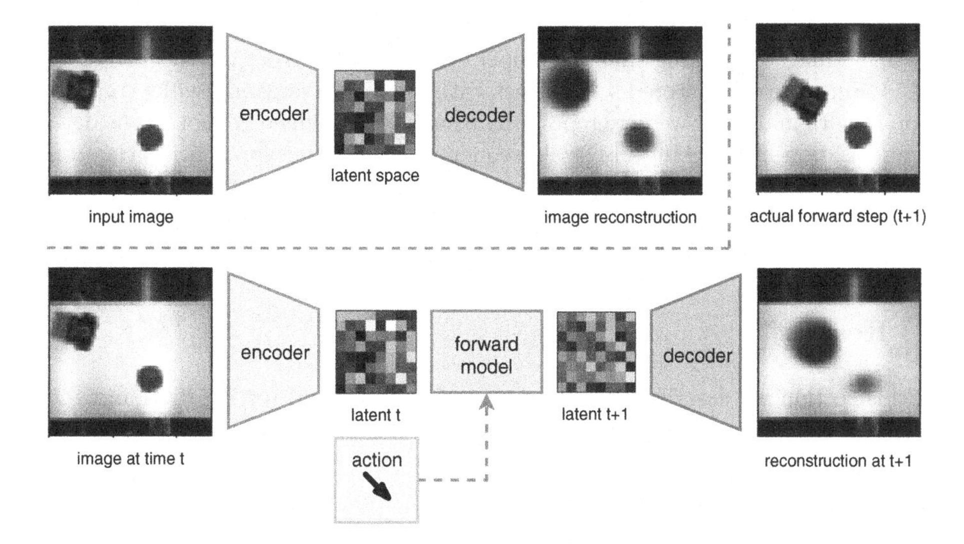

Fig. 1. Pipeline overview of our experiments. Top marked section illustrates first tier of experiments, where we evaluated the reconstruction quality of images from our scenario. Section at the bottom illustrates the second part of the experiments, where we included separately trained forward model to predict latent representation, which can be used to reconstruct image at next simulation step. Ground truth image is also available in top right corner of the figure, illustrating that reconstruction is closer to next simulated step than the original input image.

Our work includes two series of experiments, and the pipeline of the processes involved on them is displayed in Fig. 1.

3.1 Reconstruction with Autoencoders

First experiment was intended to study whether the information in the latent space can be reconstructed back into the original images (top pipeline of Fig. 1).

We tried multiple configurations of models (testing AE and VAE, and also changing the dimensions of latent spaces, attention factors of the foreground and background in the training images, object sizes). At the end of the experiments we obtained best possible AE and VAE architectures, which were then used in the second part of the experiments.

3.2 Forward Model Experiments

Second part of the experiments included introduction of forward model in between encoding and decoding part of the AE/VAE (bottom pipeline of Fig. 1). In this case, we defined an action, which denotes the angle in which the robot moves in each time step. The action and latent space, obtained from the encoder represented the input into our forward model. The expected output of the model is supposed to be the latent space in the next time step (essentially predicting, what would happen if the action at time t was executed, knowing the latent space at time t – meaning that the model needs to reconstruct the scene at time $t+1$). Since we encountered some issues with model convergence, while training it on the original data, we here report the results on simplified version of the data (segmentation-like looking grayscale sequences) without color-rich information within the training images. This second pipeline summarizes the type of state representation learning we aim to introduce in cognitive robotics, and it makes up the main contribution of this paper.

4 Results

In this section we describe the generation of training and testing data and the results obtained during first and second part of the experiments.

4.1 Dataset

Dataset images were generated using the images displayed in Fig. 2. We simulated a simple robot on a plane. The task of the robot was to find the relevant red circle on the table. For the first set of experiments, the position of the robot and the circle was placed randomly on the bright part of the background image (table area). To simulate image sequences in the second step of experiments we implemented simple, brownian-like exploration in which the robot moved around the table to explore its environment. The probability of the robot moving around in a random pattern was 1/2. We also added a direct movement of the robot to the red target with a probability of 1/2, to make it converge faster to the goal. With the color images we also constructed corresponding ground truth segmentation masks, where foreground objects (the robot and the circle) were separated from the background. The masks, visible in Fig. 3, were later used to calculate performance metric in form of Intersection over Union (IoU) on reconstructed images.

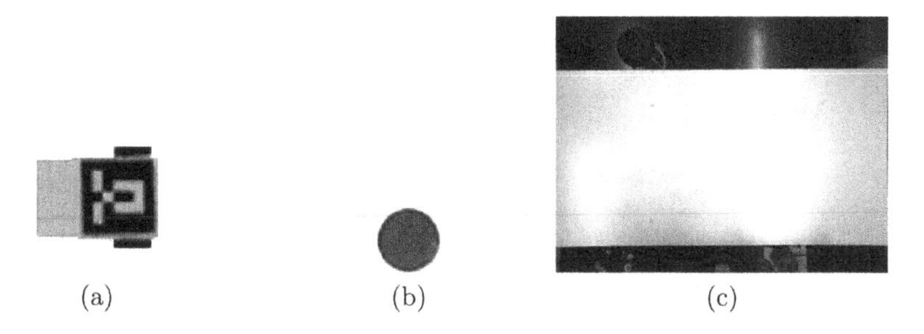

Fig. 2. Building blocks of our generated dataset: a) a robot, b) an object of interest, and c) the background image.

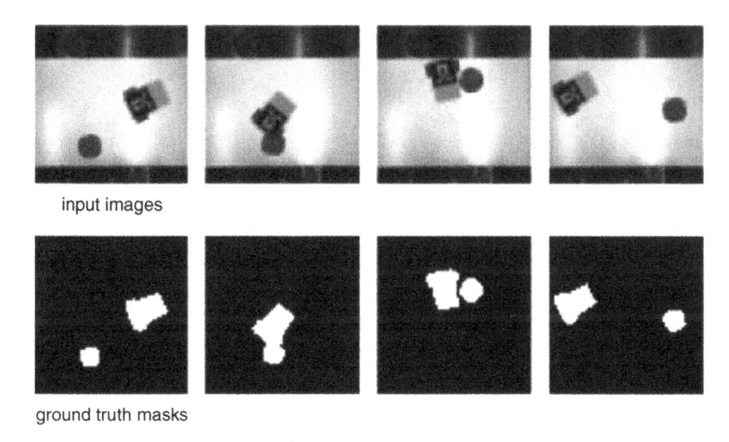

Fig. 3. Generated image examples (top) and corresponding ground truth masks (bottom).

4.2 Reconstruction Experiment

To conduct our first experiment, we trained various combinations of parameters, defining autoencoder architectures and training parameters. Common training parameters include Adam optimizer with learning rate $lr = 0.001$ with weighted mean squared error loss function (using weighted segmentation masks as balancing factors for reconstruction of the foreground objects and the background), batch size of 32 and 50 training epochs (with 5000 images per epoch). As we were training multiple variations of autoencoders, we were changing the sizes of latent space (most commonly using 4, 16, 64 with AE and 2, 4, 9, 16, 64 with VAE, see Fig. 4). The dimension of the training images was $64 \times 64 \times 3$ (3-channel RGB images).

After the training we evaluated the final reconstructions with a test set of 64 images. An example of input images, latent spaces, reconstructed images and evaluation masks is available in Fig. 4, where AE and VAE models were constructed using 16 and 64-dimensional latent spaces. Here we can observe, how latent space is represented in each model. AE keeps the spatial information

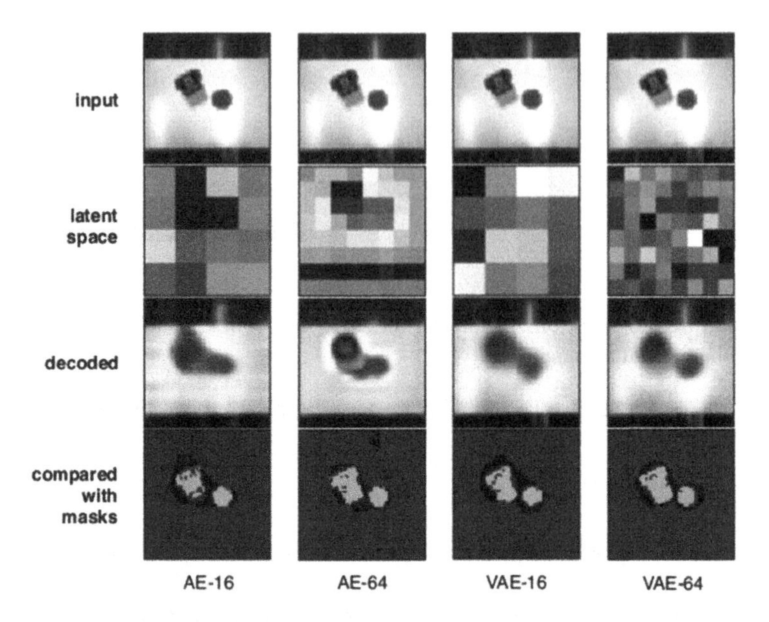

Fig. 4. Comparison between AE and VAE with 16 and 64 latent space sizes. AE yields interpretable latent spaces while VAE manages to use all available latent variables to encode information resulting in scrambled-like looking representation. (Color figure online)

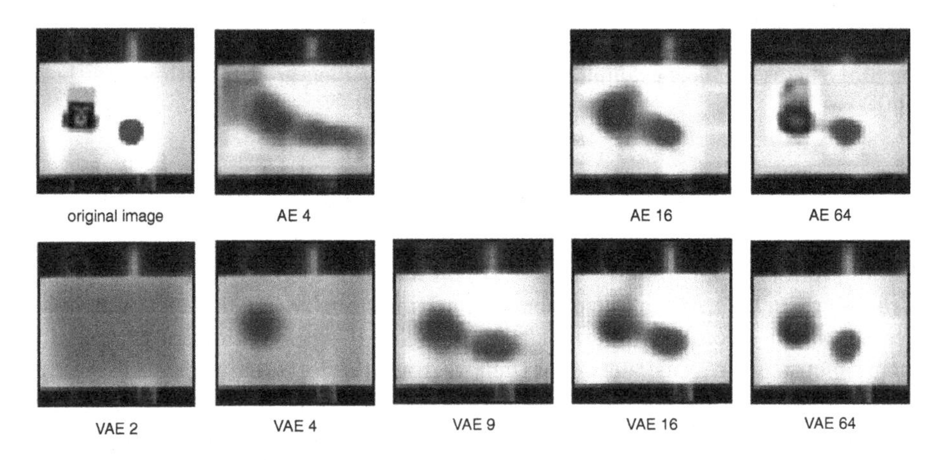

Fig. 5. Qualitative reconstruction results from first part of the experiments. In left top corner an original reference image is shown. Top row illustrates image reconstructions with different sizes of latent spaces using regular convolutional autoencoder (namely 4, 16 and 64; latent spaces with sizes 2 and 9 are ommited for regular AE due to the topological constraints of the network). Bottom row similarly illustrates image reconstructions using variational autoencoder with different latent spaces (2, 4, 9, 16 and 64).

Table 1. Top 10 rated AE/VAE models in terms of average Intersection over Union (IoU) during tests. Best results are achieved with larger latent space sizes and by increasing the object attention factor to 0.8 (denoting that robot and the object are more important for reconstruction than the background, however the background still has to be reconstructed to some degree). Models performed best, when object size was increased 3 times their original size (indicating that object size matters, when trying to reconstruct the scene as accurately as possible, as smaller regions tend to be discarded during encoding, which can lead to disappearance of smaller objects).

Model	Latent size	Back att	Obj. att	Obj. size	IoU (avg)	IoU (stdev)
VAE	64	0.2	0.8	3	0.65520	0.07533
VAE	64	0.33	0.67	3	0.61377	0.07079
AE	16	0.2	0.8	3	0.57823	0.07041
VAE	64	0.2	0.8	2	0.57033	0.11629
AE	64	0.2	0.8	1	0.56386	0.15444
VAE	64	0.33	0.67	2	0.52029	0.11642
VAE	16	0.2	0.8	3	0.50127	0.07992
AE	64	0.2	0.8	3	0.50019	0.05898
VAE	64	0.02	0.98	1	0.47663	0.06301
VAE	16	0.33	0.67	3	0.46870	0.08014

and uses downsampled image version in order to reconstruct the final image (with higher dimensions producing better visual results). In contrast with AE, VAE uses entire latent space, to encode the representation, while scrambling the spatial information (encoded information is therefore richer but we cannot really interpret it). In the last row of Fig. 4 we can also see the comparison with ground truth segmentation masks (green pixels denoting proper color classification, while blue and red represent misclassified pixels). Visual comparison of reconstructed images considering different latent space sizes is available in Fig. 5. We also present the quantitative analysis in Table 1, where we report the top 10 models with corresponding parameter combinations, which produced best accuracy in terms of IoU. In the table it is clear that larger object sizes and larger latent sizes are correlated with the overall accuracy of the models. Another important parameter is denoted as attention factor, which is in the best cases usually around 80% for foreground objects and 20% for the background. These results formed the basis for our selection of the models in the second part of the experiments.

4.3 Forward Model Experiment

In this part we used best pretrained autoencoder models (AE-64, VAE-64, AE-16, VAE-16). Forward model (FM) was trained separately on generated image sequences. The protocol of training FM included generating color images with the moving robot and red circle. Then we used pretrained encoder from autoencoder

Table 2. Results of second experiment in terms of average Intersection over Union (IoU). Various configurations were tested. VAE and AE were used to produce latent representations of the images and FM represents the forward model that was used to predict state in the next timestep. We tested latent sizes 64 and 16 with both autoencoders.

Model	Diff. learning	Latent size	Obj. size	IoU (avg)	IoU (stdev)
VAE + FM	✓	64	3	0.35866	0.21140
VAE + FM	✗	64	3	0.35050	0.20697
VAE + FM	✓	16	3	0.19372	0.12674
VAE + FM	✗	16	3	0.18675	0.14988
AE + FM	✓	64	3	0.16381	0.12321
AE + FM	✗	64	3	0.14849	0.12366
AE + FM	✓	16	3	0.12763	0.10202
AE + FM	✗	16	3	0.05069	0.05329

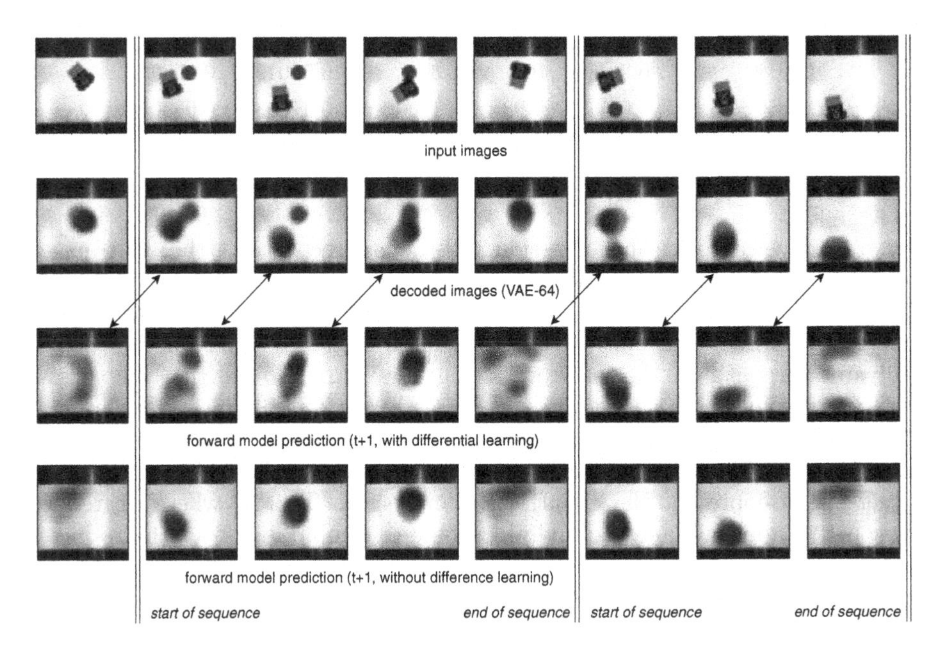

Fig. 6. Prediction example using forward model (FM). Top row displays original sequence images in. Row in the middle represents corresponding reconstructed images in each timestep. Bottom row represents reconstructed images from latent space predicted by forward model, given the action of the robot.

model to predict latent space, corresponding to each image in the generated sequence. We also generated a set of actions, each action denoting movement transition in between two consecutive image frames. The action was defined as the global orientation angle of the robot, normalized in between -1 and 1 (see the bottom row of Fig. 1). Finally we trained FM with 50 epochs and 100 iterations per epoch with batch size of 32 (resulting in total of 160.000 generated images and latent spaces used for training). We also tried to train the forward model in two distinct ways. The default way was to use the model to predict next state, based on the current state of latent space and the action (passed into the model as a tensor of the same size as the latent space, with repeated action values, to balance the network inputs). The second way of training was to predict only the difference between latent states in time t and $t+1$ (so-called difference learning). In the latter, the model only needs to predict the difference between the states as opposed to predict the complete state $t+1$ in the first variation. Results are gathered in Table 2. We can see that the difference between the proposed two ways of training the FM was not that obvious. The same observation can be made by analyzing the visual results in Fig. 6. Otherwise we can notice, that the final image reconstruction accuracy decreases after we introduce the FM, which makes sense, since FM introduces new error within its predictions. However, some predictions are quite accurate (usually in between the sequence). Forward model of course fails to predict the states at the end of the image sequence, as the robot and the red circle get randomly replaced, after the robot reaches the circle (which indicates the end of the sequence). This behaviour is illustrated in Fig. 6.

5 Conclusions

This paper presents an approach towards state representation learning for cognitive robotics. In this first work, we have tested a system based on the application of an autoencoder together with a forward model, so the latent space is evaluated with regards to the learnability of such forward model. In particular, we have focused the study on the sensitivity analysis of the main parameters of AE and VAE autoencoders. We have observed that larger latent spaces yielded best results, having larger object sizes also helped quite a lot, and VAE-64 performed best overall. VAE uses entire latent space to encode non-interpretable information, while AE performs downsample and upsample, using only the spatial area around moving robot (interpretable latent space). Forward model is able to predict the movement of the robot with some parameterization, although in many others the results were very poor. Forward model cannot predict unknown robot state after the sequence is finished, since the next robot initialization is random. This probably impacts the quantitative results the most, although there are failure cases, where the next action and next image are within the same sequence. We can conclude that the experiment was successful, and we have shown that state representation learning using autoencoders and forward model are feasible. Our next step is moving this approach towards real cognitive robotics, creating a way to learn the representation in real time and using real images. Moreover, we have started to analyze the option of training the autoencoders and the forward model concurrently, with the aim of obtaining latent spaces better suited for the forward model prediction. The first results are promising, although a deeper analysis is required due to the high number of parameters that must be adjusted, and the consequent complexity of the search process.

Acknowledgements. This work has been partially funded by the Ministerio de Ciencia, Innovación y Universidades of Spain/FEDER (grant RTI2018-101114-B-I00) and Xunta de Galicia and FEDER (grant ED431C 2017/12).

References

1. Achille, A., Soatto, S.: On the emergence of invariance and disentangling in deep representations. CoRR abs/1706.01350 (2017). http://arxiv.org/abs/1706.01350
2. Asada, M., et al.: Cognitive developmental robotics: a survey. IEEE Trans. Auton. Mental Dev. **1**(1), 12–34 (2009). https://doi.org/10.1109/TAMD.2009.2021702
3. Goodfellow, I., Bengio, Y., Courville, A.: Deep Learning. MIT Press (2016). http://www.deeplearningbook.org
4. Ha, D., Schmidhuber, J.: World models. CoRR abs/1803.10122 (2018). http://arxiv.org/abs/1803.10122
5. Higgins, I., et al.: Towards a definition of disentangled representations. CoRR abs/1812.02230 (2018). http://arxiv.org/abs/1812.02230
6. Hjelm, R.D., et al.: Learning deep representations by mutual information estimation and maximization (2018)
7. Jonschkowski, R., Brock, O.: Learning state representations with robotic priors. Auton. Robots **39**(3), 407–428 (2015). https://doi.org/10.1007/s10514-015-9459-7
8. Jonschkowski, R., Hafner, R., Scholz, J., Riedmiller, M.: PVEs: Position-velocity encoders for unsupervised learning of structured state representations (2017)
9. Kingma, D.P., Welling, M.: Auto-encoding variational bayes. CoRR abs/1312.6114 (2013). http://arxiv.org/abs/1312.6114
10. Kotseruba, I., Gonzalez, O.J.A., Tsotsos, J.K.: A review of 40 years of cognitive architecture research: focus on perception, attention, learning and applications. CoRR abs/1610.08602 (2016). http://arxiv.org/abs/1610.08602
11. Lesort, T., Rodríguez, N.D., Goudou, J., Filliat, D.: State representation learning for control: an overview. CoRR abs/1802.04181 (2018). http://arxiv.org/abs/1802.04181
12. Mnih, V., et al.: Human-level control through deep reinforcement learning. Nature **518**(7540), 529–533 (2015). https://doi.org/10.1038/nature14236
13. Munk, J., Kober, J., Babuška, R.: Learning state representation for deep actor-critic control. In: 2016 IEEE 55th Conference on Decision and Control (CDC), pp. 4667–4673, December 2016. https://doi.org/10.1109/CDC.2016.7798980
14. Rumelhart, D.E., McClelland, J.L.: Learning Internal Representations by Error Propagation. MITP (1987). https://ieeexplore.ieee.org/document/6302929

Hybridized White Learning in Cloud-Based Picture Archiving and Communication System for Predictability and Interpretability

Antonio J. Tallón-Ballesteros[1(✉)], Simon Fong[2], Tengyue Li[3], Lian-sheng Liu[4], Thomas Hanne[5], and Weiwei Lin[6]

[1] University of Huelva, Huelva, Spain
antonio.tallon.diesia@zimbra.uhu.es
[2] University of Macau, Taipa, Macau SAR
[3] ZIAT Chinese Academy of Sciences, Zhuhai, China
[4] First Affiliated Hospital of Guangzhou University of TCM, Guangzhou, China
[5] Institute for Information Systems, University of Applied Sciences and Arts Northwestern Switzerland, Olten, Switzerland
[6] South China University of Technology, Guangzhou, China

Abstract. A picture archiving and communication system (PACS) was originally designed for replacing physical films by digitizing medical images for storage and access convenience. With the maturity of communication infrastructures, e.g. 5G transmission, big data and distributed processing technologies, cloud-based PACS extends the storage and access efficiency of PACS across multiple imaging centers, hospitals and clinics without geographical bounds. In addition to the flexibility of accessing medical big data to physicians and radiologists to access medical records, fast data analytics is becoming an important part of cloud-based PACS solution. The machine learning that supports cloud-based PACS needs to provide highly accurate prediction and interpretable model, despite the model learning time should be kept as minimum as possible in the big data environment. In this paper, a framework called White Learning (WL) which hybridizes a deep learner and an incremental Bayesian network which offer the highest possible prediction accuracy and causality reasoning which are currently demanded by medical practitioners. To achieve this, several novel modifications for optimizing a WL model are proposed and studied. The efficacy of the optimized WL model is tested with empirical breast-cancer mammogram data from a local hospital.

Keywords: PACS · Machine learning · Cancer prediction · Metaheuristic optimization

1 Introduction

Healthcare has a long history of applying AI into medical systems including but not limited to e-healthcare applications, servers, mobile APPs, telemedicine, national and international interoperable electronic healthcare system [1]. With the arrival era of 5G technologies, there exists great opportunities of developing high throughput distributed

E. A. de la Cal et al. (Eds.): HAIS 2020, LNAI 12344, pp. 511–521, 2020.
https://doi.org/10.1007/978-3-030-61705-9_42

medical systems that cover users from wide and far [2]. At the same time, big data technology has reached almost maturity since a decade ago; we would be witnessing very large-scale medical information system arriving soon in the near future. Such systems usually are equipped with big data that consolidate and manage huge amount of medical data ranging from electronic health records to radiological imaging files e.g. DICOM (Digital Imaging and Communications in Medicine) which is the international standard to transmit, store, retrieve, print, process, and display medical imaging files. A DICOM file, for example, stores a typical computed tomography (CT) image of size 512 pixels wide and 512 pixels high; that is, it contains $512 \times 512 = 262{,}144$ pixels. The file size is in range of Gigabytes. Figure 1 shows a holistic big picture of how big data and information and communication technologies (ICT) could be deployed to provide online services for both medical practitioners and users.

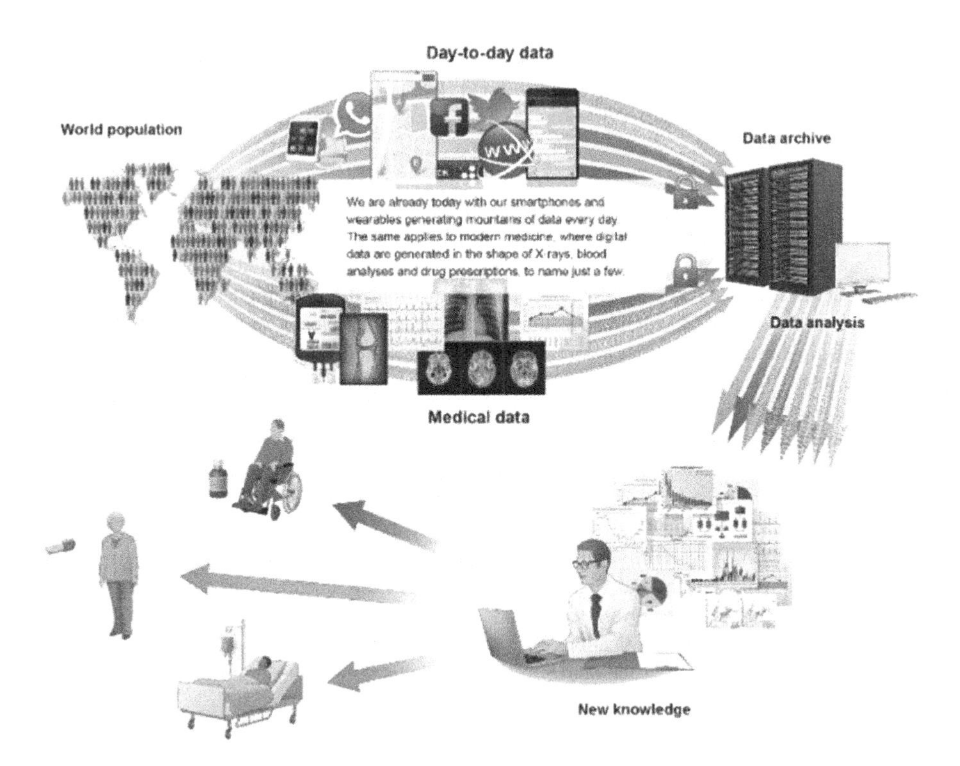

Fig. 1. Big data in medical ecosystem. Image source: courtesy of Forbes.

It can be seen that how the medical data since their generation, are being transformed, managed, extracted, analyzed and disseminated over doctors and patients. It is worth pointing out that the data analysis component is crucial in converting the raw data which come in both structured and unstructured formats into useful insights. To facilitate this important data analytics component, often large-scale data mining techniques are going to be used. A typical data mining process for medical data is shown in Fig. 2.

Our goal is to propose fusing white and black learners. The rest of this paper is organized as follows: Sect. 2 explains the proposal dealing with white and black learning; finally, Sect. 3 states the conclusions.

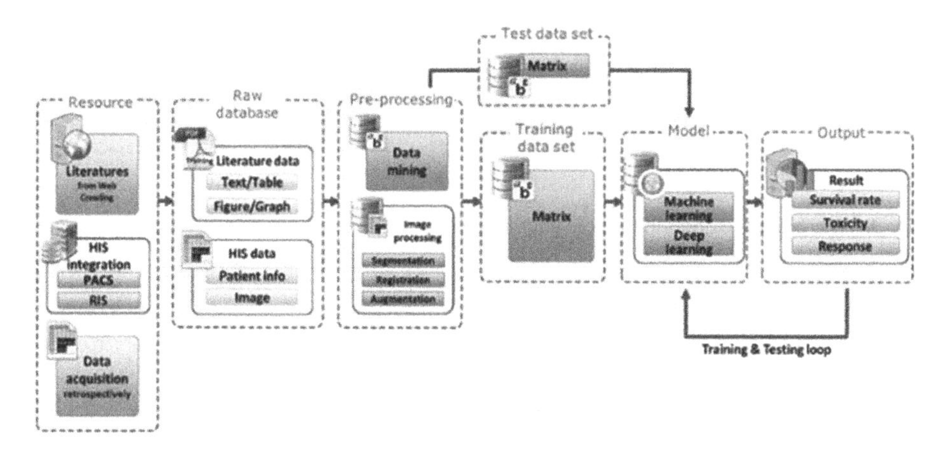

Fig. 2. A typical data mining process for medical data.

Data mining in medical domain involves large file size volumes in storage, processing and machine learning. A radiological information system (RIS) [3] is the core system for the electronic management of imaging departments. The major functions of the RIS can include patient scheduling, resource management, examination performance tracking, reporting, results distribution, and billing procedure. RIS complements HIS (hospital information systems) and PACS (picture archiving and communication system) and is critical to efficient workflow to radiology practices [4], especially for those supporting cancer treatments where RIS plays a key role. As it can be seen in Fig. 2, machine learning models including specialized deep learning and general-use predictive models embrace training and testing datasets for establishing up a mature predictive model. Due to very huge volume of medical data from the demand of high resolution in radiological imaging and massive amount of electronic records from a large population of a city or country, the training data often is very large in size and it is prone to frequent update in everyday use. Abstracting from Fig. 2, the training and testing process for traditionally data mining over medical data would be represented in the way shown in Fig. 3.

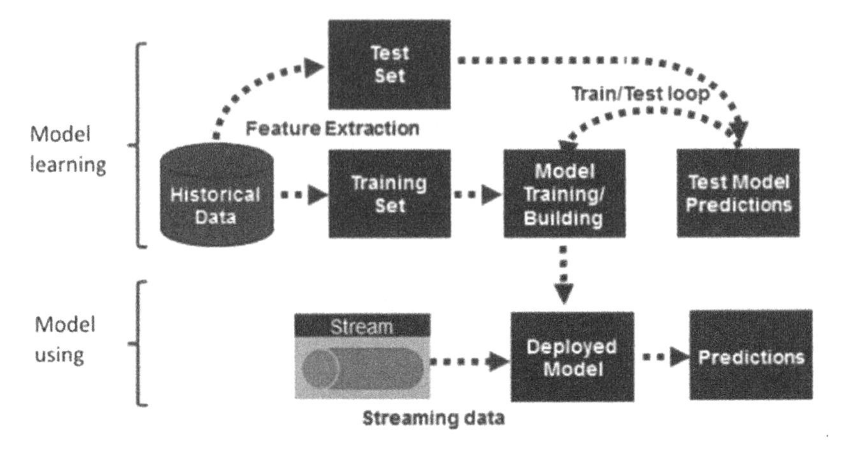

Fig. 3. The traditional training and testing process in data mining medical data. (Color figure online)

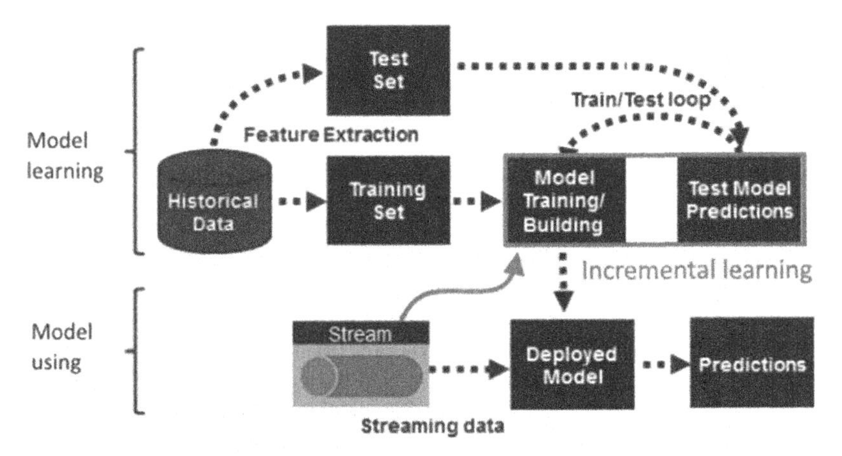

Fig. 4. The incremental training and testing process in data stream mining medical data. (Color figure online)

In the traditional approach of data mining, the full set of historical data is often loaded to the induction process which is known as the model training or building after the data is split into training data and testing data. The training and testing are divided distinctively into two separate phases where the model is first trained with all the data available for establishing up a predictive model. Once the model is evaluated to be satisfactory in performance, the model is then deployed in the subsequent Model-using phase where live data feed comes in, upon which the model makes a prediction. This approach is classical and has been used in many hospital information systems for many years.

Apparently, the model update has become the bottleneck if re-training the model requires loading in a full set of data again when fresh data arrive. There would exist certain latency in refreshing the predictive model with the latest data due to possibly a long wait for reloading and retraining the model. An alternative approach would be using data stream mining for incrementally learning and relearning for the predictive model. So that the model can learn and refresh on the spur of the moment while the new data are streaming in. Figure 4 shows a slight modification in terms of the workflow for allowing incremental learning to take place. The (orange) arrow from Stream to Model Training/Building indicates the data flow to the learning process incrementally, while the model updates itself upon the arrival of new data without the need of reloading the full dataset again.

Zooming out to the application level which is supported by the incremental data stream mining workflow, it is observed that three main performance criteria are expected from the infrastructure. A typical infrastructure is depicted in Fig. 5. The three main performance criteria are (1) accuracy and reliability, (2) real-time requirements, and (3) interpretability. The three criteria and why they are needed would be elaborated correspondingly to the services that the infrastructure provides.

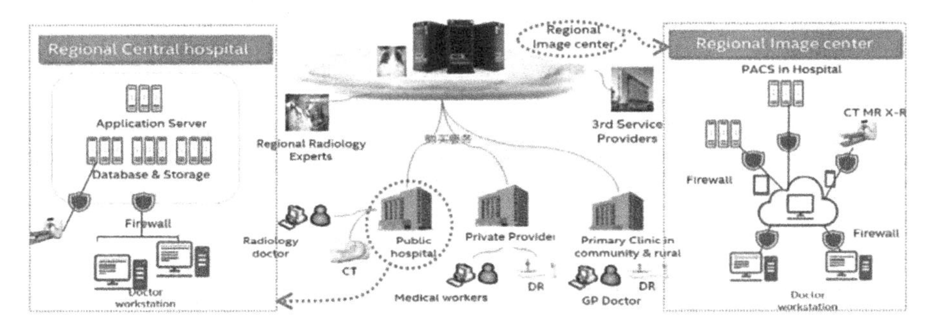

Fig. 5. The infrastructure of medical AI diagnostic big data system.

The infrastructure is an epitome of large-scale medical AI diagnostic big data system. All the imaging and medical record data are meant to be stored and managed by a central cloud which typically should be owned and supported by the national government. Heterogeneous data are continuously uploaded from regional image center that has a variety of PACS, with imaging data from CT scans, X-ray, magnetic resonance imaging (MRI), etc., which are generated from patients on a daily basis. All such data are centralized at a Cloud, which in turn offers query services to public/private hospital/clinics, for medical diagnosis and inquiries.

This type of large-scale medical information evolves from Cloud-based PACS, which was designed to replace the need to store and manage hard-copy films and reports in space-consuming shelving and rooms. Instead, medical images and non-image data can be securely stored digitally on premises or in the cloud. Cloud-based PACS store and back up an organization's medical imaging data to a secure off-site server. A cloud PACS enables medical staff to view medical imaging data from any approved devices, such as a smartphone, as an online service. The characteristics of the services that are offered by the large-scale Cloud-based PACS are summarized as follow.

- From the perspective of government:
  - Provincial cloud platform serves all clinics, centralized data aggregation.
  - Easy, secure and quick scale out business development and management.
  - Reduce the cost on deployment and maintenance via centralized management.
  - Strengthen government supervision and coordination functions.
- From the perspective of clinics:
  - Open-stack and cloud management by API, clinicians easy to access and customize.
  - Efficient data exchange through cloud, easy to get support from hospitals.
  - No need data center on each clinic, reduce IT operational costs.
- From the perspective of citizens:
  - Explore personal medical records even through different clinics.
  - Diagnosis in primary clinics but gain support by other hospital(s) through cloud.
  - Better medical decisions and advices could be offered via data analytics.

As it could be seen from the above list, most of the services hinge on the quality of the data analytics and reasonably fast service turnaround time. These requirements are typically the three criteria above-mentioned: accuracy and reliability from the data analytics, real-time accessibility and interpretable data or disease analysis, they are needed for supporting useful remote medical services in addition to the basic system reliability requirement at the data networking and technical system levels.

The need for data analytics in such large-scale and distributed medical data environment is the motivation for this research work. It is evident that by Google Trend, these three fields machine learning, medical diagnostics, and big data are converging recently, as shown in Fig. 6. We focus on devising a machine learning methodology that embraces incremental learning, accurate and fast model training, and results of data analytics that can be interpreted easily by medical practitioners. The first two criteria can be met by providing an incremental learning solution. The workflow has been already presented in Fig. 4. This is where the AI part usually comes in, by provisioning some intelligent advices and/or decision supports in the form of machine-generated predictions and reasoning results. As mentioned earlier, there are reported news about recent sentiments from doctors towards AI enabled medical diagnosis and prediction explicitly stressing that, doctors prefer to see more supporting evidences and more comprehensive information regarding how a prediction is derived, instead of just being told by a machine like a black box about a computed outcome. Figure 7 shows a combination of hardware and software which form the building blocks of the large-scale medical system. At the software side, on top of a predictive model which outputs generated prediction, doctors opt for a number of visualization tools and reports for them to inspect and analyze. This is the motivation for proposing a hybrid black and white box machine learning model, which has the benefits of both – highly accurate prediction and interpretable models for explaining how the predicted results came by.

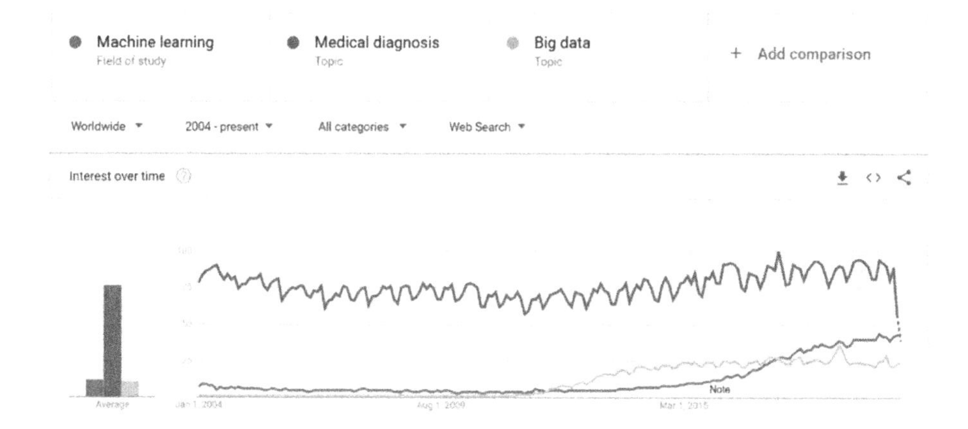

Fig. 6. Trending and convergence of the three major fields: machine learning, medical diagnostics, and big data.

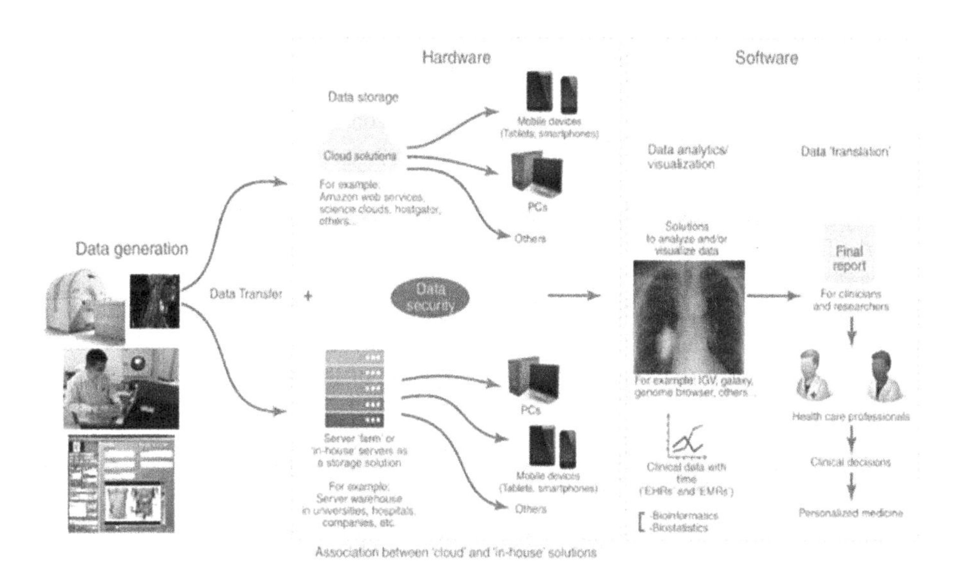

Fig. 7. A combination of hardware and software building blocks.

It can be safely concluded that a highly accurate predictive model is only a part of the AI medicine strategy. Many recent machine learning research endeavors and commercialization developments are geared towards using advanced machine learning technologies, such as deep learning. However, there are more than just about predicting a medical verdict by the machines; as shown in Fig. 6 software tools that empower doctors to analyze and interpret the data and results could be equally if not more important for clinical decision supports. In summary, the current technologies such as big data and ICT are mature. They could be put together to construct an AI infrastructure that implements a cloud-based PACS that is equipped with WL model, that have the capabilities of doing fast, accurate and interpretable prediction using big data.

2 Proposed Hybridized White Learning Methodology

In this research project, a relatively easy and feasible approach to implement white learning model is proposed and described here. There are black and white learners in the system; one is Naïve-Bayes Updateable (NBU) [5] the other is Deep Learning (DL). The two learners are connected by a filter class called "Misclassified Recall" [6] which essentially cleans up the data and using NBU which is relatively fast and passing the cleaned data to DL for refined accuracy. The White Learning (WL) model mainly works at the data level, taking a matrix of dataset, while loading the data by a sliding window (of size 1000 instances by default) at a time, the optimal features are selected, and the problematic data instances are removed progressively. In our proposed WL model, there are optimization schemes for further enhancing the prediction performance made available. Experimentation of the optimization is carried out; the preliminary results are obtained [7], and they show improvements over the naïve methods. The block diagram for our proposed WL model is shown in Fig. 8. Together with the block diagrams for individual white-learner model and individual black-learner model respectively, we can compare the outputs resulted from the three models. The individual white learner model outputs both prediction results with performance measured, and a causal graph as Bayesian network. It is noted that the Bayesian network generated by individual white-learner has full number of nodes and possible relations in the network. The individual black learner model, however, only outputs a prediction result with performance measured. Nevertheless, the WL model, outputs the sum of the outputs from the individual white-learner and black-learner; the prediction accuracy of the DL in the WL model should be higher, and the Bayesian network would be more concise in terms of network structure and the quality of the causality paths.

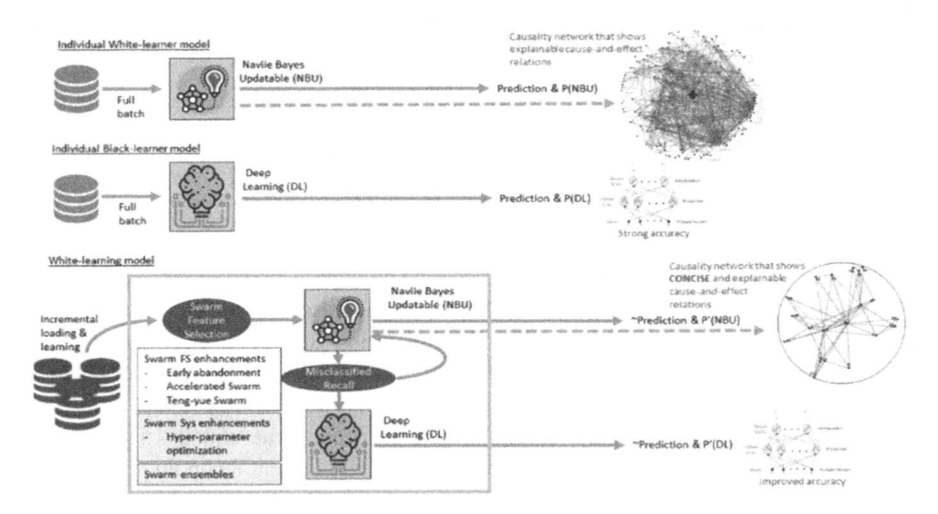

Fig. 8. Proposed hybridized white learning model.

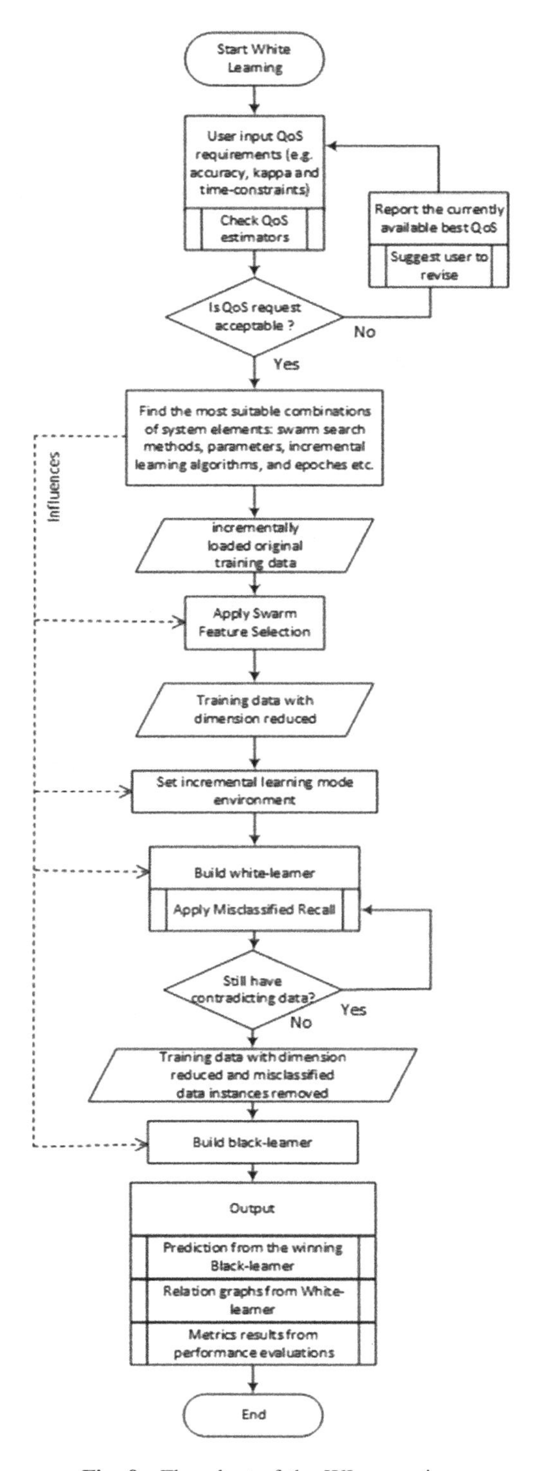

Fig. 9. Flowchart of the WL operation.

The WL model from Fig. 8 shows that it has two main learners NBU and DL; and they are enhanced by two main data processing components: swarm feature selection and misclassified recall. For the swarm feature selection, there are novel modifications such as early abandonment, accelerated swarm and new swarm algorithms for speeding up the swarm feature selection. The research of the new modifications is currently in progress. The swarm optimization aims also at enhancing the system configure by doing swarm hyper-parameter optimization. As a result, the output of the WL has two parts: one is to be used for pure prediction by DL, and the other one is a descriptive model which can reveal explainable cause-and-effect relations as a causality network. The logics of WL operation is depicted as a flow-chart, in Fig. 9. It explains how exactly the operation of WL works from loading in the data to generating the useful DL and causality network as end-result.

3 Conclusion

Cloud-based PACS is gaining popularity nowadays with the advancement of big data and 5G technologies. It demands a new type of machine learning, suitable for uses in medical diagnosis and consultation with performance criteria in accuracy, real-time constraint and interpretability. Deep learning received much attention from researchers of machine learning community because of its strong predictive power and scalability. However, deep learning as a data modeling tool is hard to be understood of how its predicted result came about from its inner working. It is generally known as a black box and is not interpretable. Often in medical applications, physicians need to understand why a model predicts a result. On the other hand, Bayesian network is a probabilistic graph with nodes representing the variables and the arcs present the conditional dependences between the variables. Prior knowledge and reasoning of how a predicted outcome come about via examining the probability distribution associate with each node and the dependencies among them can be made possible. In this paper, a white learning framework is proposed. A preliminary case of breast cancer classification is conducted in an experiment [7]. From the results, it is observed that white learning, which combines black-box and white-box machine learning has an edge in performance over individually Bayesian network alone or deep learning alone. The white learning framework has the benefits of interpretability and high predictive power, making it suitable for critical decision-making task where a reliable prediction is as important as knowing how the outcome is predicted. Furthermore, the performance of WL with respect to accuracy, real-time constraint and interpretability has been improved by swarm feature selection as an extension to WL. However, more intensive experiments are needed for validating this model, especially from the aspects of interpretability and optimization. Optimization is needed to enhance the speed and efficiency of WL that works in PACS environment where speed, accuracy and interpretability all matter.

Acknowledgment. The authors are grateful to the supports of the research grants for this work by 2018 Guangzhou Science and Technology Innovation and Development of Special Funds, 1) Grant no. EF003/FST-FSJ/2019/GSTIC, and 2) EF004/FST-FSJ/2019/GSTIC. This work has also been partially supported by TIN2017-88209-C2-R (Spanish Inter-Ministerial Commission of Science and Technology (MICYT)) and FEDER funds.

References

1. Archenaa, J., Anita, E.M.: A survey of big data analytics in healthcare and government. Proc. Comput. Sci. **50**, 408–413 (2015)
2. Benhlima, L.: Big data management for healthcare systems: architecture, requirements, and implementation. Adv. Bioinform. (2018)
3. Wang, Z., Yu, G., Kang, Y., Zhao, Y., Qu, Q.: Breast tumor detection in digital mammography based on extreme learning machine. Neurocomputing **128**, 175–184 (2014)
4. Kooi, T., van Ginneken, B., Karssemeijer, N., den Heeten, A.: Discriminating solitary cysts from soft tissue lesions in mammography using a pretrained deep convolutional neural network. Med. Phys. **44**(3), 1017–1027 (2017)
5. http://weka.sourceforge.net/doc.dev/weka/classifiers/bayes/NaiveBayesUpdateable.html. Accessed 11 Feb 2020
6. Fong, S., Li, J., Song, W., Tian, Y., Wong, R.K., Dey, N.: Predicting unusual energy consumption events from smart home sensor network by data stream mining with misclassified recall. J. Ambient Intell. Hum. Comput. **9**(4), 1197–1221 (2018). https://doi.org/10.1007/s12652-018-0685-7
7. Li, T., Fong, S., Liu, L.S., Yang, X.S., He, X., Fiaidhi, J., Mohammed, S.: White learning: a white-box data fusion machine learning framework for extreme and fast automated cancer diagnosis. IT Prof. **21**(5), 71–77 (2019)

A New Forecasting Algorithm Based on Neighbors for Streaming Electricity Time Series

P. Jiménez-Herrera, L. Melgar-García, G. Asencio-Cortés, and A. Troncoso(✉)

Division of Computer Science, Universidad Pablo de Olavide, 41013 Seville, Spain
pjimher@alu.upo.es, {lmelgar,guaasecor,ali}@upo.es

Abstract. This work presents a new forecasting algorithm for streaming electricity time series. This algorithm is based on a combination of the K-means clustering algorithm along with both the Naive Bayes classifier and the K nearest neighbors algorithm for regression. In its offline phase it firstly divide data into clusters. Then, the nearest neighbors algorithm is applied for each cluster producing a list of trained regression models, one per each cluster. Finally, a Naive Bayes classifier is trained for predicting the cluster label of an instance using as training the cluster assignments previously generated by K-means. The algorithm is able to be updated incrementally for online learning from data streams. The proposed algorithm has been tested using electricity consumption with a granularity of 10 min for 4-h-ahead predicting. Our algorithm widely overcame other four well-known effective online learners used as benchmark algorithms, achieving the smallest error.

Keywords: Forecasting · Real time · Streaming data · Electricity time series · Nearest neighbors.

1 Introduction

The current technological context has two main aspects of research and development. On the one hand, an industrial aspect, where the boom in advanced connection of devices or Internet of Things (IoT) is changing the means of production and service management systems, leading our society to a new industrial revolution known as Industry 4.0. And on the other hand, the data, as a consequence of the enormous amount of data that is generated daily in our society, coming from many different origins, including IoT between them, and leading us to a new technological revolution based on the analysis of large scale data known as Big Data.

Of the three V's that initially defined Big Data (speed, variety and volume), volume is perhaps the characteristic in which researchers have made the greatest effort. Almost all the technology developed in recent years allows to obtain approximate solutions to problems derived from the dimensionality of the data.

E. A. de la Cal et al. (Eds.): HAIS 2020, LNAI 12344, pp. 522–533, 2020.
https://doi.org/10.1007/978-3-030-61705-9_43

However, speed, despite being a feature present in many problems of data analysis, has not had the same impact, or rather, it is beginning to have it at present. Although the analysis of streaming data has been studied in the last decade, in very few cases forecasting techniques have been developed, which allow to have an updated model that is capable of giving a response in real time to obtain forecasts.

In this work, a new forecasting algorithm based on the nearest similar pattern for streaming electricity time series, named StreamNSP, is proposed. The algorithm firstly determines different patterns in historical data. Once the data stream is received, the algorithm predicts the pattern to which the data stream just arrived belongs. Then, the prediction is obtained using the nearest neighbor among the data with the same pattern to data stream. The performance of the proposed method has been tested on a real-world related to energy consumption. Finally, the results have been compared to that of the well-known prediction algorithms for streaming data.

The rest of the paper is structured as follows. Section 2 reviews of the existing literature related to the forecasting algorithms for streaming energy data. In Sect. 3 the proposed methodology to forecast streaming time series is introduced. Section 4 presents the experimental results corresponding to the prediction of the energy consumption. Finally, Sect. 5 closes the paper giving some final conclusions.

2 Related Work

Although time series forecasting have been extensively studied in the literature, there are very few works on time series forecasting for streaming big data environments. In general, the methods for predicting time series can be classified into classical methods based on Box and Jenkins [1], such as ARIMA and GARCH; and machine learning methods, such as support vector machines, nearest neighbors techniques and artificial neural networks. For a taxonomy of these techniques applied to energy time series forecasting, the reader is referred to [2].

In the last few years, some other techniques have been developed to forecast time series in the context of big data. In [3] the energy consumption in several buildings of a public university is predicted by applying a distributed k-means algorithm in Spark. The study in [4] shows that suitable accuracy predictions can be achieved by applying a deep learning algorithm to electricity consumption data in Spain. On the other hand, in [5] different scalable methods such as decision tree, gradient boosted trees and random forest, are used to also predict the electricity consumption in Spain.

One of the main challenges today is real-time decision making based on the analysis of continuous data streams usually coming from sensors in an IoT context within the new edge computing paradigm or smart grids. A new representation of energy data streams was proposed in [6] for purpose of detecting outlier consumers by applying clustering techniques in smart grids. In [7] the authors presented an energy prediction system based on an edge computing architecture.

In particular, an online deep neural network model adapted to the characteristics of IoT data was implemented for energy prediction. In [8] a new methodology for real-time forecasting of energy demand using weather predicted data was proposed. In [9] neural networks with different backpropagation algorithms was also proposed for real-time energy consumption forecasting using climate data. A combination of an online clustering algorithm with a neural-network based predictive model was presented for electricity load forecast in [10].

After a thorough review, it can be concluded that very few papers have been published to predict online streaming electricity time series and there is still a lot of research to be done.

3 Methodology

3.1 Overview

The StreamNSP algorithm has been developed for streaming of time series data, and it is based on a combination of the K-means clustering algorithm [11] along with both the Naive Bayes (NB) classifier [12] and the K nearest neighbors (KNN) algorithm [13] for regression.

The general idea behind the proposed forecasting algorithm is to take a training set in a offline phase and firstly divide it in clusters using the K-means algorithm. Then, the KNN algorithm is applied for each cluster producing a list of trained prediction models, one per each cluster. Finally, the NB classifier is trained for predicting the cluster label of an instance using as training the cluster assignments previously generated by K-means.

Once the model of StreamNSP is generated in the offline phase, it is tested and then updated online using data streams. The methodology carried out to train, test and compare StreamNSP with a set of benchmark algorithms is graphically described in the Fig. 1.

In first place, a previous process of data preparation is performed from the historical time series data. This process is described in Sect. 3.2. After the preparation of data, a model is produced for each forecasting horizon, using both the StreamNSP algorithm and a set of benchmark algorithms. Each model is evaluated using a prequential or interleaved test-then-train evaluation. Finally, a comparison of error metrics was performed. The same evaluation procedure is

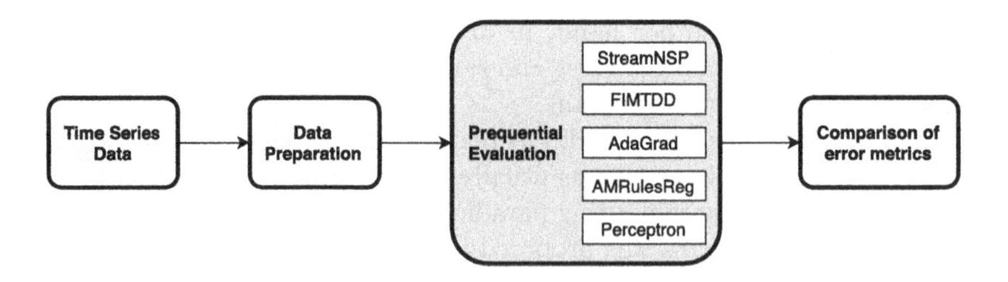

Fig. 1. Overview of the processes within the proposed methodology.

carried out for both StreamNSP and benchmark algorithms. The offline phase of StreamNSP is described in Sect. 3.3 and its online phase in Sect. 3.4. The benchmark algorithms are described in Sect. 4.3.

The algorithm StreamNSP was implemented in the Java programming language (Oracle Java 1.8.0_152-b16 SE for 64 bits) and adapted to be compatible for the MOA framework [14]. All experiments for testing and benchmarking StreamNSP were automated using the API of the MOA framework (version 19.04).

3.2 Data Preparation

The proposed forecasting algorithm is based on attributes (features) and a single numeric class to predict. However, time series data in a streaming is a sequence of numeric values. For such reason, the following data preparation process was made before to train and test the model. The Fig. 2 describes visually the procedure carried out to transform the time series data into a set of training and test for each prediction horizon. Specifically, a set of w lagged variables, $a_1, \ldots, a_w$, were extracted from a time series $x_1, \ldots, x_n$. These values reflect lagged windows of size w from the time series, as it can be seen in Fig. 2. These variables will act as input attributes for the model. Along with these attributes, a last column y representing the class was added to the so called propositional tables for each forecasting horizon from 1 to h, where h is the number of future values to predict. These column is a future value, in the time series, with respect to the past values window.

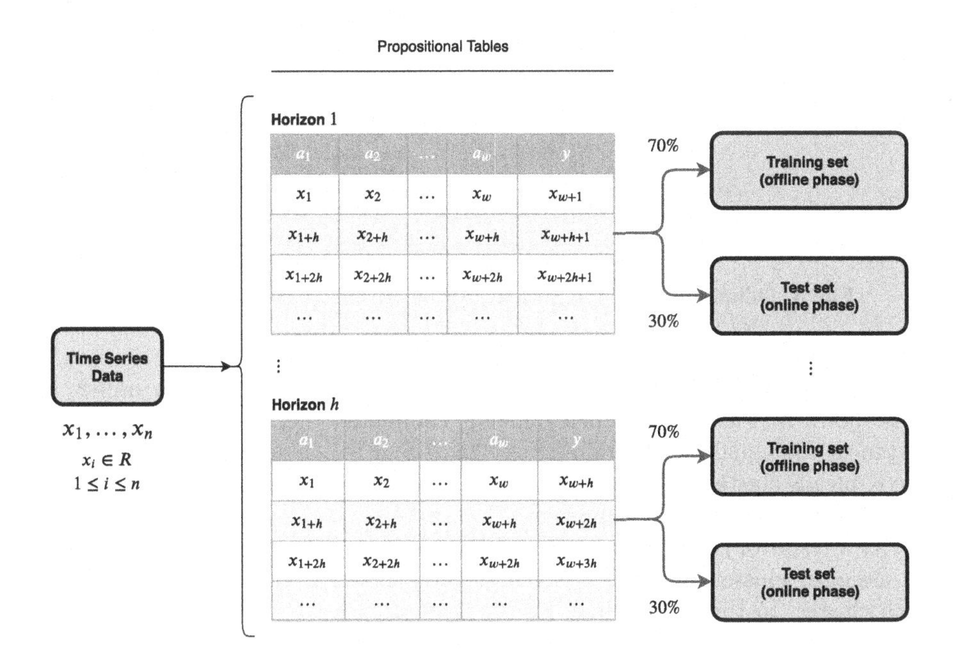

Fig. 2. Data preparation process.

Finally, for each horizon, both training and test subsets were taken from propositional tables, maintaining the original temporal order. The training set will be used to train the model in its offline phase, while the test set will be used to test and update the model in its online phase.

3.3 Offline Phase

The procedure carried out by the proposed StreamNSP algorithm in its offline phase is described in Fig. 3. As it can be seen in such figure, given a training set, each instance is extracted one by one according to its temporal order. Such instance is composed by its attributes $a_1, \ldots, a_w$ and its numeric class y.

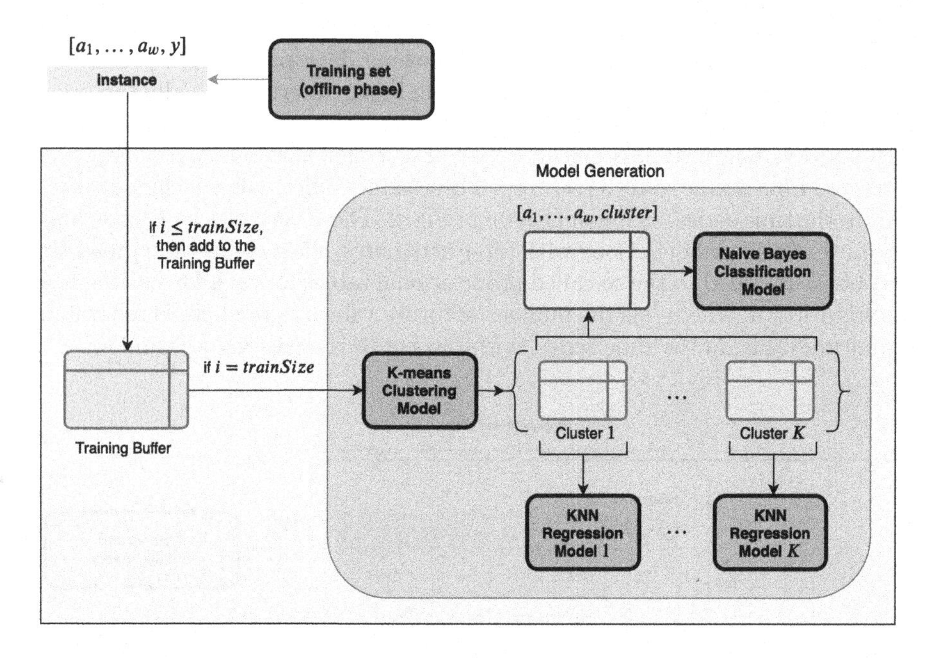

Fig. 3. Offline phase of the StreamNSP algorithm. (Color figure online)

Each instance from training set is stored in an internal training buffer, as it is shown in Fig. 3. Once such buffer is completed (i.e. when the number of instances i is equal to the training size $trainSize$) then such buffer is given to the K-means clustering algorithm. In this work, $K = 3$ clusters was set to model low, medium and high consumption.

As a result of the clustering, each instance is stored separately according to its assigned cluster. Then, a KNN regression model is trained and stored for each cluster. In this work, three KNN regression models were stored ($K = 3$). The algorithm KNN used was configured for one nearest neighbor search.

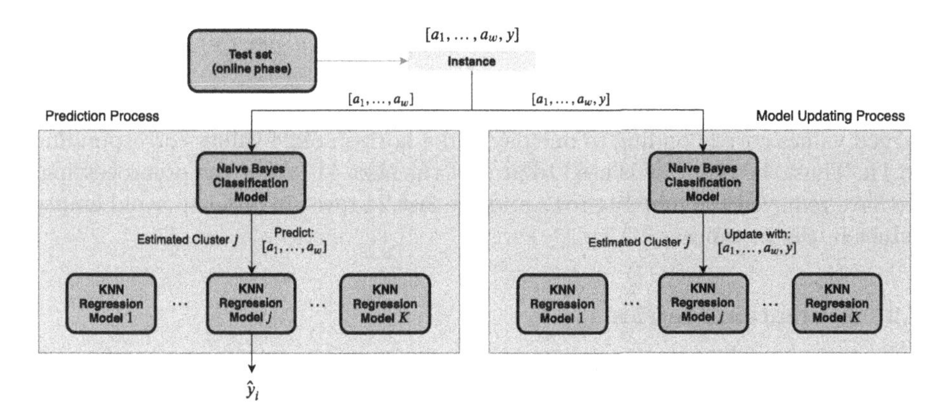

Fig. 4. Online phase of the StreamNSP algorithm.

A table containing the attributes $a_1, \ldots, a_w$ of all training instances along with their cluster assignments (the *cluster* label) is also made and stored (table coloured in orange in Fig. 3). Finally, a Naive Bayes model is trained using such table, with the aim to predict the cluster label of further test instances.

3.4 Online Phase

The procedure carried out by the proposed StreamNSP algorithm in its online phase is described in Fig. 4. As it can be seen, each instance is extracted one by one in online streaming from a test set. Such instance is composed of its attributes $a_1, \ldots, a_w$ and its numeric class y. The online phase is divided in two steps, due to the prequential evaluation performed. First, the step of predicting and, after, the step of updating the model.

The prediction step consists in receiving online the attributes $a_1, \ldots, a_w$ of the instance and use the Naive Bayes classification model previously trained. Such model returns the estimated cluster to which the test instance could belong (let be the cluster j). Then, the proper KNN regression model (the model j) is used to predict the numeric class $\hat{y}_i$ of the instance.

The model updating step consists in receiving both the attributes $a_1, \ldots, a_w$ and the actual class y of the instance. Using the Naive Bayes classification model, an estimated cluster is produced (the same cluster as the prediction step, because the instance attributes are the same). Finally, the regression model j is updated using both the attributes and class of the instance.

4 Experimentation and Results

4.1 Dataset

The time series considered in this study is related to the electricity consumption in Spain from 1 January 2007 at 00:00 to 21 June 2016 at 23:50. It is a time series of 9 years and 6 months with a high sampling frequency (10 min), resulting in 497,832 measures in total.

The time series was processed as described in Sect. 3.2 for a window of 144 lagged values corresponding to one day and a horizon of 24 values corresponding to 4 h. Thus, the past day is used to predict the next 4 h. After the preprocessing, we have removed the first 144 rows and the last 24 rows, in order to avoid empty values in the instances.

4.2 Evaluation Metrics

The MAE, RSME and MAPE errors have been used to evaluate the results of the proposed StreamNSP algorithm and the benchmark algorithms.

The MAE is the mean absolute error, which is the average of the absolute differences between actual and predictions. The MAE is defined in Eq. (1), where y_i are actual values, $\hat{y}_i$ predicted values and n is the number of predicted samples.

$$MAE = \frac{1}{n}\sum_{i=1}^{n}|y_i - \hat{y}_i| \tag{1}$$

The RMSE is the root mean square error, which represents the square root of the second sample moment of the differences between predicted values and observed values or the quadratic mean of these differences. The RMSE metric is defined in Eq. (2).

$$RMSE = \sqrt{\frac{1}{n}\sum_{i=1}^{n}(y_i - \hat{y}_i)^2} \tag{2}$$

Finally, the third evaluation metric is the MAPE, which is calculated as the average absolute percent error, that is, the average of actual values minus predicted values divided by actual values as can be seen in Eq. (3).

$$MAPE = \frac{100}{n}\sum_{i=1}^{n}\left|\frac{y_i - \hat{y}_i}{y_i}\right| \tag{3}$$

4.3 Benchmark Algorithms

In order to compare the forecasting results of the algorithm StreamNSP with other suitable approaches in the literature, four regression algorithms for online learning from data streaming were selected.

The algorithm FIMTDD [15] learns a regression tree and it is able to address time-changing data streams. The algorithm has mechanisms for drift detection and model adaptation, which enable it to maintain accurate and updated regression models at any time. The algorithm observes each example only once at the speed of arrival, and maintains at any-time a ready-to-use tree model. The tree leaves contain linear models induced online. The number of instances a leaf should observe between split attempts was set to 200. The threshold below which a split will be forced to break ties was set to 0.05.

The algorithm AdaGrad [16] is an online optimizer for learning linear regression from data streams that incorporates knowledge of the geometry of the data observed in earlier iterations to perform more informative gradient-based learning. The adaptation feature of this algorithm derives into strong regret guarantees, which for some natural data distributions achieve high performance. No regularization was used for the linear regression model and the learning rate was set to 0.01.

The algorithm AMRulesReg [17] is an adaptive model that is able to generate decision rules for regression from data streams. In this model, the antecedent of a rule is a conjunction of conditions on the attribute values, and the consequent is a linear combination of attribute values. Each rule uses a Page-Hinkley test [18] to detect changes in the process generating data and react to changes by pruning the rule set.

Finally, the algorithm Perceptron [19] is based on the algorithm Hoeffding Trees [20], but instead of using Naive Bayes models at the leaf nodes it uses perceptron regressors. The perceptron regressors use the sigmoid activation function instead of the threshold activation function and optimize the squared error.

4.4 Results

The forecasting results obtained for StreamNSP and the benchmark algorithms using the electricity time series data stream are presented and discussed in this section.

Table 1 shows the MAE, RMSE and MAPE for StreamNSP, AdaGrad, FIMTDD, Perceptron and AMRulesReg. These errors have been calculated and averaged for all predicted horizons. As it can be seen that our StreamNSP algorithm achieved better results in MAE, RMSE and MAPE than the other four benchmark learners. The MAE error of StreamNSP has been compared with the best MAE result of the other four benchmark learners, in this case AMRulesReg, and it provides an error improvement of 66.958 MW. The difference between the RMSE for AMRulesReg and StreamNSP algorithms is also high, in particular 144,315 higher for AMRulesReg. In addition, AMRulesReg obtained a MAPE of 0.313% worse than StreamNSP. Note that AdaGrad algorithm seems to be not suitable for predicting energy consumption data, because of its high errors for all the computed metrics.

Table 2 shows the errors for each prediction horizon. As it can be seen, the growth of both MAE, RMSE and MAPE errors for the proposed StreamNSP algorithm is lower and more stable across the predicted horizons than that of the other four benchmarks. The increase of the MAPE across the 24 predicted horizons is 0.816%. This value is computed by the difference between the maximum MAPE (2.336 for the horizon 24) and the minimum (1.52 for the horizon 1). The errors were always increasing across the horizons.

Table 1. Comparison of the errors ordered by MAPE.

Algorithm	MAE	RMSE	MAPE (%)
AdaGrad	3242.434	3872.137	12.052
FIMTDD	1332.544	1751.836	4.911
Perceptron	612.676	986.839	2.297
AMRulesReg	590.401	944.853	2.211
StreamNSP	523.443	800.538	1.898

Table 2. Errors of the StreamNSP algorithm for each predicted horizon.

Horizon	MAE	RMSE	MAPE (%)	Horizon	MAE	RMSE	MAPE (%)
1	421.573	568.969	1.520	13	527.449	753.941	1.907
2	428.810	578.613	1.554	14	534.718	776.120	1.942
3	435.304	590.439	1.571	15	544.480	798.651	1.976
4	443.158	604.724	1.595	16	552.460	823.934	2.008
5	454.045	621.032	1.637	17	560.636	854.281	2.050
6	466.106	635.736	1.674	18	580.300	915.053	2.116
7	470.065	640.124	1.687	19	593.585	959.358	2.166
8	473.147	644.658	1.698	20	604.592	996.627	2.214
9	477.315	650.281	1.713	21	614.681	1031.443	2.245
10	483.942	660.731	1.742	22	622.031	1051.802	2.269
11	492.637	682.344	1.783	23	627.828	1063.401	2.292
12	510.162	722.867	1.845	24	643.615	1129.542	2.336

Figure 5 shows the MAPE for each predicted horizon for both the StreamNSP and the benchmark methods. It can be observed that the StreamNSP exhibits the highest stability of MAPE across the predicted horizons with respect to the other benchmark learners. For the first 10 horizons, AMRulesReg and Perceptron methods provided a lower MAPE than StreamNSP. However, StreamNSP has the lowest average error for all horizons. StreamNSP has an error difference among horizons of 0.816%, while AMRulesReg and Perceptron have 3.217% and 3.467%, respectively. For horizons higher than 10, StreamNSP overcame the rest of algorithms, being the best method for higher horizons.

Figure 6 shows the best forecasted day according to the minimum MAPE obtained for the StreamNSP. This figure includes the actual and predicted values for each hour of the day (with 10 min of interval). This day corresponds to October 29, 2015. The x-axis is the time and the y-axis is the target variable (energy consumption in MW). The prediction fits very well at all times and it does not shows large errors for any time.

Figure 7 shows the forecasted day with the biggest MAPE for the StreamNSP. It can be seen high differences between the actual and predicted values. It seems

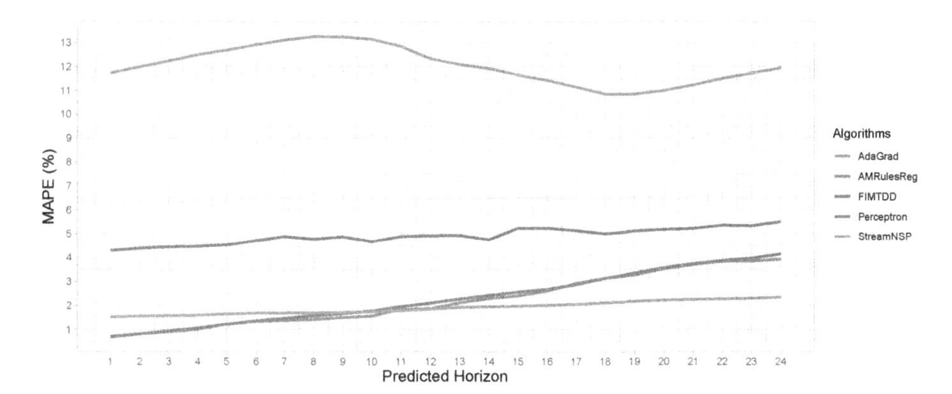

Fig. 5. Comparison of the MAPE for all algorithms along the predicted horizon.

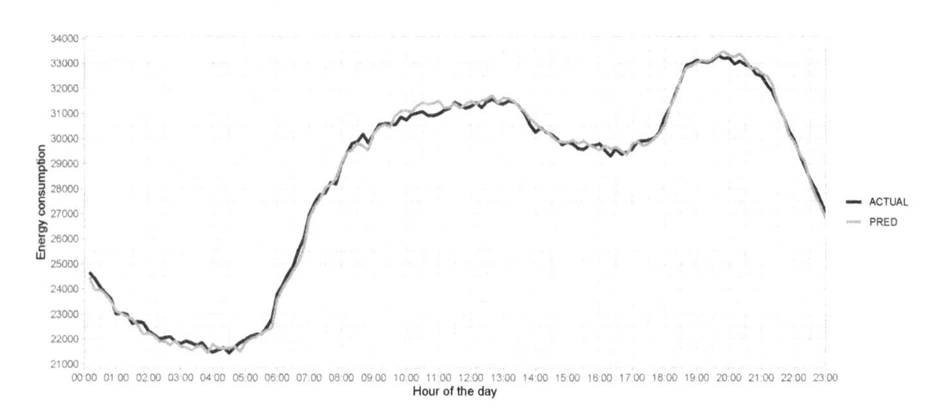

Fig. 6. Best forecasted day for the StreamNSP (day with the smallest MAPE).

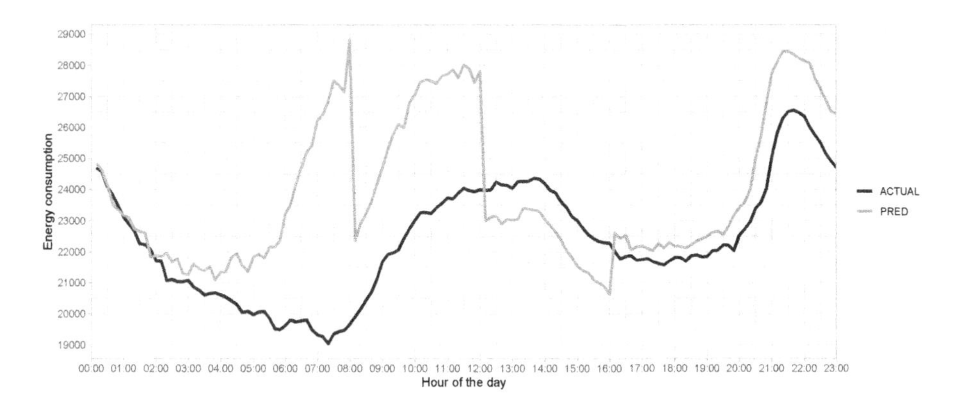

Fig. 7. Worst forecasted day for the StreamNSP (day with the maximum MAPE).

that the nearest neighbour selected to make these predictions may not represent correctly the energy consumption for such day. This day corresponds to May 1, 2014, which is a holiday in Spain (Labor day).

5 Conclusions

In this work the new StreamNSP forecasting algorithm has been proposed for online learning on streaming data. StreamNSP has an offline phase to obtain the prediction model using the historical data. This phase consists of splitting the training data into clusters using the K-means algorithm. Then, a nearest neighbors algorithm is applied for each cluster producing a list of trained regression models, one per each cluster. In addition to that, a Naive Bayes classifier is trained for predicting the cluster label of an instance using as training the cluster assignments previously generated by K-means. The algorithm can be updated incrementally for online learning from data streams including new instances into the model corresponding to its estimated cluster. StreamNSP has been tested using the electricity consumption with a granularity of 10 min for predicting a prediction horizon of four hours. The algorithm widely overcame other four online learners, such as AdaGrad, FIMTDD, Perceptron and AMRulesReg, achieving an average MAPE of 1.89% instead of 2.21%, 2.29%, 4.91% and 12.05% obtained by the other algorithms. Moreover, the StreamNSP has obtained the most accurate predictions for large forecasting horizons (11 or more values ahead).

As future work, other base algorithms will be tested for the clustering, classification and regression inner components of the StreamNSP. Furthermore, a sensitivity study of the number of clusters used in StreamNSP will be performed.

Acknowledgements. The authors would like to thank the Spanish Ministry of Science, Innovation and Universities for the support under the project TIN2017-88209-C2-1-R.

References

1. Box, G., Jenkins, G.: Time Series Analysis: Forecasting and Control. John Wiley, Hoboken (2008)
2. Martínez-Álvarez, F., Troncoso, A., Asencio-Cortés, G., Riquelme, J.C.: A survey on data mining techniques applied to electricity-related time series forecasting. Energies **8**(11), 13162–13193 (2015)
3. Pérez-Chacón, R., Luna-Romera, J.M., Troncoso, A., Martínez-Álvarez, F., Riquelme, J.C.: Big data analytics for discovering electricity consumption patterns in smart cities. Energies **11**, 683 (2018)
4. Torres, J.F., Galicia, A., Troncoso, A., Martínez-Álvarez, F.: A scalable approach based on deep learning for big data time series forecasting. Integr. Comput.-Aided Eng. **25**(4), 335–348 (2018)
5. Galicia, A., Torres, J.F., Martínez-Álvarez, F., Troncoso, A.: A novel spark-based multi-step forecasting algorithm for big data time series. Inf. Sci. **467**, 800–818 (2018)

6. Laurinec, P., Lucká, M.: Interpretable multiple data streams clustering with clipped streams representation for the improvement of electricity consumption forecasting. Data Mining Knowl. Disc. **33**(2), 413–445 (2018). https://doi.org/10.1007/s10618-018-0598-2
7. Luo, H., Cai, H., Yu, H., Sun, Y., Bi, Z., Jiang, L.: A short-term energy prediction system based on edge computing for smart city. Fut. Gener. Comput. Syst. **101**, 444–457 (2019)
8. Kwak, Y., Seo, D., Jang, C., Huh, J.-H.: Feasibility study on a novel methodology for short-term real-time energy demand prediction using weather forecasting data. Energy Build. **57**, 250–260 (2013)
9. Ahmad, T., Chen, H.: A review on machine learning forecasting growth trends and their real-time applications in different energy systems. Sustain. Cities Soc. **54**, 102010 (2020)
10. Gama, J., Rodrigues, P.P.: Stream-based electricity load forecast. In: Proceedings of the Knowledge Discovery in Databases, pp. 446–453 (2007)
11. MacQueen, J.: Some methods for classification and analysis of multivariate observations. In: Proceedings of the 5th Berkeley Symposium on Mathematical Statistics and Probability, vol. 1, pp. 281–297 (1967)
12. John, G.H., Langley, P.: Estimating continuous distributions in bayesian classifiers. In: Proceedings of the 11th Conference on Uncertainty in Artificial Intelligence, pp. 338–345 (1995)
13. Aha, D., Kibler, D.: Instance-based learning algorithms. Mach. Learn. **6**, 37–66 (1991)
14. Bifet, A., Holmes, G., Kirkby, R., Pfahringer, B.: MOA: massive online analysis. J. Mach. Learn. Res. **11**, 1601–1604 (2010)
15. Ikonomovska, E., Gama, J., Džeroski, S.: Learning model trees from evolving data streams. Data Mining Knowl. Disc. **23**(1), 128–168 (2011)
16. Duchi, J., Hazan, E., Singer, Y.: Adaptive subgradient methods for online learning and stochastic optimization. J. Mach. Learn. Res. **12**, 2121–2159 (2011)
17. Almeida, E., Ferreira, C., Gama, J.: Adaptive model rules from data streams. In: Proceedings of the Machine Learning and Knowledge Discovery in Databases, pp. 480–492 (2013)
18. Basseville, M.: Detecting changes in signals and systems-a survey. Automatica **24**(3), 309–326 (1988)
19. Bifet, A., Holmes, G., Pfahringer, B., Frank, E.: Fast perceptron decision tree learning from evolving data streams. In: Proceedings of the Advances in Knowledge Discovery and Data Mining, pp. 299–310 (2010)
20. Hulten, G., Spencer, L., Domingos, P.: Mining time-changing data streams. In: Proceedings of the Knowledge Discovery on Databases, pp. 97–106 (2001)

Effective Bin Picking Approach by Combining Deep Learning and Point Cloud Processing Techniques

Alberto Tellaeche Iglesias(✉), Iker Pastor-López, Borja Sanz Urquijo, and Pablo García-Bringas

D4K Group, University of Deusto, Avda. Universidades 24, 48007 Bilbao, Spain
{alberto.tellaeche, iker.pastor, borja.sanz, pablo.garcia.bringas}@deusto.es

Abstract. Within the concept of "Industry 4.0", one of the fundamental pillars is the concept of intelligent manufacturing. This type of manufacturing demands a high level of adaptability to design changes, greater flexibility in the adjustment of processes and an intensive use of digital information to improve them, being advanced robotics one of the key technologies to achieve this goal.

Classical industrial robotics is evolving towards another production model, which demands the rapid reconfiguration of robotic installations to manufacture different and varied products in smaller batches. In a production environment where flexibility and readjustment to the manufacture of new products must be carried out quickly, one of the fundamental tasks to be accomplished in robotics to reach these objectives efficiently is Bin Picking.

The problem of Bin Picking is one of the basic problems in artificial vision applied to robotics, and although there are numerous research studies related to this problem, it is difficult to seek the adaptability of the solutions provided to a real environment.

The present research work presents a new procedure for the solution of the Bin Picking problem, of quick configuration and execution based on artificial intelligence and point cloud processing.

Keywords: Bin picking · Deep learning · Point cloud processing

1 Introduction

In advanced robotics, one of the enabling technologies of intelligent manufacturing, and therefore, of Industry 4.0, several concepts are currently being worked on that are both different and complementary to each other, such as the direct communication of robots with integrated production systems, the use of collaborative robotics to carry out productive tasks in collaboration with workers, or the rapid reconfiguration of these systems to adapt as directly as possible to design changes or innovations made to the products being manufactured, the latter being a great competitive advantage over more traditional manufacturing systems.

In order to achieve the aforementioned objectives, a wide variety of advanced sensors are being used in addition to robotic systems, among which the artificial vision

E. A. de la Cal et al. (Eds.): HAIS 2020, LNAI 12344, pp. 534–545, 2020.
https://doi.org/10.1007/978-3-030-61705-9_44

systems are particularly noteworthy, specially the cameras or 3D sensors that provide point clouds.

Finally, to process this large amount of information that makes it possible to fulfil the aforementioned requirements of flexibility and adaptability, a variety of artificial intelligence techniques are being used, such as reinforcement learning to adapt to variations on the tasks initially programmed, or deep learning for detecting and supervising production faults that are difficult to categorize otherwise, among other examples.

However, and despite all the advances that are being made in intelligent robotics, one of the fundamental tasks to be carried out to reach these objectives efficiently is Bin Picking, and this specific problem is yet to be solved efficiently for a wide range of different cases. The main objective of this type of problem is that a robot, with the help of cameras and sensors, is able to pick up objects of different types, with random positions in space. Usually these pieces are found in a container or repository, without being ordered, and are necessary in the production process being carried out at that time. So far, numerous research works have been carried out focused on Bin Picking techniques, but without taking into account the ease of configuration and implementation of the proposed solutions in a real environment.

The main objective of the research work presented is the design of a new approach to the Bin Picking problem, so that the designed algorithm is easily reconfigurable for new parts in a changing production environment and can be used in production in the shortest time possible after being adapted to the new demands.

1.1 Related Work

In the last decade great advances have been made in artificial intelligence, more specifically in the field known as Deep Learning, making it possible to address new applications that until then could not be considered.

The use of Deep Learning has led to a new era in industrial robotics [1]. The possibility of Deep Learning to identify abstract characteristics and to recognize complex patterns has made possible advances in problems such as the one presented in this work, and has given rise to competitions such as the Amazon Picking Challenge, with challenges similar to the one presented in [2]. Likewise, [3] presents an interesting study that includes the main deep learning techniques to be applied to classify 3D objects.

The problem of Bin Picking, if simplified, is mainly reduced to two specific actions: identification of the position in space of the object to be picked (6DOF) and the optimal solution to the problem of grip. This work is focused in the first part, the correct calculation of the pose in space of the object, with respect to the sensor that acquires the 2D image and the point cloud.

There are several studies related to pose estimation in uncluttered environments. In [4], they use deep learning to perform a semantic segmentation of the scene and they use Pose Regression Networks to obtain the pose of each one of the objects. In [5], on the other hand, it is proposed the use of sparse autoencoders with RGBD data to obtain the pose of the objects from a certain view.

Another different approach to estimating objects in a Cluttered Bin Picking scenarios was presented in 2016 by the University of Bonn in the Amazon Bin Picking Challenge [6]. In this case they used a hybrid approach between object detection and segmentation using convolutional neural networks (CNNs). The same authors presented in 2017 another similar approach in which CNNs are used to perform a system that combines object location and feature extraction [7].

With respect to the processing of four dimensional data (image+point cloud), which is the case of this research work, in [8] CNNs were used for scene segmentation and feature extraction from RGBD data. Another approach to solve the same segmentation problem can be found in [9], where a PointNet network architecture was used to segment and calculate object poses in bin picking scenarios. Finally where a rapid response is needed and computation capacity is not a problem, works presented in [10] and [11] use parallel CNNs in 2D and 3D input data, using one common CNN for the extraction of characteristics subsequently used in the location of the object and in the estimation of its pose by the second network.

Although the algorithms and procedures discussed in the above pharagraphs present good results, in the industrial reality a reconfigurability and a fast and effective adaptability is required, to be able to maintain a sufficiently competitive production.

Taking into account this problem, the present research work proposes a hybrid method for the solution of the problem of identification of part pose in a bin picking problem, taking advantage of the latest trends in Deep Learning and clustering algorithms, and combining them with point cloud processing algorithms, so that this method offers a fast configuration and results robust enough to be used in a real production environment. More specifically, the proposed procedure consists of the following steps:

- Capture the scene with a camera that provides 3D information and the associated gray level image.
- Detection of the candidate parts to be extracted by means of a robust object detection using Deep Learning.
- From the detected parts, the 3D environment associated with each detection is segmented to obtain the precise partial point cloud belonging to the part.
- Once the point cloud has been obtained, the part is matched with its CAD model, by means of a modified ICP algorithm, obtaining its final pose with respect to the origin of the camera.

Section 2 presents in a general way the different steps of which the proposed algorithm is composed. Section 3 describes in detail the industrial dataset used for the validation of the method, while Sect. 4 presents the results obtained in the tests for the validation of the procedure.

Finally, Sect. 5 presents the conclusions reached during the development of this new method and the advantages that it can bring against the existing developments in the new Industry 4.0 paradigm.

2 Proposed Algorithm

The proposed algorithm to make an effective Bin Picking operation possible consists on four steps outlined in the previous section. Figure 1 presents an overall schema of the procedure, which will be explained precisely in the following subsections.

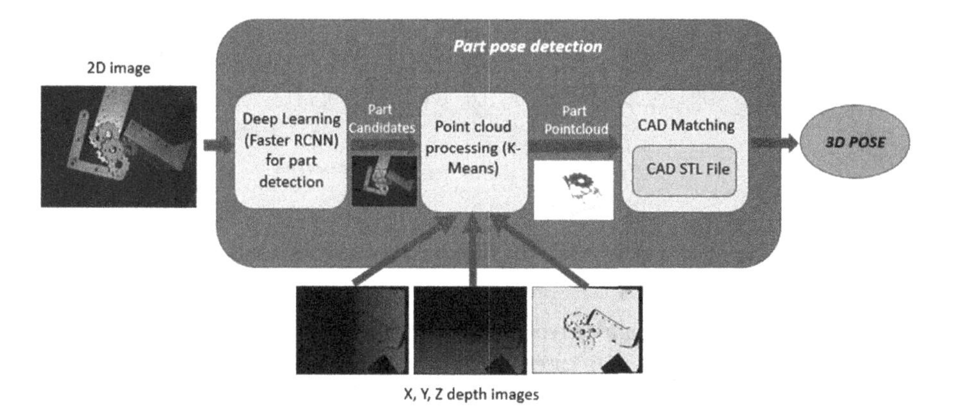

Fig. 1. General schema of the solution proposed.

2.1 Scene Capture and Initial Part Location

The images in the dataset for the validation of the proposed algorithm have been captured with a 3D sensor, which provides for each scene the spatial coordinates of each point by means of three depth images: *X, Y* and Z. It also provides the graylevel image of the scene, so that this last image has the same point of view as the *X, Y, Z* depth images. Each of the images has a resolution of 1280*960 pixels, obtaining in total, for each scene a multidimensional image of dimensions 1280*960*4 (grayscale, *X* depth, *Y* depth, *Z* depth).

To achieve a correct selection and classification of parts, Deep Learning (DL) techniques have been used, more specifically Convolutional Neural Networks (CNNs). These type of networks have proven to give promising results in complex object detection problems. In the case of use presented, the objective is to achieve is an accurate and robust detection of pieces (objects) against occlusions, changes in lighting, etc., enabling the robust selection of candidate pieces for bin picking.

There are several object detection algorithms based on DL well known in the literature. Among all them, FasterRCNN [12] has been chosen as an alternative that offers a fast and reliable response. Figure 2 shows the general architecture of the FasterRCNN algorithm:

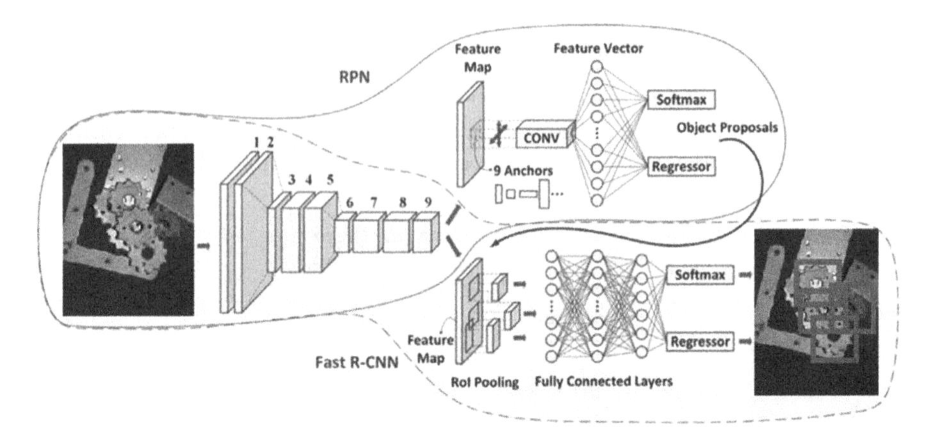

Fig. 2. General schema of the Faster-RCNN object detector. (towardsdatascience.com)

FasterRCNN is based on a convolutional neural network (CNN) architecture over which modifications are made to carry out object detection. In the present work it has been decided to use the MobileNetV2 network [13], as it is a network that offers a good compromise between training requirements, detection speed and result accuracy.

This network was created in 2018, with a total of 3.5 million trainable parameters.

For the detection of pieces, it is necessary to train the proposed architecture with the new dataset, therefore it has been necessary to label the pieces present in the dataset for the training of the object detection algorithm. Once the detector is trained, and for a new scene, the best candidate pieces to be extracted will be indicated by means of a bounding box, also indicating their class.

In Fig. 3 a sample of a scene labelling in the used dataset is shown:

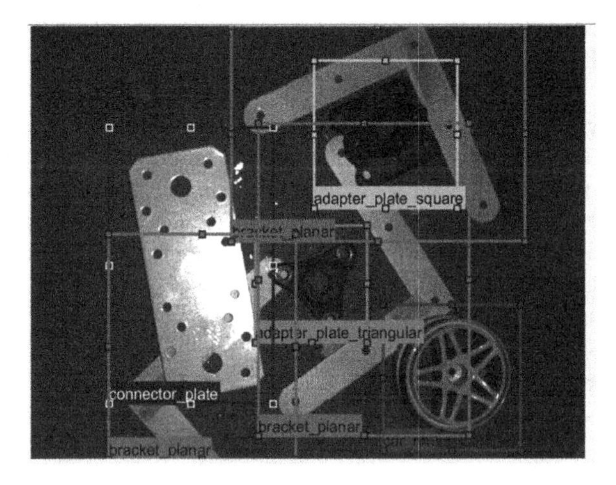

Fig. 3. Scene labelling for object detection training.

2.2 Clustering Segmentation to Obtain the Point Cloud of the Candidate Parts

Once the candidate parts have been detected in the image in the grey level image, the partial point cloud is obtained for each of them, segmenting each of the depth data of the pieces from the bounding box obtained by the piece detection algorithm applied in the previous step. In this segmentation of the spatial information of the part, there may be parts of other parts, part of the support surface, etc.

For the effective separation of the part from the rest of the elements that may appear in this preliminary segmentation of the point cloud, the k-means clustering algorithm is used applied to the previously segmented partial point cloud.

The k-means algorithm establishes that given a set of observations *(x1, x2, ..., xn)*, where each observation is a real vector of *d* dimensions, k-means constructs a partition of the observations in *k* sets ($k \leq n$) in order to minimize the sum of the squares within each group (WCSS) *S = {S1, S2,..., Sk}*. Formaly:

$$\arg\, min_S \sum_{i=1}^{k} \sum_{x \in S_i} \|x - \mu_i\|^2 = \arg\, min_S \sum_{i=1}^{k} |S_i| Var S_i \quad (1)$$

In the case presented, the dimensions will be 3, *(x, y, z)*, setting empirically k = 2.

Once the point cloud has been segmented using this clustering technique, the resulting larger cluster will be the one corresponding to the candidate piece for picking, discarding the rest of the points in the scene.

An example of this segmentation procedure can be observed in Fig. 4 (in red, segmented part, in green background):

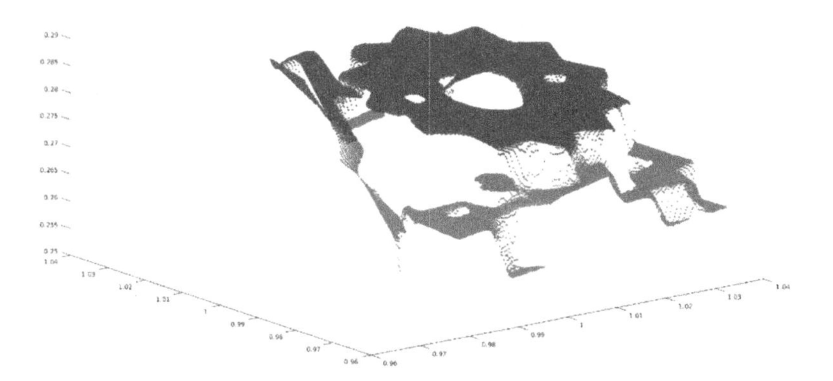

Fig. 4. Segmented object in point cloud by k-means clustering (Color figure online)

As a last step before registering the point cloud with the CAD model of the corresponding part, a smoothing of the resulting point cloud is performed using the MLS algorithm, which adjusts polynomial surfaces according to the closest *k* points in the different parts of the point cloud. At each location *P* in the point cloud, the closest neighboring points have a greater contribution than the rest of the points in the environment. This contribution is controlled by the following weighting function, which can be set on the basis of ϕ (in the case presented, $\phi = 1$):

$$w(P^*) = e^{\left(-\frac{\|P^* - P\|^2}{\varphi^2}\right)} \tag{2}$$

2.3 Point Cloud Matching with the CAD Model of the Corresponding Parts

The final registration to obtain the position of the part with respect to the 3D sensor is carried out in two well differentiated steps:

In the first of them, keypoints are calculated using the SIFT algorithm [14], for the resulting point cloud and CAD model. Using these points, an initial alignment of the part model with the previously obtained point cloud is achieved.

The second step, after the pre-alignment obtained at the previous point, is based on the application of the ICP (Iterative Closest Point) algorithm [15]. In this second step, the fine alignment of the CAD model with the point cloud is obtained so that the final position of the part with respect to the 3D sensor will be determined by the following concatenation of affine transformations:

$$H_{final} = H_{SIFT} * H_{icp} = \begin{bmatrix} R_{SIFT} & T_{SIFT} \\ 0 \;\; 0 \;\; 0 & 1 \end{bmatrix} * \begin{bmatrix} R_{icp} & T_{icp} \\ 0 \;\; 0 \;\; 0 & 1 \end{bmatrix} \tag{3}$$

3 Dataset for Part Detection

Among all existing datasets in literature, it was decided to use the MVTec Industrial 3D Object Detection Dataset (MVTec ITODD) for the development of the algorithm [16]. This dataset has been selected because it has been specifically created to be used in real industrial problems, with a main focus on Bin Picking and surface quality inspection of parts.

The dataset consists of 28 rigid objects, of different shapes and surface textures, organized in more than 800 captured scenes. For each of the scenes, the information has been captured using two industrial 3D sensors of different resolution (which provide image in gray levels, in addition to the 3D coordinates of the points), and three high-resolution cameras that capture images in gray levels from different perspectives.

To evaluate the accuracy of detection of parts of the system, from the original dataset, a subset of parts has been generated containing four small parts of those present in the dataset.

This subgroup of the dataset has been created taking into account the common casuistry presented in real industrial Bin Picking systems, which are:

- A limited number of references of pieces to be identified. It does not make sense in an industrial environment to identify multiple parts. Moreover, the identification of a smaller number of references allows a more precise training of the CNN in charge of detection.
- The different parts to be detected in a real Bin Picking problem usually have a similar size among them. It is not common to mix pieces of very different sizes and volumes in the same container.

More precisely, the four parts selected for the algorithm testing and evaluation are those labelled as "adapter_plate_square", "cap", "clamp_small" and "star" in the dataset (Fig. 5).

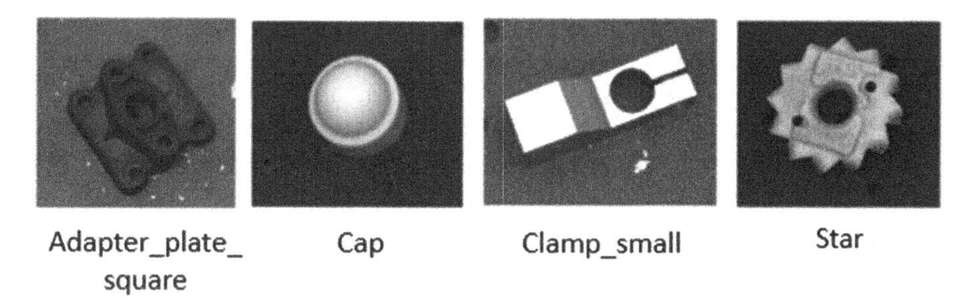

Fig. 5. Parts used to evaluate the solution proposed [16]

4 Obtained Experimental Results

In this section of the document, the results obtained for each of the stages of the algorithm will be presented, explaining the different tests and trials carried out for their validation. It is also included an analysis of the necessary processing times for each one of the stages will be made, arriving at the calculation of the total estimated time needed to calculate the 3D pose of a certain part with respect to the origin of the 3D sensor using the proposed algorithm.

4.1 Part Location Using Deep Learning

The Faster-RCNN object detector has been trained using the following configuration, with the dataset defined in Table 1. This dataset has been extracted from the original ITODD dataset:

- The solver selected to train the network in the RCNN detectors has been the stochastic gradient descent with momentum (sgdm) optimizer [17]. Empirically, the parameters for this optimizer have been $\alpha = 0.001$ and $\gamma = 0.9$.
- The loss function used has been cross entropy or multinomial logistic loss [18].
- For the training stage mini-batch size has been set to 8 and the maximum number of epochs to 40.

Table 1. Dataset details

Object	Number of scenes	Total instances
Adapter_plate_square	27	87
Cap	33	180
Clamp_small	21	144
Star	54	381

Although the dataset does not present a balanced number of samples for the four different types of pieces, it has been decided to leave this unbalance when training the system, because it reproduces the real situations that can occur in the industry, where the number of samples for each piece does not have to be the same.

A 5-fold cross validation approach has been selected for the training stage. 70% of the total instances have been selected for training, and 30% for testing. By following an n-fold approach and combining the results for each of the folds, results can be extrapolated to a situation of having n times more instances to train each part.

Table 2 shows total number of instances for training and testing with the 5-fold cross validation approach.

Table 2. Total number of instances for training and testing

Object	5-fold total instances	5-fold training instances	5-fold testing instances
Adapter_plate_square	435	304	131
Cap	900	630	270
Clamp_small	720	504	216
Star	1905	1333	572

Due to the precision needed when detecting the different parts, a part detected with a confidence of less than 90% is not considered a correct detection. Taking this into account, Table 3 shows a summary of the obtained results in terms of True Positives (Part Correctly detected), False Negatives (Part not detected when it should) and False Positives (Part detected erroneously, either by confusing the part with other, or by detecting it where there is nothing). True negatives (Part not detected where there is not a part) are not useful for evaluation metrics in this case.

Table 3. Object detection results for 5-fold cross validation

Object	True Positives	False Negatives	False Positives
Adapter_plate_square	120 (91.5%)	7	4
Cap	867(96.3%)	23	10
Clamp_small	689 (95,7%)	20	11
Star	556 (97.3%)	9	7

Although in the results it can be seen that, in general, the detection of a certain part is more accurate if there are more training instances available, in all cases a correct detection of parts above 90% has been obtained, a sufficient precision in detection to validate the chosen approach.

4.2 K Means Clustering Segmentation Results

Segmentation results using the k means technique have given good results. By applying this clustering algorithm to a previously clipped partial point cloud, this procedure effectively separates the part's point cloud from the background. After testing this process with several samples of the four parts initially selected, the number of points in the part's point cloud is between 80% and 100% higher than in the point cloud corresponding to the background.

Within the part's point cloud, 90% of the points actually correspond to the object, while the remaining 10% are spurious points that have not been correctly segmented.

4.3 Final CAD Matching and Pose Estimation

A hundred tests have been carried out for each of the pieces present in the dataset. To evaluate the accuracy of the matching algorithm, point clouds of the objects obtained in the previous section have been used, placing their center of mass in a known position in space. The matching algorithm was then applied using the CAD corresponding to the part represented by the point cloud used in each test case. Table 4 shows the mean translation and rotation errors obtained for each of the dataset parts.

Table 4. Matching procedure mean errors

Object	Traslation error (mm)	Mean rotation error (degrees)
Adapter_plate_square	8	6.3
Cap	3.4	7.8
Clamp_small	5.3	4.5
Star	6, 2	5.1

4.4 Overall Time of the Complete Procedure

When carrying out the validation tests, the average processing times for each of the stages of the algorithm were collected. The tests have been carried out on a PC with a Core i7-4770 s processor with 8 GB RAM DDR3. The average time in seconds for each of the operations that compose the algorithms have been:

- Object detection with Faster-RCNN algorithm: 0.25 s
- Segmentation by using k-means clustering = 0.04 s
- Two stage matching procedure (SIFT + ICP) = 0.07 s

Hence the overall time needed for the complete procedure is: 0.25 + 0.04 + 0.07 = 0.36 s, being this time perfectly feasible in demanding industrial bin-picking operations.

5 Conclusions

This article presents an alternative method to the existing ones for the industrial Bin-picking operation. The designed algorithm uses a combination of deep learning and point cloud processing techniques to effectively detect the 3D pose of different industrial parts in a cluttered environment.

The main advantage of this method compared to others existing in the state of the art is its ease of configuration and adaptation for new parts, since the only step required is the labelling of the new references in an image database, obtained with a 3D sensor in the new industrial configuration in which the proposed method is to be applied.

With solutions such as the one presented, we seek to advance in the direction established by the new paradigm of industry 4.0, one of whose main axioms is the rapid reconfigurability of the different production processes to adapt them to changing production demands.

References

1. Miyajima, R.: Deep learning triggers a new era in industrial robotics. IEEE Multimed. **24**, 91–96 (2017). https://doi.org/10.1109/MMUL.2017.4031311
2. Wada, K., Murooka, M., Okada, K., Inaba, M.: 3D object segmentation for shelf bin picking by humanoid with deep learning and occupancy voxel grid map. IEEE-RAS International Conference on Humanoid Robots, pp. 1149–1154 (2016). https://doi.org/10.1109/HUMANOIDS.2016.7803415
3. Griffiths, D., Boehm, J.: A review on deep learning techniques for 3D sensed data classification. Remote Sens. **11** (2019). https://doi.org/10.3390/rs11121499
4. Periyasamy, A.S., Schwarz, M., Behnke, S.: Robust 6D object pose estimation in cluttered scenes using semantic segmentation and pose regression networks. In: IEEE International Conference on Intelligent Robots and Systems, pp. 6660–6666 (2018). https://doi.org/10.1109/IROS.2018.8594406
5. Doumanoglou, A., Kouskouridas, R., Malassiotis, S., Kim, T.-K.: 6D object detection and next-best-view prediction in the crowd (2015). https://doi.org/10.1109/CVPR.2016.390
6. Schwarz, M., Behnke, S.: PointNet deep learning for RGB-D object perception in cluttered bin picking. In: IEEE International Conference on Robotics and Automation, pp. 2–4 (2017). https://doi.org/10.1109/3DV.2016.68
7. Schwarz, M., et al.: NimbRo picking: versatile part handling for warehouse automation. In: Proceedings of the IEEE International Conference on Robotics and Automation, pp. 3032–3039 (2017). https://doi.org/10.1109/ICRA.2017.7989348
8. Lin, C.M., Tsai, C.Y., Lai, Y.C., Li, S.A., Wong, C.C.: Visual object recognition and pose estimation based on a deep semantic segmentation network. IEEE Sens. J. **18**, 9370–9381 (2018). https://doi.org/10.1109/JSEN.2018.2870957
9. Dong, Z., et al.: PPR-Net: point-wise pose regression network for instance segmentation and 6D pose estimation in bin-picking scenarios, pp. 1773–1780 (2020). https://doi.org/10.1109/iros40897.2019.8967895
10. Blank, A., et al.: 6DoF pose-estimation pipeline for texture-less industrial components in bin picking applications. In: Proceedings 2019 European Conference on Mobile Robots ECMR 2019, pp. 1–7 (2019). https://doi.org/10.1109/ECMR.2019.8870920

11. Sock, J., Kim, K.I., Sahin, C., Kim, T.K.: Multi-task deep networks for depth-based 6D object pose and joint registration in crowd scenarios. In: British Machine Vision Conference 2018, BMVC 2018, pp. 1–12 (2019)
12. Ren, S., He, K., Girshick, R., Sun, J.: Faster R-CNN: towards real-time object detection with region proposal networks. IEEE Trans. Pattern Anal. Mach. Intell. **39**, 1137–1149 (2017). https://doi.org/10.1109/TPAMI.2016.2577031
13. Sandler, M., Howard, A., Zhu, M., Zhmoginov, A., Chen, L.C.: MobileNetV2: inverted residuals and linear bottlenecks. In: Proceedings of the IEEE Computer Society Conference on Computer Vision and Pattern Recognition pp. 4510–4520 (2018). https://doi.org/10.1109/CVPR.2018.00474
14. Lowe, D.G.: Distinctive image features from scale-invariant keypoints David. Int. J. Comput. Vis. **60**(2), 1–28 (2004)
15. Besl, P., McKay, N.D.: A Method for Registration of 3-D Shapes. IEEE Trans. Pattern Anal. Mach. Intell. **14**, 239–256 (1992)
16. Drost, B., Ulrich, M., Bergmann, P., Hartinger, P., Steger, C.: Introducing MVTec ITODD - a dataset for 3D object recognition in industry. In: Proceedings of the 2017 IEEE International Conference on Computer Vision Workshops (ICCVW) 2017, 2018 Janua, pp. 2200–2208 (2017). https://doi.org/10.1109/ICCVW.2017.257
17. Murphy, K.P.: Machine Learning - A Probabilistic Perspective - Table-of-Contents. MIT Press (2012). https://doi.org/10.1038/217994a0
18. Zhang, Z., Sabuncu, M.R.: Generalized cross entropy loss for training deep neural networks with noisy labels. In: Advances in Neural Information Processing Systems 2018, pp. 8778–8788 December 2018 (2018)

Forecasting Security Alerts Based on Time Series

Patrik Pekarčík, Andrej Gajdoš, and Pavol Sokol(✉)

Faculty of Science, Pavol Jozef Šafárik University in Košice, Košice, Slovakia
{patrik.pekarcik,andrej.gajdos,pavol.sokol}@upjs.sk

Abstract. As the number of devices and users connected to the Internet increases, also the number of security threats and incident increases and reactive measures are not sufficient. For this reason, the emphasis is shifting to preventive measures. The forecast of an increase or decrease in the number of security attacks or incidents in the network of an organization can be very helpful in prevention measures. In this paper, we focus on the network security situation forecasting based on time series analysis. The main objective of this paper is to determine the effect of seasonality and sliding window on network security situation forecasting, and criteria for choosing the suitable time series. Our evaluation shows that the seasonality does not play an important role in time series analysis. Also, time series analysis methods with the usage of sliding windows have comparable forecasting results. The combination of Arima and Exponential smoothing methods (ETS), which achieved the best results within the research evaluation, proves to be a suitable candidate for the real-time forecasting model.

Keywords: Cybersecurity · Network security · Situation awareness · Forecasting · Time series

1 Introduction

The number of cyber threats and attacks targeted towards all varieties of devices increases daily. The main topics in the field of cybersecurity are the detection of security incidents and the response to them. Security threats cannot be completely eliminated. Therefore, the current trend is to move from reactive to proactive activities [4]. The main goal is to prevent or mitigate security incidents before they cause harm to the organization.

Methods of predictive analysis play a significant role in predicting specific security incidents, predicting the next steps of the attacker or in predicting the security situation of the organization [11]. In this regard, we recognize three main approaches to predictive methods in cybersecurity:

- attack projection, problem being predicting the next move of an adversary in a running attack by projecting the series of actions the attacker performs [27];

E. A. de la Cal et al. (Eds.): HAIS 2020, LNAI 12344, pp. 546–557, 2020.
https://doi.org/10.1007/978-3-030-61705-9_45

- attack prediction, problem being what type of attacks are going to happen where and when [1];
- security situation forecast, problem being forecast number of attacks or vulnerabilities in the network of the organisation [18].

In this paper, we focus on the network security situation forecasting. It is based on general definition of the situational awareness: *"Perception of the elements in the environment within a volume of time and space, the comprehension of their meaning and the projection of their status in near future"* [8]. Therefore, the network security situation forecasting is a monitoring of cyber systems, understanding of the cybersecurity situation represented by modeling of cyber threats or relating security alerts and predicting the changes in cyber security situation [11].

There are a number of important issues that need to be addressed in this approach. The main problems are space and time requirements of the predictive methods, prediction window, criteria for suitable time series etc.

To summarize the problems outlined above, we emphasize the following questions that we aim to answer:

1. the effect of seasonality on network security situation forecasting,
2. the effect of the sliding window on network security situation forecasting,
3. time series selection criteria suitable for network security situation forecasting.

To answer the questions, we use predictive methods based on time series. Time series models "attempt to make use of the time-dependent structure present in a set of observations" [6]. The appropriate forecasting methods depend largely on what type of data is available. We have the choice of either qualitative forecasting methods (in cases when available data are not relevant to the forecasts) or quantitative forecasting methods. For purpose of research in this paper, we have available data from Warden system [17] and we have chosen quantitative forecasting methods, which describe the network security situation at a point in time [18].

This paper is based on the results of our previous research [21]. In previous papers, we focused on the quantitative analysis of the total number of incidents and did not pay attention to different categories of alerts. In research paper [10], we address similar issues, but only work with weekly data. This paper clarifies the issues examined and uses annual data as source data, which, in addition to the quantitative component (number), also carry a qualitative component (alert category, network protocol, or network port).

This paper is organized into five sections. Section 2 focuses on the review of published research related to predictions in cybersecurity based on time series. Section 3 focuses on the research methodology and outlines the dataset and methods used for the analysis. Section 4 states result from an analysis of the research questions and discuss knowledge obtained from the analysis. The last section contains conclusions.

2 Related Works

This section provides an overview of papers that focus on the prediction of security attacks, security incidents or security threats using time series analysis. Most of the papers focus on the detection of attacks rather than a prediction of attacks [19]. Papers [6] and [26]. Authors in [26] aim to exploit temporal correlations between the number of attacks per day in order to predict the future intensity of cyber incidents. On the other hand, [25] focuses on the prediction of attack based on ARMA time series model. In the paper, authors focused on modelling and analyzing traffic flow data by time-sequence techniques. Also, they proposed a data traffic prediction model based on the autoregressive moving average (ARMA) using the time series data.

Another research groups conduct research in the field of prediction of attack based on generalized ARCH (GARCH) models. In [24], authors propose a framework for statistically analyzing long-term vulnerability time series between January 1999 and January 2016. For this purpose, generalized ARCH (GARCH) models and SARIMA model are used for the National Vulnerability Database. Another example is [28]. Authors use grey-box FARIMA+GARCH models and discuss the integration of Extreme Value Theory (EVT) and the Time Series Theory (TST). In this paper, they show that EVT can offer long-term predictions (e.g. 24-hour ahead-of-time), while gray-box TST models can predict attack rates 1-hour ahead-of-time at an accuracy that can be deemed practical.

In the field of prediction of attacks, it is necessary to mention also paper [23]. Authors focus on the problem of forecasting attack sources based on past attack logs from several contributors. They evaluate and combine several factors - attacker-victim history using time-series, attackers and/or victims interactions using neighbourhood models and global patterns using singular value decomposition. In terms of time series analysis, they use an Exponential Weighted Moving Average (EWMA) model.

3 Methodology

3.1 Dataset

The source of data for our research is the alerts obtained from a Warden system [17]. It is a system that supports sharing information about security events on individual computer networks connected to this system. Data is stored and shared in IDEA (Intrusion Detection Extensible Alert) format [16]. IDEA format is a descriptive data model using a key-value JSON structure.

The main detection sources of data that send IDEA alerts to the Warden system can include attack detection systems, honeypots, network flow probes, system log records, and other data sources deployed in several networks (Czech national research and education network, Czech commercial network). Alert in the IDEA format contains several mandatory fields (format, ID, detect time, category) [16] and many optional fields with multiple input support. The fields we follow most in this research are the category, network traffic source data (IP address, port, protocol), network traffic target data (IP, port, protocol), detection time, and interruption time. For this research, data were collected during one year (from 2017-12-11 to 2018-12-11) by the Warden system. Collected data contain approximately one billion records from various data sources mentioned above.

For purposes of this research, we processed one-year dataset to 21 time series based on different criteria. Criteria were chosen from all possible values of category, port and protocol fields by statistical representation throughout the whole dataset. The criterion has to meet the requirement occurrence of the value in at least 1% alerts of all alerts. Chosen criteria are followings: (I) Count of all alerts; (II) Count of unique IP; (III) Category recon scanning; (IV) Category availability DDoS; (V) Category attempt login; (VI) Category attempt exploit; (VII) Category malware ransomware; (VIII) Category intrusion botnet; (IX) Port 21; (X) Port 22; (XI) Port 23; (XII) Port 25; (XIII) Port 80; (XIV) Port 443; (XV) Port 445; (XVI) Protocol TCP; (XVII) Protocol SSH; (XVIII) Protocol UDP; (XIX) Protocol ICMP; (XX) Protocol Microsoft WBT Server; (XXI) Protocol telnet. Furthermore these time series was processed to multiple version based on reference time period. We have made time series with 1 min, 10 min, 15 min, 30 min and 60 min time period.ime series is stored in PostgreSQL database with TimescaleDB extension. TimescaleDB extension is important for our future aggregations to create different views on created time series data.

3.2 Method Description

There is a wide range of quantitative forecasting methods and their usage often depends on the specific disciplines, on the nature of data or specific purposes. For choosing a particular method, properties, accuracies, and computational costs must be considered. In our research, we have considered four approaches to time series forecasting: (I) ARIMA models; (II) Exponential smoothing models (state space models); (III) the naive approach; and (IV) combination (average) of ARIMA and Exponential smoothing models.

The most commonly used classes of models in time series modelling and forecasting are ARIMA and Exponential smoothing (ETS) [13]. We compared them with the naive methods [2,3], which can process large data sets and they do not have high computational requirements. They serve as a benchmark for predictions in our research. We also added a combination (average) of the ARIMA and ETS methods to compare the standard methods with their combination. The idea of averaging or boosting is very popular in machine learning nowadays [11].

Prediction using ETS family models is characterized by a weighted combination of older observations with new ones. The new observations have a relatively higher weight compared to the older observations. Exponential smoothing reflects the fact that weights decrease exponentially as observations age [3,13].

The ARIMA models represent a generalization of the class of ARMA models that incorporate a wide range of non-stationary series. These models, by finite number of differentiations, ensure time series stationarity, allowing the use of ARMA models. ARMA models are a combination of auto-regression (AR) and moving average (MA) [2]. The ETS class provides another approach to time series modelling and forecasting. While ETS models are based on a description of the trend and seasonality in the data, ARIMA models aim to describe the autocorrelations in the data [13]. Both classes of models can reflect seasonality in the data.

3.3 Experiment Evaluation

The research questions were evaluated using above mentioned dataset from the Warden system. We evaluated the methods using the implementation presented in our previous work [10,21]. In our extensive calculations, we used R functions from one of the most common R-packages for time series predictions called *forecast* [14]. Beneficial features when working with large data sets or potentially in real-time prediction are those used to automatically fit ARIMA or ETS. These functions are designed to automatically select the best model from the considered class under given conditions, for example, taking into account information criteria [14].

For each class of models, particular models were fitted in the seasonal and non-seasonal settings. Seasonal variation, or seasonality means cycles that repeat regularly over time. A cycle structure in a time series may or may not be seasonal. If it consistently repeats at the same frequency, it is seasonal, otherwise it is not seasonal and is called a cycle. We considered one, two, five, and ten steps ahead predictions, which were compared to true values included in the test set.

Furthermore, we considered two cases of model fitting. The first one was the "classical" one; when we kept the whole training dataset and step by step, we added one more observations from the test set to training set in each round of evaluation. In the second case, we used the so-called "rolling window" or "one in, one out", which means that in each round of evaluation we remove the oldest observation from the training set and at the same time we add one new observation from the test set to training set.

At first, we calculated 95% (bootstrap) prediction intervals, and consequently, the average coverage was computed. It is the percentage of all confidence intervals which covered the true (future) value of particular time series. It should be close to 95%. The values approaching 95% indicate that the 95% prediction interval works well for a specific case (method, number of forecast steps and time interval). If the coverage is lower than 95%), it points out the lower reliability of prediction interval. Conversely, the higher the coverage (more than 95%) the wider and less informative prediction interval.

We also took a look at the average length of prediction intervals. In general, shorter prediction intervals are considered more precise (under the fixed confidence level). They give us better information about the future values of time series. We have divided our evaluation into two stages. In the first stage We evaluated forecasting methods only on the total number of alerts and did not address the qualitative component (alert category, network protocol, or network port). In previous work [10] we considered 24 hours period and four different time units (5 min, 15 min, 30 min and 60 min) considering the fact that dataset usage in this work consists of data for one week. In this paper, we extend our evaluation. Given the fact that we use one-year dataset and based on results from previous work, we considered 24 h and 7 days period with two different time units (30 min and 60 min), and two different lengths of datasets (month, two months). We decided to choose the last two months from the entire one year dataset because of the time complexity in our extensive numerical study. Moreover one can assume that time series values far in the past (with respect to time units) would not have a significant impact on predictions of future values. Main aim of this stage is to answer the issues of seasonality and the usage of rolling windows in the perspective of long-term period (one year).

In the second stage of our evaluation, we used the best combination of time interval, period, and forecasting period (30 min, 7 days, one month). In this stage, we evaluated forecasting methods on 21 attributes of alerts and we address the qualitative component (alert category, network protocol, or network port). Main aims of this stage was to analyse seasonality and the usage of rolling-windows in other time series taking into account qualitative component. Also, we analysed criteria for time series suitable for forecasting.

4 Results and Discussion

In this section, we describe in more detail both stages of experiment evaluation. We take a closer look at the individual results and discuss research questions based on them.

Results of the Second Stage of Evaluation. As a part of evaluation, in the first stage we tested all above mentioned methods in six cases (time interval, time period, time unit): (I) 30 min, 24 hours, 1 month; (II) 30 min, 7 days, 1 month; (III) 60 min, 24 hours, 2 months; (IV) 60 min, 24 hours, 1 month; (V) 60 min, 7 days, 2 months; (VI) 60 min, 7 days, 1 month.

The first approach to evaluate the predictions' quality of particular models is the so-called cross-validation [13]. We employed two variations of this approach. In the first case, we calculated the predictions at specific future times (separately for one or two or five or ten steps ahead) throughout the test set, and at the end we calculated the metric value from all the predictions for the various prediction steps separately. The metric commonly used to evaluate forecast accuracy is the mean absolute error rate (MASE) [15]. It is a prefered metric as it is less sensitive to outliers, more easily interpreted and less variable on small samples. MASE is defined as [13]:

$$\mathrm{MASE} = \mathrm{mean}(|q_j|) \tag{1}$$

where, for non-seasonal time series, q_j is:

$$q_j = \frac{e_j}{\frac{1}{T-1}\sum_{i=2}^{T}|y_i - y_{i-1}|}, \tag{2}$$

and, for seasonal time series, q_j is:

$$q_j = \frac{e_j}{\frac{1}{T-m}\sum_{i=m+1}^{T}|y_i - y_{i-m}|} \quad (3)$$

In both cases, e_j is forecast error, i.e., the difference between an observed value and its forecast, y_j represents observed value, T is the length of time series, and m is seasonality parameter (period).

In the second type of cross-validation, we considered all forecasts up to the second, fifth and tenth step ahead forecast in each round of evaluation we calculate MASE (not just the last one as in the previous case). According to this criterion, the prediction is more accurate, when the lower value (ideally below 1) of MASE is achieved. A scaled error is less than one if it arises from a better forecast than the average naive forecast computed on the training data. Conversely, it is greater than one if the forecast is worse than the average naive forecast computed on the training data [12].

Table 1. Results of the average MASE values for forecasting methods. Notes: A - ARIMA model; E - Exponential Smoothing (state space models); N - naive model; AE - ARIMA + Exponential smoothing (average); s - with seasonality; (s) - with seasonality for each model in cell; w - rolling window.

Case	30/24/1	30/7/1	60/24/2	60/24/1	60/7/2	60/7/1
Two-steps	0.4755	0.4009	0.7159	1.1612	0.5598	0.9888
	AEsw, AEw	AEsw, AEw	AEsw, AEw	AEsw, AEw	AEsw, AEw	AEsw, AEw
Five-steps	0.5539	0.4674	0.765	1.2023	0.5978	1.0249
	AEsw, AEw	AEsw, AEw	AEsw, AEw	AEsw, AEw	AEsw, AEw	AEsw, AEw
Ten-steps	0.6331	0.5369	0.8038	1.2239	0.6281	1.0453
	AEsw, AEw	AEsw, AEw	AEsw, AEw	AEsw, AEw	AEsw, AEw	AEsw, AEw

Table 1 shows the results of the average MASE values for 2-step forecasts, 5-step forecasts, and 10-step forecasts calculated over the whole training set. Except one case (60 min, 7 days, 2 months), all values were below 1. Overall, the best method seems to be the combination (average) of ARIMA and Exponential smoothing models with a sliding window. In the case of the second type of cross-validation (average MASE values), this method has the best results in all monitored cases. The ETS method appears to be a suitable method at 60-minutes intervals. In contrast, at 30-minutes, the ARIMA method has the best results for 5-steps and 10-steps forecasts.

The second approach to assessing the quality of predictions of specific models is an average coverage of 95% by prediction intervals. We used the above six cases and compared the established forecasting approaches based on different prediction steps - next, second, 5th and 10th step ahead.

The Table 2 shows the results of the average coverage of 95% prediction intervals. The values of average coverage in two cases with time unit of 30 min

Table 2. Average percentage coverage of actual (future) time series values by 95% prediction intervals. Notes: A - ARIMA model; E - Exponential Smoothing (state space models); N - naive model; AE - ARIMA + Exponential smoothing (average); ALL - all models; (-) - without; s - with seasonality; w - rolling window.

Case	30/24/1	30/7/1	60/24/2	60/24/1	60/7/2	60/7/1
One-step	96.6667	96.6667	94.0625	88.125	94.0625	88.125
	Es, E, Ar	AEs, Esr, A, Er	Asr, AEsr	Ns, Nsr, Nr	Er, AEr	Ns, Nsr, Nr
Two-steps	95.8194	95.8194	94.2006	87.4214	94.0439	87.4214
	Es, E	AEs, Esr, A, Er	AEsr	Nr	Er	Nr
Five-steps	95.1351	95.0676	95.1266	89.7436	95.1266	89.7436
	E	Er	Nsr, Nr	Nsr, Nr	Nsr, Nr	Nsr, Nr
Ten-steps	95.2234	95.189	94.5016	94.9007	94.5016	94.9007
	A	A	AEsr	Ns, Nr	Er	Ns, Nr

(monthly data) and in two cases with time unit of 60 min (bimonthly data) are close to nominal value 95 and these predictions intervals are not too wide. It implies they are quite precise. Vice versa, values of the average coverage in two cases with 60 min time intervals and bimonthly data are below the nominal value 95 so these prediction intervals are not very reliable or they can be considered as biased.

The main aim of the first stage of experimental evaluation was to determine an appropriate case. According to results mentioned above the most suitable scenario for the methodology chosen by us is the case with monthly data, time intervals of 30 min, period equal to 7 days. The suitability of the selection of the 7-day period is also confirmed by the research based on time-oriented analysis and visualization of data collected by honeypots [22]. Data set with these parameters was consequently analyzed in more details in the second stage.

Results of the Second Stage of the Evaluation. In the second stage we tested all above mentioned methods with the best result case (30 min, 7 days, 1 month) on 16 selected time series. Six time series have been removed from the evaluation process due to fact, that they contained small counts (less than 100 – e.g. category availability DDoS) or they contained mostly zeros (e.g. category malware – ransomware). If the counts are large enough (more than 100) then the difference between a continuous sample space and the discrete sample space has no perceivable effect on the forecasts [13]. However, if our data contains small counts (less than 100) then we need to use forecasting methods that are more appropriate for a sample space of non-negative integers. For instance the so called Croston's method can be considered [5,7]. On the other hand the time series with mostly zeros can be suitable for time series anomaly detection [20] and it is an interesting direction for future research.

Table 3 shows the results of the average MASE values for 2-step forecasts, 5-step forecasts and 10-step forecasts calculated for 16 time series. In this table the significant time series for discussion are showed. The results from the 2nd stage

Table 3. Results of the average MASE values for forecasting methods. Notes: A - ARIMA model; E - Exponential Smoothing (state space models); N - naive model; AE - ARIMA + Exponential smoothing (average); s - with seasonality; (s) - with seasonality for each model in cell; w - rolling window.

Time series	Count	Recon Scanning	Attempt Login	Attempt Exploit	Intrusion Botnet	Port 80	Protocol SSH	Protocol Telnet
Two-steps	0.397	0.449	0.1457	0.8304	0.1985	0.1764	0.1662	0.8983
	AEsw	AEsw	AEsw	AEsw	Aw	AEsw	AEsw	AEsw
	AEw	AEw	AEw	AEw		AEw	AEw	AEw
Five-steps	0.4633	0.5151	0.2078	0.8271	0.2112	0.1868	0.2221	0.9726
	AEsw	AEsw	AEsw	AEsw	As	AEsw	AEsw	AEsw
	AEw	AEw	AEw	AEw	Asw, A	AEw	AEw	AEw
Ten-steps	0.5335	0.5839	0.2595	0.8191	0.2133	0.1975	0.2697	0.9832
	AEsw	AEsw	AEsw	AEsw	As	AEsw	AEsw	AEsw
	AEw	AEw	AEw	AEw	Asw, A	AEw	AEw	AEw

of research evaluation confirm the findings from the first stage. The best method seems to be the combination (average) of ARIMA and Exponential smoothing models. Although the methods with sliding window do not have the best results in all cases (16-time series), their results in the average MASE value are close to the best method.

Example of usage of forecasting method based on time series is shown in Fig. 1 and Fig. 2, where we can see one-step forecasting based on the combination of ARIMA and ETS (30 min time unit) for attribute "category attempt login" (Fig. 1) and for attribute "category attempt exploit" (Fig. 2). These two categories of security alerts show the difference between time series based on security data, which we should consider. Both time series have a relatively sufficient number of data (Attempt login - 46.709.781 (7.74% of the total number of alerts) and Attempt exploit - 27.695.575 (4.59% of total alerts)). The difference lies in the nature of data. The second time series is hardly predictable [9] (you can see that predictions are far away from true values many times) because it looks like a white noise (random walk process). In such situation it is difficult to find something reliable and better than naive forecasting methods due to the lack of correlation structure or some other patters which could be captured by sophisticated models. On the contrary the time series in Fig. 1 shows some kind of structure and patterns and also the predictions are better compared to the previous case.

Discussion of Research Questions. As mentioned above, seasonal variation or seasonality means cycles that repeat regularly over time. We selected both ETS and ARIMA methods since they are able to reflect seasonality in the data. Our assumption is that seasonality does not need to be taken into account, as the patterns in data (number of security alerts) do not repeat regularly (just irregularly in few cases) over time, but they depend on other factors. As the

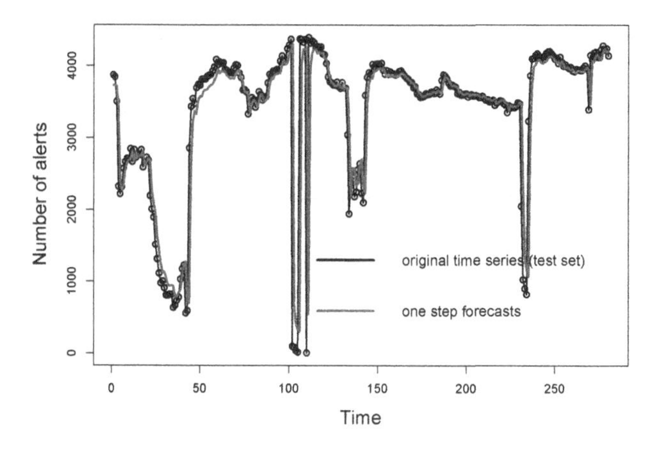

Fig. 1. One-step forecasting for attribute "category attempt login".

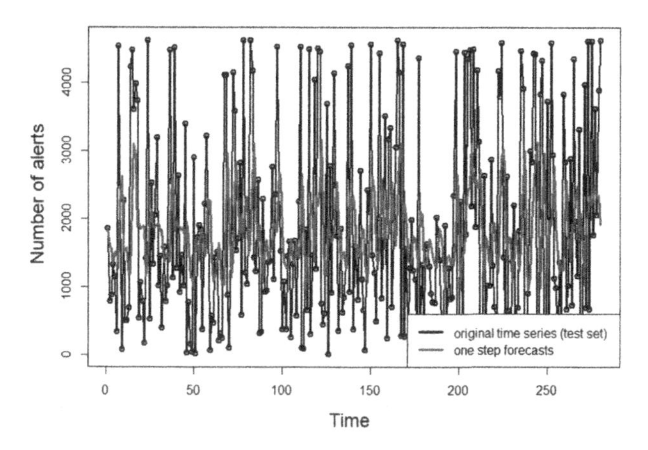

Fig. 2. One-step forecasting for attribute "category attempt exploit".

results show, the best values for individual forecasting are always achieved by the method in both its forms - taking into account, resp. disregarding seasonality. From this point of view, we can state that in time series based only on the total number of attacks, the seasonality does not play an important role in forecasting.

As it can be seen from our results (Table 1 and Table 2) the best performing forecasting approaches were those, which employed the so called rolling window technique. It is a good outcome because from the practical point of view it is not necessary to keep the whole dataset in memory and there is no need to fit models, make computations and predictions using the entire data set. It makes sense to find a reasonable window which is usually much shorter than the length of original data set. Again this can be an advantage when it comes to real-time predictions. In our numerical study we considered the length of window to be the 80% of monthly data (time unit – 30 min.) or 80% of bimonthly data (time unit – 60 min.).

5 Conclusion and Future Works

As we mentioned in this paper several times, forecasting methods for this research were chosen so that they could find a suitable model themselves. The reason is the fact that the aim of the on-coming research is the real-time forecasting of security alerts. For this purpose, it is necessary to solve several issues, e.g. issue of seasonality or the issue of the sliding window usage. In this paper, we focus on these issues and verify our assumptions using four methods and one-year dataset of security alerts. The results confirmed the assumption that seasonality is not necessarily taken into account, as well as the possibility of using a time window. These results are important for selecting an appropriate method for real-time processing. The combination of Arima and ETS methods, which achieved the best results within the research evaluation, proves to be a suitable candidate for the real-time forecasting model.

Acknowledgment. This research is funded by the VVGS projects under contracts No. VVGS-PF-2020-1423 and No. VVGS-PF-2020-1427 and Slovak Research and development agency project under contract No. APVV-17-0561.

References

1. Abdlhamed, M., Kifayat, K., Shi, Q., Hurst, W.: Intrusion prediction systems. In: Alsmadi, I.M., Karabatis, G., AlEroud, A. (eds.) Information Fusion for Cyber-Security Analytics. SCI, vol. 691, pp. 155–174. Springer, Cham (2017). https://doi.org/10.1007/978-3-319-44257-0_7
2. Box, G.E., Jenkins, G.M., Reinsel, G.C., Ljung, G.M.: Time Series Analysis: Forecasting and Control. Wiley, Hoboken (2015)
3. Brockwell, P.J., Davis, R.A.: Introduction to Time Series and Forecasting. Springer, Cham (2016). https://doi.org/10.1007/978-3-319-29854-2
4. Cho, J.H., et al.: Toward proactive, adaptive defense: a survey on moving target defense. IEEE Commun. Surv. Tutor **22**(1), 709–745 (2020)
5. Christou, V., Fokianos, K.: On count time series prediction. J. Stat. Comput. Simul. **85**(2), 357–373 (2015)
6. Condon, E., He, A., Cukier, M.: Analysis of computer security incident data using time series models. In: 19th International Symposium on Software Reliability Engineering, 2008. ISSRE 2008, pp. 77–86. IEEE (2008)
7. Croston, J.D.: Forecasting and stock control for intermittent demands. J. Oper. Res. Soc. **23**(3), 289–303 (1972)
8. Endsley, M.R.: Situation awareness global assessment technique (SAGAT). In: Proceedings of the IEEE 1988 National Aerospace and Electronics Conference, pp. 789–795. IEEE (1988)
9. Hendry, D.F., et al.: Dynamic econometrics. In: Advanced Texts in Econometrics, Oxford University Press on Demand (1995)
10. Husak, M., Bartos, V., Sokol, P., Gajdos, A.: Predictive methods in cyber defense: current experience and research challenges. Future Gener. Comput. Syst. **115**, 517–530 (2021)
11. Husák, M., Komárková, J., Bou-Harb, E., Čeleda, P.: Survey of attack projection, prediction, and forecasting in cyber security. IEEE Commun. Surv. Tutor. **21**(1), 640–660 (2018)

12. Hyndman, R.J.: Measuring forecast accuracy. Business forecasting: practical problems and solutions, pp. 177–183 (2014)
13. Hyndman, R.J., Athanasopoulos, G.: Forecasting: Principles and Practice. OTexts (2018)
14. Hyndman, R.J., Khandakar, Y., et al.: Automatic time series for forecasting: the forecast package for R. No. 6, Monash University, Department of Econometrics and Business Statistics (2007)
15. Hyndman, R.J., Koehler, A.B.: Another look at measures of forecast accuracy. Int. J. Forecast. **22**(4), 679–688 (2006)
16. Kacha, P.: Idea: security event taxonomy mapping. In: 18th International Conference on Circuits, Systems, Communications and Computers (2014)
17. Kacha, P., Kostenec, M., Kropacova, A.: Warden 3: security event exchange redesign. In: 19th International Conference on Computers: Recent Advances in Computer Science (2015)
18. Leau, Y.-B., Manickam, S.: Network security situation prediction: a review and discussion. In: Intan, R., Chi, C.-H., Palit, H.N., Santoso, L.W. (eds.) ICSIIT 2015. CCIS, vol. 516, pp. 424–435. Springer, Heidelberg (2015). https://doi.org/10.1007/978-3-662-46742-8_39
19. Liu, Y., et al.: Cloudy with a chance of breach: forecasting cyber security incidents. In: 24th USENIX Security Symposium 2015, pp. 1009–1024 (2015)
20. Mehrotra, K.G., Mohan, C.K., Huang, H.: Anomaly Detection Principles and Algorithms. TSC. Springer, Cham (2017). https://doi.org/10.1007/978-3-319-67526-8_9
21. Sokol, P., Gajdoš, A.: Prediction of attacks against honeynet based on time series modeling. In: Silhavy, R., Silhavy, P., Prokopova, Z. (eds.) CoMeSySo 2017. AISC, vol. 662, pp. 360–371. Springer, Cham (2018). https://doi.org/10.1007/978-3-319-67621-0_33
22. Sokol, P., Kleinová, L., Husák, M.: Study of attack using honeypots and honeynets lessons learned from time-oriented visualization. In: IEEE International Conference on Computer as a Tool (EUROCON), pp. 1–6. IEEE (2015)
23. Soldo, F., Le, A., Markopoulou, A.: Blacklisting recommendation system: using spatio-temporal patterns to predict future attacks. IEEE J. Sel. Areas Commun. **29**(7), 1423–1437 (2011)
24. Tang, M., Alazab, M., Luo, Y.: Exploiting vulnerability disclosures: statistical framework and case study. In: Cybersecurity and Cyberforensics Conference (CCC) 2016, pp. 117–122. IEEE (2016)
25. Wei, M., Kim, K.: Intrusion detection scheme using traffic prediction for wireless industrial networks. J. Commun. Netw. **14**(3), 310–318 (2012)
26. Werner, G., Yang, S., McConky, K.: Time series forecasting of cyber attack intensity. In: Proceedings of the 12th Annual Conference on Cyber and Information Security Research, p. 18. ACM (2017)
27. Yang, S.J., Du, H., Holsopple, J., Sudit, M.: Attack projection. In: Kott, A., Wang, C., Erbacher, R.F. (eds.) Cyber Defense and Situational Awareness. AIS, vol. 62, pp. 239–261. Springer, Cham (2014). https://doi.org/10.1007/978-3-319-11391-3_12
28. Zhan, Z., Xu, M., Xu, S.: Predicting cyber attack rates with extreme values. IEEE Trans. Inf. Forensics Secur. **10**(8), 1666–1677 (2015)

Hybrid Artificial Intelligence Applications

A Real Time Vision System Based on Deep Learning for Gesture Based Human Machine Interaction

Alberto Tellaeche Iglesias(✉), Iker Pastor-López, Borja Sanz Urquijo, and Pablo García-Bringas

D4K Group, University of Deusto, Avda. Universidades 24, 48007 Bilbao, Spain
{alberto.tellaeche, iker.pastor, borja.sanz, pablo.garcia.bringas}@deusto.es

Abstract. The use of gestures is one of the principal ways of communication among human beings when other forms, such as speech, are not possible. Taking this as a basis, the use of gestures has become also a principal form of human machine interaction in many different fields, ranging from advanced industrial setups where robots are commanded by gestures, to the use of hands to remotely control multimedia devices present at home.

The majority of the systems for gesture detection are based on computer vision, either color images, depth images or point clouds, and have to overcome the inherent problems of image processing: light variations, occlusions or change of color. To overcome all these problems, recent developments using deep learning techniques have been presented, using Convolutional Neural Networks.

This work presents a hand gesture recognition system based on Convolutional Neural Networks and RGB images that is robust against environmental variations, fast enough to be considered real time in embedded interaction applications, and that overcomes the principal drawbacks of the state of the art hand gesture recognition systems presented in previous works.

Keywords: Real time · Deep learning · Gesture detection · Embedded systems

1 Introduction

Among the different forms of interaction, understanding and communicating by gestures is a key element.

Gestures are natural movements performed by humans and, as such, present a lot of variability in their execution, either in the case of the same person doing the same gesture repeatedly or in the case of different people performing it. Occlusions, perspective and variations in lighting conditions add more challenges to the gesture detection process.

Gesture recognition involves complex processes (e.g., motion modeling, motion analysis, pattern recognition and machine learning). In this way, Darrell and Pentland [1] adapted Dynamic Time Wrapping (DTW) to recognize dynamic gestures. Later,

E. A. de la Cal et al. (Eds.): HAIS 2020, LNAI 12344, pp. 561–572, 2020.
https://doi.org/10.1007/978-3-030-61705-9_46

Starner et al. [2] proposed the use of Hidden Markov Models (HMM) to classify orientation, trajectory information and resultant shape.

Wearable approaches based on physical sensors, such as accelerometers and gyroscopes have also been developed. In [3] a data glove captures the motion of the arm and hand by inertial and magnetic sensors. In [4], the authors propose a stretch-sensing soft glove to interactively capture hand poses with high accuracy and without requiring an external optical setup. In [5], Gesture information is derived by segmentation of depth images and skeleton tracking, while in [6], color segmentation in 2D images (detection of hands, head or tags) has been used. Ge et al. [7] presented a novel method for real-time 3D hand pose estimation from single depth images using 3D Convolutional Neural Networks (CNNs). In the same way, there are some methods that use CNNs, like the ones presented in [8, 9]. Another good example that uses deep learning for gesture detection is the recently launched Google Media Pipe framework that, among other capabilities, allows the tracking and detection of gestures performed with both hands [10].

Many research works focus the efforts on detecting hands and head of the person doing the specific gesture. Examples of this type of procedures are described in [11], where head and hands of the user are tracked in the 3D space. Another example using color segmentation in 2D images to detect the user´s hand is presented in [12].

Deep Learning technology for image processing was re-launched in 2012, when the research group of the Toronto University, leaded by Geoffrey E. Hinton, presented a Convolutional Neural Network (CNN) named AlexNet winning the ImageNet Large Scale Visual Recognition Challenge [13].

In image processing problems, the CNNs have represented a big advance for the resolution of problems such as scene identification, object detection or image segmentation, where good results were impossible to achieve when the complexity of the scene augmented [14].

After AlexNet CNN, many models have been developed for image processing tasks. Some of the most relevant are GoogLeNet from Google [15], VGG-16 network from Oxford University [16], ResNet, engineered by Microsoft [17] or the region based CNNs (RCNNs).

The RCNNs are possibly the most common approach of CNN for object detection tasks. To solve this problem, there are mainly two approaches: region proposal-based methods, such as RCNN and its variations, SPP-net or FPN, and regression/classification methods as YOLO, Multibox, G-CNN, AttentionNet, etc. [18].

RCNN model and its derivatives are examples of the region proposal methods [19]. In the case of the RCNN network, it has had three principal evolutions to obtain faster results in object detection: RCNN, Fast RCNN, and Faster RCNN.

The original RCNN detector first generates region proposals using image processing algorithms such as Edge Boxes [20].

A further development of the RCNN detector, with the intention of making it faster, led to the Fast-RCNN detector [21]. The main difference with the previous approach is that, while using a region proposal function like RCNN, after it, Fast-RCNN detector processes the entire image. The Fast-RCNN algorithm pools the features of the proposed regions using a CNN.

Faster-RCNN is the latest evolution of the RCNN detectors [22], shown in Fig. 1. In this case, instead of using an external algorithm to detect the regions to analyze, Faster-RCNN uses a region proposal network. This network is faster and better tuned for the training data, offering faster and better results.

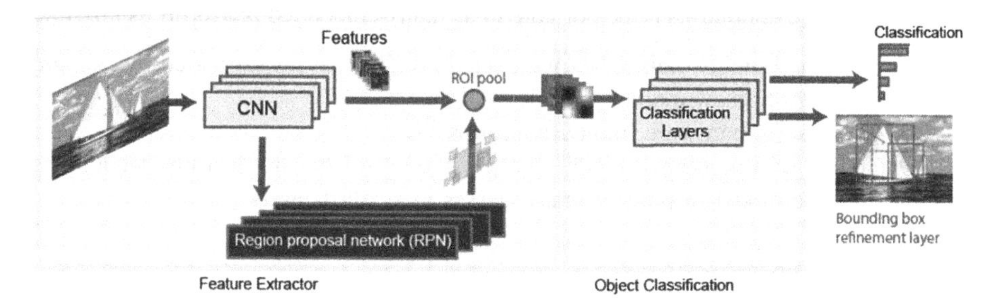

Fig. 1. General schema of the Faster RCNN detector

This paper presents a study to assess the feasibility of the different variations of the RCNN object detectors to detect hand gestures in real time. Section 2 formulates the problem to solve. In Sect. 3, the dataset used for the training stage is proposed. Section 4 explains the proposed approach in this paper in terms network architecture. In Sect. 5 the training procedure of the different RCNN alternatives is explained, and Sect. 6 presents the results obtained after the evaluation tests. The Sect. 7 lists the conclusions of this work, highlighting the strong points of the method proposed.

2 Problem Formulation

CNNs require quite demanding computational capabilities to achieve good results, and this is a problem presented in works such as [23] and [24].

In gesture recognition for Human Machine Interaction (HMI), where a rapid response is needed, small CNNs are the suitable approach in the RCNN detectors to test the system validity. Among the different networks present in state of the art research, these nets have been selected: Squeezenet [25], GoogleNet [26] and Mobilenetv2 [27].

Three are the main characteristics that a gesture detection system must fulfill to be usable in many different tasks. These are:

- Flexible and rapid definition of new gestures.
- Robustness to different ways of performing the same gesture by different people (orientation, hand position, size of the hand, skin color…), and to environmental conditions (light variations, different distances to the camera, partial occlusions…).
- Fast response, enough to be considered real time depending on the application that uses this way of interation.

This work aims to obtain a real time and lightweight system that can be deployed in desktop PCs, but also in embedded systems such as Nvidia Jetson platforms, Google Coral, or Intel Neural Compute Stick 2 powered by a Myriad X VPU processor.

These embedded systems, despite having enough computation power to deploy systems based on small sized CNNs, are programmed using frameworks that do not support all the CNNs layer types present in current literature, as the case of OpenVino (Intel) or Tensorflow Lite.

According to these limitations the design of the CNN architecture in this research must fullfil these conditions to be portable to as many embedded platforms as possible:

- Use of a small, lightweight CNN with standard CNN layers supported by as many deep learning frameworks as possible.
- Fast response in hardware limited platforms.
- Availability of a pretrained model to allow the use of transfer learning techniques, adjusting the model response to new classes in small datasets.

3 Dataset for Gesture Recognition

Many gesture datasets are already publicly available for research, However, they do not correctly represent the real environmental conditions that occur in human machine interaction tasks. Examples of these type of datasets can be the dataset created by the University of Padova using Kinect and Leap Motion devices [28], The Hand Gesture Detection Dataset from the Video Processing and Understanding Lab [29], or the Hand Gesture Database [30]. In all these datasets the hands are already segmented performing gestures, and do not need to be located in the overall scene. In a real time gesture detection system, the environment has to be constantly monitored.

Also, the main application that this research covers in the human machine interaction (HMI). In HMI applications the need of many different gestures is usually limited. The use of a high variety of classes (gestures) makes the learning curve of these systems hard and their practical usability decreases.

The created dataset in this work for human machine gesture interaction consists on four different gestures, defined assuming the common interaction that occurs between a collaborative robot and an industrial worker in an assembling operation [31], named Agree, Halt, Ok and Run. Each gesture is a different position of the hand. Table 1 summarizes the four different hand positions for each gesture.

Table 1. Hand position for each gesture

AGREE	HALT	OK	RUN
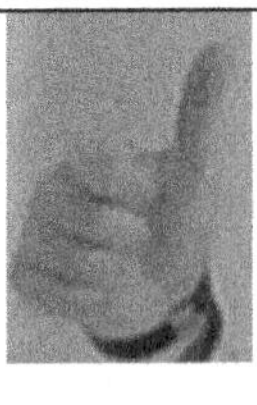	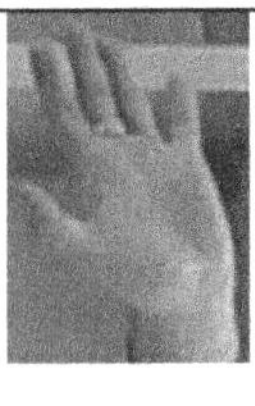	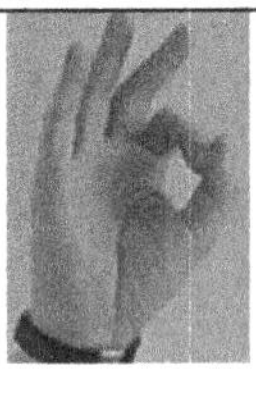	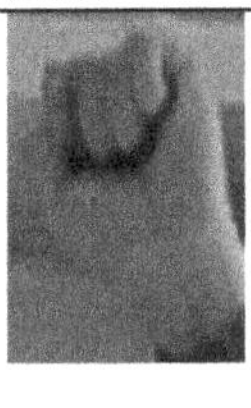

For each gesture, 100 images have been recorded and labelled. In each image, the same gesture has been performed with both hands, so a total of 200 gestures have been labelled for each class, summing up a training dataset of 800 gestures. The gestures have also been labelled at different distances from the camera, adding more variability. Figure 2 shows an example of image labelling for the Halt gesture.

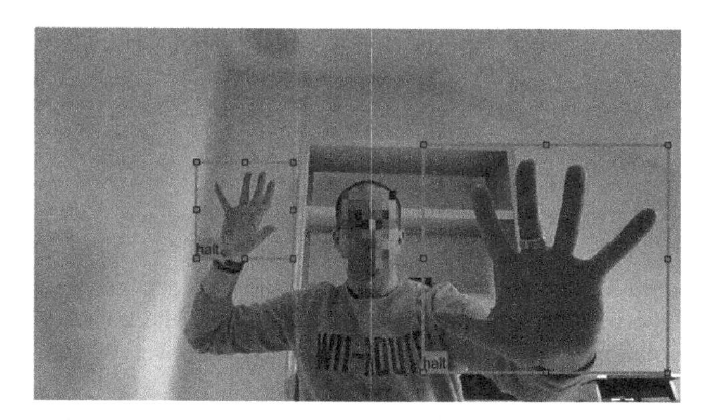

Fig. 2. Labelling for the Halt gesture

For each of the 400 images, the dataset stores the image name and the coordinates of each labelled gesture as bounding boxes, in the form (X, Y, W, H), where X and Y are the coordinates of the upper left corner, W is the width and H the height of the bounding box. The images have a resolution of 1280 * 720 pix.

4 Proposed Approach

This work proposes a new small CNN architecture, modifying the Darknet reference model presented in [32]. This is a well-known model for its speed on detection, while maintaining a relatively small size, making it suitable for our application after considering the limitations exposed in Sect. 2. This model offers its convolutional weights pre-trained with the ImageNet dataset [33].

The Darknet network consists on 32 layers, with the schema presented in Fig. 3.

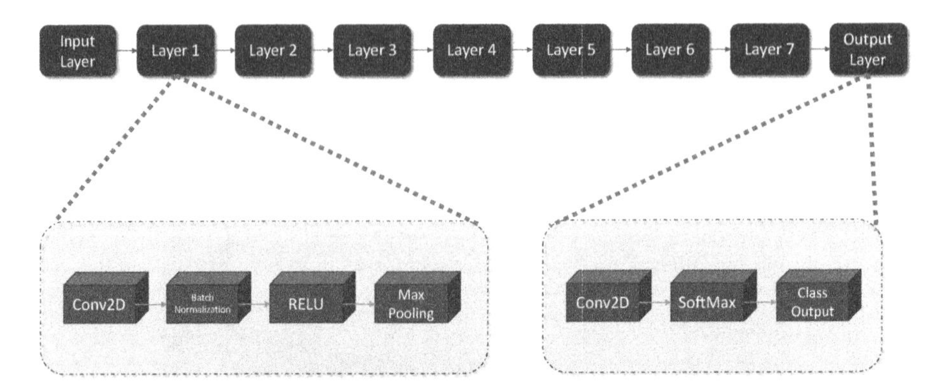

Fig. 3. Architecture of the Darknet network model

The proposed CNN in this work simplifies the Darknet model, and also takes advantage of the transfer learning approach, maintaining the trained weights of the Darknet convolutional layers. The changes carried out over the original Darknet architecture have been:

- Simplification of the intermediate convolutional layers (Fig. 5). This simplification of layers is justified by the embedded platforms framework limitations stated in Sect. 2. These changes make the network faster, smaller and more portable to many different systems.
- Change in the output stage of the network, to adapt it to the Faster RCNN object detector (Fig. 4), using a fully connected layer of 5 outputs (number of classes plus one extra to adapt the model to the RCNN detectors)

The proposed network has 25 layers instead the original 32:

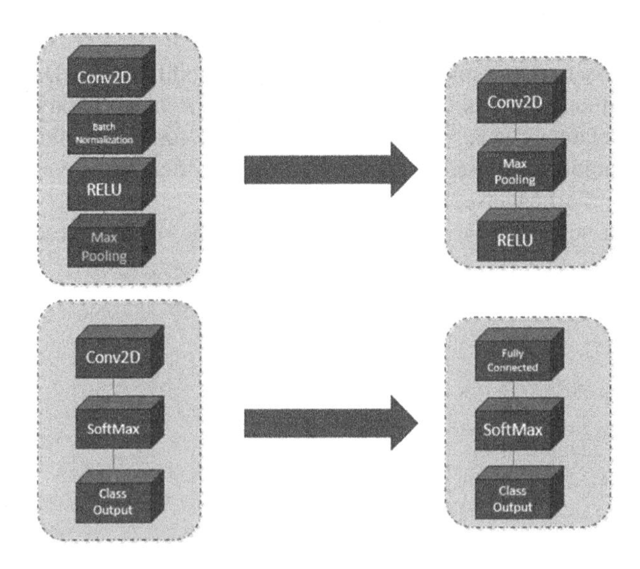

Fig. 4. Changes in the Darknet CNN model (left) to create the new CNN (right)

Table 2 shows the proposed network in this work in relation to the state of the art small CNNs, created specifically to be efficient in limited devices.

Table 2. Main characteristics of CNN networks used in RCNN detector

Network	Year	Layers	Parameters (Millions)
SqueezeNet	2016	68	1.24
GoogleNet	2015	144	7.0
Mobilenetv2	2018	155	3.5
Proposed CNN	2019	24	6.3

The proposed approach has a similar number of parameters when compared to the small existent CNNs, however, has a much lower number of layers. Taking into account that the calculations needed for each layer can be parallelized, the proposed network turns out to be much efficient in terms of computation time. This can be stated in Sect. 6.

5 Training Stage

The training parameters have been selected and adjusted empirically, according to the literature. The following section explains more precisely the internals of network parameter setting in the training stage.

5.1 Solver, Cost Function and Parameters for Network Training

The solver selected to train the network in the RCNN detectors has been the stochastic gradient descent with momentum (sgdm) optimizer. The original sgd was defined originally in [34].

The gradient descent algorithm updates the network parameters, weights and biases, to minimize the loss function by taking small steps in the direction of the negative gradient of the loss:

$$\theta_i = \theta_i - \alpha \nabla E(\theta_i) \tag{1}$$

Where l stands for the iteration number, $\alpha > 0$ is the learning rate, θ is the parameter vector and $E(\theta)$ is the loss function.

The problem with this original algorithm is that it can oscillate along the path of steepest descent in direction to the optimum.

Adding a momentum term to the original sgd algorithm can mitigate this oscillation [35]. The final expression for the sgdm is then:

$$\theta_i = \theta_i - \alpha \nabla E(\theta_i) + \gamma(\theta_i - \theta_{i-1}) \tag{2}$$

Where γ is the momentum and determines the contribution of the previous gradient step to the current iteration.

In this work, the following values have been used: $\alpha = 0.001$, $\gamma = 0.9$. A small enough learning rate allows the correct convergence of the training stage. The loss function used is cross entropy or multinomial logistic loss, shown in Eq. 3.

$$H(P_n, Q_n) = -\sum_i P_n(i) log Q_n(i) \tag{3}$$

Where P_n is the multiclass predicted vector for the sample n and Qn is the expected output vector. i is the number of classes in the classification problem.

In this case, the sgdm algorithm is evaluated using mini-batches to evaluate the gradient. Due to memory constraints, the mini-batch size has been set to 8 and the maximum number of epochs, to 10 in the case of the classical RCNN algorithm and to 40 in the Fast-RCNN and Faster-RCNN.

Finally, the number of regions proposed in the RCNN detectors′ algorithms has been lowered from their original value of 2000 to 1000. Lowering this value to its half, does not compromise the effectiveness of the detection, and memory and computation time are saved.

6 Obtained Results

The training of the different gesture recognition approaches has been carried out using a Nvidia GeForce 1080 Ti, in a PC running Ubuntu Linux 18.04 LTS and MATLAB R2019b.The Deep Learning Toolbox, along with its available tools such as the Network Designer has been used for network prototyping and testing.

6.1 Initial Validation of the Proposed CNN Architecture

The dataset has been split in two subsets: training and testing. To do it, the indexes of the 400 available images (800 gestures) have been shuffled and then, 60 (15% of the dataset, 120 gestures) have been extracted for testing. The remaining 340 labelled images (680 gestures) have been used in the training stage.

Finally, for the pre-trained models and proposed CNN a transfer learning approach has been followed.

The following table presents the results for the Faster RCNN gesture detection approach. The numerical results presented are:

- Percentage of correctly classified instances: The gesture is correctly detected and located in the image. Not detecting a gesture of detect a different one is considered the same error.
- Precision obtained in correctly detected gestures: Confidence obtained in correctly detected gestures.
- Time for gesture detection in a given instance (image). This time has been obtained as the average detection time in the 60 testing images.

Table 3. Results for Faster RCNN detector

CNN	% correct classified instances	Mean confidence	Mean detection time
Squeezenet	100%	99.83%	0.16 s
Googlenet	100%	99.85%	0.37 s
Mobilenetv2	98.33%	99.86%	0.26 s
Proposed CNN	98.33%	94.19%	0.145 s

In the Faster RCNN detector, the proposed architecture is faster than any other tested network, and the classification capabilities are comparable to those that the reference networks have.

The mean detection time is 0.14 s, which means that up to 7 images can be analyzed per second. This speed along with a 98.33% of correct classified instances, make this combination suitable for real time gesture recognition.

6.2 Performance Evaluation of the Proposed CNN Architecture

In the previous section it has been demonstrated that the proposed network architecture based on the Darknet model has a comparable performance to those of the selected reference networks, being at the same time smaller and faster.

With the proposed architecture validated, this section carries out a more in-depth training and validation of results using a 10-fold cross validation approach, to obtain more precise measurements of correct classification instances, confidence in detection and detection time.

Table 3 shows the results obtained for each iteration and the average results of the network performance, using the Faster RCNN detector.

Table 4. 10 fold cross validation of the proposed network architecture.

Fold	% correct classified instances	Mean confidence	Mean detection time (s)
1	97.56%	99.75%	0.124 s
2	98.45%	97.34%	0.147 s
3	95.3%	95%	0.152 s
4	100%	99.3%	0.161 s
5	96.34%	92.47%	0.153 s
6	98.5%	96.15%	0.139 s
7	94.3%	94.56%	0.17 s
8	97%	99.4%	0.142 s
9	92.8%	97.83%	0.122 s
10	99%	95.8%	0.151 s
Mean	96.92%	96.76%	0.1461 s

According to results present in Table 3 and Table 4, the proposed CNN offers a good balance among precision in detection, confidence in detected gestures and speed, and can be considered as a valid architecture for HMI systems in real time.

7 Conclusions and Future Work

CNNs have demonstrated in the last decade that result incredibly powerful when it comes to solve complex image processing problems where a high variability in the dataset is present. This variability can appear in several forms, such as partial occlusions, perspective changes, different sizes of the same object due to distance, changes in color and in lighting, etc.

It has been demonstrated that, for certain applications where the problem to solve is not extremely complicated and does not require the classification of a high number of different output classes, the use of a small CNN offers many advantages over the state of the art published CNN network architectures in terms of training time, computation speed and accuracy. The use of small networks allows the use of embedded systems for computation. The system is able to detect the almost the 100% (96.92%) of the gestures correctly (with the testing dataset), and it is robust to variations that can make other alternative approaches fail. These variations are very difficult to solve with skin segmentation approaches for gesture detection. In addition to this, and using a small CNN in the Faster-RCNN object detector, the average computation time for a 1Mpix image is 0.14 s using GPU computation, a time that can be considered real time for systems that use gestures as a form of interaction.

References

1. Darrel, T., Pentland, A.: Space-time gestures. In: Proceedings of IEEE Conference on Computer Vision and Pattern Recognition, pp. 335–340. IEEE (1993)
2. Starner, T., Weaver, J., Pentland, A.: Real-time American sign language recognition using desk and wearable computer-based video. IEEE Trans. Pattern Anal. Mach. Intell. **20**(1998), 1371–1375 (1998)
3. Bin, F., Fuchun, S., Huaping, L., Di, G.: Novel data glove using inertial and magnetic sensors for motion capture and robotic arm-hand teleoperation. Ind. Robot Int. J. **44**(2), 155–165 (2017)
4. Glauser, O., Wu, S., Panozzo, D., Hilliges, O., Sorkine-Hornung, O.: Interactive hand pose estimation using a stretch-sensing soft glove. ACM Trans. Graph. (TOG) **38**(4), 41 (2019)
5. Suarez, J., Murphy, R.: Hand gesture recognition with depth images: a review. In: Proceedings of RO-MAN, pp. 411–417. IEEE (2012)
6. Yan, M.H., Ahuja, N., Tabb, M.: Extraction of 2D motion trajectories and its application to hand gesture recognition. IEEE Trans. Pattern Anal. Mach. Intell. **24**, 1061–1074 (2002)
7. Ge, L., Liang, H., Yuan, J., Thalmann, D.: Real-time 3D hand pose estimation with 3D convolutional neural networks. IEEE Trans. Pattern Anal. Mach. Intell. **41**(4), 956–970 (2018)
8. Ge, L., Liang, H., Yuan, J., Thalmann, D.: Robust 3D hand pose estimation in single depth images: from single view CNN to multi-view CNNs. In: 2016 IEEE Conference on Computer Vision and Pattern Recognition (CVPR) (2016)
9. Tang, D., Chang, H.J., Tejani, A, Kim, T K.: Latent regression forest: structured estimation of 3D articulated hand posture. In: 2014 IEEE Conference on Computer Vision and Pattern Recognition (CVPR), pp. 3786–3793 (2014)

10. Google media pipeline. Google. https://github.com/google/mediapipe/. Visited on March 2020
11. Triesch, J., Von der Malsburg, C.: A gesture interface for human robot interaction. In: Proceedings of FG 1998, Nara, Japan (1998)
12. Van den Bergh, M., Van Gool, L.: Combining RGB and ToF cameras for real-time 3D hand gesture interaction. In: IEEE Workshop on Applications of Computer Vision (WACV 2011), Kona, USA (2011). https://doi.org/10.1109/wacv.2011.5711485
13. Krizhevsky, A., Sutskever, I., Hinton, G.E.: ImageNet classification with deep convolutional neural networks. In: NIPS Proceedings (2012)
14. Lin, T.Y., Maire, M., et al.: Microsoft COCO: Common Objects in Context. arXiv:1405.0312v3 (2015)
15. Szgedy, C., Liu, W., et al.: Going deeper with convolutions. arXiv:1409.4842v1 (2014)
16. Simonyan, K., Zisserman, A.: Very Deep Convolutional Networks for large-scale Image Recognition. arXiv:1409.1556v6. (2015)
17. He, K., Zhang, X., et al.: Deep residual learning for image recognition. arXiv:1512.03385v1 (2015)
18. Zhao, Z.Q, Xu, S.T., Wu, X.: Object detection with deep learning: a review. arXiv:1807.05511 (2018)
19. Girshick, R., Donahue, J., et al.: Rich feature hierarchies for accurate object detection and semantic segmentation. arXiv:1311.2524v5 (2014)
20. Zitnick, C.L., Dollár, P.: Edge boxes: locating object proposals from edges. In: Fleet, D., Pajdla, T., Schiele, B., Tuytelaars, T. (eds.) ECCV 2014. LNCS, vol. 8693, pp. 391–405. Springer, Cham (2014). https://doi.org/10.1007/978-3-319-10602-1_26
21. Girshick, R.: Fast R-CNN. In: Proceedings of the IEEE International Conference Computer Vision (2015)
22. Shaoqing, R., He, K., et al.: Faster R-CNN: towards real-time object detection with region proposal networks. In: Advances in Neural Information Processing Systems 28 (2015)
23. Ma, Y., Wang, C.: SdcNet: a computation-efficient CNN for object recognition. arXiv:1805.01317v2 (2018)
24. Cong, J., Xiao, B.: Minimizing computation in convolutional neural networks. International Conference on Artificial Neural Nets, Hamburg, Germany (2014)
25. Iandola, F.N., Han, S., et al.: SqueezeNet: AlexNet-level accuracy with 50x fewer parameters and < 0.5 MB model size. arXiv:1602.07360v4 (2016)
26. Szegedy, C., et al.: Going deeper with convolutions. arXiv preprint arXiv:1409.4842. (2014)
27. Sandler, M., Howard, A., et al.: MobileNetV2: inverted residuals and linear bottleneks. In: IEEE Conference Computer Vision and Pattern Recognition (CVPR), Salt Lake City, USA, pp. 4510–4520 (2018)
28. Marin, G., Dominio, F., Zanuttigh, P.: Hand gesture recognition with leap motion and kinect devices. IEEE International Conference Image Processing, Paris, France (2014)
29. Molina, J., Pajuelo, J.A., Escudero-Viñolo, M., Bescós, J., Martínez, J.M.: A natural and synthetic corpus for benchmarking of hand gesture recognition systems. Mach. Vis. Appl. **25** (4), 943–954 (2013). https://doi.org/10.1007/s00138-013-0576-z
30. Maqueda, A.I., del Blanco, C.R., Jaureguizar, F., García, N.: Human-computer interaction based on visual hand-gesture recognition using volumetric spatiograms of local binary patterns. Comput. Vis. Image. Und. **141**, 126–137 (2015)
31. Maurtua, I., et al.: Natural multimodal communication for human-robot collaboration. Int. J. Adv. Robot. Syst. **10**(1), 53–62 (2017)
32. Redmon, J.: Darknet: Open Source Networks in C. http://pjreddie.com/darknet/ (2016)

33. ImageNet Large Scale Visual Recognition Challenge (ILSVRC). http://www.image-net.org/challenges/LSVRC/
34. Robbins, H., Monro, S.: A stochastic approximation method. Ann. Math. Stat. **22**(3), 400–407 (1951)
35. Murphy, K.P.: Machine Learning: A Probabilistic Perspective. The MIT Press, Cambridge (2012)

Tourists Movement Analysis Based on Entropies of Markov Process

Naohiro Ishii[1(✉)], Kazuya Odagiri[2], Hidekazu Iwamoto[3], Satoshi Takahashi[4], Kazunori Iwata[5], and Tokuro Matsuo[1]

[1] Advanced Institute of Industrial Technology, Tokyo, Japan
nishii@acm.org, matsuo@aiit.ac.jp
[2] Sugiyama Jyogakuen University, Nagoya, Japan
kodagiri@sugiyama-u.ac.jp
[3] Josai International University, Tokyo, Japan
iwamoto@jiu.ac.jp
[4] Electro-Communication University, Tokyo, Japan
takahashi@uec.ac.jp
[5] Aichi University, Nagoya, Japan
kazunori@vega.aichi-u.ac.jp

Abstract. Tourist movement studies have been carried out for understanding tourists decisions for visiting and sightseeing. Knowing tourist interests and wayfinding decision-making affect tourists routes and facilities since the planners and hotel facilities will do planning their hospitality and every service plans using their information. To make the model of the tourist movements, an effective mathematical description will be expected for their systematic analysis. In this paper, Markov process model of the tourist movements are newly developed using information theory. Then, it is shown that the order of Markov process of the movements is estimated using conditional entropies, efficiently and the shuffling operation of Markov process is newly proposed to verify conditional entropies of the Markov process. The stochastic simulation model based on the analysis is useful for the verification of the Markov process with the estimated order of the behavior of tourists movement.

Keywords: Movement of tourists · Conditional entropies · Order of Markov process · Shuffling for Markov process

1 Introduction

The tourists visit and travel sightseeing spots in the domestic or foreign countries. Tracking tourists movement patterns plays a fundamental role in understanding tourist behavior, which is applicable to management activities, planning and tour product development [1, 2]. Spatio-temporal movement of tourists has useful information for the management to satisfy their aims and minds and the majority of tourist movement modelling studies have been focused on spatial movement patterns of tourists [3–5]. The movement study using systematic approach is expected to develop tourists behavior, effectively, which means the analysis, modeling and its validation. It is useful for the tourist movements whether the successive events depend on one or more immediately

E. A. de la Cal et al. (Eds.): HAIS 2020, LNAI 12344, pp. 573–584, 2020.
https://doi.org/10.1007/978-3-030-61705-9_47

preceding ones, which are described in the model of Markov process. The movement of tourists using Markov process will show their effective actions and essential behavior for their systematic analysis. Conventional modeling of tourists movements is studied using Markov chains which are assumed to be the first order dependence [1]. Relatively little attention has been paid to the estimation of the order of Markov process, since it takes much data statistically to estimate and test the transition probabilities for their higher order transition matrices [8]. In this paper, it is shown that the Shannon's conditional entropies play an important role to estimate the Markov properties of the movement of tourists, systematically. Further, the Markov model of the movement is developed, systematically, which is based on the conditional entropies [6, 7]. To make sure their entropy values, shuffling operations of the Markov process is proposed and carried out to confirm the Markov process with the estimated order. It is clarified that the entropies approach is effective for the systematic study of the movement of tourists. This study will be applicable also to the management system for the convention participants [10].

2 Statistical Dependent Relations Using Entropies

Statistical dependent relations of the stochastic events are described in the Shannon's entropies [5, 6], as follows.

Let $\{X_n,\ n \in I\}$ be a stochastic process, where X_n is a stochastic variable at time n and I shows a set of discrete time. The stochastic process is defined to be the m-th order Markov process using conditional entropies, if and only if the following equations hold,

$$\begin{aligned} &p(X_{m+1} = x_{m+1}|X_1 = x_1, X_2 = x_2 \cdots, X_m = x_m) \\ &\neq p(X_{m+1} = x_{m+1}|X_2 = x_2 \cdots, X_m = x_m) \end{aligned}$$

and

$$\begin{aligned} &p(X_{m+1} = x_{m+1}|X_{-i} = x_{-i}, X_{-i+1} = x_{-i+1} \cdots, X_m = x_m) \\ &= p(X_{m+1} = x_{m+1}|X_{-i+1} = x_{-i+1} \cdots, X_m = x_m) \qquad (i = 1, 2, \cdots), \end{aligned} \tag{1}$$

where $p(a|b)$ implies the occurrence probability a under the occurrence b.

The following inequality (2) of arithmetic and geometric means [2] is useful for the entropies.

$$\left(\frac{q_1}{p_1}\right)^{p_1}\left(\frac{q_2}{p_2}\right)^{p_2}\cdots\left(\frac{q_n}{p_n}\right)^{p_n} \le p_1\left(\frac{q_1}{p_1}\right) + p_2\left(\frac{q_2}{p_2}\right)\cdots + p_n\left(\frac{q_n}{p_n}\right), \tag{2}$$

where the equality, = in the Eq. (2) holds for $p_i = q_i$, $(i = 1, 2, \ldots, n)$. By log transformation of the Eq. (2) becomes

$$-\sum_{i=1}^{n} p_i \log p_i \le -\sum_{i=1}^{n} p_i \log q_i, \tag{3}$$

where the equality, = in the Eq. (3) holds for $p_i = q_i$, $(i = 1, 2, \ldots, n)$. By replacing p_i to $p(i, j, k)$ and q_i to $p(i, j) \cdot p(k|j)$ in the Eq. (3), the following equation is obtained.

$$-\sum_i \sum_j \sum_k p(i,j,k) \log p(i,j,k) \leq -\sum_i \sum_j \sum_k p(i,j,k) \log p(i,j) \cdot p(k|j), \quad (4)$$

where the equality, = in the Eq. (4) holds for $p(k|i,j) = p(k|j)$.

From the Eq. (4), the following Eq. (5) is derived.

$$-\sum_i \sum_j \sum_k p(i,j,k) \log p(k|i,j) \leq -\sum_j \sum_k p(j,k) \log p(k|j) \quad (5)$$

The left side of the Eq. (5) shows the second order conditional entropy, while the right side of that equation shows the first order one. The Eq. (5) is extended to the general inequality inductively as follows,

the n-th order conditional entropy $\leq$ the (n − 1) th order conditional entropy (6)

Then, the necessary and sufficient condition for the m-th order Markov process is to satisfy the following Eq. (7) based on the conditional entropies,

$$H_0 \geq H_1 \geq H_2 \geq \cdots H_{m-1} \geq H_m = H_{m+1} = \cdots, \quad (7)$$

where H_i is the m-th order conditional entropy shown in the following,

$$H_i = -\sum_{l_1} \sum_{l_2} \cdots \sum_{l_{i+1}} p(l_1, l_2, \ldots, l_{i+1}) \log p(l_{i+1}|l_1, l_2, \cdots, l_i), \quad i = 0, 1, 2, \ldots \quad (8)$$

Since the joint entropy Z_{i+1} is represented as follows,

$$Z_{i+1} = -\sum_{l_1} \sum_{l_2} \cdots \sum_{l_{i+1}} p(l_1, \cdots, l_{i+1}) \log p(l_1, l_2, \cdots, l_{i+1}), \quad (9)$$

the conditional entropy H_i is represented using the joint entropies $\{Z_i\}$. Using the joint entropies $\{Z_i\}$, the m-th order Markov process is defined as follows.

The necessary and sufficient condition to be m-th order Markov process is given,

For all the integers n's less than the integer m,

$$Z_{n-1} - Z_{n-2} \geq Z_n - Z_{n-1}$$

For the integer n equal to the integer m,

$$Z_{n-1} - Z_{n-2} > Z_n - Z_{n-1} \quad (10)$$

For all the integer n's more than the integer m,

$$Z_{n-1} - Z_{n-2} = Z_n - Z_{n-1}$$

3 Application of Markov Process to Tourists Movement

Tourists visit several sightseeing places. Are there any stochastic properties for their sightseeing behaviors? Tourists movements show some properties from their routes. The Hokkaido island is well known, in which areas of the Hokkaido island are classified as A, B, C and D in Fig. 1. The tourists movement is reported officially in the Hokkaido Tourism Bureau in Fig. 2[9]. The alphabets shown in Fig. 2 are assigned as the areas of the sightseeing places in Hokkaido: the A implies the central area of the Hokkaido, the B for the northern area, the C for the southern area, the D for the

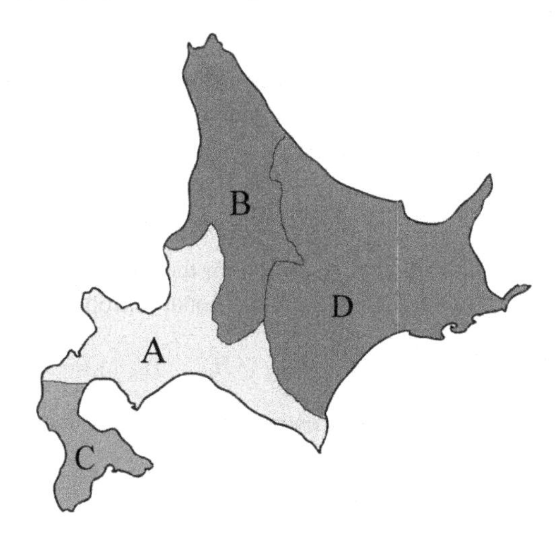

Fig. 1. Hokkaido island (A: Central, B: North, C: South, D: East)

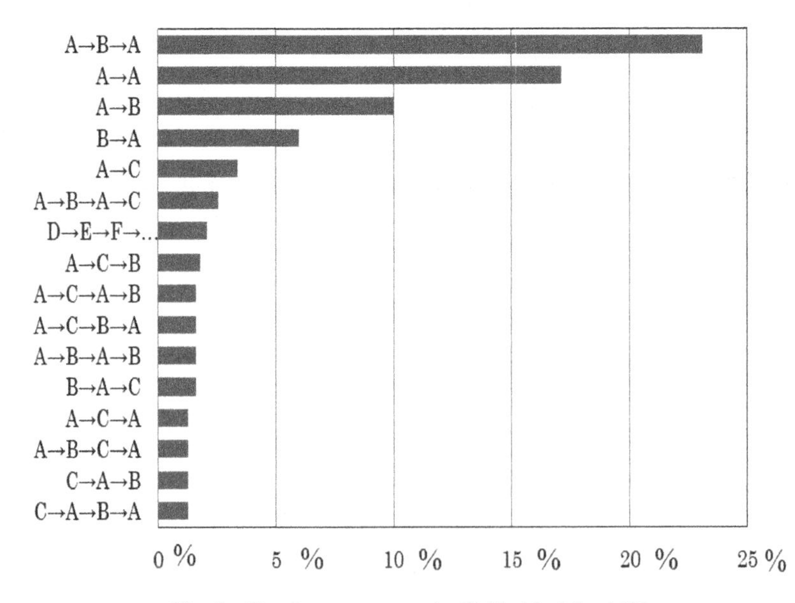

Fig. 2. Tourists movement in Hokkaido island [9]

Ohotsuku ocean area, the E for the Eastern area and the F for the west of the Hokkaido, respectively [9]. Tourist routes are given in Table 1. From Table 1, the dendrogram is made in Fig. 3 as shown in the following.

Table 1. Ratio of tourists movements in Fig. 1

Tourists routes	Ratio
A→B→A	23.1%
A→A	17.1%
A→B	10.0%
B→A	6.0%
A→C	3.4%
A→B→A→C	2.6%
D→E→F→.	2.1%
A→C→B	1.8%
A→C→A→B	1.6%
A→C→B→A	1.6%
A→B→A→B	1.6%
B→A→C	1.6%
A→C→A	1.3%
A→B→C→A	1.3%
C→A→B	1.3%
C→A→B→A	1.3%

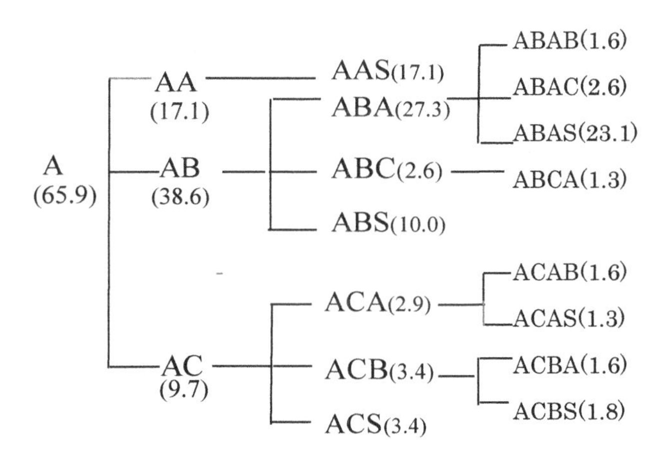

Fig. 3. Dendrogram of tourists movements from Fig. 2

The dendrogram in Fig. 3 is made in the following steps. First, the tourists routes including A in Table 1 consist of the set of the sequences A → B → A(23.1%), A → A(17.1%), A → B(10.0%), A → C(3.4%), A → B → A → C(2.6%), A → C → B(1.8%), A → C → A → B(1.6%), A → C → B → A(1.6%), A → B → A → B(1.6%), A → C → A(1.3%) and A → B → C → A(1.3%). Second, the ratio of the first A becomes the summation of ratios of these sequences, that is, 65.9%. Thus, the root of the dendrogram of the A is 65.9% in Fig. 3. Third, the branches from the root A is AA, AB and AC. The ratio of branch AA becomes that of the summation of the sub-sequence A $\rightarrow$ A in the above sequences becomes 17.1%. Thus, AA in Fig. 3 becomes 17.1%. Further, the ratios of branches AAS, ABA, ABC, ABS, ACA, ACB, ACS are computed. From the data of tourists routes in Table 1, the ratios of branches of 4 tuples are computed as shown in Fig. 3. Similar dendrograms of the roots B, C and D are made. Here, the ABS in Fig. 3 is the stopped state of the AB.

3.1 Estimation of the First and Second Order Transition Probabilities

The transition probabilities of tourists routes are computed from the dendrogram in Fig. 3. The transition probability is fundamental transition numerical value from the previous event to the present event. As an example, $p(B|A)$ shows the first order transition probability from the previous (conditional) event, A, to the present event, B. The dendrogram shows the first order transition probabilities: the transition probability $p(A|A) = p(A,A)/p(A) = 17.1/65.4 = 0.2614$, which is shown in AA(17.1) and A(65.9) in Fig. 2, also $p(B|A) = p(A,B)/p(A) = 38.6/65.4 = 0.590$ shown in AB(38.6) and A(65.9) in Fig. 3, $p(C|A) = p(A,C)/p(A) = 9.7/65.4 = 0.148$. Similarly, $p(A|B) = 1.0$ and $p(A|C) = 1.0$ are derived. Next, the second order transition probability $p(B|A,A)$ shows the probability from two step previous event, A and one step one, A to the present event, B. The second order transition probability $p(A|A,A) = p(A,A,A)/p(A,A) = 1.0$ is assumed, which is shown in AAS(17.1) and AA(17.1) in Fig. 2. Here, the stopping state event is assumed to be one step continuation of the previous event. The second order transition probability $p(A|A,B) = p(A,B,A)/p(A,B) = 27.3/38.6 = 0.707$ is also derived from the dendrogram ABA(27.3) and AB(38.6) in Fig. 3. All the other second order transition probabilities are derived from the dendrogram in Fig. 3.

The 0-th order entropy H_0, the first order entropy H_1 and the second order entropy H_2 are computed as follows,

$$
\begin{aligned}
H_0 &= -\sum_{i=A,B,C,D} p(i)\log_2 p(i) \\
&= -0.654\log_2 0.654 - 0.076\log_2 0.076 - 0.026\log_2 0.026 - 0.021\log_2 0.021 \\
&= 0.940
\end{aligned}
$$

$$
H_1 = -\sum_i \sum_j p(i,j)\log_2 p(j|i) = 0.892
$$

and

$$
H_2 = -\sum_i \sum_j \sum_k p(i,j,k)\log_2 p(k|i,j) = 0.605
$$

These entropy values for the tourists movements are graphed in Fig. 4.

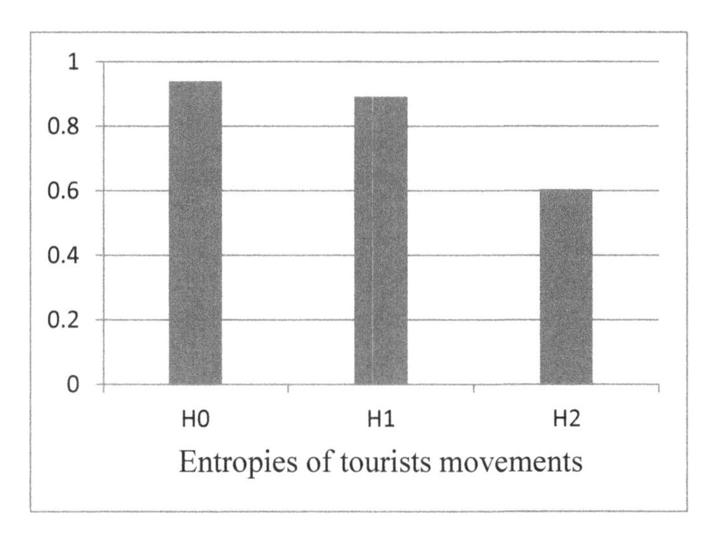

Fig. 4. Entropies of tourists movements, H_0, H_1 and H_2

From Fig. 4, Markov order for the tourists movements seems to be more than the order 2, since the value of entropies decreases from H_1 to H_2. To estimate Markov order for the tourists movements, a stochastic Markov model for tourists routes are generated using transition probabilities derived from the dendrogram of tourists routes in Fig. 3.

4 Stochastic Model Based on Conditional Entropies for Tourists Movement

In order to extract characteristic information from the tourist movements, some stochastic model will be useful generated the real observed data. The observed data are often not sufficient for the estimation of the higher order characteristics of the tourists movements in this study. Since the behavior of the higher order Markov properties are computed using sufficient data, it is often difficult to compute them by the real few observed data. To solve these insufficient data problems, any simulated models are expected to estimate the higher order Markov properties. The stochastic simulated models are generated using probability transition matrices computed from the tourists movement data. The stochastic movement model is made as shown in Fig. 5.

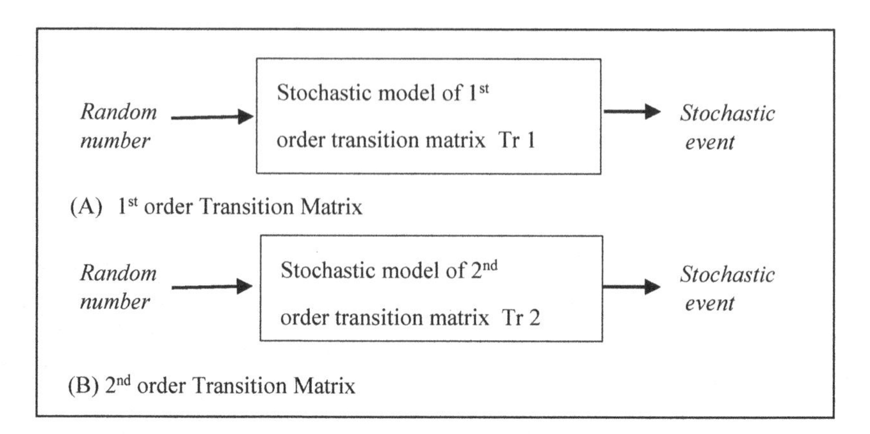

Fig. 5. Simulated stochastic models for tourist movements

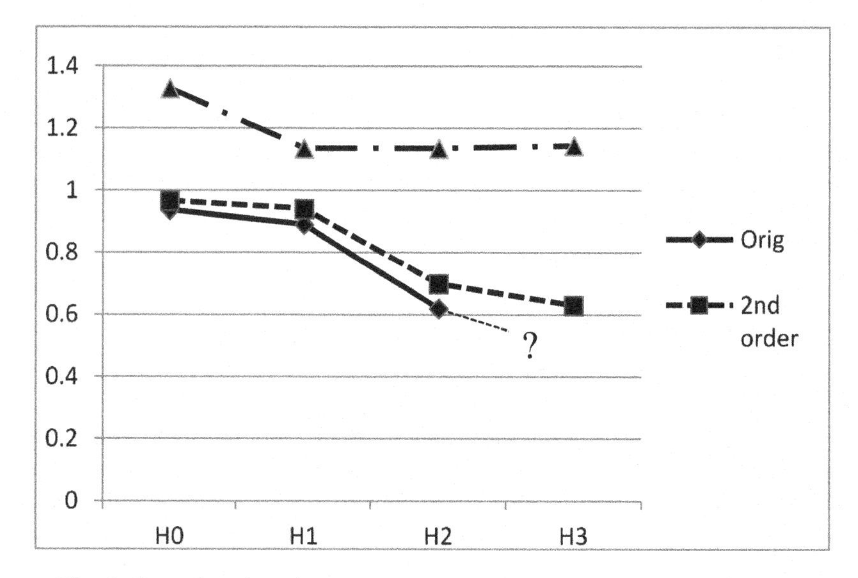

Fig. 6. Entropies of tourist movement data and its simulated stochastic models

In Fig. 6, entropies values of the tourists movements are shown in solid line, in which H_0, H_1 and H_2 are computed, while those of the models with the 1st order transition matrix and the 2nd order transition matrix are shown in the large dotted line and the small one, respectively. Figure 6 shows the model with the 2nd order transition matrix is fitted to the original tourist movements data, while one of the 1st order transition matrix, Tr1 does not interpret the original movement data. Further, since the model with the 2nd order transition matrix, Tr2 can estimate the 3rd order entropies, this Markov process is estimated to be the 2nd order Markov one. This is because the value of the 3rd order entropy, H_3 is not decreased largely than that of the 2nd order one, H_2 in Fig. 6. Thus, the original tourist movement is estimated to have the 2nd order Markov process. Occurrence of some three consecutive events {A, B, C} of original data is compared with those of the 2nd order model and the 1st order model in Fig. 7. Each bar graph in Fig. 7 shows the value with %. In Fig. 7, the first black bar in the three consecutive events, 'AAA' shows the occurrence of the original data, while the second white bar shows the occurrence generated by the transition matrix of the 2nd order Markov model. The third dotted line bar in Fig. 7 shows those generated by the transition matrix of the 1-st order Markov model. The 2nd order Markov model shows to be near to the original events than the 1st order Markov model.

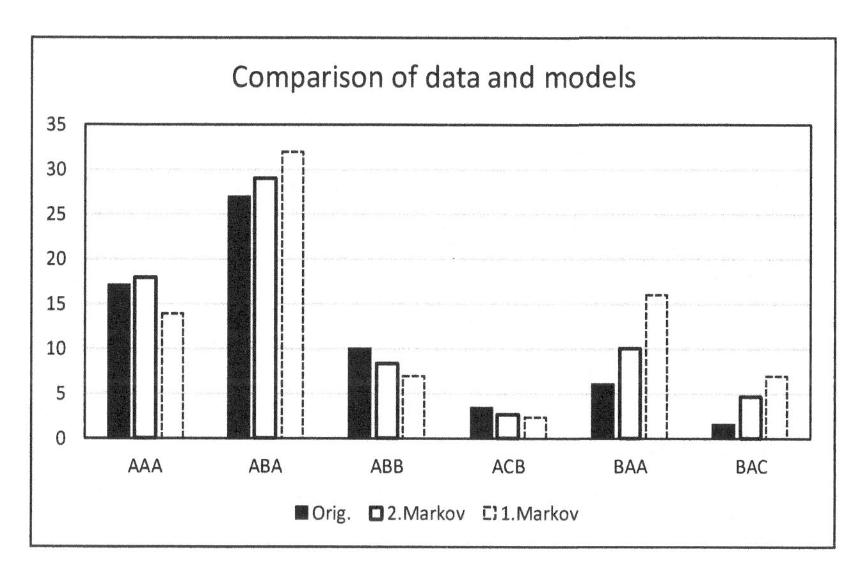

Fig. 7. Comparison of some consecutive three events among data and models

5 Shuffling Operations for Markov Model

When the observed experimental data are insufficient as the sampling data, the higher order properties are not computed by their small samples. Then, these models using transition matrices made from the observed small data can estimate their Markov properties of the observed data. In the previous studies, card shuffling is studied [11], in which the times of a deck of shuffled cards are discussed until it is close to random. The given computed entropy in this paper, has its value between the value of the lower order entropy and that of the higher order one. Then, the respective order entropy has its occurrence distribution of the stochastic events. Is it possible to realize the shuffling for the Markov process under these conditions? The shuffling of the second order Markov process is realized in the following subsequence. First, the subsequence is assumed to be the following stochastic events with second order Markov process.

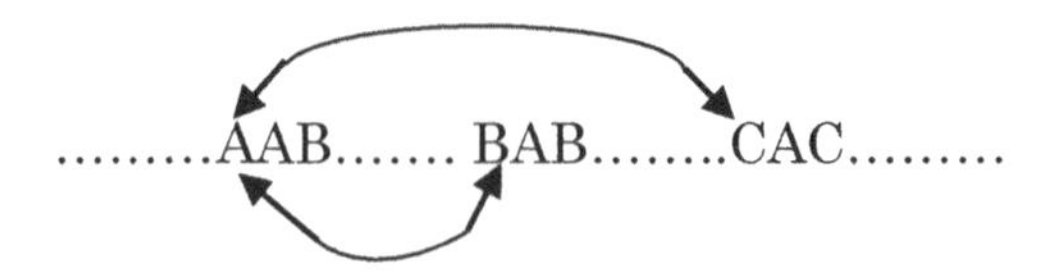

Fig. 8. Shuffling the second order Markov process

The second order Markov process implies the present state is affected from the states of the previous two steps before and one step before. When the present event 'B' in the 'AAB' in Fig. 8 is taken, the 'AA' consists of the event, 'A' of the previous two steps and also the event, 'A' of the previous one step before the event, 'B'. Similar event sequences, 'BAB' and 'CAC' have the same properties of Markov process. To remove the second order Markov properties under the condition of preserving the first order Markov properties, a shuffling method using random number is shown in arrowed lines in Fig. 8. The first event, 'A' in the 'AAB' is interchanged with the first one, 'C' in the 'CAC' or with the first one, 'B' in the 'BAB'. By the above shuffling, the occurrence 'AB', 'BA' and 'CA' does not change. This shuffling is formulated as follows. The joint probability of the above three successive events is shown in $p(i, j, k)$. Then, the interchanged variable is assumed to be i''. Thus, the joint probability with the interchanged variable i'' is shown in $p(i'', j, k)$. The problem here is to make clear the range of the shuffled second order entropy. First, the comparison is between the 1st order entropy, H_1 and the shuffled 2nd order entropy, $H_{2shuffled}$, which is generated using the shuffled operation in Fig. 8.

$$\begin{aligned} H_1 - H_{2shuffled} &= -\sum_i \sum_j p(i,j)\log(p(i,j)/p(i)) + \sum_i \sum_j \sum_k p(i'',j,k)\log(p(i'',j,k)/p(i,j)) \\ &= +2\sum_i p(i)\log p(i) - \sum_i \sum_j p(i'',j)\log p(i,j) \\ &\geq +2\sum_i p(i)\log p(i) \sum_i \sum_j p(i'',j)\log p(i'',j) = 0, \end{aligned} \tag{11}$$

where the inequality between the 2nd and 3rd equations holds using the Eq. (3) with two variables, i and j. By the Eqs. (11), the following equation holds.

$$H_1 \geq H_{2shuffled} \tag{12}$$

Next, the comparison is between the shuffled 2nd order entropy, $H_{2shuffled}$ and the 2nd order entropy.

$$
\begin{aligned}
H_{2shuffled} - H_2 &= -\sum_i \sum_j \sum_k p(i'',j,k) \log(p(i'',j,k)/p(i,j)) \\
&+ \sum_i \sum_j \sum_k p(i,j,k) \log(p(i,j,k)/p(i,j)) \\
&= -\sum_i p(i) \log p(i) - 2\sum_i \sum_j p(i,j) \log p(i,j) \\
&+ \sum_i \sum_j p(i'')p(i) \log p(i,j) + \sum_i \sum_j \sum_k p(i,j,k) \log(p(i,j,k)) \\
&\geq -\sum_i \sum_j p(i,j) \log(p(i,j)/p(i)) - \sum_i \sum_j \sum_k p(i,j,k) \log(p(i,j,k)/p(i,j)) \\
&= H_1 - H_2 \geq 0,
\end{aligned}
\tag{13}
$$

where the inequality between the 4th and 5th equations holds using the Eq. (3) with two variables, i and j. Further, the 6th equation is derived from the Eq. (7). By the Eqs. (13), the following equation holds.

$$H_{2shuffled} \geq H_2 \tag{14}$$

Thus, from Eqs. (12) and (14), the range of is obtained.

$$H_{2shuffled} H_1 \geq H_{2shuffled} \geq H_2 \tag{15}$$

The shuffled values are shown in Fig. 9. In Fig. 9, the shuffling ratio 5% and 15% are shown, in which the ratio implies the shuffling number/total number of data. These shuffling values are greater than the second order entropy, H_2 of the model.

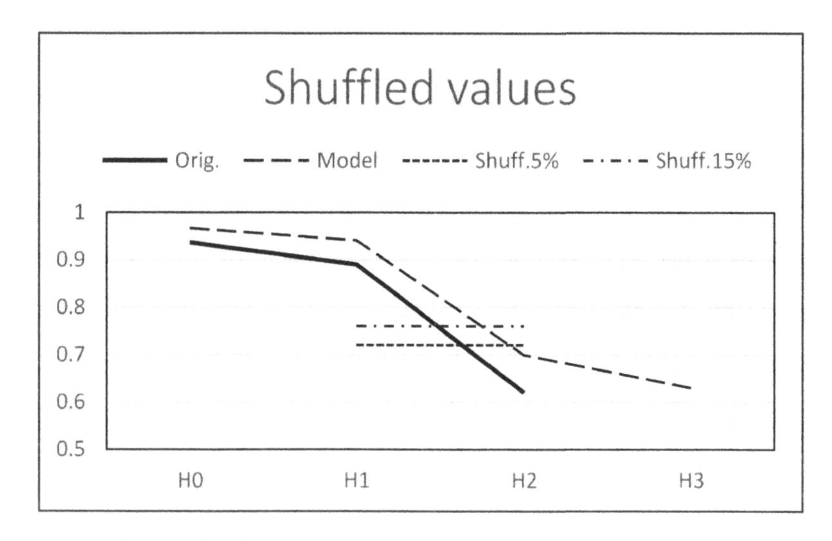

Fig. 9. Shuffled value for the tourist movement Markov model

6 Conclusion

Tourists movement is a complex process, represented in the spatio-temporal stochastic events. This paper develops how to describe the tourists movement for their analysis and modeling using the Markov process, which is based on the conditional entropies. In this paper, it is shown that the Shannon's conditional entropies play an important role to estimate the Markov properties of the movement of tourists, to generate the movement model and to validate entropy values, systematically. To make sure their entropy values, shuffling operations of the Markov process is proposed and carried out. It was clarified for the tourists movement analysis and modeling to develop based on the conditional entropies of the Markov process.

References

1. Xia, J.C., Zeephongsekul, P., Packer, D., Arrowsmith, C.: Modelling spatio-temporal movement of tourists using finite Markov chains. Math. Comput. Simul. **79**, 1544–1553 (2009)
2. McKercher, B., Lau, G.: Movement patterns of tourists within a destination. Tourism Geograph. **10**(5), 355–374 (2008)
3. Dumont, B., Ropvers, P., Gulink, H.: Estimation of off-track visits in a nature reserve: a case study in central Belgium. Landscape Urban Plann. **71**(2–4), 311–321 (2005)
4. O'Connor, A., Zerger, A., Itami, B.: Geo-temporal tracking and analysis of tourist movement. Math. Comput. Simul. **69**(1–2), 135–150 (2005)
5. Lew, A., McKercher, B.: Modeling tourist movements: a local destination analysis. Ann. Tourism Res. **33**(2), 403–423 (2006)
6. Shannon, C., Weaver, W.: The Mathematical Theory of Communication. Univ. of Illinois Press, Urbana (1949)
7. Cover, T., M., Thomas, J.A.: Elements of Information Theory, Wiley (2006)
8. Nakahama, H., Ishii, N., Yamamoto, M.: Markov process of maintained impulse activity in central single neurons. Kybernetik **11**, 61–72 (1972)
9. Hokkaido Tourism Bureau (2018). 9Thttp://www.pref.hokkaido.lg.jp/kz/kkd/h28-cs06.pdf9T
10. Matsuo, T., Iwamoto, H.: Analysis of motivation of convention participants and proposal of attendance management system. In: Proceedings of the IEEE-ACIS SNPD, pp. 621–626. IEEE Computer Society (2017)
11. Aldous, D., Diaconis, P.: Shuffling cards and stopping times. Am. Math. Mon. **93**(5), 333–348 (1986)

Clustering Imputation for Air Pollution Data

Wedad Alahamade[1,3](✉), Iain Lake[1], Claire E. Reeves[2], and Beatriz De La Iglesia[1]

[1] University of East Anglia, Norwich Research Park, Norwich NR4 7TJ, UK
{W.Alahamade,i.lake,B.Iglesia}@uea.ac.uk
[2] Centre for Ocean and Atmospheric Sciences, School of Environmental Sciences, University of East Anglia, Norwich, UK
c.reeves@uea.ac.uk
[3] Taibah University, Medina, Saudi Arabia
https://www.uea.ac.uk/
https://www.taibahu.edu.sa/

Abstract. Air pollution is a global problem. The assessment of air pollution concentration data is important for evaluating human exposure and the associated risk to health. Unfortunately, air pollution monitoring stations often have periods of missing data or do not measure all pollutants. In this study, we experiment with different approaches to estimate the whole time series for a missing pollutant at a monitoring station as well as missing values within a time series. The main goal is to reduce the uncertainty in air quality assessment.

To develop our approach we combine single and multiple imputation, nearest neighbour geographical distance methods and a clustering algorithm for time series. For each station that measures ozone, we produce various imputations for this pollutant and measure the similarity/error between the imputed and the real values. Our results show that imputation by average based on clustering results combined with multiple imputation for missing values is the most reliable and is associated with lower average error and standard deviation.

Keywords: Air quality · Uncertainty · Time series clustering · Imputation

1 Introduction

Air is one of the essential natural resources not only for humans but for all life on this planet. With the development of economies throughout the world and population increases in cities, environmental problems involving air pollution have attracted increasing attention. Air pollution is defined as the contamination of the atmosphere by substances called *pollutants.* According to Kampa and Castanas [11], the air pollutants that negatively affect human health and

E. A. de la Cal et al. (Eds.): HAIS 2020, LNAI 12344, pp. 585–597, 2020.
https://doi.org/10.1007/978-3-030-61705-9_48

the environment include carbon monoxide (CO), particulate matter ($PM_{2.5}$ and PM_{10}), ozone (O_3), nitrogen dioxide (NO_2) and sulfur dioxide (SO_2).

There are several detrimental effects of air pollution on health and the environment and its effect on human health in particular attracts considerable research effort.

For example, several epidemiological studies have proven the associations between air pollutants and asthma e.g. [6], mortality e.g. [28] and morbidity e.g. [7]. The World Health Organization [26], estimated that 4.2 million premature deaths per year are linked to air pollution.

The air pollutant concentrations that are used to determine the air quality index in the UK are O_3, NO_2, SO_2, PM_{10}, and $PM_{2.5}$. These are measured at the Automatic Urban and Rural Network (AURN), which has 168 stations distributed around the UK. There are 165 stations that measure NO_2, 86 stations that measure $PM_{2.5}$, 82 stations that measure PM_{10}, and 83 stations that measure O_3. Stations are categorized by their environmental type to one of the following: rural, urban background, roadside, and industrial. Not all the AURN stations report all pollutants, as this mainly depends on the purpose of the monitoring station. Even though a station measures a particular air pollutant there are times them no data are reported, for example during periods of instrument failure or servicing. Together this results in high levels of missing data. Therefore current air quality assessments are based on high levels of uncertainty. This may lead to incorrect policy decisions, with further negative environmental and health consequences [8]. Our aim is therefore to investigate robust methods for estimating the missing observations.

In this study we focus on imputation of ozone (O_3), one of the main pollutants influencing pollution levels in the UK. We apply two different approaches to estimate the missing pollutant in a station: an imputation based on geographical distance, and one based on clustering. We then assess which results in more robust and accurate imputation. In the long term we hope that our imputed pollutant values, if accurate, will enable us to calculate new air quality indices and to show where more measurements may be beneficial.

2 Related Work

In the context of environmental data various techniques have been proposed to impute missing values using single imputation such as mean [14,16]; Nearest Neighbor (NN) algorithms [3,29]; linear interpolation [2] and Expectation Maximization (EM) [10]. Other authors [16,18] have replaced each missing value of PM_{10} by the mean of the two data points before and after the missing value. In a similar study, Luong et al. [14] used the daily mean of each variable to replace the missing values. Their dataset contains temperature, PM_{10}, $PM_{2.5}$, NO_2, and SO_2.

Zheng et al. [29] used station spatial or temporal neighbours to fill the missing values in each monitoring station. Then, they built a model to forecast the readings of an air quality monitoring station over the next 48 hours for $PM_{2.5}$. Azid et al. [3] used NN based on distance to impute the missing data.

Arroyo et al. [2] used multiple regression techniques (linear and nonlinear) and artificial neural network models to impute the missing values in the daily data averages of ozone based on the concentrations of five other pollutants: NO, NO_2, PM_{10}, SO_2, and CO. Jhun et al. [9] estimated the missing data for an O_3 hourly trend dataset using criteria in the dataset such as the hour of the day, season at each region, and the seasonal pattern of the trend. The Expectation Maximization (EM) algorithm is often used to fill the missing data using available data in the cases when the missing data has a linear relation with the available data [10]. Some other studies deleted any incomplete data and only considered data that are captured between 50% to 75% of the time [9,27].

3 Problem Definition

3.1 Air Quality

The quality of air is negatively affected by particles and gases which can be influenced by several factors including location, time, and other variables [12]. In the UK, air quality is quantified using the Daily Air Quality Index (DAQI) which is calculated using the concentrations of five air pollutants namely nitrogen dioxide (NO_2), sulphur dioxide (SO_2), ozone (O_3), particles <2.5 ($PM_{2.5}$), and particles <10 (PM_{10}). This index is numbered from 1 to 10, and divided into four bands: 'low' (1–3), 'moderate' (4–6), 'high' (7–9) and 'very high' (10). An index value is initially assigned for each pollutant depending on its measured concentration. Then the DAQI is taken to be the highest value assigned to a pollutant. Periods of poor air quality can be identified using this index. Air quality is negatively correlated with the DAQI index, meaning that a higher DAQI index represents worse air quality (for more details https://uk-air.defra.gov.uk/air-pollution/).

There are DAQI values calculated for different stations and geographical areas. However, sufficient data must be available for this. For example, to calculate the particles (PM_{10}, $PM_{2.5}$) daily mean contributing to the index, 75% of the daily observations must be captured; otherwise, the pollutant is considered as missing that day. Moreover if there is no measurement for a pollutant, then the DAQI is based on the concentrations of just those pollutants measured. This means that if, for example, the PM10 concentration was such that it had the highest index for an individual pollutant, but it's concentration was not measured, then the DAQI, which would be determined by the measured pollutant with highest index, would give an unrealistically low value. This would give the impression that the air quality is better than it actually is.

3.2 Data Imputation Methods

To impute the missing data, there are two main methods available: single imputation and multiple imputation. In single imputation each missing value is imputed by only one estimated value. An easy though naive imputation is to replace with the mean or most commonly occurring value [1]. The main drawback of this method is that does not reflect the uncertainty inherent in missing data [21].

Multiple imputation is a statistical technique, that replaces each missing value with a set of plausible (n) values. The results of the multiple imputation methods are (n) datasets [22]. The differences between these datasets reflect the uncertainty of the missing values [25].

One of the most effective multiple imputation methods is Multivariate Imputation via Chained Equations (MICE), also known as Sequential Regression multiple imputation [19]. It is based on Fully Conditional Specification (FCS). Each incomplete variable is imputed by a separate model on a variable-by-variable basis so each variable can be modeled according to its distribution. For example, continuous variables can be modeled using linear regression, binary variables modeled using logistic regression and categorical data using polytomous regression [25]. For a time series (TS), predictive mean matching (pmm) can be used in the imputation process [4].

3.3 Imputation of Air Quality Measurements

For any given station, j, and pollutant i we can approximate the pollutant concentration P_i^j over time using a number of methods. For example, since geographical distance or similarity in the type of station may be relevant we could construct a nearest-neighbour approach based on similarity or distance measures. Alternatively, we can use a form of clustering or grouping of stations to obtain values from other stations in the same cluster which appear to be most similar to the j station.

3.4 Evaluation

If real values are known, we can compare our imputation to those real values in order to evaluate which imputation method works best. Hence, for our experimental set up we take each existing Time Series (TS) for a given pollutant and station, P_i^j in turn, and impute it by the various methods to obtain an imputed TS, PI_i^j. This enables evaluation with a 'ground truth'.

We can compare the real values to the imputed values by a number of measures including distance and regression error measures. We used the Root mean squared error (RMSE), which measures the average magnitude of the errors between the actual and the imputed data. The RMSE is defined as:

$$RMSE = \sqrt{\frac{1}{N}\sum_{i=1}^{N}(\hat{x}_i - x_i)^2} \quad (1)$$

where in our case x_i represent the observed data points and $\hat{x}_i$ represent the imputed values.

The method that gives the lowest error on average for all stations (i.e. imputed TS) will be the considered the best method. Note that the best methods may change from one pollutant to another and may be affected by other factors such as station type (e.g. urban background, rural and roadside) or frequency of data measurement (e.g. hourly, daily).

To provide a more robust testing scenario we separate the 'model building' stage for the imputation from the testing stage. We use an initial data period of three years as a training set to build the imputations, and then impute on the next year of the TS to evaluate goodness of fit.

4 Proposed Methods

We have two levels of missing data in our TS: partial and total. The first corresponds to missing observations within the TS for a given pollutant. The second corresponds to a pollutant not being measured at all for the station.

4.1 Imputing Missing Observations

We imputed the missing observations of a measured pollutant in each station using single and multiple imputation methods; then we applied a TS clustering algorithm to each complete dataset. For single imputation, we used a Simple Moving Average (SMA) method. This method replaces each missing value using a weighted moving average. The mean value in this method is calculated from an equal number of observations on either side of a central missing value; the user can identify the length of that window [15]. In our experiment, we set the window length to 30, so the missing value is replaced by the monthly moving average before and after the missing value.

For multiple imputations, we used MICE to impute the missing value with n different values. In our experiment, we set $n = 5$.

4.2 Imputing Missing Pollutant Time Series

4.2.1 Nearest (Geographical) Neighbours Imputation

To impute the missing pollutant P_i at station j, we first looked at geographically close stations. For this, we measured the geographic distance between station j and all other stations that measure pollutant P_i using the Harvison metric which calculates geographic distance on earth based on longitude and latitude as follows:

$$\begin{aligned} a &= \sin^2(\Delta\varphi/2) + \cos\varphi_1.\cos\varphi_2.\sin^2(\Delta\lambda/2) \\ c &= 2.(\sqrt{a}, \sqrt{1-a}) \\ d &= R.c \end{aligned} \tag{2}$$

where φ represents latitude, λ represents longitude, and R is earth's radius (mean radius = 6,371 km).

Then to impute pollutant P_i for station j we use:

- The nearest neighbour (**1NN**) using the Harvison distance to station j.
- The average of the two nearest neighbours (**2NN**) to station j.

4.2.2 Clustering for Imputation

Clustering requires a measure of similarity or distance between objects, points, groups, or TS. In this exercise, we experimented with two distance metrics suited to TS.

Dynamic Time Warping (DTW) is a distance measure that is used to find the optimal alignment (shortest path) that minimizes the sum of distances between two TS. It was proposed by Sakoe and Chiba [23]. It is an extension of the Euclidean Distance measure (ED) that offers a non-linear alignment between two series.

Shape-Based Distance (SBD) is a faster alternative to DTW, and is based on the cross-correlation with coefficient normalization (NCCc) sequence between two series. It was proposed as part of the k-Shape clustering algorithm by Paparrizos et al. [17] and for its application the TS data should have appropriate amplitudes, or be z-normalized in order to get better clustering results using SBD metric. The SBD distance is calculated by the following formula:

$$SBD(X,Y) = 1 - \frac{max(NCC_c(x,y))}{\|x\|_2\|y\|_2} \tag{3}$$

where $\|.\|_2$ is the l_2 norm of the series calculated as the square root of the sum of the squared vector values. SBD range lies between 0 and 2, with 0 indicating perfect similarity [24].

In our experiment, SBD gave well separated clusters that were more compact than those obtained using DTW, so we report it in our results.

Once we have defined a distance measure a clustering algorithm will group objects according to their distance/similarity. Partition clustering algorithms divide the data points into non-overlapping subsets/clusters. The best-known partitioning algorithm is the k-medoids, also called Partitioning Around Medoids (PAM). It was proposed by Kaufman and Rousseeuw [13]. The cluster medoids act as the cluster 'centers', which are the most representative objects of a cluster. The average dissimilarity between medoids and all data points in the cluster is minimised. The concept of cluster medoids is similar to cluster centroids, but medoids are always members of the data set and may not be located at the center of the cluster, whereas centroids may not correspond to real objects.

PAM requires us to identify the number of the cluster (K) before running the algorithm. To do that, we used Silhouette index (Sil), which is a well-known measurement for estimating the number of clusters in a dataset proposed by Rousseeuw et al. [20].

Hence we used PAM as a clustering algorithm to produce a clustering of the stations. If station j belongs to cluster C_i, given the measured pollutant over time, then, to impute pollutant P_i based on the clustering results, we use:

- The cluster medoid, (**CM**), to impute the missing pollutants at station j, P_i^j.
- The average of pollutant P_i in cluster C_i, (**CA**) which is the daily average of pollutant P_i in all the stations that fall in this cluster.

4.3 Experimental Framework

All our proposed methods were implemented in R. We divide our experiment into two phases: the first phase is imputation of missing observations and clustering process based on the training set as shown in Fig. 1. In general, the clustering results obtained from each individual dataset created by MICE are slightly different hence we merged them into one final clustering result using the majority voting. Majority voting [5] is a simple ensemble technique which chooses the cluster for a station chosen by the majority of the clustering results. The first stage results in a set of complete TS and clustering results.

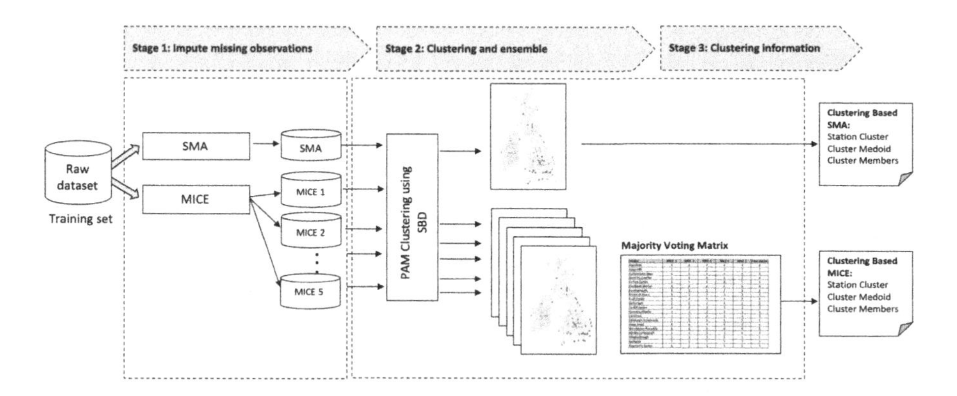

Fig. 1. Phase 1: TS missing observations imputation and clustering process.

The second phase is our proposed imputation method for TS in the test period, as shown in Fig. 2. The imputation of missing observations takes place for the test data as it did for the train data, however in the test set we combined the MICE datasets into one by averaging the n imputed values for each individual observation creating one value. Then, based on the clustering results from the first phase, we assigned a cluster number and cluster medoids for each station. Then the clustering results and NN imputation (1NN and 2NN) are used to produce whole imputed TS for each station.

5 Air Pollutants Concentrations Dataset

The dataset generated at AURN stations include multivariate TS data that show the hourly concentrations of different air pollutants. In this study we only focused on stations that measure ozone. The data can be obtained from https://uk-air.defra.gov.uk/data/data_selector. The observations we download from each station included date, time, hourly pollutant concentration for each pollutant measured at the station, and Status (R = Ratified, P = Provisional, P* = As supplied).

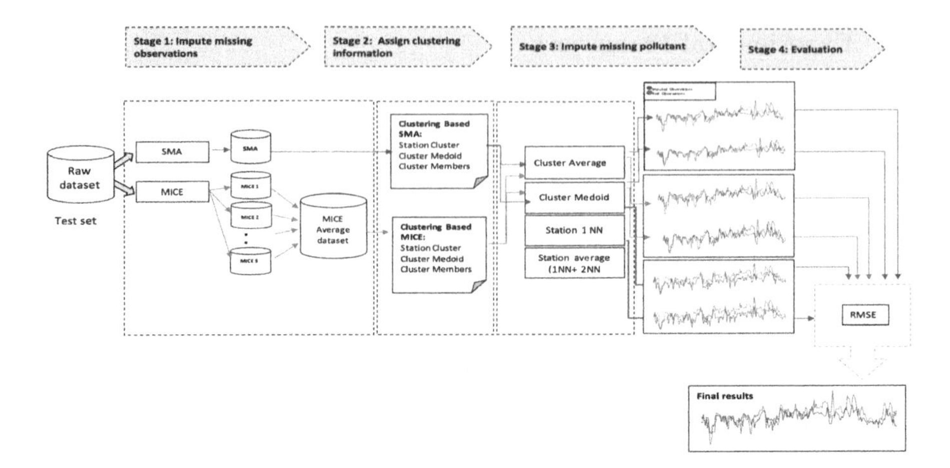

Fig. 2. Phase 2: air pollutant imputation methods.

In total, there are 83 stations around the UK, in which the ozone (O_3)is measured. We removed 18 stations that have more than 25% of missing data. In total we included 65 stations in our analysis. Figure 3, shows the geographical distribution of these stations. We divided the dataset into two parts: the training set including observations for a period of three years (2015–2017); and the test set including the observations of the following year (2018).

Fig. 3. Geographical distribution of ozone monitoring stations in the UK used in the experiment.

6 Results

Although the optimal number was always 2, this did not provide us with a sufficiently granular clustering result. We used in each case the second best number of clusters which was 13 using SMA and 7 using MICE. For MICE, the optimal number of clusters did not vary for the 5 datasets.

The visualisation of the clusters obtained are shown in Fig. 4. As can be observed, even though we only used the pollutant concentrations as TS to cluster the stations using the temporal similarity as measured by SBD, the results of the clustering show that there is a spatial (geographical) correlation between stations in each cluster.

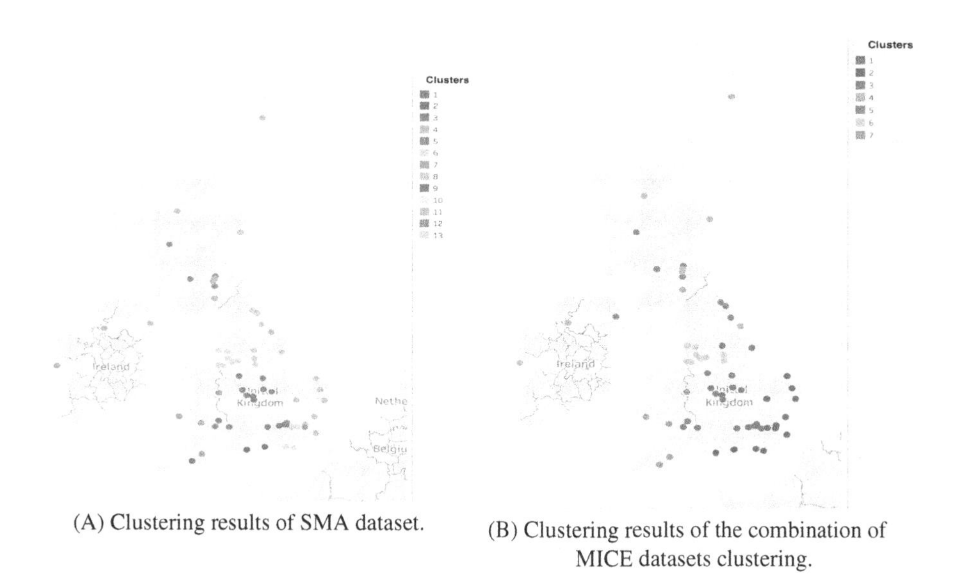

(A) Clustering results of SMA dataset.

(B) Clustering results of the combination of MICE datasets clustering.

Fig. 4. Clustering results of training datasets using SMA and MICE imputation methods.

According to our 4 described methods, using the Cluster Medoid (**CM**), the Cluster average (**CA**), the 1NN (**1NN**) and the average of the 2NN (**2NN**), we created 8 different imputed TS, 4 for the SMA dataset and 4 for the combined MICE datasets. We evaluate those by calculating the RMSE to measure the difference between the imputed and the real data for each station. For each station, we ranked our imputation methods for each dataset based on the value of RMSE from smallest to largest, hence the best imputation method for SMA will have a rank of 1, etc., and similarly for the MICE combined dataset. We then compare these methods based on the average ranks to select the best imputation method. Table 1 shows the comparison of the average of RMSE and the average rank for all methods from all stations for both the MICE and SMA datasets, respectively, using the Cluster Average (**CA**) is associated with the minimum average rank (2.25, 2.37), the minimum average of error (10.003, 10.315), and the minimum standard deviation (3.901, 4.218). This is followed by **2NN** and then **CM** with **1NN** providing the worst results.

An example of the 4 imputed TS for one station (Glasgow Townhead) for the period of six months (Jan-Jul of 2018) using SMA (top) and MICE (bottom) datasets is shown in Fig. 5. It shows that all the imputations reproduce the trend well, though they may generate slightly higher values. Some periods, early in the year appear to show more deviation and this may be due to temperatures having an effect. MICE with CA appears to produce the closest results.

Figure 6 shows a different station, "Glazebury". In this figure, the red TS represents the real observations at the stations with some missing values in the middle of the TS. The green TS represents imputed missing observations using SMA (Top), and MICE (bottom). On the other hand, the blue TS is the result of imputing the whole pollutant TS using the Cluster Average **CA**.

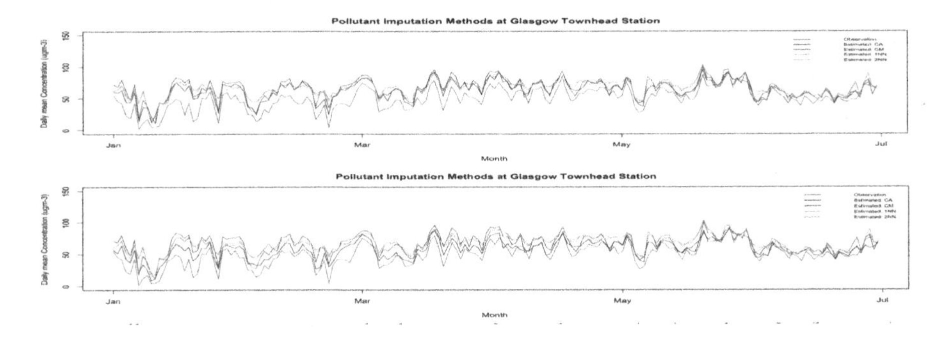

Fig. 5. Pollutant imputation methods using SMA dataset (top) and MICE (bottom) at Glasgow Townhead station.

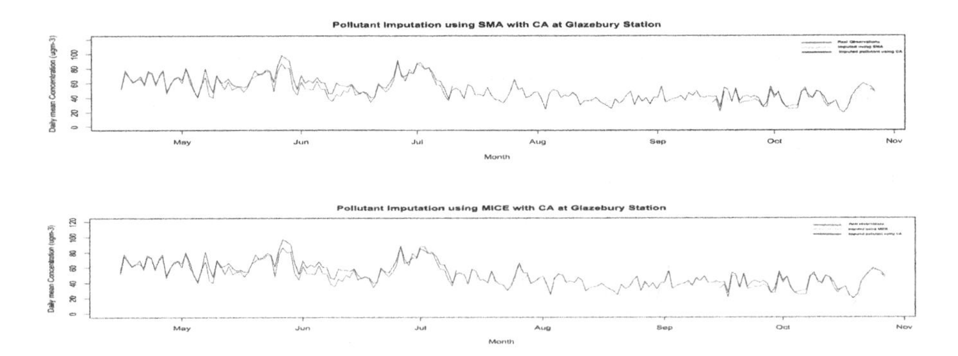

Fig. 6. Observations and **CA** imputed TS using SMA (top) and MICE (bottom) at Glazebury station. (Color figure online)

It is worth noting that using the Cluster Medoid (**CM**) to impute the missing pollutant is not possible in some cases. If the station we are going to impute is itself the medoid of the cluster, or if the cluster has only one station then we have no feasible imputation hence we record how many stations the imputation was possible for as the last column of Table 1. As we can see from the table, it is not possible to create a cluster average for the SMA dataset at "Rochester Stoke" station, because the cluster has only that station. In this case we cannot use the Cluster Average and the Cluster Medoid in the imputation process.

Table 1. The average RMSE and rank comparison for each methods in the two datasets.

Methods	Average rank	Average errors (RMSE)	Standard deviation (std)	Station contributing
MICE Dataset				
Cluster Average (CA)	**2.25**	**10.003**	**3.901**	65
Cluster Medoid (CM)	2.78	11.410	4.544	58
First neighbor (1NN)	2.86	12.116	5.417	65
Average of 2NN	2.41	10.784	5.272	65
SMA Dataset				
Cluster Average (CA)	2.37	10.315	4.218	64
Cluster Medoid (CM)	2.61	11.692	4.404	52
First neighbor (1NN)	3.05	12.641	5.263	65
Average of 2NN	2.53	11.266	5.121	65

7 Conclusions and Future Work

We have proposed and compared a number of techniques to impute ozone values for a station when missing partially or completely. We found that using the clustering average as obtained by clustering the stations on the pollutant values over time using SBD and PAM to impute the missing pollutants gave better results compared to other techniques. This was true regardless of the method used to impute missing observations (partial imputation). However, the combination of multiple imputation for partial missing values and cluster average for pollutant imputation gave the best results.

Our future work is to apply this method to all air pollutants that contribute to the DAQI, then calculate the DAQI from the imputed pollutants and compare it with the historical reported DAQI based on datasets with missing data. From that we can identify any deviations between DAQI values calculated with more information (i.e. the imputed information) and the historical reported DAQI, and this may highlight stations where more measurements will be beneficial, for example where inclusion of the measurement of another pollutant at an AURN station will likely lead to a more accurate DAQI.

References

1. Allison, P.D.: Missing Data, vol. 136. Sage Publications, Thousand Oaks (2001)
2. Arroyo, Á., Herrero, Á., Tricio, V., Corchado, E., Woźniak, M.: Neural models for imputation of missing ozone data in air-quality datasets. Complexity **2018**, 14 (2018)
3. Azid, A., et al.: Prediction of the level of air pollution using principal component analysis and artificial neural network techniques: a case study in Malaysia. Water Air Soil Pollut. **225**(8), 2063 (2014). https://doi.org/10.1007/s11270-014-2063-1
4. Buuren, S., Groothuis-Oudshoorn, K.: MICE: multivariate imputation by chained equations in R. J. Stat. Softw. 1–68 (2010)
5. Dimitriadou, E., Weingessel, A., Hornik, K.: Voting-merging: an ensemble method for clustering. In: Dorffner, G., Bischof, H., Hornik, K. (eds.) ICANN 2001. LNCS, vol. 2130, pp. 217–224. Springer, Heidelberg (2001). https://doi.org/10.1007/3-540-44668-0_31
6. Gass, K., Klein, M., Chang, H.H., Flanders, W.D., Strickland, M.J.: Classification and regression trees for epidemiologic research: an air pollution example. Environ. Health **13**(1), 17 (2014). https://doi.org/10.1186/1476-069X-13-17
7. Gore, R.W., Deshpande, D.S.: An approach for classification of health risks based on air quality levels. In: 2017 1st International Conference on Intelligent Systems and Information Management (ICISIM), pp. 58–61. IEEE (2017)
8. Holnicki, P., Nahorski, Z.: Emission data uncertainty in urban air quality modeling–case study. Environ. Model. Assess. **20**(6), 583–597 (2015). https://doi.org/10.1007/s10666-015-9445-7
9. Jhun, I., Coull, B.A., Schwartz, J., Hubbell, B., Koutrakis, P.: The impact of weather changes on air quality and health in the united states in 1994–2012. Environ. Res. Lett. **10**(8), 084009 (2015)
10. Junninen, H., Niska, H., Tuppurainen, K., Ruuskanen, J., Kolehmainen, M.: Methods for imputation of missing values in air quality data sets. Atmos. Environ. **38**(18), 2895–2907 (2004)
11. Kampa, M., Castanas, E.: Human health effects of air pollution. Environ. Pollut. **151**(2), 362–367 (2008)
12. Kang, G.K., Gao, J.Z., Chiao, S., Lu, S., Xie, G.: Air quality prediction: big data and machine learning approaches. Int. J. Environ. Sci. Dev. **9**(1), 8–16 (2018)
13. Kaufman, L., Rousseeuw, P.J.: Finding Groups in Data: An Introduction to Cluster Analysis, vol. 344. Wiley, Hoboken (2009)
14. Luong, L.M., Phung, D., Sly, P.D., Morawska, L., Thai, P.K.: The association between particulate air pollution and respiratory admissions among young children in Hanoi, Vietnam. Sci. Total Environ. **578**, 249–255 (2017)
15. Moritz, S., Bartz-Beielstein, T.: Imputets: time series missing value imputation in R. R J. **9**(1), 207–218 (2017)
16. Norazian, M.N., Shukri, Y.A., Azam, R.N., Al Bakri, A.M.M.: Estimation of missing values in air pollution data using single imputation techniques. ScienceAsia **34**(3), 341–345 (2008)
17. Paparrizos, J., Gravano, L.: k-shape: efficient and accurate clustering of time series. In: Proceedings of the 2015 ACM SIGMOD International Conference on Management of Data, pp. 1855–1870. ACM (2015)
18. Plaia, A., Bondi, A.: Single imputation method of missing values in environmental pollution data sets. Atmos. Environ. **40**(38), 7316–7330 (2006)
19. Raghunathan, T.E., Lepkowski, J.M., Van Hoewyk, J., Solenberger, P., et al.: A multivariate technique for multiply imputing missing values using a sequence of regression models. Surv. Methodol. **27**(1), 85–96 (2001)

20. Rousseeuw, P.J.: Silhouettes: a graphical aid to the interpretation and validation of cluster analysis. J. Comput. Appl. Math. **20**, 53–65 (1987)
21. Rubin, D.B.: An overview of multiple imputation. In: Proceedings of the Survey Research Methods Section of the American Statistical Association. Citeseer (1988)
22. Rubin, D.B.: Multiple Imputation for Nonresponse in Surveys, vol. 81. Wiley, Hoboken (2004)
23. Sakoe, H., Chiba, S.: Dynamic programming algorithm optimization for spoken word recognition. IEEE Trans. Acoust. Speech Signal Process. **26**(1), 43–49 (1978)
24. Sardá-Espinosa, A.: Comparing time-series clustering algorithms in R using the dtwclust package. R Development Core Team, Vienna (2017)
25. Van Buuren, S., Oudshoorn, K.: Flexible Multivariate Imputation by MICE. TNO, Leiden (1999)
26. WHO: Ambient air pollution: health impacts (2019). https://www.who.int/airpollution/ambient/health-impacts/en/
27. Wong, C.M., Vichit-Vadakan, N., Kan, H., Qian, Z.: Public health and air pollution in Asia (PAPA): a multicity study of short-term effects of air pollution on mortality. Environ. Health Perspect. **116**(9), 1195–1202 (2008)
28. Yang, Y., et al.: The association between ambient air pollution and daily mortality in Beijing after the 2008 olympics: a time series study. PLoS ONE **8**(10), e76759 (2013)
29. Zheng, Y., et al.: Forecasting fine-grained air quality based on big data. In: Proceedings of the 21th ACM SIGKDD International Conference on Knowledge Discovery and Data Mining, pp. 2267–2276. ACM (2015)

Identifying and Counting Vehicles in Multiple Lanes by Using a Low-Cost Vehicle-Mounted Sensor for Intelligent Traffic Management Systems

Elnaz Namazi[1(✉)], Jingyue Li[1(✉)], Rudolf Mester[1], and Chaoru Lu[2]

[1] Department of Computer Science, Norwegian University of Science and Technology (NTNU), Trondheim, Norway
{elnaz.namazi,jingyue.li,rudolf.mester}@ntnu.no
[2] Department of Civil and Environmental Engineering, Norwegian University of Science and Technology (NTNU), Trondheim, Norway
chaoru.lu@ntnu.no

Abstract. There is evidence that accessing online traffic data is a key factor to facilitate intelligent traffic management, especially at intersections. With the advent of autonomous vehicles (AVs), new options for collecting such data appear. To date, much research has been performed on machine learning to provide safe motion planning and to control modern vehicles such as AVs. However, few studies have considered using the sensing features of these types of vehicles to collect traffic information of the surrounding environment. In this study, we developed new algorithms to improve a traffic management system when the traffic is a mixture of human-driven vehicles (HDVs) and modern vehicles with different levels of autonomy. The goal is to utilize the sensing ability of modern vehicles to collect traffic data. As many modern vehicles are equipped with vehicle-mounted sensors by default, they can use them to collect traffic data. Our algorithms can detect vehicles, identify their type, determine the lane they are in, and count the number of detected vehicles per lane by considering multi-lane scenarios. To evaluate our proposed approach, we used a vehicle-mounted monocular camera. The experimental work presented here provides one of the first investigations to extract real traffic data from multiple lanes using a vehicle-mounted camera. The results indicate that the algorithms can identify the detected vehicle's type in the studied scenarios with an accuracy of 95.21%. The accuracy of identifying the lane the detected vehicle is in is determined by two proposed approaches, which have accuracies of 91.01% and 91.73%.

Keywords: Lane detection · Multiple lanes · Vehicle detection · Intelligent traffic management · Vehicle-mounted monocular camera

E. A. de la Cal et al. (Eds.): HAIS 2020, LNAI 12344, pp. 598–611, 2020.
https://doi.org/10.1007/978-3-030-61705-9_49

1 Introduction

There is a growing body of literature that recognizes the importance of collecting traffic data in intelligent traffic management systems. Developments in machine learning techniques and sensors' capabilities have led to proposing various approaches for collecting different types of traffic data (e.g., [1]). These data can be used to manage traffic safely and efficiently, especially at intersections [2]. When focusing on intersection management systems, detecting vehicles' types [3], identifying the lanes they are in, and counting the number of vehicles per lane are vital to provide a global view of the intersection to manage the traffic with high performance.

Previous research on collecting traffic data has mostly used stationary sensors, which are affected by the brightness and weather condition, besides having high installation and maintenance costs. Moreover, equipping all streets with these types of sensors can be costly. The main contribution of our research is taking advantage of the sensing capabilities of modern vehicles, e.g., AVs, which are equipped with various types of sensors, to collect data of the surrounding vehicles to manage traffic. Moreover, this idea is reachable in pure AVs traffic and mixed traffic (a combination of HDVs and AVs), as managing mixed traffic is one of the most important issues for the near future, since changing all vehicles to autonomous versions will be a time-consuming process. Even after this period, traffic might include HDVs as well, because some people enjoy driving. Another contribution of this research is proposing an approach which is generalizable with various levels of vehicle autonomy. Therefore, we used a vehicle-mounted monocular camera, which is one of the cheapest sensors, so there is a high probability that most modern vehicles will be equipped with one. Moreover, by using the camera vision, we are able to record video from multiple lanes. Therefore, we used the camera data to analyze the surrounding traffic. Our developed algorithms are able to detect and classify vehicles in multiple lanes, detect the lanes next to the equipped vehicle, determine the location of the detected vehicles, and count the number of vehicles in each lane. By accessing this information and sharing it with traffic management systems, these systems would have a better global view of the environment and would be able to make better traffic management decisions, especially at intersections.

Our proposed algorithms attempt to answer two research questions:

- **RQ1.** How can we enhance the accuracy of detected vehicles' types based on existing object detection algorithms?
- **RQ2.** How can we identify the lane the detected vehicle is in on multi-lane streets to estimate the number of vehicles in each lane?

The remainder of the paper proceeds as follows. The next section summarizes related works. Section 3 explains the research methodology used in this study. The implementation to answer the proposed RQs is described in Sect. 4. Section 5 presents the experimental results on real traffic data. The last chapter discusses the findings and concludes.

2 State of the Art

In the past few years, a considerable amount of literature has been published on vehicle detection, lane detection, lane-keeping, and tracking for driver assistant systems (e.g., [4]).

Target detection algorithms can be classified into three categories [5]. The first category is the digital image processing approach, such as the frame difference (FD) approach. The second one is a machine learning approach, which is usually based on an AdaBoost classifier or support vector machine (SVM). The last category is based on deep learning approaches. The proposed algorithms in this group are based on convolution neural networks (CNN), Fast-RCNN, Faster-RCNN, YOLO (You Only Look Once), etc. [5].

To improve the object detection performance, Tian et al. [5] proposed a hybrid method, which combined the FD method and YOLO. The results show that this approach can improve the bounding boxes' precision. Moreover, they introduced a model to estimate the distance and speed of the targets based on video from a stationary monocular camera in real time. To detect and track objects and estimate distance and motion in real time, Chen et al. [4] proposed an approach based on deep learning. First, they compared YOLOv3 with a single shot detector (SSD). Second, their object distance estimation was developed based on the Monodepth algorithm. Third, they proposed a new method to analyze object behavior based on SSD. To validate the proposed methodology, they used real traffic from a city center and a railway.

Moreover, different methodologies have been proposed for lane detection. Hillel et al. classified the purpose of lane understanding into lane departure warning, adaptive cruise control (ACC), lane keeping, lane centering, lane change assist, turn assist, fully autonomous driving for paved roads, and fully autonomous driving for cross-country trips [6]. Lane boundary tracking generally includes three major steps [7]. The first step is lane marking detection. In this step, various types of sensors, such as a camera (e.g., [8]), lidar (e.g., [9]), radar, GPS (e.g., [10]), and a line sensor camera (e.g., [11]), can be used. The second step is lane boundary estimation, which includes position, object type, lane information, and vehicle information. The last step is lane boundary tracking. In this step, different filtering approaches such as a Kalman filter, extended Kalman filter, unscented Kalman filter, and particle filter are used [7].

Jo et al. [12] proposed a new method to build an accurate lane-level road map based on a stereo camera, GPS, and in-vehicle sensors. The lane map generation process includes two main steps. The first step is pre-processing, which includes global optimization, ego-motion estimation, and lane detection. The second step includes coordination conversion, clustering, and polyline fitting. Jia et al. [13] proposed a sequential monocular road detection algorithm. The algorithm is classified into sequential road modeling, probabilistic segmentation, and boundary refinement. The current image, previous image, and previous road maps are the input to this process, and the current road map is its output. The multi-lane detection approach is proposed by Chao et al. based on the deep convolutional neural network. The full connected network (FCN) is applied to the captured image by the monocular camera to extract the lane boundary feature. On the image, perspective transform, Hough transform, and the least square method are applied for the lane fitting [14].

Cao et al. [15] proposed a lane detection algorithm that considered dynamic environments and complex road conditions. It is based on the superposition threshold algorithm and the random sample consensus (RANSAC) algorithm. Another approach proposed color-based segmentation for lane detection; it used global convolution networks (GCN), residual-based boundary refinement, and Adam optimization [16]. Yuan et al. introduced a new approach to segmentation and lane detection [17]. It was based on a normal map, an adaptive threshold segmentation method, denoising operations, Hough transform, and the vanishing point.

3 Research Methodology

3.1 Research Strategy

A case study approach was chosen to evaluate the effectiveness of the proposed algorithms with real traffic in an urban area. A vehicle-mounted monocular camera was driven on a predefined path in Trondheim, Norway. For the purpose of data analysis, the recorded video was divided into smaller scenarios. Five scenarios were selected by considering the situation coverage and the research scope. The studied scenarios are presented in Table 1.

Table 1. Scenarios.

Scenarios	Description	Total frames
S1	Includes streets with 4 lanes and 3 lanes (1 left and 2 right)	994
S2	Includes streets with 4 lanes and 1 reserved lane in the center, 1 four-way intersection with a red traffic light and 2 traffic lights at two-way intersections	533
S3	Includes a 4-lane street, 1 red traffic light at a four-way intersection, 1 green traffic light at a four-way intersection, and 1 red traffic light at a two-way intersection	2249
S4	Includes a 4-lane street with a guardrail in the center, 1 green traffic light at a curved four-way intersection, 1 red traffic light at a curved intersection, and 1 red traffic light at a four-way intersection	1819
S5	Includes 4-lane and 2-lane streets and 1 red traffic light at a three-way intersection	2278

3.2 Data Collection

To test our proposed algorithms with real traffic, we decided to record our own footage. Therefore, we equipped a vehicle with a front-facing GoPro Hero 7 camera [18]. The video resolution and frame rate were 1920 × 1080 and 30 frames per second (FPS), respectively. The GPS information includes latitude, longitude, altitude, speed, and a UTC stamp.

The equipped vehicle was driven along the predefined path in Trondheim, Norway, between 9 and 10 a.m. on a typical workday. In this experiment, we focused on city traffic with various numbers of lanes, intersections, and traffic lights.

The recorded video was split into small scenarios to be analyzable, and one frame was analyzed in every 30. The experiments were run using a desktop computer with an Intel Core i7-4770 k CPU 3.40 GHz × 8 and Intel Haswell Desktop graphics.

The data telegram is defined as follows:

- Type of the detected vehicles
- Location of the detected vehicles on the multi-lane streets
- Number of vehicles in each lane

4 Implementation

By extending existing vehicle detection and lane detection algorithms, the proposed method is able to extract the information of the traffic surrounding the camera-mounted vehicle. Several existing algorithms and libraries have been widely applied for vehicle detection and classification, such as YOLO ([24, 25]), PyTorch [19], and OpenCV [20]. Since YOLO is able to run in real-time vehicle detection and classification based on the global context in the image and a single network evaluation [27], it has the potential to provide traffic information to help with real-time traffic management systems [5]. In order to detect lanes, the results of comparing three different edge detection algorithms—Sobel edge detection, Canny edge detection, and Prewitt edge detection—show that Canny edge detection is able to detect the required lanes with less noise than the other two [3]. Therefore, in this paper, we used Canny edge detection [21] and progressive probabilistic Hough transform [22, 23] to deal with lane detection.

The major goal of this paper is to propose a method which can provide lane-based traffic information by extracting data from video via a vehicle-mounted monocular camera. In our last paper [3], we proved that a vehicle-mounted monocular camera can collect traffic data, such as the speed and distance of the detected vehicles. However, traffic management systems need more detailed information on each lane. In this paper, we focused on localizing the detected vehicles in each lane.

4.1 RQ1. Vehicle Type Detection

As we mentioned before, we used YOLO to do vehicle detection and classification. YOLO was originally trained on the COCO dataset, which includes 80 object categories, such as car, cat, umbrella, cell phone, etc. Therefore, the accuracy of the model is not good enough to extract real-world traffic data [3]. Since the traffic management only requires traffic objects, a pre-trained weight on the KITTI dataset was used to train YOLO to enhance its accuracy in classifying traffic objects. The KITTI dataset focuses on traffic objects and contains eight categories named car, van, truck, pedestrian, person_sitting, cyclist, tram, and misc. [28]. The proposed system architecture is shown in Fig. 1. As shown in Fig. 1, the input of the system is the recorded videos from real-world traffic, as described in Sect. 3.2. The algorithm is based on YOLO trained on the

KITTI dataset. Moreover, the output of the system is the processed videos. In these videos, bounding boxes are drawn around the detected vehicles, and the types of detected vehicles are identified. Moreover, lane markers are detected and highlighted. This information is recorded in JSON files for further analysis.

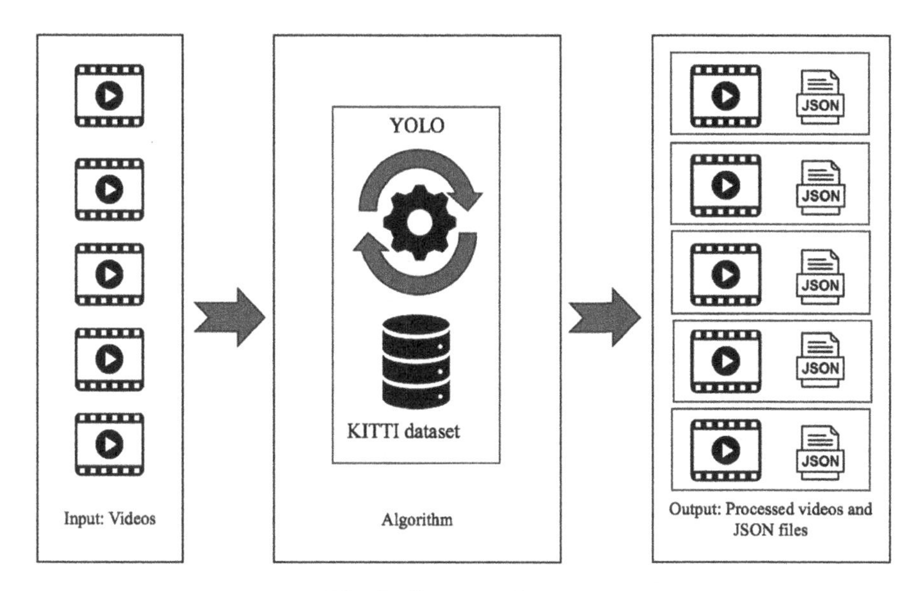

Fig. 1. System architecture.

4.2 RQ2. Extracting Traffic Data

To answer this research question, we followed three steps, as shown in Fig. 2. The first step was to identify the nearby lanes on both sides of the equipped vehicle. To do this we converted the extracted frames to grayscale to reduce the processing time. To remove the noise, frames were blurred. After that, as we mentioned in Sect. 4, we used Canny edge detection [21], and the regions of interest (RoI) [29] to reduce the computation time. Moreover, progressive probabilistic Hough transform [22, 23] is applied to detect lines. After that, lines were drawn on top of the frames, which are shown in green in Fig. 3 and Fig. 4. The parametrization for the detected lines is based on the starting point (x_1, y_1) and ending point (x_2, y_2) of the line in the defined RoI.

The second step is detecting vehicles and dividing them into three groups. To do this, based on the distance between a central point on the bottom side of the bounding boxes around the detected vehicles and detected lanes, we classified vehicles into three groups, named left, middle, and right. To classify the vehicles, we followed these rules: If the vehicles were driven in the same lane as the equipped vehicle, we classified them as middle; if they were to the left side of that vehicle, we classified them as left; and others were classified as right. The conditions to make these decisions are shown in Table 2. This table includes three figures, in which green lines are the detected lanes on both sides of the equipped vehicle; they are named the left line (LL) and right line (RL).

Bounding boxes around the detected vehicle are shown as a red rectangle. The central point on the bottom side of the bounding box is named "central point" (CP). Blue arrows represent the conditions, which are called left of the left line (LoL), left of the right line (LoR), right of the left line (RoL), and right of the right line (RoR).

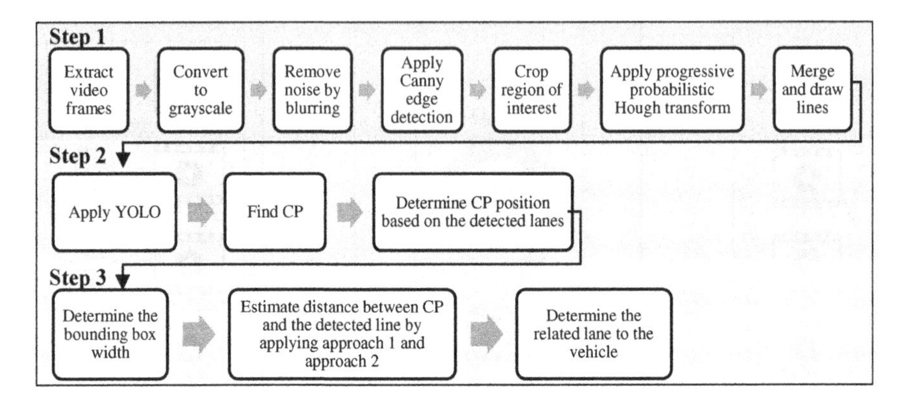

Fig. 2. Lane detection, object detection, and location estimation.

In the third step, we identify the location of each vehicle in multiple lanes. The idea is based on the assumption that vehicle size is less than the lane width. So, the vehicle location is identified based on the distance between the CP in the bounding box around the detected vehicle and the detected lane which that vehicle is in. The distance is measured by two proposed approaches as follows.

Approach 1.

In the first approach, we estimate the location of the detected vehicle based on the shortest path between the CP and the related lane. The shortest distance between a point and a line which is defined by two points, is presented in Eq. (1) [30]. The distance (D_i) of the point CP on the bounding box around the vehicle i, which is expressed by $(x_{vi,0}, y_{vi,0})$ from the line which passes through two points, $P_1 := (x_1, y_1)$ and $P_2 := (x_2, y_2)$, is as follows:

$$\text{distance}\left((P_1, P_2), (x_{vi,0}, y_{vi,0})\right) = \frac{\left|(x_2 - x_1)(y_1 - y_{vi,0}) - (x_1 - x_{vi,0})(y_2 - y_1)\right|}{\sqrt{(x_2 - x_1)^2 + (y_2 - y_1)^2}} \quad (1)$$

This approach is presented in Fig. 3. In this figure, similar to Table 2, green lines are the detected lanes on both sides of the equipped vehicle, called LL and RL. Red rectangles are bounding boxes around the detected vehicle. CP represents the central point on the bottom side of the bounding box. Blue arrow which is called D_i, shows the shortest distance between a CP on vehicle i and a related line. W_{vi} shows the width of the vehicle i.

Approach 2.
In this approach, we propose a solution to estimate the vehicle distance (d_i) to the related line in the horizontal direction, as shown in Fig. 4. Other variables are named as in Fig. 3.

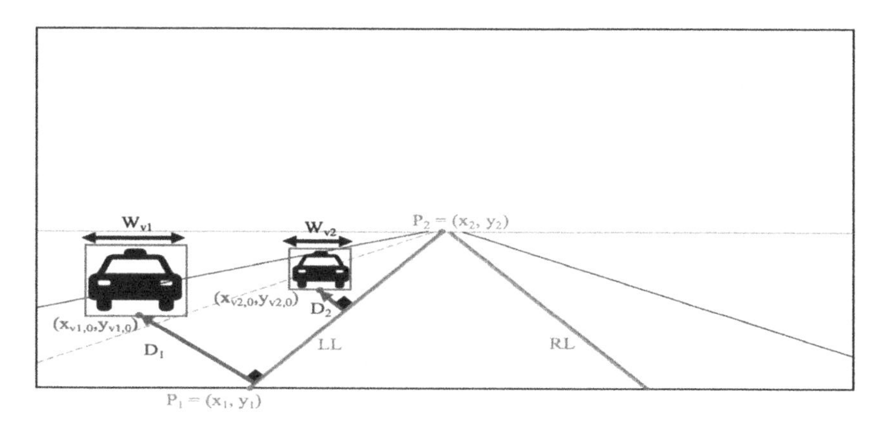

Fig. 3. The first approach to estimating the lane the detected vehicle is in.

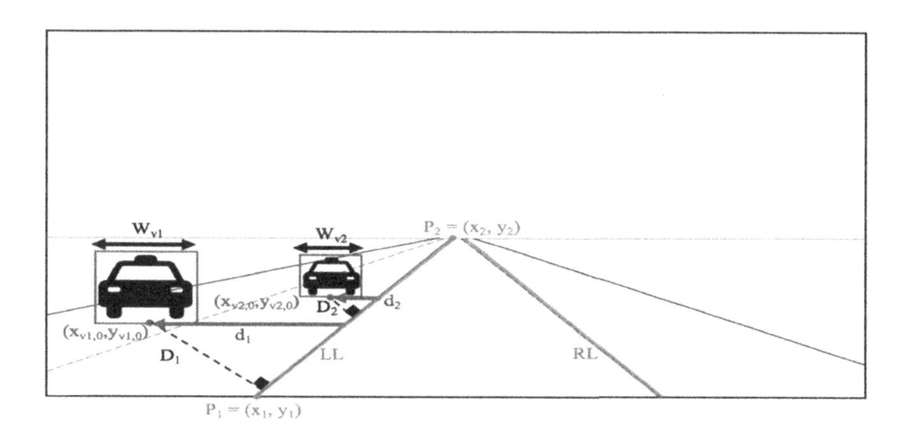

Fig. 4. The second approach to estimating the lane the detected vehicle is in.

Table 2. Dividing vehicles into three main groups, left, middle, and right.

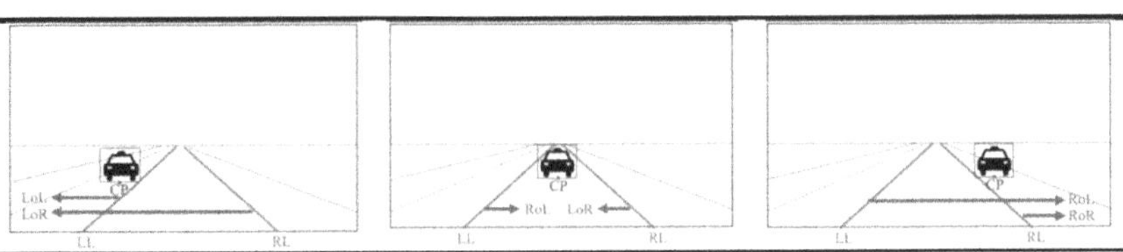

If the CP is located on the left side of the left line and on the left side of the right line, then the vehicle is on the left side.	If the CP is located on the right side of the left line and on the left side of the right line, then the vehicle is in the middle.	If the CP is located on the right side of the left line and on the right side of the right line, then the vehicle is on the right side.

To measure d_i, our proposed approach consists of the following steps.

1- Measuring the slope of the related line (jL, j := L or R), which passes through two points, P_1 and P_2 [31].

$$\mathrm{Slope}_{jL} = \frac{(y_2 - y_1)}{(x_2 - x_1)} \tag{2}$$

2- Converting the line's slope to an angle in degrees [31].

$$jL_{degree} = \arctan\left(\mathrm{Slope}_{jL}\right) \tag{3}$$

3- Estimating d_i by using triangulation formulas, as shown in Fig. 5.

Based on Euclidean parallelism [26],

$$L \parallel d_i \Rightarrow \beta = \propto = \gamma = N_{degree} \tag{4}$$

$$D_i \perp N \Rightarrow \lambda = 90^\circ \tag{5}$$

By considering the triangle rules [32],

$$\theta + \lambda + \gamma = 180^\circ \Rightarrow \theta = 180^\circ - 90^\circ - \gamma \Rightarrow \theta = 90^\circ - N_{degree} \tag{6}$$

Based on the trigonometric ratios, the hypotenuse (d_i) is calculated by the following formula [33]:

$$d_i = \frac{D_i}{\cos(\theta)} \Rightarrow d_i = \frac{D_i}{\cos\left(90^\circ - N_{degree}\right)} \tag{7}$$

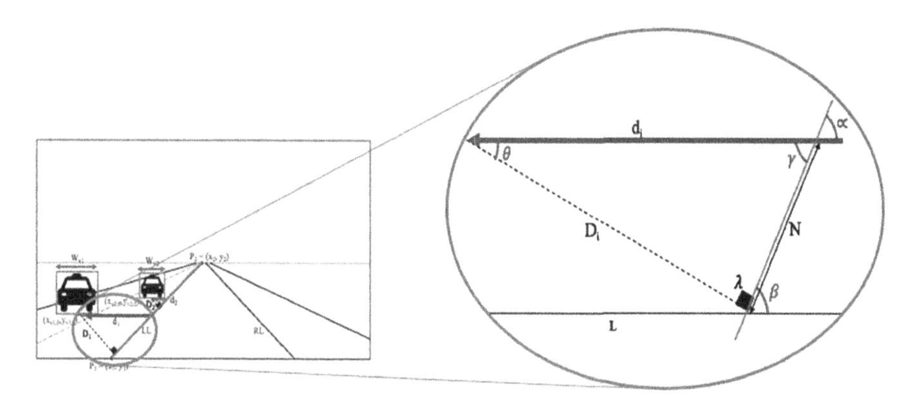

Fig. 5. Identifying the vehicle's lane by the second approach.

Finally, as the last step, the location of the vehicle is estimated by considering the distance and vehicle size, as shown in Table 3, in which $Distance_i$ is the distance calculated for a vehicle i by following approach 1 and approach 2, and S_{vi} is the size of vehicle i.

Table 3. Conditions for finding the detected vehicle's location in multiple lanes.

Condition	Output
$0 < Distance_i < S_{vi}$	1st lane on the left/right
$S_{vi} < Distance_i < 2 \times S_{vi}$	2nd lane on the left/right
$2 \times S_{vi} < Distance_i < 3 \times S_{vi}$	3rd lane on the left/right
$(n - 1) \times S_{vi} < Distance_i < n \times S_{vi}$	nth lane on the left/right

We ran our algorithms on predefined scenarios and extracted the frames. Out of every 30 frames, we analyzed one frame manually as a ground truth. In this study, the scenarios include 7873 frames in total, and we analyzed 262 frames. Then, the outputs of the algorithms were compared with the manually extracted data.

5 Results

The purpose of the first experiment was to determine the accuracy of the improved algorithms in identifying the type of the detected vehicles. Table 4 illustrates our results. It is apparent from this table that the accuracy of identifying the detected vehicles' type is higher than 90.74% for all lanes in the studied scenarios.

Table 4. Vehicle type detection in the predefined scenarios.

		2nd lane on the left	1st lane on the left	Middle	Right	Total
Scenario 1	Manual	5.00	19.00	22.00	2.00	48.00
	System	5.00	19.00	22.00	0.00	46.00
	Correct (%)	100.00	100.00	100.00	0.00	95.83
	Error (%)	0.00	0.00	0.00	100.00	4.17
Scenario 2	Manual	0.00	12.00	9.00	0.00	21.00
	System	0.00	12.00	9.00	0.00	21.00
	Correct (%)	100.00	100.00	100.00	100.00	100.00
	Error (%)	0.00	0.00	0.00	0.00	0.00
Scenario 3	Manual	0.00	70.00	24.00	1.00	95.00
	System	0.00	68.00	24.00	1.00	93.00
	Correct (%)	100.00	97.14	100.00	100.00	97.89
	Error (%)	0.00	2.86	0.00	0.00	2.11
Scenario 4	Manual	1.00	2.00	44.00	7.00	54.00
	System	1.00	1.00	42.00	5.00	49.00
	Correct (%)	100.00	50.00	95.45	71.43	90.74
	Error (%)	0.00	50.00	4.55	28.57	9.26
Scenario 5	Manual	10.00	11.00	5.00	48.00	74.00
	System	9.00	10.00	5.00	45.00	69.00
	Correct (%)	90.00	90.91	100.00	93.75	93.24
	Error (%)	10.00	9.09	0.00	6.25	6.76

In the second experiment, we analyzed the identified location of the detected vehicles in each lane. The results obtained from the selected scenarios are shown in Table 5. App 1 and App 2 indicate approach 1 and approach 2, respectively. The results obtained from the experiments show that the accuracy of vehicle location identification is between 71.43% and 90.54% with the first approach, and between 71.43% and 94.59% with the second approach, for all lanes.

Table 5. Vehicle location detection in the predefined scenarios.

Scenarios	Outputs	2nd lane on the left		1st lane on the left		Middle		Right		Total	
		App 1	App 2	App 1	App 2	App 1	App 2	App 1	App 2	App 1	App 2
Scenario 1	Correct (%)	80.00	100.0	94.74	84.21	86.36	86.36	100.0	100.0	89.58	87.50
	Error (%)	20.00	0.00	5.26	15.79	13.64	13.64	0.00	0.00	10.42	12.50
Scenario 2	Correct (%)	100.0	100.0	75.00	75.00	66.67	66.67	100.0	100.0	71.43	71.43
	Error (%)	0.00	0.00	25.00	25.00	33.33	33.33	0.00	0.00	28.57	28.57
Scenario 3	Correct (%)	100.0	100.0	80.00	80.00	95.83	95.83	100.0	100.0	84.21	84.21
	Error (%)	0.00	0.00	20.00	20.00	4.17	4.17	0.00	0.00	15.79	15.79
Scenario 4	Correct (%)	100.0	100.0	100.0	100.0	90.91	90.91	71.43	71.43	88.89	88.89
	Error (%)	0.00	0.00	0.00	0.00	9.09	9.09	28.57	28.57	11.11	11.11
Scenario 5	Correct (%)	70.00	100.0	72.73	72.73	100.0	100.0	97.92	97.92	90.54	94.59
	Error (%)	30.00	0.00	27.27	27.27	0.00	0.00	2.08	2.08	9.46	5.41

Table 6. Total accuracy for all scenarios.

	Type identification	Localization based on App 1	Localization based on App 2
Correct (%)	95.21	91.01	91.73
Error (%)	4.79	8.99	8.27

In total, the accuracy of the vehicle type detection and location identification for the vehicles with the correct type detection in all scenarios when considering all lanes is shown in Table 6. As this table shows, the accuracy of the second approach for estimating the lanes the detected vehicles are in is higher than that of the first approach.

6 Discussion and Conclusion

The main objective of this research was to study modern vehicles' sensing abilities for collecting traffic data to improve traffic management systems. To achieve this objective, we have developed a system and done experiments with real traffic data. Some of the prior studies that have noted the importance of collecting traffic data used stationary sensors to achieve this goal (e.g., [5]). As using stationary sensors are costly to equip all streets, we have used a vehicle-mounted sensor, as modern vehicles are equipped with various types of sensors, which are powerful and free resources to use.

As we have mentioned, modern vehicles are equipped with various types of sensors, but we decided to use a monocular camera to make our solution more feasible in the real world. Due to lidars are more expensive than cameras, the possibility of equipping all vehicles with a lidar is low, which will limit the generalizability of the proposed approach in reality. Therefore, we decided to use a monocular camera, which is cheap and likely to be mounted on most modern vehicles. Moreover, the camera's field of view gives us the possibility to collect data from multiple lanes to provide a better understanding of the traffic situation.

Our proposed algorithms are a combination of a deep learning algorithm called YOLO, which was trained on the KITTI dataset to detect vehicles and identify their type, and image processing approach to provide robust vehicle location estimation for multiple lanes. Although most of the existing papers in this scope have focused on lane detection (e.g., [15]) or object detection (e.g., [5]), we have combined both methodologies to extract more data types. In reviewing the literature, we found that more recent studies have been limited to lane detection and tracking for driver assistance systems (e.g., [17]). No approaches were found on the dependency between vehicle detection and the related lane, as it is vital for traffic management systems, especially at intersections, to access the traffic volume per lane.

One of the most significant findings from our proposed algorithms is that a vehicle-mounted monocular camera is able to extract traffic data, such as the detected vehicles' type, what lanes they are in, and the number of detected vehicle in each lane. Our experiments on real traffic data with five scenarios confirmed that our algorithms can identify the detected vehicles' type with an accuracy higher than 90.74%. The accuracy of vehicle location identification for all lanes with the first and second approaches is between 71.43% and 90.54%, and between 71.43% and 94.59%, respectively. The observed low accuracy of the second scenario can be explained by the fact that the lane marks on the right side almost vanished, which had a direct effect on the accuracy of the vehicle location detection. Moreover, the accuracy of identifying the lane the detected vehicle with the correct determined type was in by considering the total lanes was 91.01% for the first approach, and 91.73% for the second approach. Although this study was limited by driving an equipped vehicle in the middle lane, the findings prove that this idea would be feasible in reality. However, further experimentation to consider various scenarios is recommended. Moreover, as our proposed algorithms are based on object detection and lane detection algorithms, therefore, by enhancing the accuracy of the object detection and lane detection algorithms, the performance of our proposed algorithm would be enhanced. Our future work will improve the performance and accuracy of our approach further.

References

1. Lamouik, I., Yahyaouy, A., Sabri, M.A.: Smart Multi-Agent Traffic Coordinator for Autonomous Vehicles at Intersections, pp. 1–6. IEEE (2017)
2. Namazi, E., Li, J., Lu, C.: Intelligent intersection management systems considering autonomous vehicles: a systematic literature review. IEEE Access pp. 91946–91965 (2019)
3. Namazi, E., Holthe-Berg, R.N., Lofsberg, C.S., Li, J.: Using vehicle-mounted camera to collect information for managing mixed traffic. In: 15th International Conference on Signal-Image Technology & Internet-Based Systems, pp. 222–230 (2019)
4. Chen, Z., Khemmar, R., Decoux, B., Atahouet, A., Ertaud, J.-Y.: Real time object detection, tracking, and distance and motion estimation based on deep learning: application to smart mobility, pp. 1–6. IEEE (2019)
5. Tian, S., et al.: An improved target detection and traffic parameter calculation method based on YOLO with a monocular camera. In: CICTP, pp. 5696–5708 (2019)
6. Hillel, A.B., Lerner, R., Levi, D., Raz, G.: Recent progress in road and lane detection: a survey. Mach. Vis. Appl. 727–745 (2014)
7. Keatmanee, C., Jakborvornphan, S., Potiwanna, C., San-Uml, W., Dailey, M.N.: Vision-based lane keeping—a survey, pp. 1–6. IEEE (2018)
8. Andrade, D.C., et al.: A novel strategy for road lane detection and tracking based on a vehicle's forward monocular camera. IEEE Trans. Intell. Transp. Syst. 1497–1507 (2018)
9. von Reyher, A., Joos, A., Winner, H.: A lidar-based approach for near range lane detection, pp. 147–152. IEEE (2005)
10. Goldbeck, J., Hürtgen, B., Ernst, S., Kelch, L.: Lane following combining vision and DGPS. Image Vis. Comput. 425–433 (2000)
11. Narita, Y., Katahara, S., Aoki, M.: Lateral position detection using side looking line sensor cameras, pp. 271–275. IEEE (2003)
12. Jo, Y., Han, S.-J., Lee, D., Min, K., Choi, J.: An autonomous lane-level road map building using low-cost sensors. In Eleventh International Conference on Machine Vision. (ICMV 2018), vol. 11041 (2019)
13. Jia, B., Chen, J., Zhang, K., Wang, Q.: Sequential monocular road detection by fusing appearance and geometric information. IEEE/ASME Trans. Mechatronics **24**(2), 633–643 (2019)

14. Chao, F., Yu-Pei, S., Ya-Jie, J.: Multi-lane detection based on deep convolutional neural network. IEEE Access 150833–150841 (2019)
15. Cao, J., Song, C., Song, S., Xiao, F., Peng, S.: Lane detection algorithm for intelligent vehicles in complex road conditions and dynamic environments. Sensors 3166 (2019)
16. Zhang, W., Mahale, T.: End to end video segmentation for driving: Lane detection for autonomous car. arXiv preprint (2018)
17. Yuan, C., Chen, H., Liu, J., Zhu, D., Xu, Y.: Robust lane detection for complicated road environment based on normal map. IEEE Access 49679–49689 (2018)
18. GoPro hero7 black. https://gopro.com/en/us/shop/cameras/hero7-black/CHDHX-701-master.html. Accessed 2020
19. Paszke, A., et al.: Automatic differentiation in PyTorch. In: 31st Conference on Neural Information Processing Systems (NIPS 2017) (2017)
20. Bradski, G.: The opencv library. Software Tools 120–125 (2000)
21. Ding, L., Goshtasby, A.: On the Canny edge detector. Pattern Recogn. 721–725 (2001)
22. Galamhos, C., Matas, J., Kittler, J.: Progressive probabilistic Hough transform for line detection. IEEE 554–560 (1999)
23. Matas, J., Galambos, C., Kittler, J.: Robust detection of lines using the progressive probabilistic Hough transform. Comput. Vis. Image Understand. 119–137 (2000)
24. Redmon, J., Divvala, S., Girshick, R., Farhadi, A.: You only look once: unified, real-time object detection. In: The IEEE Conference on Computer Vision and Pattern Recognition (CVPR), pp. 779–788 (2016)
25. Redmon, J., Farhadi, A.: YOLOv3: An incremental improvement. arXiv preprint (2018)
26. Geometry. https://en.wikipedia.org/wiki/Parallel. Accessed 2019
27. YOLO. https://pjreddie.com/darknet/yolo/. Accessed 2019
28. Use YOLOv3 PyTorch to train KITTI. https://github.com/packyan/PyTorch-YOLOv3-kitti. Accessed 2019
29. Deng, G., Wu, Y.: Double lane line edge detection method based on constraint conditions Hough transform, pp. 107–110. IEEE (2018)
30. Point-Line Distance–2-Dimensional. https://mathworld.wolfram.com/Point-LineDistance2-Dimensional.html. Accessed 2020
31. Slope. https://en.wikipedia.org/wiki/Slope. Accessed 2019
32. Sum of angles of a triangle. https://en.wikipedia.org/wiki/Sum_of_angles_of_a_triangle. Accessed 2019
33. Trigonometry. https://en.wikipedia.org/wiki/Trigonometry. Accessed 2019

Minimizing Attributes for Prediction of Cardiovascular Diseases

Roberto Porto Solano[1] and Jose M. Molina[2](✉)

[1] Corporación Universitaria Americana, Barranquilla, Colombia
rporto@coruniamericana.edu.co
[2] Universidad Carlos III de Madrid, Madrid, Spain
molina@ia.uc3m.es

Abstract. This study is aimed at the early detection of cardiovascular diseases using predictions learning with a high percentage of successes using the lowest possible number of attributes. Results are comparable to other techniques. Applying the learning system through the reduction of attributes, a tree was obtained with the same classification result of 85.8% that appears in the literature, but it was obtained with 5 variables using the decision tables technique (Decisions Table) and Bayesian Networks.

Keywords: A.I. · Reliable · Attributes reduction · Correlation index · Correct decisions

1 Introduction

Cardiovascular diseases (CVD) are a group of conditions in the heart and blood vessels of the human body that have been classified and analyzed in many works [1, 2, 3]. Predictions of various cardiovascular diseases vary depending on the population [4]. Many investigations that work on the Data Science line (e.g., [5, 6, 7, 8]), proximate the work done in this study, since they use the relatively small set of Cardiovascular disease data composed of 14 attributes and 303 patient records and seek to recognize patterns or diagnoses based on clinical test results established for each population (i.e., data), to explain symptoms presented in patients. It should be noted that it is possible to diagnose risk factors based on the analysis of data from patients who may or may not suffer from diseases (e.g., liver, diabetes mellitus, heart attacks, cancer, dengue among other infectious diseases) that can be treated even cured, from early detection through machine learning techniques [9, 10, 11, 12]. These data are consolidated as a whole, which are used to create models that allow classifying or predicting diseases.

Traditional statistics are not enough to handle large quantities of variables, it is important to process the data with machine learning techniques to detect previously ignored properties and then perform the respective interpretations of the results [13].

This work was funded by public research projects of Spanish Ministry of Economy and Competivity (MINECO), reference TEC2017-88048-C2-2-R.

E. A. de la Cal et al. (Eds.): HAIS 2020, LNAI 12344, pp. 612–619, 2020.
https://doi.org/10.1007/978-3-030-61705-9_50

This research arises from the interest to assist cardiologists of non-profit organizations that help enrich the quality of patients who may or may not suffer from cardiovascular diseases (CVD) by examining and verifying the results obtained in an agile and efficient way, generating knowledge and expectation in doctors about how to increase the accuracy of diagnoses from the prediction, to control or prevent risk factors of CVD from an interpretable system, using a simple and agile methodology. Therefore, data from the free repository of the University of California (UCI) will be used, more specifically from the Statlog heart disease data set, since it is the most used and the one with the most articles on the application of Machine Learning techniques (ML), which is explained in subsect. 3.1, so that we can classify any type of cardiac abnormality from the analysis of this data set.

Interpreting the results after applying ML techniques to dataset with many attributes is usually complicated, although the techniques that are theoretically used are interpretable as is the case with decision trees, particularly the use of so many attributes and so much data division makes the interpretation of the results difficult, so a methodology is proposed that allows the reduction of characteristics (i.e., variables) in order to find information that can be learned. On the other hand, the relationships that can be understood or interpreted from the attributes, allow to improve the prediction of the proposed methodology or at least allow to obtain results that are similar to the best ones, in terms of tests of classification, precision, sensitivity, specificity, with a smaller quantity of attributes from the proposed methodology. Additionally, this study is oriented so that its application can be used directly on other medical data groups, so that the knowledge extracted from the dataset from the applicability of a new methodological proposal, which can be used in any data sets without regard in its area or that the procedure can be applied to other medical datasets that allow a better approach to disease prediction and at some point, giving another approach to traditional ML techniques to build information on the structure of these types of medical data sets.

2 Literature Review

One of main approaches to this problem would be the research carried out in [14], in which they propose a model to predict heart disease from a set of private data, reducing the amount of attributes from 14 to 6, by using a genetic algorithm that allows the selection of categorical attributes, to subsequently use traditional classifiers for the prediction and diagnosis of heart disease, obtaining a classification percentage of 99.2% using the Decision Tree technique, out of 96.5% classification using the Naive Bayes technique. On the other hand, in [15] a classification model of heart disease is presented using the Statlog data set. This is composed of 2 systems, the first system uses the RelieF algorithm to extract the superior characteristics, discarding the features that offer less information, to later use the RS reduction heuristic for feature elimination, then the new data set is trained with the reduction of attributes, to perform tests with the different traditional classifiers, obtaining better results using the C4.5 technique with a classification percentage of 92.59% with the 7 attributes that presented the strongest qualities in distinction and of greater value.

Some aspects presented with the previous studies are consistent in some aspects with the proposal presented in this research, such as the reduction of attributes [16], and the selection of attributes based on the definition of criteria based on characteristics (e.g., more information, less information, correlation) [17].

Currently, in the field of machine learning, predictions about various types of diseases are addressed using different tools. In the review we carried out, the investigations are grouped based on machine learning techniques such as decision trees, Naïve Bayes, vector support machine, Bagging, neural networks, k-neighbors and fuzzy logic, which are among the most used for the classification and prediction of diseases according to recent literature. On the other hand, they are subclassified according to the data set, whether they are free to use (e.g., ICU) or private. Additionally, data extraction methods and methodologies used to increase their results, important for comparing their results with those obtained when using the methodology proposed in this research, are highlighted.

3 Methodology

The objective of this methodology is to find an interpretable system for the early detection of cardiovascular diseases, seeking the maximization of the percentage of successes with the minimum number of attributes for prediction. The first step is the analysis of the Pearson correlation statistical coefficient performed using the R software, to determine the attributes that more and less correlate from the Pearson coefficient. Subsequently, performance evaluations of the classification techniques found in the classifiers section of the Weka data analysis and exploration tool are performed, based on criteria such as the correct classification of instances, incorrect classification of instances, execution time of the model, and accuracy of the classification, considering not balancing the data due to the small difference between the classes and the cross-validation parameterization for small data not exceeding 10%. Additionally, the estimation of the criteria as Average absolute error, Calculation of kappa concordance, Mean square error, Relative absolute error and Relative square error to select the best classification techniques to be presented in section 3.3.

3.1 Selection of Heart Disease Dataset (Statlog)

This section presents a set of data used for the experiments, which belongs to the open repository of the University of California which has the name Heart Disease and is composed of 76 attributes, 270 instances and 2 classes (present and absent). It should be noted that this is one of the most used open data sets in machine learning publications applied to the medical field [5]. For this investigation they only take 14 attributes including the class attribute, whose distribution is as follows: the class absent is made up of 150 instances corresponding to 55.5% and the class present, which is made up of 120 instances that corresponds to 44.5% of the data set.

3.2 Statistical Correlation Experiments

This section shows a breakdown of the attributes of the Statlog data set and their statistical relationship in terms of effectiveness displayed independently, in order to distinguish the attributes in a first observation. The graphs of the composition of the data set attributes presented in Fig. 1 show that there are attributes that do not separate well, in addition to the classes being unbalanced as mentioned in subsect. 3.1.

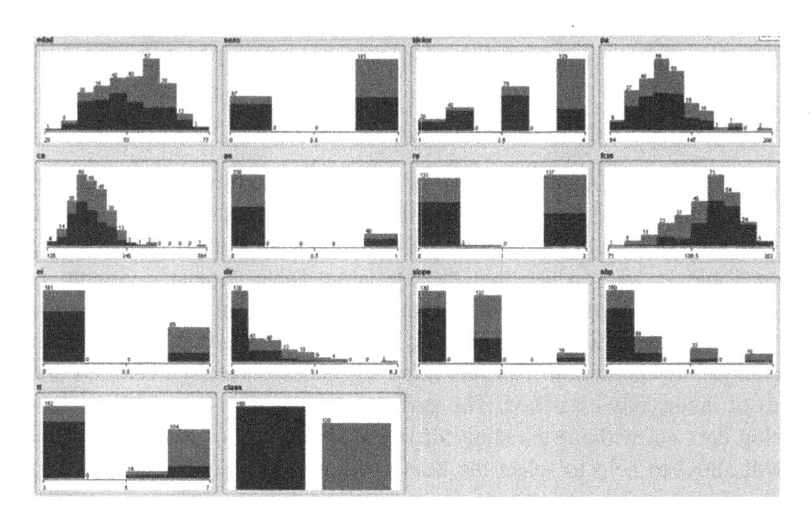

Fig. 1. Graph of the statistics of the attributes of the heart disease data set

In order to estimate how the attributes are directly or inversely proportional in the first instance, Pearson's correlation coefficient was calculated with the R software, which resulted in the variables that are most proportionally correlated are Dir (depression induced by rest) and Pd (pending depression) with a coefficient of 0.61 followed by sex with Tt (thallium tomography) with a coefficient of 0.39 and Sex with Nbp (number of main loops) with a coefficient of 0.35. Likewise, the variables that are most inversely correlated are Fcm (maximum heart rate) with Age, Fcm with Pd and Fcm with Ei (Induced exercise) with coefficients of −0.40, −0.386 and −0.38 respectively as shown in Fig. 2.

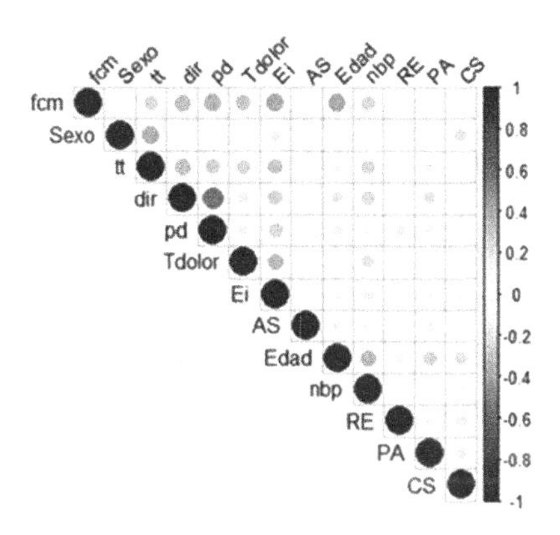

Fig. 2. Pearson's correlation of all attributes of the heart disease dataset.

In Fig. 2, the upper diagonal of a correlation matrix is presented, where the correlations by color are shown, the positive ones being in blue and negative in red, the size of the circle and the intensity of the color being proportional with the coefficient of correlation. This section is a fundamental part to determine the relationship of the variables and to be able to choose the attributes that are most correlated to reduce (e.g., Slope, Dir, Sex, etc.) according to the methodology outlined in this article.

3.3 Performance Evaluation Methods

A cross validation by 10 was performed for each of the experiments with different classifying algorithms. Table 1 shows the results of the tests. Tests have been conducted to evaluate the performance of the different classification algorithms to predict heart disease.

From Table 1, we can see that the Decision Table, Logistic, Simple Logistic, TreeLMT, HoeffdingTree and the minimum sequential optimization (SMO) techniques have a percentage accuracy of the classification above 83%. Being DecisionTable the best technique to classify, it also has more instances correctly classified and fewer instances of incorrectly classified. The performance comparison of ML techniques in the Statlog data set without the study of the methodology of reduction of characteristics, will allow to help to select the best traditional techniques for the study of the technique of elimination of attribute.

Table 1. Comparison of classifier performance

Algorithms	Correctly classified instances	Incorrectly classified instance	Timing to build model	Accuracy
AdaBoostM1	216	54	0,01	80
AtributeSelectedClassifier	218	52	0,11	80,8
Bagging	214	56	0,02	79,3
Classification via Regression	216	54	0,05	80
FilteredClassifier	221	49	0,14	81,8
InteractiveClassifierOptimizer	223	47	0,02	82,6
J48	207	63	0,02	76,6
LogiBoost	222	48	0,01	82,2
Logistic	226	44	0,03	83,7
MultiClassClasiffier	226	44	0,36	83,7
MultilayerPerceptron	211	59	0	78,4
NaiveBayes (NB)	226	44	0,01	83,7
RandomForest	220	50	0,09	81,5
RandomSubSpace	221	49	0,01	82
SGD	224	46	0,03	82,9
SimpleLogistic	225	45	0,09	83,3
SMO	227	43	0,01	84,1
TreeLMT	225	45	0,2	83,33
HoeffdingTree	225	45	0.02	83.3
DecissionTable (DT)	229	41	0.04	84.81

4 Learning System Through Attribute Reduction

A previous analysis was performed to determine the variables that were most correlated in subsect. 3.2, as well as the review of the best techniques (i.e., DecisionTable, C4.5, SMO, Naive Bayes, Logistic and Simple Logistic) to classify in order to determine whether it is possible to have the same accuracy in the classification by decreasing the number of attributes of the set in subsect. 3.3. The first classification was carried out without the reduction of variables obtaining a correct classification of 84.81% using the Decision Table technique, subsequently, the variables were reduced taking into account the variables with the highest correlation coefficient for what they generated in the following order: dp (Depression pending) obtaining a correct classification of 84.81% using the NaiveBayes technique, then Dir obtaining a correct classification of 84.81% using the Decision Table technique, subsequently sex obtaining a correct classification of 84.81 using the Decision Table technique, then the variable As was reduced, obtaining a correct classification of 85.18% using the SGD technique, thus continuing with the Fcm variable obtaining a correct classification of 84.4 using the SGD and SMO technique, then the Age variable was reduced obtaining a classification of 85.18% using the NaiveBayes technique, later the variable Ei was reduced, obtaining a correct classification of 85.5% using the NaiveBayes technique, so we was continued with the variable Pa, obtaining a classification of 84.81% using the Decision Table technique, then the variable Cs was reduced, obtaining a correct classification of 85.56%, subsequently, the classification percentage dropped to 78.8% by reducing the Tdolor variable using the NaiveBayes technique, as shown in the following Table 2.

Table 2. Attribute reduction vs. correct classification of techniques

Variables /Techniques	DT	NB	DT	DT	SGD	SGD/ SMO	NB	NB	DT	NB/ DT	NB
Age	O	O	O	O	O	O	X	X	X	X	X
Sex	O	O	O	X	X	X	X	X	X	X	X
Tdolor	O	O	O	O	O	O	O	O	O	O	X
Pa	O	O	O	O	O	O	O	O	X	X	X
Cs	O	O	O	O	O	O	O	O	O	X	X
As	O	O	O	O	X	X	X	X	X	X	X
Re	O	O	O	O	O	O	O	O	O	O	O
Fcm	O	O	O	O	O	X	X	X	X	X	X
Ei	O	O	O	O	O	O	O	X	X	X	X
Dir	O	O	X	X	X	X	X	X	X	X	X
Slope	O	X	X	X	X	X	X	X	X	X	X
Nbp	O	O	O	O	O	O	O	O	O	O	O
Tt	O	O	O	O	O	O	O	O	O	O	O
Class	O	O	O	O	O	O	O	O	O	O	O
Number of variables	14	13	12	11	10	9	8	7	6	5	4
Correctly classified instances	84,8	84,8	84,8	84,8	85,1	84,4	85,2	85,5	84,8	85,5	78,8

The most outstanding technique used in the attribute reduction methodology is Decision Table with a correct classification of 85.5%, but this technique does not allow us to extract classification rules that show us the dependencies of the attributes, so the J48 technique is used, obtaining a result equal to the first classification corresponding to the first experiment without reducing attributes of 84.8% in addition to being a result very close to that obtained when using the Decision Table technique.

Using the J48 technique, the following rules are obtained, and the reduced tree generated with the C4.5 algorithm after attribute reduction, as shown in Fig. 3.

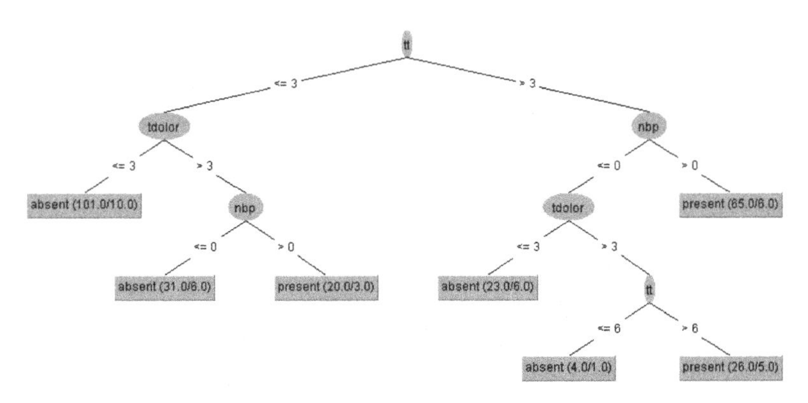

Fig. 3. Tree generated by Weka's J48 technique for rule extraction. Source: developed by author

5 Conclusions

This research has demonstrated the robustness of the attribute reduction methodology when determining the minimum number of attributes that allowed to predict with a high success rate using a set of medical data, for the early detection of cardiovascular diseases (Statlog), and to obtain better or similar results, without applying the proposed methodology; which was achieved, and even the results obtained were similar to those found in literature.

When experimenting with different methods such as learning rules, combining learning techniques, lazy learning, statistical functions, mathematics, through the generation of trees and based on Bayes learning, it was observed that the classification algorithm that works best when reducing the attributes of the data set is Decision Table. This study did not pretend to be better than the other investigations, it only seeks to verify the performance of this new methodology of attribute reduction, and how it can be used as explanatory mechanisms and presentation of the results.

References

1. OPS/OMS Chile-Cardiovascular diseases. https://www.paho.org/chi/index.php?option=com_content&view=article&id=172:enfermedades-cardiovasculares&Itemid=1005, Accessed 09 Sep 2019
2. Cardiovascular diseases (CVDs). https://www.who.int/news-room/fact-sheets/detail/cardiovascular-diseases-(cvds), Accessed 20 ene 2019
3. Beatriz, The figures of cardiovascular disease , Spanish Heart Foundation. https://fundaciondelcorazon.com/blog-impulso-vital/3264-las-cifras-de-la-enfermedad-cardiovascular.html, Accessed 30 Sep 2019
4. Fagard, R.H.: Predicting risk of fatal cardiovascular disease and sudden death in hypertension. J. Hypertens. **35**(11), 2165 (2017). https://doi.org/10.1097/hjh.0000000000001485
5. King, R.D., Feng, C., Sutherland, Y.A.: Statlog: comparison of classification algorithms on large real-world problems. Appl. Artif. Intell. **9**(3), 289–333 (1995). https://doi.org/10.1080/08839519508945477
6. Sharmila, S.: Analysis of heart disease prediction using datamining techniques, **08**(05), 3 (2017)
7. Turki, T., Wei, Y.Z.: Boosting support vector machines for cancer discrimination tasks. Comput. Biol. Med. **101**, 236–249 (2018). https://doi.org/10.1016/j.compbiomed.2018.08.006
8. Nilashi, M., Bin Ibrahim, O., Mardani, A., Ahani, A., Jusoh, A.: A soft computing approach for diabetes disease classification. https://journals.sagepub.com/doi/abs/10.1177/1460458216675500, Accedido 22 ago 2019
9. Leslie, H.H., Zhou, X., Spiegelman, D., Kruk, Y.M.E.: Health system measurement: harnessing machine learning to advance global health. PLoS One **13**(10), e0204958 (2018). https://doi.org/10.1371/journal.pone.0204958
10. Masethe, H.D., Masethe, Y.M.A.: Prediction of heart disease using classification algorithms, p. 4 (2014)
11. Fatima, M., Pasha, Y.M.: Survey of machine learning algorithms for disease diagnostic. J. Intell. Learn. Syst. Appl. **09**, 1 (2017). https://doi.org/10.4236/jilsa.2017.91001
12. El Houby, E.M.F.: A survey on applying machine learning techniques for management of diseases. J. Appl. Biomed. **16**(3), 165–174 (2018). https://doi.org/10.1016/j.jab.2018.01.002
13. Puth, M.-T., Neuhäuser, M., Ruxton, Y.G.D.: Effective use of Spearman's and Kendall's correlation coefficients for association between two measured traits. Anim. Behav. **102**, 77–84 (2015). https://doi.org/10.1016/j.anbehav.2015.01.010
14. Bahadur, Y.S.: Research Scholar, Department of Computer Science and Mathematics, Govt. P.G. Science College Rewa (M.P.), India. Predict the Diagnosis of Heart Disease Patients Using Classification Mining Techniques. IOSR J. Agric. Vet. Sci. 4(2), 60–64 (2013). https://doi.org/10.9790/2380-0426164
15. Liu, X., et al.: A Hybrid Classification System for Heart Disease Diagnosis Based on the RFRS Method. Computational and Mathematical Methods in Medicine (2017). https://www.hindawi.com/journals/cmmm/2017/8272091/abs/, Accedido: 29 Jul 2019
16. Pita, S., Fernández, Y.S.: Pértegas Díaz, Pruebas diagnósticas: Sensibilidad y especificidad (2010)
17. Delgado, C., Araneda, A., Behrens, Y.M.I.: Validación del instrumento Montreal Cognitive Assessment en español en adultos mayores de 60 años. Neurología, March 2017. https://doi.org/10.1016/j.nrl.2017.01.013

A Neural Approach to Ordinal Regression for the Preventive Assessment of Developmental Dyslexia

Francisco J. Martinez-Murcia[1](✉), Andres Ortiz[1], Marco A. Formoso[1], Miguel Lopez-Zamora[2], Juan Luis Luque[2], and Almudena Gimenez[2]

[1] Department of Communications Engineering, University of Málaga, Málaga, Spain
fjmm@ic.uma.es
[2] Department of Developmental and Educational Psychology, University of Málaga, Málaga, Spain

Abstract. Developmental Dyslexia (DD) is a learning disability related to the acquisition of reading skills that affects about 5% of the population. DD can have an enormous impact on the intellectual and personal development of affected children, so early detection is key to implementing preventive strategies for teaching language. Research has shown that there may be biological underpinnings to DD that affect phoneme processing, and hence these symptoms may be identifiable before reading ability is acquired, allowing for early intervention. In this paper we propose a new methodology to assess the risk of DD before students learn to read. For this purpose, we propose a mixed neural model that calculates risk levels of dyslexia from tests that can be completed at the age of 5 years. Our method first trains an auto-encoder, and then combines the trained encoder with an optimized ordinal regression neural network devised to ensure consistency of predictions. Our experiments show that the system is able to detect unaffected subjects two years before it can assess the risk of DD based mainly on phonological processing, giving a specificity of 0.969 and a correct rate of more than 0.92. In addition, the trained encoder can be used to transform test results into an interpretable subject spatial distribution that facilitates risk assessment and validates methodology.

Keywords: Autoencoder · Deep learning · Dyslexia · Prevention · Ordinal regression

1 Introduction

The Developmental Dyslexia (DD) is a learning disability that hinders the acquisition of reading skills, affecting roughly a 5% of the population [15]. It is characterized by difficulties in reading, unreadable handwriting, letter migration and common misspelling, that can affect the intellectual and personal development

E. A. de la Cal et al. (Eds.): HAIS 2020, LNAI 12344, pp. 620–630, 2020.
https://doi.org/10.1007/978-3-030-61705-9_51

of affected children [18]. A variety of learning methodologies exist that can positively impact the reading abilities of affected children. However, the diagnosis is generally associated to reading, and therefore it limits the minimum age, which may be of fundamental impact to apply preventive treatments.

In the last years, many works are pointing to common biological underpinnings that may cause this disability. Specifically, an incorrect phonological processing may lay behind some problems associated with DD, causing an abnormal encoding of words in memory [4–6]. These symptoms may be identifiable before the subjects acquire the ability to read, allowing for a preventive intervention that favours the reading competence in those in risk for DD.

Data decomposition is often used in machine learning both for dimensionality reduction and interpretation of the methodology. Many methodologies exist, among then the very popular Principal Component Analysis (PCA) [17] or Independent Component Analysis (ICA) [1,11]. In contrast to these techniques, whose model of the data is a linear combination of hidden variables, there exist manifold learning techniques that allow to discover more complex combinations. Some of them have been widely used in the literature, such as Isomap, the t-distributed stochastic neighbour embedding (t-SNE) or more recently, autoencoders [3,10]. Autoencoders are a powerful and versatile tool used in many works to yield a data-driven distribution of the data, allowing for correlation with continuous variables and classification, e.g. in Alzheimer's Disease [10].

Typically, machine learning is often thought of as a variety of methods for classification and regression. Moreover, most methodologies that deal with any kind of diagnosis tend to make use of classifiers, whereas those dealing with continuous assessment –e.g., cognitive tests– make use of regression. However, there is an intermediate problem, for which there are not so many alternatives available: risk assessment [9]. In the case of DD, there exist an arbitrary scale ranging from 0 to 4, in which no intermediate values are available. The risk scale is not continuous in nature, but in contrast to multi-class classification the outcomes still depend on each other: level 3 implies a higher risk than 2, but smaller than 4. There is an ordinal nature in these problems, and that is why we use ordinal regression to tackle the problem.

Many ordinal regression methods have been proposed. The most widespread consists on dividing the grading problem in a series of binary classifiers, each of which indicates if a certain threshold has been surpassed [9,13]. However, most of these systems deal with inconsistency in the classifier when the training complexity increases. That is, some binary classifiers may indicate the grade is above a given threshold, whereas others may not. In [2], the authors propose a Consistent Rank Logits (CORAL) ordinal regression to implement the binary classifiers with parameter sharing in the weights of the last layers, but with individual biases in each neuron, accomplishing theoretical classifier consistence.

In this paper, we present a novel methodology to predict the risk of DD in 5 year old individuals based on the outcomes of tests designed by expert psychologists. These subjects were followed over 4 years (from 5 to 8 years old), until a consistent DD risk evaluation was performed at age 7. We apply autoencoders for obtaining a feature modelling of the test outcomes and then a ordinal neural regressor that tries to predict the risk levels using the data at age 7. The dataset and the complete methodology is introduced at Sect. 2, the results are presented at Sect. 3 and discussed at Sect. 4. Finally, conclusions about this work are drawn at Sect. 5.

2 Materials and Methods

2.1 The LEEDUCA Study

The LEEDUCA project is a study for the assessment of specific learning difficulties of reading -dyslexia- and their evolution during infancy [12]. It implements a Response to Intervention (RtI) system that has been applied for 20 years in the US and 10 years in Finland. The system applies a dynamic evaluation three times a year from 4 to 8 years to large population samples. Specifically, the control and experimental groups came from a cohort from different schools in the south of Spain, following evaluation from 5 to 8 years, via the standard criteria used in similar studies and the Special Education School Services (SESS).

2.2 Data and Preprocessing

The data from the LEEDUCA study comprises a battery of tests spanning from 5 to 8 years old children at school. These tests are adapted to the age and educational level of the students (e.g., when they cannot read at 5 years), and therefore it is difficult to establish any longitudinal processing. As stated, we only use the 33 tests performed at 5 years –when students cannot read– to predict the risk of DD at 7 years. The risk grades were set in function of the number and grade of the scores in assessments of four major categories: Phonological Route, Visual Route, Text Fluidity and Text Comprehension. Anomalous values were set based on percentile (p) values, in which $p < 30$, $p < 20$ and $p < 30$ were set to grade 1, 2 and 3. Afterwards, these abnormality grades were averaged over all assessments and categories, and the final risk was estimated according to this average value, in a scale of 0 to 4, depending on the intervals where it laid $(-\infty, 0), (0, 0.5), (0.5, 1.5), (1.5, 2.5), (2.5, \infty)$. In the end, the number of subjects in each grade is 5, 331, 270, 50 and 10 for grades 0, 1, 2, 3 and 4.

All subjects lacking more than 5 test results in the tests were deleted from the set. That left us with 572 subjects with evaluations at 5 and 7. K-Nearest-Neighbour (KNN) imputation [19] with the two closest neighbours was used to generate valid values for those missing less than 5 results. Finally, the data was scaled to the range $[0, 1]$, estimating the minimum and maximum values from the training subset.

2.3 Denoising Autoencoder

Autoencoders (AEs) are a specific type of neural encoder-decoder architecture. It consists of a feed-forward neural network that reduces dimensionality (encoder), directly connected to a inverse network (a decoder, usually symmetric with the encoder) that increases dimensionality to reconstruct the original shape. Then, the network is trained to minimize the error between the input and the output. A typical variation is the denoising AE (DAE), in which the input is corrupted with noise and the network is expected to provide the original input, without noise, which is sometimes considered a regularization procedure. No further regularization was used.

In this work, we propose a hybrid model that trains the autoencoder and then reuses the encoder part to perform dimensionality reduction, as in [10]. The precise architecture uses symmetric encoder and decoder modules. There are three layers of N, 64 and 3 neurons for the encoder and 3, 64 and N for the decoder (where N is the number of tests included). We used 3 neurons in the Z-layer to favour a visual interpretation of the results in a three-dimensional space, and 64 neurons in the intermediate layers of the encoder and decoder were chosen after a careful systematic test of accuracy and visualization, in powers of 2. A higher number of neurons led to overfitting and lower explainability of the representation, and a smaller number of neurons yielded lower performance. Batch normalization is used for speeding up the convergence and the activation function for layers 1, 2, 4 and 5 is ELU. The intermediate layer (usually known as Z-layer) and output layers have linear activation. For training we use the Mean Squared Error (MSE) between the input and output data as loss, and the Adamax optimizer [7].

2.4 Ordinal Neural Regression

To perform ordinal regression, we use the Consistent Rank Logits (CORAL) approach proposed in [2]. CORAL is devised to create an ordinal regression framework with theoretical guarantees for classifier consistency, in contrast to other methods in the literature [13]. The procedure consists of two major contributions. First, a label extension, by which the rank level y_i is extended into $K-1$ binary labels $\{t_{i,0}, \dots t_{i,K-1}\}$ such that $t_{i,j} \in \{0,1\}$ indicates whether y_i exceeds a given rank ($y_i > r_k$), as in [13]. This is implemented at the output layer of the regression network, via a layer with $K-1$ binary neuron classifiers sharing the same weight parameter but independent bias units, which according to [2] solves the inconsistency problem among predicted binary responses. The predicted rank is obtained as:

$$r_i = \sum_{j=0}^{K-2} o_{i,j} \tag{1}$$

where $o_{i,j}$ is the output (linear activation) of the jth neuron for the ith subject, also known as logit.

The second key aspect of the CORAL regression is the loss function. To calculate the loss between $o_{i,j}$ and the target level $t_{i,j}$, the authors propose:

$$\mathcal{L}(\mathbf{o},\mathbf{l}) = \sum_{n}\sum_{j} t_{n,j} \log\left[s(o_{n,j})\right] + (1-t_{n,j})(\log\left[s(o_{n,j})\right] - o_{n,j}) \tag{2}$$

where $s(\cdot)$ is the sigmoid function. An optional feature importance variable could multiply the second term to adjust for label prevalence, although adding it did not increased the performance significantly. Furthermore, since it also implied making assumptions about the real distribution of subjects, we chose not to use this importance term.

2.5 Full Model: Architecture and Training

The resulting model is a combination of the encoder part of a DAE and an ordinal neural regressor, a 3-layer feed-forward network that uses the CORAL framework. The model architecture is displayed in more detail at Fig. 1a), b) and c).

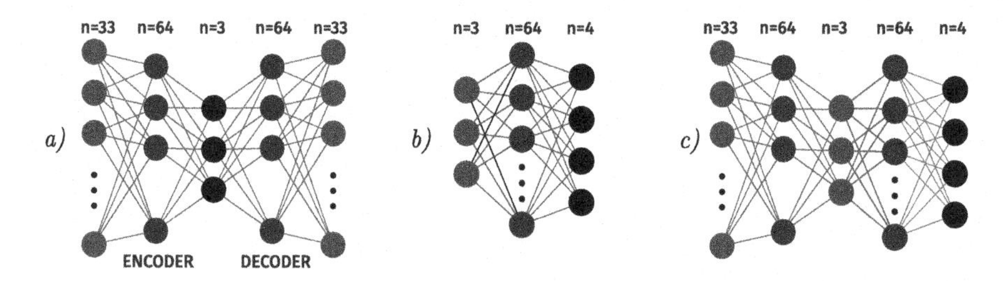

Fig. 1. Schema of the a) Autoencoder for pre and re-training, b) Feed-forward network for CORAL ordinal regression, c) complete model.

The cost functions for the encoder and the regressor are defined at Sects. 2.3 and 2.4, and Adam with $lr = 0.01$ is used to train the whole system (with or without locking the encoder). We applied early stopping in both cases, that is, the training was stopped after 150 epochs if there was no improvement in validation loss, in order to retain the best model.

2.6 Evaluation

The models have been tested under a 10-fold stratified cross-validation (CV) scenario [8]. A large variety of performance measures were obtained, specifically: correct rate, per-class correct rate (for multi-class classification), sensitivity, specificity, precision and F1-score, and their corresponding standard deviation (STD) over all cross-validation folds. Finally, the balanced accuracy is defined as the average correct rate over all classes [10], which is the most representative measure in such an imbalanced problem.

For evaluating the relative contribution of each variable to the final outcome (either the manifold distribution, risk estimation or classification), we use a randomization procedure based on Permutation Importance (PI) [14]. We iteratively set each variable to zero, and re-tested the trained regressor obtaining a performance estimation in each CV fold. Afterwards, we compare those performances to the regressor using all variables. In this framework, a larger performance loss implies a larger influence of that variable in the model.

Finally, we define the following models to be compared in our work:

- **PCA.** A model composed of a decomposition of the dataset using Principal Component Analysis and a CORAL regression (Fig. 1b) on the component scores for each subject. Note that only the training subset is used to create the PCA model and project the test set.
- **Pretraining.** The proposed model in which the autoencoder (Fig. 1a) is first trained, and then the model is built with the neural regressor (Fig. 1b) and the pre-trained encoder (Fig. 1c). The encoder is locked and only the neural regressor is trained.
- **Retraining.** The AE is pre-trained as in the previous model (Fig. 1a), but this time, the full model (Fig. 1c) including the encoder and the neural regressor are trained simultaneously.

3 Results

After training and testing the models defined in Sect. 2.6, we measured first the multi-level performance; that means, we provide the accuracy for the different DD risk levels, the overall correct rate and the balanced accuracy. These results are presented at Table 1.

Table 1. Results for the ordinal regression, including accuracy per level, balanced accuracy and overall correct rate for the PCA, pre- and re-training models.

	PCA	Pre-training	Re-training
Level 0 (acc.)	0.000 [0.00]	**0.143 [0.14]**	0.067 [0.14]
Level 1 (acc.)	**0.822 [0.13]**	0.633 [0.17]	0.615 [0.15]
Level 2 (acc.)	**0.433 [0.18]**	0.376 [0.09]	0.395 [0.13]
Level 3 (acc.)	0.058 [0.12]	0.225 [0.26]	**0.442 [0.14]**
Level 4 (acc.)	0.000 [0.00]	0.000 [0.00]	0.000 [0.00]
Correct rate [STD]	**0.575 [0.06]**	0.481 [0.07]	0.484 [0.08]
Balanced acc.	0.309 [0.05]	0.321 [0.05]	**0.357 [0.06]**

Regarding the per-level accuracy, we observe that PCA is good in general for obtaining a fair overall correct rate (0.575) when compared to the pre-training model (0.481) and the re-trained model (0.484). However, the PCA fails to account for the less-prevalent levels (3 and 4, the ones associated with high risk of DD), which is precisely the main objective of this paper. When looking at this, the pre-training model at least detects a small proportion (0.225) of level 3 subjects and also level 0, but failing to account for level 4, whereas the re-trained model detects a larger amount (0.442) of these levels, at the cost of mistaking some level 1 and 2 subjects. This is reflected on the balanced accuracy, which is higher in the case of the re-training model, but also can be seen in more detail at the confusion matrices, displayed at Fig. 2.

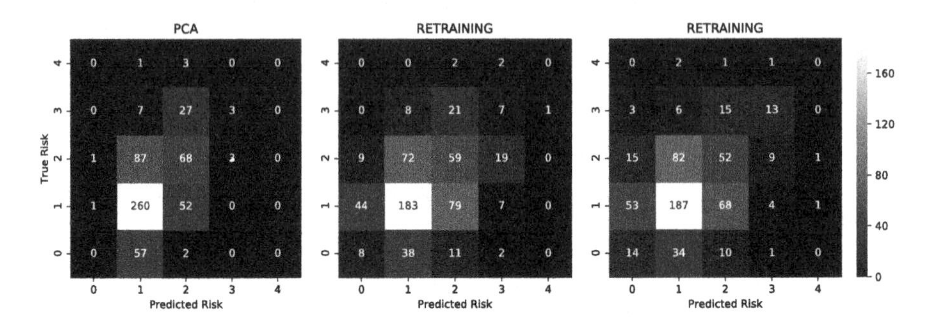

Fig. 2. Confusion matrices for the three models evaluated.

There we see how the re-training model is the best in grading extreme-level subjects (levels 0, 3 and 4) correctly. This is far more evident in the case of the levels more associated to dyslexia (3 and 4), which are far better in the DAE + ordinal regression models than in the PCA.

However, there is another approach to the problem: the one that considers only the detection of subjects in high risk of DD (a risk level $\geq$3). Derived from the same model, the results of this binary scenario are presented at Table 2.

Table 2. Performance results for binary classification of the highest levels ($r_i \geq 3$)

	PCA	Pre-training	Re-training
Correct rate	**0.934 [0.012]**	0.898 [0.052]	0.927 [0.041]
Sensitivity	0.050 [0.110]	0.225 [0.281]	**0.442 [0.153]**
Specificity	**0.998 [0.006]**	0.946 [0.059]	0.962 [0.037]
Precision	0.667 [0.580]	0.446 [0.482]	**0.909 [0.091]**
F1-score	0.400 [0.000]	0.572 [0.193]	**0.585 [0.150]**
Balanced acc.	0.524 [0.053]	0.586 [0.131]	**0.702 [0.086]**

The overall correct rate in this case is astounding, over 90% in all cases. However, this is again due to the lower prevalence of DD. When digging deeper into the measures, we observe that the sensitivity and specificity, as well as the balanced accuracy, offer a clearer sight of the performance of each model. Particularly, the larger specificity is achieved again by the PCA model (it is the best in discarding subjects with no risk of DD). However, the sensitivity of the model is 0.050, close to labelling all subjects as low risk. The DAE+Regressor models offer larger sensitivity (over 0.2), again with the re-training model the one achieving better results, with a sensitivity of 0.442, and a precision of 0.909, and a total balanced accuracy of 0.702, which is fairly good for this application. Furthermore, the specificity of this method (0.927) is excellent, indicating that the system hardly misses any subject in risk of DD. Given that our purpose is to perform a preventive intervention on subjects in risk, a good trade-off between high specificity and the best possible sensitivity is a sensible approach.

4 Discussion

The results of evaluating the model show that it is possible to predict DD when students are 5 years old, before they have learnt to read. This is a fundamental advance in preventive treatment, allowing for an earlier detection of this learning disability and making it possible to apply a prevention program.

Since the LEEDUCA study has a large cohort that has been repeatedly evaluated over the years, many subjects are available for our study. Thus, neural network architectures may be applied to the problem. The combination of a representation modelling approach (the DAE) that has been applied to other data analysis pipelines [10], and the flexibility of neural regression seems to be informative enough to automatically grade the risk of DD and provide a set of subjects to which the preventive program could be applied. Moreover, this methodology gives us larger insight into which tests are more predictive of future reading disability, at the same time that it provides a deeper insight into the data, revealing a self-supervised data decomposition via the autoencoder that allows for a bi- and tri-dimensional representation of the dataset.

When exploring this projection onto a two-dimensional space, and comparing the three models, we obtain Fig. 3. There we can see that all three methods project the subjects (each point) in a spatial coordinate related to the DD risk. However, these distributions differ. In the case of PCA, the risk increases with component 0 (the first PCA component), but individuals are sparsely located, and the levels are very mixed, which was expected for a linear approach. For the DAE + regressor models, the levels are more distinguishable. In the case of the pre-training model, it resembles the PCA model with an increasing risk over neuron 0, but this time, the levels are clustered together. However, the subjects at higher level are still very mixed, making it difficult for the regressor to correctly assign risk levels. The re-training model, however, is forming a manifold that resembles a curve starting at subjects with risk 0–1 and relatively increasing up to the furthest subjects, those with risk level 3 and 4. This proves that there exist a relationship between the test outcomes and the risk of developing DD that is better modelled by the re-training model, generating more accurate predictions of risk.

Focusing on this model, it may be very useful to assess which input variables cause larger changes in the overall balanced accuracy and sensitivity. To do so, we use the PI algorithm (see Sect. 2.6) that helps us to visualize the relative influence of each variable. This importance is shown at Fig. 4.

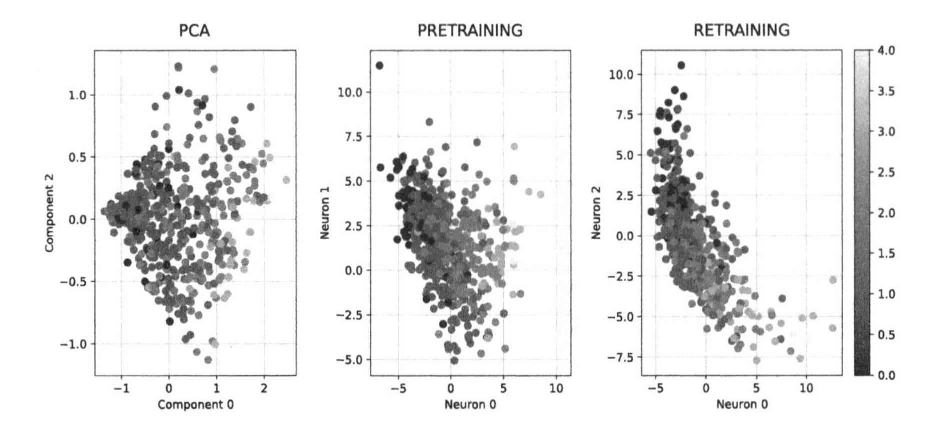

Fig. 3. Distribution of the points at the output of the PCA (for the baseline system) and the AE (for the pre- and re-training systems). Note the self-supervised distribution of the gradings in the later models.

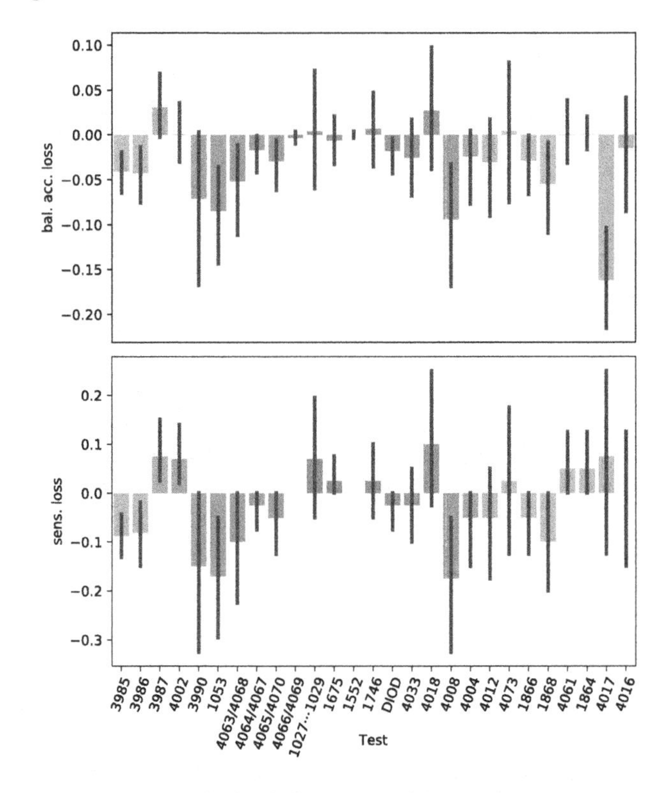

Fig. 4. Relative importance of the different variables in the re-training system, computed using the sensitivity and balanced accuracy loss.

In Fig. 4 the behaviour is consistent in most variables, regardless of how the loss is measured (balanced accuracy or sensitivity in the binary classification, DD detection), except for two relevant cases, test variables 4017 and 4002. Those correspond respectively to a test to label Arabic numerals and a test for verbal memory according to the phonological hypothesis. For the remaining variables, the larger performance loss is for variables 3990, 1053, 4063/4068 and 4008. The last one corresponds to an evaluation of the 'sustained attention', within the category of executive functions. All the remaining correspond to the phonological hypothesis, specifically for trials that evaluate the Lexical access speed in colours (3990), numbers (1053) and objects in syllables (4063/4068). This is consistent with the current scientific understanding of DD in the literature. In fact, an incorrect phonological processing is one of the most accepted causes of DD in the scientific community [16], causing an abnormal encoding of words in memory.

In summary, we developed a novel methodology intended to accurately grade subjects two years before the first DD risk evaluations. It uses a self-supervised decomposition via denoising autoencoders plus a neural ordinal regression following the CORAL methodology. The results prove that the methodology is useful for an early screening, achieving high values of specificity that could lead to non-invasive preventive methodologies that allow a more efficient development of reading skills.

5 Conclusions

In this work, we have developed a neural system that combines a denoising autoencoder with the theoretical guarantees of the Consistent Rank Logits (CORAL) neural regression, allowing for a model that is able to predict the risk of Developmental Dyslexia two years before first assessing the reading abilities. The system combines a pre-training of the autoencoder, and then connecting the output of the encoder to a neural perceptron that uses parameter sharing at the output as in the CORAL ordinal regression framework, yielding a specificity of 0.969 and correct rate of over 0.92. The system outputs risk level values similar to the ones assessed at age 7 using just the test outcomes at age 5, based mainly on phonological processing. The system proved its ability in detecting non-affected and yielding a subset of candidates for preventive –non invasive– language teaching modalities, allowing a visual interpretation by transforming the battery of tests into a manifold related to the risk levels of dyslexia, validating the methodology.

Acknowledgements. This work was partly supported by the MINECO/FEDER under RTI2018-098913-B-I00, PSI2015-65848-R and PGC2018-098813-B-C32 projects. Work by F.J.M.M. was supported by the MICINN "Juan de la Cierva - Formación" FJCI-2017-33022.

References

1. Bartlett, M., Movellan, J., Sejnowski, T.: Face recognition by independent component analysis. IEEE Trans. Neural Netw. **13**(6), 1450–1464 (2002)

2. Cao, W., Mirjalili, V., Raschka, S.: Rank-consistent ordinal regression for neural networks. arXiv:1901.07884 [cs, stat], August 2019
3. Chen, M., Shi, X., Zhang, Y., Wu, D., Guizani, M.: Deep features learning for medical image analysis with convolutional autoencoder neural network. IEEE Trans. Big Data (2017). https://doi.org/10.1109/TBDATA.2017.2717439
4. Goswami, U.: A neural oscillations perspective on phonological development and phonological processing in developmental dyslexia. Lang. Linguist. Compass **13**(5), e12328 (2019). https://doi.org/10.1111/lnc3.12328
5. Goswami, U.: Speech rhythm and language acquisition: an amplitude modulation phase hierarchy perspective. Ann. N. Y. Acad. Sci. **1453**(1), 67–78 (2019). https://doi.org/10.1111/nyas.14137
6. Kimppa, L., Shtyrov, Y., Partanen, E., Kujala, T.: Impaired neural mechanism for online novel word acquisition in dyslexic children. Sci. Rep. **8**(1), 1–12 (2018). https://doi.org/10.1038/s41598-018-31211-0
7. Kingma, D.P., Ba, J.: Adam: a method for stochastic optimization. arXiv preprint arXiv:1412.6980 (2014)
8. Kohavi, R.: A study of cross-validation and bootstrap for accuracy estimation and model selection. In: Proceedings of International Joint Conference on AI, pp. 1137–1145 (1995)
9. Li, L., Lin, H.T.: Ordinal regression by extended binary classification. In: Advances in Neural Information Processing Systems, pp. 865–872 (2007)
10. Martinez-Murcia, F.J., Ortiz, A., Gorriz, J., Ramirez, J., Castillo-Barnes, D.: Studying the manifold structure of Alzheimer's disease: a deep learning approach using convolutional autoencoders. IEEE J. Biomed. Health Inform. **24**(1), 17–26 (2020). https://doi.org/10.1109/JBHI.2019.2914970
11. Martínez-Murcia, F.J., Górriz, J., Ramírez, J., Puntonet, C.G., Illán, I., Initiative, A.D.N., et al.: Functional activity maps based on significance measures and independent component analysis. Comput. Methods Programs Biomed. **111**(1), 255–268 (2013). https://doi.org/10.1016/j.cmpb.2013.03.015
12. Martinez-Murcia, F.J., et al.: Periodogram connectivity of EEG signals for the detection of dyslexia. In: Ferrández Vicente, J.M., Álvarez-Sánchez, J.R., de la Paz López, F., Toledo Moreo, J., Adeli, H. (eds.) IWINAC 2019. LNCS, vol. 11486, pp. 350–359. Springer, Cham (2019). https://doi.org/10.1007/978-3-030-19591-5_36
13. Niu, Z., Zhou, M., Wang, L., Gao, X., Hua, G.: Ordinal regression with multiple output CNN for age estimation. In: Proceedings of the IEEE Conference on Computer Vision and Pattern Recognition, pp. 4920–4928 (2016)
14. Olden, J.D., Jackson, D.A.: Illuminating the "black box": a randomization approach for understanding variable contributions in artificial neural networks. Ecol. Model. **154**(1), 135–150 (2002). https://doi.org/10.1016/S0304-3800(02)00064-9
15. Peterson, R., Pennington, B.: Developmental dyslexia. Lancet **379**, 1997–2007 (2012)
16. Shaywitz, S.E., Morris, R., Shaywitz, B.A.: The education of dyslexic children from childhood to young adulthood. Ann. Rev. Psychol. **59**, 451–475 (2008)
17. Spetsieris, P.G., Ma, Y., Dhawan, V., Eidelberg, D.: Differential diagnosis of parkinsonian syndromes using functional PCA-based imaging features. Neuroimage **45**(4), 1241–52 (2009)
18. Thompson, P.A., Hulme, C., Nash, H.M., Gooch, D., Hayiou-Thomas, E., Snowling, M.J.: Developmental dyslexia: predicting individual risk. J. Child Psychol. Psychiatry **56**(9), 976–987 (2015)
19. Troyanskaya, O., et al.: Missing value estimation methods for DNA microarrays. Bioinformatics **17**(6), 520–525 (2001). https://doi.org/10.1093/bioinformatics/17.6.520

Fall Detection Based on Local Peaks and Machine Learning

José R. Villar[1(✉)], Mario Villar[2], Mirko Fañez[3], Enrique de la Cal[1], and Javier Sedano[3]

[1] University of Oviedo, Oviedo, Spain
{villarjose,delacal}@uniovi.es
[2] University of Granada, Granada, Spain
mario.villarsanz@gmail.com
[3] Instituto Tecnológico de Castilla y León, Burgos, Spain
{mirko.fanez,javier.sedano}@itcl.es

Abstract. This research focuses on Fall Detection (FD) using on-wrist wearable devices including tri-axial accelerometers performing FD autonomously. This type of approaches makes use of an event detection stage followed by some pre-processing and a final classification stage. The event detection stage is basically performed using thresholds or a combination of thresholds and finite state machines. In this research, we extend our previous work and propose an event detection method free of thresholds to tune or adapt to the user that reduces the number of false alarms; we also consider a mixture between the two approaches. Additionally, a set of features is proposed as an alternative to those used in previous research. The classification of the samples is performed using a Deep Learning Neural Network and the experimentation performs a comparison of this research to a published and well-known technique using the UMA Fall, one of the publicly available simulated fall detection data sets. Results show the improvements in the event detection using the new proposals.

1 Introduction

The study of Fall Detection (FD) represents a challenge in many different domains, from the monitoring of patients to the improvement of the autonomous living of elderly people. There are many different solutions, including video systems [1], intelligent tiles [2], sound detection [3], etc. Wearables play an important role in FD as they can be easily deployed, allowing care institutions to optimize their services with a relatively low cost [4,5]. More specifically, autonomous on-wrist wearable devices may be crucial in helping the elder population to continue living by their own. With autonomous on-wrist wearable devices we are referring to smart devices, such as smart-watches, that can be extended to detect any possible fall event using their own computational capabilities, without the assessment of any external service. In this research, we focus on smart-watches with built-in tri-axial acceleromenters (3DACC), which is by far the most chosen option [6–10]. Reviews on FD can be found in [11,12].

E. A. de la Cal et al. (Eds.): HAIS 2020, LNAI 12344, pp. 631–643, 2020.
https://doi.org/10.1007/978-3-030-61705-9_52

The main part of the solutions make use of Machine Learning (ML) to classify the current instance as a fall. Some examples of these methods are those presented in [6,8], where a feature extraction stage and Support Vector Machines classifies the Time Series (TS) windows. However, thresholds have been also used in FD [9,13,14], labelling the instance according to whether or not the magnitude of the acceleration surpass the pre-defined values. Thresholds have also been used in FD to define simple rules that drive the final decision [9,10,15]. Refer to [7] for a comparison of these type of methods.

Currently, it could be said that there are two main research approaches: using deep learning solutions and using classical ML solutions. Concerning the former, there are several published studies [16,17], but the capacity of current wearable devices is still far from that desired to include this type of models [18]. This study focuses on the second type of solutions; more specifically, in those studies concerned with the dynamics in a fall event [19,20]. These studies includes a FD method, a pre-processing stage and a classification stage using an ML method. For instance, Abbate et al. proposed the use of these dynamics as the basis of the FD algorithm [19], with moderate computational constraints but a high number of thresholds to tune. The proposal of Abbate et al has been modified in a series of papers [21–23] to adapt the sensor placement on a wrist. We refer to this event detection as *on-wrist Abbate*. Recently, local peak detection was proposed to identify the fall events together with a different set of transformations of the acceleration magnitude [24], which represents the starting point of this research.

The main contribution in this study consist of introducing a Finite State Machine (FSM) to the event detection mechanism proposed in [24]. Interestingly, this new event detection makes use of no user predefined threshold, which represents a step ahead in the event detection mechanisms in the literature. We refer to this event detection mechanism as *MAX-PEAK-FSM*. Alternatively, we evaluate a mixture of both approaches, denoted as *ABBATE-MAX-PEAK*. Furthermore, several new features are computed for the acceleration data window surrounding each detected peak; a study on this topic is performed. Finally, a comparison with different solutions in the literature are presented.

The structure of the paper is as follows. The next section deals with the description of both the MAX-PEAK and the new proposal MAX-PEAK-FSM together with the ABBATE-MAX-PEAK. The feature description and how these features are processed is included in this section as well. Section 3 details the experimentation set up and includes the results and discussion. Finally, the conclusions are drawn.

2 Fall Detection Using Local Maximum Peaks

Figure 1 shows the block diagram proposed to detect the fall events. Firstly, the magnitude of the acceleration is calculated. The first stage is the event detection method, which signals whether a TS sample includes a candidate of a fall event. The second stage is the feature extraction from a peak window surrounding the found peak. Finally, the set of features is classified either as a Fall or as a

Not_Fall peak. This classification stage is performed with a feed-forward Neural Network (NN) following the studies in [19,22,24]. This section deals with the event detection which is described in the next subsection, while the FSM is described in Subsect. 2.2.

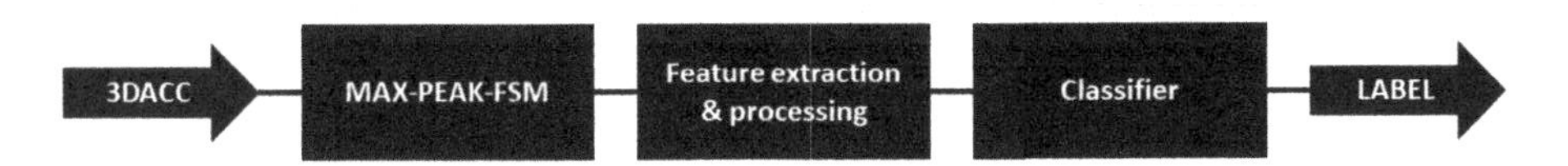

Fig. 1. Block diagram of the proposal. The local maximum peaks are filtered and only those found relevant are anylized. The feature extraction aims to represent the most interesting characteristics of the TS surrounding the peak. Finally, a feed-forward NN classifies the instance.

2.1 Event Detection Using Local Maximum Peaks

The block diagram of the event detection stage is presented in Fig. 2. The values within the Time Series (TS) of the magnitude of the acceleration are smoothed using the mean value within sliding window of size $\frac{1}{4}$ of second and shift 1 sample. From now on, the TS contains the mean values computed from the smooth step.

Afterwards, we apply the S_1 transformation proposed in [25]. S_1 is calculated using Eq. 1, where k is the predefined number of samples and t is the current sample time-stamp. It is worth noticing that, although we analyze the window $[a_{t-2k-1}, a_t]$ at time t, the peak candidate is a_{t-k}, the center of the interval. The S_1 transformation represents a scaling of the TS, which makes the peak detection easier using a predefined threshold α. The algorithm for detecting peaks is straightforward: a peak occurs in time t if the value S_t is higher than α and is the highest in its $2k$ neighborhood. The value of k is determined as the inverse of the sampling frequency.

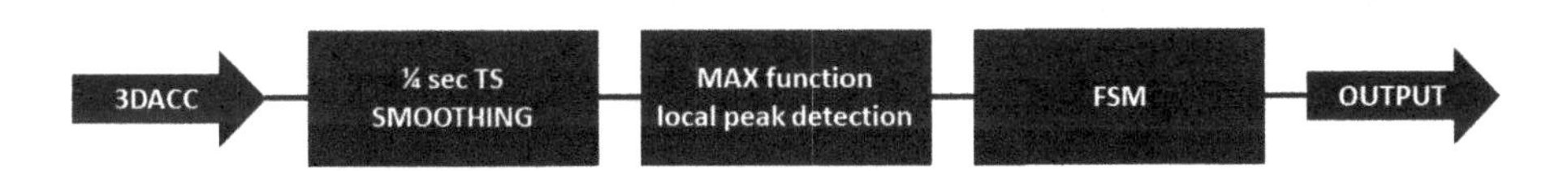

Fig. 2. Event detection mechanism. The 3DACC signal is smoothed using a $\frac{1}{4}$ second window. The filtered signal is analyzed using the local maximum peak proposed in [25]. When a local maximum peak is detected the FSM filters those repetitive peaks that appears in certain activities, such as walking or running. The output is whether a peak might be a fall event candidate (thus, needing further processing) or not.

$$S_1(t) = \frac{1}{2} \times \{\max_{i=t-2k}^{t-k-1} (a_{i+1} - a_i) + \max_{i=t-k+1}^{t} (a_i - a_{i-1})\} \quad (1)$$

As stated in [24], using statistics theory avoids the problem of the defining α. To do so, we defined walking as the reference activity (henceforth subindex

w). Each user u needs to perform this activity during a short period of time, where the mean μ^u_w and the standard deviation σ^u_w are computed; the TS is then normalized using $<\mu^u_w, \sigma^u_w>$. S_1 is calculated for the normalized TS during this walking period, calculating its mean ($\mu^u_{wS_1}$) and standard deviation ($\sigma^u_{wS_1}$). Then we set $\alpha = 3 \times \sigma^u_{wS_1}$, which means (for a normal distribution) that *a high value that is statistically the upper limit for S_1 when walking is a peak candidate.*

2.2 A Finite State Machine Labelling the Relevant Peaks

The FSM proposed in [19] was designed considering the dynamics of a fall event; it has been found that in good percentage of the cases the FSM certainly detects the fall dynamics. However,this proposal makes use of thresholds to determine the magnitude of the acceleration peak and the time window around the peak value. Thus, we simplify this FSM (see left part of Fig. 3. Each detected local maximum peak changes the state to *Timing*, starting a timer of 2.5 seconds as was suggested in [19]. If the timer fires, the state moves into *Is a Peak*, where the feature extraction and further processing together with the classification takes place. The state changes to *No Peak* once the peak is labelled.

Moreover, we merged the two FSMs, the one proposed in [19] and the one proposed before. This solution, called ABBATE-MAX-PEAK, uses the S1 value and the concept of statistically out of range wrt the acceleration value when walking instead of the acceleration and a predefined threshold. However, the timers and the calculation of the peak window is performed as stated in the work of Abbate et al.

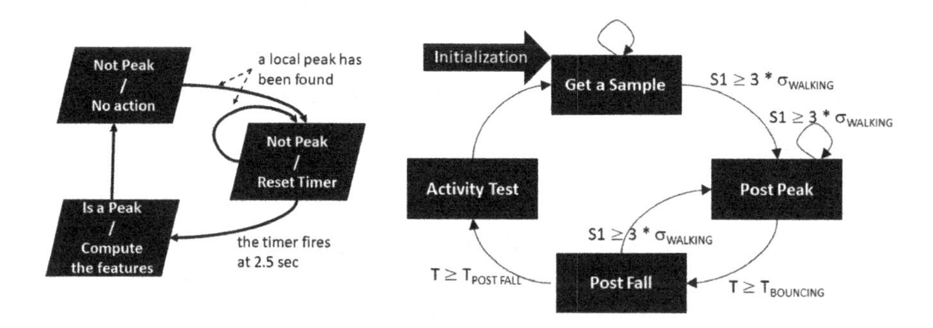

Fig. 3. The proposed FSMs. To the left, the FSM used in the MAX-PEAK solution. To the right, the FSM used in the ABBATE-MAX-PEAK approach. This latter makes use of the same FSM as proposed in Abbate et al. [19], but using the S1 and the concept of statistically out of range proposed in the previous section.

2.3 Extended Feature Subset

The research in [19] introduced up to 8 features that were computed in the context of the dynamic window around each detected peak; these features includes too many parameters and predefined thresholds and tuning them becomes a hard task. In [24] 4 different well-known transformations were proposed; the main novelty were that these 4 features were computed for both the pre-peak and post-peak parts of the peak window. The rationale was that, provided there are differences in the human behavior before and after a fall, the differences must be reflected on these features as well. Therefore, the $[a_{t-2k-1}, a_t]$ window is split in two: before ($I_B = [a_{t-2k-1}, a_{t-k-1}]$) and after ($I_A = [a_{t-k+1}, a_t]$) the peak, respectively. For each of these sub-intervals the following transformations were calculated, with s and e meaning the bounds of the corresponding intervals:

- Average Absolute Acceleration Magnitude Variation, **AAMV**, computed as $AAMV = \sum_{t=s}^{e-1} |a_{t+1} - a_t|/N$, with N the number of samples in the interval $[s, e]$.
- Energy of the Acceleration Magnitude, **E**, calculated as $E = \sum_{t=s}^{e} a_t^2/N$
- Mean of the acceleration magnitude, **MN**, in the interval $[s, e]$.
- Standard Deviation of the acceleration magnitude, **SD**, in the interval $[s, e]$.

In this research we propose 3 more features from [26] together with the S_1 function proposed in [25] and adapted to this specific problem. This is the listing of these features.

- Amount of Movement, **AoM**, computed as $AoM = |max_{t=s}^{e}(a_t) - min_{t=s}^{e}(a_t)|$.
- Mean Absolute Deviation, **MAD**, computed as $MAD = \frac{1}{N} \sum_{t=s}^{e} |a_t - MN_{t=s}^{e}|$.
- Maximum of the differences, $\mathbf{S_1}$, proposed in [25] and computed using Eq. 1.

When using the MAX-PEAK, the 4 features from [24] plus the 2 first features from [26] are computed for i) the subinterval before the peak, ii) the subinterval after the peak and iii) for the whole peak window. The S_1 feature will be computed for the current peak and used as an input feature as well. For the MAX-PEAK we have a total of 19 features. In the case of ABBATE-MAX-PEAK, the same features as proposed in [19,22] are used.

3 Experiments and Results

3.1 Data Sets and Experimentation Set up

This research makes use of UMA Fall [27], a public staged falls data set. A total of 17 participants contributed to this data set, with up to 208 TS of simulated falls and a total of 531 TS. The TS were sampled at 20 Hz; in this research, we focus on the TS from the 3DACC sensor placed on a wrist. Each participant performed a non-fixed number of Activities of Daily Living (ADL) and falls.

The experimentation is divided in two parts. The first one is devoted to compare fall event detection, while the second one compares the performance of this study. In both of them, this study is compare with the proposals in [19,24].

The first part compares the methods using the well-known counters True Positive -TP-, True Negative -TN-, False Positive -FP- and False Negative -FN- in order to evaluate the performance of the event detection methods; we count a positive as a fall while a negative as non-fall. These counters are updated according to whether there are or not peaks detected in each of the participant's TS and the label this TS has. For each participant, the walking activity TS are used to set up its α value.

The second part makes use of densely connected neural network using Keras. The model includes, in all the cases, 3 layers (with 150 neurons each and a ReLU activation) plus one final layer of 1 neuron using a sigmoid activation and L2 regularizer with 0.001 as updating coefficient. A 0.4 % dropout layer is included between each two layers to avoid the overfitting. In all the cases, the models were allowed 30 epochs with a batch size computed as the number of instances divided by the number of epochs. The features extracted from the detected peaks are scaled to the interval [0.0, 1.0]. All the instances are labelled as FALL or NOT_FALL.

In this second part, we perform Leave-one-PARTICIPANT-out cross validation: we keep the data from the current participant for validation; the remaining instances are used to train and test the Deep Learning NN. A 10-fold cross validation is performed then using the train and test part. The mean Sensitivity and mean Specificity obtained for the validation data set are the metrics used in the comparison of the methods.

3.2 Comparison of Event Detection Methods

Table 1 shows the counters for each of the event detection methods. The performance of the on-wrist Abbate is much worse than that of MAX-PEAK and MAX-PEAK-FSM if we consider the undetected alarms: 56 undetected falls for the on-wrist Abbate, 2 for the MAX-PEAK and MAX-PEAK-FSM and 3 for the ABBATE-MAX-PEAK. Besides, the on-wrist Abbate performs really well with the TN, perhaps due to the relatively high threshold used in detecting the fall events. The MAX-PEAK-FSM and the ABBATE-MAX-PEAK clearly outperform the MAX-PEAK in terms of reducing the false alarms.

On the other hand, when analyzing the UMA Fall data set, the number of peaks detected by each method were 201 for the on-wrist Abbate, 3073 for the MAX-PEAK, 449 for the MAX-PEAK-FSM and 531 for the ABBATE-MAX-PEAK. This means that for several TS the event detection considered more than one peak. Obviously, the sensitiveness of MAX-PEAK is much higher than those of on-wrist Abbate and MAX-PEAK-FSM, producing by far more false alarms than the other methods. Hence, the MAX-PEAK produces highly imbalanced data sets and we are not going to use it the next experimentation concerning with instances classification. A priory, the MAX-PEAK-FSM and the ABBATE-MAX-PEAK seem the best event detection methods.

Table 1. Event detection results for each participant.

Pid	on-wrist Abbate				MAX-PEAK				MAX-PEAK-FSM				ABB-MAX-PEAK			
	TN	FP	FN	TP	TN	FP	FN	TP	TN	FP	FN	TP	TN	FP	FN	TP
1	16	2	5	15	7	11	0	20	9	9	0	20	10	8	0	20
2	15	3	2	10	7	11	0	12	13	5	0	12	13	5	0	12
3	17	2	2	16	5	14	0	18	8	11	0	18	9	10	0	18
4	18	3	7	10	4	17	1	16	10	11	1	16	11	10	1	16
5	15	0	0	6	5	10	0	6	8	7	0	6	9	6	0	6
6	4	0	2	4	0	4	0	6	0	4	0	6	0	4	0	6
7	20	2	0	0	2	20	0	0	3	19	0	0	3	19	0	0
8	16	3	0	0	3	16	0	0	6	13	0	0	7	12	0	0
9	16	2	2	16	5	13	0	18	12	6	0	18	12	6	0	18
10	19	2	0	0	7	14	0	0	9	12	0	0	10	11	0	0
11	19	0	1	0	4	15	0	1	8	11	0	1	8	11	0	1
12	22	1	9	0	0	23	0	9	5	18	0	9	7	16	0	9
13	7	0	5	7	4	3	0	12	6	1	0	12	6	1	0	12
14	5	0	0	6	1	4	0	6	2	3	0	6	2	3	0	6
15	9	1	8	3	3	7	0	11	6	4	0	11	7	3	0	11
16	56	8	5	51	8	56	0	56	27	37	0	56	27	37	1	55
17	12	6	8	10	3	15	1	17	7	11	1	17	7	11	1	17
Total	**286**	**35**	**56**	**154**	**68**	**253**	**2**	**208**	**139**	**182**	**2**	**208**	**148**	**173**	**3**	**207**

3.3 Classification of Time Series

Results from the different configurations are shown in Table 2 and in the box plots in Fig. 4 and Fig. 5. Although paying attention to the figures in the Table the two approaches MAX-PEAK-FSM and ABBATE-MAX-PEAK dominates the on-wrist Abbate, if we pay attention to the box plots there is no clear winner.

On the one hand, the ABBATE-MAX-PEAK shows a surprising no variation performance, either for good (with the specificity) or for bad (the sensitivity). Nevertheless, we can not say the sensitivity of this configuration is worse than for the other methods: the results vary differently for each participant.

With all these figures and graphs we can state that perhaps more features need to be extracted and a better feature set must be needed in order to obtain a good robust performance for all the participants.

Table 2. Classification results in this leave one participant out cross validation. SEN and SPE stand for Sensitivity and Specificity, while AVRG refers to the average of the metrics over all the participants. An hyphen (-) stands when the participant did not perform any staged fall, thus the value of the sensitivity becomes not calculable.

Pid	on-wrist Abbate		MAX-PEAK-FSM		ABBATE-MAX-PEAK	
	SEN	SPE	SEN	SPE	SEN	SPE
1	0.6667	0.9888	0.7633	0.9813	0.6850	0.8889
2	0.8391	1.0000	0.7696	1.0000	0.9231	1.0000
3	0.9027	0.9893	0.8676	0.9946	1.0000	1.0000
4	0.7730	1.0000	0.7676	1.0000	0.8882	1.0000
5	0.6000	1.0000	0.5923	1.0000	0.8571	1.0000
6	0.6167	0.9462	0.5958	0.9769	0.3750	0.9200
7	-	0.9551	-	0.9561	-	0.8842
8	-	0.9720	-	0.9764	-	0.9467
9	0.7085	0.9972	0.6872	0.9962	0.8429	0.7750
10	-	0.9608	-	0.9598	-	0.9250
11	0.5667	0.9799	0.4667	0.9871	0.5000	1.0000
12	0.6111	0.9825	0.6667	0.9796	0.5444	0.9167
13	0.7688	0.9985	0.7937	0.9970	1.0000	1.0000
14	0.8182	1.0000	0.8182	1.0000	0.6000	0.9000
15	0.7368	0.9946	0.7263	0.9957	0.8000	1.0000
16	0.8250	0.9900	0.7984	0.9909	0.9436	0.9442
17	0.6560	0.8949	0.6600	0.8782	0.7824	0.8923
AVRG	0.7207	0.9794	0.7124	0.9806	0.7673	0.9408
AVRG	**0.7207**	**0.9794**	**0.7124**	**0.9806**	**0.7673**	**0.9408**

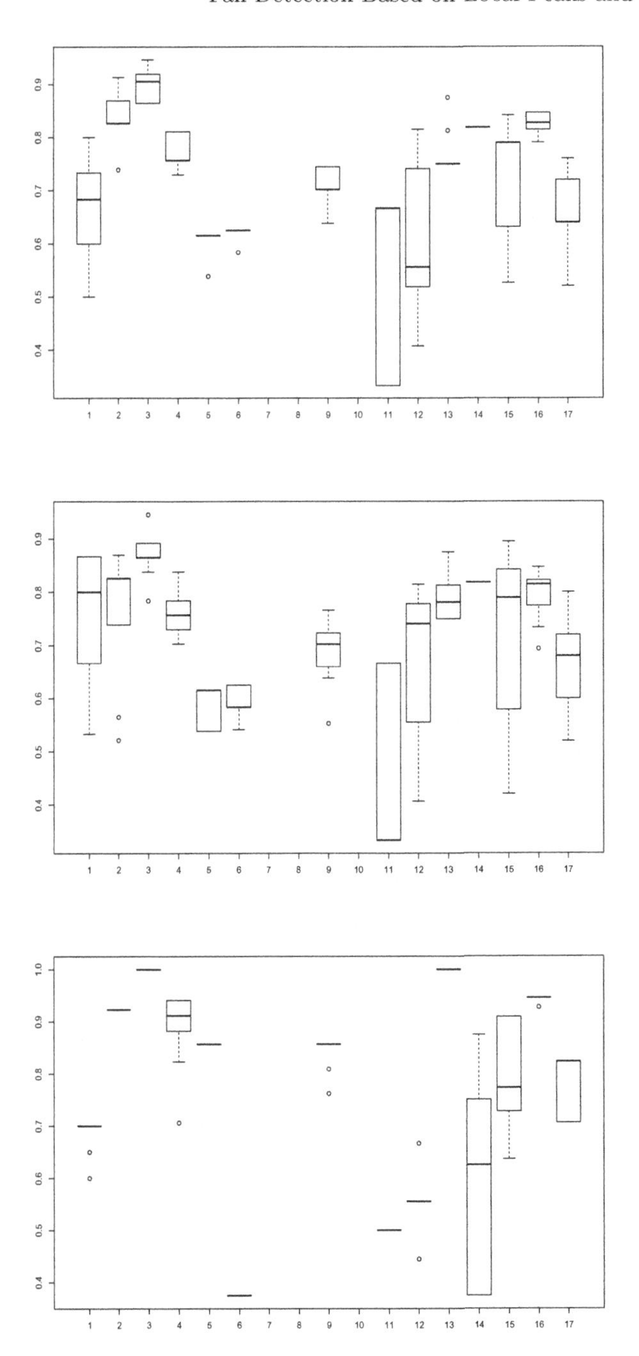

Fig. 4. Box plot of the sensitivity for the validation data set per participant. Upper, central and lower parts are for the on-wrist Abbate, the MAX-PEAK-FSM and the ABBATE-MAX-PEAK, correspondingly.

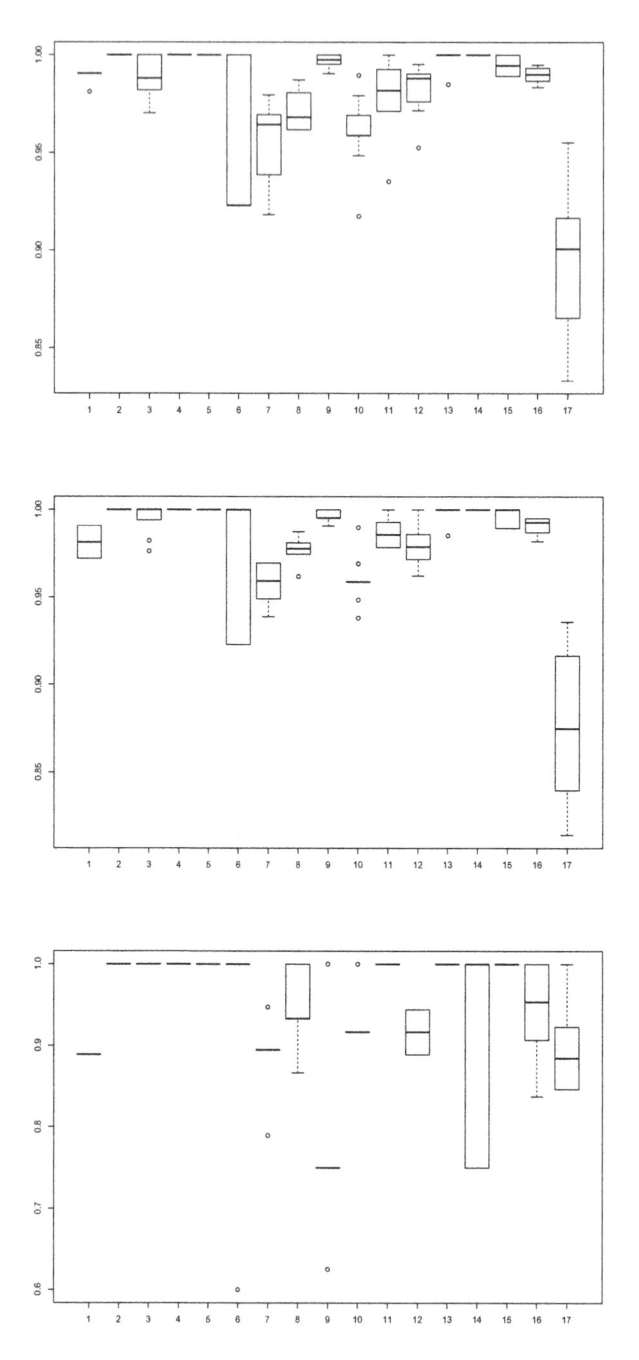

Fig. 5. Box plot of the specificity for the validation data set per participant. Upper, central and lower parts are for the on-wrist Abbate, the MAX-PEAK-FSM and the ABBATE-MAX-PEAK, correspondingly.

4 Conclusions

This research is focused on FD using wearable devices using a 3DACC sensor located on a wrist. The study has analyzed different event detection methods together with different transformations of the acceleration windows when an event is detected. The comparison has been performed using densely connected layers in a Deep Learning configuration using the Keras framework.

Results show that the two proposed event detection methods were much better than the previously used method because i) there is no need of a predefined threshold and ii) because the number of undetected falls is almost negligible. While the baseline method fails detecting 56 out of 210 falls, the proposals detect 207 or 208 out of 210 falls. However, the transformations that have been studied did not improve the results obtained from the on-wrist Abbate solution. This might be due to an inefficient set of features that becomes redundant. Extra transformations (in the domain of the frequency and others) might be needed in order to enhance the results. Additionally, the use of other Deep Learning models, such as Long Short Term Memory or GA networks, can lead to better results at the cost of draining battery in case of being run in the wearable device or in a Smartphone.

Acknowledgment. This research has been funded by the Spanish Ministry of Science and Innovation, under project MINECO-TIN2017-84804-R, and by the Grant FC-GRUPIN-IDI/2018/000226 project from the Asturias Regional Government.

References

1. Zhang, S., Wei, Z., Nie, J., Huang, L., Wang, S., Li, Z.: A review on human activity recognition using vision-based method. J. Healthc. Eng. **2017**, article ID 3090343, 31 p. (2017). https://doi.org/10.1155/2017/3090343
2. Rimminen, H., Lindström, J., Linnavuo, M., Sepponen, R.: Detection of falls among the elderly by a floor sensor using the electric near field. IEEE Trans. Inf. Technol. Biomed. **14**, 1475–1476 (2010)
3. Principi, E., Droghini, D., Squartinia, S., Olivetti, P., Piazza, F.: Acoustic cues from the floor: a new approach for fall classification. Exp. Syst. Appl. **60**, 51–61 (2016)
4. Igual, R., Medrano, C., Plaza, I.: Challenges, issues and trends in fall detection systems. BioMed. Eng. OnLine **12**, 66 (2013). https://doi.org/10.1186/1475-925X-12-66
5. Godfrey, A.: Wearables for independent living in older adults: gait and falls. Maturitas **100**, 16–26 (2017)
6. Zhang, T., Wang, J., Xu, L., Liu, P.: Fall detection by wearable sensor and one-class SVM algorithm. In: Huang, D.S., Li, K., I.G. (ed.) Intelligent Computing in Signal Processing and Pattern Recognition. Volume 345 of Lecture Notes in Control and Information Systems, pp. 858–863. Springer, Berlin Heidelberg (2006). https://doi.org/10.1007/978-3-540-37258-5_104
7. Hakim, A., Huq, M.S., Shanta, S., Ibrahim, B.: Smartphone based data mining for fall detection: analysis and design. Proc. Comput. Sci. **105**, 46–51 (2017)

8. Wu, F., Zhao, H., Zhao, Y., Zhong, H.: Development of a wearable-sensor-based fall detection system. Int. J. Telemed. Appl. **2015**, 11 (2015)
9. Bourke, A., O'Brien, J., Lyons, G.: Evaluation of a threshold-based triaxial accelerometer fall detection algorithm. Gait Posture **26**, 194–199 (2007)
10. Huynh, Q.T., Nguyen, U.D., Irazabal, L.B., Ghassemian, N., Tran, B.Q.: Optimization of an accelerometer and gyroscope-based fall detection algorithm. J. Sens. **2015**, article ID 452078, 8 p. (2015). https://doi.org/10.1155/2015/452078
11. Chaudhuri, S., Thompson, H., Demiris, G.: Fall detection devices and their use with older adults. J. Geriatr. Phys. Therapy **37**, 178–196 (2014)
12. Casilari-Pérez, E., García-Lagos, F.: A comprehensive study on the use of artificial neural networks in wearable fall detection systems. Exp. Syst. Appl. **138**, 112811 (2019)
13. Fang, Y.C., Dzeng, R.J.: A smartphone-based detection of fall portents for construction workers. Proc. Eng. **85**, 147–156 (2014)
14. Fang, Y.C., Dzeng, R.J.: Accelerometer-based fall-portent detection algorithm for construction tiling operation. Autom. Constr. **84**, 214–230 (2017)
15. Kangas, M., Konttila, A., Lindgren, P., Winblad, I., Jämsaä, T.: Comparison of low-complexity fall detection algorithms for body attached accelerometers. Gait Posture **28**, 285–291 (2008)
16. Casilari, E., Lora-Rivera, R., García-Lagos, F.: A wearable fall detection system using deep learning. In: Wotawa, F., Friedrich, G., Pill, I., Koitz-Hristov, R., Ali, M. (eds.) IEA/AIE 2019. LNCS (LNAI), vol. 11606, pp. 445–456. Springer, Cham (2019). https://doi.org/10.1007/978-3-030-22999-3_39
17. Wu, X., Cheng, L., Chu, C.-H., Kim, J.: Using deep learning and smartphone for automatic detection of fall and daily activities. In: Chen, H., Zeng, D., Yan, X., Xing, C. (eds.) ICSH 2019. LNCS, vol. 11924, pp. 61–74. Springer, Cham (2019). https://doi.org/10.1007/978-3-030-34482-5_6
18. Santos, G.L., Endo, P.T., de Carvalho Monteiro, K.H., da Silva Rocha, E., Silva, I., Lynn, T.: Accelerometer-based human fall detection using convolutional neural networks. Sensors **19**, 1–12 (2019)
19. Abbate, S., Avvenuti, M., Bonatesta, F., Cola, G., Corsini, P.: AlessioVecchio: a smartphone-based fall detection system. Pervasive Mobile Comput. **8**(6), 883–899 (2012)
20. Delahoz, Y.S., Labrador, M.A.: Survey on fall detection and fall prevention using wearable and external sensors. Sensors **14**(10), 19806–19842 (2014)
21. Khojasteh, S.B., Villar, J.R., de la Cal, E., González, V.M., Sedano, J., YAZG̈AN, H.R.: Evaluation of a wrist-based wearable fall detection method. In: 13th International Conference on Soft Computing Models in Industrial and Environmental Applications, pp. 377–386 (2018). https://doi.org/10.1007/978-3-319-92639-1_31
22. Khojasteh, S.B., Villar, J.R., Chira, C., González, V.M., de la Cal, E.: Improving fall detection using an on-wrist wearable accelerometer. Sensors **18**, 1350 (2018)
23. Villar, J.R., de la Cal, E., Fañez, M., González, V.M., Sedano, J.: User-centered fall detection using supervised, on-line learning and transfer learning. Prog. Artif. Intell. **8**(4), 453–474 (2019). https://doi.org/10.1007/s13748-019-00190-2
24. Villar, M., Villar, J.R.: Peak detection enhancement in autonomous wearable fall detection. In: 19th International Conference on Intelligent Systems Design and Applications (2019)
25. Palshikar, G.K.: Simple algorithms for peak detection in time-series. Technical report, Tata Research Development and Design Centre (2009)

26. Villar, J.R., González, S., Sedano, J., Chira, C., Trejo-Gabriel-Galán, J.M.: Improving human activity recognition and its application in early stroke diagnosis. Int. J. Neural Syst. **25**(4), 1450036–1450055 (2015)
27. Casilari, E., Santoyo-Ramón, J.A., Cano-García, J.M.: Umafall: a multisensor dataset for the research on automatic fall detection. Proc. Comput. Sci. **110**(Supplement C), 32–39 (2017)

Neural Networks for Background Rejection in DEAP-3600 Detector

Iñaki Rodríguez-García, Vicente Pesudo(✉), Roberto Santorelli, Miguel Cárdenas-Montes, and on behalf of the DEAP-3600 Collaboration

Department of Fundamental Research, Centro de Investigaciones Energéticas Medioambientales y Tecnológicas, Madrid, Spain
{inaki.rodriguez,vicente.pesudo,roberto.santorelli, miguel.cardenas}@ciemat.es

Abstract. Understanding the nature of dark matter is a major challenge in modern Physics. During the last decades, several detectors have been built to detect the signal of interactions between dark matter and ordinary matter. DEAP-3600 is a liquid-argon detector with 3.3 tons of active volume placed at SNOLAB (Canada), 2.1 km underground. This detector aims at searching for weakly interacting massive particles (WIMP) as dark matter candidate. The interaction of WIMPs with a nucleus of argon is expected to produce scintillation light with a particular signature. In this work, a Multilayer Perceptron is used for separating this signature from other background signatures, and specifically from a frequent background originated in the neck of the detector. As a consequence of this work, an improvement in the classification of neck events is achieved, reaching a mean acceptance of 44.4% for a background rejection power of 99.9% of neck events for the same sample of simulated events.

Keywords: Multilayer perceptron · DEAP-3600 · Classification · Background signal discrimination

1 Introduction

Deep Learning algorithms are being widely used to solve scientific and technical problems. The application of these techniques in particle physics and high energy physics aim at overcoming the difficulties associated with the larger and more complex datasets produced at higher pace than ever.

Weakly interacting massive particles (WIMPs) have been proposed as dark matter (DM) candidates for solving the astrophysical evidences of missing mass. They are believed to be a relic from the Big Bang without electrical charge and interacting only weakly with ordinary matter.

Typically there are three different approaches for DM searches: direct detection in shielded underground detectors; indirect detection with satellites, balloons, and ground-based telescopes looking for signals of dark matter annihilation or decay; detection at particle colliders where DM particles may be produced

E. A. de la Cal et al. (Eds.): HAIS 2020, LNAI 12344, pp. 644–654, 2020.
https://doi.org/10.1007/978-3-030-61705-9_53

in high-energy collisions. Direct searches aim at observing the interaction of DM particles from the galactic halo with nuclei in the detector target. The low interaction probability requires of large detectors and environments with very low radioactive backgrounds.

DEAP-3600 (Fig. 1(a)) is a detector situated at SNOLAB (Canada) that aims for direct detection of dark matter [5,7]. It consists of an acrylic sphere of 850 mm radius filled with 3.3 tons of liquid argon (LAr). In the active volume of detector—the LAr volume—elastic collisions between Ar nuclei and WIMPs would produce a nuclear recoil. In this process the recoiling Ar atom releases energy that other Ar atoms in its path use to form excimers (excited dimers). Such excimers produce scintillation light when deexciting within few microseconds. This light is seen by 255 photomultiplier tubes (PMT), mounted 50 cm away from the LAr using acrylic lightguides. These lightguides maximize the light collection while minimizing the background introduced by radioactivity from the PMTs. The top of the sphere and the neck volume are filled with argon gas, thus there are some PMTs in the top of the detector that are facing the gas phase, whereas most are directly facing the liquid phase.

Above the acrylic vessel there is a neck where the argon is liquefied via external contact with a liquid nitrogen cooling coil (Fig. 1(b)). Flow guides are placed in the intersection of the neck and the acrylic vessel to guide the liquid argon back from the cooling coil to the main vessel. It is conjectured that a LAr film is present on the flow guide surfaces. Rarely, alpha decays can occur on the acrylic flow guide surface, where the LAr film generates scintillation light which arrives to the PMTs. Because of shadowing effects, the resulting light pattern can mimic in some cases the low-energy interactions we expect after WIMP interactions.

There are other sources of background, like neutrons, the beta decay of ^{39}Ar present in natural Ar and surface activity from the spherical acrylic vessel. However the use of fiducialization (removing the outer layers of the active volume from the analysis), pulse shape discrimination [6] and other discrimination techniques allow us to identify and reject those events. Hence, the α decays ocurring in the neck constitute the most persistent background after the standard cut-based analysis. As a consequence, the conditions imposed to safely reject these events are the ones reducing most importantly the acceptance of potencial signal events [8].

In this work, a Multilayer Perceptron architecture (MLP) implementation is used for improving the event identification and the rejection of background. The algorithm is fed with the normalized light patterns of simulated neck events (background, tagged as 0) and nuclear recoil events (signal, tagged as 1). In the simulated samples, the MLP implementation presented here achieves a mean acceptance of 44.4% for a background rejection of 99.9%, which surpasses the performance of the cut-based event selection [8].

The rest of the paper is organized as follows: a brief description of the data and the algorithm developed in this work are presented in Sect. 2; The results obtained are presented and analyzed in Sect. 3 and Sect. 4 contains the conclusions of this work.

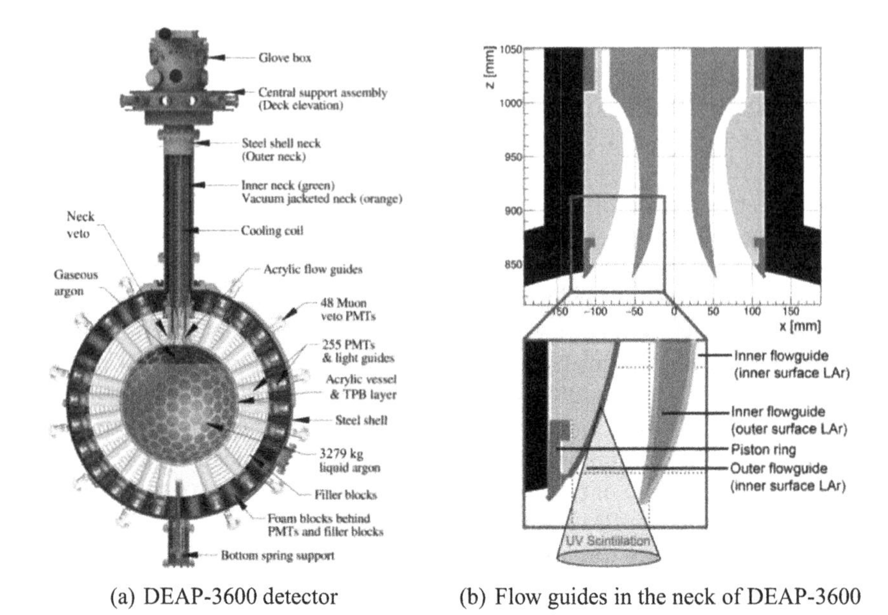

(a) DEAP-3600 detector (b) Flow guides in the neck of DEAP-3600

Fig. 1. (a) Schematic of the DEAP-3600 detector. (b) Detailed view of the flow guides, where neck events originate [8].

2 Methods

2.1 Neck Events

Neck events originate in the flow-guides of the neck (Fig. 1(b)), with the photons travelling down in gas phase first, and later in liquid. On the other hand, WIMP-nucleus recoils would be produced in the main LAr volume. The paths of the light produced by the nuclear recoils that we look for and these pathological peripheric events are different, leading to topological features that can make the two populations distinguishable. Some examples are: the difference in the speed of light in gas and liquid, the isotropic emission from events originating in the LAr versus the particular topological distribution of photons originating from the neck, or the reflectivity of the liquid-gas interface to neck photons. The underlying idea to both currently implemented analysis and this work, is exploiting these features to efficiently reject this background while keeping detector acceptance as high as possible.

The conditional clauses used to reject neck events in the cut-based analysis are:

- If the light of the two top PMT rings is larger than 4% of the total light. The PMTs that are at the same height are said to belong to the same ring. The neck is filled with gas and a certain proportion of photons will be reflected in the gas-liquid interface, so the two top rings will receive a larger proportion of photons compared to events in the LAr.

- If one of the three first photons of an event are captured in the gas subtented area. This feature exploits the higher speed of light in gas with respect to LAr.
- If different position reconstruction algorithms disagree in the reconstructed height (Z) more than what would be expected for 90% of the LAr events, or in radius (R) in more than what would be expected for 85% of the LAr events. Two position reconstruction algorithms are used, one based on light only and another one on light plus time patterns—arrival time of photons to PMTs. While the two algorithms are in good agreement with each other for events originating in the LAr volume, for neck events the reconstructed positions tend to be different.

For this work, a specific set of simulated events was generated using Geant4 [1], a simulation toolkit where detectors and physics processes can be described with a lot of detail. The events in the dataset were required to leave an amount of light within the region of interest for WIMP searches and to be reconstructed at least 220 mm away of the acrylic vessel surface ($R < 630$ mm) and inside the liquid ($Z < 550$ mm) by the light-based position reconstruction algorithm.

The effectiveness of selection cuts against neck events is evaluated through the background rejection power and the acceptance. The background rejection power is calculated as $R_f = 1 - \frac{N_{bg,s}}{N_{bg}}$, where $N_{bg,s}$ is the number of neck event passing the cuts and N_{bg} the total number of neck events.

The acceptance is defined as the ratio between the accepted nuclear recoil events after the cuts $N_{nr,s}$, and the total number of nuclear recoil events N_{nr}, $A = \frac{N_{nr,s}}{N_{nr}}$.

A total of 190020 simulated events were used to train and test the Multilayer Perceptron, 95010 nuclear recoil events, and 31760 events for each of the three surfaces which compose the neck (Fig. 1(b)). The final goal of this work is maximising the acceptance for a background rejection power of 99.9%, which is a more stringent condition than the one used in the currently published analysis [8].

Acceptance and background rejection power can be linked to the more usual True Positive Rate (TPR) and False Positive Rate (FPR) of a binary classification as $A = TPR = \frac{TP}{TP+FN}$, and $R_f = 1 - FPR = \frac{FP}{FP+TN}$, TP is the number of true positive outcomes, TN the true negative cases, FN the false negative ones, and FP is the false positive ones.

2.2 Multilayer Perceptron

A Multilayer Perceptron (MLP) is a biological-inspired neural network composed of neurons, as fundamental elements, grouped in layers (Eq. 1). The output of each node is a non-linear combination of non-linear functions from the outputs of the previous layer. There is one input layer, which receives the input data, one output layer, which produces the output, and a fixed number of intermediate or hidden ones, which map input into output. The input of any neuron can be expressed as $f(\mathbf{W}, \mathbf{x})$, where $\mathbf{x}$ is the input vector to the neuron, and $\mathbf{W}$ is the matrix of weights, which is optimized through the training process. By increasing the number of the hidden layers, more complicated relationships can be established between the input and the output. In the context of this analysis, MLP can be used to approximate non-linear relationships between dependent variables (the observations to be predicted) and independent variables (a set of previous observations, which can be used to predict), in such a way they can be assimilated as extensions of generalized linear models [2,9].

The hidden layers and their output are parametrized as follows:

$$\begin{aligned} \mathbf{h} &= \sigma_1(\mathbf{W}_h\, \mathbf{x}_i) \\ \hat{\mathbf{y}}_i &= \sigma_2(\mathbf{W}_y\, \mathbf{h}) \end{aligned} \tag{1}$$

where $\mathbf{x}_i$ is the input vector, $\mathbf{W}_h$ is the matrix of weights of the hidden layer—a network with an unique hidden layer is considered in this example—, σ_1, σ_2 are non-linear activation functions, $\mathbf{W}_y$ is matrix of weights of the output layer, and $\hat{\mathbf{y}}$ is the prediction.

The light pattern of the 255 photomultipliers is used as input for the MLP architecture. This light pattern is normalized to promote the learning from the pattern and not from the amount of light, which is higher for the more energetic events. This has the advantage of using normalized variables for training and also allows to train the classifier for a wide range of energy of the events.

The MLP configuration has been selected after a reduced optimisation process, greedy process, freezing all the hyperparameters except the one being optimized in that particular step. Therefore it can be considered as a high-quality sub-optimal configuration. The range of parameters investigated are:

- Number of neurons per layer, ranging from 16 to 320 in steps of 16, conserving a lower number of neurons in later layers.
- Activation function, with `relu`, `tanh` and `sigmoid`. `Relu` in the hidden layers and `sigmoid` in the output layer proved to be best both in terms of time and performance.
- Size of batch, ranging from 16 to 256 in steps of 16.
- Number of hidden layers. All the mentioned process was done for 2 and 3 hidden layers, and some less stringent tests with 4 hidden layers. The performance with 2 hidden layers was at the same level as with 3, with a marginal improvement.
- The introduction of drop out does not worsen the performance of the MLP and allows us to perform some statistical analysis.

The architecture we adopted after this process is, hence, two hidden layers of 256 and 32 neurons with `relu` activation function, and a single neuron in the output layer with `sigmoid` activation function. The batch size is 32, the loss function is `binary crossentropy`, `adam` as optimizer, and a dropout of 0.10 in the hidden layers is also applied. The network is trained with 6 epochs, since a larger number of epochs produced overfitting. A fixed 70% of the dataset is used as training set, and the remaining 30% as test set. The evolution of the loss function used to optimize the algorithm with the epochs can be seen in Fig. 2. This architecture is implemented in *keras* [4].

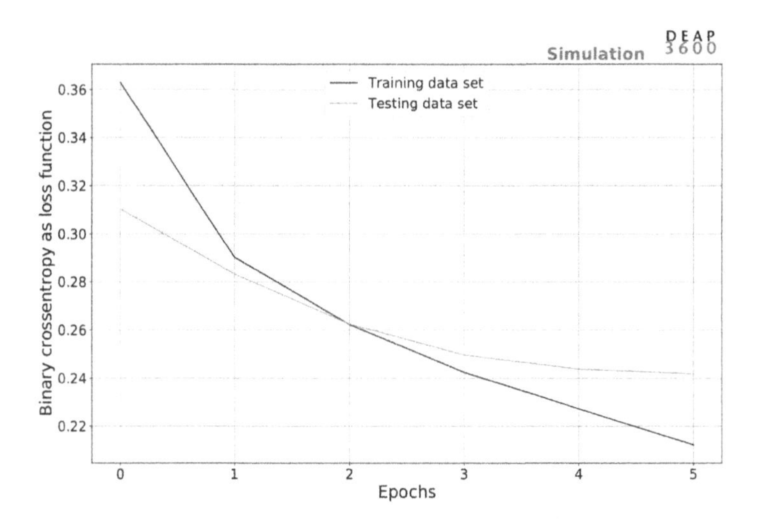

Fig. 2. Loss values for training and test sets as function of the number of epochs.

3 Experimental Results and Analysis

The mean acceptance and standard deviation for a background rejection power of 99.9% is (42.2 ± 1.5)%. The standard deviation is calculated from the statistical analysis of the output of 15 independent executions of the MLP. For this work we pick the execution maximizing the acceptance for such background rejection goal, which is 44.4%. Fig. 3 shows a detailed view of the predicted scores for the test set (containing labelled nuclear recoil and neck events) for the best execution of a MLP implementation, and the corresponding ROC curve is depicted in Fig. 4. With this choice, an acceptance of 44.4% is achieved by setting a threshold on 0.993. This performance improves by a factor of $\approx$2 (systematic uncertainties not yet evaluated) the cut-based discrimination devoted to neck alpha rejection [8] while increasing the background rejection from 0.99 to 0.999, so the improvement is two-fold.

The performance can be appreciated in Fig. 3, where two large set of events are well predicted although long tails towards the incorrect labels are also produced. The aim of this kind of classification is to produce the highest possible peaks with no tails, being particularly important the tail of neck events towards the score equal to 1.

A detailed inspection of the correctly and incorrectly classified events versus the vertical coordinate of the detector evidences the presence of an underlying pattern (Fig. 5). It can be observed that nuclear recoil events (True recoil) are likely to be correctly classified when the interaction takes place in the top hemisphere of the detector, i.e. positive values of vertical coordinate. Conversely, the nuclear recoils are more probably classified as neck events (False neck) when the interaction takes place in the bottom hemisphere. Since neck events tend to reconstruct in the bottom hemisphere, it is natural that the MLP has less

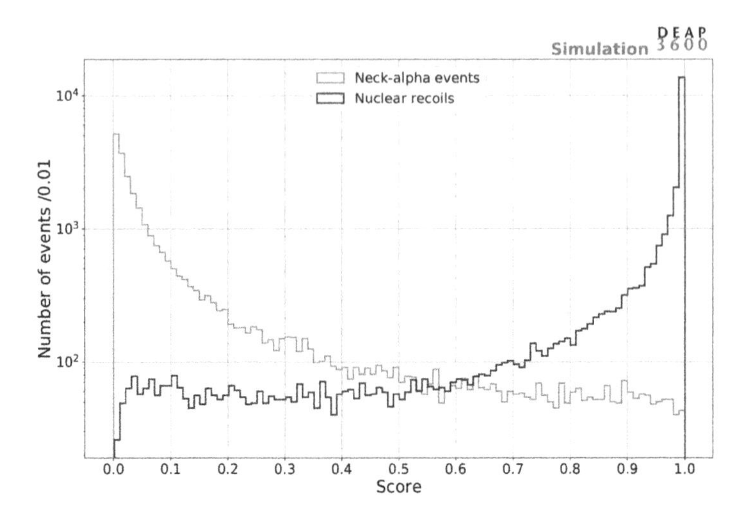

Fig. 3. Scores of simulated neck events and nuclear recoil events predicted by MLP implementation. The best case of 15 independent runs is presented. For a background rejection power of 99.9%, this execution achieves an acceptance of 44.4%. The score imposed as threshold to fulfill the requirement is 0.993.

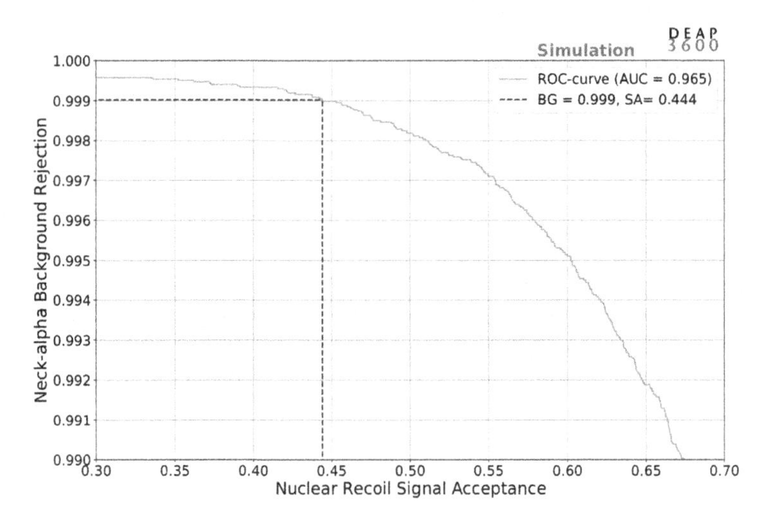

Fig. 4. ROC curve for neck (background) and nuclear recoil events (signal) produced by the MLP implementation. The best case of 15 independent runs of the MLP implementation is presented. The acceptance for 99.9% rejection rate is shown.

success reconstructing nuclear recoil events in that region. However, setting a cut in Z that rejects background as efficiently as the MLP (99.9%) would leave a very small active volume and, hence, low acceptance. The neck events misclassified as nuclear recoil events are few, due to the stringent background rejection goal, and are compatible to a homogeneous distribution along the z-coordinate.

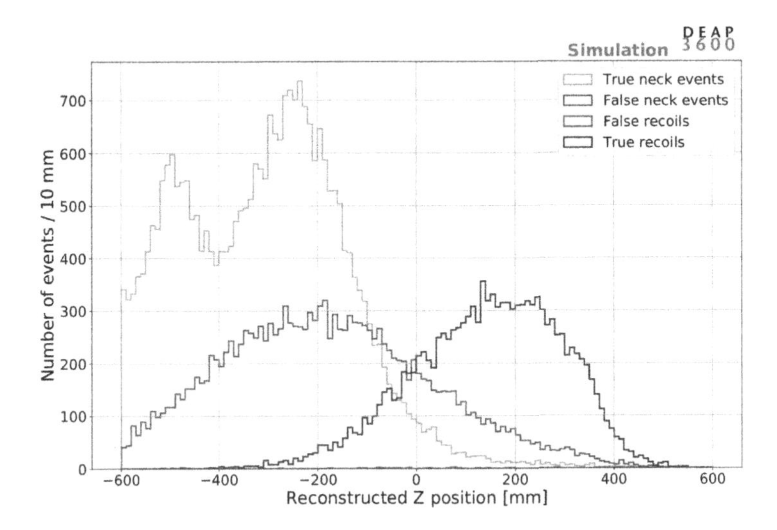

Fig. 5. Distribution of predicted events by a MLP as a function of the reconstructed Z coordinate. The plot shows that most of the events accepted by the algorithm (True recoils, blue line) are in the top hemisphere of the detector, while the events incorrectly rejected (False neck, green line) are closer to the bottom. False recoils events are scarce given the high background rejection imposed.

The application of machine learning techniques in the field of rare event searches in physics relies strongly on Monte Carlo simulations [3]. Hence, it is fundamental to design a validation procedure to ensure that the response of the trained algorithm is based on properly simulated features instead of unphysical artifacts. In this case we used the decay of ^{39}Ar present in natural argon and introducing slightly above 3 kHz of signal. This rate makes it an ideal candidate because both experimental and simulated data are abundant, and we can compare the output of our MLP using the two sets of inputs.

The MLP implementation—trained with neck and nuclear recoil events—was used to classify a dataset composed of 17260 simulated ^{39}Ar decays and 100874 real ^{39}Ar decays identified in data. The acceptances for both dataset are: 44.1% for real data and 44.3% for simulated data. Figure 6 shows that the MLP implementation trained with neck and nuclear recoil events predicts the electronic recoils of ^{39}Ar in a very similar way to the nuclear recoils. This is natural because of two reasons: first, both ^{39}Ar decays and the expected nuclear recoils are produced homogeneously within the LAr volume as opposed to the neck events, and second, no time information is used for the training. The difference between electronic and nuclear recoils is based on the deexcitation time associated to the two processes, so this feature is invisible to the algorithm. It is evident that the algorithm performs very similarly to both inputs, so training on simulation can be used for classification of experimental data. For this reason, this validation test is considered satisfactory for the MLP.

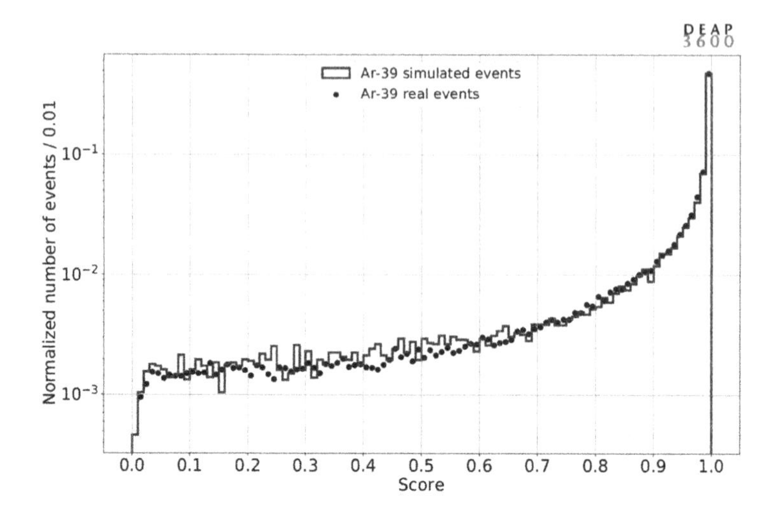

Fig. 6. Score distributions for simulated and real ^{39}Ar decays. The MLP passes this validation test since it cannot distinguish both populations and training on simulations is applicable on real data.

4 Conclusions

In this paper, an example of application of deep learning architectures for background discrimination in particle physics experiments is presented. Particularly, the application focuses on the DEAP-3600 experiment, aiming at the direct detection of WIMPs, which have been postulated as the constituent of missing matter in the Universe. The binary classification problem is to discriminate the signal interactions between WIMPs and argon nuclei, from background alpha decays originating in the neck of the detector.

The effort based on a MLP architecture and using the light pattern of the events as input has demonstrated its efficiency increasing the ratio signal to background. In comparison with the previous cut-based discriminator, a relevant improvement in the discrimination capacity has been achieved. Currently, this effort is being incorporated to the mainstream data analysis of DEAP-3600's data.

As future work, two working lines are proposed. On one hand, to benefit from the 2-dimensional spatial correlation by generating full images from the events and using a 2D CNN architecture. And, on the other hand, to exploit the information in the time pattern of the signals by implementing sequence-learning architectures. A characterization of the uncertainties associated with the classification process is also in progress.

Acknowledgment. The research leading to these results has received funding by the Spanish Ministry of Economy and Competitiveness (MINECO) for funding support through the grants FPA2017-82647-P and "Unidad de Excelencia María de Maeztu": CIEMAT - FÍSICA DE PARTÍCULAS through the grant MDM-2015-0509.

We thank the Natural Sciences and Engineering Research Council of Canada, the Canadian Foundation for Innovation (CFI), the Ontario Ministry of Research and Innovation (MRI), and Alberta Advanced Education and Technology (ASRIP), Queen's University, the University of Alberta, Carleton University, the Canada First Research Excellence Fund, the Arthur B. McDonald Canadian Astroparticle Research Institute, DGAPA-UNAM (PAPIIT No. IA100118) and Consejo Nacional de Ciencia y Tecnología (CONACyT, Mexico, Grants No. 252167 and A1-S-8960), the European Research Council Project (ERC StG 279980), the UK Science and Technology Facilities Council (STFC ST/K002570/1 and ST/R002908/1), the Russian Science Foundation (Grant No 16-12-10369), the Leverhulme Trust (ECF-20130496) and the International Research Agenda Programme AstroCeNT (MAB/2018/7) funded by the Foundation for Polish Science (FNP) from the European Regional Development Fund. Studentship support from the Rutherford Appleton Laboratory Particle Physics Division, STFC and SEPNet PhD is acknowledged. We would like to thank SNOLAB and its staff for support through underground space, logistical, and technical services. SNOLAB operations are supported by the CFI and Province of Ontario MRI, with underground access provided by Vale at the Creighton mine site. We thank Vale for support in shipping the acrylic vessel underground. We gratefully acknowledge the support of Compute Canada, Calcul Québec, the Center for Advanced Computing at Queen's University, and the Computation Center for Particle and Astrophysics (C2PAP) at the Leibniz Supercomputer Center (LRZ) for providing the computing resources required to undertake this work.

References

1. Agostinelli, S., et al.: Geant4 - a simulation toolkit. Nucl. Inst. Meth. A **506**(3), 250–303 (2003). https://doi.org/10.1016/S0168-9002(03)01368-8
2. Bishop, C.M.: Neural Networks for Pattern Recognition. Oxford University Press Inc., New York (1995)
3. Cárdenas-Montes, M., Montes, B., Santorelli, R., Romero, L.: Evaluation of decision trees algorithms for position reconstruction in argon dark matter experiment. In: Martínez-Álvarez, F., Troncoso, A., Quintián, H., Corchado, E. (eds.) HAIS 2016. LNCS (LNAI), vol. 9648, pp. 575–587. Springer, Cham (2016). https://doi.org/10.1007/978-3-319-32034-2_48
4. Chollet, F., et al.: Keras (2015). https://github.com/fchollet/keras
5. DEAP-3600 Collaboration: DEAP-3600 dark matter search at SNOLAB. J. Phys.: Conf. Ser. **375**(1), 012027 (2012). https://doi.org/10.1088/1742-6596/375/1/012027
6. DEAP-3600 Collaboration: Measurement of the scintillation time spectra and pulse-shape discrimination of low-energy β and nuclear recoils in liquid argon with deap-1. Astropart. Phys. **85**, 1–23 (2016). https://doi.org/10.1016/j.astropartphys.2016.09.002
7. DEAP-3600 Collaboration: Design and construction of the deap-3600 dark matter detector. Astropart. Phys. **108**, 1–23 (2019). https://doi.org/10.1016/j.astropartphys.2018.09.006

8. DEAP-3600 Collaboration: Search for dark matter with a 231-day exposure of liquid argon using deap-3600 at snolab. Phys. Rev. D **100**, 022004 (2019). https://doi.org/10.1103/PhysRevD.100.022004
9. Goodfellow, I., Bengio, Y., Courville, A.: Deep Learning. MIT Press, Cambridge (2016). http://www.deeplearningbook.org

Dyslexia Detection from EEG Signals Using SSA Component Correlation and Convolutional Neural Networks

Andrés Ortiz[1(✉)], Francisco J. Martínez-Murcia[1], Marco A. Formoso[1], Juan Luis Luque[2], and Auxiliadora Sánchez[2]

[1] Department of Communications Engineering, University of Malaga, Malaga, Spain
aortiz@ic.uma.es

[2] Department of Developmental Psychology, University of Malaga, Malaga, Spain

Abstract. Objective dyslexia diagnosis is not a straighforward task since it is traditionally performed by means of the intepretation of different behavioural tests. Moreover, these tests are only applicable to readers. This way, early diagnosis requires the use of specific tasks not only related to reading. Thus, the use of Electroencephalography (EEG) constitutes an alternative for an objective and early diagnosis that can be used with pre-readers. In this way, the extraction of relevant features in EEG signals results crucial for classification. However, the identification of the most relevant features is not straighforward, and predefined statistics in the time or frequency domain are not always discriminant enough. On the other hand, classical processing of EEG signals based on extracting EEG bands frequency descriptors, usually make some assumptions on the raw signals that could cause indormation loosing. In this work we propose an alternative for analysis in the frequency domain based on Singluar Spectrum Analysis (SSA) to split the raw signal into components representing different oscillatory modes. Moreover, correlation matrices obtained for each component among EEG channels are classfied using a Convolutional Neural network.

Keywords: Singular Spectrum Analysis · Dyslexia diagnosis · Convolutional Neural Network

1 Introduction

Developmental dyslexia (DD) is a difficulty in the acquisition of reading skills, whose prevalence is estimated between 5% and 12% of the population [13]. It has an important social impact, since it may determine school failure and has harmful effects in the self-esteem of affected children. Prevention programs and individualized intervention tasks may help to mitigate behavioural aspects in dyslexic children, when they are applied in the early stages. Nevertheless, early

E. A. de la Cal et al. (Eds.): HAIS 2020, LNAI 12344, pp. 655–664, 2020.
https://doi.org/10.1007/978-3-030-61705-9_54

diagnosis is currently a challenging task since most behavioural tests developed to this end include reading or writing tasks.

Alternatively, the use of biomedical signals directed to measure brain activity, constitutes a powerful tool to develop differential and objective diagnosis methods. These signals can be acquired under a specific experimental setup that may not neccesary require any action from the subject. In this work we use Electroencephalography (EEG) acquired during a non-interactive task consisting of the application of auditory stimuli that resemble the sampling processes performed in the brain for language processing. This segmentation proccess aims to extract features for recognising patterns related to different phonemes, sylabes or words. Thus, in this work we propose a method for the extraction of EEG features to be used in differential diagnosis. Moreover, these features may help to identify biomarkers to figure out unknown aspects of the DD related to its neural basis. This can offer valuable information for a better understanding of the differences between dyslexic and non-dyslexic subjects, with special application to the design of individualized intervention tasks [15].

Usually, frequency features are used in EEG processing, specifically those related to the power distribution in different frequency bands (Delta, Theta, Alpha, Beta and Gamma). Frequency-based descriptors have been used in BCI and EVP experiments [2,8,11], by means of Fourier or Wavelet Analysis to estimate the average power in each band. These descriptors allowed to differentiate brain states or responses to diverse stimuli. As a matter of fact, different studies conducted in the search for DD-related patterns in EEG signals [4,14] have shown differences in readers due to cognitive impairment of the phonological representation of word forms. Speech encoding which is related to speech prosody and sensorimotor synchronization problems can be revealed by finding patterns at different sub-bands. In this work, we used EEG signals recorded by a 32 active electrodes BrainVision (Brain Products GmhH) equipment during 5 min sessions, while presenting an auditive stimulus to the subject. These signals are then pre-processed and analyzed in the frequency domain by means of Singular Spectrum Analysis (SSA), which allows to decompose the raw signal into additive components representing different oscillatory modes.

The rest of the paper is organized as follows. Section 2 presents details of the database and signal preprocessing. Then, Sect. 3 describes the auditory stimulus and the post-processing using SSA to extract features, as well as the classification method. Section 4 presents and discusses the classification results, and finally, Sect. 5 draws the main conclusions.

2 Materials and Methods

2.1 Database

The present experiment was carried out with the understanding and written consent of each child's legal guardian and in the presence thereof. Forty-eight participants took part in the present study, including 32 skilled readers (17 males) and 16 dyslexic readers (7 males) matched in age ($t(1) = -1.4, p > 0.05$, age range: 88–100 months). The mean age of the control group was $94,1 \pm 3.3$ months, and $95,6 \pm 2.9$ months for the dyslexic group. All participants were right-handed Spanish native speakers with no hearing impairments and normal or corrected–to–normal vision. Dyslexic children in this study had all received a formal diagnosis of dyslexia in the school. None of the skilled readers reported reading or spelling difficulties or had received a previous formal diagnosis of dyslexia. Each subject was measured twice for each stimulus.

3 Methods

DD is a reading disorder characterized by reduced awareness of speech units [10]. Recent models of neuronal speech coding suggest that dyslexia originates from the atypical dominant neuronal entrainment in the right hemisphere to the slow-rhythmic prosodic (Delta band, 0.5–4 Hz), syllabic (Theta band, 4–8 Hz) or the phoneme (Gamma band, 12–40 Hz), speech modulations, which are defined by the onset time (i.e., the envelope) generated by the speech rhythm [1,5].

According to [1,5], different brain rhythms involved in language processing are associated to neural oscillations that control the sampling processes developed to split auditory stimulus into its constituent parts, neccesary to recognise patterns at phoneme, syllabe and word. These neurophysiological responses should explain the manifestations of the temporal processing deficits described in dyslexia. In this work, EEG signals were obtained for auditory stimulus consisting in amplitude modulated (AM) white-noise at the rate of 8Hz. EEG signals were acquired at a sampling rate of 500 Hz, using a 32 active electrodes (Brain-Products actiCAP) while presenting the auditory stimulus.

3.1 Signal Preprocessing

EEG signals were pre-processed in order to remove artefacts related to eye blinking and impedance variations due to movements. Since eye blinking signal is recorded along with EEG signals, these artefact are removed by blind source separation using Independent Component Analysis (ICA) [9]. Then, EEG signal of each channel is normalized independently to zero mean and unit variance to unify the scale in the subsequently processing carried out (for instance, Power Spectral Density calculation). In addition, a number of samples at the beginning and at the end of the signals were removed in order to obtain the same number of samples for each subject. Specifically, 136 s of EEG recording per subject and for each experiment were stored. It is worth noting that these 136 s signals were split into 40 s segments to speed up the post processing (such as SSA computation). Moreover, 40 s is enough time to capture the lowest EEG frequency considered (corresponding to Delta band ([0.5–4] Hz)) with a reasonable frequency resolution. Finally, all segments are band-pass filtered to keep only the frequencies of interest ([0.5, 40] Hz). Each segment is processed and used independently to generate samples for training the classifier.

3.2 Singular Spectrum Analysis

Singular Spectrum Analysis (SSA) is a non-parametric spectral estimation method that decomposes the original time series into a sum of K series. Formally, a time series $\{X = x_1, x_2, ..., x_N\}$ is embedded into a vector space of dimension $\mathbb{K}$, composed of the eigenvectors of the covariance matrix C_x computed for the L-lagged vectors. Lagged vectors $\overline{X_i}$ are defined as:

$$\overline{X_i} = \{x_i, ..., x_{i+L-1}\} \in \mathbb{R}^L \tag{1}$$

where $K = N - L + 1$. Thus, the covariance matrix :

$$X_x = \frac{1}{N-L} \sum_{t=1}^{N-L} \overline{X(t)X(t+L)} \tag{2}$$

The K eigenvectors E_k of the lag-covariance matrix C_x are called temporal empirical orthogonal functions (EOFs). Moreover, the eigenvalues λ_k corresponding to each eigenvector account for the contribution of the direction E_k to total variance. This way, the projection of the original time series on the k-component can be computed as:

$$Y_k(t) = \overline{X}(t+n-1)E_k(n) \tag{3}$$

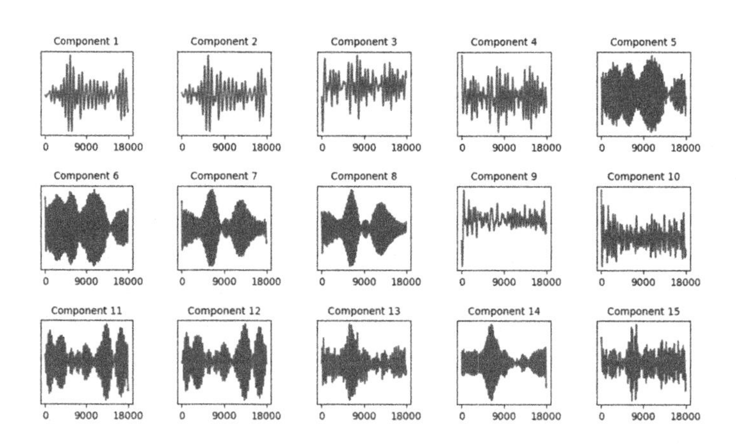

Fig. 1. Example of 15 first SSA components extracted for channel 0

Each component extracted from SSA accounts for a part of the variance of the original signal. As these components are sorted according to the associated eigenvalues (in descending order), the first components will account for more variance than later components. Later, in Sect. 4, we show the variance explained by the computed components.

On the other hand, as can be seen in Fig. 1, some of the extracted components are highly correlated. These correlated components can be grouped without losing interpretability. In this work, correlated EOFs were grouped to finally compose 5 components.

3.3 Feature Extraction by Component Correlation

The feature extraction stage in this work consists in the computation of the Pearson's correlation between channels for the PSD of each SSA component. This way, the PSD of each component is estimated using a modification of the Welch's method [16], a robust estimator that improves the standard periodogram by reducing the noise, but at the cost of reducing the spectral resolution. To perform the original method, the signal is divided into different segments overlapping semgents. Then, a modified periodogram is computed for each windowed segment, and the resulting periodograms are averaged. In our case, since a number of EEG segments are available per subject and electrode, we compute the modified periodogram over every segment. Here, the *Hanning* window is used, and then the average periodogram is used to compute the correlation matrices.

As shown in Fig. 2, there appear SSA components presenting very similar channel correlation matrices. This is the result of the computation of PSDs of highly correlated SSA components, as their PSD profile is very similar. These components can be grouped together since it indicates poorly separated components. On the contrary, well separated components generally exhibit low correlation. In fact, it is usual to group highly correlated components (in the time domain) by means of the so called *weighted correlation matrix* (w-correlation), which allows identifying correlated components.

This way, highly correlated SSA components are grouped together in the time domain and then, the PSD of the group is computed again. Since SSA produces additive components, they can be grouped by simply adding them. The resulting correlation matrices are then classified using a Convolutional Neural Network.

3.4 Classification Using an Ensemble of CNNs

Once the correlation matrices for the PSD of the grouped components are computed, they are classified using a convolutional neural network. Convolutional neural networks are widely used to clasify image data with one or more channels (i.e. RGB images or even hyperspectral images) with important applications in the Machine Learning community [3,7,12], especially within the artificial vision and image analysis fields. CNNs are bioinspired by the convolutional response of neurons, and combine feature extraction and classification in one single architecture. The combination of different convolutional layers is able to recognize different patterns, from low-level features to higher abstractions, depending on the net depth. The set of fully connected layers (dense), similar to a perceptron, placed after convolutional layers, the classification. On the other hand, all neurons in any convolutional layer share the same weights, saving memory and

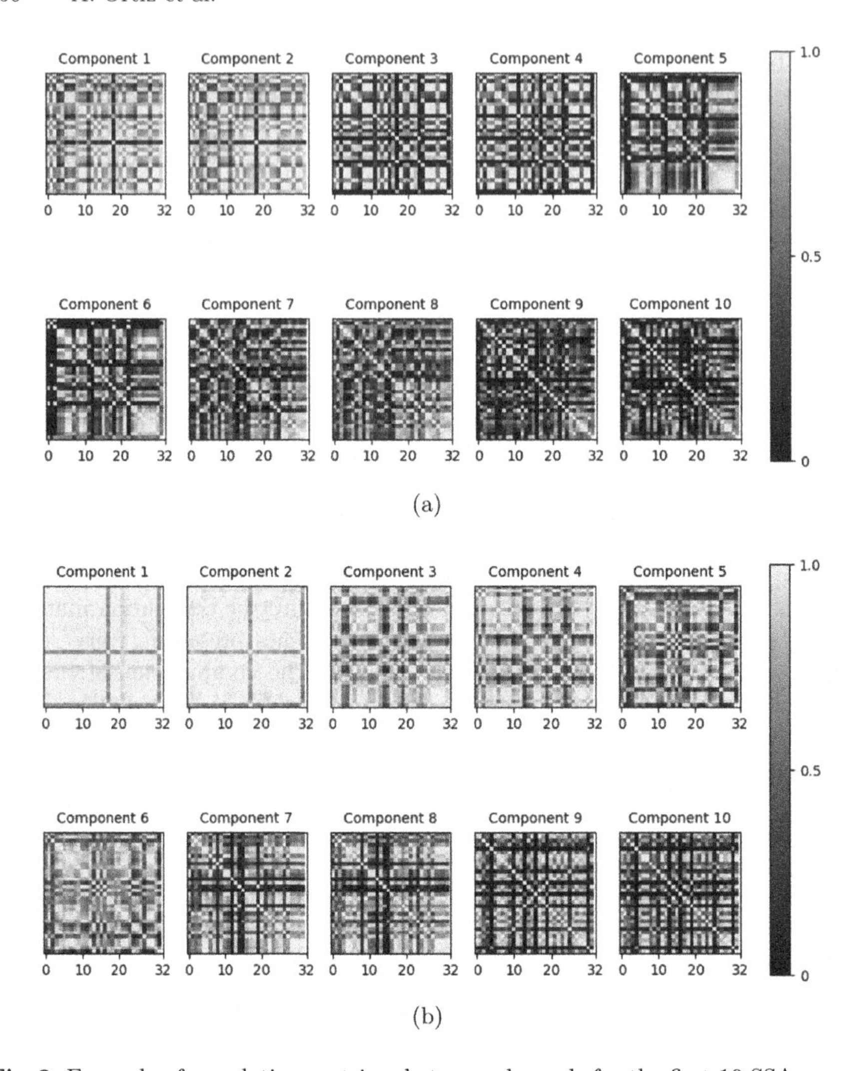

Fig. 2. Example of correlation matrices between channels for the first 10 SSA components computed for Control (a) and DD (b) subjects.

easing the computation of the convolutions. This considerably reduces the number of trainable parameters in the network in comparison to a perceptron-like network designed for the same classification task.

CNN architectures have evolved over time, including new layers and connections among layers that have outperformed previous image classification approaches. An example of improvement for CNN is the use of residual blocks [6], consisting in adding to the input of a convolutional layer the input of a previous convolutional layer. Other improvements include the use of batch normalization layers or the use of strides >1 in convolutional layers instead of poolings.

In this work, a CNNs are used to classify the subjects by means of their channel correlation matrices explained in Sect. 3.3. Since a matrix correlation is computed for each grouped component, we used a CNN with the architecture shown in Fig. 3 for each one. Subsequently, the output of all CNN-based classifiers are combined by a majority voting strategy. The use of ensebles of CNNs have demonstrated their effectivity in image classification tasks, increasing the performance obtained by a single CNN while diminishing the overfitting effects [7].

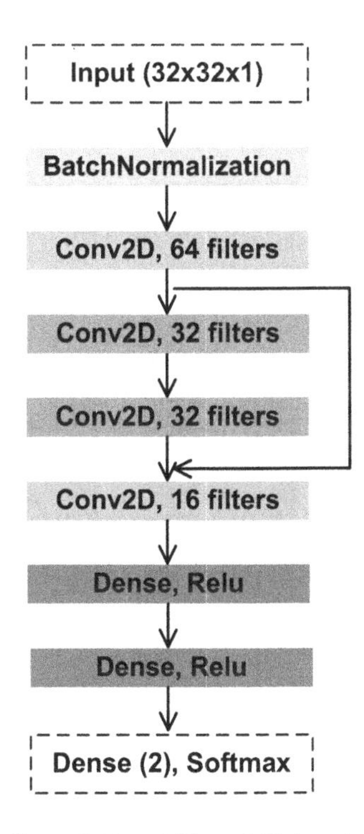

Fig. 3. Architecture of the Convolutional Neural Network used for classifying subjects by means of their channel correlation matrices

4 Experimental Results

In this section, we show the results of the classification experiments carried out to demonstrate the discriminative capabilities of the features extracted from EEG signals. As explained in Sect. 3, the input to each of the CNNs consists of a channel correlation matrix for a specific grouped component. Moreover, since components showing a high correlation between them are guessed to belong to the same source, they can be added up. This way, 5 clusters in the *w-correlation*

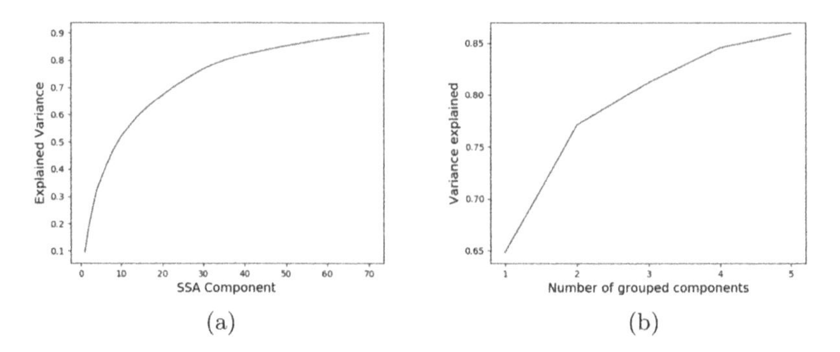

Fig. 4. Variance explained by SSA (a) individual components, (b) grouped components (5 groups)

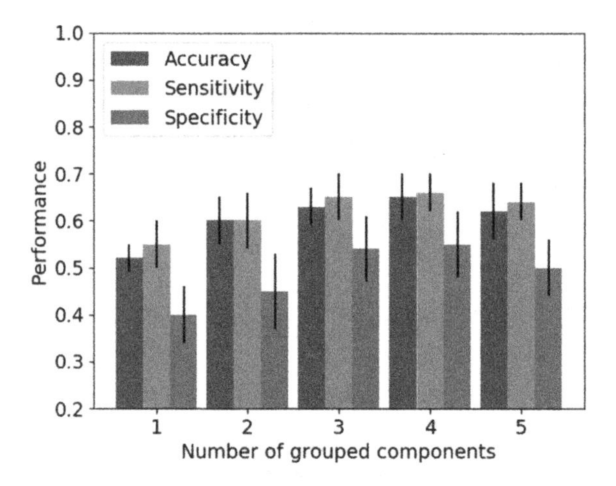

Fig. 5. Classification performance obtanied for different number of grouped components. Accuracy, Sensitivity and Specificity are shown

matrix have been computed by the hierarchical clustering of the pairwise distances among entries in the w-correlation matrix. Indeed, Fig. 4a show the variance explained by 70 components and Fig. 4b the variance explained by the 5 groups of components.

Grouping components has two main advantages. On the one hand, the classifier architecture is simpler. On the other hand, components with lower variance that could cause missclassifications (as they are not informative enough) are added together in a group explaining a larger part of the variance than those individual components.

Figure 5 show the classification performance obtained when a different number of grouped components are considered. As shown, the use of 4 grouped components provide the best performance. It is worth noting that 3 components (for instance) in Fig. 5 indicates that an ensemble composed of 3 CNNs is used.

As shown in Fig. 5 (a), since grouped components are sorted indescending order of the variance explained, first grouped components explain the most part of the variance, and therefore, provide the best classffication results. However, the last grouped component are most likely to contain noisy components, causing missclassifications.

5 Conclusions and Future Work

In this work we present a classification method for EEG signals based on SSA and CNN. The core idea in this work is the use of between channel correlation of the PSD of different oscillatory modes contained in the EEG signals. These oscillatory modes are represented by SSA components. An analysis of the components was performed and those showing higher correlations are grouped to compose a reduced set of components that accumulates a higher part of the variance. The use of grouped components reduces the number of CNN stages in the ensemble (since one CNN per component is used) and removes highly correlated components from the input of the classifier, improving the performance. The approach shown in this work shows its effectivity for extracting informative features for the differential diagnosis of DD. As a future work, we plan to continue exploring the SSA components searching for single oscillatory modes in EEG channels, represented by the fundamental frequency of a component or from harmonics, that could be synchronized among channels. This way, instead of using the correlation matrix, a matrix containing a synchronizaton index among channels could be used. This also have important and interpretable biological implications regarding the identificaton of cooperative brain areas - and the analysis of differences in the cooperation between controls and DD subjects - in language processing task.

Acknowledments. This work was partly supported by the MINECO/FEDER under PGC2018–098813-B-C32 project. We gratefully acknowledge the support of NVIDIA Corporation with the donation of one of the GPUs used for this research. Work by F.J.M.M. was supported by the MICINN "Juan de la Cierva - Formación" Fellowship. We also thank the *Leeduca* research group and Junta de Andalucía for the data supplied and the support.

References

1. Di Liberto, G.M., Peter, V., Kalashnikova, M., Goswami, U., Burnham, D., Lalor, E.C.: Atypical cortical entrainment to speech in the right hemisphere underpins phonemic deficits in dyslexia. NeuroImage **175**(1), 70–79 (2018)
2. Bradley, A., Wilson, W.: On wavelet analysis of auditory evoked potentials. Clin. Neurophysiol. Official J. Int. Fed. Clin. Neurophysiol. **115**, 1114–28 (2004)

3. Cireşan, D.C., Meier, U., Masci, J., Gambardella, L.M., Schmidhuber, J.: Flexible, high performance convolutional neural networks for image classification. In: Proceedings of the Twenty-Second International Joint Conference on Artificial Intelligence - Volume Volume Two, pp. 1237–1242. IJCAI'11, AAAI Press (2011). https://doi.org/10.5591/978-1-57735-516-8/IJCAI11-210. https://doi.org/10.5591/978-1-57735-516-8/IJCAI11-210
4. Cutini, S., Szũcs, D., Mead, N., Huss, M., Goswami, U.: Atypical right hemisphere response to slow temporal modulations in children with developmental dyslexia. NeuroImage **143**, 40–49 (2016)
5. Flanagan, S., Goswami, U.: The role of phase synchronisation between low frequency amplitude modulations in child phonology and morphology speech tasks. J. Acoust. Soc. Am. **143**, 1366–1375 (2018). https://doi.org/10.1121/1.5026239
6. He, K., Zhang, X., Ren, S., Sun, J.: Deep residual learning for image recognition, pp. 770–778, June 2016
7. Krizhevsky, A., Sutskever, I., Hinton, G.E.: ImageNet classification with deep convolutional neural networks. In: Proceedings of the 25th International Conference on Neural Information Processing Systems - Volume 1, pp. 1097–1105. NIPS'12, Curran Associates Inc., USA (2012)
8. León, J., Ortega, J., Ortiz, A.: Convolutional neural networks and feature selection for BCI with multiresolution analysis. In: Advances in Computational Intelligence, pp. 883–894 (2019)
9. Li, R., Principe, J.C.: Blinking artifact removal in cognitive EEG data using ICA. In: 2006 International Conference of the IEEE Engineering in Medicine and Biology Society, pp. 5273–5276 (2006)
10. Molinaro, N., Lizarazu, M., Lallier, M., Bourguignon, M., Carreiras, M.: Out-of-synchrony speech entrainment in developmental dyslexia. Hum. Brain Mapp. **37**, 2767–2783 (2016)
11. Ortega, J., Asensio-Cubero, J., Gan, J., Ortiz, A.: Classification of motor imagery tasks for BCI with multiresolution analysis and multiobjective feature selection. BioMed. Eng. OnLine **15**(73), 1–12 (2016)
12. Ortiz, A., Martínez-Murcia, F.J., García-Tarifa, M.J., Lozano, F., Górriz, J.M., Ramírez, J.: Automated diagnosis of parkinsonian syndromes by deep sparse filtering-based features. In: Chen, Y.-W., Tanaka, S., Howlett, R.J., Jain, L.C. (eds.) Innovation in Medicine and Healthcare 2016. SIST, vol. 60, pp. 249–258. Springer, Cham (2016). https://doi.org/10.1007/978-3-319-39687-3_24
13. Peterson, R., Pennington, B.: Developmental dyslexia. Lancet **379**, 1997–2007 (2012)
14. Power, A.J., Colling, L.J., Mead, N., Barnes, L., Goswami, U.: Neural encoding of the speech envelope by children with developmental dyslexia. Brain Lang. **160**, 1–10 (2016). https://doi.org/10.1016/j.bandl.2016.06.006. http://www.sciencedirect.com/science/article/pii/S0093934X15301681
15. Thompson, P.A., Hulme, C., Nash, H.M., Gooch, D., Hayiou-Thomas, E., Snowling, M.J.: Developmental dyslexia: predicting individual risk. J. Child Psychol. Psychiatry **56**(9), 976–987 (2015)
16. Welch, P.: The use of fast fourier transform for the estimation of power spectra: a method based on time averaging over short, modified periodograms. IEEE Trans. Audio Electroacoust. **15**(2), 70–73 (1967). https://doi.org/10.1109/tau.1967.1161901

Local Binary Pattern Features to Detect Anomalies in Machined Workpiece

Lidia Sánchez-González(✉), Virginia Riego, Manuel Castejón-Limas, and Laura Fernández-Robles

Departamento de Ingenierías Mecánica, Informática y Aeroespacial, Universidad de León, 24071 León, Spain
{lidia.sanchez,manuel.castejon,l.fernandez}@unileon.es

Abstract. Quality standards involve objective procedures that guarantee the criteria keep constant during the process. In manufacturing, an important task that operators do by visual inspection is the evaluation of the surface finish of a machined workpiece. In this paper, a vision-based system that represents the image texture by a Local Binary Pattern vector is proposed. As the machined parts that present a regular pattern correspond with no wear surfaces, texture descriptors give such information making possible to determine automatically the presence of wear along the workpiece surface. Four different classification techniques are considered so as to determine the best approach. Among them, Random Forest classification algorithm yields the best hit rate with a 86.0%. Such results satisfies the expert demands.

Keywords: Quality estimation · Milling machined parts · Local binary pattern descriptors · Wear detection

1 Introduction

Intelligent systems based on artificial vision are widely employed in diverse fields such as medicine [17], security [3], food industry [2] or manufacturing [7]. As Industry 4.0 is currently adopted in manufacturing processes, collaborative robots can be dotted by intelligence to assist the operators in daily tasks. Among them, one is the quality maintenance of the milling workpiece, which has been traditionally measured by visual inspection of the operator. That yields problems of subjectivity or criteria changing, among others. To solve that, an intelligent system based on artificial vision can be employed to acquire images of the machined workpiece and analyze them in order to determine if the roughness and texture they present achieve the quality standards previously established.

In this sense, some works have been carried out to predict surface roughness [4] or defects [10]. In manufacturing processes, some researchers use image processing to analyze tool condition [8], considering flank wear area [7] or different parameters as the area of the wear region and the crater front distance and width [19]. Texture descriptors are also employed very often to evaluate the

E. A. de la Cal et al. (Eds.): HAIS 2020, LNAI 12344, pp. 665–673, 2020.
https://doi.org/10.1007/978-3-030-61705-9_55

roughness, regularity or smoothness of a region [1] such as the ones based on the Gray Level Co-ocurrence Matrix (GLCM) since they give information about tool wear related to the workpiece surface texture [12] or assess the quality of the machined workpiece by analyzing its surface [6].

In order to identify tool wear automatically, other approaches use Convolutional Neural Networks [5,20] or wavelet and statistical features extracted from sound signals [16]. These recent works in this area, among others, show that this is still a challenging matter in this field.

This work continues the one published in [6] by proposing a method that uses texture descriptors local binary patterns so as to determine the quality of a workpiece by analyzing its surface and the presence of wear.

The rest of the paper is organized as follows. In Sect. 2 the proposed method and the employed descriptors are explained. Section 3 presents the results of the experiments in order to validate the method. Lastly, in Sect. 4 the achieved conclusions and future works are gathered.

2 Vision System

In this paper, the same infrastructure considered in previous works [6] is employed. In short, inner and outer surface of machined parts are visualized by using an industrial boroscope and captured with a microscope camera attached to it. An image of the employed vision-based system is shown in Fig. 1. The image acquisition employs white LED light. Thanks to this system, images present enough information about the surface finish what makes possible to estimate automatically the quality of the produced part.

From the machined parts, like the ones shown in Fig. 2, images of their inner and outer surfaces along the complete part are obtained. Some samples are presented in Fig. 3. The resolution of these images is 300 ppp and its size is 2592 $\times$ 1944 pixels.

Firstly, there is a preprocessing step where original images are converted to grey level images (see Fig. 4 left); then they suffer an histogram enhancement by applying CLAHE (Contrast-Limited Adaptive Histogram Equalisation) as it is shown in Fig. 4 [15,21]. After that, a Sobel edge filter is applied [11] so as to leverage the lines presented in the image since they give information about the surface finish of the machined workpiece (see Fig. 4 right).

In [6], a global representation of the presented texture in the machined workpiece based on the Grey Level Coocurrence Matrix and the Haralick features [9] is computed in order to form the feature vector.

Fig. 1. Vision-based system formed by a boroscope and a microscope camera connected to it [14].

Fig. 2. Examples of the machined parts analyzed in this paper.

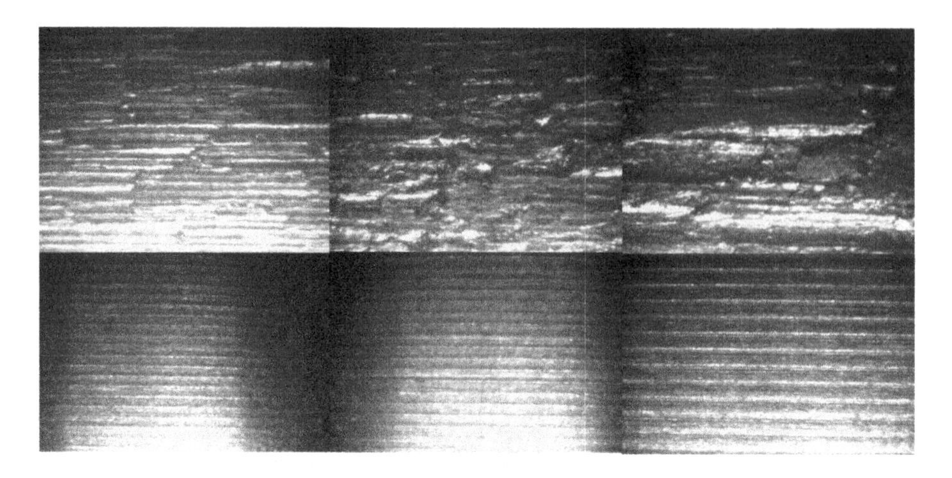

Fig. 3. Samples of inner and outer surfaces where surface finish is determined as wear (upper row) or not (bottom row).

Unlike that approach, in this paper a local texture descriptor named Local Binary Pattern (LBP) is employed so as to describe the texture considering just the neighborhood of a given pixel [13]. To do this, after converting the image to grey scale I, LBP is calculated for each pixel of the image as follows [18]:

$$LBP_{P,R}(x_0) = \sum_{k=1}^{P} s\{I(x_k) - I(x_0)\} \cdot 2^{k-1} \tag{1}$$

being

$$s(z) = \begin{cases} 1, z \geq 0 \\ 0, z < 0 \end{cases} \tag{2}$$

the information between the differences from the value of the central pixel $I(x_0)$ and the value of the pixels along the neighborhood $I(x_k)$. The considered neighborhood is circularly symmetric with radius 8 and it has 24 points. LBP results yield an histogram that makes possible to classify texture patterns.

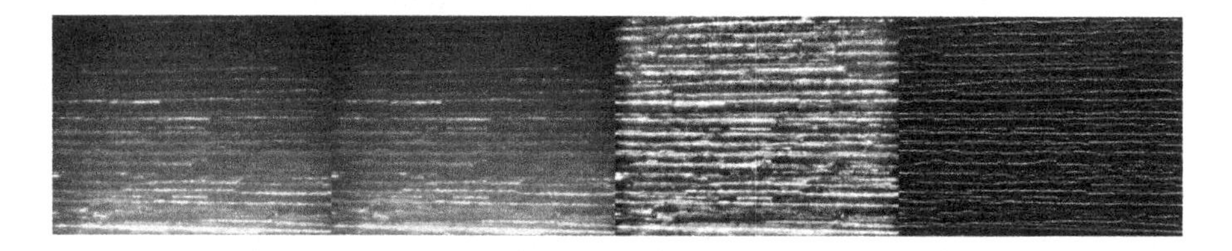

Fig. 4. Obtained images in each step of the procedure. First the real-coloured image is converted to a gray scale; then the histogram is enhanced. Finally a sobely filter is applied in order to leverage lines.

Once the feature vector is formed by the LBP descriptors, several classification algorithms are evaluated in order to identify the best approach. A scheme of the complete procedure is shown in Fig. 5.

3 Experimental Results

In order to validate the proposed method, the same dataset than [6] is considered. It is formed by 587 images, where 437 present some wear and 152 fulfilled the quality standards, free of wear (some examples are presented in Fig. 3). After the preprocessing stage explained previously, the feature vector formed by the mentioned LBP descriptors is computed for each sample.

Experiments are carried out by considering a 70% of the dataset for training in order to determine the different parameters of the model and the other 30% for testing.

Four different classification algorithms are employed in order to carry out a supervised classification of the feature vector: Decision Trees, K-Nearest Neighbors, Random Trees and Support Vector Classification.

A study of the correlation amongst the considered descriptors is carried out, as it is shown in Fig. 6, It is noticeable that descriptors 4, 5 and 6 are highly correlated.

Taking into account the collinearities obtained, the feature vector is reduced to 4 elements, the first four LBP descriptors.

Once the most significant features are identified, a pairs plot is obtained in order to visualize the behavior of the selected features in wear detection. As Fig. 7 shows, there is an important overlapping area among the distributions.

Table 1 gathers the hit rates achieved by the different classifiers for the original dataset. As it is explained previously, the datased is formed by feature vectors of 6 LBP descriptors; from the whole dataset, a reduced dataset with just the 4 first LBP descriptors is obtained. As it is shown, three of the approaches present hit rates higher than 80%, being the Random Forest the classifier that yields the best results. The obtained results are adequate to assess the wear area of the machined workpiece.

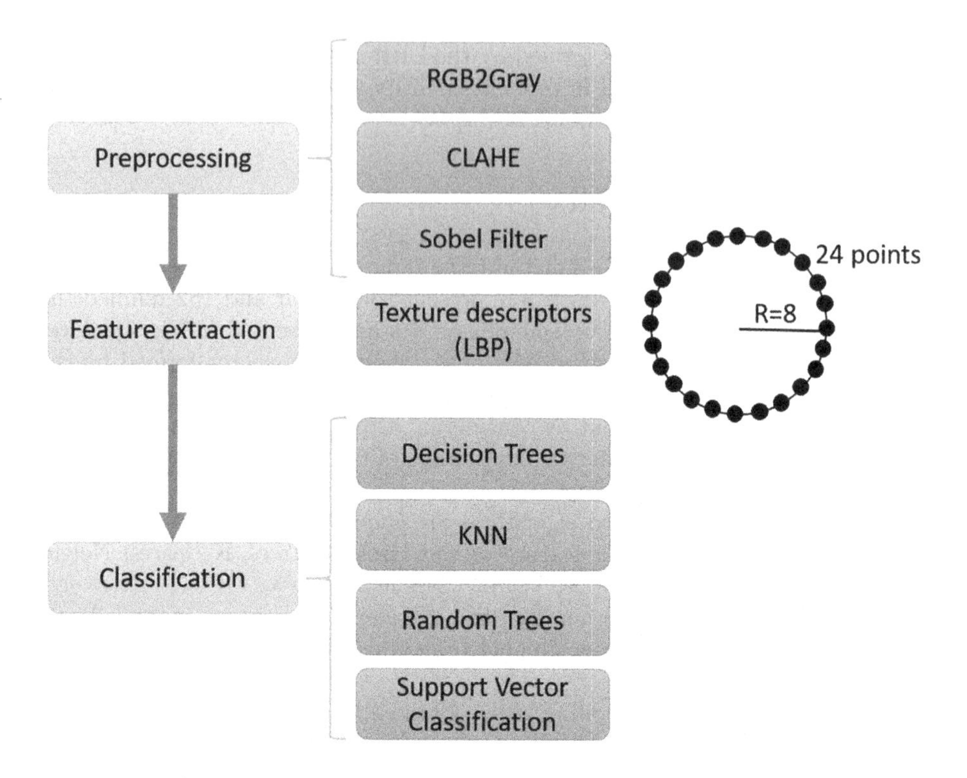

Fig. 5. Scheme of the proposed method.

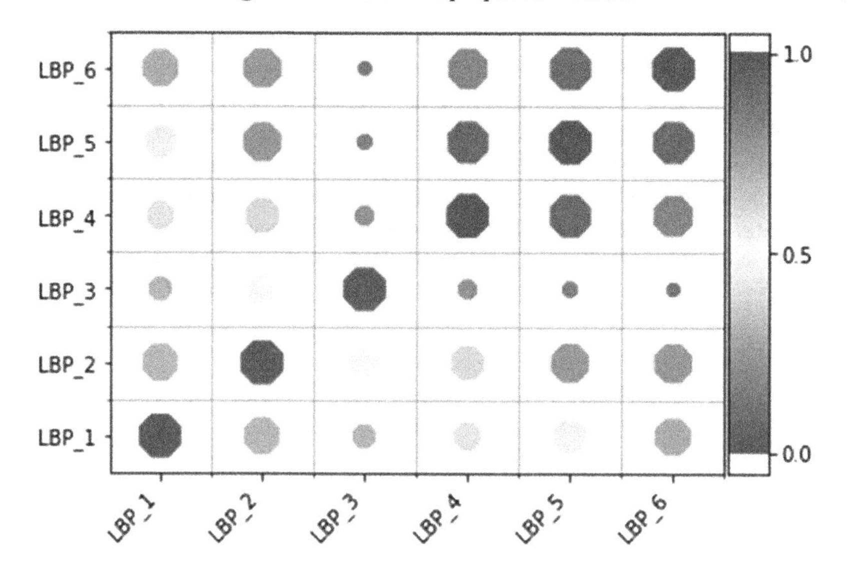

Fig. 6. Calculated correlation of the considered LBP descriptors

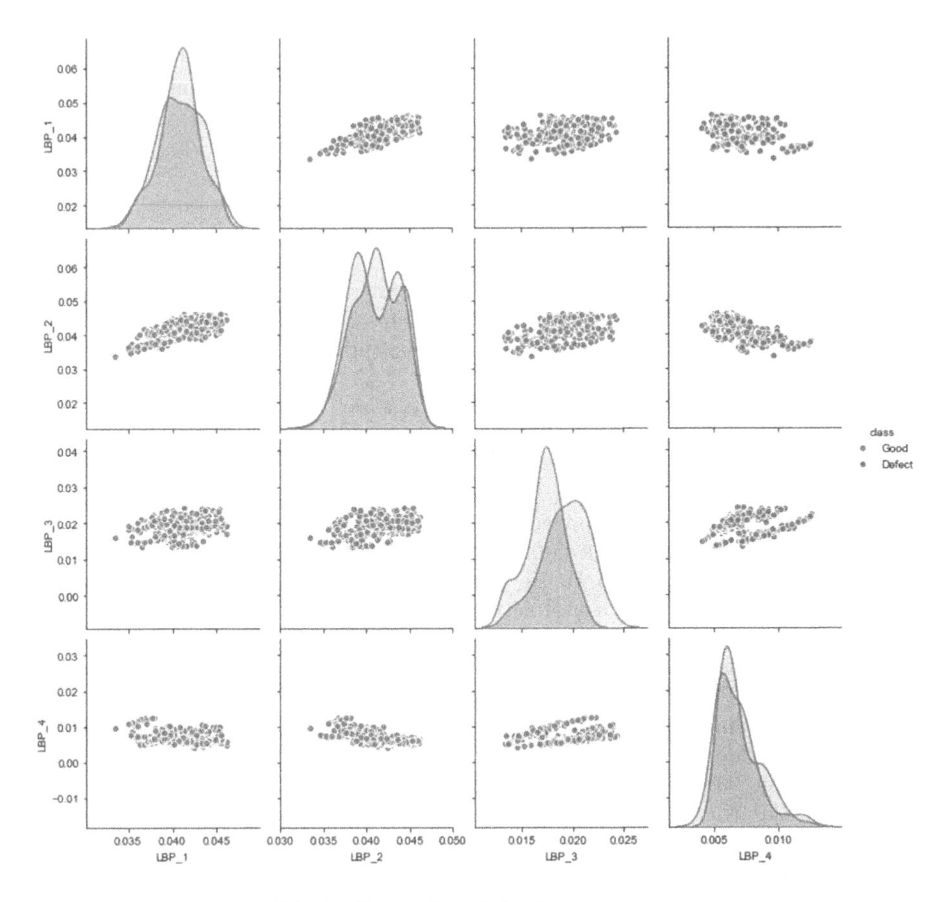

Fig. 7. Pairs plot of the feature vector

Table 1. Hit rates of the different classifiers identifying wear surfaces in workpiece

# Features	Decision tree	K Neighbors	Random forest	Support vector
6 features	81.5	84.8	**86.0**	74.2
4 features	81.5	84.3	84.3	74.2

4 Conclusions

This paper presents a vision-based system that analyses the texture of machined workpiece in order to detect wear and, consequently, determine if the quality of the machined part satisfies the requirements. Images acquired by a microscope camera are represented by calculating Local Binary Pattern descriptors that make possible to determine if the texture of the surface presents some defects. After feature extraction, different classification algorithms are considered in order to compare their accuracy and identify the best approach. According to the results, although Decision Trees and K Neighbors outperforms a hit rate of 80%, the best results are obtained using Random Forest, since a hit rate of 86.0% is achieved. This hit rate fulfills the expected requirements.

References

1. Arivazhagan, S., Ganesan, L.: Texture classification using wavelet transform. Pattern Recogn. Lett. **24**(9–10), 1513–1521 (2003)
2. Belan, P.A., Araújo, S.A., Alves, W.A.L.: An intelligent vision-based system applied to visual quality inspection of beans. In: Campilho, A., Karray, F. (eds.) Image Analysis and Recognition, pp. 801–809. Springer International Publishing, Cham (2016)
3. Bu, F., Gharajeh, M.S.: Intelligent and vision-based fire detection systems: a survey. Image Vis. Comput. **91**, 103803 (2019). https://doi.org/10.1016/j.imavis.2019.08.007. http://www.sciencedirect.com/science/article/pii/S0262885619301222
4. Bustillo, A., Correa, M.: Using artificial intelligence to predict surface roughness in deep drilling of steel components. J. Intell. Manufact. **23**(5), 1893–1902 (2012). https://doi.org/10.1007/s10845-011-0506-8
5. Cao, X.C., Chen, B.Q., Yao, B., He, W.P.: Combining translation-invariant wavelet frames and convolutional neural network for intelligent tool wear state identification. Comput. Ind. (2019). https://doi.org/10.1016/j.compind.2018.12.018
6. Castejón-Limas, M., Sánchez-González, L., Díez-González, J., Fernández-Robles, L., Riego, V., Pérez, H.: Texture descriptors for automatic estimation of workpiece quality in milling. In: Pérez García, H., Sánchez González, L., Castejón Limas, M., Quintián Pardo, H., Corchado Rodríguez, E. (eds.) Hybrid Artificial Intelligent Systems, pp. 734–744. Springer International Publishing, Cham (2019)
7. Dai, Y., Zhu, K.: A machine vision system for micro-milling tool condition monitoring. Precis. Eng. **52**, 183–191 (2018). https://doi.org/10.1016/j.precisioneng.2017.12.006. http://www.sciencedirect.com/science/article/pii/S0141635917302817
8. Dutta, S., Pal, S., Mukhopadhyay, S., Sen, R.: Application of digital image processing in tool condition monitoring: a review. CIRP J. Manuf. Sci. Technol. **6**(3), 212–232 (2013). https://doi.org/10.1016/j.cirpj.2013.02.005. http://www.sciencedirect.com/science/article/pii/S1755581713000072
9. Haralick, R., Shanmugan, K., Dinstein, I.: Texture features for image classification. IEEE Syst. Man Cybern. **3**(6), 610–621 (1973)
10. Hu, H., Liu, Y., Liu, M., Nie, L.: Surface defect classification in large-scale strip steel image collection via hybrid chromosome genetic algorithm. Neurocomputing **181**, 86–95 (2016). https://doi.org/10.1016/j.neucom.2015.05.134. http://www.sciencedirect.com/science/article/pii/S0925231215018482. big Data Driven Intelligent Transportation Systems
11. Kanopoulos, N., Vasanthavada, N., Baker, R.L.: Design of an image edge detection filter using the sobel operator. IEEE J. Solid-State Circuits **23**(2), 358–367 (1988)
12. Li, L., An, Q.: An in-depth study of tool wear monitoring technique based on image segmentation and texture analysis. Measurement, **79**, 44–52 (2016). https://doi.org/10.1016/j.measurement.2015.10.029. http://www.sciencedirect.com/science/article/pii/S0263224115005631
13. Ojala, T., Pietikäinen, M., Mäenpää, T.: Multiresolution gray-scale and rotation invariant texture classification with local binary patterns. IEEE Trans. Pattern Anal. Mach. Intell. **24**(7), 971–987 (2002). https://doi.org/10.1109/TPAMI.2002.1017623

14. Olivera, D.C.: Using a borescope prototype: specifications, virtual modelling and practical application. Master's thesis, University of León, Spain (2019)
15. Park, G.H., Cho, H.H., Choi, M.R.: A contrast enhancement method using dynamic range separate histogram equalization. IEEE Trans. Consum. Electron. **54**(4), 1981–1987 (2008)
16. Ravikumar, S., Ramachandran, K.I.: Tool wear monitoring of multipoint cutting tool using sound signal features signals with machine learning techniques. Mater. Today: Proc. **5**(11), 25720–25729 (2018). https://doi.org/10.1016/j.matpr.2018.11.014
17. Shen, L., Margolies, L.R., Rothstein, J.H., Fluder, E., McBride, R., Sieh, W.: Deep learning to improve breast cancer detection on screening mammography. Sci. Rep. **9**(1), 12495 (2019). https://doi.org/10.1038/s41598-019-48995-4
18. Smolka, B., Nurzynska, K.: Power lbp: a novel texture operator for smiling and neutral facial display classification. Procedia Comput. Sci. **51**, 1555–1564 (2015). https://doi.org/10.1016/j.procs.2015.05.350
19. Szydłowski, M., Powałka, B., Matuszak, M., Kochmański, P.: Machine vision micro-milling tool wear inspection by image reconstruction and light reflectance. Precis. Eng. **44**, 236–244 (2016). https://doi.org/10.1016/j.precisioneng.2016.01.003. http://www.sciencedirect.com/science/article/pii/S0141635916000052
20. Wu, X., Liu, Y., Zhou, X., Mou, A.: Automatic identification of tool wear based on convolutional neural network in face milling process. Sensors **19**(18), 3817 (2019). https://doi.org/10.3390/s19183817
21. Zuiderveld, K.: Contrast limited adaptive histogram equalization. In: Heckbert, P.S. (ed.) Graphics Gems IV, pp. 474–485. Academic Press Professional Inc, San Diego, CA, USA (1994). http://dl.acm.org/citation.cfm?id=180895.180940

Early Fully-Convolutional Approach to Wavefront Imaging on Solar Adaptive Optics Simulations

Francisco García Riesgo[2,4], Sergio Luis Suárez Gómez[2,3], Jesús Daniel Santos Rodríguez[2,4(✉)], Carlos González Gutiérrez[2,5], Enrique Díez Alonso[2], Francisco Javier Iglesias Rodríguez[1,2], Pedro Riesgo Fernández[2,6], Laura Bonavera[2,4], Susana del Carmen Fernández Menéndez[2,7], and Francisco Javier De Cos Juez[1,2]

[1] Department of Prospecting and Exploitation of Mines, University of Oviedo, Independencia 13, 33004 Oviedo, Spain

[2] Instituto Universitario de Ciencias y Tecnologías Espaciales de Asturias (ICTEA), Independencia 13, 33004 Oviedo, Spain

jdsantos@uniovi.es

[3] Department of Mathematics, University of Oviedo, Federico García Lorca 18, 33007 Oviedo, Spain

[4] Department of Physics, University of Oviedo, Federico García Lorca 18, 33007 Oviedo, Spain

[5] Department of Computer Science, University of Oviedo, Campus of Viesques s/n, 33024 Gijón, Spain

[6] Department of Business Administration, University of Oviedo, Campus of "El Cristo", Avenida de El Cristo s/n, 33071 Oviedo, Spain

[7] Department of Geology, University of Oviedo, Jesús Arias Velasco St. s/n, 33005 Oviedo, Spain

Abstract. Aberrations are presented in the wave-front images from celestial objects taken with large ground-based telescopes, due to the effects of the atmospheric turbulence. Therefore, different techniques, known as adaptive optics techniques, have been developed to correct those effects and obtain new images clearer in real time. One part of an adaptive optics system is the Reconstructor System, it receives information of the wavefront given by the wavefront sensor and calculates the correction that will be performed by the Deformable Mirrors. Typically, only a small part of the information received by the wave-front sensors is used by the Reconstructor System. In this work, a new Reconstructor System based on the use of Fully-Convolutional Neural Networks is proposed. Due to the features of Convolutional Neural Networks, all the information received by the wavefront sensor is then used to calculate the correction, allowing for obtaining more quality reconstructions than traditional methods. This is proved in the results of the research, where the most common reconstruction algorithm (the Least-Squares method) and our new method are compared for the same atmospheric turbulence conditions. The new algorithm is used for Solar Single Conjugated Adaptive Optics (Solar SCAO) with the aim of simplifying the system since all the needed calculations are performed with the network. The found improvements can be stated around at 0.4 rad of mean WFE over the recovered wavefront.

E. A. de la Cal et al. (Eds.): HAIS 2020, LNAI 12344, pp. 674–685, 2020.
https://doi.org/10.1007/978-3-030-61705-9_56

Keywords: Solar adaptive optics (Solar AO) · Fully-Convolutional Neural Networks (FCNN) · Single Conjugated Adaptive Optics (SCAO) · Durham Adaptive optics Simulation Platform (DASP)

1 Introduction

One of the main problems of ground-based telescopes is that the wavefronts received from celestial objects are deformed by the Earth's atmosphere in their way [1, 2]. It is caused by two reasons; firstly, the atmosphere is opaque for some electromagnetic waves, depending on its wavelength. Due to that fact, ground-based telescopes receive less information than space telescopes. Secondly, the wavelengths which can cross the atmosphere will suffer different aberrations caused by the atmospheric turbulence.

Adaptive Optics (AO) are a set of techniques developed to improve the precision of optical systems by means of correcting the possible distortions suffered by the wavefronts [1]. It also may be used in fields like medicine (correction of ocular aberrations), communication (possible aberrations in the wavefronts of laser communication), microscopy, etc. In this study, AO is used to correct the aberrations caused by the atmospheric turbulence in the received wavefronts in ground-based solar observations.

Previously, different reconstructors based on Artificial Neural Networks (ANNs) had been developed for night observations [3–5]. The main improvement included in this research is the fact that solar observations are corrected, whose difficulty relies on the observed object (the sun, a wide object for the field of view usually used) and also these observations are made during diurnal hours, implying higher turbulence.

Nowadays, the totality of big telescopes, both for diurnal and nocturnal observations, have at least a slight correction performed by an AO system. However, a perfect correction cannot be expected when using these systems; they are not able to measure all the aberrations of the wavefront and the systems neither would make a perfect correction, even if they could measure perfectly all the parameters, considering the physical limitations of the system.

In this paper, we present the results from an implementation of an Artificial Neural Network (ANN) as an SCAO reconstructor. They are compared with the results obtained by the Least-Squares method, which is nowadays the state of art reconstructor for Solar AO. All the results have been obtained in simulated situations performed with the Durham Adaptive optics Simulation Platform (DASP).

2 Materials and Methods

2.1 Solar Adaptive Optics

The atmospheric turbulence is a random phenomenon which is continuously varying, for that reason the reconstructions should be done in real time [6]. In a schematic representation, the atmosphere works as a mixture of air mass layers at different altitudes. The height of each layer depends on the its air density, which relies on the temperature; Solar observations must be done in diurnal hours, when the temperature is higher and the atmosphere is receiving solar energy, which implies two key factors [2].

In one hand the atmospheric turbulence layers have more energy providing more aberrations in the obtained images. On the other hand, the air temperature is higher, so it is easier to mix all the layers, having more variations in the atmospheric turbulence in shorter periods of time.

2.2 Solar Single Conjugated Adaptive Optics System

In general, an AO system measures the incoming wavefront with one or more wavefront sensors (WFS), being the Shack-Hartmann (SH) WFS the most common one [7]; its main idea consists in the slopes of the incoming wavefront being measured in different subapertures. Each one is focused the incoming light using convergent lens. In nocturnal AO, each subaperture estimates the distortions with a light spot called centroid, via the local slope of the incoming wavefront determined by the position of the centroid. However, in diurnal AO, when the Sun is the objective of the observations, the result of the convergent lent is a new image; the focused image of each subaperture is saturated by the Sun, as is shown in Fig. 1. To calculate the local slope of the received wavefront a new algorithm is needed, the correlation calculation that is made by the SH. The algorithm consists in a comparison between the image of each subaperture with one of them, the result is a value represented by a spot on each subaperture, that then is used as the centroid from the night observations.

Information measured by the WFS is used by the reconstructor system (RS) [1, 2] that calculates how the incoming wavefront should be corrected. Usually, the most common algorithm in solar AO for correction is the Least Squares (LS) technique [8]. Other algorithms that are used in night observations are Learn and Apply (L + A) [9] or the Linear-Quadratic Gaussian Control (LQG) [10], this algorithms could be hybridized with other systems, for example combining it with a k-nearest neighbor algorithm [11]. Another reconstruction algorithm for night observation based on ANNs called Complex Atmospheric Reconstructor based on Machine lEarNing (CARMEN) [12, 13]. In this work, the research is continued for solar AO by developing a RS based on fully-Convolutional ANNs.

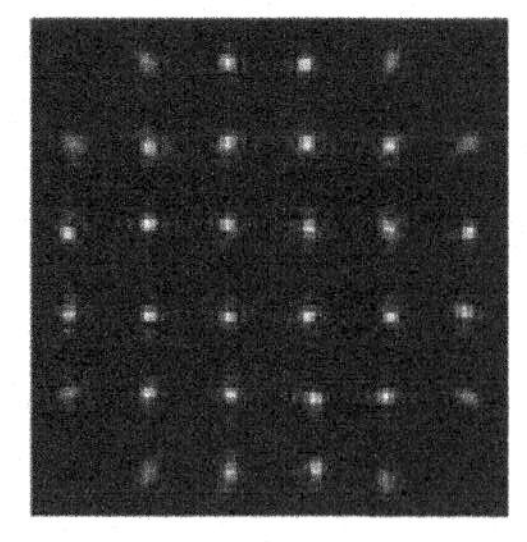

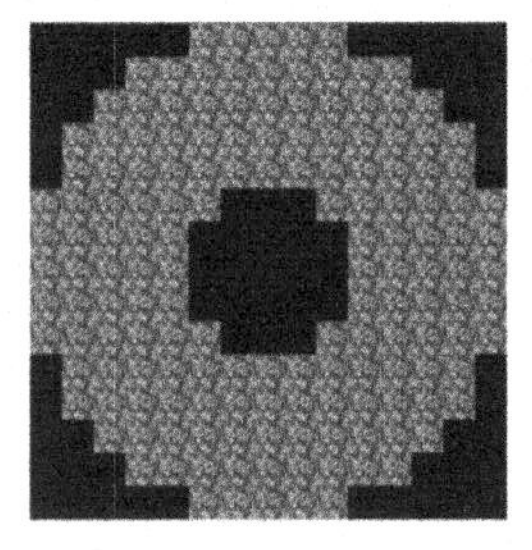

Fig. 1. Difference on the information received by the SH WFS subapertures between night and diurnal observations. The left image is from a nocturnal SH of 6×6 subapertures, while the right one corresponds to the data received by 15×15 subapertures from solar observations.

Finally, the correction of the received wavefront is the last step of an AO system, that is made by one or more Deformable Mirrors (DM) [2, 14]. They consist in mirrors that can take different shape to compensate the aberrations presented on the incoming light. They are made with piezoelectric materials, so they are modeled modifying the voltage applied to some mechanical actuators situated behind the surface of the mirror.

In this work, SCAO configuration is considered, one of the simplest for AO. It is characterized by using only a one WFS associated to a unique DM. All the process is done in close-loop, so the last reconstruction is used in the calculation of the next one.

2.3 Simulation Platform: DASP

The Durham Adaptive Optics Simulation Platform [15] was chosen for doing the needed simulations. It models and simulates different AO systems for nocturnal and diurnal observations, where all the parameters can be modified: the number of WFSs, DMs, parameters of the turbulence, etc. The RS is included on the software, so it can perform reconstructions for each simulation. The LS method is the one used in DASP, allowing a straightforward comparison for results obtained with new techniques.

The turbulences are generated by DASP using the Kolmogorov Atmospheric Model [16] implemented with Monte-Carlo simulations. DASP calculates the physical propagation of the wavefront when it travels the atmospheric turbulence, along with the aberration effect that it will made.

The atmospheric turbulence is determined by a few numbers of parameters, as the Fried's coherence length (r_0) [2], which determines the intensity of the turbulence. The higher is the value of r_0, the lower is the intensity of the turbulence. In a real situation an observation wouldn't be done if the value of r_0 is less than 9-8 cm.

2.4 Artificial Neural Networks as Solar RS: Fully-Convolutional Neural Networks (FCNN)

Artificial neural network are mathematical algorithms that try to mimic de behavior of biological neural networks [17], it is formed by an interconnected group of processing units called neurons.

The simplest architecture of an ANN is the Multi-Layer Perceptron (MLP), characterized by having the neurons distributed in different layers, where each neuron applies an activation function to the information that is received as input and the output is passed to the neurons of the next layer. The connections between neurons are regulated by different weights.

All ANNs systems can learn from the data and approximate nonlinear systems [18]. Different algorithms that measure the error are used for the learning process. ANNs require a training process before their use, where they need information of the input and the correct outputs to modify the weights between the layers and learn to give an answer to the problem. Different math algorithms can be used in this process, in this case backpropagation algorithm was used [19], that is the most common used one.

The first RS based in ANNs was an MLP called CARMEN. It was developed for AO for night observations [20], obtaining promising results. Due to that fact, more RS based on ANNs were developed later, continuing the work, as the Convolutional

CARMEN reconstructor [5]. In that case a different kind of ANN was chosen, using a Convolutional Neural Network (CNN) [17].

Convolutional Neural Networks (CNN). CNNs are other kind of ANNs developed for solving more complex problems, especially when there is a big amount of data to process [17, 21]. They are very useful in image processing, considering that images are constituted by a matrix of data. A CNN is composed by different convolutional layers with their own kernels that extract the main characteristics of an image working as filters, so the output is given by processing and reducing the size of the inputs given. CNNs has shown good results in other techniques as document recognition, image classification, speech recognition and others [22–24].

CNNs usually combine convolutional layers with pooling layers, the last ones reduce the size of the information that traverses the ANN by extracting the maximum or the mean value of a local region of pixels instead of maintaining the original dimensions.

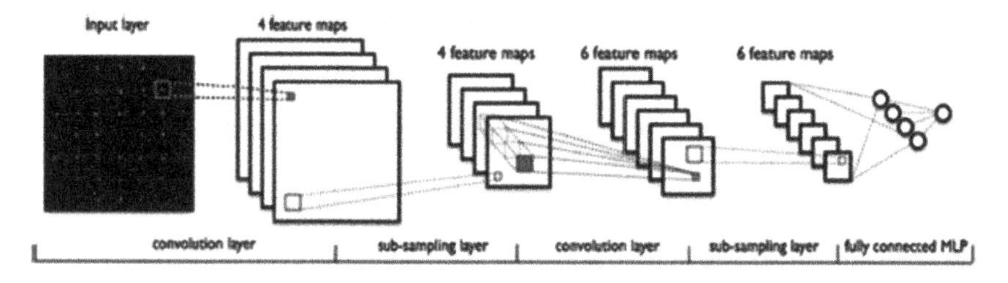

Fig. 2. Schematic representation of a CNN used as RS for Solar AO [4], the input of the ANN is the original image received by the WFS. At the end of the convolutional and sub-sampling layers an MLP is located.

Commonly, an MLP is included at the end of the CNN, its inputs are the features computes by the CNN, which have much smaller size than the original inputs. The training process of a CNN includes the modification of the weights of the different filters of the convolutional layers just as the weights of the interconnections of the MLP.

Fully-Convolutional Neural Networks FCNs. This type of ANN is a continuation of the previous ones, where the final part of the system that was formed by an MLP, is substituted by a deconvolutional block, also called transposed-convolutional block [25].

Once the inputs have traversed the different convolutional and pooling layers, their main features have already been obtained. According to the characteristics extracted, the final output is generated in the deconvolutional process where some layers with its own kernels generate a dense response, like an image.

In this work, the RS based on FCNs extracts directly the image of the atmospheric turbulence phase at each moment from the initial image received in the subapertures of the SH, avoiding the loss of information that usually is presented in the preprocessing data process needed in the other kinds of RSs.

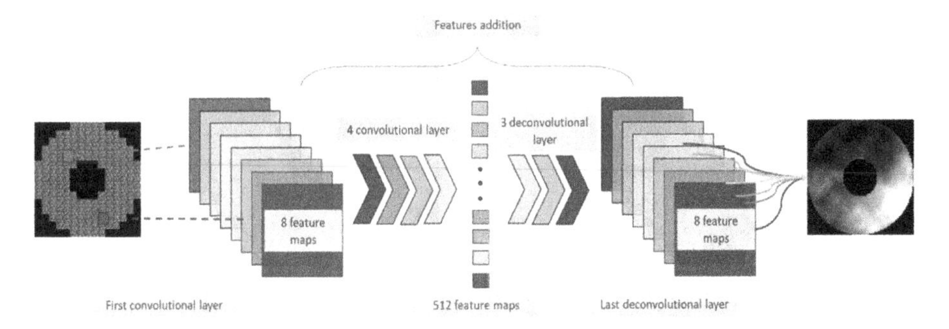

Fig. 3. Schematic representation of the FCN used in this work, both convolutional and deconvolutional block are also represented.

3 Experimental Setup

The experiments were performed on a computer running on Ubuntu LTS 14.04.3, with an Intel Xeon CPU E5-1650 v3 @ 3.50 GHz, 128 Gb DDR4 memory, Nvidia GeForce GTX TitanX, and SSD hard drive. Python was the computer language used, the same as DASP is implemented.

The simulations were performed trying to replicate the conditions of the AO system of the Gregor Solar Telescope [26], with a pupil of 1.5 m. The WFS consists in an SH WFS of 15 subapertures associated with a CCD of 24 pixels per subaperture. The reconstructed phased has 90×90 pixels of size, this parameter was imposed by the DASP simulator due to the conditions of the WFS.

The network used in this work was chosen via a searching process, where much FCNs with different topologies were tested. The picked topology is explained as follows (see Fig. 3):

- Convolutional block: This first part of the ANN consists in five convolutional layers with 8, 8, 2, 2, 2 kernels respectively. The kernels sizes are of 9, 7, 5, 5, 3 pixels of size. The strides in both directions are of two in all the layers except in the fourth one, where it value is 3, and padding is added too.
- Deconvolutional block: It consists in four deconvolutional layers with 2, 2, 2 and 8 kernels respectively. Their correspondent kernel sizes are of 3, 5, 5, 5 and 5 of size. The strides horizontally and vertically have the values 2, 1, 3, 1 and 3 for each layer. Padding has been added.

The hyperbolic tangent function is chosen for all the layers of the both blocks of the ANN. For the training process a Train Set of 60,000 images of the same region of the Sun with different atmospheric turbulence was simulated. The set contains the images received by the WFS, which conform the inputs of the ANN, and the related image of the turbulence phase for each input, intended to be the desired output (see Fig. 4).

The ANN was trained with different topologies before the most adequate was set. Each training process was done for approximately 50 epochs (depending on each case), requiring one hour per epoch.

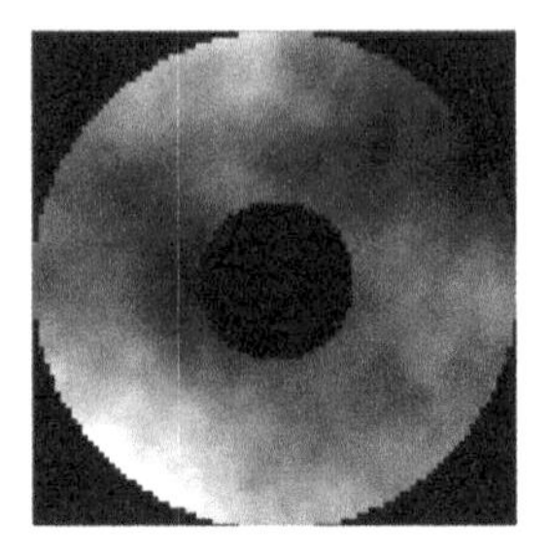

Fig. 4. Information contained in the Train Set. The image on the lefts shows the information received by the SH WFS, it is given as input to the RS. On the left the desired output of the FCN is showed, it consists on the image of the turbulence phase simulated by DASP for the first image.

4 Results and Discussion

Three different test set of images were made to obtain the quality of the reconstructions made by the ANN. The reconstruction made by DASP based on the Least-Squares method is also simulated in the test, avoiding us to compare in this work which method obtain the best results. Therefore, each test set has three different simulated images, the image received by the WFS (the input of the ANN), the original phase simulated by DASP (the desired output of the ANN) and the phase of the turbulence reconstructed by DASP using the Least-Squares method (LS).

The difference between these three tests is the r0 value. All the tests have 400 simulations, with turbulence layers with height from 0 m to 16 km. Three different r0 values were chosen, 8 cm for the first test, 10 cm for the second test and 12 cm for the latest test.

The quality of the reconstructions is measured by using the RMS Wavefront Error (RMS WFE). That error is calculated by doing the root-mean-square-error over the values of each image. For obtaining the RMS WFE in terms of wavelength:

$$WFE = RMSE \cdot \frac{\lambda}{2 \cdot \pi} \tag{1}$$

Where λ is wavelength of the celestial body. In this work 500 nm is taken as Sun's wavelength. Then the WFE of both reconstructions is compared with the WFE of the original phase to obtain the residual WFE. The method which had the minimum value of residual WFE would be the best one, since it means that the reconstructed image and the original image are the most similar.

4.1 $r_0 = 8\,\text{cm}$.

This value of r_0 corresponds with a day with very bad turbulence conditions, no observations would be taken in a real telescope in similar situations. The results for the first test set are presented in Table 1.

Table 1. Result obtained for $r_0 = 8\,\text{cm}$.

r_0 cm	Residual WFE ANN		Residual WFE LS		WFE Original Image		WFE ANN Image		WFE LS Image	
	rad	nm	rad	nm	rad	nm	rad	nm	rad	nm
8	2.14	170.3	2.60	207.2	7.48	595.8	6.51	518.5	8.42	670.6

The residual WFE values were calculated by doing the mean value of the residual WFE for each simulation, over the 400 simulations of the test. The same for the WFE values of the images. In Fig. 5 a visual comparison between the both reconstructors are showed for the same image of the test set.

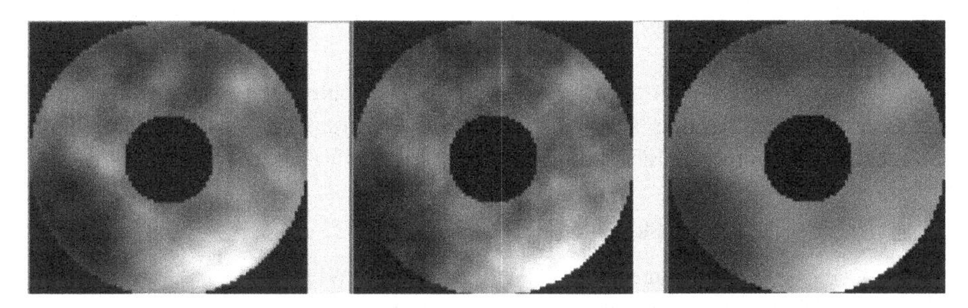

Fig. 5. Visual study of the reconstruction for a case with $r_0 = 8$ cm. The original phased is showed in the center of the image, being the ANN reconstruction the one on the left and the LS reconstruction the one on the right. At first sight, it is seen how the reconstruction made by the ANN is much clearer than the LS one, according to the Table 1, where the ANN one has the best results too.

4.2 $r_0 = 10\,\text{cm}$

Now the results for an atmospheric turbulence of 10 cm of r_0 are showed. It corresponds with bad turbulence conditions where no telescope observations are normally made (Fig.6, Table 2).

Table 2. Result obtained for $r_0 = 10\,\text{cm}$.

r_0 cm	Residual WFE ANN		Residual WFE LS		WFE Original Image		WFE ANN Image		WFE LS Image	
	rad	nm	rad	nm	rad	nm	rad	nm	rad	nm
10	1.81	144.5	2.09	167.0	6.84	544.7	6.09	485.3	7.51	597.8

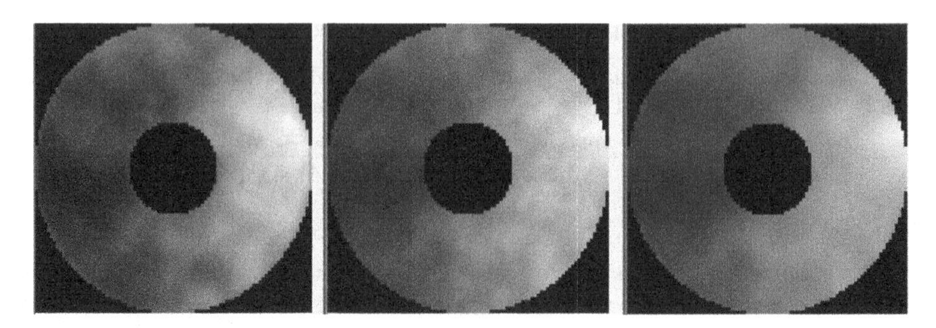

Fig. 6. Visual study of the reconstruction for a case with $r_0 = 10\,\text{cm}$. The original phased is showed in the center of the image, being the ANN reconstruction the one on the left as in Fig. 5

4.3 $r_0 = 12\,\text{cm}$

This case corresponds with a turbulence layer of a turbulent day where observations can be performed. As it is showed, the ANN reconstructor has been tested in bad turbulence conditions, that are the most demanding for it (Fig.7, Table 3).

Table 3. Result obtained for $r_0 = 12\,\text{cm}$.

r_0 cm	Residual WFE ANN		Residual WFE LS		WFE Original Image		WFE ANN Image		WFE LS Image	
	rad	nm	rad	nm	rad	nm	rad	nm	rad	Nm
12	1.52	121.0	1.91	152.0	6.14	488.6	5.64	448.8	6.71	534.0

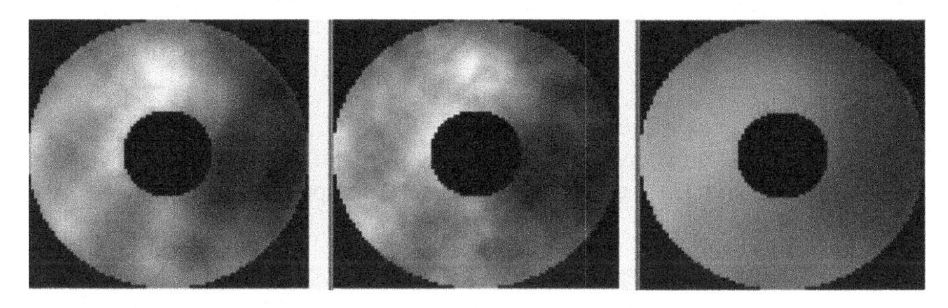

Fig. 7. Visual study of the reconstruction for a case with $r_0 = 12\,\text{cm}$. The original phased is showed in the center of the image, being the ANN reconstruction the one on the left and the LS reconstruction the one on the right.

4.4 Discussion

Results for the artificial intelligence model improving significantly in all cases the LS reconstructions, working approximately in real time as it only takes 30 s to reconstruct 30,000 images. As it is showed in the tables, the ANN RS improves in the approximately the same quantity the reconstructions, independently of the intensity of the turbulence, so it could be used for common days of observations.

The principal improvement of the ANN RS resides in the information contained on the input data. The input of the FCN is all the image receive by the WFS (see Fig. 2), so preprocessed data is not required. The correlation algorithm and the centroid algorithm is needed by common RS as the LS method; therefore, in that cases a lot of information is lost before the information is passed to the reconstructor.

5 Conclusion

In this work a hybrid artificial system is presented where different equipment as a telescope, deformable mirrors, wavefront sensors and reconstructor system are used together for correcting the atmospheric turbulence.

The main advantage of the new reconstructor presented is the good quality and sharpness of the phase turbulence reconstructions, due to use of all the information received by the WFS as input avoiding the loss of information that usually is presented in the commonly used preprocessing data process.

The results are showed in terms of numeric data to compare in an analytical approach the improvements of the research, but they are also exhibited some visual examples. The presented research improves around the 15% the quality of the reconstruction compared with the LS method, depending on the turbulence conditions. This value is higher for days with normal atmosphere turbulence for observation and can achieve 20%.

Considering future improvements of the reconstructor system based on FCN, the next step would be to obtain good results in Sun's regions where the system had not been trained before and in order to its future implementation in a real telescope, test it with real images of the Sun. Another future enhancement could be to design a RS based on FCNs for different more complex Solar AO systems, as Multi-Conjugate adaptive optics (MCAO), and compare our results with other existing RSs.

References

1. Roddier, F.: Adaptive Optics in Astronomy; Cambridge university press (1999)
2. Rimmele, T.R.: Solar adaptive optics. Adapt. Opt. Syst. Technol. **4007**, 218–232 (2000)
3. Osborn, J., et al.: Open-loop tomography with artificial neural networks on CANARY: on-sky results. Mon. Not. R. Astron. Soc. **441**, 2508–2514 (2014). https://doi.org/10.1093/mnras/stu758
4. Suárez Gómez, S.L., et al.: Improving adaptive optics reconstructions with a deep learning approach. In: de Cos Juez, F.J., et al. (eds.) Hybrid Artificial Intelligent Systems, pp. 74–83. Springer International Publishing, Cham (2018). https://doi.org/10.1007/978-3-319-92639-1_7
5. García Riesgo, F., Suárez Gómez, S.L., Sánchez Lasheras, F., González Gutiérrez, C., Peñalver San Cristóbal, C., de Cos Juez, F.J.: Convolutional CARMEN: tomographic reconstruction for night observation. In: Pérez García, H., Sánchez González, L., Castejón Limas, Ml, Quintián Pardo, H., Corchado Rodríguez, E. (eds.) HAIS 2019. LNCS (LNAI), vol. 11734, pp. 335–345. Springer, Cham (2019). https://doi.org/10.1007/978-3-030-29859-3_29

6. Zilberman, A., Golbraikh, E., Kopeika, N.S.: Propagation of electromagnetic waves in Kolmogorov and non-Kolmogorov atmospheric turbulence: three-layer altitude model. Appl. Opt. **47**, 6385 (2008). https://doi.org/10.1364/AO.47.006385
7. Neal, D.R., Copland, J., Neal, D.A.: Shack-Hartmann wavefront sensor precision and accuracy. Adv. Charact. Tech. Opt. Semicond. Data Storage Compon.ents **4779**, 148–161 (2002)
8. Ellerbroek, B.L.: First-order performance evaluation of adaptive-optics systems for atmospheric-turbulence compensation in extended-field-of-view astronomical telescopes. JOSA A **11**, 783–805 (1994)
9. Vidal, F., Gendron, E., Rousset, G.: Tomography approach for multi-object adaptive optics. JOSA A **27**, A253–A264 (2010)
10. Sivo, G., et al.: First on-sky SCAO validation of full LQG control with vibration mitigation on the CANARY pathfinder. Opt. Express **22**, 23565–23591 (2014)
11. Matei, O., Pop, P.C., Vălean, H.: Optical character recognition in real environments using neural networks and k-nearest neighbor. Appl. Intell. **39**(4), 739–748 (2013). https://doi.org/10.1007/s10489-013-0456-2
12. Osborn, J., et al.: First on-sky results of a neural network based tomographic reconstructor: carmen on Canary. In: Adaptive Optics Systems IV; Marchetti, E., Close, L.M., Véran, J.-P., Eds.; International Society for Optics and Photonics. **9148**, p. 91484 M (2014)
13. Suárez Gómez, S.L., et al.: Compensating atmospheric turbulence with convolutional neural networks for defocused pupil image wave-front sensors. In: de Cos Juez F. et al. (eds) Hybrid Artificial Intelligent Systems. HAIS 2018. Lecture Notes in Computer Science, vol 10870. Springer, Cham (2018) https://doi.org/10.1007/978-3-319-92639-1_34
14. Dainty, J.C., Koryabin, A.V., Kudryashov, A.: V Low-order adaptive deformable mirror. Appl. Opt. **37**, 4663–4668 (1998)
15. Basden, A., et al.: DASP the Durham adaptive optics simulation platform: modelling and simulation of adaptive optics systems. SoftwareX (2018)
16. Zilberman, A., Golbraikh, E., Kopeika, N.S.: Propagation of electromagnetic waves in Kolmogorov and non-Kolmogorov atmospheric turbulence: three-layer altitude model. Appl. Opt. **47**, 6385–6391 (2008)
17. Habibi Aghdam, H., Jahani Heravi, E.: Guide to Convolutional Neural Networks. Springer, Cham (2017). https://doi.org/10.1007/978-3-319-57550-6
18. Hornik, K., Stinchcombe, M., White, H.: Multilayer feedforward networks are universal approximators. Neural Netw. **2**, 359–366 (1989). https://doi.org/10.1016/0893-6080(89)90020-8
19. LeCun, Y., Boser, B., Denker, J.S., Henderson, D., Howard, R.E., Hubbard, W., Jackel, L. D.: Backpropagation applied to handwritten zip code recognition. Neural Comput. **1**, 541–551 (1989)
20. Gómez, S.L.S., Gutiérrez, C.G., Rodríguez, J.D.S., Rodríguez, M.L.S., Lasheras, F.S., de Cos Juez, F.J.: Analysing the performance of a tomographic reconstructor with different neural networks frameworks. In: Madureira, A.M., Abraham, A., Gamboa, D., Novais, P. (eds.) ISDA 2016. AISC, vol. 557, pp. 1051–1060. Springer, Cham (2017). https://doi.org/10.1007/978-3-319-53480-0_103
21. Suárez Gómez, S.L.: Técnicas estadísticas multivariantes de series temporales para la validación de un sistema reconstructor basado en redes neuronales (2016)
22. Mirowski, P.W., LeCun, Y., Madhavan, D., Kuzniecky, R.: Comparing SVM and convolutional networks for epileptic seizure prediction from intracranial EEG. In: 2008 IEEE Workshop on Machine Learning for Signal Processing, pp. 244–249 (2008)

23. Nagi, J., et al.: Max-pooling convolutional neural networks for vision-based hand gesture recognition. In: 2011 IEEE International Conference on Signal and Image Processing Applications (ICSIPA), pp. 342–347 (2011)
24. Nguen, N.T., Sako, S., Kwolek, B.: Deep CNN-based recognition of JSL finger spelling. In: Pérez García, H., Sánchez González, L., Castejón Limas, M., Quintián Pardo, H., Corchado Rodríguez, E. (eds.) HAIS 2019. LNCS (LNAI), vol. 11734, pp. 602–613. Springer, Cham (2019). https://doi.org/10.1007/978-3-030-29859-3_51
25. Long, J., Shelhamer, E., Darrell, T.: Fully convolutional networks for semantic segmentation. In: Proceedings of the IEEE conference on computer vision and pattern recognition, pp. 3431–3440. IEEE (2015)
26. Berkefeld, T., Schmidt, D., Soltau, D., von der Lühe, O., Heidecke, F.: The GREGOR adaptive optics system. Astron. Nachrichten **333**, 863–871 (2012). https://doi.org/10.1002/asna.201211739

Modeling a Specific Commercial Single Proton Exchange Membrane Fuel Cell

Jose Manuel Lopez-Guede[1,4], Julian Estevez[2,4], and Manuel Graña[3,4](✉)

[1] Dept. of Systems Engineering and Automatic Control, Faculty of Engineering of Vitoria, Basque Country University (UPV/EHU), Nieves Cano 12, 01006 Vitoria-Gasteiz, Spain
jm.lopez@ehu.es
[2] Dept. of Mechanics, Faculty of Engineering of Gipuzkoa, Basque Country University (UPV/EHU), Plaza Europa 1, 20018 Donostia-San Sebastian, Spain
[3] Dept. of Computer Science and Artificial Intelligence, Faculty of Informatics, Basque Country University (UPV/EHU), Paseo Manuel de Lardizabal 1, 20018 Donostia-San Sebastian, Spain
manuel.grana@ehu.es
[4] Computational Intelligence Group, Basque Country University (UPV/EHU), Leioa, Spain

Abstract. Within the different modeling possibilities to describe the behavior of complex dynamic systems, Artificial Neural Networks (ANN) are one of the most outstanding approaches. In this paper authors have used that approach to model the electrical performance of a specific commercial single proton exchange (PEM) fuel cell (FC). More specifically, a 2 KW device has been studied obtaining real data that have been used to generate a neural model with only one input and one output, i.e., the current and the voltage of the PEM fuel cell respectively. After following the steps described in the experimental design part of the paper, very promising results were reached with the test dataset, even using ANNs with one hidden layer.

1 Introduction

Nowadays Fuel Cell (FC) energy generation has been classified as a renewable energy technology to control the environment pollution and to contribute in solving the petrol energy crisis. Among the different FC options, Proton Exchange Membrane (PEM) FCs are considered as one the best alternatives since its structure is simple and it has high power density, superior reliability and durability, low operating temperature, quick start and no moving parts.

Due to the increasing interest in PEM FC research and development, its operational performances are focused on a number of mathematical models covering the dynamic and steady-state conditions. So, the PEM FC systems behavior can be analyzed starting even with the design step by different pathways with respect to computer simulations in different operational conditions [1,2].

E. A. de la Cal et al. (Eds.): HAIS 2020, LNAI 12344, pp. 686–697, 2020.
https://doi.org/10.1007/978-3-030-61705-9_57

It is possible to find out in the state of the art a number of successful methods to model the electrical characteristics of PEM FCs obtaining the voltage provided, however, such previous works usually rely on complex models using many input variables. For example, in [3] three input variables are used (partial pressures of oxygen and hydrogen, as well as cell operating current). A model of similar complexity is obtained in [4], where the temperature of the fuel cell and one sample time delayed values of the current and voltage are used. More complex models of four inputs are also used. In [5] authors consider the oxygen and hydrogen flows, stack current and stack temperature as inputs, while in [6] the oxygen and hydrogen pressures, room temperature and stack current are taken. It is possible to find models with five inputs as in [7], where oxygen and hydrogen inlet pressures, oxygen relative humidity, stack temperature and the stack current are the inputs of the model. Finally, there are even more complex models taking six inputs as in [8], where authors consider anode and cathode relative humidity, anode and cathode flow rate temperatures, current density and cell temperature. In [9] there are also six inputs, i.e., air and hydrogen humidification temperatures, air and hydrogen flow rates, cell temperature and current density.

The objective of the work developed in this paper is to obtain a model as simple as possible (as least simpler than the previously described approaches) of a commercial PEM FC from the point of view of the inputs needed, but it should be accurate enough. Following this, a simple model with the current I_{FC} at the input and the voltage V_{FC} at the output has been obtained using a neural network [10], showing promising accuracy values. The real motivation to use this neural network based approach is that authors pursue to establish a modeling framework that allows dealing with complex dynamics like fuel starvation phenomena. This modeling task should be taken a previous step in order to generate control algorithms to optimize the internal operation of fuel cells, paying special attention to its performance. The obtaining of those control algorithms and its optimization is not faced in this paper.

The structure of the paper is as follows. A general description of PEM FC and the details of a specific commercial PEM FC is given in Sect. 2, Sect. 3 describes the experimental design while Sect. 4 discusses the obtained results. Finally, Sect. 5 summarizes the main conclusions and the future work.

2 PEM Fuel Cells

The content of this section provides a general description about PEM fuel cells in subsection 2.1 and a more specific description focusing in a commercial device in subsection 2.2.

2.1 General Description

These devices are developed to work at low temperatures (50–80 °C) and within a low pressures range (0–2 bar) using a special polymer electrolyte membrane. They are developed mainly for transport applications and in general, for both stationary and portable FC applications. PEM fuel cells are composed of two main structural parts:

1. Membrane electrode assemblies (MEA) consisting in electrodes, solid membrane electrolyte, catalyst, and gas diffusion layers
2. Bipolar and electrical plates.

The reactants are oxygen (O_2) supplied at cathode and hydrogen (H_2) supplied at anode. The chemical reaction is based on the dissociation of hydrogen molecules into electrons and ionized atoms in form H+. The oxygen picks up the electrons and completes the external circuit. The electrons go through this circuit thus providing the electrical current. The oxygen then combines with the H^+ hydrogen, obtaining water (H_2O) as waste product leaving the FC. The electrolyte allows the appropriate ions to pass between the electrodes [11]. The most important feature in a single FC is that depending on operational conditions, it typically produces a small potential difference (0.5–1 V). Due to this reason, fuel cells are usually connected in series in order to form a fuel cell assembled system. The stack is the system used in moving elements as cars, generators, or other electrochemical devices that produce power.

2.2 Commercial PEM FC Description

Fig. 1. PEM fuel cell test station (Arbine Instruments FCTS-20kW)

In this paper authors have used a commercial device manufactured by Nedstack. More specifically, it is a 2 kW PEM fuel cell stack with 16 cells of a

230 cm^2 surface area. The PEM FC stack was connected to a test bench station manufactured by Arbin Instruments as shown in Fig. 1, where the MITS Pro-FCTS software was used to control and monitorize the operation. It is located at National Center for Hydrogen and Fuel Cell of Romania. The assembly is composed of five modules that could be described as the gas input and control module, humidifier module, cooling water module, power and control module. The gas input and control module included mass flow controls (MFC), installed into both fuel and oxidant lines sensors (in order to assure wide power range capacities from very small to 20 kW power output), temperature and pressure regulators. The temperature was maintained through a specific cooling water system. The humidifier module allows the required humidity in both fuel and oxidant channels. The power and control module assures mainly the monitoring of environmental and experimental conditions, electronic programmable load, emergency and main power switches, and heat coil control.

3 Experimental Setup

In this section authors describe the experimental design that has been carried out in the paper. The data obtaining and modification processes are given in subsection 3.1 and subsection 3.2 respectively, while in subsection 3.3 the modeling assumptions and process are introduced.

3.1 Data Obtaining

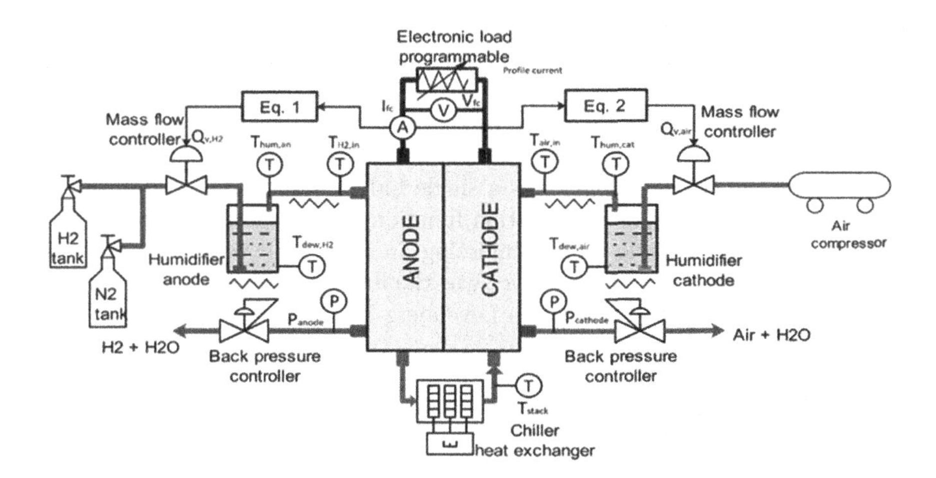

Fig. 2. PEM fuel cell testing system

The data obtaining process can be described by the schematic of Fig. 2. For the experiments that have been carried out, the purity of the fuel hydrogen that was supplied at anode was 99.998% and the inlet pressure was 60 psi. At cathode air was supplied. Both fuel and air were humidified using deionized water before entering into the test fuel cell. The excess of hydrogen and air were exhausted to the atmosphere.

A number measurements were carried out through the test system using the MITS PRO software. A typical fuel cell polarization of current and voltage curve was obtained in following conditions: stack temperature 338 K, anode hydrogen stoichiometry 1.25, cathode air stoichiometry 2.0, anode compartment pressure 18 psi and cathode compartment pressure 14.7 psi.

3.2 Dataset Modification

After the dataset obtaining process described in the previous subsection, an additive noise has been added. The magnitude of the noise has been 2%, and the final aim is to carry out a learning process leading to a model that could be robust in production time. This means that the predictions generated by the learned model should not be affected by small errors reading the sensors of the input signals.

3.3 Model Generation

In this paper, as stated previously, we are dealing with the problem of obtaining a model to obtain the voltage (V_{FC}) given by the PEM FC from the current (I_{FC}). The first step is to chose the structure of the artificial neural network that will be tuned through a training process. For that training purpose, the data obtained following the process described in the previous subsection have been used for the training and test steps. The whole dataset has been divided them into three subsets, more specifically a 60% is used for training, a 20% is used for validating and the last 20% is used as a independent test of network generalization. Given the input/output specification of the model, the trained ANN has only one neuron at both the input and output layers, and in order to maintain the simplicity requested by the specifications, it is a single hidden layer ANN containing 250 neurons with the log sigmoid activation function in that hidden layer. This size was determined as feasible after completing an systematic search process. The activation function of the output layer was the linear function. Finally, the used training algorithm is the well known Levenberg-Marquardt.

4 Results

This section is devoted to explain the results achieved following the experimental design described in Sect. 3, dividing the discussion in the results obtained with train and test datasets independently. During this discussion, we will focus on the final results, overlooking details of the training process itself. As described previously, it was mandatory that the model was as simple as possible. That requirement was met since the ANN has only one hidden layer.

4.1 Experimental Results with the Training Dataset

Table 1. Results of the best trained model (train data)

Magnitude	Value	Percentage of the minimum voltage	Percentage of the mean voltage
MSE	0.0011 V^2	0.0127 %	0.0105 %
Maximum error	0.2952 V	3.2960 %	2.7070 %
Mean error	0.0176 V	0.1965 %	0.1614 %

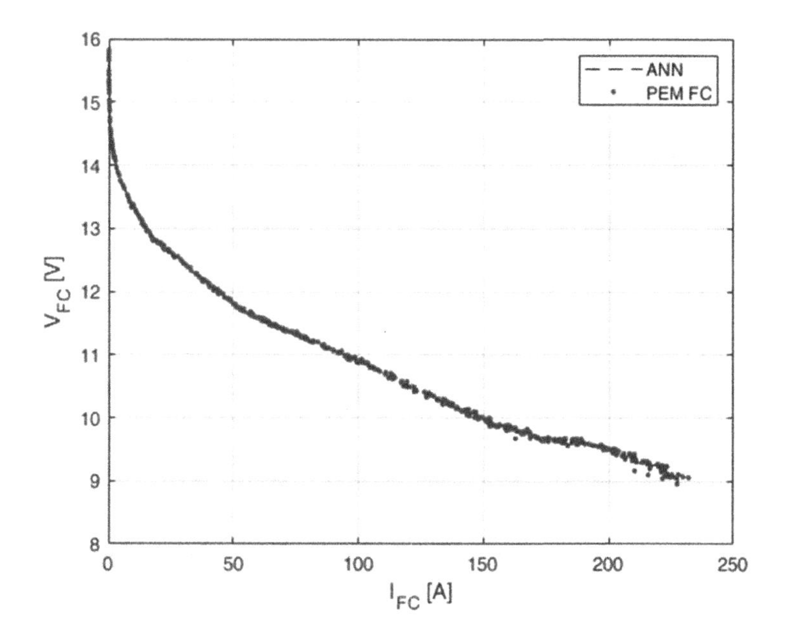

Fig. 3. PEM FC behavior vs ANN output (train data)

After training the neural model, the achieved accuracy results with the training dataset are shown in Table 1. In that table we can see that the trained model shows absolute values of medium squared error (MSE) of 0.011 V^2, maximum error of 0.2952 V and mean error of 0.0176 V. These absolute values are also expressed as the percentage of the minimum and mean voltage V_{FC} supplied by the PEM FC device, with the aim of helping to understand the meaning of these values.

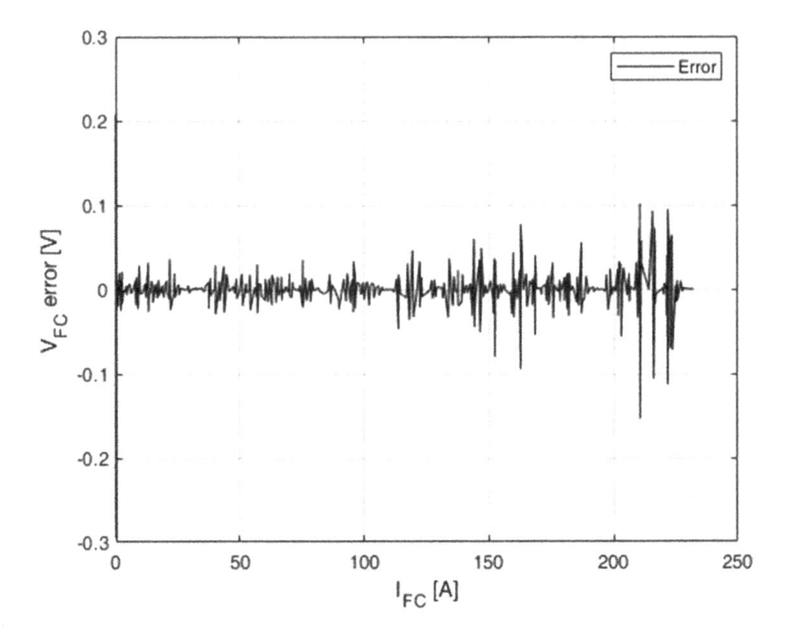

Fig. 4. ANN errors (train data)

In order to provide more insight we have added a number of figures showing the prediction capabilities of the obtained model with training dataset. In Fig. 3 the polarization curve of the PEM fuel cell is shown, comparing the original train data (as were gathered from the device and modified with the additive noise) to the outputs generated by the ANN after the training process, in such a way that it is possible to obtain an intuitive idea about the accuracy of the model, since the prediction of V_{FC} is accurate along all range of I_{FC} values.

On the other hand, Fig. 4 shows the original data to be learned as well as the modeling error, i.e., the difference between the curves of Fig. 3. One can notice that the curve that describes the behavior to learn is not linear at the beginning an end, which justifies the use of ANNs, even more if we keep in mind that this is a first attempt to establish a systematic modeling framework to reach a good description of complex phenomena as fuel starvation. Since the original and the learned curves for the train dataset are very close, Fig. 4 contains the augmented the difference between them. There we can see that for all values of I_{FC} the error is smaller than 0.15 V, and for the most part of the range of I_{FC} values, the error is less than 0.05 V, meeting a mean error of 0.0176 V.

Finally, Fig. 5 shows the correlation value obtained when the result of the trained ANN is evaluated taking into account the training dataset. It is possible to assess that the quality of obtained ANN is very high, given that the correlation coefficient is very close to 1.

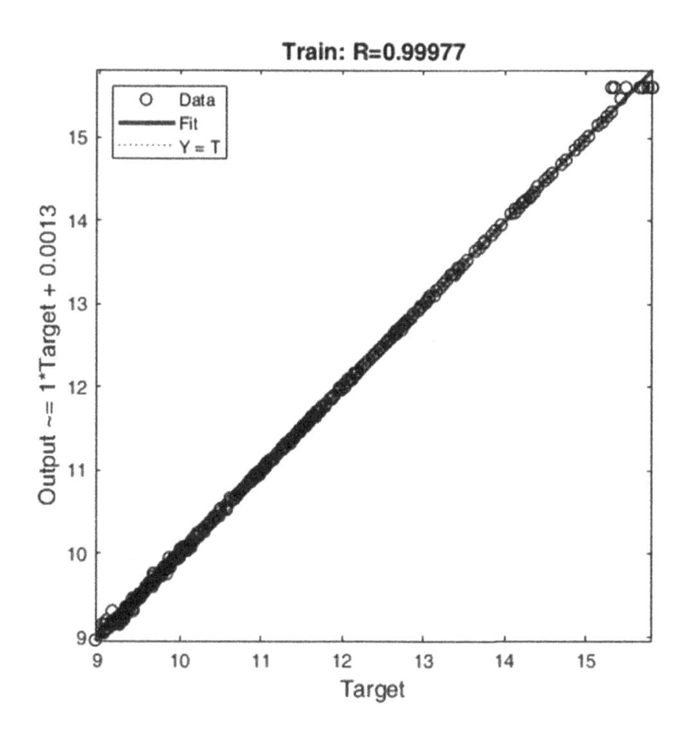

Fig. 5. Correlation values (train data)

Table 2. Results of the best trained model (test data)

Magnitude	Value	Percentage of the minimum voltage	Percentage of the mean voltage
MSE	0.0351 V^2	0.3905%	0.3218%
Maximum error	1.2638 V	14.0658%	11.5889%
Mean error	0.0626 V	0.6967%	0.5740%

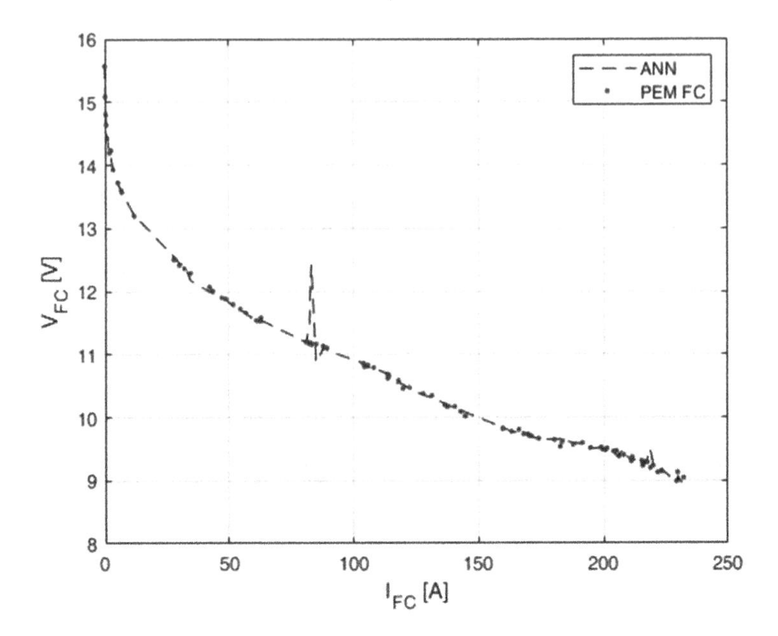

Fig. 6. PEM FC behavior vs ANN output (test data)

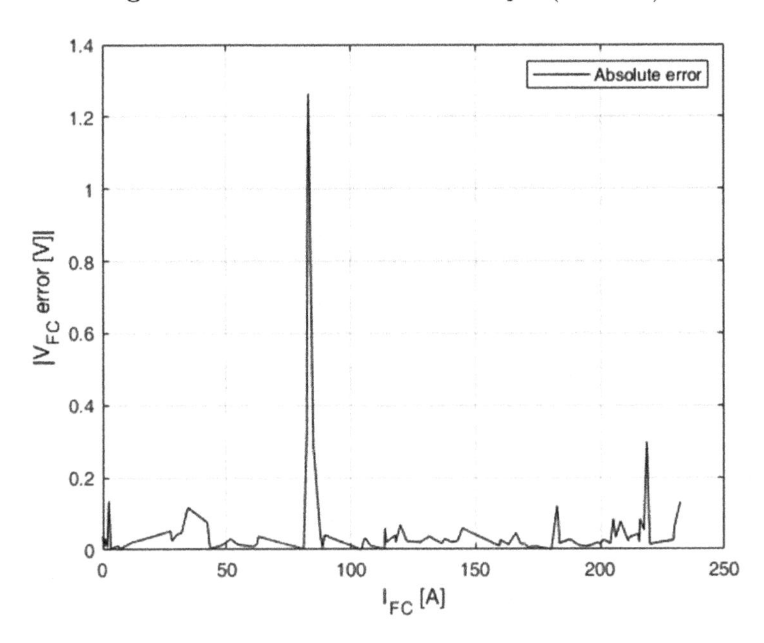

Fig. 7. ANN output absolute errors (test data)

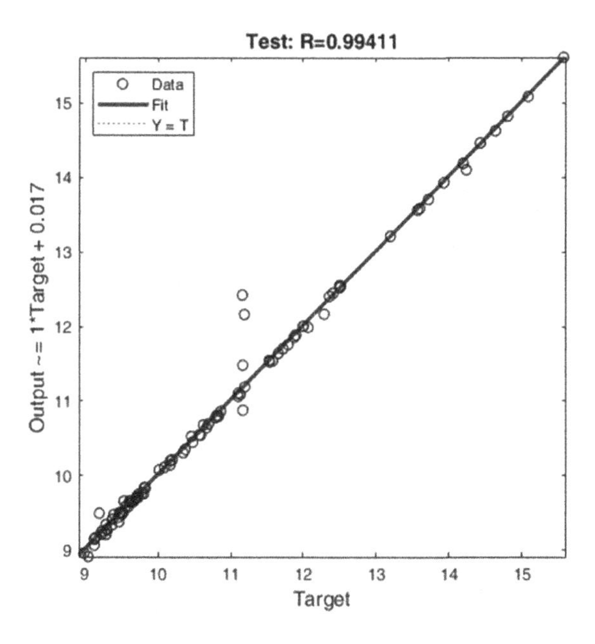

Fig. 8. Correlation values (test data)

4.2 Experimental Results with the Test Dataset

This subsection is devoted to discuss the results obtained using only the test dataset.

Some numeric result describing the accuracy obtained with the test dataset are in shown in Table 2. There it is possible to see that with the test dataset, the MSE is 0.0351 V^2, the maximum error is 1.2638 V and mean error is 0.0626 V. These absolute values are expressed again, as in the case of the previous subsection, as percentage of the minimum and mean voltage V_{FC} supplied by the PEM FC device.

We have included Fig. 6 and Fig. 7, where the polarization curve of the PEM fuel cell is shown comparing the modified test data (with noise) to the outputs generated by the trained ANN, as well as the absolute error between these two series. It is possible to see that the training process has been successful since the model prediction of V_{FC} is accurate along all range of I_{FC} values, excepting for one value around $I_{FC} = 80$ A. The presence of this artifact must be analyzed in future works.

Finally, Fig. 8 shows the correlation value obtained when the result of the trained ANN is evaluated taking into account the test dataset. The correlation coefficient value is 0.99411, which means again that the quality of obtained ANN is very high.

5 Conclusions

This paper has dealt with the problem of obtaining a simple model of a commercial proton exchange membrane fuel cell (PEM FC). More specifically, we have based our work on artificial neural networks due to their special characteristics. The first part of the paper explains both the basic concepts of PEM FC devices and the specific characteristics of one concrete commercial PEM FC. Then the experimental design of the modeling process has been detailed, giving information about the data obtaining and modification process and about the structure of the chosen ANN, their parameters and its training algorithm. Finally, the obtained results have been discussed finding that the achieved accuracy is very promising.

As future work, the following problem to address is to obtain an even more accurate model. There are two obvious ways to pursue that objective. The first one is to obtain more data after executing the data obtaining procedure described in subsection 3.1, while the second one is to increase the number of the inputs of the model up to two, in order to keep the model simpler than those described in the state-of-the-art, but in such a way that hidden effects not covered by the magnitude I_{FC} could be taken into account.

Acknowledgments. The work in this paper has been partially supported by FEDER funds for the MINECO project TIN2017-85827-P and grant IT1284-19 as university research group of excellence from the Basque Government.

References

1. Asl, S.S., Rowshanzamir, S., Eikani, M.H.: Modelling and simulation of the steady-state and dynamic behaviour of a pem fuel cell. Energy. **35**(4), 1633–1646 (2010). http://www.sciencedirect.com/science/article/pii/S0360544209005301
2. Daud, W.R.W., Rosli, R.E., Majlan, E.H., Hamid, S.A.A., Mohamed, R., Husaini, T.: Pem fuel cell system control: a review. Renew. Energy **113**, 620–638 (2017)
3. Mammar, K., Chaker, A.: Neural network-based modeling of pem fuel cell and controller synthesis of a stand-alone system for residential application. Int. J. Comput. Sci. Issues (IJCSI) **9**, 244–253 (2012)
4. Belmokhtar, K., Doumbia, M., Agboussou, K.: Pem fuel cell modelling using artificial neural networks (ann). Int. J. Renew. Energy Res. **4**, 725–730 (2014)
5. Hatti, M., Tioursi, M., Nouibat, W.: Static modelling by neural networks of a pem fuel cell. In: IECON 2006–32nd Annual Conference on IEEE Industrial Electronics, pp. 2121–2126 (2006)
6. Puranik, S.V., Keyhani, A., Khorrami, F.: Neural network modeling of proton exchange membrane fuel cell. IEEE Trans. Energy Convers. **25**(2), 474–483 (2010)
7. Han, I.S., Chung, C.B.: Performance prediction and analysis of a pem fuel cell operating on pure oxygen using data-driven models: a comparison of artificial neural network and support vector machine. Int. J. Hydrogen Energy **41**(24), 10202–10211 (2016). http://www.sciencedirect.com/science/article/pii/S036031991530389X

8. Falcão, D., Pires, J.C.M., Pinho, C., Pinto, A., Martins, F.: Artificial neural network model applied to a pem fuel cell. In: IJCCI 2009: PROCEEDINGS OF THE INTERNATIONAL JOINT CONFERENCE ON COMPUTATIONAL INTELLIGENCE, pp. 435–439 (2009)
9. Bhagavatula, Y.S., Bhagavatula, M.T., Dhathathreyan, K.S.: Application of artificial neural network in performance prediction of PEM fuel cell. Int. J. Energy Res. **36**(13), 1215–1225 (2012). https://doi.org/10.1002/er.1870
10. Widrow, B., Lehr, M.A.: 30 years of adaptive neural networks: perceptron, madaline, and backpropagation. Proc. IEEE **78**(9), 1415–1442 (1990)
11. Jayakumar, A., Sethu, S.P., Ramos, M., Robertson, J., Al-Jumaily, A.: A technical review on gas diffusion, mechanism and medium of PEM fuel cell. Ionics **21**(1), 1–18 (2014). https://doi.org/10.1007/s11581-014-1322-x

Deep Learning for House Categorisation, a Proposal Towards Automation in Land Registry

David Garcia-Retuerta[1(✉)], Roberto Casado-Vara[1], Jose L. Calvo-Rolle[2], Héctor Quintián[2], and Javier Prieto[1]

[1] BISITE Research Group, University of Salamanca, Edificio Multiusos I+D+i, Calle Espejo s/n, 37007 Salamanca, Spain
dvid@usal.es

[2] Department of Industrial Engineering, University of A Coruña, Ferrol, A Coruña, Spain

Abstract. Land typology classification is one of the main challenges of Land Registries all around the world. This process has historically been carried out by hand, requiring a large workforce and long processing times. Satellite imagery is shaking up the information retrieval methods for rural areas, where automatic algorithms have also been developed for land categorisation, but never for urban areas. This study provides an algorithm which can potentially speed up the decision-making process, reduce and detect biases; by automatically classifying images of houses facades into land registry categories. Convolutional Neural Networks are combined with a SVM and trained with over 5,000 labelled images. Success rate is above 85% and single image processing time is of the order of milliseconds. Results make it possible to reduce operating costs and to improve the classification performance by taking the human factor out of the equation.

Keywords: Deep learning · Land registry · Data analysis · Software tool

1 Introduction

Before explaining the research process, it is interesting to make an introduction to some questions of context, in addition to the techniques themselves, which help to understand the current moment, as well as to be able to draw conclusions

Supported by the project "Intelligent and sustainable mobility supported by multi-agent systems and edge computing (InEDGEMobility): Towards Sustainable Intelligent Mobility: Blockchain-based framework for IoT Security", Reference: RTI2018–095390-B-C32, financed by the Spanish Ministry of Science, Innovation and Universities (MCIU), the State Research Agency (AEI) and the European Regional Development Fund (FEDER).

E. A. de la Cal et al. (Eds.): HAIS 2020, LNAI 12344, pp. 698–705, 2020.
https://doi.org/10.1007/978-3-030-61705-9_58

beyond coldly exposing the reliability of an algorithm. The aim of this study is to provide a tool capable of classifying the typology and construction category of urban dwellings automatically.

A long time ago, Vitruvius already grouped the temples of the Roman empire (I century B.C.) into five categories so as to synthesise the architecture knowledge [28]. It is the beginning of a train of thought which uses the classification as a method to understand the reality. Moving forward into the future, and based on this idea, land registries began to be used all around the world due to their positive impact on agricultural production. One of their main advantages is the juridical safety they provide to farmers, which can lead to investments for improving productivity, usage of advanced technologies, land transfers and easier access to credit [22]. For example, same areas of Africa are currently developing their own systems in order to tackle critical situations [1].

According to statistics, land and read estates value, together with mortgages on properties, account to around 60–65% of the national assets in developed countries. Furthermore, 30–35% of the GDP in such a countries is generated by land and property related activities [21,27]. Because of all of the previous factors, cadastres hold a great importance at the present and will likely maintain it in the future.

Land registry faced major changes with the birth of the World Wide Web as it provided new revolutionary ways of storing, capturing and analysing the information. Adaptation to new techniques took place at that time and history is set to repeat itself once more, this time due to the revolutionary possibilities of databases, Big Data and machine learning. Databases provide a solution for the ever-increasing amount of generated land information [15], Big Data surges as the perfect way of analysing it [7,8,25] and machine learning can deal with the hardest processing processes [16,17].

Machine Learning is a powerful tool which enables computers to infer patters and relationships from data [2,23]. In particular, Convolutional Neural Networks (CNN) have rapidly improved object detection and semantic segmentation [12]. It could be said that some advanced networks have learnt to "understand" the world which is shown to them through images [9,11]. Based on this idea, we have used an advanced CNN (which "understands" the world), taken out its very last layer (which translates the inner knowledge/the general features to the human languages) and re-trained the last part so that it summaries all the information from an image into certain categories. This method has been previously used by other authors to develop and action recognition system [3,24] and an object detection architecture [10], achieving good performance with the famous MNIST dataset (handwritten digits classification) [5].

This research study is focused on automating dwelling classification in the context of urban land registries. Classification efforts are nowadays carried out manually which makes them time-consuming and expensive. Our aim is to provide a cheaper and faster solution which can eventually be used in the real-world. State-of-the-art machine learning techniques are used for dealing with images of the dwellings. A dataset provided by the land registry of Salamanca (Spain) has been used for training the neural networks and for measuring their success rate. Over 85% of the images were correctly labelled and single image processing time is of the order of milliseconds. As a result, this work has the potential of setting a breeding ground for a future implementation with real-life applications.

This article is organised as follows: Sect. 2 provides a description of the used data and the developed model, in Sect. 3 we discuss about the model performance and the suitability of using it as part of a real-life program, Sect. 4 presents some of the drawn conclusions.

2 Materials and Methods

2.1 Dataset

The aim of this study is to categorise the typology and category of different urban dwellings based solely on images of them. It should be noted that no metadata of the dwellings have been used, which adds extra difficulty to the considered problem.

In order to develop effective techniques in this study, a database of the land registry of Salamanca (Spain) has been used. It contains 5802 images of dwellings with their respective building categories. There are examples of three different building categories, although one category ("1.2.1 single or semi-detached building") has been discarded because it does not have a significant number of samples. The remaining categories are: "1.1.2 collective houses in a closed bloc" and "1.2.2 single-family houses in line or closed bloc". Several other categories can be found in the Spanish cadastre books they do not refer to urban dwellings or they are too outdated to be found in cities nowadays.

The data has been divided into two groups: training and test. 80% of the images are randomly selected to create the training group, and the remaining 20% will form the testing dataset. The former is shown with its labels to the developed network+SVM (for training the SVM), and the latter is used to compare real labels against predicted labels (providing a measure of the prediction error).

Several tests have been carried out to verify that there are no biases when calculating the accuracy of the model, and all of them have given satisfactory results (such as using training and testing datasets of different proportions, classifying a set of images belonging to the same neighbourhood but having different categories and classifying defective images). Therefore, it can be affirmed that the program is indeed capable of classifying the dwellings by their typology and category, instead of classifying them based on neighbourhood/environmental/lighting characteristics/etc. This is due to the variety and diversity of the images on the dataset. Figure 2 shows an example of the carried out classification.

2.2 Developed Model

Convolutional neural networks have been used to extract several features from the images, and subsequently an SVM (Support Vector Machine) has been

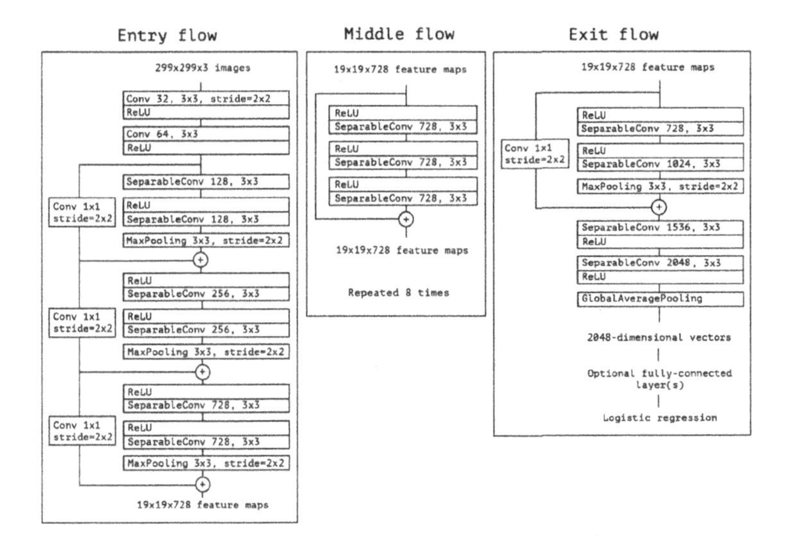

Fig. 1. Basic structure of the used CNN for the image classification. Xception (2016).

trained to perform a classification based on the features obtained. Its suitability for this problem is explained below.

The SVM algorithm is used to divide the solution space based on the desired categories. The new images are represented in this space and classified based on the previous division. This method was invented in 1963 by Vapnik and its first applications already obtained good results for the classification of images [4]. Since then it has become a common technique in machine learning due to its simplicity and good performance.

Artificial neural networks are a bio-inspired mathematical algorithm that has been used in recent years to solve many real-world problems. A very powerful type of neural network for image analysis are convolutional neural networks (CNN), which have been successfully used to find contours automatically [12] and to perform an automatic classification of objects in any image [14]. In the latter aspect, ResNet set a milestone in 2015 by achieving a better classification than humans in the ImageNet competition [13]. On the basis of these results and its good past performance we decided to implement a model for cadastre classification based on dwelling images.

The proposed model makes use of both techniques, SVM and CNN, to achieve a correct classification of the images obtained. This method is based on recent state-of-the-art researches such as [6,20,26,29]. For this study, an already-trained convolutional neural network has been used. It was previously trained in image classification with the structure of Fig. 1. The last layer has been replaced by the SVM, which has been trained with the available images. Building categories that contain few examples have not been included as it cannot expected to obtain relevant knowledge from them.

Several trained networks have been tested. The best overall performance was obtained by Xception, both in accuracy (Table 1) and processing time. It is formed by 36 convolutional layers which are structured into 14 modules (a detailed description of the structure is shown in Fig. 1).

Table 1. Performance of the different trained networks+SVM

	Inception ResNet V2	Inception V.3	VGG16	Xception
Accuracy	0.6442	0.6809	0.6354	0.8557
MSE	0.3557	0.319	0.3645	0.1442

3 Results and Discussion

The developed system has achieved a 85% success rate in the collected dataset. The results have been satisfactory, with a processing time of the order of milliseconds for classifying new images. An example of the obtained classification can be found in Figure casado2020iot2, and the result's confusion matrices in Fig. 3.

Fig. 2. Obtained results for building classification. Images in red show errors in classification, images in green show successful cases. (Color figure online)

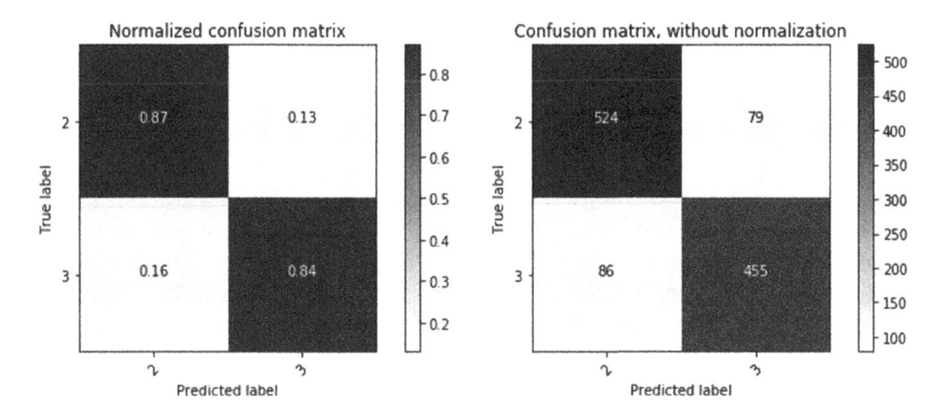

Fig. 3. Confusion matrices of the best performing combination: Xception+SVM.

The program obtained is capable of automatically classifying the typology and category of a dwelling with a significant degree of confidence. Verification by a human assistant is still necessary to obtain a definitive classification, but the programme has great potential as a support tool for operators.

It could be applied both to verify the classification of human operators and to improve their productivity. In the first case, the machine would analyse the classifications already carried out and accept as good those that coincide with the prediction. The cases that differ will have to be analyzed by another operator different from the original one to obtain a definitive verdict. This can be very useful when performing quality control or preventing internal fraud, as it allows to focus on anomalous cases before carrying out an in-depth analysis. In the second case, they would be told which photographs they should pay more or less attention to. The easier classifications would only have to be accepted, while the more complicated ones would have to be examined in detail. The workload would be considerably reduced, while maintaining the quality of the final classification. Furthermore, it would allow quality control of external work to be carried out.

It would be feasible to scale up the scope of the proposed method. With access to more categorised images it is likely that better training of the neural network will be achieved, thus improving the success rate. In addition, all other typologies and categories could be included so that the model would be able to correctly classify an image of any building presented to it. This could be complemented by a classification system based on orthophotographs for rural environments [18,19].

It is also possible to scale up the use of the method. Most of the processes it performs are highly parallelizable so it can be implemented on a server for large-scale use. Training is the only computationally expensive process in the program, but this only has to be done once.

4 Conclusions

At present we are in the moment in which the mathematical classification of the machine surpasses the capacity of human comprehension. There are two aspects to this situation: The first is to accept a classification that is not understood and does not respond to traditional patterns, although it is shown to be optimal for the purpose proposed. The second is the uncertainty of the administration caused by state-of-the-art methods which are hard to justify. The future lies not in reducing the mathematical capacity of the machine, but in increasing the capacity to understand and control that the processes that are carried out are adequate. This is already happening in other administrative fields where they have faced similar situations when facing the virtual world, such as the current wide-spread usage of digital signatures and the implementation of online method to carry out many administrative tasks.

References

1. Atwood, D.A.: Land registration in africa: the impact on agricultural production. World Dev. **18**(5), 659–671 (1990)
2. Casado-Vara, R., Chamoso, P., De la Prieta, F., Prieto, J., Corchado, J.M.: Non-linear adaptive closed-loop control system for improved efficiency in iot-blockchain management. Inf. Fusion **49**, 227–239 (2019)
3. Casado-Vara, R., Martin-del Rey, A., Affes, S., Prieto, J., Corchado, J.M.: IoT network slicing on virtual layers of homogeneous data for improved algorithm operation in smart buildings. Future Gener. Comput. Syst. **102**, 965–977 (2020)
4. Cortes, C., Vapnik, V.: Support-vector networks. Mach. Learn. **20**(3), 273–297 (1995)
5. Deng, L.: The mnist database of handwritten digit images for machine learning research [best of the web]. IEEE Signal Process. Mag. **29**(6), 141–142 (2012)
6. Elleuch, M., Maalej, R., Kherallah, M.: A new design based-svm of the cnn classifier architecture with dropout for offline arabic handwritten recognition. Procedia Comput. Sci. **80**, 1712–1723 (2016)
7. García-Retuerta, D., Bartolomé, Á., Chamoso, P., Corchado, J.M., González-Briones, A.: Original Content Verification Using Hash-Based Video Analysis. In: Novais, P., Lloret, J., Chamoso, P., Carneiro, D., Navarro, E., Omatu, S. (eds.) ISAmI 2019. AISC, vol. 1006, pp. 120–127. Springer, Cham (2020). https://doi.org/10.1007/978-3-030-24097-4_15
8. García-Retuerta, D., Bartolomé, Á., Chamoso, P., Corchado, J.M.: Counter-terrorism video analysis using hash-based algorithms. Algorithms **12**(5), 110 (2019)
9. Garg, R., B.G., V.K., Carneiro, G., Reid, I.: Unsupervised CNN for single view depth estimation: geometry to the rescue. In: Leibe, B., Matas, J., Sebe, N., Welling, M. (eds.) ECCV 2016. LNCS, vol. 9912, pp. 740–756. Springer, Cham (2016). https://doi.org/10.1007/978-3-319-46484-8_45
10. Gidaris, S., Komodakis, N.: Object detection via a multi-region and semantic segmentation-aware CNN model. In: Proceedings of the IEEE International Conference on Computer Vision, pp. 1134–1142 (2015)

11. Goyal, Y., Khot, T., Summers-Stay, D., Batra, D., Parikh, D.: Making the v in VQA matter: Elevating the role of image understanding in visual question answering. In: Proceedings of the IEEE Conference on Computer Vision and Pattern Recognition, pp. 6904–6913 (2017)
12. He, K., Gkioxari, G., Dollár, P., Girshick, R.: Mask r-cnn. In: Proceedings of the IEEE International Conference on Computer Vision, pp. 2961–2969 (2017)
13. He, K., Zhang, X., Ren, S., Sun, J.: Deep residual learning for image recognition. In: Proceedings of the IEEE Conference on Computer Vision and Pattern Recognition, pp. 770–778 (2016)
14. Hu, J., Shen, L., Sun, G.: Squeeze-and-excitation networks. In: Proceedings of the IEEE Conference on Computer Vision and Pattern Recognition, pp. 7132–7141 (2018)
15. Hunter, G.J., Williamson, I.P.: The development of a historical digital cadastral database. Int. J. Geogr. Inf. Syst. **4**(2), 169–179 (1990)
16. Kotsiantis, S.B., Zaharakis, I., Pintelas, P.: Supervised machine learning: a review of classification techniques. Emerg. Artif. Intell. Appl. Comput. Eng. **160**, 3–24 (2007)
17. Li, T., Prieto, J., Fan, H., Corchado, J.M.: A robust multi-sensor phd filter based on multi-sensor measurement clustering. IEEE Commun. Lett. **22**(10), 2064–2067 (2018)
18. Matikainen, L., Hyyppä, J., Kaartinen, H.: Automatic detection of changes from laser scanner and aerial image data for updating building maps. Int. Arch. Photogramm. Remote Sens. Spat. Inf. Sci. **35**, 434–439 (2004)
19. Müller, S., Zaum, D.W.: Robust building detection in aerial images. Int. Arch. Photogram. Remote Sens. **36**(B2/W24), 143–148 (2005)
20. Niu, X.X., Suen, C.Y.: A novel hybrid CNN-SVM classifier for recognizing handwritten digits. Pattern Recogn. **45**(4), 1318–1325 (2012)
21. Osskó, A.: Advantages of the unified multipurpose land registry system. In: International Conference on Enhancing Land Registration and Cadastre for Economic Growth in India, vol. 31 (2006)
22. Payne, G.: Urban land tenure policy options: titles or rights? Habitat Int. **25**(3), 415–429 (2001)
23. Prieto, J., Mazuelas, S., Win, M.Z.: Context-aided inertial navigation via belief condensation. IEEE Trans. Signal Process. **64**(12), 3250–3261 (2016)
24. Ravanbakhsh, M., Mousavi, H., Rastegari, M., Murino, V., Davis, L.S.: Action recognition with image based CNN features. arXiv preprint arXiv:1512.03980 (2015)
25. Sagiroglu, S., Sinanc, D.: Big data: a review. In: 2013 International Conference on Collaboration Technologies and Systems (CTS), pp. 42–47. IEEE (2013)
26. Sampaio, W.B., Diniz, E.M., Silva, A.C., De Paiva, A.C., Gattass, M.: Detection of masses in mammogram images using CNN, geostatistic functions and SVM. Comput. Biol. Med. **41**(8), 653–664 (2011)
27. Sánchez, A.J., Rodríguez, S., de la Prieta, F., González, A.: Adaptive interface ecosystems in smart cities control systems. Future Gener. Comput. Syst. **101**, 605–620 (2019)
28. Vitruvius, M.P.: The ten books on architecture, translated by morris hicky morgan (1960)
29. Xue, D.X., Zhang, R., Feng, H., Wang, Y.L.: CNN-SVM for microvascular morphological type recognition with data augmentation. J. Med. Biol. Eng. **36**(6), 755–764 (2016)

On the Identification of Critical Questions in the PISA for Schools Program

Noelia Rico[1(✉)], Pedro Alonso[2], Laura Muñiz-Rodríguez[3], Raúl Pérez-Fernández[3,4], Luis J. Rodríguez-Muñiz[3], and Irene Díaz[1]

[1] Department of Computer Science, University of Oviedo, Oviedo, Spain
{noeliarico,sirene}@uniovi.es

[2] Department of Mathematics, University of Oviedo, Oviedo, Spain
palonso@uniovi.es

[3] Department of Statistics and O.R. and Mathematics Education, University of Oviedo, Oviedo, Spain
{munizlaura,perezfernandez,luisj}@uniovi.es

[4] KERMIT, Department of Data Analysis and Mathematical Modelling, Ghent University, Ghent, Belgium

Abstract. PISA for Schools is an OECD (Organization for Economic Cooperation and Development) program designed to provide results on students' performance in Mathematics, Reading and Science at school level. In order to achieve this purpose, participants are asked to answer a content-based test together with a background questionnaire. Answers are next evaluated by a group of reviewers using a coding guide defined in terms of an ordinal qualitative scale. Although guarantying consistency among reviewers is key, differences may arise on a particular question due to different interpretations of the coding guide for some specific answers. In order to identify the origin of the discrepancies and ensure consistency in the evaluation process of forthcoming editions of the program, this work aims at identifying critical questions that lead to the largest disagreements among reviewers. Ultimately, this critical questions should be examined in detail by performing some qualitative analysis of both the answers provided by the participants and the instructions on the coding guide.

Keywords: PISA · Ordinal scale · Degrees of proximity · Dispersion

1 Introduction and Context

In the context of decision-making, experts usually have to express their preferences on a set of alternatives. Many decision-making problems use ordinal qualitative scales formed by linguistic terms since very often data are expressed at an ordinal level. In fact, words are more natural than numbers [10] and more

Supported by Grants TIN2017–87600-P from Spanish Government and IDI/2018/000176 from the Principality of Asturias. Raúl Pérez-Fernández acknowledges the support of the Research Foundation of Flanders (FWO17/PDO/160).

E. A. de la Cal et al. (Eds.): HAIS 2020, LNAI 12344, pp. 706–717, 2020.
https://doi.org/10.1007/978-3-030-61705-9_59

appropriate for dealing with imprecision and uncertainty in human decisions [5]. According to [8], ordinal qualitative scales used in decision-making problems are, in general, Likert-type scales. These scales are characterized by ordered response categories in which there is a balanced number of positive and negative categories and a numerical value is assigned to each category.

These scales are often applied to measure perceived quality, which is a task arising in many fields such as health and education. For example, in the context of education, Cerchiello *et al.* [4] propose to summarize students' perceived quality data using non parametric indices based on the observed frequency distribution that are able to exploit efficiently the ordinal nature of the analyzed variables. Thus, they obtain a ranking of the taught courses and produce indicators used to design plan actions on the organizational component and on the relationship between didactics and adequacy of the resources.

PISA is the well-known OECD Program for International Student Assessment. In particular, PISA for Schools is a voluntary assessment program that aims to provide valuable information on the learning climate within a school and to measure key components of 21st century skills mainly based on Mathematics, Reading and Science. The assessment has been successfully administered over 2200 times in schools in 11 countries around the world [9]. From these assessments valuable information for national education systems is provided. Thus, the evaluation process should be as accurate as possible. For that purpose, the pilot study is especially important and, thus, reviewers should be trained on the use of the coding guides and their interpretation. Reviewers are strongly requested to apply the coding guides with a high level of consistency. However, some answers could be difficult to interpret, and consequently they would lead to different marks if they were evaluated by different reviewers.

Clearly, PISA for Schools evaluation constitutes a decision-making problem where different reviewers express an evaluation by using an ordinal scale. How to deal with ordinal scales is somehow a complex problem. Initially, it was common to transform the scale into several dichotomous variables or to arbitrarily associate each linguistic term with a number. However, it is now known that standard measures of the spread of a distribution are inappropriate when dealing with qualitative data [1]. In this work, we follow a different approach based on dispersion measures in the context of ordinal qualitative scales [6]. More precisely, this work aims at identifying the questions that lead to the largest disagreement among reviewers, the ultimate goal being to improve the training process for reviewers in future editions of the program.

The paper is organized as follows: Sect. 2 describes the data used in this study. Section 3 details the method employed to identify critical questions. The method is applied to the PISA for Schools data in Sect. 4. Finally, in Sect. 5 some results and conclusions are drawn.

2 Problem Description

The here-evaluated data have been retrieved from the pilot phase of PISA for Schools undertook in Spain. In the PISA for Schools program, students are asked to complete a booklet that holds different items, which are taken by a semi-randomized procedure from a previously designed dataset of PISA-based questions. Although the program was undertaken in 11 countries, booklets are the same for all of them (adapted to each national language). Different stimuli are presented in the booklet, and one or more items are related to each stimulus. Furthermore, items are classified into one of the three following domains: **Mathematics**, **Reading**, and **Science**.

These items are made up of questions, which can be classified based on the nature of their possible answer. Some of them are multiple choice questions, in which the students have to select the only correct answer from a closed set of options. These questions are considered *original* because student's genuine answer is straightforwardly translated to its mark. Obviously, these questions are out of the present study, because different marks for one pair of student/question could only obey to mistakes in typing or coding. On the other hand, there are questions that do require the students to write their own answer. These are known as *coded* questions because, in order to mark the question, the student's answer has to be previously interpreted by an expert reviewer. For some of these questions the students must write a short answer but sometimes they are required to construct a more elaborated answer or even to justify their reasoning. Hence, depending on the length of the answer, *coded* questions can be split into two different subcategories: coded questions with short answer and coded questions with long answer.

The reviewers are provided with coding guides with strict criteria and guidelines for evaluating the questions. Although *coded* questions with short answer may appear difficult to evaluate, the coding guides make clear enough how to mark them in relation to different possible answers of the students, and thus it is immediate to obtain their mark too. The most challenging questions for the reviewers are ***coded* questions with long answer**. Despite the effort on making the guidelines in the coding guide as precise as possible, sometimes there still could be subjectivity on the evaluation. Therefore, the latter are the object of interest in this work, since it is in their evaluation process where reviewers are more likely to disagree.

The PISA for Schools pilot study consists of a total of 141 questions, specifically there are 40 questions defined for Mathematics, 47 for Reading and 54 for Science. *Coded* questions with long answer requiring to be codified by experts are a total of 44 (more specifically: 7 for Mathematics, 17 for Reading and 20 for Science). Coding guides provided to the reviewers clarify how the answers of the students should be encoded and marked with one of following mutually exclusive categories: *unanswered*, *incorrect*, *semi-correct* or *correct*. Note that not all of the questions have so many categories available. More concretely, there are answers that only can be *unanswered*, *incorrect* or *correct*. The former are here referred to as Type B questions, whereas the latter are referred to as Type A questions.

These coded questions for which the students are required to write a more elaborated answer are more suitable to be misunderstood and thus their codification is thoroughly done by a total of four reviewers, which are randomly taken from a pool of reviewers following an experimental design made by the organization of the program. From now on, the term *question* will refer only to one of the coded questions with long answer, as they will be the material for our study.

Therefore, the sample size of our study consists of 44 questions which are answered by 1568 different students. Note that not all the 1568 students answered the 44 questions. More precisely, each student completed only one of the seven available booklets (whose number of questions varies between 15 and 24). To sum up, we have data of 672 different answers for each of the 44 questions and each answer is reviewed by 4 different reviewers.

3 Methodology

The purpose of this analysis is to identify critical questions in the PISA for Schools program. By providing the reviewers with a coding guide with strict instructions for marking the answers of the students, the subjectivity in the evaluation should be minimized. Unfortunately, despite the efforts to make the coding guide as explicit as possible, it seems that reviewers do not always agree on their evaluations. For this very reason, it is necessary to find a method to describe how much the reviewers disagree with regard to their evaluation of a precise question for a precise student. We aim to determine which are the questions that, despite the guidelines on the coding guide, lead to the largest disagreements among reviewers. The key points of the method proposed in this work are the following:

- Fix the considered ordinal scale and establish the degrees of proximity between the elements of this scale (see Subsection 3.1).
- Obtain all the possible **combinations** of marks given by r independent reviewers. Each combination has a vector of degrees of proximity associated, hereinafter referred to as **vector of dispersion** (see Subsection 3.2).
- Identify combinations leading to the same vector of degrees of proximity. Each set of combinations with the same vector of degrees of proximity is referred to as a **tier** (see Subsections 3.2 and 3.3).
- Establish a hierarchy of tiers (see Subsection 3.3).
- Rank the questions (see Subsection 3.3).

3.1 The Ordinal Scale

To model the present problem we will work with ordinal scales. An **ordinal scale** $\mathscr{L} = \{L_1, \ldots, L_\ell\}$ is a tool of measurement where the elements of $\mathscr{L}$ are linearly ordered such that $L_i \leq L_j$ if $i \leq j$. Each ordinal scale is associated with a set of degrees of proximity $\Delta = \{\delta_1, \ldots, \delta_h\}$ representing how distant the elements of the ordinal scale $\mathscr{L}$ are with respect to each other (see [7]). Here, we do consider uniform ordinal scales, meaning that the degree of proximity between any two elements L_i and L_j is given by $|i - j| + 1$.

3.2 The Vector of Dispersion

Assuming that each reviewer uses the same ordinal scale $\mathscr{L}$, a **dispersion measure** on $\mathscr{L}^r$ (being r the number of reviewers evaluating each question) can be used for measuring the **disagreement among reviewers**.

One of the most prominent dispersion measures for ordinal scales is based on the Gini index [7]. The dispersion associated with the evaluations given by the r independent reviewers is obtained from comparing head-to-head all elements L_i given by each reviewer for an answer. A total of $p = \frac{r(r-1)}{2}$ degrees of proximity representing these pairwise comparisons are obtained. These degrees are gathered in a vector sorted in ascending order. Example 1 illustrates the procedure.

Example 1. Consider an answer given by a student to a question. The question is evaluated by 4 independent reviewers (R_1, R_2, R_3, R_4) using an ordinal scale $\mathscr{L} = \{L_1, L_2\}$. Consider that the degree of proximity of L_1 and L_1 is δ_1; the degree of proximity of L_1 and L_2 is δ_2; and the degree of proximity of L_2 and L_2 is δ_1.

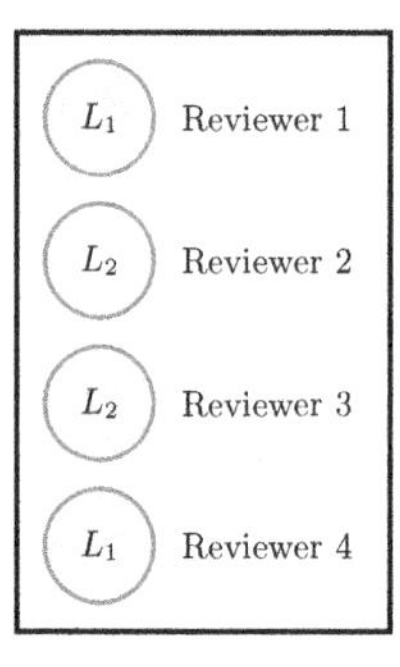

Fig. 1. Example of combination of marks given by four independent reviewers using an ordinal scale $\mathscr{L} = \{L_1, L_2\}$ to a student's answer of a question.

Table 1. Head-to-head degrees of proximity for the combination of marks shown in Fig. 1

Reviewer	R_1 (L_1)	R_2 (L_2)	R_3 (L_2)	R_4 (L_1)
R_1 (L_1)	–	δ_2	δ_2	δ_1
R_2 (L_2)	–	–	δ_1	δ_2
R_3 (L_2)	–	–	–	δ_2
R_4 (L_1)	–	–	–	–

The degrees of proximity obtained in the comparison head-to-head of the marks shown in Fig. 1 are specified in Table 1. These degrees are sorted in ascending order, thus obtaining the six-element vector of dispersion $(\delta_1, \delta_1, \delta_2, \delta_2, \delta_2, \delta_2)$.

3.3 Application of the Method of Majority Judgement

Once the vector of dispersion is obtained, it is necessary to rank the combinations of marks according to its associated dispersion. The method selected in this work to perform this task is similar to Balinski and Laraki's majority judgment [2,3], but with the correction described by García-Lapresta and Borge [6].

More precisely, Balinski and Laraki's majority judgment ranks (frequency) distributions of elements on an ordinal scale in terms of their couple of medians. In case two distributions have the same couple of medians, it is necessary to break the tie between them by removing this couple of each distribution and, subsequently, choosing the couple of medians of the new vector as the couple for the comparison. This procedure is repeated until all distributions are ranked. The correction described by García-Lapresta and Borge [6] considers both elements of the couple of medians (instead of the smallest among both elements, as originally proposed by Balinski and Laraki). This method is briefly described below.

- Consider an ordinal scale $\mathscr{S} = \{S_1, \ldots, S_s\}$. Consider two different vectors of elements $\mathbf{s}_1 = (s_{11}, \ldots, s_{1n}), \mathbf{s}_2 = (s_{21}, \ldots, s_{2n}) \in \mathscr{S}^n$ such that $s_{1i} \leq s_{1j}$ and $s_{2i} \leq s_{2j}$ if $i \leq j$. These vectors are ranked according to their associated couples of medians (L_i, L_j) (for $\mathbf{s}_1$) and $(L_{i'}, L_{j'})$ (for $\mathbf{s}_2$).
- The vector with couple of medians (L_i, L_j) is ranked below the vector with couple of medians $(L_{i'}, L_{j'})$ if either
  - $i + j < i' + j'$ or
  - $i + j = i' + j'$ and $j - i \leq j' - i'$.
- If $\mathbf{s}_1$ and $\mathbf{s}_2$ share the same couple of medians, it is necessary to break the tie between the vectors. To that end, the couple is removed from both vectors and the new couples of medians of the new vectors are selected to perform the comparison. The vectors are ranked according to the two rules defined in the previous step. This procedure is repeated until the two vectors are ranked.

Note that this method is applied in this work twice: firstly, to establish a hierarchy of tiers (considering as input vectors the vector of degrees of proximity associated with each combination of marks); secondly, to rank the questions (considering as input vectors the vectors of tiers associated with the evaluations for all the students). Example 2 illustrates the procedure for ranking the questions.

Example 2. Consider the ordinal scale given by the tiers $\{T_0, T_1, T_2\}$ and three questions Q1, Q2 and Q3. For this example, ten students answer to these questions Q1, Q2 and Q3 and their answers are marked by four different reviewers. The number of times that the combination of the marks falls in each tier is shown in Table 2 together with their cumulative frequencies.

These three questions share the same couple of medians (T_0, T_0). Thus, this couple is removed from the vector representing each question and a new couple of medians is computed for each question. The next three lines of Table 2 show the new couple of medians. Note that (T_0, T_0) is smaller than (T_0, T_1). Thus, Q2 is the least critical question. As Q1 and Q3 share the same couple of medians (T_0, T_1), this couple is removed from the combination, obtaining the pair (T_0, T_2) for Q1 and (T_0, T_1) for Q3. As (T_0, T_1) is smaller than (T_0, T_2), the resulting ranking from most critical to least critical is Q1 $\succ$ Q3 $\succ$ Q2.

Table 2. Example of answers of 10 students to 3 different questions and the distribution of the combination of their evaluation among tiers.

QuestionID	Combination	Distribution			Cumulative frequency		
		T_0	T_1	T_2	T_0	T_1	T_2
Q1	$(T_0, T_0, T_0, T_0, \mathbf{T_0}, \mathbf{T_0}, T_1, T_2, T_2, T_2)$	6	1	3	0.6	0.7	1
Q2	$(T_0, T_0, T_0, T_0, \mathbf{T_0}, \mathbf{T_0}, T_0, T_1, T_1, T_2)$	7	2	1	0.7	0.9	1
Q3	$(T_0, T_0, T_0, T_0, \mathbf{T_0}, \mathbf{T_0}, T_1, T_1, T_2, T_2)$	6	2	2	0.6	0.8	1
Removing (T_0, T_0)							
Q1	$(T_0, T_0, T_0, \mathbf{T_0}, \mathbf{T_1}, T_2, T_2, T_2)$	4	1	3	0.5	0.125	0.375
Q2	$(T_0, T_0, T_0, \mathbf{T_0}, \mathbf{T_0}, T_1, T_1, T_2)$	5	2	1	0.625	0.25	0.125
Q3	$(T_0, T_0, T_0, \mathbf{T_0}, \mathbf{T_1}, T_1, T_2, T_2)$	4	2	2	0.5	0.125	0.375
Removing (T_0, T_1)							
Q1	$(T_0, T_0, \mathbf{T_0}, \mathbf{T_2}, T_2, T_2)$	3	0	3	0.5	0	0.5
Q3	$(T_0, T_0, \mathbf{T_0}, \mathbf{T_1}, T_2, T_2)$	3	1	2	0.5	0.167	0.333

4 Ranking PISA for Schools Questions

The method described in Sect. 3 is then applied to identify critical questions in the PISA for Schools program. Recall that, as already stated in Sect. 2, the questions of interest are the ones in which the students write a long answer that the reviewers should mark according to the criteria given by a coding guide. In particular, there are two different types of questions within this group.

- Type A questions are the ones whose answers can be marked as *unanswered*, *incorrect* or *correct*.
- Type B questions are those which refine their possible marks adding an extra category so the question can be marked as *unanswered*, *incorrect*, *semi-correct* or *correct*.

Since the two types of questions have a different number of possible answers, the considered ordinal scale must differ.

On the one hand, for Type A questions we define $\mathscr{L}^A = \{L_1^A, L_2^A\}$ ($\ell = 2$), i.e., the answer of the student is marked as L_1^A if it is *incorrect* or *unanswered*; or as L_2^A if it is *correct*. Two possible degrees of proximity ($\Delta^A = \{\delta_1^A, \delta_2^A\}$) are obtained for Type A questions. The ordinal scale is illustrated in Fig. 2.

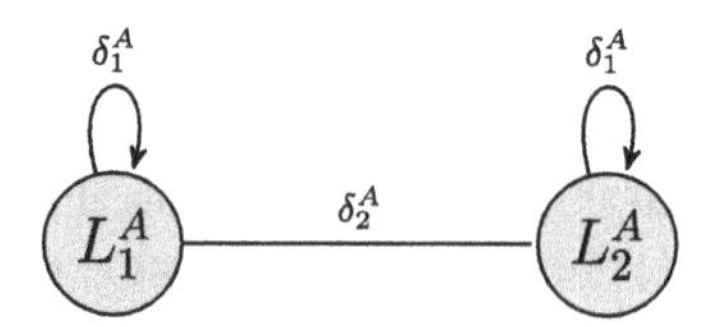

Fig. 2. Ordinal scale for Type A questions.

On the other hand, for Type B questions we define the ordinal scale $\mathscr{L}^B = \{L_1^B, L_2^B, L_3^B\}$ ($\ell = 3$), i.e., the answer of the student is marked as L_1^B if it is *incorrect* or *unanswered*; as L_2^B if it is *semi-correct*; or as L_3^B if it is *correct*. Here, we assume the scale used for Type B questions to be uniform[1]. Intuitively, this means that (for instance) for Type B questions we assume that *semi-correct* (L_2^B) is as close to being *correct* (L_3^B) as it is to being *incorrect* (L_1^B). Formally, this is the reason why the degree of proximity for L_i and L_j is given by $\delta_{|i-j|+1}$. Three possible degrees of proximity ($\Delta^B = \{\delta_1^B, \delta_2^B, \delta_3^B\}$) are obtained for Type B questions. The resulting ordinal scale for these questions is illustrated in Fig. 3.

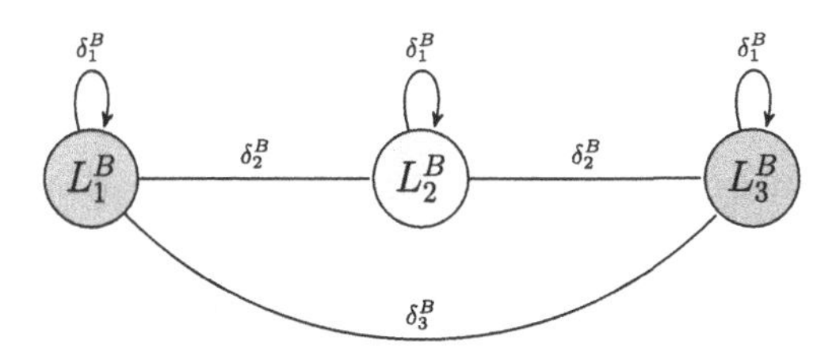

Fig. 3. Ordinal scale for Type B questions.

Once the scales are defined for each type of question, for each combination of marks provided by 4 reviewers the vector of dispersion is computed as described in Subsection 3.2 (see also Example 1). The total number of different combinations that can be obtained given ℓ different marks in a combination of length r with possible repetitions is $CR_{\ell,r} = \binom{\ell+r-1}{r}$. Thus, in our problem:

- For Type A where the scale is $\{L_1^A, L_2^A\}$ ($\ell = 2$) and $r = 4$, there are 5 different combinations of marks.
- For Type B where the scale is $\{L_1^B, L_2^B, L_3^B\}$ ($\ell = 3$) and $r = 4$, there are 15 different combinations of marks.

Following the process illustrated in Example 1 with all the 5 possible combinations for Type A questions and 15 combinations for Type B questions, it becomes clear that some of these combinations are represented by the same dispersion vector and, thus, can be considered equivalent. As the questions will be later ranked based on their dispersion, equivalent combinations with the same associated vector of dispersion are grouped into the same **tier**. Table 3 and Table 5 show the tiers obtained respectively for Type A ($\mathscr{T}^A = \{T_0^A, T_1^A, T_2^A\}$) and Type B questions ($\mathscr{T}^B = \{T_0^B, T_1^B, T_2^B, T_3^B, T_4^B, T_5^B, T_6^B\}$).

The tiers are then ranked according to the method described in Subsection 3.3. Thus, the couple of medians for each dispersion vector is computed for each tier (see Table 4 and Table 6 for Type A and Type B questions respectively).

[1] Note that the scale used for Type A questions is necessarily uniform since it contains only two elements.

Table 3. Combinations of the marks expressed by four different reviewers for Type A questions and their associated vector of dispersion.

Combination	Vector of dispersion
$L_1^A, L_1^A, L_1^A, L_1^A$ $L_2^A, L_2^A, L_2^A, L_2^A$	$(\delta_1^A, \delta_1^A, \delta_1^A, \delta_1^A, \delta_1^A, \delta_1^A)$
$L_1^A, L_2^A, L_2^A, L_2^A$ $L_2^A, L_1^A, L_1^A, L_1^A$	$(\delta_1^A, \delta_1^A, \delta_1^A, \delta_2^A, \delta_2^A, \delta_2^A)$
$L_1^A, L_1^A, L_2^A, L_2^A$	$(\delta_1^A, \delta_1^A, \delta_2^A, \delta_2^A, \delta_2^A, \delta_2^A)$

Table 4. Tiers of combinations for Type A questions.

Tier	Vector of dispersion	Couple of median degrees of proximity
T_0^A	$(\delta_1^A, \delta_1^A, \delta_1^A, \delta_1^A, f\delta_1^A, \delta_1^A)$	(δ_1^A, δ_1^A)
T_1^A	$(\delta_1^A, \delta_1^A, \delta_1^A, \delta_2^A, \delta_2^A, \delta_2^A)$	(δ_1^A, δ_2^A)
T_2^A	$(\delta_1^A, \delta_1^A, \delta_2^A, \delta_2^A, \delta_2^A, \delta_2^A)$	(δ_2^A, δ_2^A)

Table 5. Combinations of the marks expressed by four different reviewers for Type B questions and their associated vector of dispersion.

Combination	Vector of dispersion
$L_1^A, L_1^A, L_1^A, L_1^A$ $L_2^A, L_2^A, L_2^A, L_2^A$ $L_3^A, L_3^A, L_3^A, L_3^A$	$(\delta_1^B, \delta_1^B, \delta_1^B, \delta_1^B, \delta_1^B, \delta_1^B)$
$L_1^A, L_2^A, L_2^A, L_2^A$ $L_3^A, L_2^A, L_2^A, L_2^A$ $L_2^A, L_1^A, L_1^A, L_1^A$ $L_2^A, L_1^A, L_1^A, L_1^A$	$(\delta_1^B, \delta_1^B, \delta_1^B, \delta_2^B, \delta_2^B, \delta_2^B)$
$L_1^A, L_1^A, L_2^A, L_2^A$ $L_3^A, L_3^A, L_2^A, L_2^A$	$(\delta_1^B, \delta_1^B, \delta_2^B, \delta_2^B, \delta_2^B, \delta_2^B)$
$L_1^A, L_2^A, L_2^A, L_3^A$	$(\delta_1^B, \delta_2^B, \delta_2^B, \delta_2^B, \delta_2^B, \delta_3^B)$
$L_1^A, L_2^A, L_2^A, L_3^A$ $L_1^A, L_1^A, L_2^A, L_3^A$	$(\delta_1^B, \delta_2^B, \delta_2^B, \delta_2^B, \delta_3^B, \delta_3^B)$
$L_1^A, L_1^A, L_1^A, L_3^A$ $L_3^A, L_3^A, L_3^A, L_1^A$	$(\delta_1^B, \delta_1^B, \delta_1^B, \delta_3^B, \delta_3^B, \delta_3^B)$
$L_1^A, L_1^A, L_2^A, L_2^A$	$(\delta_1^B, \delta_1^B, \delta_3^B, \delta_3^B, \delta_3^B, \delta_3^B)$

Table 6. Tiers of combinations for Type B questions.

Tier	Vector of dispersion	Couple of median degrees of proximity
T_0^B	$(\delta_1^B, \delta_1^B, \delta_1^B, \delta_1^B, \delta_1^B, \delta_1^B)$	(δ_1^B, δ_1^B)
T_1^B	$(\delta_1^B, \delta_1^B, \delta_1^B, \delta_2^B, \delta_2^B, \delta_2^B)$	(δ_1^B, δ_2^B)
T_2^B	$(\delta_1^B, \delta_1^B, \delta_2^B, \delta_2^B, \delta_2^B, \delta_2^B)$	(δ_2^B, δ_2^B) and subsequently (δ_1^B, δ_2^B)
T_3^B	$(\delta_1^B, \delta_2^B, \delta_2^B, \delta_2^B, \delta_2^B, \delta_3^B)$	(δ_2^B, δ_2^B) and subsequently (δ_2^B, δ_2^B)
T_4^B	$(\delta_1^B, \delta_2^B, \delta_2^B, \delta_2^B, \delta_3^B, \delta_3^B)$	(δ_2^B, δ_2^B) and subsequently (δ_2^B, δ_3^B)
T_5^B	$(\delta_1^B, \delta_1^B, \delta_1^B, \delta_3^B, \delta_3^B, \delta_3^B)$	(δ_1^B, δ_3^B)
T_6^B	$(\delta_1^B, \delta_1^B, \delta_3^B, \delta_3^B, \delta_3^B, \delta_3^B)$	(δ_3^B, δ_3^B)

Obtaining a ranking of tiers from least to most disperse for Type A questions is immediate since considering the subindices of the median degrees $(1+1) < (1+2) < (2+2)$ a ranking without ties is generated. Nevertheless, for Type B questions, tiers $\{T_2^B, T_3^B, T_4^B\}$ have the same couple of median degrees of proximity (δ_2^B, δ_2^B). To further rank these tiers it is necessary to remove this couple of the vector of dispersion, thus obtaining a new couple of median degrees of proximity. For example, for T_2 the vector of dispersion after removing the initial couple of median degrees of proximity is $(\delta_1^B, \delta_1^B, \delta_2^B, \delta_2^B)$ with couple of median degrees of proximity (δ_1^B, δ_2^B). This is repeated for each tier, resulting in the couples shown in Table 6. Figures 4 and 5 show the combinations that belong to each tier.

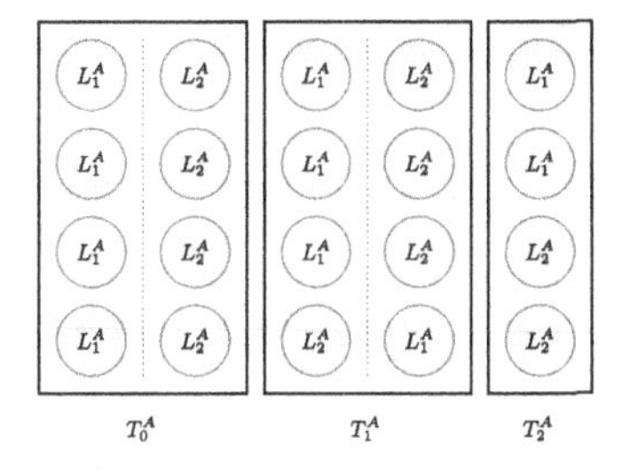

Fig. 4. Hierarchy of dispersion among reviewers for all possible combinations of elements L_i^A expressed by the $r = 4$ reviewers for Type A questions. The instances of L_1^A are pictured in red and the instances of L_2^A are pictured in green. (Color figure online)

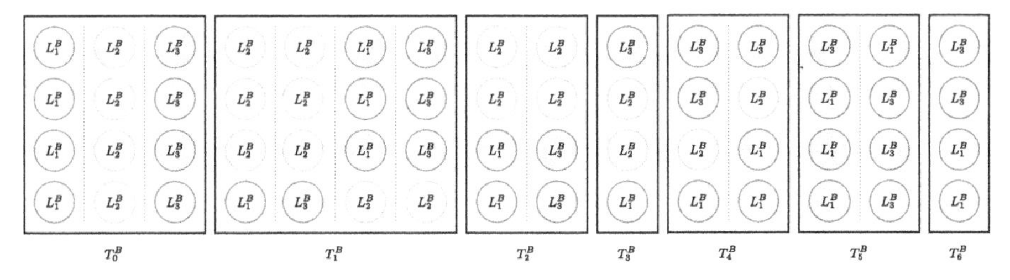

Fig. 5. Hierarchy of dispersion among reviewers for all possible combinations of elements L_i^B expressed by the $r = 4$ reviewers for Type B questions. The instances of L_1^B are pictured in red, the instances of L_2^B are pictured in yellow and the instances of L_3^B are pictured in green. (Color figure online)

Once the tiers are ranked, it is possible to rank the questions, which is the ultimate goal of this work. Hence, for each question, the number of combinations in each tier is counted and Balinski and Laraki's majority judgement described in Subsection 3.3 is again applied. Thus, questions are ranked according to their respective distribution of frequencies of tiers. In order to rank the questions according to their disagreement among reviewers, all tiers obtained for a question throughout all students are gathered together.

Notice that, the answers of at least half of the students fall in tier T_0. This tier accumulates all the answers for which the four reviewers give the same mark. Hence, the first couple of median degrees will always be (T_0, T_0) and, still when this couple is removed, the left value of the couple will always be T_0. Thus, the question with least dispersion will be the one that changes earlier from tier T_0 to a tier associated with more dispersion. This very much simplifies the method because questions are actually ranked lexicographically according to their cumulative frequency in tier T_0, and subsequently in T_1, and so on.

Figure 6 represents the distribution of frequencies of tiers for the questions in the three categories (Mathematics, Reading and Science) covered by the PISA for Schools program. Mathematics questions are indicated with the prefix PM, Reading questions are indicated with the prefix PR and Science questions are indicated with the prefix PS.

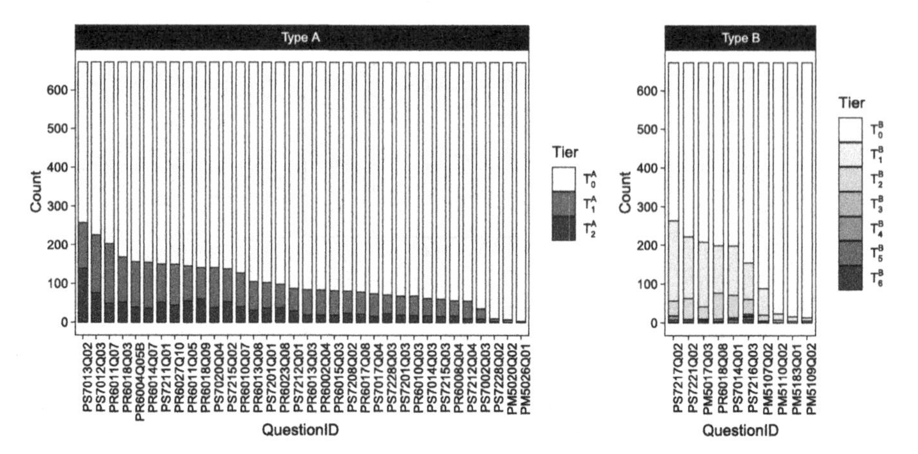

Fig. 6. Graphical representation of the distributions of frequencies for the questions of the PISA for Schools program.

At the light of the results, we infer that the obtained ranking indicates the questions for which the coding guide appears to be less precise. As it can be seen in Fig. 6 questions with more discrepancy are related to Science, whereas Mathematics questions tend to be be associated with less discrepancy, especially when the granularity of the ordinal scale is greater. In particular, the coding guide of Question PS7013Q02 should be the first one to be further improved among Type *A* questions and the coding guide of Question PS7217Q02 should be the first one to be further improved among Type *B* questions.

5 Conclusions and Future Work

The method proposed in this work has enabled to identify questions that lead to the largest disagreements among reviewers during an evaluation process. After using data from the pilot study of PISA for Schools program, the method is proved to be valid, since its outcome can be interpreted as a ranking of the questions from most critical to least critical in terms of the disagreement among reviewers.

We should underline that, at the present stage of our study, we are not focusing on discussions concerning the content and the coding guides that reviewers may hold after a discrepancy is detected. This is something we plan to do in a forthcoming study. Primarily, we have developed a method for detecting critical questions, that is, questions being liable to produce controversies in reviewers' interpretations. Starting by these questions identified as critical, the next step will lie in qualitatively analyzing both the answers provided by the participants and the instructions on the coding guide. The latter will provide valuable feedback in view of improving the training process for reviewers and, therefore, guarantying a higher consistency in the evaluation process of the PISA for Schools program.

References

1. Allison, R.A., Foster, J.E.: Measuring health inequality using qualitative data. J. Health Econ. **23**(3), 505–524 (2004)
2. Balinski, M., Laraki, R.: A theory of measuring, electing and ranking. Proc. Natl. Acad. Sci. US Am. **104**, 8720–8725 (2007)
3. Balinski, M., Laraki, R.: Majority Judgment: Measuring, Ranking, and Electing. MIT press, Cambridge (2010)
4. Cerchiello, P., De Quarti, E., Giudici, P., Magni, C.: Scorecard models to evaluate perceived quality of academic teaching. Stat. Applicazioni **8**(2), 145–155 (2010)
5. Fasolo, B., Bana, C.A., Costa, E.: Tailoring value elicitation to decision makers' numeracy and fluency: expressing value judgments in numbers or words. Omega **44**, 83–90 (2014)
6. García-Lapresta, J.L., Borge, L.: Measuring dispersion in the context of ordered qualitative scales. In: Gil, E., Gil, E., Gil, J., Gil, M. (eds) The Mathematics of the Uncertain. Studies in Systems, Decision and Control, vol. 142. Springer, Cham (2018)
7. García-Lapresta, J.L., Pérez-Román, D.: Ordinal proximity measures in the context of unbalanced qualitative scales and some applications to consensus and clustering. Appl. Soft Comput. **35**, 864–872 (2015)
8. García-Lapresta, J.L., González del Pozo, R.: An ordinal multi-criteria decision-making procedure under imprecise linguistic assessments. Eur. J. Oper. Res. **279**(1), 159–167 (2019)
9. PISA for Schools Brochure. (https://www.oecd.org/pisa/pisa-for-schools/PISA-for-Schools-Brochure-(Digital).pdf). Accessed 3 Feb 2020
10. Windschitl, P.D., Wells, G.L.: Measuring psychological uncertainty: verbal versus numeric methods. J. Exp. Psychol. Appl. **2**, 343–364 (1996)

Exploratory Analysis of Radiomics Features on a Head and Neck Cancer Public Dataset

Oier Echaniz[1,2], Carlos M. Chiesa-Estomba[3], and Manuel Graña[1,2](✉)

[1] Grupo de Inteligencia Computacional (GIC),
Universidad del País Vasco (UPV/EHU), San Sebastián, Spain
manuel.grana@ehu.eus

[2] Asociación de Ciencias de la programación Python San Sebastian (ACPYSS),
San Sebastián, Spain

[3] Otorhinolaryngology-Head and Neck Surgery Department,
Hospital Universitario Donostia, San Sebastián, Spain

Abstract. The prediction of the stage and evolution of cancer is a matter of strong social interest. The head and neck cancer is not one of the most prevalent and deathly cancers, but it is quite challenging due to its morphological variability and the risk of proliferation. In this paper we report results on a radiomics features based machine learning approaches trying to predict (a) the stage of the cancer, (b) the need for surgery, and (c) the survival after 2000 days. Results are encouraging, but a lot of work need to be done in order to attain an accuracy leading to clinical use.

1 Introduction

Head and neck cancer represents the sixth most common malignancy worldwide, with around 800,000 new cases and 320,000 deaths in 2015 [12]. Laryngeal squamous cell carcinoma (LSCC) represents between 30–50% of all neoplasms in the head and neck, with 157,000 new cases diagnosed worldwide in 2012 [6]. Their treatment is quite difficult due to the complexity of the head and neck anatomy, where a lot of critical structures are concentrated, and the variability of the tumors. Contrast-enhanced computed tomography (CT), magnetic resonance imaging (MRI), and positron emission tomography (PET) imaging are routinely acquired during the diagnosis and staging process of head and neck cancer patients. Radiomics is a comprehensice image analysis approach extracting large amounts of quantitative information from radiological medical images, which include measurements of intensity, shape, and texture [14]. Specifically, texture analysis represents a set of tools to improve characterization of tumor heterogeneity consisting of extracting texture indices from different imaging modalities [10]. Radiomics techniques are also able to non-invasively characterize the overall tumor accounting for heterogeneity, and quantitative imaging features can work as a prognostic or predictive biomarker [1,4,8], which can be

E. A. de la Cal et al. (Eds.): HAIS 2020, LNAI 12344, pp. 718–728, 2020.
https://doi.org/10.1007/978-3-030-61705-9_60

derived from routine standard-of-care imaging data, providing clinicians with a fast, low-cost, and repeatable instrument for longitudinal monitoring [7,11].

Recently Parmar et al. [13] assessed a large panel of machine-learning methods for overall survival prediction of head and neck cancer patients. They investigated 12 machine-learning classifiers [5,9] belonging to the 12 classifier families: Bagging (BAG), Bayesian (BY), boosting (BST), decision trees (DT), discriminant analysis (DA), generalized linear models (GLM), multiple adaptive regression splines (MARS), nearest neighbors (NN), neural networks (Nnet), partial least square and principle component regression (PLSR), random forests (RF), and support vector machines (SVM). In this study the authors demonstrated high prognostic performance and stability of machine learning methods applied to Radiomics features measured by Area under the Receiver Operating Curve (AUC). They used two independent cohorts, one for training (101 head and neck cancer patients) and the other (95 patients) for testing. Three classifers BY (AUC = 0.67), RF (AUC = 0.61), and NN (AUC = 0.62) showed highest prognostic performance and stability.

In this article we focus in massive feature extraction over a open dataset with available open and free tools testing machine leaning tools to predict stage, surgery, and survival. We hope that this work will help to create decision making tools that physicians require in order to reproduce them in a local hospital afterwards. The paper is structured as follows: Sect. 2 reports the data source and the processing pipeline. Section 3 reports our computational results, and Sect. 4 gives some conclusions of our work.

2 Materials and Methods

2.1 Data

We have used for the experiments in this paper the data published in the cancer imaging archive[1] [3], specifically the head and neck cancer data from Head-Neck-Radiomics-HN1[2] [2,16], which contains clinical data and computed tomography (CT) from 137 head and neck squamous cell carcinoma (HNSCC) patients treated by radiotherapy, Fig. 1 provides an example visualization of the 3D rendering of the CT. For these patients the gross tumor volume was manual delineated over a pre-treatment CT scan by an experienced radiation oncologist. Figure 2 shows a slice with its corresponding gold standard segmentation, after alineation of the images. The data also contains .csv files with anonymized patient data and disease information, which we use it to determine different classes for predictions and data analysis.

2.2 Methods

We have used the Pyradiomics[3] [15] open-source python package for the extraction of Radiomics features from medical imaging. The package offers several

[1] https://www.cancerimagingarchive.net.
[2] https://wiki.cancerimagingarchive.net/display/Public/Head-Neck-Radiomics-HN1.
[3] https://www.radiomics.io/pyradiomics.html.

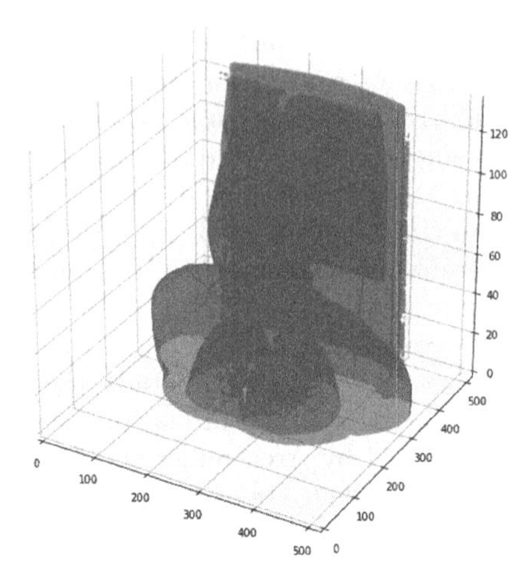

Fig. 1. Example of CT Scan 3D rendering.

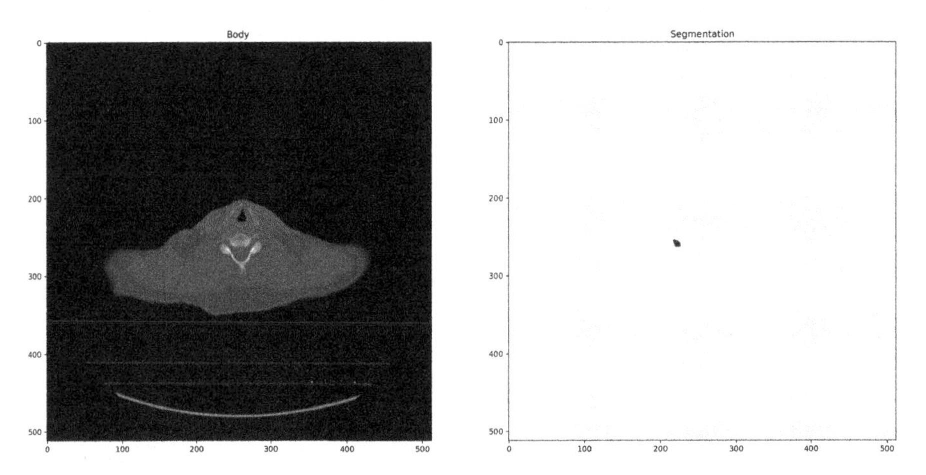

Fig. 2. Example of a CT scan and its gold standard segmentation, after the spatial registration preprocessing is done.

facilities for image preprocessing and registration, image filtering, such as wavelet analysis and others, texture and morphological feature extraction and the generation of reproducibility information, which is summarized in Fig. 3. The overall process pipeline is as follows:

Preprocesing We have to change the file format, and ensure that the CT images and the segmented gold standard are properly aligned in order to do meaningful feature extraction. Figure 2 shows an example CT slice and its gold standard segmentation after registration.

Feature-extraction We apply the conventional Radiomics approach, computing all kinds of features from the 3D images after filtering with diverse

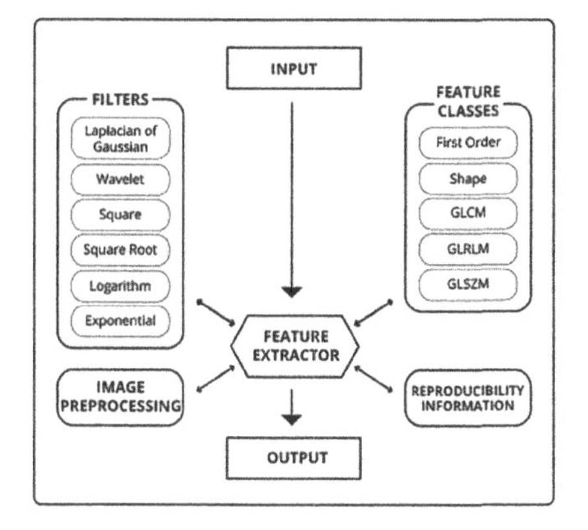

Fig. 3. Features extraction in the pyradiomics package.

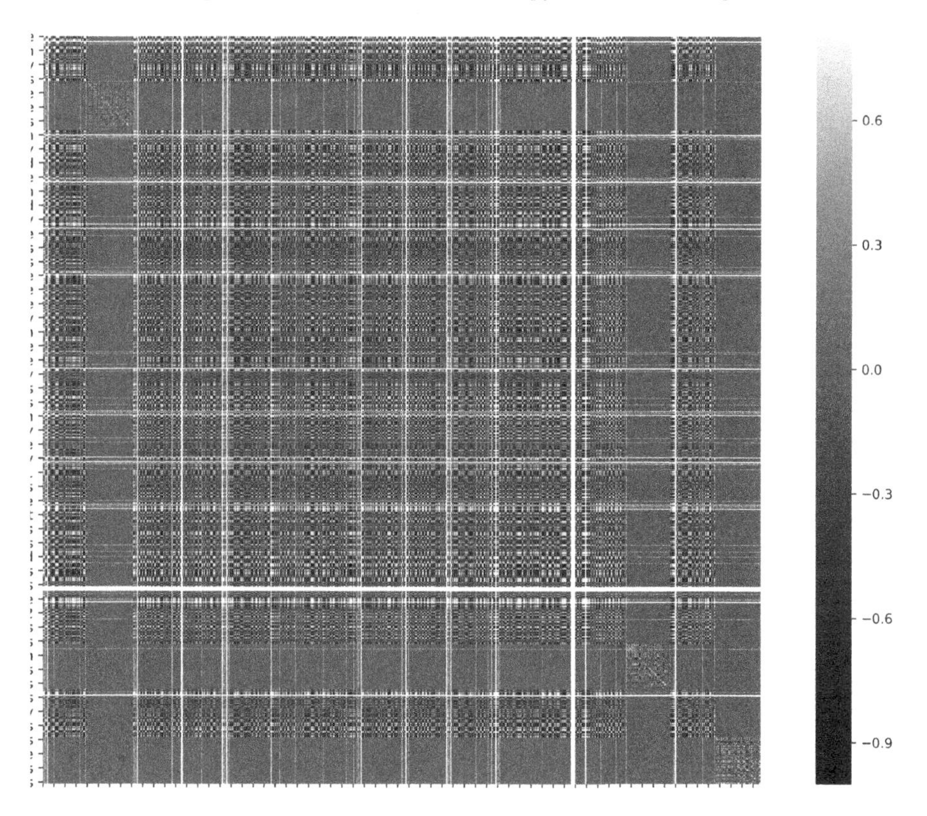

Fig. 4. Correlations between radiomics features.

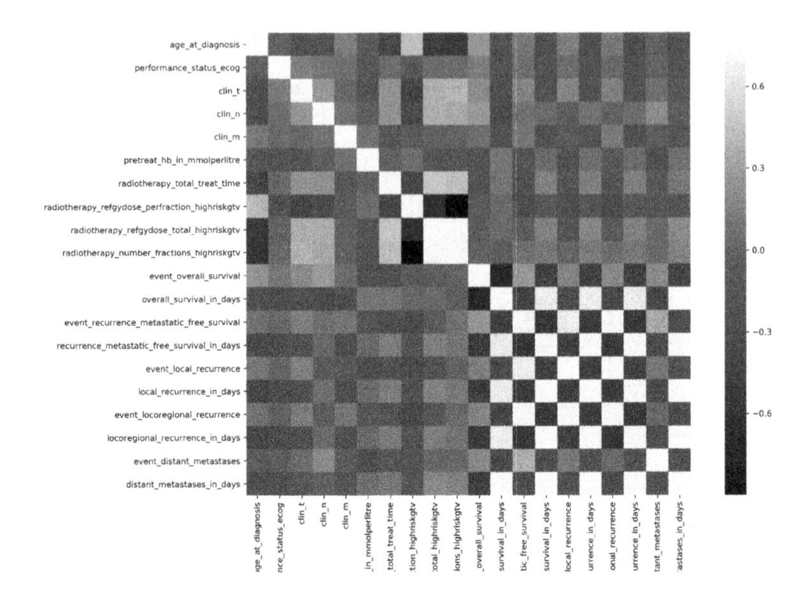

Fig. 5. Correlations between demographic and clinical patient variables.

Table 1. Top 20 features with highest variance.

Filter name	Feature	Variance
AdditiveGaussianNoise	original_gldm_LargeDependenceLowGrayLevelEmphasis	0.896
AdditiveGaussianNoise	original_glszm_LargeAreaLowGrayLevelEmphasis	0.759
AdditiveGaussianNoise	original_glszm_SmallAreaLowGrayLevelEmphasis	0.626
AdditiveGaussianNoise	original_glrlm_LongRunLowGrayLevelEmphasis	0.409
AdditiveGaussianNoise	original_gldm_SmallDependenceLowGrayLevelEmphasis	0.399
AdditiveGaussianNoise	original_gldm_LowGrayLevelEmphasis	0.340
AdditiveGaussianNoise	original_glrlm_LowGrayLevelRunEmphasis	0.309
AdditiveGaussianNoise	original_glrlm_ShortRunLowGrayLevelEmphasis	0.288
AdditiveGaussianNoise	original_glszm_LowGrayLevelZoneEmphasis	0.248
AdditiveGaussianNoise	original_glszm_GrayLevelNonUniformity	0.114
AdditiveGaussianNoise	original_glszm_GrayLevelNonUniformityNormalized	0.106
AdditiveGaussianNoise	original_glszm_GrayLevelVariance	0.101
AdditiveGaussianNoise	original_glszm_SizeZoneNonUniformity	0.088
AdditiveGaussianNoise	original_glszm_SizeZoneNonUniformityNormalized	0.070
AdditiveGaussianNoise	original_ngtdm_Strength	0.063
AdditiveGaussianNoise	original_glszm_ZoneVariance	0.060
AdditiveGaussianNoise	original_gldm_DependenceVariance	0.060
AdditiveGaussianNoise	original_glszm_SmallAreaHighGrayLevelEmphasis	0.054
AdditiveGaussianNoise	original_glszm_LargeAreaEmphasis	0.054
AdditiveGaussianNoise	original_glszm_LargeAreaHighGrayLevelEmphasis	0.053

filters, such as AdditiveGaussianNoise, Bilateral, BinomialBlur, BoxMean, BoxSigmaImageFilter, CurvatureFlow, DiscreteGaussian, LaplacianSharpening, Mean, Median, Normalize, RecursiveGaussian, ShotNoise, SmoothingRecursiveGaussian, SpeckleNoise. We also apply, image transformations such as

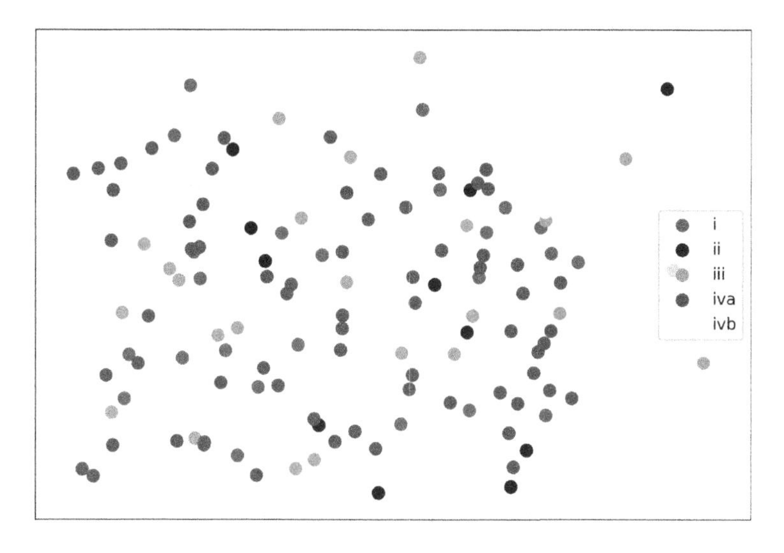

Fig. 6. Stage of the tumor (color) of the patients. The axes are the first two principal components of radiomics features.

Fig. 7. Did the patient survive more than 2000 days? True (Red), False (Blue). The axes are the first two principal components of radiomics features. (Color figure online)

the wavelet analysis, and the local binary patter (LBP) in two and three dimensions. We compute image features, such as energy, and other statistics, and some texture descriptors, such as grey level coocurrence matrices, grey level run length matrices, neighbouring gray tone differences, and morphological shape features, such as elongation, diameter, and others. Overall, we compute 1488 features.

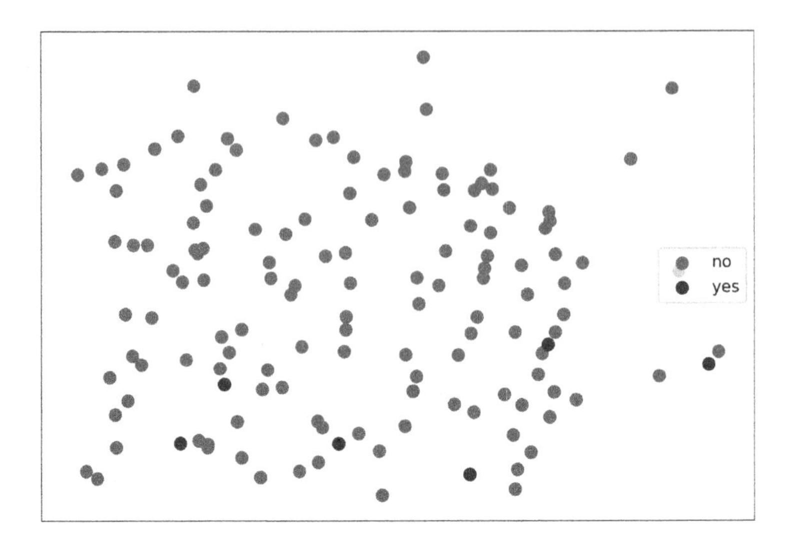

Fig. 8. Did the patient need surgery? Yes (blue), No (Red). The axes are the first two principal components of radiomics features. (Color figure online)

Feature-selection We apply a variance and correlation analysis for the selection of the most informative features. Table 1 gives the top variance features with their variance values. We found that the AditiveGaussian Filter is the image source for them. This means more separation exist between values in the features taken with this filter, which may be indicative of greater discriminant power. Also, Fig. 4 visualizes the correlation among the extracted radiomics features. The greater correlation implies that taking into account these variables simultaneously does not improve our classification accuracy, they are redundant and may be dismissed. Similarly, Fig. 5 shows the correlation among demographic and clinical variables with the same motive. We select one of the highly correlated variables and dismiss the others.

Sample-labeling We have to select a way to label the samples in order to apply the machine learning approaches. We have considered the following classification problems:

- a multi-class labeling given by stage of the tumor (i, ii, ii, iva and ivb), Fig. 6 shows the distribution of the stage tumor of the patiens over the 2D space spanned by the two first principal components of the selected features. It can be assessed qualitatively that the problem is not easy.
- a survival threshold to define two classes of patients (<2000 days, >=2000 days), Fig. 7 shows the distribution of the survival of the patiens over the 2D space spanned by the two first principal components of the selected features. It can be assessed qualitatively that the problem is not easy.
- the need for surgical procedure, Fig. 8 shows the distribution of the survival of the patiens over the 2D space spanned by the two first principal components of the selected features. No only the cases are spatially inter-

mixed, but also the yes class is much more scarce, so we have a strongly imbalanced dataset.

Machine-Learning We have used the Scikit Learn python package, which is becoming a standard in many areas of science. We have exploited a selection of the wide spectrum of classifiers offered by the package, namely k Nearest Neighbor, radial basis function (RBF) suppport vector machines (SVM), Gaussian Processes, Decision Tree, Random Forest, Neural Network, and AdaBoost. We have used the default parameters. Regarding the validation methodology, we have carried out a 6-fold cross-validation reporting the test for each folder, plus a random partition

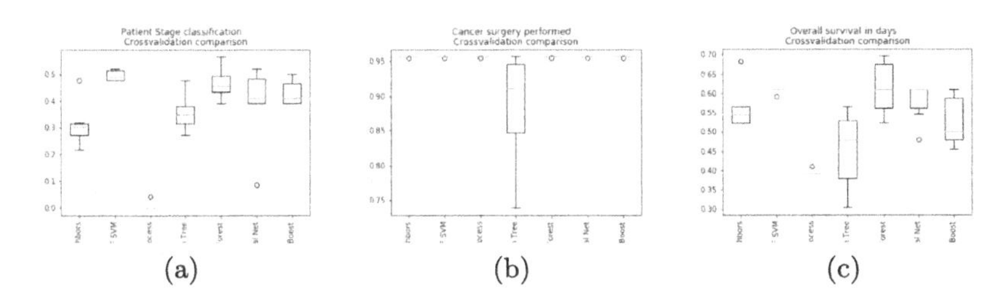

Fig. 9. Cross validation scores for different machine learning algorithms. (a) classification into patient stage (b) surgery prediction, (c) survival after 2000 days prediction.

3 Results

3.1 Tumor Stage

The first set of results refer to the multi-class problem of cancer stage classification. We have five classes, hence accuracy results such as those shown in Table 2 are relatively good because pure chance classification would result in accuracies near 0.15. In this exploratory results we do not have space to do a detailed examination of results per class. Figure 9(a) provides a box plot of the results *per* classifier, showing that the RBF-SVM is the one that improves over all in this case.

3.2 Surgery Prediction

Surgery prediction results in Table 3 are very good, but as the dataset is very strongly class imbalanced, it is possible that these results are biased towards the majority class. Further examination and experimental results would confirm this suspicion. Figure 9(b) provides a box plot of results *per* classifier. The worst response corresponds to the decision trees, all other classifiers are almost identical in top accuracy response.

Table 2. Cross validation accuracy scores for different machine learning algorithms predicting cancer stage fase *per* folder. Random fold is a random fold taken from data 66% used for train and 33% for test. Same random fold is used for all algorithms.

Classifier	Fold 1	Fold 2	Fold 3	Fold 4	Fold 5	Fold 6	Random fold
Nearest neighbors	0.260	0.478	0.217	0.304	0.304	0.318	0.326
RBF SVM	0.521	0.521	0.478	0.478	0.478	0.5	0.543
Gaussian process	NA	NA	NA	NA	0.043	NA	NA
Decision tree	0.347	0.347	0.478	0.304	0.391	0.272	0.304
Random forest	0.434	0.565	0.434	0.391	0.478	0.5	0.521
Neural net	0.086	0.521	0.434	0.391	0.391	0.5	0.173
AdaBoost	0.391	0.478	0.434	0.391	0.391	0.5	0.391

Table 3. Cross validation accuracy scores for different machine learning algorithms predicting surgery outcome *per* folder. Random fold is a random fold taken from data 66% used for train and 33% for test. The same random fold is used for all algorithms.

Classifier	Fold 1	Fold 2	Fold 3	Fold 4	Fold 5	Fold 6	Random fold
Nearest neighbors	0.956	0.956	0.956	0.956	0.956	0.954	0.934
RBF SVM	0.956	0.956	0.956	0.956	0.956	0.954	0.934
Gaussian process	0.956	0.956	0.956	0.956	0.956	0.954	0.934
Decision tree	0.956	0.956	0.913	0.869	0.826	0.863	0.869
Random forest	0.956	0.956	0.956	0.956	0.956	0.954	0.934
Neural net	0.956	0.956	0.956	0.173	0.956	0.954	0.934
AdaBoost	0.956	0.956	0.956	0.956	0.956	0.954	0.934

Table 4. Cross validation scores for different machine learning algorithms for survival prediction *per* folder. Random fold is a random fold taken from data 66% used for train and 33% for test. Same random fold is used for all algorithms.

Classifier	Fold 1	Fold 2	Fold 3	Fold 4	Fold 5	Fold 6	Random fold
Nearest neighbors	0.565	0.521	0.565	0.521	0.521	0.681	0.543
RBF SVM	0.608	0.608	0.608	0.608	0.608	0.590	0.695
Gaussian process	0.391	0.391	0.391	0.391	0.391	0.409	0.304
Decision tree	0.478	0.391	0.347	0.521	0.478	0.5	0.5
Random forest	0.565	0.652	0.565	0.478	0.652	0.409	0.608
Neural net	0.391	0.608	0.608	0.608	0.608	0.409	0.369
AdaBoost	0.478	0.608	0.521	0.608	0.478	0.454	0.391

3.3 Survival Prediction

Survival prediction results are presented in Table 4 and in Fig. 9(c). It can be appreciated that our results are in bad shape, only the random forest classifier shows results clearly above random choice. These results may be due to a bad feature selection relative to the task at hand, i.e. selected variables are irrelevant ot this survival event. Other feature selection processes and longitudinal studies maybe required in order to improve results in this regard.

4 Conclusions

We report in this paper the application of radiomics feature extraction and machine learning techniques to three different prediction tasks: (a) the stage of a head and neck cancer, (b) the realization of surgery, and (c) the survival after 2000 days. We have carried out the experiments over a well know dataset published in the cancer imaging archive. Results are encouraging but show the need for additional research on feature selection, and the need for longitudinal studies in the case of the survival prediction. We are continuing the exploration of this dataset aiming for the definition and implementation or more informative features and the application of modern deep learning approaches, though the limited data impedes their straightforward application.

References

1. Aerts, H.J.W.L.: The potential of radiomic-based phenotyping in precision medicine: a review. JAMA Oncol. **2**(12), 1636–1642 (2016)
2. Aerts, H.J.W.L., et al.: Decoding tumour phenotype by noninvasive imaging using a quantitative radiomics approach. Nat. Commun. **5**(1), 4006 (2014)
3. Cardenas, C., Mohamed, A., Sharp, G., Gooding, M., Veeraraghavan, H., Yang, J.: Data from AAPM RT-MAC grand challenge 2019. Technical report, The Cancer Imaging Archive (2019)
4. Chiesa-Estomba, C.M., Echaniz, O., Larruscain, E., Gonzalez-Garcia, J.A., Sistiaga-Suarez, J.A., Graña, M.: Radiomics and texture analysis in laryngeal cancer. Looking for new frontiers in precision medicine through imaging analysis. Cancers **11**(10), 1409 (2019)
5. De Lope, J., Graña, M.: Behavioral activity recognition based on gaze ethograms. Int. J. Neural Syst. **30**(07), 2050025 (2020). PMID: 32522069
6. Ferlay, J., et al.: Cancer incidence and mortality worldwide: sources, methods and major patterns in globocan 2012. Int. J. Cancer **136**(5), E359–E386 (2015)
7. Gillies, R.J., Kinahan, P.E., Hricak, H.: Radiomics: Images are more than pictures, they are data. Radiology **278**(2), 563–577 (2016). PMID: 26579733
8. Giraud, P., et al.: Radiomics and machine learning for radiotherapy in head and neck cancers. Front. Oncol. **9**, 174 (2019)
9. Górriz, J.M., et al.: Artificial intelligence within the interplay between natural and artificial computation: advances in data science, trends and applications. Neurocomputing (2020)
10. Guezennec, C., et al.: Prognostic value of textural indices extracted from pretherapeutic 18-F FDG-PET/CT in head and neck squamous cell carcinoma. Head Neck **41**(2), 495–502 (2019)
11. Kumar, V., et al.: Radiomics: the process and the challenges. Magn. Reson. Imaging **30**(9), 1234–1248 (2012). Quantitative Imaging in Cancer
12. Global Burden of Disease Cancer Collaboration: Global, regional, and national cancer incidence, mortality, years of life lost, years lived with disability, and disability-adjusted life-years for 32 cancer groups, 1990 to 2015: a systematic analysis for the global burden of disease study. JAMA Oncol. **3**(4), 524–548 (2017)
13. Parmar, C., Grossmann, P., Rietveld, D., Rietbergen, M.M., Lambin, P., Aerts, H.J.W.L.: Radiomic machine-learning classifiers for prognostic biomarkers of head and neck cancer. Front. Oncol. **5**, 272 (2015)

14. Scheckenbach, K.: Radiomics: big data statt biopsie in der Zukunft? Laryngo-Rhino-Otol **97**(S 01), S114–S141 (2018)
15. van Griethuysen, J.J.M., et al.: Computational radiomics system to decode the radiographic phenotype. Cancer Res. **77**(21), e104–e107 (2017)
16. Wee, L., Dekker, A.: Data from head-neck-radiomics-HN1 [data set]. Technical report, The Cancer Imaging Archive (2019)

Stroke Rehabilitation: Detection of Finger Movements

Diego Aranda-Orna[1], José R. Villar[2(✉)], and Javier Sedano[1]

[1] Instituto Tecnológico de Castilla y León, Burgos, Spain
{diego.aranda,javier.sedano}@itcl.es
[2] Computer Science Department, University of Oviedo, Oviedo, Spain
villarjose@uniovi.es

Abstract. For several stroke cases, rehabilitation focuses on the pincer movements and grasps with the index and thumb fingers. The improvements in the coordination between these fingers guides the recovery of the subject. Obtaining a good measurement of these opening and closing movements is still unsolved, with robotic based high cost solutions. This research includes a preliminary study that analyses the use of tri-axial accelerometers to measure these movements and to evaluate the performance of the subjects. Under certain constraints, the solution has been found valid to detect the finger opening-closing pincer movements.

Keywords: Stroke rehabilitation · Pincer movements · Hybrid artificial intelligent systems

1 Introduction

Stroke rehabilitation includes many different aspects according to the development of the onset itself and its consequences on the patient [1]. Indeed, the impact of the new technologies and developments has promoted a wide variety of methods and techniques using portable and relatively low-cost equipment that allows the patients to perform the rehabilitation in their own homes [2–4]. However, the main part of the rehabilitation is still carried out on health care centers, with or without specialized equipment. For instance, a robotic equipment was employed to perform and evaluate the rehabilitation of upper limbs (including the wrists and hands) [5]. Similarly, robotic systems were proposed for rehabilitation in [6]. In [7,8], the authors proposed the combination of virtual reality with robot-assisted therapy to improve the adaptive control.

The rehabilitation includes exercises such as cone stacking [9], as well as many other types of exercises according to the part of the body that needs to be tackled. On this study, we focus on the rehabilitation of the hand fingers

This research has been funded by the Spanish Ministry of Science and Innovation under project MINECO-TIN2017-84804-R and by the Grant FCGRUPIN-IDI/2018/000226 project from the Asturias Regional Government.

E. A. de la Cal et al. (Eds.): HAIS 2020, LNAI 12344, pp. 729–738, 2020.
https://doi.org/10.1007/978-3-030-61705-9_61

with patients that had suffered from a stroke [10,11]. This type of exercises has been analyzed in depth for Parkinson Disease patients [12,13]. In this context, there have been published some studies proposing robotic-based rehabilitation. In some cases, the authors focused on acute paralyzed patients [14] using a robotic glove that assists the patient in moving the fingers. A similar study analyzes how to develop a robotic-assisted globe to help in the rehabilitation of the hand fingers [15].

The solution of exoskeletons are mainly expensive and difficult to deploy; therefore, low complexity exoskeleton alternatives have also been proposed [16]. A completely different option is to assist the physiotherapist in measuring the performance of the rehabilitation patients. As an example, the authors proposed using rope-embedded strain sensors to measure the performance of the patients when closing or extending the index and thumb fingers, comparing the measurements with video recording [17].

In this study, we focus on assisting the physiotherapists in the rehabilitation of the patients when producing the pincer movement with the index and thumb fingers. To do so, we propose a simple sensing device to measure the improvements in the coordination between the index and thumb fingers. The sensing device includes a tri-axial accelerometer (3DACC) to register the changes in the acceleration of the index finger in order to decide whether the movement is being correct or not. This approach has been found valid with a specific configuration of the hand and fingers, tracking the movements of the user. For a specific participant, the use of thresholds were found valid, although not general.

This study is organized as follows. The next Section deals with the description of the device and the basis of the calculations, the data gathering and the experimental set up is also detailed. Section 3 copes with the results and the discussion on these results. Finally, the main conclusions and future work are detailed.

2 Material and Method

This section copes with the description of the device that is proposed in this study to determine the finger movements and the initial experimentation performed to validate the idea. The next Subsection describes the device, then the simple algorithm to detect the finger movements is detailed and finally the experimental set-up is explained.

2.1 A 3DACC Device to Measure the Finger Movements

This research proposes the use of 3DACC to detect the angular movement of the index and thumb fingers when performing the activity of pincer grasping, that is, closing and opening the arc between those fingers. 3DACC based wearable devices have been profusely employed in the detection or diagnosing of illnesses as well as human activities of daily living [18–21]. Basically, they are cheap, do not require much effort in deploying and the measurement is reliable.

The developed prototype is shown in the left part of Fig. 1, where a 3DACC is placed on each finger end. The right part of Fig. 1 depicts the orientation of the 3DACC axes when properly placed on a participant. Each of the two external elements consists of a MEMS (microelectromechanical system) 3DACC sensor, configured with a full scale of $\pm 2g$ and a sampling frequency of 16 Hz.

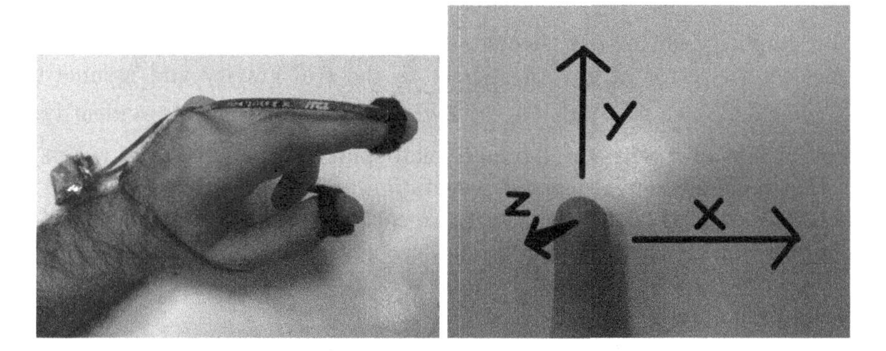

Fig. 1. Left part: The prototype sensing unit, with two 3DACC located on each finger end. Right part: 3DACC axes orientation relative to its finger. The z-axis is perpendicular to the finger, positive to the outside of the hand.

There are restrictions when using this first release of the prototype. Firstly, only opening and closing finger movements are allowed, with the hand steadily immobilized. The fingers must point to the positive y-axis, while the x-axis should be kept parallel to the rotation axis. Finally, the planes containing the angular movements of each finger should not form an angle higher than 60° with the vertical direction (i.e., a rotation plane that is almost orthogonal to the gravity direction should be avoided); this can be achieved with the hand initially pointing upwards or downwards.

2.2 Detection of the Movements

The angle function will be defined to have nice properties: it will increase when fingers move in the opening direction and decrease for movements in the closing direction. Its values will only depend on the current orientation of the rotation axis, so that its calculation will produce no error propagation; also this dependence will be continuous and stable. Having no error propagation is a very desirable property which implies that we do not need additional information (from other sensors or additional restrictions) to compensate the propagating errors. Error propagation usually arises from integration methods, which is why we have used a different approach.

In order to construct our model, we will deal first with the information coming from one 3DACC. Under the assumptions explained before, the acceleration measured by a 3DACC is given in Eq. (1), where $\mathbf{g}$, $\mathbf{a}_f$ and $\mathbf{n}$ denote the gravity, the acceleration of the finger during the angular movement, and some noise, respectively. The noise $\mathbf{n}$ will be assumed to be negligible, and for simplicity we will consider that $\mathbf{n} = 0$. For our purposes, a good enough estimation of $\mathbf{g}$ at a time instant t_i can be obtained via the simple moving average filter of the last three samples.

$$\mathbf{a} = (a_x, a_y, a_z) = \mathbf{g} + \mathbf{a}_f + \mathbf{n} \tag{1}$$

For simplicity during our theoretical construction of the angle function, we will neglect the error of $\mathbf{g}$ with respect to the real gravity and assume that these coincide. Since $g := ||\mathbf{g}|| = \sqrt{g_x^2 + g_y^2 + g_z^2}$ is constant, we can identify the possible values of $\mathbf{g}$ with the 2-dimensional sphere surface $S^2(g)$ of radius $1g$. Note that a significant part of the orientation of the accelerometer during the movement is perfectly determined by $\mathbf{g}$, except for a possible rotation around the axis of direction $\mathbf{g}$ (which will not be the case under our assumptions), and when the accelerometer is not moving we have $\mathbf{a} = \mathbf{g}$, so that the partial orientation is known with good precision.

Our assumptions force the x-axis to coincide with the rotation axis, and g_x to be constant. Therefore, Eq. (2) keeps constant, and the point (g_y, g_z) lies on the circumference $S^1(r)$ of radius r and axes (y, z). We define the *angle function* $\theta(t)$ at the time instant t as the corresponding angle of the point (g_y, g_z) in $S^1(r)$ (Eq. (3)). Note that, with the corresponding identification via the inclusion $S^1(r) \subseteq S^2(r)$, the angle $\theta = 0$ corresponds to the direction given by the projection of $\mathbf{g}$ on the rotation plane.

$$r := \sqrt{g^2 - g_x^2} = \sqrt{g_y^2 + g_z^2} \tag{2}$$

$$\theta(t) := \operatorname{arctan2}\big(g_z(t), g_y(t)\big) \tag{3}$$

An important detail is that, in order to preserve the continuity of $\theta(t)$, we need to choose its value at the corresponding turn, just by adding or subtracting 2π as many times as necessary. Note that when we modify $\theta(t_i)$ in that way, we have a new function that not only depends on t_i but also on the previous value $\theta(t_{i-1})$; but by abuse of notation we will still denote it as $\theta(t)$.

We can sum the contributions of the two angle functions, θ_I and θ_T, of the index finger and thumb, which gives an angle function with intensified slopes (Eq. (4)), which can be used to detect the opening-closing movements.

$$\theta_S(t) := \theta_I(t) + \theta_T(t) \tag{4}$$

Note that if $r = 0$, the direction of $\mathbf{g}$ does not have enough information to determine the orientation and θ is not well-defined. In the case that the angle between the rotation axis and the direction of the gravity is *too small*, or equivalently, if r becomes *too small*, then θ becomes unstable because of the nearby discontinuity, and therefore this model would not work properly. In practice, we smoothen θ_S

with a simple moving average filter of 5 terms, and then use it to detect the movements in later steps of our algorithm.

The real-time algorithm proposed in this study aims to detect significant peaks on the angle function. Since significant peak detection is a very studied problem in the literature, we claim no innovation about our peak detection algorithm, although it was obtained as a result of this work. Significant peaks, also called real peaks, are usually a subjective concept whose parameters depend on the context and the measurement unit, so that we are not concerned with giving a formal definition.

At each instant t_i, the algorithm first checks if there is a local peak, and then decides to classify it, or not, as a significant peak. After a consecutive sequence minimum-maximum-minimum of significant peaks is found, if the differences between their instants t_i and values $\theta_S(t_i)$ satisfy certain upper and lower threshold bounds, the algorithm notifies that a movement was detected in that interval and then some values (like the duration of the movement) can be calculated and returned as output. Some of the threshold values used are dynamic and updated in real time. Algorithm 1 outlines the developed algorithm.

Algorithm 1: An outline of the algorithm to detect movements.

Input: Receives a Time Series (TS)
Result: A list with the detected movements
Set sequence as an empty list;
Set movements as an empty list;
for *each sample s at time t in TS* **do**
    if *s is a relative peak* **then**
        Add ¡peak(s,t)¿ to sequence;
    else
        if *s is a relative valley* **then**
            Add ¡valley(s,t)¿ to sequence;
            if *last 3 elements in sequence are valley, peak and valley* **then**
                if *the time and value constraints are accomplished* **then**
                    Add ¡movement(t_2,t)¿ to movements;
                end
            end
        end
    end
end
Return the movements list;

2.3 Data Gathering and Experimentation Set Up

All the samples were gathered by a stroke rehabilitation specialist who simulated the movements of the patients. The duration of each sample corresponds to 1 min. The hand was not completely immobilized, which may have worsen the results. The 9 samples used in our statistics correspond to a downwards position of the hand, where only one type of movement is performed on each case, and for all possible cases including movement durations of 1 s, 2 s and 5 s, and opening distances of 1 cm, 3 cm and 5 cm.

Other samples where the hand orientation was invalid were gathered too, but these have not been included in the statistical calculations since our initial assumptions were not satisfied. The invalid samples that simulated strong tremblings gave always bad results (only noise was observed in the angle functions). For the invalid samples without trembling simulation, both good and bad results were obtained, depending on the duration and opening angle of each case.

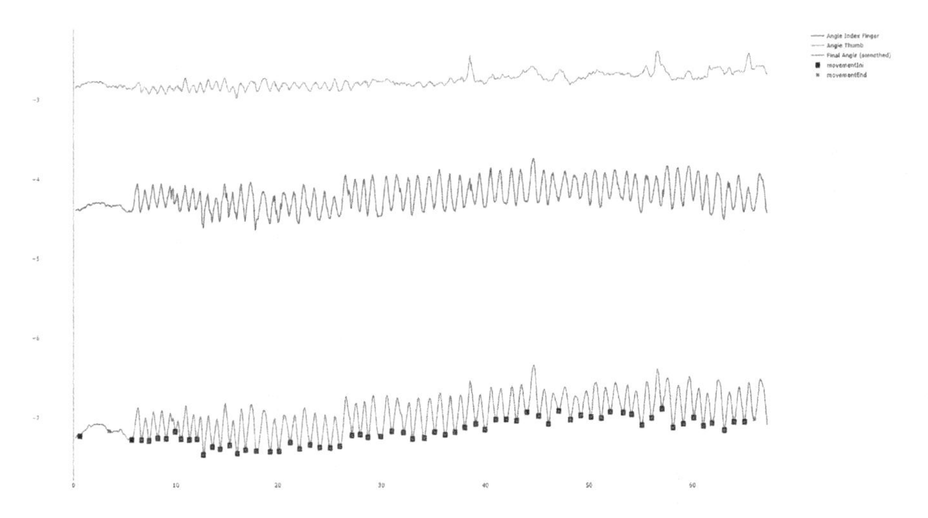

Fig. 2. Angle obtained for the movements in case of 1 s, 3 cm. The orange line is the angle in the thumb, the blue line is the angle in the index finger, the green line is the smoothed final angle, the black square dot is the starting point of a movement while the red cross is its ending point. The x-axis measures time, while the y-axis shows the angle. (Color figure online)

In most part of the samples, for both valid and invalid cases, the thumb rotation movement was performed in wrong direction (laterally or even in opposite direction); due to these movements in wrong direction, the error of the angle function θ_S has been found greater than it was expected.

3 Results and Discussion

The obtained results are shown in Figs. 2, 3 and 4 and Tables 1 and 2. The figures correspond with 2 of the 9 instances used. Each figure shows the angle functions for both fingers, index and thumb, and the sum of both angle functions (i.e. θ_S) where the movements are detected. In general and contrary to our assumptions, the hand was not immobilized and was allowed to slightly move during the

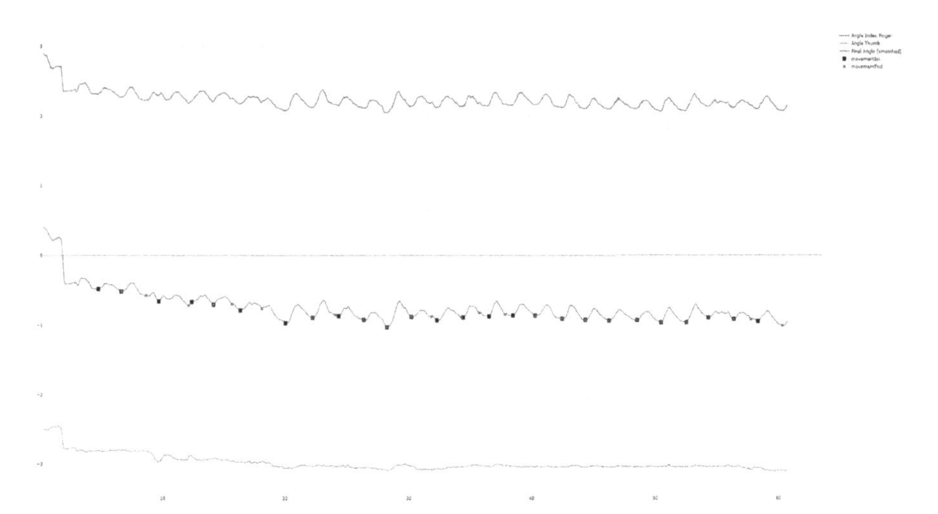

Fig. 3. Angle obtained for movements in case of 2 s, 1 cm. The orange line is the angle in the thumb, the blue line is the angle in the index finger, the green line is the smoothed final angle, the black square dot is the starting point of a movement while the red cross is its ending point. The x-axis measures time, while the y-axis shows the angle. (Color figure online)

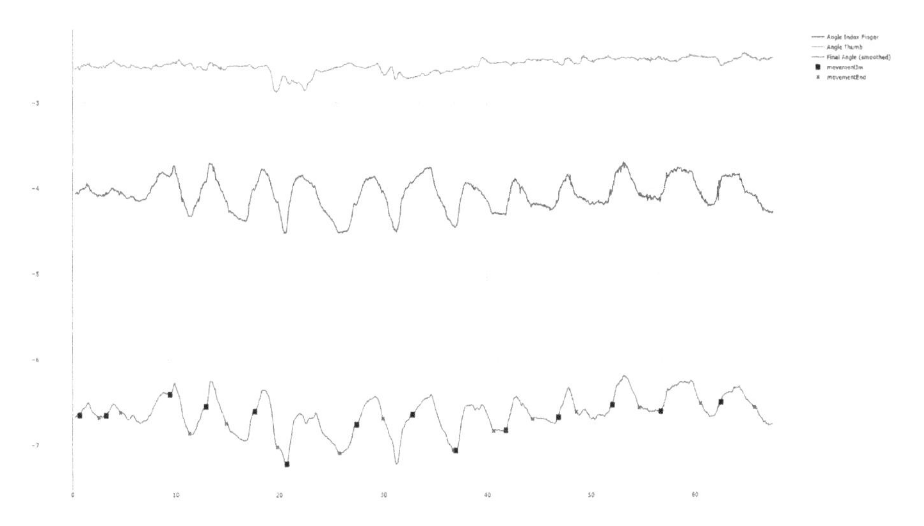

Fig. 4. Angle obtained for movements in case of 5 s, 5 cm. The orange line is the angle in the thumb, the blue line is the angle in the index finger, the green line is the smoothed final angle, the black square dot is the starting point of a movement while the red cross is its ending point. The x-axis measures time, while the y-axis shows the angle. (Color figure online)

experiment, and the thumb sometimes moved laterally or even backwards. As can be seen in the Figures, the movements were clearly identified even though the ratio signal/noise is about 0.5 rad, that is, the angle is even of smaller order of magnitude than the noise.

We can see the good results in the cases of fast pincer movements with duration of 1 and 2 s, while the performance were poorer when using 5 s although still acceptable. In this case, the detected movements were shorter than actually they were, probably because of some noise due to movements of the hand. Apart from the main 9 instances used in this study, other samples with non-valid orientations were studied as well but were not found useful: wrong finger orientations (with unsteady response) and strong tremblings cases, where the angle functions consisted primarily of noise and no peaks to be detected, were unacceptable.

In Tables 1 and 2, we compare the parameters calculated by the algorithm with the real data for the 9 instances with valid orientation.

Table 1. Algorithm performance for each case.

Distance (cm)	Real average length (s)	Estimated average length (s)	Average length error (s)
1	1	0.95	−0.05
3	1	0.98	−0.02
5	1	1.01	0.01
1	2	1.88	−0.12
3	2	1.76	−0.24
5	2	1.97	−0.03
1	5	2.38	−2.62
3	5	2.04	−2.96
5	5	2.73	−2.27

Table 2. Algorithm performance in terms of the number of detected movements. NoM stands for Number of Movements, while AMA stands for averaged maximum acceleration.

Actual NoM	Estimated NoM	Error in NoM	AMA
64	56	−8	475
64	64	0	760
60	57	−3	1021
30	26	−4	371
32	31	−1	602
32	31	−1	658
14	11	−3	1189
14	17	3	981
13	14	1	530

4 Conclusions

This study is a preliminary research to measure the finger movements in the stroke rehabilitation. To do so, a device with two 3DACC sensors are placed on the tip outer face of the index and thumb fingers. With a sequence of transformations and angle measurements, we show that we can classify sequences of movements as valid or not. This research represents a proof of concept and a very simple decision mechanism based on thresholds is proposed. The experimentation with data gathered from a specialist in stroke rehabilitation mimicking the real movements the normal patients have shows this solution as very promising.

However, there is space for improvements. Firstly, current thresholds may not be suitable for any participant and more intelligent modelling techniques could be applied and developed to enhance the classification of the movements. We think that Deep Learning might be a good starting point, but we do not discard the use of Hidden Markov Models as well. Moreover, to reduce the number of constraints in the use of this solution we propose the use of more sensory elements, such as a magnetometer, so better experimental set up can be automatically detected; this approach would allow to construct a complete reference system for the orientation of the fingers relative to the hand, giving better detection of movements, and angles for pincer movements may be calculated with good precision even if the hand is moving and changing its orientation.

References

1. Miura, S., et al.: Quality management program of stroke rehabilitation using adherence to guidelines: a nationwide initiative in japan. J. Stroke Cerebrovasc. Dis. **28**(9), 2434–2441 (2009)
2. Kim, H., Lee, S.H., Cho, N.B., You, H., Choi, T., Kim, J.: User-dependent usability and feasibility of a swallowing training mhealth app for older adults: mixed methods pilot study. JMIR mHealth and uHealth **8**(7), e19585 (2020)
3. Chi, N.F., Huang, Y.C., Chiu, H.Y., Chang, H.J., Huang, H.C.: Systematic review and meta-analysis of home-based rehabilitation on improving physical function among home-dwelling patients with a stroke. Arch. Phys. Med. Rehab. **101**(2), 359–373 (2020)
4. Veisi-Pirkoohi, S., Hassani-Abharian, P., Kazemi, R., Vaseghi, S., Zarrindast, M.R., Nasehi, M.: Efficacy of RehaCom cognitive rehabilitation software in activities of daily living, attention and response control in chronic stroke patients. J. Clinical Neurosci. **71**, 101–107 (2019)
5. Wolf, S.L., et al.: The HAAPI (Home Arm Assistance Progression Initiative) trial: A novel robotics delivery approach in stroke rehabilitation. Neurorehabil. Neural Repair **29**(10), 958–968 (2015). PMID: 25782693
6. Zhang, H., Austin, H., Buchanan, S., Herman, R., Koeneman, J., He, J.: Feasibility studies of robot-assisted stroke rehabilitation at clinic and home settings using rupert. In: Proceedings of the 2011 IEEE International Conference on Rehabilitation Robotics, IEEE press (2011)
7. Bartnicka, J., et al.: The role of virtual reality and biomechanical technologies in stroke rehabilitation. In: Nazir, Salman, Teperi, Anna-Maria, Polak-Sopińska, Aleksandra (eds.) AHFE 2018. AISC, vol. 785, pp. 351–361. Springer, Cham (2019). https://doi.org/10.1007/978-3-319-93882-0_34

8. Huang, X., Naghdy, F., Naghdy, G., Du, H., Todd, C.: The combined effects of adaptive control and virtual reality on robot-assisted fine hand motion rehabilitation in chronic stroke patients: a case study. J. Stroke Cerebrovasc. Dis. **27**(1), 221–228 (2018)
9. Chen, M.-H., Huang, L.-L.: Design suggestions of the clinical upper extremity rehabilitation equipment for stroke patients. In: Bagnara, S., Tartaglia, R., Albolino, S., Alexander, T., Fujita, Y. (eds.) IEA 2018. AISC, vol. 824, pp. 682–687. Springer, Cham (2019). https://doi.org/10.1007/978-3-319-96071-5_72
10. McPherson, L.M., Dewald, J.P.: Differences between flexion and extension synergy-driven coupling at the elbow, wrist, and fingers of individuals with chronic hemiparetic stroke. Clinical Neurophysiol. **130**(4), 454–468 (2019)
11. Wolbrecht, E.T., Rowe, J.B., Chan, V., Ingemanson, M.L., Cramer, S.C., Reinkensmeyer, D.J.: Finger strength, individuation, and their interaction: Relationship to hand function and corticospinal tract injury after stroke. Clinical Neurophysiol. **129**(4), 797–808 (2018)
12. Kwon, D.Y., Kwon, Y., Kim, J.W.: Quantitative analysis of finger and forearm movements in patients with off state early stage Parkinson's disease and scans without evidence of dopaminergic deficit (SWEDD). Parkinsonism Relat. Disord. **57**, 33–38 (2018)
13. Stegemöller, E., Zaman, A., MacKinnon, C.D., Tillman, M.D., Hass, C.J., Okun, M.S.: Laterality of repetitive finger movement performance and clinical features of Parkinson's disease. Hum. Movement Sci. **49**, 116–123 (2016)
14. Patar, M.N.A.A., Komeda, T., Low, C.Y., Mahmud, J.: System integration and control of finger orthosis for post stroke rehabilitation. Procedia Technol. **15**, 755–764 (2014)
15. Oliver-Salazar, M., Szwedowicz-Wasik, D., Blanco-Ortega, A., Aguilar-Acevedo, F., Ruiz-González, R.: Characterization of pneumatic muscles and their use for the position control of a mechatronic finger. Mechatronics **42**, 25–40 (2017)
16. Bataller, A., Cabrera, J., Clavijo, M., Castillo, J.: Evolutionary synthesis of mechanisms applied to the design of an exoskeleton for finger rehabilitation. Mech. Mach. Theory **105**, 31–43 (2016)
17. Lu, S., Chen, D., Liu, C., Jiang, Y., Wang, M.: A 3-D finger motion measurement system via soft strain sensors for hand rehabilitation. Sens. Actuator A Phys. **285**, 700–711 (2019)
18. Murphy, M.A., Andersson, S., Danielsson, A., Wipenmyr, J., Ohlsson, F.: Comparison of accelerometer-based arm, leg and trunk activity at weekdays and weekends during subacute inpatient rehabilitation after stroke. J. Rehab. Med. **18**, 426–433 (2019)
19. Carús, J.L., Peláez, V., López, G., Lobato, V.: Jim: a novel and efficient accelerometric magnitude to measure physical activity. Stud. Health Technol. Inform. **177**, 283–288 (2012)
20. Lee, J.Y., Kwon, S., Kim, W.S., Hahn, S.J., Park, J., Paik, N.J.: Feasibility, reliability, and validity of using accelerometers to measure physical activities of patients with stroke during inpatient rehabilitation. PLoS ONE **13**(12), e0209607 (2018)
21. Villar, J.R., González, S., Sedano, J., Chira, C., Trejo-Gabriel-Galan, J.M.: Improving human activity recognition and its application in early stroke diagnosis. Int. J. Neural Syst. **25**(04), 1450036 (2015)

A Hybrid Bio-inspired Clustering Approach for Diagnosing Children with Primary Headache Disorder

Svetlana Simić[1], Slađana Sakač[2], Zorana Banković[3], José R. Villar[4], Svetislav D. Simić[5], and Dragan Simić[5(✉)]

[1] Faculty of Medicine, University of Novi Sad, Hajduk Veljkova 1–9, 21000 Novi Sad, Serbia
svetlana.simic@mf.uns.ac.rs
[2] Clinical Centre of Vojvodina, Hajduk Veljkova 1–9, 21000 Novi Sad, Serbia
sladjanasakac@yahoo.com
[3] Frontiers Media SA, Paseo de Castellana 77, Madrid, Spain
zbankovic@gmail.com
[4] University of Oviedo, Campus de Llamaquique, 33005 Oviedo, Spain
villarjose@uniovi.es
[5] Faculty of Technical Sciences, University of Novi Sad, Trg Dositeja Obradovića 6, 21000 Novi Sad, Serbia
simicsvetislav@uns.ac.rs, dsimic@eunet.rs

Abstract. Half of the general population experiences a headache during any given year. Medical data and information in turn provide knowledge based on which physicians make scientific decisions for diagnosis and treatments. It is, therefore, very useful to create diagnostic tools to help physicians make better decisions. This paper is focused on a new approach based on a model for combining fuzzy partition method and bat clustering algorithm for diagnosing children with primary headache disorder. The proposed hybrid system is tested on data set collected from hospitalized children in Clinical Centre of Vojvodina, Novi Sad, Serbia.

Keywords: Headache classification · Attribute selection · Bat clustering algorithm · Diagnosis

1 Introduction

In recent times, data is the raw material from all information. This data and information in turn provide knowledge through modelling, analysis, interpretation, and visualization. It is not easy for a decision maker in decision-making processes to handle too much data, information and knowledge.

Headache disorders are the most prevalent of all the neurological conditions and are among the most frequent medical complains seen in a general practice. More than 90% of the general population report experiencing a headache during any given year [1]. The common practice is to pay attention to the health of working population which is the carrier and the backbone of every society when it comes to the risky occupations,

E. A. de la Cal et al. (Eds.): HAIS 2020, LNAI 12344, pp. 739–750, 2020.
https://doi.org/10.1007/978-3-030-61705-9_62

and to perform regular medical checkups [2]. Primary headaches can also be experienced by children. On the one hand, a busy primary care consultation, the use of a headache symptom diary, may provide important information for the evaluation of children presenting chronic headaches [3]. On the other hand, when the children are hospitalized, it is possible to apply a series of diagnostic procedures for determining cues and headache type.

In general, it is necessary to gain solid evidence through data selection and even transformation measure in order to learn the important data for the forthcoming prediction of unseen data, to support decision making, necessary actions, and treatment of a disease. Data selection is usually divided into two phases. First, the experts – physicians select the variables from the enterprise database according to their experience, and in the second phase, the optimal number of variables is sought with the use of attribute selection method [4].

The International Classification of Headache Disorders – The Third Edition (ICHD-3) uses the same Classification and the same Questionnaire for children, young population (teenagers), working population, and elderly population. This is one of the challenges in researching different populations and the usage of the same Questionnaire and established features in it. Some features could be important for working population though less important or unimportant for children and young population. There are challenges in the research of the standardized ICHD-3 Questionnaire and criteria – these are features defined in it. There are motivations for this research and new challenges for future research to find the most important features and to help physicians make better decisions in order to classify the primary headache disorders in children and young population and prepare the best treatment for them.

This paper continues the authors' previous researches [5, 6, 7] where some of useful techniques, algorithms, automatic methods, expert systems, and knowledge–based systems for data and attribute selection helping physicians make diagnosis of primary headache based on ICHD are presented. This paper presents bio-inspired clustering system for diagnosing children with primary headache disorder combining *Fuzzy Partition Method* (FPM) and *Bat Clustering Algorithm* (C-Bat). The proposed hybrid system is tested on data set collected from hospitalized children in Clinical Centre of Vojvodina, Novi Sad, Serbia. Also, this paper continues the authors' previous research in medical domain, especially in computer-assisted diagnosis and machine learning methods presented in research papers [8, 9, 10, 11]. This paper presents a clustering system for diagnosing children with primary headache with respect to authors' previous researches which were focused on diagnosing working population with primary headaches. In general, the classification methods are much more implemented in previous researches than in clustering methods. However, in the real-world setting, the physicians do not know the type of primary headache in advance and therefore it is more important to research and, finally, implement clustering methods than it is to use classification methods.

The rest of the paper is organized in the following way: Sect. 2 provides an overview of the related work. Section 3 presents primary headache classification, and comparison of different approaches of attribute selection. Modelling the bio-inspired diagnosis, fuzzy partition method and bat clustering algorithm are presented in Sect. 4.

The preliminary experimental results are presented in Sect. 5. Section 6 provides conclusions and some directions for future work.

2 Related Work

A new migraine analysis method was proposed by using electroencephalography (EEG) signals under flash stimulation in time domain. These types of signals are commonly pre-processed before the analysis procedure, and pre-processing techniques affect the analysis results. Histogram differences in the case of flash stimulation are calculated and used as features for the healthy subjects and migraine patients. These features are applied to a *k-means* clustering algorithm, and silhouette clustering results have shown correct clustering rate for migraine patients with 86.6% [12].

In the research paper [13], a goal was to evaluate the classification accuracy of the ant colony optimization (ACO) algorithm for the diagnosis of primary headaches using a website questionnaire expert system on headache diagnosis that was completed by patients. The cross-sectional study was conducted with 850 headache patients who randomly applied to hospitals from three cities in Turkey. Finally, neurologists' diagnosis results were compared with the classification results. The ACO for diagnosis classified patients with 96.9% overall accuracy. Diagnosis accuracies of migraine, tension-type headache (TTH), and cluster headaches were 98.2%, 92.4%, and 98.2% respectfully.

The use of machine learning is recruited for the classification of primary headache disorders, for which a dataset of 832 records of patients with primary headaches was considered, originating from three medical centers located in Turkey, as presented in [14]. Three main types of primary headaches were derived from the data set including TTH in both episodic and chronic forms, migraine without aura, migraine with aura, and cluster headache. Six machine-learning based classifiers, including linear and non-linear ensemble learning, in addition to one regression-based procedure, have been evaluated for the classification of primary headaches within a supervised learning setting, achieving highest aggregate performance outcomes of *Area under the ROC Curve* 92.3%, sensitivity 89.7%, and overall classification accuracy of 84.3%.

To evaluate diagnosis accuracy of Artificial Immune Systems (AIS) algorithms for the classification of migraine, tension-type and cluster-type of headaches by using the website-based diagnosis survey expert system was researched. The headache diagnoses of 850 patients from three different cities in Turkey were evaluated by using AIS algorithms and it is presented in [15]. According to the results, AIS algorithms for diagnosis have the maximum accuracy of 71%.

One of the leading reasons that make migraine a larger issue is that it cannot be diagnosed easily by physicians due to numerous overlapping symptoms with other diseases, such as epilepsy and TTH [16]. Flash stimulation is used during the recording of EEG signals. To achieve this, different machine learning algorithms on the EEG signal features extracted by using discrete wavelet transform are tested. The real-world dataset, recorded in the laboratory, displays that the flash stimulation can improve the classification accuracy for more than 10%.

3 Primary Headache Classification

The International Classification of Headache Disorders – The Third Edition (ICHD-3) established the uniform terminology and consistent operational diagnostic criteria for a wide range of headache disorders around the world [17]. The ICHD-3 provides a hierarchy of diagnoses with varying degrees of specificity. Headache disorders are identified with three or sometimes five-digit codes which is, in details, presented in [17]; short identification for just two important digit codes is presented in Table 1. All headache disorders are classified into two major groups: A) Primary headaches from ICHD-3 code 1. to 4.; and B) Secondary headaches ICHD-3 code from 5. to 12. The first digit specifies the major diagnostic categories (i.e. Migraine). The second digit indicates a disorder within the category (i.e. Migraine without aura). Each category is then subdivided into groups, types, subtypes and sub-forms. Subsequent digits permit more specific diagnosis for some headache types.

Table 1. The international classification of headache disorders – the third edition [17]

	ICHD-3 code		Diagnosis - Primary headache disorders
A	**1.**	1.1	Migraine without aura
		1.2	Migraine with aura
		¦	
		1.6	Episodic syndromes that may be associated with migraine
	2.		**Tension-type headache (TTH)**
		2.1	Infrequent episodic tension-type headache
		¦	
		2.4	Probable tension-type headache
	3.		**Trigeminal autonomic cephalalgias (TACs)**
	4.		**Other primary headache disorders**
B	**5.**		**Secondary headache disorders**
	¦		
	12.		

The starting point of an accurate diagnosis is differentiating primary headaches, without organic cause, from secondary headaches, where etiological cause can be determined. Headache diagnosing is usually based on: anamnesis, clinical examination and additional examinations. The physicians, who are more concerned with the detailed anamnesis and clinical examinations, apply ICHD-3 criteria – features, and can easily establish the primary headache diagnosis. If the criteria are not satisfied, the physicians will have to suggest an additional examination to a patient.

3.1 Comparing Different Approaches of Attribute Selection

This sub-section analyzes different studies which are all based on ICHD-3 recommendations, and therefore comparable to each other. These studies deal with different approaches to data and attribute selection based on automatic methods, expert systems, knowledge–based systems and physicians' expert knowledge as well, as depicted in Table 2. In general, attribute selection – feature selection – feature reduction approaches are widely used in data mining and machine learning. Feature selection could be divided into *Stochastic* and *no-Stochastic Feature Selection* methodologies, a refinement of an initial stochastic feature selection task with a no-stochastic method to additionally reduce the subset of features which is to be retained [18].

Consistency measure filter is based on the idea that the selected subset of features should be consistent and self-contained, and there should be no conflicts between the objects described by similar features [19]. **Relief algorithm** is proposed in [20] and it selects the statistically relevant features and usually it is within 95% confidence interval. **Genetic algorithm wrapper** is a nature-inspired algorithm, which uses an evolutionary optimization for finding the best subset of features. This approach starts with generating some random population representing the solution space, and through operations of cross-over and mutation into population it searches for an optimal solution [21]. The **Ant Colony Optimization** (ACO) based classification algorithm process is basically discovering classification rules by simulating ants' foraging [22]. **Rule Based Fuzzy Logic** (RBFL) model based on knowledge mining, means extracting information in the form of "if - then" statements made by surveying people [2]. The columns from 1 to 7, in Table 2, present different techniques and/or algorithms used in the observed research: (1) Consistency measure filter [8]; (2) ReliefF Greedy [8]; (3) ReliefF top10 [8]; (4) Genetic algorithm wrapper [8]; (5) Ant colony optimization based classification algorithm [23]; (6) Rule Based Fuzzy Logic System [2]; (7) Physician's expert choice; and, finally, column RES shows the final decision for data and attributes selection. Simple plus (+) denotes important selected attribute – feature by the considered method. **Bold red pluses** (+) indicate features denoted as very important by the expert – neurologist; and a simple plus (+) indicates less important features that are used as an additional decision support. Additionally, one feature according to the physician is important for recognizing TTH. In the column RES the feature marked by **blue bold pluses** (+) represents the final decision for important data and attributes selection.

This decision is based on the fact that at least six of seven observed studies consider the observed attribute as significant for deciding upon important attributes that can help physicians–neurologists to decide on a type of primary headache. The assessment "at least six of seven" presents more than 85% of observed sample and can, therefore, be considered as a reliable percentage for the observed empirical approximation. It could be concluded that the most important features based on ICHD-3 criteria are: **(4)**, **(5)**, **(6)**, **(7)**, **(8)**, **(10)**, **(12)**, **(13)** and **(15)** which are highlighted with **blue bold pluses** (+). .

Table 2. Comparison of a selection attribute for primary headache based on ICHD-3 diagnostic criteria: **No.** Line number; **Attributes** from Questionnaire; **Decision**: **1.** Consistency measure filter, **2.** ReliefF Greedy, **3.** ReliefF top10, **4.** Genetic algorithm wrapper, **5.** Ant Colony Optimization based classification algorithm, **6.** Rule Based Fuzzy Logic System, **7.** Physician's expert choice, **8.** column RES – final decision for important attributes selection

No.	Attributes	1	2	3	4	5	6	7	RES
1.	Sex								
2.	1. How old were you when the headache occurred for the first time?								
3.	2. How often do you have headache attacks?	+							
4.	3. How long do headache attacks last?	+	+	+	+		+	+	+
5.	4. Where is headache located?	+	+		+	+	+	+	+
6.	5. How intense is the pain?	+	+	+	+	+	+	+	+
7.	6. What is the quality of the pain you experience?	+	+	+	+	+	+	+	+
8.	7. Do your headaches worsen after physical activities such as walking?	+	+	+	+		+	+	+
9.	8. Do you avoid routine physical activities because you are afraid they might trigger your headache?		+	+				+	
10.	9.a) Are the headaches accompanied by? a) Nausea	+	+	+	+		+	+	+
11.	9.b) Are the headaches accompanied by? b) Vomiting		+	+			+	+	
12.	9.c) Are the headaches accompanied by? c) Photophobia	+	+	+	+	+	+	+	+
13.	9.d) Are the headaches accompanied by? d) Phonophobia		+	+		+	+	+	+
14.	10. Do you have temporary visual, sensory or speech disturbance?								
15.	11. Do you, during a headache attack, have tension and/or heightened tenderness of head or neck muscles?	+	+	+	+			+ TTH	+
16.	12. Do you have any body numbness or weakness?								
17.	13. Do you have any indications of oncoming headache?	+	+		+				
18.	14. Headache is usually triggered by: Menstrual periods	+							
19.	15. In the half of my visual field, lasting 5 minutes to an hour, along with the headache attack or an hour before.								
20.	16. Along with the headache attack or an hour before one I have sensory symptoms.								

4 Modelling the Bio-inspired Diagnosis Model

The proposed bio-inspired diagnosis model for Diagnosing Primary Headache Disorder implemented in this research is presented in Fig. 1. It consists of two phases. First phase includes: fuzzy partitioning step, where elements of input data set are divided into two groups; yet, only one of them is appropriate for further analysis, it is called *Selected data* and it includes two clusters. *Selected data* are provided according to the appropriate value in questions 6 and 8, marked in black bold, from Table 2.

The second phase is realized with Bat clustering algorithm. The patients whose diagnosis undoubtedly confirms types of primary headache are selected and they are called Solutions marked in **red bold** in Fig. 1. The rest of patients are "unclassified" and they are marked in **green bold**.

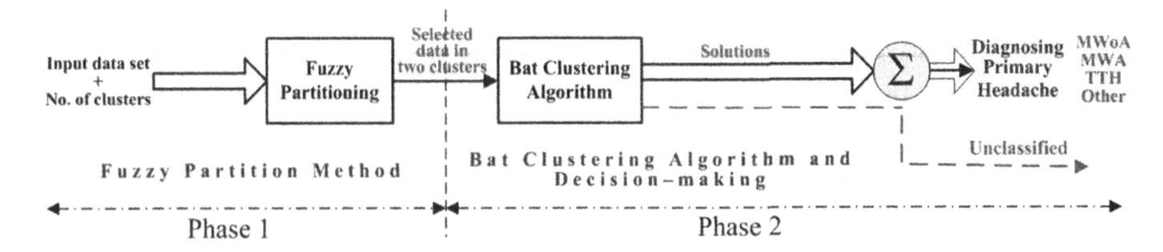

Fig. 1. A Bio-inspired clustering model for *Diagnosing Children with Primary Headache Disorder* (**MWoA** – Migraine without aura; **MWA** – Migraine with aura; **TTH** – Tension Type Headache; **Other** – Other primary headaches)

4.1 Fuzzy Partition Method

The data set is typically an observation of some physical process. Each observation consists of n measured variables, grouped into an n-dimensional row vector $x_k = [x_{k1}, x_{k2}, \ldots, x_{kn}]^T$, $x_k \in R^n$. A set of N observations is denoted by $X = \{x_k \mid k = 1, 2, \ldots, N\}$, and is represented as an N x n matrix, a data set. Since clusters can formally be viewed as subsets of the data set, the number of subsets (clusters) is denoted by c. Fuzzy partition can be seen as a generalization of hard partition, and it allows μ_{ik} to attain real values in [0, 1]. A N x c matrix $U = [\mu_{ik}]$ represents the fuzzy partitions, and its conditions are given by:

$$\mu_{ij} \in [0, 1],\ 1 \leq i \leq N,\ 1 \leq k \leq c \tag{1}$$

$$\sum_{k=1}^{c} \mu_{ik} = 1,\quad 1 \leq i \leq N \tag{2}$$

$$0 < \sum_{i=1}^{N} \mu_{ik} < N,\quad 1 \leq k \leq c \tag{3}$$

Let $X = [x_1, x_2, \ldots, x_N]$ be a *finite set* and let $2 \leq c < N$ be an integer. The *fuzzy partitioning space* for X is the set

$$M_{fc} = \left\{ U \in \Re^{N x c} \mid \mu_{ik} \in [0, 1], \forall i, k; \sum_{k=1}^{c} \mu_{ik} = 1, \forall i;\ 0 < \sum_{k=1}^{c} \mu_{ik} < N, \forall k \right\} \tag{4}$$

The i-th column of U contains values of the *membership function* of the i-th fuzzy subset of X. The Eq. (5) constrains the sum of each column to 1, and thus the total membership of each x_k in X equals one. The distribution of memberships among the c fuzzy subsets is not constrained.

4.2 Bat Clustering Algorithm

The *Bat algorithm* is a metaheuristic algorithm for global optimization. It was inspired by the echolocation behavior of microbats, with varying pulse rates of emission and loudness. The Bat algorithm was developed by Xin-She Yang and presented for the first time in [24]. A novel bat algorithm (BA)-based clustering approach for solving crop type classification problems using a multispectral satellite image is presented for the first time in 2016 [25], and demonstrated the robustness of the proposed algorithm. In subsequent research papers this algorithm is called *Bat Clustering Algorithm* (C-Bat).

The workflow proposed *Bat Clustering Algorithm* and its basic steps are presented in Fig. 2. It can be described in the following way. Each bat has its own unique ID, position, and fitness attributes. However, in the bat algorithm, each bat is assigned the same loudness, pulse frequency, and wave length. The position of a bat is represented by a solution x. Its location is determined by the values of D dimensions. The solution x uses a $(N, K \otimes D)$ matrix, where N is the population, and K is the number of clusters. The second term $K \otimes D$ identifies the location of the bat, and Q, V, and A present *Frequency*, *Velocity*, and *Loudness* respectively.

In the initialization phase, the population of n host nests x_i, where $i = 1, 2, \ldots, n$, is generated. The cluster centers are represented by the means of the attributes. The centroid is represented as a paired tuple, $cen(i, :)$, where i is the central point of the cluster. The tuple has the format of (k, d), where k is the k-th cluster and d is the coordinate in $K \otimes D$ or higher dimensions. The objective functions are defined with Eqs. (5) and (6).

$$\text{MIN}\,\{x - \text{cen}\} \tag{5}$$

$$cen = \frac{1}{N}\sum\nolimits_{x_i \in cluster_i} x_i\,,\quad i = 1, \ldots, K \tag{6}$$

Each bat has a velocity v_i and the bat's position is partly determined by its velocity. At first, the bats are randomly distributed. After initialization, the bats move to a better place according to set functions presented by Eq. (7).

$$\begin{aligned} f_i &= f_{\min} + (f_{\max} - f_{\min}) \times \beta \\ v_i^t &= v_i^{t-1} + (v_i^{t-1} - x_*) \times f_i \\ x_i^t &= x_i^{t-1} + v_i^t \end{aligned} \tag{7}$$

A random number is then produced: if it is larger than the current bat rate, the algorithm selects a solution from those calculated and generates a local solution. The centroids are the averages of the nearby data points. The distances are then minimized according to the direction of the optimization goal following objective functions shown by Eqs. (5) and (6). The convergence process then starts to iterate based on the Eq. (8):

$$\beta = Q \times rand(\,) \tag{8}$$

where Q presents *Frequency*, *rand*() is a random value generator, and the random values are distributed over [0, 1].

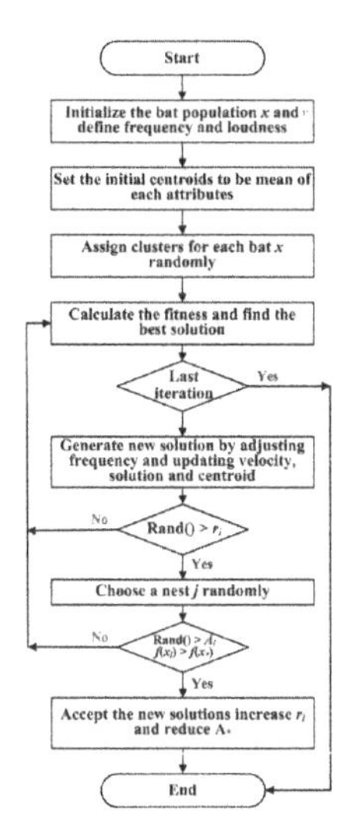

Fig. 2. Workflow of *Bat Clustering Algorithm*

The positions of the bats are then updated. *f* represents the frequency of echolocation. When the frequency equals the sum of the minimum frequency and the difference between the maximum and minimum frequencies, the speed of the bat is updated. The new speed is set to the previous speed plus the product of the previous frequency and the difference between the current position and the previous position. A variable called the pulse rate is also used in the algorithm. When the pulse rate is exceeded, the following formula is updated:

$$x_i^t = x_* + 0.01 \times rand() \quad (9)$$

Equation (9) serves as the updating function, where x_* is taken as the best solution. It is also used to represent the best position for the bat to move towards. If the loudness value is not high enough and the new solution is better than the old one, the better one becomes the solution.

5 Experimental Results and Discussion

The proposed bio-inspired clustering approach for diagnosing children with primary headache disorder, in our research, is tested on the data set collected from Clinical Centre of Vojvodina, Novi Sad, Serbia. This data set is a part of a larger study [6], encompassing hospitalized children. The most important features **(4)**, **(5)**, **(6)**, **(7)**, **(8)**, **(10)**, **(12)**, and **(15)** based on ICHD-3 criteria are presented in Table 2. The headache data set has thirteen features – attributes; and four classes – types of primary headache: *Migraine without aura* (**MWoA**), *Migraine with aura* (**MWA**), *Tension-type headache* (**TTH**), *Other primary headaches* (**Other**); and missing data – *No*.

Table 3. Pairwise comparison for *Children Headache Data Set* – for nine ICHD-3 attributes

Com.	MWoA	MWA	TTH	Other	Unclassified
1	17/25 **68.00 %**			27/35 **77.14 %**	(8+8)=16/60 **26.66 %**
2	19/25 **76.00 %**		21/29 **72.41 %**		(6+8)=14/54 **25.92 %**
3		18/21 **85.71 %**		24/35 **68.57 %**	(3+11)=14/56 **25.00 %**
4		10/21 **47.61 %**	15/29 **51.72 %**		(11+14)=25/50 **50.00 %**
5	4/25 **16.00 %**	18/21 **85.71 %**			(21+3)=24/46 **52.17 %**
Total	**25**	**21**	**29**	**35**	
	Overall accuracy		**65.17 %**		**34.83 %**

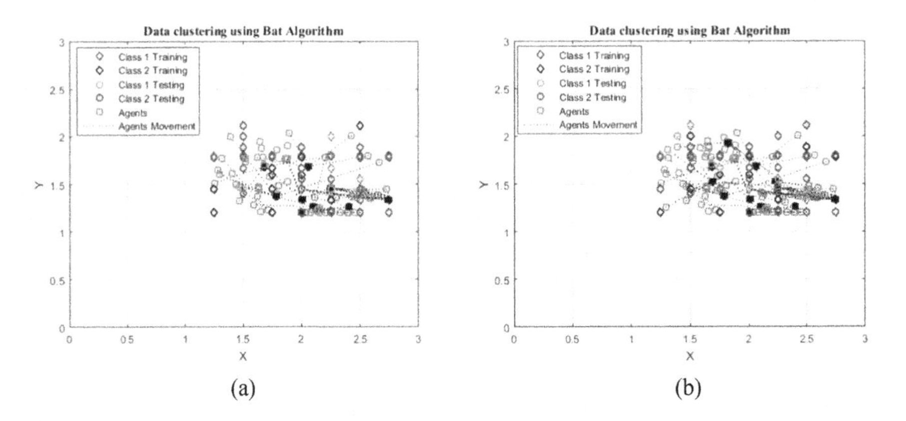

Fig. 3. Bio-inspired clustering model for *Diagnosing Children with Primary Headache Disorder* presented with two clusters - Pairwise comparison for nine ICHD-3 attributes

The *Children Headache Data Set* consists of 110 instances. After *Fuzzy Partition* process, for nine ICHD-3 attributes, 60 *Selected Data* are selected for pairwise comparison classes (MWoA – Other). After 250 iterations, 17 instances are patients who suffer from MWoA, 27 are categorized as Other, and the remaining 16 are *Unclassified.* The optimal cluster centroids are: Centroid 1: 2.75, 2.05; Centroid 2: 1.33, 1.68 given in Fig. 3(a). Figure 3(b) presents pairwise comparison for nine ICHD-3 attributes for (MWoA – TTH). Experimental results for pairwise comparison for nine ICHD-3 attributes are presented in Table 3. Overall accuracy for the entire *Children Headache Data Set* in pairwise comparison is 65.17%, while the particular accuracy for **MWoA** is 53.33%; **MWA** is 73.01%; **TTH** is 62.06%; **Other** headaches is 74.31%; and "*Unclassified*" is 34.83%.

6 Conclusion and Future Work

The aim of this paper is to propose the new bio-inspired clustering approach for diagnosing children with primary headache disorder. The new proposed mode is obtained by combining fuzzy partition method and bat clustering algorithm. The proposed hybrid system is tested on a data set collected from hospitalized children in Clinical Centre of Vojvodina, Novi Sad, Serbia. The headache data set has four classes – types of primary headache: Migraine without aura, Migraine with aura, Tension-type headache, and Other primary headaches.

This study analyzes the most important ICHD-3 attributes. Preliminary experimental results encourage further research by the authors, since the overall accuracy for nine attributes is 65.17%. Our future research will focus on creating new hybrid model which will combine other evolutionary techniques in order to efficiently solve different well-known data sets and real-world medical data sets as well.

References

1. Hagen, K., Zwart, J.-A., Vatten, L., Stovner, L.J., Bovin, G.: Prevalence of migraine and non-migrainous headache – head-HUNT, a large population-based study. Cephalalgia **20** (10), 900–906 (2000). https://doi.org/10.1046/j.1468-2982.2000.00145.x
2. Simić, S., Simić, D., Slankamenac, P., Simić-Ivkov, M.: Computer-assisted diagnosis of primary headaches. In: Corchado, E., Abraham, A., Pedrycz, W. (eds.) HAIS 2008. LNCS (LNAI), vol. 5271, pp. 314–321. Springer, Heidelberg (2008). https://doi.org/10.1007/978-3-540-87656-4_39
3. How, C.H., Chan, W.S.D.: Headaches in children. Singapore Med. J. **55**(3), 128–131 (2014). https://doi.org/10.11622/smedj.2014029
4. Relich, M., Bzdyra, K.: Knowledge discovery in enterprise databases for forecasting new product success. In: Jackowski, K., Burduk, R., Walkowiak, K., Woźniak, M., Yin, H. (eds.) IDEAL 2015. LNCS, vol. 9375, pp. 121–129. Springer, Cham (2015). https://doi.org/10.1007/978-3-319-24834-9_15
5. Simić, S., Banković, Z., Simić, D., Simić, S.D.: Different approaches of data and attribute selection on headache disorder. In: Yin, H., Camacho, D., Novais, P., Tallón-Ballesteros, A. J. (eds.) IDEAL 2018. LNCS, vol. 11315, pp. 241–249. Springer, Cham (2018). https://doi.org/10.1007/978-3-030-03496-2_27
6. Sakač, S., Simić, S., Sekulić, S., Jovin, Z., Gebauer-Bukurov, K., Božić, K.: Neuroimaging in children and adolescents with recurrent headaches, yes or no? In: IX/XV Neurology Congress of Serbia, Summary Collection, S60 ("Neuroimaging kod dece i adolescenata sa rekurentnim glavoboljama, da ili ne?") ("IX/XV Kongres neurologa Srbije, Zbornik sažetaka, S60") (2013)
7. Simić, S., Simić, D., Slankamenac, P., Simić-Ivkov, M.: Rule-based fuzzy logic system for diagnosing migraine. In: Darzentas, J., Vouros, G.A., Vosinakis, S., Arnellos, A. (eds.) SETN 2008. LNCS (LNAI), vol. 5138, pp. 383–388. Springer, Heidelberg (2008). https://doi.org/10.1007/978-3-540-87881-0_37
8. Krawczyk, B., Simić, D., Simić, S., Woźniak, M.: Automatic diagnosis of primary headaches by machine learning methods. Open Med. **8**(2), 157–165 (2013). https://doi.org/10.2478/s11536-012-0098-5

9. Simić, S., Milutinović, D., Sekulić, S., Simić, D., Simić, S.D., Đorđević, J.: A hybrid case-based reasoning approach to detecting the optimal solution in nurse scheduling problem. Logic J. IGPL **28**(2), 226–238 (2020). https://doi.org/10.1093/jigpal/jzy047jzy047
10. Jackowski, K., Jankowski, D., Simić, D., Simić, S.: Migraine diagnosis support system based on classifier ensemble. In: Bogdanova, A.M., Gjorgjevikj, D. (eds.) ICT Innovations 2014. AISC, vol. 311, pp. 329–339. Springer, Cham (2015). https://doi.org/10.1007/978-3-319-09879-1_33
11. Simić, S., Banković, Z., Simić, D., Simić, S.D.: A hybrid clustering approach for diagnosing medical diseases. In: de Cos Juez, F., et al. (eds.) Hybrid Artificial Intelligent Systems. Lecture Notes in Computer Science, vol. 10870, pp. 741–752. Springer, Cham (2018). https://doi.org/10.1007/978-3-319-92639-1_62
12. Alkan, A., Akben, S.B.: Use of k-means clustering in migraine detection by using EEG records under flash stimulation. Int. J. Phys. Sci. **6**(4), 641–650 (2011)
13. Celik, U., Yurtay, N.: An ant colony optimization algorithm-based classification for the diagnosis of primary headaches using a website questionnaire expert system. Turk. J. Electric. Eng. Comput. Sci. **25**(5), 4200–4210 (2017). https://doi.org/10.3906/elk-1612-17
14. Kaky, A.J.M.: Intelligent Systems Approach for Classification and Management of Patients with Headache. Ph.D. thesis, Liverpool, John Moores University (2017)
15. Celik, U., Yurtay, N., Koc, E.R., Tope, V., Gulluoglu, H., Ertas, M.: Diagnostic accuracy comparison of artificial immune algorithms for primary headaches. Comput. Math. Methods Med. **2015**, Article ID 465192 (2015). https://doi.org/10.1155/2015/465192
16. Subasi, A., Ahmed, A., Aličković, E., Hassan, A.R.: Effect of photic stimulation for migraine detection using random forest and discrete wavelet transform. Biomed. Signal Process. Control **49**, 231–239 (2019) https://doi.org/10.1016/j.bspc.2018.12.011
17. The International Classification of Headache Disorders 3rd edition. https://www.ichd-3.org/
18. Tallón-Ballesteros, A.J., Correia, L., Cho, S.-B.: Stochastic and Non-Stochastic Feature Selection. In: Yin, H., et al. (eds.) IDEAL 2017. LNCS, vol. 10585, pp. 592–598. Springer, Cham (2017). https://doi.org/10.1007/978-3-319-68935-7_64
19. Arauzo-Azofra, A., Benitez, J.M., Castro, J.L.: Consistency measures for feature selection. J. Intell. Inf. Syst. **30**(3), 273–292 (2008)
20. Kira, K., Rendell, L.A.: A practical approach to feature selection. In: Ninth International Workshop on Machine Learning, pp. 249–256 (1992). https://doi.org/10.1016/b978-1-55860-247-2.50037-1
21. Guyon, I., Gunn, S., Nikravesh, M., Zadeh, L.: Feature Extraction, Foundations and Applications. Springer, Heidelberg (2006). https://doi.org/10.1007/978-3-540-35488-8
22. Michelakos, I., Mallios, N., Papageorgiou, E., Vassilakopoulos, M.: Ant colony optimization and data mining. In: Studies in Computational Intelligence, vol. 352, pp. 31–60. Springer, Heidelberg (2011). https://doi.org/10.1007/978-3-642-20344-2_2
23. Tallón-Ballesteros, A.J., Riquelme, J.C.: Tackling ant colony optimization meta-heuristic as search method in feature subset selection based on correlation or consistency measures. In: Corchado, E., Lozano, J.A., Quintián, H., Yin, H. (eds.) IDEAL 2014. LNCS, vol. 8669, pp. 386–393. Springer, Cham (2014). https://doi.org/10.1007/978-3-319-10840-7_47
24. Yang, X.S.: A new metaheuristic bat-inspired algorithm. In: Studies in Computational Intelligence, vol. 284, pp. 65–74. Springer, Heidelberg (2010). https://doi.org/10.1007/978-3-642-12538-6_6
25. Senthilnath, J., Kulkarni, S., Benediktsson, J.A., Yang, X.S.: A novel approach for multi-spectral satellite image classification based on the bat algorithm clustering problems. IEEE Geosci. Remote Sens. Lett. **13**(4), 599–603 (2016). https://doi.org/10.1109/LGRS.2016.2530724

Artificial Neural Networks for Tours of Multiple Asteroids

Giulia Viavattene(✉) and Matteo Ceriotti

James Watt School of Engineering,
James Watt (South) Building, Glasgow G12 8QQ, UK
G.Viavattene.1@research.gla.ac.uk, Matteo.Ceriotti@glasgow.ac.uk

Abstract. Designing multiple near-Earth asteroid (NEA) rendezvous missions is a complex global optimization problem, which involves the solution of a large combinatorial part to select the sequences of asteroids to visit. Given that more than 22,000 NEAs are known to date, trillions of permutations between asteroids need to be considered. This work develops a method based on Artificial Neural Networks (ANNs) to quickly estimate the cost and duration of low-thrust transfers between asteroids. The capability of the network to map the relationship between the characteristics of the departure and arrival orbits and the transfer cost and duration is studied. To this end, the optimal network architecture and hyper-parameters are identified for this application. An analysis of the type of orbit parametrization used as network inputs for best performance is performed. The ANN is employed within a sequence-search algorithm based on a tree-search method, which identifies multiple rendezvous sequences and selects those with lowest time of flight and propellant mass needed. To compute the full trajectory and control history, the sequences are subsequently optimized using an optimal control solver based on a pseudospectral method. The performance of the proposed methodology is assessed by investigating NEA sequences of interest. Results show that ANN can estimate the cost or duration of optimal low-thrust transfers with high accuracy, resulting into a mean relative error of less than 4%.

Keywords: Neural network · Space mission · Trajectory optimization · Near-Earth asteroids

1 Introduction

In the last decades, Near-Earth Asteroids (NEAs) have caught the attention of the scientific community for planetary defense, technology demonstration, and resource exploitation. The irregularity of their shape, size, gravity and magnetic fields, composition makes each of them unique and worth to be studied [7]. Multiple NEA rendezvous missions allow to visit a larger number of asteroids than single-NEA missions, while reducing the cost for each observation. Low-thrust propulsion systems, such as solar electric propulsion (SEP), are a more

E. A. de la Cal et al. (Eds.): HAIS 2020, LNAI 12344, pp. 751–762, 2020.
https://doi.org/10.1007/978-3-030-61705-9_63

efficient technology than chemical propulsion in terms of fuel consumption. The higher specific impulse of low-thrust systems makes them an attractive solution for multi-target missions since they require less propellant for a given velocity increment ΔV [18].

The design of multiple NEA missions requires the solution of a complex global optimization problem to compute the optimal trajectory that meets the mission requirements, such as type of propulsion system and propellant mass available. This problem consists mainly of two sub-problems which are tightly coupled: a large combinatorial part, aiming at the identification of the most convenient asteroid sequences; and a continuous part to identify the optimal trajectory and control history to fly from asteroid to asteroid. The final purpose is to determine an optimal trajectory, which requires the least amount of fuel mass and maximizes the number of asteroids visited within a given time of flight (TOF).

To identify the most promising sequences of asteroids, all the permutations among them need to be considered. Given that more than 22,000 NEAs are known to date, according to the NASA's database[1], trillions of permutations should be analyzed. Moreover, since low-thrust propulsion produces little thrust continuously for a long time, the problem is continuous, thus computationally very intensive to obtain solutions for each asteroid-to-asteroid transfer.

Several methodologies have been proposed to solve this complex problem. The solution advanced by the majority of them requires the use of a simplified model to determine the most convenient asteroid sequences and, successively, convert it into feasible trajectories by means of a low-thrust optimization. For instance, Peloni et al. [10] approximate the low-thrust legs using a shape-based method and find the sequence with a search-and-prune algorithm; while a homotopic approach was used for approximating transfers in Ref. [15].

Previous works show that artificial intelligence can be applied to solve complex problems in aerospace sciences. A method based on an evolutionary algorithm and an artificial neural network (ANN) was employed to determine trajectories to a single NEA using solar sailing as propulsion system [3]. It was proved that this method can find a solution more efficiently than traditional optimal control methods. Machine learning was also successfully used in identifying low-thrust trajectories with minimum fuel consumption between main belt asteroids [5] and in estimating the final mass of the spacecraft after a transfer between two NEAs [8]. Other applications include the accuracy enhancement for pinpoint landing [13] and orbit prediction [11].

This paper investigates the use of ANNs within a sequence-search algorithm to solve the global optimization problem of multiple asteroid missions, by identifying the most convenient asteroid sequences and providing estimates of the cost and duration of each transfer. In essence, the goal of the analysis is to demonstrate that ANN can *quickly* estimate the cost and TOF of low-thrust transfers between NEAs. When trained appropriately, using a neural network

[1] Data available through the link https://cneos.jpl.nasa.gov/orbits/elements.html (accessed on 2020/01/10).

can potentially eliminate the need to prune the database of asteroids as it can generalize the network function to asteroids and departure dates not included in the training.

The ANN design for the tour of multiple asteroids presents multiple challenges. First, a method to compute the training database needs to be identified. With the goal of including a sufficient number of samples in the database, direct and indirect optimization methods result to be very expensive in terms of computational effort. Instead, analytic methods can help in the initial phase of the design, thus when training the network, to provide a quick and reliable, but approximated, description of the trajectory. Secondly, since the network inputs influence the accuracy of the network output with respect to the targets, different parametrizations of the orbits and their effect on the network performance are studied. Also, the extended close-up observation of the NEAs requires that velocity and position of the asteroids are matched by the spacecraft at the departure and arrival point of each transfer; thus, the asteroid phasing should be carefully considered in the inputs. It is paramount to define the topology and hyper-parameters of the network for this application. This is not straightforward and needs to be investigated.

The structure of the paper is the following. In Sect. 2 the optimal control problem is described, followed by the generation of the ANN training database. The input vector, architecture and hyper-parameters of the network are optimized in Sect. 3 to achieve the highest performance. The trained ANN is then integrated into a sequence search algorithm, which is detailed in Sect. 4. Among the sequences obtained, one is optimized, highlighting the main results of the methodology. Finally, Sect. 6 completes this paper with the conclusions.

2 Optimal Low-Thrust Trajectories

In the following, an optimal control problem (OCP) for low-thrust trajectories is formulated. This identifies the optimal trajectory for each body-to-body leg, i.e., Earth-to-asteroid or asteroid-to-asteroid. For a spacecraft orbiting the Sun, the state vector, $\mathbf{x}$, is expressed in modified equinoctial elements (MEE) [2], adjoined by the spacecraft mass:

$$\mathbf{x} = [p, f, g, h, k, L, m]^T \tag{1}$$

The following set of ordinary differential equations of motion can be defined:

$$\dot{\mathbf{x}}(t) = \mathbf{A}(\mathbf{x})\mathbf{a} + \mathbf{b}(\mathbf{x}) \tag{2}$$

with $\mathbf{a}$ being the acceleration generated by the propulsion system, and $\mathbf{A}(\mathbf{x})$ and $\mathbf{b}(\mathbf{x})$ being, respectively, the matrix and the vector of the dynamics. A full definition of $\mathbf{A}(\mathbf{x})$ and $\mathbf{b}(\mathbf{x})$ can be found in Ref. [1]. The SEP propulsive acceleration can be described as follows:

$$\mathbf{a} = \frac{T_{max}}{m}\mathbf{N} \tag{3}$$

where T_{max} is the maximum thrust that can be generated and $\mathbf{N} = [N_r, N_\theta, N_h]^T$ indicates the acceleration direction and magnitude vector in radial, transverse, out-of-plane frame. The mass of the spacecraft m changes with time while thrusting as described by the following mass differential equation:

$$\dot{m} = -\frac{T_{max}||\mathbf{N}||}{I_{sp} g_0} \tag{4}$$

with $||\mathbf{N}||$ being the magnitude of $\mathbf{N}$ and I_{sp} is the specific impulse of the propulsion system. For the remainder of this work, a solar electric propulsion system with $I_{sp} = 3000$ s and $T_{max} = 0.3$ N is adopted for a spacecraft with initial mass of 1500 kg.

In this case the objective of the optimization is to find the optimal control history $\mathbf{u}(t) \equiv \mathbf{N}(t)$ so that the least amount of propellant mass is used to visit the highest number of NEAs. Thus, the performance index to minimize is:

$$J = \int_{t_0}^{t_f} m(t) \, \mathrm{d}t \tag{5}$$

subject to the constraint:

$$\begin{aligned} &||\mathbf{N}(t)|| \leq 1 \qquad \forall t \in [t_0, t_f] \\ &\mathbf{r}(t_0) = \mathbf{r}_0 \\ &\mathbf{v}(t_0) = \mathbf{v}_0 \\ &\mathbf{r}(t_f) = \mathbf{r}_f \\ &\mathbf{v}(t_f) = \mathbf{v}_f \end{aligned} \tag{6}$$

where $\mathbf{N}$ can vary in magnitude to allow for thrust throttling, with N_r, N_θ, $N_h \in [-1, 1]$. Moreover, to satisfy the rendezvous conditions, the position $\mathbf{r}$ and velocity $\mathbf{v}$ of the spacecraft have to match with the position $\mathbf{r}_0$ and velocity $\mathbf{v}_0$ of the departure body at the departure time t_0, and with the the position $\mathbf{r}_f$ and velocity $\mathbf{v}_f$ of the arrival body at the arrival time t_f.

Several methodologies were proposed to solve the low-thrust OCP. Indirect methods solve the OCP by transforming the problem into a two-boundary value problem, using the Pontryagin's principle [12]. Direct methods transcribe the continuous OCP into a non-linear programming (NLP) problem which discretizes the trajectory into smaller arcs of constant thrust magnitude and direction [14]. Both methods are computationally intensive, thus not efficient to generate the network training database where thousands of samples are included.

It is chosen to use a shape-based approach, which can produce a trajectory solution while reducing the required computational effort. This method approximates the shape of the rendezvous trajectory with minimum-cost for the given range of launch dates, TOF, and number of revolutions [4]. The required control history to fly the calculated trajectory is retrieved from the acceleration profile. A genetic algorithm is employed to search for the optimal shaping parameters for the transfer with minimum time of flight.

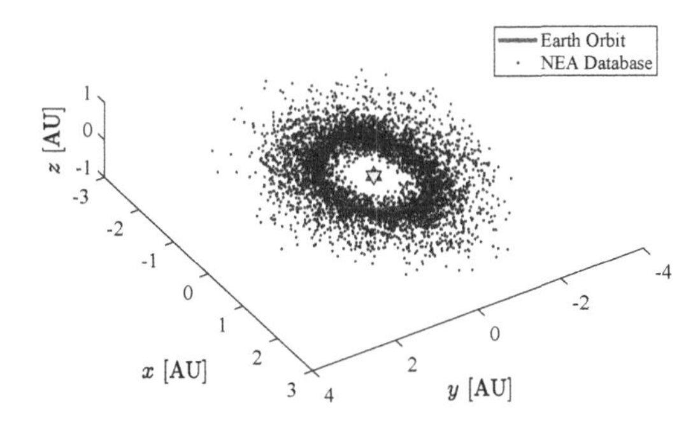

Fig. 1. Visualization of all the asteroids in the training database.

2.1 Database Generation

The training database contains the network inputs and the desired outputs, which are the orbital characteristics of the departure and arrival orbits and the position of the objects along their orbits (*input vector* $\mathbf{x}$) and the cost ΔV and TOF of the transfer between them (*output vector* $\mathbf{y}$), defined as follows:

$$\mathbf{x} = [p_0, f_0, g_0, h_0, k_0, L_0, p_f, f_f, g_f, h_f, k_f, L_f] \tag{7}$$

$$\mathbf{y} = [\Delta V, t_{0,f}] \tag{8}$$

where $p_0, f_0, g_0, h_0, k_0, L_0$ and $p_f, f_f, g_f, h_f, k_f, L_f$ are the modified equinoctial elements [19] describing the departure and arrival orbits, respectively, ΔV indicates the velocity increment and $t_{0,f}$ the time of flight.

The NEA orbital characteristics are obtained from the NASA's Near-Earth Object Program[2]. NEAs that are interesting for scientific reasons, their composition and orbital dynamics are included in the database.

To improve the converge rate of low-thrust OCPs, the highly-inclined ($i \geq 20°$) and highly-eccentric ($e \geq 0.4$) asteroids are excluded. Transfers to those asteroids would have been excluded by the network anyway since they require a longer TOF and considerable amount of propellant. This results in 6286 asteroids, with about 300 Potentially Hazardous Asteroids (PHA) and about 1450 Near-Earth Object Human Space Flight Accessible Targets Study (NHATS). PHAs have an Earth minimum orbit intersection distance lower than 0.05 AU and estimated diameter greater than 150 m, while NHATS are selected by NASA because they might be accessible by future human space flight missions.

Figure 1 shows the Earth's orbit (in red) and all the asteroids included in the database (blue dots), showing their position with respect to the Earth's orbit on 27 April 2019.

For the generation of the training database, the permutations among a subset of NEAs including 100 objects are considered for a total of 10,100 transfer samples. The goal is to verify the *generalization* property of the neural network: a

[2] Data available through the link https://cneos.jpl.nasa.gov/orbits/elements.html (accessed on 2019/06/17).

successfully trained ANN is able to generalize estimating transfer costs between NEAs not included in the database and with different launch dates.

To verify the generalization property during the training, the database is divided into training set, validation set and test set. The training set is used for the training, while the validation and test sets contain samples that are not included in the training. The validation set is used to verify the overfitting does not occur during the training and the test set is used to test the performance of the network after the training with totally new cases.

For each transfer between two selected bodies, the shape-based method is used to find the ΔV and TOF of the transfer. The training database is generated by storing for each transfer the parametrization of the departure and arrival orbits, the angular position of the relative asteroids at a reference time, and the cost and TOF of the minimum-cost transfer. The launch window is set in the period 01/01/2020 and 30/12/2030. A maximum time of flight of 1500 days per transfer is set as transfers longer than four years are not of interest.

3 Neural Network Design

The topology and the hyper-parameters of the network can affect its performance. Since their best values are not known a priori, it is essential to analyze the ANN performance with respect to its parameters so that the correlation between network outputs and targets is maximized and the network error in the identification of transfer cost and time mapping is minimized. In a regression analysis, the correlation identifies how well the outputs fit the targets, with one and zero indicating perfect or zero fit, respectively. The network error can be defined as the mean square error (MSE) between the output of the network $\mathbf{y}$ and the targets $\mathbf{y}_t$:

$$\mathcal{E}_{MSE} = \frac{1}{N} \sum_{i=1}^{N} ||\mathbf{y}_i - \mathbf{y}_{t,i}||^2 \tag{9}$$

with N being the number of outputs. Since the validation set has samples which are not included in the training database, the validation-set MSE is often used.

3.1 Input Vector Analysis

The input vector of the network needs to define completely the departure and arrival orbits. To this end the orbital parameters can be used. However, several orbit parametrizations exist. Among these, the classical orbital elements (COE), modified equinoctial elements (MEE), equinoctial elements (EE), Cartesian coordinates, Delaunay elements, and eccentricity and angular momentum vector (eH). The interested reader is referred to Ref. [19] for the main differences between these orbit parametrizations. In this section, the effect of using different orbit parametrization on the network performance is investigated.

These parametrizations are used as input to a network, whose architecture is taken from Ref. [8], with two hidden layers and 80 neurons per layer to evaluate

Table 1. Network performance for different parametrizations of the orbit.

ANN input	Correlation	Validation-set MSE
COE	0.855	0.530
EE	0.856	0.487
MEE	0.925	0.236
Cartesian	0.551	0.761
Delaunay	0.694	0.862
eH	0.908	0.221

how the performance changes. The sigmoid is used as activation function and the stochastic gradient-descent algorithm is adopted for the training. The learning rate is set to 0.01, which is the highest value that does not cause divergence in the training process, and the database is divided in 70% training set, 15% validation set, and 15% test set. The performance of the network, in terms of correlation and validation-set MSE, is presented in Table 1 for each orbit parametrization.

The highest correlation is obtained when MEE are used as inputs ($C_{MEE} = 0.925$), which presents also a low validation-set error ($e_{MEE} = 0.236$). The latter is slightly lower when the eH parametrization is used, but a poorer correlation is registered in this case. However, priority is given to the highest correlation since this represents the performance of the network in all the three training, validation and test phases. Thus, for the remaining of this paper, MEE are used to describe the departure and arrival orbits as input to the network.

3.2 Architecture Optimization

In this subsection, we aim at finding the best values of the network hyper-parameters. To this end, the response of the network to each of these parameters is analyzed. The architecture of the network is defined by the number of hidden layers and the number of neurons. Other hyper-parameters that can affect the performance are the learning algorithm, activation function for each hidden layer, learning rate or gradient constant and its increase or decrease factor.

To determine the optimal values of the network architecture and hyper-parameters, an optimization procedure needs to be carried out. In theory, the most systematic option would be to optimize all the parameters at the same time by using, for instance, a genetic algorithm. However, the number of parameters to optimize and the need to train the network at every trial make the computational time extremely extensive. For this reason, one parameter at a time is tuned. First, the parameter's values are set to their default values taken from Ref. [8]. Secondly, one parameter is varied individually and the effect on the ANN performance is studied. The parameter is then set equal to the optimal value found, and the next parameter is considered for the same procedure. The default values and search space for each network parameter are detailed in Table 2, where the parameters are presented in the same order of analysis.

Table 2. Default values, search space and optimal values for the network hyper-parameters.

ANN parameter	Default	Search space	Optimal
Number of hidden layers	2	[2, 8]	4
Number of neurons	80	[40, 100]	80
Learning algorithm	Gradient descent	Levenberg-Marquardt Resilient back-propagation Scaled conjugate gradient Gradient descent	Levenberg-Marquardt
Activation function	sigmoid	tansig, sigmoid, ReLu	sigmoid

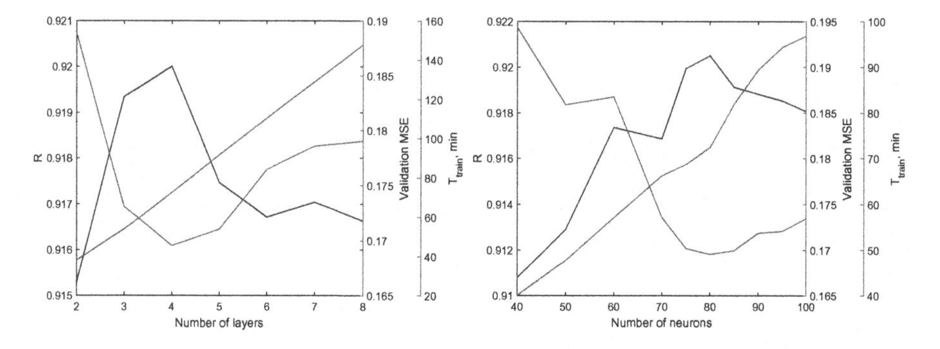

Fig. 2. Effect of varying the network parameters on its performance.

A neural network with an appropriate number of layers and neurons per each layer can approximate any continuous linear or non-linear function [6]. A larger number of neurons and layers will increase the flexibility of the network introducing more weights. However, more flexibility can induce to an overfitting of the data, thus to a bad generalization of the network function.

The samples are divided in 75% training set, 15% validation set, and 15% testing set. For the analysis the datasets, weights and biases are initialized with same seed at every evaluation. The effect of changing the number of layers and neurons on the correlation coefficient R, MSE of the validation set and training time T_{train} is shown in Fig. 2. Increasing the number of layers and neurons improves the network performance up to certain number of layers and neurons (*peak*), after which the performance starts to degrade. As expected, the time required for the training process increases significantly as the depth of the network grows. The highest correlation coefficient and lowest validation-set MSE occur with number of layers of four and number of neurons of 80.

Different training algorithms and activation functions of the hidden layers are studied. As shown in Table 3, each of them induces some differences in the accuracy and the training speeds. Among the training algorithms, the Levenberg-Marquardt backpropagation offers the best performance at cost of a larger

Table 3. Effect of different values of the network parameters on its performance.

Training algorithm	R	Validation MSE	T_{train} [min]
Levenberg-Marquardt	0.9732	0.1211	59.79
Resilient back-propagation	0.9258	0.1598	2.39
Scaled conjugate gradient	0.9386	0.1467	4.67
Gradient descent	0.9205	0.1584	76.93
Activation function	R	Validation MSE	T_{train} [min]
tanh	0.9489	0.1609	34.31
sigmoid	0.9732	0.1211	59.79
ReLu	0.9210	0.2295	52.42

training time, while the sigmoid function performs better as activation function. For the chosen training algorithm, the gradient constant μ influences the state vector $\mathbf{x}$ as follows:

$$\mathbf{x}_{k+1} = \mathbf{x}_k - [\mathbf{J}^T\mathbf{J} + \mu\mathbf{I}]^{-1}\mathbf{J}^T\mathbf{e} \tag{10}$$

where $\mathbf{J}$ is the Jacobian matrix of the network error vector $\mathbf{e}$ with respect to the current k-th weights and biases. The initial value of μ is set to 0.001. When μ is large, the algorithm becomes a gradient descent with small step size. However, after each successful step (i.e., the cost function is reduced) μ is reduced of a decrease factor μ_{dec}. The closest μ is to zero, the more the algorithm moves towards the Newton's method, which has a faster convergence and is more accurate. The decrease factor is set equal to 0.1.

From the investigation of all the parameters the optimal structure of the network is defined and detailed in Table 2. As a verification, the algorithm is run again but this time using the optimal values as default values. The test confirms that the obtained values allow the network to achieve the highest performance, with correlation coefficient of 0.9732 and validation-set MSE of 0.1211.

4 Sequence Search

The sequence search identifies the most convenient sequences of asteroids. It starts at the Earth at a fixed departure date. Once the full NEA database is loaded, the asteroid ephemerides are updated at departure time $t_{0,i}$, with i indicating the ith leg of the sequence. The trained ANN is employed to calculate the cost and the TOF of transfers from the Earth to all the NEAs available in the database. Only $N_{max} = 200$ of the best transfers, in terms of largest number of objects visited with lower ΔV, are stored. To ensure close-up observation, a 100-days stay time is added at the arrival asteroid. At this point, the arrival asteroid becomes the departure asteroid of the following transfer, for which the same procedure is iterated, following a *tree-search method.* The sequence is complete when the total mission time reaches 10 years.

Table 4. Orbital characteristics of the NEAs visited in the optimized sequence.

Designation	2011 WU2	2014 WU200	2013 DA1	2004 FM32	2007 SQ6	2019 FU2
Classification	NHATS	NHATS	NHATS	NHATS	NHATS	PHA
a, AU	1.182	1.028	1.168	1.099	1.043	1.069
e, -	0.0439	0.0715	0.1365	0.1623	0.1456	0.1116
i, deg	3.02	1.27	1.89	3.76	9.10	7.79
Ω, deg	236.78	265.69	142.45	183.99	191.40	189.55
ω, deg	198.59	226.51	348.42	298.55	283.77	287.42
M, deg	341.04	43.17	290.34	66.42	224.21	82.30

Note: M is calculated at 2019/04/27

The departure date 01/01/2035 is chosen outside of the time frame used to build the network training database, so that the generalization property can be tested. In [16] it is shown that, in the context of the global optimization problem, using a trained ANN allows a faster evaluation of the best asteroid sequences. The algorithm is 25 times faster than other methodologies [10] previously used, where the same type of machine was used to compute the same search.

5 Tour of Multiple Asteroids

The sequence search algorithm identifies 200 asteroid sequences in less than 15 h. Once all the sequences have been characterized, one of the sequences that visits six asteroids, which are NHATS and at least one PHA, in 10 years is chosen to be fully optimized. The algorithm implements the OCP detailed in Sect. 2, optimizing the trajectory leg by leg. It requires an initial guess which is generated by solving a Lambert problem [2] and uses the departure and arrival orbits and TOF identified by the network. To allow for close-up observations and avoid overlapping between legs, a minimum stay time of 20 days is enforced. The OCP is solved by using a discrete NLP together with a variable-order adaptive Radau collocation method [9] and the NLP solver IPOPT [17].

The orbital characteristics of the encountered bodies are detailed in Table 4 for the selected sequence. The characteristics of the multiple NEA rendezvous mission are reported in Table 5. It presents the departure and arrival dates, the cost and TOF resulted from the optimization, in brackets the cost and TOF calculated by the ANN, and the stay time at each object.

To evaluate how well the network performs with respect to the optimization procedure, the values of ΔV and TOF from ANN are compared to the optimal ones. The deviation is quantified by calculating the average percentage error:

$$\mathcal{E}_{\Delta V} = \frac{1}{N}\sum_{i}^{N}\left(\frac{\Delta V_{opt} - \Delta V_{ANN}}{\Delta V_{opt}}\right) \cdot 100 = 2.19\% \qquad (11)$$

Table 5. Mission parameters of the optimized NEA sequence.

Leg	Departure Arrival	TOF [days]	ΔV [km/s]	Stay time [days]
Earth - 2011 WU2	2035/08/24	553	5.71	20
	2037/02/27	(503)	(4.96)	
2011 WU2 - 2014 WU200	2037/03/19	661	5.31	100
	2039/01/09	(631)	(4.87)	
2014 WU200 - 2013 DA1	2039/04/19	530	4.78	20
	2040/09/30	(580)	(4.92)	
2013 DA1 - 2004 FM32	2040/10/20	515	4.24	20
	2042/03/19	(518)	(4.28)	
2004 FM32 - 2007 SQ6	2042/04/09	637	5.27	20
	2044/01/06	(657)	(5.44)	
2007 SQ6 - 2019 FU2	2044/01/26	650	5.08	–
	2045/11/06	(670)	(4.23)	

(.) Results from ANN.

$$\mathcal{E}_{TOF} = \frac{1}{N}\sum_{i}^{N}\left(\frac{TOF_{opt} - TOF_{ANN}}{TOF_{opt}}\right) \cdot 100 = 4.97\% \tag{12}$$

with N being the number of legs in the trajectory.

The low average percentage error for both ΔV and TOF indicates that the network was able to learn the complicated non-linear relationship between the inputs (i.e., departure and arrival orbits and position of the bodies at a reference time) and outputs, which are an estimation of the cost and duration of the low-thrust transfer between these two orbits. Considering also the drastic reduction of computational time that ANN allows, it is possible to conclude that using ANN to search for preliminary multiple-asteroid rendezvous missions improves the speed of the search and guarantees a high accuracy of the results.

6 Conclusions

An artificial neural network is designed to estimate the cost and time of flight of transfers between asteroids with the final purpose of computing low-thrust tours of multiple asteroids. Tuning the architecture and hyper-parameters of the network as well as choosing the best inputs for this application is essential to optimize the network performance.

Employing an ANN within a sequence search algorithm offers a high accuracy with a relative error of less than 4% on average. In addition, it vastly improves the speed of the algorithm, reducing the computational time of 25 times.

To obtain the flight trajectory and control history, an optimal control problem needs to be solved. However, using this methodology allows to reduce the problem to solve the OCP only for the sequences of interest.

References

1. Betts, J.T.: Practical Methods for Optimal Control and Estimation Using Nonlinear Programming, 2nd edn. SIAM Press, Philadelphia (2010)
2. Curtis, H.: Orbital Mechanics for Engineering Students. Elsevier, Amsterdam (2005)
3. Dachwald, B.: Optimization of interplanetary solar sailcraft trajectories. J. Guid. Control Dyn. **27**(1), 66–72 (2004)
4. De Pascale, P., Vasile, M.: Preliminary design of low-thrust multiple gravity-assist trajectories. AIAA J. Spacecr. Rockets **43**(5), 1065–1076 (2006). https://doi.org/10.2514/1.19646
5. Hennes, D., Izzo, D., Landau, D.: Fast approximators for optimal low-thrust hops between main belt asteroids. In: IEEE Symposium Series on Computational Intelligence (SSCI) (2016). https://doi.org/10.1109/SSCI.2016.7850107
6. Kůrková, V.: Kolmogorov's theorem and multilayer neural networks. Neural Netw. **5**(3), 501–506 (1992). https://doi.org/10.1016/0893-6080(92)90012-8
7. Lissauer, J.J., de Parter, I.: Fundamental Planetary Science. Cambridge University Press, Cambridge (2013)
8. Mereta, A., Izzo, D., Wittig, A.: Machine learning of optimal low-thrust transfers between near-earth objects. In: Martínez de Pisón, F.J., Urraca, R., Quintián, H., Corchado, E. (eds.) HAIS 2017. LNCS (LNAI), vol. 10334, pp. 543–553. Springer, Cham (2017). https://doi.org/10.1007/978-3-319-59650-1_46
9. Patterson, M.A., Rao, A.V.: GPOPS-II: a MATLAB software for solving multiple-phase optimal control problems using hp-adaptive Gaussian quadrature collocation methods and sparse nonlinear programming. ACM Trans. Math. Softw. **41**(1) (2014). https://doi.org/10.1145/2558904
10. Peloni, A., Ceriotti, M., Dachwald, B.: Solar-sail trajectory design for a multiple near-earth-asteroid rendezvous mission. J. Guid. Control Dyn. **39**(12), 2712–2724 (2016). https://doi.org/10.2514/1.G000470
11. Peng, H., Bai, X.: Artificial neural network-based machine learning approach to improve orbit prediction accuracy. AIAA J. Spacecr. Rockets **55**(5), 1–13 (2018). https://doi.org/10.2514/1.A34171
12. Pontryagin, L.S., Boltyanskii, V.G., Gamkrelidze, R.V., Mishchenko, E.F.: The Mathematical Theory of Optimal Processes. Wiley, New York (1963)
13. Sánchez-Sánchez, C., Izzo, D.: Real-time optimal control via Deep Neural Networks: study on landing problems. J. Guid. Control Dyn. (3), 1122–1135. https://doi.org/10.1023/B:CJOP.0000010527.13037.22
14. Sims, J., Flanagan, S.: Preliminary design of low-thrust interplanetary missions. In: AAS/AIAA Astrodynamics Specialist Conference, AAS paper 99-0328 (1999)
15. Tang, G., Jiang, F., Li, J.: Trajectory optimization for low-thrust multiple asteroids rendezvous mission. In: AIAA/AAS Astrodynamics Specialist Conference (2015). https://doi.org/10.1515/jnum-2014-0003
16. Viavattene, G., Ceriotti, M.: Artificial neural network for preliminary multiple NEA rendezvous mission using low thrust. In: 70th International Astronautical Congress (IAC), Washington, D.C., USA (2019)
17. Wachter, A., Biegler, L.T.: On the implementation of an interior-point filter line-search algorithm for large-scale nonlinear programming. Math. Program. **106**(1), 25–57 (2006). https://doi.org/10.1007/s10107-004-0559-y
18. Wertz, J.R.: Orbit & Constellation Design & Management. Springer, Heidelberg (2009)
19. Wiesel, W.: Spaceflight Dynamics, 3rd edn. CreateSpace, Scotts Valley (2010)

Deep Learning for Scene Recognition from Visual Data: A Survey

Alina Matei, Andreea Glavan, and Estefanía Talavera(✉)

Bernoulli Institute for Mathematics, Computer Science and Artificial Intelligence, University of Groningen, Nijenborgh 9, 9747 AG Groningen, The Netherlands
e.talavera.martinez@rug.nl

Abstract. The use of deep learning techniques has exploded during the last few years, resulting in a direct contribution to the field of artificial intelligence. This work aims to be a review of the state-of-the-art in scene recognition with deep learning models from visual data. Scene recognition is still an emerging field in computer vision, which has been addressed from a single image and dynamic image perspective. We first give an overview of available datasets for image and video scene recognition. Later, we describe ensemble techniques introduced by research papers in the field. Finally, we give some remarks on our findings and discuss what we consider challenges in the field and future lines of research. This paper aims to be a future guide for model selection for the task of scene recognition.

Keywords: Scene recognition · Ensemble techniques · Deep learning · Computer vision

1 Introduction

Recognizing scenes is a task that humans do on a daily basis. When walking down the street and going from one location to the other, tends to be easy for a human to identify where s/he is located. During the past years, deep learning architectures, such as Convolutional Neural Networks (CNNs) have outperformed traditional methods in many classification tasks. These models have shown to achieve high classification performance when large and variety datasets are available for training. Nowadays, the available visual data is not only presented in a static format, as an image, but also in a dynamic format, as video recordings. The analysis of videos adds an additional level of complexity since the inherent temporal aspect of video recordings must be considered: a video can capture scenes which suffer temporal alterations. Scene recognition with deep learning has been addressed by ensemble techniques that combine different levels of semantics extracted from the images, e.g. recognized objects, global information, and context at different scales.

A. Matei and A. Glavan—Both authors contributed equally to this study.

E. A. de la Cal et al. (Eds.): HAIS 2020, LNAI 12344, pp. 763–773, 2020.
https://doi.org/10.1007/978-3-030-61705-9_64

Developing robust and reliable models for the automatic recognition of scenes is of importance in the field of intelligent systems and artificial intelligence since it directly supports real-life applications. For instance, *Scene and event recognition* has been previously addressed in the literature [1,29]. *Scene recognition for robot localization* with indoor localization for mobile robots is one of the emerging application scopes of scene recognition [2,5,21]. According to the authors of [21], in the following two decades, every household could own a social robot employed for housekeeping, surveillance or companionship tasks. In the field of lifelogging, collections of photo-sequences have proven to be a rich tool for the understanding of the behaviour of people. In [9,19] methods were develop for the analysis of egocentric image collected by wearable cameras. The above-mentioned approaches address the recognition of scenes either following an image-based approach or a video or photo-sequence based approach.

As contributions, (i) to the best of our knowledge, this is the first survey that collects works that address the task of scene recognition with deep learning from visual data, both from images and videos. Moreover, (ii) we describe available datasets which assisted the fast advancement in the field.

This paper is structured as follows: in Sect. 2 we discuss the available datasets supporting scene and object focused recognition. Section 3 addresses the methodology of the state-of-the-art techniques and approaches discussed in the paper at hand. Furthermore, in Sect. 4 we discuss the presented approaches. Finally, in Sect. 5 we draw some conclusions.

2 Datasets for Scene Recognition

The latest advancements in deep learning methods for scene recognition are motivated by the availability of large and exhaustive datasets and hardware that allows the training of deep networks. Thus, deep learning CNNs are applied to tackle the complexity and high variance of the task of scene recognition.

The inherent difficulty of scene recognition is related to the nature of the images depicting a scene context. Two major challenges were described in [30]:

- *Visual inconsistency* refers to low inter-class variance. Some scene categories can share similar visual appearances which create the issue of class overlaps. Since images belonging to two different classes can be easily confused with one another, the class overlap cannot be neglected.
- *Annotation ambiguity* describes a high intra-class variance of scene categories. Demarcation of the categories is a subjective process which is highly dependent on the experience of the annotators, therefore images from the same category can showcase significant differences in appearance.

The majority of the available datasets are focused on object categories providing labels [6,10,13,20], bounding boxes [15] or segmentations [15,18]. ImageNet [6], COCO (Common Objects in Context) [18], and Open Images [15] are well known in the field of object recognition. Even though these dataset were built

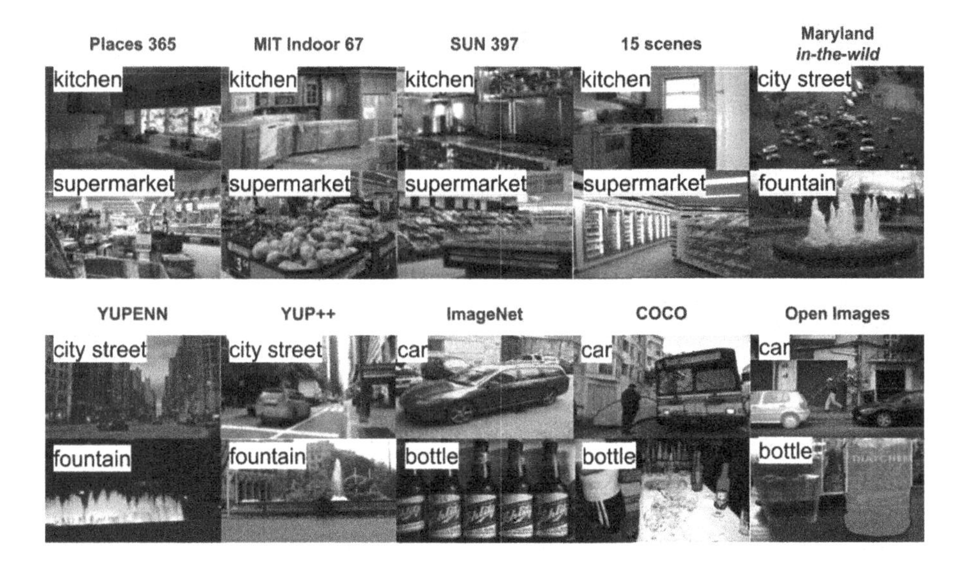

Fig. 1. Example of samples of the publicly available datasets as described in Table 1. Samples are presented from the same classes amongst similar datasets (i.e. scene, video and object centric) in order to emphasize the diversity of the image and video data. For the video-centric datasets (i.e. Maryland "in-the-wild", YUPENN, YUP++) representative video frames are presented.

for object recognition, transfer learning has shown to be an effective approach when aiming to apply them for scene recognition.

In the literature we can find the 15-scenes [16], MIT Indoor67 [23], SUN397 [32], and Places365 [35] as scene-centered datasets. More specifically, the Places project introduced Places365 as a reference dataset, which is composed of 434 scenes which account for 98% of the type of scenes a person can encounter in the natural and man-made world. A total of 10 million images were gathered, out of which 365 scene categories were chosen to be part of the dataset. Several annotators were asked to label every image and images with contradicting labels were discarded. Currently, the dataset is available in the Places365-standard format (i.e. 365 categories, roughly 1 million images training set, validation set with 50 images per class and test with 900 images per class) and the Places365-challenge format which extends the training set to 8 million image samples in total. With a dataset of this magnitude, the training of CNNs exclusively on data describing scenes becomes feasible.

Scene recognition also encloses dynamic scene data; due to the limited amount of available datasets which include such data, most of the research efforts in this sub-field also include gathering suitable experimental data. Here we highlight the Maryland 'in-the-wild' [24], YUPENN [7] , YUP++ [8] datasets. The dataset in [8] poses new challenges by introducing more complex data, i.e. videos with camera motion. The scope of the categories that are being recorded

Table 1. An overview of publicly available datasets for the task of scene recognition.

Dataset	Data	#Classes	Classification of		Labelled as	
			Images	Streams	Object	Scenes
Places365 [35]	1M images	365	✓			✓
MIT Indoor67 [23]	15620 images	67	✓			✓
SUN397 [32]	108754 images	397	✓			✓
15 scene [32]	4000 images	15	✓			✓
Maryland 'in-the-wild' [24]	10 videos	13		✓		✓
YUPENN [7]	410 videos	14		✓		✓
YUP++ [8]	1200 videos	20		✓		✓
Imagenet [6]	3.2M images	1000	✓		✓	
COCO [18]	1.5M images	80	✓		✓	
Open Images [15]	1.7M images	600	✓		✓	

amongst the three datasets presented is not nearly as exhaustive as in the case of the objects and scenes datasets mentioned above. This is an indicator of the incipient status of research in this particular area of scene recognition.

The original models proposed by the authors of the [24] and [7] datasets were not based on deep learning techniques. The authors of the Maryland 'in-the-wild' [24], introduced a chaotic system framework for describing the videos. The authors' proposed pipeline extracts a 960-dimensional Gist descriptor per videoframe. Each dimension is considered a time-series, from which the chaotic invariants are computed. Traditional classifiers, such as KNN and SVM, are used for the final classification. In [7], the authors introduced the YUPENN dataset and for its analysis, they proposed a spatiotemporal oriented energy feature representation of the videos which they classify using KNN.

An overview of the described datasets is provided in Table 1. In Fig. 1 we complete the quantitative overview of the datasets by presenting representative image samples for each of the datasets described.

3 Frameworks for Scene Recognition

In this section, we describe relevant aspects of the state-of-the-art methods on scene recognition with deep learning. The choice for deep architectures is motivated by the complexity of the task: since the images are not described semantically the models used are aimed at learning generic contextual features of the scenes, which are captured by the high-level convolutional layers.

Previous to deep learning, visual recognition techniques have made extensive use of object recognition when faced with such problems [4,17]. The scenes would be recognized based on exhaustive lists of objects identified in the scene. However, other challenges appear such as object detection and their high appearance variability. The combination of object detection and overall context recognition [28] showed promising results.

Focusing on deep learning research papers, we group them based on the type of the analysed datasets, images or videos. We present their performances and limitations in the context of the evaluated datasets.

3.1 Static Scene Recognition

Several works have addressed the recognition of scenes based on single image analysis. The best well-known work on scene recognition was introduced in [35], which relied on the Places365 dataset.

Table 2. Top-5 classification accuracy of the trained networks on the validation and test splits of the Places365 dataset. Apart from the ResNet architecture which has been fine-tuned over Places365, the other architectures are trained from scratch.

Architectures trained on Places365	Top-5 accuracy	
	Validation set	Test set
Places365 AlexNet [35]	82.89%	82.75%
Places365 GoogleNet [35]	83.88%	84.01%
Places365 VGG [35]	84.91%	85.01%
Places365 ResNet [35]	85.08%	85.07%

Deep learning architectures have been trained over the Places365 dataset. The approach proposed by the authors of literature [35] is to exploit the vast dataset at hand by training three popular CNNs architectures (i.e. AlexNet [14], GoogLeNet [26], VGG16 [25]) on the Places dataset. The performance of these architectures over the validation and test splits of the Places365 dataset are presented in Table 2. When introducing a new dataset, it became a ritual to test the generalization capabilities of weights trained over Places365. Thus, authors fine-tune these specialised networks trained on Places365 over newly available datasets. For instance, the VGG16 [25], pre-trained on the Places365 dataset, achieved a 92.99% accuracy on the SUN Attribute dataset [31]. To compare the performance of the above approaches for static scene recognition, the following datasets are considered: 15 scenes dataset [16], MIT Indoor 67 [23] and SUN 397 [32]. An overview of the comparison of the quantitative results is presented in Table 3.

Furthermore, in [11] the authors experimented with the ResNet152 residual network architecture, fine-tuned over the Places365. This work achieved a top-5 accuracy of 85.08% and 85.07% on the validation and, respectively, the test set of the Places365 dataset, as shown in Table 2.

The use of the semantic and contextual composition of the image has been proposed by various approaches. For instance, in [29], the authors proposed the Hybrid1365 VGG architecture, a combination of deep learning techniques trained for object and scene recognition. The method uses different scales at

Table 3. An overview of the quantitative comparison in terms of accuracy between methods for single image classification for the 15 scenes, MIT Indoor, SUN 397 datasets.

	15 scenes	MIT Indoor	SUN 397
Places365 AlexNet [35]	89.25%	70.72%	56.12%
Places365 GoogleNet[35]	91.25%	73.20%	58.37%
Places365 VGG [35]	91.97%	76.53%	**63.24%**
Hybrid1365 VGG [35]	**92.15%**	**79.49%**	61.77%
7-scale Hybrid VGG [12]	**94.08%**	80.22%	63.19%*
7-scale Hybrid AlexNet [12]	93.90%	**80.97%**	**65.38%**

which objects appear in a scene can facilitate the classification process by targeting distinct regions of interest within the image. Objects usually appear at lower scales. Therefore, the object classifier should target local scopes of the image. In contrast, the scene classifier should be aimed at the global scale, in order to capture contextual information. They concluded that it is possible to extend the performance obtained individually by each method. The Hybrid1365 VGG architecture [29] scores the highest average accuracy of 81.48% over all the experiments conducted for the place-centric CNN approach (has the highest performance for 2 out of 3 comparison datasets as shown in Table 3).

The dataset biases which arise under different scaling conditions of the images is addressed in [12], by involving a multi-scale model which combines various CNNs specialized either on object or place knowledge. The authors combined the training data available in the Places and ImageNet datasets. The knowledge learned from the two datasets is coupled in a scale-adaptive way. In order to aggregate the extracted features over the architectures used, simple max pooling[1] is adopted in order to down-sample the feature space. If the scaling operation is significant, the features of the data can drastically change from describing scene data to object data. The architectures are employed to extract features in parallel from patches, which represent the input image at increasingly larger scale versions. The multi-scale model combines several AlexNet architectures [14]. The hybrid multi-scale architecture uses distinctive models for different scale ranges; depending on the scale range, the most suitable model is chosen from object-centric CNN (pre-trained on ImageNet), scene-centric CNN (pre-trained on Places365) or a fine-tuned CNN (adapted to the corresponding scale based on the dataset at hand). In total, seven scales were considered; the scales were obtained by scaling the original images between 227 $\times$ 227 and 1827 $\times$ 1827 pixels. For the final classification given by the multi-scale hybrid approach, the concatenation of the fc7 features (i.e. features extracted by the 7th fully connected layer of the CNN) from the seven networks are considered. Principal

[1] Max pooling is a pooling operation which computes the maximum value in each patch of a feature map; it is employed for down-sampling input representations.

Component Analysis (PCA) is used to reduce the feature space. This model obtained the highest accuracy of 95.18% on the 15 scenes dataset [16].

The hybrid approaches presented in [29] and [12] achieve higher accuracy than a human expert, which was quantified as 70.60%. This indicates that the combination of object-centric and scene-centric knowledge can potentially establish a new performance standard for scene recognition.

3.2 Dynamic Scene Recognition

While early research in the field of scene recognition has been directed at single images, lately attention has been naturally drawn towards scene recognition from videos. CNNs have shown promising results for the general task of scene recognition in single images and have the potential to be also generalized to video data [33,34]. To achieve this generalization, the spatio-temporal nature of dynamic scenes must be considered. While static scenes (depicted as single images) only present spatial features, videos also capture temporal transformations which affect the spatial aspect of the scene. Therefore, one challenge related to the task of scene classification from videos is creating a model which is powerful enough to capture both the spatial and temporal information of the scene. However, there are few works on video analysis for scene recognition.

In the works introduced in [3,22], the authors relied on Long Short Term Memory networks (LSTMs) for video description. However, they did not focus on recognizing the scenes.

Table 4. Overview of the results achieved by the spatio-temporal residual network (T-ResNet) proposed in [8] over the YUP++ dataset.

	YUP++ static	YUP++ moving	YUP++ complete
ResNet	86.50%	73.50%	85.90%
T-ResNet	**92.41%**	**81.50%**	**89.00%**

In [8], the authors introduced the T-ResNet architecture, alongside the YUP++ dataset, which established a new benchmark in the sub-field of dynamic scene recognition. The T-ResNet is based on a residual network [27] that was pre-trained on the ImageNet dataset [6]. It employs transfer learning to adapt the spatial-centric residual architecture to a spatio-temporal-centric network. The results achieved by the architecture were only compared with the classical ResNet architecture as shown in Table 4. The superiority of the T-ResNet is evident: it achieves an accuracy of 92.41% on the YUP++ static camera partition, 81.50% on the YUP++ moving camera partition and finally 89.00% on the entire YUP++ dataset. This demonstrates the superiority of the spatio-temporal approach. The T-ResNet model exhibits strong performance for classes with linear motion patterns, e.g. classes 'elevator', 'ocean', 'windmill farm'. However, for scene categories presenting irregular or mixed defining motion patterns the performance is negatively impacted, e.g. classes 'snowing' and 'fireworks'. The authors of [8] observed that T-ResNet exhibits difficulties distinguishing intrinsic scene dynamics from the additional motion of the camera. Further research is required to account for this difference.

4 Discussion

The novel availability of large, exhaustive datasets, such as the Places Database, is offering significant support for further research for the challenge of scene recognition. The combination of scene-centric and object-centric knowledge has proven superior to only considering the scene context. Dynamic scene recognition reached new state-of-the-art performance through the approach of adapting spatial networks to the task, transforming the network to also consider the temporal aspect of the scenes. These emerging spatio-temporal networks are suitable for video data captured with a static camera. However, it still faces difficulties in the case of added camera motion.

One observation arising from methods addressing single image analysis scene recognition is that deeper CNN architectures such as GoogLeNet [26] or VGG [25] are not superior in all cases. For the hybrid multi-scale model combining scene-centric and object-centric networks in [12], experiments using VGG architecture for more than two-scales (two VGG networks) obtained disappointing results, inferior to the baseline performance achieved with one single scale (one network). Since the multi-scale hybrid model entails seven different scales, it can be inferred that VGG becomes noisy when applied on small input image patches.

Addressing the task of scene recognition from the global features that describe an image, the CNNs are expected to learn deep features that are relevant for the contextual clues present in the image. Literature [35] observers that the low-level convolutional layers detect low-level visual concepts such as object edges and textures, while the high-level layers activate on entire objects and scene parts. Even though the model has been previously trained on an exclusively places-centric dataset, the network still identifies semantic clues in the image by detecting objects alongside contextual clues. Therefore, CNNs trained on the Places Database (which does not contain object labels) could still be employed for object detection.

Another aspect arising from training the same architecture on datasets with a different number of scene categories (i.e. and Places365) proves that having more categories leads to better results as well as more predicted categories. We can observe that the architecture AlexNet trained on Places205 (version prior to Places365) obtains 57.2% accuracy, while the same architecture trained on Places365 obtains 57.7% accuracy. For the places CNN approach two main types of miss-classifications occur: on one hand, less-typical activities happening in a scene context (e.g. taking a photo at a construction site) and on the other hand, images depicting multiple scene parts. A possible solution, as proposed by [35], would be assigned multiple ground-truth labels in order to capture the content of an image more precisely.

The results achieved by the T-ResNet model illustrate the potential of spatio-temporal networks for video analysis. The transformation from a purely spatial network to a spatio-temporal one can succeed on the basis of a very small training set (i.e. only 10% of the YUP++ dataset introduced) as proven by [8]. Well-initialized spatial networks can be efficiently transformed to extract spatio-temporal features, therefore, in theory, most networks that perform well on single image analysis could be easily adapted to video analysis.

5 Conclusions

In this work, we describe the state-of-the-art on deep learning for scene recognition. Furthermore, we presented some of the applications of scene recognition to emphasize the importance of this topic. We argue that the main factor to consider is the type of data on which recognition and classification are applied. Since the task of scene recognition is not entirely subjective due to the nature of the scene images and the scene categories overlap, no one particular method can be generalized to all scene recognition tasks. This paper will aid professionals in making an informed decision about which approach best fits their scene recognition challenge. We have found room for research in the field of video analysis and expect that numerous works will emerge in the coming years.

References

1. Bacha, S., Allili, M.S., Benblidia, N.: Event recognition in photo albums using probabilistic graphical models and feature relevance. J. Vis. Commun. Image Represent. **40**, 546–558 (2016)
2. Baumgartl, H., Buettner, R.: Development of a highly precise place recognition module for effective human-robot interactions in changing lighting and viewpoint conditions. In: Proceedings of the 53rd Hawaii International Conference on System Sciences (2020)
3. Bin, Y., Yang, Y., Shen, F., Xie, N., Shen, H.T., Li, X.: Describing video with attention-based bidirectional LSTM. IEEE Trans. Cybern. **49**(7), 2631–2641 (2018)
4. Bosch, A., Muñoz, X., Martí, R.: Which is the best way to organize/classify images by content? Image Vis. Comput. **25**(6), 778–791 (2007)
5. Chaves, D., Ruiz-Sarmiento, J.R., Petkov, N., Gonzalez-Jimenez, J.: Integration of CNN into a robotic architecture to build semantic maps of indoor environments. In: Rojas, I., Joya, G., Catala, A. (eds.) IWANN 2019. LNCS, vol. 11507, pp. 313–324. Springer, Cham (2019). https://doi.org/10.1007/978-3-030-20518-8_27
6. Deng, J., Dong, W., Socher, R., Li, L.J., Li, K., Fei-Fei, L.: ImageNet: a large-scale hierarchical image database. In: 2009 IEEE Conference on Computer Vision and Pattern Recognition, pp. 248–255. IEEE (2009)
7. Derpanis, K.G., Lecce, M., Daniilidis, K., Wildes, R.P.: Dynamic scene understanding: the role of orientation features in space and time in scene classification. In: IEEE Conference on Computer Vision and Pattern Recognition, pp. 1306–1313 (2012)

8. Feichtenhofer, C., Pinz, A., Wildes, R.P.: Temporal residual networks for dynamic scene recognition. In: Proceedings of the IEEE Conference on Computer Vision and Pattern Recognition, pp. 4728–4737 (2017)
9. Furnari, A., Farinella, G.M., Battiato, S.: Temporal segmentation of egocentric videos to highlight personal locations of interest. In: Hua, G., Jégou, H. (eds.) ECCV 2016. LNCS, vol. 9913, pp. 474–489. Springer, Cham (2016). https://doi.org/10.1007/978-3-319-46604-0_34
10. Griffin, G., Holub, A., Perona, P.: Caltech-256 object category dataset (2007)
11. He, K., Zhang, X., Ren, S., Sun, J.: Deep residual learning for image recognition. In: Proceedings of the IEEE Conference on Computer Vision and Pattern Recognition, pp. 770–778 (2016)
12. Herranz, L., Jiang, S., Li, X.: Scene recognition with CNNs: objects, scales and dataset bias. In: Proceedings of the IEEE Conference on Computer Vision and Pattern Recognition, pp. 571–579 (2016)
13. Krizhevsky, A., Hinton, G., et al.: Learning multiple layers of features from tiny images (2009)
14. Krizhevsky, A., Sutskever, I., Hinton, G.E.: ImageNet classification with deep convolutional neural networks. In: Advances in Neural Information Processing Systems, pp. 1097–1105 (2012)
15. Kuznetsova, A., et al.: The open images dataset v4: unified image classification, object detection, and visual relationship detection at scale. IJCV (2020)
16. Lazebnik, S., Schmid, C., Ponce, J.: Beyond bags of features: spatial pyramid matching for recognizing natural scene categories. In: 2006 IEEE Computer Society Conference on Computer Vision and Pattern Recognition (CVPR 2006), vol. 2, pp. 2169–2178. IEEE (2006)
17. Li, L.-J., Su, H., Lim, Y., Fei-Fei, L.: Objects as attributes for scene classification. In: Kutulakos, K.N. (ed.) ECCV 2010. LNCS, vol. 6553, pp. 57–69. Springer, Heidelberg (2012). https://doi.org/10.1007/978-3-642-35749-7_5
18. Lin, T.-Y., et al.: Microsoft COCO: common objects in context. In: Fleet, D., Pajdla, T., Schiele, B., Tuytelaars, T. (eds.) ECCV 2014. LNCS, vol. 8693, pp. 740–755. Springer, Cham (2014). https://doi.org/10.1007/978-3-319-10602-1_48
19. Martinez, E.T., Leyva-Vallina, M., Sarker, M.K., Puig, D., Petkov, N., Radeva, P.: Hierarchical approach to classify food scenes in egocentric photo-streams. IEEE J. Biomed. Health Inform. **24**, 866–877 (2019)
20. Nene, S.A., Nayar, S.K., Murase, H., et al.: Columbia object image library (1996)
21. Othman, K.M., Rad, A.B.: An indoor room classification system for social robots via integration of CNN and ECOC. Appl. Sci. **9**(3), 470 (2019)
22. Peris, Á., Bolaños, M., Radeva, P., Casacuberta, F.: Video description using bidirectional recurrent neural networks. In: Villa, A.E.P., Masulli, P., Pons Rivero, A.J. (eds.) ICANN 2016. LNCS, vol. 9887, pp. 3–11. Springer, Cham (2016). https://doi.org/10.1007/978-3-319-44781-0_1
23. Quattoni, A., Torralba, A.: Recognizing indoor scenes. In: 2009 IEEE Conference on Computer Vision and Pattern Recognition, pp. 413–420. IEEE (2009)
24. Shroff, N., Turaga, P., Chellappa, R.: Moving vistas: exploiting motion for describing scenes. In: 2010 IEEE Computer Society Conference on Computer Vision and Pattern Recognition, pp. 1911–1918. IEEE (2010)
25. Simonyan, K., Zisserman, A.: Very deep convolutional networks for large-scale image recognition. arXiv preprint arXiv:1409.1556 (2014)
26. Szegedy, C., et al.: Going deeper with convolutions. In: Proceedings of the IEEE Conference on Computer Vision and Pattern Recognition, pp. 1–9 (2015)

27. Thorpe, M., van Gennip, Y.: Deep limits of residual neural networks. arXiv preprint arXiv:1810.11741 (2018)
28. Viswanathan, P., Southey, T., Little, J., Mackworth, A.: Place classification using visual object categorization and global information. In: 2011 Canadian Conference on Computer and Robot Vision, pp. 1–7. IEEE (2011)
29. Wang, L., Wang, Z., Du, W., Qiao, Y.: Object-scene convolutional neural networks for event recognition in images. In: CVPR, ChaLearn Looking at People (LAP) challenge (2015)
30. Wang, L., Guo, S., Huang, W., Xiong, Y., Qiao, Y.: Knowledge guided disambiguation for large-scale scene classification with multi-resolution CNNs. IEEE Trans. Image Process. **26**(4), 2055–2068 (2017)
31. Xiao, J., Ehinger, K.A., Hays, J., Torralba, A., Oliva, A.: SUN database: exploring a large collection of scene categories. Int. J. Comput. Vis. **119**(1), 3–22 (2014). https://doi.org/10.1007/s11263-014-0748-y
32. Xiao, J., Hays, J., Ehinger, K.A., Oliva, A., Torralba, A.: Sun database: large-scale scene recognition from abbey to zoo. In: 2010 IEEE Computer Society Conference on Computer Vision and Pattern Recognition, pp. 3485–3492. IEEE (2010)
33. Xu, Z., Yang, Y., Hauptmann, A.G.: A discriminative CNN video representation for event detection. In: Proceedings of the IEEE Conference on Computer Vision and Pattern Recognition, pp. 1798–1807 (2015)
34. Yue-Hei Ng, J., Hausknecht, M., Vijayanarasimhan, S., Vinyals, O., Monga, R., Toderici, G.: Beyond short snippets: deep networks for video classification. In: Proceedings of the IEEE Conference on Computer Vision and Pattern Recognition, pp. 4694–4702 (2015)
35. Zhou, B., Lapedriza, A., Khosla, A., Oliva, A., Torralba, A.: Places: a 10 million image database for scene recognition. IEEE Trans. Pattern Anal. Mach. Intell. **40**, 1452–1464 (2017)

Cost-Efficiency of Convolutional Neural Networks for High-Dimensional EEG Classification

Javier León[1(✉)], Andrés Ortiz[2], Miguel Damas[1], Jesús González[1], and Julio Ortega[1]

[1] Department of Computer Architecture and Technology, University of Granada, Granada, Spain
jaleon@correo.ugr.es, {mdamas,jesusgonzalez,jortega}@ugr.es

[2] Department of Communications Engineering, University of Málaga, Málaga, Spain
aortiz@ic.uma.es

Abstract. Deep learning approaches have been at the forefront of machine learning problem-solving for the last decade. Although computationally more intensive than traditional techniques, the performance of artificial neural networks has justified their adoption for a wide array of applications. However, for small and high-dimensional datasets the large amount of learnable parameters is often a disadvantage. In this situation, the relationship between model complexity and quality gains relevance, since overfitting issues play a more central role. This is the case for Electroencephalography (EEG) classification, where it is usual to only have a small number of trials comprised of many electrode readings. In this paper, we optimize three Convolutional Neural Networks (CNNs) of different depths and evaluate them on three EEG Motor Imagery (MI) datasets in terms of classification accuracy, while also paying close attention to time consumption. The results show that the shallower ones tend to perform better at a lower cost than the deeper ones, which suggests that efforts in the direction of cost-saving may be aligned with model accuracy for small, high-dimensional datasets such as those often found in EEG.

Keywords: Convolutional Neural Networks · Brain-Computer Interfaces · Electroencephalography · Cost analysis

1 Introduction

Electroencephalography (EEG), along with other applications in the field of bioinformatics, often deals with high-dimensional datasets and a great scarcity of training samples since the process of data acquisition is cumbersome: Brain-Computer Interface (BCI) subjects are required to repeatedly perform tasks so that the brain activity associated with those tasks can be recorded. Motor Imagery (MI), the focus of this paper, works with data from imagined movements.

E. A. de la Cal et al. (Eds.): HAIS 2020, LNAI 12344, pp. 774–785, 2020.
https://doi.org/10.1007/978-3-030-61705-9_65

Deep learning approaches to EEG classification have been fairly common in recent years. Various kinds of neural networks are employed in the state-of-the-art; for instance, Feed-Forward neural Networks (FFNNs) can be found in [8], Convolutional Neural Networks (CNNs) in [2,3,17], Recurrent Neural Networks (RNNs) in [19], and a recurrent-convolutional hybrid in [18].

However, a large part of the research efforts is devoted only to the improvement of classification accuracy, in search of reliable enough frameworks to open up the possibility of real-world solutions. As a consequence, efficiency concerns tend to be relegated to the background, if they are even mentioned at all. In [18], the authors assess the choice between two models of similar accuracy by means of a real-time experiment where the bigger model has a delay of 2.5 seconds, against 1.4 of the smaller one. This highlights the need to also consider practicality, because prohibitive operational times and costs are as much of a disadvantage as poor accuracy. While there are many ways to tackle cost-saving, this paper looks at the accuracy-cost trade-off of different CNN depths in the context of EEG classification, with small and high-dimensional training sets where the curse of dimensionality [16] is likely to occur. We optimize the hyperparameters of three CNNs of fixed structure using a Genetic Algorithm (GA) and analyze their differences in accuracy, size, and training time.

The remaining sections are organized as follows: Sect. 2 describes the datasets; Sect. 3 explains the CNN model, the optimization procedure, the performance measurements, and the statistical analysis; Sect. 4 presents and discusses the experimental results; finally, the conclusions drawn from this work can be found in Sect. 5.

2 The Datasets

In the present paper, three EEG datasets are used to evaluate the accuracy and cost of the three CNN alternatives. The datasets, corresponding to three subjects (104, 107, and 110), were recorded in the BCI Laboratory of the University of Essex, UK [4]. A total of 12 healthy subjects between 24 and 50 years old (58% female, half of them naïve to BCI) were recruited for the experiment. The subjects gave their written informed consent before the experiment and were paid for their participation.

The EEG data corresponds to the MI paradigm, which takes advantage of the brief amplifications and attenuations (Event-Related Desynchronization and Synchronization, respectively), that limb movement imagination produces. 15 electrodes were used to record EEG trials (placement shown in Fig. 1) at a sampling rate of 256 Hz. These trials were used to build patterns through a type of Multiresolution Analysis [11], the Discrete Wavelet Transform, as seen in [4].

To build each pattern, the signal obtained from each electrode was divided into 20 consecutive and partially overlapping segments. For every segment, MRA was performed with 6 wavelet levels to produce sets of coefficients. These sets are of two types, approximation and details, and have decreasing size in powers of two (128, 64, 32, 16, 8, and 4 coefficients for levels 6 to 1). In total, an EEG

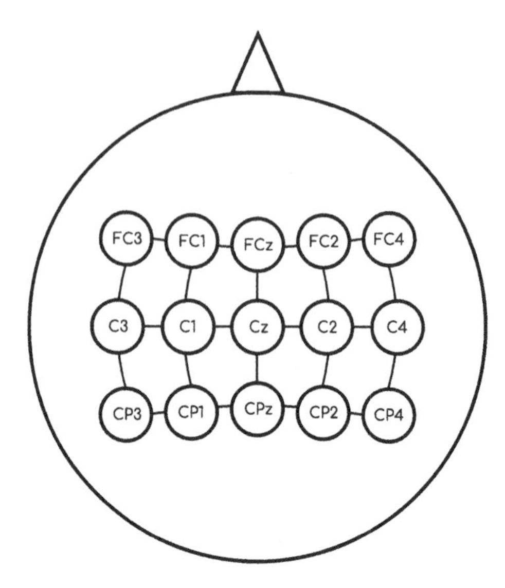

Fig. 1. Electrode placement in the extension of the International 10–20 system.

pattern has $2 \times S \times E \times L$ sets of coefficients, where S indicates the number of segments, E is the number of electrodes, and L is the number of wavelet levels. Therefore, with $S = 20$, $E = 15$, and $L = 6$, there are $3,600$ sets of coefficients and a total of $151,200$ coefficients. This number can be reduced to $3,600$ coefficients by computing the within-set variance [4]. The resulting patterns are also normalized between 0 and 1, with no missing values present.

For each of the three datasets, there are 178 patterns available for training, and a further 178 for testing, with every one of them containing $3,600$ features. The datasets have three balanced classes that correspond to imagined left and right hand movements and imagined feet movement.

3 Methodology

3.1 Convolutional Neural Networks and Structure Optimization

Whereas the CNN shares the standard fully-connected layers with other types of networks such as FFNN, its main element is the convolution operator. The convolution operator takes two functions and outputs a third one. In this paper, the one-dimensional finite discrete convolution ($\star$), defined in Eq. 1 and depicted in Fig. 2, is used.

$$H[i] = \sum_{u=-k}^{k} F[u] \cdot G[i-u], \forall i \in \{1, ..., n\}, \tag{1}$$

where H is the result of the convolution of F and G ($F \star G$), i is an index pointing to discrete values, and n represents the size of G. In the context of CNNs, G can be seen as an input vector and F as a convolutional filter.

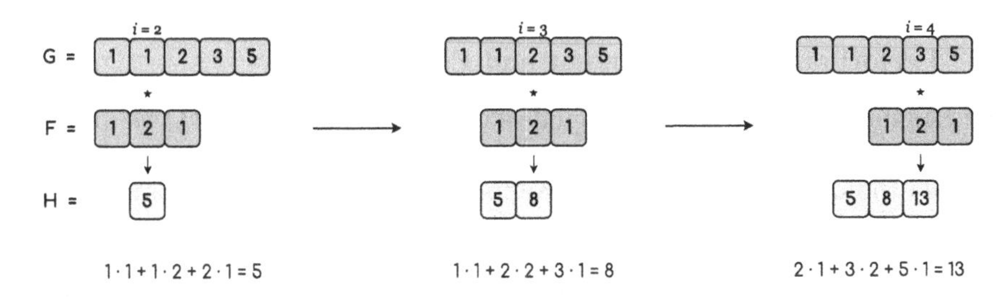

Fig. 2. Illustration of 1-D convolution. A filter of size 3 is convolved with each element of the top row to produce the bottom row. Border values are ignored.

In practice, the aim of using convolutional layers is to hierarchically process the input in different levels of detail, so that the network can find useful abstractions that generalize well to unseen data. The convolutional filters applied to the inputs have parameters that are learned during the training stage. Pooling layers, which summarize the input by regions (size can be tuned), are used with the goal of reducing dimensionality and adding translation invariance.

An overview of a CNN with one convolutional layer can be seen in Fig. 3.

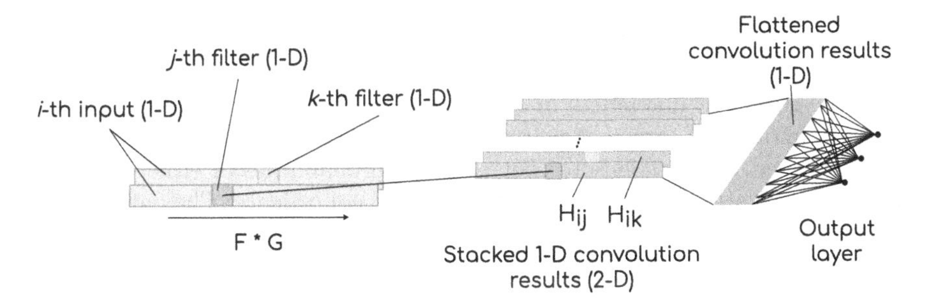

Fig. 3. Several filters are applied on a 1-D input, creating a 2-D stack of convolution results. This data structure is then transformed back into 1-D before the fully-connected output layer.

The structure of each one of the three CNNs considered in this paper is optimized by finding two values for every convolutional layer: the number of filters, and the size of the filters. The parameters of the pooling layers are kept fixed. The optimization is carried out by a GA, which performs an iterative search using a population of candidate parameter combinations that compete through a set number of generations on the basis of a certain fitness measure (in this case, cross-validation as defined in Sect. 3.2). Parent selection is done by binary tournament and population replacement is elitist. For more details on GAs and evolutionary computation in general, refer to [12].

3.2 Performance Measurement and Estimation

The classification accuracy of the models is evaluated according to two different performance measures: 5-fold cross-validation accuracy is used inside the GA to guide the optimization, and the Kappa coefficient is used to compare final models to each other:

- Cross-validation accuracy: the training set is split into n partitions, iteratively using $n-1$ of them for model training and the remaining one for testing. The final value is the average of the n test accuracies, with a range of possible values of $[0, 1]$.
- Cohen's Kappa coefficient [10]: it is similar to the accuracy metric, but it also takes into account the possibility of correctly classifying by chance. It is computed as:

$$\kappa = \frac{p_0 - p_c}{1 - p_c}, \tag{2}$$

where p_0 is the measured accuracy, and p_c is the sum of the probabilities of random agreement for all possible classes. The range of values is $[-1, 1]$.

3.3 Analysis of Results

Since there are three alternatives, a Friedman test [13] is performed to know if there are significant differences in quality among them.

Then, in order to carry out pairwise comparisons, the Bayesian Signed-Rank test [5] is used, which computes not only the probabilities of either algorithm prevailing, but also the probability of a practical equivalence. The output of the test is displayed as a point cloud in barycentric coordinates within a triangle, where each vertex is associated with a possibility (i.e., one of them wins, the other one wins, or they are equivalent). The closer the point cloud is to a vertex, the higher the probability given to that possibility.

More formally, the test calculates the distribution (assumed to be a Dirichlet distribution) of a parameter z. Let A and B be the sets of measurements of two alternatives. By counting the occurrences in the sample of $b - a > 0$, $b - a < 0$, and $b - a \approx 0$, where a and b are elements of A and B, the test is able to build a Dirichlet distribution. $b - a \approx 0$ represents the Region of Practical Equivalence (rope), which contains non-significant differences within the interval $[\text{rope}_{\text{min}}, \text{rope}_{\text{max}}]$. The distribution is then sampled to obtain triplets of the form shown in Eq. 3:

$$[P(z < \text{rope}_{\text{min}}), P(z \in \text{rope}), P(z > \text{rope}_{\text{max}})]. \tag{3}$$

The elements of these triplets are treated as barycentric coordinates, so that every triplet can be seen as a point in the aforementioned triangle.

4 Experimental Results

4.1 Experimental Setup

The code was written in *Python 3.4.9*. Some of the state-of-the-art machine learning libraries available for the language are used here: *Scikit-Learn 0.19.2* [15], *NumPy 1.14.5* [14], and *TensorFlow 1.10.1* [1] as a backend for *Keras 2.2.2* [9]. The Friedman test is provided by the R library `scmamp` [6]. Bayesian tests are implemented in the R library `rNPBST` [7].

The experiments have been carried out on a cluster node with the following hardware specifications:

- Intel® Xeon® E5-2620 v4 @ 2.10 GHz: 16 cores/32 threads and a Thermal Design Power (TDP) of 85 W.
- NVIDIA TITAN Xp: 3,840 CUDA cores, 12 GB of GDDR5X RAM memory, and a TDP of 250 W.

No feature selection is performed as a previous step, and thus the CNNs work with 3,600 features per dataset. The GA uses, in all cases, 40 individuals evolved through 10 generations. Selection is done by binary tournament, replacement is elitist, and fitness evaluation uses 5-fold cross-validation of networks trained for 25 epochs. Initialization is done by sampling from a normal distribution centered at the middle of the allowed value ranges.

The individuals of the population contain two values for each convolutional layer: number of convolutional filters and filter size. All convolutional layers use *ReLU* activation. Recombination is done by Single-point crossover, where a cutoff point divides the parents into two halves and the offspring inherits one half from each parent. The mutation operator multiplies each element of the individual by a value sampled from a Gaussian distribution centered at 1.

The experiments have been repeated 5 times for each structure alternative and dataset to enable statistical analysis.

4.2 Results

In order to analyze the effect of depth in model accuracy and cost, three different structures are compared: CNN-1L, which has one convolutional layer; CNN-2L, which has two convolutional layers, each followed by a Max Pooling layer; and CNN-3L, which has three convolutional layers, all of them followed by a Max Pooling layer. The three alternatives also have the standard input layer, with 3,600 units, and output layer, which is a fully connected softmax layer for three-class classification. Table 1 holds average and peak values obtained in the three datasets. Figure 4 depicts this information.

Table 1. Test-set Kappa comparison for CNN-1L, CNN-2L, and CNN-3L. SD: Standard Deviation.

Dataset	Measure	CNN-1L	CNN-2L	CNN-3L
104	Avg. ± SD	0.7431 ± 0.0098	0.6462 ± 0.0150	0.6574 ± 0.0161
	Best	0.7550	0.6678	0.6789
107	Avg. ± SD	0.7274 ± 0.0094	0.6596 ± 0.0095	0.5676 ± 0.0183
	Best	0.7390	0.6715	0.5959
110	Avg. ± SD	0.6595 ± 0.0075	0.6580 ± 0.0045	0.6259 ± 0.0141
	Best	0.6713	0.6629	0.6378

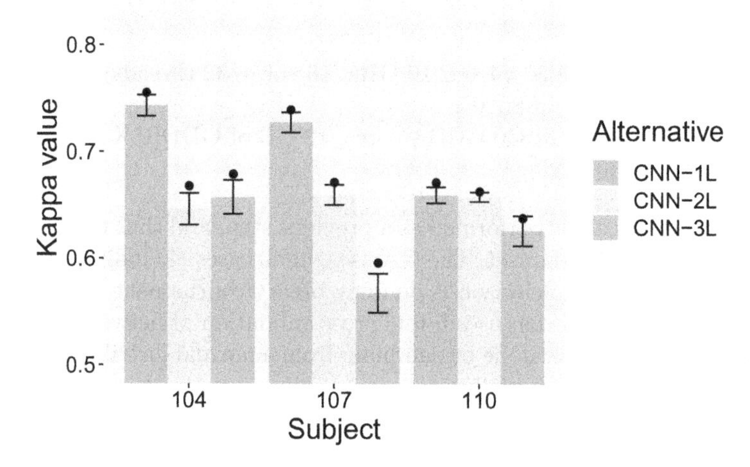

Fig. 4. Comparison of test-set Kappa values for CNN-1L, CNN-2L, and CNN-3L.

As can be seen, CNN-1L, which is the shallowest of the three, achieves by far the highest accuracy. The other two are somewhat comparable, although there is a wide gap between them in dataset 107. The difference between CNN-1L and the rest can be attributed to the presence of overfitting for CNN-2L and CNN-3L, since the training examples are vastly outnumbered by the features and a general decline in quality is observed as the depth increases. However, it is also worth mentioning that the Max Pooling layers inserted after the convolutional layers in CNN-2L and CNN-3L may have also affected quality in a significant way: their use is widespread when building deep CNNs, but it does not mean that they are always useful.

The Friedman test, predictably, finds statistically significant differences ($p = 6.773 \cdot 10^{-5}$) among the three alternatives. The post-hoc pairwise Bayesian Signed-Rank tests (posterior probabilities in Table 2 and heatmaps in Fig. 5) confirm the major differences already observed. The probability of CNN-1L being worse than CNN-2L or CNN-3L is deemed null, as the test does the calculations based on the available data, which contains no instances of CNN-1L losing to them. This is represented in Figures 5a and 5b by two point clouds compressed against the right border. The comparison between CNN-2L and CNN-3L also assigns a considerable advantage to CNN-2L, but, as illustrated by Fig. 5c, the outcome is not entirely one-sided.

Table 2. Probabilities calculated by the Bayesian Signed-Rank test for the pairwise comparisons. In each pair, the first alternative corresponds to a, and the second to b.

Comparison	$P(b - a < 0)$	$P(b - a \approx 0)$	$P(b - a > 0)$
CNN-2L vs. CNN-1L	0.000	0.203	0.797
CNN-3L vs. CNN-1L	0.000	0.070	0.930
CNN-3L vs. CNN-2L	0.068	0.216	0.716

According to classification accuracy alone, the conclusions suggested by the data are straightforward: CNN-1L, the shallowest of the CNNs analyzed here, is the best. Moreover, depending on the particular dataset, some doubts could exist in the choice between CNN-2L and CNN-3L, but overall the former seems to perform better. Nonetheless, as stated previously in this paper, the cost of the models is another relevant factor to consider. For instance, see Table 3, where the average running times of the optimization algorithm is displayed. As readily observed, each alternative needs on average a distinct amount of time to be completed. If the above were not enough to pick one between CNN-2L or CNN-3L, Table 3 could also be used to support CNN-2L, given that it is roughly 14% cheaper than CNN-3L. The contrast could be further accentuated when talking about energy consumption, owing to factors such as the differences in continued device usage over time for the duration of the evaluated procedures.

In addition to comparing proposals, it is also possible to look into the variance of the solutions pertaining to the same proposal. In particular, the question of whether a narrow neural network can compete with a wide one is legitimate, because neural networks are known to be strongly affected by initialization. Just as valid as looking for competitive, shallower networks is looking for competitive, narrower networks. Although no universal guideline exists, these options are worth exploring for economic, environmental, or purely practical reasons.

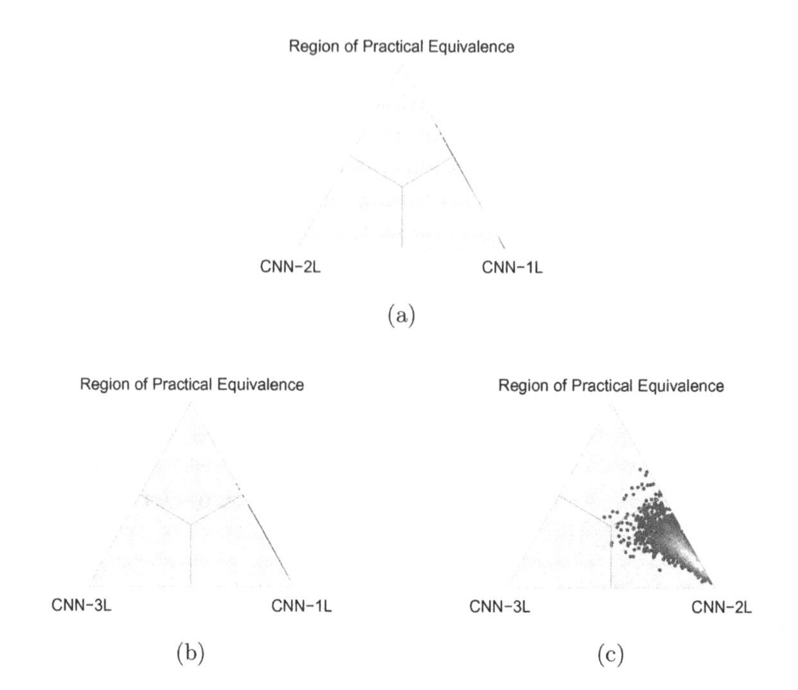

Fig. 5. Heatmaps for the Bayesian pairwise comparisons of the three alternatives. a) CNN-2L and CNN-1L. b) CNN-3L and CNN-1L. c) CNN-3L and CNN-2L. The left vertex is associated with $b - a < 0$, the right vertex with $b - a > 0$, and the top vertex with $b - a \approx 0$. 2,000 points sampled from the Dirichlet distribution. Red means lower density, and brighter colors reflect higher densities. (Color figure online)

Table 3. Average time consumption for CNN-1L, CNN-2L, and CNN-3L. SD: Standard Deviation.

Alternative	Time (s) ± SD
CNN-1L	$5,237 \pm 167$
CNN-2L	$7,207 \pm 387$
CNN-3L	$8,386 \pm 427$

In this case, Figs. 6, 7, and 8 exemplify how there does not appear to be a clear direct relationship between wider CNNs and more quality. For CNN-1L, Fig. 6 displays such a trend for dataset 104, but not for datasets 107 and 110, where a pattern cannot be identified; in fact, the best CNN-1L solution for dataset 110 is the second narrowest network. The same can be said about CNN-2L (Fig. 7), which shows many of the solutions with a similar performance and even one outlier with very few convolutional filters. In Fig. 8, CNN-3L is no

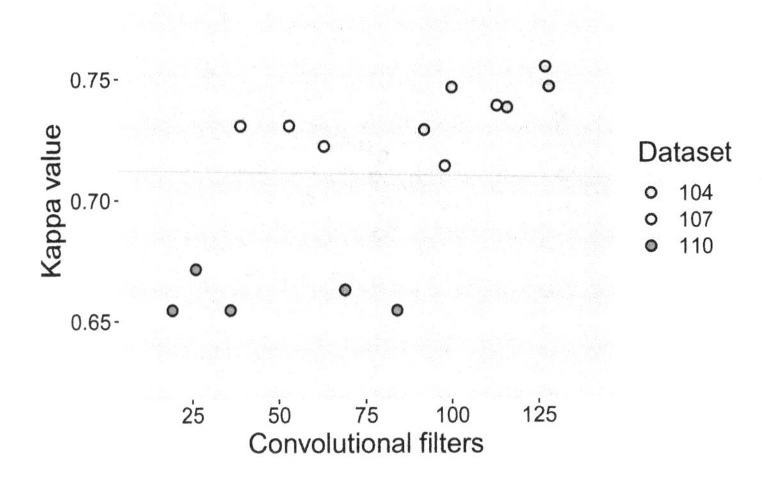

Fig. 6. Test-set Kappa values against amount of convolutional filters in CNN-1L.

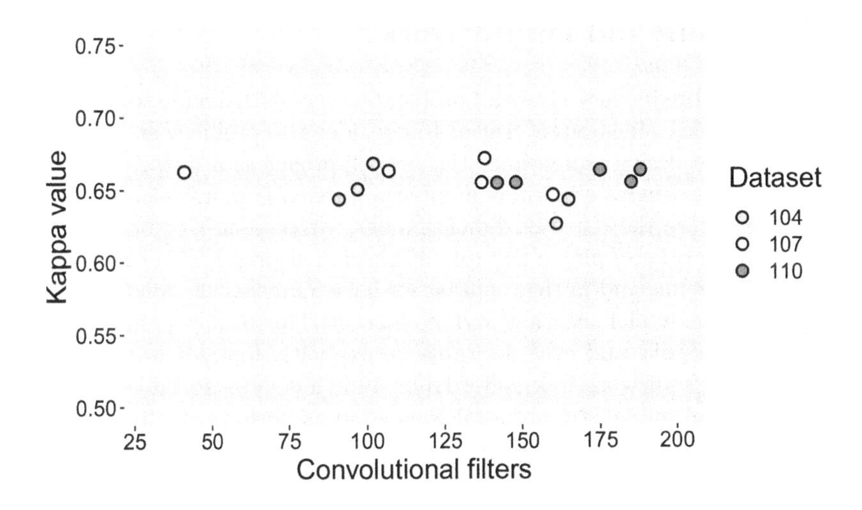

Fig. 7. Test-set Kappa values against amount of convolutional filters in CNN-2L.

exception, with the best solutions for each dataset being predominantly in the middle to lower size range for each dataset.

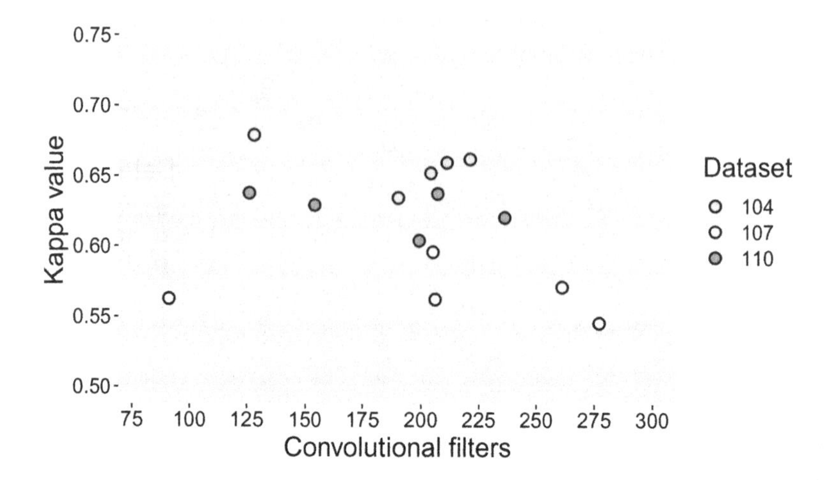

Fig. 8. Test-set Kappa values against amount of convolutional filters in CNN-3L.

5 Conclusions and Future Work

CNNs are undoubtedly very powerful problem solvers with a wide scope of application. Nevertheless, it is often crucial to consider the problem at hand at the time of structure design: sometimes the best approach is a deep network, but some other times a more efficiency-oriented approach is more beneficial. There are problems where the curse of dimensionality, or economic or environmental concerns (among others) play a key role. High-dimensional EEG classification is one of such problems, and in that context we have analyzed the relationship and trade-offs between model accuracy and model cost. This has brought to light the fact that it is possible, and even desirable, to explicitly look for ways to make a problem-solving framework more affordable, and thus more suitable for the real world. Because an unrealistic proposal is as good as nothing at all.

There are shortcomings to this work that could be tackled in the future work. The conclusions that can be drawn from this kind of analysis would be better supported with a larger scale in the number of datasets, network structures compared, and repetitions. Energy consumption could be a very informative addition. An assessment of the influence of pooling layers would enrich the discussion on CNNs as well. A comparison with classic machine learning algorithms would also serve as a baseline for the potential of CNNs. Lastly, this could be generalized to other types of neural networks that are common lately in EEG classification, such as RNNs.

Acknowledgements. This work was supported by projects PGC2018-098813-B-C31 and PGC2018-098813-B-C32 (Spanish "Ministerio de Ciencia, Innovación y Universidades"), and by European Regional Development Funds (ERDF).

References

1. Abadi, M., et al.: TensorFlow: large-scale machine learning on heterogeneous systems (2015). https://www.tensorflow.org/guide
2. Acharya, U.R., Oh, S.L., Hagiwara, Y., Tan, J.H., Adeli, H.: Deep convolutional neural network for the automated detection and diagnosis of seizure using EEG signals. Comput. Biol. Med. **100**, 270–278 (2018)
3. Amin, S.U., Alsulaiman, M., Muhammad, G., Mekhtiche, M.A., Shamim Hossain, M.: Deep Learning for EEG motor imagery classification based on multi-layer CNNs feature fusion. Future Gener. Comput. Syst. **101**, 542–554 (2019)
4. Asensio-Cubero, J., Gan, J.Q., Palaniappan, R.: Multiresolution analysis over simple graphs for brain computer interfaces. J. Neural Eng. **10**(4), 046014 (2013)
5. Benavoli, A., Corani, G., Demšar, J., Zaffalon, M.: Time for a change: a tutorial for comparing multiple classifiers through Bayesian analysis. J. Mach. Learn. Res. **18**(1), 2653–2688 (2017)
6. Calvo, B., Santafé Rodrigo, G.: scmamp: statistical comparison of multiple algorithms in multiple problems. R J. **8/1** (2016)
7. Carrasco, J., García, S., del Mar Rueda, M., Herrera, F.: rNPBST: an R package covering non-parametric and bayesian statistical tests. In: Martínez de Pisón, F.J., Urraca, R., Quintián, H., Corchado, E. (eds.) HAIS 2017. LNCS (LNAI), vol. 10334, pp. 281–292. Springer, Cham (2017). https://doi.org/10.1007/978-3-319-59650-1_24
8. Chiarelli, A.M., Croce, P., Merla, A., Zappasodi, F.: Deep learning for hybrid EEG-fNIRS brain-computer interface: application to motor imagery classification. J. Neural Eng. **15**(3), 036028 (2018)
9. Chollet, F., et al.: Keras (2015). https://keras.io
10. Cohen, J.: A coefficient of agreement for nominal scales. Educ. Psychol. Measur. **20**(1), 37–46 (1960)
11. Daubechies, I.: Ten Lectures on Wavelets, vol. 61. Siam (1992)
12. Eiben, A.E., Smith, J.E., et al.: Introduction to Evolutionary Computing, 2 edn., vol. 53. Springer, Heidelberg (2015)
13. Friedman, M.: The use of ranks to avoid the assumption of normality implicit in the analysis of variance. J. Am. Stat. Assoc. **32**(200), 675–701 (1937)
14. Oliphant, T.E.: A guide to NumPy, vol. 1. Trelgol Publishing USA (2006). https://docs.scipy.org/doc/numpy/reference/
15. Pedregosa, F., et al.: Scikit-learn: machine learning in Python. J. Mach. Learn. Res. **12**, 2825–2830 (2011). https://scikit-learn.org/stable/documentation.html
16. Raudys, S., Jain, A.: Small sample size effects in statistical pattern recognition: recommendations for practitioners. IEEE Trans. Pattern Anal. Mach. Intell. **13**(3), 252–264 (1991)
17. Sakhavi, S., Guan, C., Yan, S.: Learning temporal information for brain-computer interface using convolutional neural networks. IEEE Trans. Neural Netw. Learn. Syst. **29**(11), 5619–5629 (2018)
18. Tayeb, Z., et al.: Validating deep neural networks for online decoding of motor imagery movements from EEG signals. Sensors **19**(1), 210 (2019)
19. Wang, P., Jiang, A., Liu, X., Shang, J., Zhang, L.: LSTM-based EEG classification in motor imagery tasks. IEEE Trans. Neural Syst. Rehabil. Eng. **26**(11), 2086–2095 (2018)

Author Index

Aguilar-Moreno, Marina 25
Alahamade, Wedad 585
Alaíz, Carlos M. 221
Alaiz-Moretón, Héctor 329
Aledo, Juan A. 410
Alejo, R. 195
Alfaro, Juan C. 410
Alonso, Enrique Díez 674
Alonso, Pedro 706
Álvarez, Martín 477
Álvarez, Rubén 273
Andrades, José Alberto Benítez 329
Aquino, Pâmella A. 465
Aranda-Orna, Diego 729
Argente, Estefanía 486
Argüeso Gómez, Francisco 73
Arrieta, Unai 61
Arroyo, Ángel 86
Asencio-Cortés, G. 522
Atchade Adelomou, Parfait 245

Banković, Zorana 739
Baruque, Bruno 341
Basurto, Nuño 86
Bella, Juan 233
Bellas, Francisco 499
Bonavera, Laura 73, 674
Butakov, Nikolay 284

Calvo-Rolle, José Luis 329, 341, 698
Cambra, Carlos 86
Cano, José-Ramón 424
Carballido, Jessica A. 172
Cárdenas-Montes, Miguel 147, 644
Carvalho, André C. P. L. F. 397
Casado-Vara, Roberto 341, 698
Castañeda, Ángel Luis Muñoz 183
Castejón-Limas, Manuel 665
Casteleiro-Roca, José-Luis 329, 341
Cecchini, Rocío L. 172
Ceriotti, Matteo 751
Chiesa-Estomba, Carlos M. 718
Cho, Sung-Bae 3
Clark, Patrick G. 387
Concepción-Morales, Eduardo René 261
Cuellar, Carmen Benavides 329

Damas, Miguel 774
De Cos Juez, Francisco Javier 674
de Cos Juez, Francisco Javier 73
de la Cal, Enrique 631
de la Cal, Enrique A. 95
de Lope, Javier 132
De La Iglesia, Beatriz 585
DeCastro-García, Noemí 183
del Carmen Fernández Menéndez, Susana 674
Díaz, Hernán 209
Díaz, Irene 209, 450, 706
Díez, Fidel 477
Díez-González, Javier 273
Dorronsoro, José R. 221, 233
Duro, R. J. 362

Echaniz, Oier 718
Edeghere, Obaghe 160
Edo-Osagie, Oduwa 160
Estevez, Julian 686

Faina, A. 362
Fáñez, Mirko 95, 631
Fernández Menéndez, Susana del Carmen 73
Fernández, Ángela 233
Fernández, Pedro Riesgo 674
Fernández-Robles, Laura 665
Fernández-Rodríguez, Mario 183
Ferrero-Guillén, Rubén 273
Fong, Simon 511
Formoso, Marco A. 620, 655

Gajdoš, Andrej 546
Gámez, José A. 410
García Nieto, Paulino José 73
García, Ander 61
García, Salvador 424
García-Bringas, Pablo 534, 561
García-Gonzalo, Esperanza 73
García-Ordás, María Teresa 329

Garcia-Retuerta, David 698
Garrido-Merchán, Eduardo C. 13
Gimenez, Almudena 620
Glavan, Andreea 763
Golobardes Ribé, Elisabet 245
Gómez, Marisol 49
Gómez, Sergio Luis Suárez 674
Gómez-Sancho, Marta 374
González, Jesús 774
González-Almagro, Germán 424
González-Nuevo, Joaquín 73
González-Rodríguez, Inés 209
Graña, Manuel 25, 132, 686, 718
Granda-Gutiérrez, E. E. 195
Gritsenko, Vyacheslav 312
Grzymala-Busse, Jerzy W. 387
Gutiérrez, Carlos González 674
Gutiérrez-Naranjo, Miguel A. 147
Guzmán-Ponce, A. 195, 299

Hanne, Thomas 511
Hernández-Lobato, Daniel 374
Herrero, Álvaro 86
Hippe, Zdzislaw S. 387

Ibaseta, Daniel 477
Ichise, Ryutaro 107
Iglesia, Beatriz De La 160
Iglesias, Alberto Tellaeche 534
Ishii, Naohiro 573
Iwamoto, Hidekazu 573
Iwata, Kazunori 573

Jiménez-Herrera, P. 522
Jorajuría, Tania 49
Jove, Esteban 329, 341

Khodorchenko, Maria 284
Kim, Jin-Young 3

Lake, Iain 160, 585
León, Javier 774
Li, Jingyue 598
Li, Tengyue 511
Lim, Kyung-Hyun 3
Lin, Weiwei 511
Liu, Lian-sheng 511
López, David 221
López, Vivian F. 465
Lopez-Guede, Jose Manuel 686
Lopez-Zamora, Miguel 620
Lorente, Mikel 61
Lu, Chaoru 598
Luengo, Julián 424
Luque, Juan Luis 620, 655

Maleta, Ángel 61
Marcial-Romero, J. R. 195
Martínez-Murcia, Francisco J. 620, 655
Matei, Alina 763
Matsuo, Tokuro 573
Meden, Blaž 499
Melgar-García, L. 522
Méndez-Pérez, Juan Albino 341
Merchán, Eduardo C. Garrido 350
Mester, Rudolf 598
Molina, Jose M. 612
Molina, Martin 350
Molleda, Julio 477
Moreno, María N. 465
Moreno-García, M. N. 437
Mroczek, Teresa 387
Mundim, Leandro R. 397
Muñiz-Rodríguez, Laura 706
Munne, Rumana Ferdous 107
Muñoz, María D. 465

Namazi, Elnaz 598
Naya-Varela, M. 362
Nechepurenko, Liudmyla 312
Niemiec, Rafal 387

Odagiri, Kazuya 573
Olszewski, Dominik 36
Ortega, Julio 774
Ortiz, Andrés 620, 655, 774

Palacios, Juan José 209
Palacios, Rafael 13
Pastor-López, Iker 534, 561
Peer, Peter 499
Pekarčík, Patrik 546
Peluffo-Ordóñez, D. H. 437
Pérez, Daniel 486
Pérez, Hilde 273
Pérez-Cañedo, Boris 261
Pérez-Fernández, Raúl 450, 706
Pesudo, Vicente 644

Ponzoni, Ignacio 172
Prieto, Abraham 499
Prieto, Javier 698
Puente, Cristina 13

Quintián, Héctor 329, 341, 698

Reeves, Claire E. 585
Riascos, J. A. 437
Rico, Noelia 450, 706
Riego, Virginia 665
Riesgo, Francisco García 674
Rodríguez Iglesias, Francisco Javier 73
Rodríguez, Francisco Javier Iglesias 674
Rodríguez, Jesús Daniel Santos 674
Rodríguez, Sara 465
Rodríguez-García, Iñaki 644
Rodríguez-Muñiz, Luis J. 706
Rosete, Alejandro 261

Sakač, Slađana 739
Sánchez Lasheras, Fernando 73
Sánchez, Auxiliadora 655
Sánchez, J. S. 299
Sánchez, María Luisa 73
Sánchez-González, Lidia 665
Santorelli, Roberto 644
Santos Rodríguez, Jesús Daniel 73
Santos, Moisés R. 397
Sanz Urquijo, Borja 561
Sedano, Javier 631, 729
Simić, Dragan 739
Simić, Svetislav D. 739
Simić, Svetlana 739
Sokhin, Timur 284
Sokol, Pavol 546
Solano, Roberto Porto 612
Suárez Sánchez, Ana 73
Suarez, Juan Luis 424
Suárez, Victor 95

Takahashi, Satoshi 573
Talavera, Estefanía 763
Tallón-Ballesteros, Antonio J. 511
Tamayo-Quintero, J. D. 437
Tellaeche Iglesias, Alberto 561
Teryoshkin, Sergey 284
Toffolatti, Luigi 73
Troncoso, A. 522

Umaquinga-Criollo, A. C. 437
Urquijo, Borja Sanz 534

Valdovinos, R. M. 195, 299
Vasco-Carofilis, Roberto A. 147
Vela, Camino R. 209
Verdegay, José Luis 261
Viavattene, Giulia 751
Vidaurre, Carmen 49
Vilasís Cardona, Xavier 245
Villar, José R. 95, 631, 729, 739
Villar, Mario 95, 631
Voss, Viktor 312

Wojciechowski, Szymon 120
Woźniak, Michał 120

Zayas-Gato, Francisco 341

Printed in the United States
By Bookmasters